THE PROCESS

THE PROCESS
A New Foundation in Art and Design

Judith Wilde
Richard Wilde

Laurence King Publishing

AUTHORS' ADVICE

The Process can be used as a practice to engage in moving toward a new way of problem solving.

Regardless of what creative endeavor one might be involved with, *The Process* can be used for inspiration to jumpstart one's own problem-solving ventures, and also acts as a reminder that there can be numerable solutions to any given problem.

The Process contains thousands of images, which can easily lead to visual fatigue.
The authors recommend that in order to fully absorb any given problem, no more than one or two chapters should be viewed at a sitting.

CONTENTS

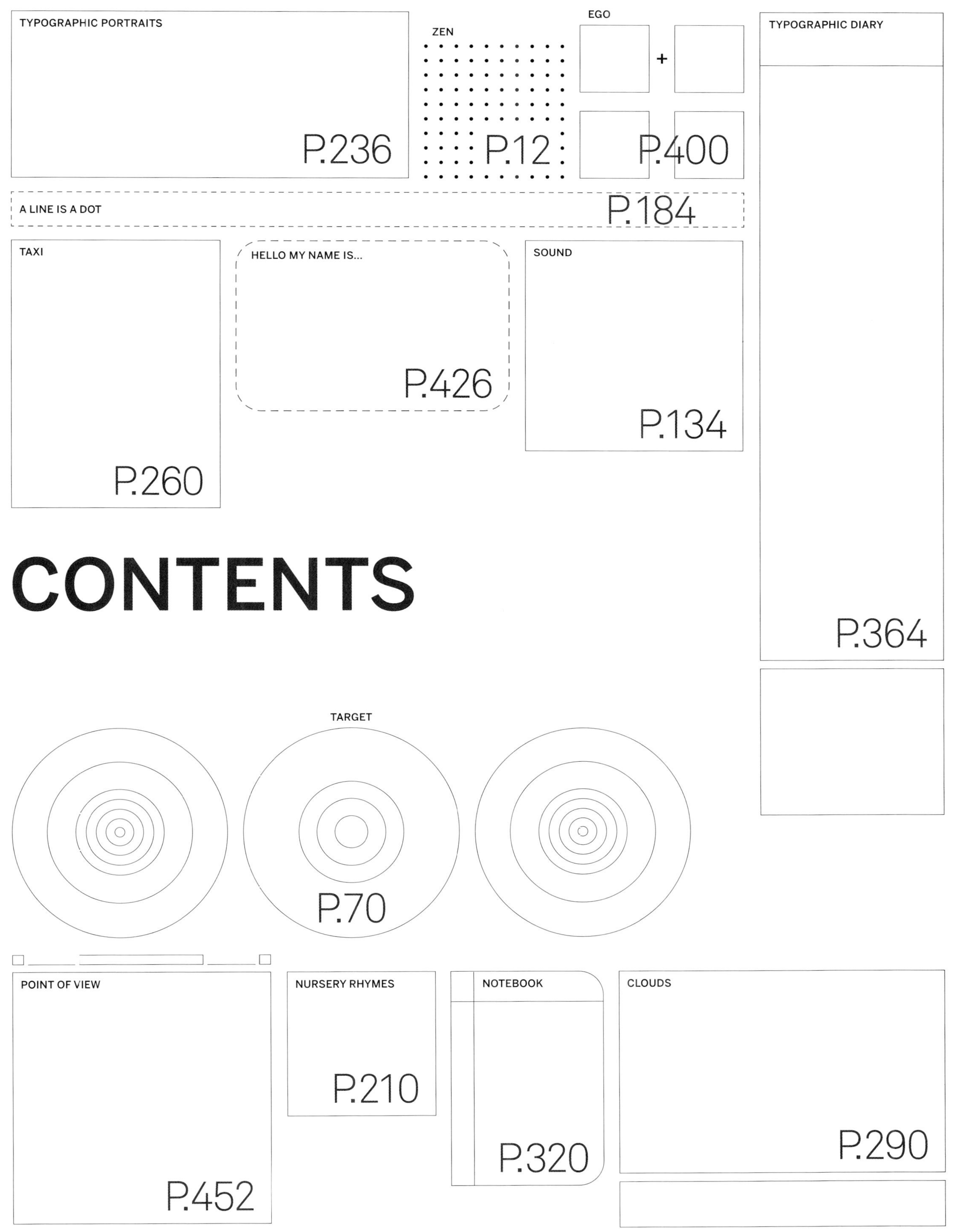

FOREWORD

CONCEPTUAL FEARLESSNESS

There are few things in life of which I am certain, particularly in the ever-changing field of graphic design, where media and aesthetic parameters change by the day. Yet certainty courses through my body and mind whenever I reflect on the visual literacy exercises "invented" by Judith and Richard Wilde that await you in this volume. What I am entirely certain of – because I've seen the results first hand – is that the myriad solutions demanded by these simple yet rigorously crafted visual language skill tests guarantee that students – and there have been thousands of them – will come away exponentially more literate and better design thinkers. I am certain that literacy is the fundamental goal of all education, especially design education, and the Wildes' process is essential.

What I am uncertain of is this: Could I meet the Wildes' challenge? Have I the chops to take any three of these problems, for example the ones that appeal to my conceptual vigor, "Targets," "Sound" or "Hey Taxi," and devise solutions that transcend my safe bank of clichés? Maybe! But not without trouble at first. Consistent with the Wildes' plan, however, difficulty is the fuel that ignites the proverbial engine of creativity. The exercises do indeed become increasingly difficult as the assignments progress throughout a semester. But at the same time, the students' ability to smartly solve these problems increases – and not simply to get it over with, but to proudly display the intelligence they've garnered from exercising their conceptual and aesthetic muscles.

I am not one for magic bullets and miracle growth enhancements, but it is uncanny how this process of visual thinking and making awakens that part of the brain that stimulated students to study art and design in the first place. It doesn't matter what design media – digital or analog – they will enter after graduation, or even whether they stay or leave the art and design disciplines for other careers. These exercises engage and enhance the skills and tools for creative thinking with long-term effect. How?

Each problem is thematically outlined with certain limitations (and what doesn't have self- or externally imposed limitations?), yet the outcome is designed to be as free as air. Students are asked to push the boundaries: their own boundaries, not those of some arbitrary standard or competition imperative. Students draw, paint, and collage. They write, letter, and typographically assemble their responses. There is an imponderable yet palpable surge of energy (or magic, or some other force) when faced with the tabloid-sized assignment page with the empty grid of boxes waiting impatiently to be filled. Reading the problem, carefully spelled out to avoid confusion, the student is faced with the sudden realization that virtually anything is possible – that creativity is about accepting limits along with freedom. The inevitable transformation from nothing into something – whatever the thing – will be the most satisfying, possibly ecstatic, feeling in the world. Having multiple chances to iterate on the core idea is the genius that underpins this process.

Of course, there are many degrees of success. Some projects are more appealing than others. For me, "Targets" opened up more opportunities than "Zen." But that too is the brilliance of these exercises (and others that are sadly not included here): There are many ways to activate the creative vortex and enter the talented mind. Judith and Richard Wilde have been inventing, reinventing and, ultimately, refining this process for four decades. Not only is it a perfect way to draw out the best in students, but it also urges the most intrepid creation possible. The act of teaching conceptual fearlessness must be supported by a fearless act. These exercises work every time. I promise!

Steven Heller
Co-Chair MFA Design,
Designer as Author + Entrepreneur,
SVA NYC

INTRODUCTION

The Process is a compendium of 13 experimental art and design projects, all geared toward teaching college art students what is needed to become an artist.

The projects in this book, created by Judith Wilde and Richard Wilde, are given primarily to students starting at the School of Visual Arts in a course titled "Visual Literacy," which sets the stage for becoming an artist. They are also given to students in experimental workshops throughout the world.

Projects focus on developing formal excellence: a strong sense of aesthetics coupled with the ability to generate new ideas. It is the balance between form (image making) and content (conceptual thinking) that must be reconciled. This is the dilemma that presents itself in all creative endeavors.

Although there is no hard and fast rule for how these projects are administered in terms of order, we've discovered that those dealing primarily with form are more tangible at the onset in terms of teaching, and early success in this area tends to empower students to then take on more conceptually driven projects.

The premise of this book is predicated on the belief that everyone is born creative, with an openness and a spontaneity that has been smothered by societal demands. If one examines children's drawings, it can be seen that they possess an instinctive, uninhibited quality, and consequently have a real life to them. Yet, as one becomes educated and socialized, this essence-bearing gift is replaced by memorization, do's and don'ts, social norms, in effect an education that inhibits growth. So, by the time one begins college, the unknown has been replaced by the known.

Mystery, wonder, and spontaneity have been replaced by false assumptions, ideas, conceits, and beliefs in the form of baggage that can be understood as layers of habitual reactions to most any endeavor. One has lost the ability to respond and instead one merely reacts in a mechanical, automatic way, without grappling with the problem at hand.

Struggle is what is needed, in the form of questioning and pondering, and with sensitivity to what might present itself. The enemy is the baggage that we all carry, which always leads to cliché solutions that live in the known. It is this very baggage, this learned robotic approach to making art, that *The Process* tries to eradicate.

Another factor that hampers creative growth is that, at the onset, one finds that having generated a few ideas, one unfortunately cannot go further as a visual problem solver. But at this very juncture, it is necessary to overcome this inertia and not be at the mercy of a false belief that all possibilities have been exhausted. That is why, in all the projects that appear in this book, multiple solutions are required, which help one get past this blockage and the lie that one's capabilities have been maximized. It is when playing and doodling, experimentation and invention are encouraged, that one is urged past this interval to enter the unknown, the world of questioning where one's real possibilities lie.

An important element in solving problems is to have a clear set of parameters that can be understood as the hallmark of the condition required to solve visual communication problems. One's initial response to parameters is most often to envision them as an impediment to creativity, while in truth they lay the groundwork for successful solutions to emerge.

It is the combination of the constraints of each assignment along with the restraints of the medium, coupled with the spirit of embracing and trusting the process of experimentation and play, that sets the stage for original work.

THOUGHTS ON THE CREATIVE PROCESS 1

Remember, the ability to come up with new ideas is already present within you. It's your birthright. It doesn't have to be invented, it has to be rediscovered. Over the years, we've developed layers and layers of habitual reactions to most any situation. We react when we should respond. Learning how to respond is the directive of self-discovery.

Zen and the creation of images. In an attempt to touch one's inner self, be present to where ideas arise and to develop a more intuitive and insightful creative process which enhances your capabilities for problem solving, experiment on the twelve grids you see below by creating images without thinking. Rely on your feelings. This is an activity to bypass habitual thought where playing with the freedom of a child becomes paramount. Allow yourself to enter a way of working where one form dictates the next in a spontaneous and unpremeditated way. Before you begin, try not to predetermine what your solutions will be. See where the exercise takes you. Let your hand lead you, rather than your head. There are no limitations on color or medium.

PROBLEMS : SOLUTIONS SERIES

CREATED BY RICHARD WILDE / JUDITH WILDE, PRODUCED BY VISUAL ARTS PRESS, LTD. ART DIRECTORS: RICHARD WILDE / JUDITH WILDE

ZEN PROBLEM:

In an attempt to touch one's inner self, be present to where ideas arise and to develop a more intuitive and insightful process that enhances one's capabilities at problem solving, experiment with the twelve grids printed on the assignment sheet in an effort to create images without predetermined ideas. This assignment is one of pure experimentation.

AIM:
To bypass habitual thought, and begin to play with the freedom of a child. To allow oneself to enter a way of working in an unpremeditated way, where unexpected imagery emerges. The hope is to connect to a level of consciousness rarely perceived, which is not subject to habitual thinking. On a broader scale, this assignment allows one to develop trust in one's instincts and create a dialogue between the emerging elements, as each subsequent form is introduced.

SUGGESTIONS:
Before beginning, try not to predetermine the solutions. Respond to the dictates of the grid to see where the exercise takes you. Trust your inner impulses and let your hand lead, rather than your head. Ideally, this type of investigation will set the conditions for a sensibility to emerge that becomes the foundation of one's personal signature. In this type of formal investigation, there are no right or wrong answers.

SPECIFICATIONS:
There are no limitations on color or medium, although pen and ink is a good starting point.

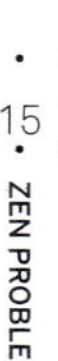

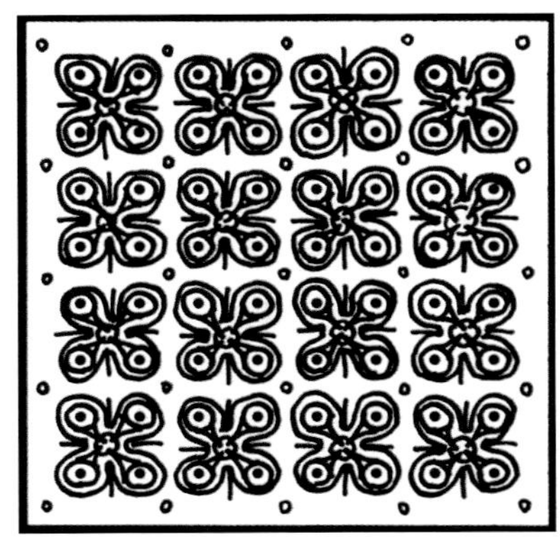
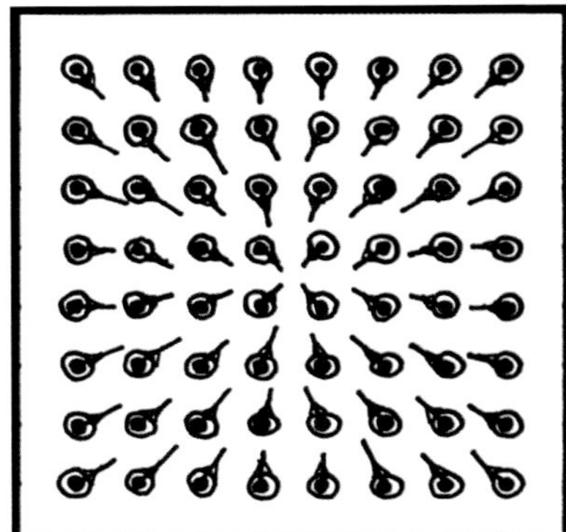
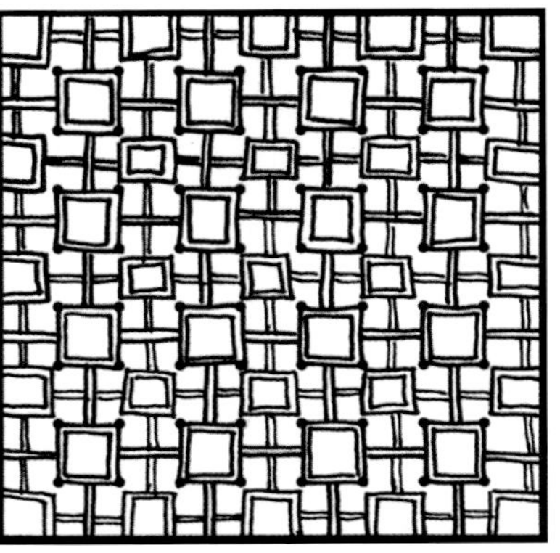
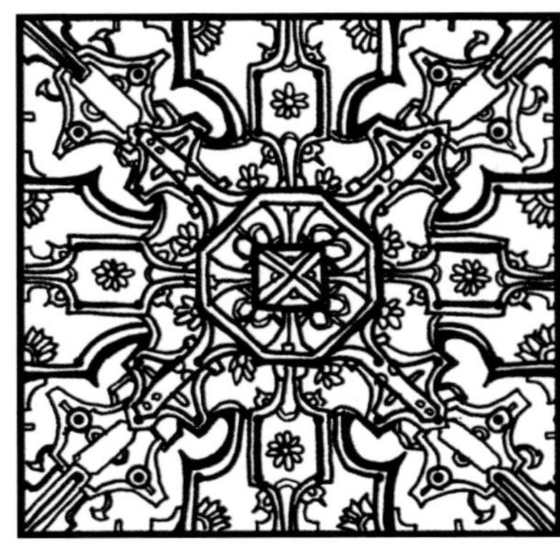
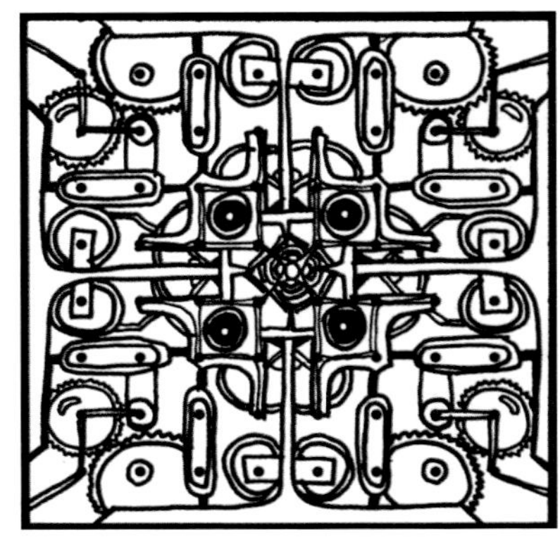
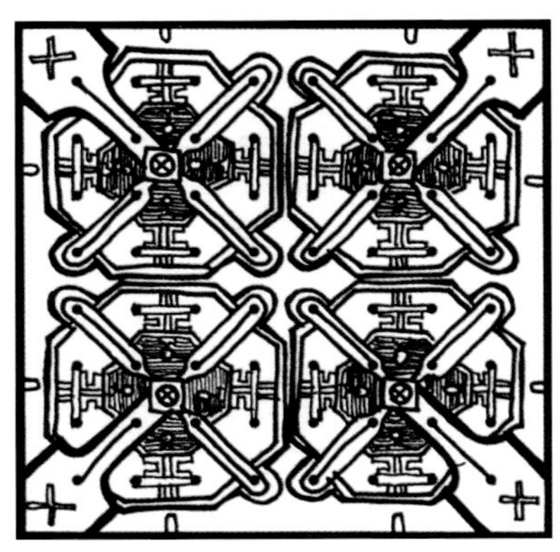
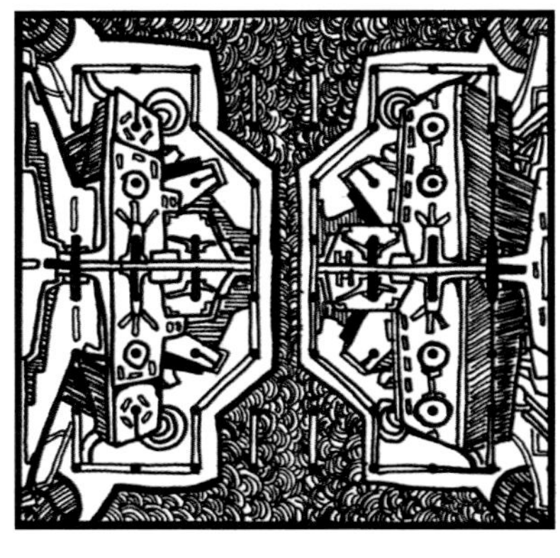
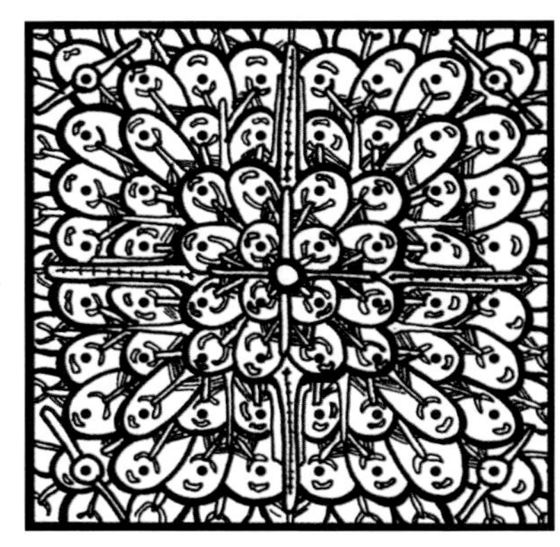
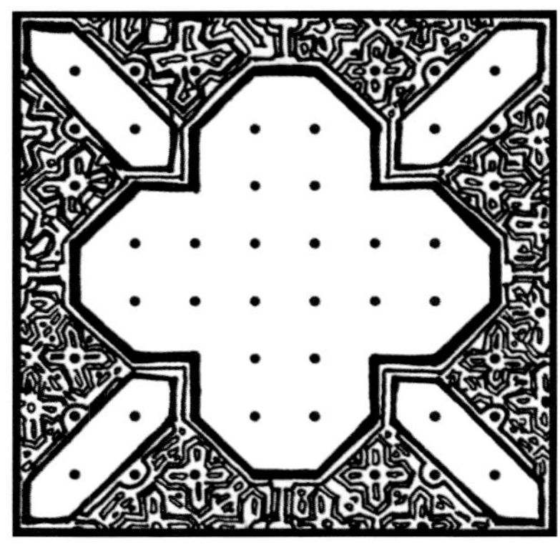
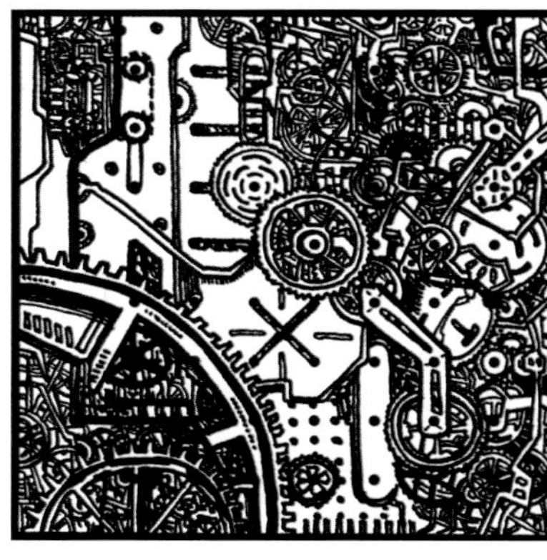

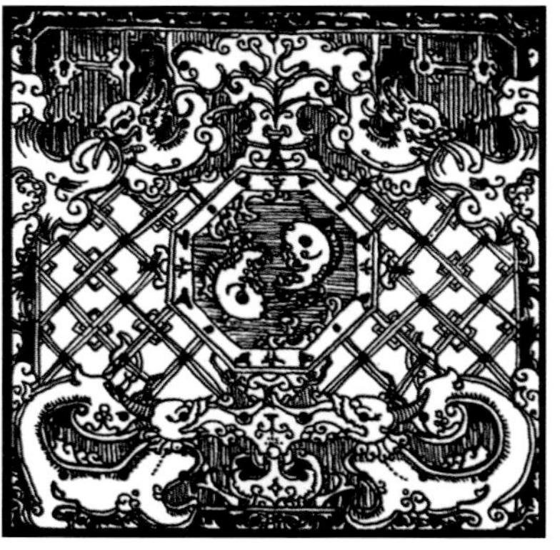

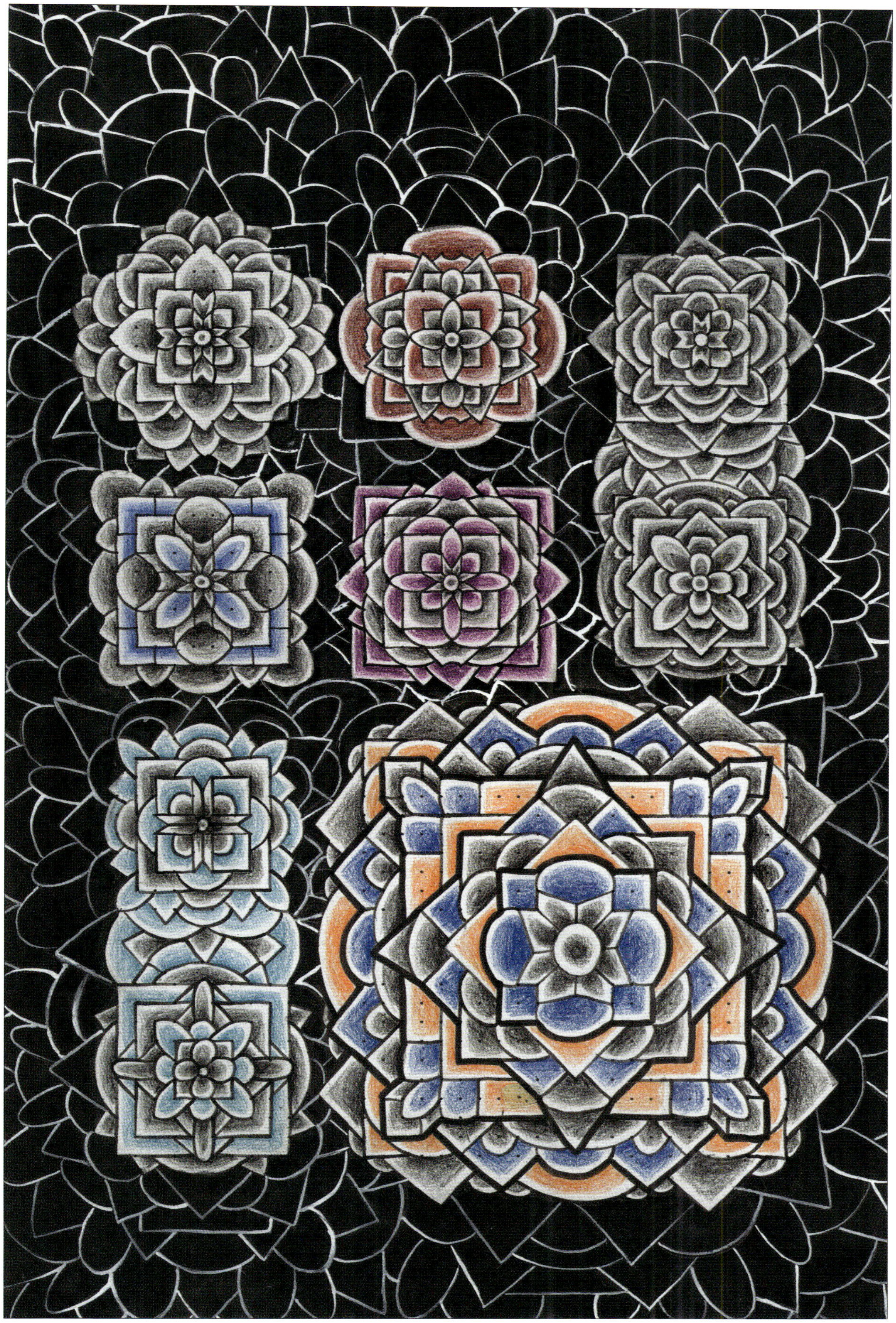

ZEN SOLUTIONS:

Figure 1 is the entire assignment addressed by one student, in a structured mannered style, where precision, symmetry, and a clear adherence to the underlying grid is followed.

Figure 2, in certain areas, exhibits a connection to the gridlike page, but follows a more abstract expressionistic sensibility.

The left-hand page represents a classic approach where geometry and formal composition dominate, while the right-hand page has similar attributes, but follows a more romantic line of expression.

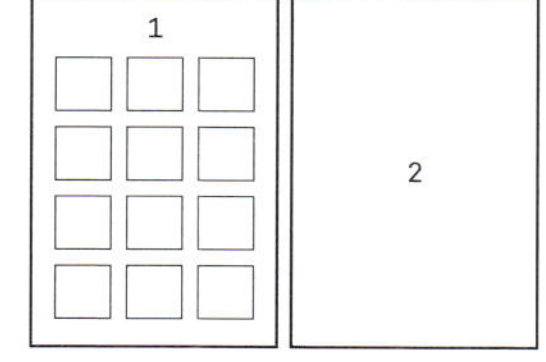

1. *Chi Hung Ku*
2. *Brianna DiFelice*

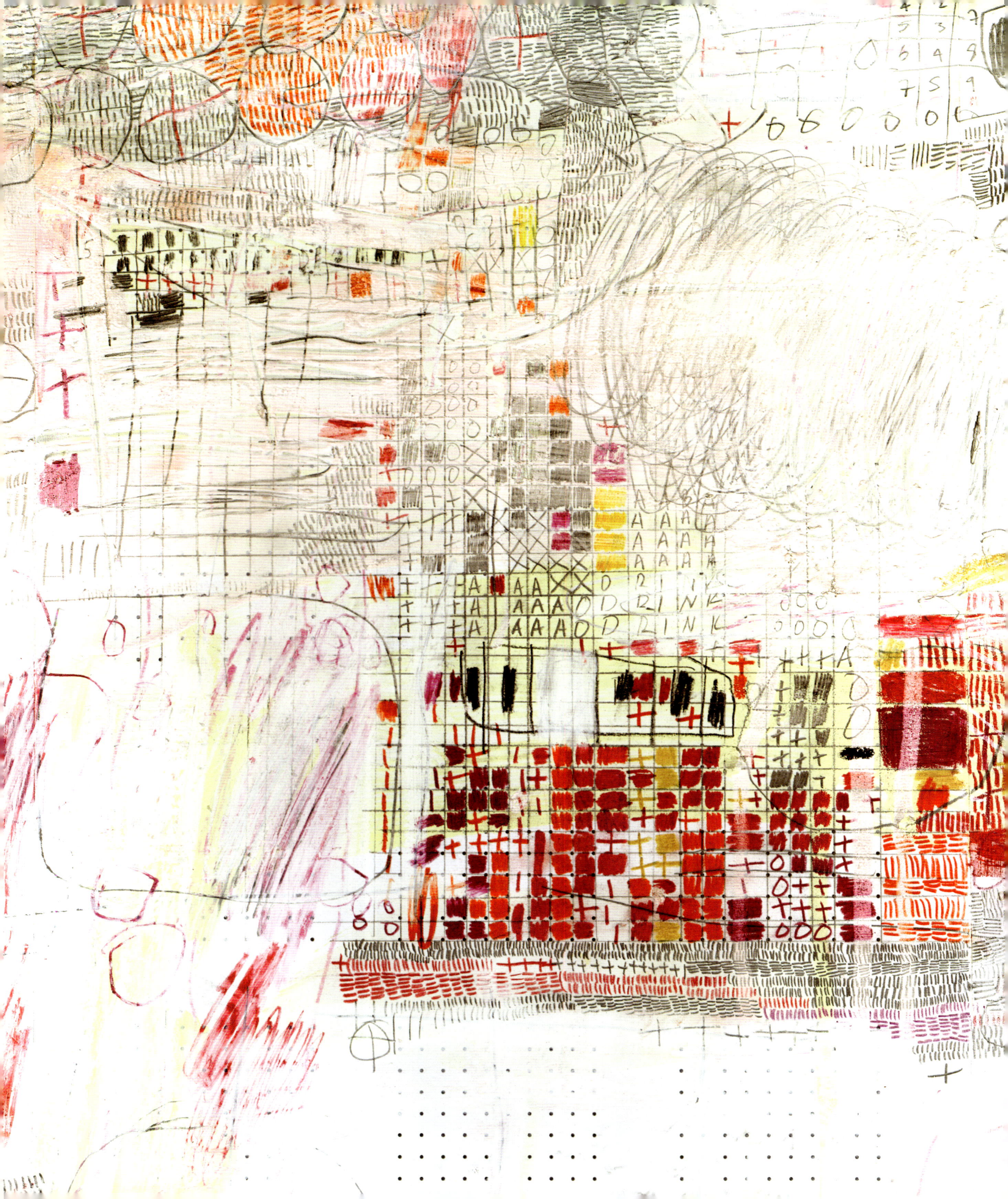
DRINK
DRINK

ZEN SOLUTIONS:

Figure 1 uses the project as a point of departure to work in a highly spontaneous abstract expressionistic manner. Yet upon closer observation, certain areas reference the underlying grid pattern.

Figures 2 through 6 follow a more structured approach in discovering unique imagery, by incorporating a sense of movement through the use of line. In some cases the grid is apparent, while in others the grid has been obliterated.

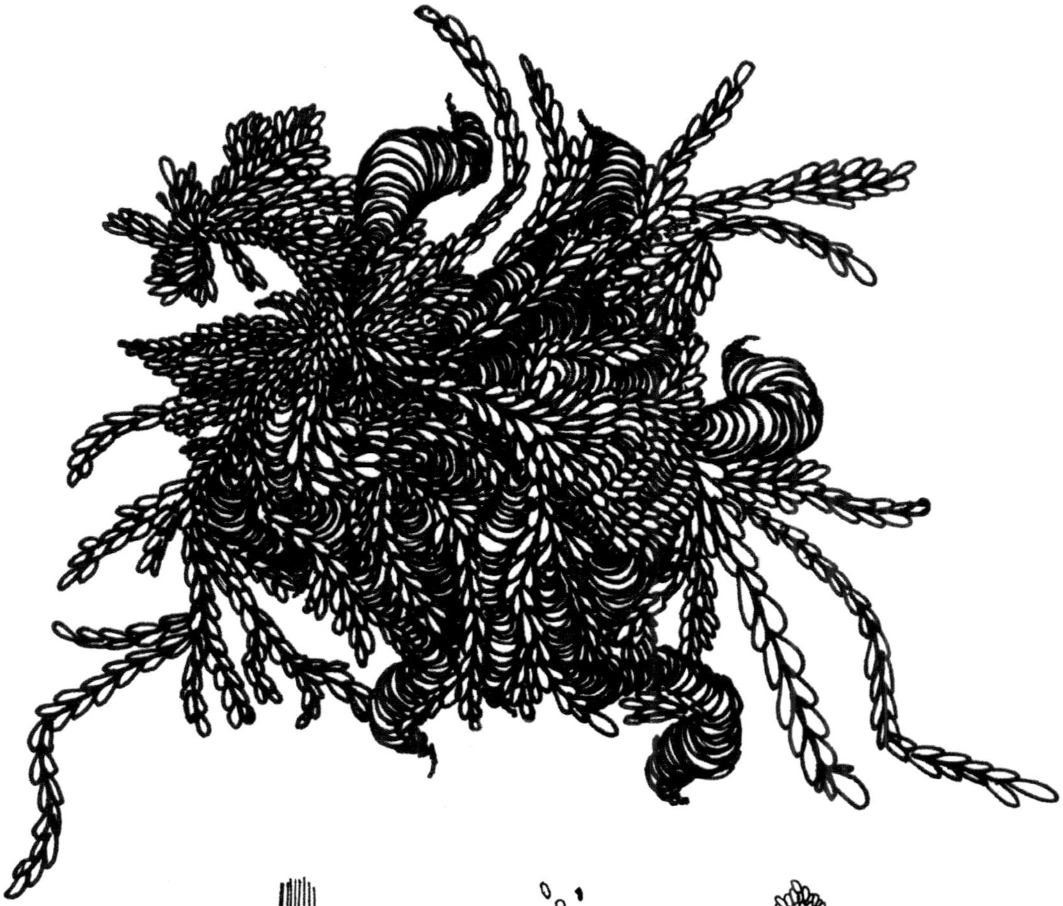

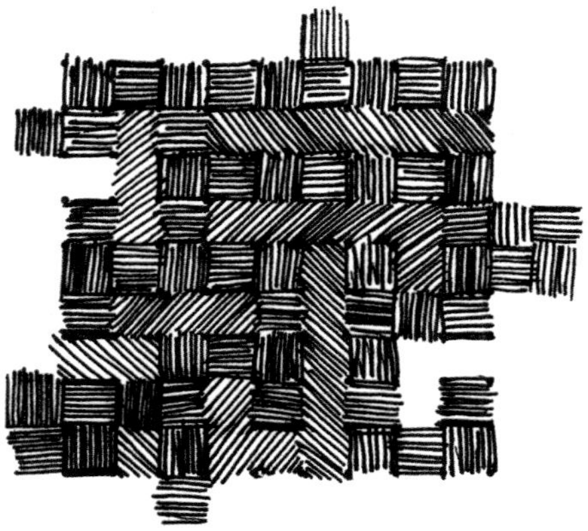

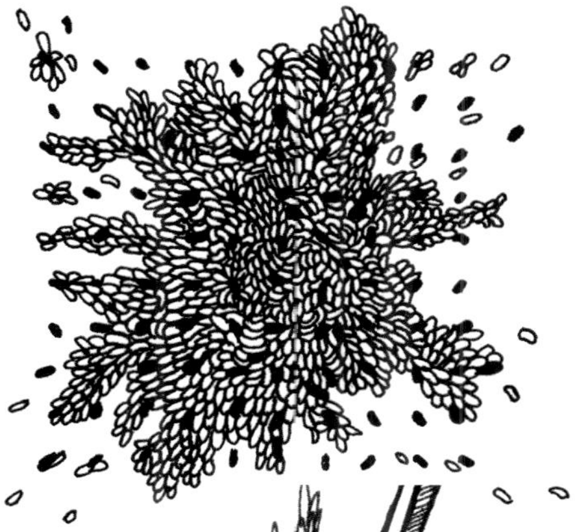

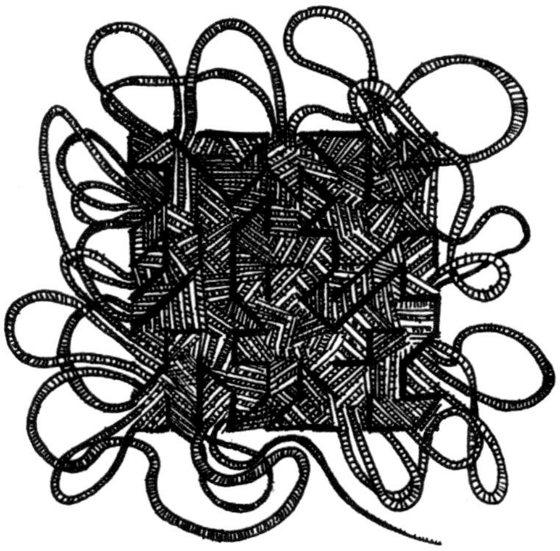

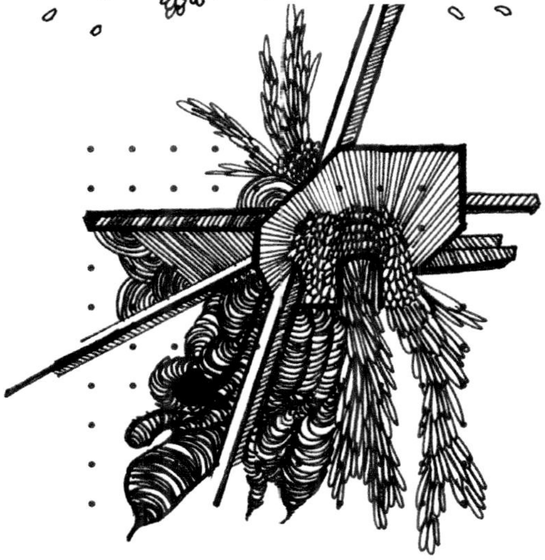

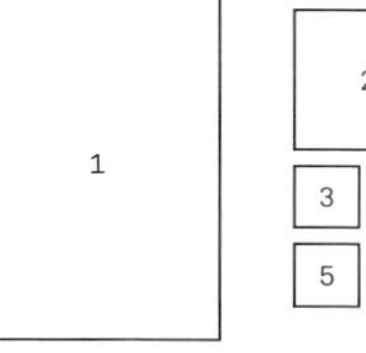

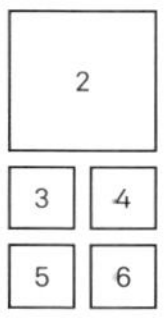

1. *Holly Jarrett*
2–6. *Huimin Lee*

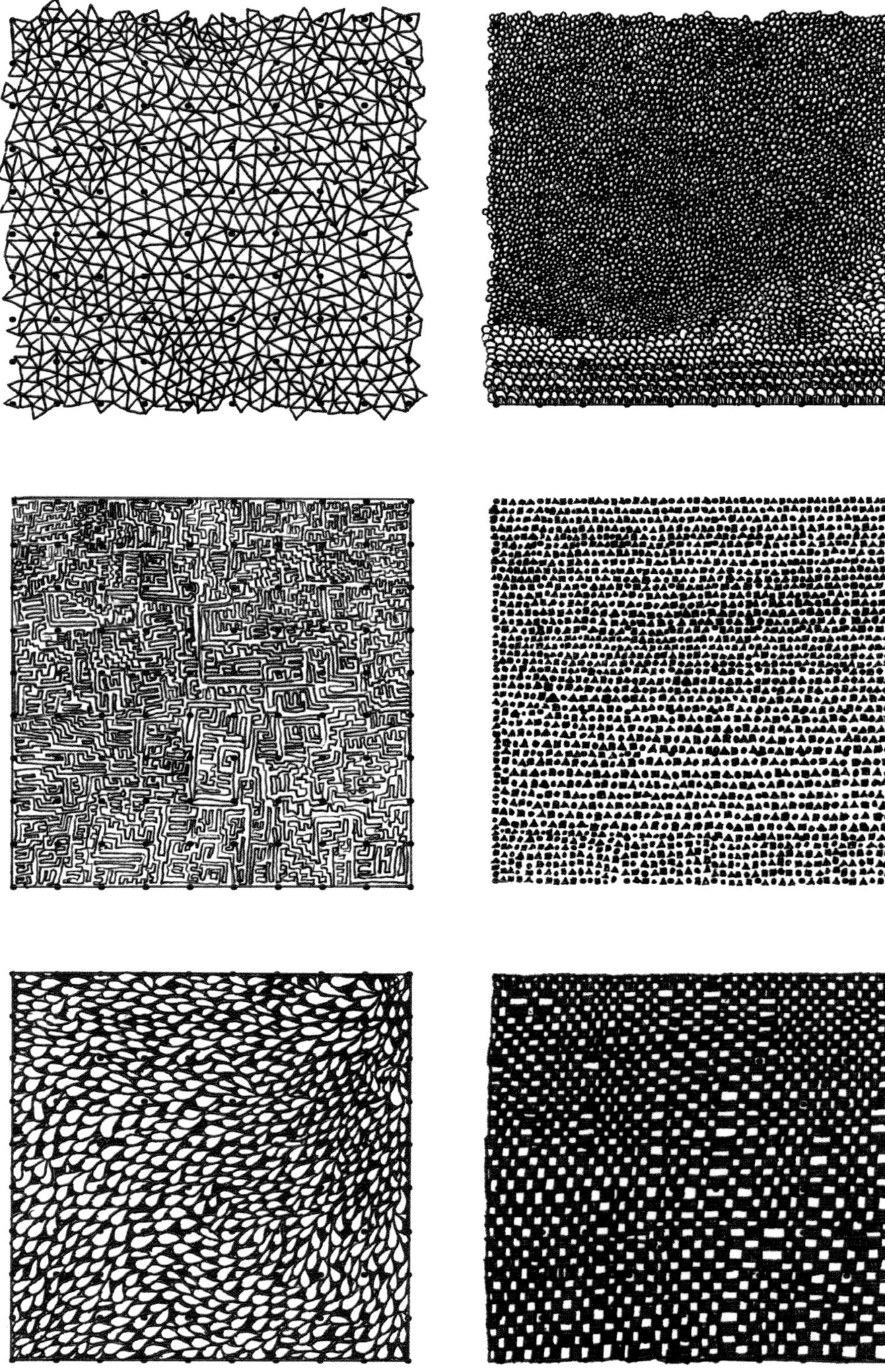

ZEN SOLUTIONS:

Figures 1 through 9 are created by one student. All images represent an obsessive approach, where detail, rhythm, pattern, and movement dictate the journey of complexity.

For the most part, figures 1 through 6 maintain the integrity of the square grid, while figures 7 and 8 follow another impulse, and figure 9 lies somewhere between these two sensibilities.

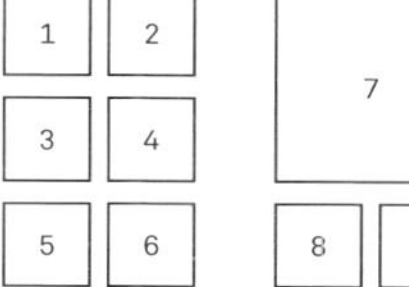

1–9. *Boyeon Jenna Kim*

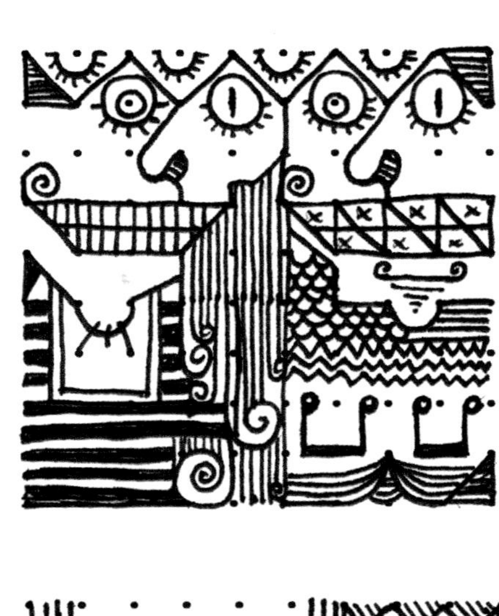

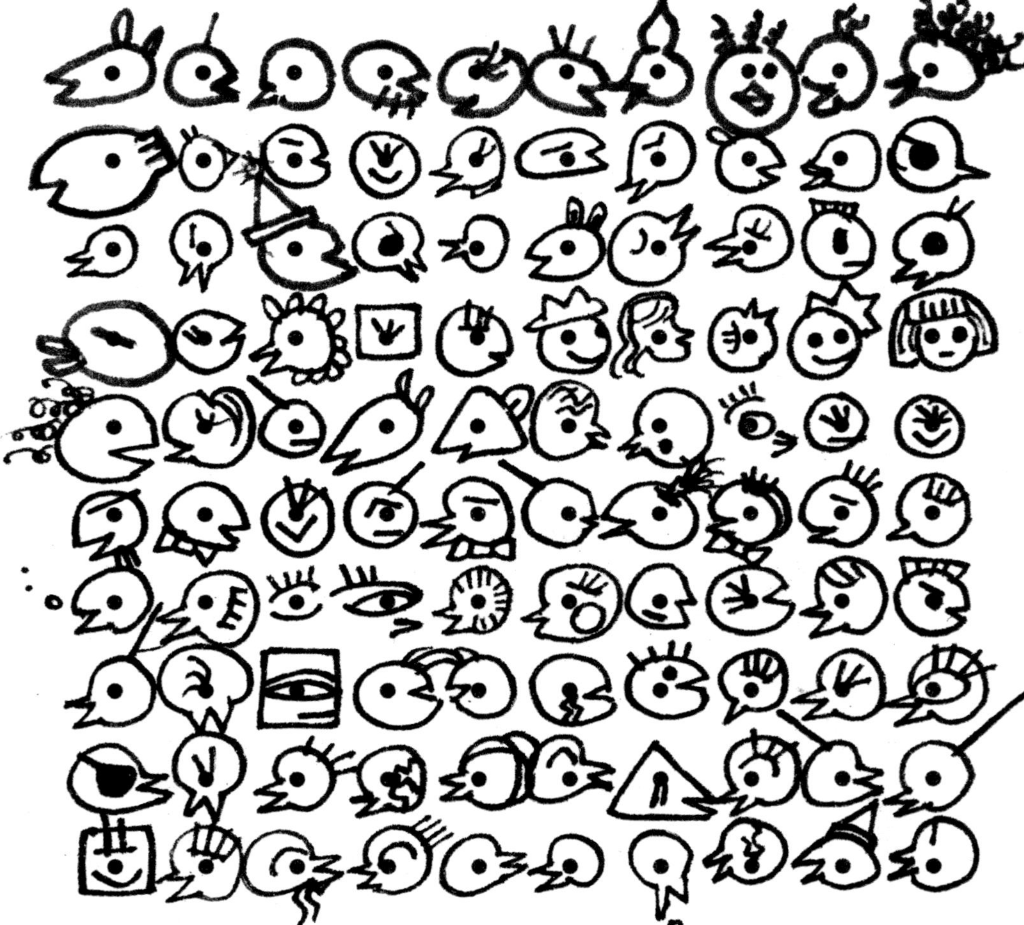

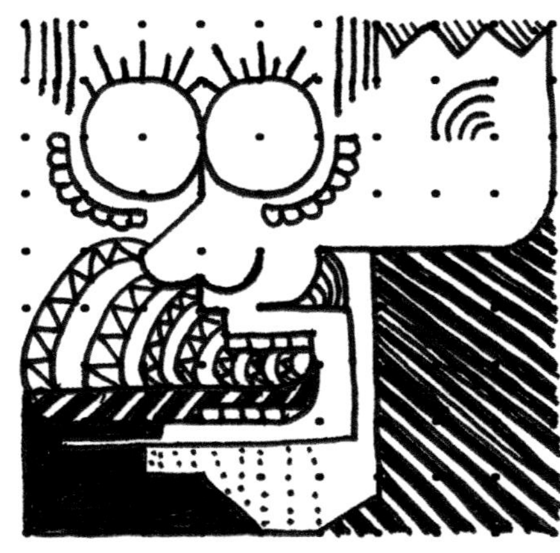

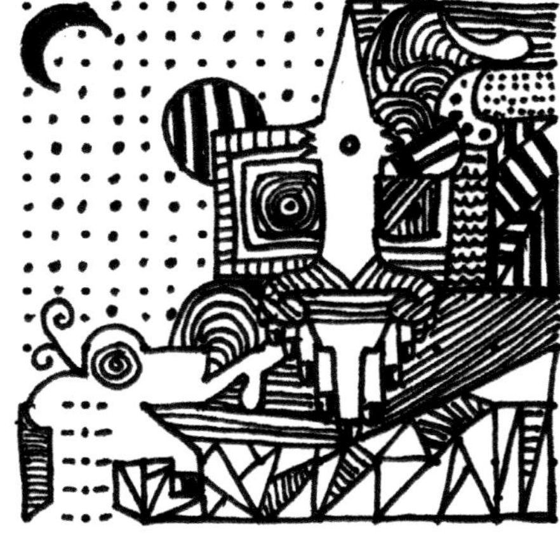

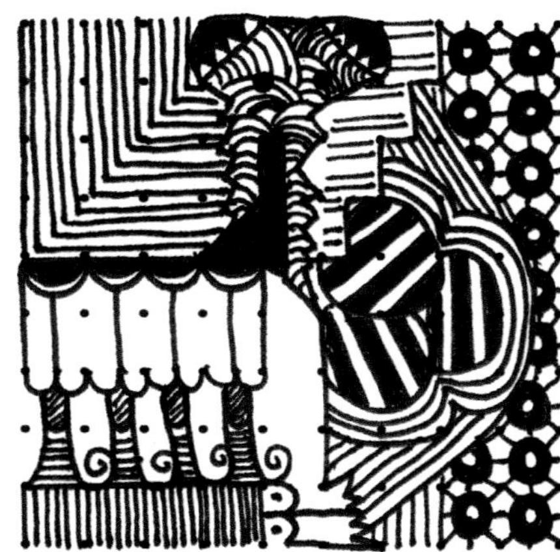

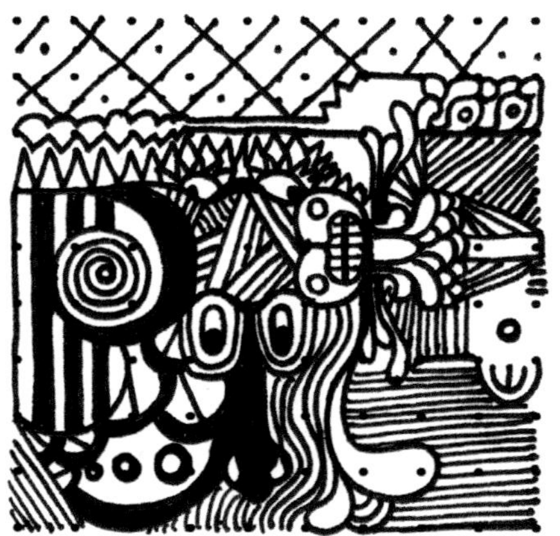

ZEN SOLUTIONS:

Figures 1 through 5 are linear experiments with patterning.

Figure 6 and figures 9 through 12 use each dot of the grid to create studies of faces, eyes, breasts, lady bugs, and insects.

Figures 7 and 8 are the creation of a complex narrative of warring factions.

In contrast, figure 10 is a humorous social comment depicting eyes all looking toward a central focal point of breasts, which speaks of the nature of male behavior.

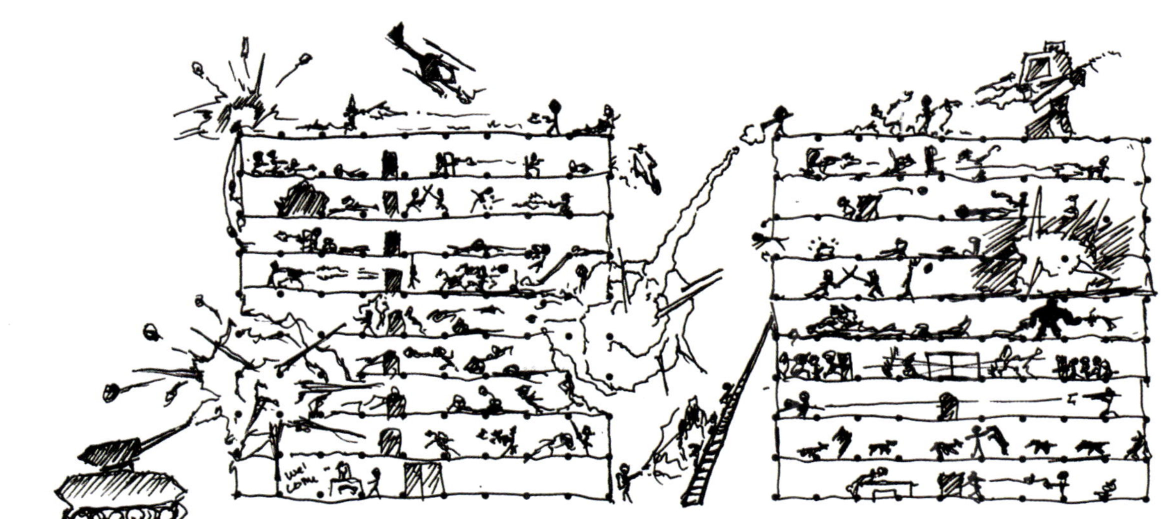

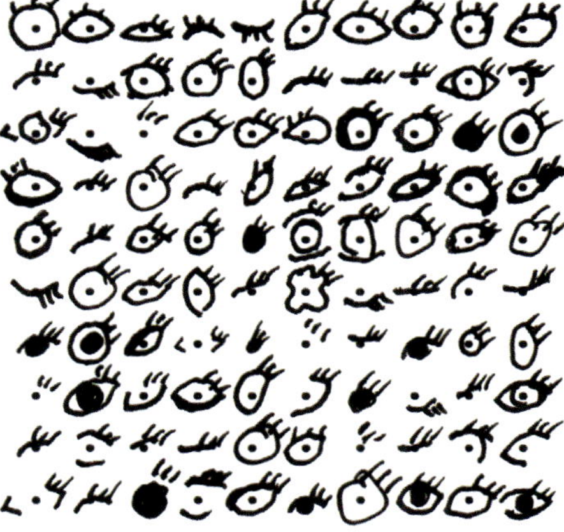

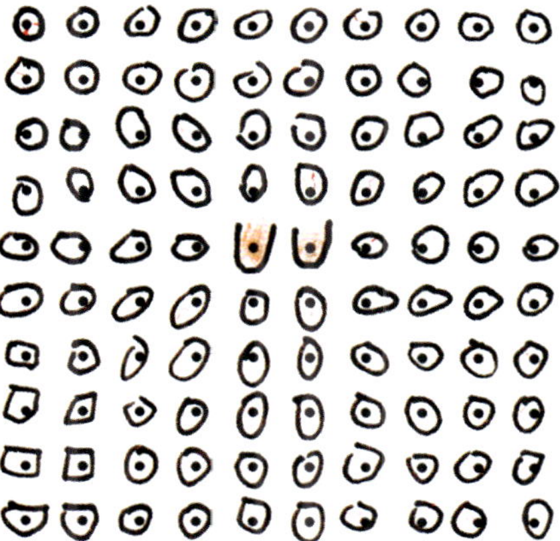

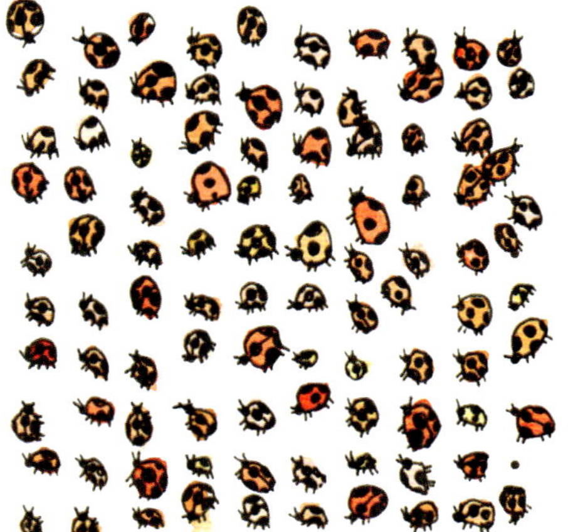

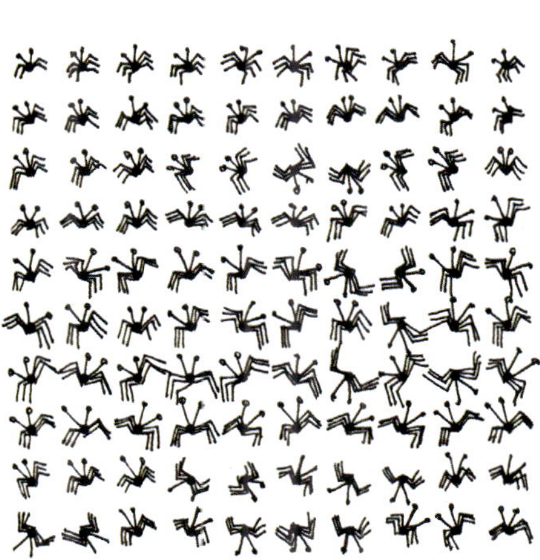

1	6	7	8
2		9	10
3 4 5		11	12

1–5. *Alex Morel*
6. *Youjin Kim*
7–8. *Eun Kim*
9. *Michael Chang*
10. *Jill Brody*
11. *Jaewook Lee*
12. *Yunhaing Kwak*

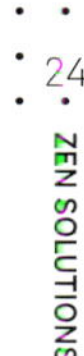

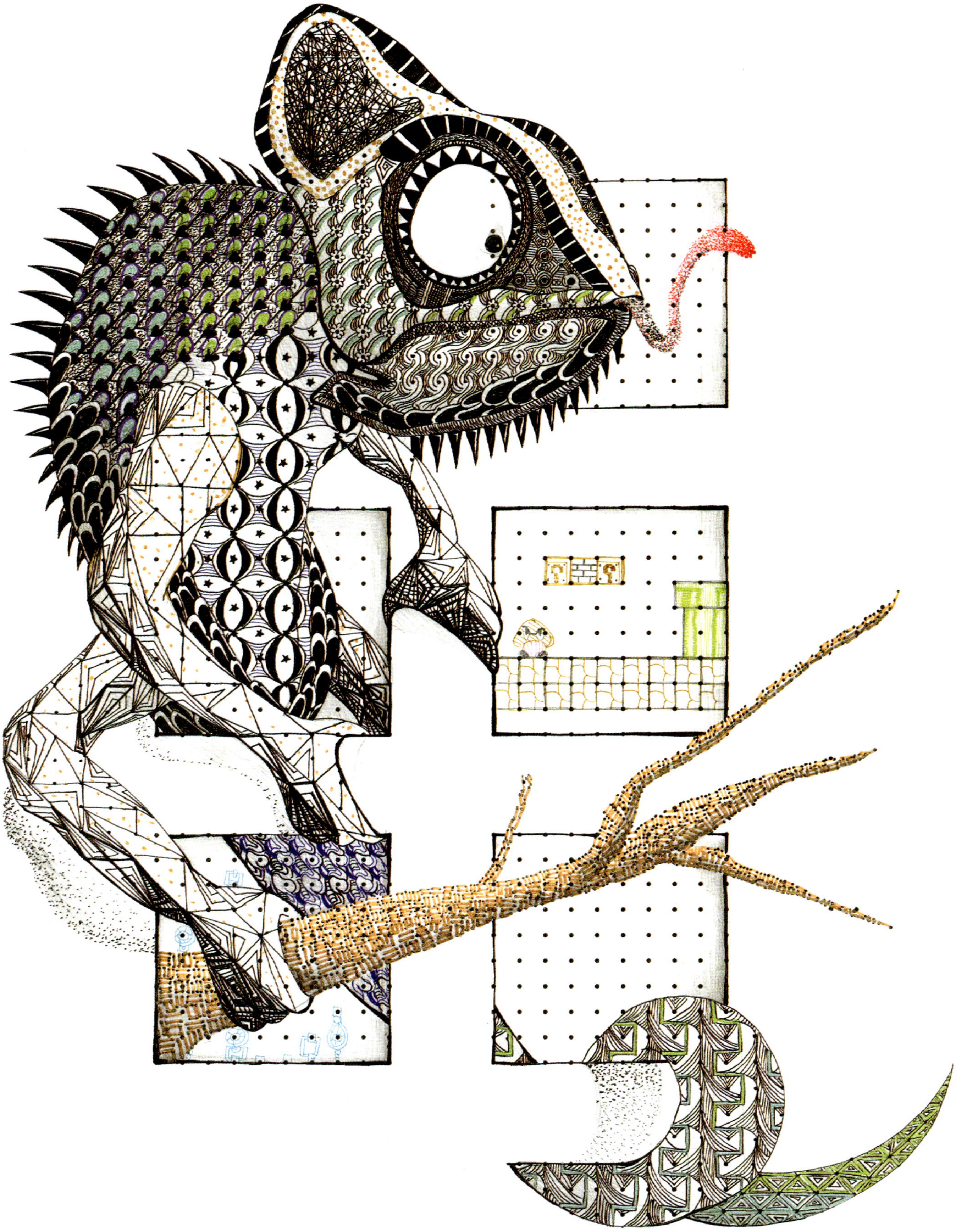

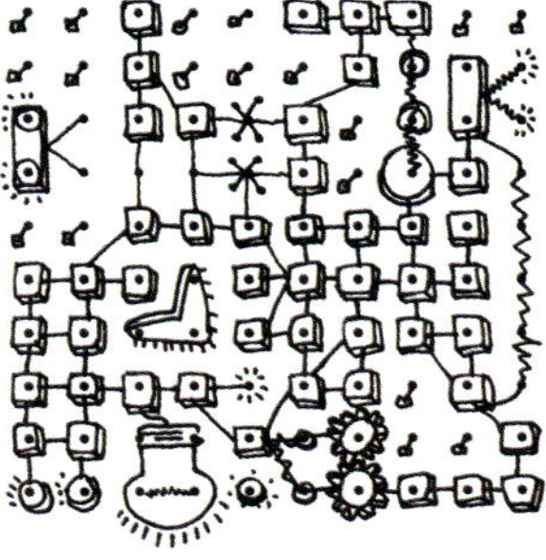
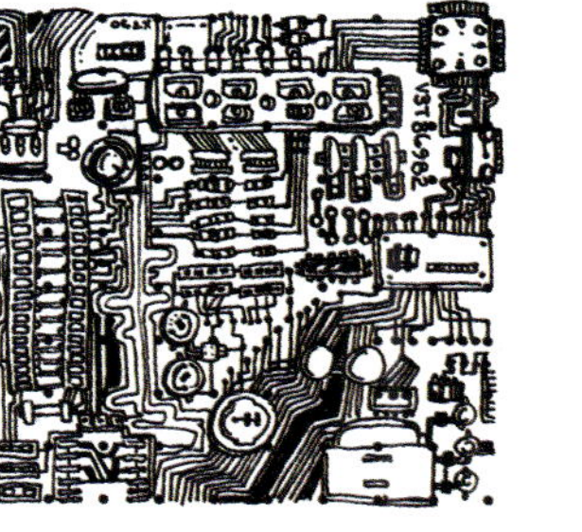
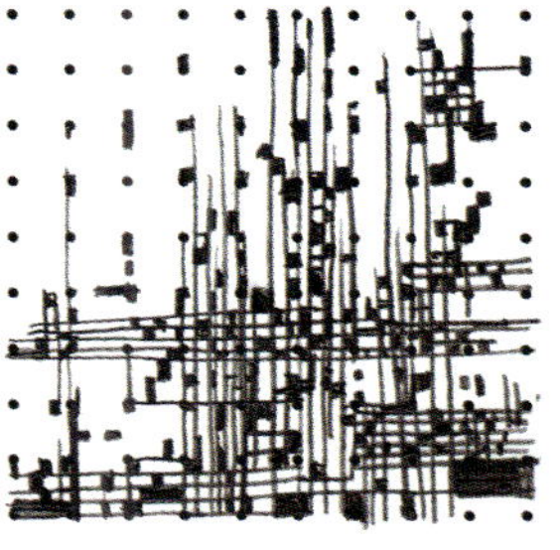
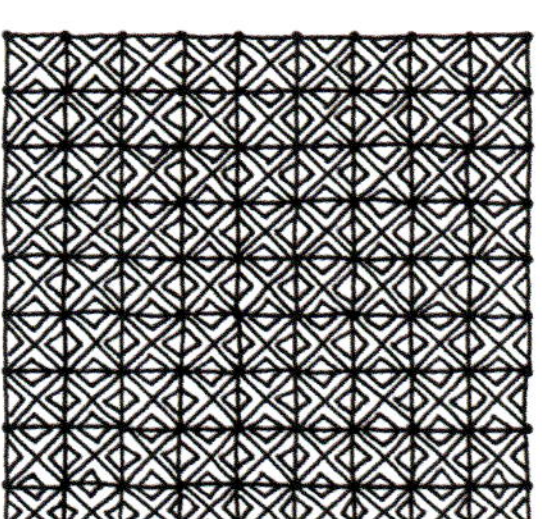
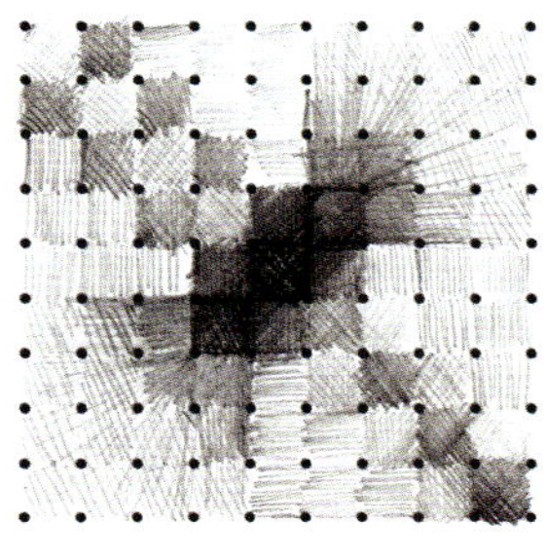
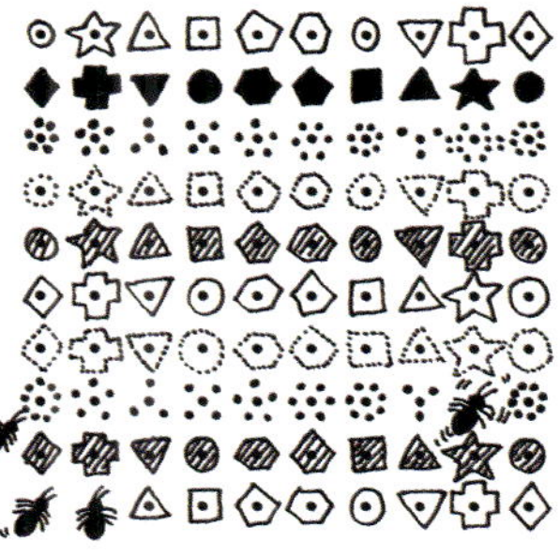
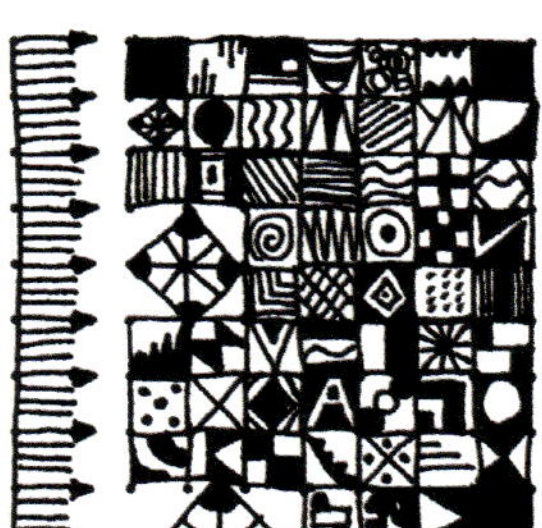
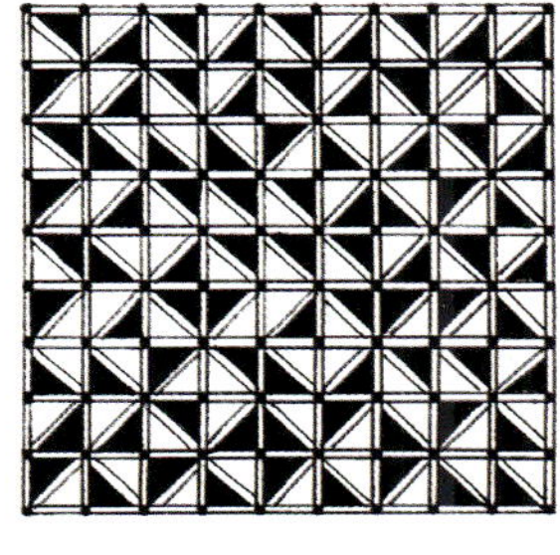
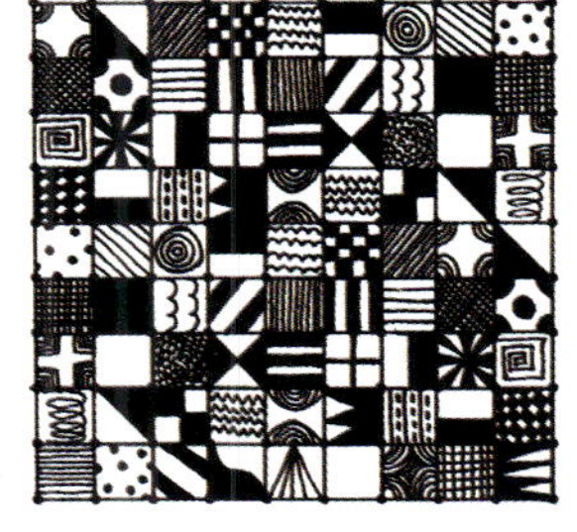

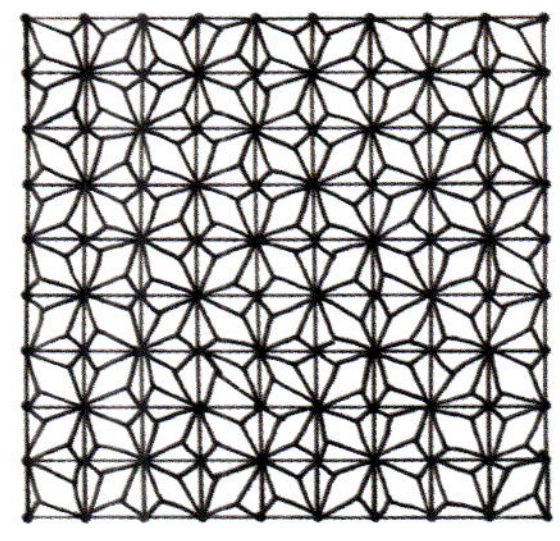

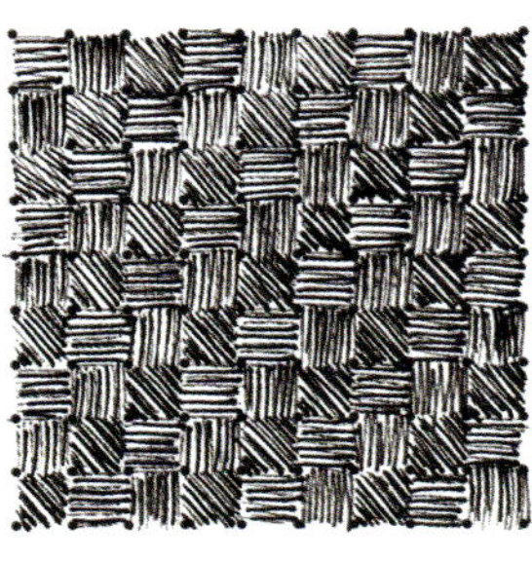
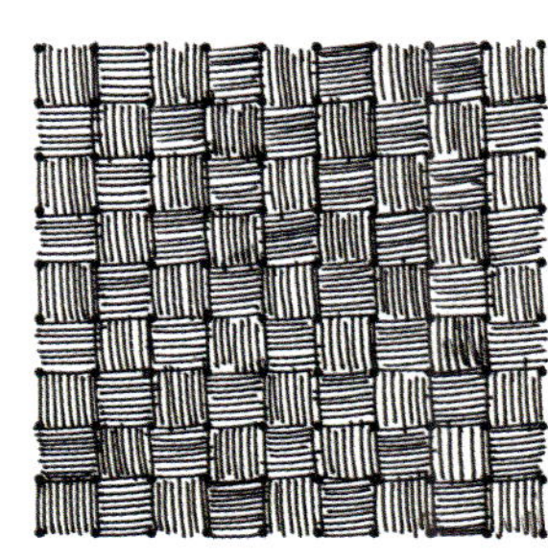
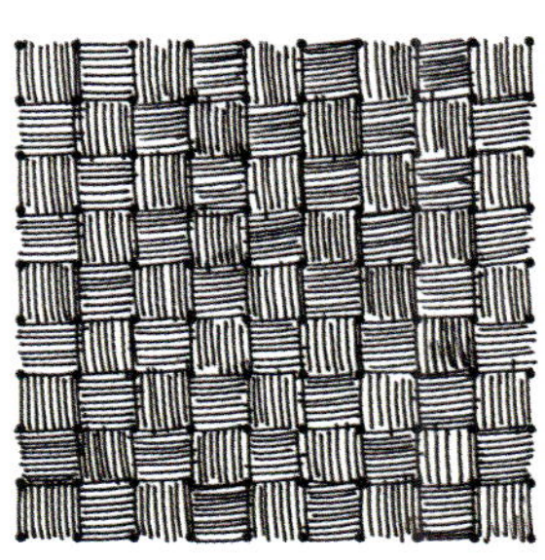
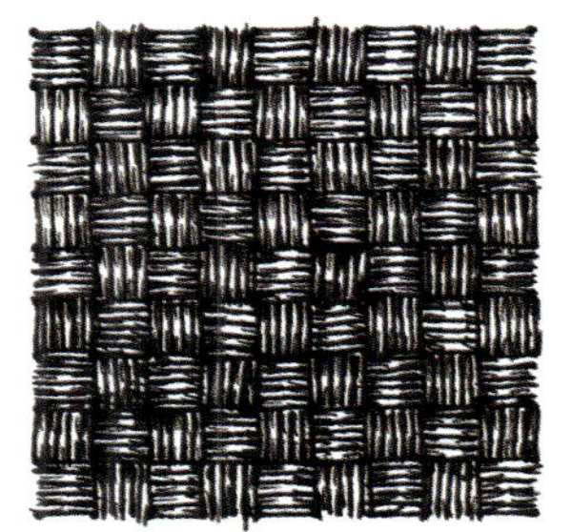

ZEN SOLUTIONS:

In figure 1, the lizardlike creature breaks out of the grid in terms of the head and upper body, though at the same time, the grid is used as an integral part of the patterning.

Figures 2 through 16 use line in their experimenting with pattern and the emergence of form to create an array of highly diverse imagery.

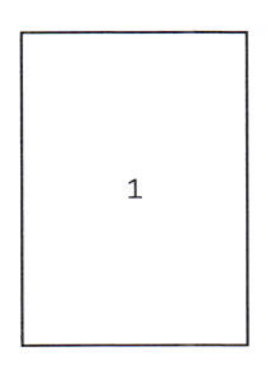

1. *Jaewon Park*
2. *Sangwook Song*
3. *Alexander Wager*
4. *Haemin Lim*
5. *Nakkyu Oh*
6. *Justin Bernard*
7. *Nakkyu Oh*
8. *Hyojoo Kim*
9. *Julia Kim*
10. *Hana Yoo*
11. *Nicole Lapenta*
12. *Jinkyung Myung*
13. *Hana Yoo*
14. *Ekaterina Boulakhova*
15. *Chiyoung Choo*
16. *Keith Cayea*

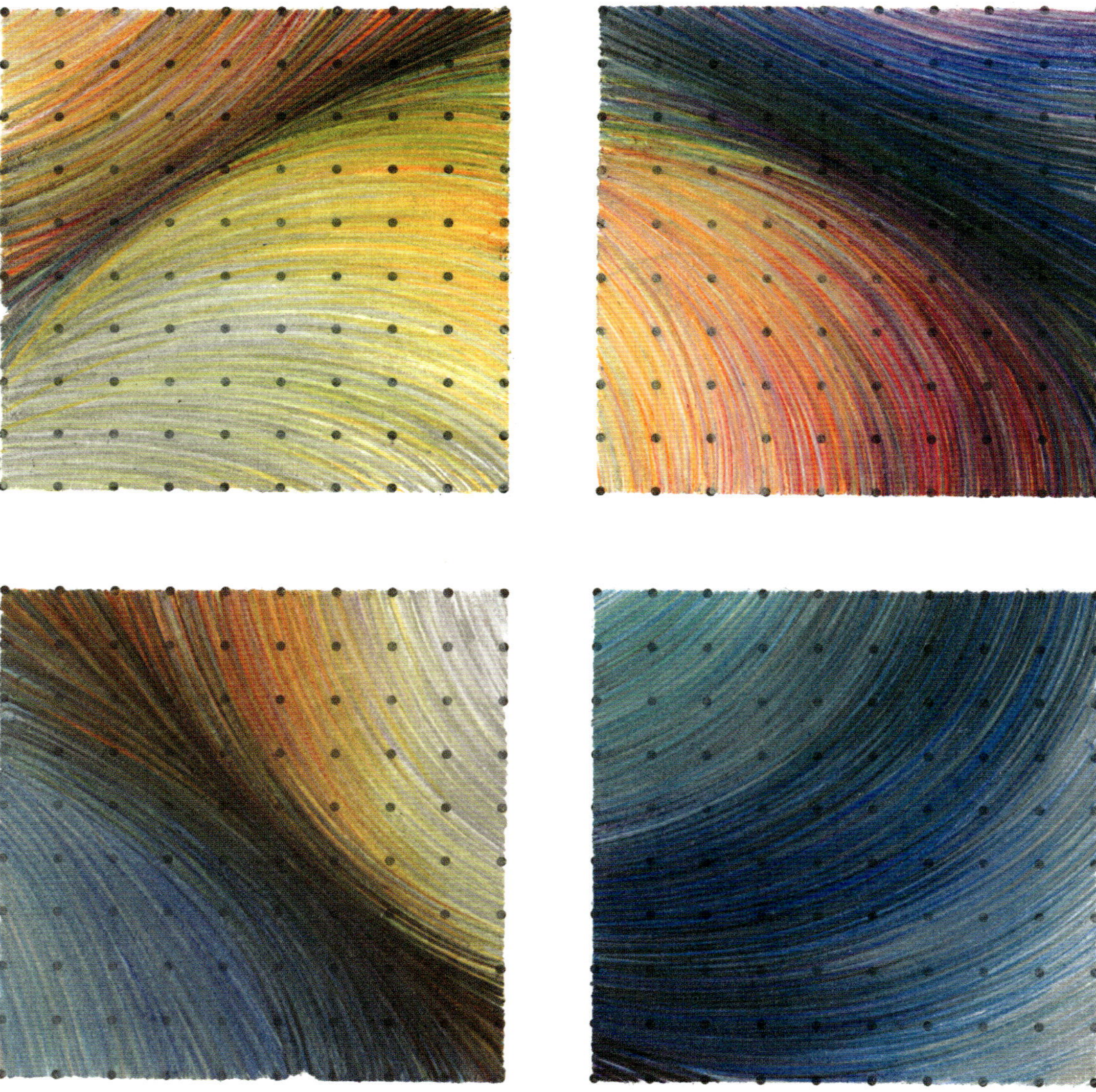

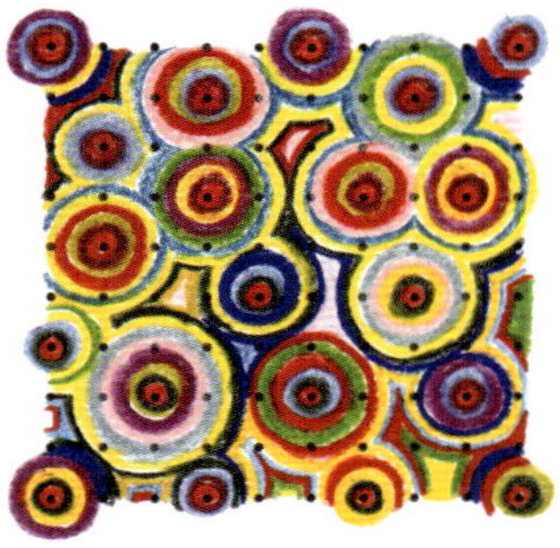

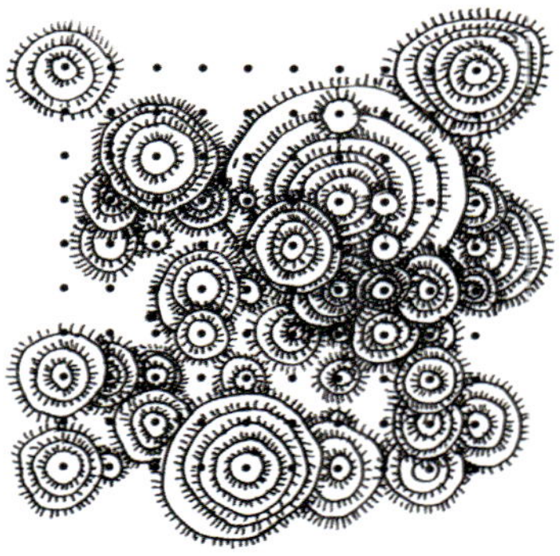

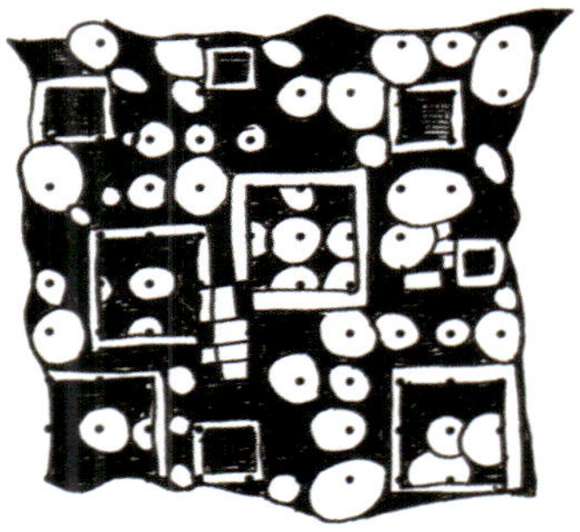

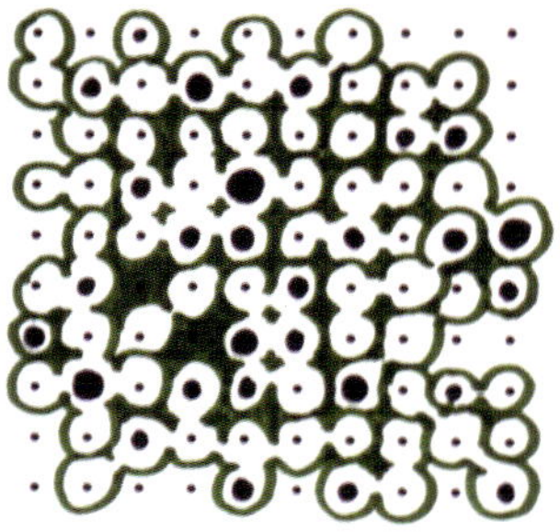

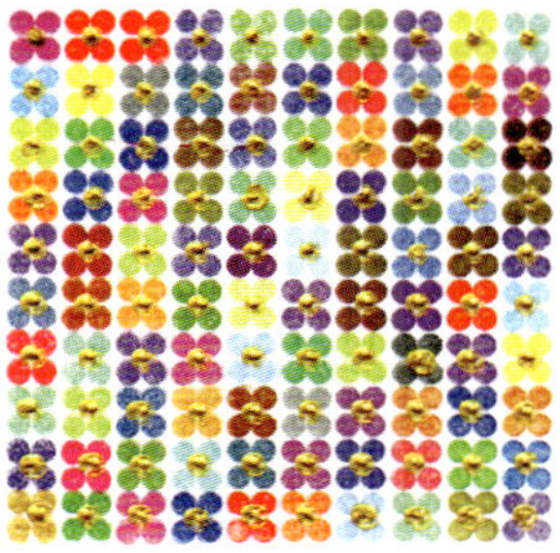

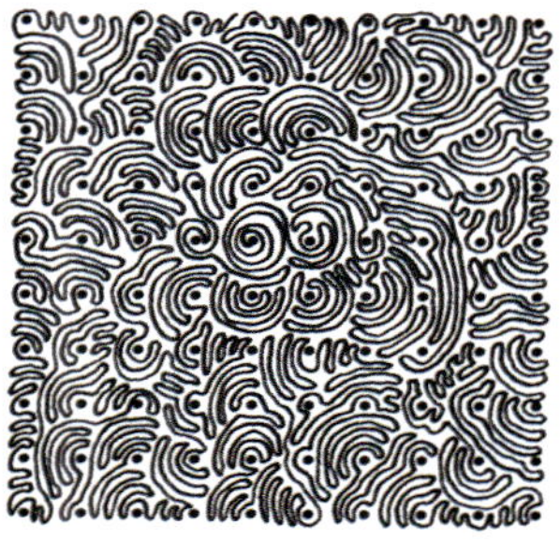

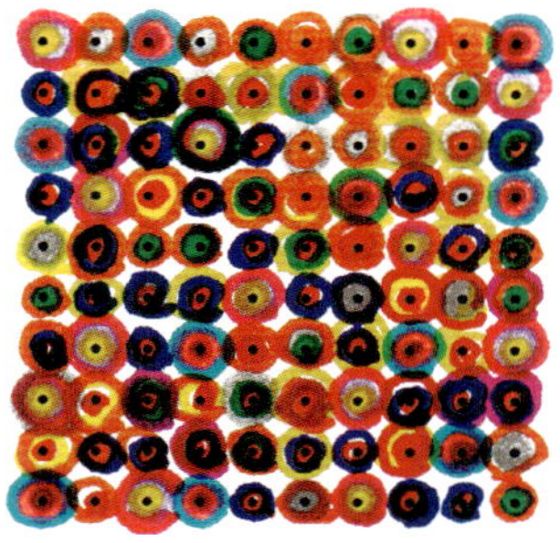

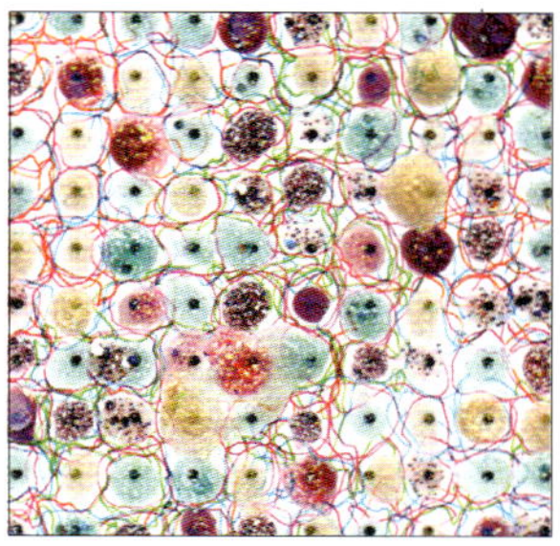

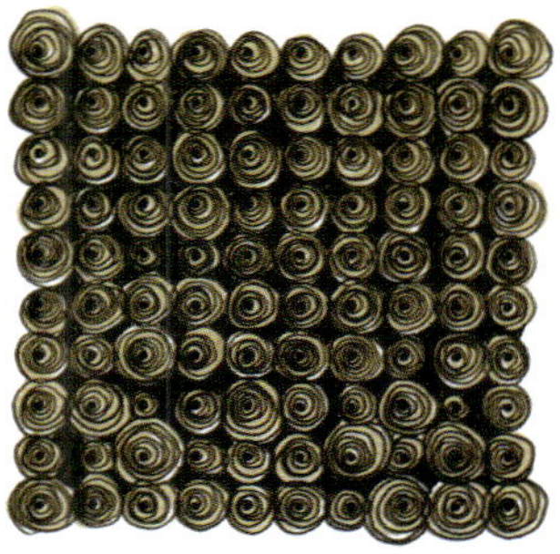

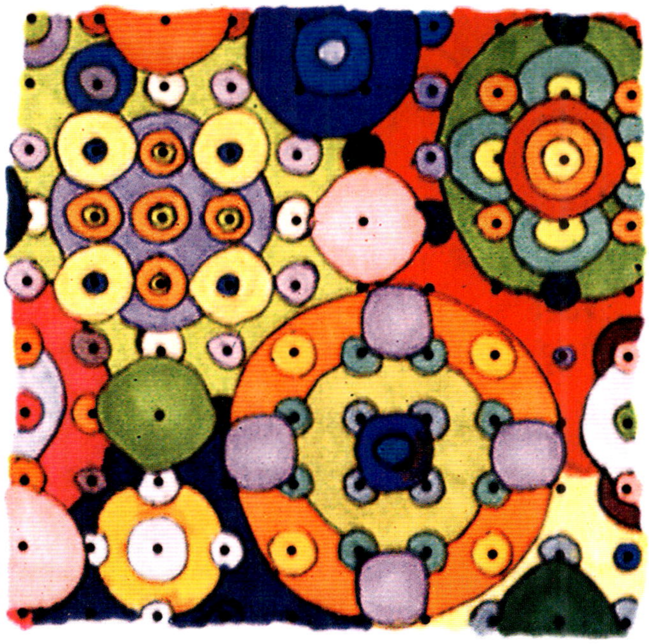

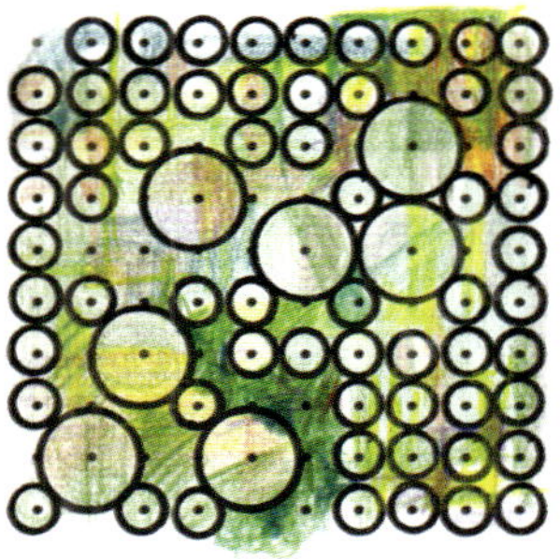

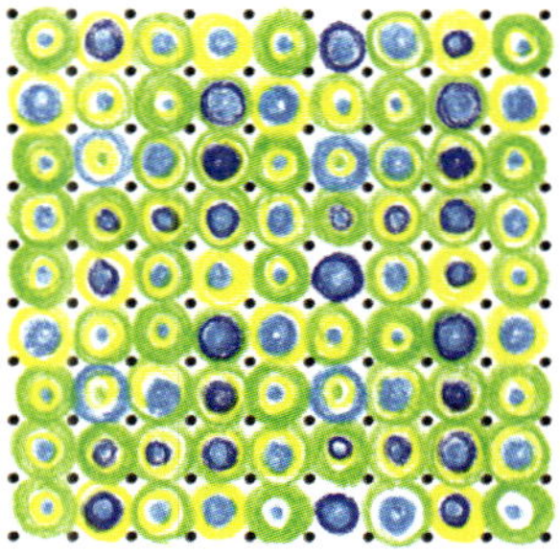

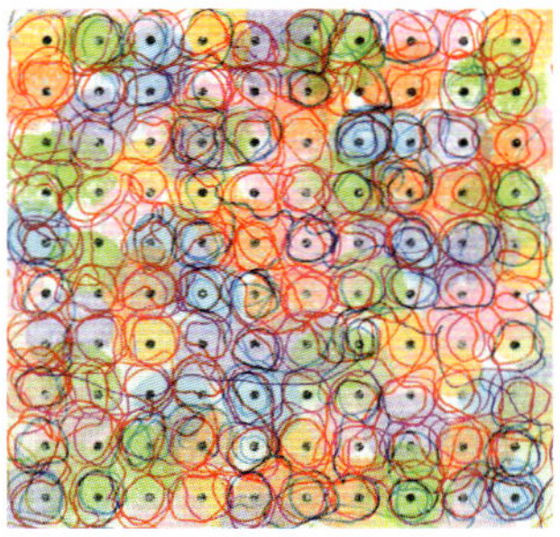

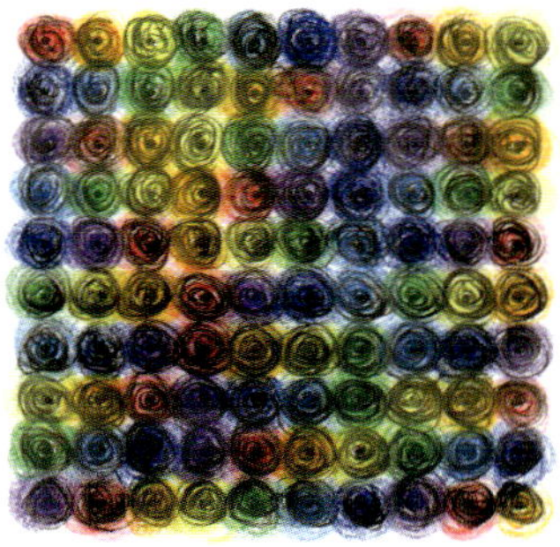

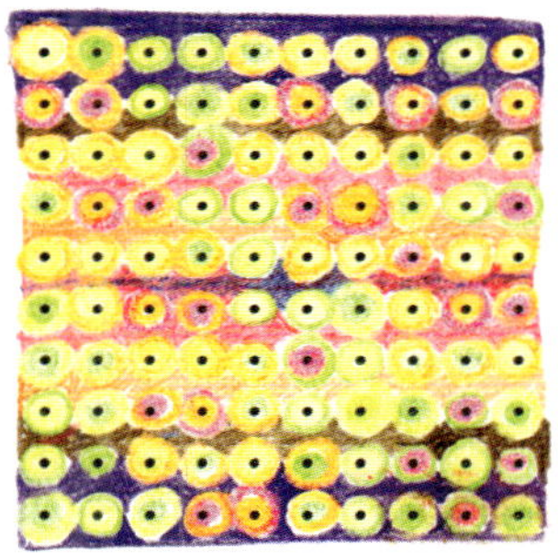

ZEN SOLUTIONS:

Figures 1 through 4 deal with movement, pattern, color, and dimensionality, while at the same time, given their similarities and positioning to one another, function as a single image.

Figures 5 through 19 use the common element of circles as a motif. The solutions vary greatly from one another, which signals the multiplicity of emerging avenues of expression using a common theme

Given that the grid is a representation of one hundred mechanically drawn circles, to extend this very form seems a natural response to the problem.

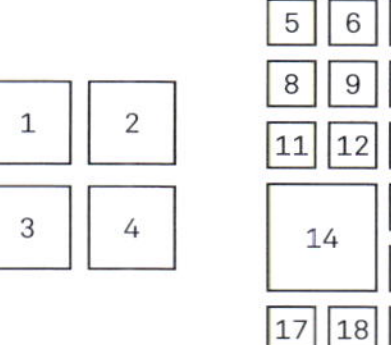

1–4. Yeonwoo Jung
5. Ryan DeCarlo
6. Daisy Millard
7. Jessica Pietrafeso
8. Jane Goldman
9. Najung Kim
10. Nakkyu Oh
11. Hisa Ide
12. Takako Saegusa
13. Nicole Lapenta
14. Brenton Dashevsky
15. Kim Foster
16. Seyoung Park
17. Takako Saegusa
18. Carlotta Merzari
19. Y. Kim

Yet, in all of these solutions, the circles have a sense of spontaneity, which is in direct opposition to the starting point of the grid.

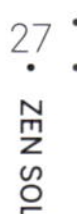

zen and the creation of images. In a
one's inner self, be present to wh
to develop a more intuitive an
process which enhances yo
problem solving, experiment in
see below by creating image
Rely on your feelings. This is a
habitual thought, where pl
of a child becomes para
enter a way of worki
the next in a spo
way. Before yo
what your soluti
takes you. Let y
head. There ar

[illegible] ATED BY RICHARD W[illegible] JUDITH [illegible] ©2001, [illegible] BY VISUAL [illegible] PRESS, LTD. [illegible] DIRECTORS: [illegible] JUDITH [illegible], DES[illegible]ER: [illegible]SWITHA RODRI[illegible]

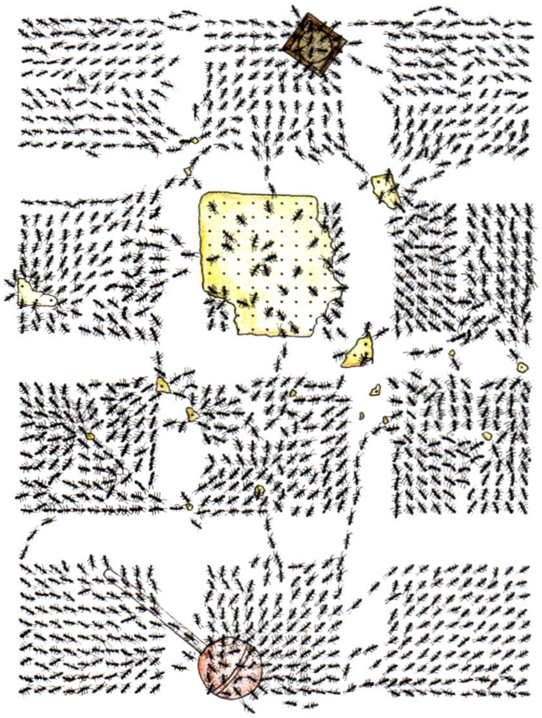

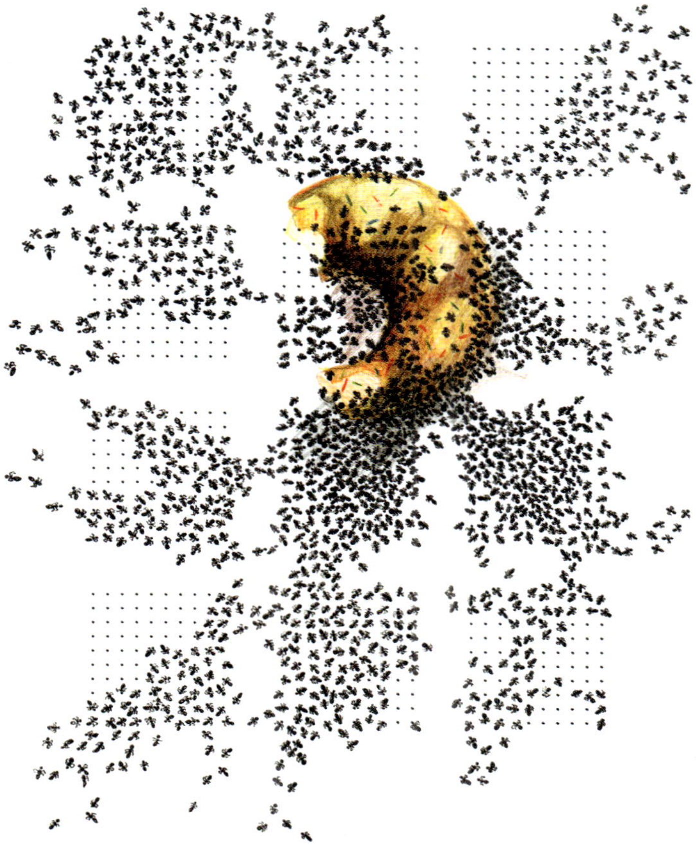

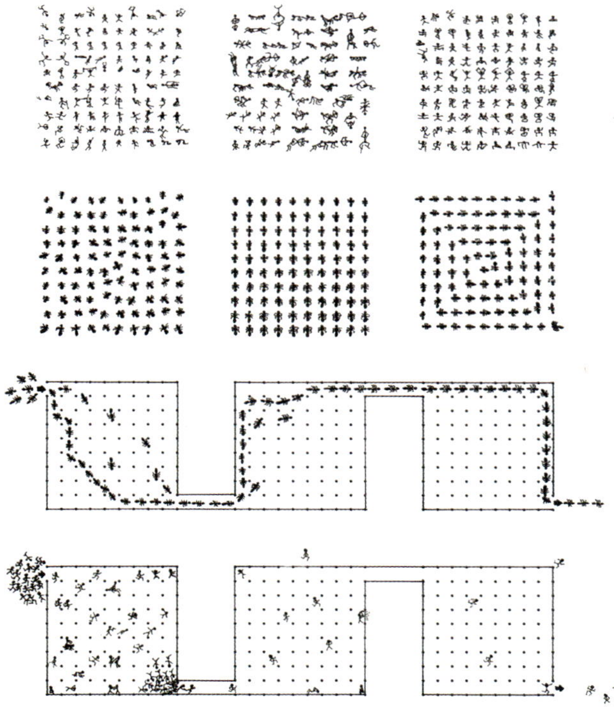

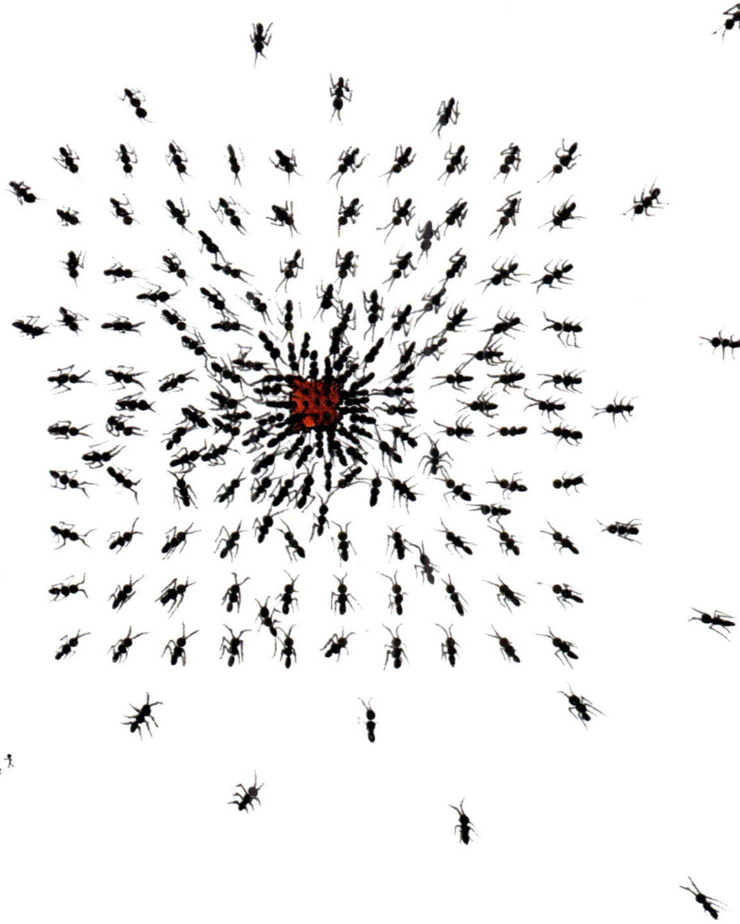

ZEN SOLUTIONS:

Using ants as a theme, figures 1 through 4 represent the interaction of all twelve grids.

Figure 5 represents a single grid on the assignment sheet that incorporates a red square as the focal point. In this solution, as in figures 1 through 4, the dots became the point of departure in the creation of different ant colonies.

In figures 2 through 4 each of the twelve gridded areas can stand alone as single narratives.

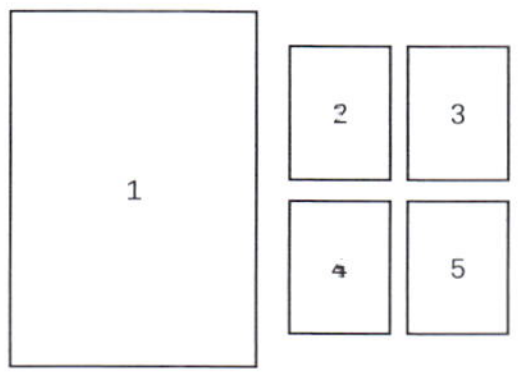

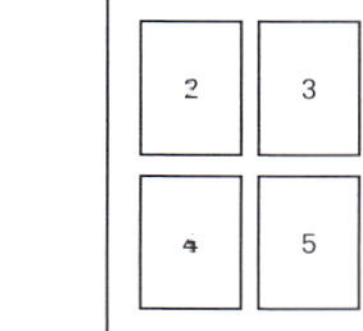

1. *You Kim*
2. *Minyeong Park*
3. *Hyunjeon Kim*
4. *Alfred Park*
5. *S. Kim*

ZEN SOLUTIONS:

Often, connecting the dots creates linear solutions that result in intricate patterns, or mazelike configurations.

Figures 1 and 2 reflect the influence of Keith Haring.

Figures 3 and 4 incorporate different narratives. In figure 3, the student began investigating patterning, then the project shifted from the abstract to the literal.

Figure 4 uses Christmas trees to create a maze using a geometric approach to patterning. Upon closer observation one can find a figure in the maze.

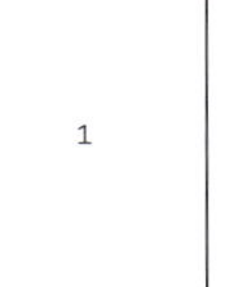

1. *Martha Guadarrama*
2. *Seonghye Kim*
3. *Christopher Breuer*
4. *Min Choi*

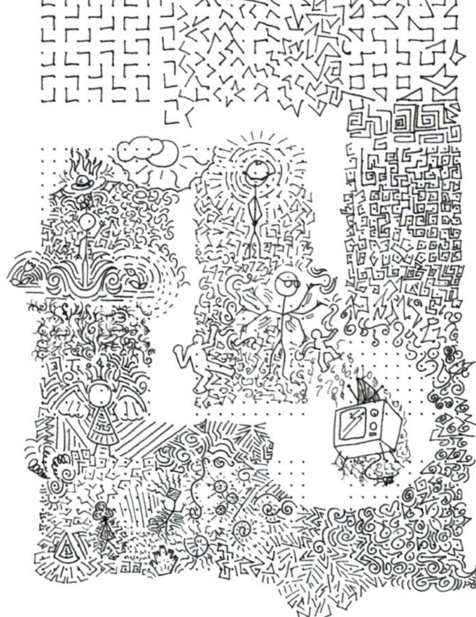

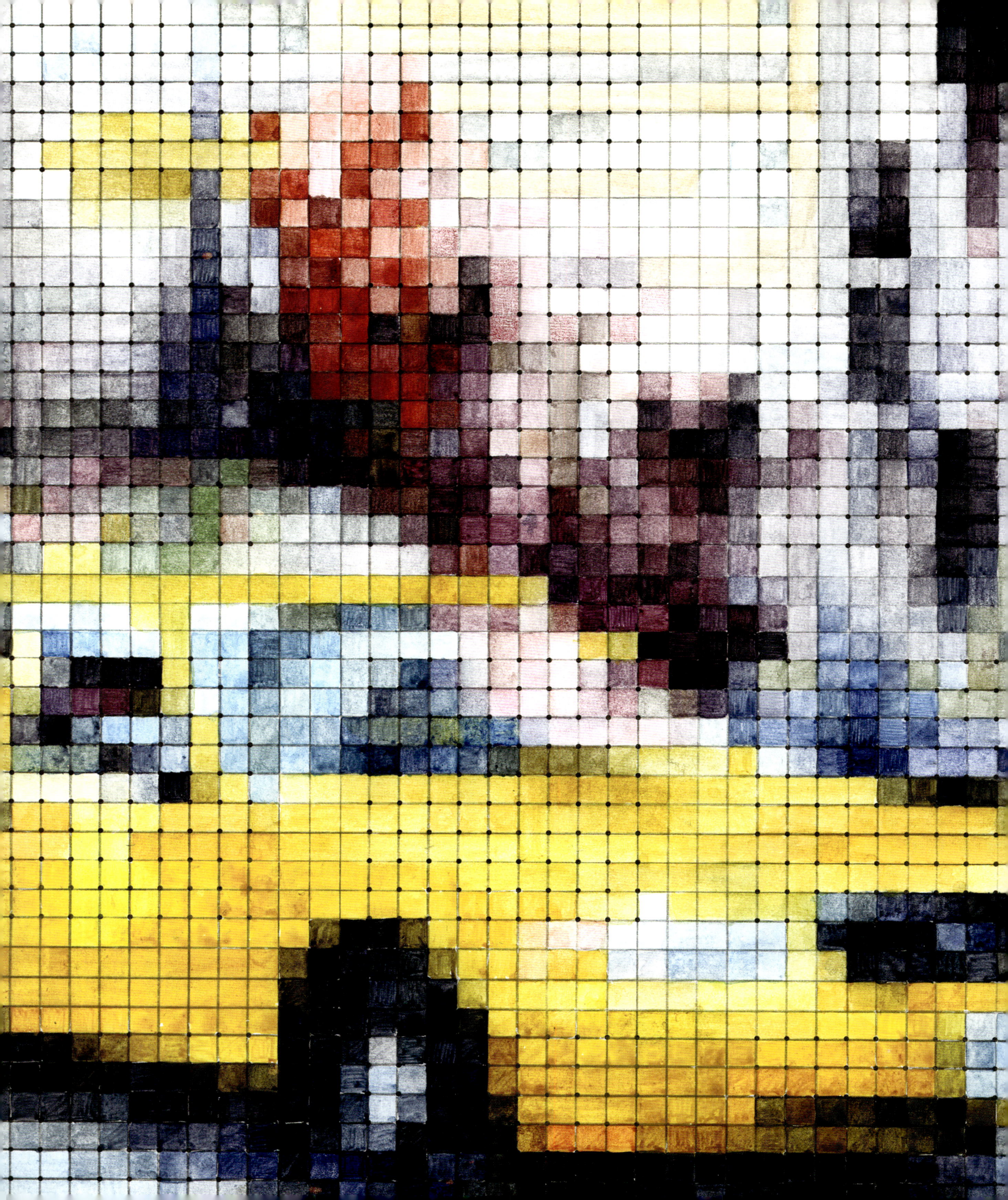

ZEN SOLUTIONS:

The contrast between a classical approach, as seen in figure 1, and the spontaneous romantic investigations as seen in figures 2 through 10, give rise to the enormity of possibilities inherent in this assignment within the space between these two genres.

One of the secrets in creating original imagery is to adhere to the formal restrictions of the grid, but also by experimenting with the restrictions of the grid, or negating the grid, one can be led into uncharted territory by reinterpreting the given conditions to create expressionistic work.

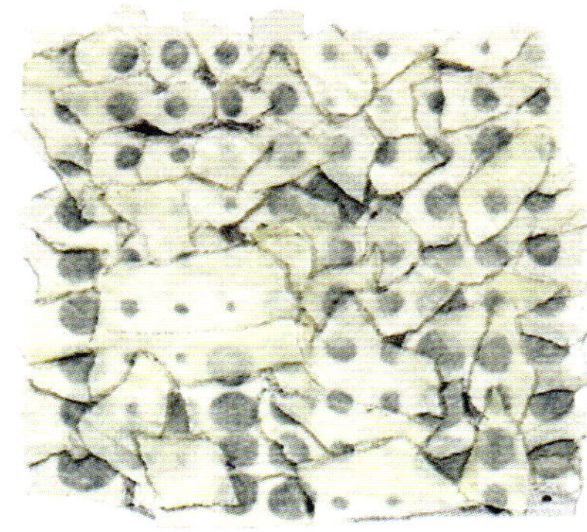

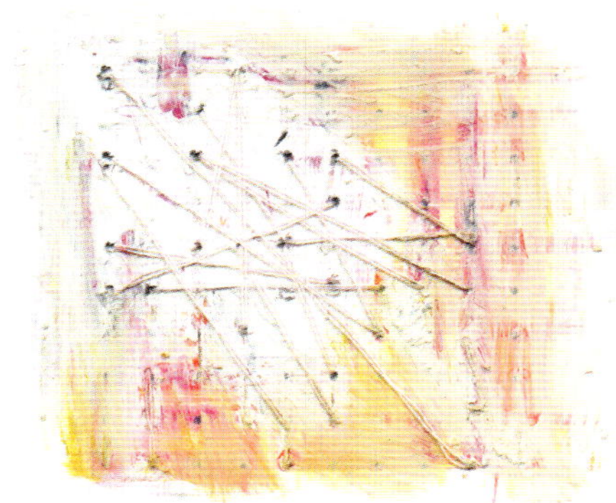

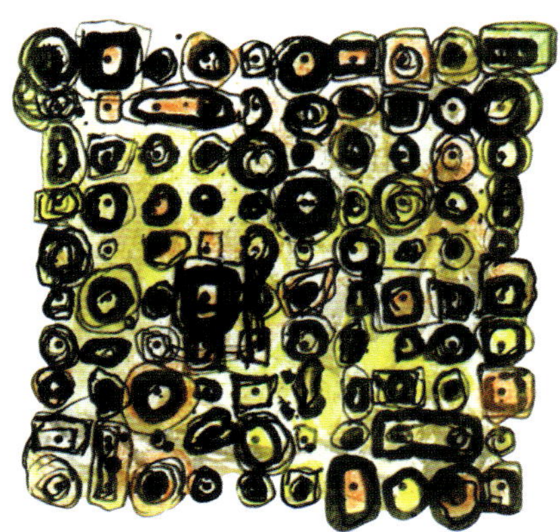

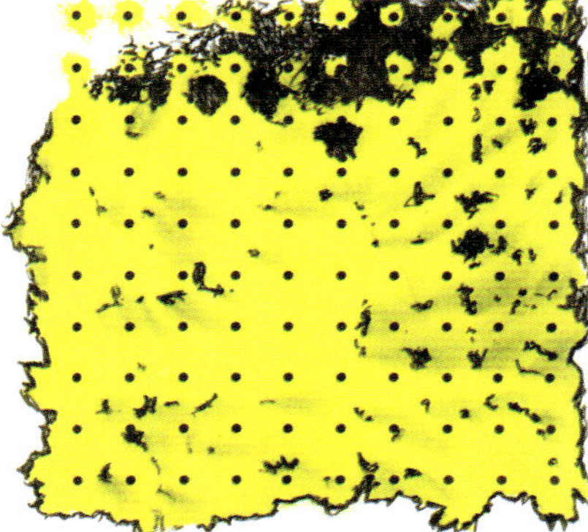

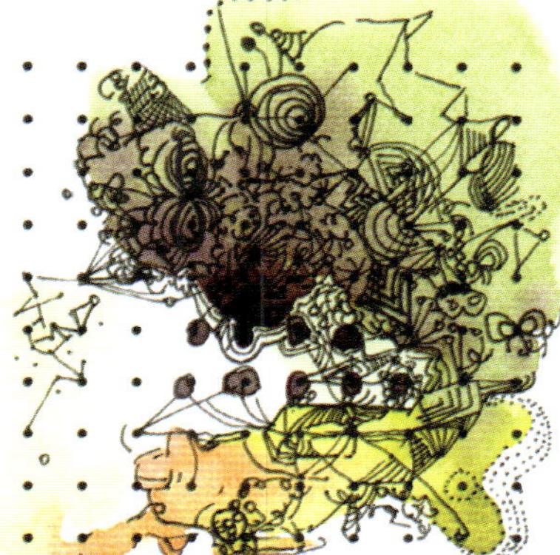

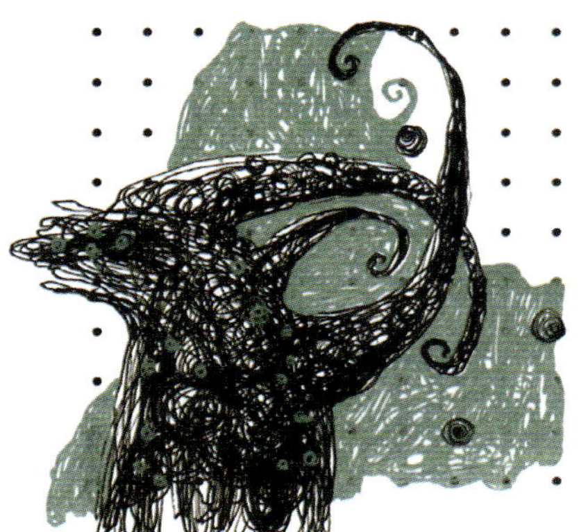

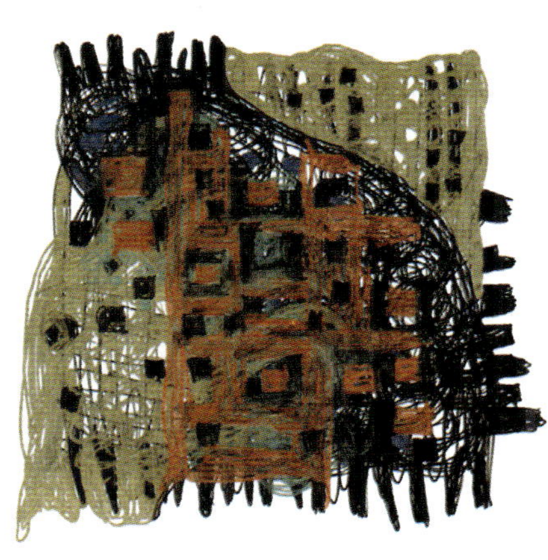

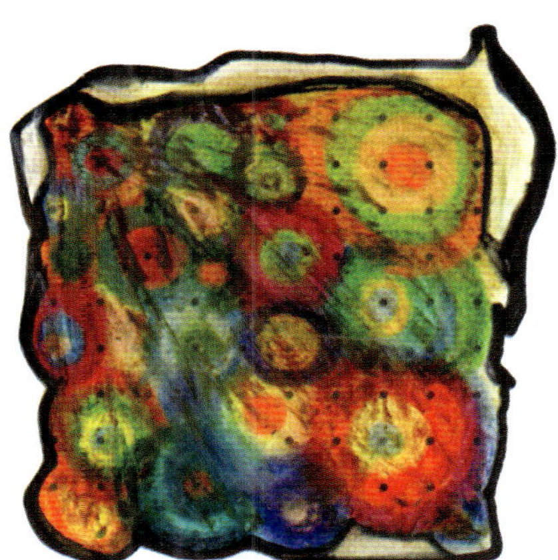

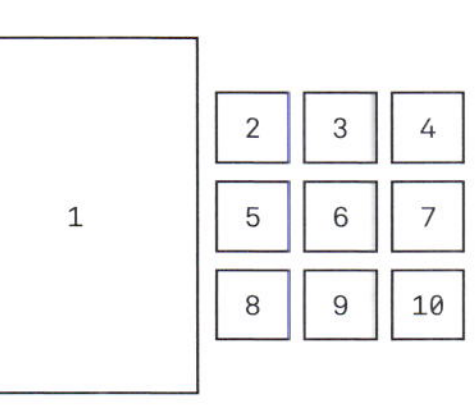

1. *Seunghee Lee*
2. *Najung Kim*
3. *Myungsun Jang*
4. *Chei Park*
5. *Sarah Macreading*
6. *Carlotta Merzari*
7. *Juhee Lim*

8-9. *Nataliya Hats*

10. *Lyanne Dubon*

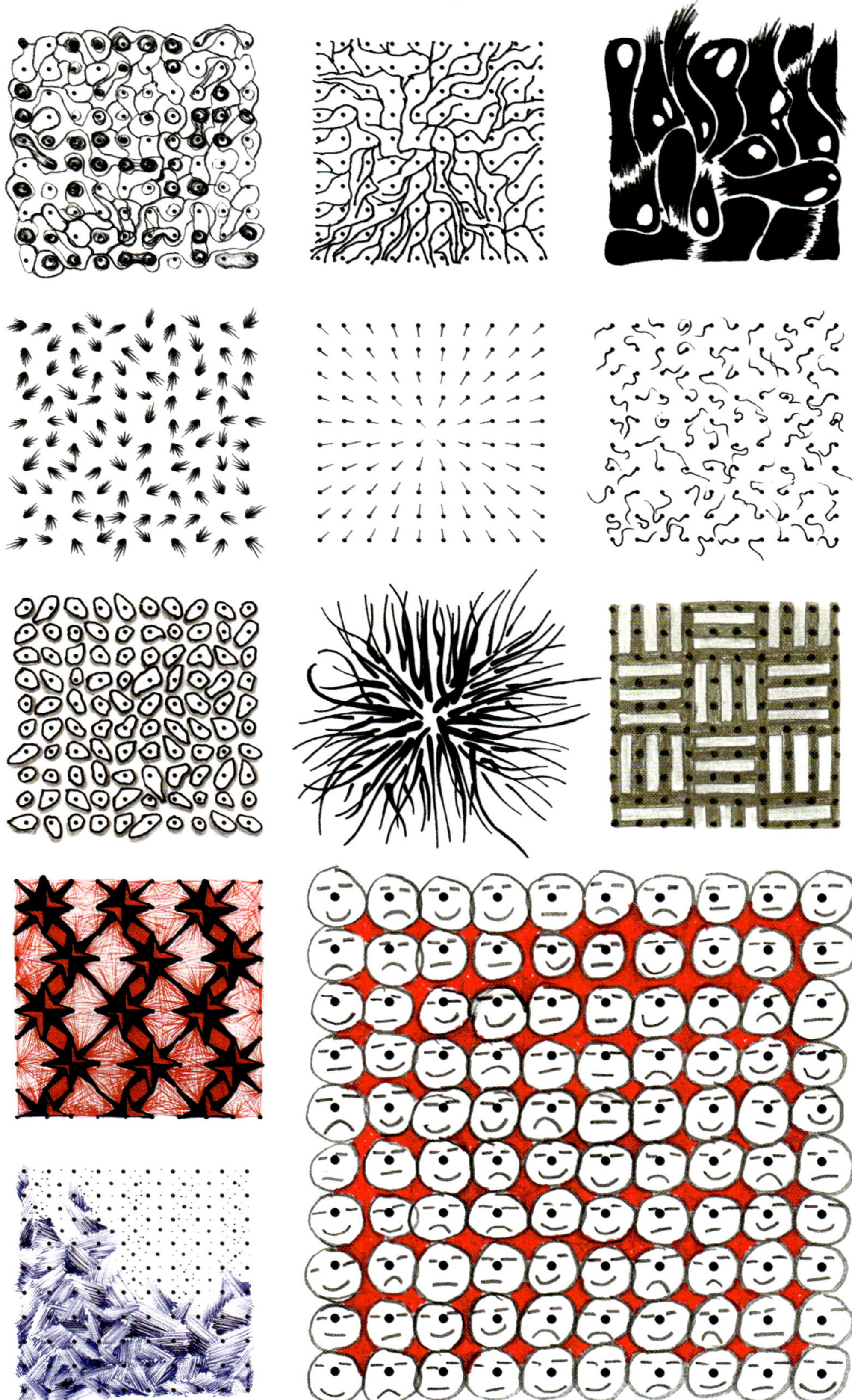

zen and the creation of images. In an attempt to touch one's inner self, be present to where ideas arise and to develop a more intuitive and insightful creative process which enhances your capabilities for problem solving, experiment in the twelve grids you see below by creating images without thinking. Rely on your feelings. This is an activity to bypass habitual thought, where playing with the freedom of a child becomes paramount. Allow yourself to enter a way of working where one form dictates the next in a spontaneous and unpremeditated way. Before you begin, try not to predetermine what your solutions will be. See where the exercise takes you. Let your hand lead you, rather than your head. There are no limitations on color or medium.

ZEN SOLUTIONS:

Figures 1 through 13 exhibit a range of varied executions using primarily black and white and, at times, the support of an additional color.

Figure 6, which appears to be a random composition of sperm, in fact adheres strictly to the structure of the grid pattern creating a dichotomy that reconciles two divergent genres.

Figure 13 is a highly personal abstract reconfiguration of the grid.

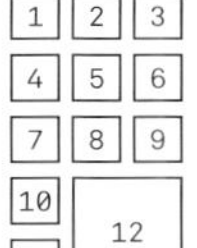

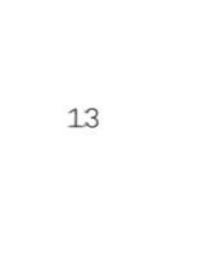

1–2. *Myungsun Jang*
3. *Louis Rivera*
4. *Nicole Lapenta*
5. *Jaesung Jung*
6. *Angela Fan*
7. *Najung Kim*
8. *Jaesung Jung*
9. *Sira Kim*
10. *Rigel Ferrin*
11. *Stephen Myers*
12. *Whitney Young*
13. *Eunhye Ro*

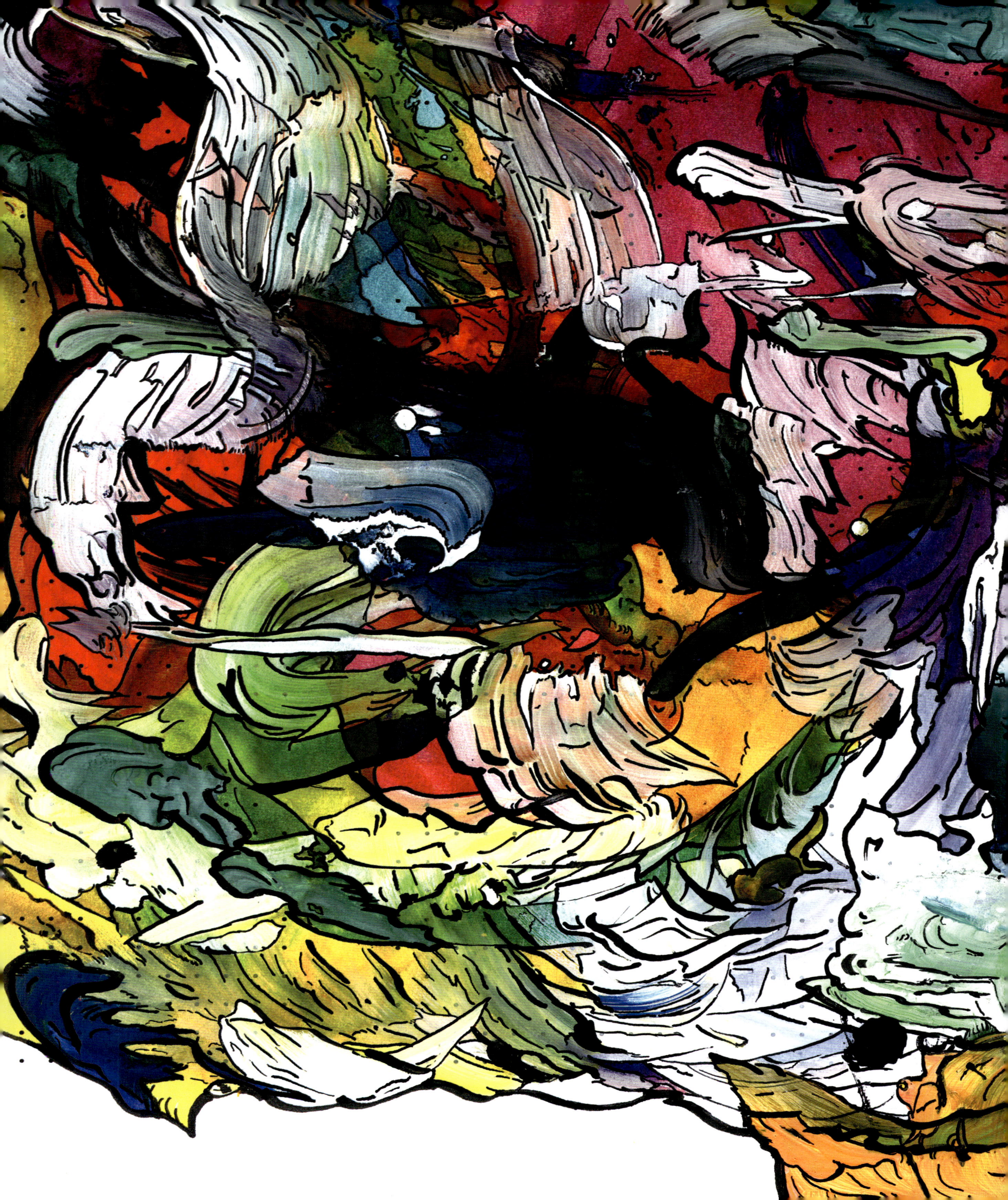

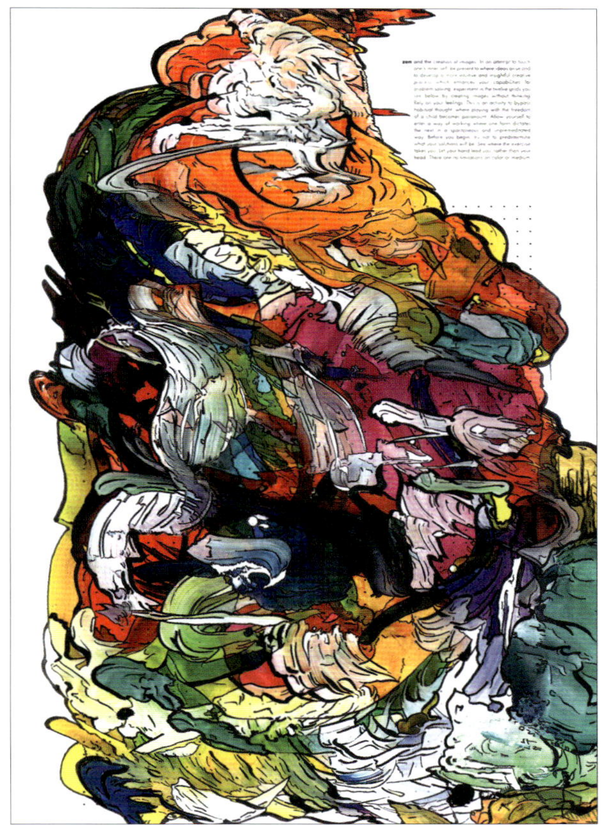

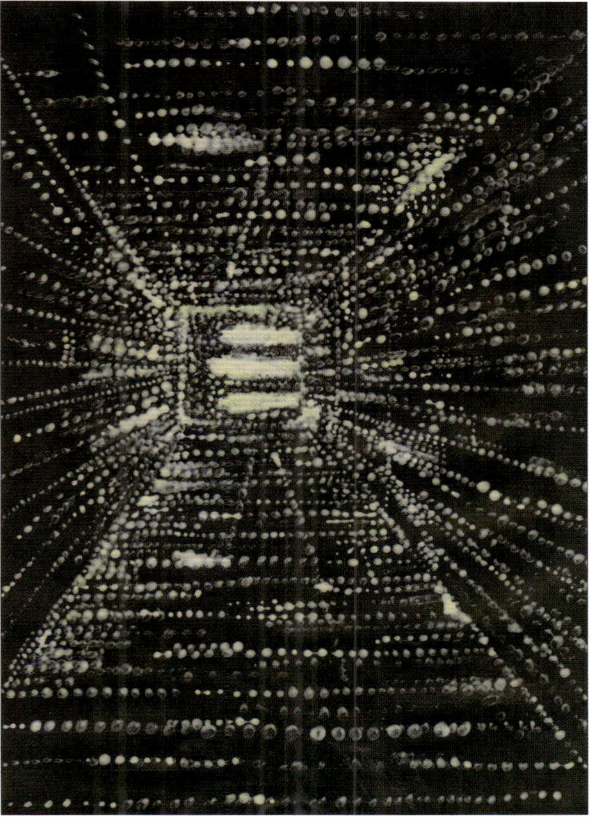

ZEN SOLUTIONS:

Figure 1 is a magnification of a section of figure 2. This solution was executed by applying color first, which then suggested the areas to be delineated by black ink. This highly abstract personal investigation into form deals with space, tension, pattern, line, and the interaction of color.

Figures 3 through 5 are primarily black and white investigations of form that deal with abstraction and fantasylike storytelling.

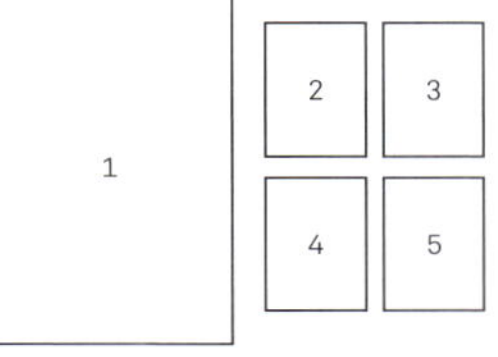

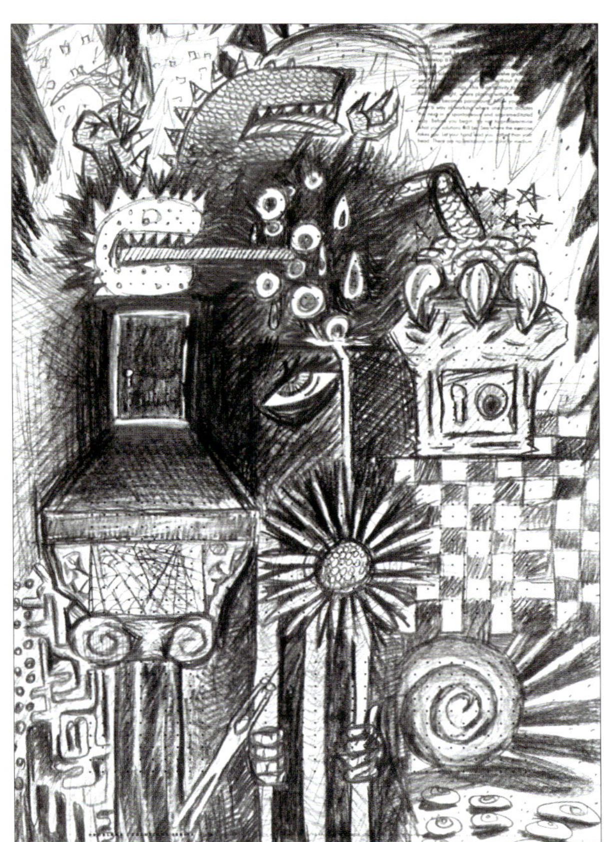

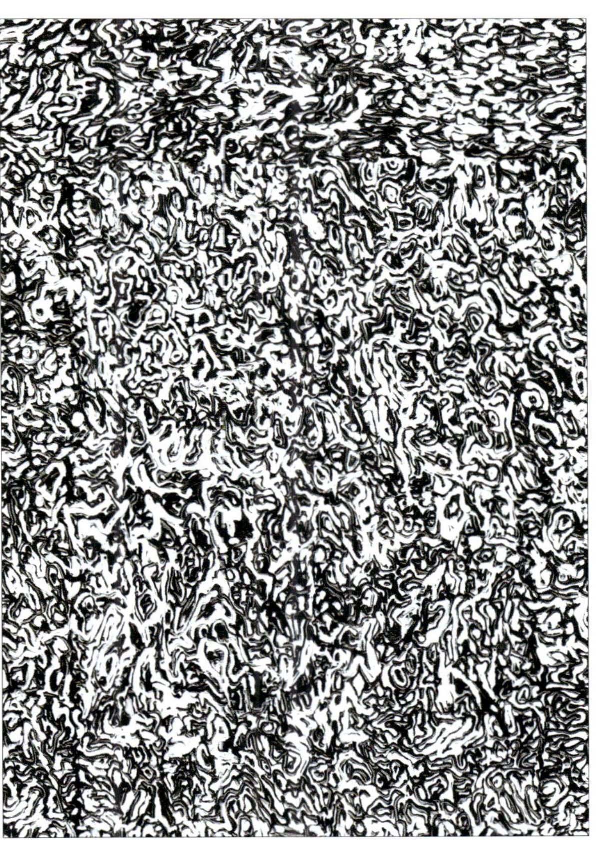

1–2. Sarah O'Conor
3. Gisung Lee
4. Christopher Lee
5. Nicholas Gray

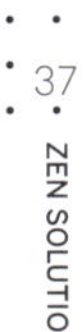

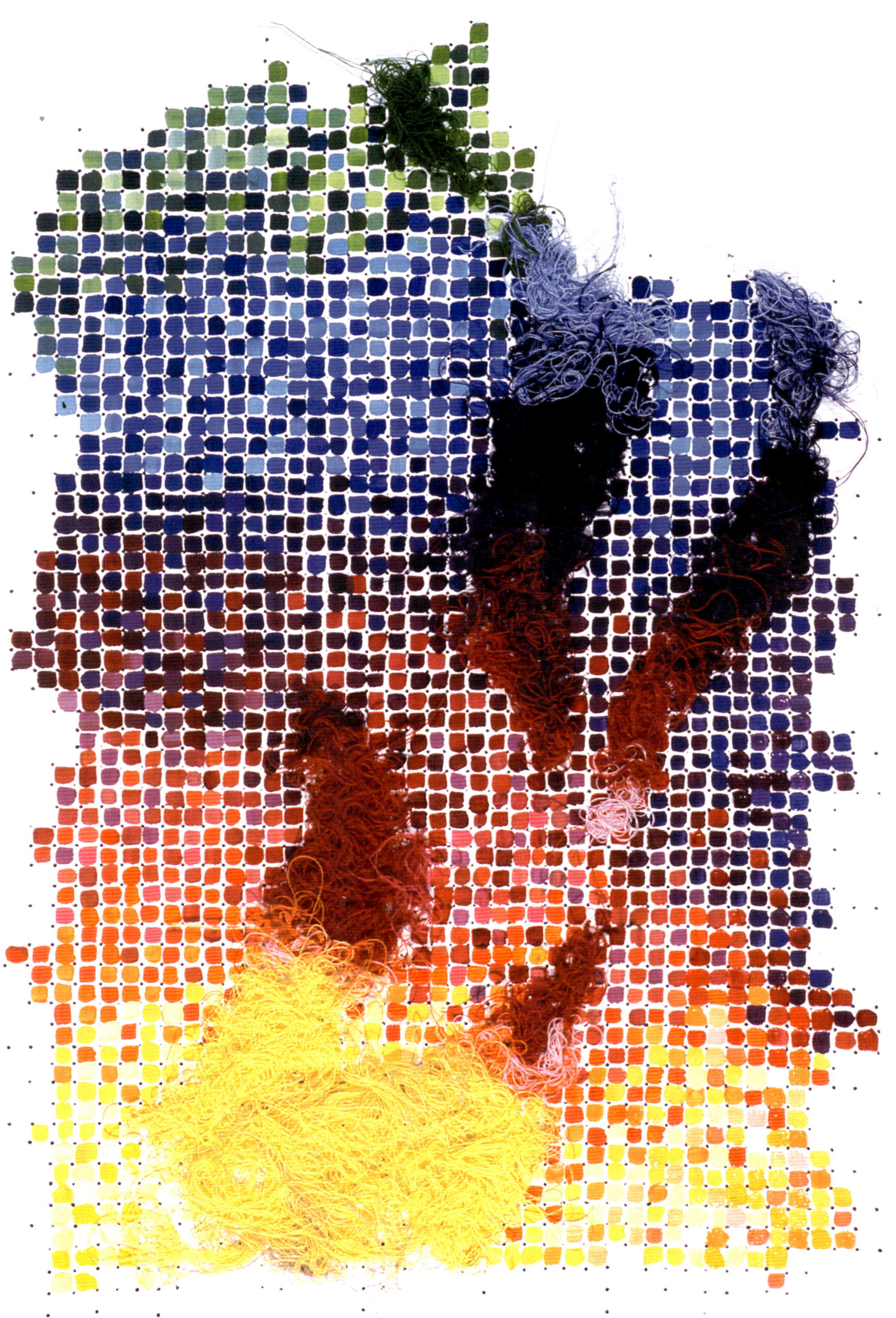

ZEN SOLUTIONS:

For all these solutions, pattern is the overarching element.

Figure 1 uses three-dimensional materials in executing the solution.

Figures 2 through 4 utilize the gridded sheet to create a narrative involving corn, while figures 3 and 4 use this organic image to reference a video game.

Figure 5 expresses a curious pictoral execution, where each of the screws that appear to be dimensional are carefully rendered, while the red linear portion is an actual piece of thread, which is sewn throughout the solution.

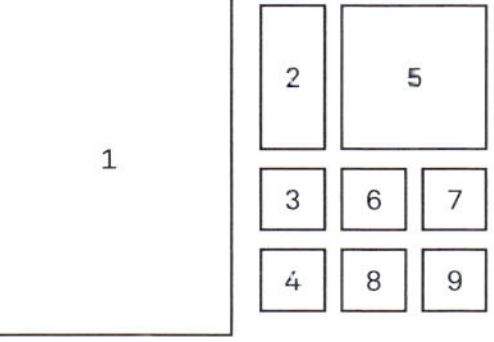

1. *Amanda Pastenkos*
2–4. *Elizabeth Bucholz*
5. *Sunyoung Koo*
6. *Amanda Pastenkos*
7. *Najung Kim*
8. *Kristen Hoge*
9. *Najung Kim*

Figures 6 through 9 strictly adhere to the given grid using a blue palette.

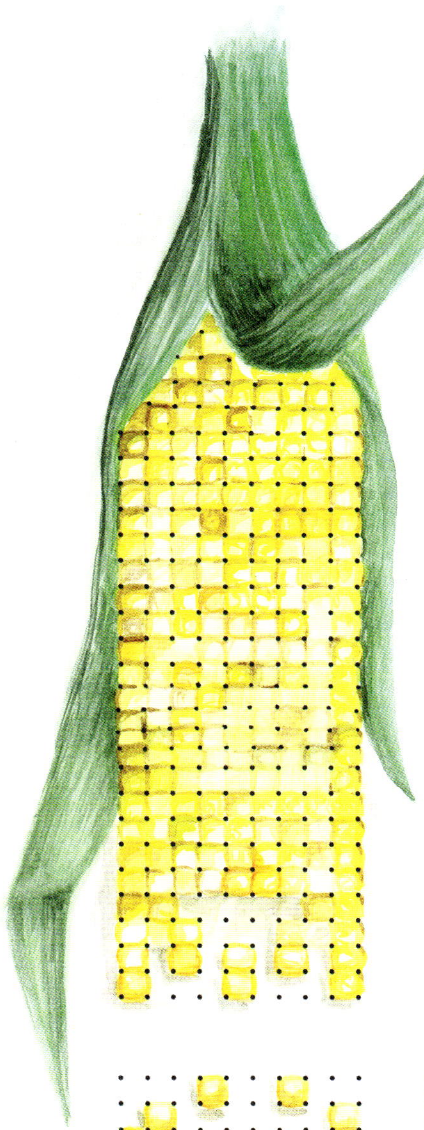

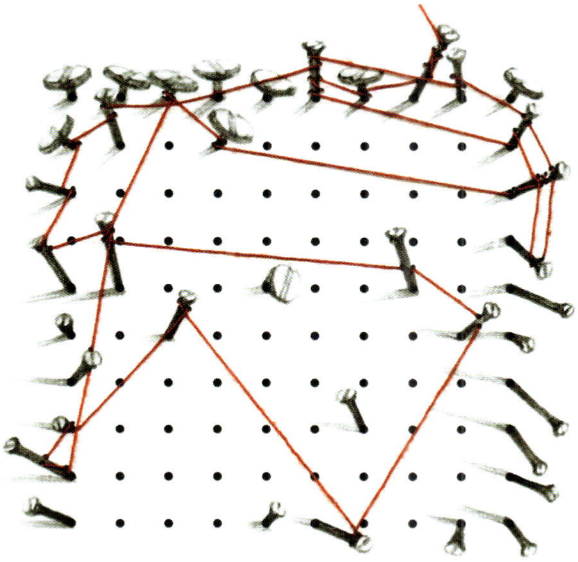

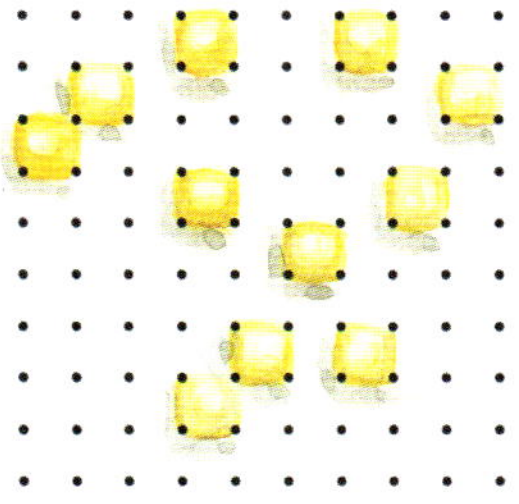

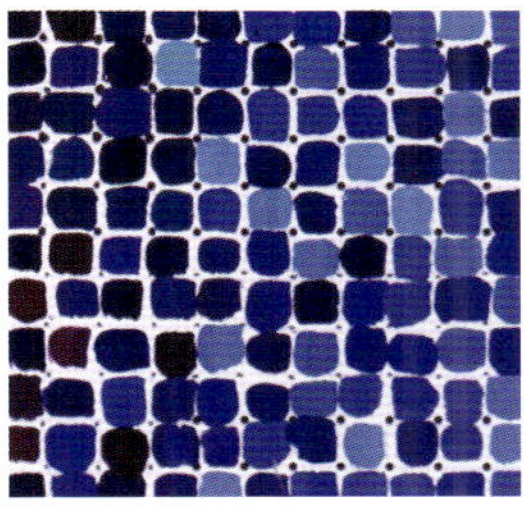

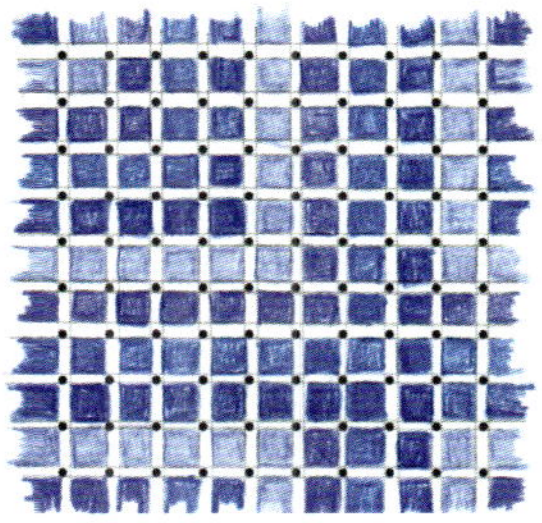

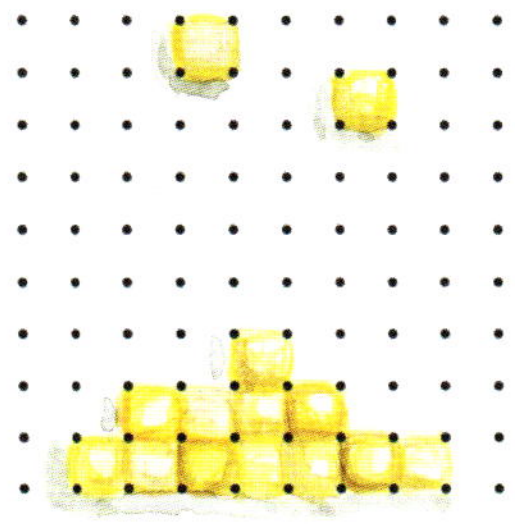

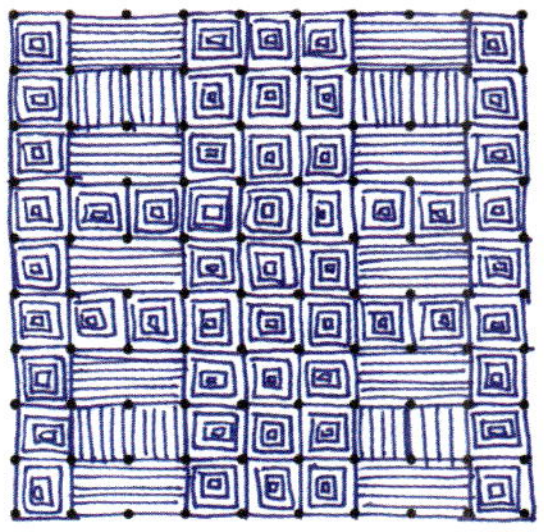

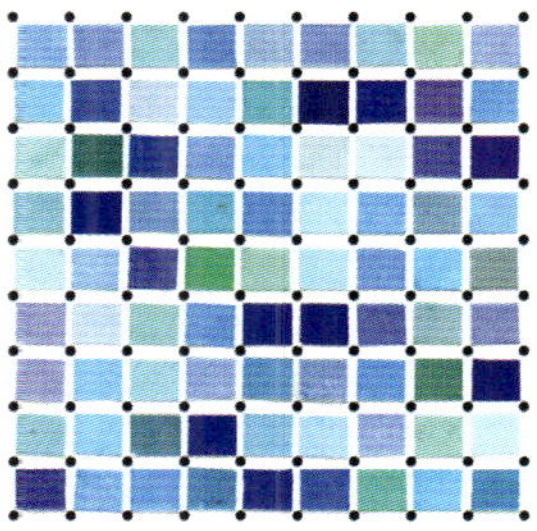

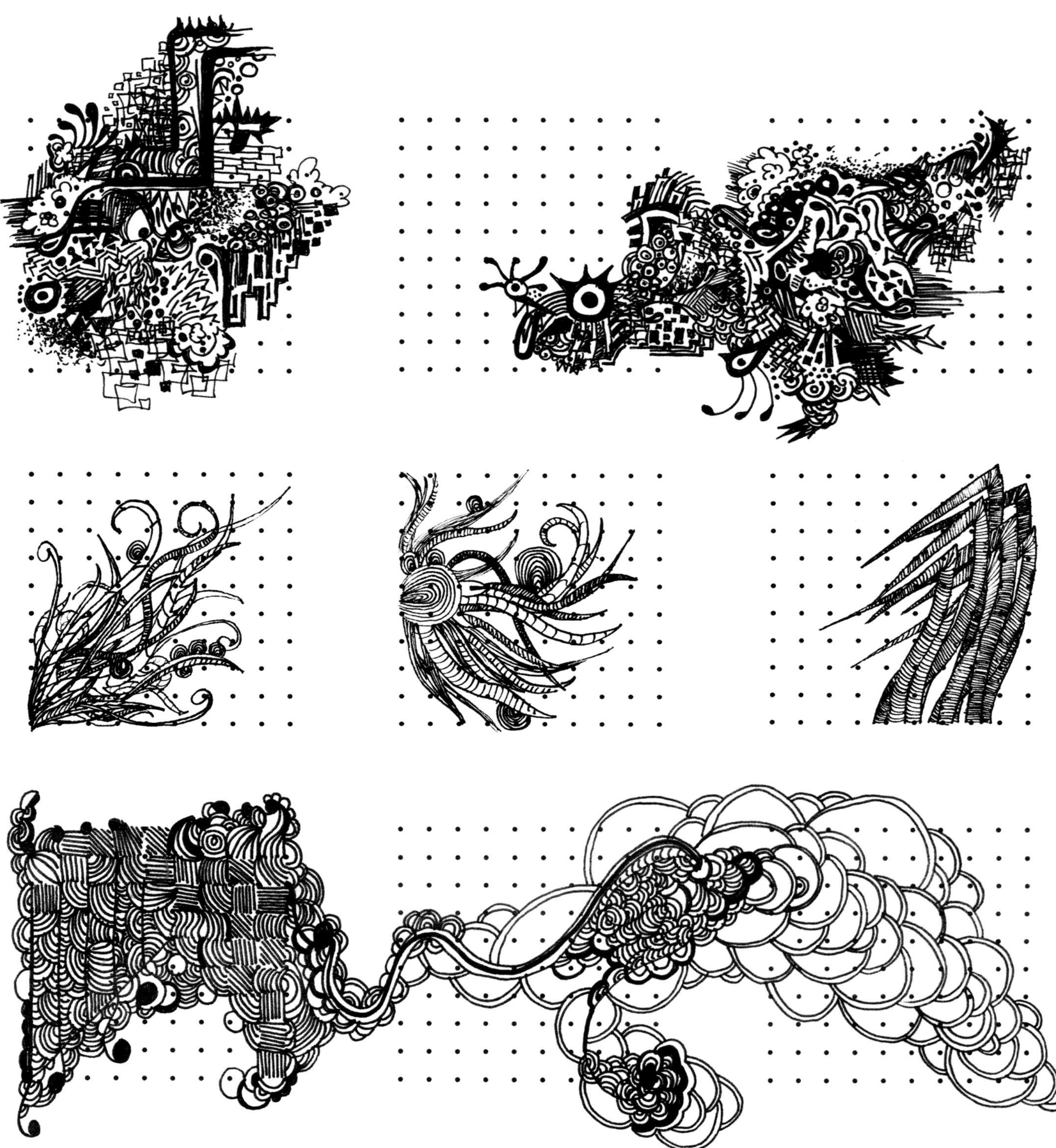

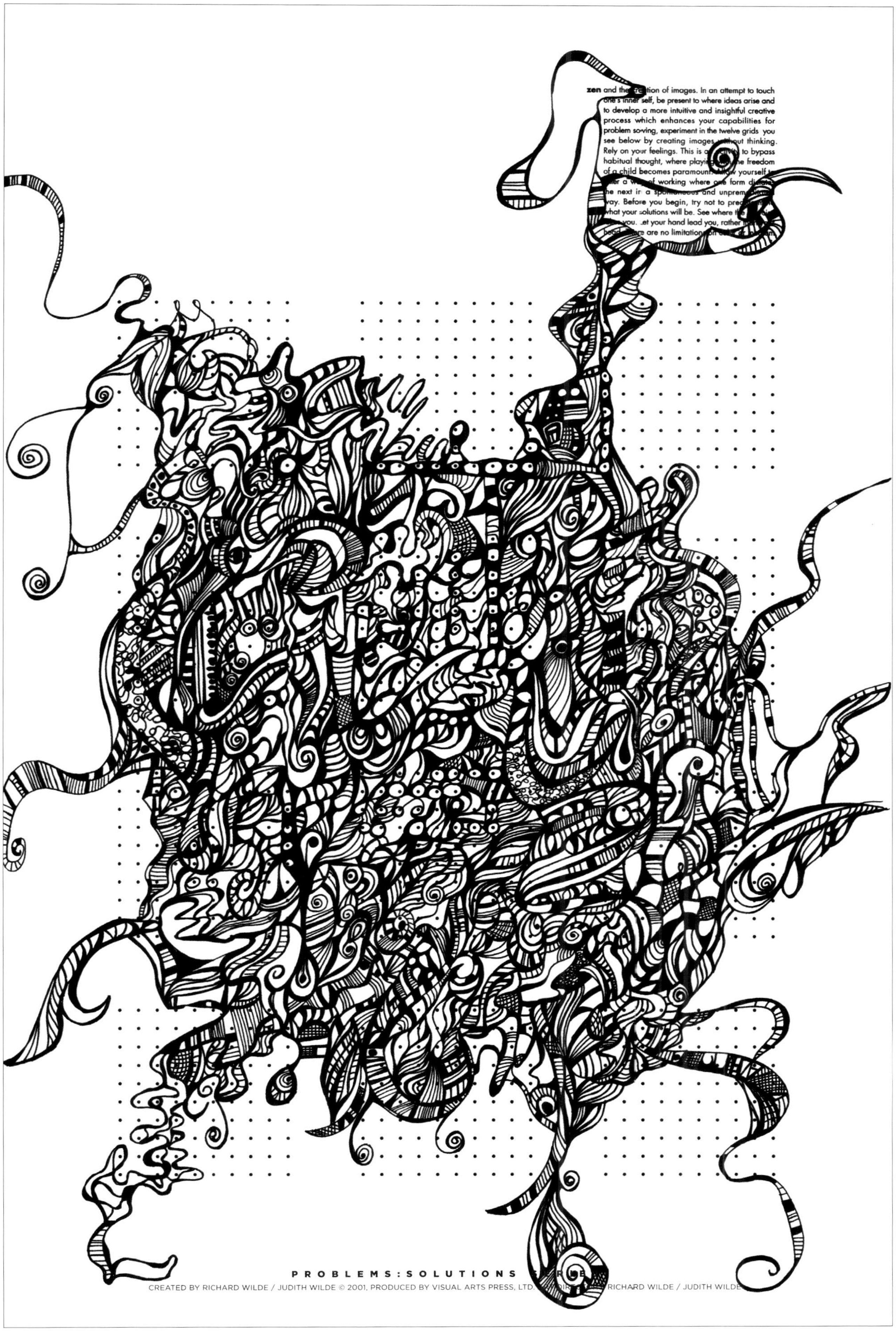

ZEN SOLUTIONS:

The highly linear organic solutions in figures 1 through 9 are depictions that at times appear in more than one gridded area of the assignment sheet.

Curiously, figures 2 and 3 are transformed into a bird with a black circle serving as its eye, although the initial intent was to simply create abstract configurations of line and form. Figures 4 through 6 also infer literal imagery, that initially began as abstract investigations.

Figure 10 utilizes all twelve grids in the creation of a meandering stylized doodle that deals with line and complex patterning.

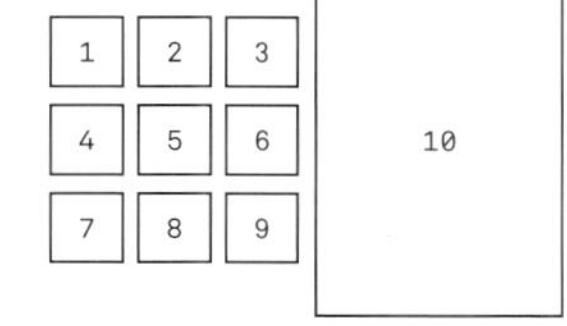

1–3. *Christine Dempsey*
4–6. *Seiji Hori*
7–9. *Erica Knauss*
10. *Marie-Yan Morvan*

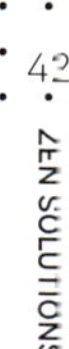

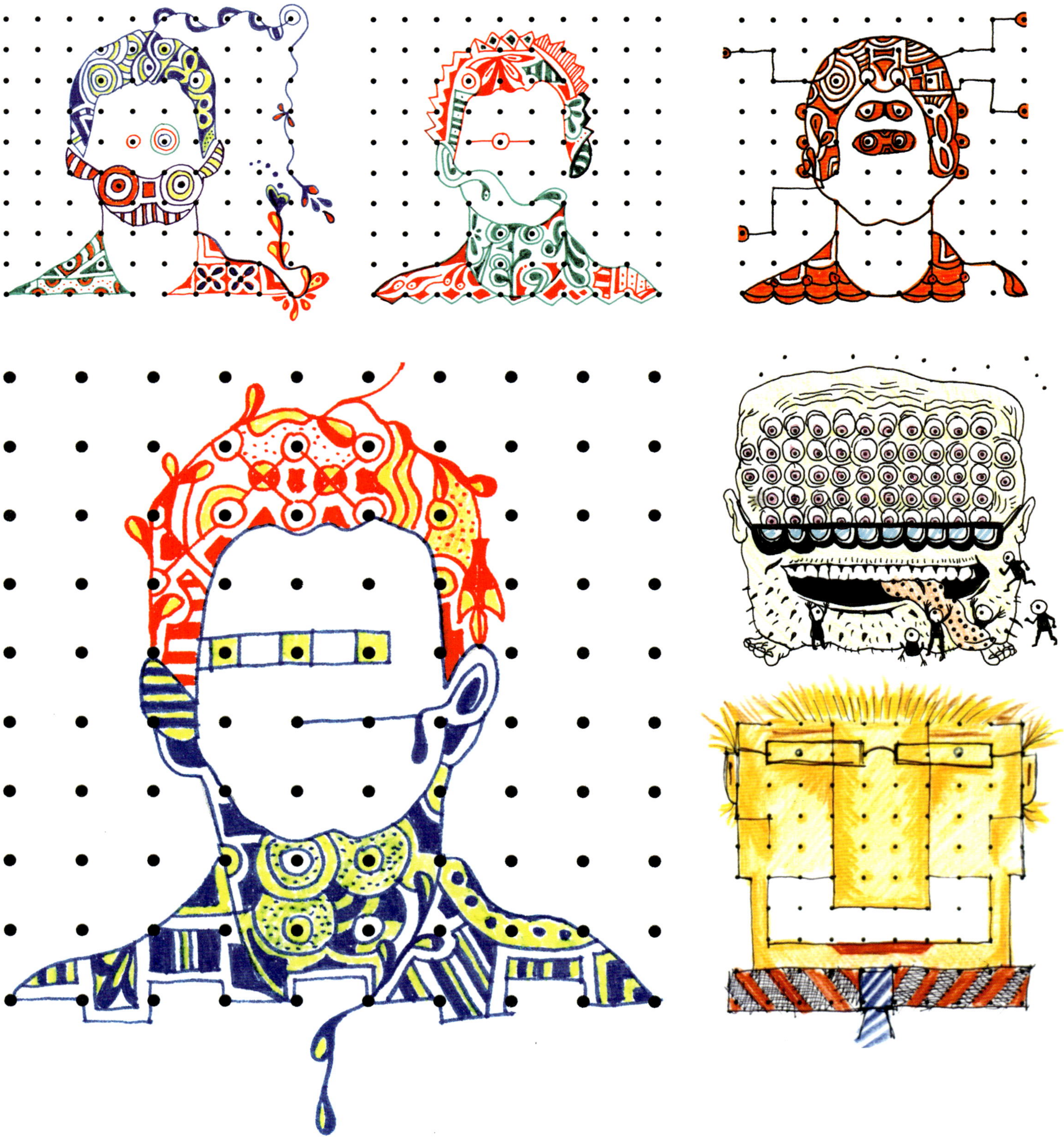

ZEN SOLUTIONS:

Creating a face is a popular response to this project. Adhering to the rigid grid, while at the same time being true to one's nature in terms of form, color, line, and patterning, one can achieve innovative imagery.

Figures 1 through 4 are drawn by the same student and exhibit a variation of a single theme.

Figures 5 and 6 deal with exaggeration and humor, while figures 7 through 10, done by one student, have a thematic quality, and only marginally follow the dictates of the grid. Each solution transcends one's habitual nature in creating original imagery.

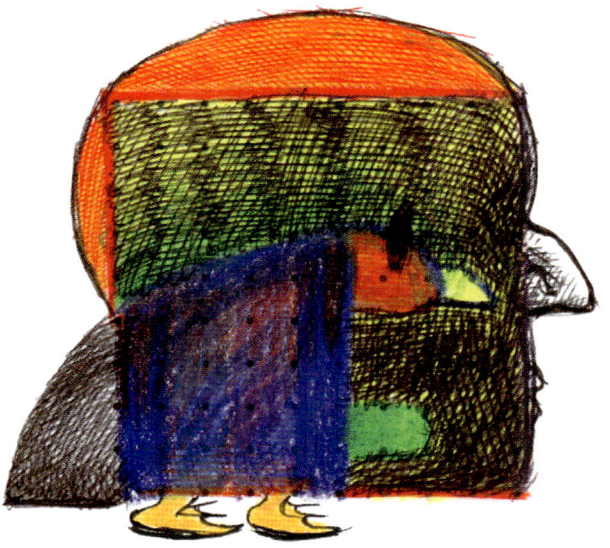

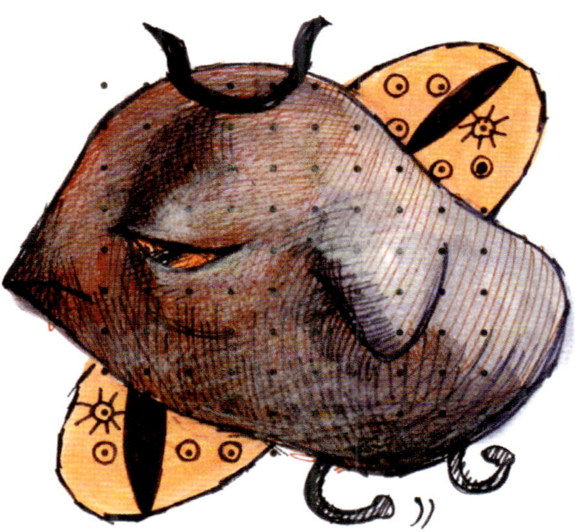

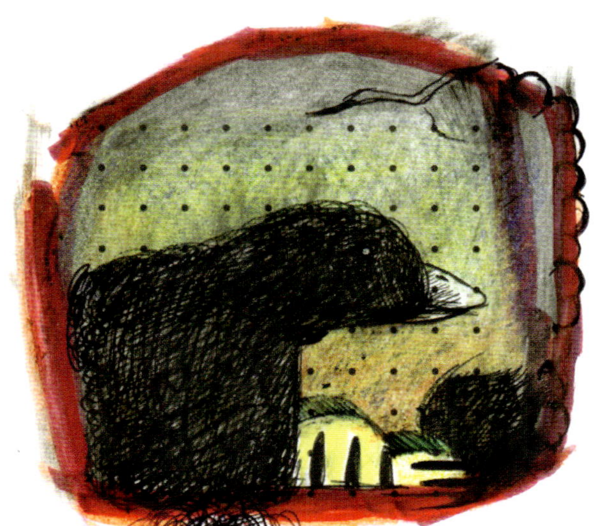

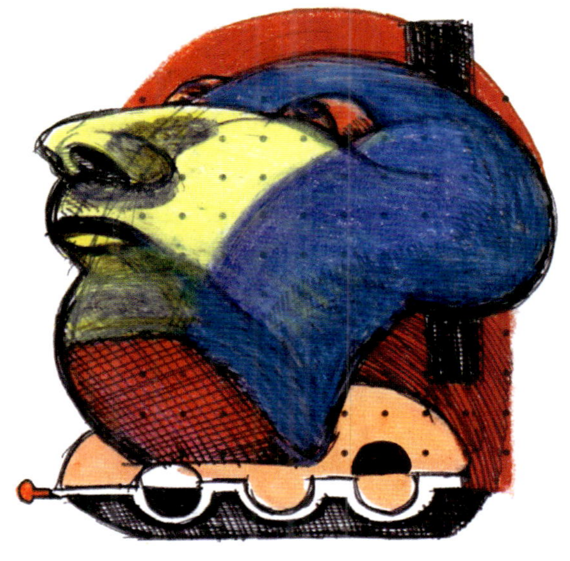

1	2	3
4		5
		6

7	8
9	10

1–4. *Fnu Herry*
5. *Choon Teoh*
6. *Chris Mohr*
7–10. *Soyoung Huh*

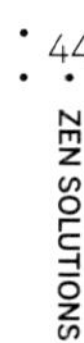

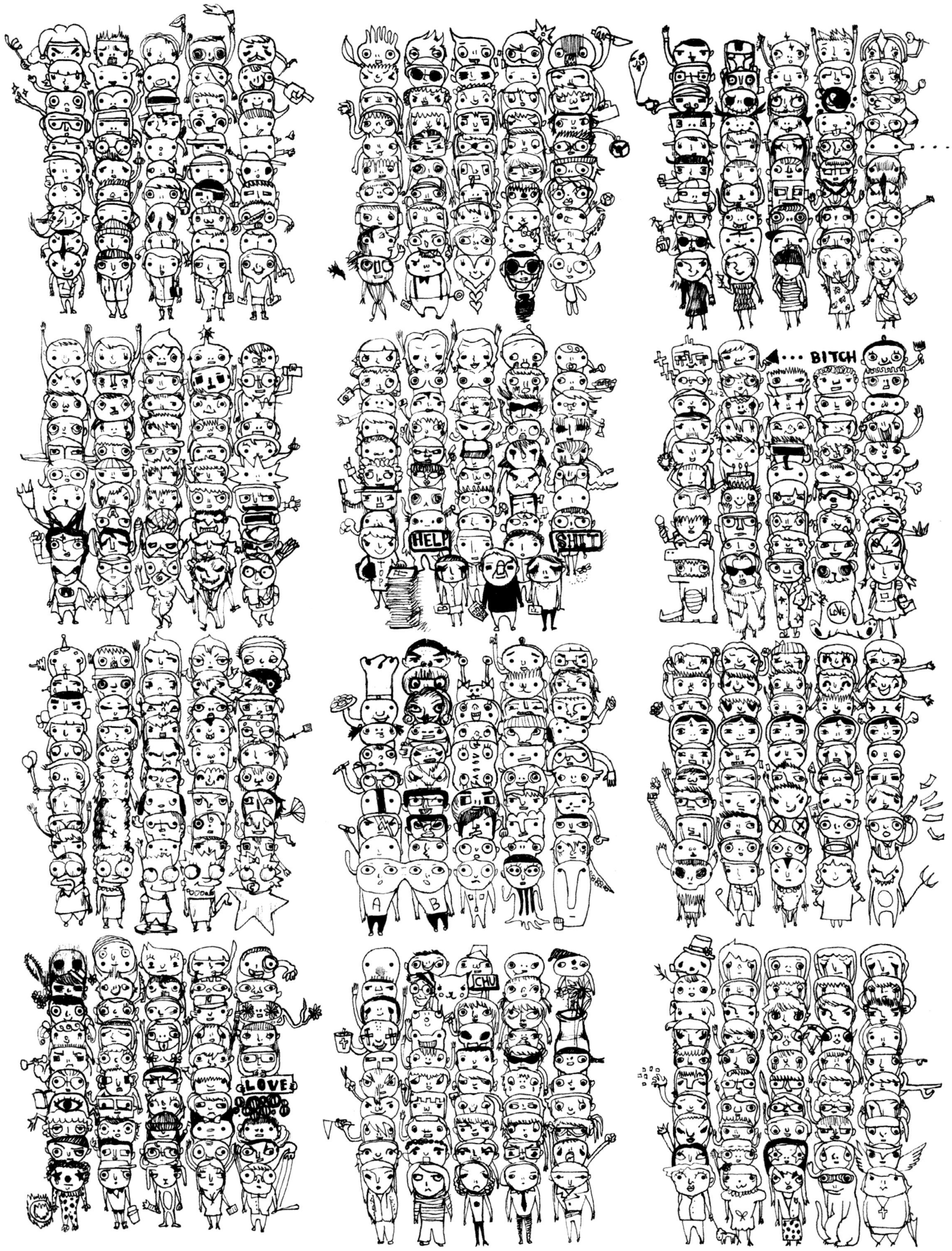

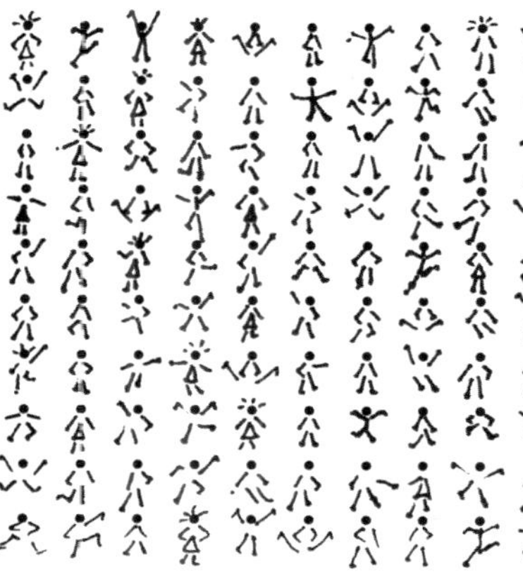

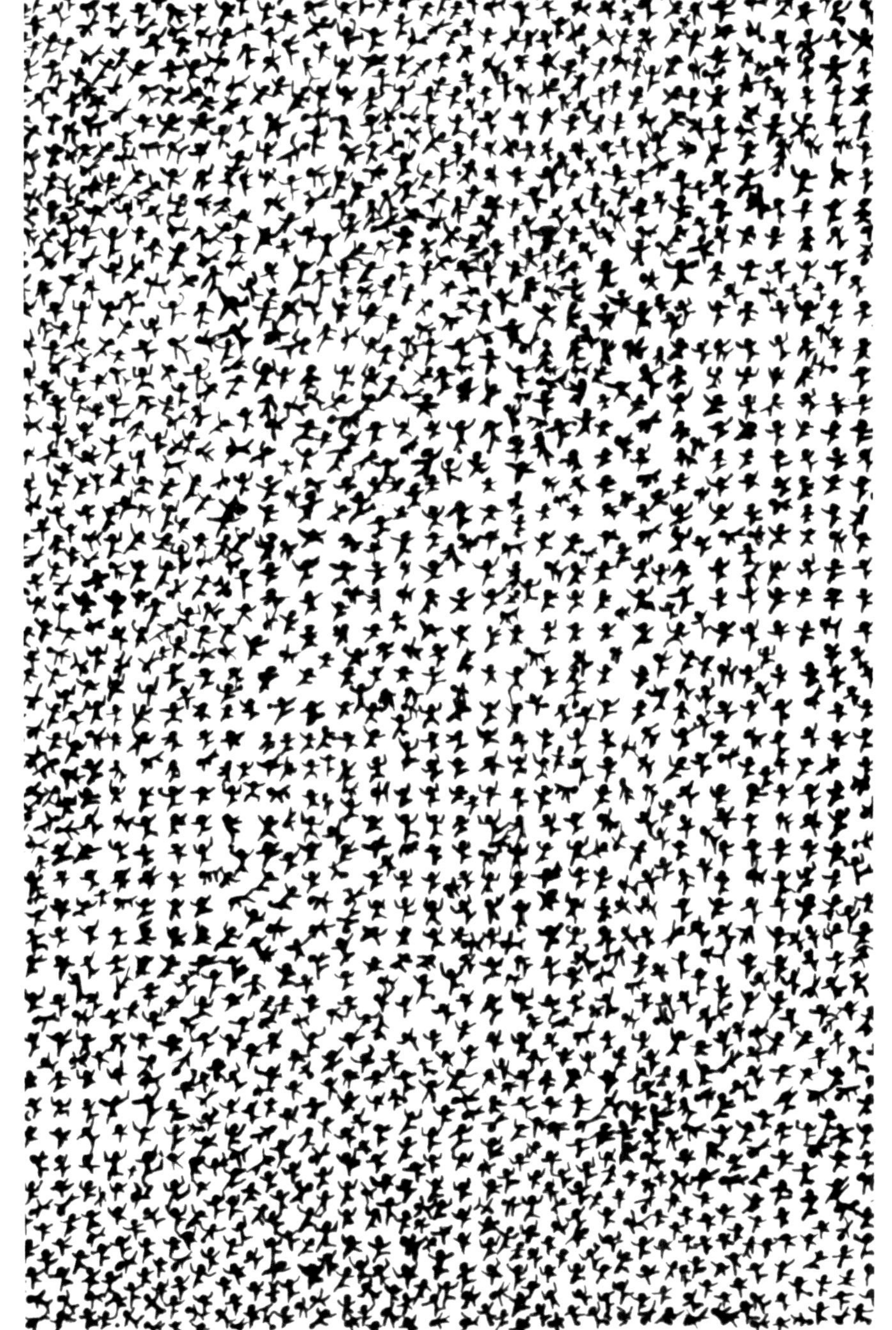

ZEN SOLUTIONS:

Figures 1 through 8 represent the human form by utilizing the dots as a starting point for either the head or eyes of the figures depicted.

Figure 1 is a creation of approximately six hundred humorous characters.

Figures 2 through 7 each represent one hundred active figures, which in some cases exhibit a hieroglyphic, typographic sensibility.

Figure 8 represents the entire assignment sheet using a similar approach, creating a distinct surface pattern with the illusion of constant movement.

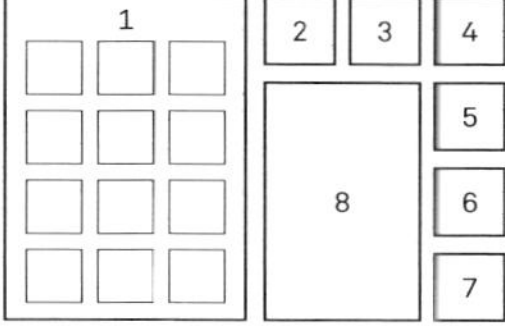

1. *Somyi Yang*
2. *Eunjung Park*
3. *Jungho Oh*
4. *Jungeun Cho*
5. *Dana Coor*
6. *Junghyun Ko*
7. *Jaehyun Park*
8. *Isabel Radetsky*

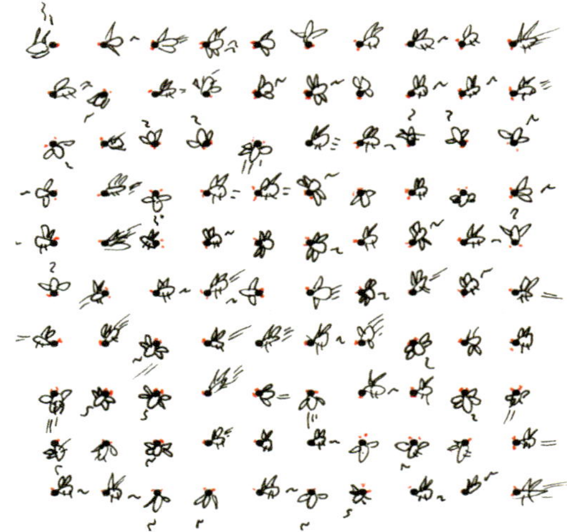

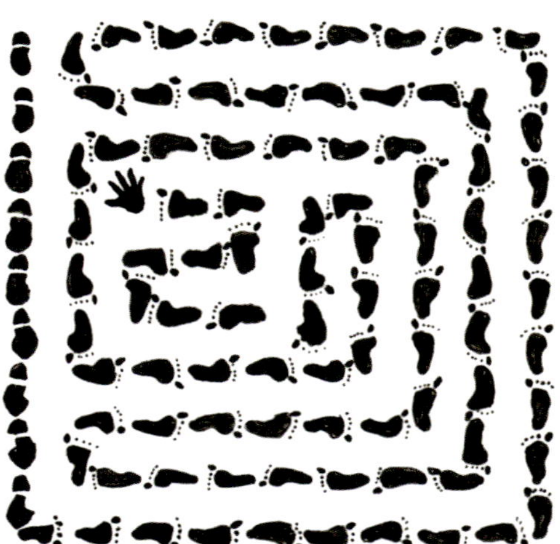

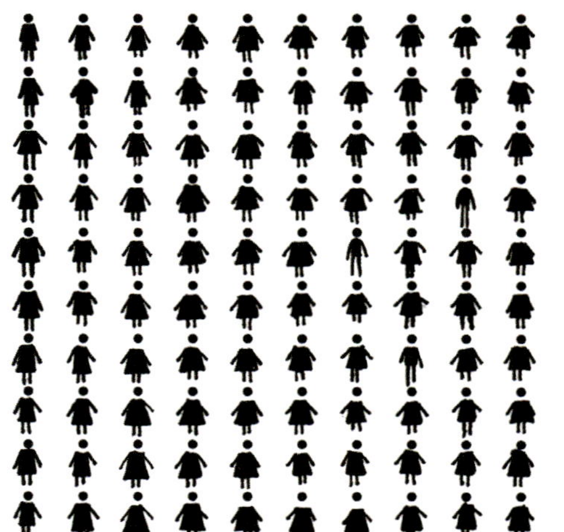

ZEN SOLUTIONS:

Figures 1 through 7 each represent one hundred images, which include an aerial view of people doing exercise with outstretched arms, ants, footprints, bows, insects, and characters that reflect human postures. Although each image has its own distinct character, it is the pattern that they create that functions as a single entity.

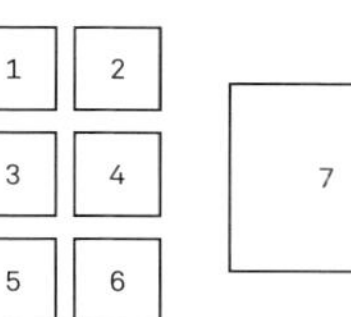

1. *Haejeon Lee*
2. *Jaehoon Moon*
3. *Haejeon Lee*
4. *Haeyun Jee*
5. *Haejeon Lee*
6. *David Fishman*
7. *Jaehoon Moon*

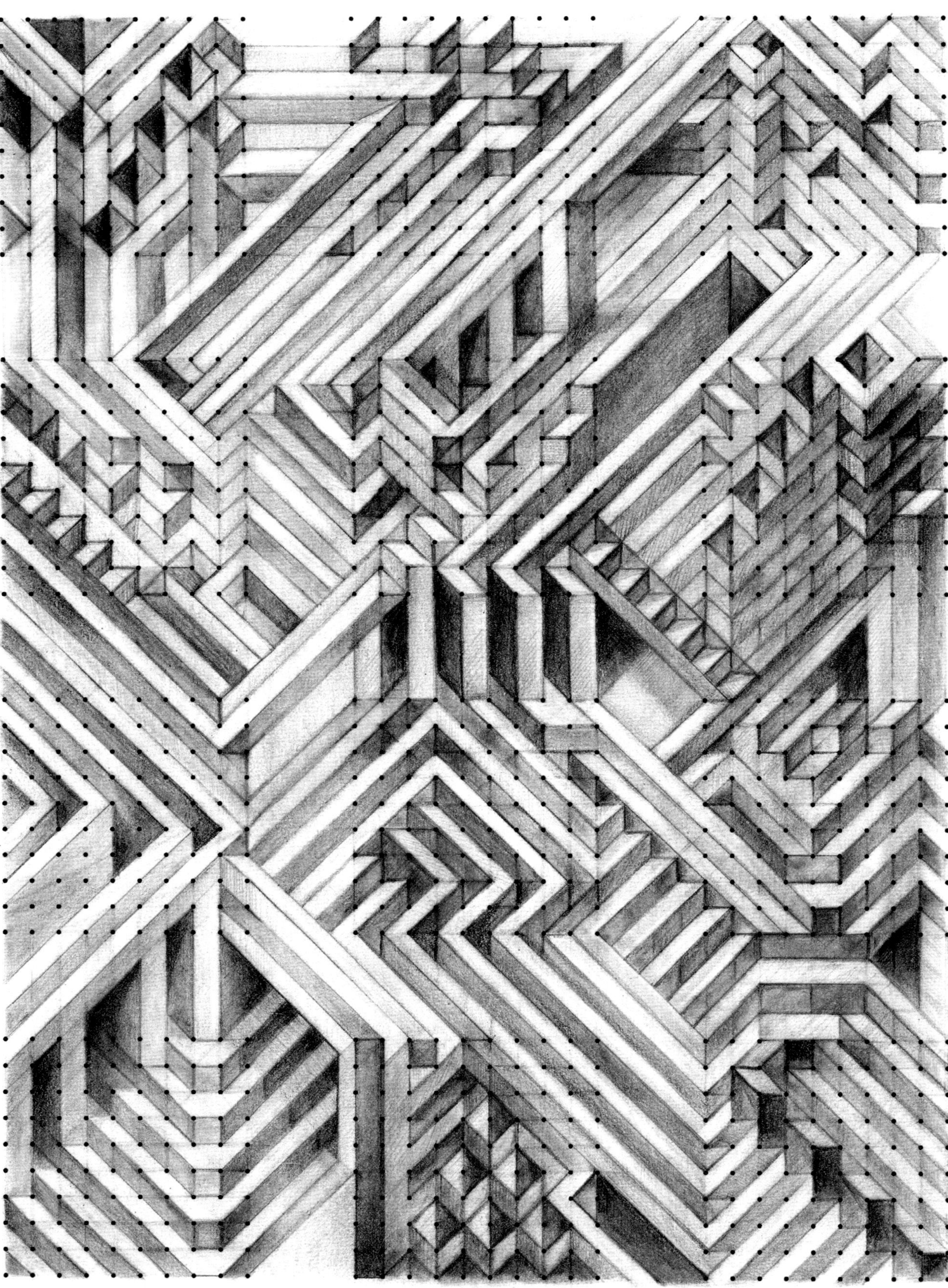

ZEN SOLUTIONS:

The images shown here adhere to a geometric vernacular principle.

Figure 1 uses an isometric perspective that references an Escher-esque dynamic. All twelve hundred dots are carefully considered in creating this single image.

Figures 2 through 6, and 8, 10 and 11, create a pyramid configuration that can be viewed as an image either coming forward, or receding in space.

Figures 7 and 9 are patterned interacting triangles that create a stylized cubistic space.

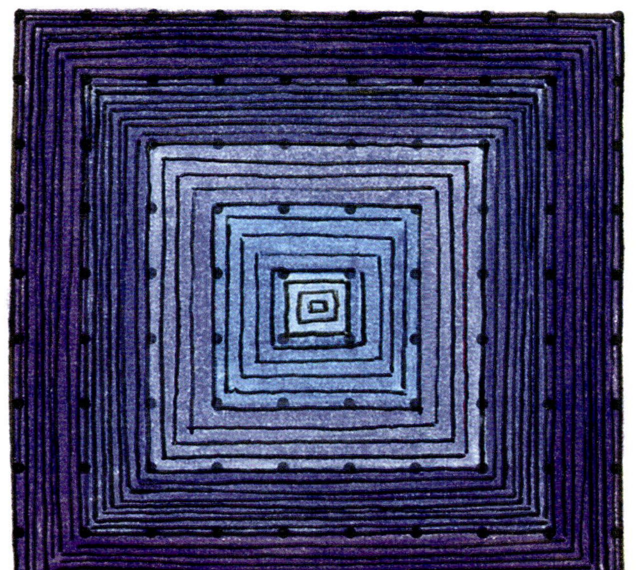

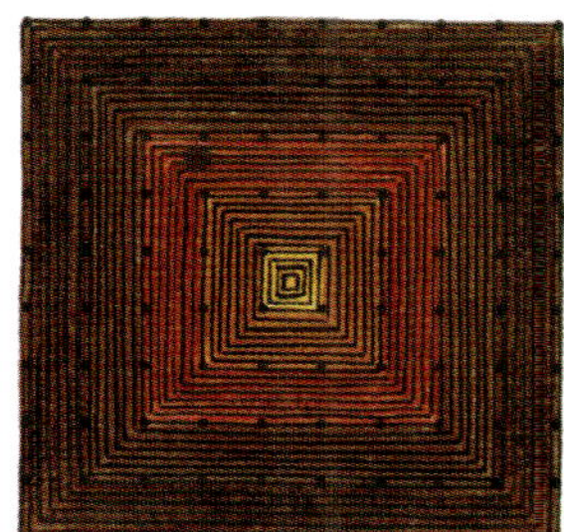

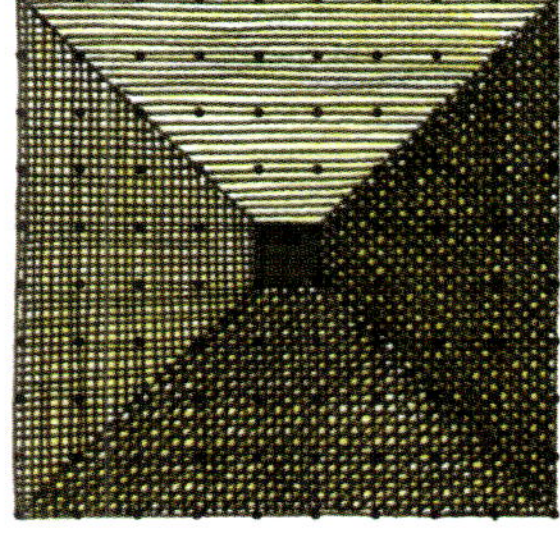

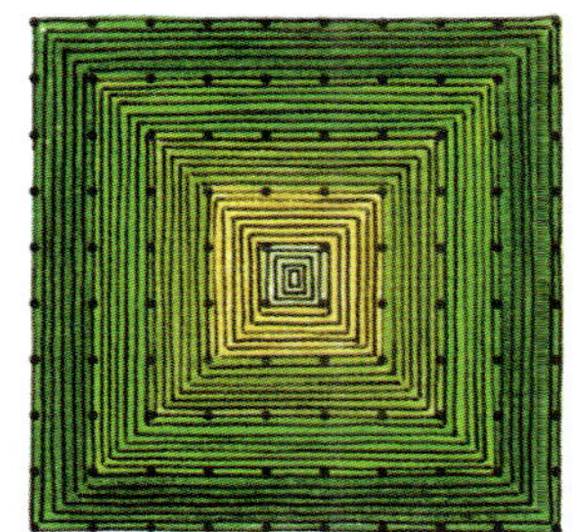

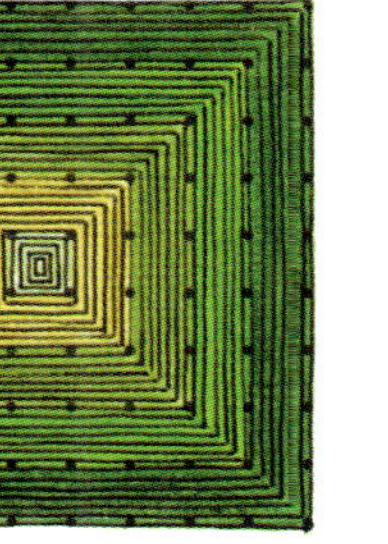

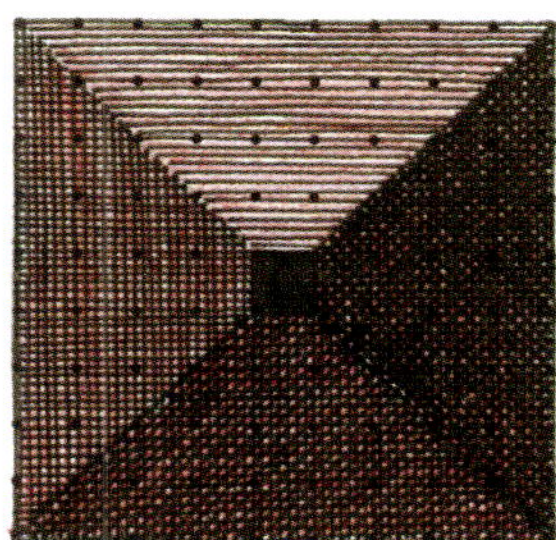

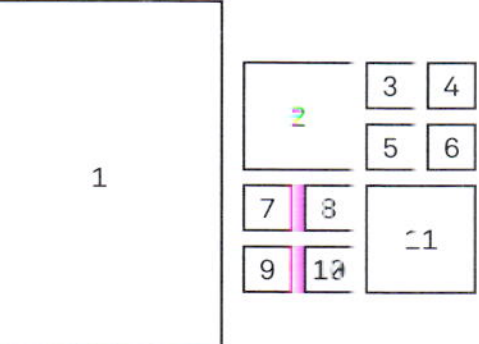

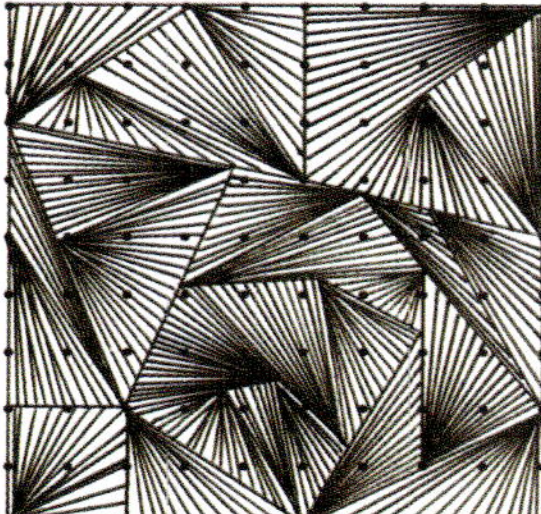

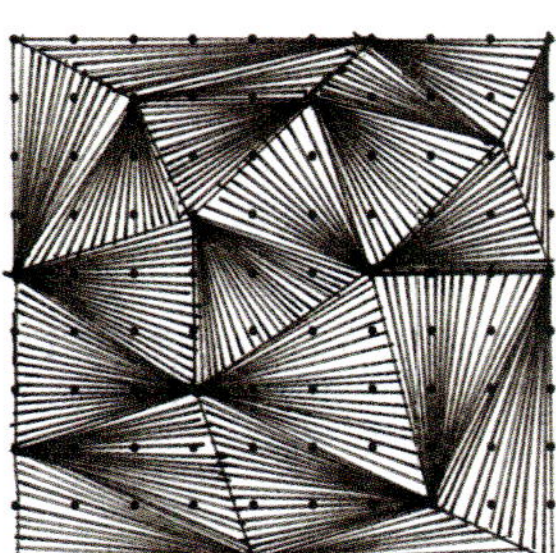

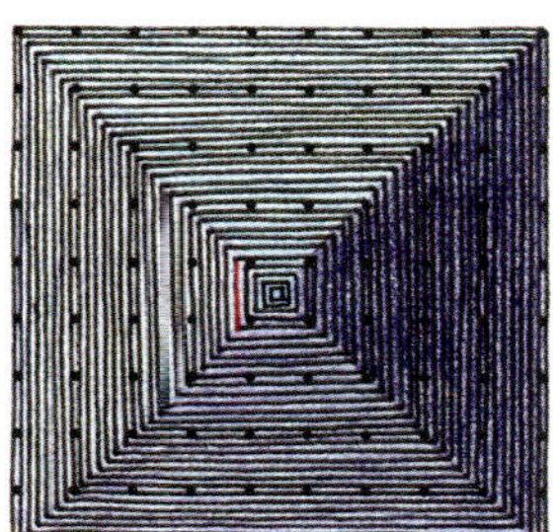

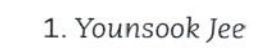

1. *Younsook Jee*
2–6. *Claudio Barra*
7. *Jeewon Kim*
8. *Claudio Barra*
9. *Jeewon Jay*
10. *Claudio Barra*
11. *Yumi Nakamura*

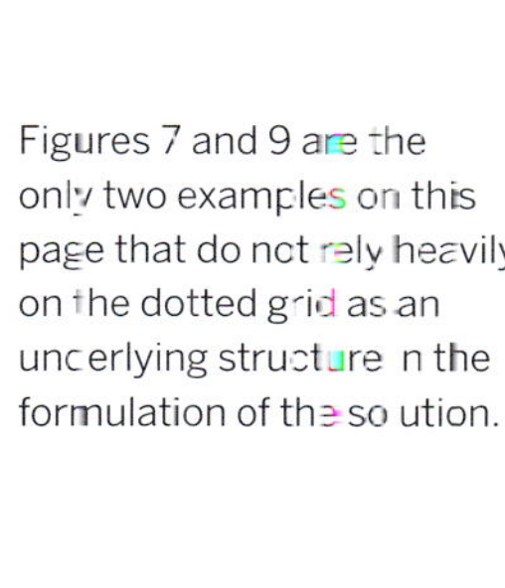

Figures 7 and 9 are the only two examples on this page that do not rely heavily on the dotted grid as an underlying structure in the formulation of the solution.

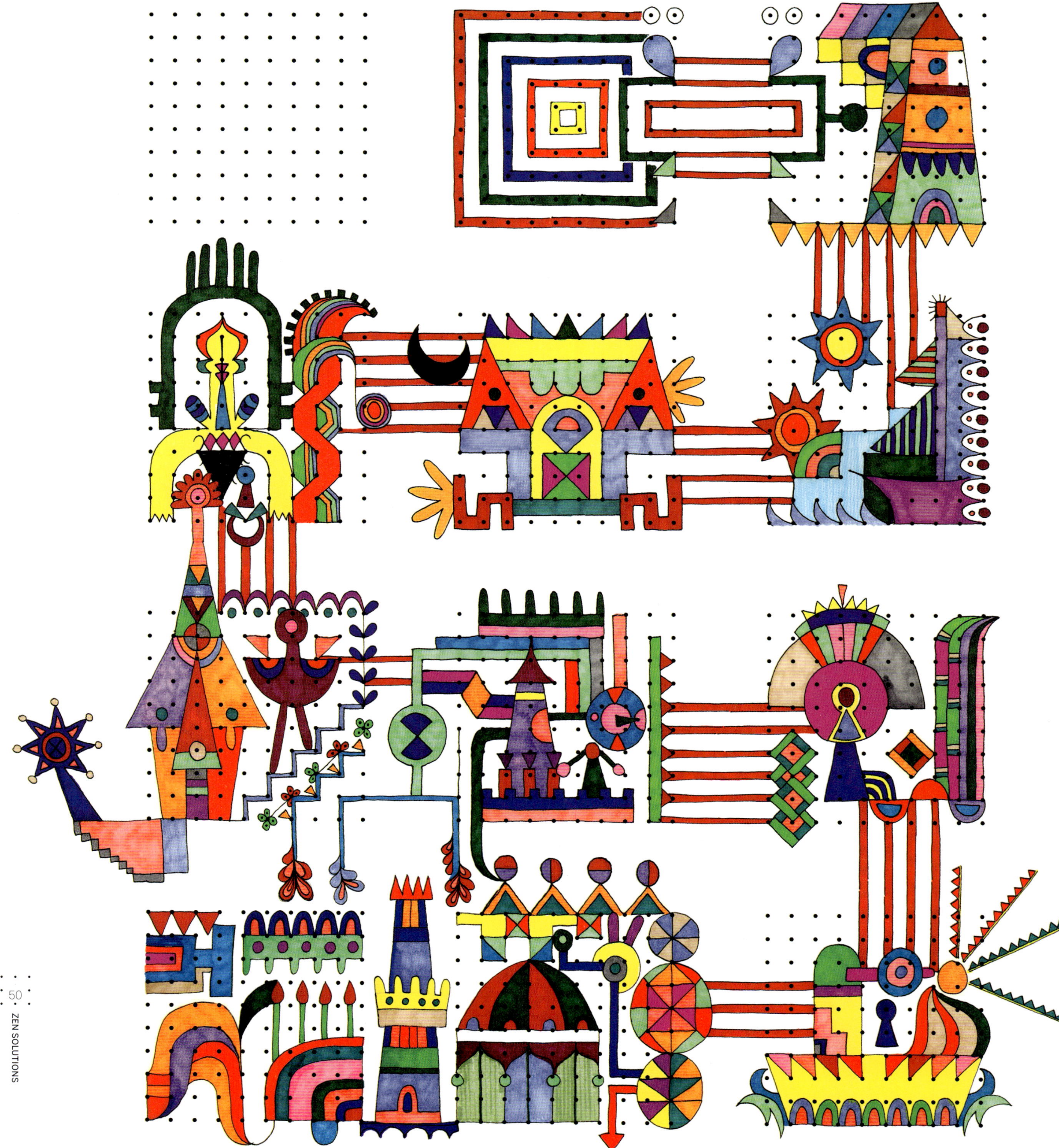

ZEN SOLUTIONS:

Figure 1 represents a decorative storybook narrative, where each solution morphs into the next. Color, form, flat geometric shapes, patterning, and movement create an attitude of playfulness.

The investigations in figures 2 through 11 are explorations of patterning in an obsessive manner, that deal with the interaction of repeated forms in highly personal ways.

Figure 8 is a sewn solution that uses red thread.

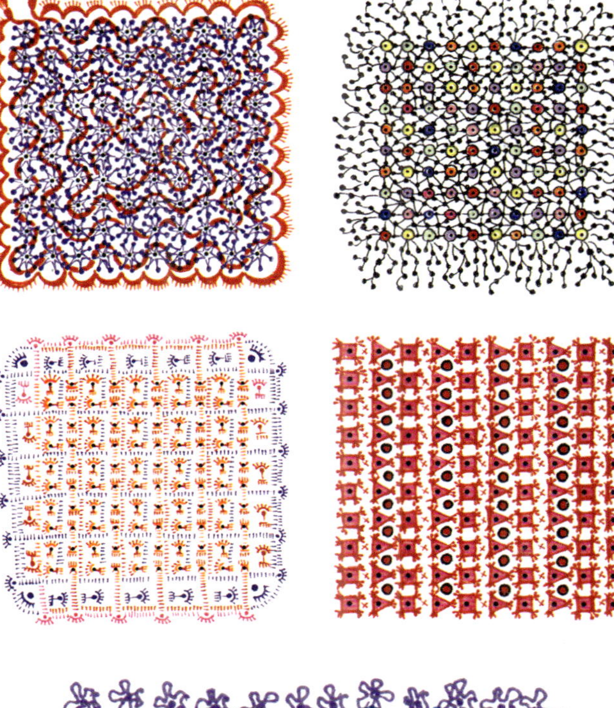

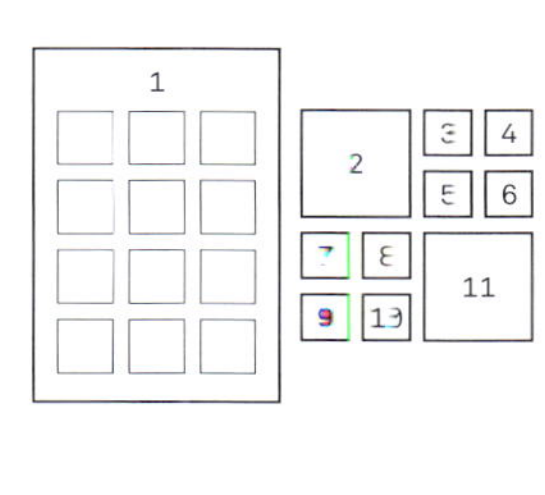

1. Ege Dalaman
2–7. Regina Kushnir
8. Jacqueline Carbajal
9. Nicole Lapenta
10–11. Regina Kushnir

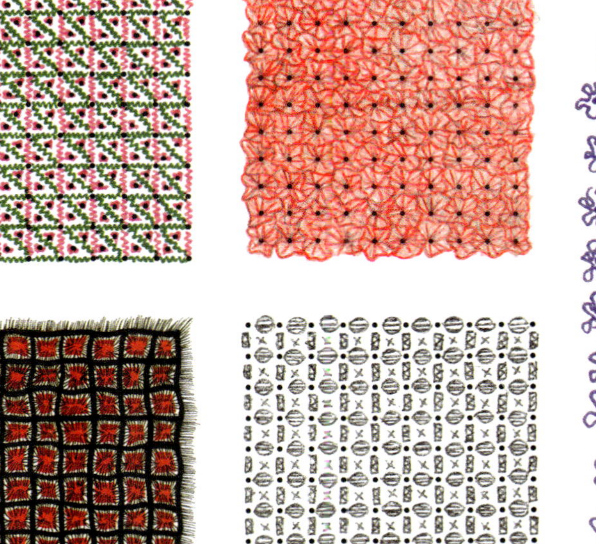

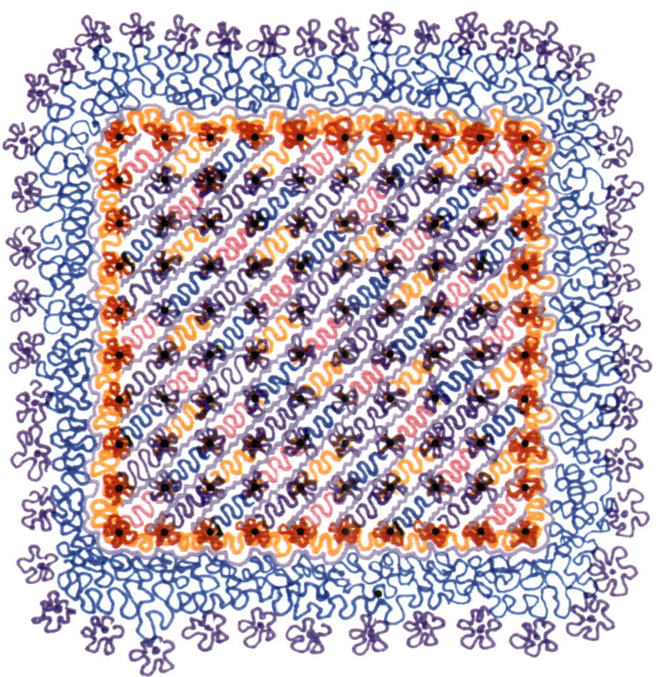

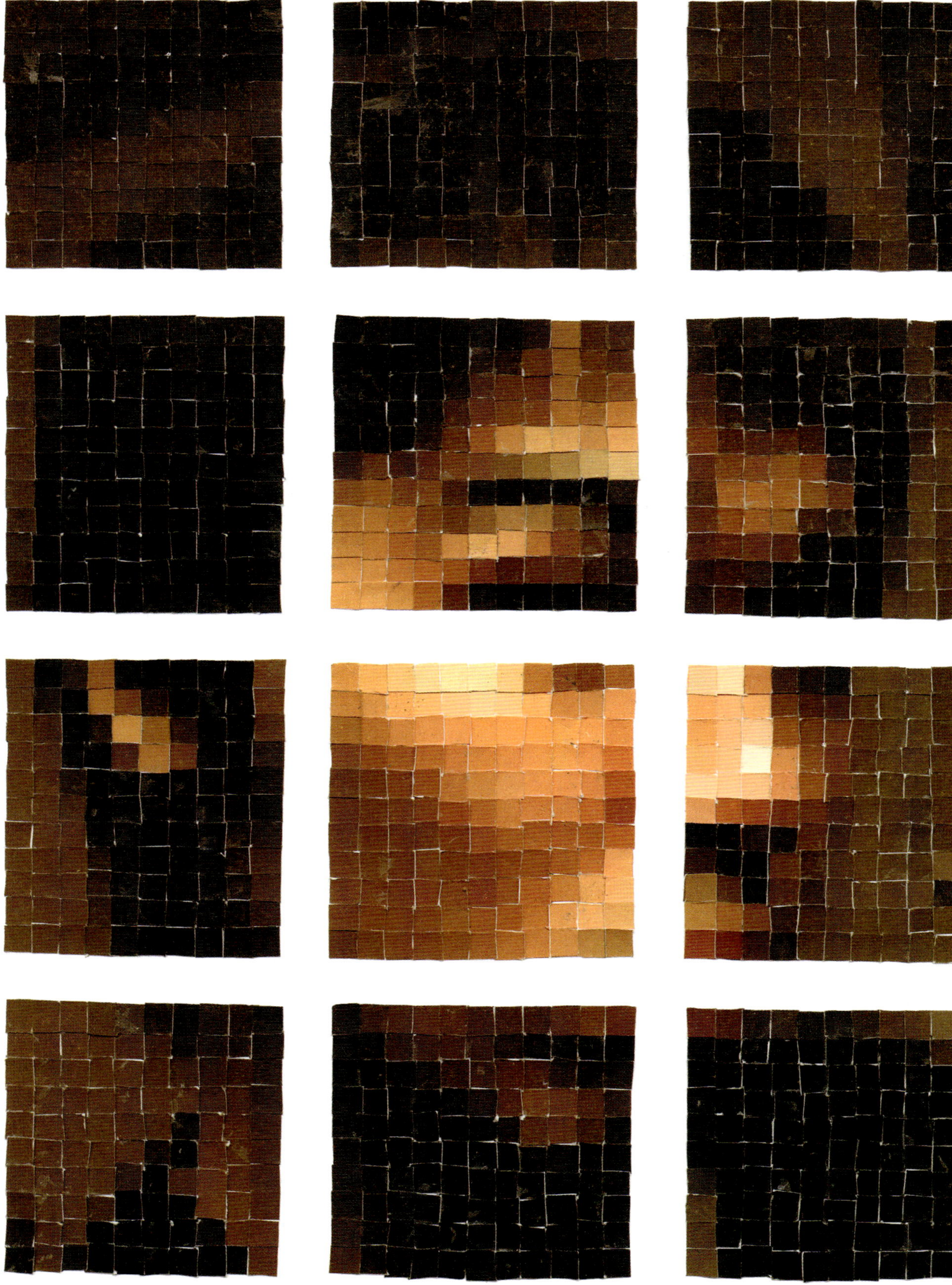

ZEN SOLUTIONS:

Figure 1 consists of twelve hundred individual squares of color paper carefully pasted next to one another. Each of the twelve individual areas serve as abstract imagery, yet when viewed together the portrait appears.

Figures 2 through 7 reflect the given gridlike pattern, where each solution has its own distinct character.

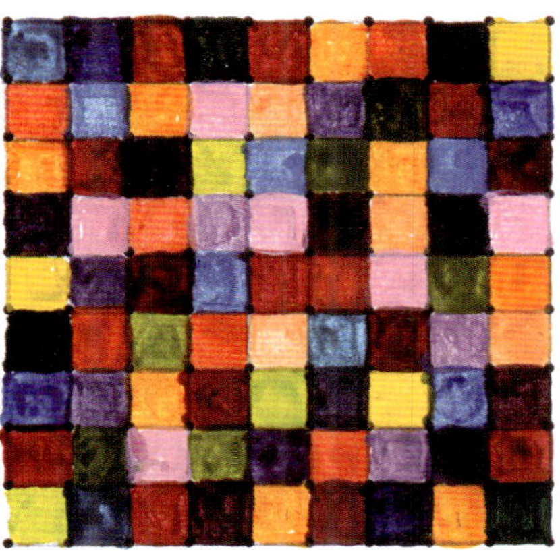

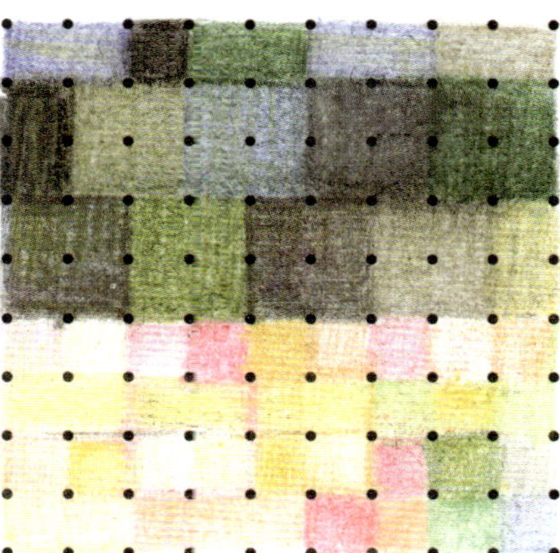

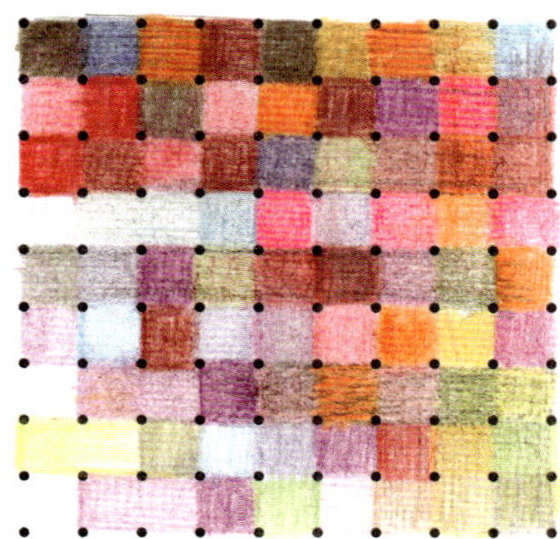

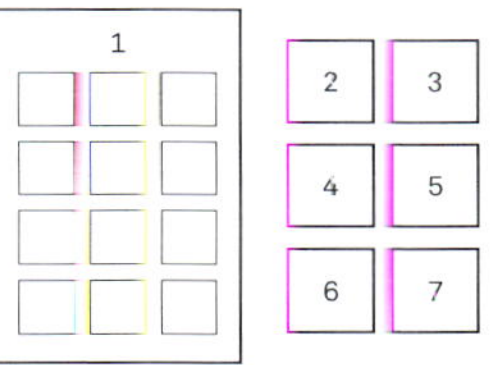

1. *Duesung Byun*
2. *Cathy Wang*
3. *Jessica Sachs*

4–5. *Allan Weiss*

6–7. *Richard Epstein*

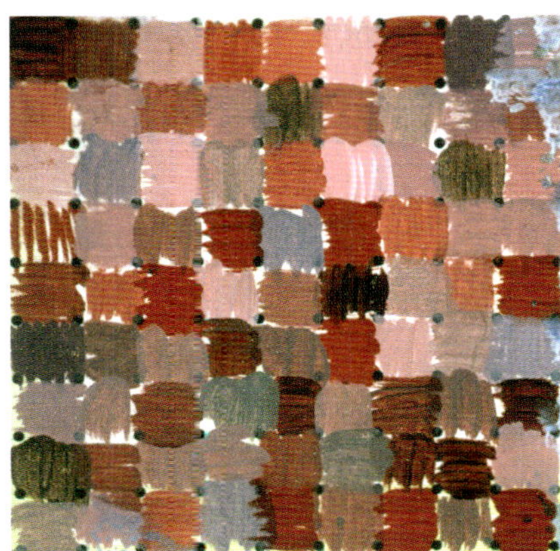

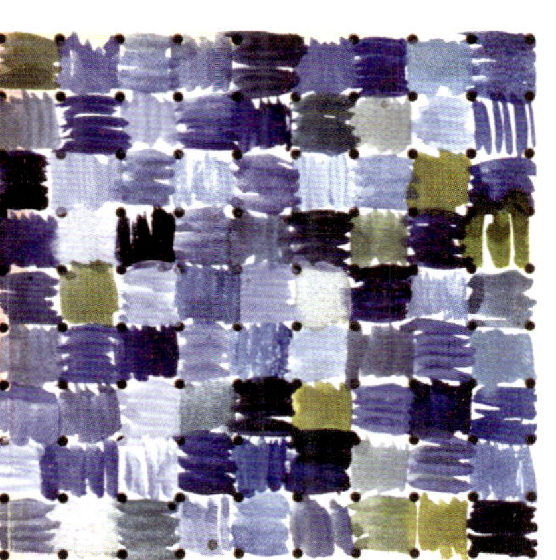

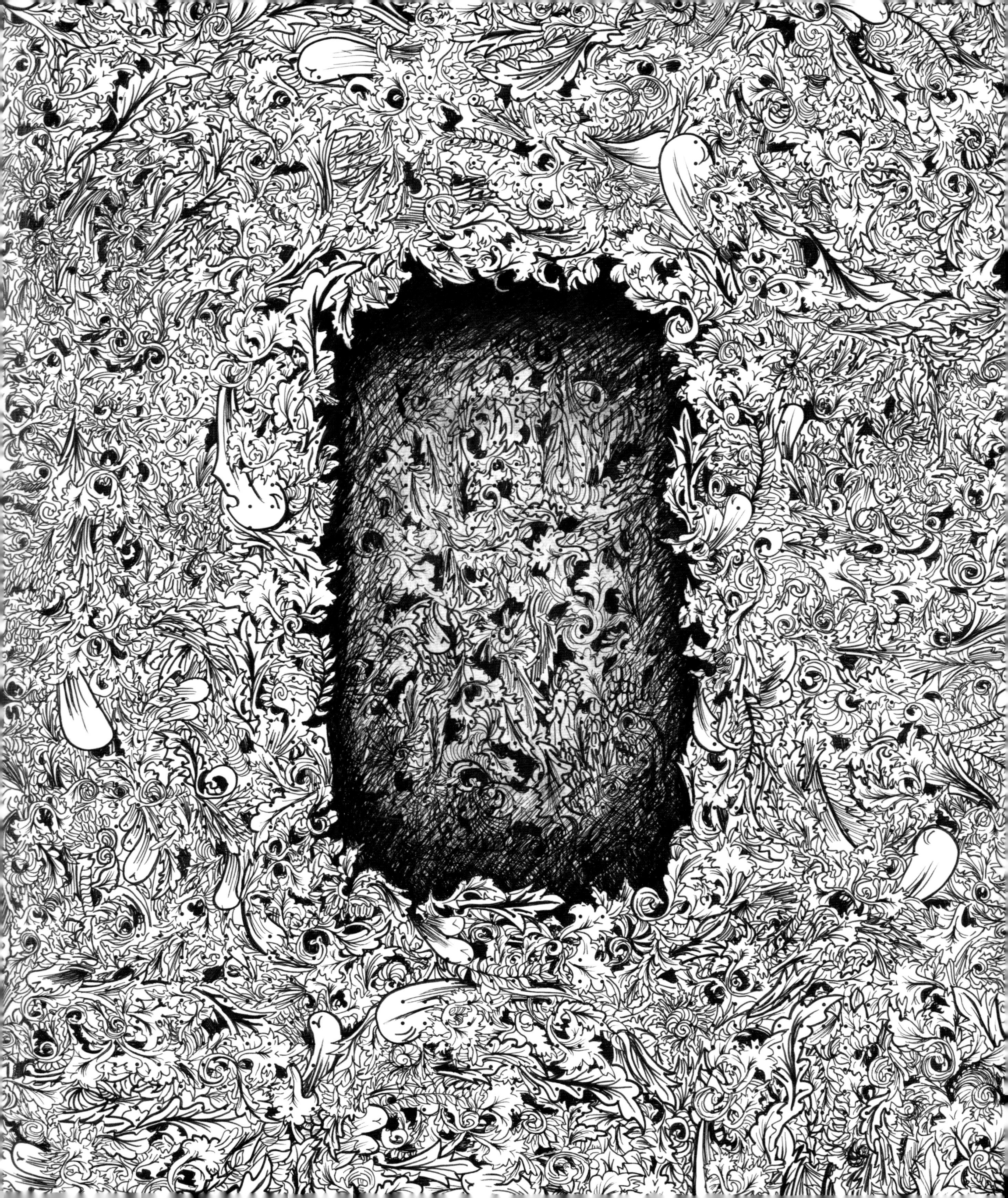

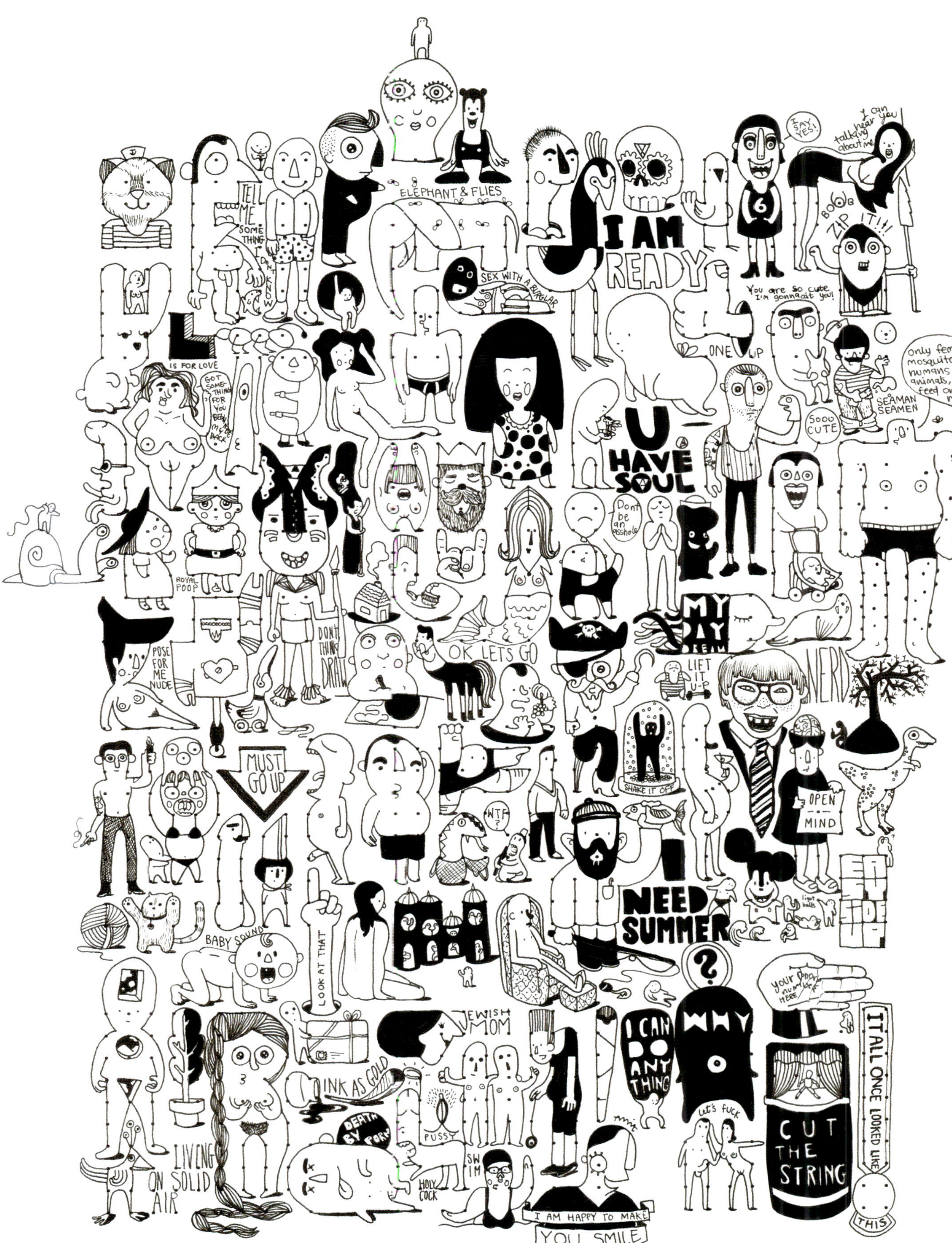

ZEN SOLUTIONS:

Figures 1 and 2 represent two distinctly different approaches to problem solving.

Figure 1 is an organically drawn exploration of form that trusts an emotional impulse where a more essential voice emerges.

Figure 2 represents an idea-oriented approach to problem solving, based on an elaborate cast of highly stylized characters.

Many of the solutions to the Zen Problem fall between these two approaches to problem solving. Access to this caliber of creative exploration is an ongoing search for all artists.

1 2

1. Enle Li
2. Amit Greenberg

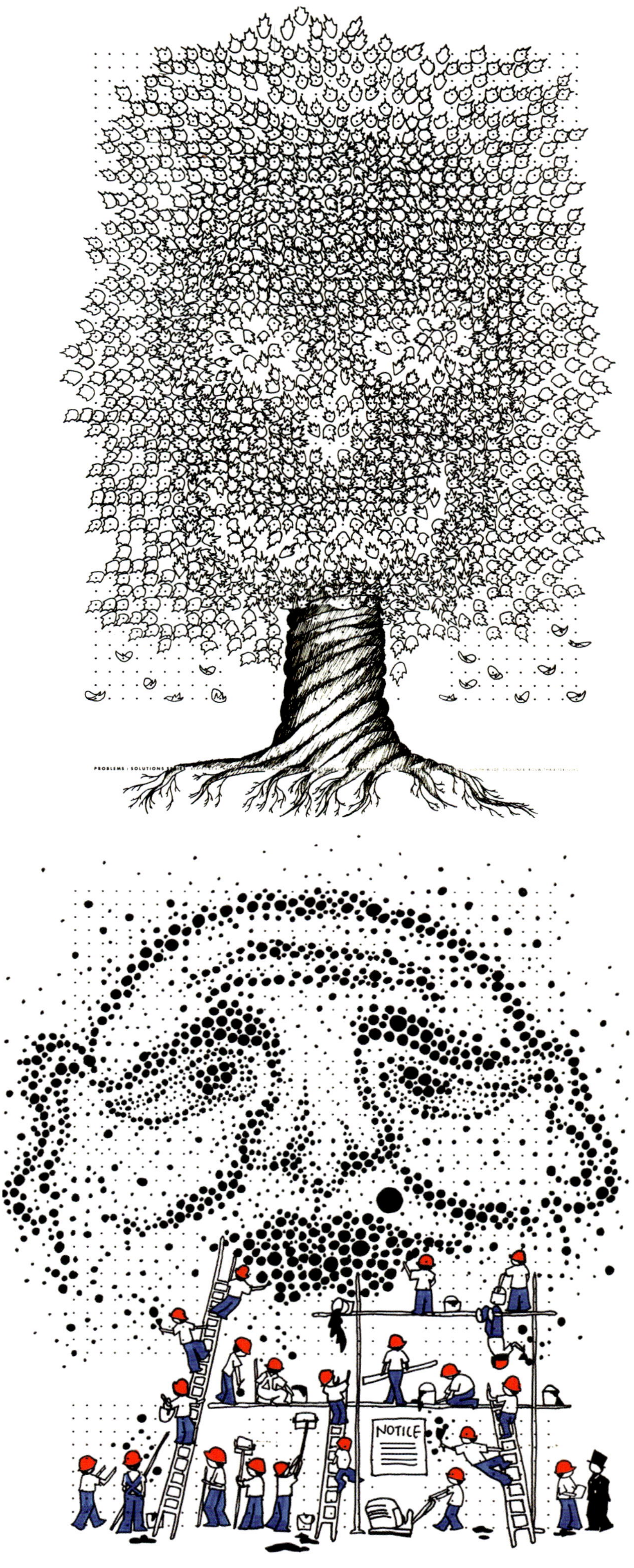
PROBLEMS : SOLUTIONS SERIES
NOTICE

ZEN SOLUTIONS:

Figures 1 and 3 use a theme of skulls to create a narrative solution.

Figure 2 is an extension of the dot pattern that uses dots of different sizes to create a face. The narrative is furthered by including a scaffolding with workers involved in the act of its implementation.

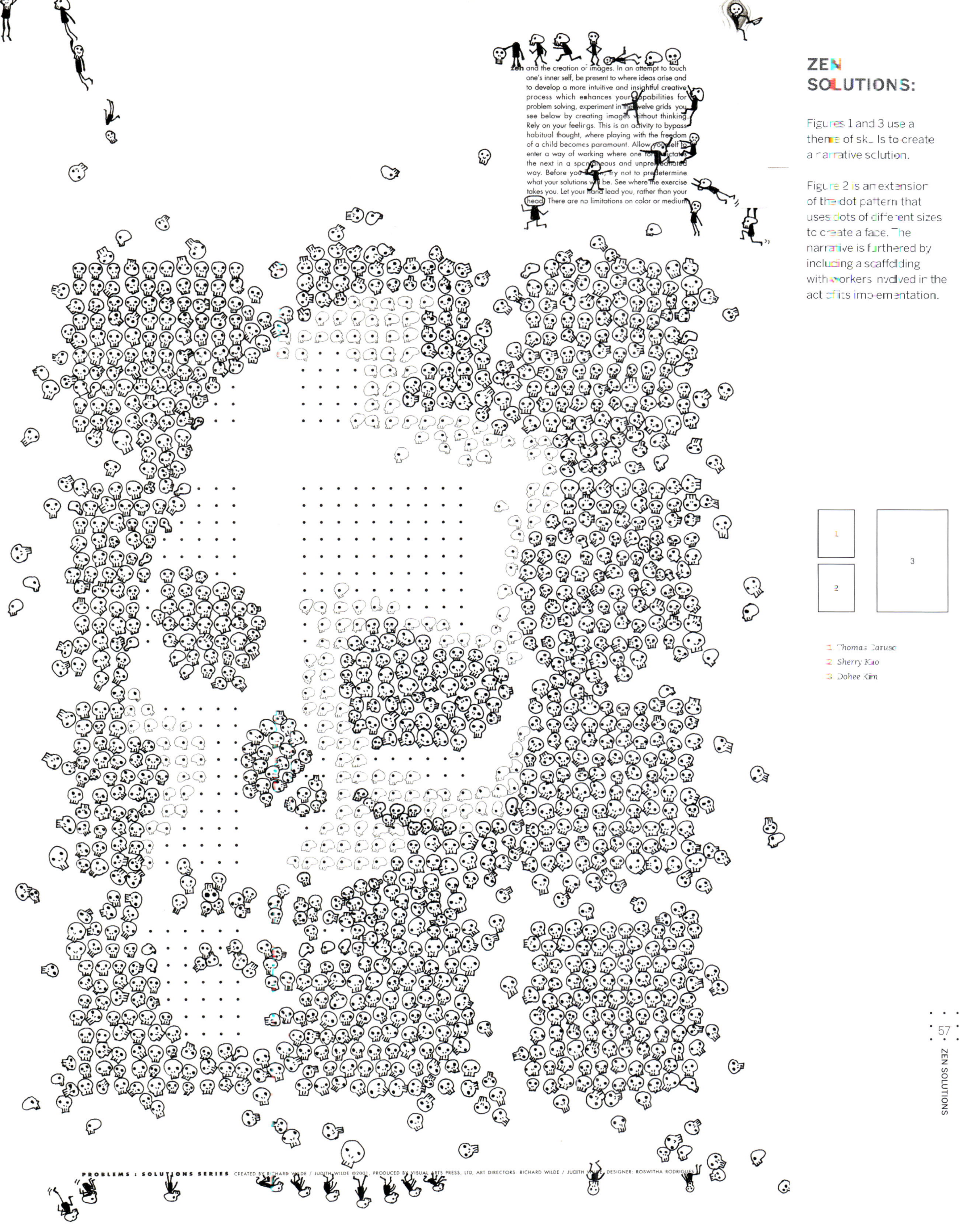

1 Thomas Caruso
2 Sherry Kao
3 Dohee Kim

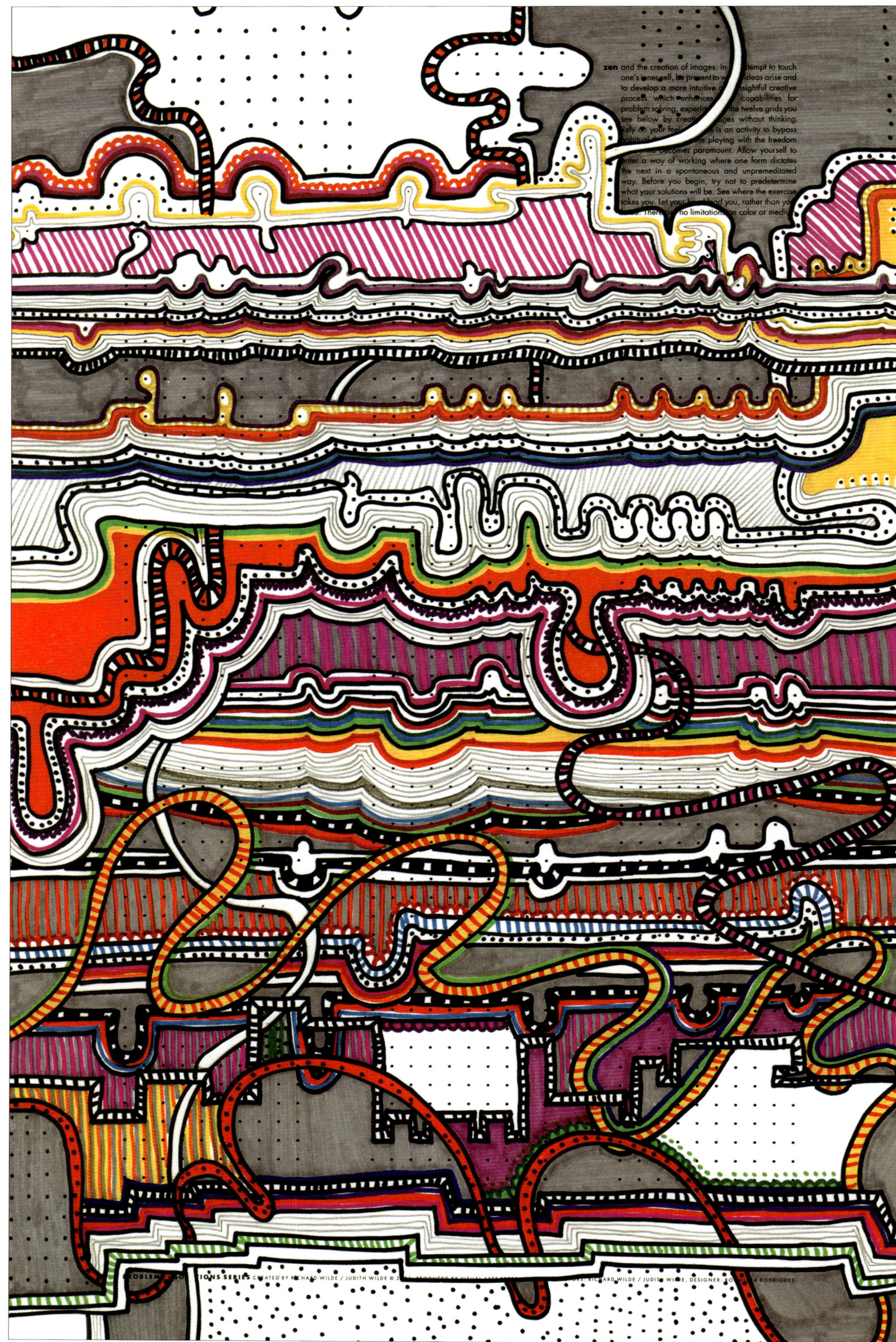
zen and the creation of images. In tempt to touch
one's inner self, be present to ideas arise and
to develop a more intuitive sightful creative
process which enhances capabilities for
problem solving, experi the twelve grids you
see below by creati ges without thinking.
Rely on your feel is an activity to bypass
playing with the freedom
becomes paramount. Allow yourself to
enter a way of working where one form dictates
the next in a spontaneous and unpremeditated
way. Before you begin, try not to predetermine
what your solutions will be. See where the exercise
takes you. Let your ad you, rather than yo
There no limitations on color or mediu
ROBLEM IONS SERIES CREATED BY RICHARD WILDE / JUDITH WILDE
RICHARD WILDE / JUDIT WI E, DESIGNER: RO A RODRIGUES

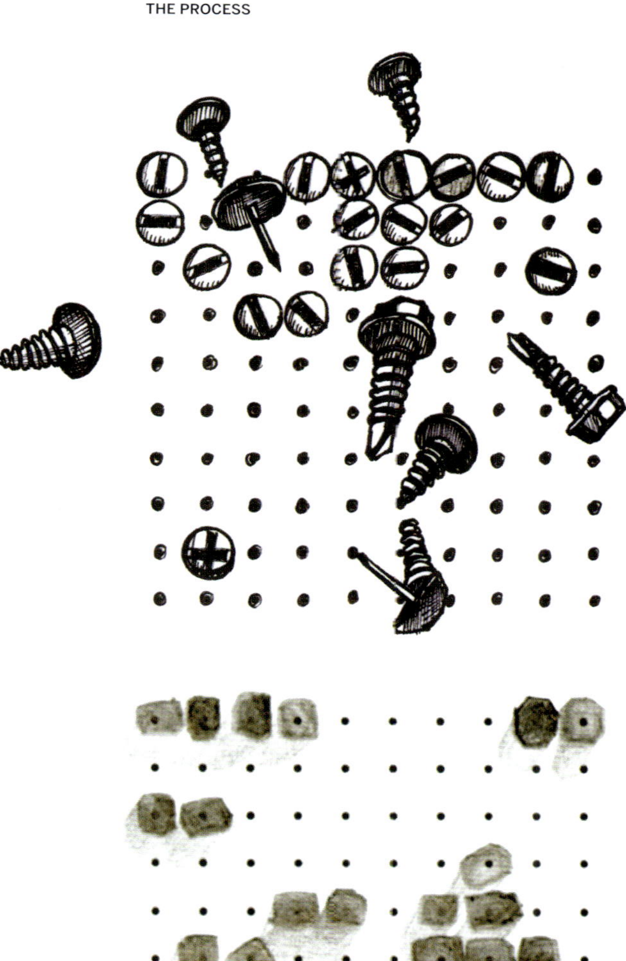

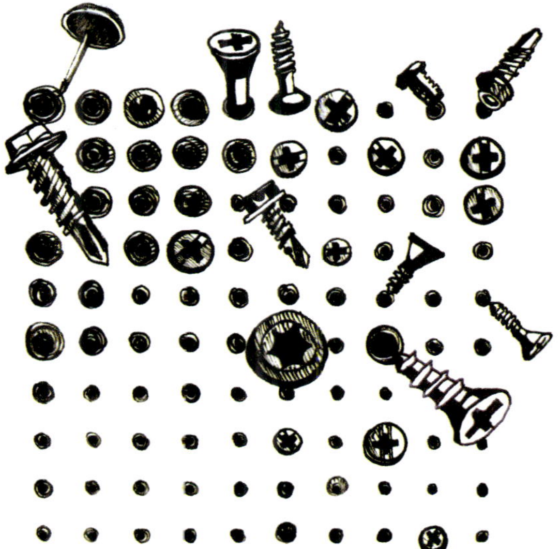

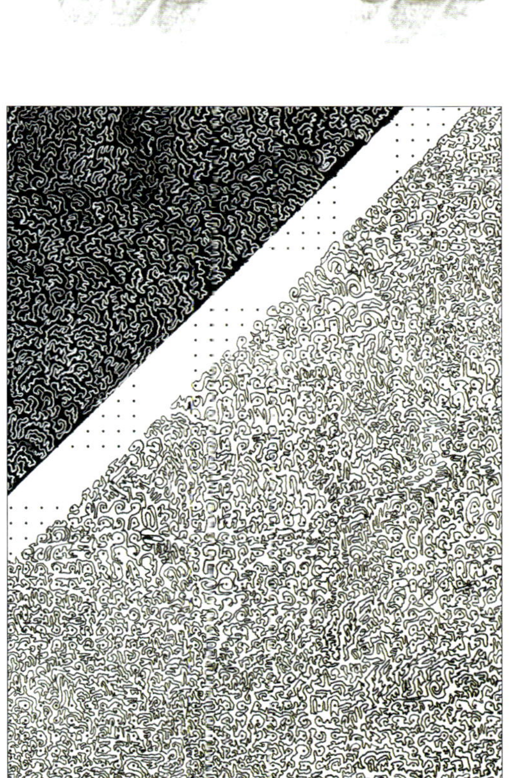

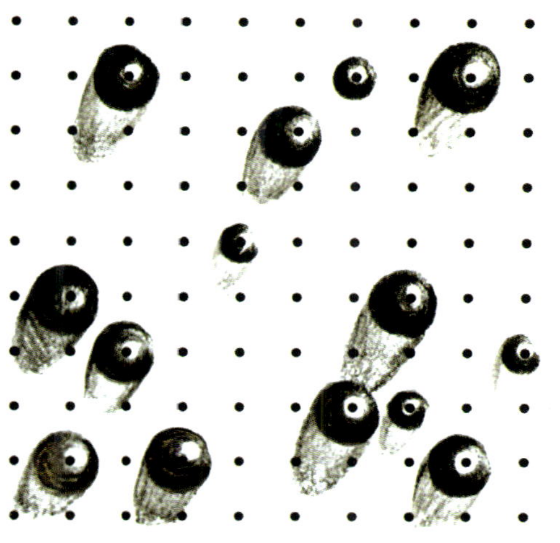

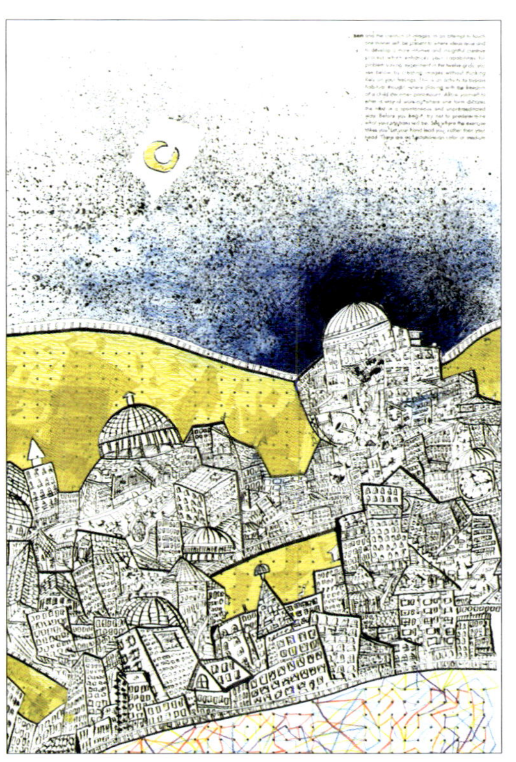

ZEN SOLUTIONS:

Figure 1 represents a 'controlled' spontaneous approach where the given dots play a minor role in this linear, patterned exploration that integrates line and movement. This type of form-making cannot be preconceived but evolves organically as each additional form and color dictates the next incarnation.

Figures 2 through 5 depict a more literal expression in creating tangible objects that utilize perspective and dimensionality.

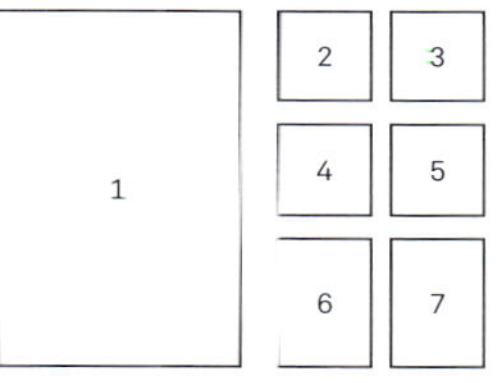

1 Maria Jose Herrada
2–3 Seokmin Hong
4–5 Ahhyun Kim
6 Derrick Barreiro
7 Yoojeong Kim

Figures 6 and 7 use intricate linear patterning dealing with abstraction and storytelling respectively.

In figure 6 there is a frenetic energy within the two contrasting geometric shapes.

Figure 7 consists of a cityscape of contrasting genres.

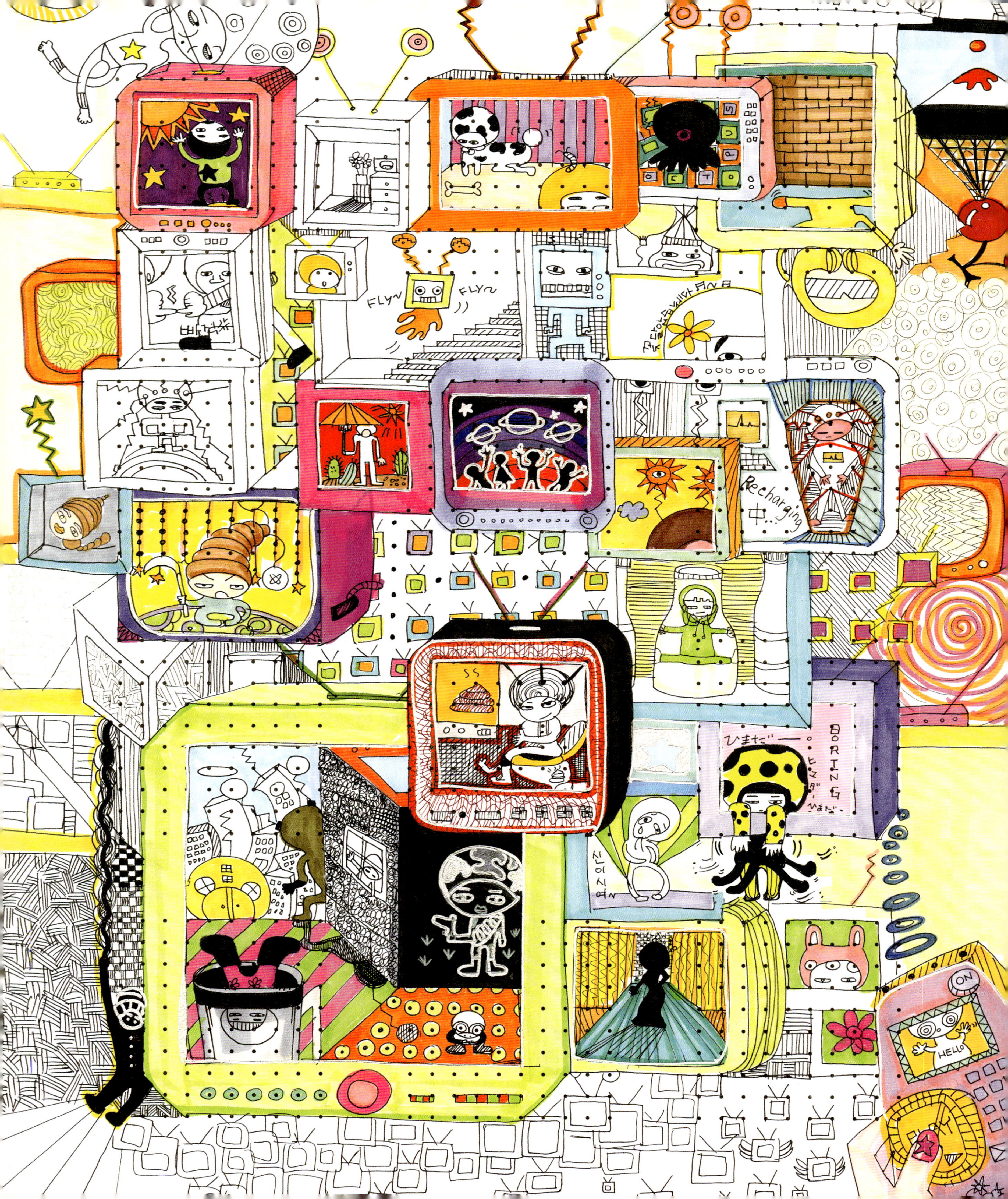
FLY~
FLY~
Recharging 中...
ひまだ———。
BORING
ヒマダ~
ひまだ~
신이시여~
ON
HELLO

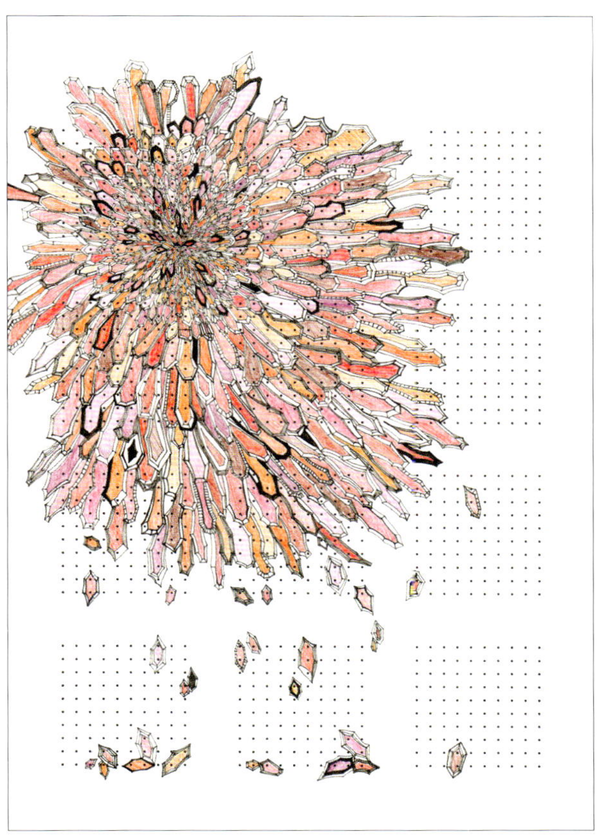

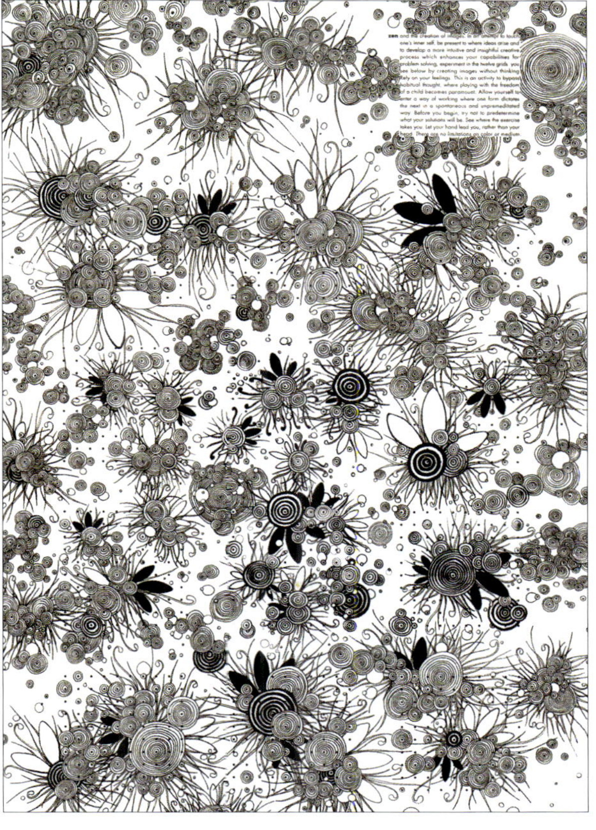

ZEN SOLUTIONS:

Figures 1 through 5 represent single solutions utilizing all twelve grids on the assignment sheet.

Figure 1 uses overlapping dimensional geometric shapes in creating a lighthearted world of cartoonlike imagery.

Figures 2 and 3 address literal narratives, while figures 4 and 5 are abstract in nature.

Figure 5 uses the technique of quilting to create a dimensional geometric solution.

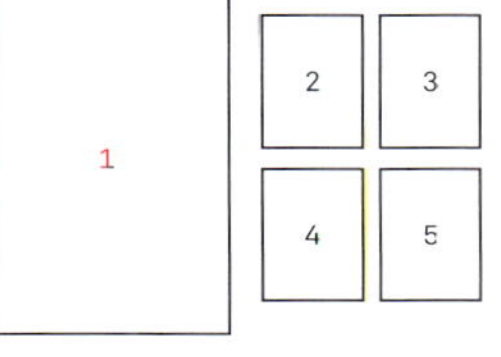

. Haejun Moon
. Jiyoon Yeom
. Jaewon Park
. Hyunhwa Lee
. Elaine Park

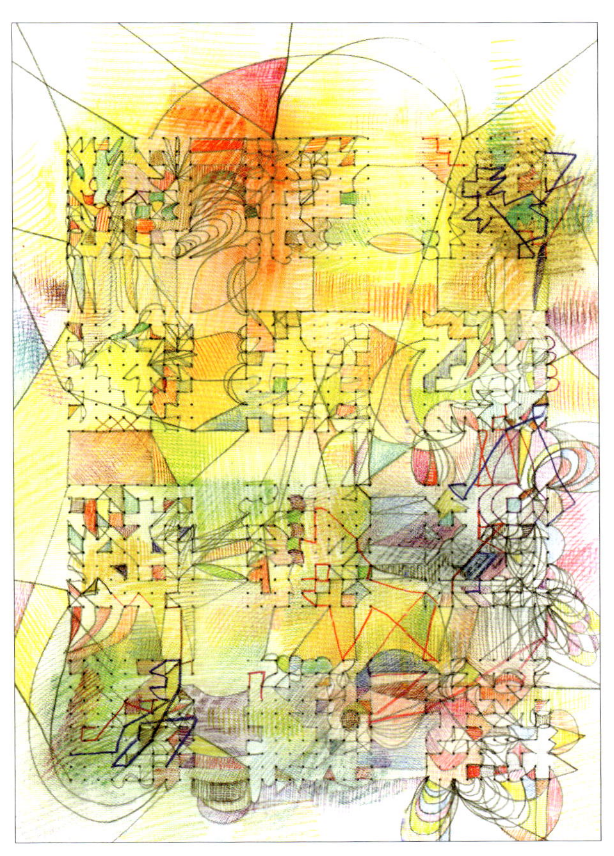

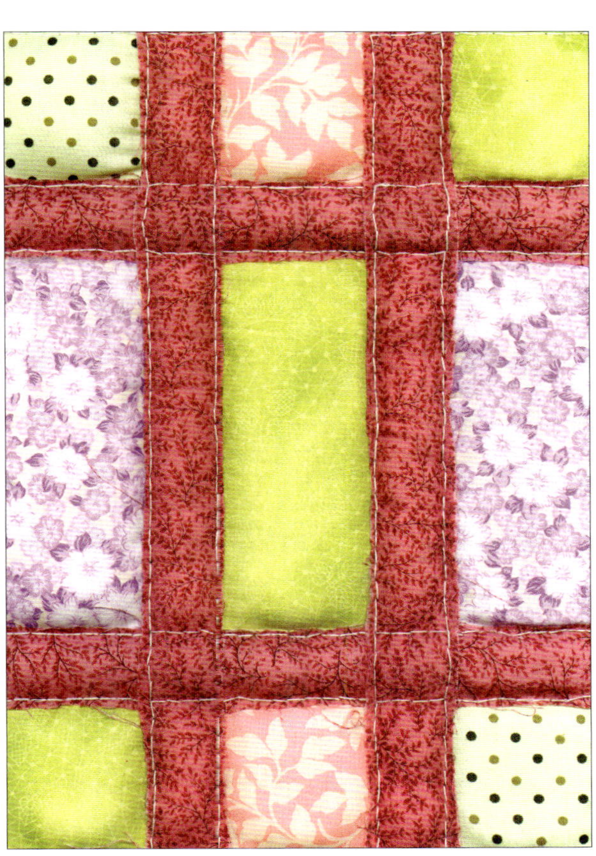

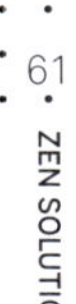

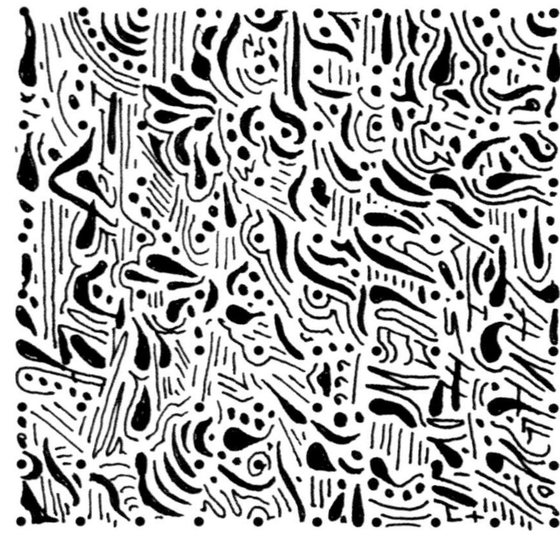

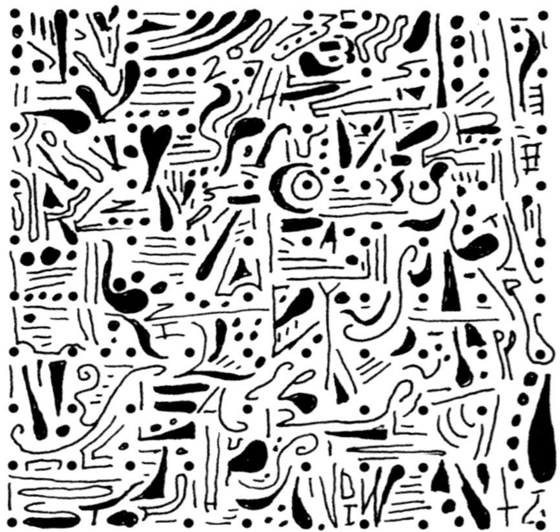

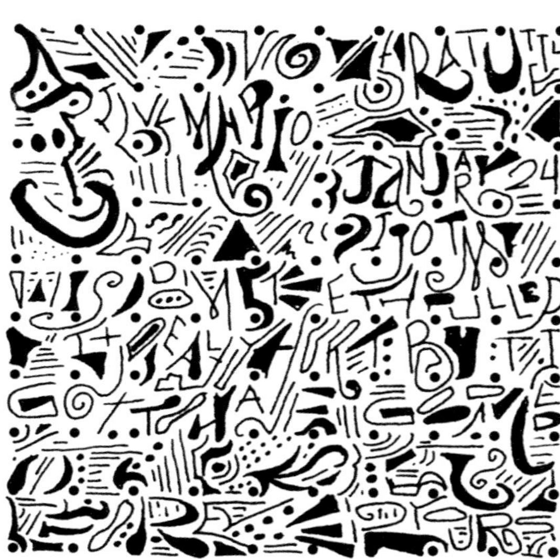

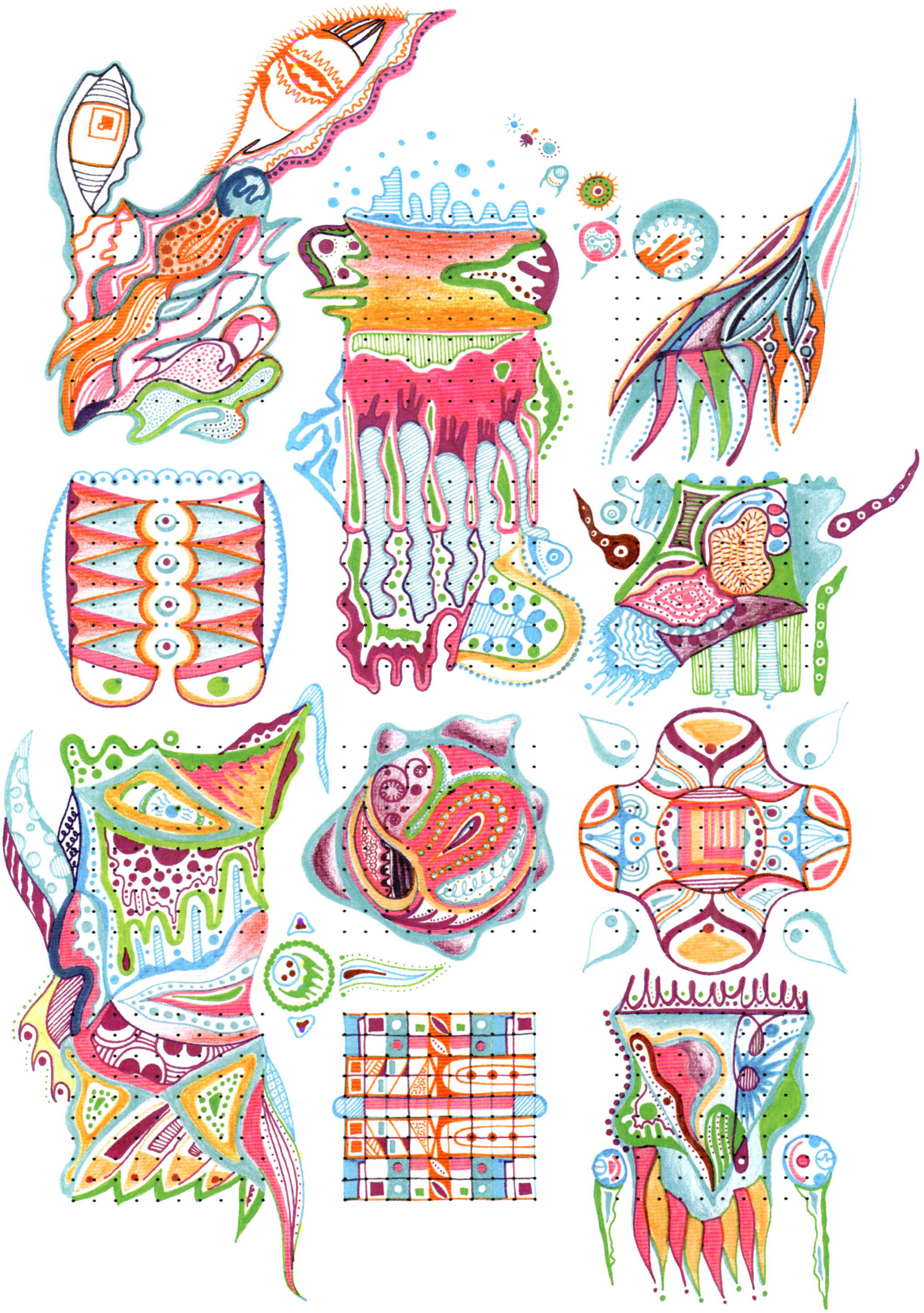

ZEN SOLUTIONS:

Figures 1 through 4 incorporate line, where flat amorphous shapes work with the dots of the grid to create patterns of seemingly haphazard compositions. The images adhere closely to the underlying configuration of the grid, creating a dichotomy of form resulting in a highly personal abstract language, which speaks of one's stream of consciousness.

Figure 5 is a playful investigation using color, form, tonality, texture, line, and pattern in the creation of a decorative world of fantasy that results from trusting the unknown.

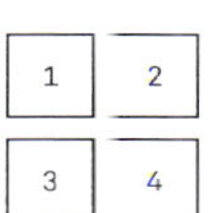

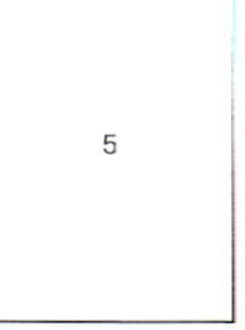

1–4. Tara Tuttle
5. Sebastian Plaza

Although the risk is in confronting the realm of not knowing, one must get past this fear and trust the journey.

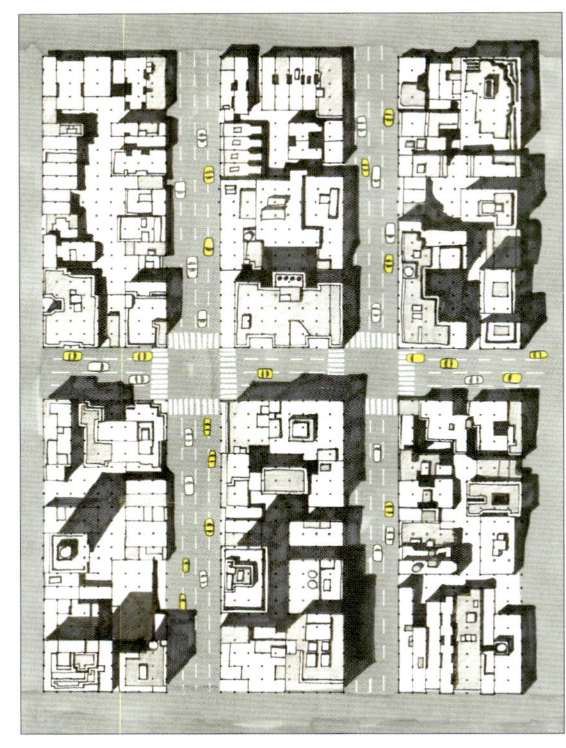

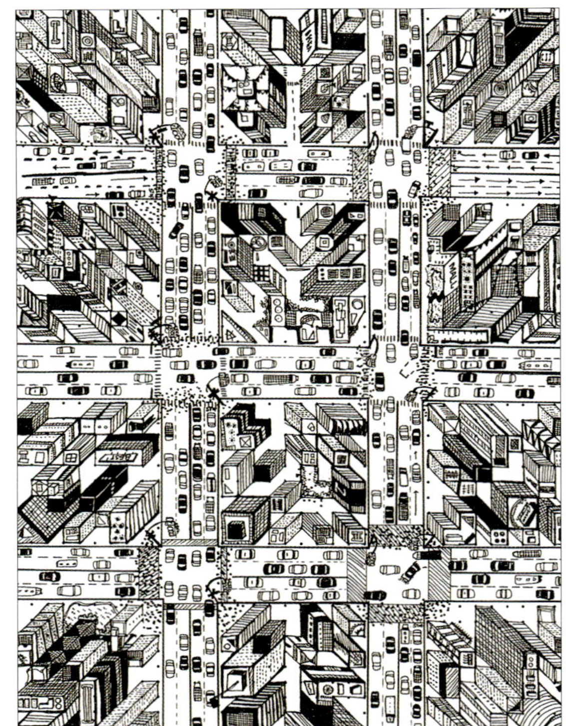

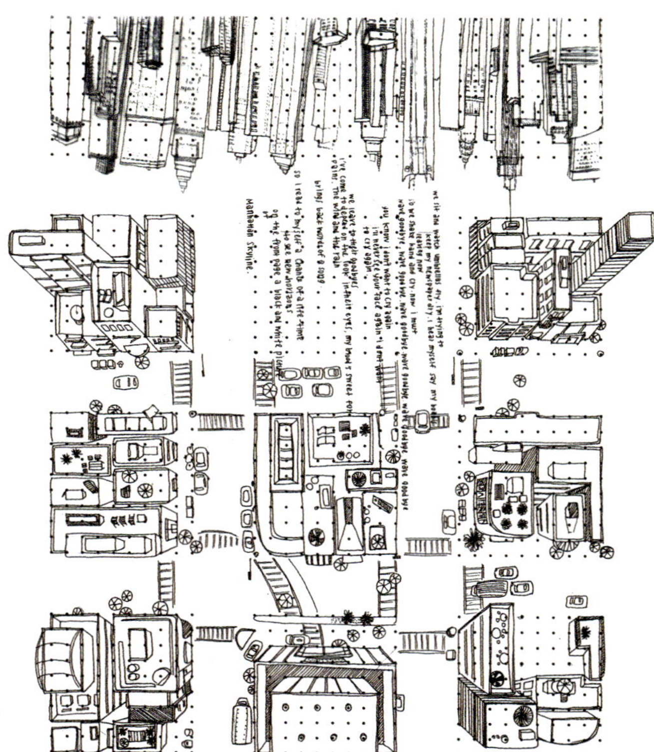

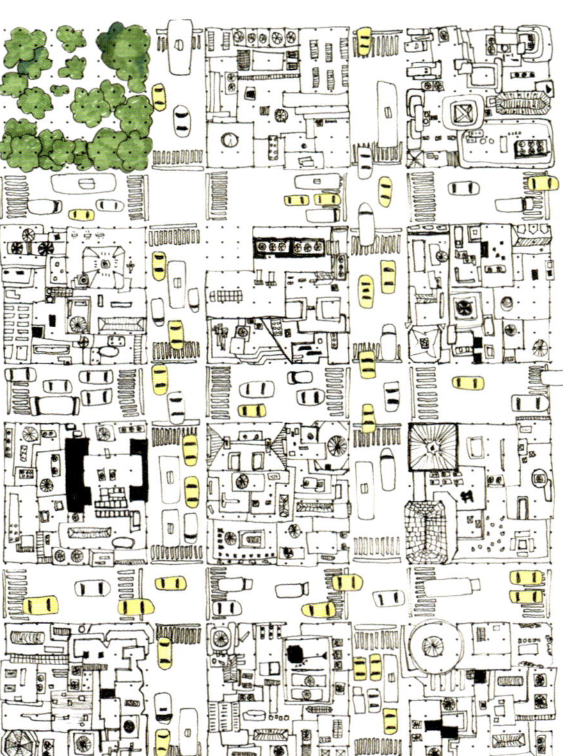

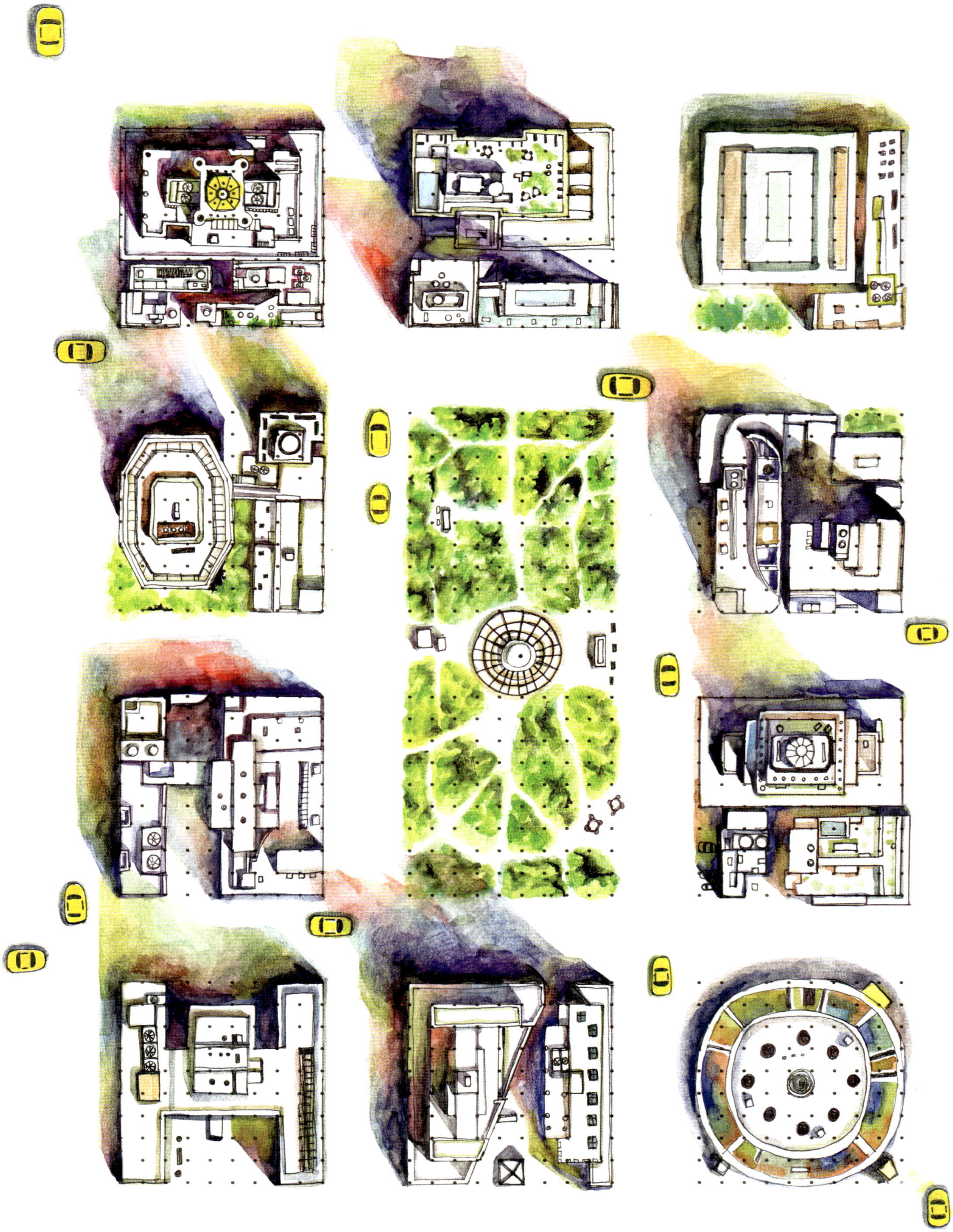

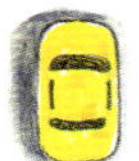

ZEN SOLUTIONS:

Figures 1 through 5 represent aerial views of cityscapes. Stylistically, they embody distinct avenues of expression.

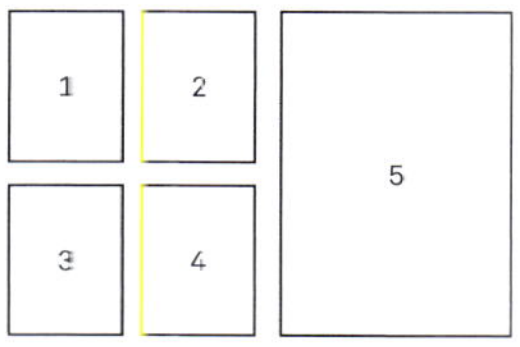

1	2	5
3	4	

1. *Youngyoon Kim*
2. *Chengwen Fung*
3. *Sebit Min*
4. *Hanbyul Lee*
5. *Jungeun Kwak*

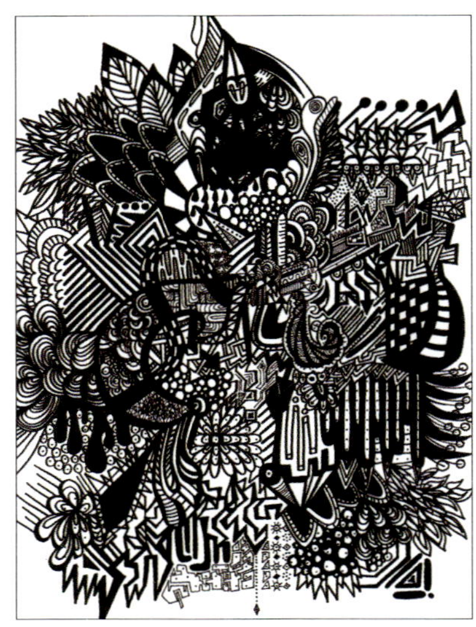

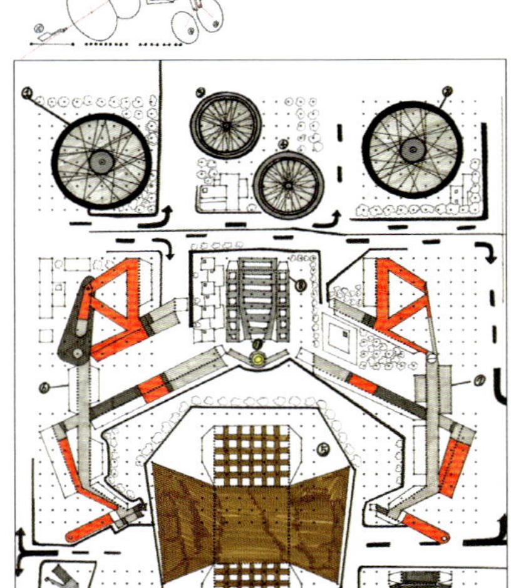

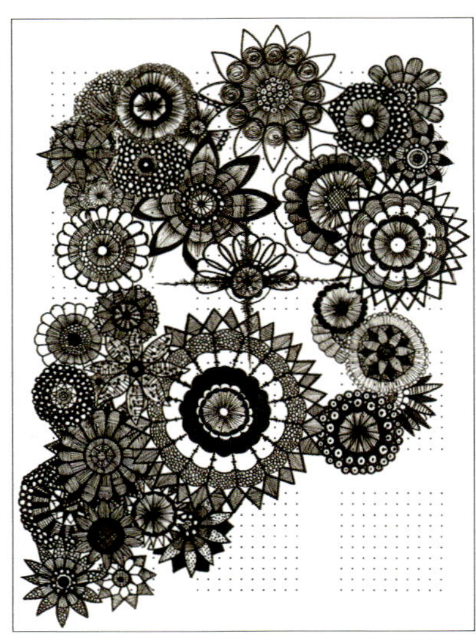

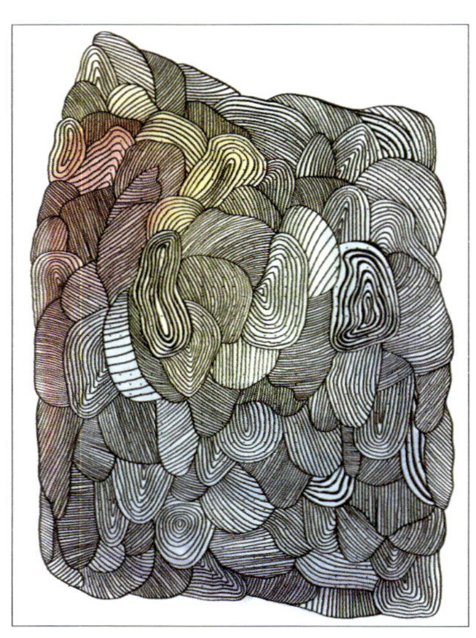

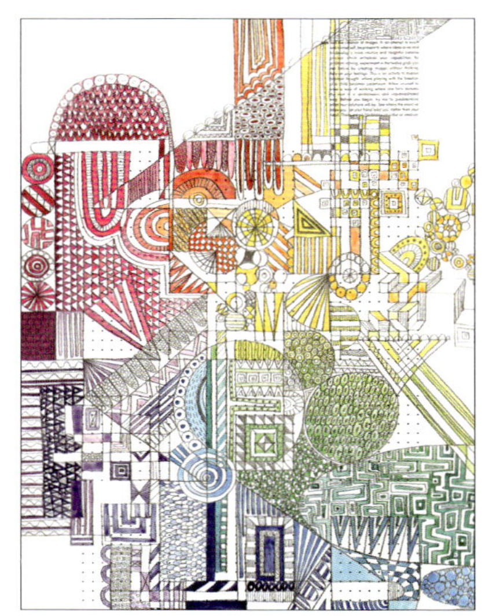

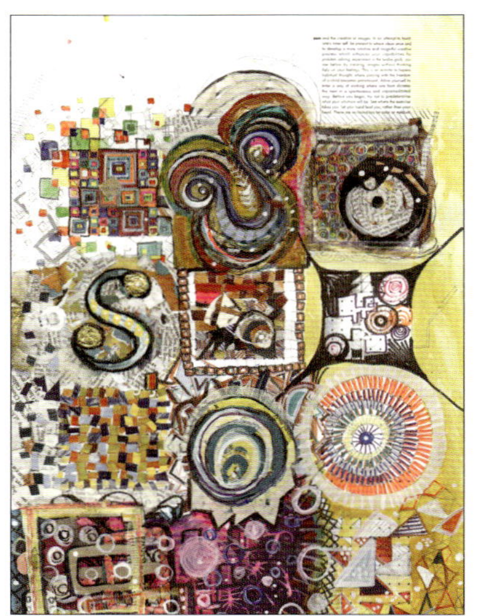

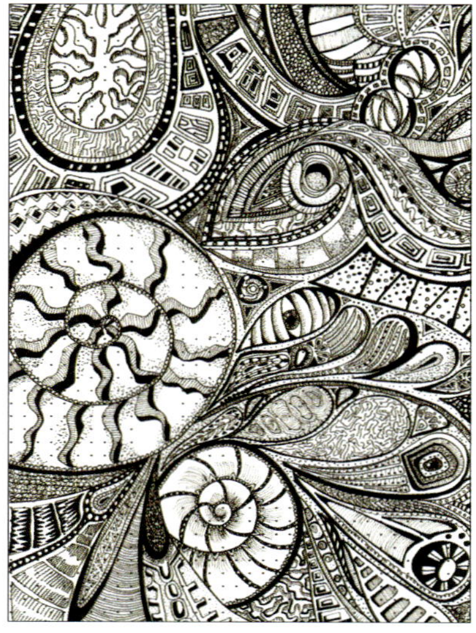

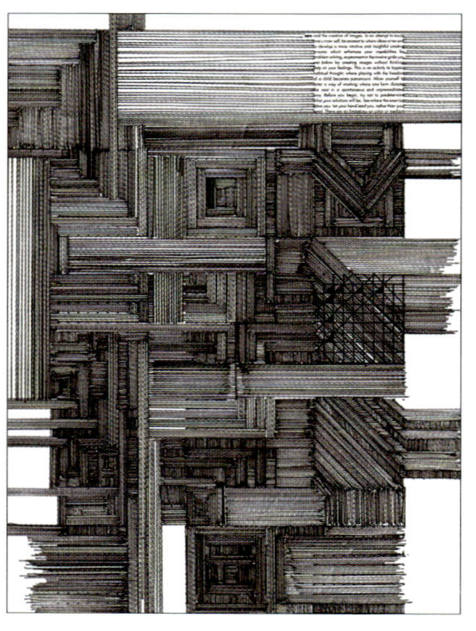

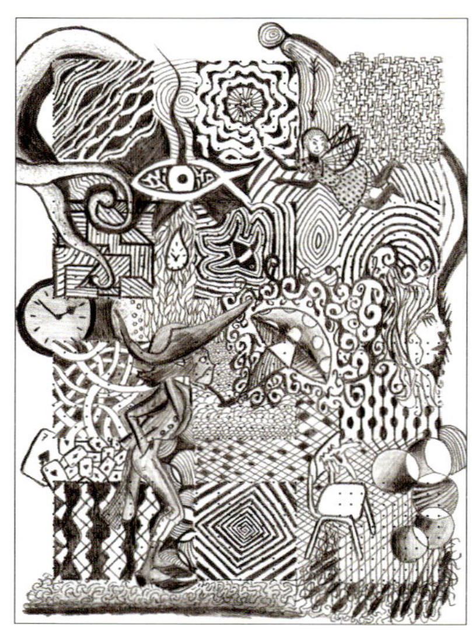

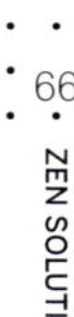

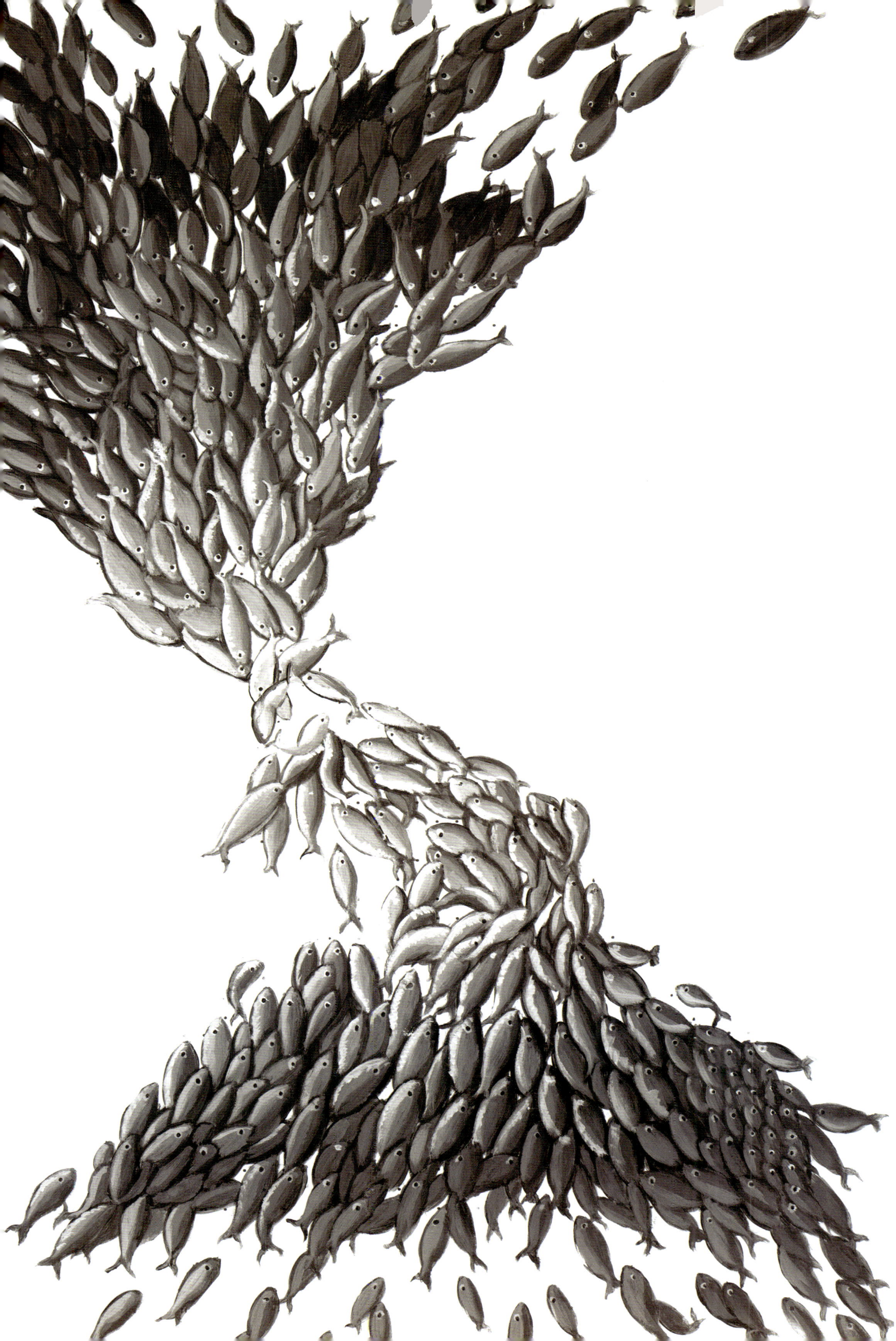

ZEN SOLUTIONS:

Figures 1 through 10 use the assignment to create a single image that explores patterning and complexity in executing abstract and narrative solutions.

Solutions range from an adherence to the grid system to having an imperceptible reference to the given restraints of the dot diagram.

Figure 10 uses the dots as fish eyes as a point of departure where the grid has been obliterated.

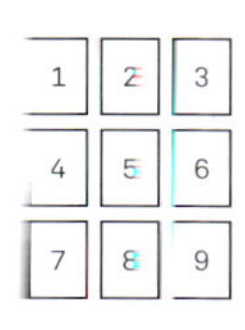

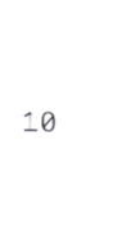

1. *Angela Kim*
2. *Dalhee Lee*
3. *Anna Prince*
4. *Rebecca Lim*
5. *Yuna Lee*
6. *Michele Clark*
7. *Yerang Wi*
8. *Chris Minho Kwon*
9. *Frank Olivo*
10. *Heejae Choi*

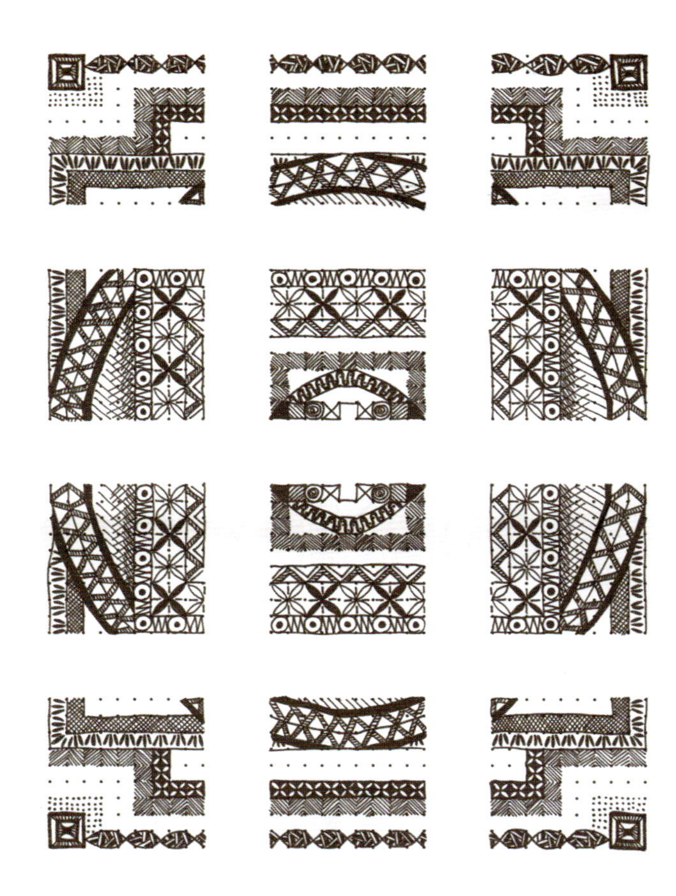

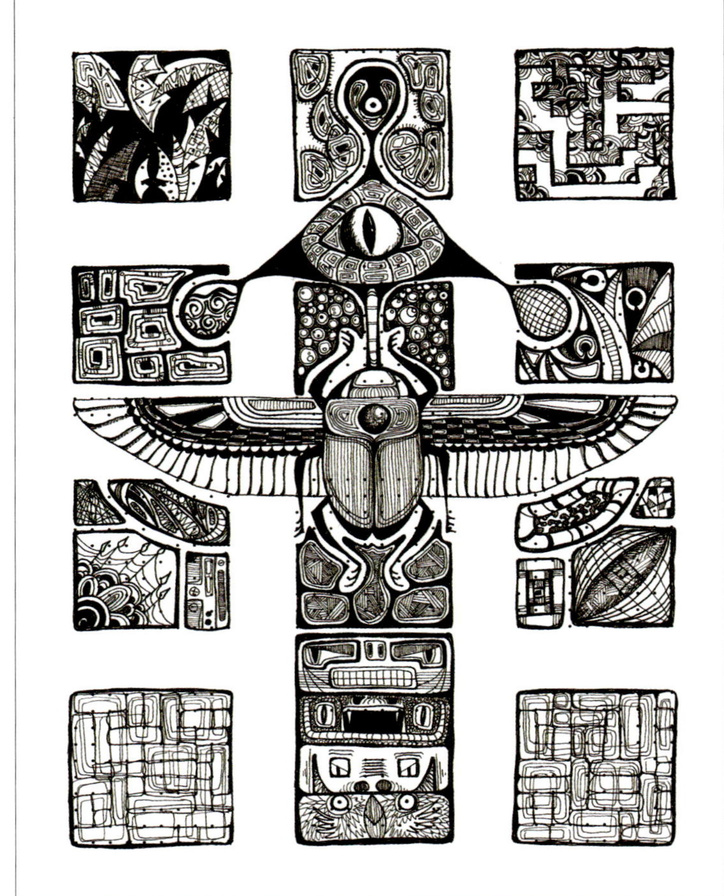

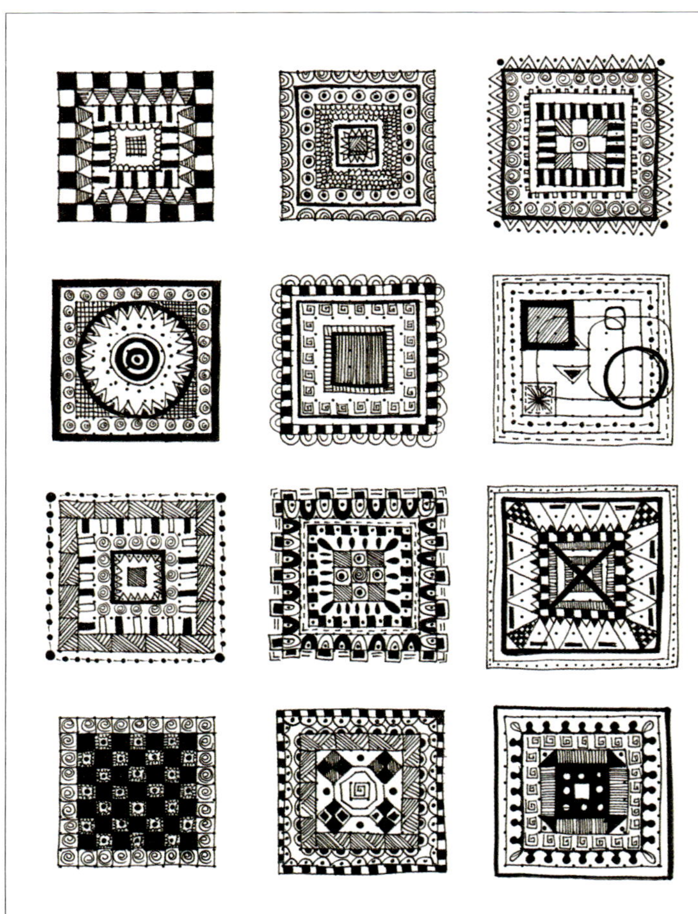

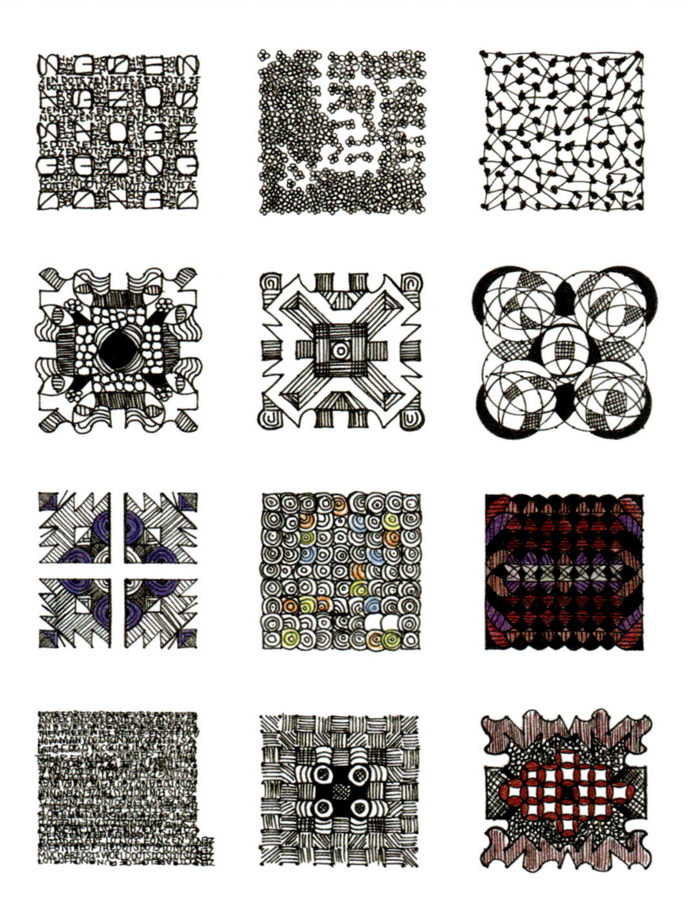

ZEN SOLUTIONS:

Figures 1 through 5 represent single-themed solutions, where for the most part the integrity of all twelve areas on the assignment sheet has been maintained.

Figures 1 through 4 focus on patterning and linear explorations that are transformed into highly stylized design solutions.

Figure 5 incorporates color and animates a story of ants devouring an Oreo cookie.

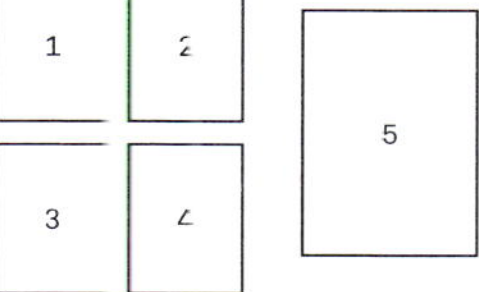

1. Hsaio Pin Lin
2. Alex Lieblein
3. Jaewoon Park
4. Daniel e Debiasio
5. Daseul Ahn

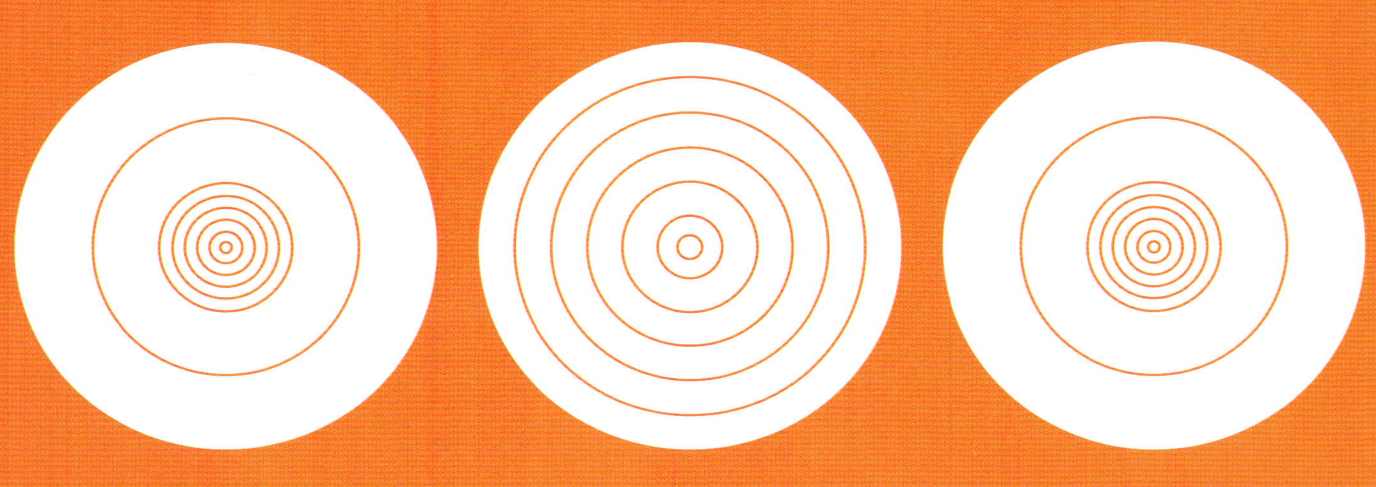

THOUGHTS ON THE CREATIVE PROCESS 2

During the design process one should remain sensitive to all that is given. In the case of formal problems, each stage of the project dictates its next incarnation. A design might call for the use of intense color, less complexity, the reproportioning of form, the introduction of balance or asymmetry, as well as a multitude of other aesthetic decisions.

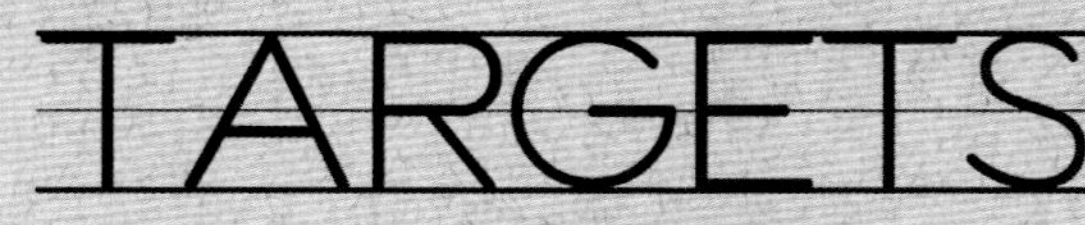

TRADITIONALLY, A TARGET IS AN OBJECT MARKED WITH CONCENTRIC CIRCLES, TO BE AIMED AT IN SHOOTING PRACTICE OR IN CONTESTS. IT REPRESENTS PRECISION AS WELL AS A GOAL TO BE STRIVED FOR, OR AN OBJECT OF SCORN OR ABUSE. BECAUSE WE LIVE IN A VERY GOAL ORIENTED WORLD, THE TARGET MOST OFTEN SYMBOLIZES LEVELS OF SUCCESS AND ACCURACY. ON THE OTHER HAND, THE MORE OMINOUS SYMBOLISM REFLECTS WEAPONRY, WHICH IS ASSOCIATED WITH DEATH. USING THE SEVEN TARGETS ON THE ASSIGNMENT SHEET MAKE A PERSONAL, POLITICAL OR PURELY GRAPHIC STATEMENT, IN WHATEVER WAY INTERESTS YOU.

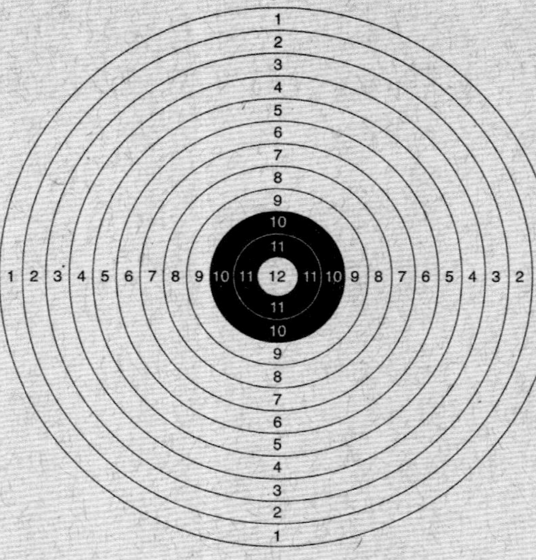

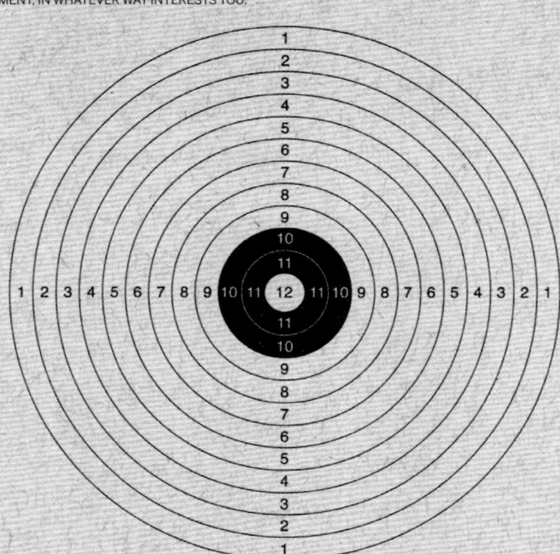

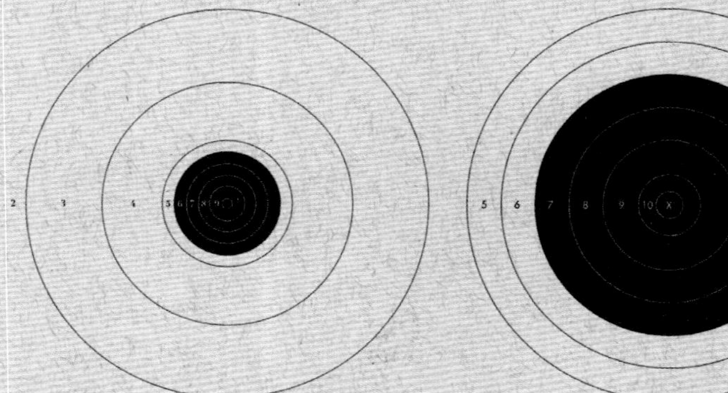

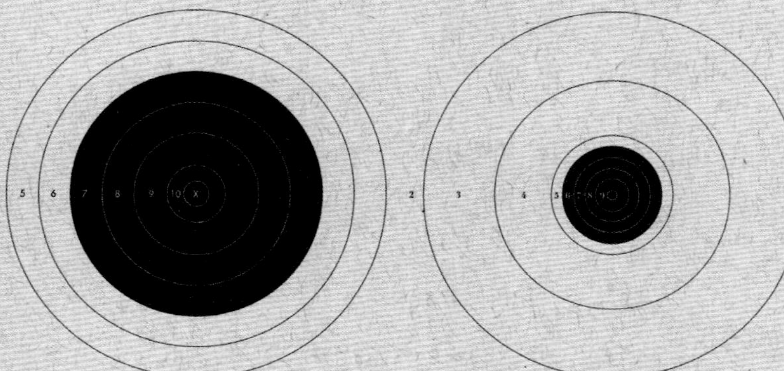

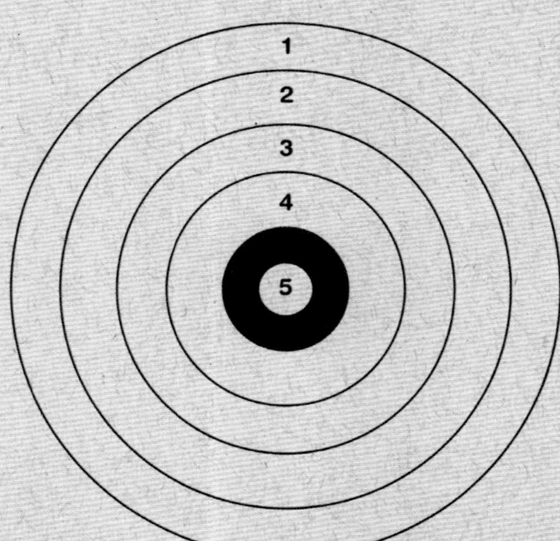

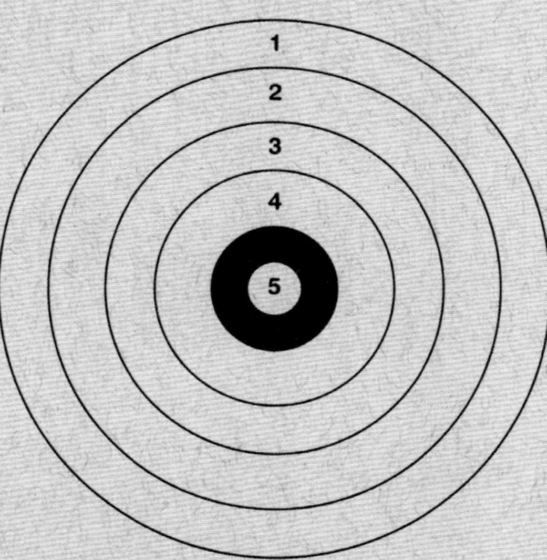

COMPETITOR ______________________________

PROBLEMS : SOLUTIONS SERIES

CREATED BY RICHARD WILDE / JUDITH WILDE, PRODUCED BY VISUAL ARTS PRESS, LTD. ART DIRECTORS: RICHARD WILDE / JUDITH WILDE

TARGET PROBLEM:

A target is a recognizable, symmetrical graphic iconic image in popular culture. Its intent is for developing accuracy in weaponry, specifically for guns, bow and arrow, and the recreational activity of playing darts.

Use the seven targets printed on the assignment sheet to make a personal, political, social or purely graphic statement.

AIM:
The concentric circles serve as a starting point in creating either recognizable imagery or patterns, executed spontaneously or carefully mannered. As in most of the assignments appearing in this book, the underlying intent is for one to have the opportunity to find one's own voice for personal expression. This project, given its parameters, sets the stage for invention.

SUGGESTIONS:
Given the wide range of directions one can take in solving this problem, it is helpful at the onset to determine a course of action. Doodling, which can very well lead to a direction, can be a way to begin one's investigation in setting the stage for original imagery to appear.

SPECIFICATIONS:
Either address all seven areas as individual explorations, or try to combine the seven areas into one cohesive statement. There are no limitations on color or medium.

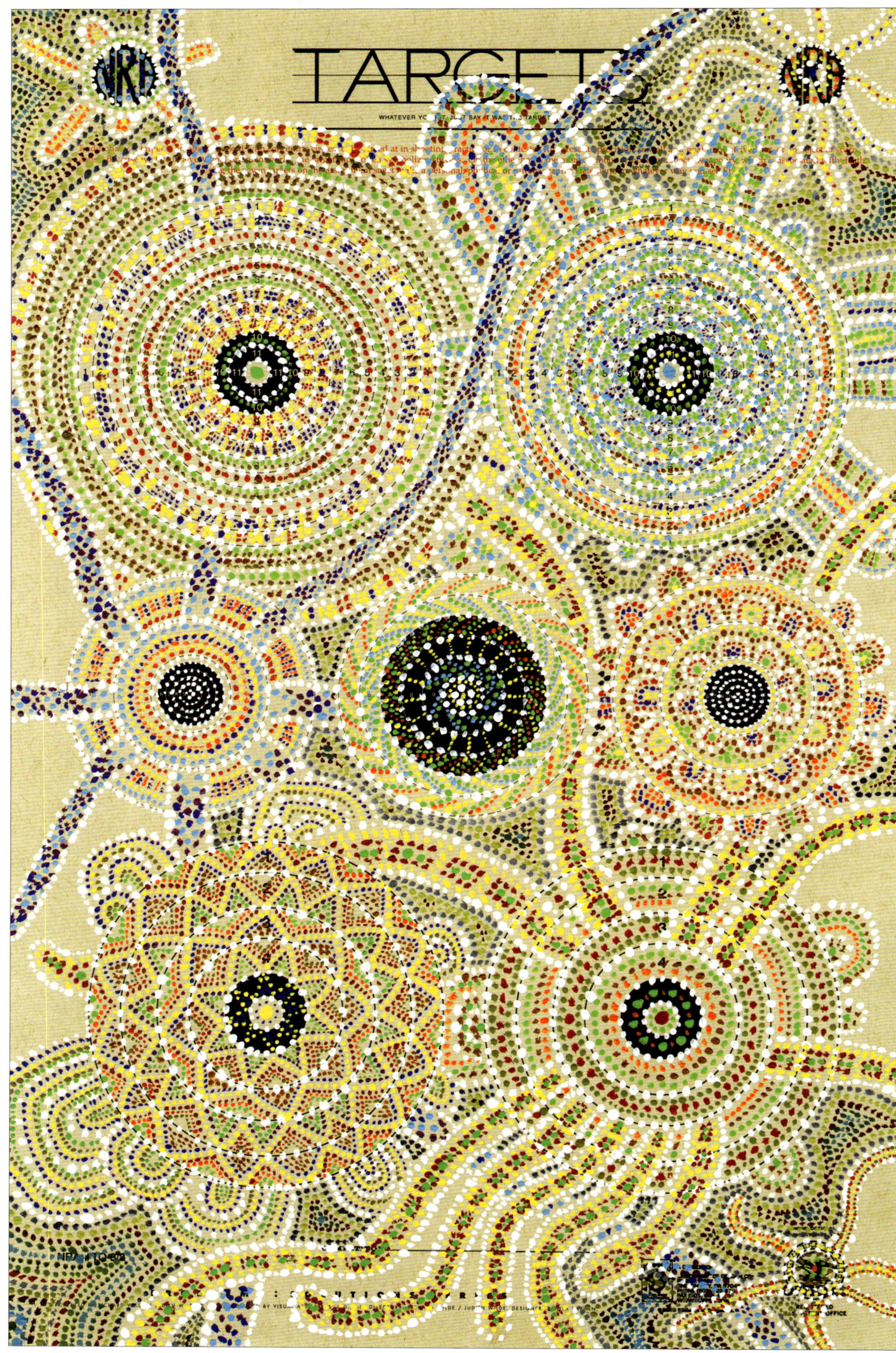
TARGETS

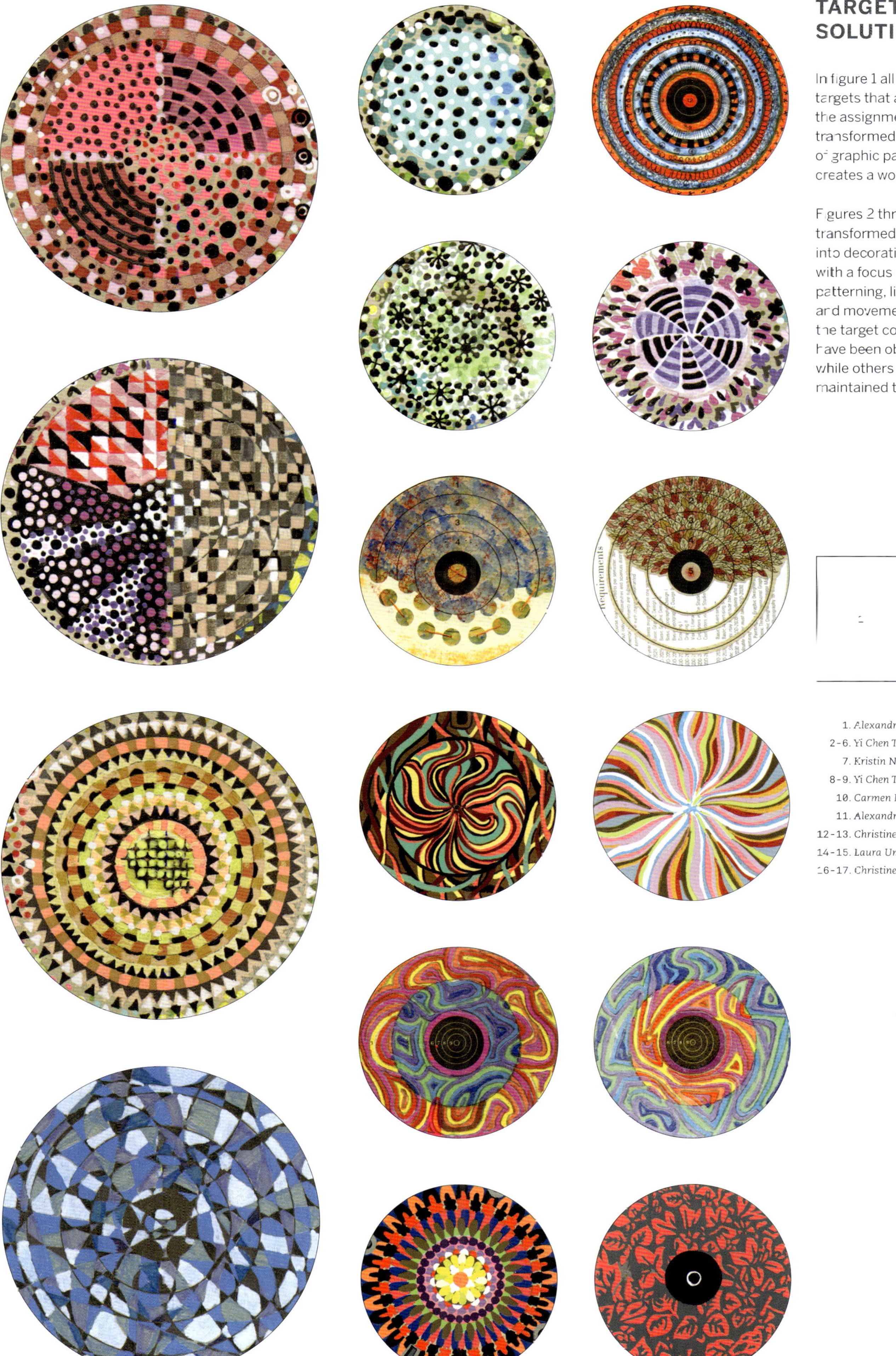

TARGET SOLUTIONS:

In figure 1 all seven targets that appear on the assignment sheet are transformed into a mosaic of graphic patterning that creates a world unto itself.

Figures 2 through 17 have transformed the targets into decorative motifs with a focus on color, patterning, line, texture, and movement. For some, the target configurations have been obliterated, while others have maintained their integrity.

1. *Alexandra Stikeleather*
2–6. *Yi Chen Tsai*
7. *Kristin Naranjo*
8–9. *Yi Chen Tsai*
10. *Carmen Ng*
11. *Alexandra Barron*
12–13. *Christine Lee*
14–15. *Laura Umbach*
16–17. *Christine Lee*

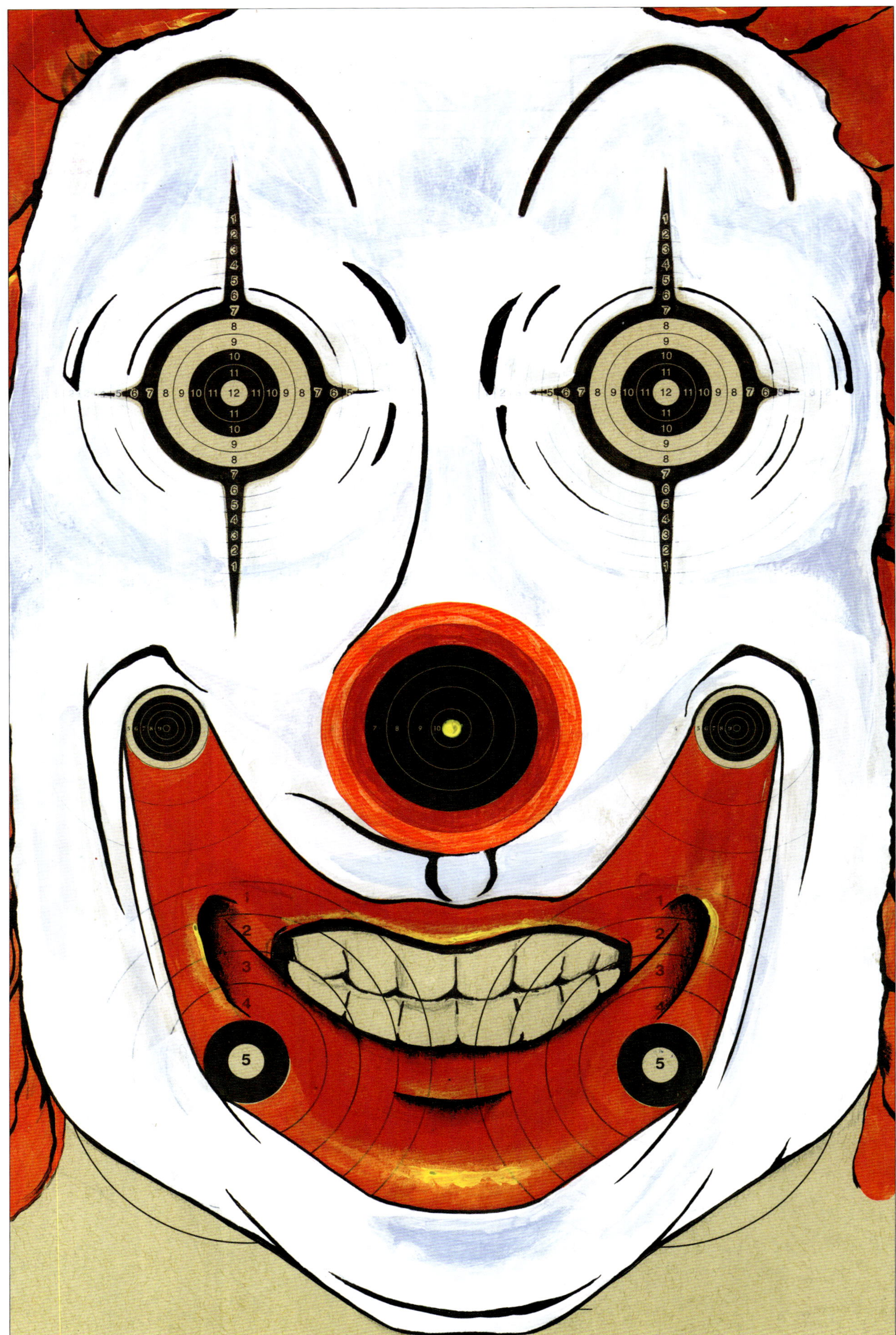

TARGET SOLUTIONS:

Both figures 1 and 3 use the dictates of the targets to create a composition by freely incorporating artistic license as a way of adaptation. The challenge to expand one's visual problem-solving capabilities has been undertaken within the given constraints.

Figure 2 addresses the subject of hunting by incorporating a rabbit's face into a target, while both the target and rabbit maintain their integrity.

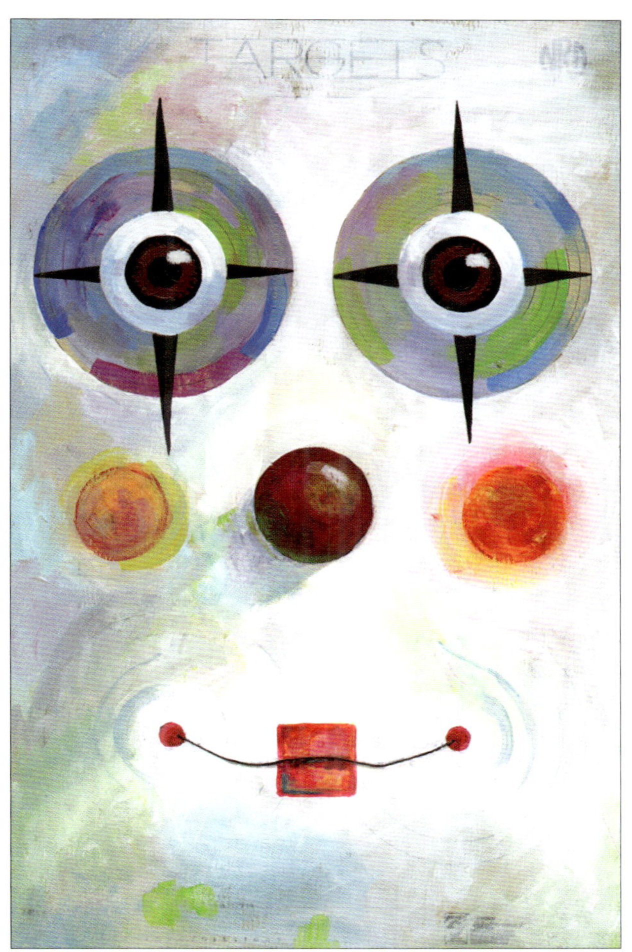

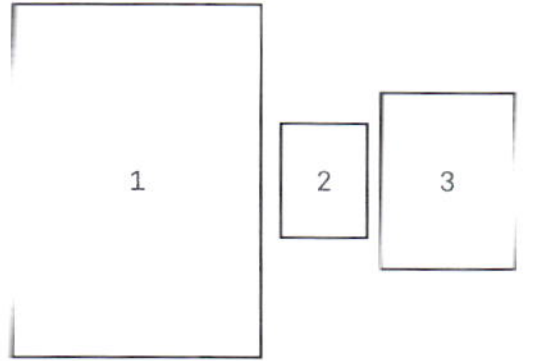

1. *Hyungkyu Choi*
2. *Lauren Harju*
3. *Suwon Paek*

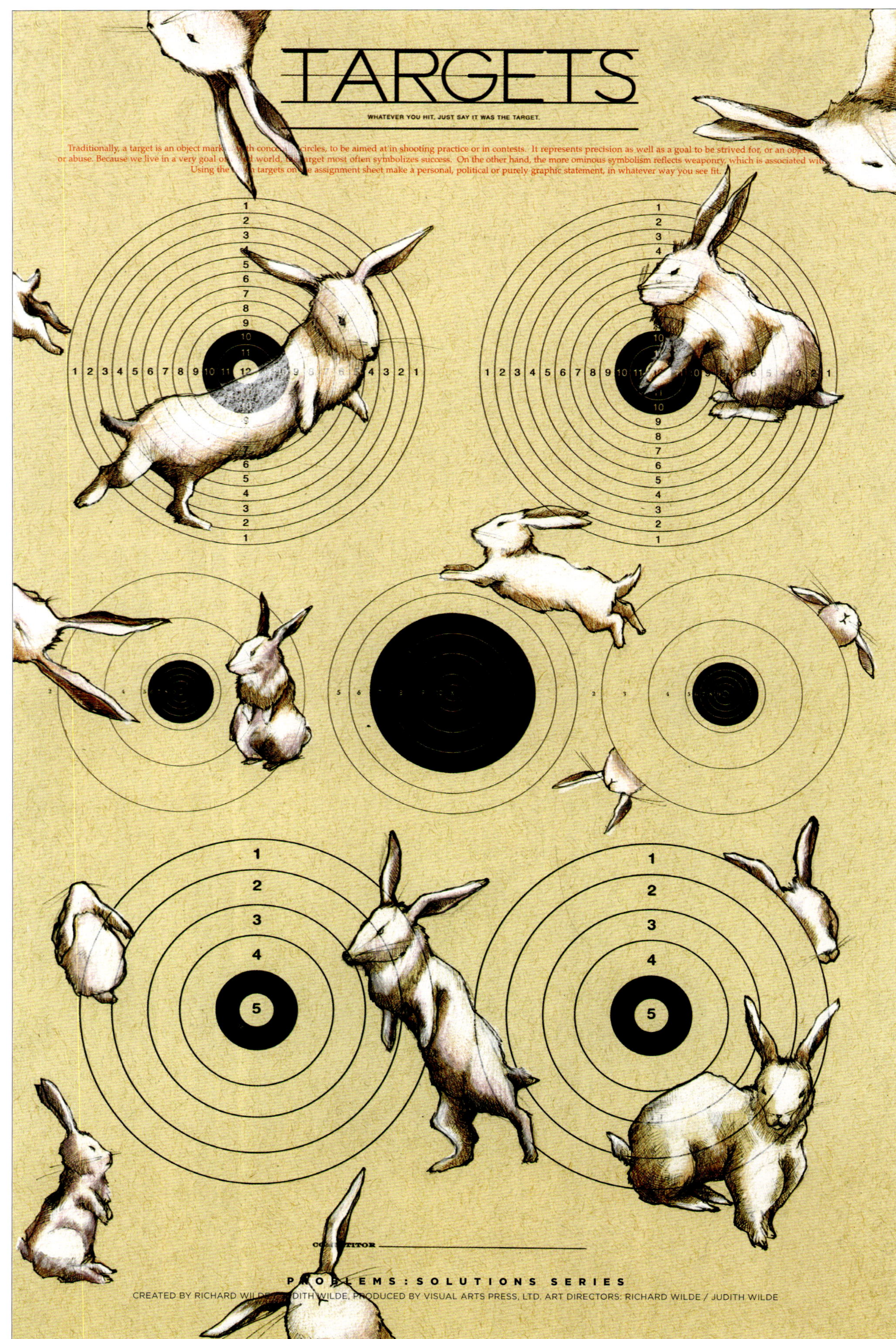
TARGETS
WHATEVER YOU HIT, JUST SAY IT WAS THE TARGET.
Traditionally, a target is an object mark circles, to be aimed at in shooting practice or in contests. It represents precision as well as a goal to be strived for, or an
or abuse. Because we live in a very goal world, arget most often symbolizes success. On the other hand, the more ominous symbolism reflects weaponry, which is associated
Using the targets on e assignment sheet make a personal, political or purely graphic statement, in whatever way you see fit.
PROBLEMS : SOLUTIONS SERIES
CREATED BY RICHARD WIL DITH WILDE, PRODUCED BY VISUAL ARTS PRESS, LTD. ART DIRECTORS: RICHARD WILDE / JUDITH WILDE

TARGET SOLUTIONS:

Figure 1 juxtaposes playfully frolicking rabbits against a background of targets, giving rise to both the joy of life and the threat of death. This solution raises one's consciousness to the activity of hunting.

Figures 2 through 25 are abstract compositions exhibiting a range of invention, exploration, and risk taking.

1. *Jinyi Roh*
2–4. *Cindy Kang*
5. *Dongmin Kim*
6. *Cindy Kang*
7. *Kirsten Karkanen*
8. *Haenara Im*
9. *Longo Chen*
10. *Jinkyung Myung*
11. *Alex Morel*
12. *Jeni Moon*
13. *Jin Byeolyi*
14. *Laura Umbach*
15. *Vincent DiGangi*
16. *Jeni Moon*
17–18. *Romina Leiva*
19. *Joonmo Kang*
20–21. *June Lim*
22. *Haenara Im*
23. *June Lim*
24. *Christine Lee*
25. *Vincent DiGangi*

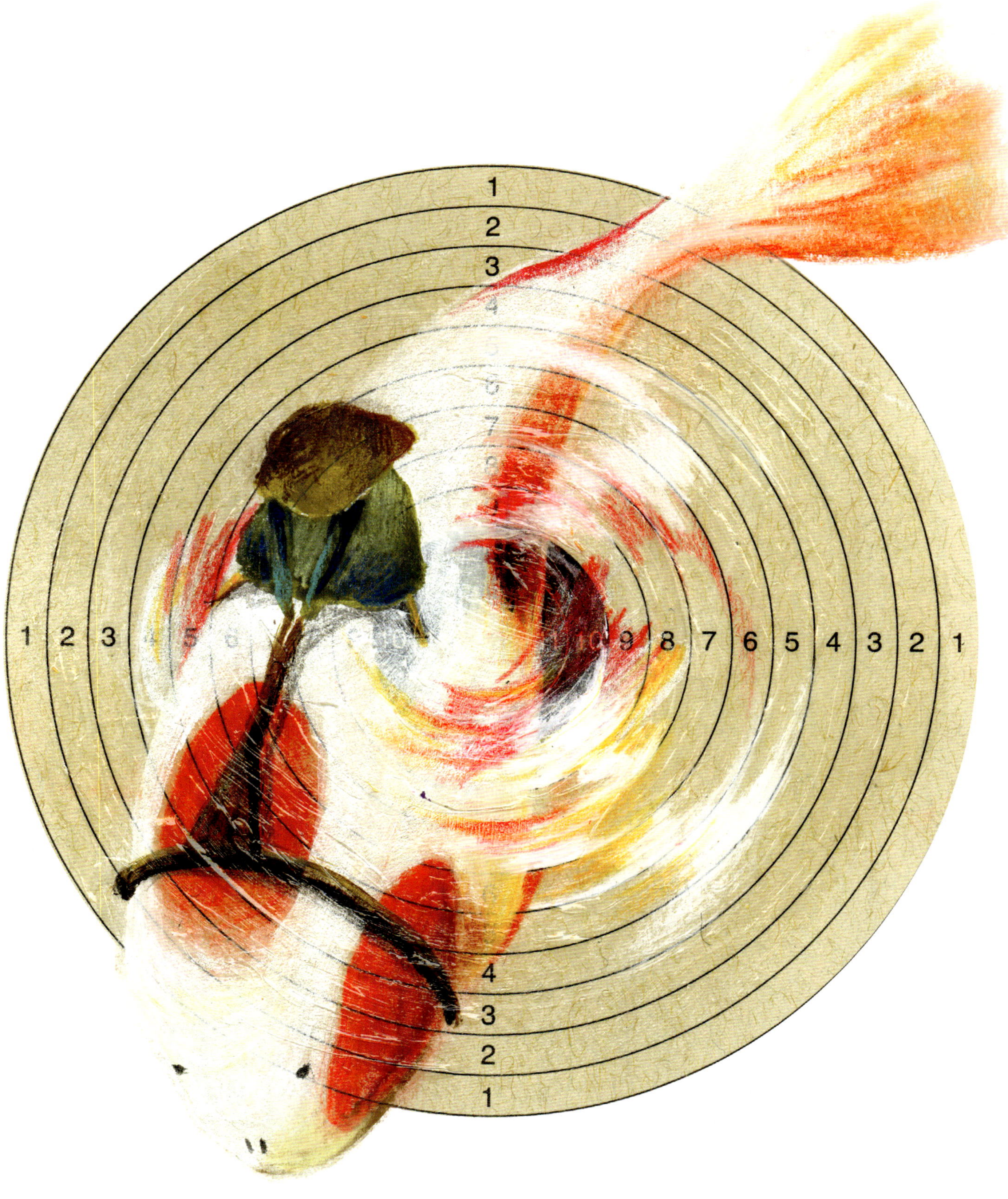

TARGET SOLUTIONS:

Figures 1 through 7 deal with storytelling and fantasy, and are viewed from an aerial perspective, while maintaining the concentric circles.

Figures 1 through 3 are playful solutions that include a child riding on the back of a fish by holding onto a harness, a child peering into a cup with a fish in it, as well as a fish swimming in a circular motion.

Figures 4 through 7 evolved from the idea of dropping a pebble into a pond and seeing concentric circles emerge, unhampered by a fish swimming there.

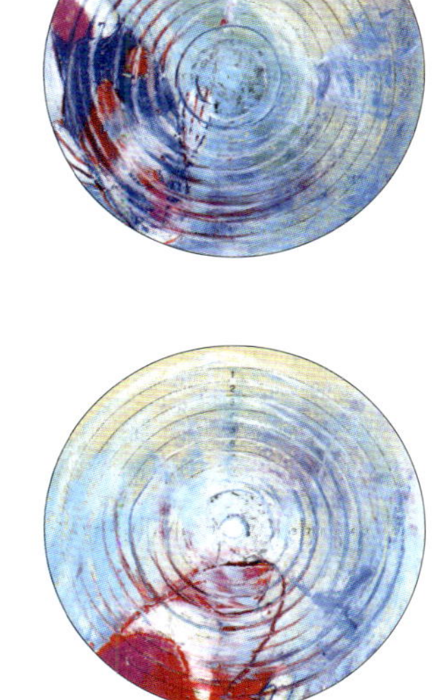

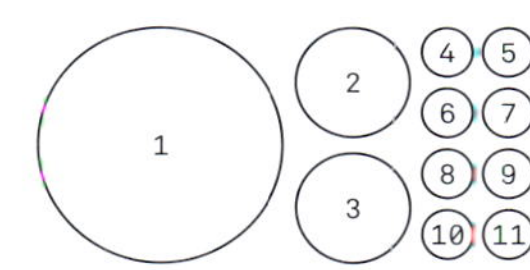

1–3. *Minhee Choi*
4–7. *Aurelie Joly*
8–9. *Pablo Delcan*
10–11. *Dinami Moda*

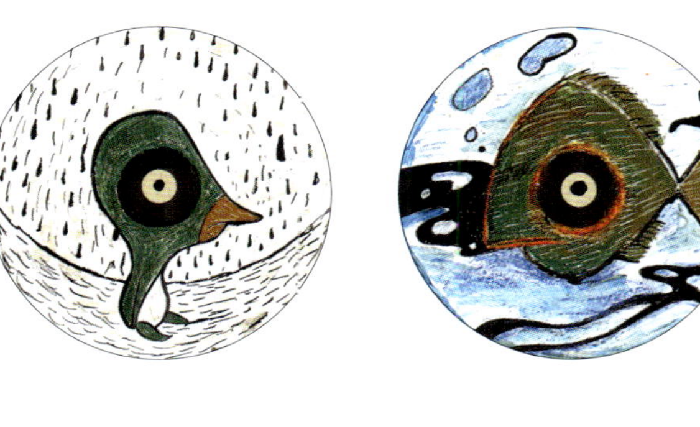

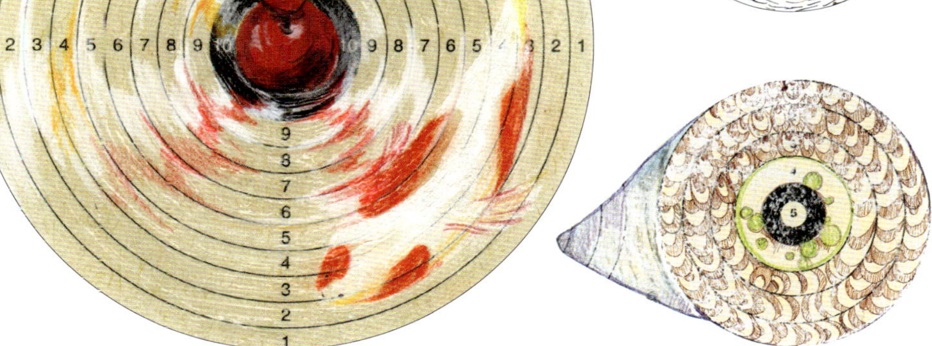

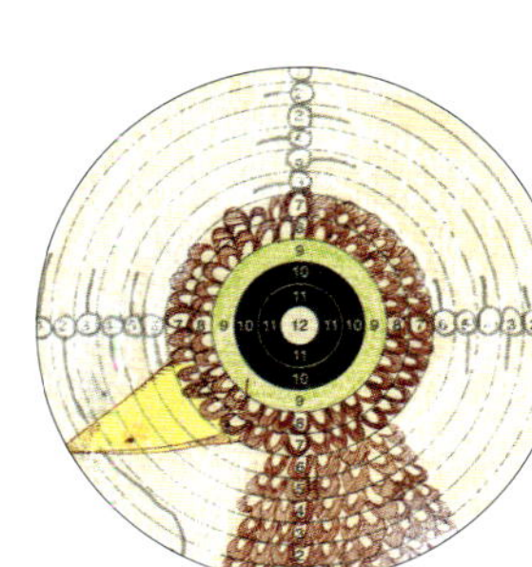

Figures 8 through 11 use the center of the target as an eye and as the focal point in the creation of strange creatures, which vary in terms of execution.

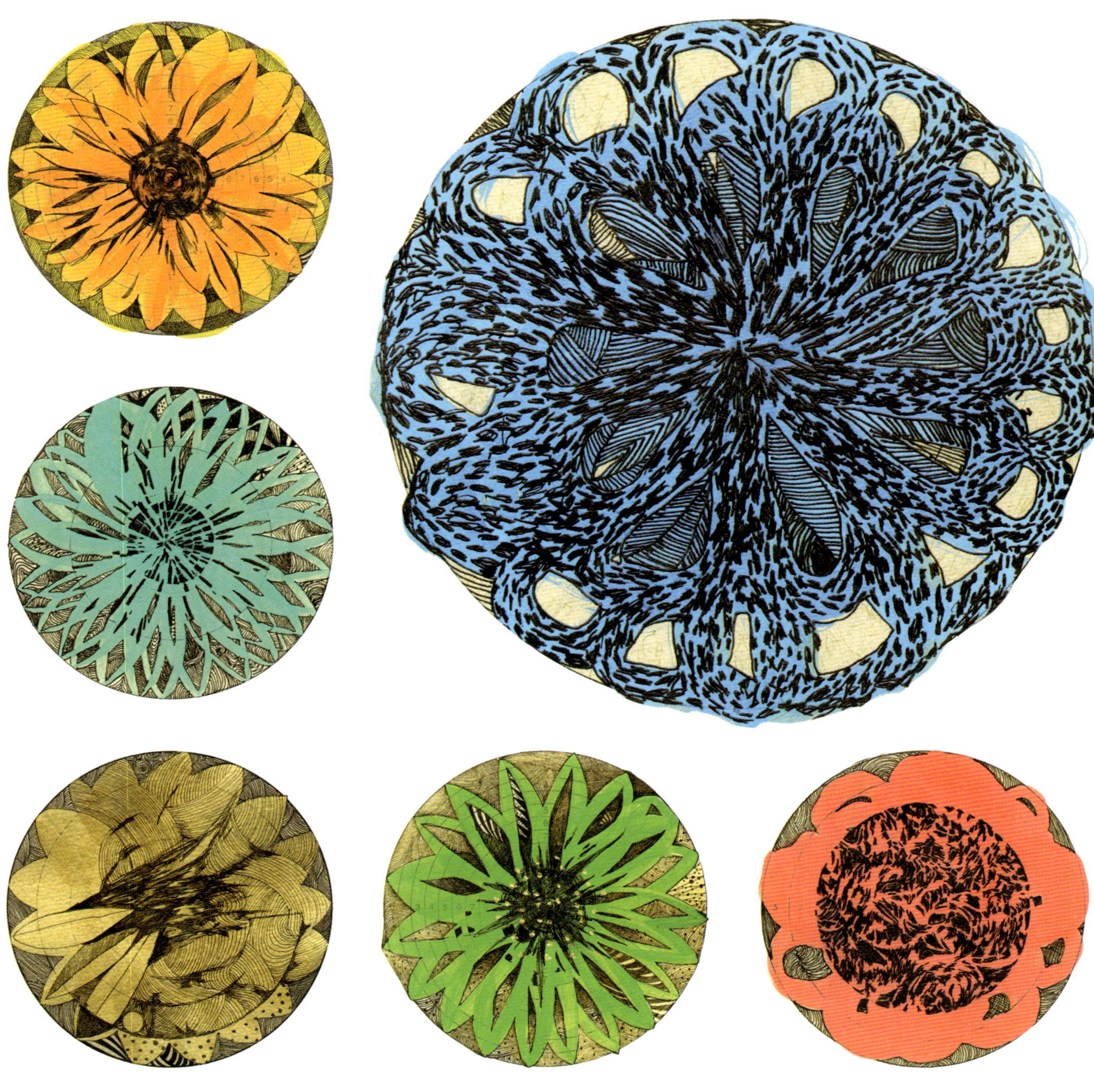

TARGET SOLUTIONS:

Flowers are the theme in figures 1 through 6. Several solutions have transcended the literal concept of a flower, by inventing abstract forms as a point of departure in an effort to create new imagery.

Figures 7 through 9 are thematic solutions that deal with organic imagery, all adhering to the circular grid, where the organic and geometric have been reconciled.

Figures 10 through 12 depict seafaring imagery that includes a highly personalized interpretation of a fish, a lifesaver ring, and a coil of rope.

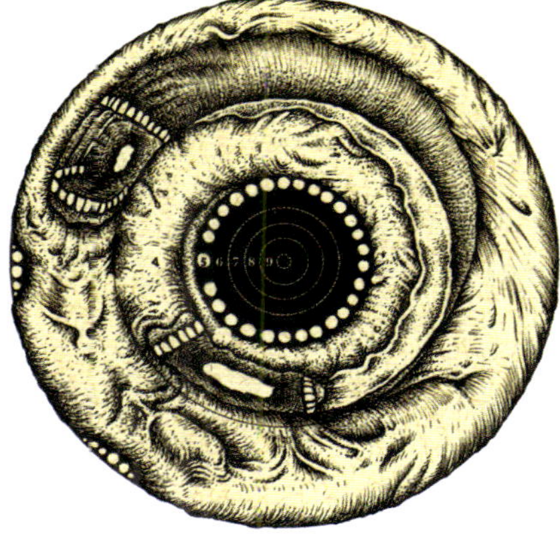

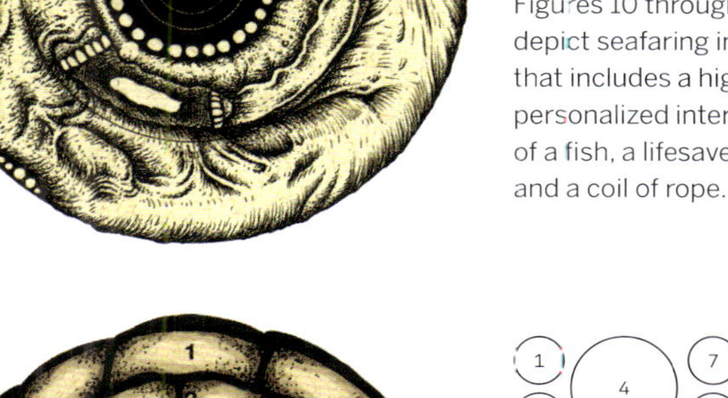

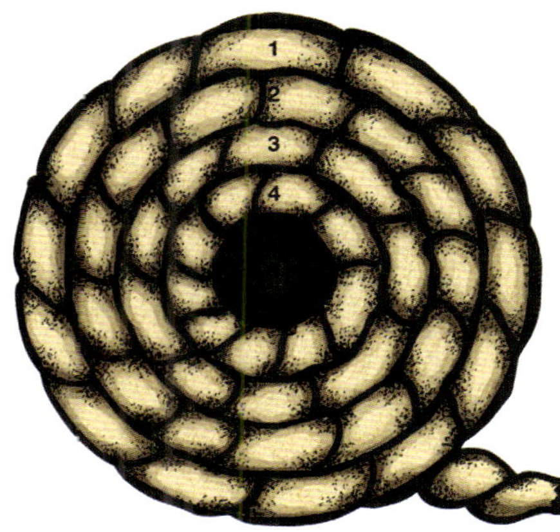

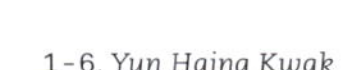

1-6. Yun Haing Kwak
7-9. Sam Ba
10-12. Sebastian Pino
13. Narae Lee
14-15. Yi Chieh Jen

Figures 13 through 15 are designed with a limited palette of black, and in some cases black and gold, using flat geometric forms, spatial relationships and patterning that emanates from a central focal point.

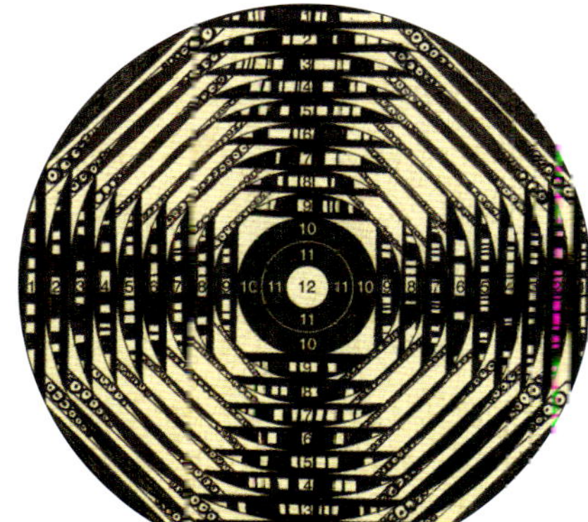

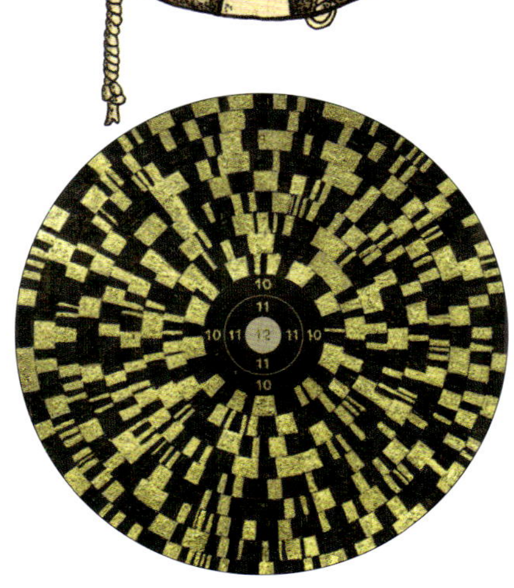

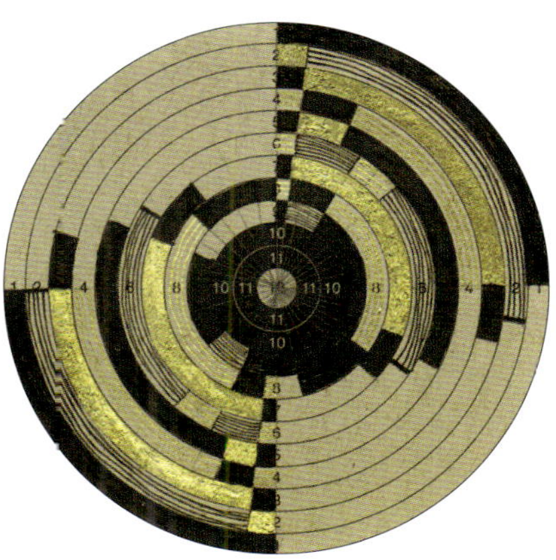

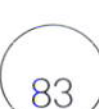

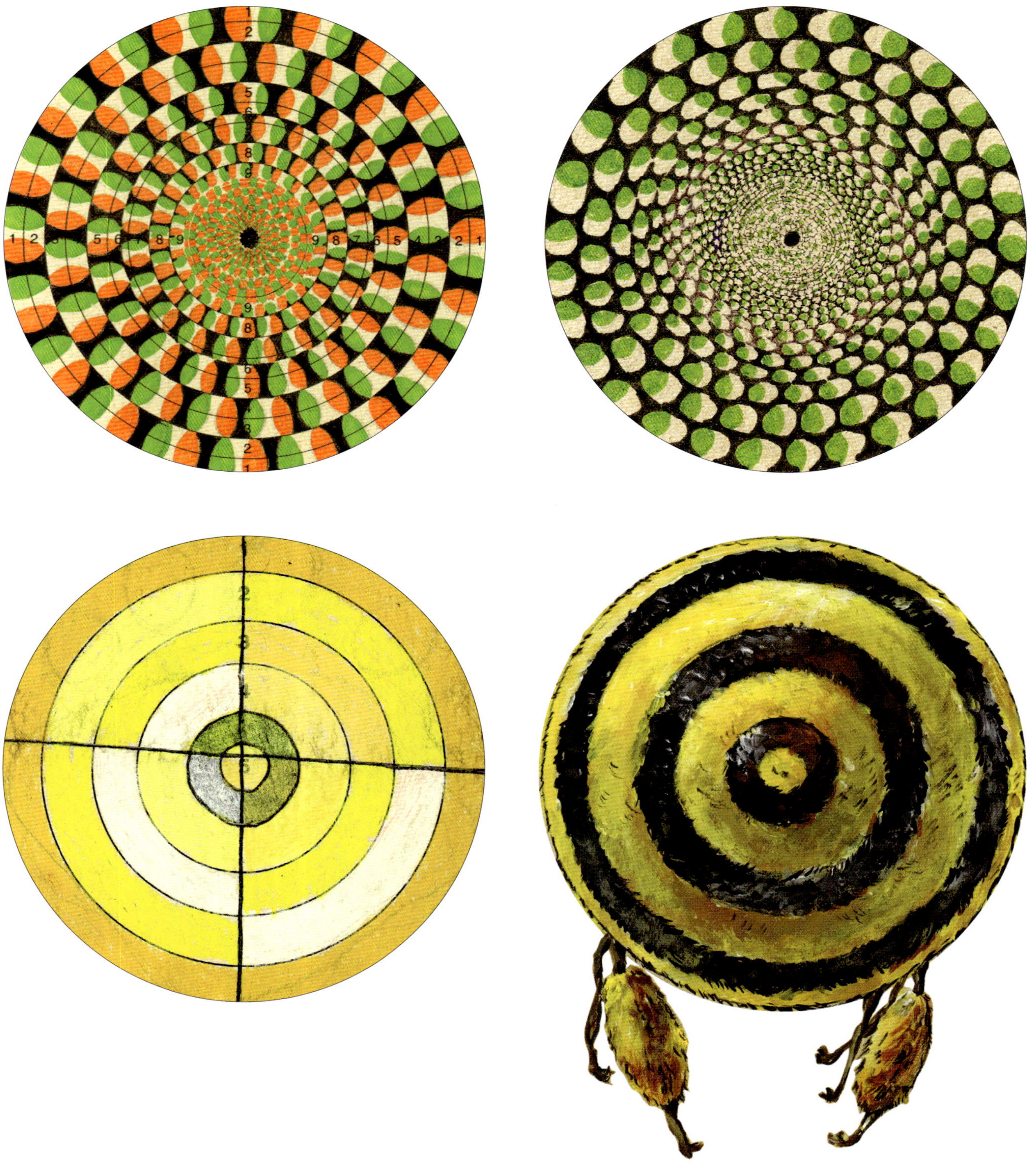

TARGET SOLUTIONS:

Figures 1 and 2 deal with the optical effect of receding space, using a center focal point and diminishing size.

Figure 3 is a personal color study, while figure 4 functions both as a target and a bumblebee. The target appears on the rear end of a bumblebee, creating an allegorical solution.

Figures 5 and 6 are organically drawn flowers which are in direct contrast to the precise geometry of a target.

Figures 7 through 12 are executed in pencil, incorporating continuous tone.

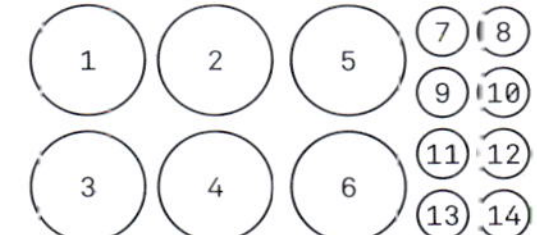

1–2. Yunhaing Kwak
3. Haenara Im
4. Dongmin Kim
5–6. Elaine Park
7. Seunghyeon Im
8–12. Eunji Kim
13–14. Rebecca Lim

Figure 13 was created by burning the exposed areas of the target with a match, which is juxtaposed against the unaffected areas that were initially covered by sticks and then removed.

Figure 14 is a dimensional solution that uses burnt wooden matchsticks as a form of expression.

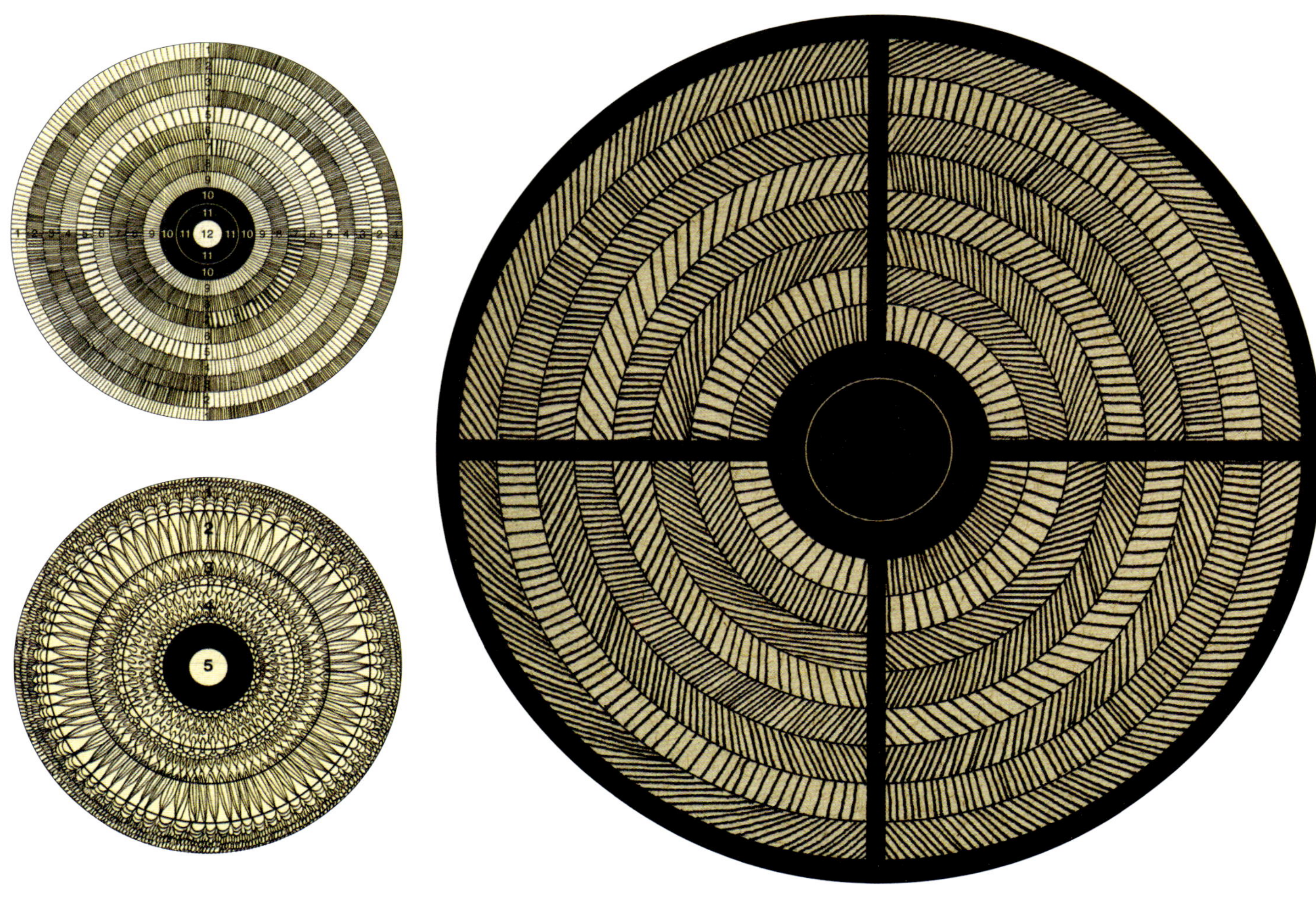
12
5

TARGET SOLUTIONS:

Figures 1 through 15 express an array of black and white solutions, many of which deal with inventive patterning through the use of line. Symmetry plays a major role in most solutions.

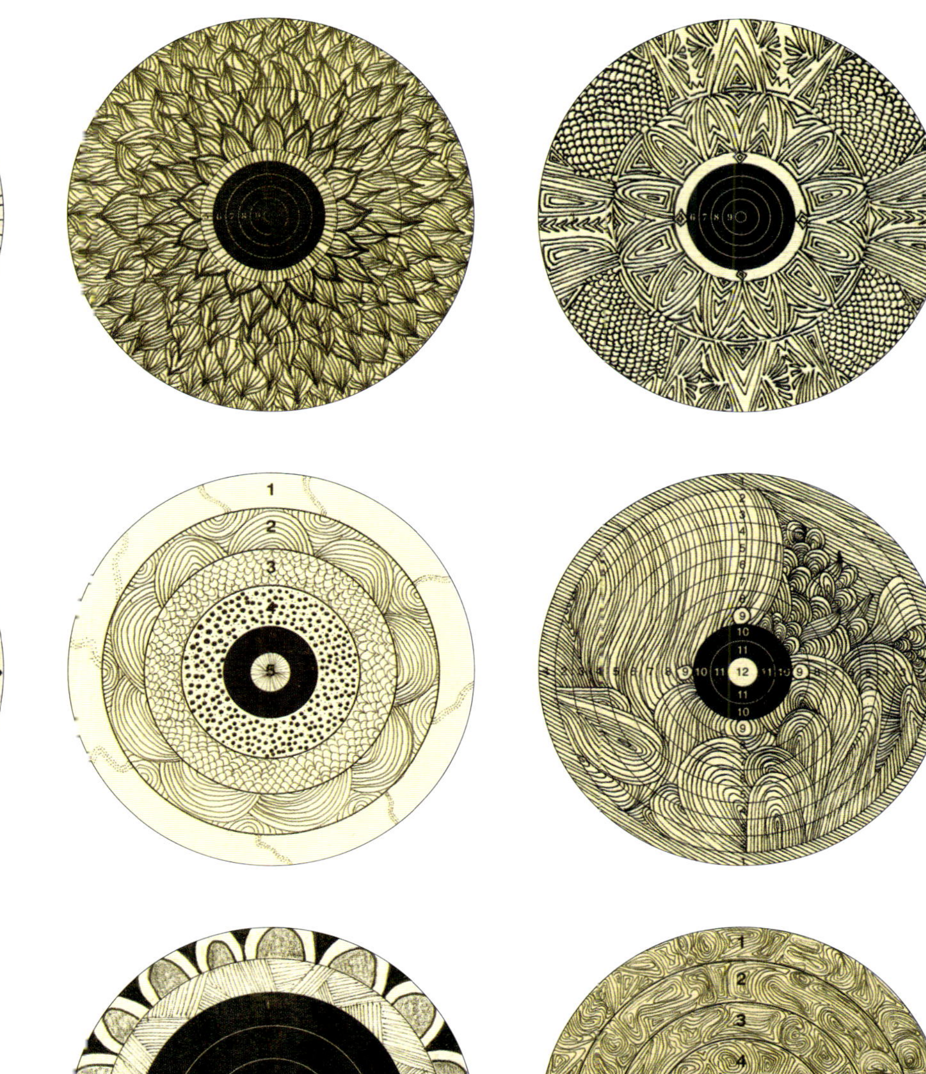

1. *Emily Bonnet*
2. *Roza Gazarian*
3. *Susanne Soum*
4. *Aerial Chen*
5. *Chantal Durante*
6. *Roza Gazarian*
7. *Jiwon Kim*
8. *Chantal Durante*
9. *Roza Gazarian*
10. *Haewon Park*
11. *Lauren Hom*
12. *Chantal Durante*
13. *Kim Capers*
14. *Aerial Chen*
15. *Youngwoon Choi*

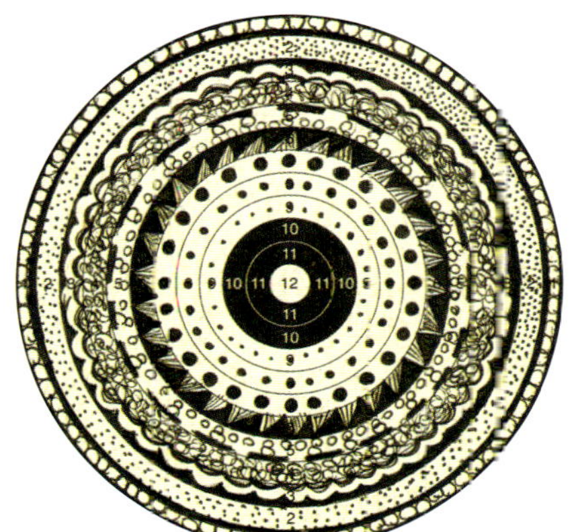

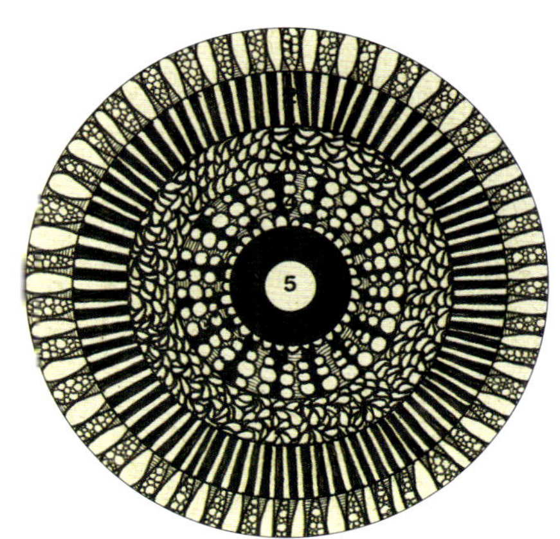

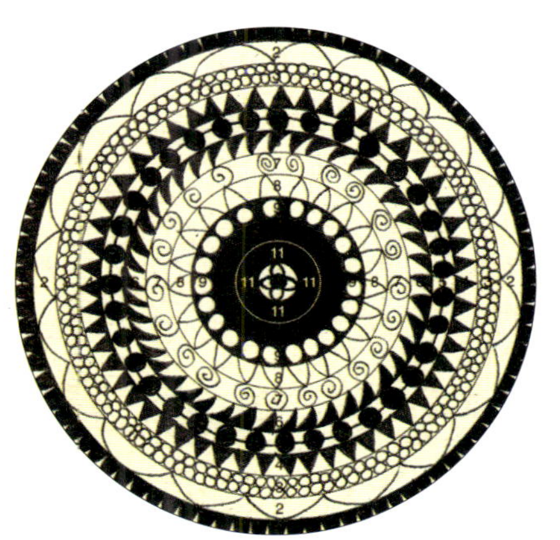

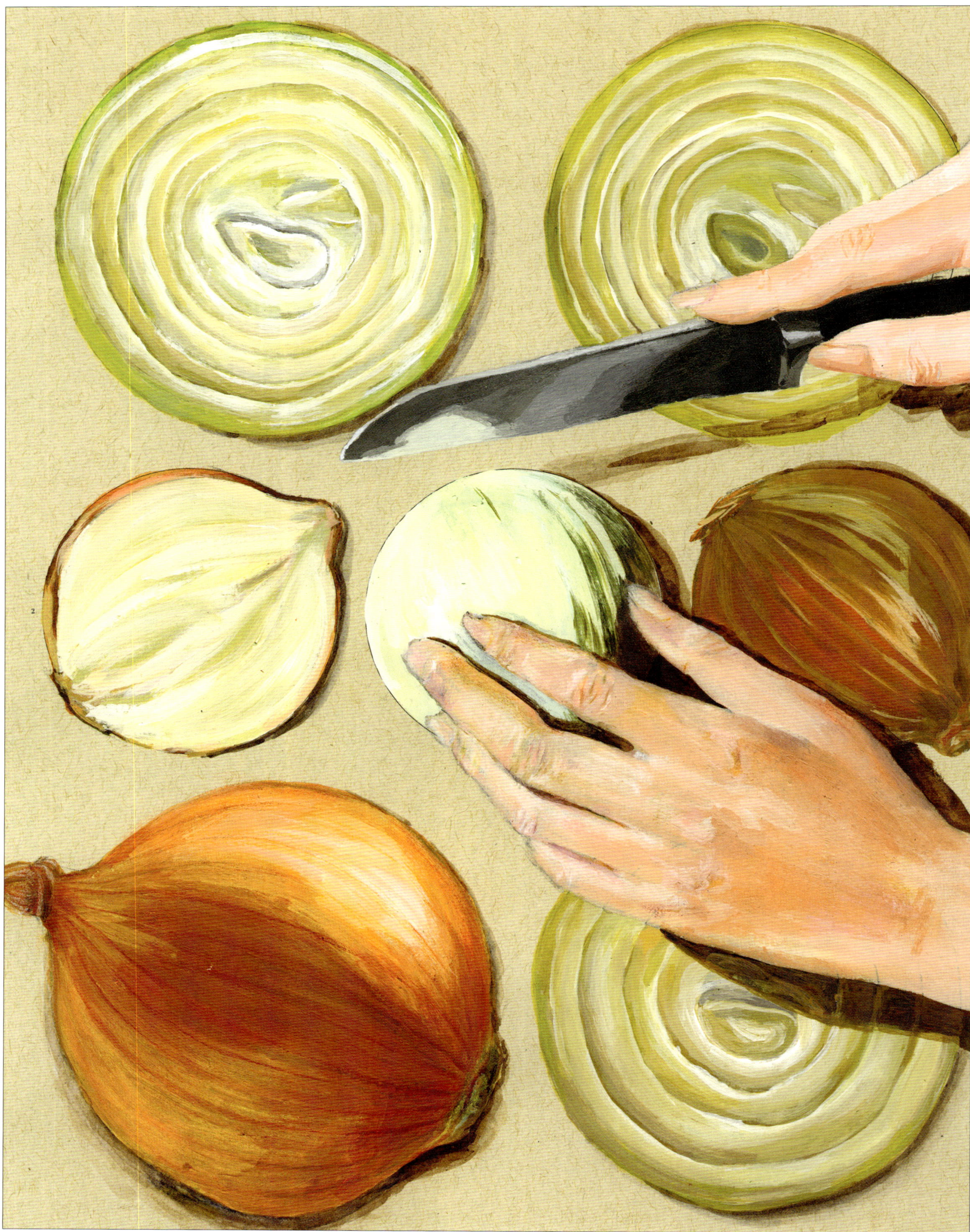

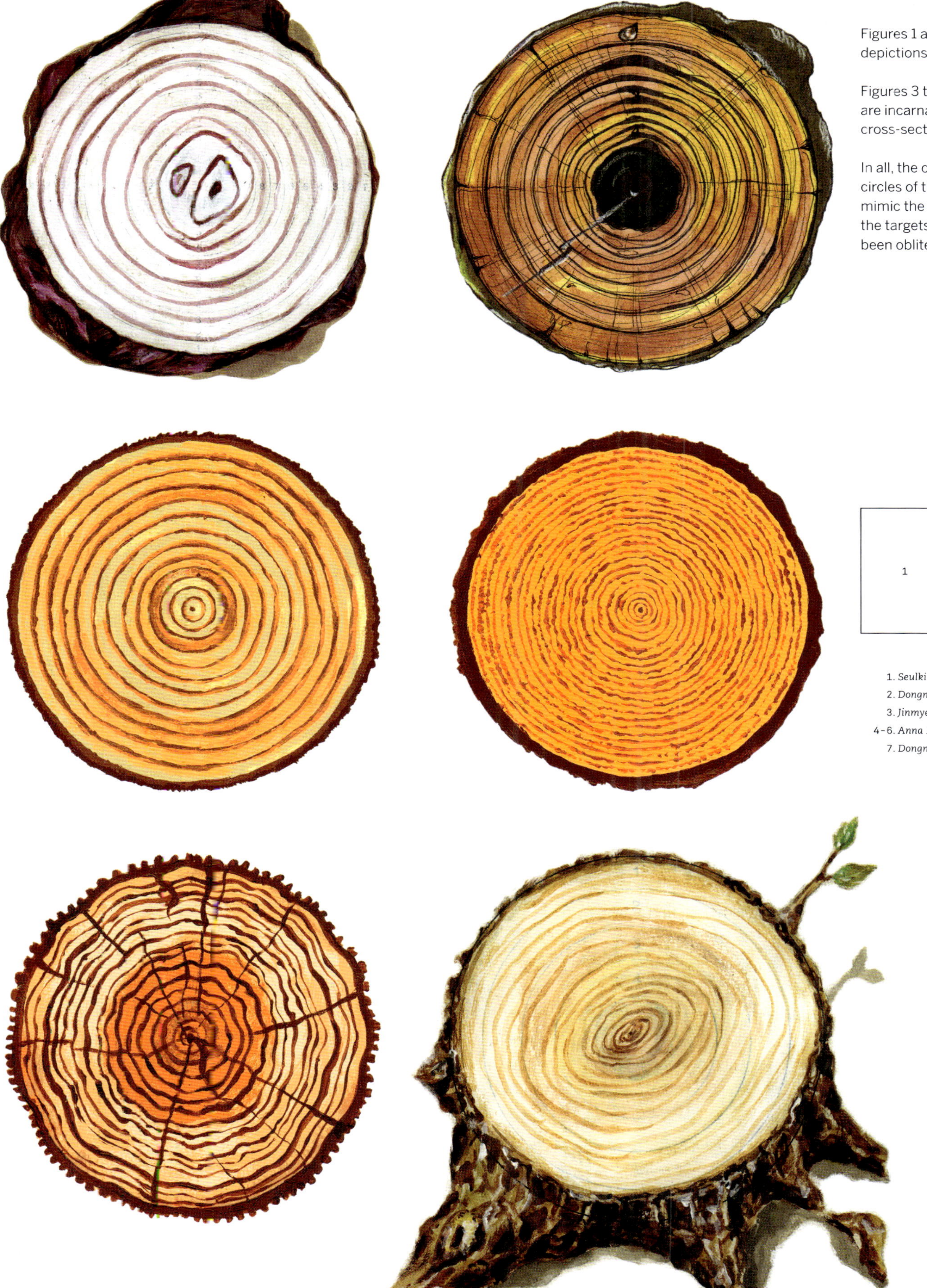

TARGET SOLUTIONS:

Figures 1 and 2 are depictions of onions.

Figures 3 through 7 are incarnations of cross-sections of trees.

In all, the concentric circles of the subjects mimic the circles from the targets that have been obliterated.

1. *Seulki Song*
2. *Dongmin Kim*
3. *Jinmyeong Shin*

4–6. *Anna Laytham*

7. *Dongmin Kim*

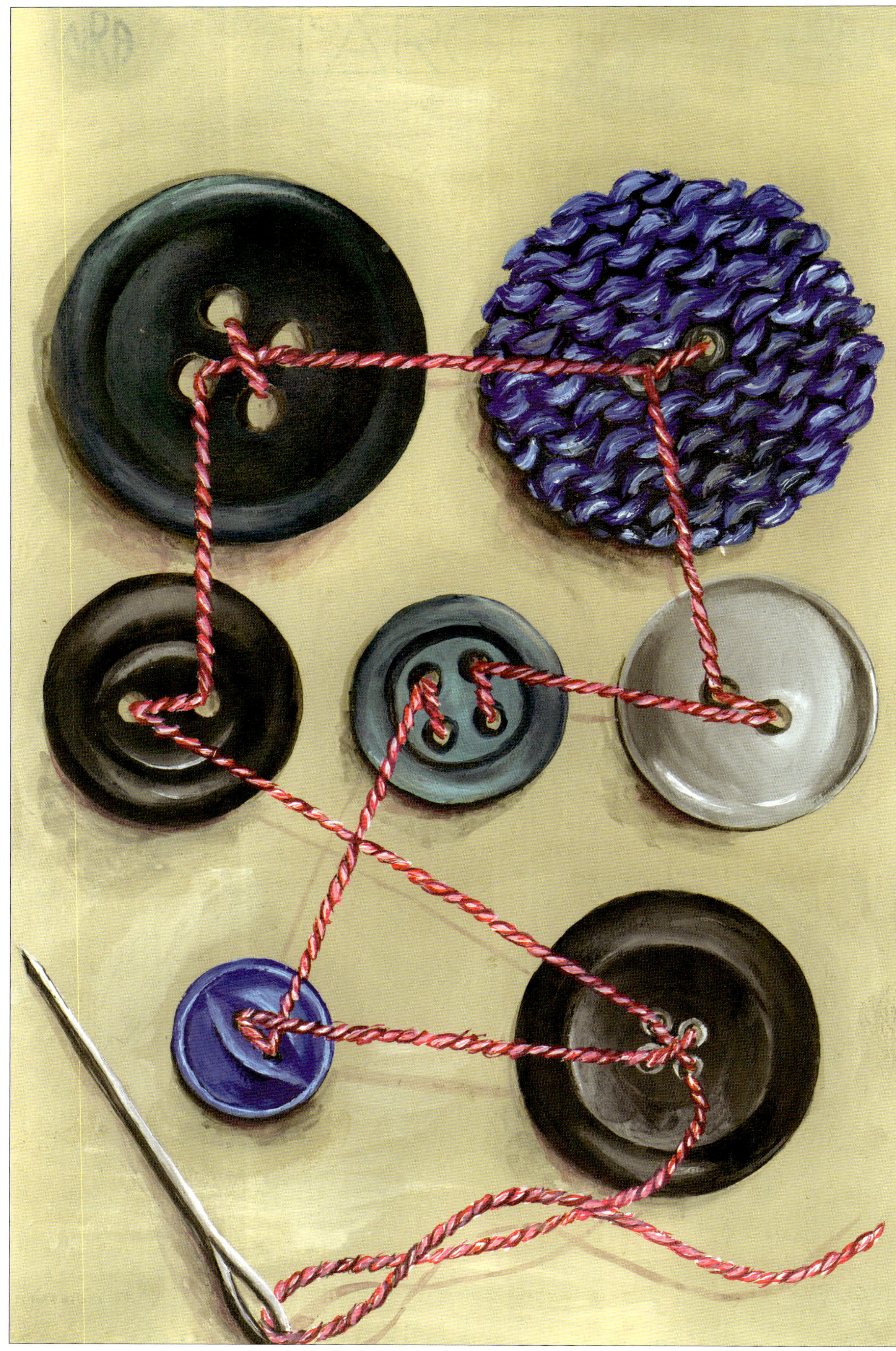

TARGET SOLUTIONS:

In figure 1, seven buttons are threaded together to create a personal narrative; their placement is all that remains of the target format.

Figures 2 through 6 represent variations of flowers, ranging from realism to graphic patterning.

Figure 7 transforms the targets into a woman's breasts covered by a bra.

These solutions illustrate the unpredictability of where an assignment can lead if one is open to risk taking, which allows creativity to emerge.

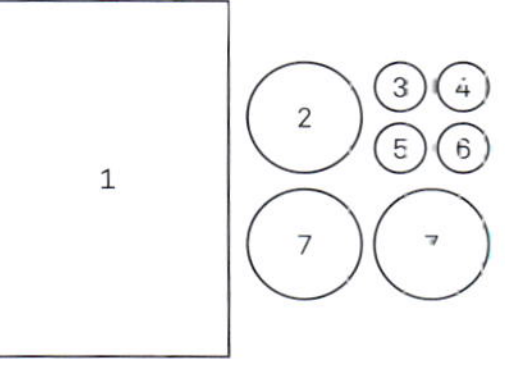

1. *Mytran Dang*
2. *Sebit Min*
3. *Seol Choi*

4–5. *Fumiko Hagano*

6. *Andrew Haupt*
7. *S. Kim*

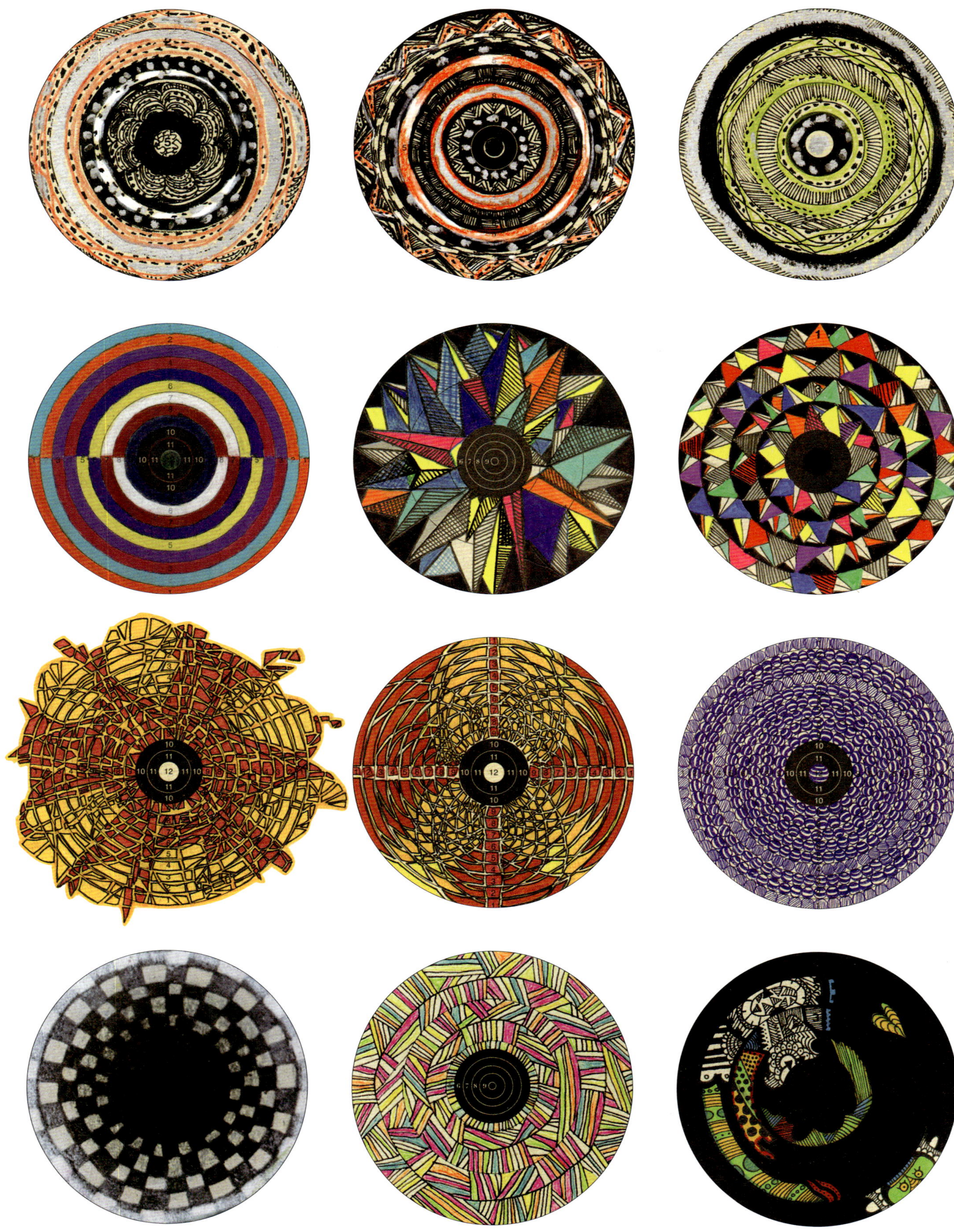

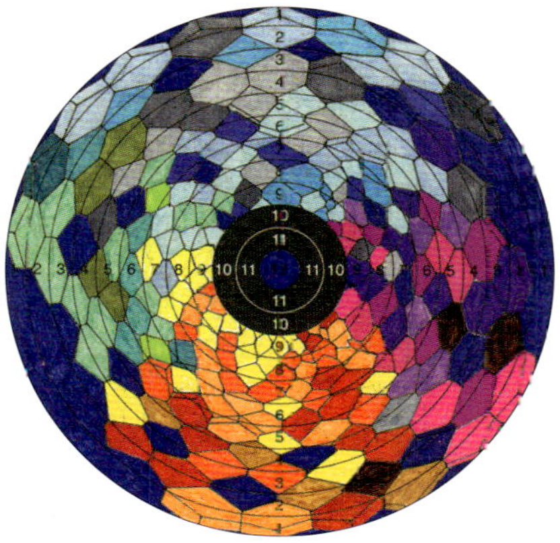

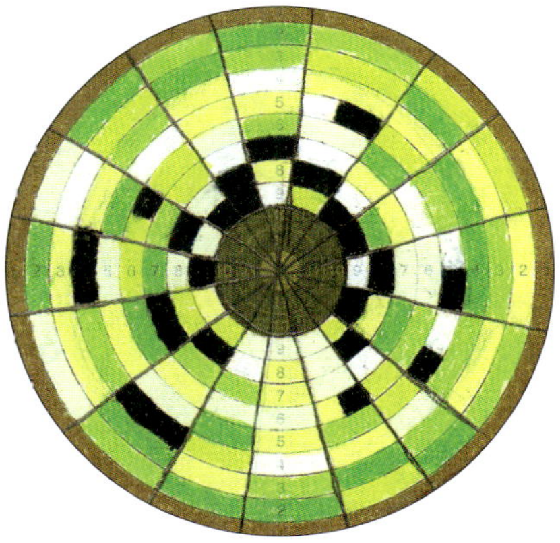

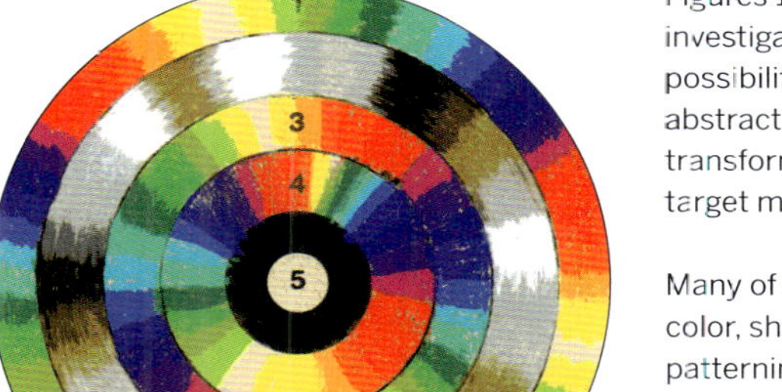

TARGET SOLUTIONS:

Figures 1 through 24 investigate the infinite possibilities of personal abstract graphic transformations of a target motif.

Many of the images utilize color, shape, form, line, patterning, complexity, and spatial relationships.

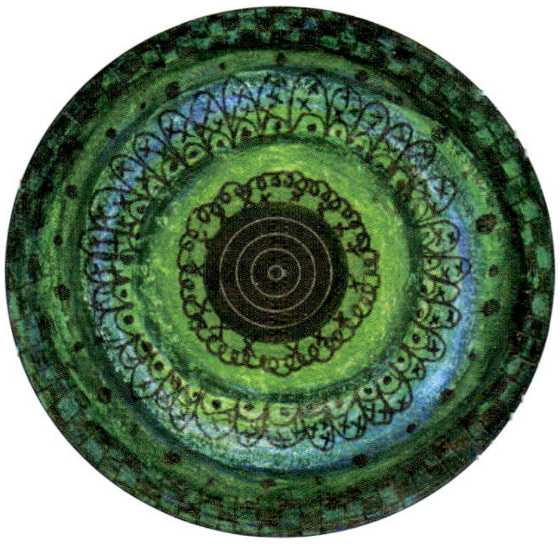

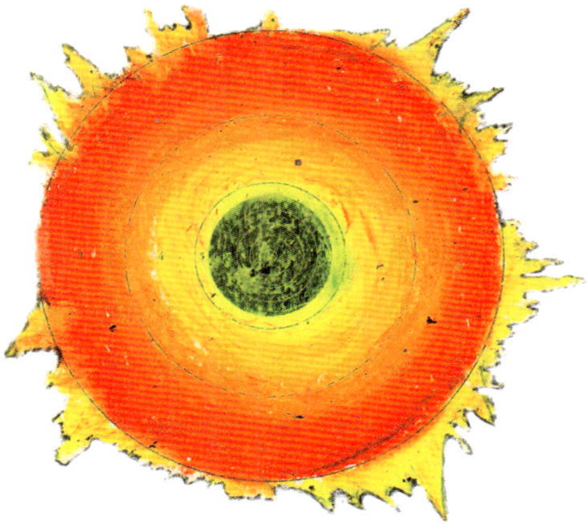

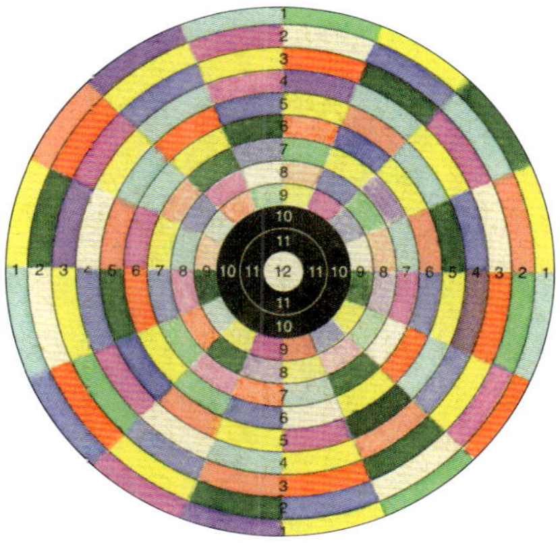

1	2	3	13	14	15
4	5	6	16	17	18
7	8	9	19	20	21
10	11	12	22	23	24

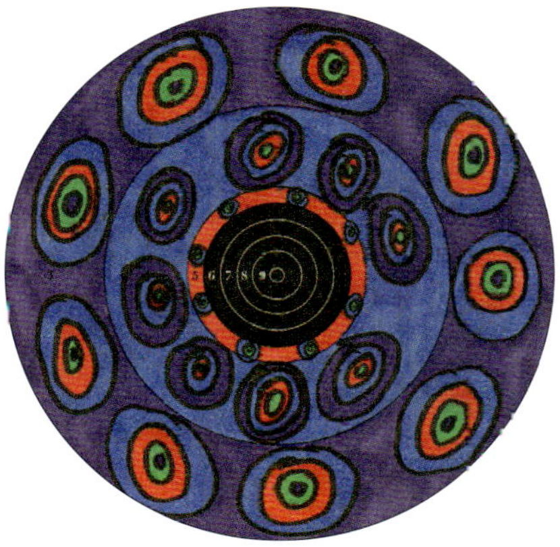

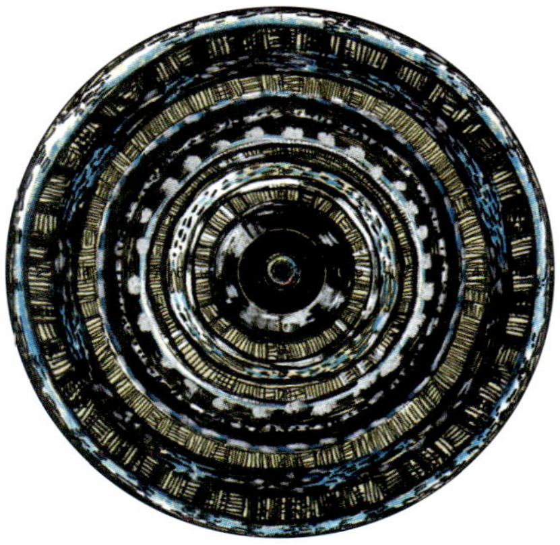

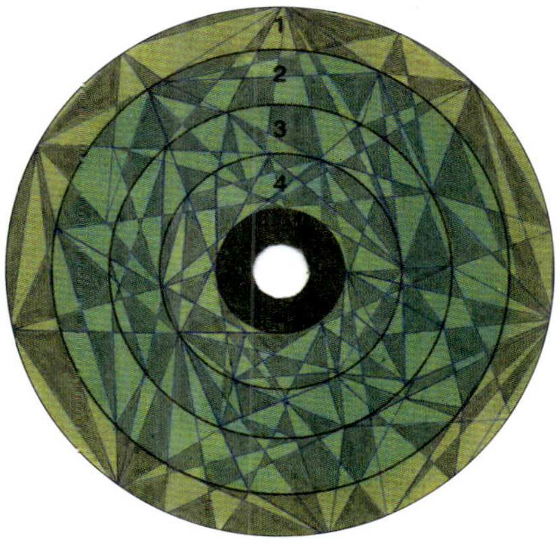

1–3. *Jin So*
4. *Jesus Lopez*
5–6. *Claudia Silva Goppert*
7–8. *Catherine Lee*
9. *Heekyung Cho*
10. *Soyoon Lee*
11. *Borim Kim*
12. *Alex Morel*
13. *Emily Bonnet*
14. *Haenara Im*
15. *Kyung Moon*
16. *Kristin Naranjo*
17. *Angie Talavera*
18. *Hoonjong Suh*
19. *Jongsang Lee*
20. *Jin So*
21. *Donghee Choo*
22. *Tahui Lee*
23–24. *Jessie Gang*

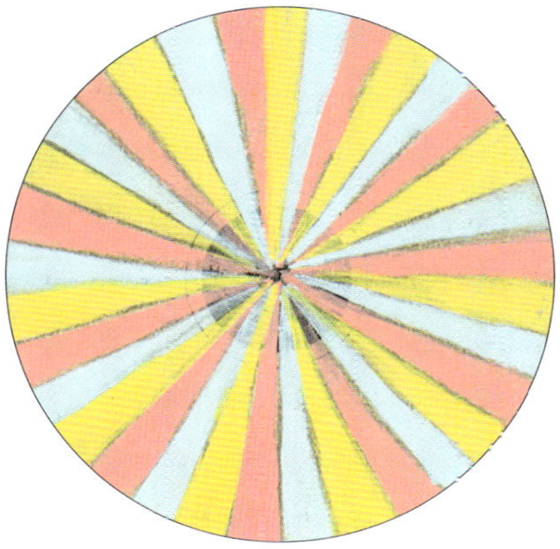

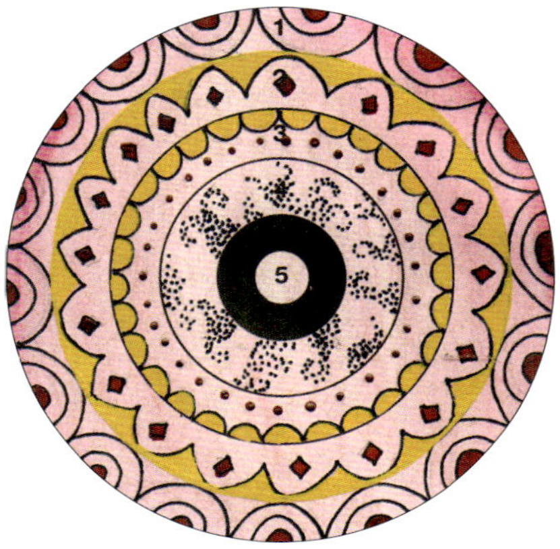

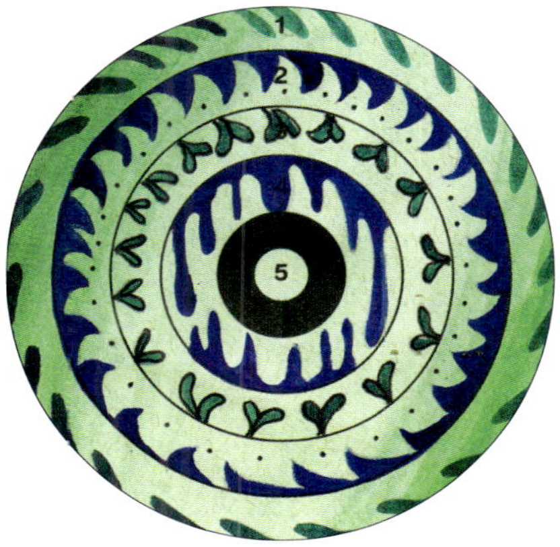

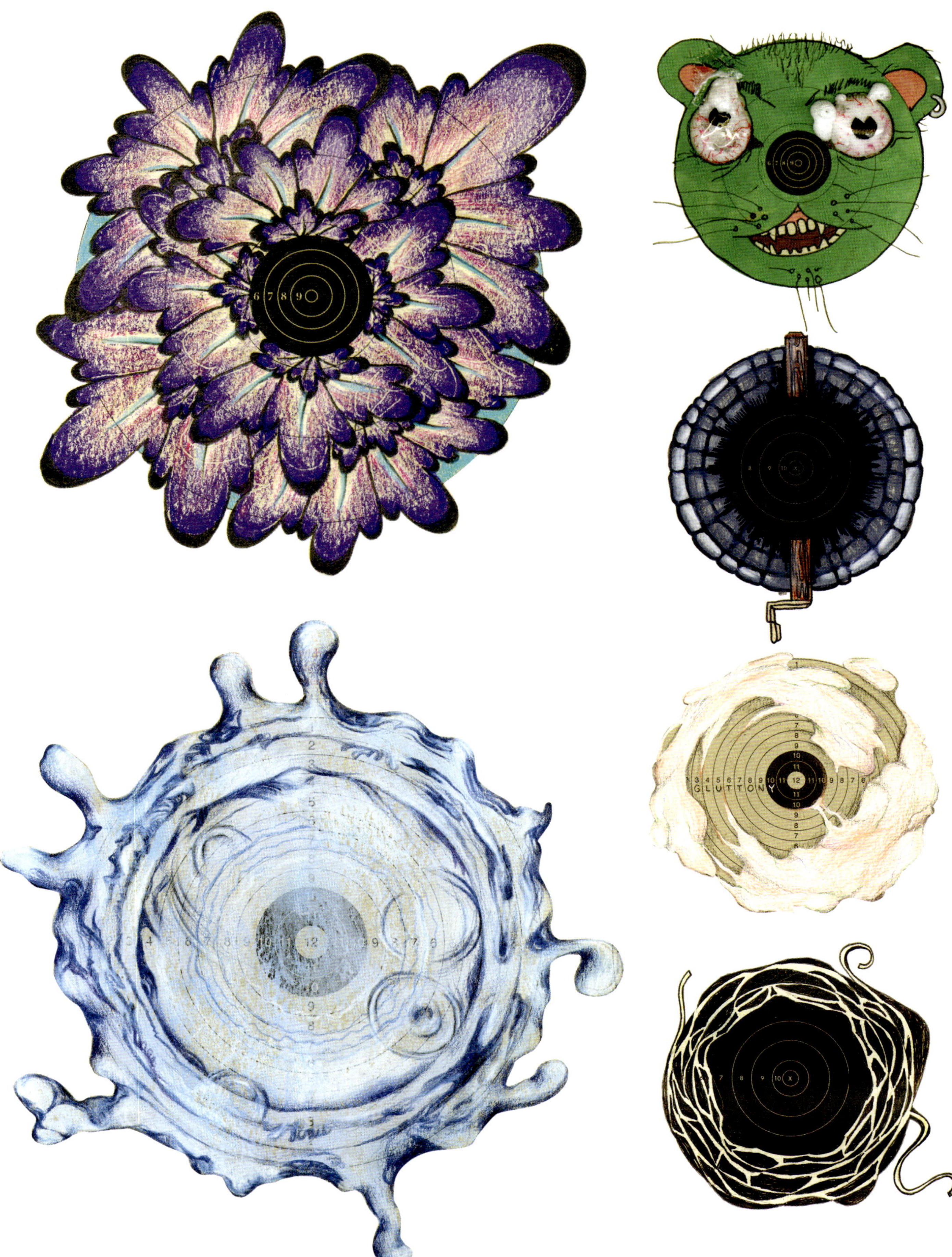
GLUTTONY

TARGET SOLUTIONS:

Figures 1 through 15 range from the literal to the abstract.

Figures 1 through 6 break out of the circular design of the target to further extend their concepts.

All solutions are viewed from an aerial perspective, with the exception of figure 3.

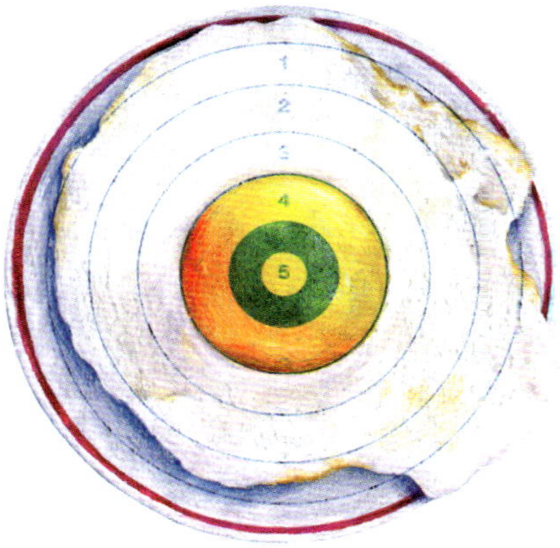

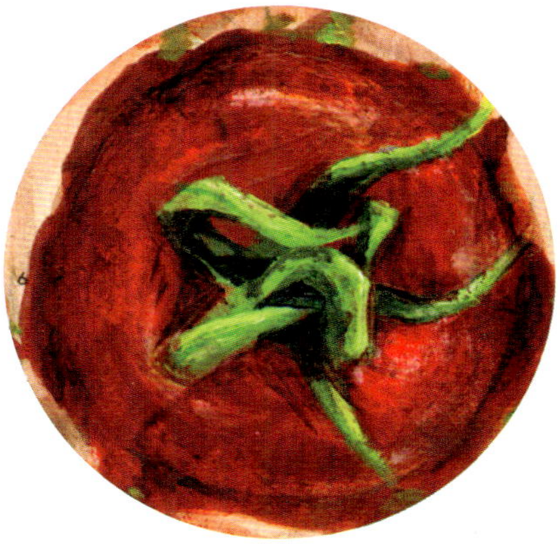

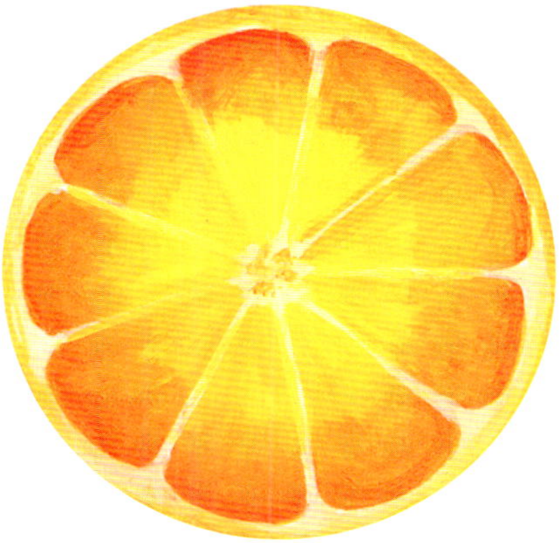

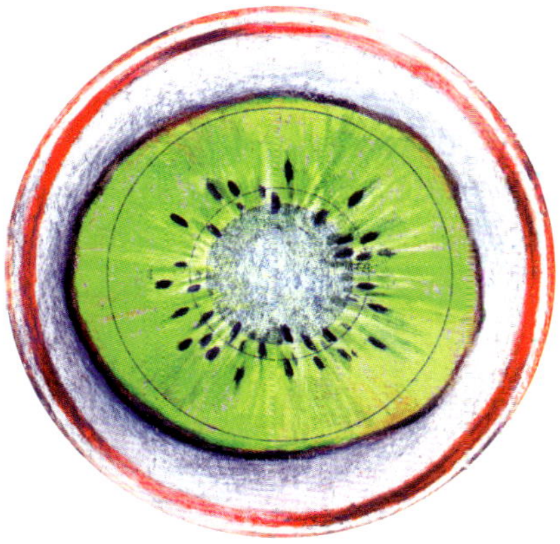

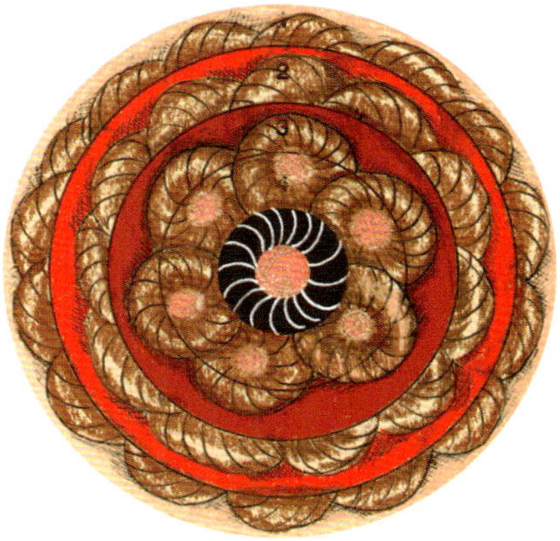

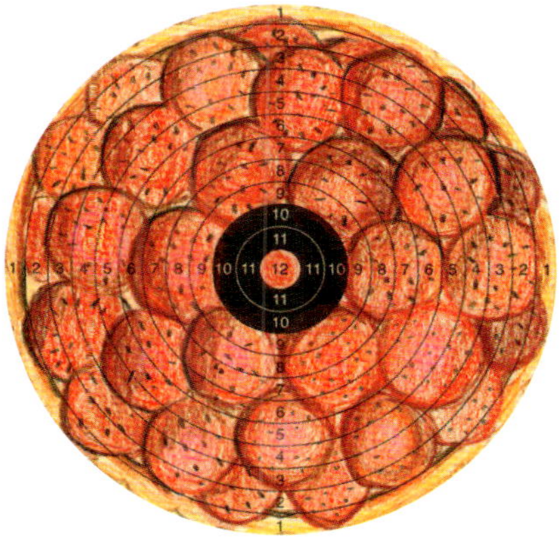

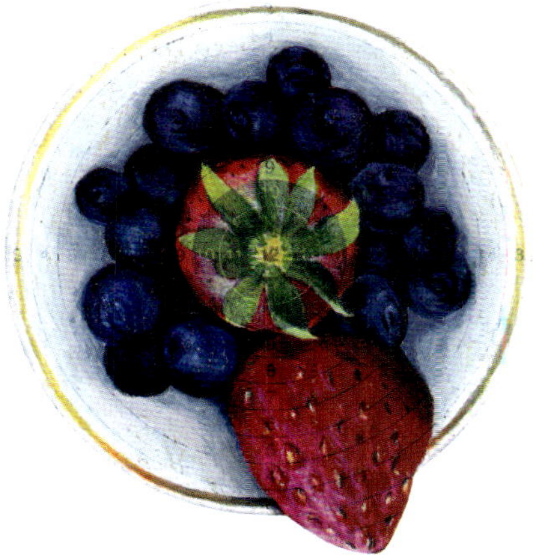

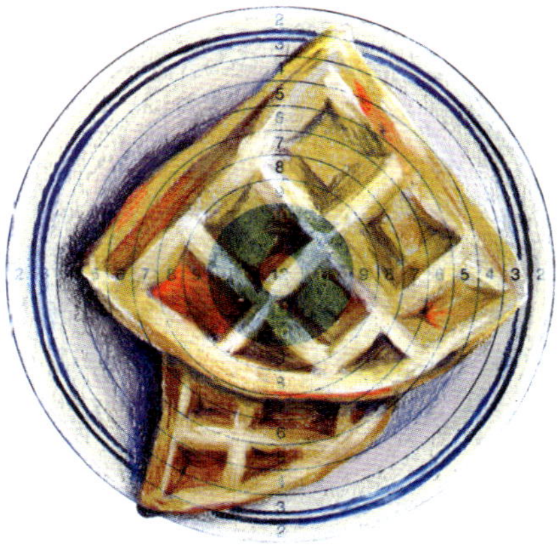

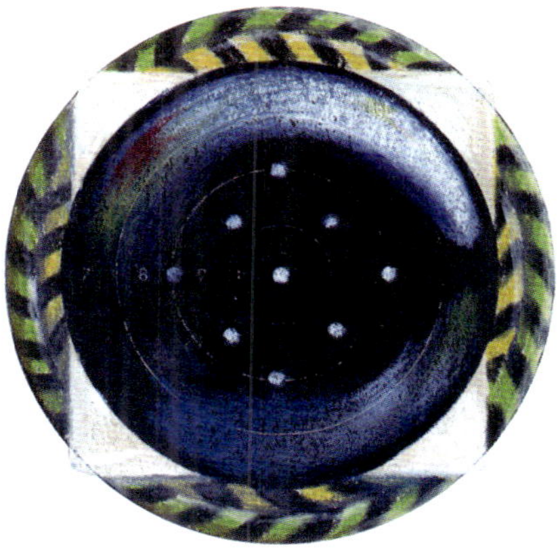

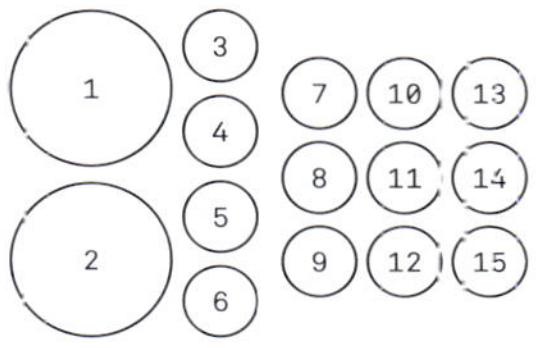

1. *Melanie Chernock*
2. *Borim Kim*
3. *Danielle Guzman*
4. *Andrew Lee*
5. *Maxine Taylor*
6. *Soojin Jung*

7-9. *Bora Kim*

10. *Eunseo Kang*
11. *Laura Ng*
12. *Bora Kim*
13. *Liz Margulies*
14. *M. Tanizaki*
15. *Bora Kim*

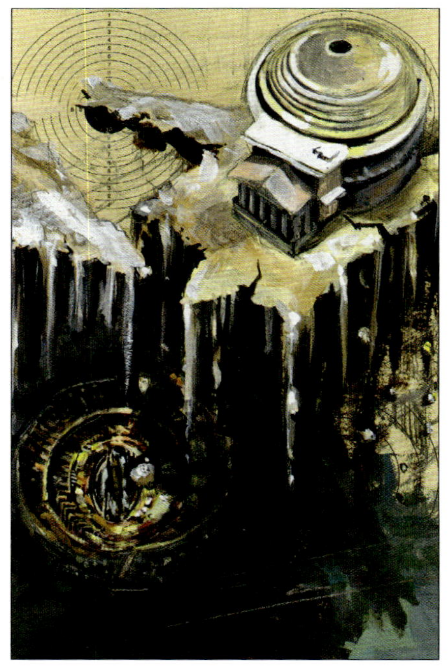

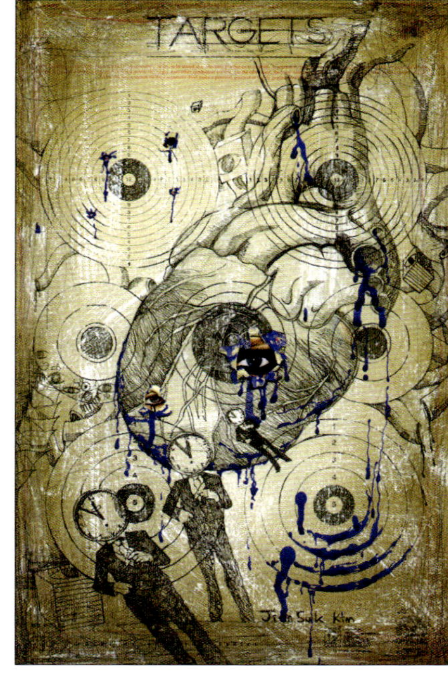
TARGETS

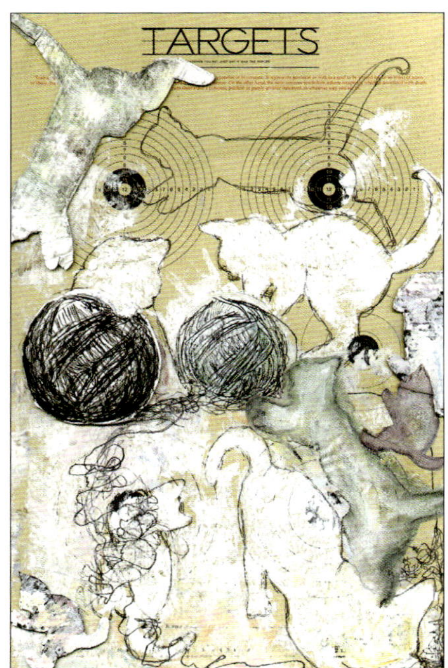
TARGETS

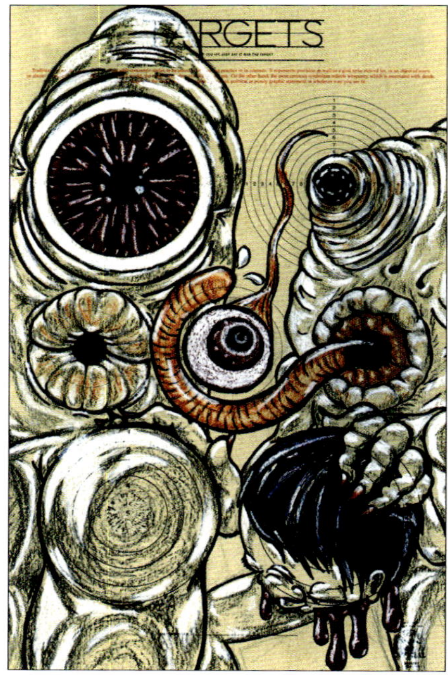

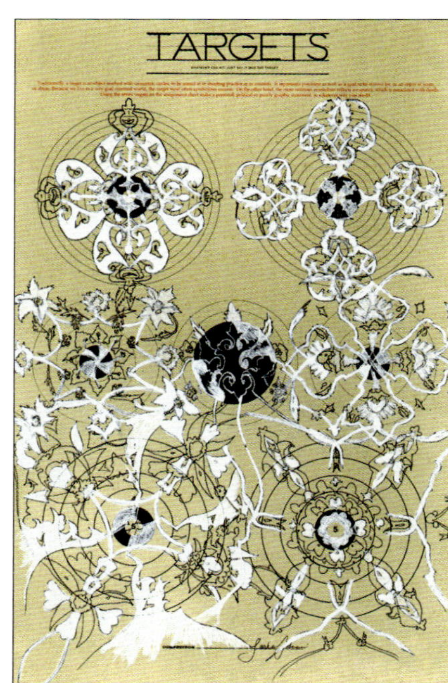
TARGETS

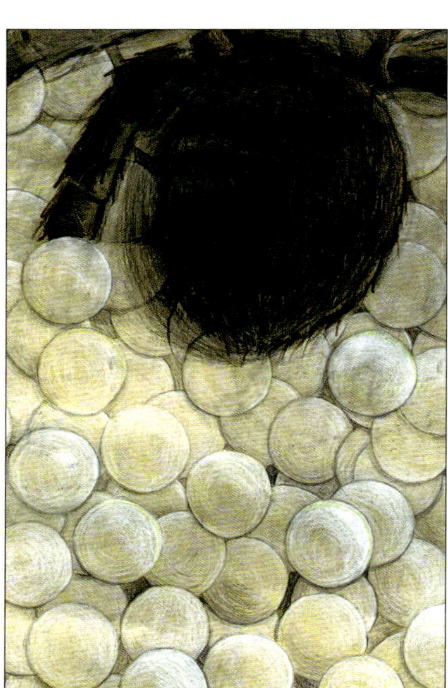

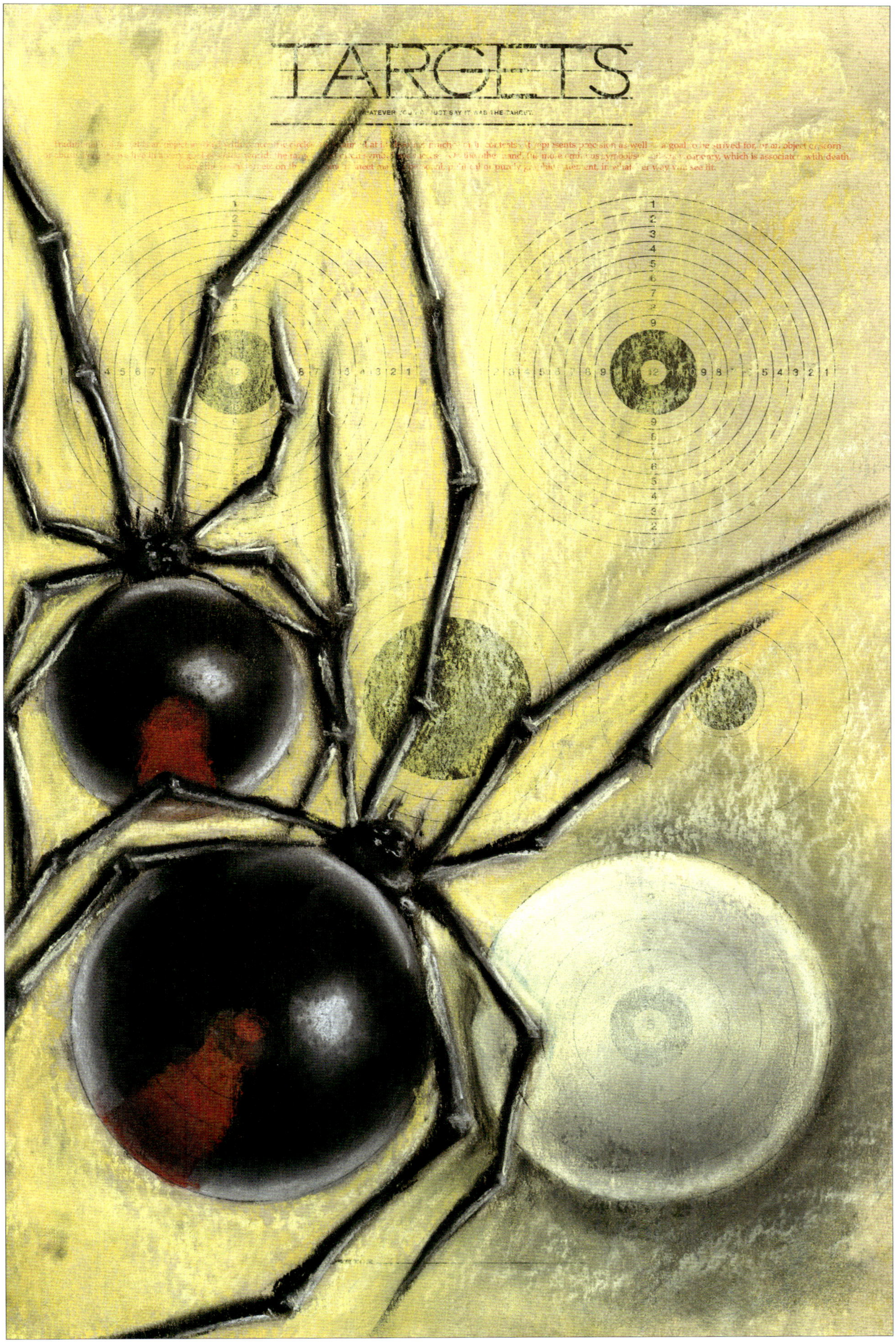

TARGET SOLUTIONS:

Figures 1 through 7 approach the assignment as illustration, relying on drawing and painting skills. Themes include highly complex narratives, where to varying degrees, the targets are still visible, except in figure 6, where the target is completely obscured.

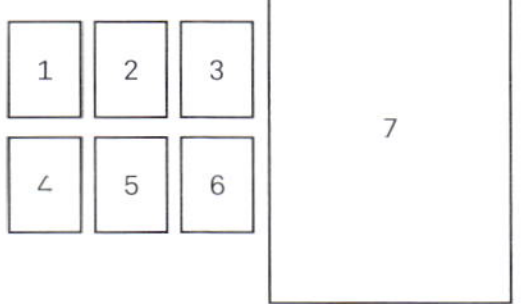

1. *Xing Pei Wang*
2. *Jinsuk Kim*
3. *Alexandra Rosano*
4. *Larissa Stephens*
5. *Sasha Jefemin*
6. *Akil Grant*
7. *Leonardo Laurenceau*

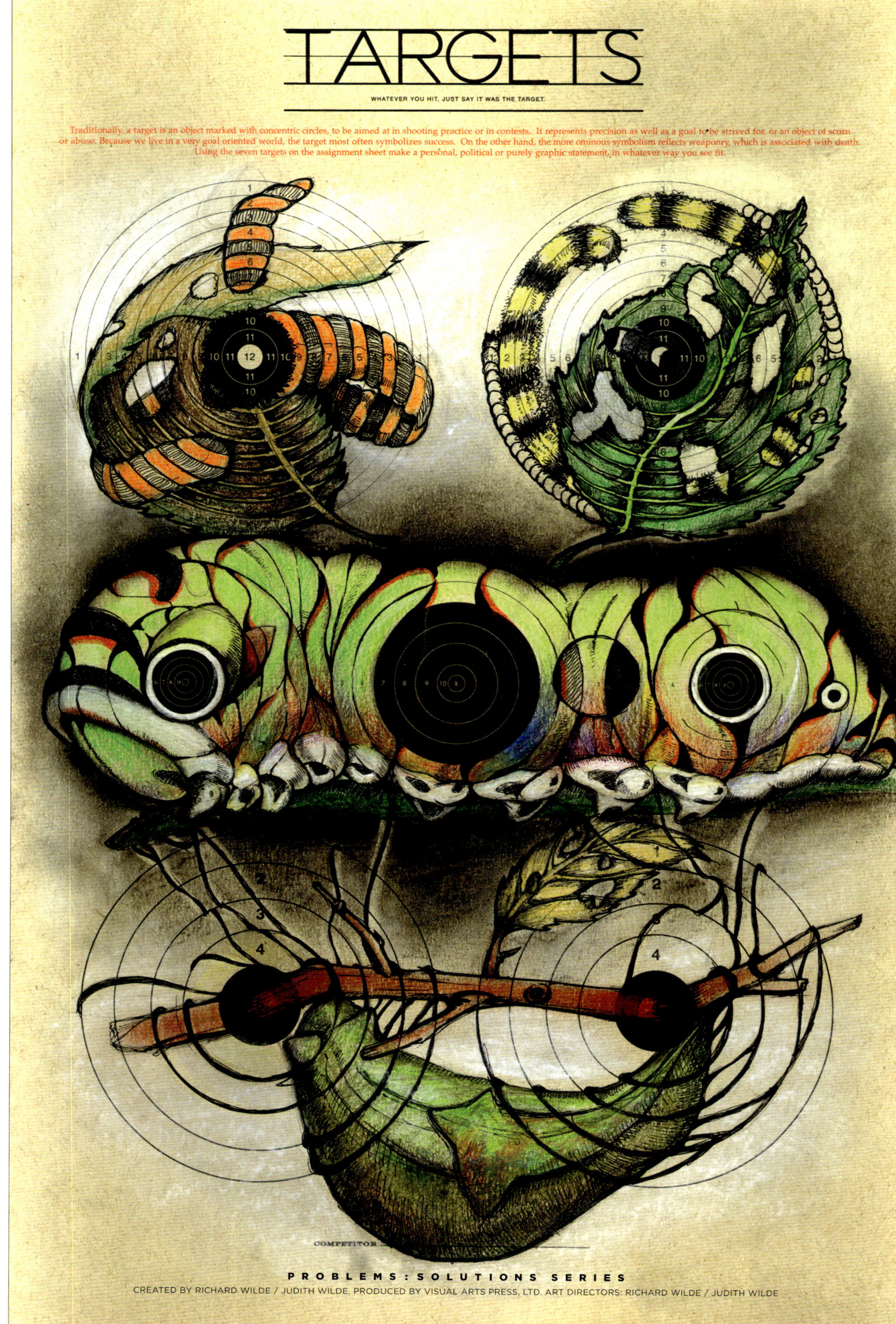
TARGETS
WHATEVER YOU HIT, JUST SAY IT WAS THE TARGET.
Traditionally, a target is an object marked with concentric circles, to be aimed at in shooting practice or in contests. It represents precision as well as a goal to be strived for, or an object of scorn or abuse. Because we live in a very goal oriented world, the target most often symbolizes success. On the other hand, the more ominous symbolism reflects weaponry, which is associated with death. Using the seven targets on the assignment sheet make a personal, political or purely graphic statement, in whatever way you see fit.
COMPETITOR
PROBLEMS:SOLUTIONS SERIES
CREATED BY RICHARD WILDE / JUDITH WILDE, PRODUCED BY VISUAL ARTS PRESS, LTD. ART DIRECTORS: RICHARD WILDE / JUDITH WILDE

TARGET SOLUTIONS:

Figure 1 addresses the life cycle of caterpillars, from devouring leaves, to their inherent nature of camouflage, to the metamorphic stage of a cocoon.

Figures 2 through 4 investigate aquatic life. These three solutions use a radiating effect to evoke the movement of water, which mimics the target pattern.

Figure 5 is an undulating abstract solution that references forms of organic life.

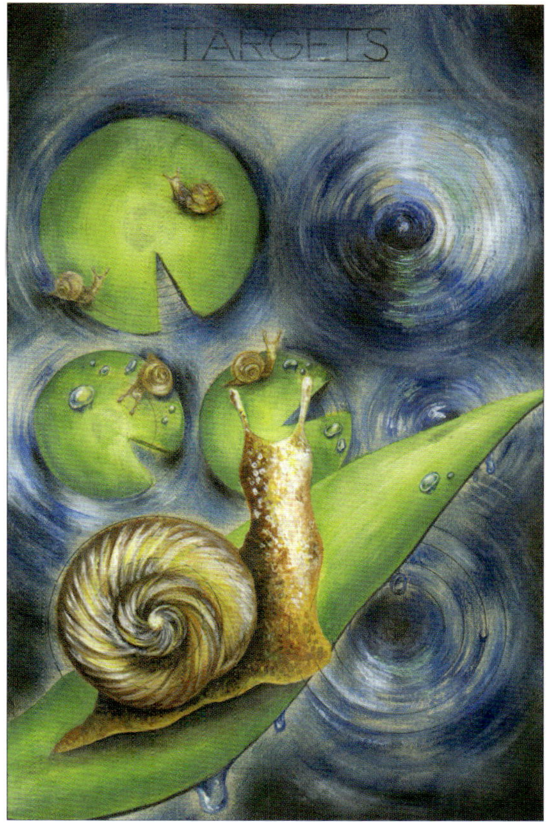

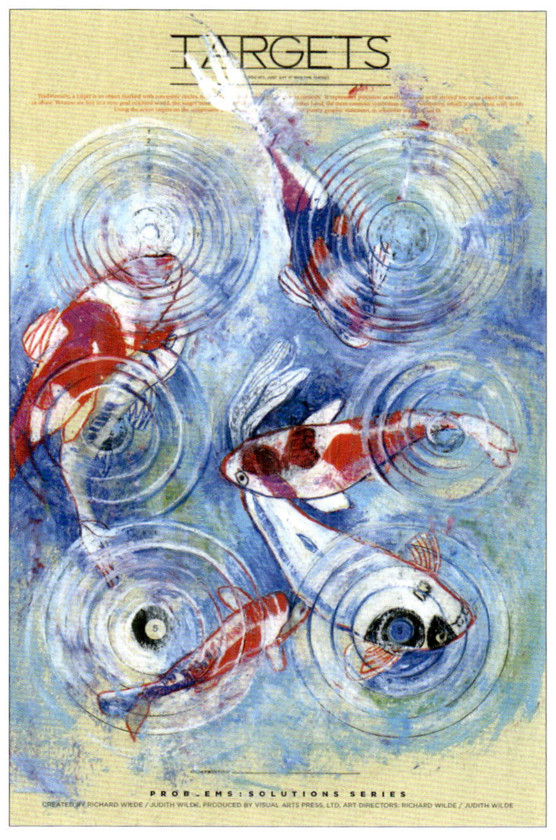

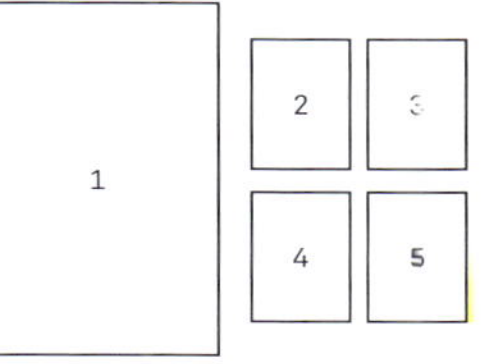

1. *Dayoung Mun*
2. *Hyeyoon Park*
3. *Aurelie Joly*
4. *Jaedon Lee*
5. *Minah Kim*

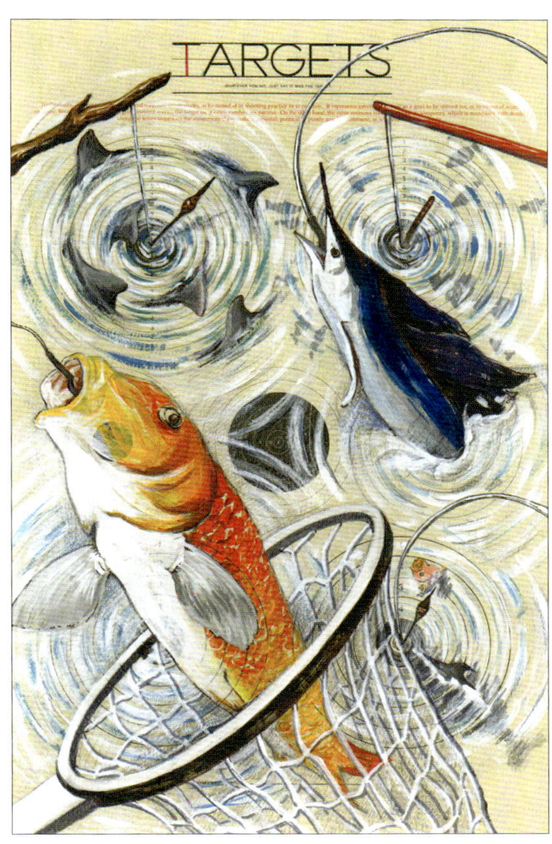

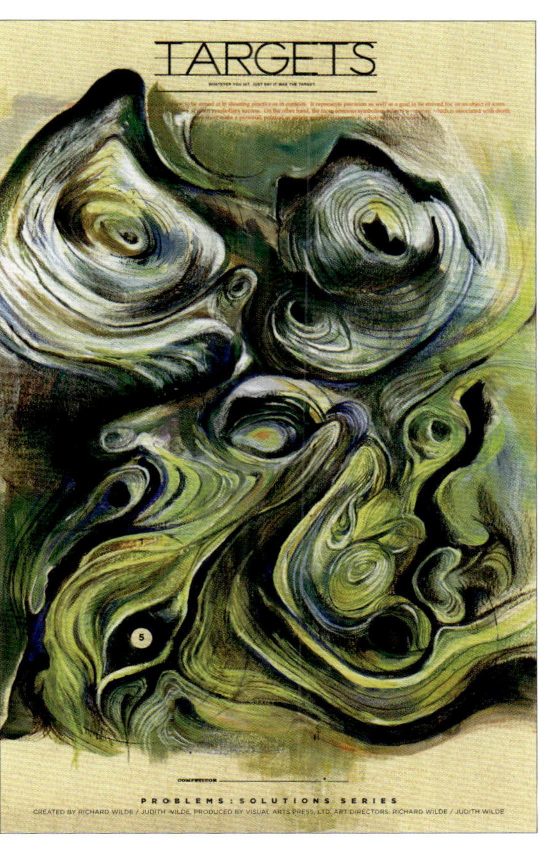

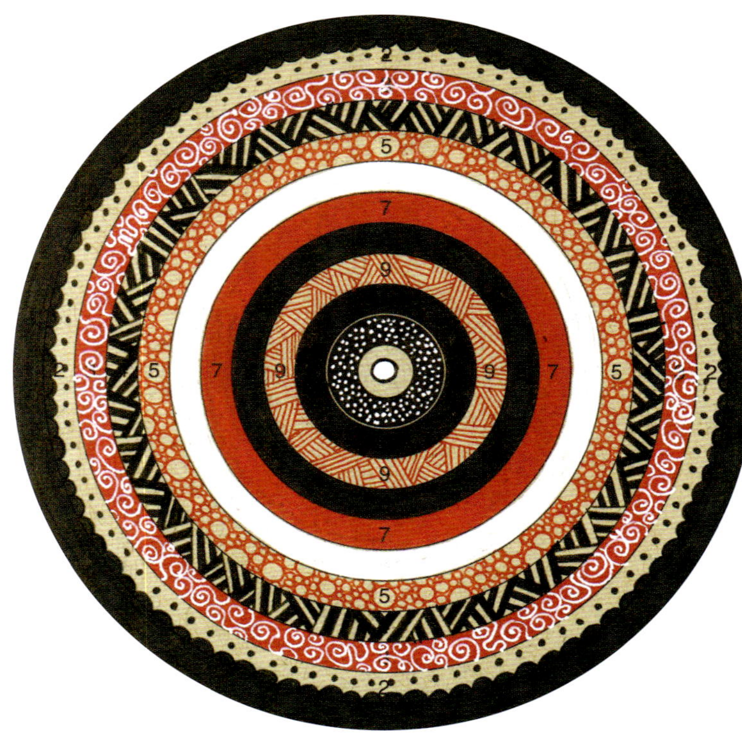
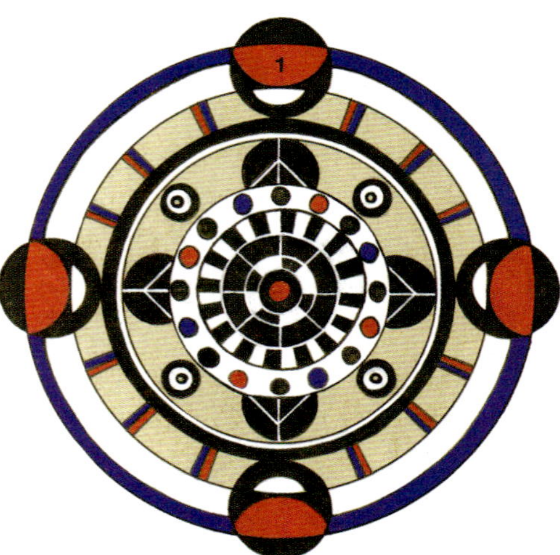
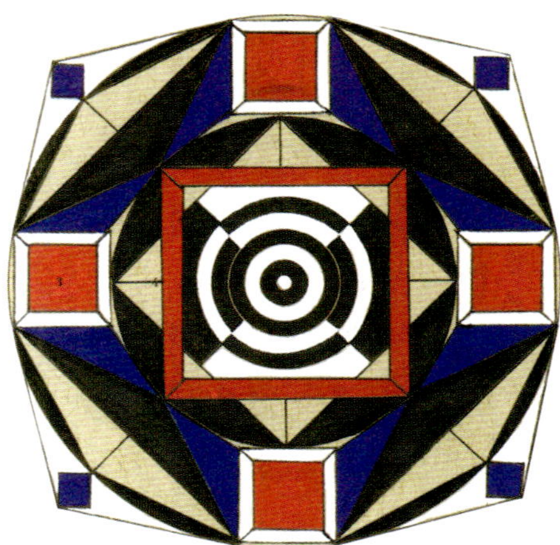
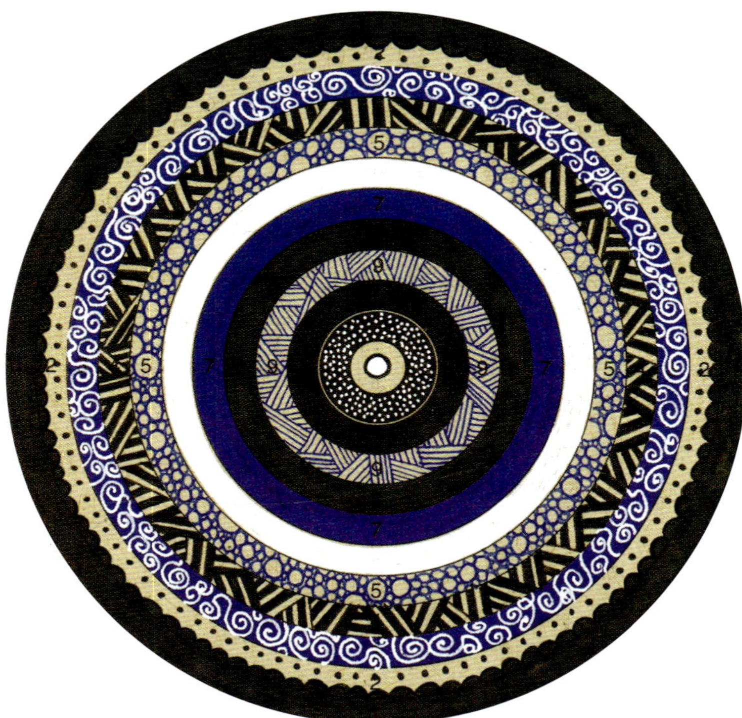
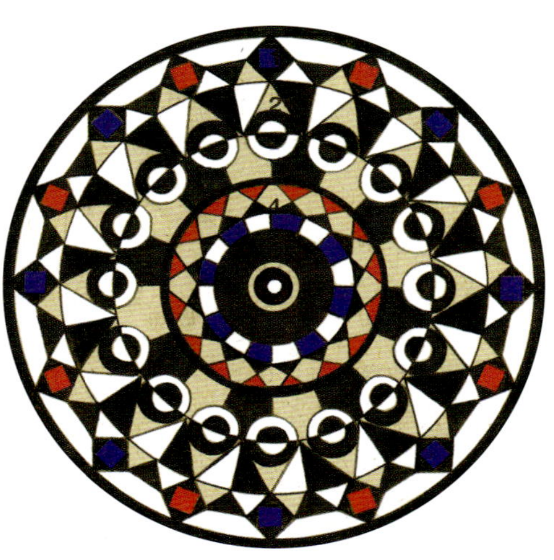

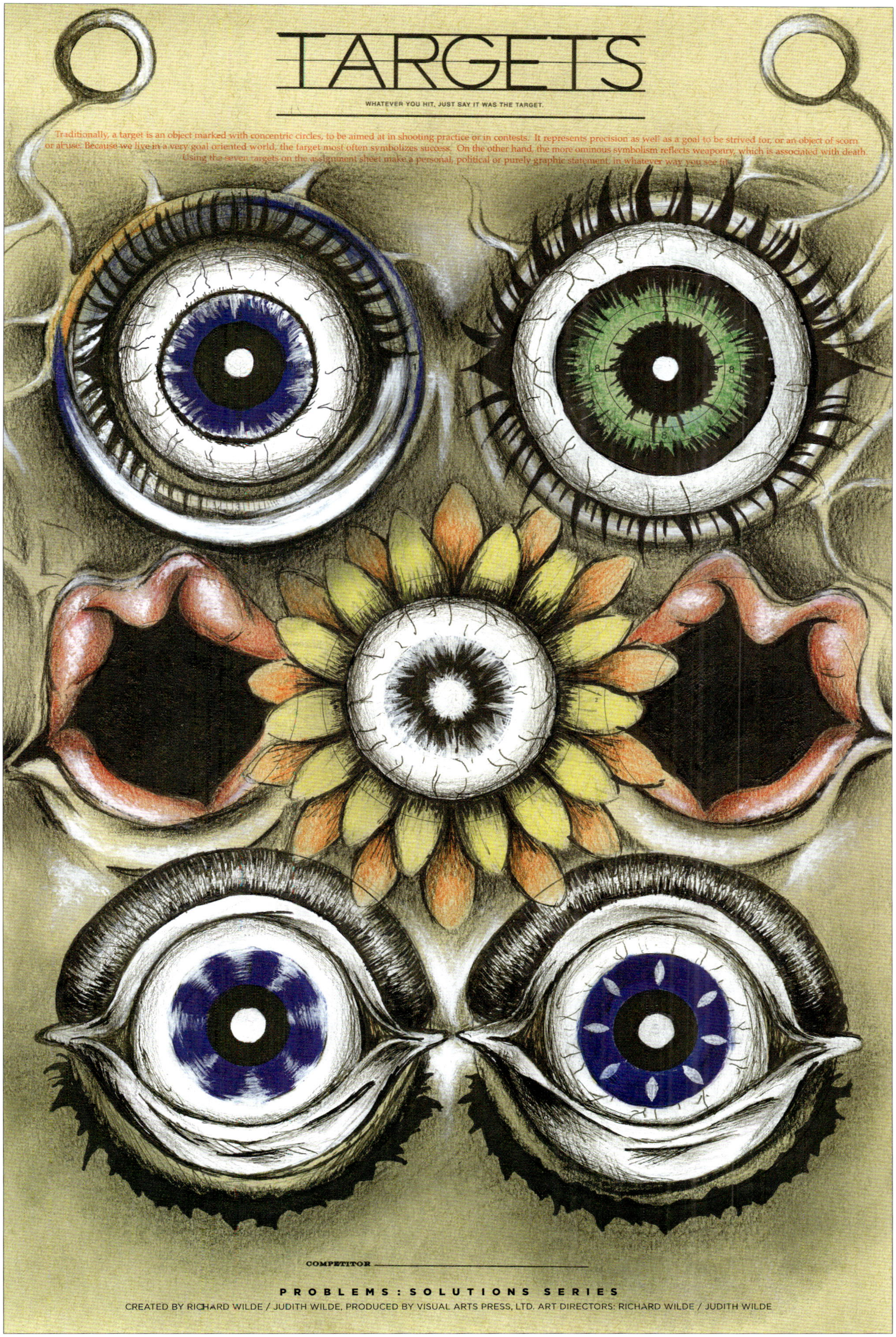

TARGETS

WHATEVER YOU HIT, JUST SAY IT WAS THE TARGET.

Traditionally, a target is an object marked with concentric circles, to be aimed at in shooting practice or in contests. It represents precision as well as a goal to be strived for, or an object of scorn or abuse. Because we live in a very goal oriented world, the target most often symbolizes success. On the other hand, the more ominous symbolism reflects weaponry, which is associated with death. Using the seven targets on the assignment sheet make a personal, political or purely graphic statement, in whatever way you see fit.

COMPETITOR

PROBLEMS: SOLUTIONS SERIES

CREATED BY RICHARD WILDE / JUDITH WILDE, PRODUCED BY VISUAL ARTS PRESS, LTD. ART DIRECTORS: RICHARD WILDE / JUDITH WILDE

TARGET SOLUTIONS:

Figures 1 through 5 are graphic explorations in patterning using a palette of red, blue, black, and white on the target's beige ground.

Figures 1 and 2 deal with textured linear patterns that are juxtaposed against flat graphic forms.

Figures 3 through 5 deal solely with symmetrical geometric patterning.

Figure 6 is a highly personal solution with surrealistic undertones.

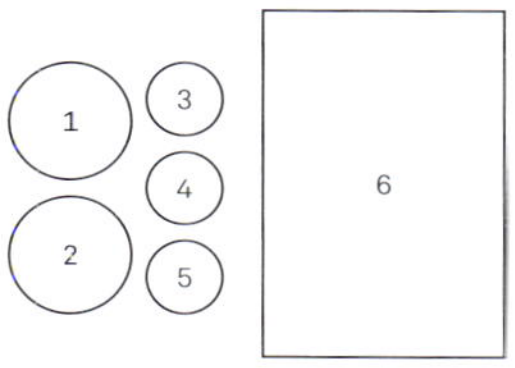

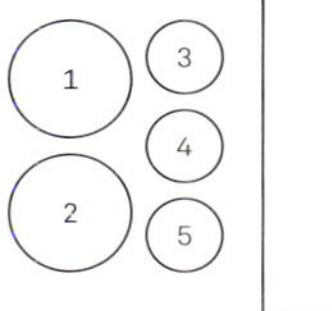

1–5. *Hannah Hyeona Ahn*
6. *Stephanie Tin*

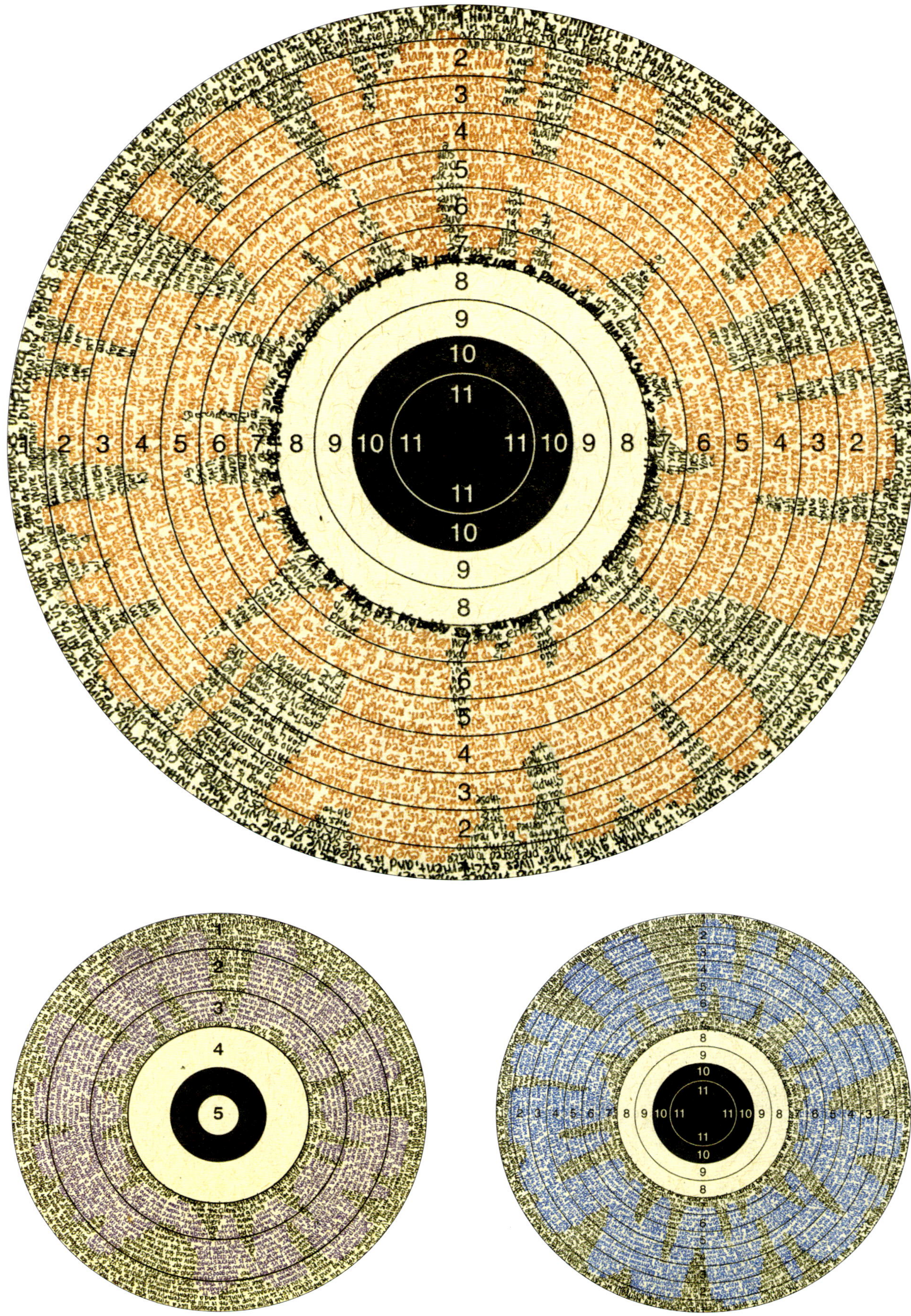

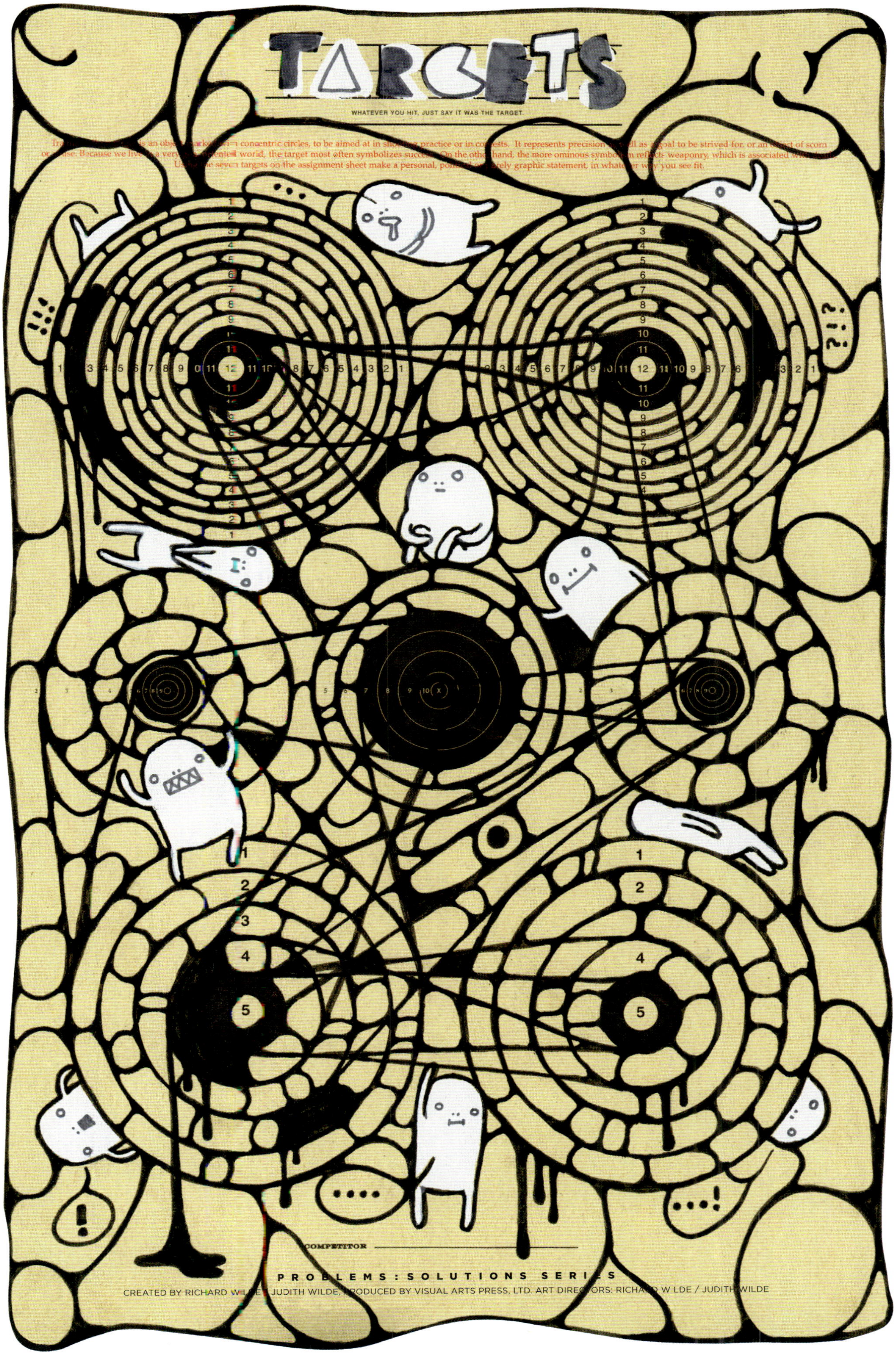

TARGET SOLUTIONS:

A popular theme that was used in solving this assignment was superimposing a variety of gearlike mechanisms onto the targets. Most were executed in black and white, using either pen and ink or pencil. The strength of many of the solutions lies in their interpretation of the intricacies of the gears.

In figure 1 there is a direct reference to the classic film *Modern Times*, depicting the memorable scene in which Charlie Chaplin moves through a series of gears.

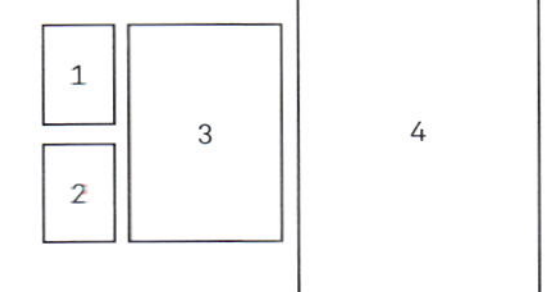

1. *Hyunseung Im*
2. *Joonmo Kang*
3. *Jeongok Kim*
4. *Thomas Shim*

In figure 2, colorful abstract imagery moves through a gearlike assembly line resulting in a car, while figure 3 deals with the complexity of overlapping gears.

Figure 4 contrasts playful characters against the gearlike structure, which gives a humorous overtone to the solution.

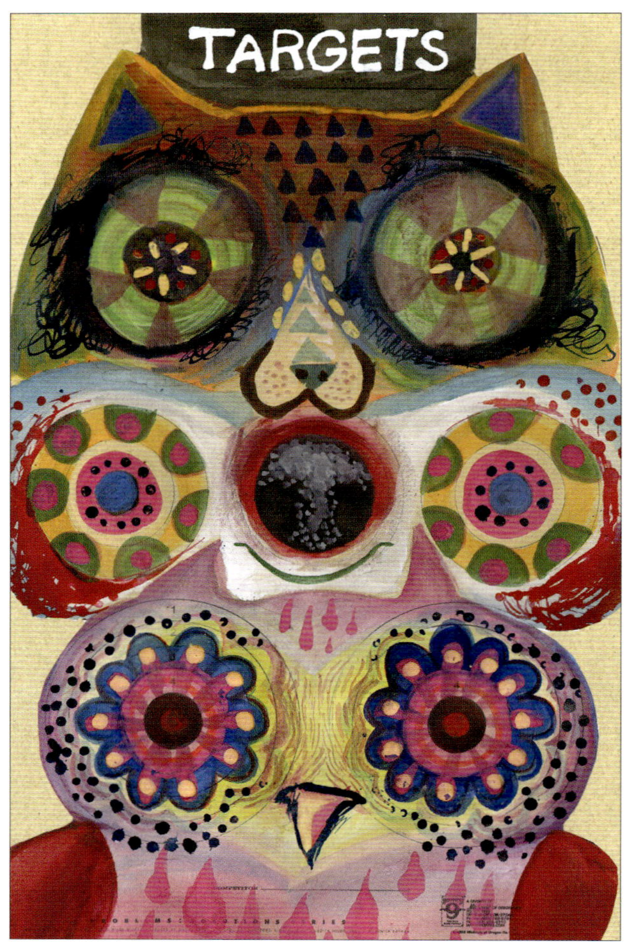
TARGETS

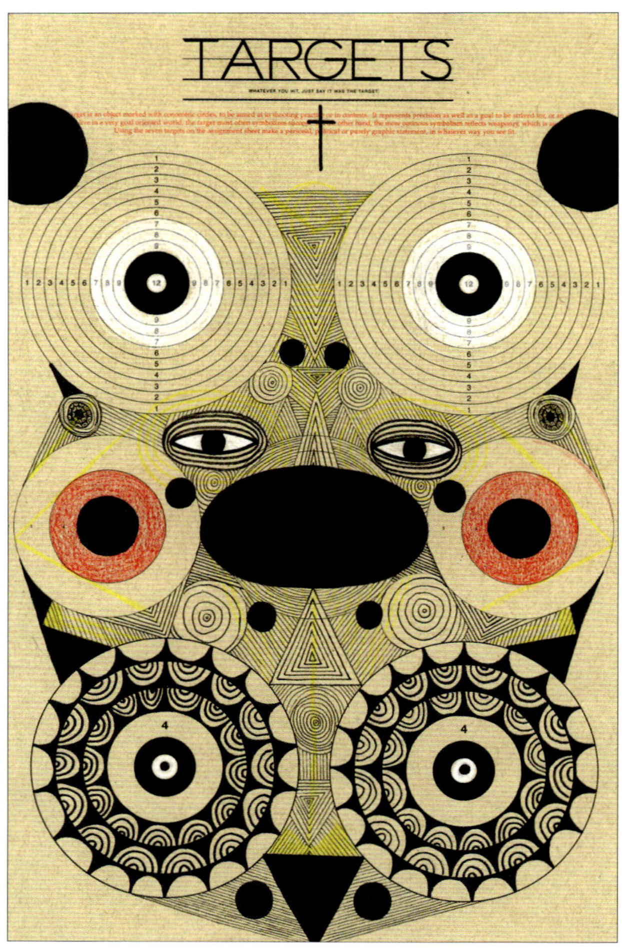
TARGETS
WHATEVER YOU HIT, JUST SAY IT WAS THE TARGET!

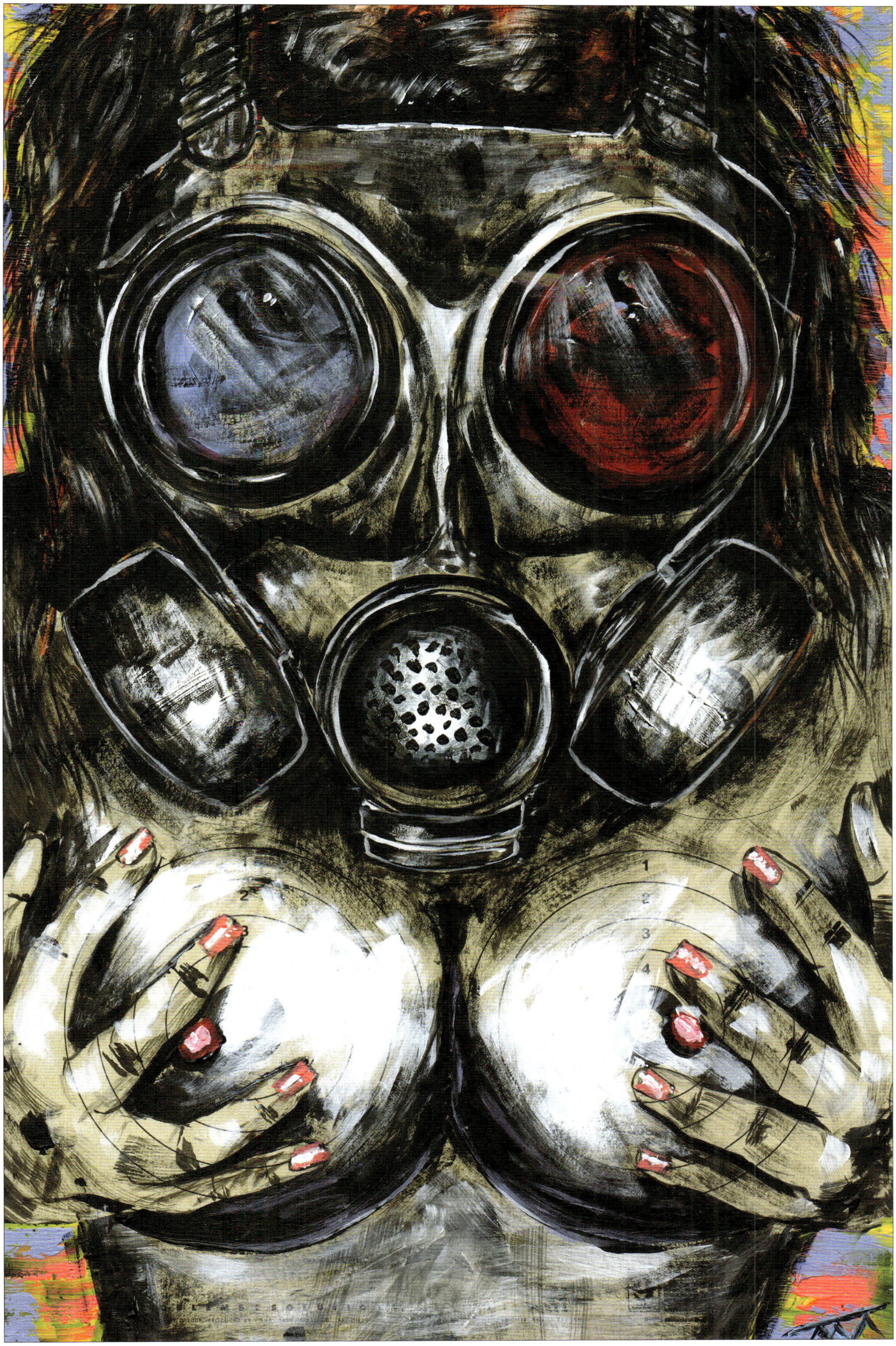

TARGET SOLUTIONS:

Figure 1 utilizes a naïve approach in the creation of three separate characters, executed in a spontaneous and decorative way.

In contrast, figure 2 is a carefully mannered image using linear and geometric forms. In both figures 1 and 2, which are executed in a totem pole fashion, faces of humans and animals appear stacked one on top of another.

Figure 3 uses an expressionistic style to juxtapose a gas mask against a female body, creating an eerie, unsettling image. It is evident that all of the target motifs serve as the underpinnings of each of these solutions.

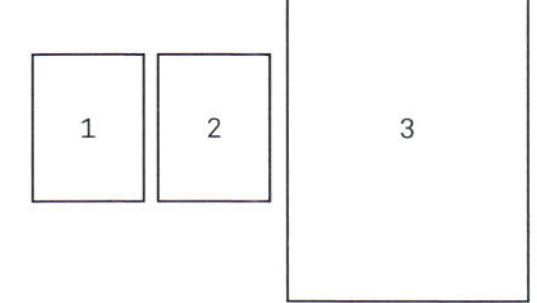

1. *Amy Churchwell*
2. *Claudio Barra*
3. *Junhyeok Chang*

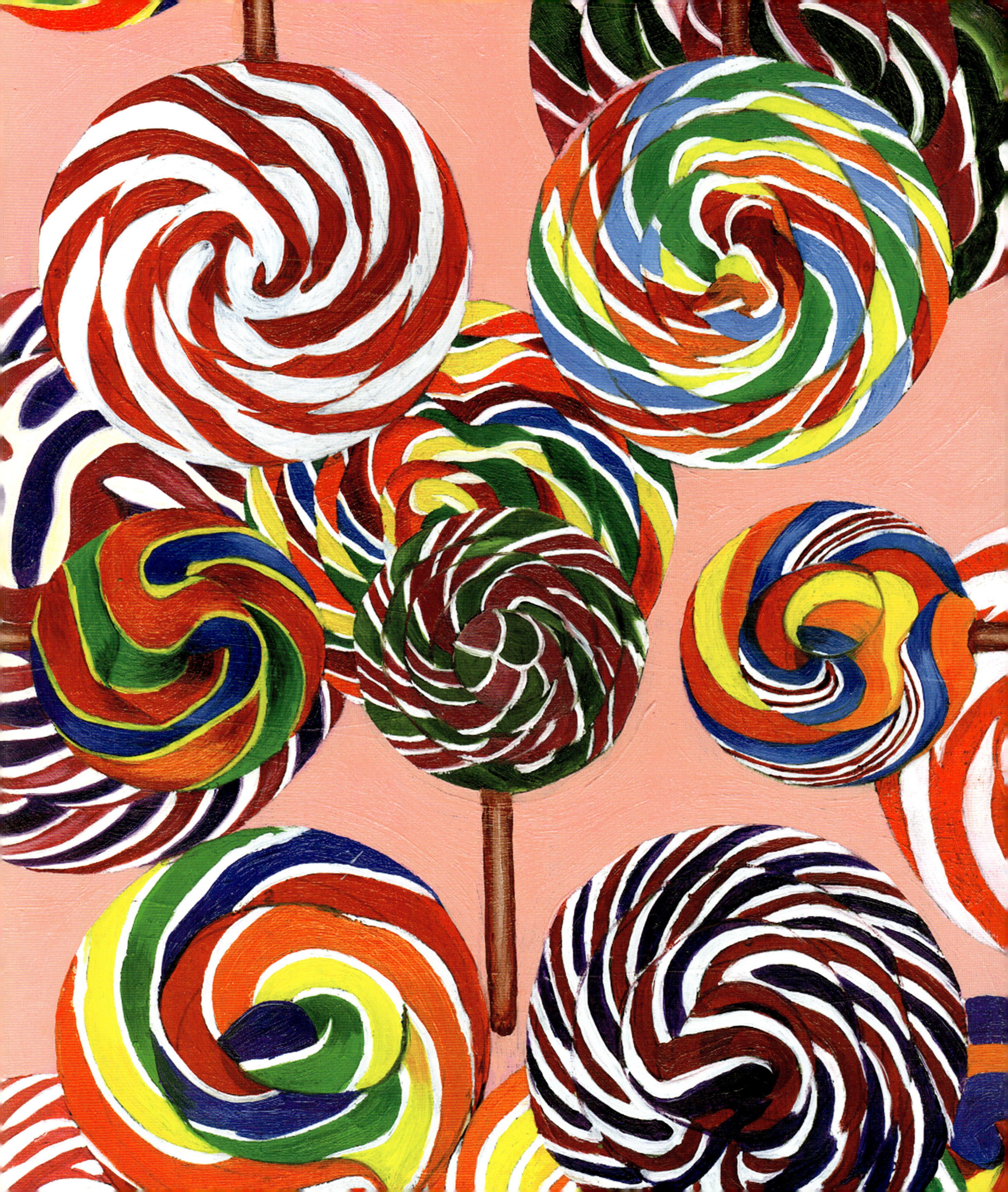

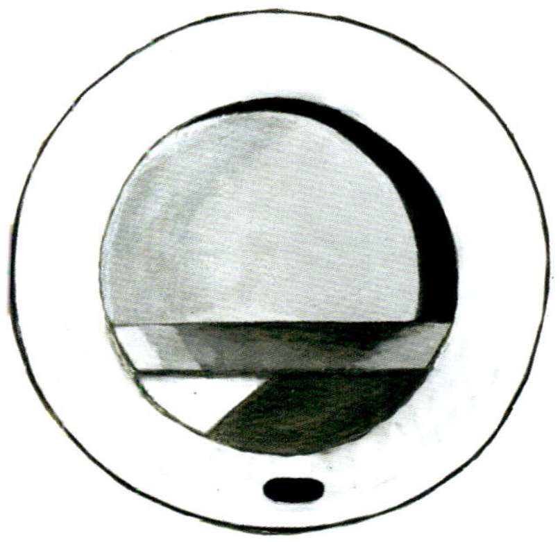

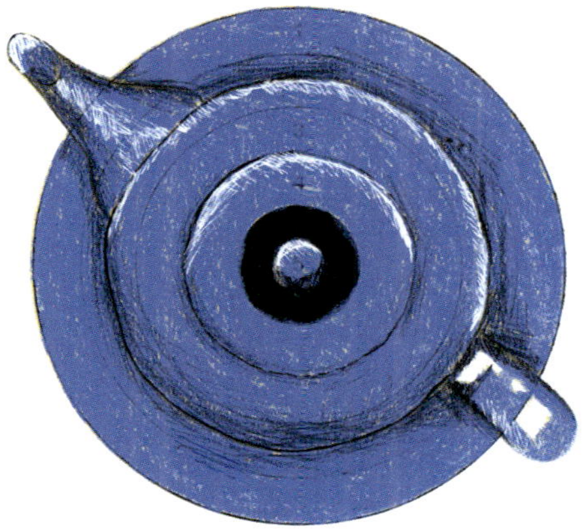

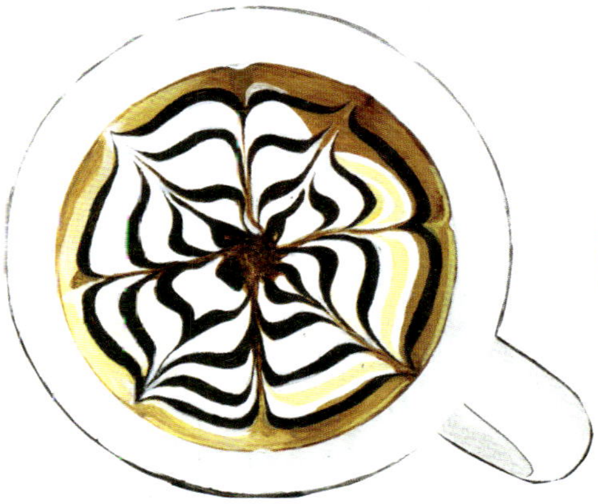

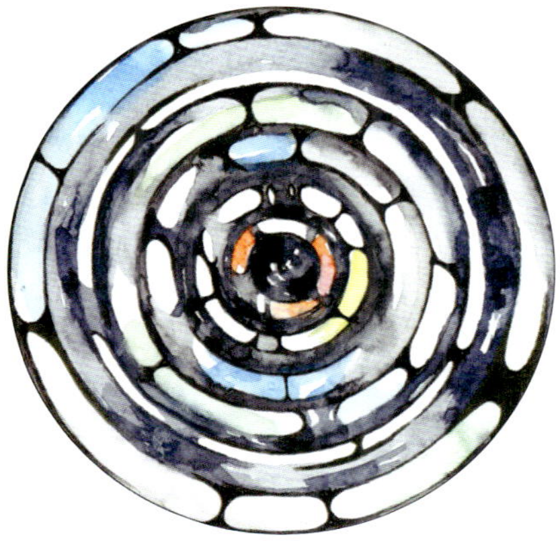

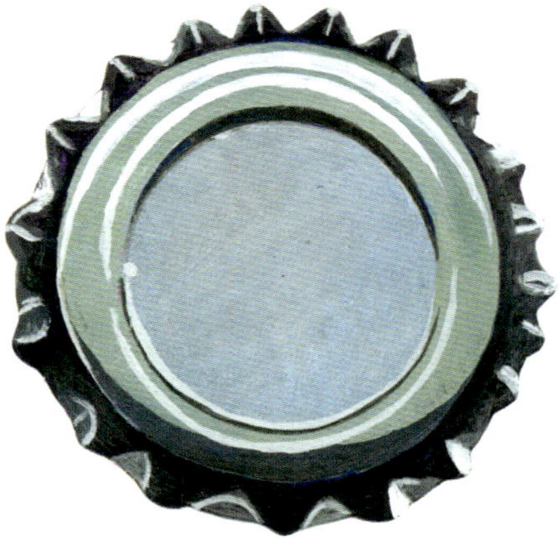

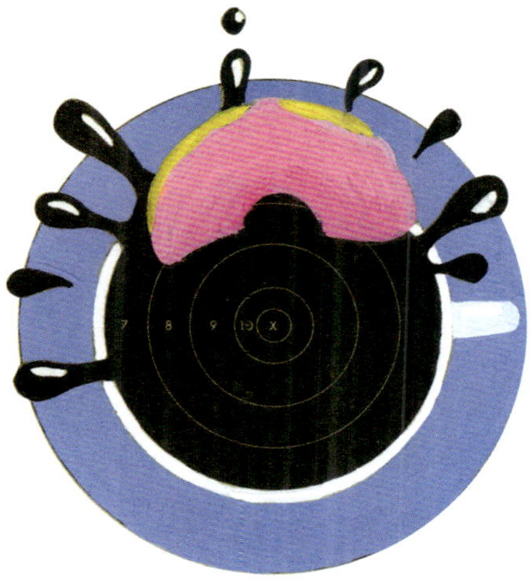

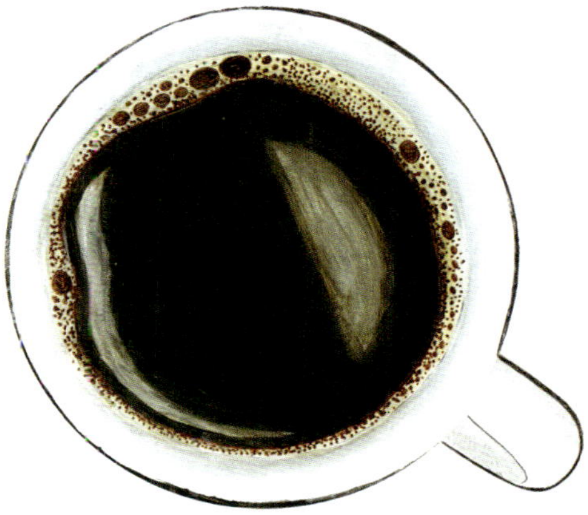

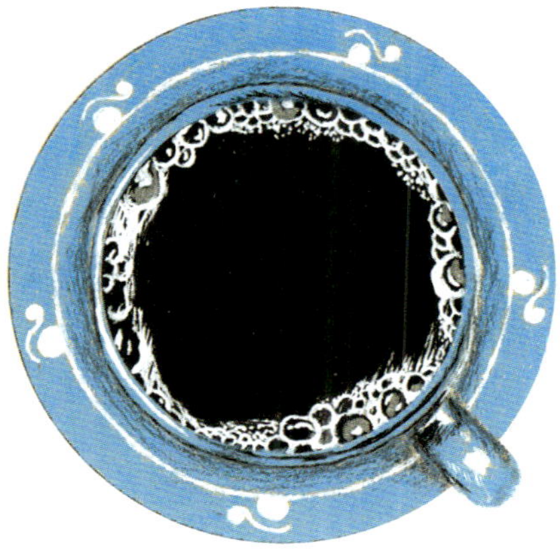

TARGET SOLUTIONS:

Figure 1 is an investigation into the patterning seen in lollipops. Through overlapping and varying sizes juxtaposed against a flat ground, spatial relationships are created. Some images appear on the surface of the picture plane, while others recede back into space.

Figures 2 through 9 are food items and objects viewed from an aerial vantage point.

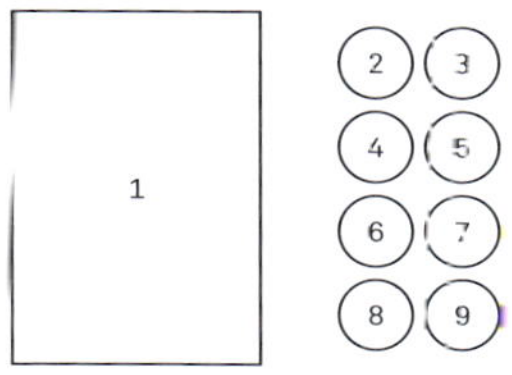

1

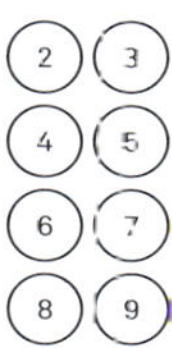

1. *Jiyoon Byun*
2. *Yoonha Chung*
3. *Laura Ng*
4. *Yoonha Chung*
5. *Eunjung Kim*
6. *Yoonha Chung*
7. *S. Kim*
8. *Liz Margulies*
9. *Laura Ng*

TARGETS

WHATEVER YOU HIT, JUST SAY IT WAS THE TARGET.

Traditionally, a target is an object marked with concentric circles, to be aimed at in shooting practice or in contests. It represents precision as well as a goal to be strived for, or an object of scorn or abuse. Because we live in a very goal oriented world, the target most often symbolizes success. On the other hand, the more ominous symbolism reflects weaponry, which is associated with death. Using the seven targets on the assignment sheet make a personal, political or purely graphic statement, in whatever way you see fit.

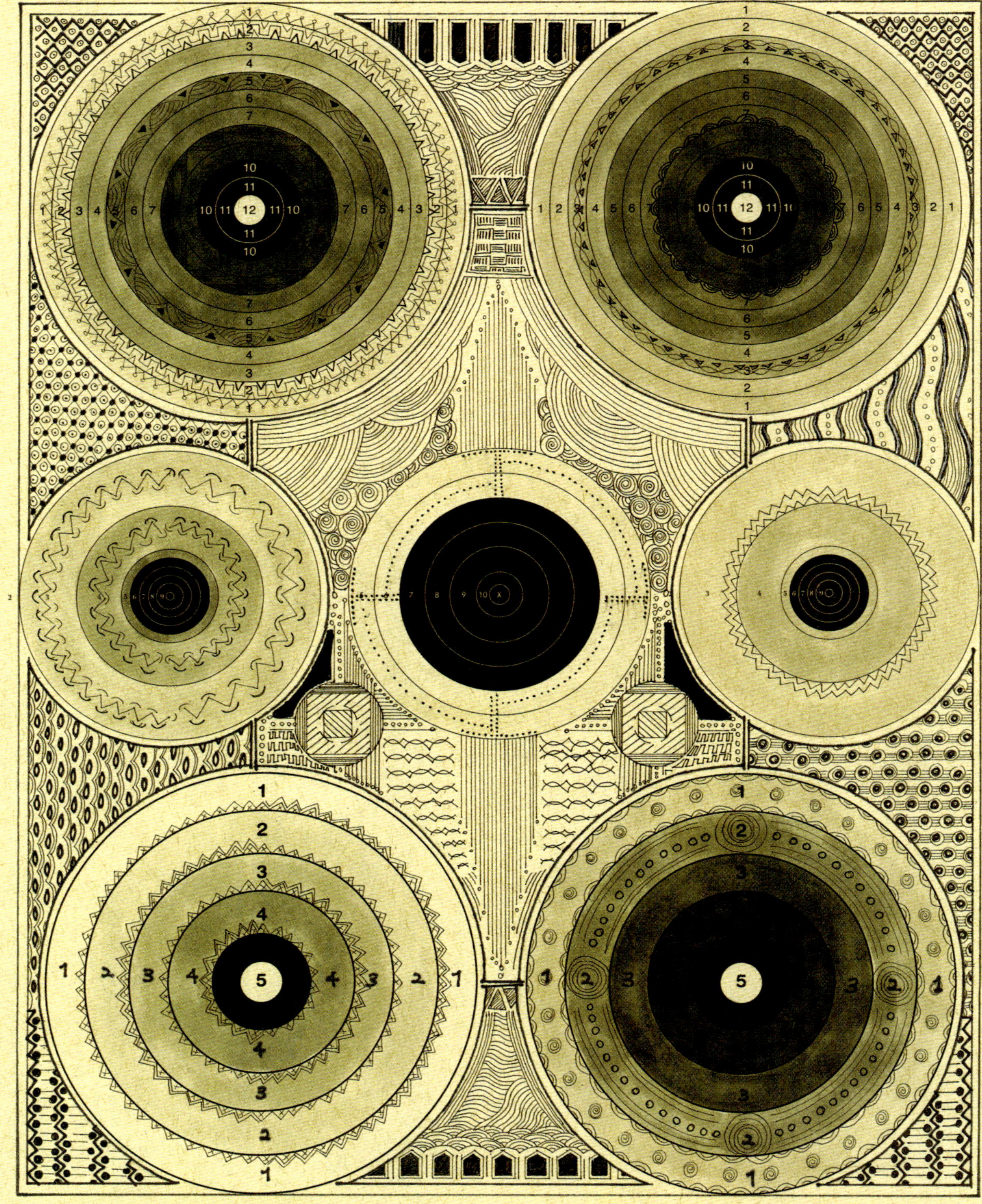

COMPETITOR ______________________

PROBLEMS : SOLUTIONS SERIES

CREATED BY RICHARD WILDE / JUDITH WILDE, PRODUCED BY VISUAL ARTS PRESS, LTD. ART DIRECTORS: RICHARD WILDE / JUDITH WILDE

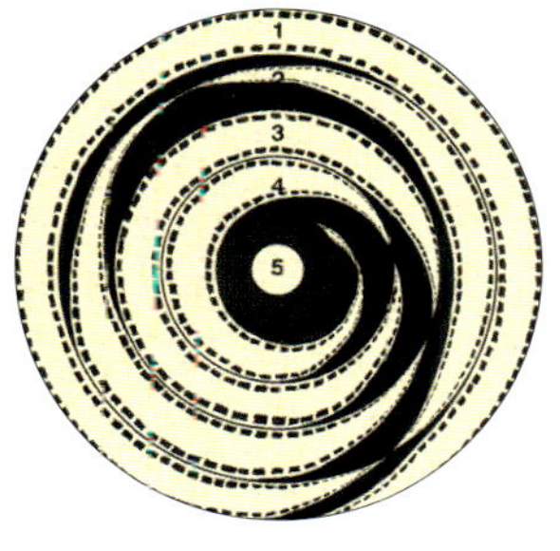
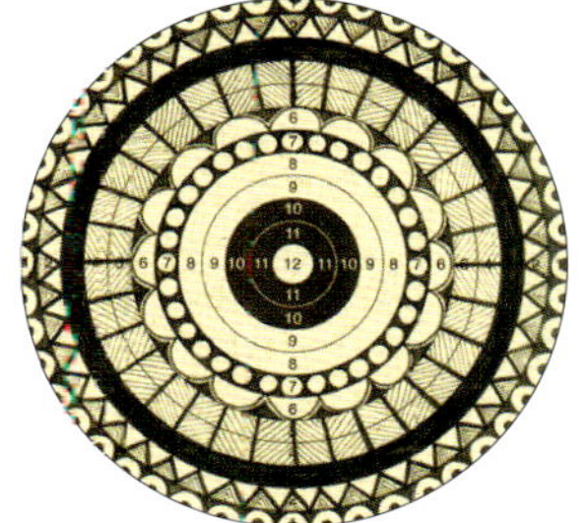
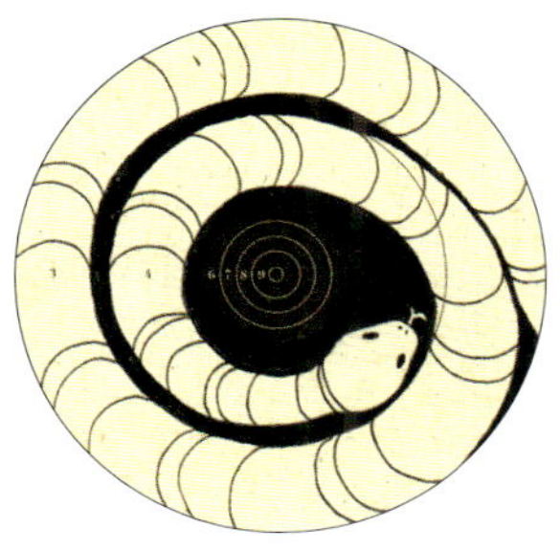
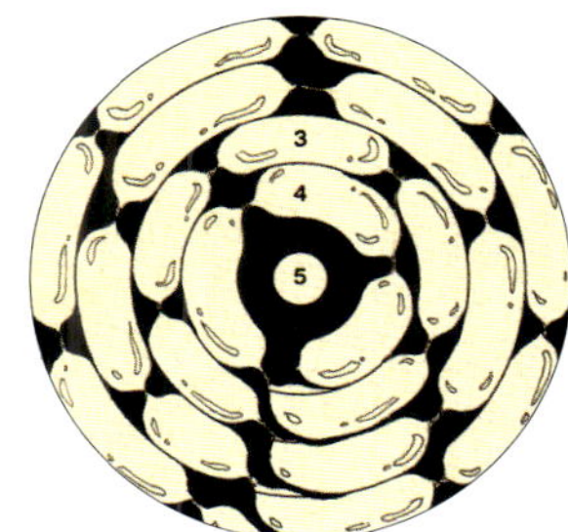

TARGET SOLUTIONS:

Figure 1 is a highly decorative solution that works as a single image and explores line, pattern, and texture.

Figures 2 through 25 are executed either with black ink, pencil, and white pencil and are purely graphic solutions, most of which use the concentric circles of the target as the underlying compositional structure. Attention to detail is an overriding factor in most of these solutions.

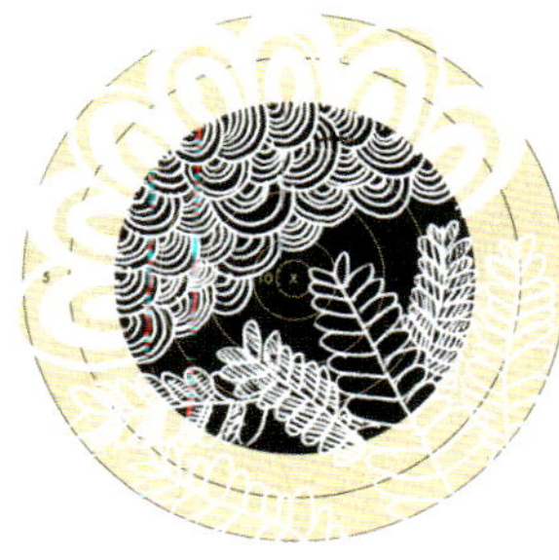
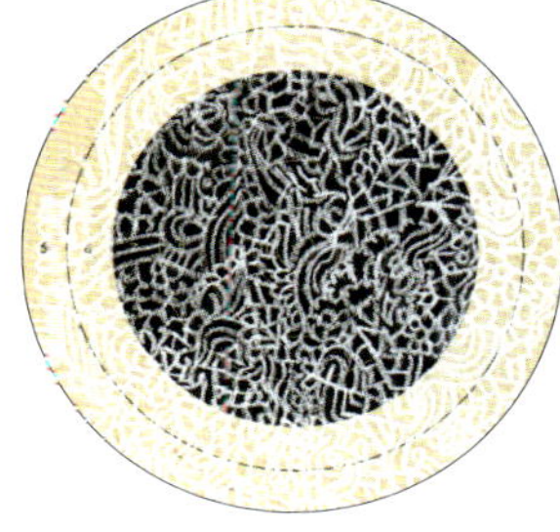
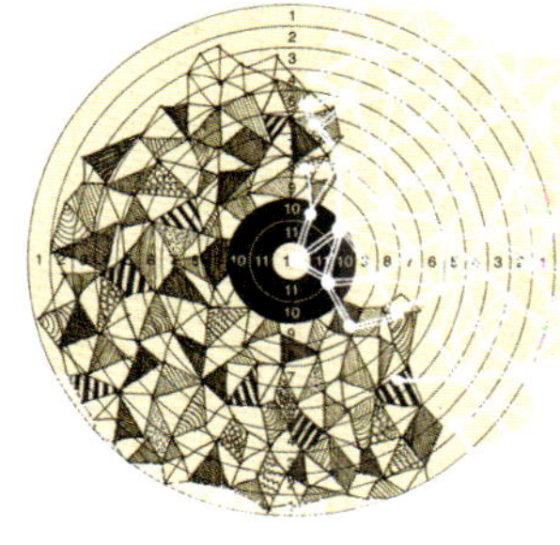
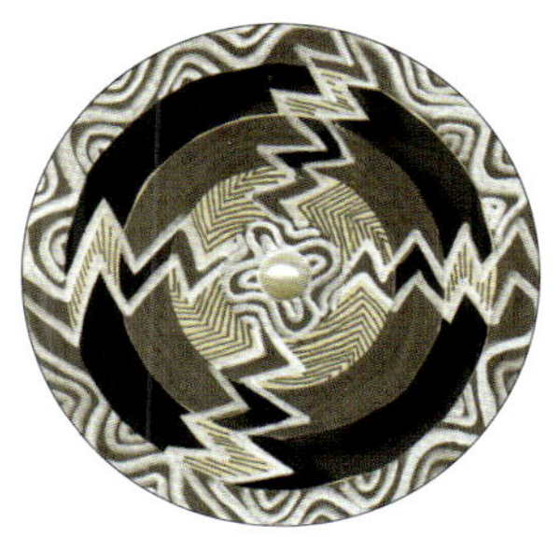
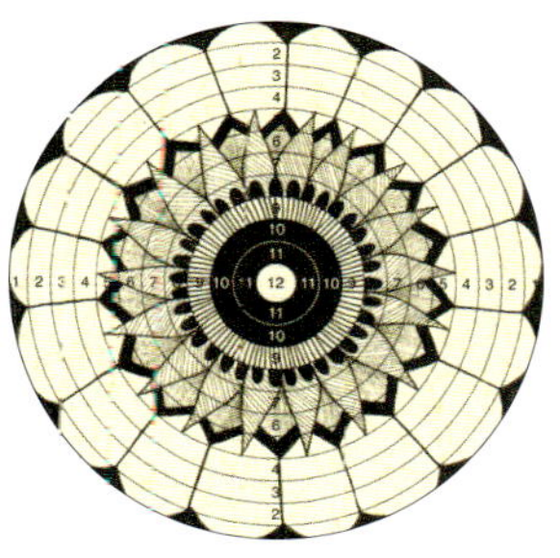
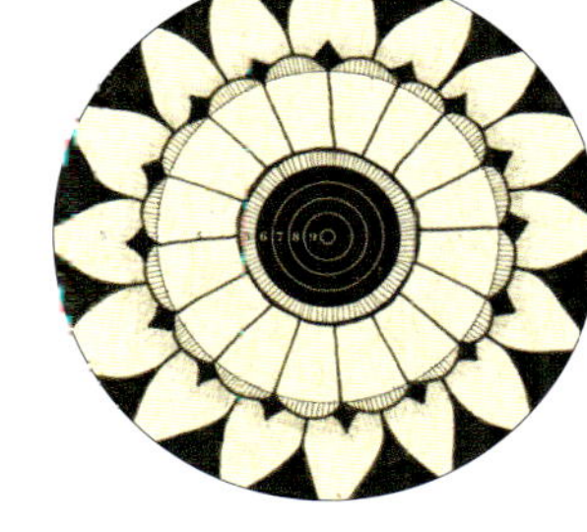
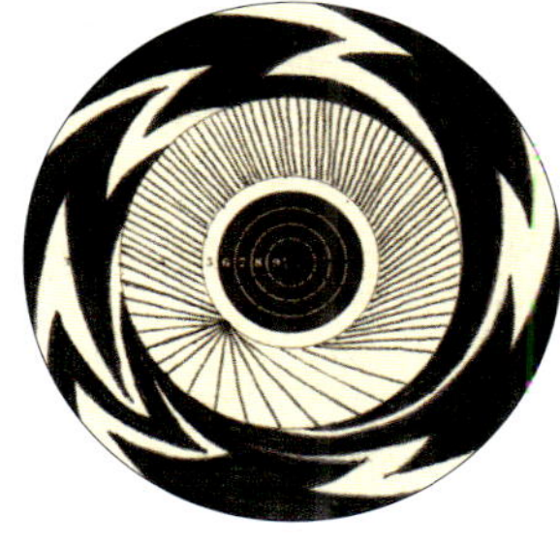
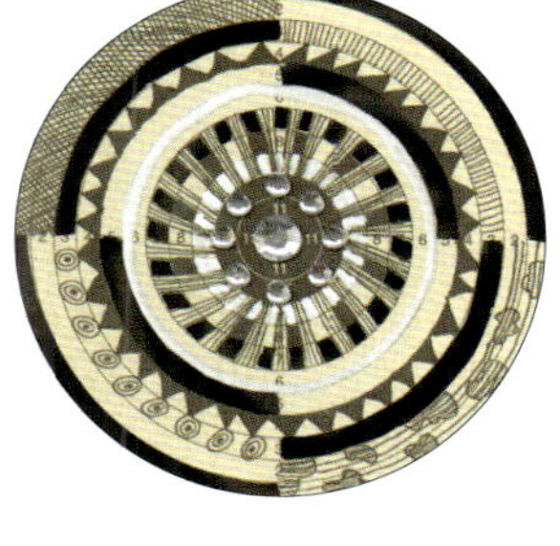
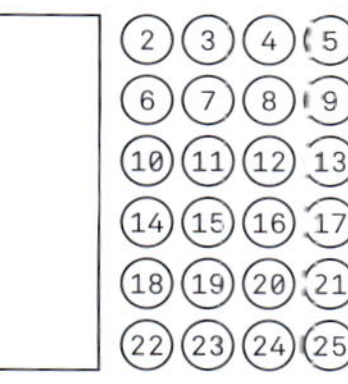

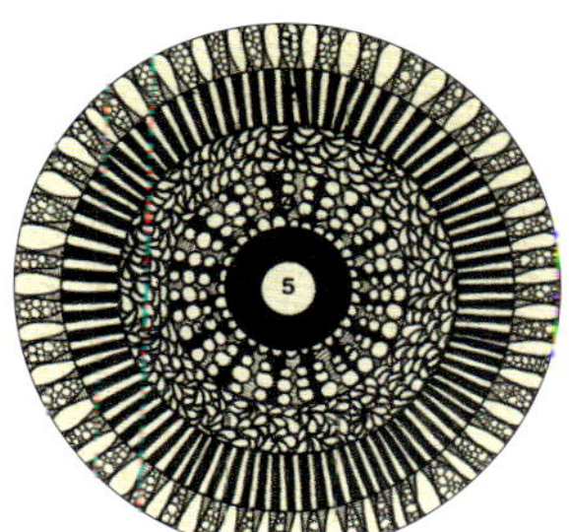
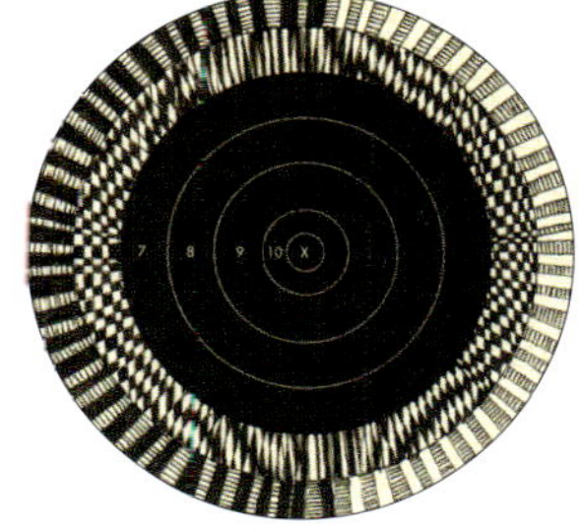
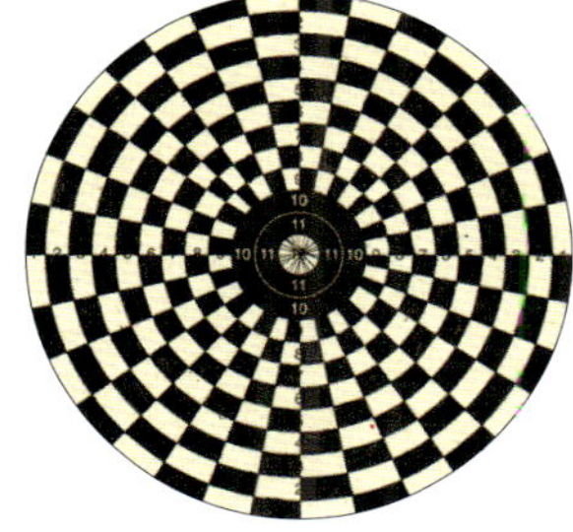
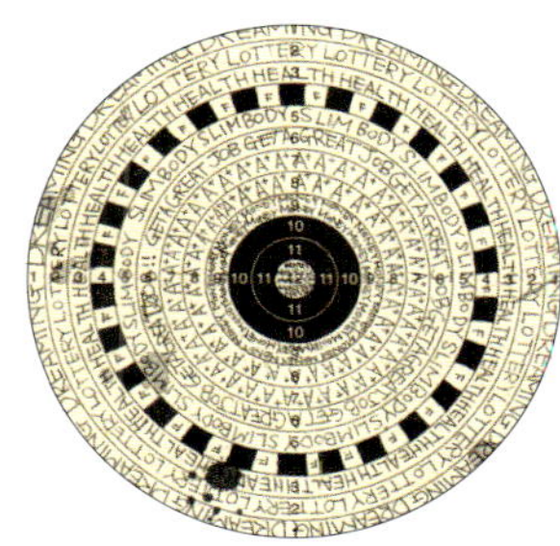
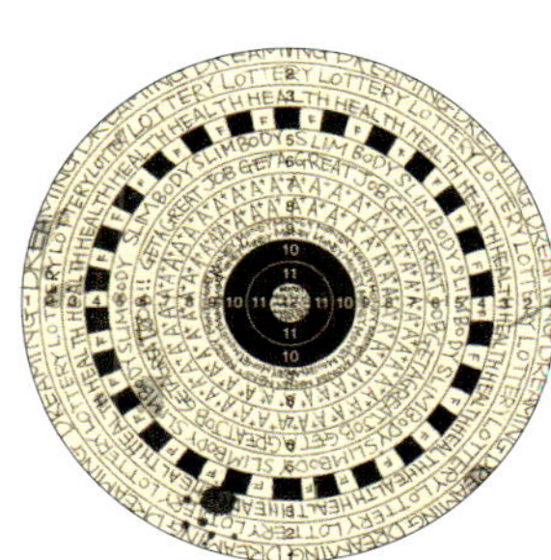
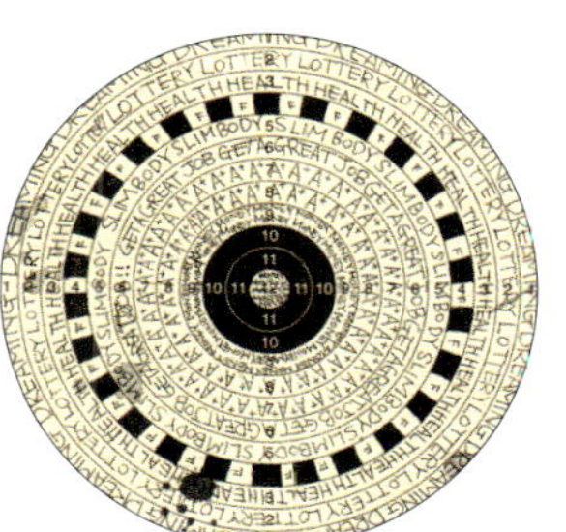
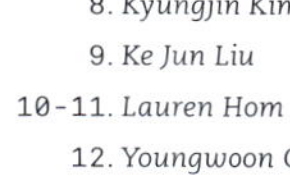

1. *Yeryung Ko*
2. *Dohee Kim*
3. *Yoojung Kang*

4–5. *Dohee Kim*

6. *Kyungjin Kim*
7. *Moe Nakamura*
8. *Kyungjin Kim*
9. *Ke Jun Liu*

10–11. *Lauren Hom*

12. *Youngwoon Choi*
13. *Ke Jun Lui*

14–15. *Aerial Chen*

16–17. *Jinsook Bae*

18–19. *Roza Gazarian*

20. *Susanne Soum*

21–23. *Roza Gazarian*

24. *Youngwoon Choi*
25. *Hye Ok Row*

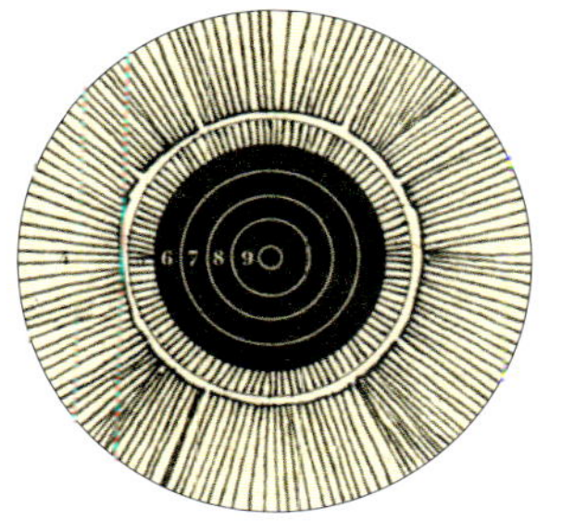
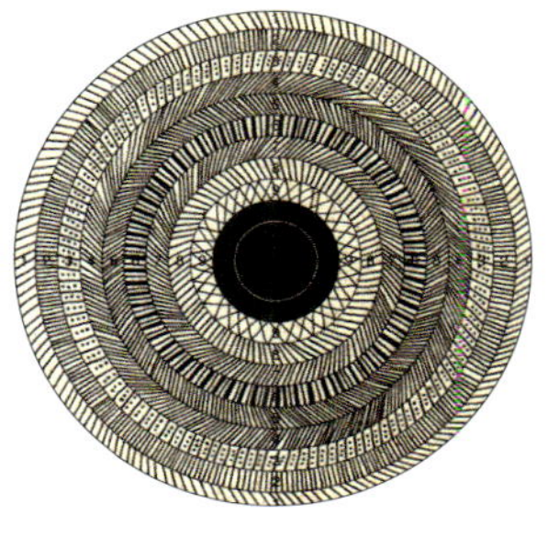
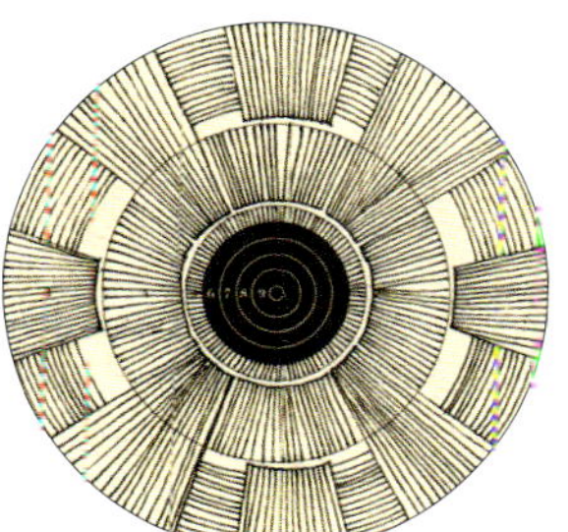
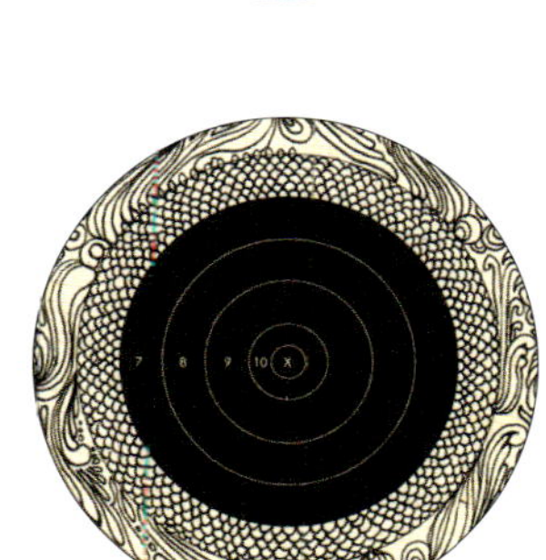
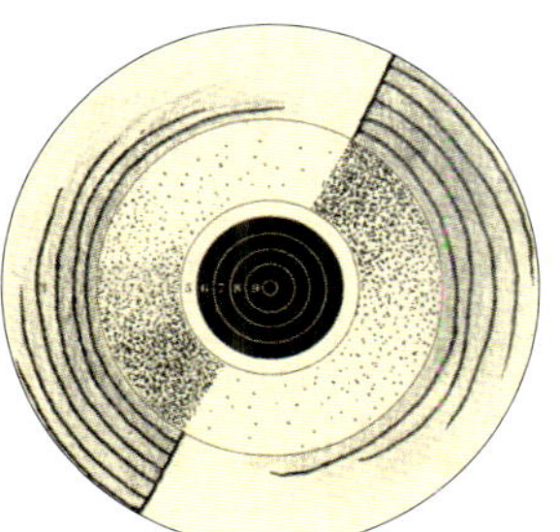
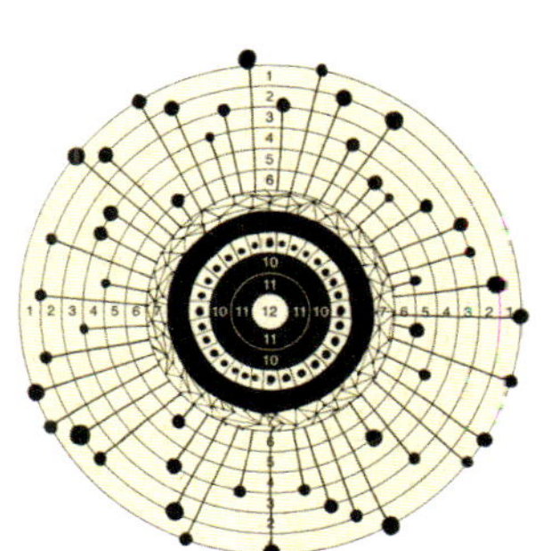
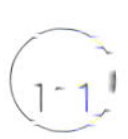

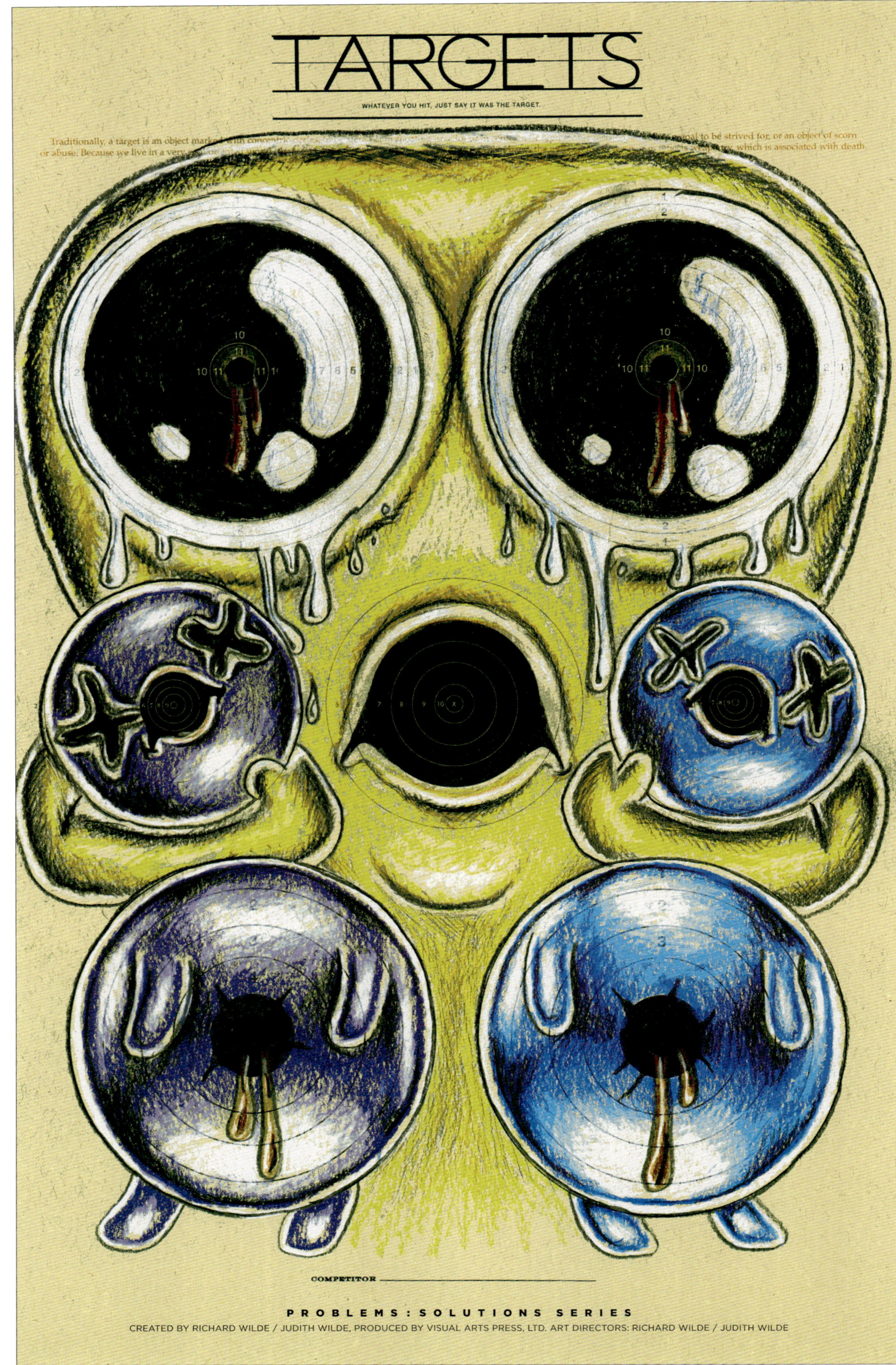
TARGETS
WHATEVER YOU HIT, JUST SAY IT WAS THE TARGET.
COMPETITOR
PROBLEMS : SOLUTIONS SERIES
CREATED BY RICHARD WILDE / JUDITH WILDE, PRODUCED BY VISUAL ARTS PRESS, LTD. ART DIRECTORS: RICHARD WILDE / JUDITH WILDE

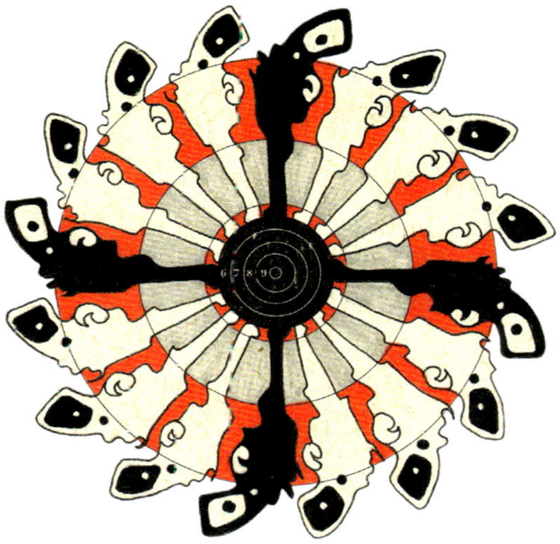

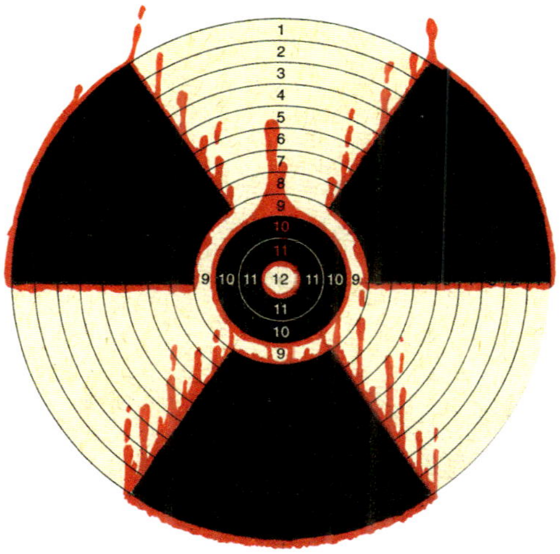

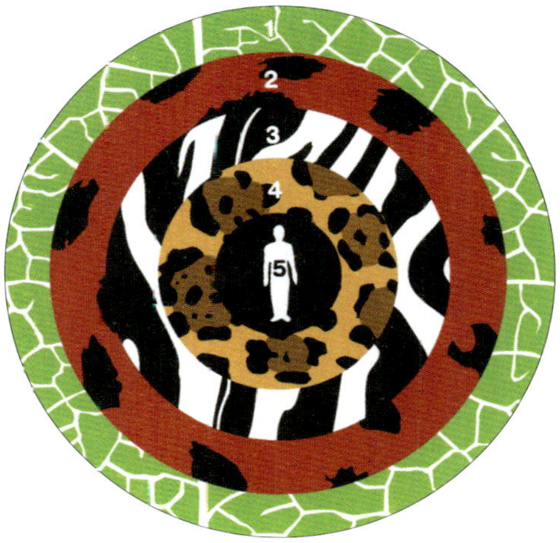

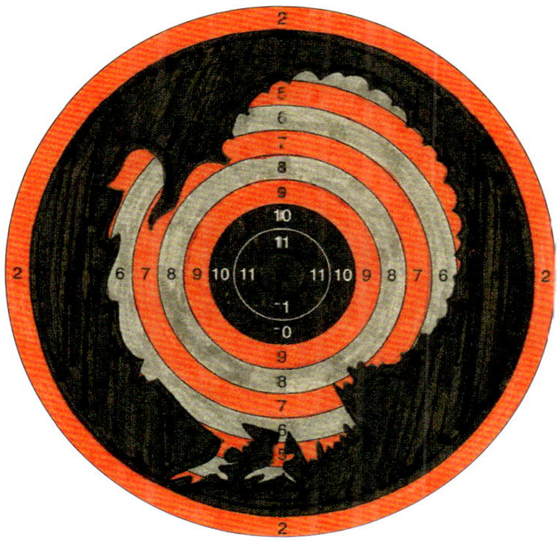

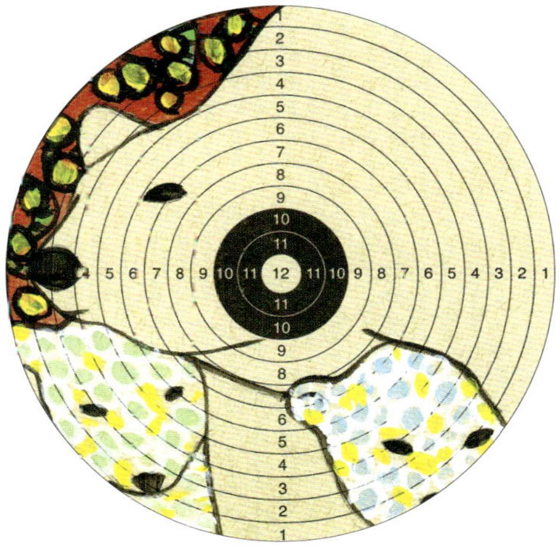

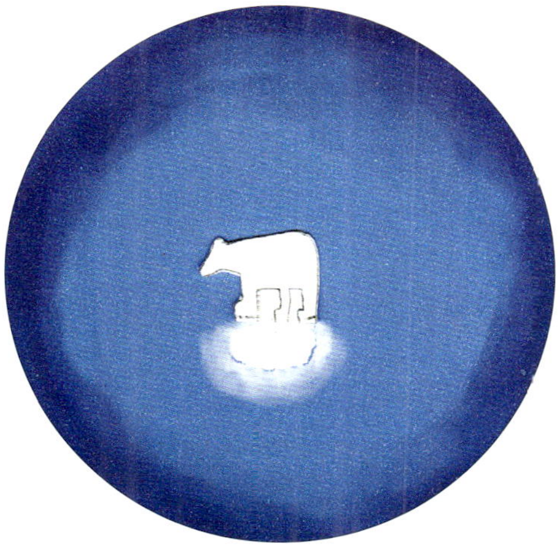

TARGET SOLUTIONS:

At the onset, figure 1 is not necessarily comprehended in terms of its intent. But upon closer observation, it is a depiction of a yellow person with large black eyes holding purple and blue children who have been shot in their stomachs. The difficulty in reading the images of the children is that one does not view the circular head and body portions of the children as single entities. This is because the yellow person's arms separate the heads from the bodies. In essence, the image is a statement about gun control.

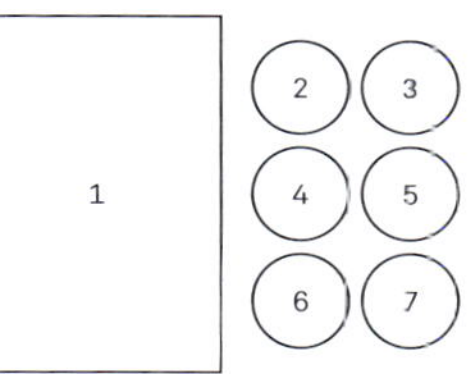

1. *Davide Illiano*
2. *Kirsten Karkanen*
3. *Jerry Rosen*
4. *Duesung Byun*
5. *Kirsten Karkanen*
6. *Daon Kim*
7. *Yoejin Kim*

There is a sense of movement in figure 2, which uses the motif of guns to create a decorative pattern referencing a sideshow shooting gallery.

Figures 3 through 5 symbolically depict social messages regarding nuclear waste, guns, and the killing of animals and people.

Figure 6 deals with death, in the depiction of a mother bear and two cubs that are camouflaged and not apparent at first sight, which makes the message more poignant.

Figure 7 references the melting of the polar ice caps.

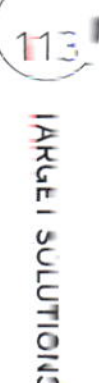

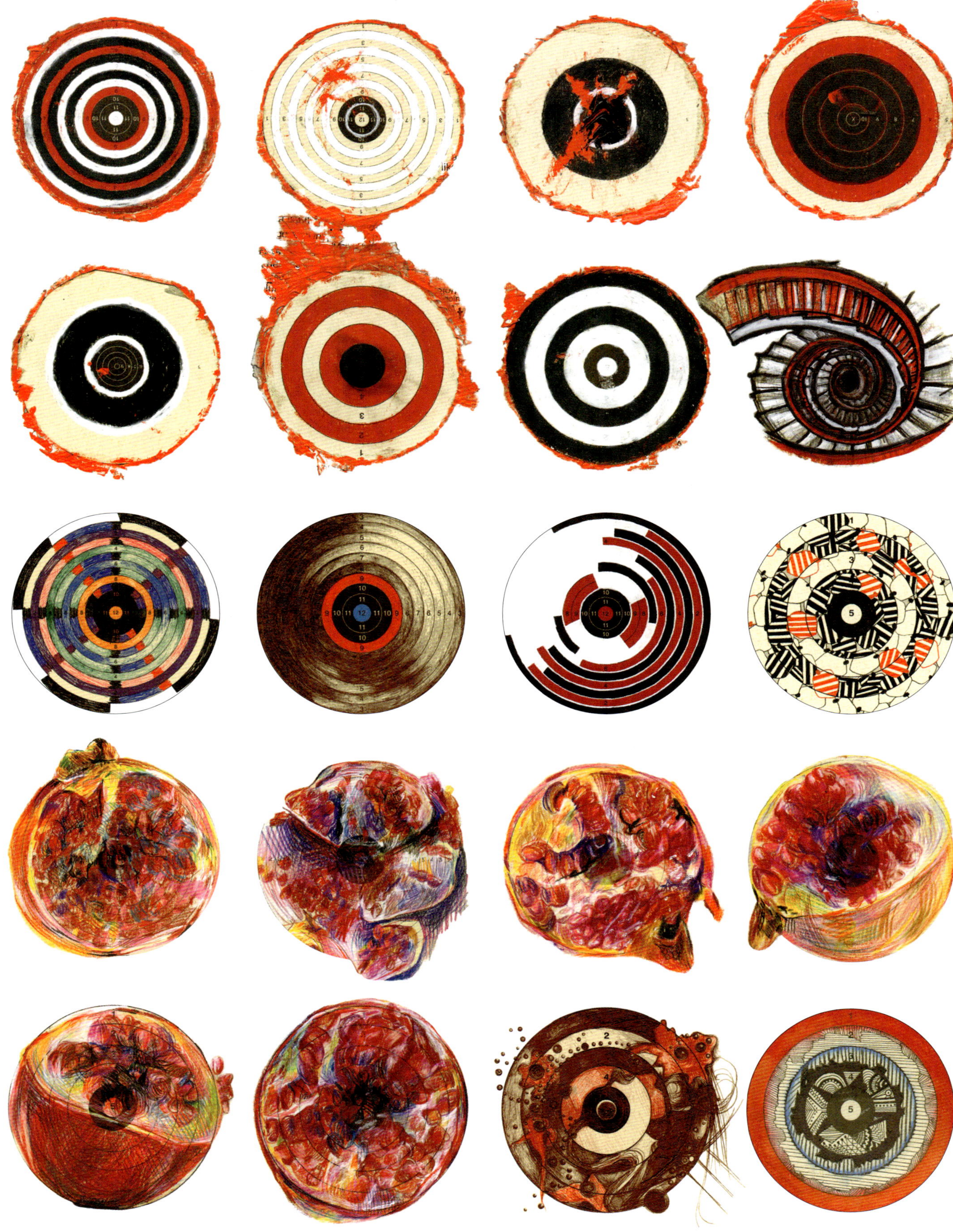

TARGET SOLUTIONS:

The color red is a common denominator in figures 1 through 21. Images range from purely abstract, to reconfigured targets, to literal explorations.

Figures 13 through 18 are expressively drawn interpretations of a pomegranate.

Figure 21 is an optical study of a radiating image.

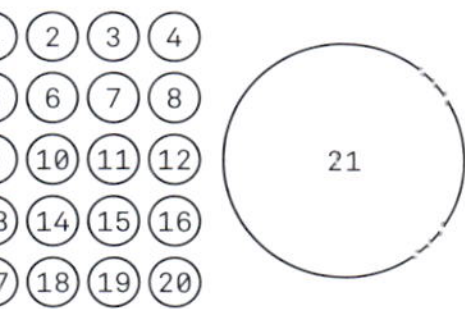

1–7. Najeebah Al Ghadban
8. Stephanie Hartman
9–10. Eva Cheung
11. Soyeon Lee
12. Kirsten Karkanen
13–16. Yujin Lee
17. Eva Cheung
18. Yujin Lee
19. Eva Cheung
20. Alex Morel
21. S. Kim

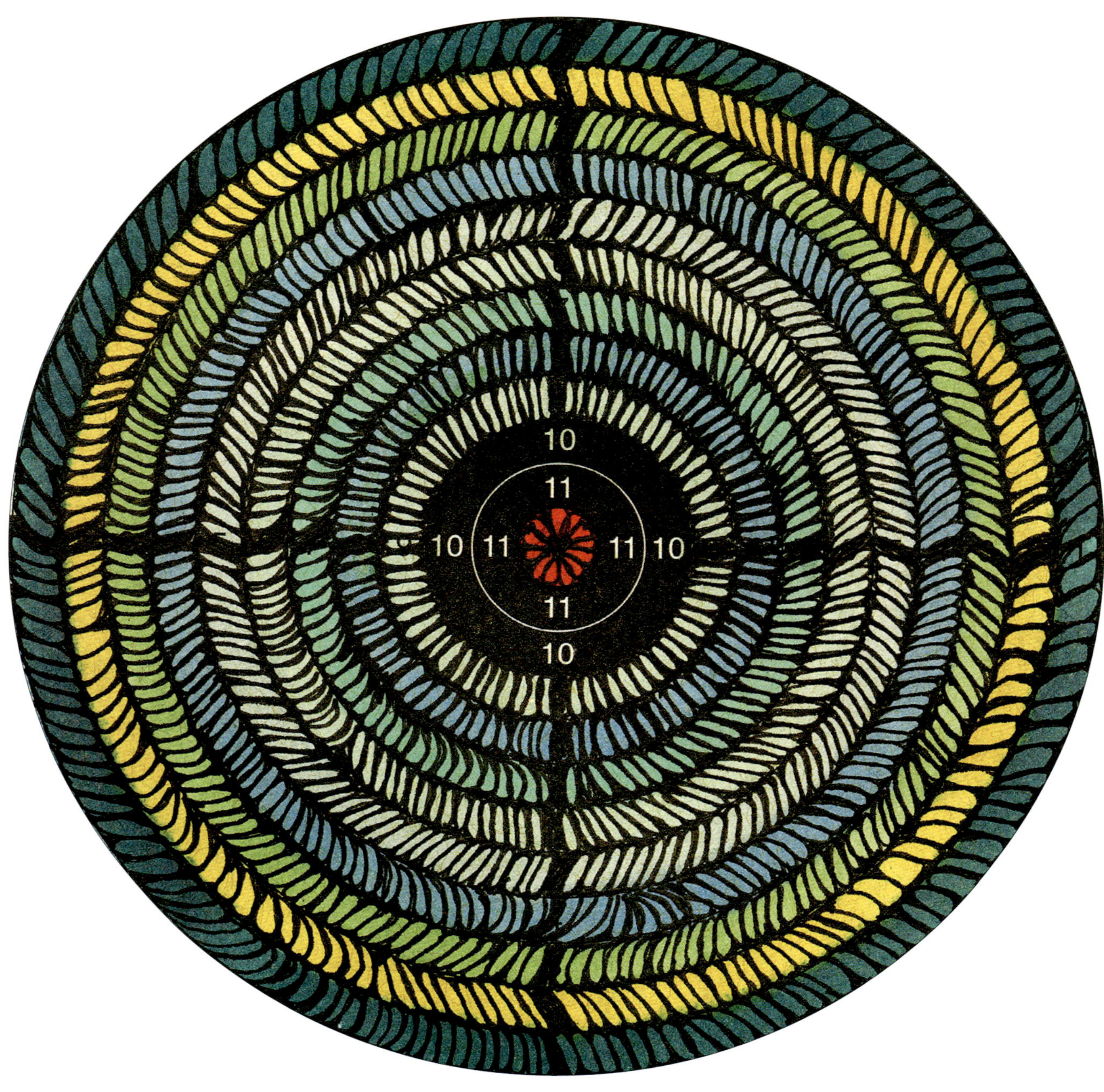
10
11
10 11 11 10
11
10

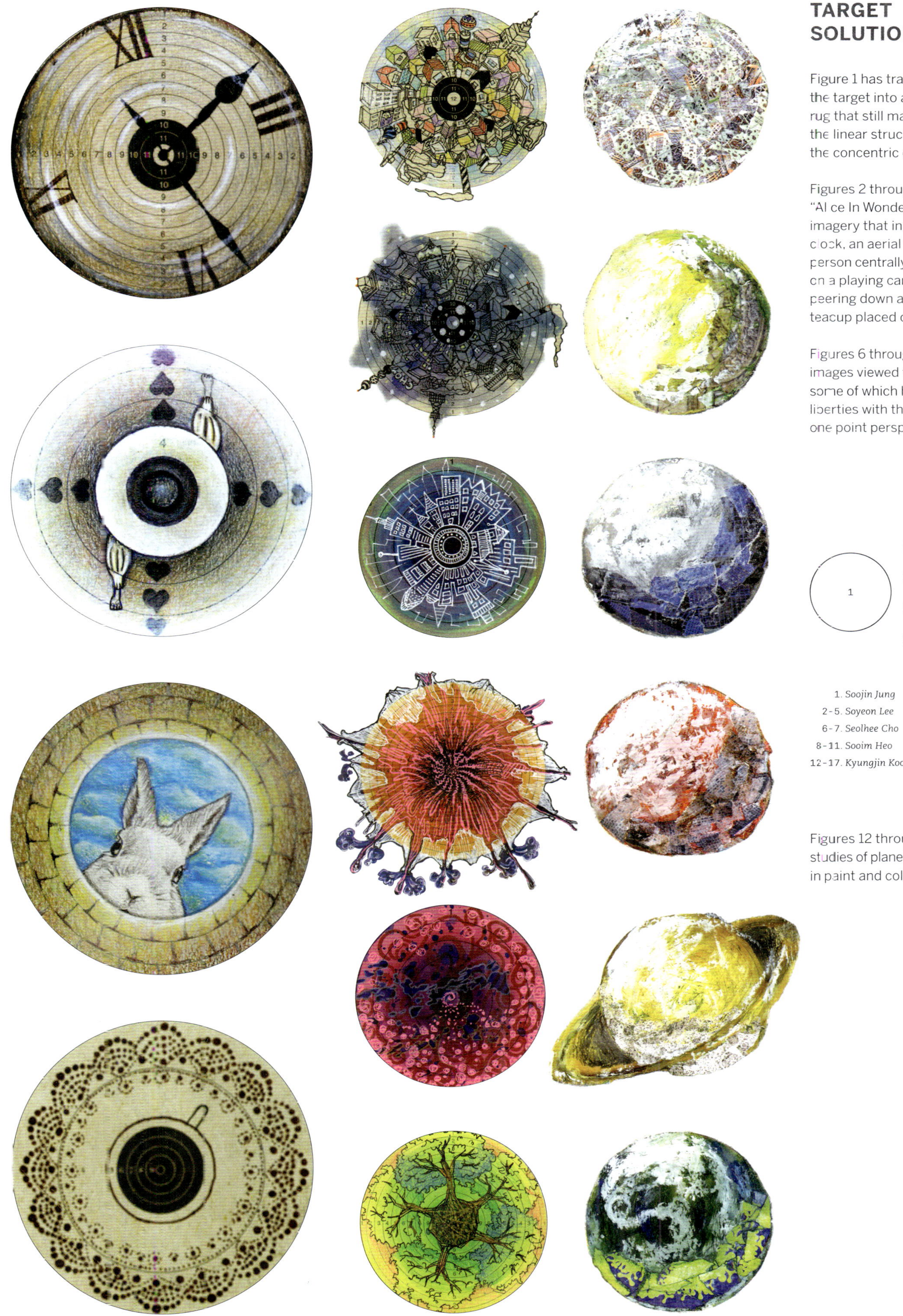

TARGET SOLUTIONS:

Figure 1 has transformed the target into a braided rug that still maintains the linear structure of the concentric circles.

Figures 2 through 5 depict "Alice In Wonderland" imagery that includes a clock, an aerial view of a person centrally positioned on a playing card, a rabbit peering down a well, and a teacup placed on a doily.

Figures 6 through 11 are images viewed from above, some of which have taken liberties with the use of one point perspective.

1. *Soojin Jung*
2-5. *Soyeon Lee*
6-7. *Seolhee Cho*
8-11. *Sooim Heo*
12-17. *Kyungjin Kook*

Figures 12 through 17 are studies of planets, executed in paint and collage.

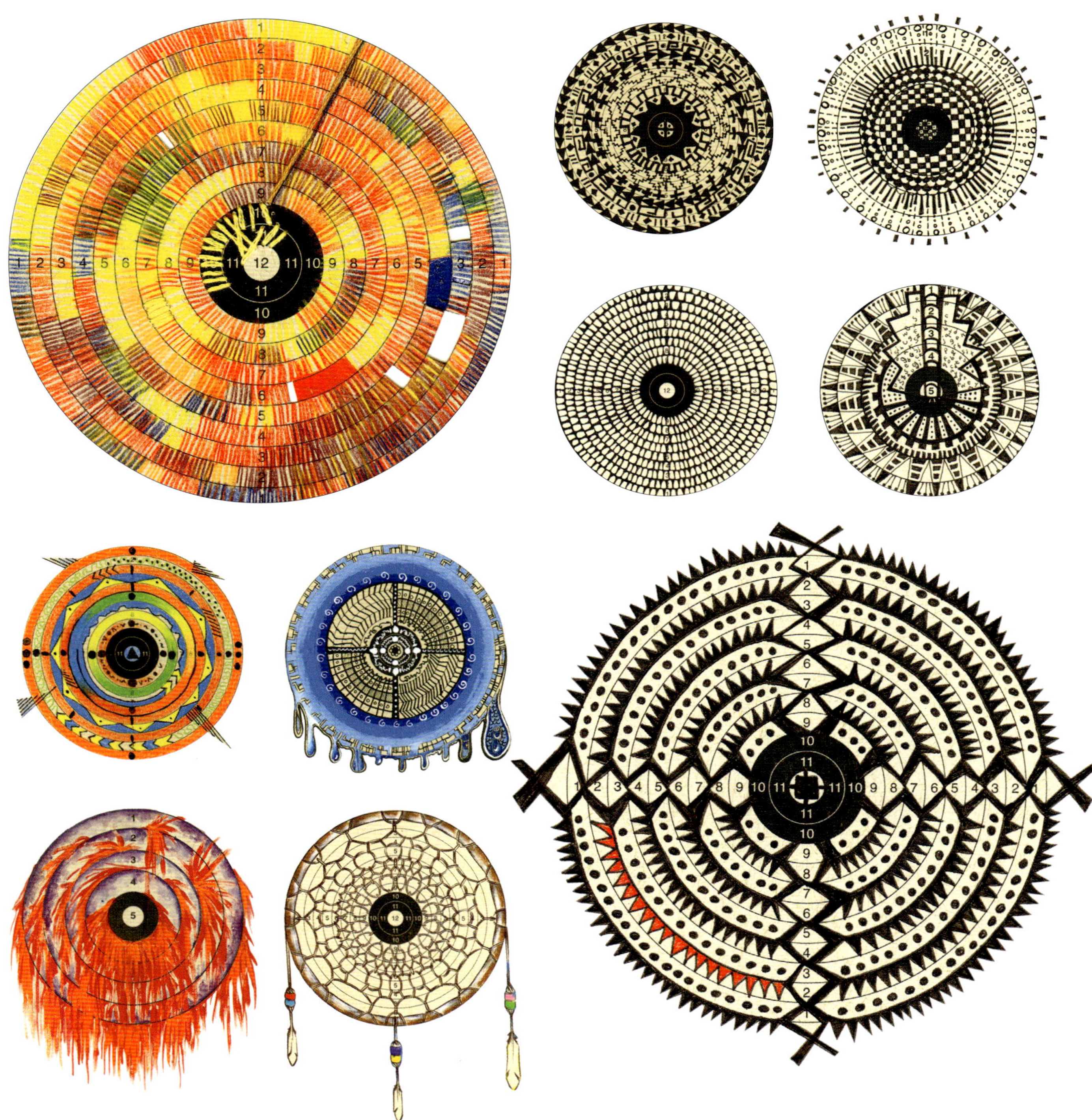

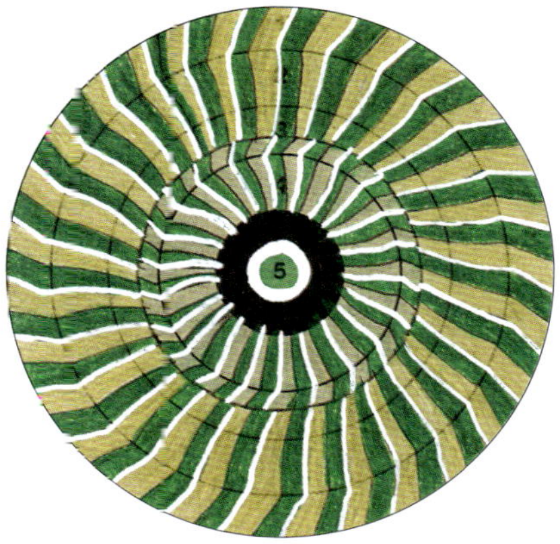

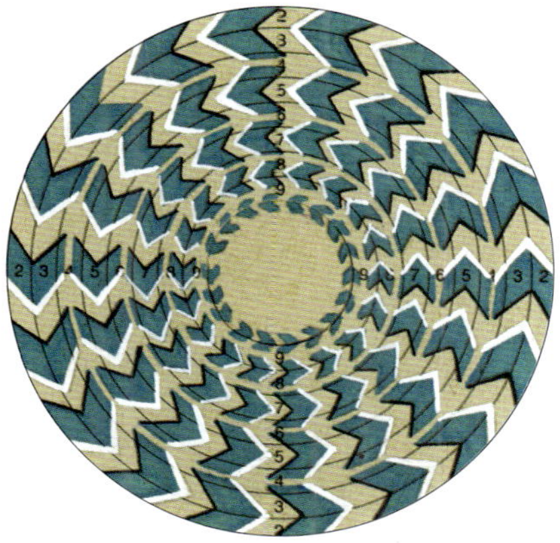

TARGET SOLUTIONS:

Figures 1 through 10 deal with intricate abstract explorations that reference Native American imagery.

Figures 11 through 18 concern themselves with optical illusions that exhibit a pulsating effect.

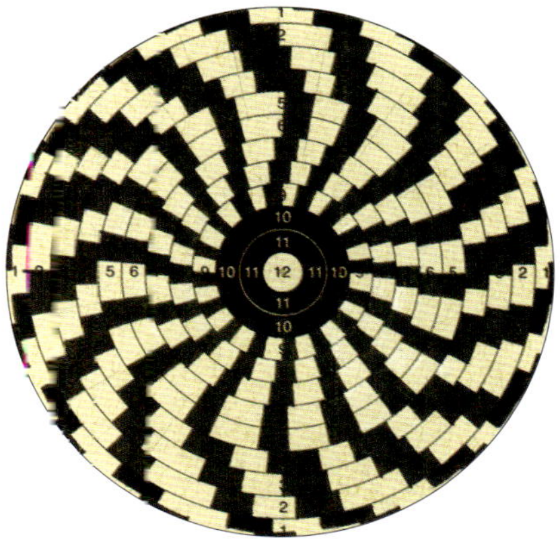

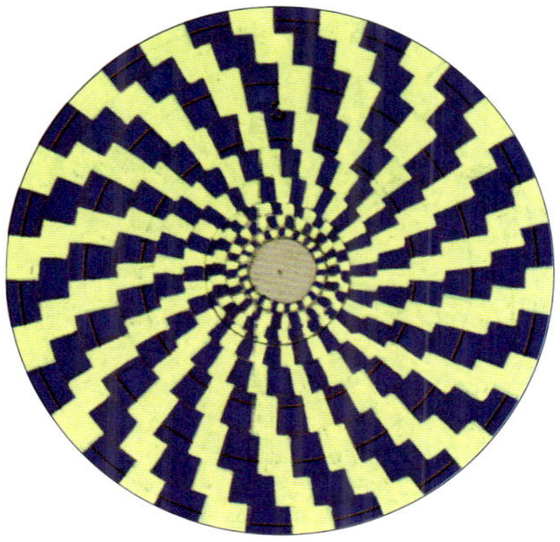

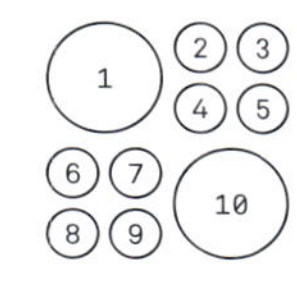

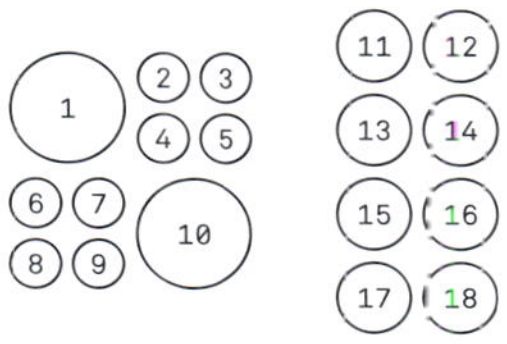

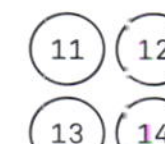

1. *Tess Lee*
2. *Deborah Gruber*
3. *Jiwon Kim*
4. *Yungwoon Choi*
5. *Jiwon Kim*
6. *Colin Smight*
7. *Hea Kim*
8. *Daisy Millard*
9. *Vu Do*
10. *Jiwon Kim*
11. *Minyeong Park*
12. *Kyunggin Jun*
13. *Rochelle Jiang*
14. *Kyunggin Jun*

15-16. *Duesung Byun*

17-18. *Minyeong Park*

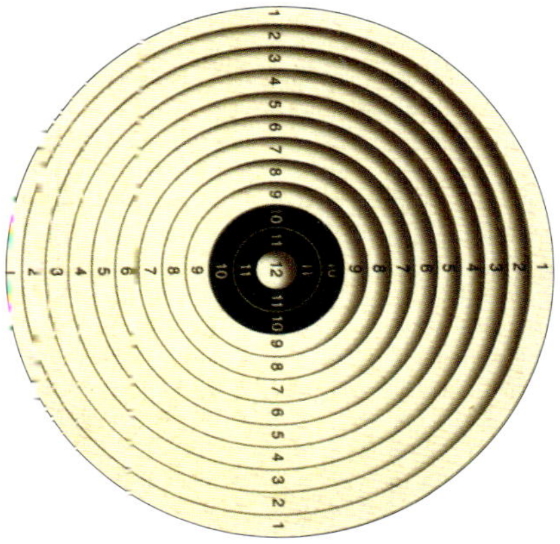

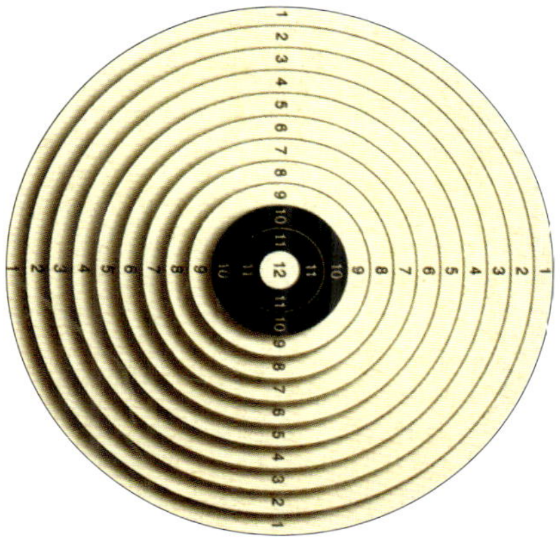

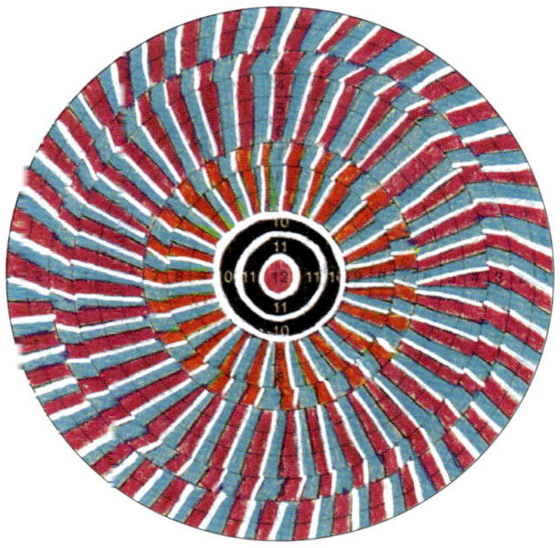

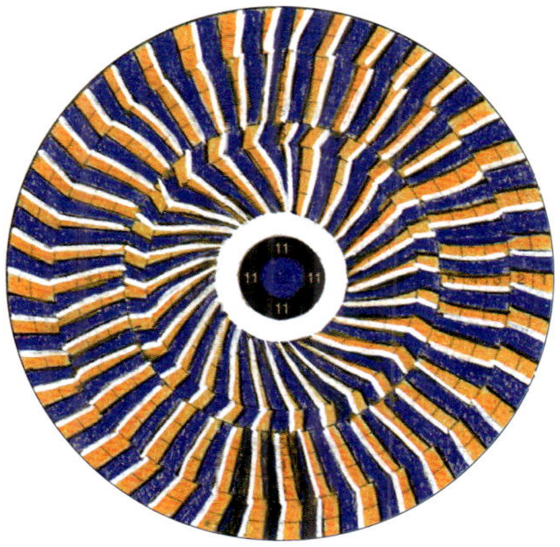

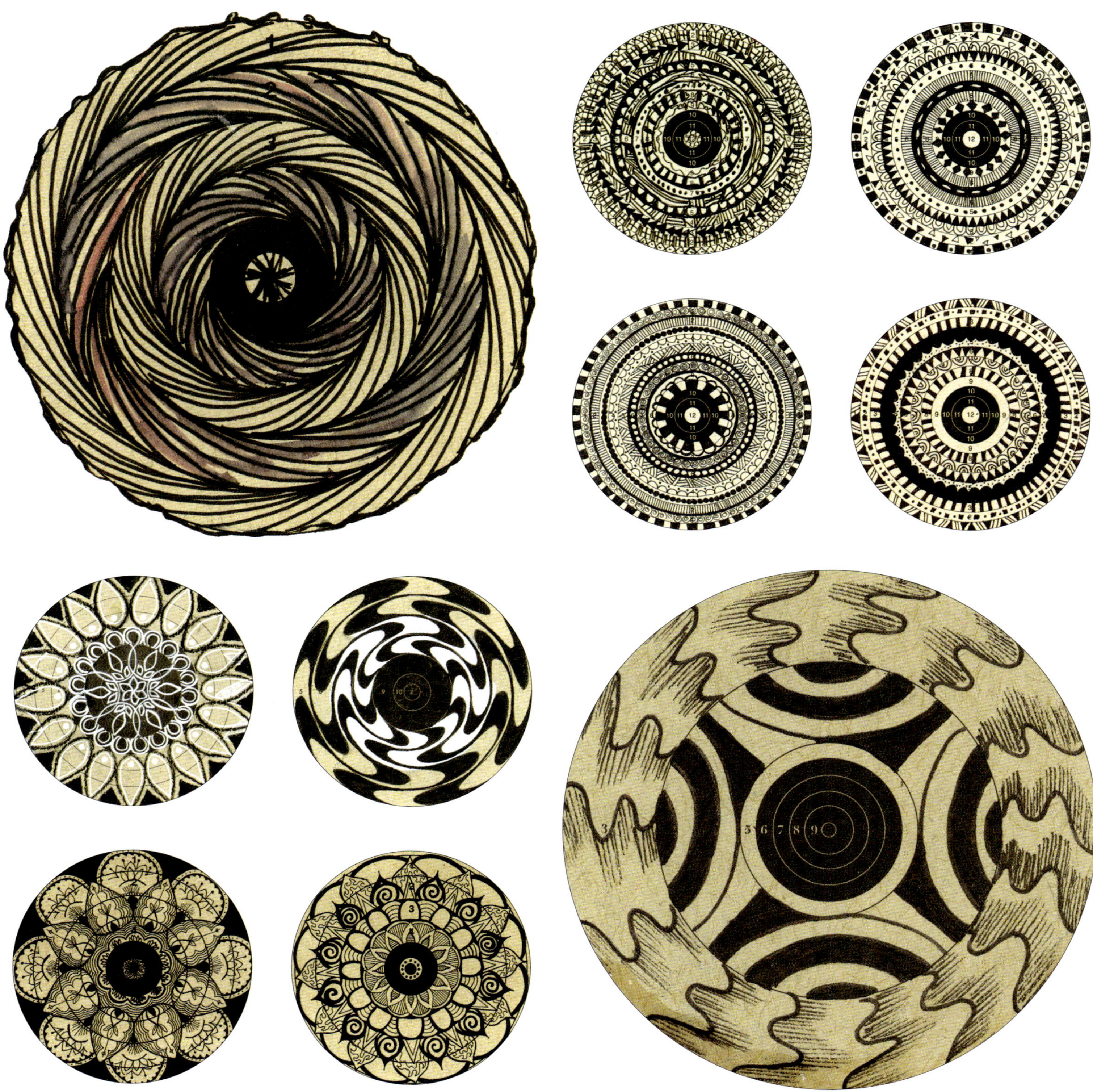

TARGET SOLUTIONS:

Figures 1 through 10 represent a range of single solutions that focus on patterning, referencing leaded glass windows to abstract explorations.

In figures 6 and 7, white pencil is used to heighten the visual impact.

Figures 11 through 13 are spontaneously executed, in a process where each image informs the next incarnation. They deal with overlapping and highly detailed patterning in the creation of an active intricate surface.

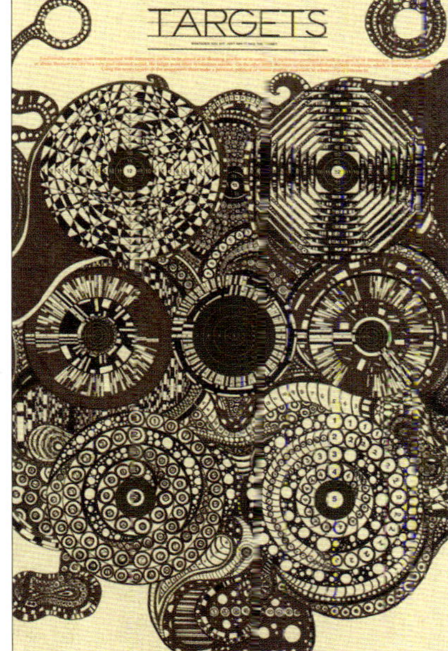

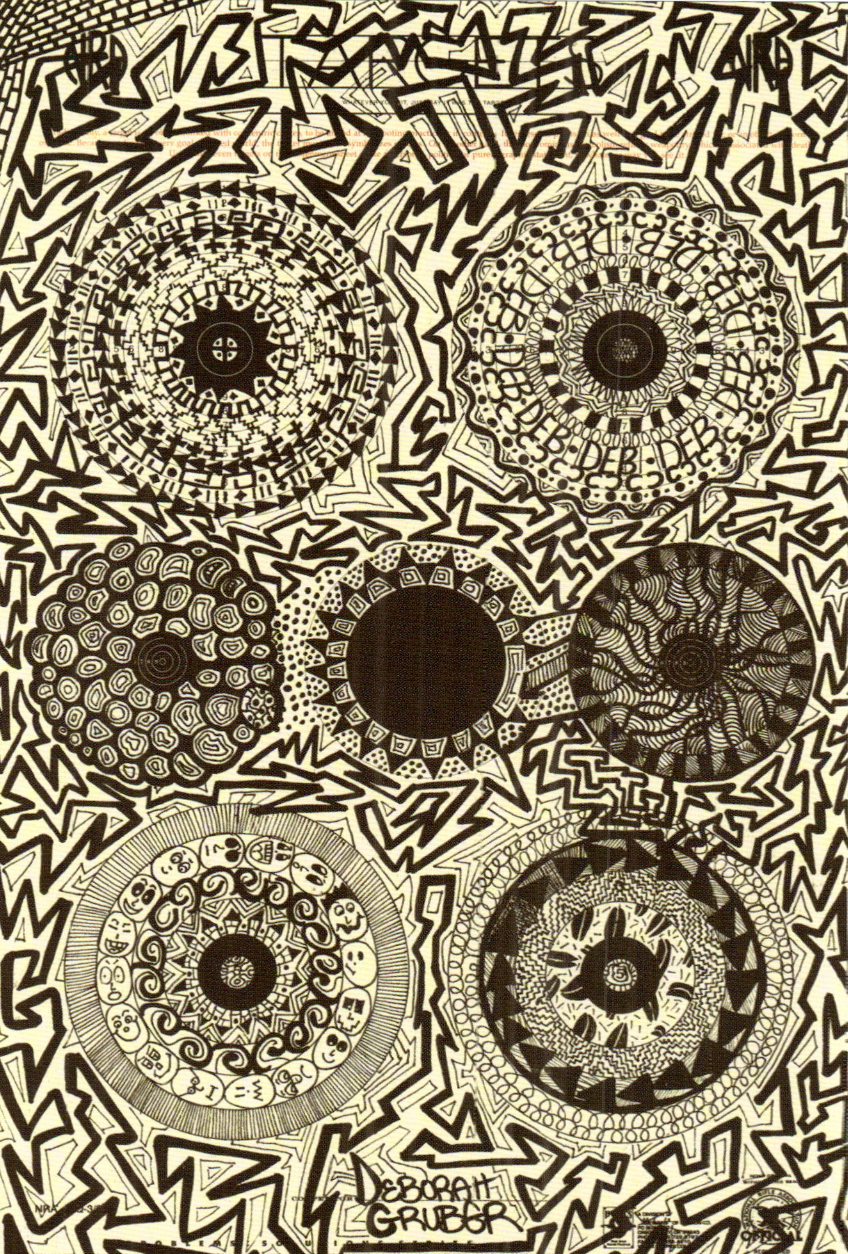

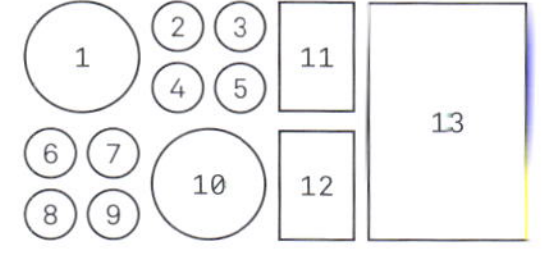

1. Dahee Kim
2. Minjung Kim
3–4. Haewon Park
5. Jewon Moon
6. Kyunghwa Kim
7. Sara Chaudhuri
8–9. Kristen Sorace
10. Guilet Libby
11. Seulki Heo
12. Narae Lee
13. Deborah Gruber

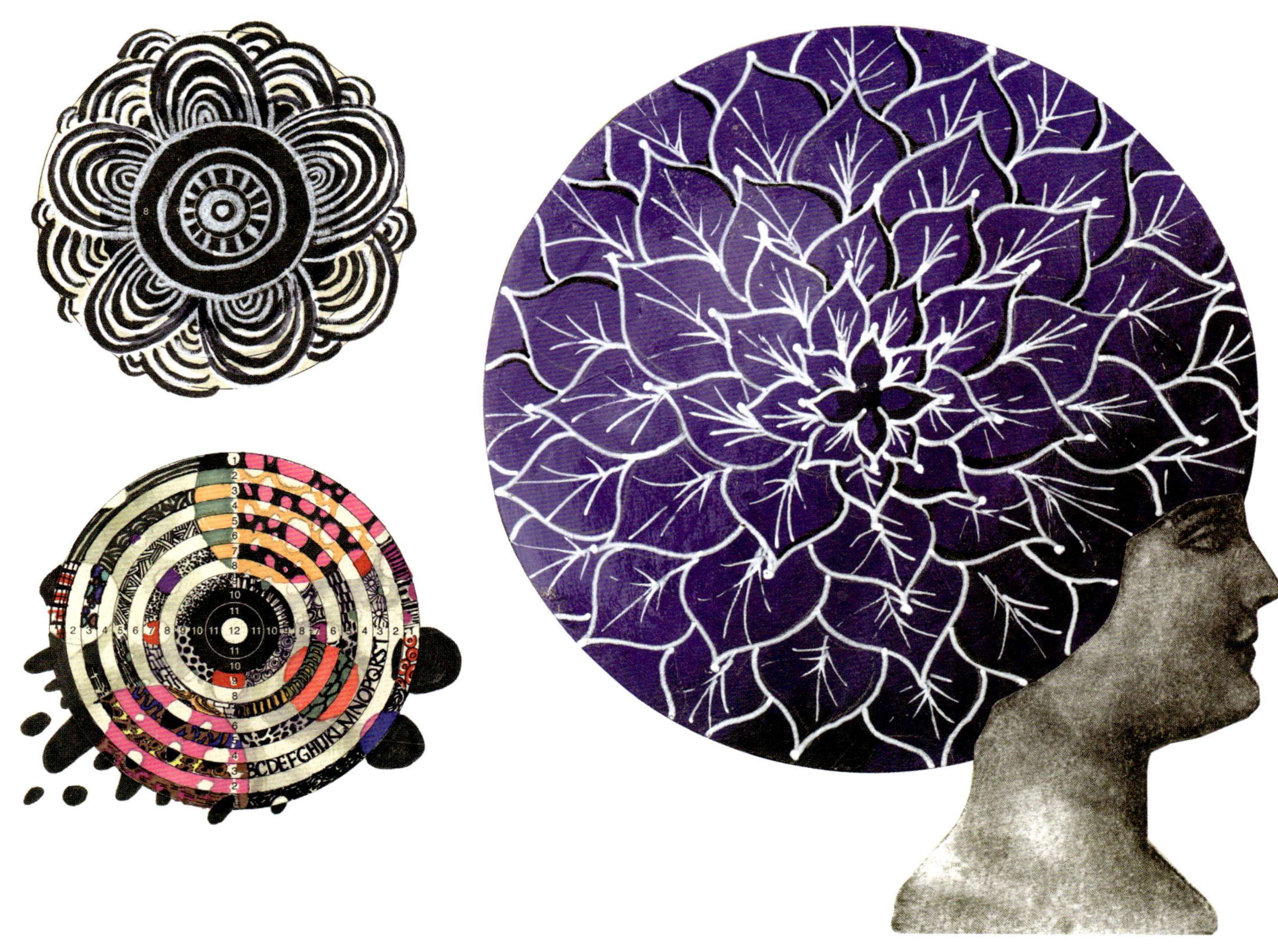

TARGET SOLUTIONS:

Figures 1 and 2 deal with abstraction, while figures 3 through 15 deal with literal interpretations.

Figure 3 transforms the target into a flowering hat that is placed on a person in profile.

Figures 4 through 6 address the deconstruction of automobile logos.

In figure 7, the target is turned into a spider's web.

Figure 8 uses concentric circles to depict a chain, while figure 9 uses a spiral to illustrate a rope.

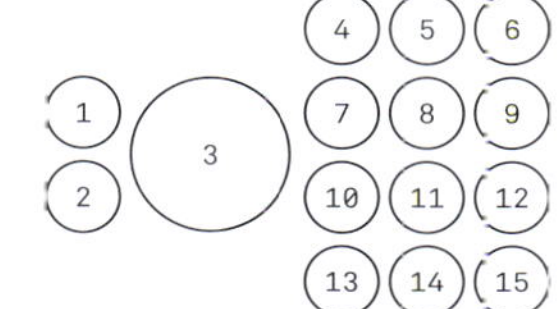

1. Boram Lee
2. Eunyoung Cho
3. Annjeong Hyun
4–6. Jung Yoon
7. Jaewon Park
8–9. Dohee Kim
10. Michael Domondon
11. Stephanie Hartman
12. A. Fazzolari
13. Hyo Han
14. Jeongwoo Kim
15. H. Kim

Figures 10 through 15 use various subjects whose design was derived from a central focal point.

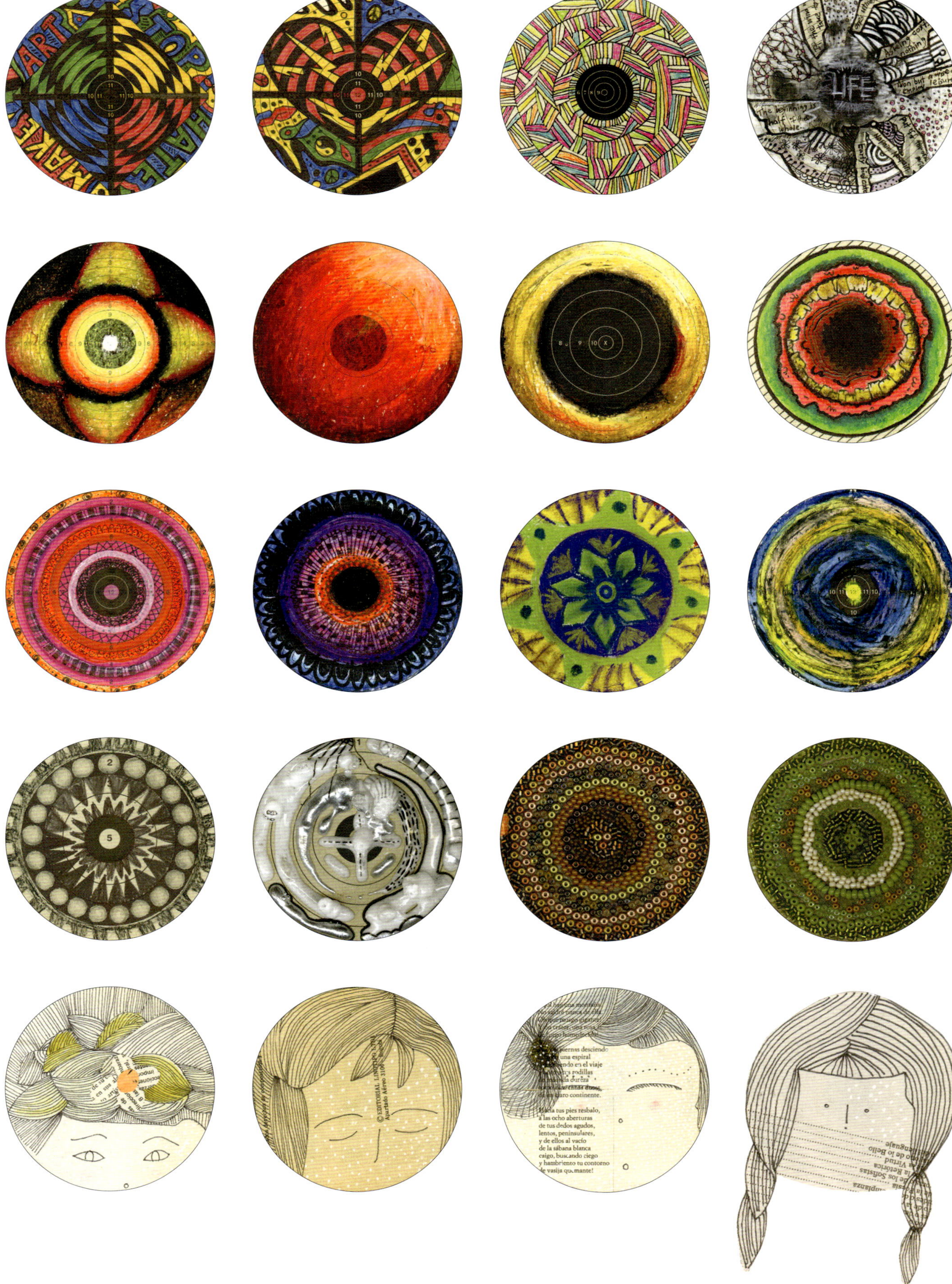

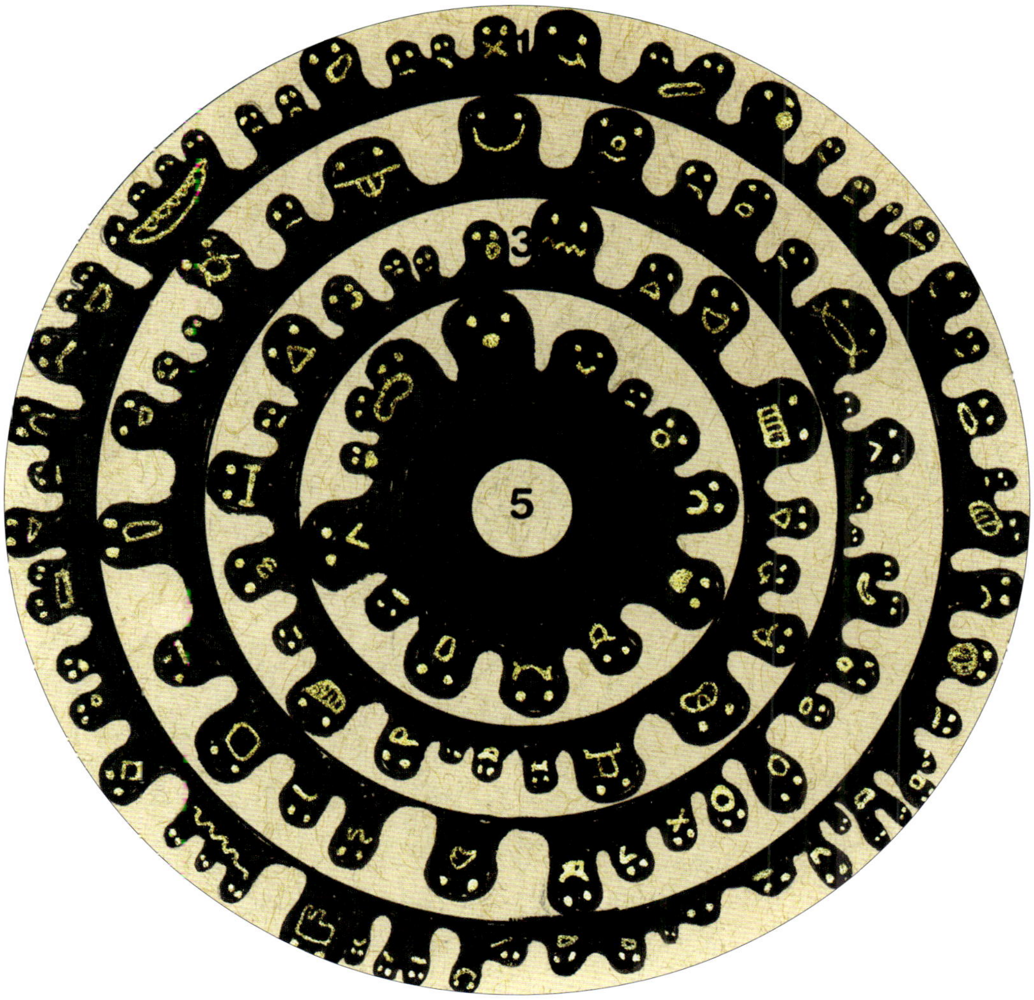

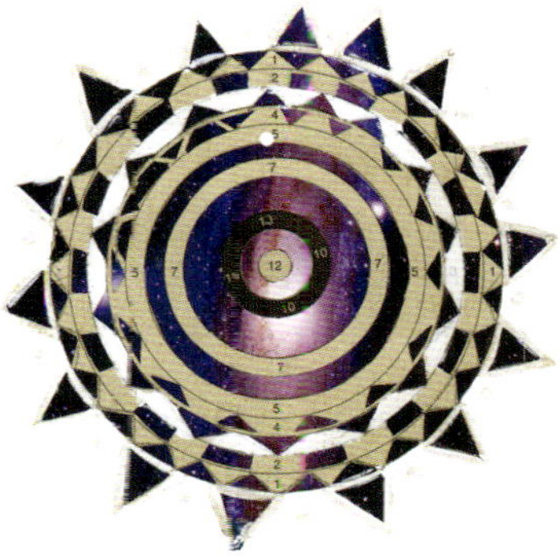

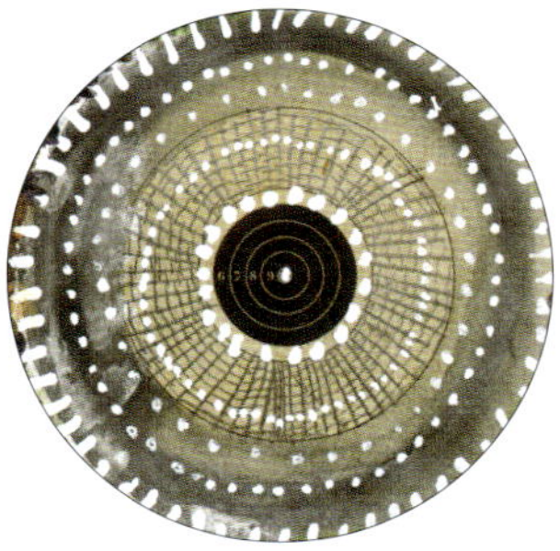

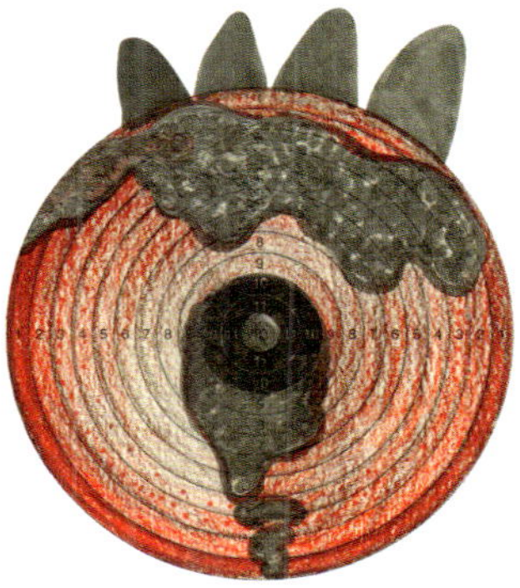

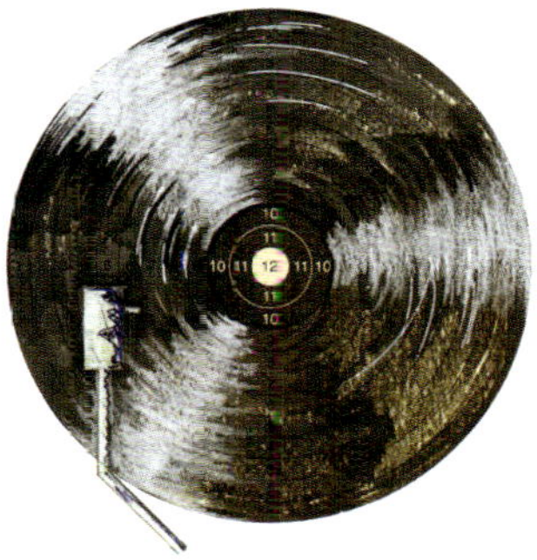

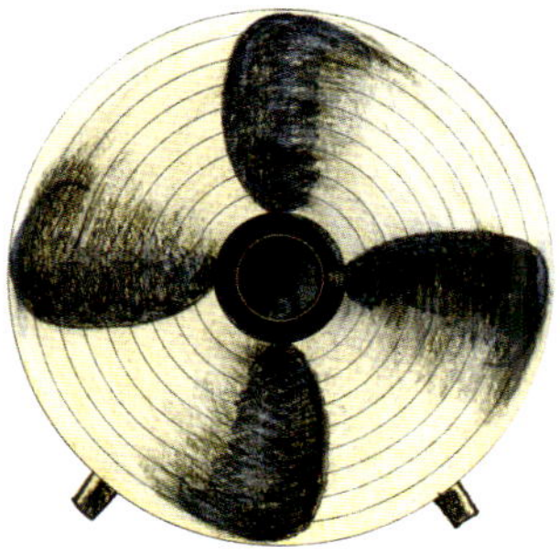

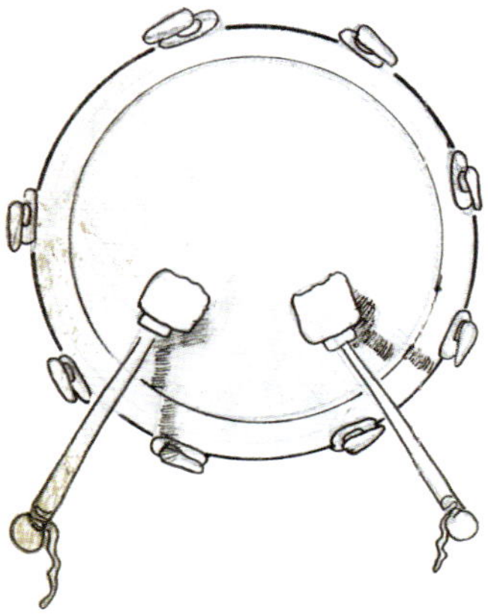

TARGET SOLUTIONS:

Figures 1 through 13 feature various forms of abstract imagery to convey expression.

Figures 14 through 16 are dimensional executions. Figure 14 uses paste and figures 15 and 16 use colored beads to create circular patterns.

Figures 17 through 20 use line and typography to create highly personal portraits.

Figure 21 is a humorous solution featuring a variety of facial expressions within the concentric circles of the target. At first glance the image echoes a bicycle gear.

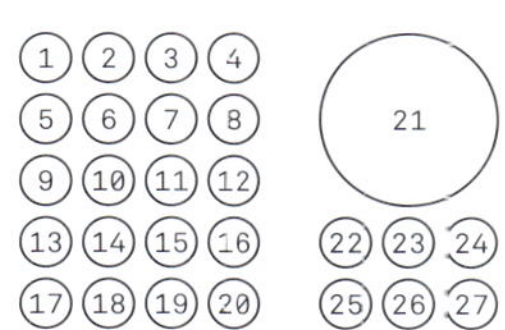

1–2. *Brent Philhower*
3. *Borim Kim*
4. *Jihye Cho*
5–7. *Jasmin Valcourt*
8. *Alex Morel*
9–10. *Kristin Naranjo*
11. *Sarah Liriano*
12. *Dan Reisman*
13. *Mikhail Abramov*
14. *Danielle Guzman*
15–16. *Yoonjoo Lee*
17–20. *Karen Montero*
21. *Jen Yi Chieh*
22. *S. Kim*
23. *Michele Demis*
24. *Camila Tramon*
25. *Anna Kim*
26. *Jaehyun Park*
27. *Jordan Wess*

Figures 22 through 24 are abstractions, while figures 25 through 27 are narrative solutions depicting commonplace objects.

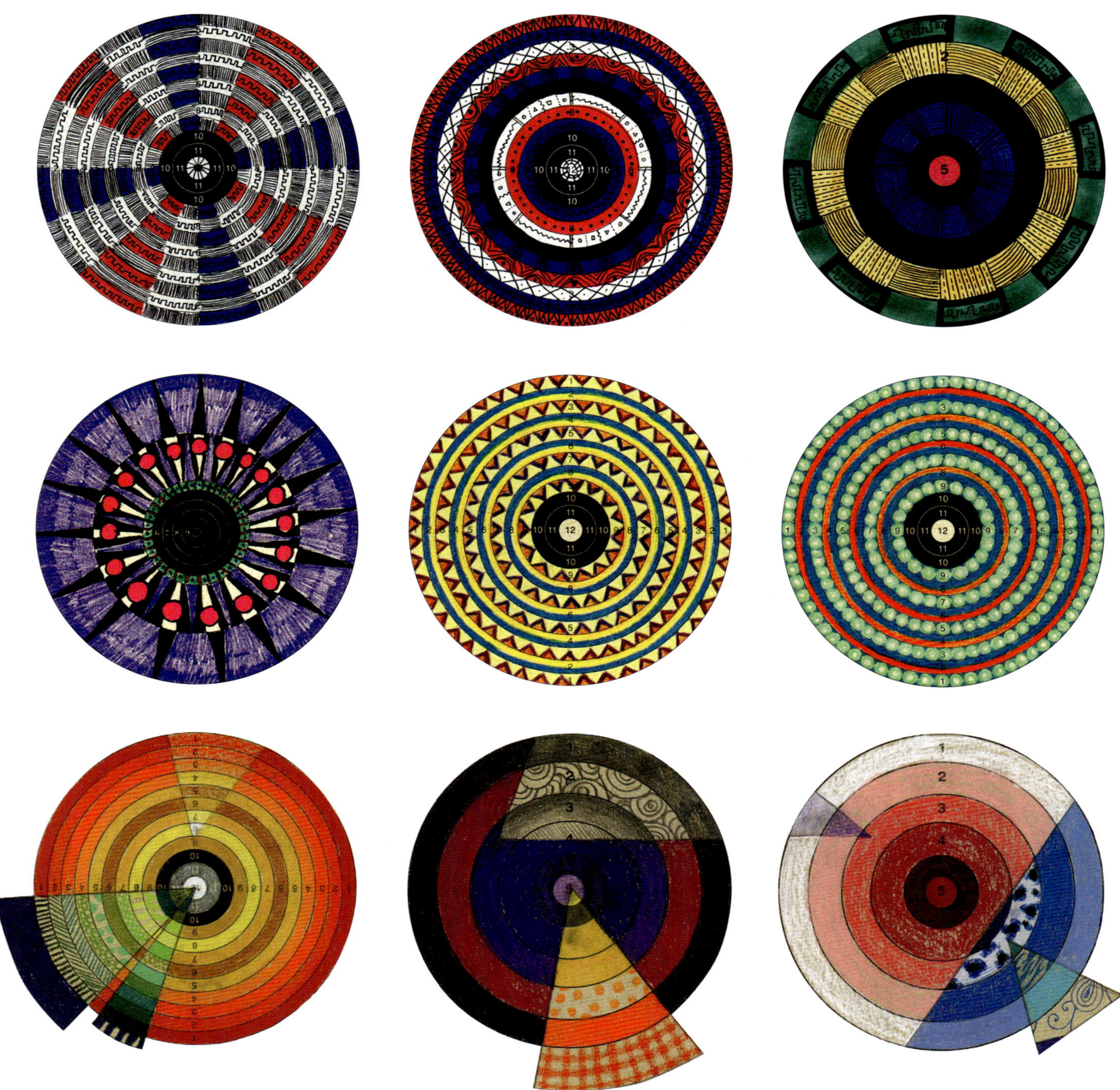

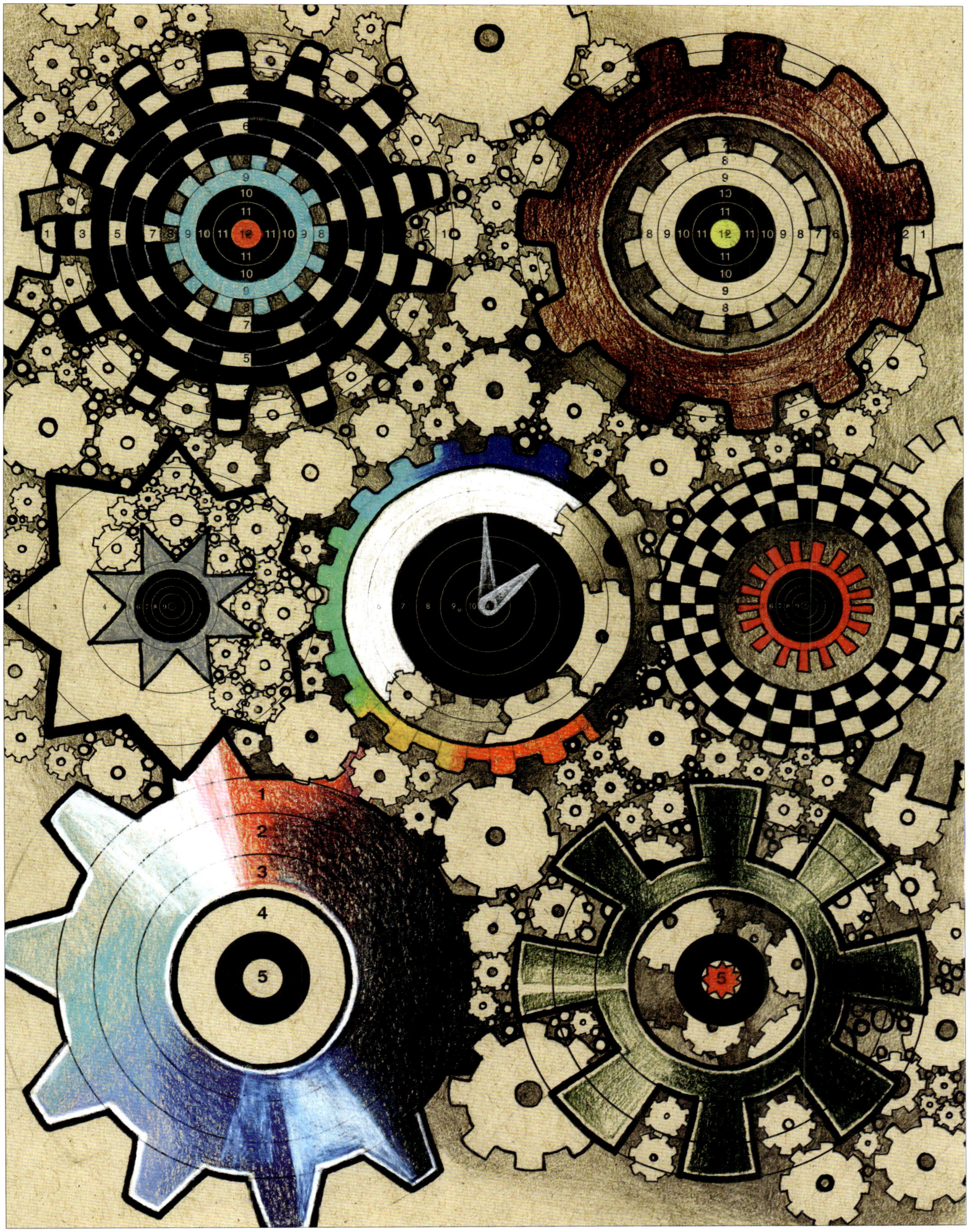

TARGET SOLUTIONS:

Figures 1 through 6 are heavily patterned geometric solutions that pay homage to the concentric circles that appear on the assignment sheet.

In figures 7 through 9, triangular shapes, as well as changes in color, interrupt the symmetry of the circles.

Figure 10 represents an entire assignment sheet that takes liberties in breaking out of the confinement of the given targets, creating a highly personal interpretation of the interaction of gears.

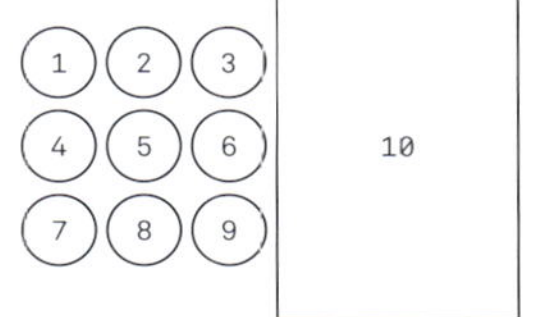

1–3. *Soohee Cho*
4. *Romina Leiva*
5–6. *Minji Han*
7–9. *Dasol Kim*
10. *Dongwoo Sohn*

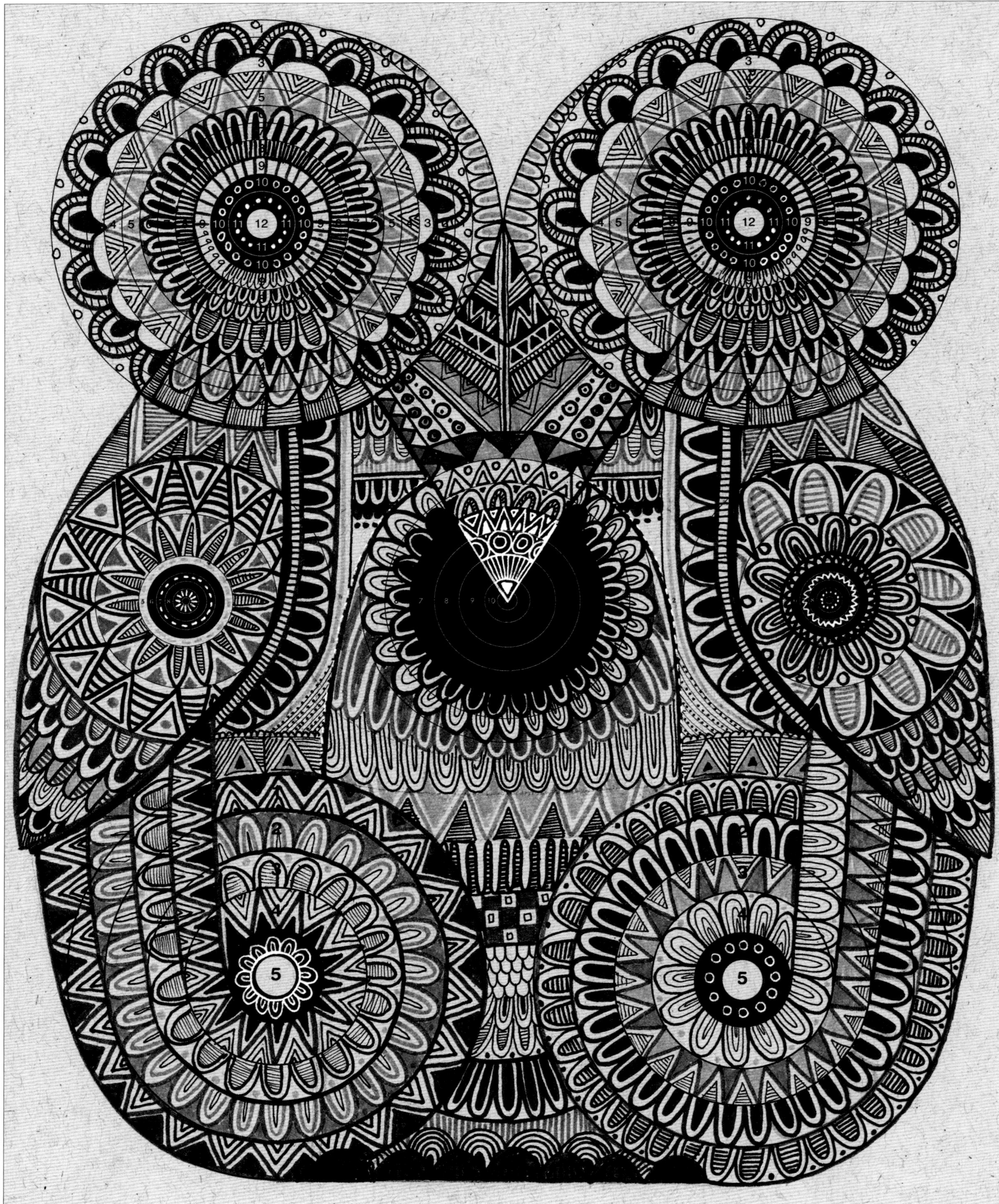

TARGET SOLUTIONS:

Figures 1 through 3 deal primarily with pattern, line tonality, and texture.

In figure 1 various linear, geometric shapes have been juxtaposed against one another in the creation of an owl. White is used against a circular black ground to accentuate the beak of the bird. Although the owl is essentially flat, the top portion of the beak appears dimensional.

In figure 2 hands are used as a pictorial element as well as a vehicle to depict the process of the development of the piece.

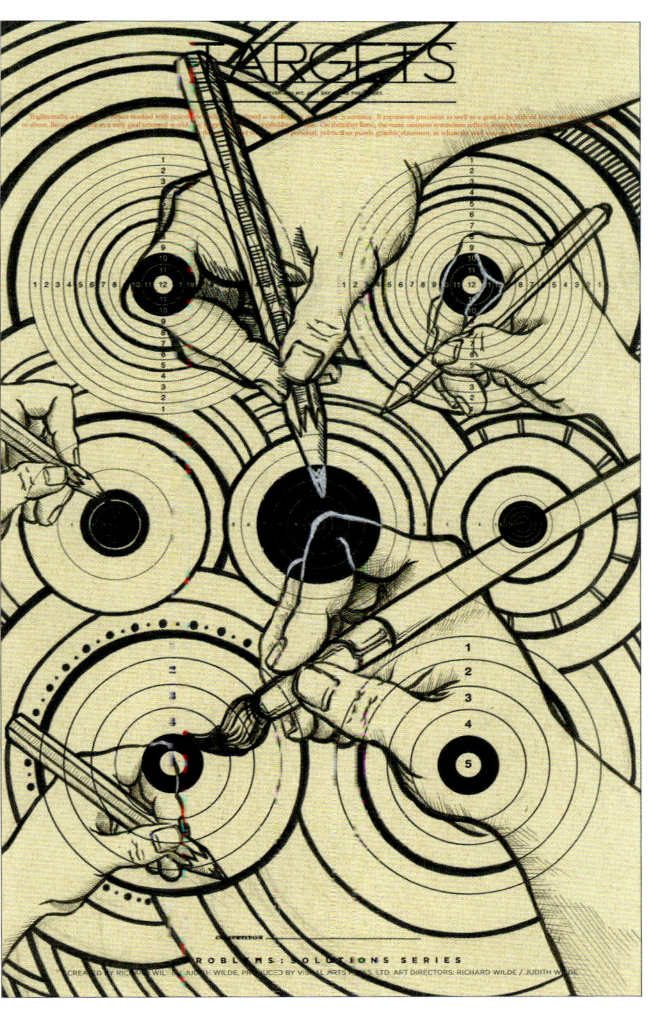

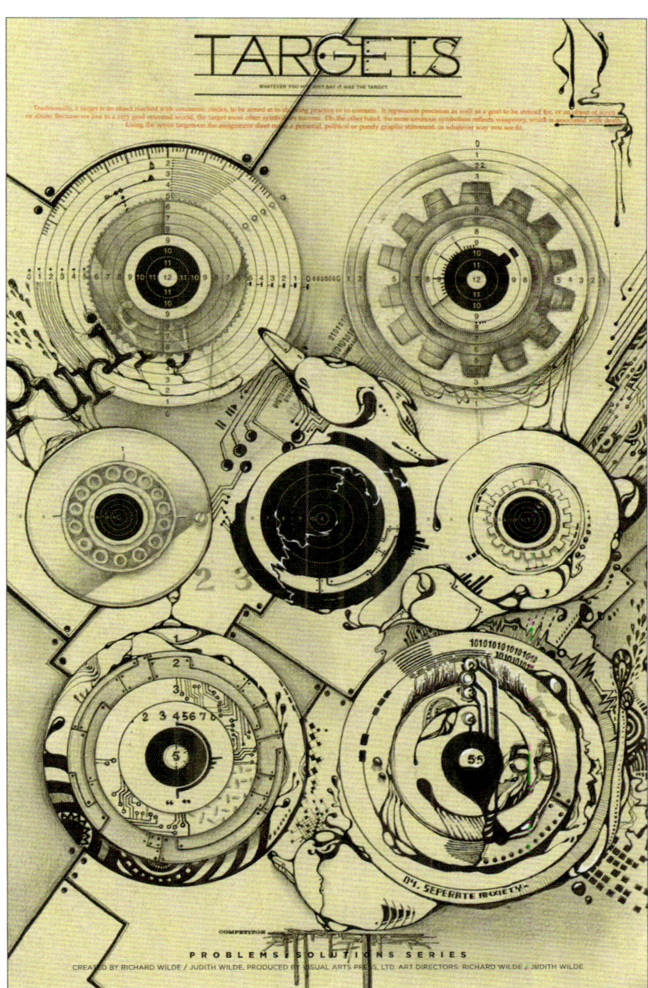

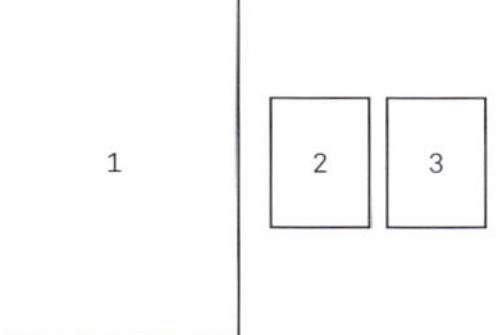

1. *Lucia Paul*
2. *Jill Brody*
3. *Monica Kim*

In figure 3, ink is coupled with pencil to give the targets a greater range of tonalities. The solution integrates both abstract and literal imagery.

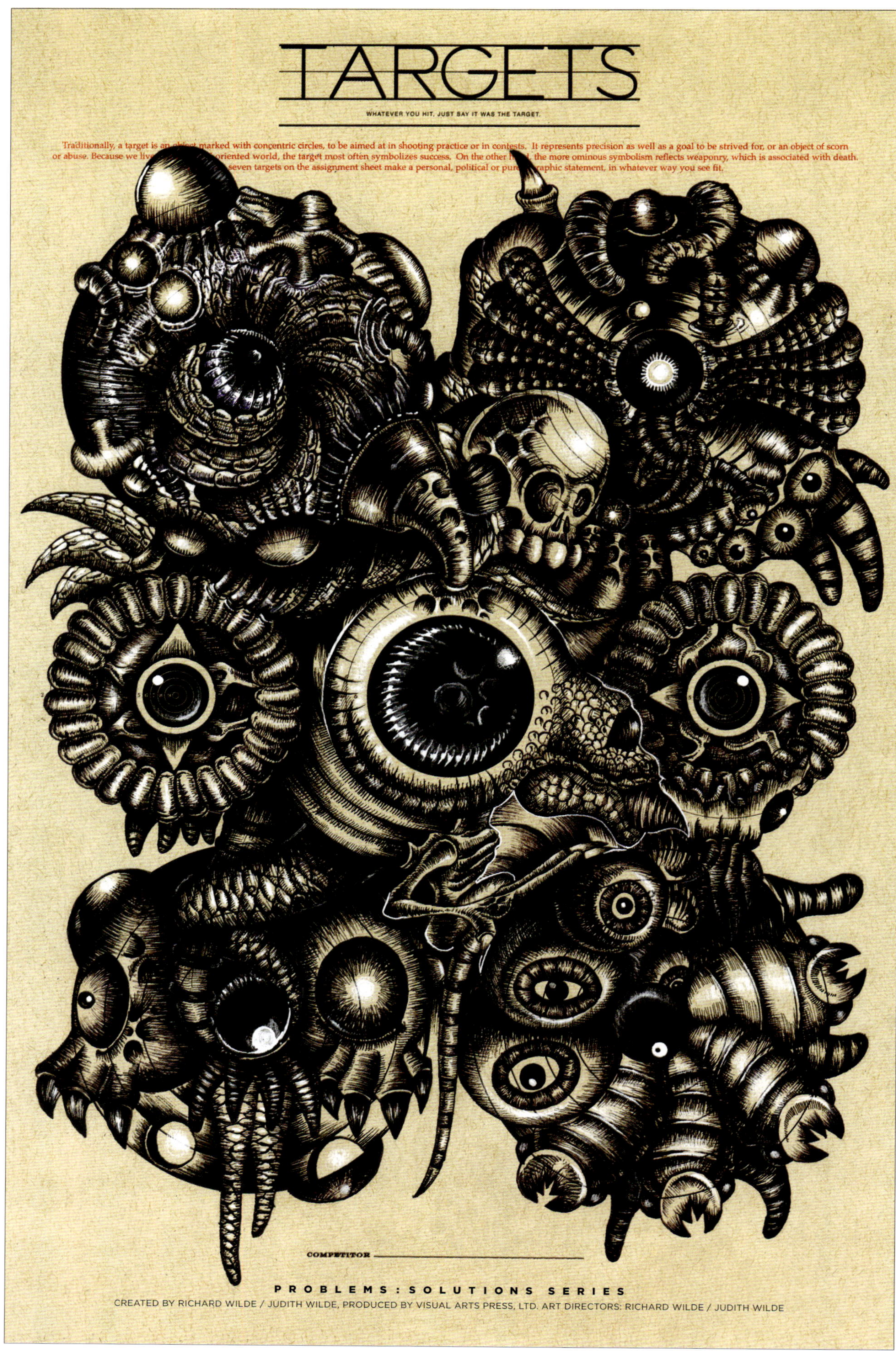
TARGETS
WHATEVER YOU HIT, JUST SAY IT WAS THE TARGET.
Traditionally, a target is an
marked with concentric circles, to be aimed at in shooting practice or in contests. It represents precision as well as a goal to be strived for, or an object of scorn
or abuse. Because we liv
oriented world, the target most often symbolizes success. On the other h
the more ominous symbolism reflects weaponry, which is associated with death.
seven targets on the assignment sheet make a personal, political or pur
raphic statement, in whatever way you see fit.
COMPETITOR
PROBLEMS : SOLUTIONS SERIES
CREATED BY RICHARD WILDE / JUDITH WILDE, PRODUCED BY VISUAL ARTS PRESS, LTD. ART DIRECTORS: RICHARD WILDE / JUDITH WILDE

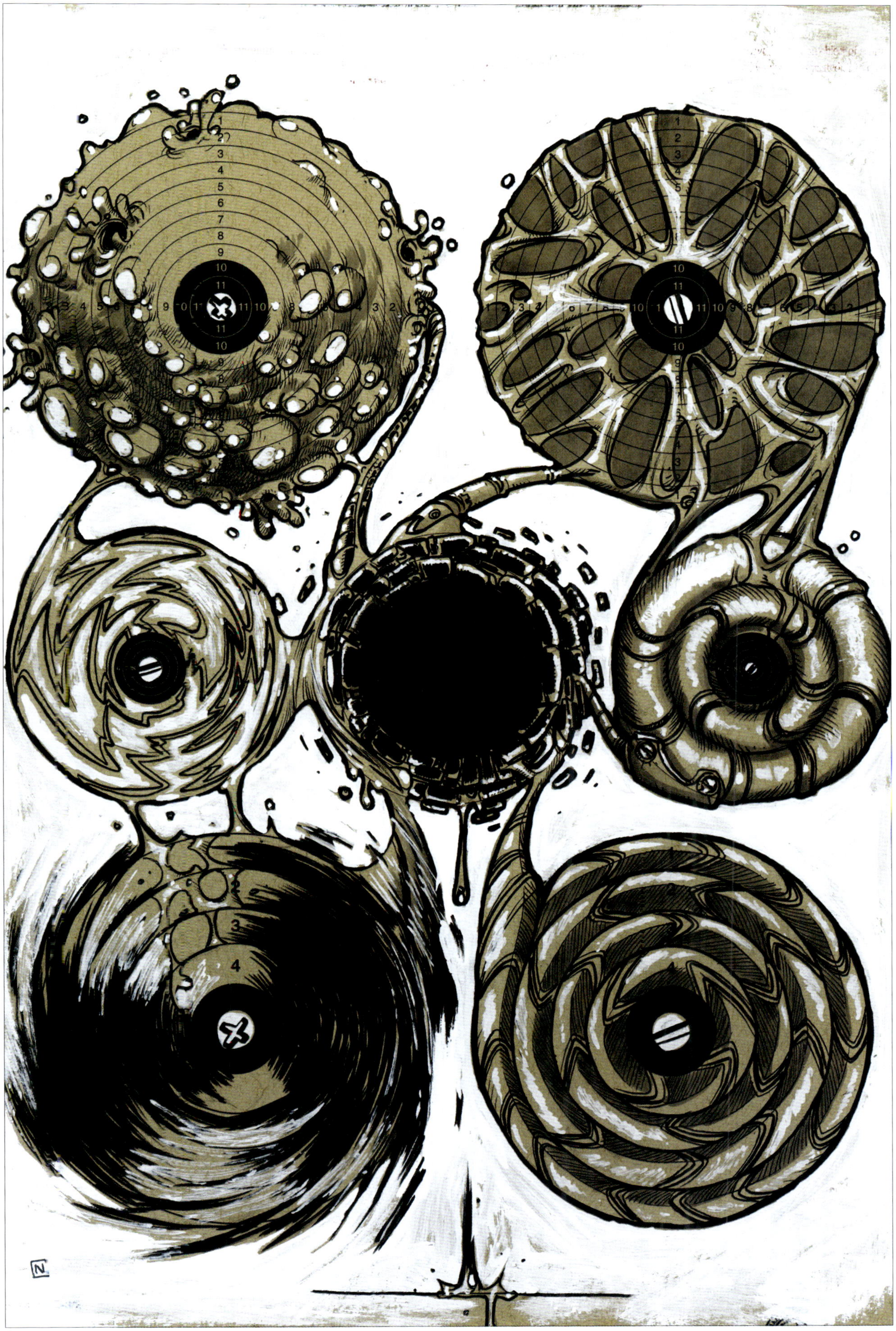

TARGET SOLUTIONS:

Figures 1 and 2 are both highly illustrative organic solutions.

Figure 1 investigates patterning that alludes to the allegorical imagery of a macabre world.

Figure 2 explores abstraction, while referencing organic life forms.

Both use white to dramatize the dimensionality of the drawn images.

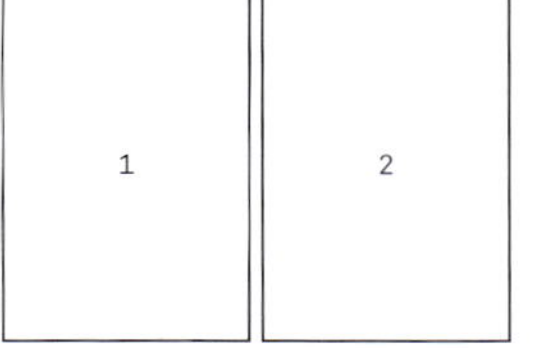

1. *Hao Yen Chuang*
2. *Fernando Pinto*

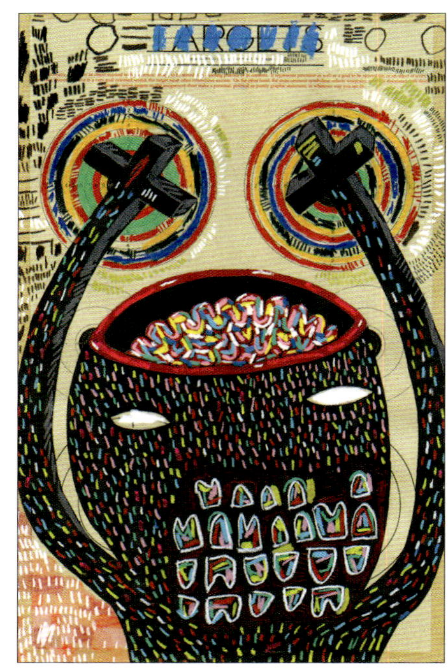

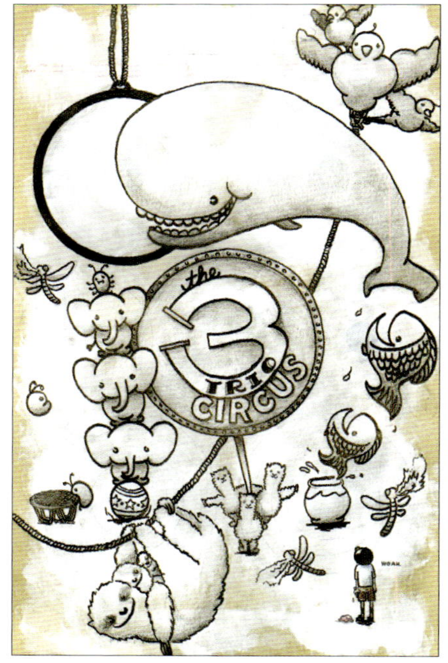
the
3
TRIO
CIRCUS

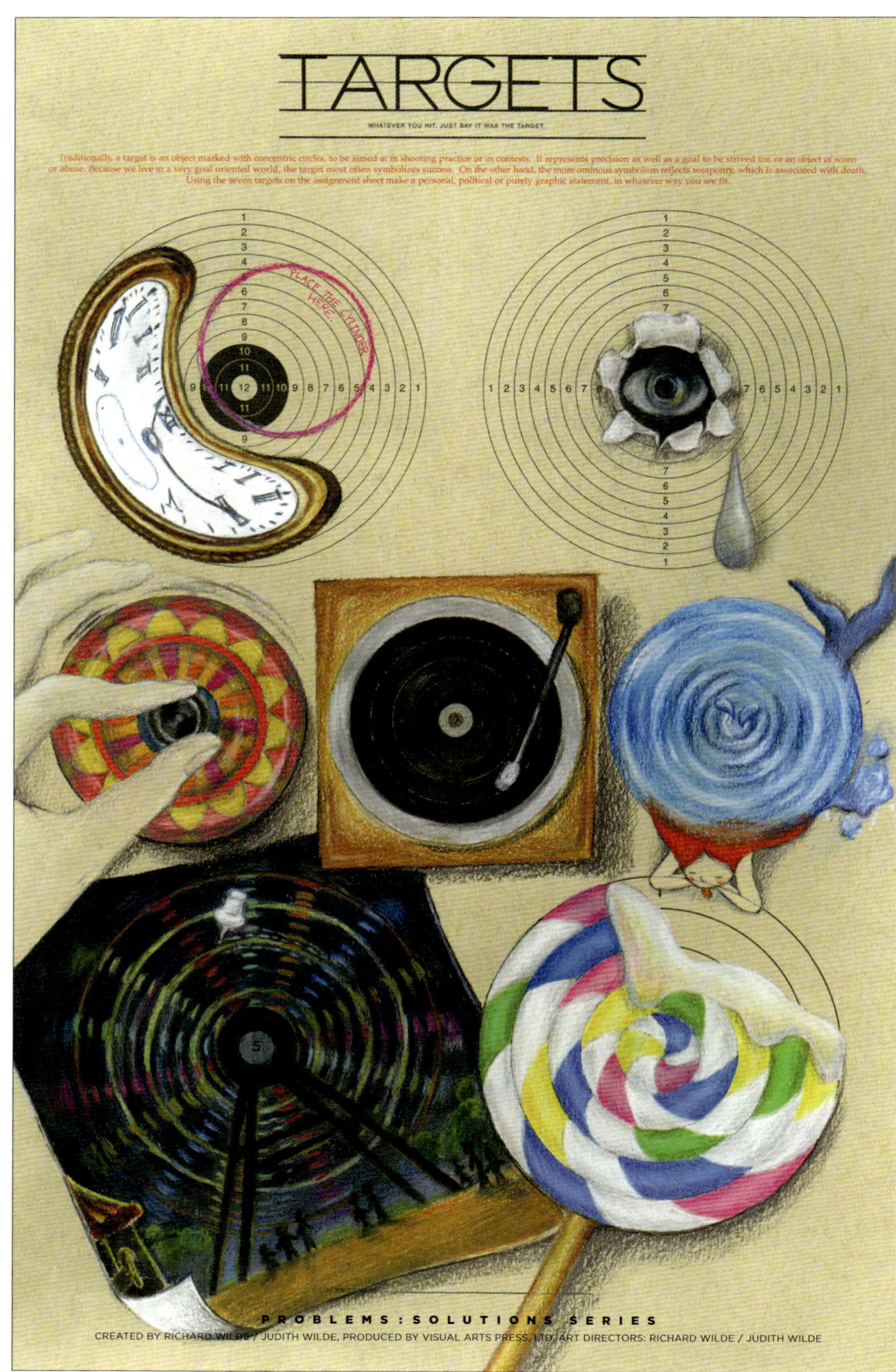
TARGETS
WHATEVER YOU HIT, JUST SAY IT WAS THE TARGET.
Traditionally, a target is an object marked with concentric circles, to be aimed at in shooting practice or in contests. It represents precision as well as a goal to be strived for, or an object of scorn or abuse. Because we live in a very goal oriented world, the target most often symbolizes success. On the other hand, the more ominous symbolism reflects weaponry, which is associated with death. Using the seven targets on the assignment sheet make a personal, political or purely graphic statement, in whatever way you see fit.
PLACE THE CYLINDER HERE
PROBLEMS : SOLUTIONS SERIES
CREATED BY RICHARD WILDE / JUDITH WILDE, PRODUCED BY VISUAL ARTS PRESS, LTD. ART DIRECTORS: RICHARD WILDE / JUDITH WILDE

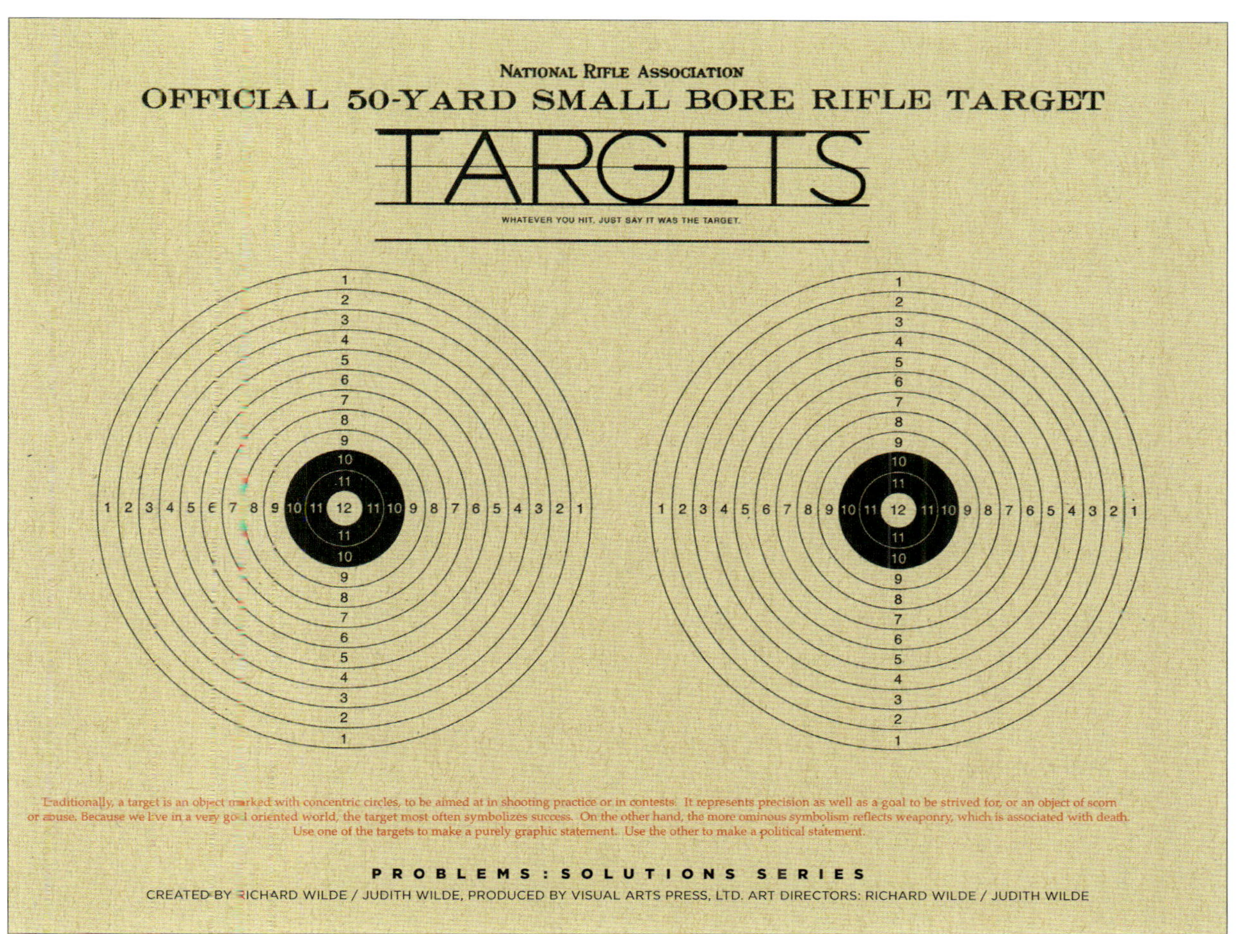

TARGET SOLUTIONS:

Figures 1 through 3 are narrative solutions. Yet, they represent distinctly different approaches to the given assignment.

In figure 1, only two targets are visible, and the assignment sheet has been transformed into a personal fantasy dominated by a strange colorful character.

Figure 2, "The 3 Trio Circus," is a black, white, and gray interpretation of animals playfully performing circus acts that has taken the liberty of referencing the given targets only minimally.

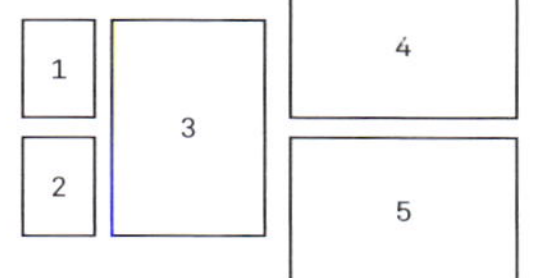

1. *Anna Richter*
2. *Emily Matsuno*
3. *Aemin Shim*
4. *Richard Wilde/Judith Wilde*
5. *Pablo Verdugo*

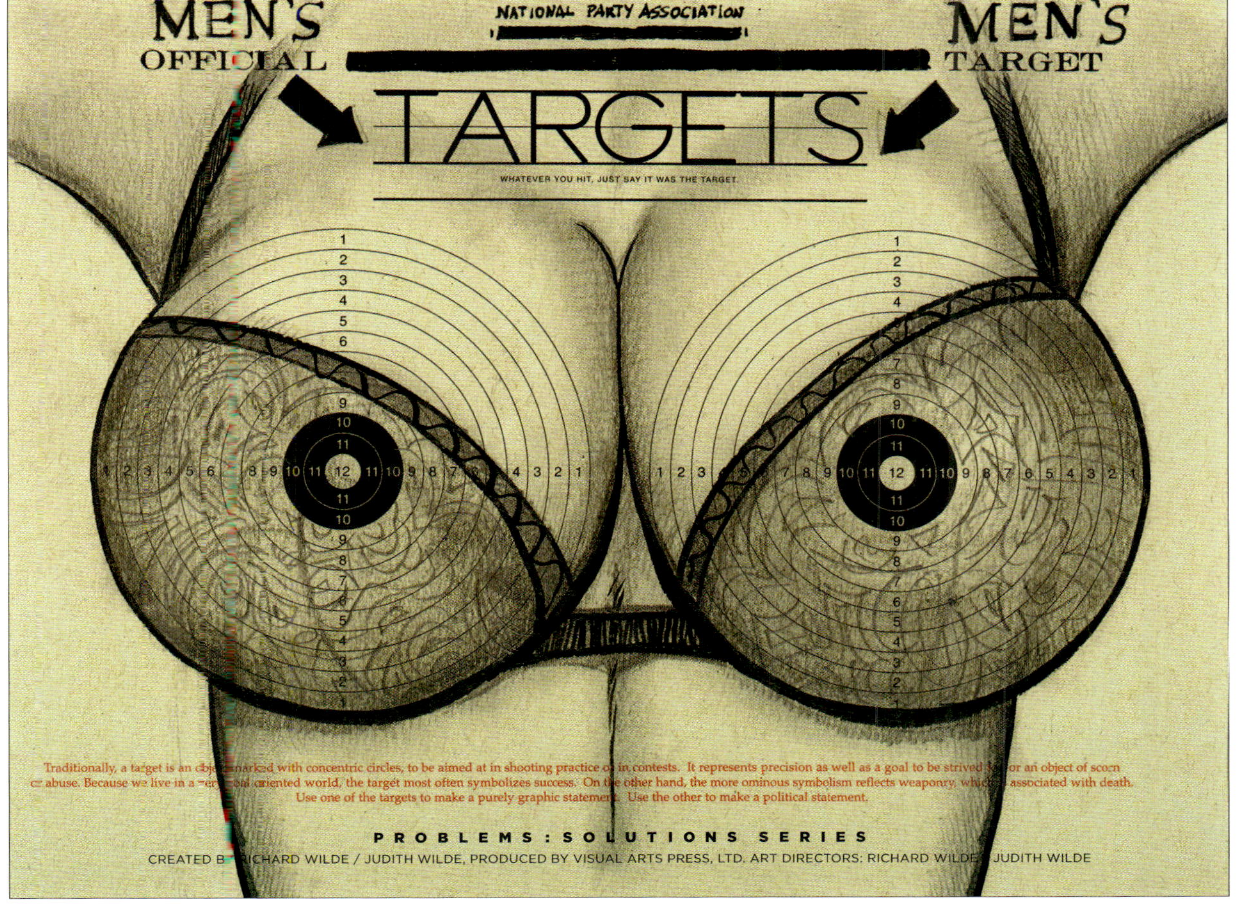

Figure 3, in contrast, focuses on seven different subjects, while maintaining the integrity of each target.

Figure 4 is a modified version of the assignment that is often given as preparation for the larger assignment.

Figure 5 uses tonality, line, and texture to create a dimensional image.

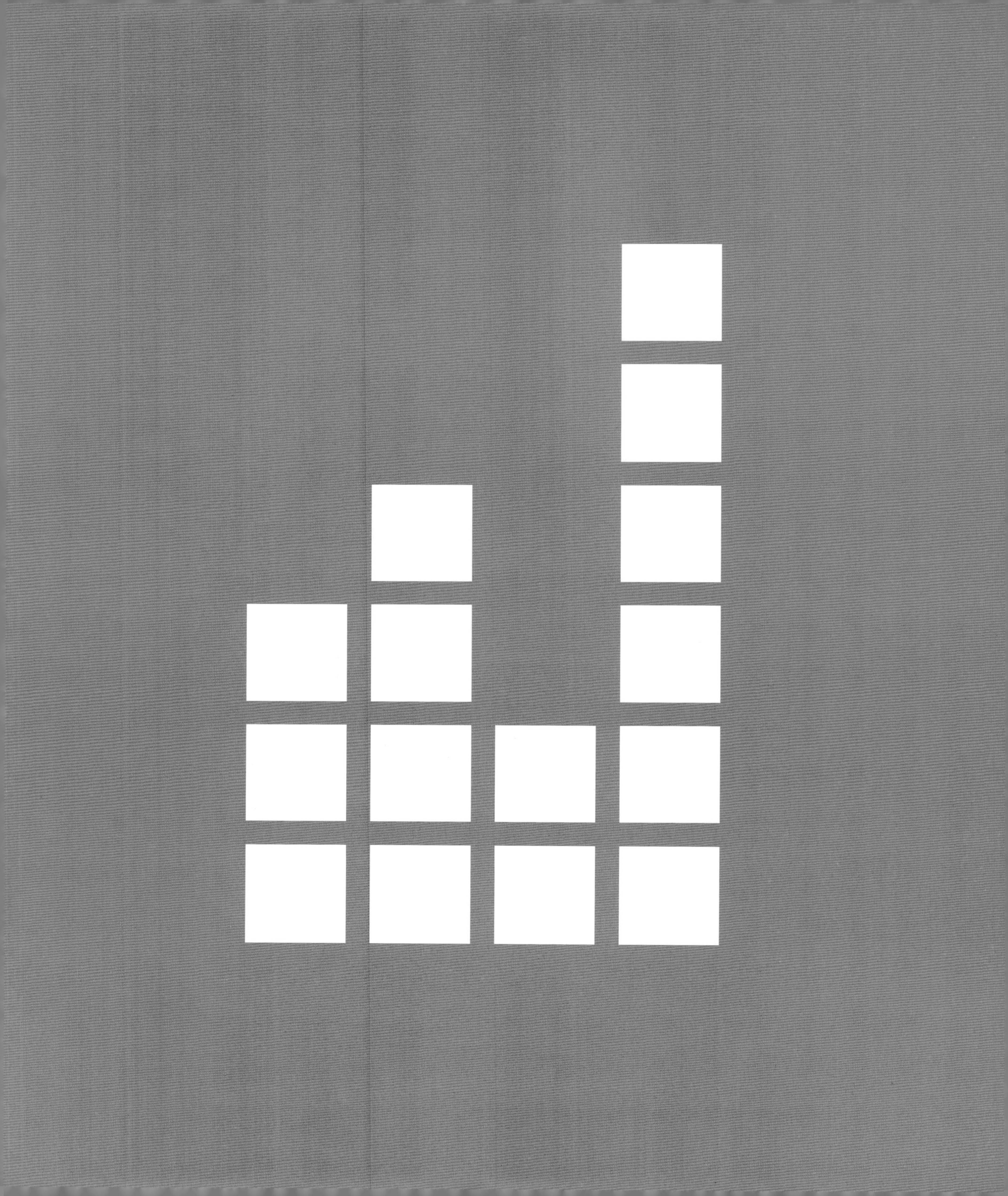

THOUGHTS ON THE CREATIVE PROCESS 3

One must overcome one's inability to begin. The blank page is the great pitfall of creativity. One must get past one's resistance, which takes the form of daydreaming, habitual reactions, procrastination and the feeling of incompetence in not knowing how to engage. One must simply begin.

SOUND PROBLEM

IN THE SPACES PROVIDED BELOW, GRAPHICALLY REPRESENT THE SOUNDS OF THE TOPICS INDICATED. CONSIDERATION OF THE CHARACTER OF THE SOUND IN TERMS OF ITS TEMPO, VOLUME, DURATION, CONTEXT AND COLOR IS ESSENTIAL. ALTHOUGH LITERAL PROBLEM SOLVING HAS ITS PLACE IN DESIGN, A GRAPHIC VOCABULARY MUST BE EXPANDED BEYOND A NARRATIVE VOICE. THE USE OF METAPHOR, SYMBOLISM, ABSTRACTION, AND TYPOGRAPHY ARE ENCOURAGED.

FRUSTRATION	INDIGESTION	BARNYARD
SHORT ORDER COOK	AVALANCHE	GUILLOTINE
REJECTION	A HABIT	LOUD PERSON
TAP DANCER	BIRTHDAY	SUBWAY

PROBLEMS : SOLUTIONS SERIES

CREATED BY RICHARD WILDE / JUDITH WILDE, PRODUCED BY VISUAL ARTS PRESS, LTD. ART DIRECTORS: RICHARD WILDE / JUDITH WILDE

SOUND PROBLEM:

Visually represent the specific sounds of the subjects listed on the assignment sheet by distilling the character of each sound into a formal equivalent. Consider the tempo, volume, duration, line, form, texture, tension, color, space, and context. Keep in mind that one has the benefit of text, which offers a wider range of executional directions.

AIM:
Although literal problem solving has its place in design, one's graphic vocabulary must be expanded beyond the narrative voice.

The subjects on the assignment sheet can be solved using abstraction, metaphor, symbolism, and typography.

While there are no right or wrong solutions, one still needs to find a balance between an overly abstract solution, which might embody new form but is lacking in terms of communication, and an obvious clichéd solution, which may communicate well but lacks visual impact.

SUGGESTIONS:
It is important to remember that the Sound Problem, with its vast array of subjects, forces one into the unknown where one is being called upon to create a visual interpretation for the sound of a specific subject, rather than the subject itself.

SPECIFICATIONS:
There are no limitations on medium or color.

NOTES:
The assignment sheet shown represents twelve of the subjects given for the Sound Problem; however, there are sixty subjects in all reviewed in this chapter.

3

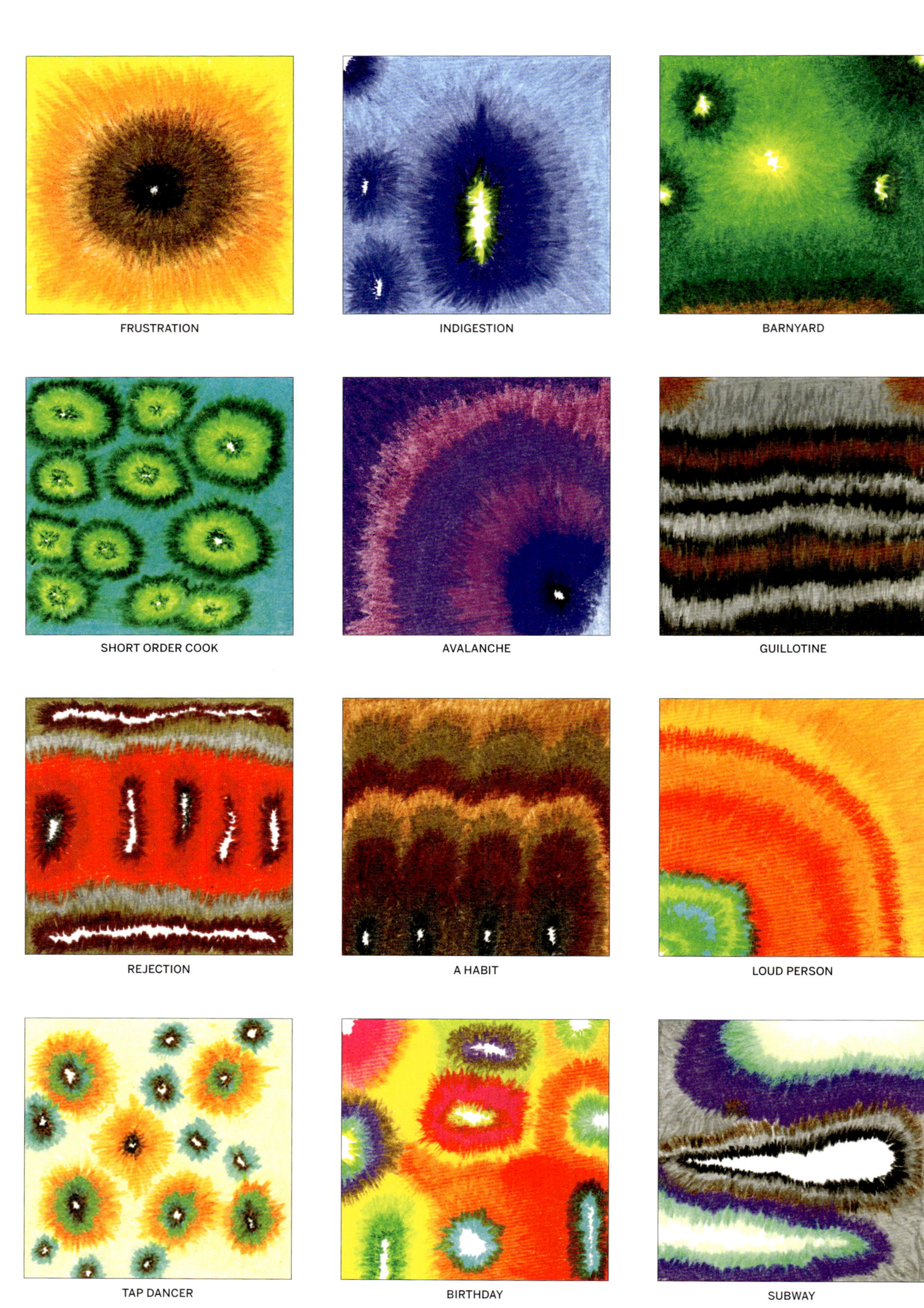
FRUSTRATION
INDIGESTION
BARNYARD
SHORT ORDER COOK
AVALANCHE
GUILLOTINE
REJECTION
A HABIT
LOUD PERSON
TAP DANCER
BIRTHDAY
SUBWAY

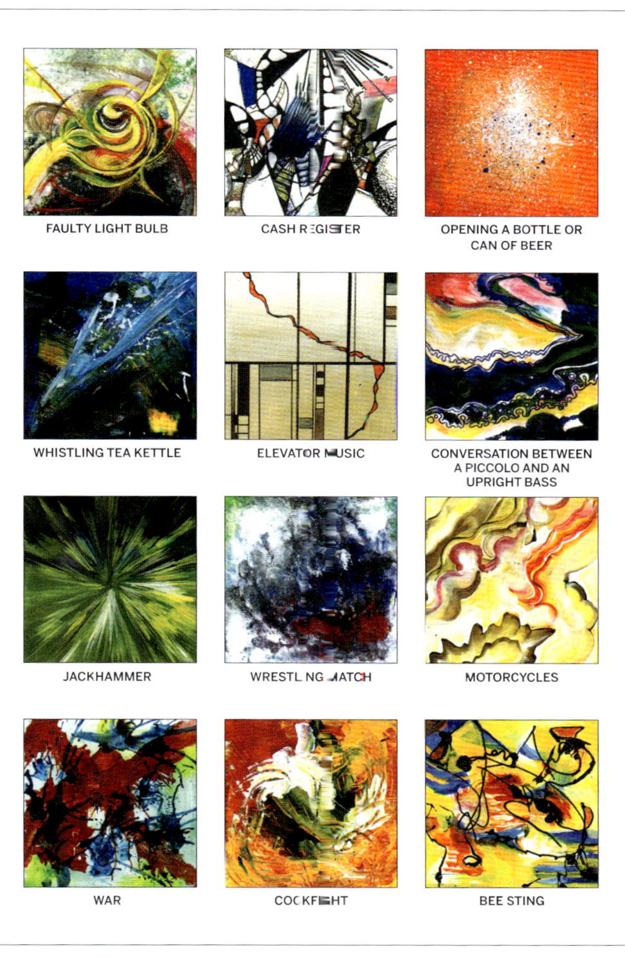

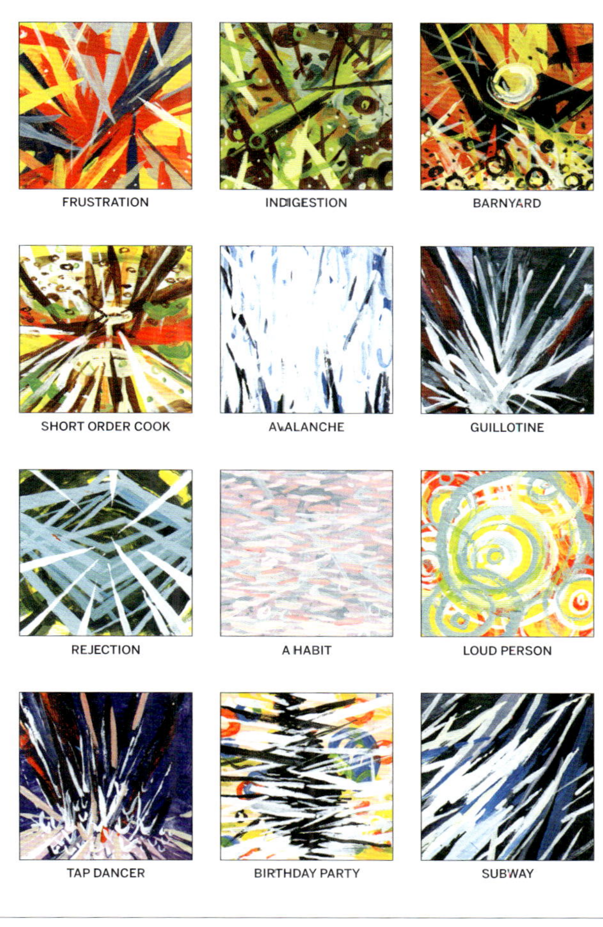

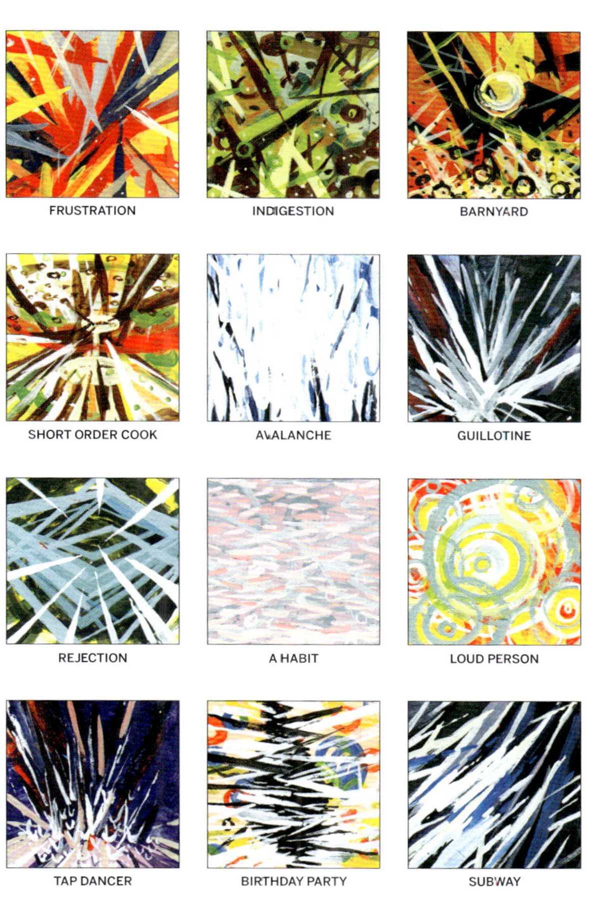

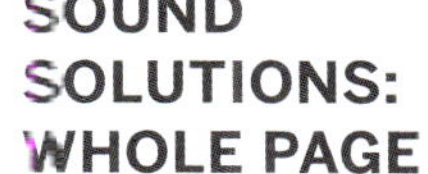

SOUND SOLUTIONS: WHOLE PAGE

Figures 1 through 5 represent the problem as given in this assignment to express the sounds of twelve different subjects. The following are various personal solutions that move one toward an inner voice, and in turn empower one's openness to invention. Each of the five solutions exhibits a clear stylization.

Figures 1 through 3 express an emotional response to the project.

Figure 4 is a mannered solution that utilizes geometry, reductive form, and flat imagery.

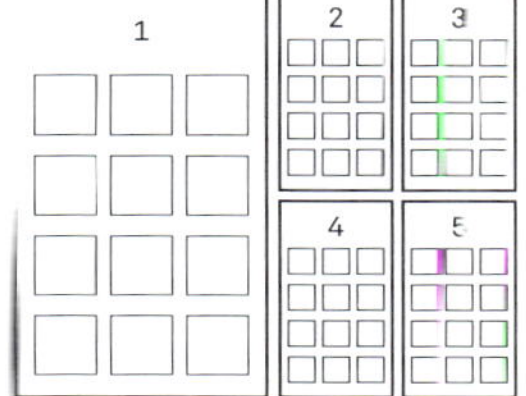

1. *Estefania Ferrand*
2. *Eunjung Yoo*
3. *Caleb Brown*
4. *Scott Buchan*
5. *Angela Ham*

Figure 5 straddles the two worlds of classicism and romanticism.

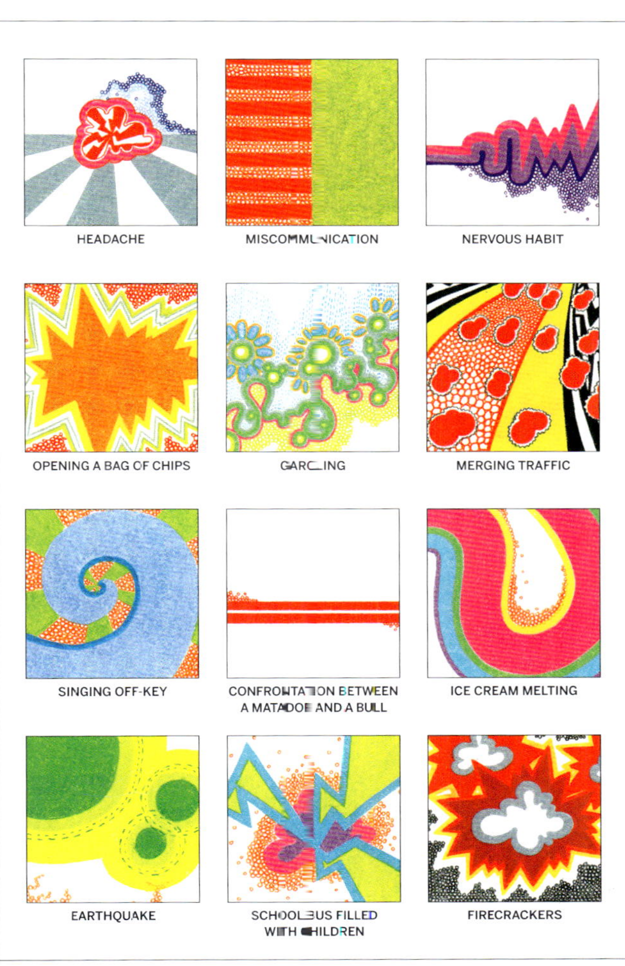

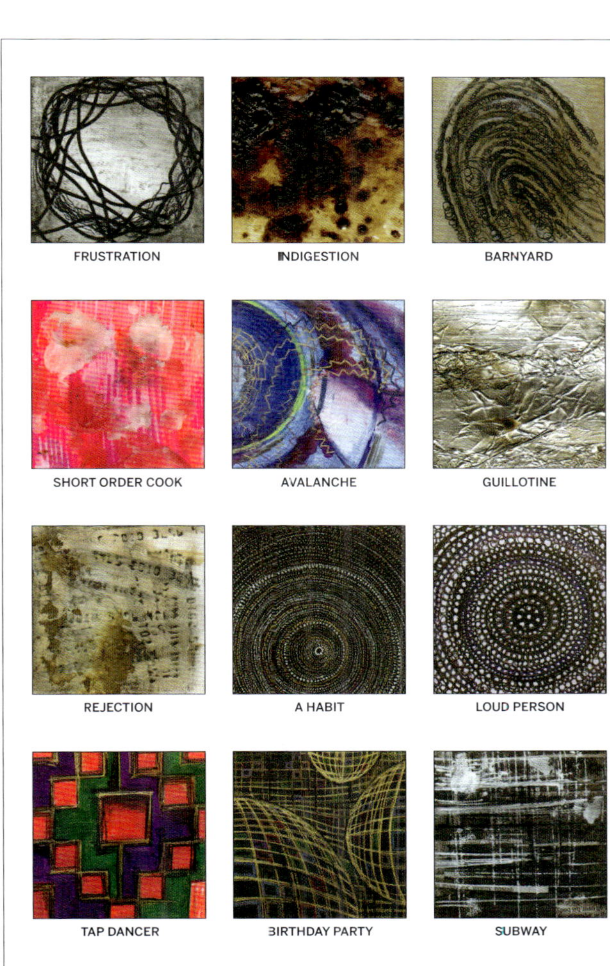

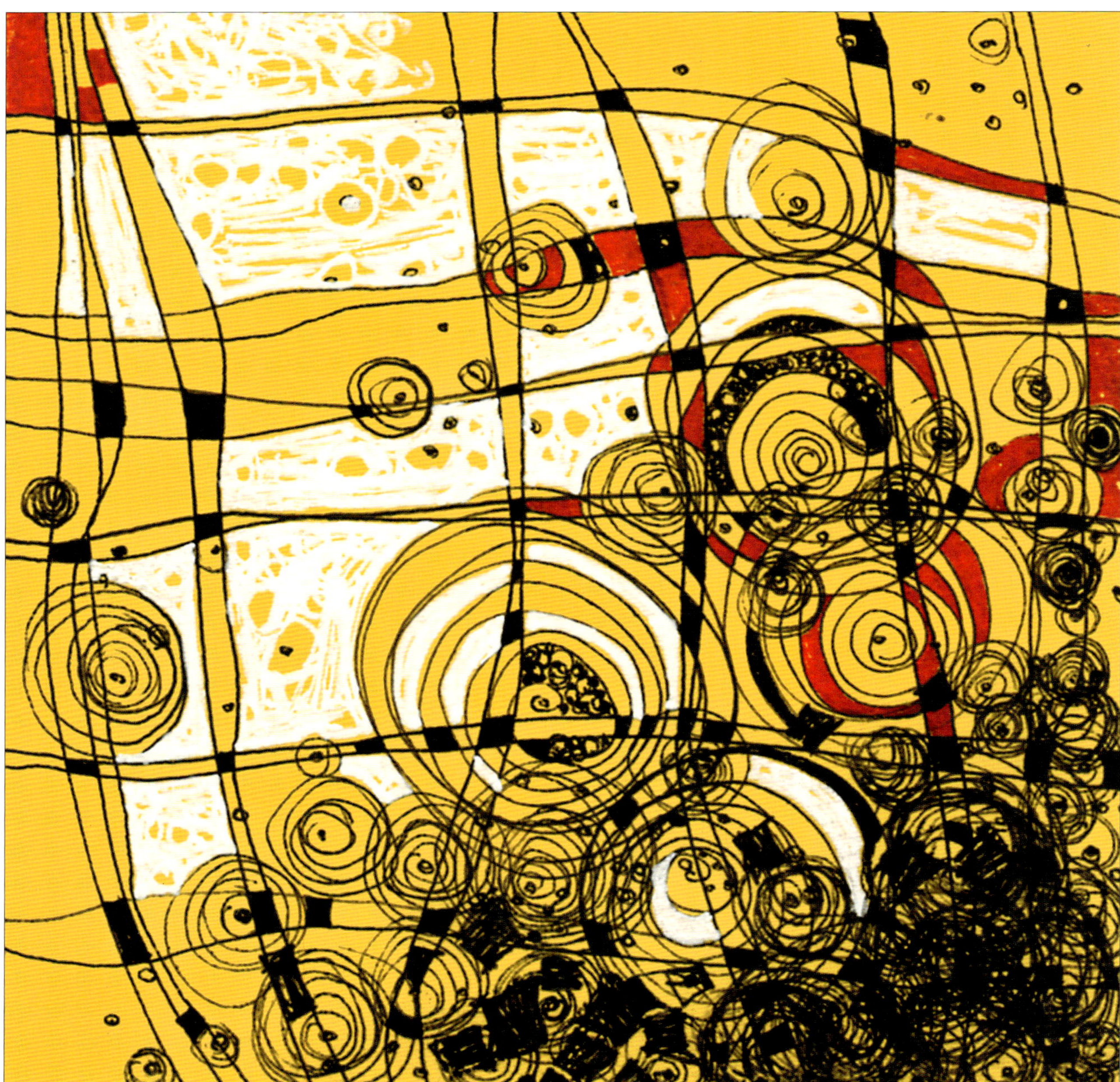

BEE STING

SOUND SOLUTIONS: BEE STING

Although an actual bee sting is silent, one can draw from this event to include: the puncture wound, the buzzing sound prior to being stung, and the cry of pain. These elements can all be used as a starting point for expressing one's idea of what the sound might entail.

Figure 1 uses a limited palette that is representational of a bee's coloring. Here the color red references blood or swelling associated with the pain of a bee sting. Spontaneity and movement add drama to this solution.

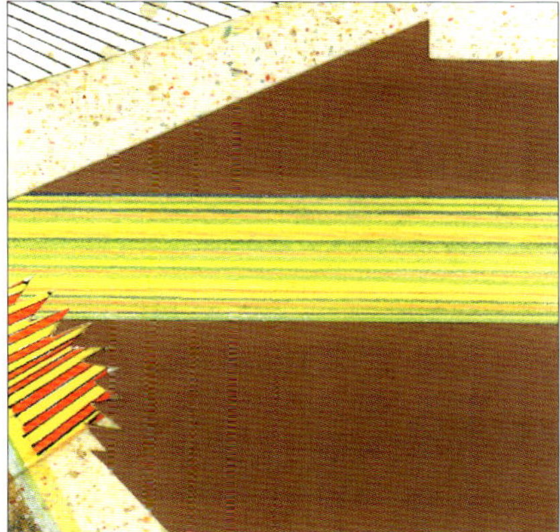

BEE STING

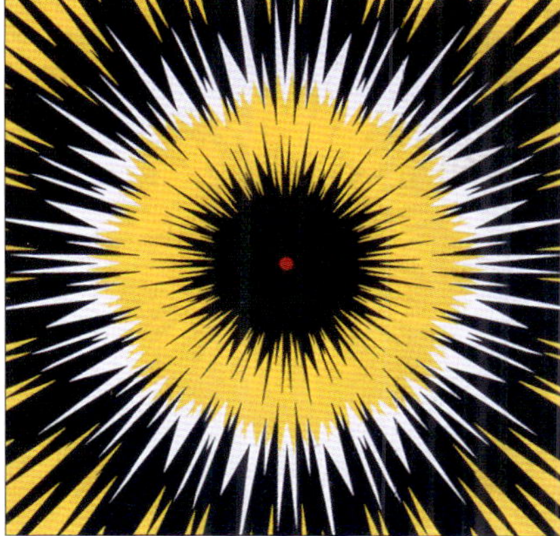

BEE STING

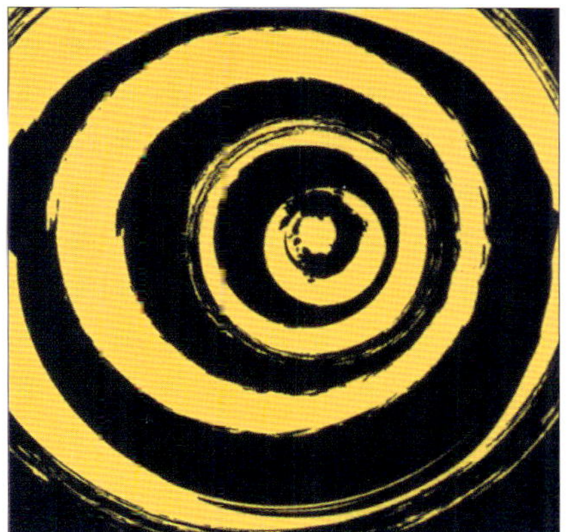

BEE STING

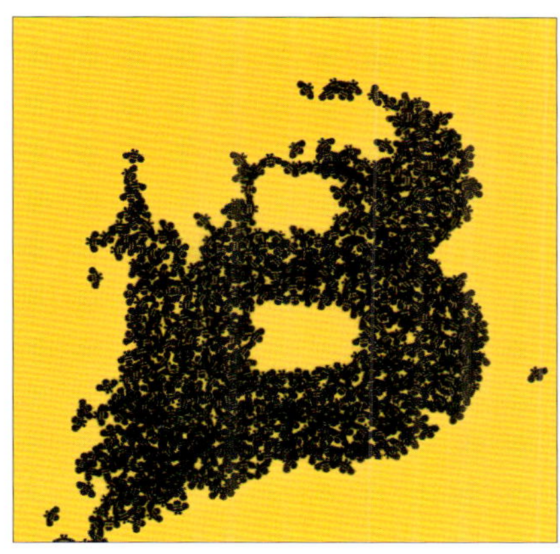

BEE STING

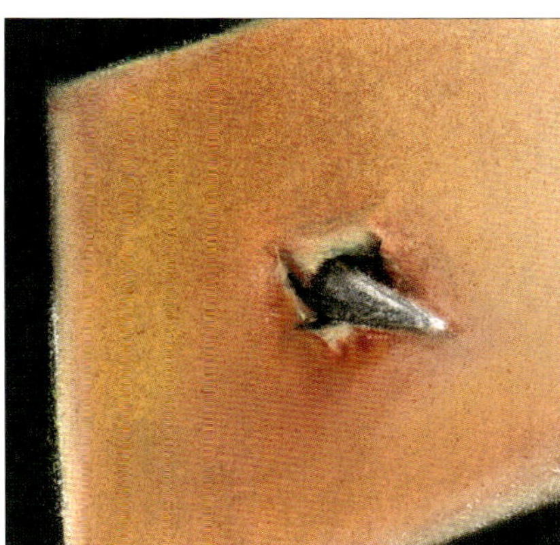

BEE STING

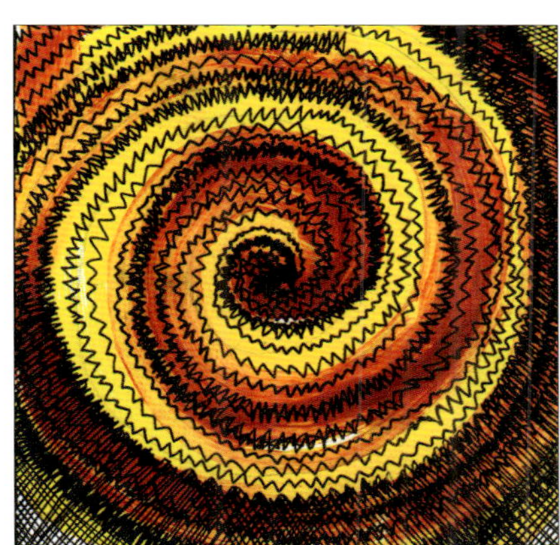

BEE STING

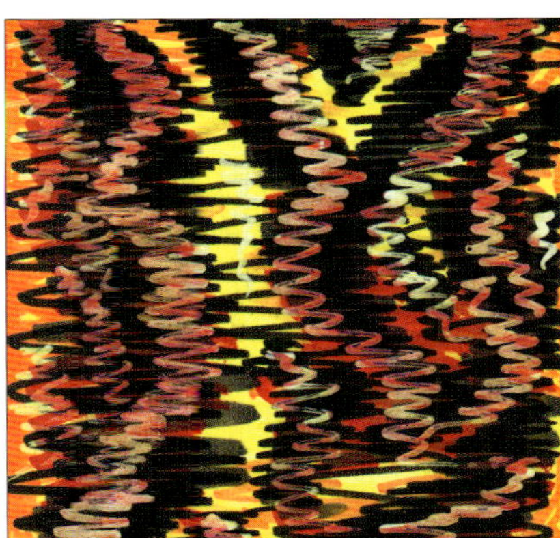

BEE STING

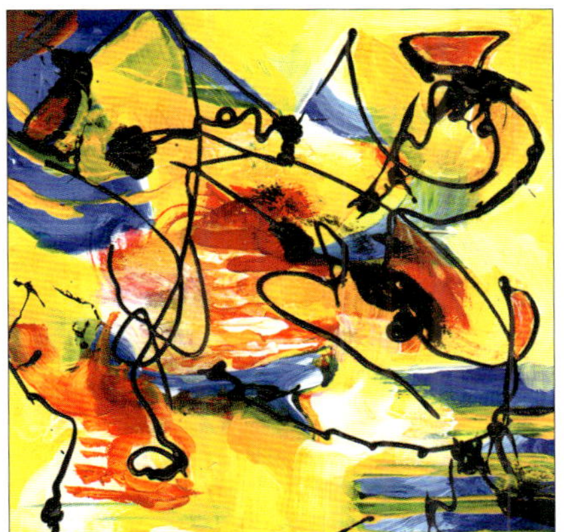

BEE STING

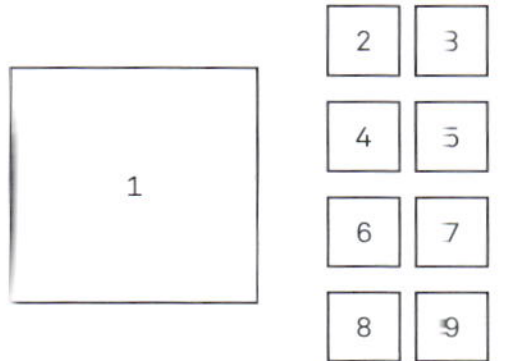

1. *Nataliya Hats*
2. *Yueh Lu*
3. *Wei Lieh Lee*
4. *Matthew Sablan*
5. *Sunwoo Ann*
6. *M. Takagi*
7. *J. Kim*
8. *Cherry Moon*
9. *Eunjung Yoo*

In solutions 2 through 9 black, yellow, and red are the dominant colors used to depict the subject.

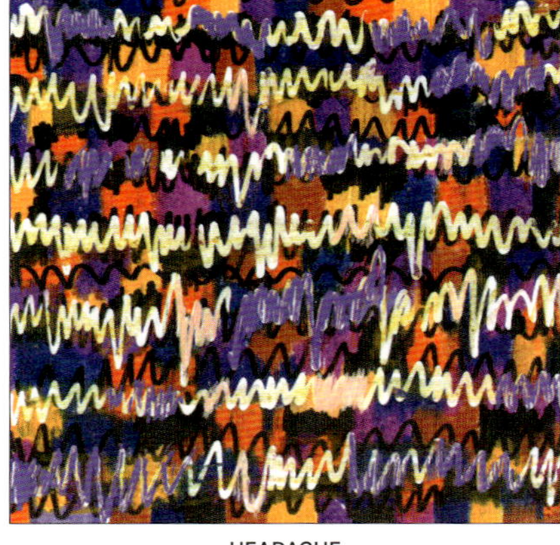
HEADACHE

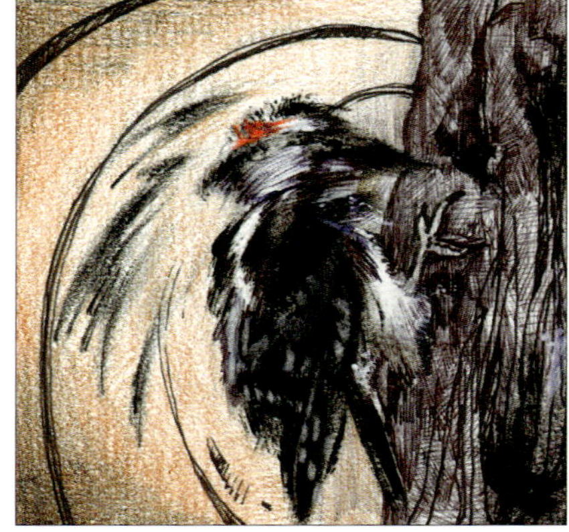
HEADACHE

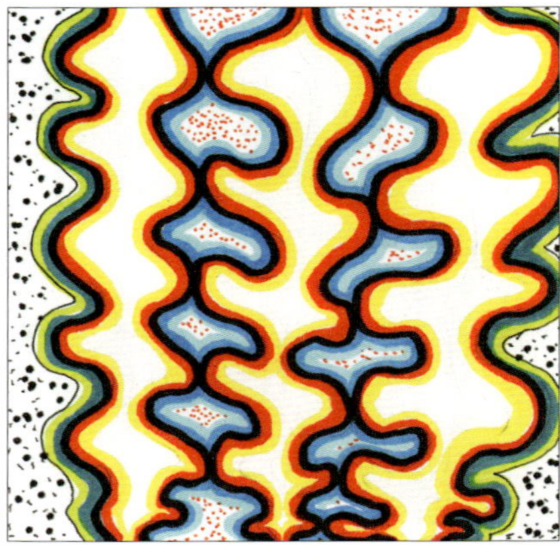
HEADACHE

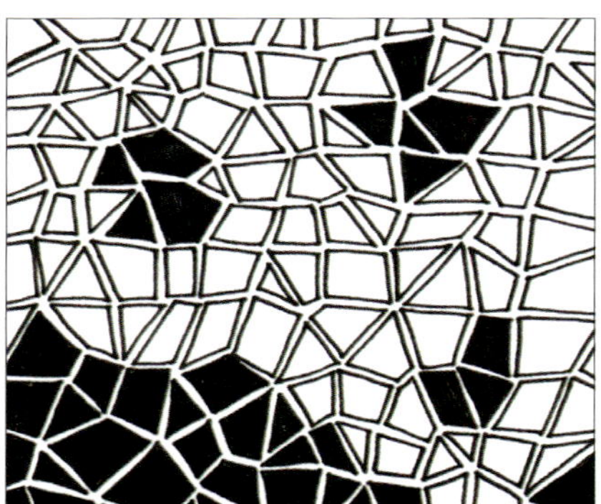
HEADACHE

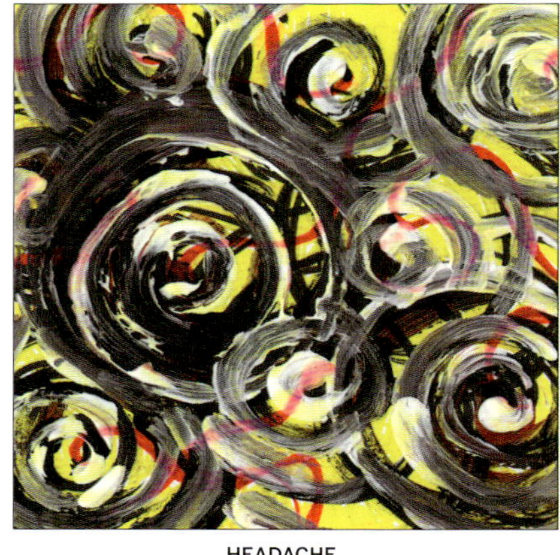
HEADACHE

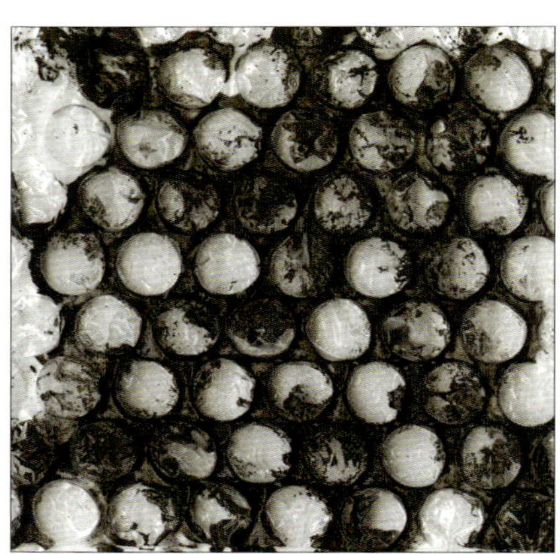
HEADACHE

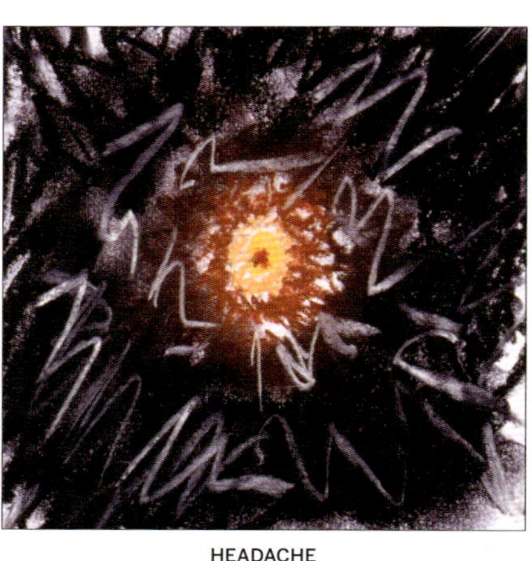
HEADACHE

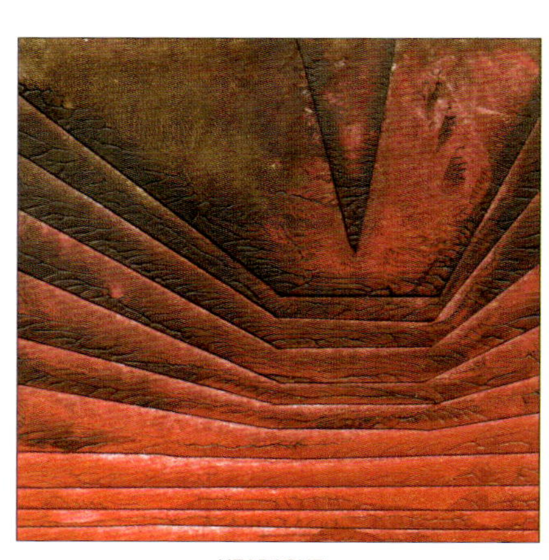
HEADACHE

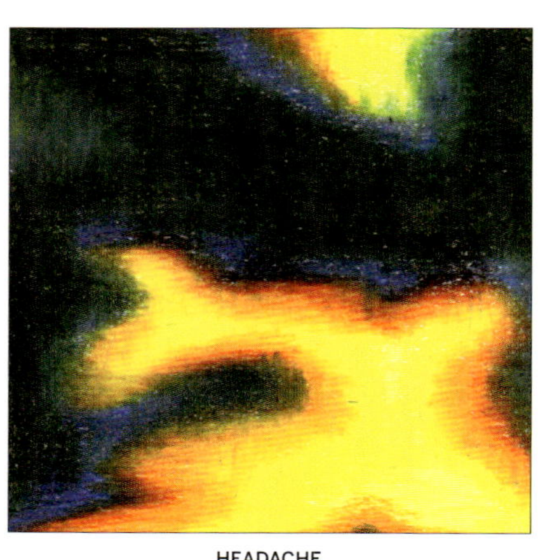
HEADACHE

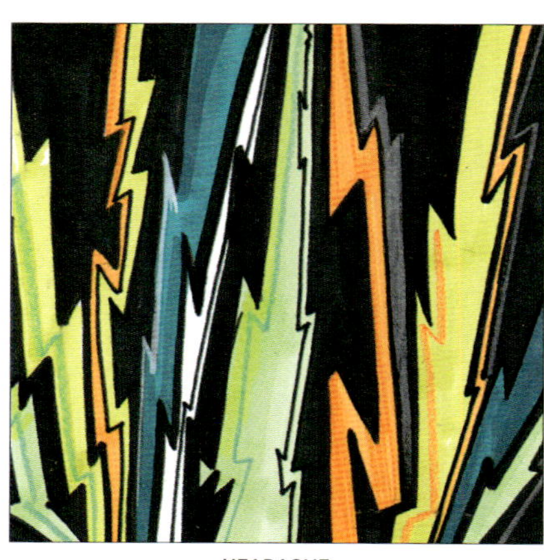
HEADACHE

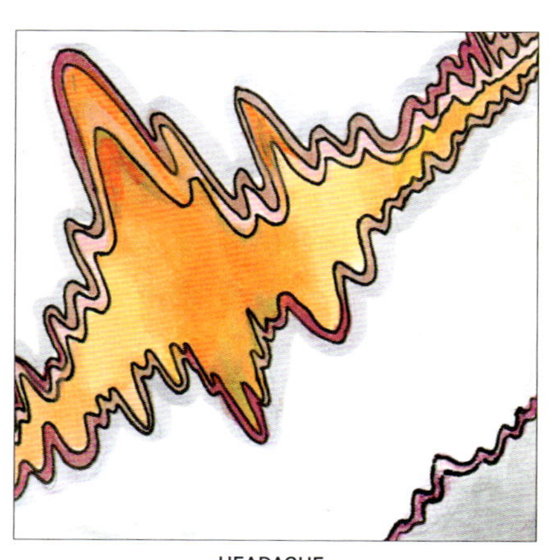
HEADACHE

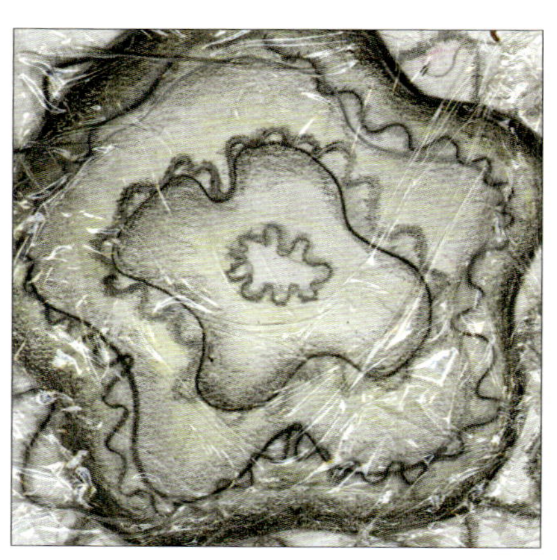
HEADACHE

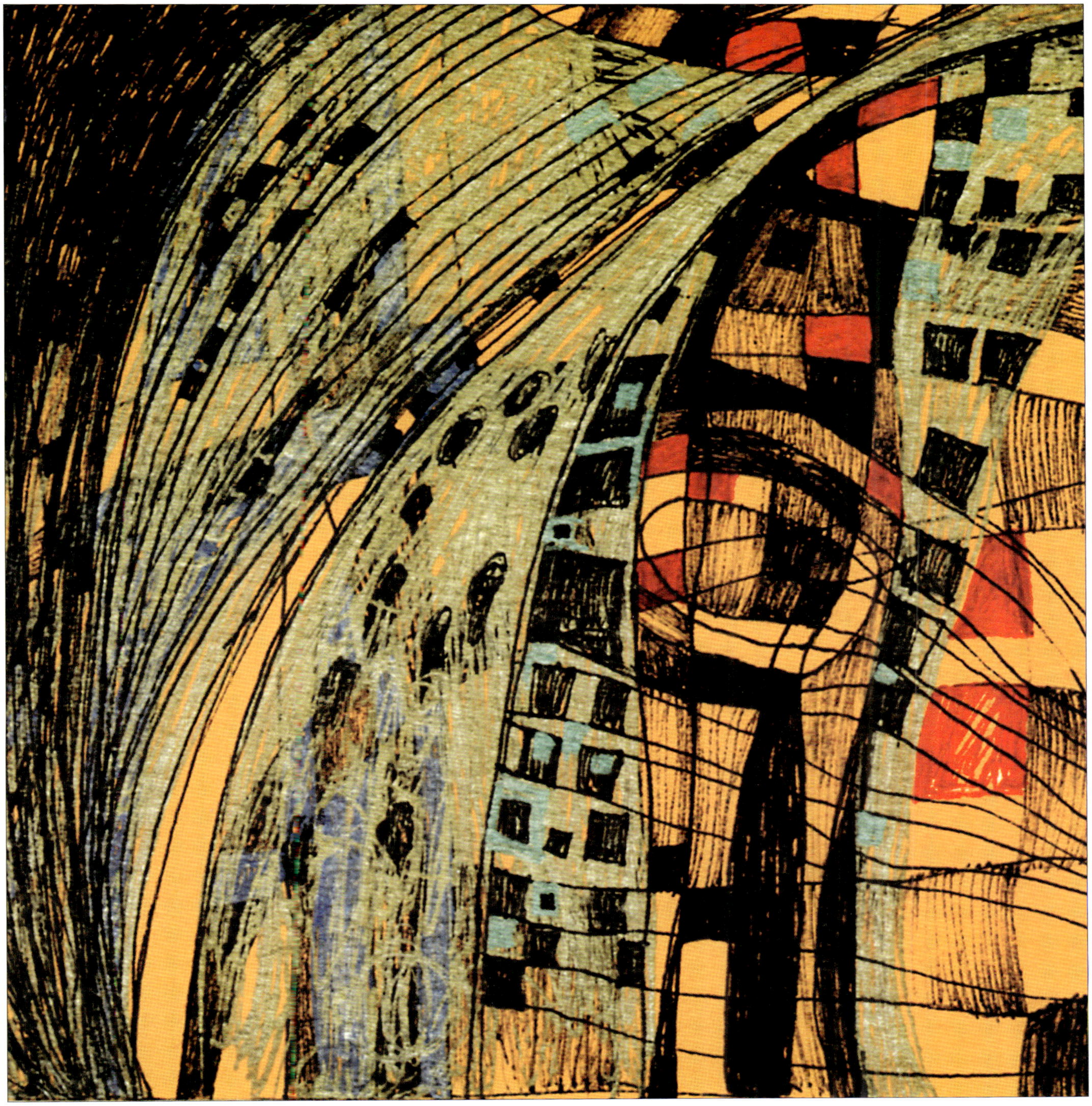

WHISTLING TEA KETTLE

SOUND SOLUTIONS: HEADACHE & WHISTLING TEA KETTLE

Figures 1 through 12 incorporate various techniques and approaches in depicting the sound associated with a headache.

Forms range from hard edge to amorphous shapes, where tension is used as a common denominator to express frenetic energy.

Figure 2, which depicts a woodpecker in motion, is indicative of a metaphoric solution.

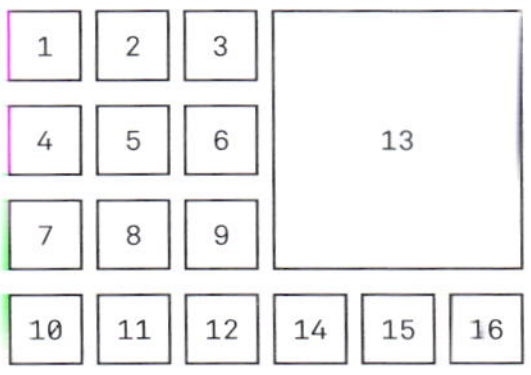

1	2	3	13		
4	5	6			
7	8	9			
10	11	12	14	15	16

1. *Yi Chen Tsai*
2. *Yeonsoo Kim*
3. *Sueyeon Park*
4. *Hye Ok Row*
5. *Shiella Pesik*
6. *Shaw Fay Guo*
7. *Rhonda Lehr*
8. *Dominika Kramerova*
9. *John Allen*
10. *Jieun Jeon*
11. *Hea Kim*
12. *Carolina Caicedo*
13. *Nataliya Hats*
14. *Hyman Richter*
15. *Hyunju Park*
16. *Jeroen de Korte*

Figures 13 through 16 are interpretations of the sound of a whistling tea kettle. Abstract solutions dominate, except for figure 14, which is a clear narrative of anthropomorphizing a tea kettle.

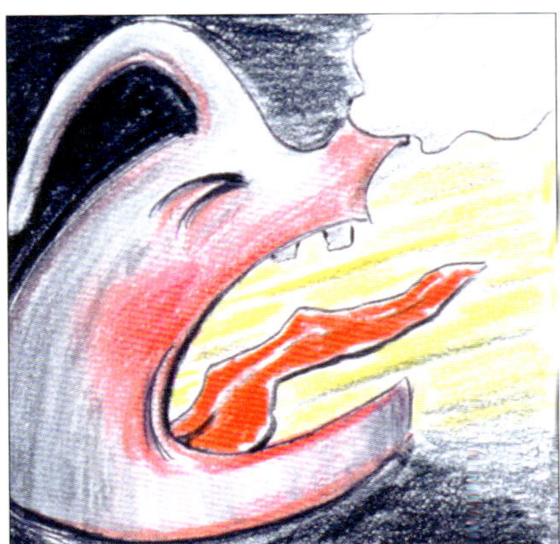

WHISTLING TEA KETTLE

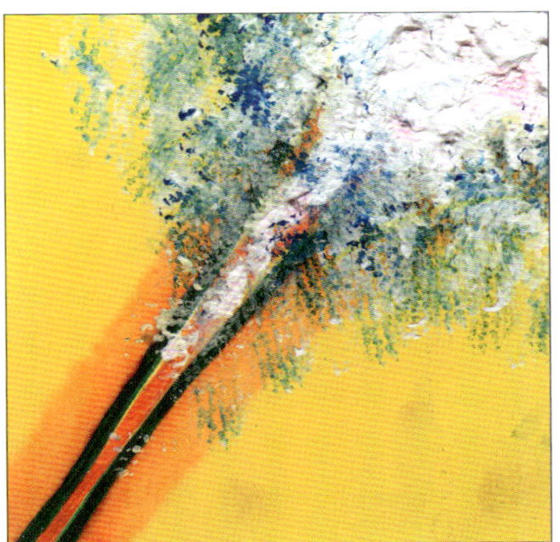

WHISTLING TEA KETTLE

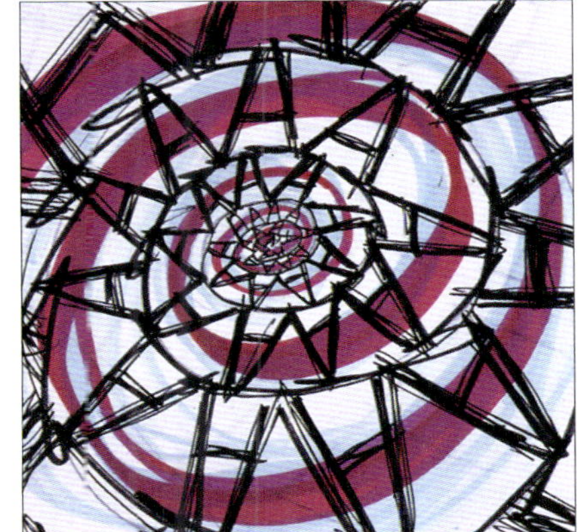

WHISTLING TEA KETTLE

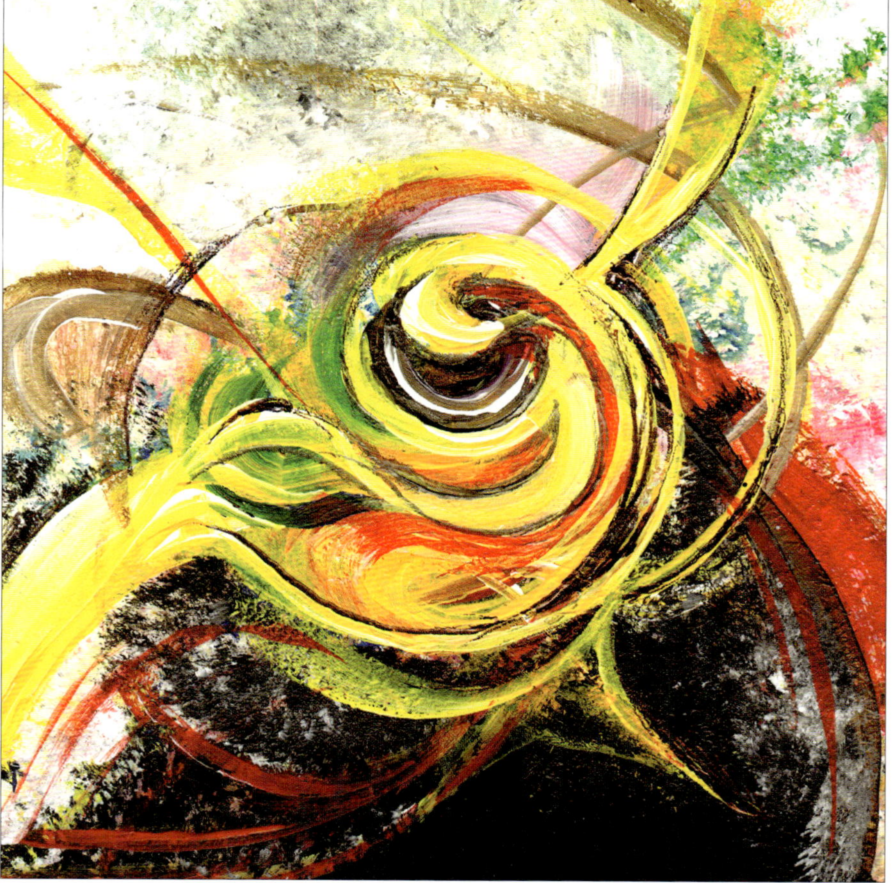

FAULTY LIGHT BULB

FAULTY LIGHT BULB

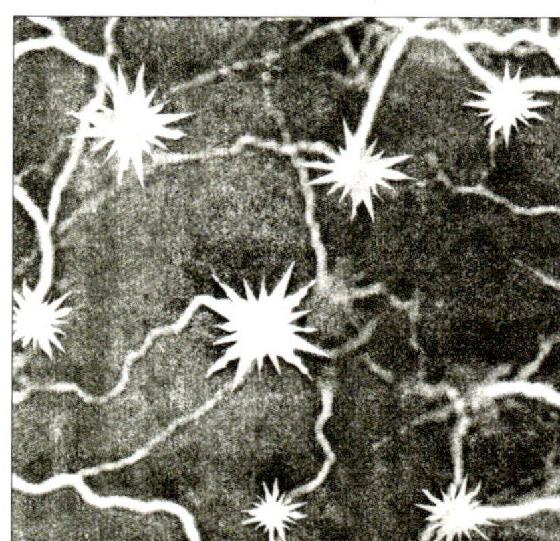

FAULTY LIGHT BULB

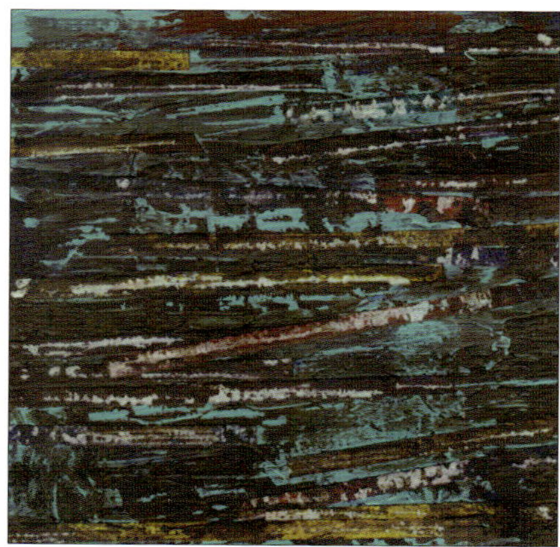

FAULTY LIGHT BULB

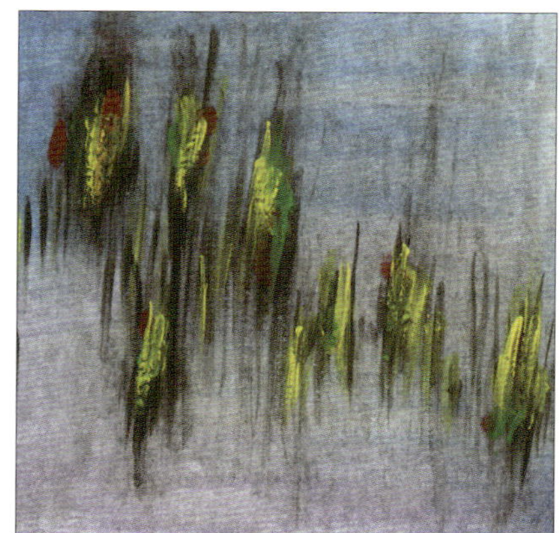

FAULTY LIGHT BULB

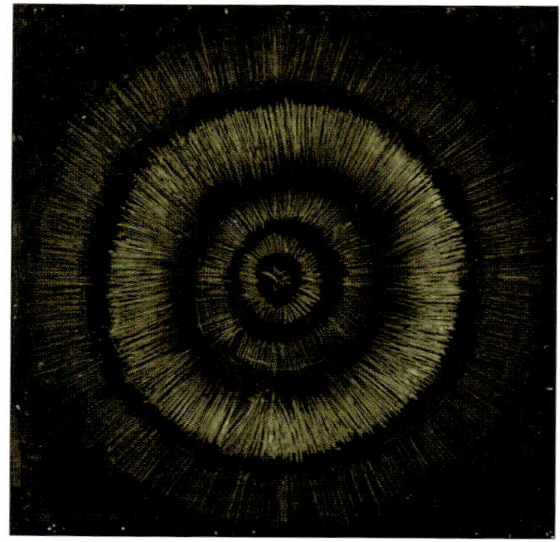

FAULTY LIGHT BULB

SOUND SOLUTIONS: FAULTY LIGHT BULB & ICE CREAM MELTING

The topic of a faulty light bulb is depicted in figures 1 through 6.

Figure 1 deals with spontaneous movement in the form of a spiral pattern, while figures 2 and 3 represent interruption, pulsation, and static as it pertains to the intermittent flickering of a light bulb.

Figures 7 through 30 are depictions of the sound of melting ice cream, which in truth is silent.

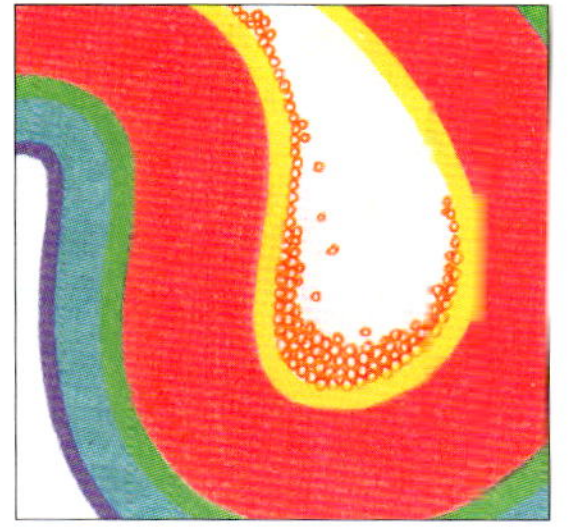
ICE CREAM MELTING

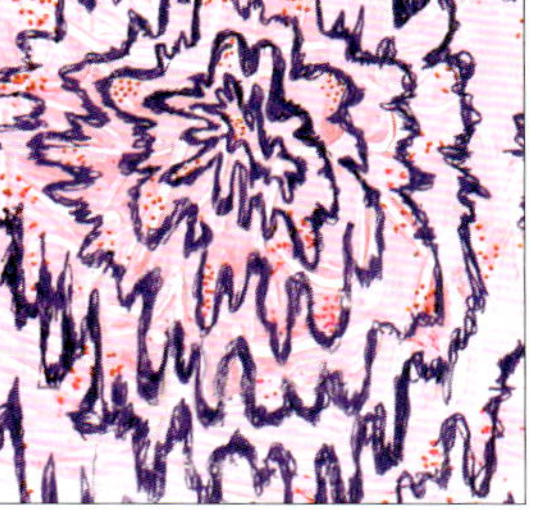
ICE CREAM MELTING

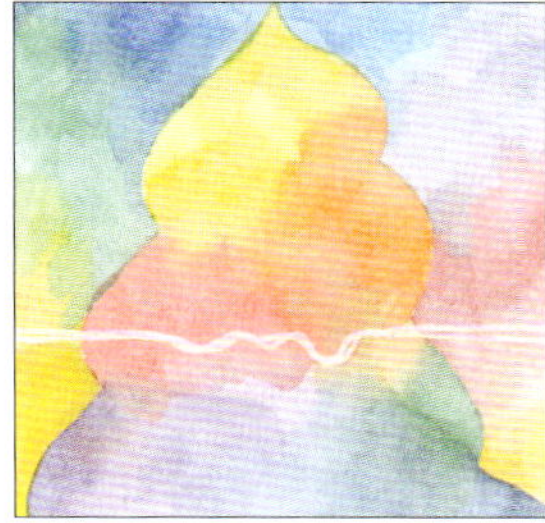
ICE CREAM MELTING

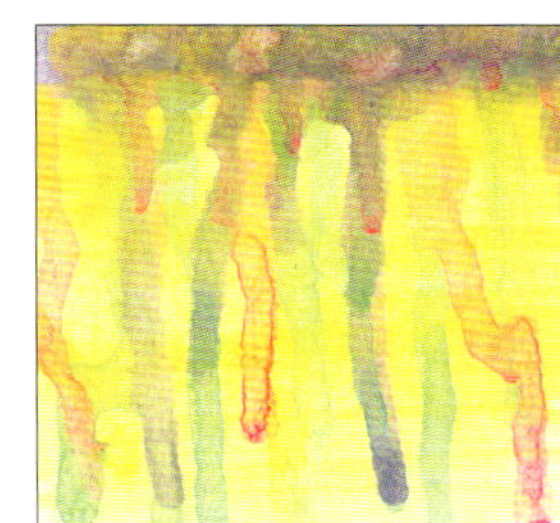
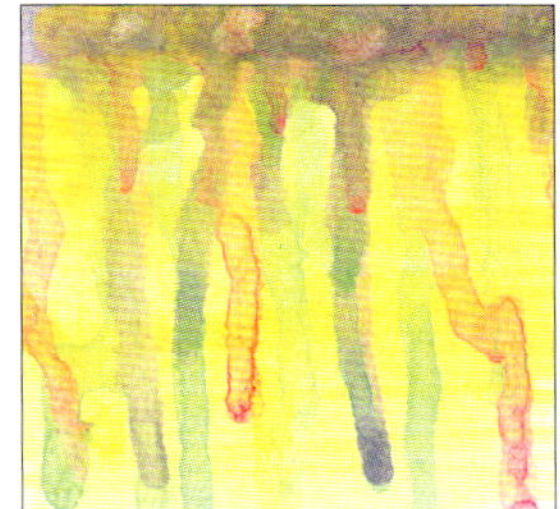
ICE CREAM MELTING

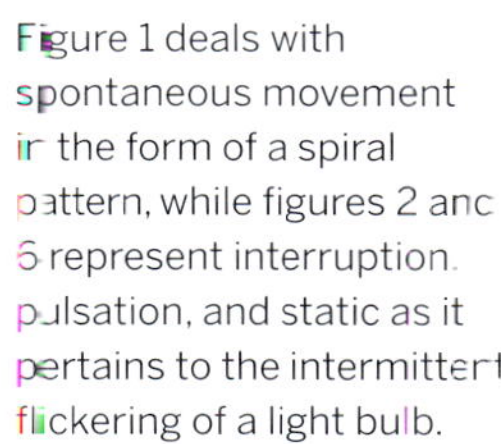

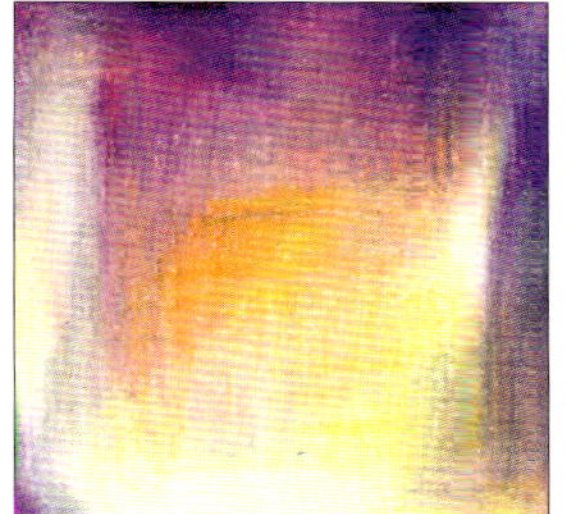
ICE CREAM MELTING

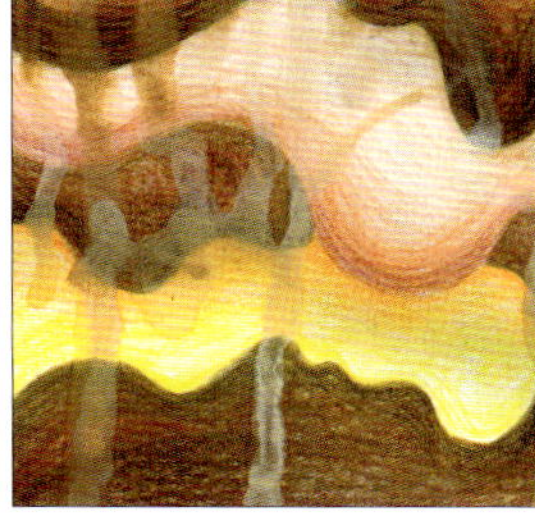
ICE CREAM MELTING

ICE CREAM MELTING

ICE CREAM MELTING

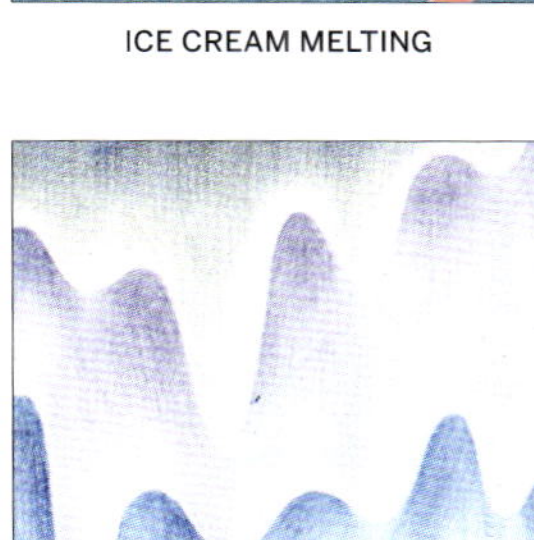
ICE CREAM MELTING

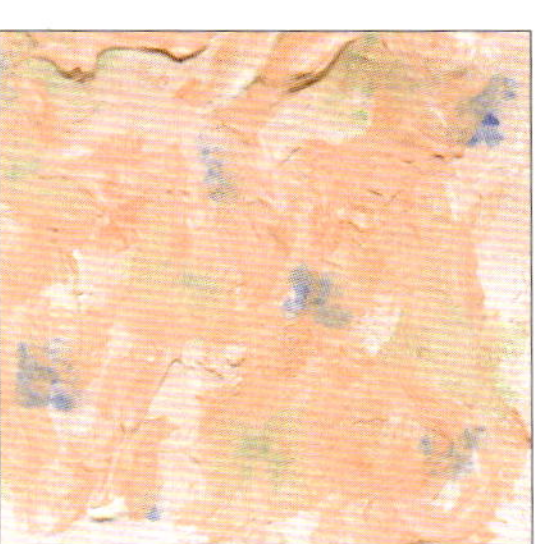
ICE CREAM MELTING

ICE CREAM MELTING

ICE CREAM MELTING

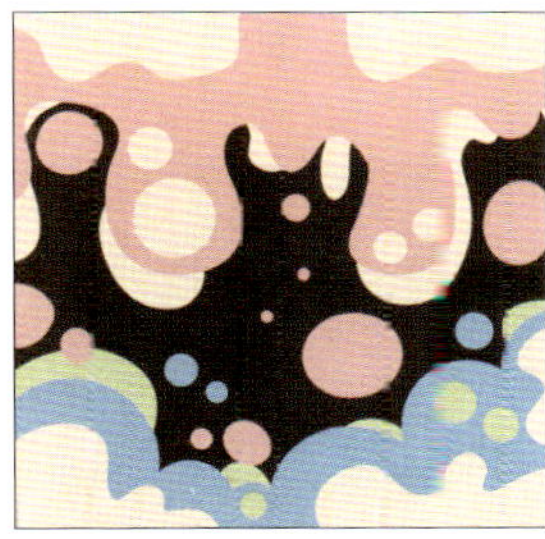
ICE CREAM MELTING

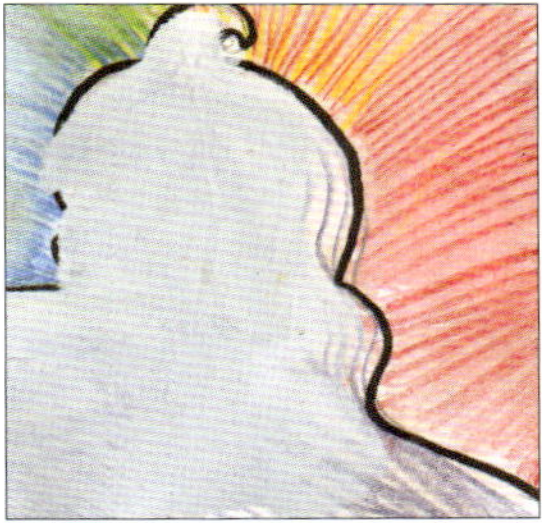
ICE CREAM MELTING

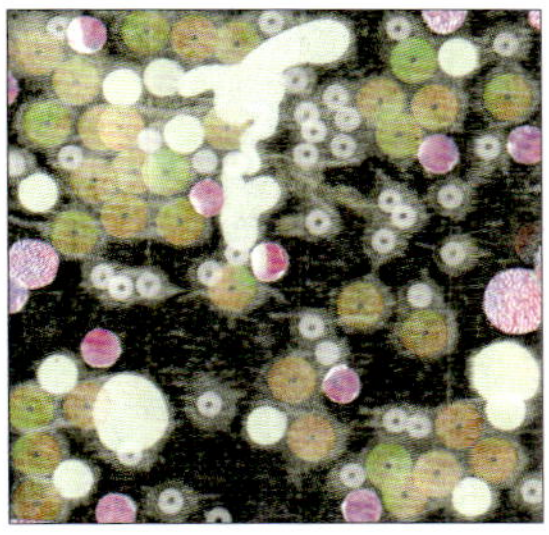
ICE CREAM MELTING

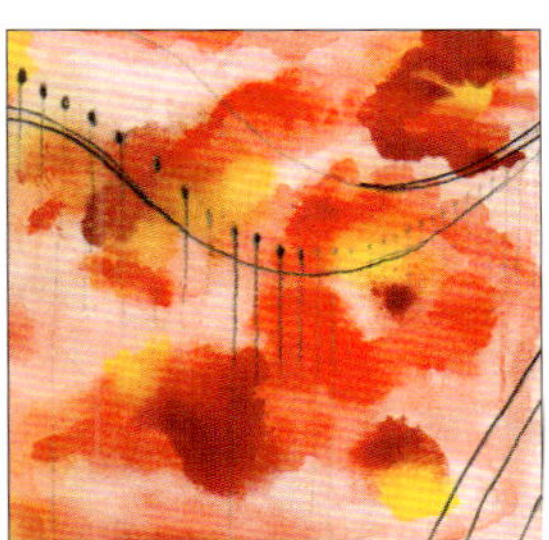
ICE CREAM MELTING

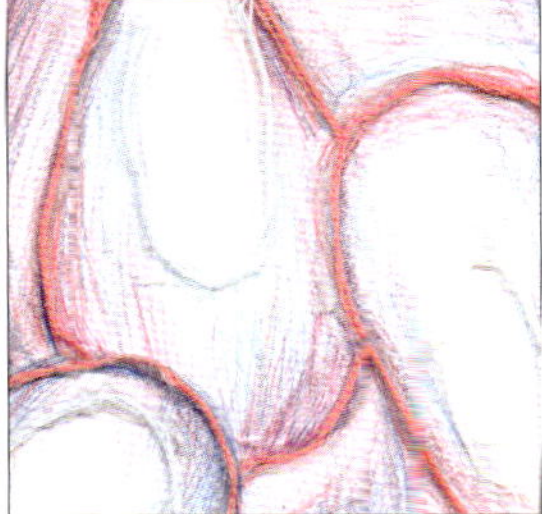
ICE CREAM MELTING

ICE CREAM MELTING

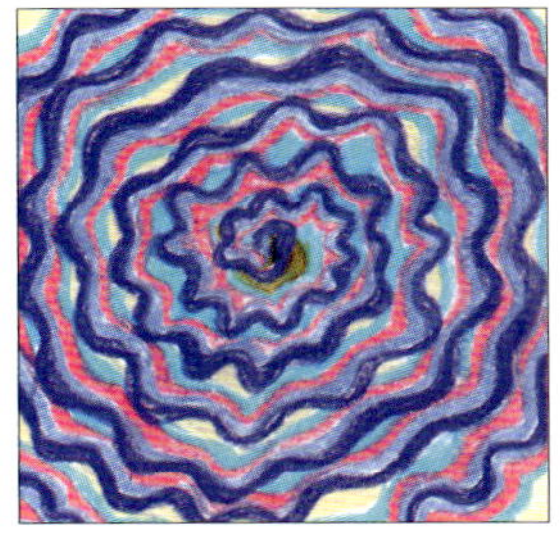
ICE CREAM MELTING

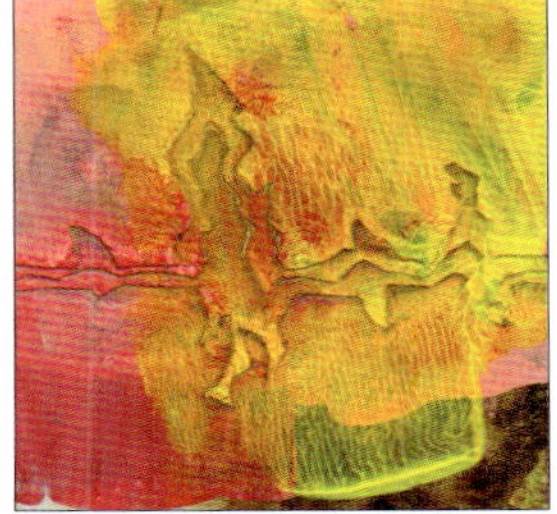
ICE CREAM MELTING

ICE CREAM MELTING

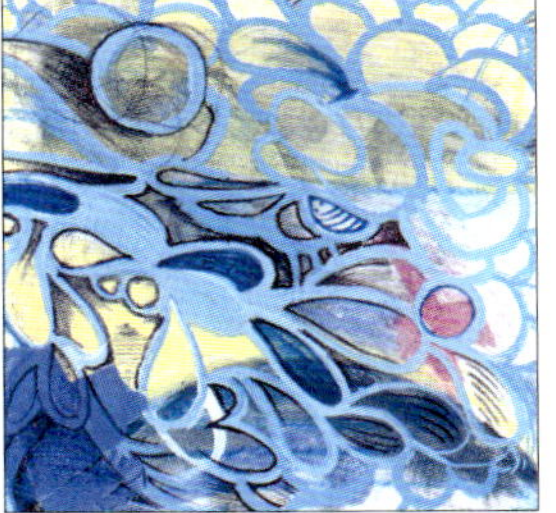
ICE CREAM MELTING

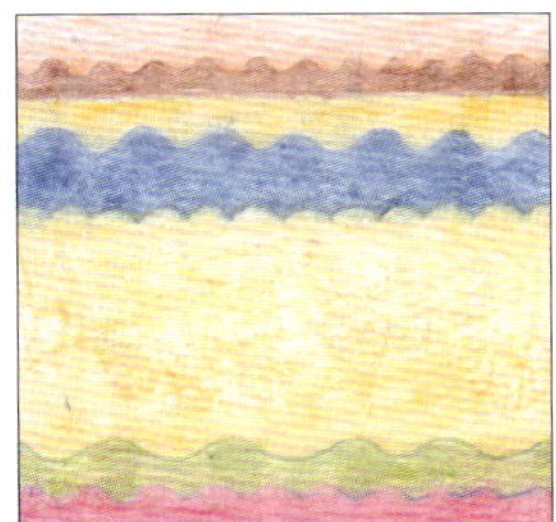
ICE CREAM MELTING

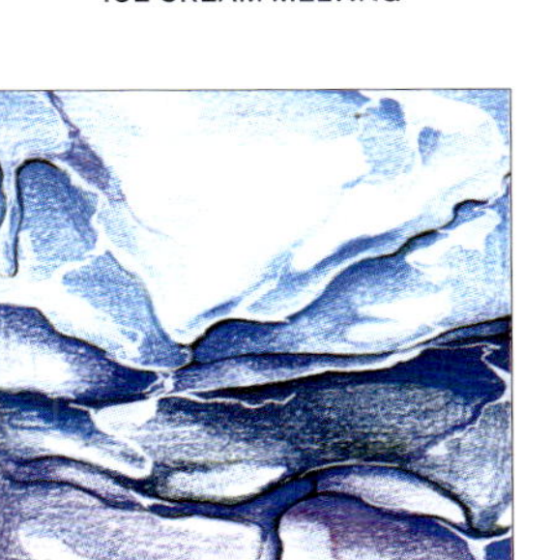
ICE CREAM MELTING

1. *Eunjung Yoo*
2. *Jiyoon Kim*
3. *Jarrod Barretto*
4. *Woomin Han*
5. *Jessica Gibson*
6. *Hyun Jung Ra*
7. *Scott Buchan*
8. *Moonee Kim*
9. *Soomin Yoo*
10. *Hye Ok Row*
11. *John Allen*
12. *Minjoo Han*
13. *Yoojung Kang*
14. *Jeehye Noh*
15. *Luree Lee*
16. *Yi Yi Shao*
17. *Lingxiao Tan*
18. *Y. Ryabov*
19. *K. Capers*
20. *N. Saint Onge*
21. *Jiyoung Lee*
22. *Matthew Peters*
23. *Kelly Shami*
24. *M. Jaramillo*
25. *Jeong Kang*
26. *D. Kramerova*
27. *Minjoo Han*
28. *Pablo De [illegible]an*
29. *S. Merley*
30. *Jieun Jeon*

The sound of this movement is imperceptible. Here, as in some of the other subjects, one needs to take artistic license in executing one's solution. In this instance, one can reference undulating amorphous form and a downward movement that references melting.

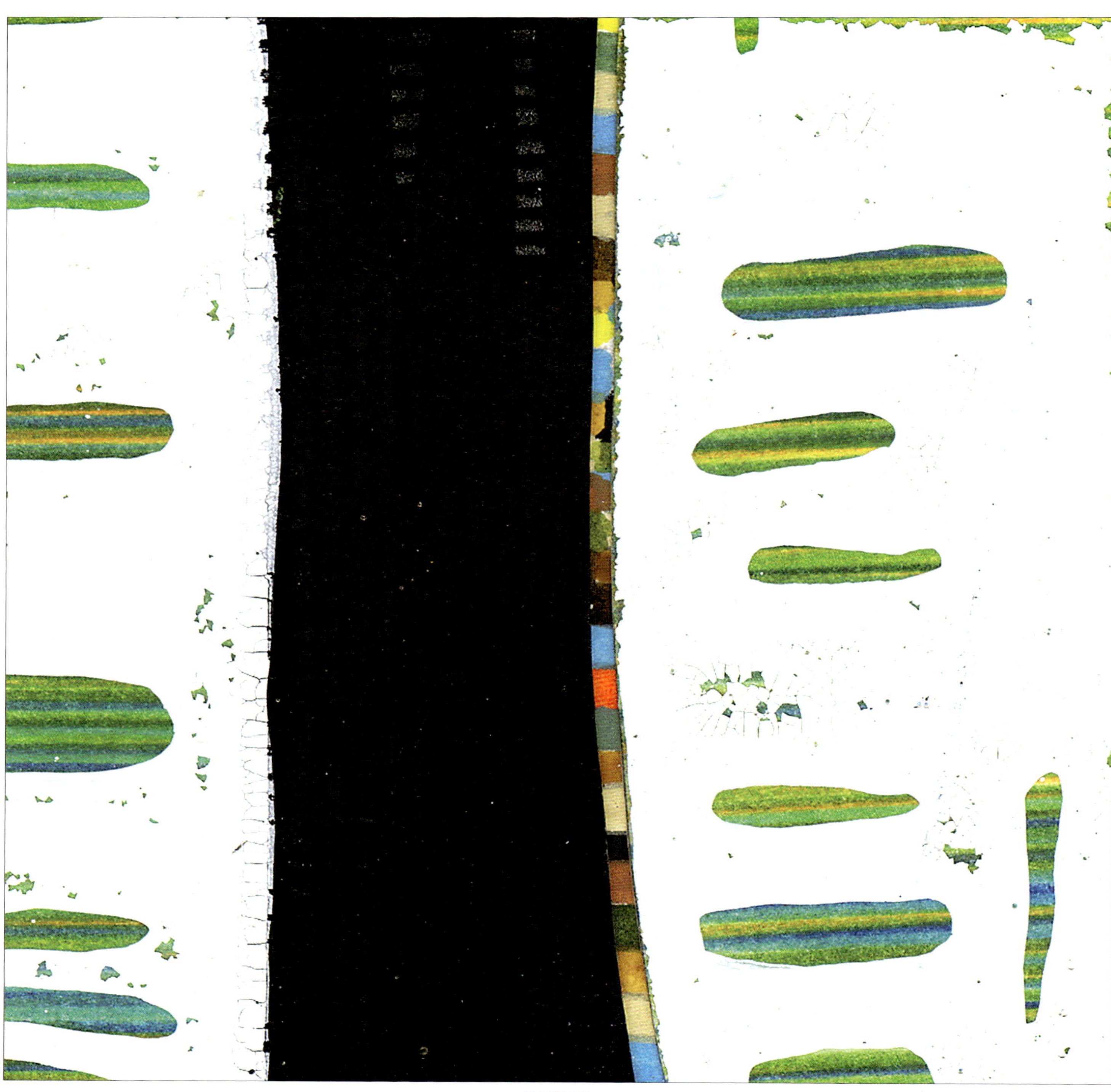

GARGLING

SOUND SOLUTIONS: GARGLING

The common denominator in all these abstract solutions is organic formulations that are almost cell-like in structure, referencing the movement of the throat and the microscopic organisms associated with gargling.

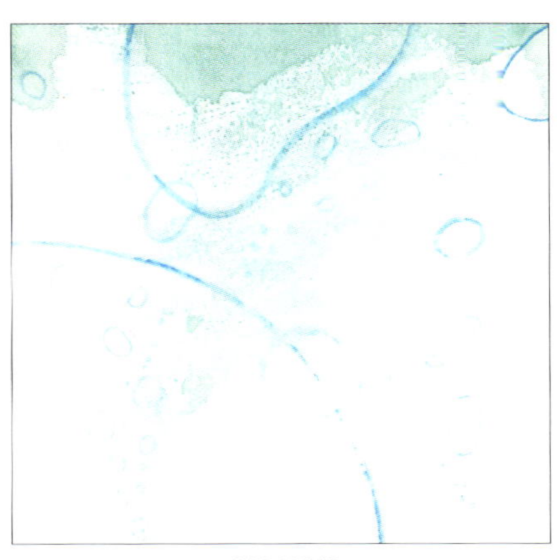
GARGLING

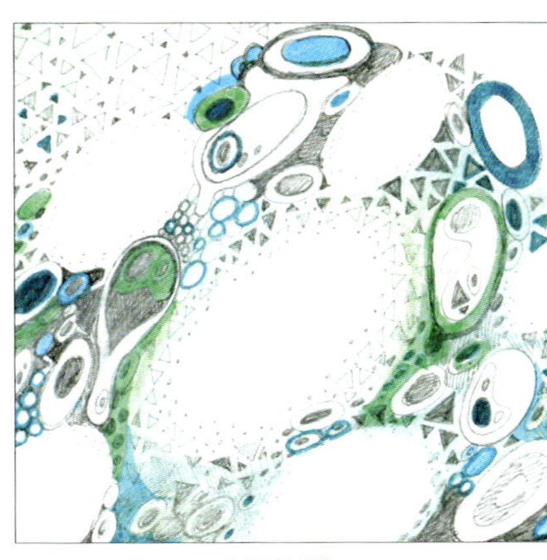
GARGLING

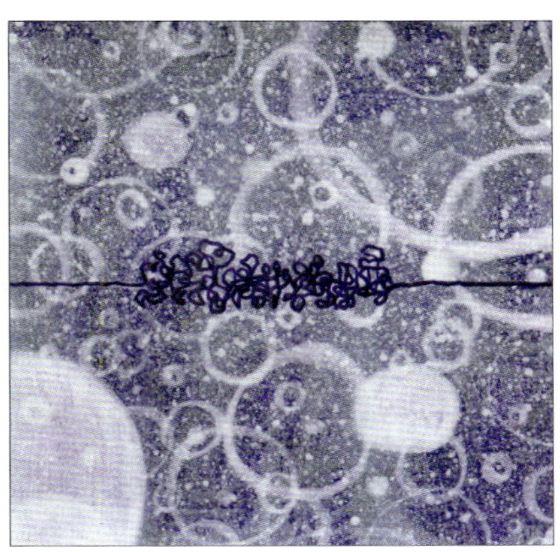
GARGLING

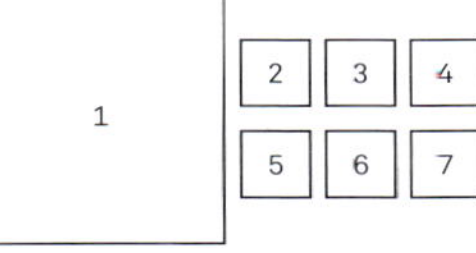

1. *Yueh Lu*
2. *Yulsoo Sung*
3. *Yeojin Tak*
4. *Soomin Yoo*
5. *S. Kim*
6. *Hyejin Yoon*
7. *Vera Gorbunova*

GARGLING

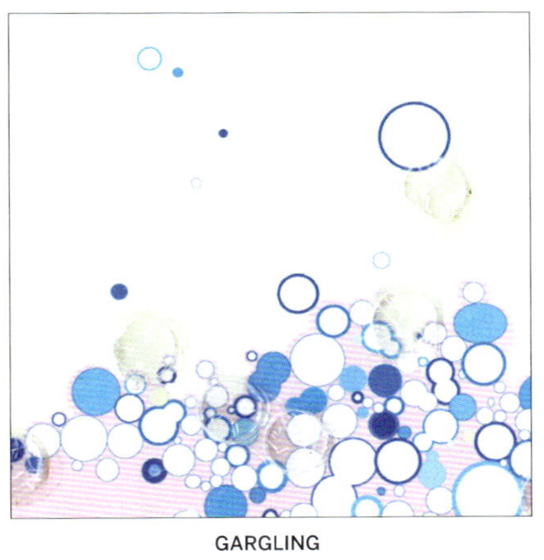
GARGLING

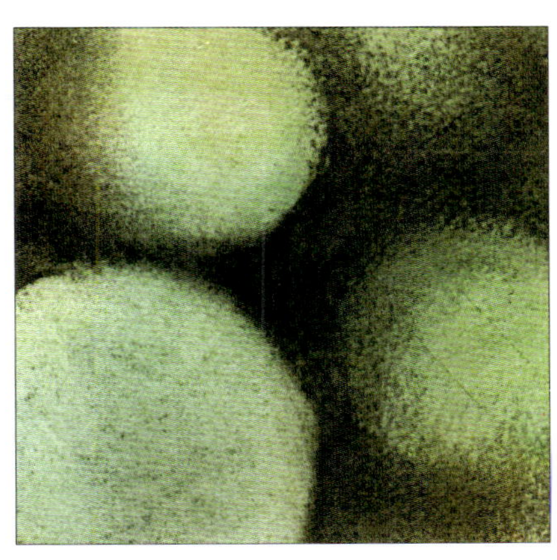
GARGLING

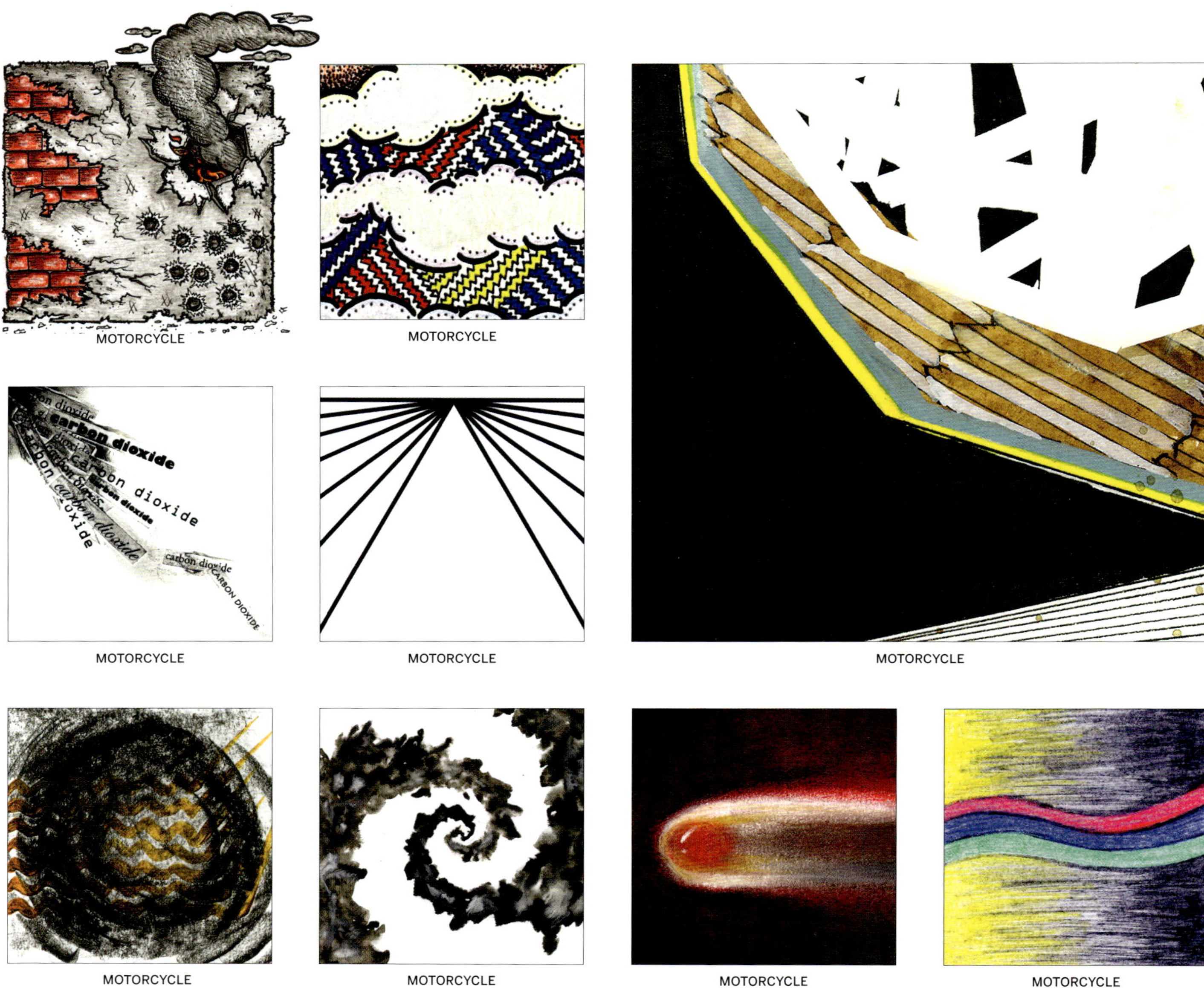

MOTORCYCLE MOTORCYCLE
MOTORCYCLE MOTORCYCLE MOTORCYCLE
MOTORCYCLE MOTORCYCLE MOTORCYCLE MOTORCYCLE

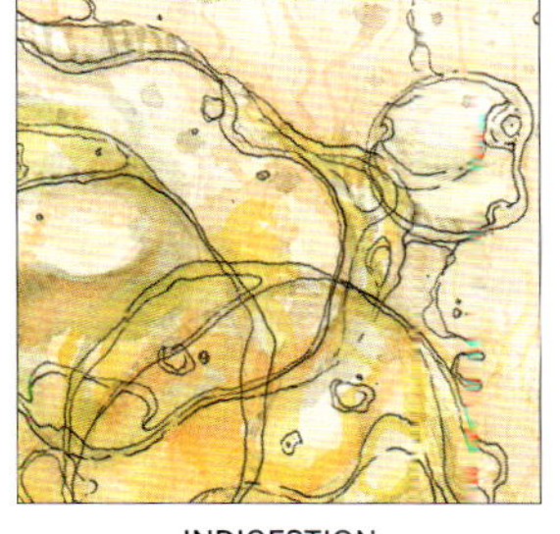
INDIGESTION

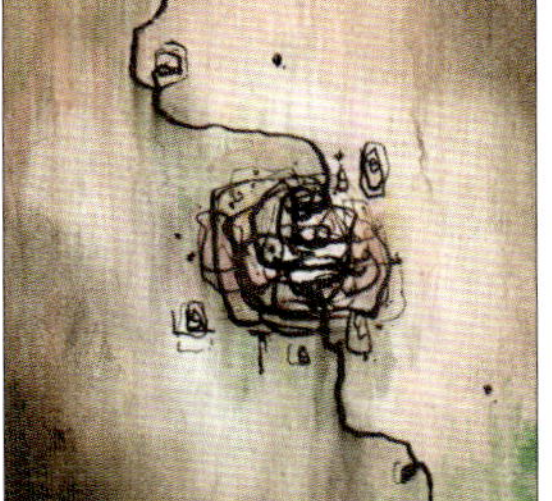
INDIGESTION

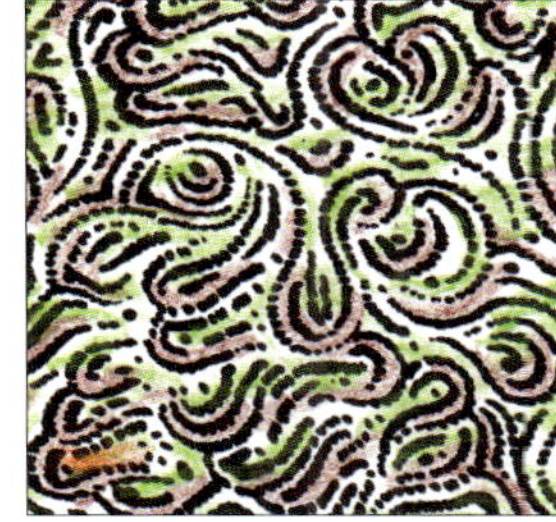
INDIGESTION

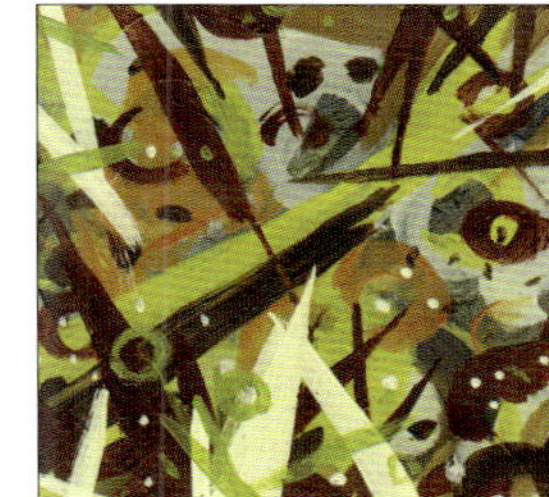
INDIGESTION

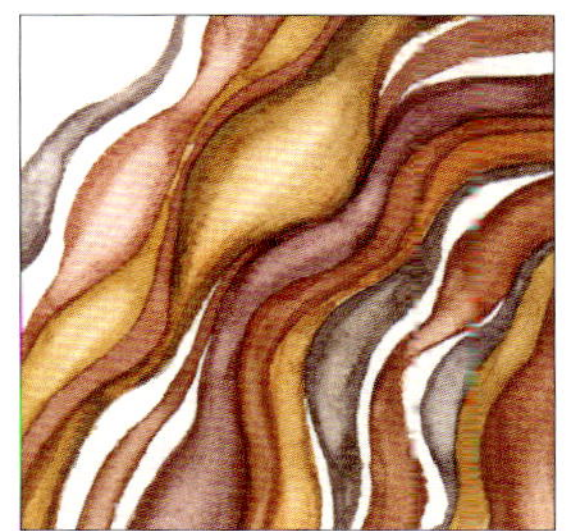
INDIGESTION

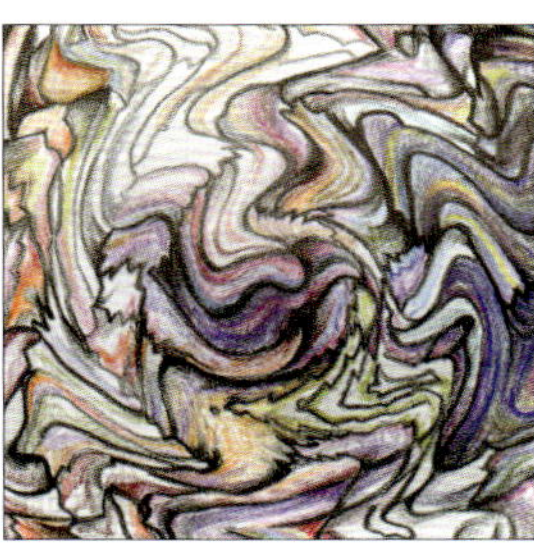
INDIGESTION

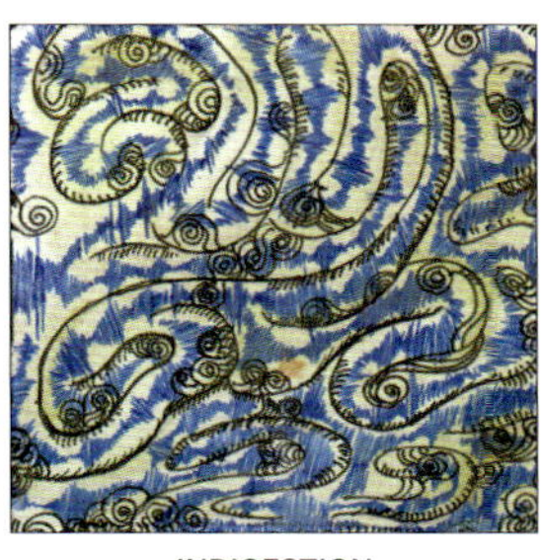
INDIGESTION

INDIGESTION

INDIGESTION

INDIGESTION

INDIGESTION

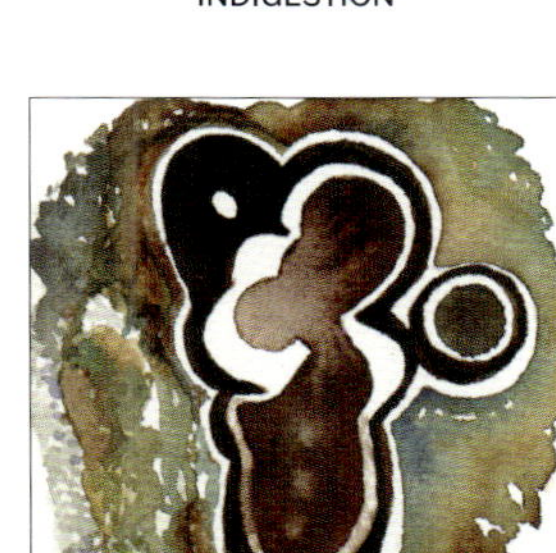
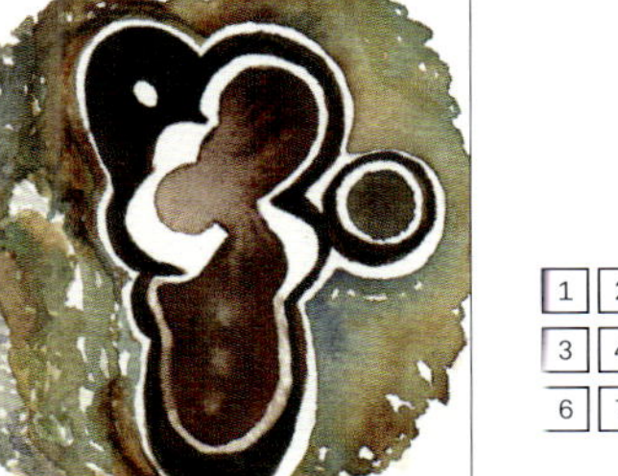
INDIGESTION

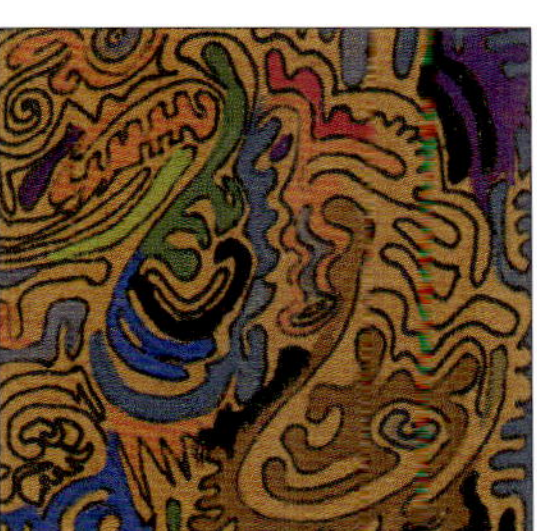
INDIGESTION

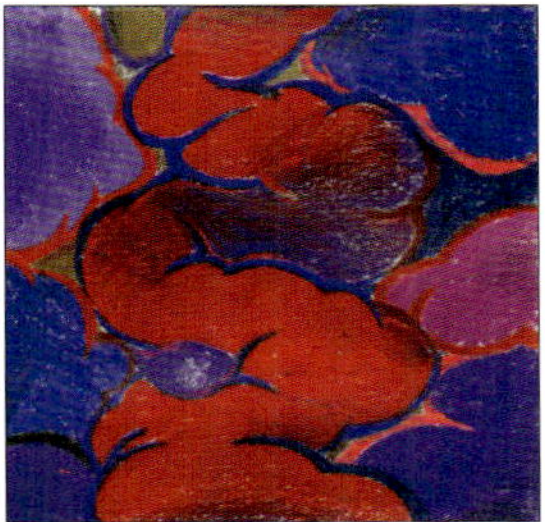
INDIGESTION

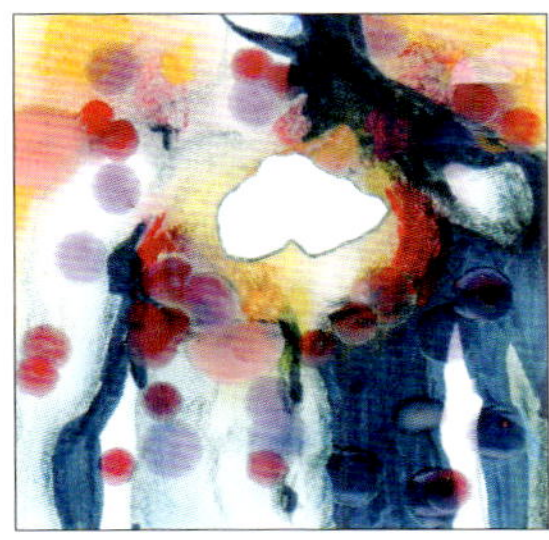
INDIGESTION

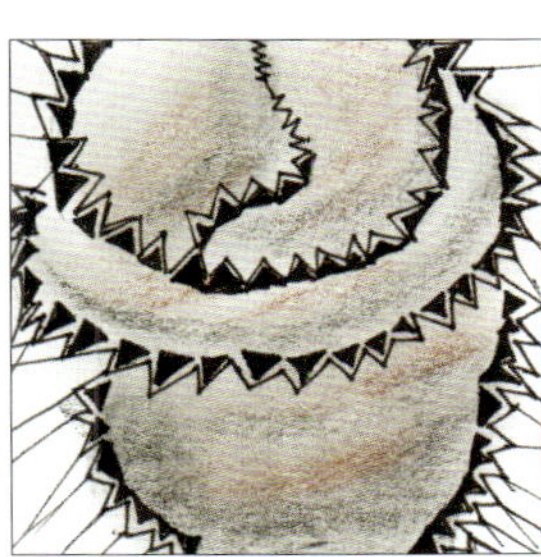
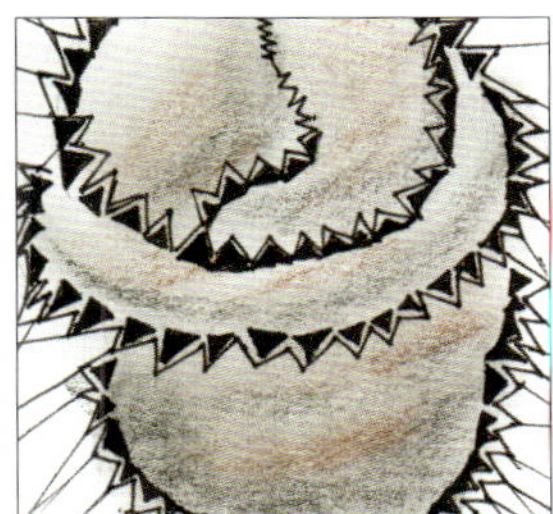
INDIGESTION

INDIGESTION

INDIGESTION

INDIGESTION

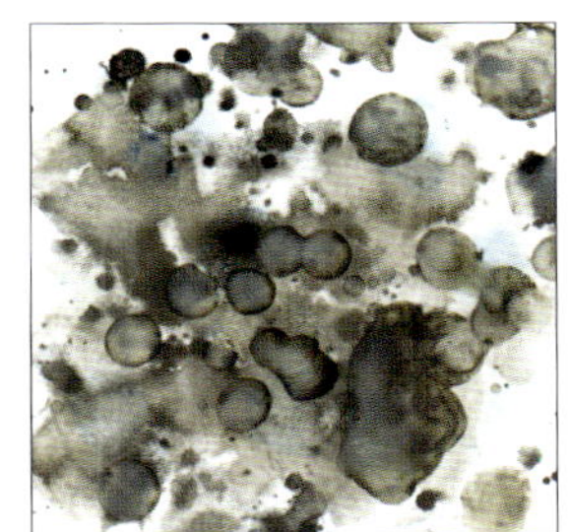
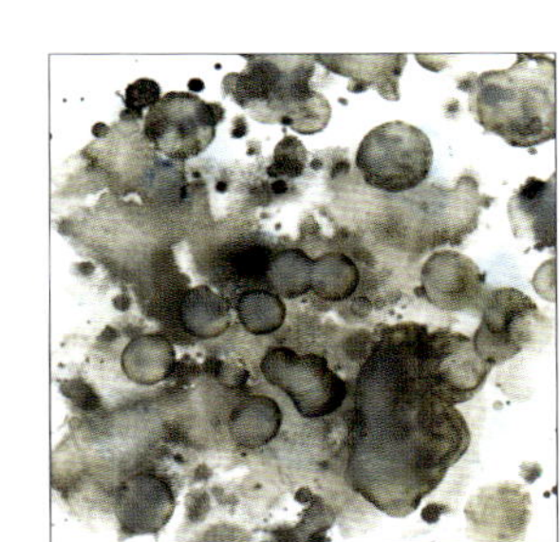
INDIGESTION

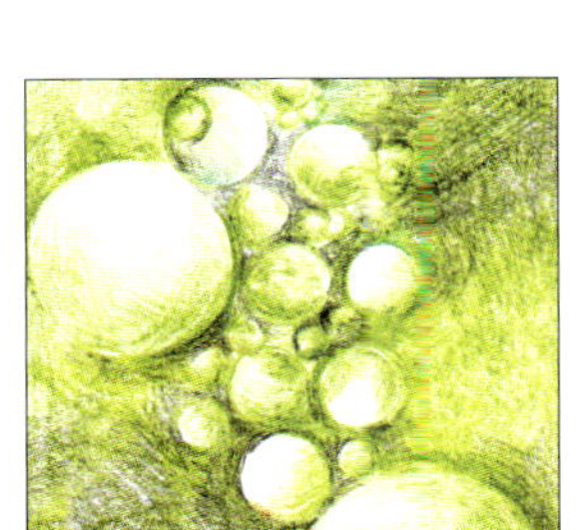
INDIGESTION

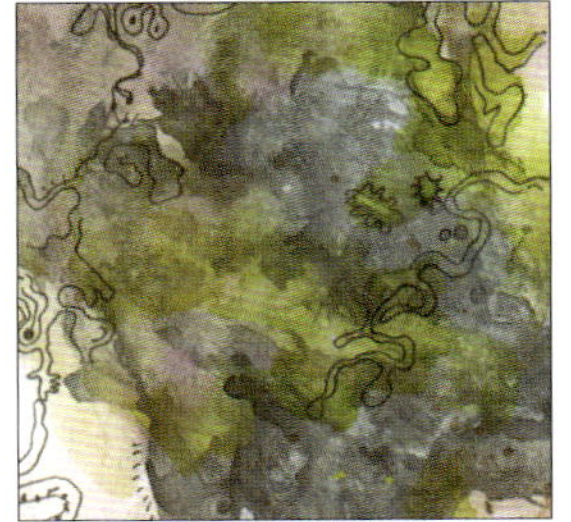
INDIGESTION

INDIGESTION

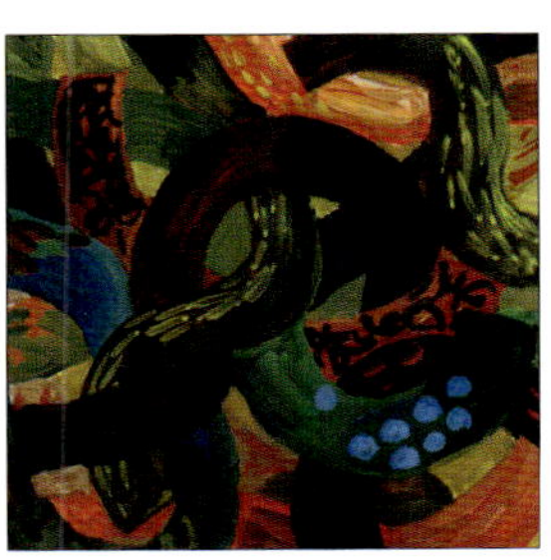
INDIGESTION

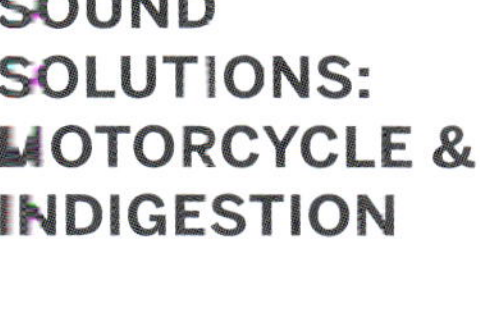

SOUND SOLUTIONS: MOTORCYCLE & INDIGESTION

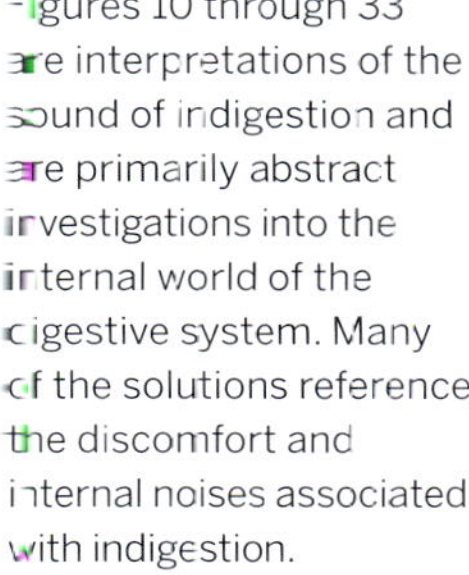

Figures 1 through 9 deal with the sound of motorcycles, utilizing the principle of movement to infer the sound of an explosive activity. At times literal imagery is referenced.

Figures 10 through 33 are interpretations of the sound of indigestion and are primarily abstract investigations into the internal world of the digestive system. Many of the solutions reference the discomfort and internal noises associated with indigestion.

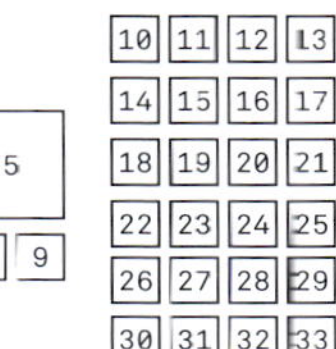
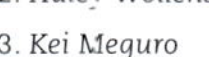

1. Adam Kostman
2. Haley Wollens
3. Kei Meguro
4. Jiseong Jang
5. Yueh Lu
6. Kayo Ono
7. Jungho Oh
8. M. Takagi
9. Catalina Argomedo
10. Elaine Park
11. Donghwi Shim
12. Kevin Harris
13. Caleb Brown
14. Jinsuk Kim
15. Jaewon Park
16. Deukgyu Lee
17. Heejung Kim
18. Jaeyoon Song
19. Haejun Moon
20. Carlotta Merzari
21. Hyunjin Kim
22. Karolina Pietrynczak
23. Steve Choi
24. Jihye Yoon
25. Nari Kim
26. Jaeyeong Kim
27. Manoil Tzonev
28. Sanghyun Lee
29. Soyeon Kim
30. Hyunah Choi
31. Christine Choi
32. Amy Churchwell
33. Hsing Kyo

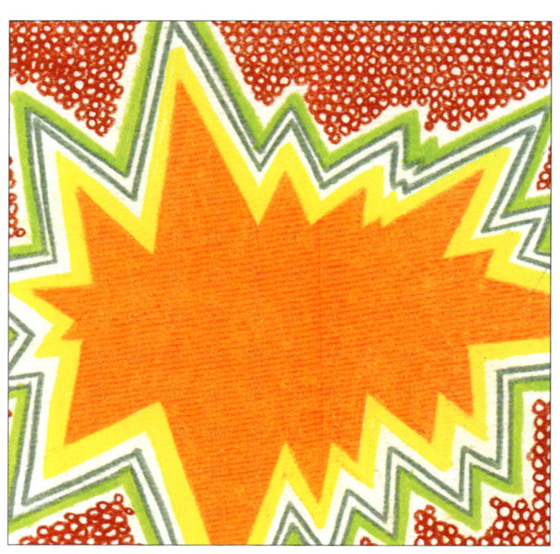
OPENING A BAG OF CHIPS

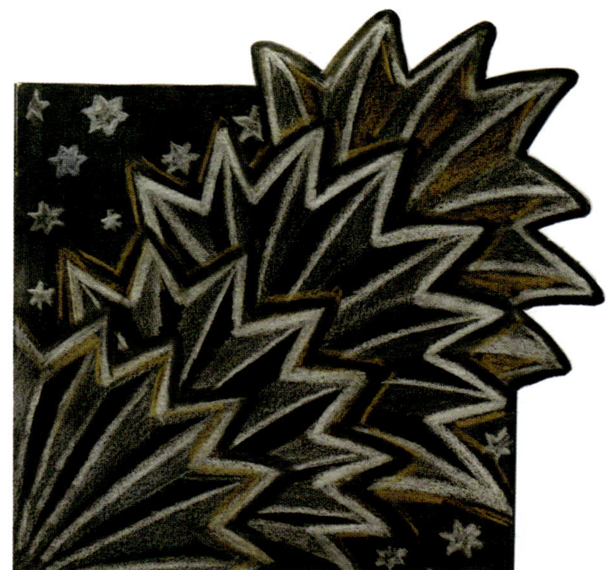
OPENING A BAG OF CHIPS

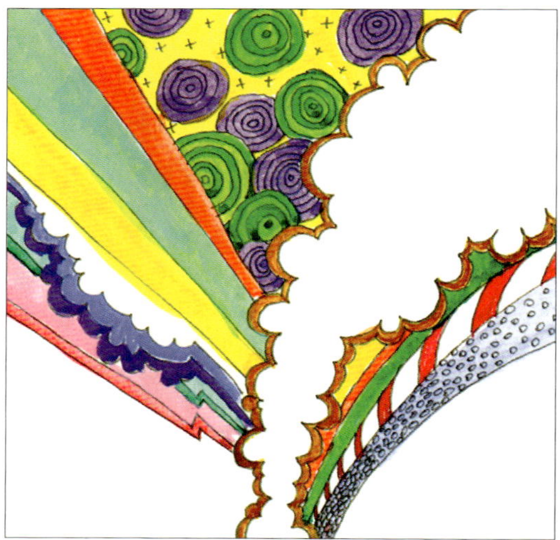
OPENING A BAG OF CHIPS

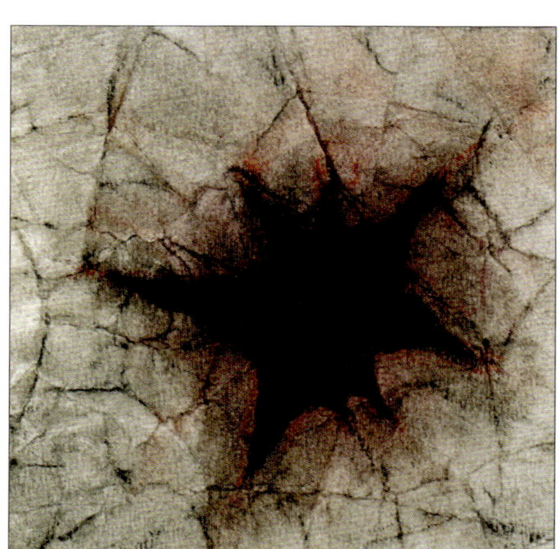
OPENING A BAG OF CHIPS

SOUND SOLUTIONS: OPENING A BAG OF CHIPS & JACKHAMMER

Figures 1 through 4 represent the popping sound made when opening a bag of chips, conveyed by a sense of explosive movement emanating from various focal points. Certain solutions reference a cartoon vernacular.

Figures 5 through 14 depict the sound of a jackhammer. This pounding, vibrating activity addresses the high decibel level of noise that is most unpleasant to the ear. Curiously, many of these solutions, which at first are viewed as abstractions, do in fact have underlying narratives.

JACKHAMMER

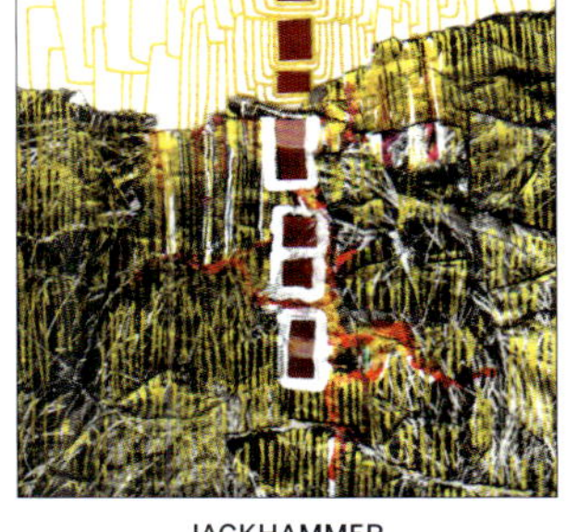

JACKHAMMER

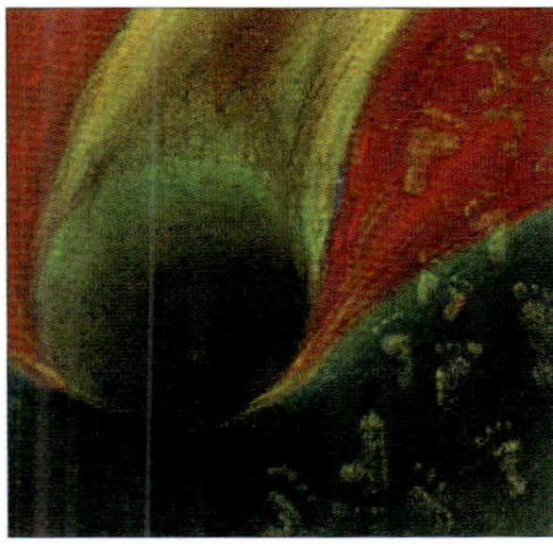

JACKHAMMER

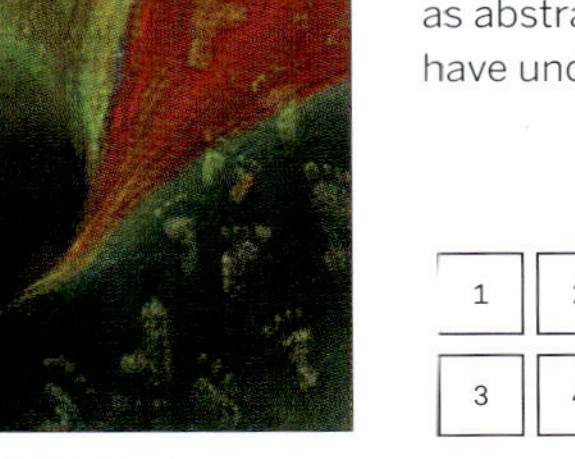

JACKHAMMER

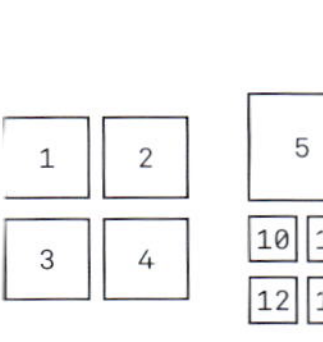

JACKHAMMER

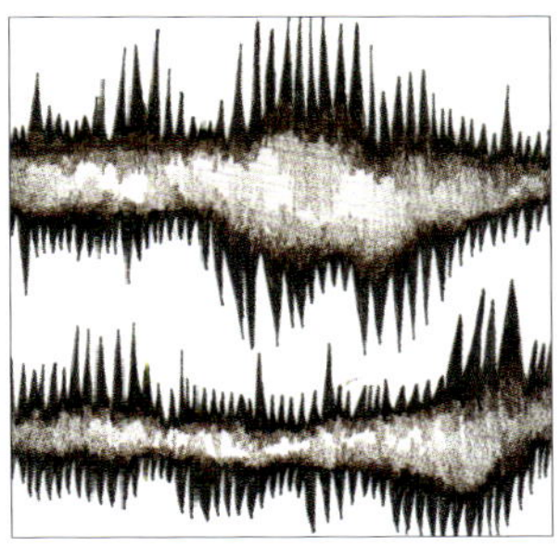

JACKHAMMER

1. Scott Buchan
2. Aemin Shim
3. Yulsoo Sung
4. Alan Tung
5. Jesse Goldman
6. Haley Wollens
7. Hyewon Shim
8. George Skoufas
9. M. Takagi
10. Najung Kim
11. Inyoung Kim
12. Adam Kostman
13. Jinyong Yang
14. Elliot Friedland

JACKHAMMER

JACKHAMMER

JACKHAMMER

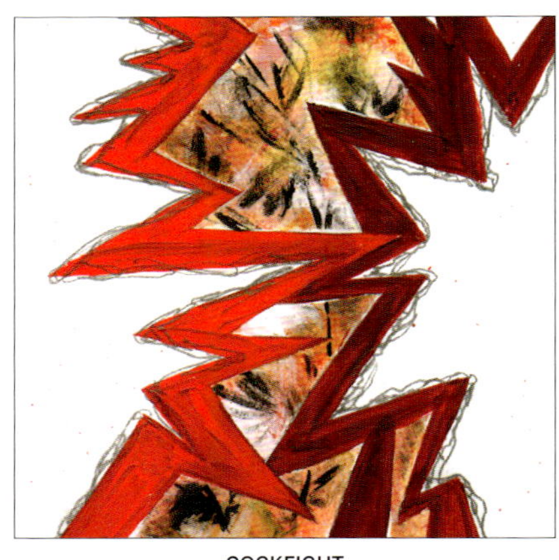
COCKFIGHT

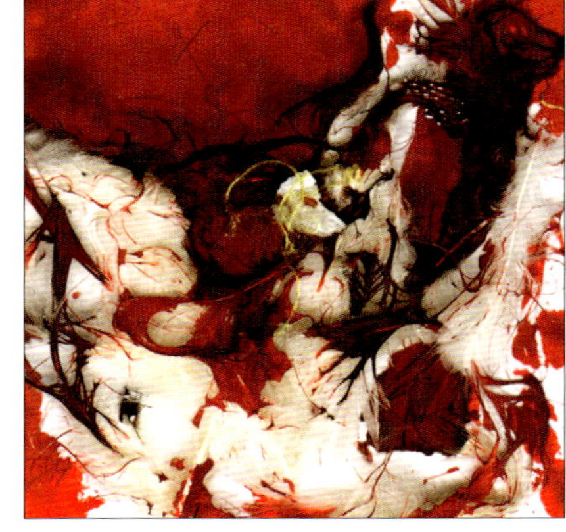
COCKFIGHT

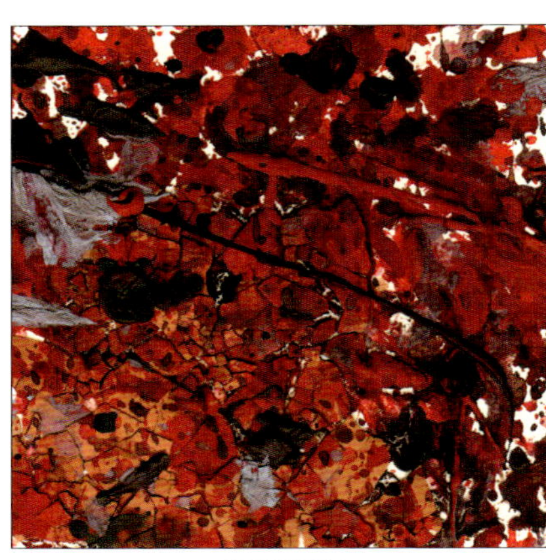
COCKFIGHT

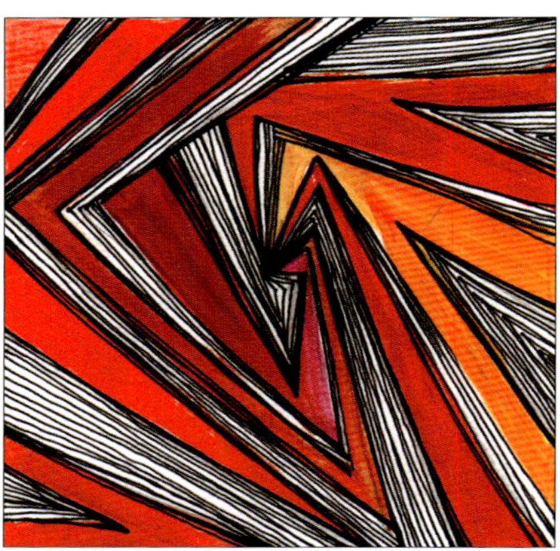
COCKFIGHT

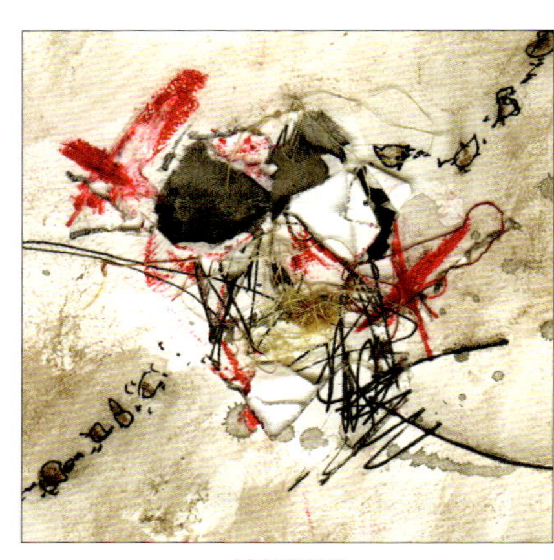
COCKFIGHT

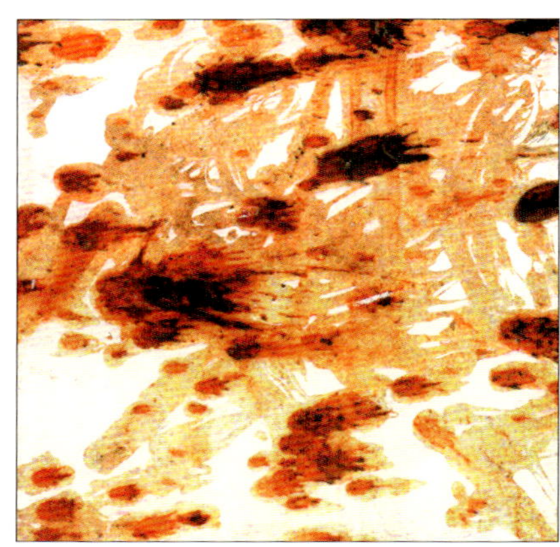
COCKFIGHT

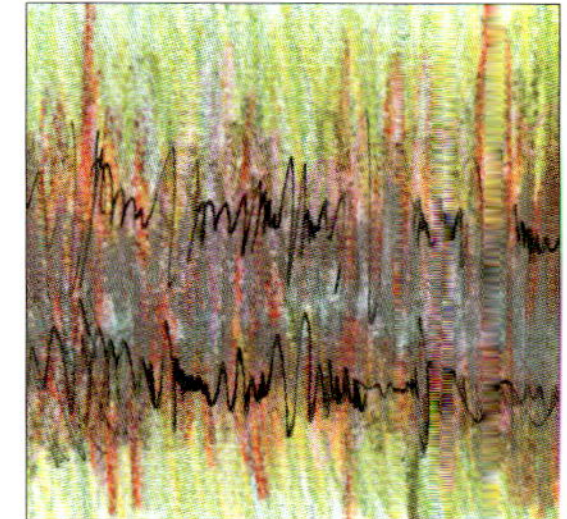

NERVOUS HABIT

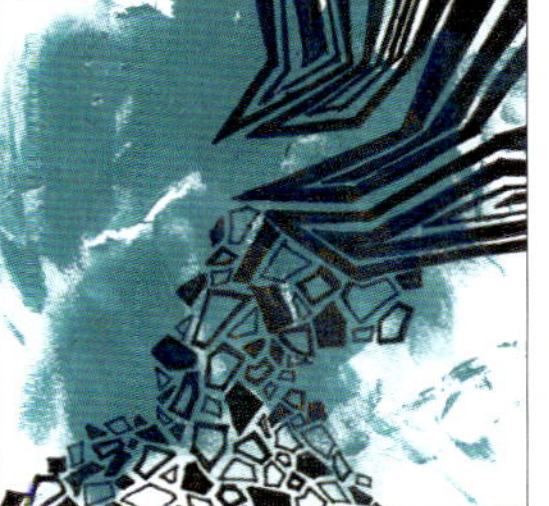

NERVOUS HABIT

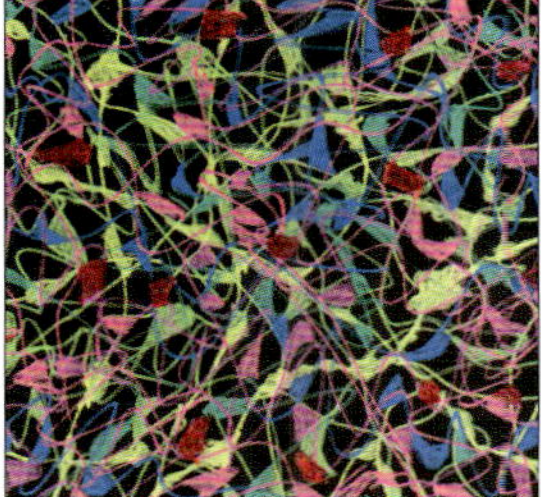

NERVOUS HABIT

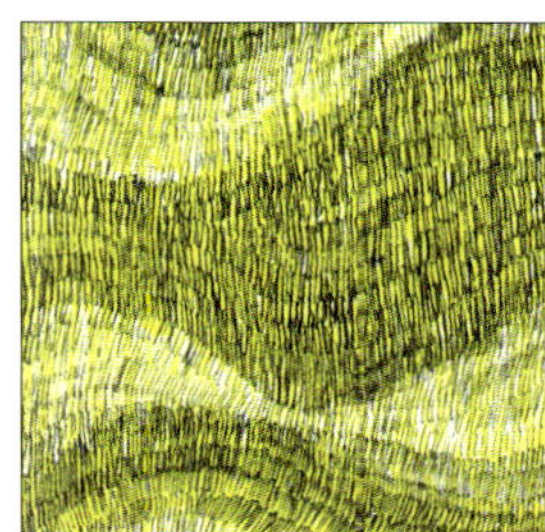
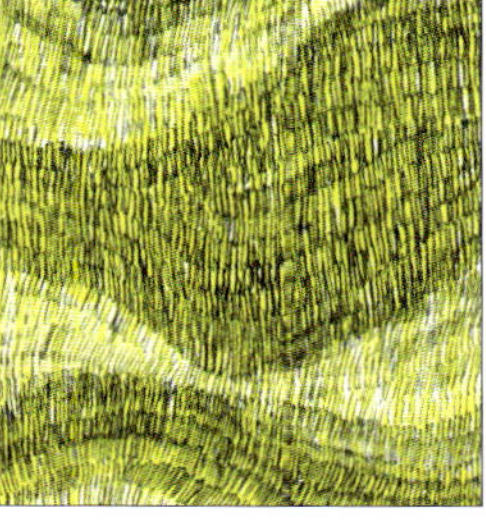

NERVOUS HABIT

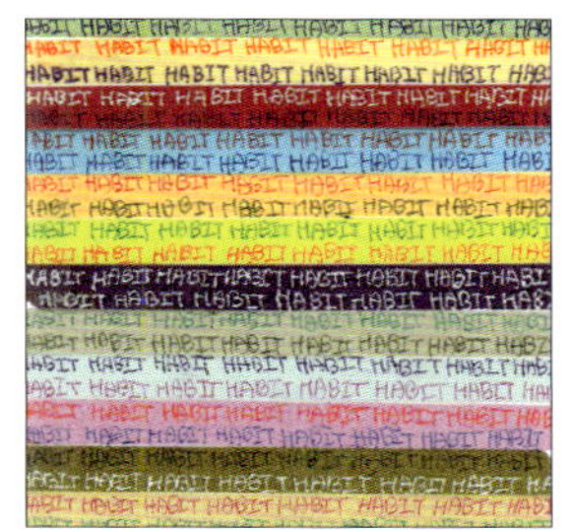

NERVOUS HABIT

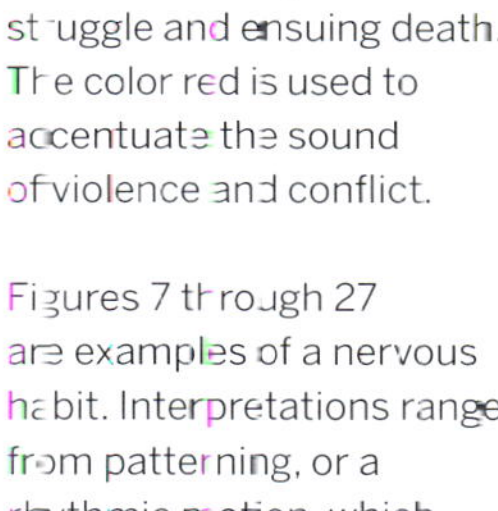

NERVOUS HABIT

NERVOUS HABIT

NERVOUS HABIT

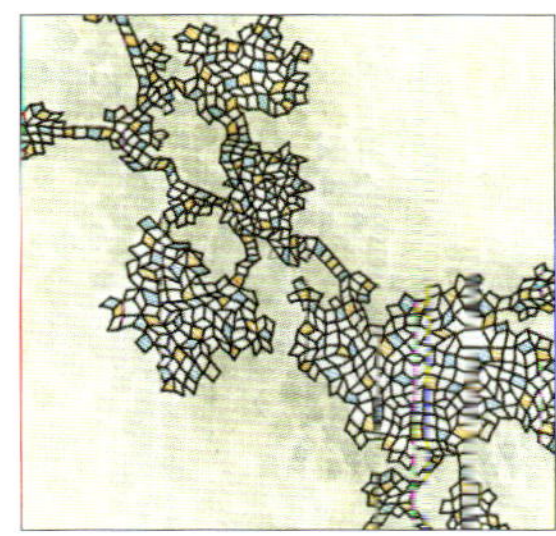

NERVOUS HABIT

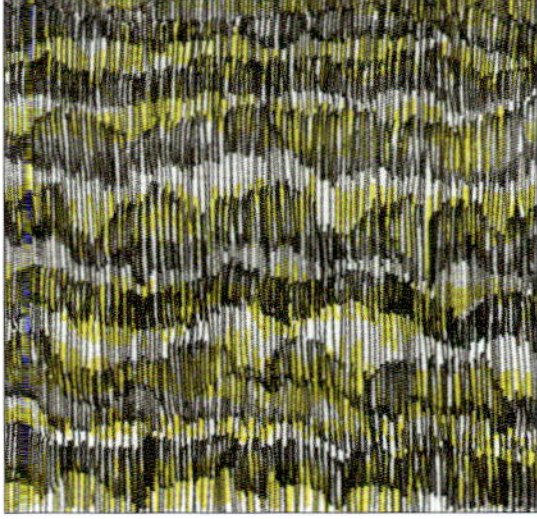

NERVOUS HABIT

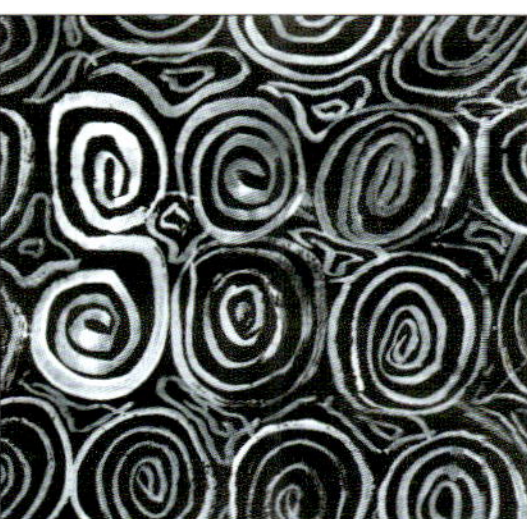

NERVOUS HABIT

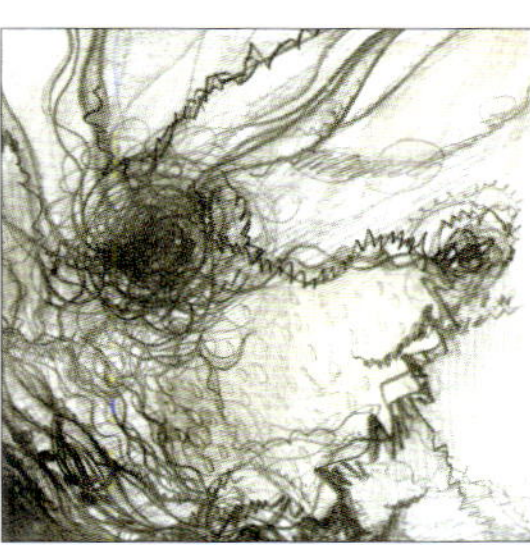

NERVOUS HABIT

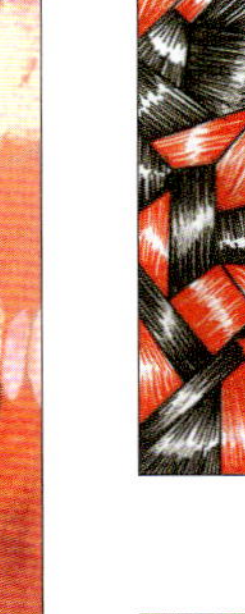

NERVOUS HABIT

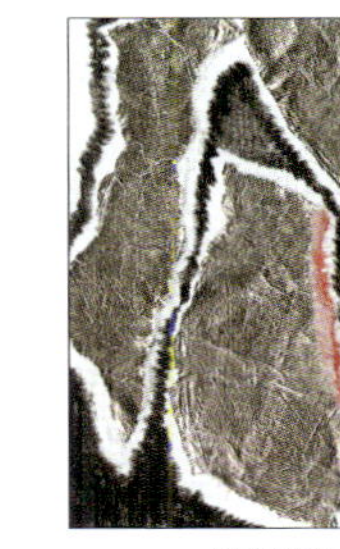
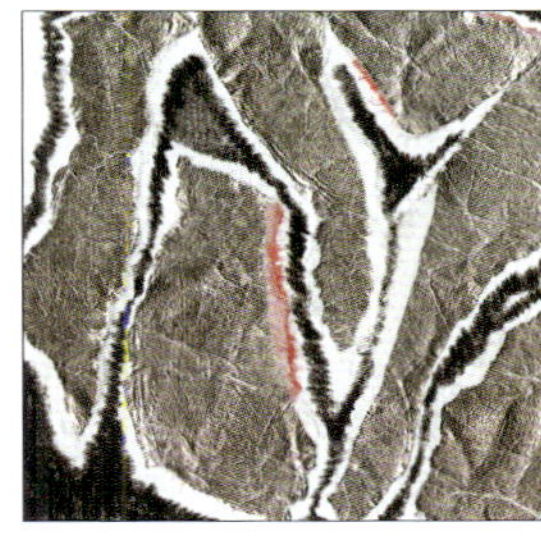

NERVOUS HABIT

NERVOUS HABIT

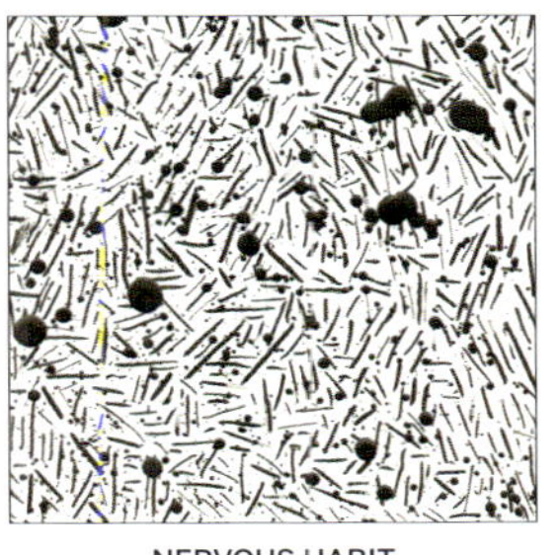
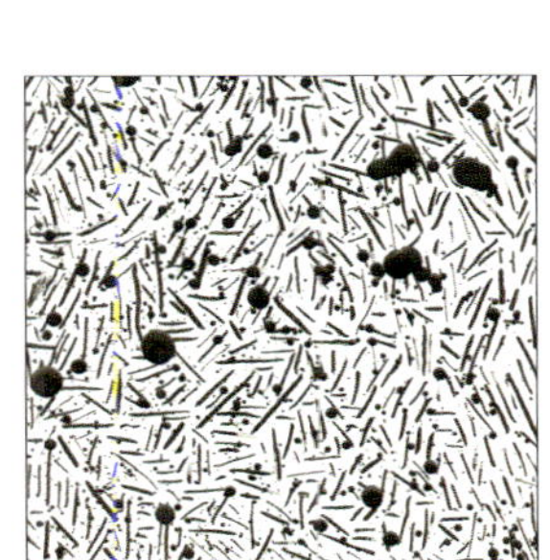

NERVOUS HABIT

NERVOUS HABIT

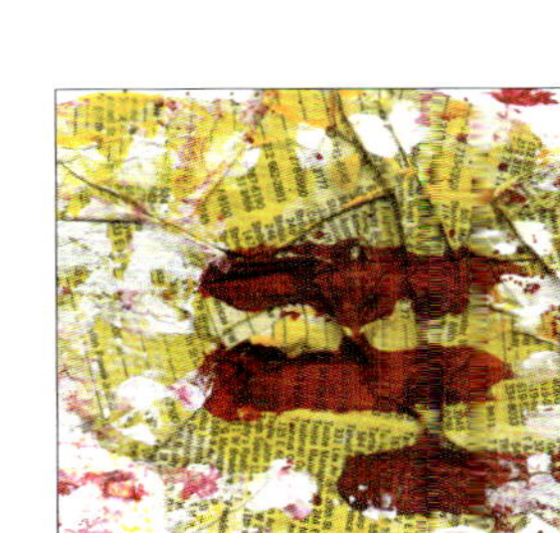

NERVOUS HABIT

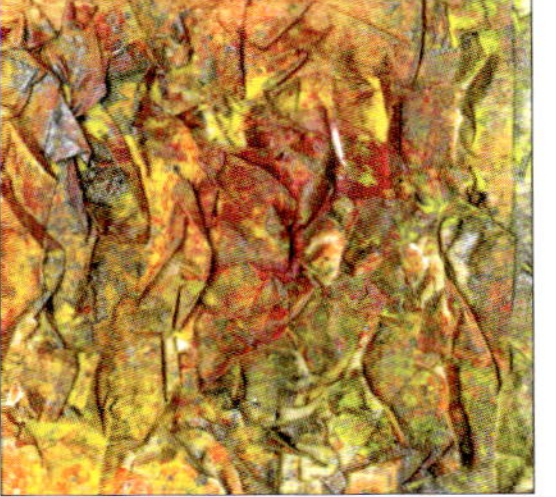

NERVOUS HABIT

NERVOUS HABIT

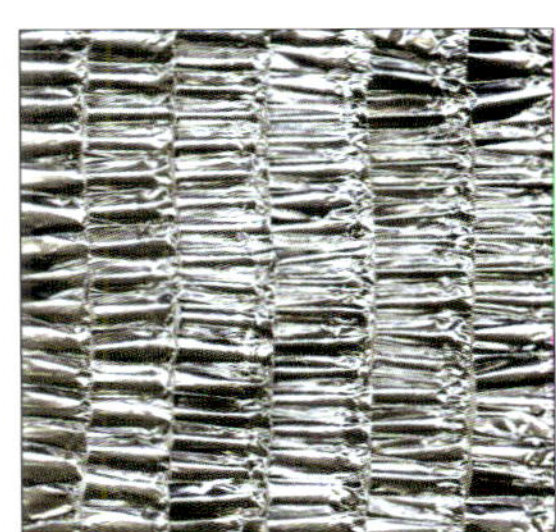

NERVOUS HABIT

SOUND SOLUTIONS: COCKFIGHT & NERVOUS HABIT

Figures 1 through 6 are investigations into the bloody world of cockfighting, which is an illegal activity in the USA. They deal with struggle and ensuing death. The color red is used to accentuate the sound of violence and conflict.

Figures 7 through 27 are examples of a nervous habit. Interpretations range from patterning, or a rhythmic motion, which infers an habitual repetitive movement, to personal abstract idiosyncratic behaviors.

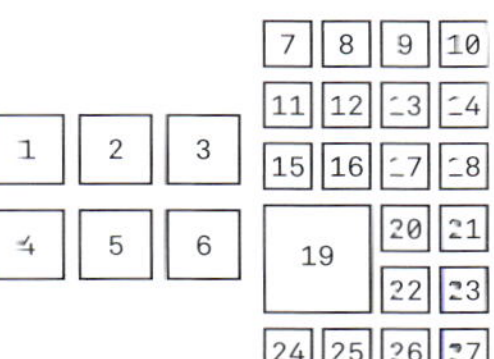

1. *Sunyoung Koo*
2. *Samantha Zahabian*
3. *Yoonbin Lee*
4. *J. Kim*
5. *Sarah Macreading*
6. *Chelsey Chapman*
7. *Jeffrey Teets*
8. *Moonee Kim*
9. *Yi Chen Tsai*
10. *Aimée Hunt*
11. *Thomas Caruso*
12. *David Freiman*
13. *Fanny Sping Artursson*
14. *Bomi Jo*
15. *Elaine Park*
16. *Minjoo Han*
17. *Kato Kie*
18. *Euna Lee*
19. *Christopher Wright*
20. *Nicole Lapenta*
21. *Yeonsoo Kim*
22. *Yeojin Tak*
23. *Santiago Carrasquilla*
24. *Joohee Hong*
25. *Katie Lim*
26. *Rachelle Browers*
27. *Brianna Hussey*

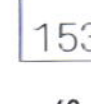

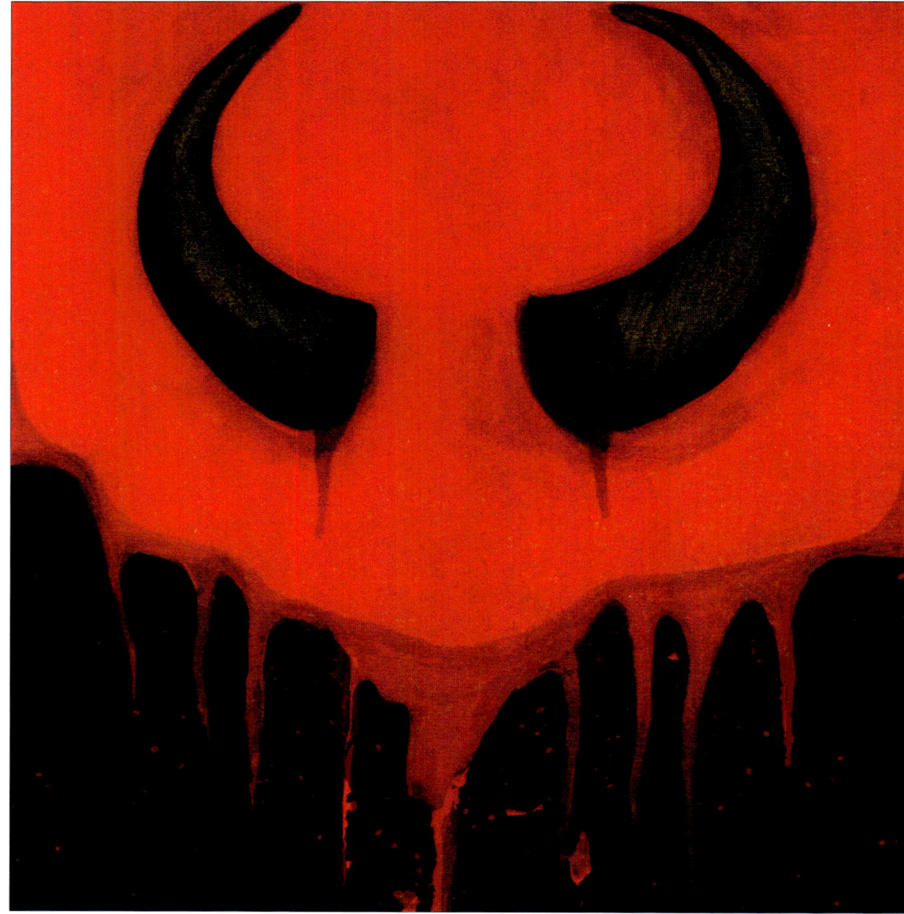

CONFRONTATION BETWEEN A MATADOR AND A BULL

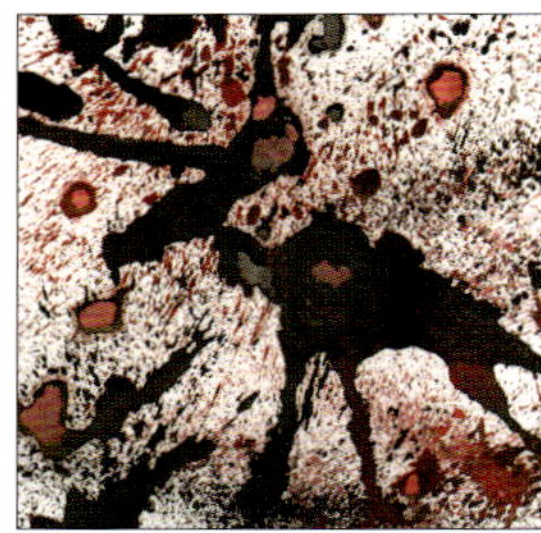

CONFRONTATION BETWEEN A MATADOR AND A BULL

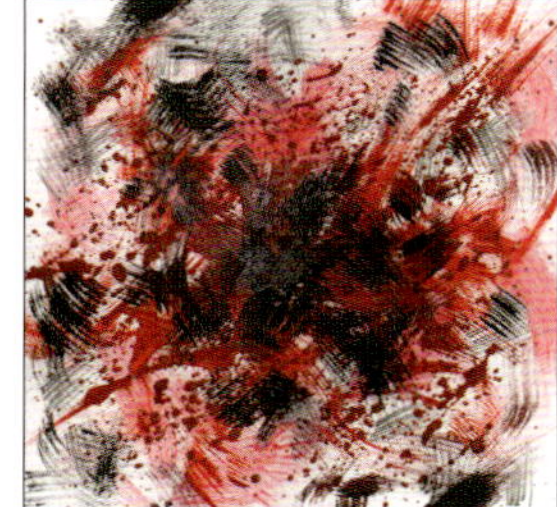

CONFRONTATION BETWEEN A MATADOR AND A BULL

CONFRONTATION BETWEEN A MATADOR AND A BULL

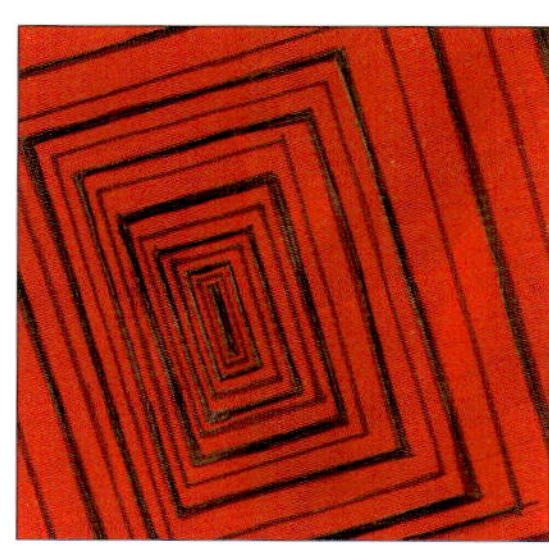

CONFRONTATION BETWEEN A MATADOR AND A BULL

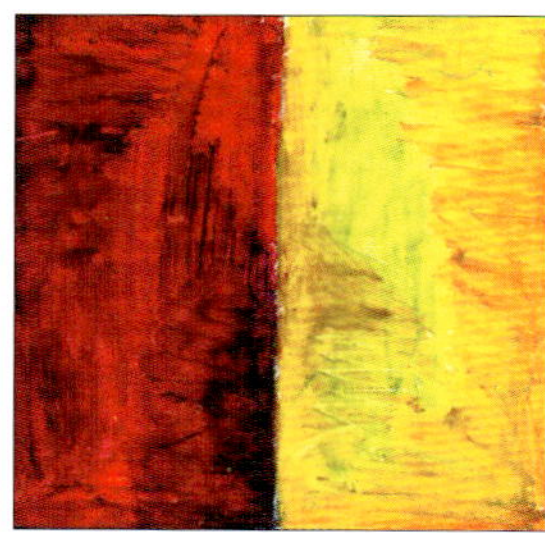

CONFRONTATION BETWEEN A MATADOR AND A BULL

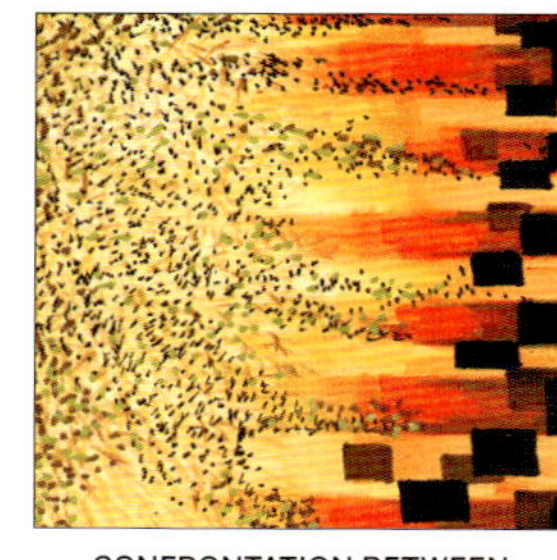

CONFRONTATION BETWEEN A MATADOR AND A BULL

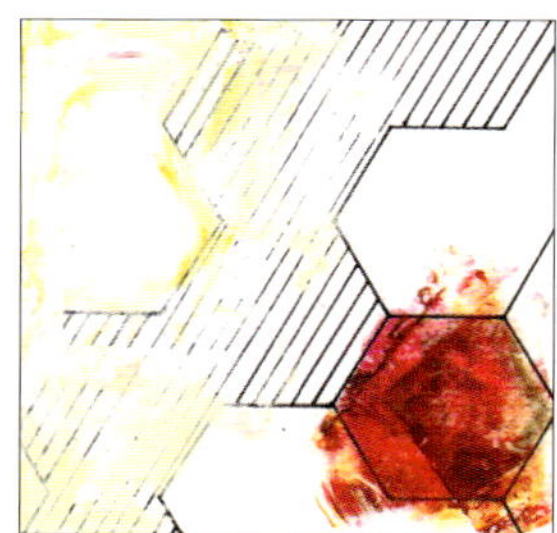

CONFRONTATION BETWEEN A MATADOR AND A BULL

SOUND SOLUTIONS: CONFRONTATION BETWEEN A MATADOR AND A BULL & EARTHQUAKE

The dramatic tension of a bullfight and the occurrence of an earthquake share certain similarities that can be drawn from these interpretations.

The bullfight is depicted in figures 1 through 8, and all exhibit a sense of violence. The color red, which references blood, is utilized in every solution.

Given its almost symmetrical composition, figure 1 is symbolic in its representation, while figures 2 and 3 clearly show the goriness of this confrontation.

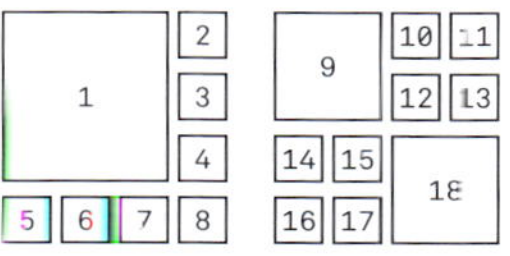

1. Inga Kolta-Mnich
2. Vera Gorbunova
3. Nicole Lapenta
4. Joohee Hong
5. Moonee Kim
6. Nayoung Kim
7. Yi Chen Tsai
8. Donna Kwon
9. Aemin Shim
10. Minjung Lee
11. Tess Lee
12. A. Martinez
13. Yi Chen Tsai
14. Yulsoo Sung
15. Jieun Jeon
16. Hayun Moon
17. D. Guzman
18. D. Kramerova

The solutions for an earthquake in figures 9 through 18 evoke a sound that many people have never heard. Here, the intent was to place students in a similar situation to Albrecht Dürer when he portrayed a rhinoceros that had only been described to him. What transpired was an interpretation of a creature that lived in both reality and fantasy at the same time. Invention was the modus operandi.

EARTHQUAKE

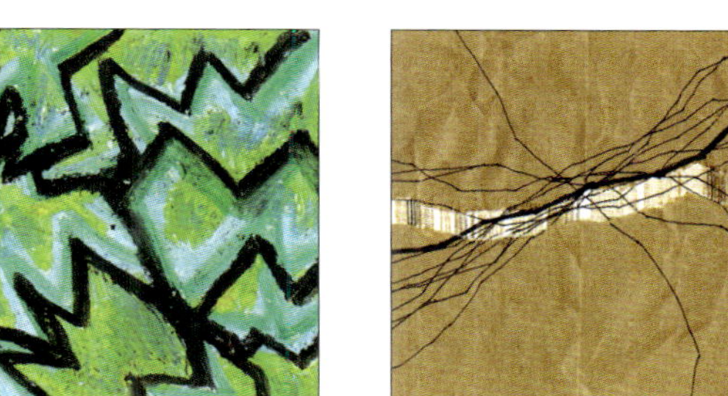

EARTHQUAKE

EARTHQUAKE

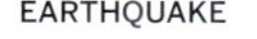

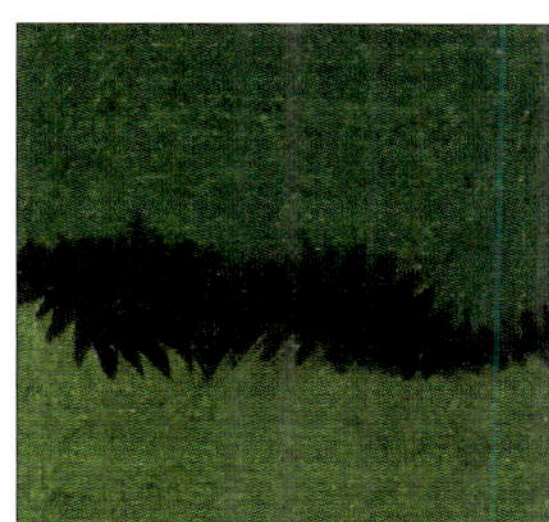

EARTHQUAKE

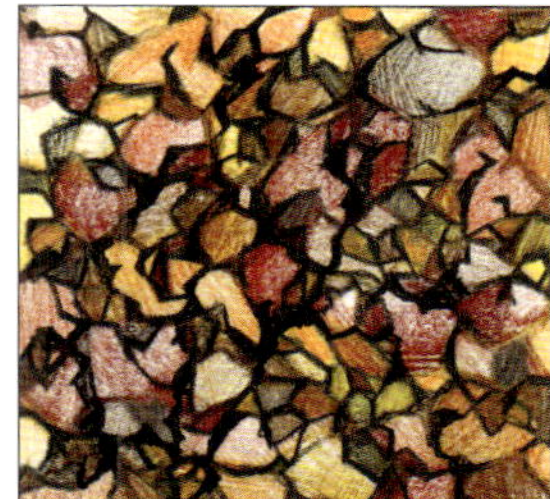

EARTHQUAKE

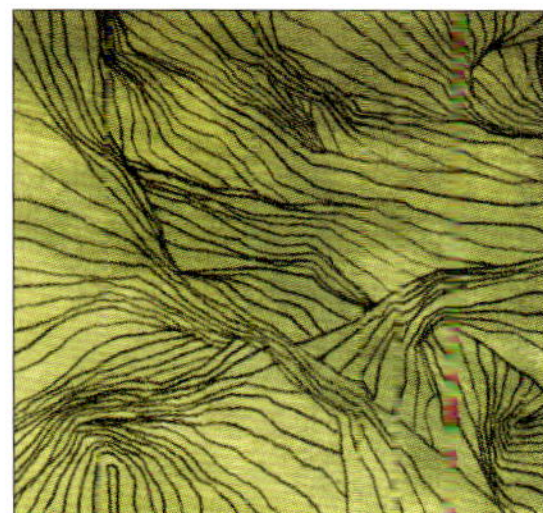

EARTHQUAKE

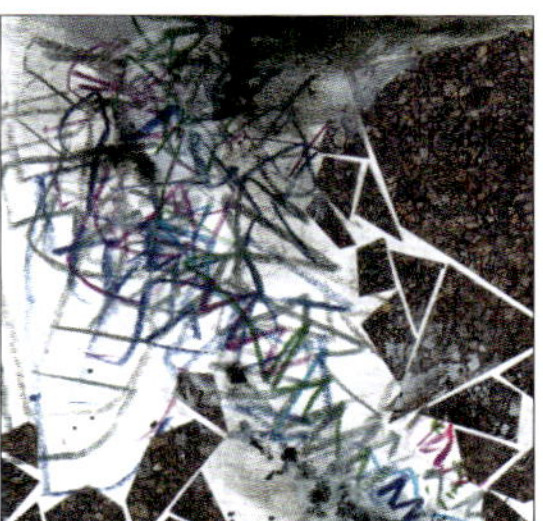

EARTHQUAKE

EARTHQUAKE

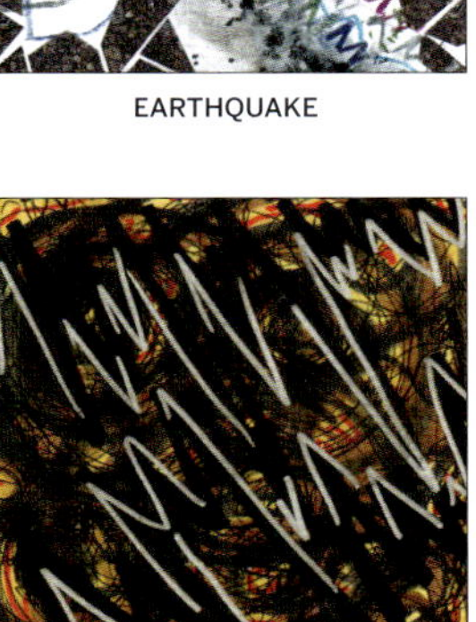

EARTHQUAKE

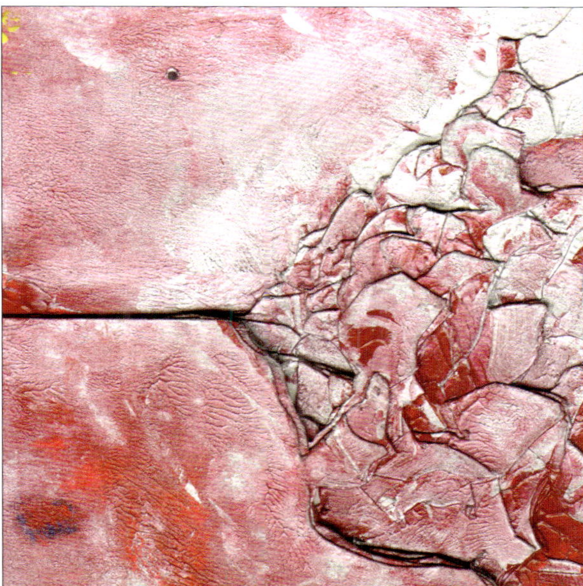

EARTHQUAKE

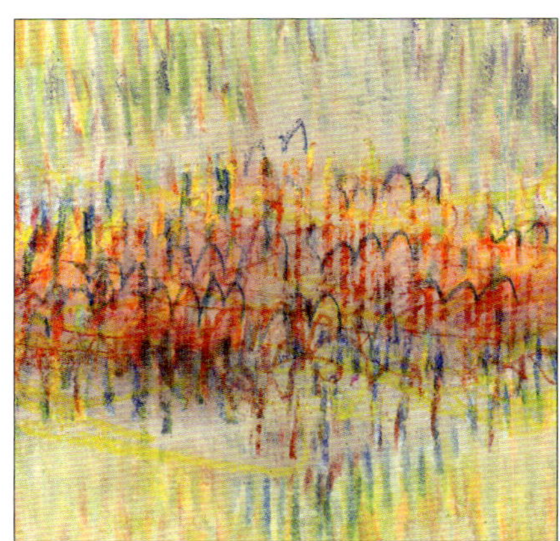
ELEVATOR MUSIC

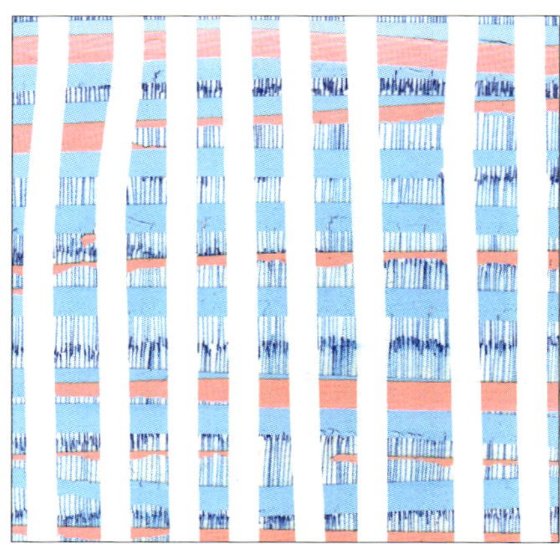
ELEVATOR MUSIC

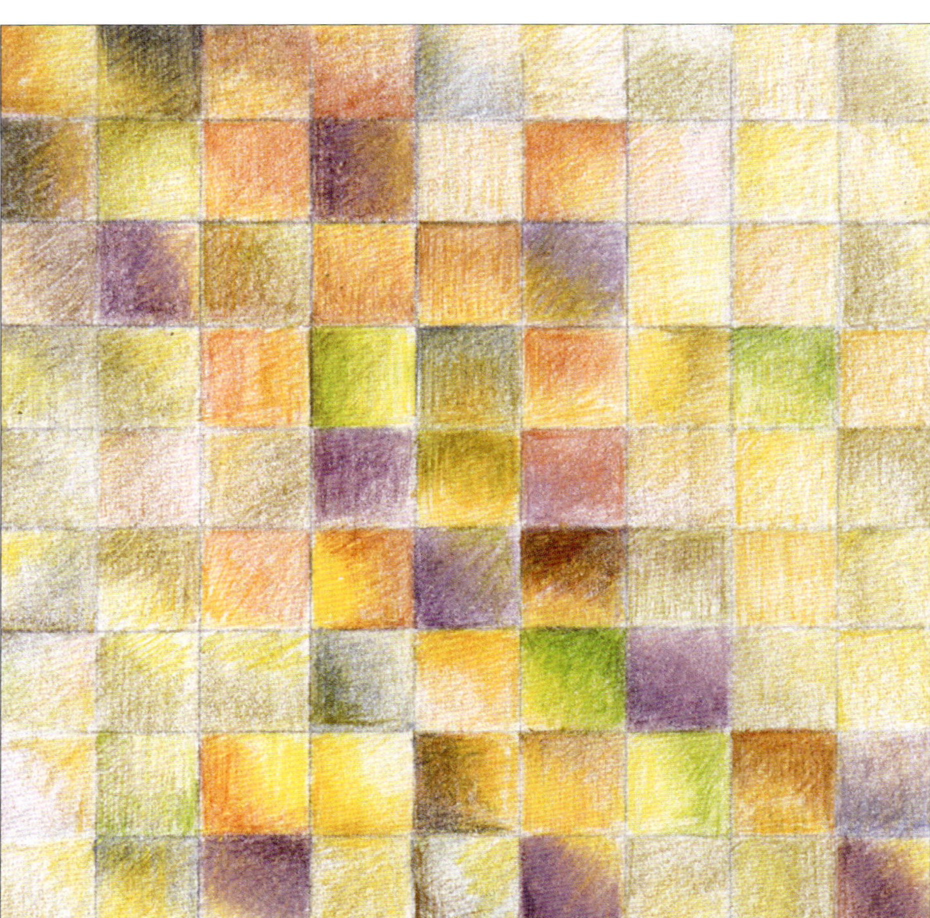
ELEVATOR MUSIC

SOUND SOLUTIONS: ELEVATOR MUSIC & SCHOOL BUS FILLED WITH CHILDREN

Figures 1 through 3 express the benign, barely inaudible music played in elevators.

Figures 4 through 12 represent a school bus filled with children. All solutions depict the colorful, lighthearted sensibility of this cacophony of sound. Movement and primary colors dominate in each composition.

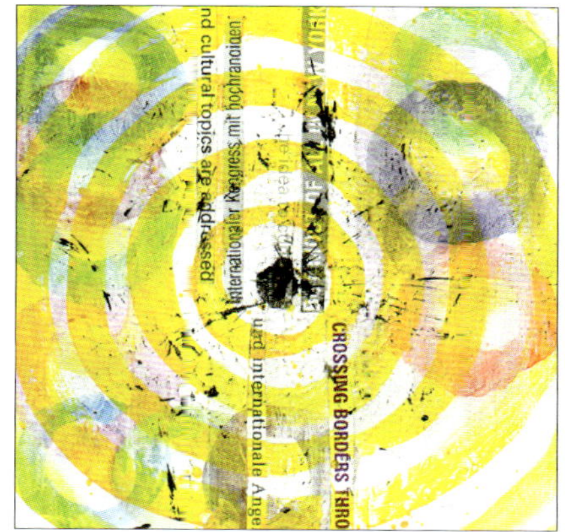

SCHOOL BUS FILLED WITH CHILDREN

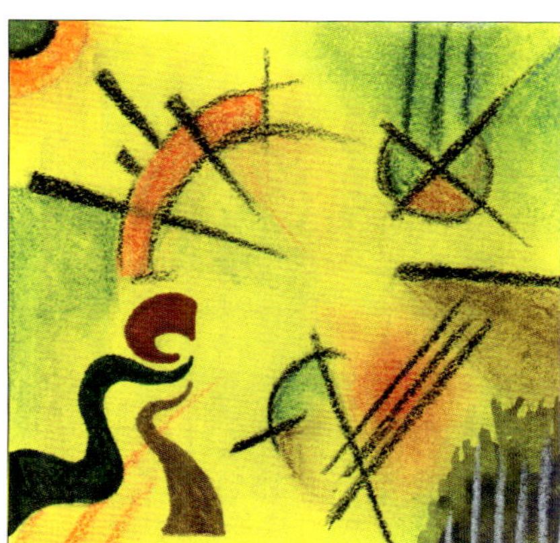

SCHOOL BUS FILLED WITH CHILDREN

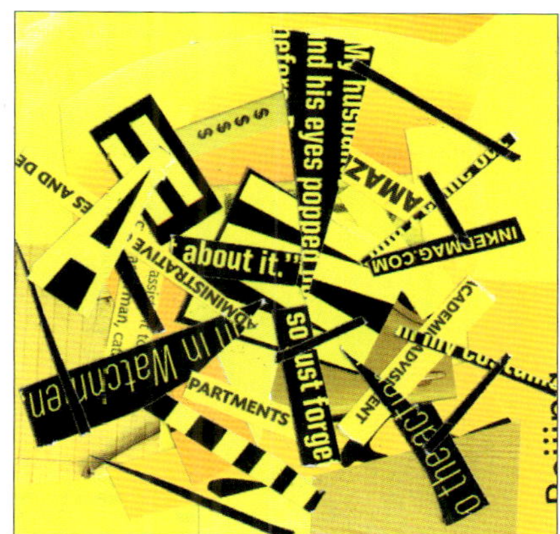

SCHOOL BUS FILLED WITH CHILDREN

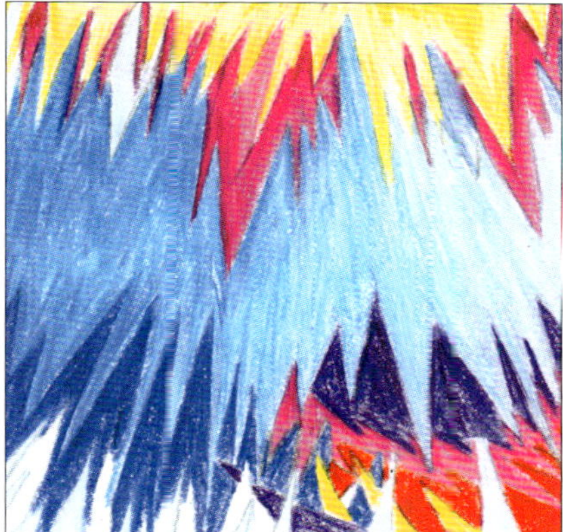

SCHOOL BUS FILLED WITH CHILDREN

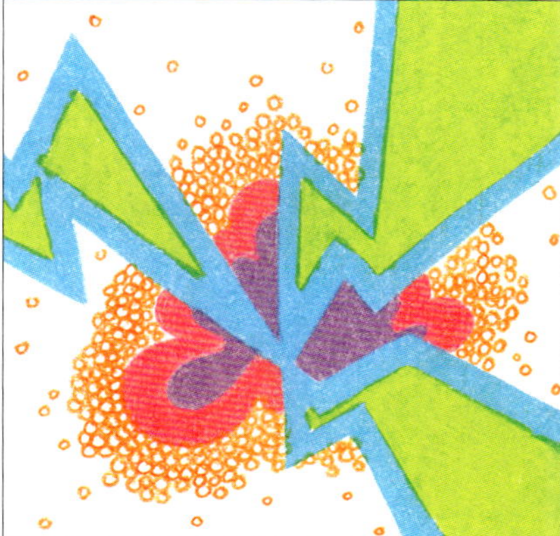

SCHOOL BUS FILLED WITH CHILDREN

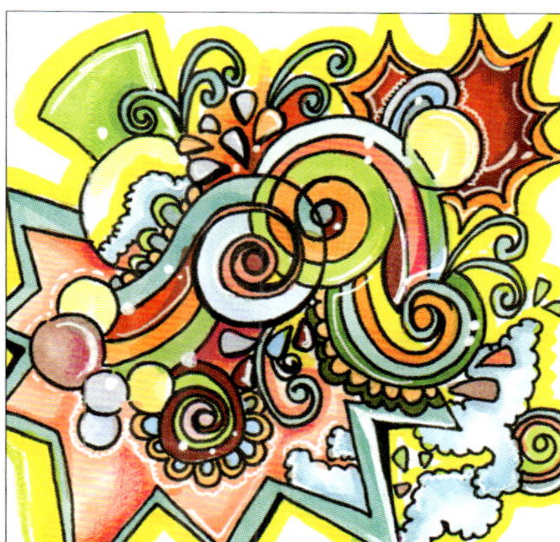

SCHOOL BUS FILLED WITH CHILDREN

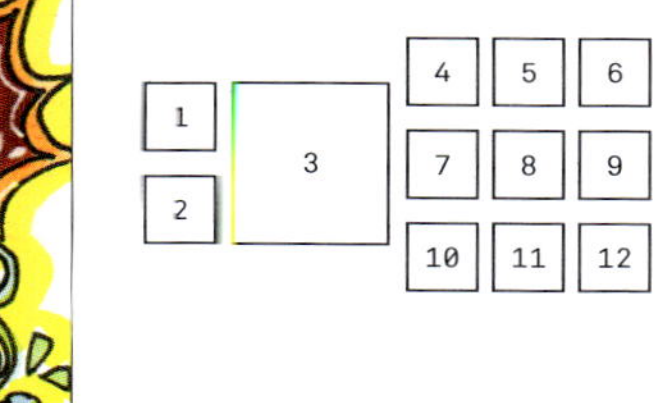

1. *Madeleine Arnoucd*
2. *Yueh Lu*
3. *Regina Kushnir*
4. *Joohee Hong*
5. *Fedro Dos Santos*
6. *Deokjang Yoon*
7. *John Allen*
8. *Scott Buchan*
9. *Hea Kim*
10. *Dominika Kramerova*
11. *Aemin Shim*
12. *Junewon Han*

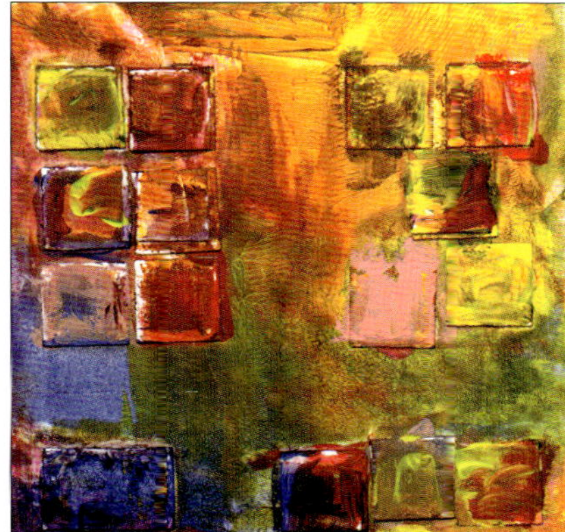

SCHOOL BUS FILLED WITH CHILDREN

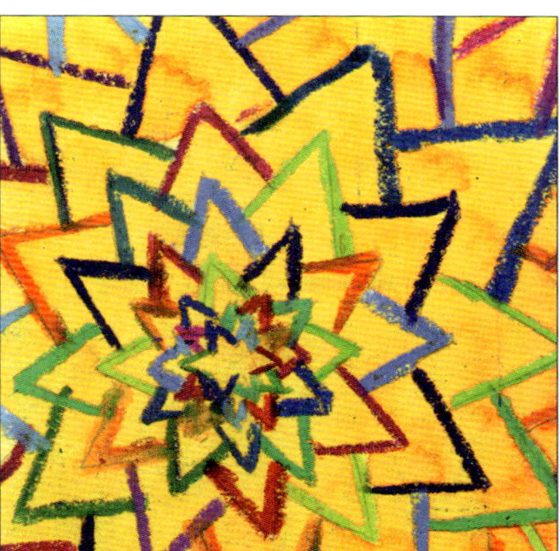

SCHOOL BUS FILLED WITH CHILDREN

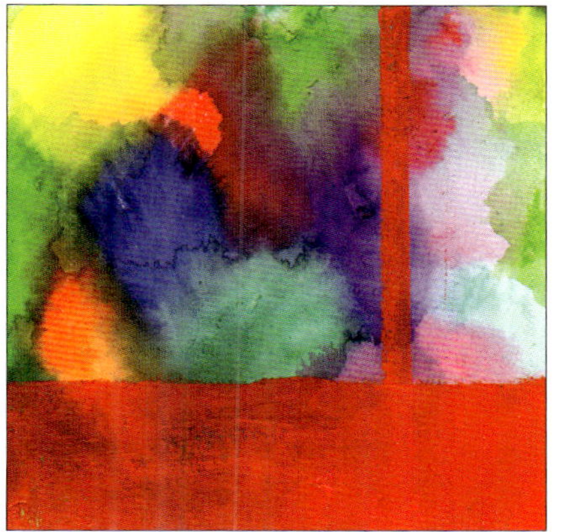

SCHOOL BUS FILLED WITH CHILDREN

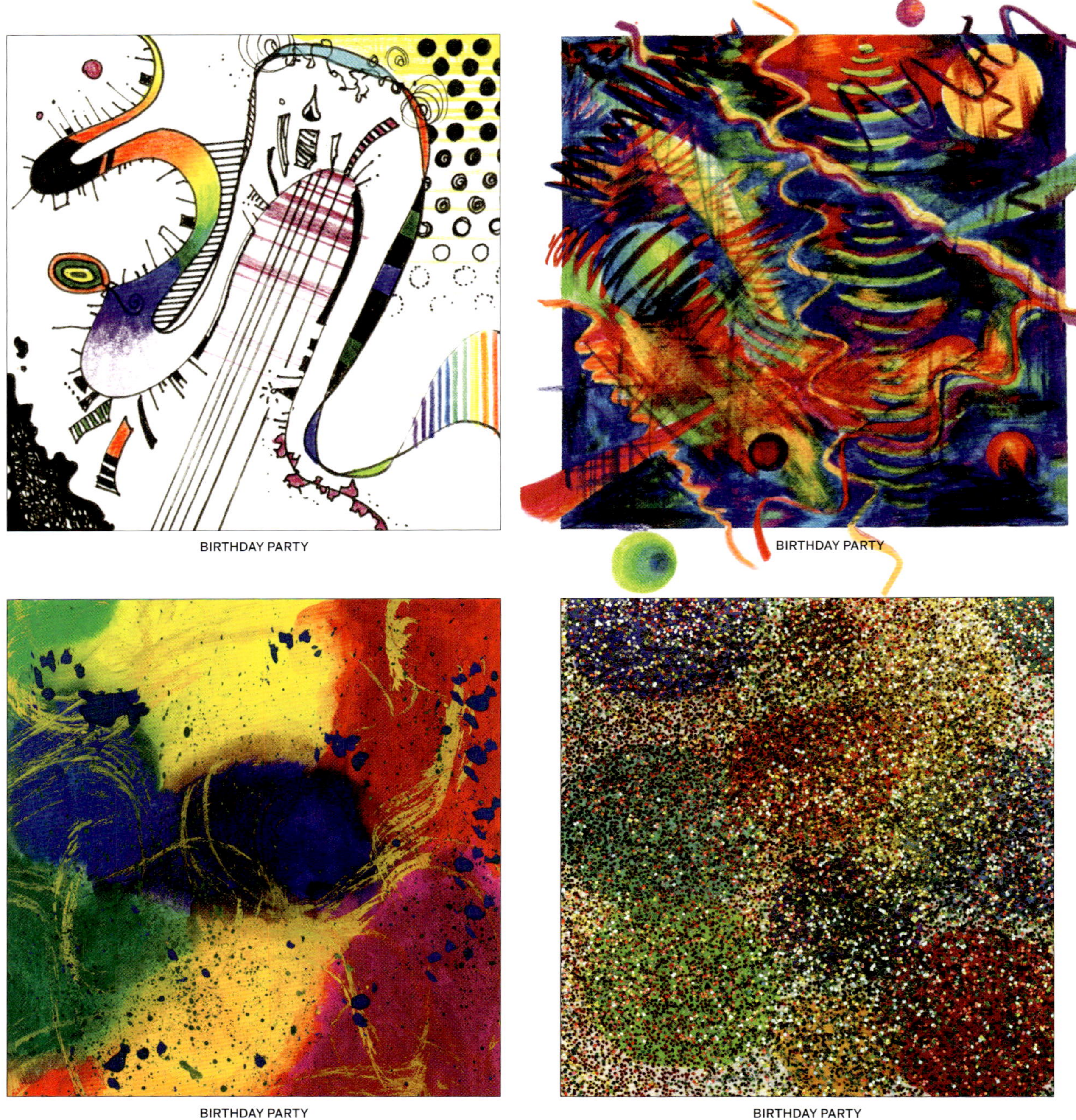

BIRTHDAY PARTY

BIRTHDAY PARTY

BIRTHDAY PARTY

BIRTHDAY PARTY

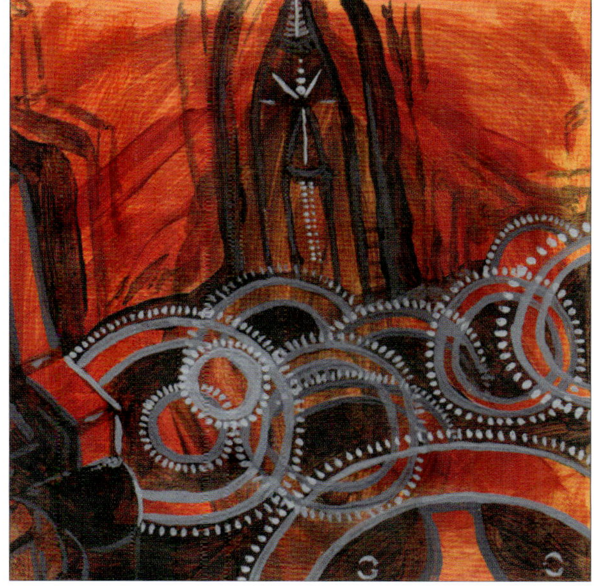

SUBWAY

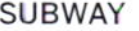

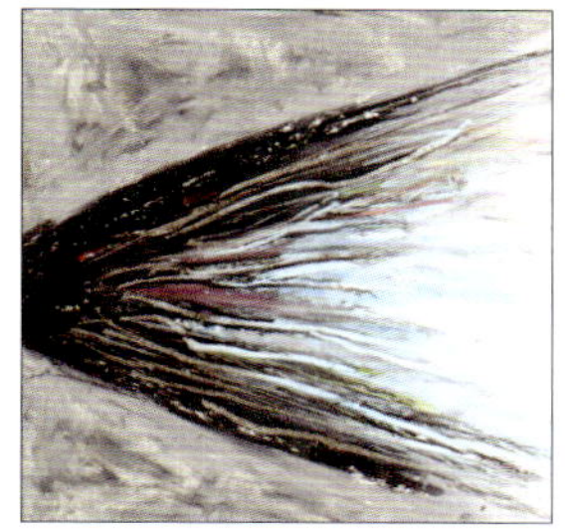

SUBWAY

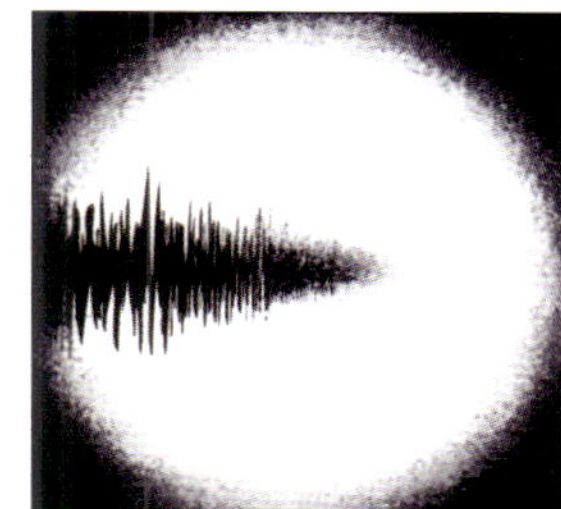

SUBWAY

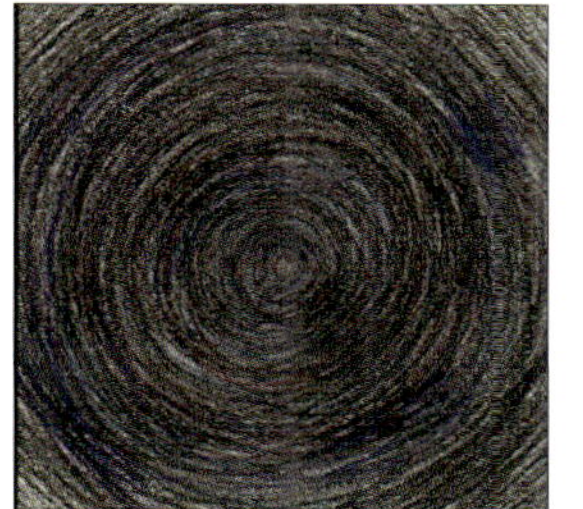

SUBWAY

SUBWAY

SUBWAY

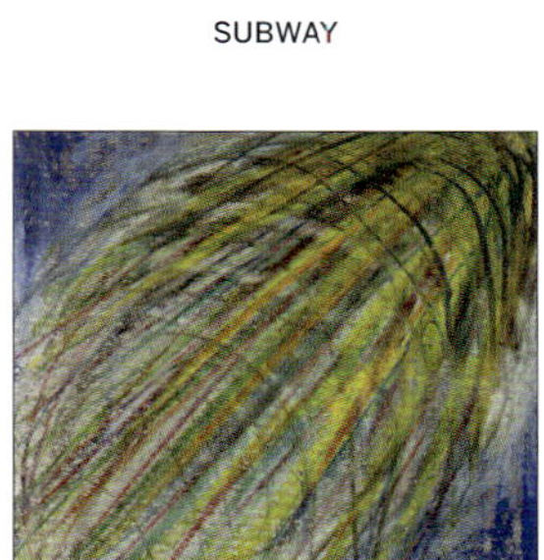

SUBWAY

SUBWAY

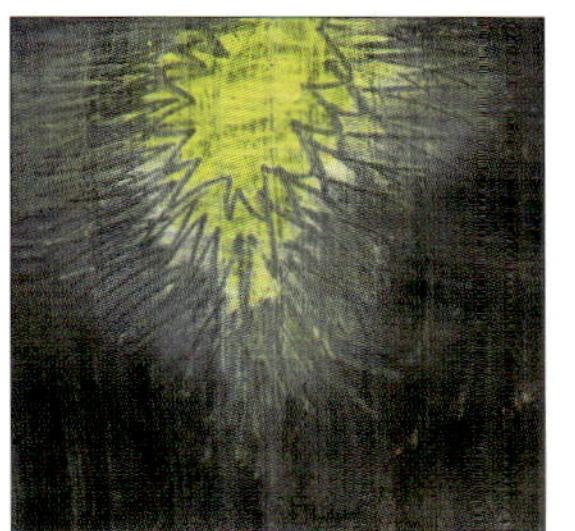

SUBWAY

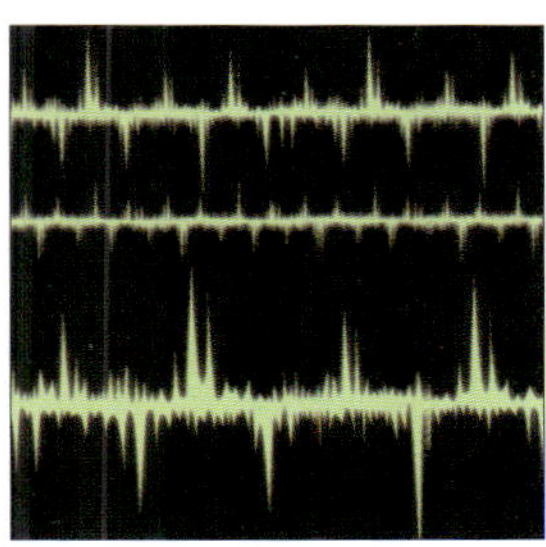

SUBWAY

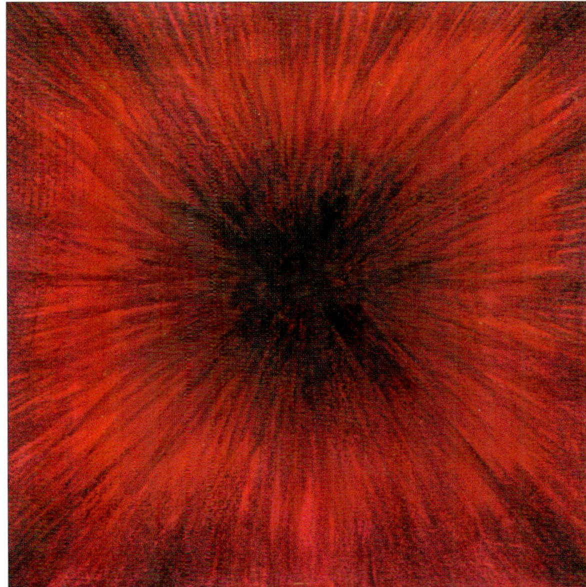

SUBWAY

SUBWAY

SUBWAY

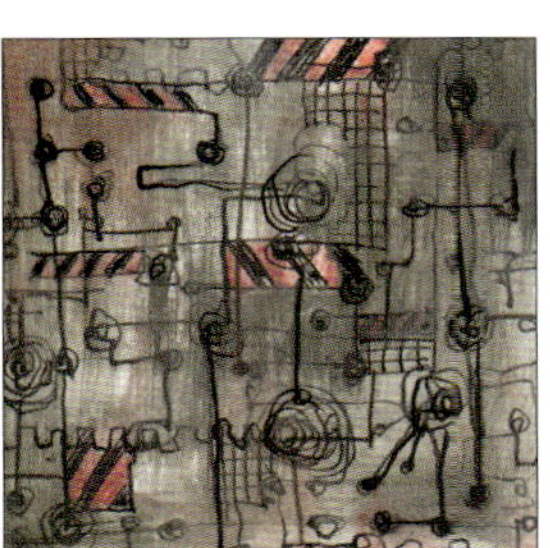

SUBWAY

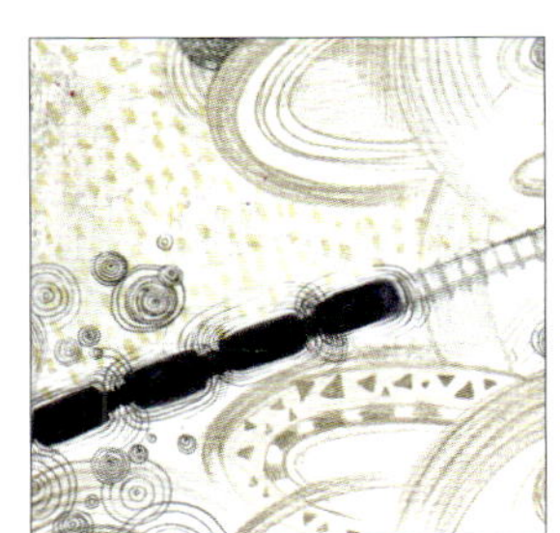

SUBWAY

SOUND SOLUTIONS: BIRTHDAY PARTY & SUBWAY

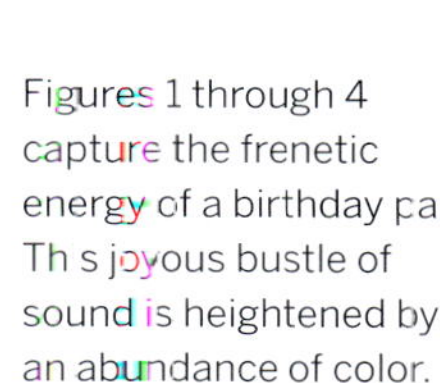

Figures 1 through 4 capture the frenetic energy of a birthday party. This joyous bustle of sound is heightened by an abundance of color.

Figure 4 uses color glitter as a medium.

The New York City subway is depicted in figures 5 through 19, which capture the sound in varying degrees of intensity. For some, the ominous nature of New York's underground subway, with its often deafening decibel level, is grappled with in these explorations.

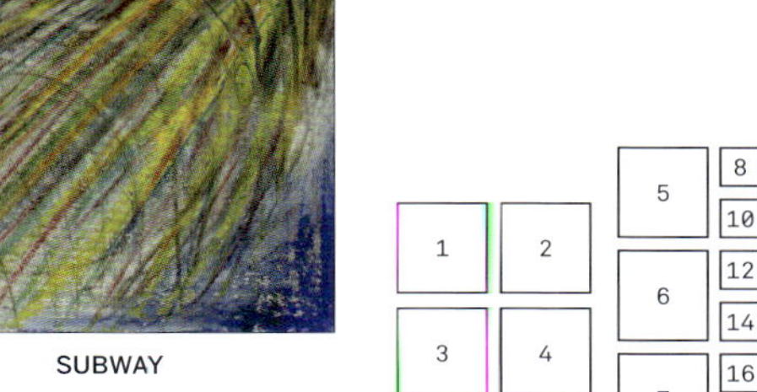

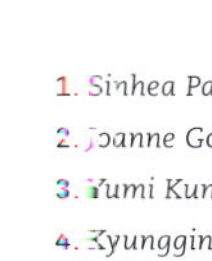

1. Sinhea Park
2. Joanne Gonzales
3. Yumi Kunz
4. Kyunggin Jun
5. Chris Foxx
6. Mina Kwon
7. Seunghun Lee
8. Gabriella Pugachevsky
9. Igor Langshteyn
10. Rosa Jung
11. Conner Fitzgerald
12. Alyssa Leary
13. Borim Kim
14. Joshua Pforsich
15. Duesung Byun
16. Erika Yost
17. Soobin Park
18. Thomas Shim
19. Heejung Kim

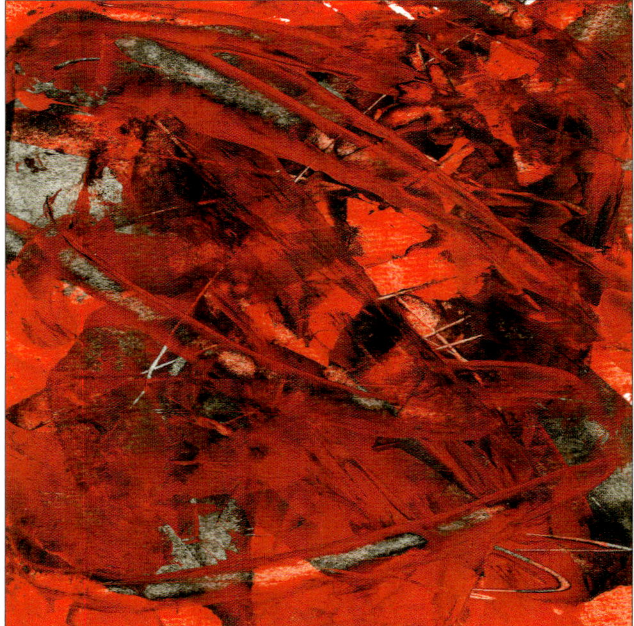
FRUSTRATION

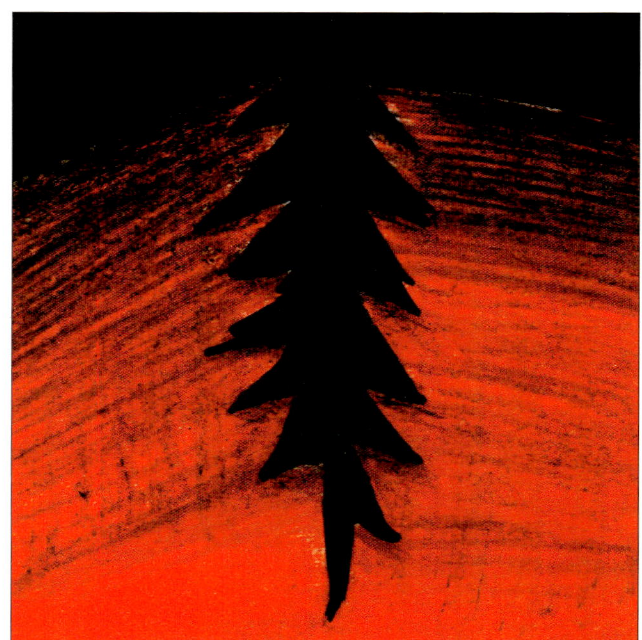
FRUSTRATION

SOUND SOLUTIONS: FRUSTRATION

Figures 1 through 8 deal with the subject of frustration, which has no audible sound connected to it. The constraints of this problem put one in the position to be inventive and use expressions of frustration as a starting point to simulate its possible sound. The activity of angst, turmoil, agitation, and tension are addressed throughout this assignment.

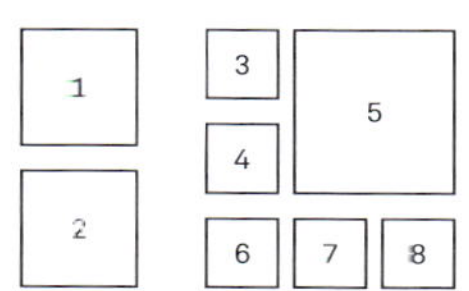

1. *Yuki Murata*
2. *Thomas Caruso*
3. *Nyong Ha Chang*
4. *Caleb Brown*
5. *Shanelle Ingante*
6. *Igor Langshteyn*
7. *Madeleine Arnoucd*
8. *Emily Bertone*

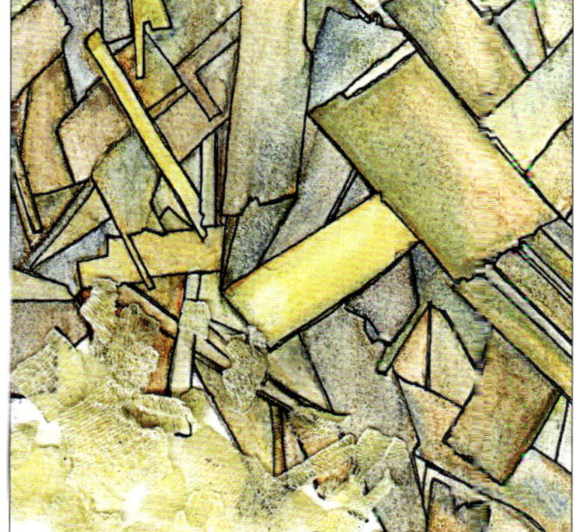

FRUSTRATION

FRUSTRATION

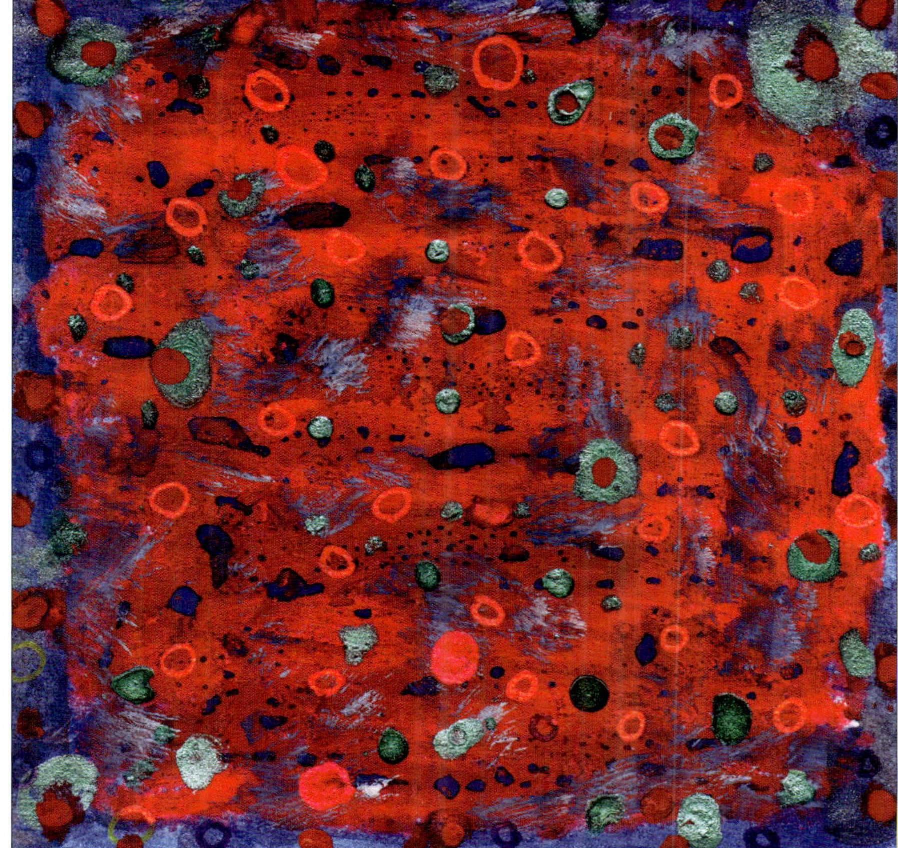

FRUSTRATION

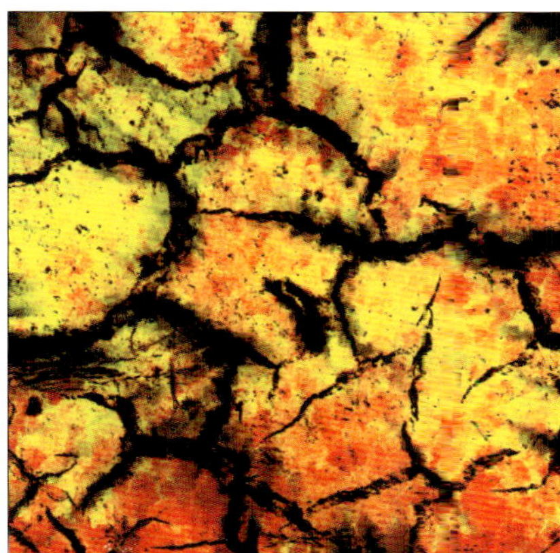

FRUSTRATION

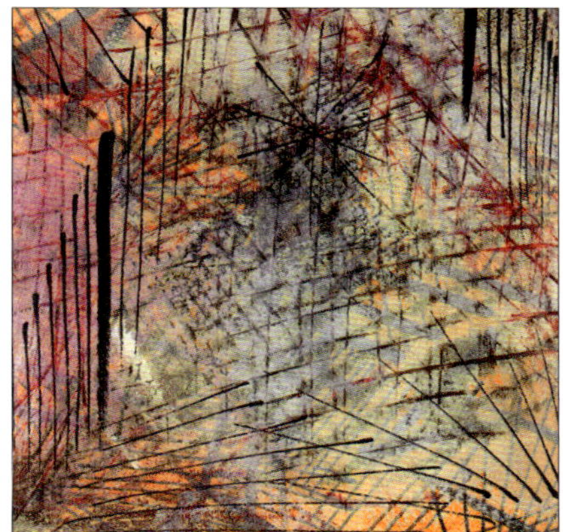

FRUSTRATION

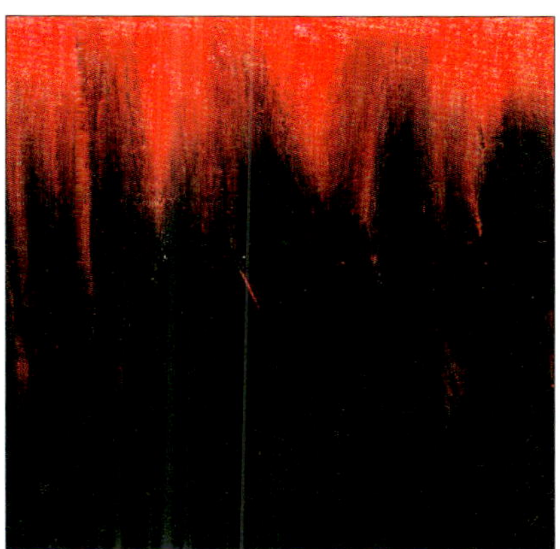

FRUSTRATION

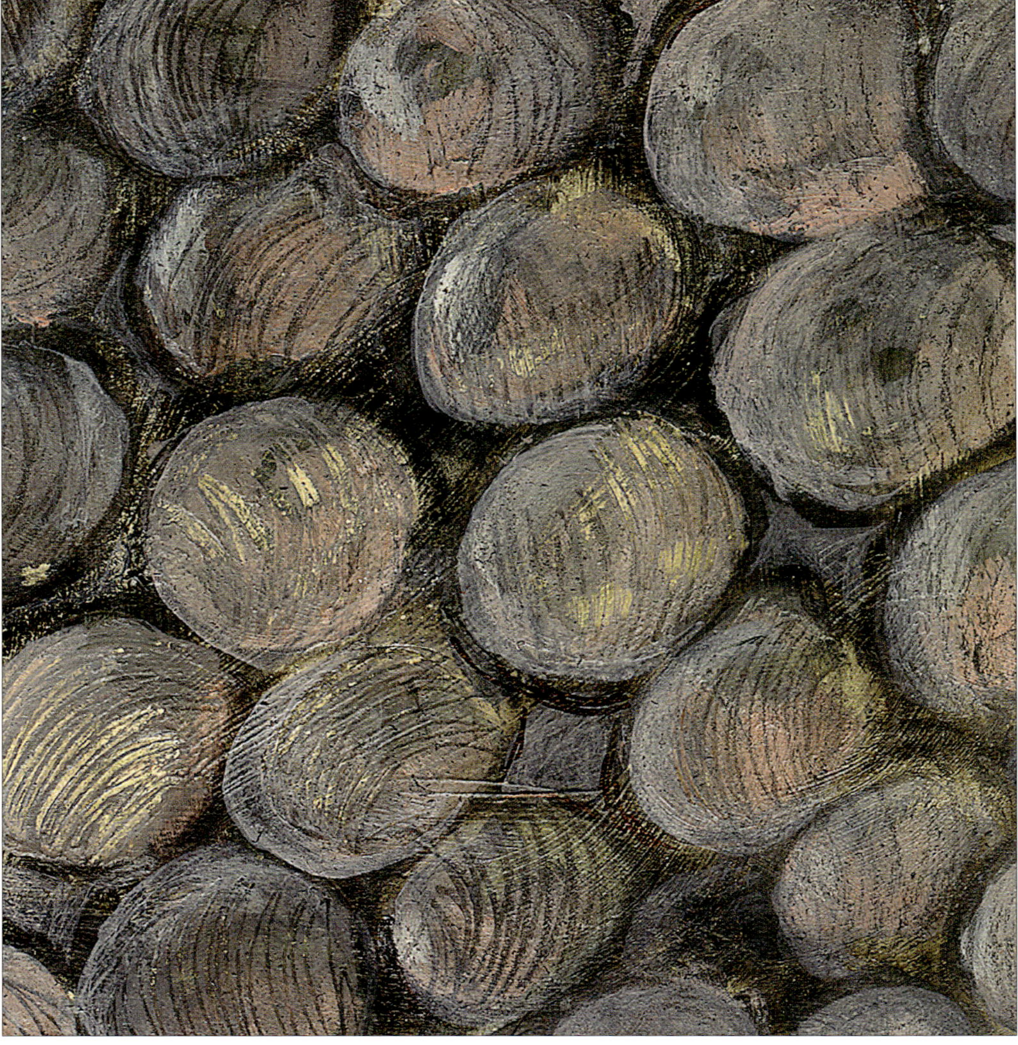
BARNYARD

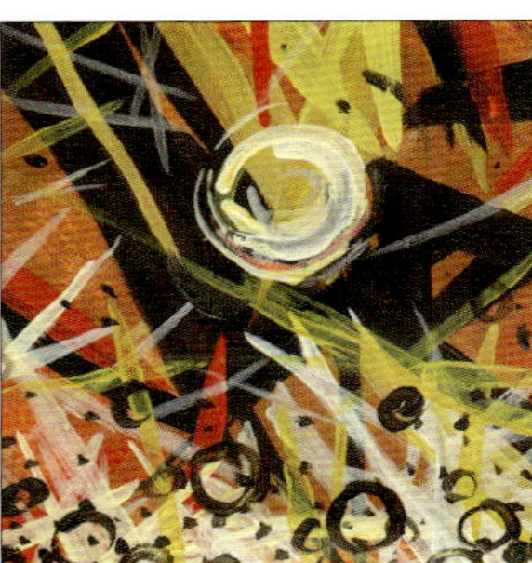
BARNYARD

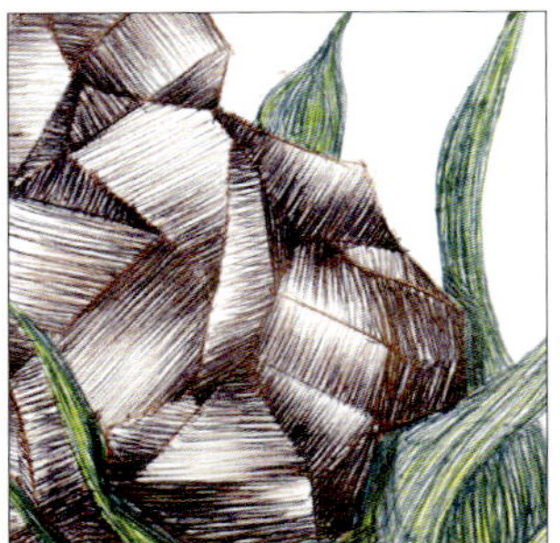
BARNYARD

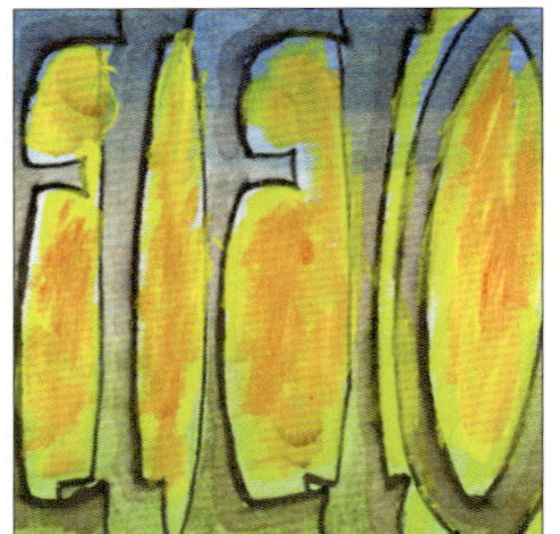
BARNYARD

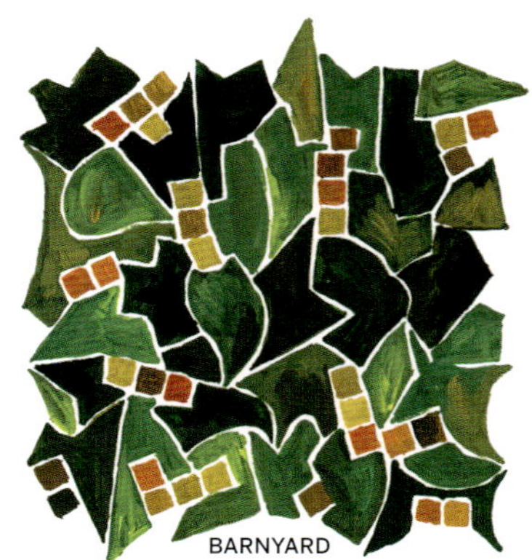
BARNYARD

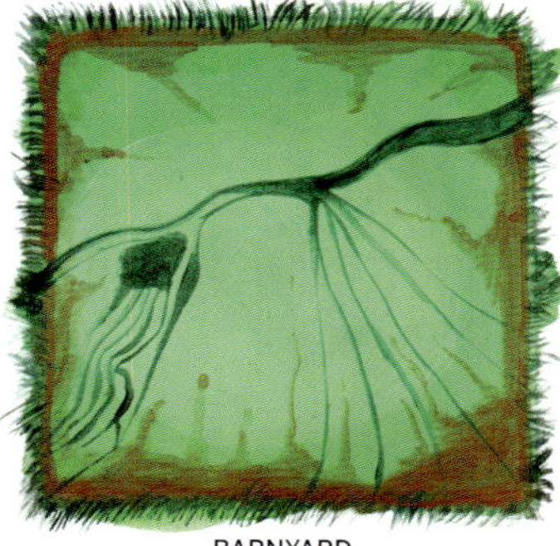
BARNYARD

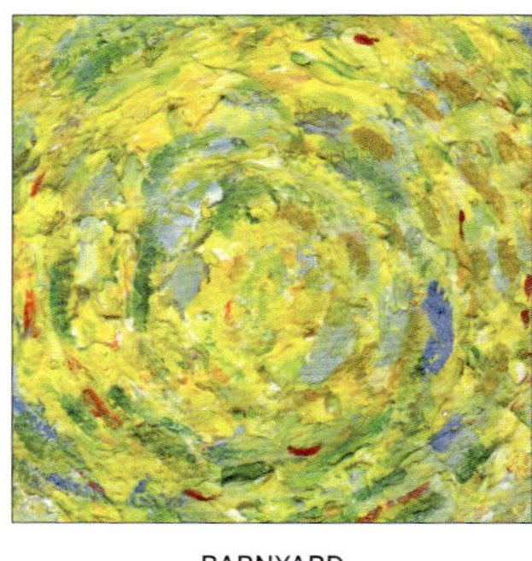
BARNYARD

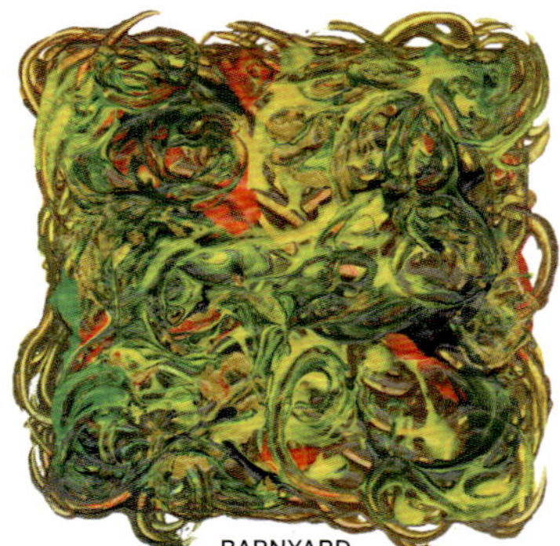
BARNYARD

SOUND SOLUTIONS: BARNYARD & TAP DANCER

Barnyard is addressed in figures 1 through 8, where a multiplicity of sounds ranging from animals, birds, insects, and farm machinery have been explored. Greens, browns and muted colors dominate the palette for these organic solutions.

Figure 4 is a typographic solution that uses the negative space to spell out the letters E, I, E, I, O, referencing a phrase from the classic children's nursery rhyme "Old MacDonald Had A Farm."

Figures 9 through 18 depict tap dancing, which mainly deals with rhythm.

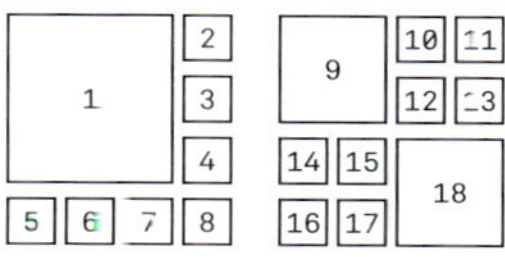

1. *Jhonny Tufino*
2. *Caleb Brown*
3. *Chien Wei Huang*
4. *Colleen Yessman*
5. *Hsing-Ting Kuo*
6. *Alberto Reyes*
7. *Yasmin Malki*
8. *Yoon Ha Chung*
9. *Yookyoung Kim*
10. *Heesang Lee*
11. *Lily Tran*
12. *Yunhaing Kwak*
13. *Haein Kim*
14. *Caleb Brown*
15. *Gouhea Park*
16. *Seongmi Park*
17. *Sooyoon Lee*
18. *Chien Wei Huang*

TAP DANCER

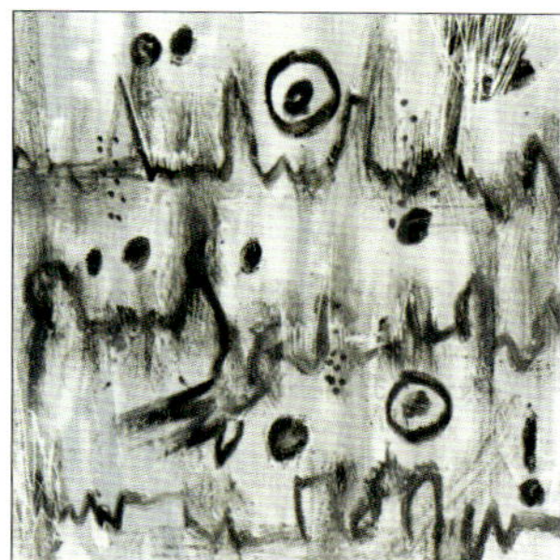

TAP DANCER

TAP DANCER

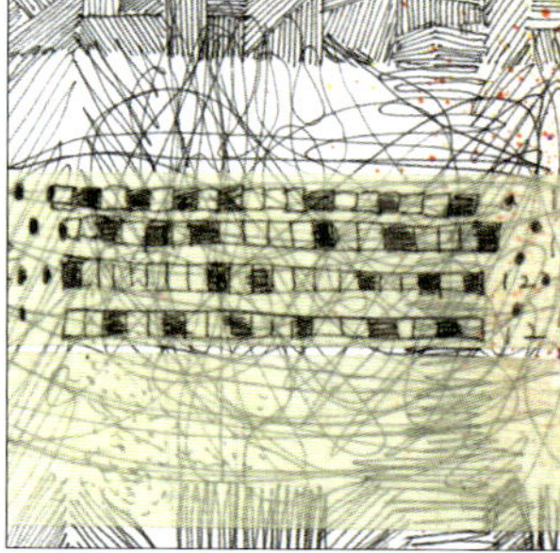

TAP DANCER

TAP DANCER

TAP DANCER

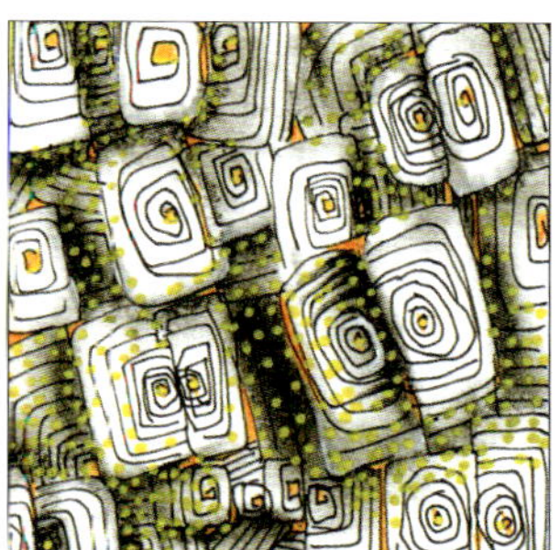

TAP DANCER

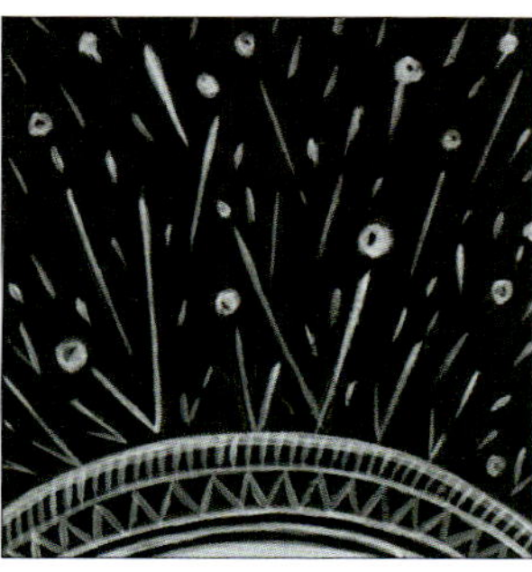

TAP DANCER

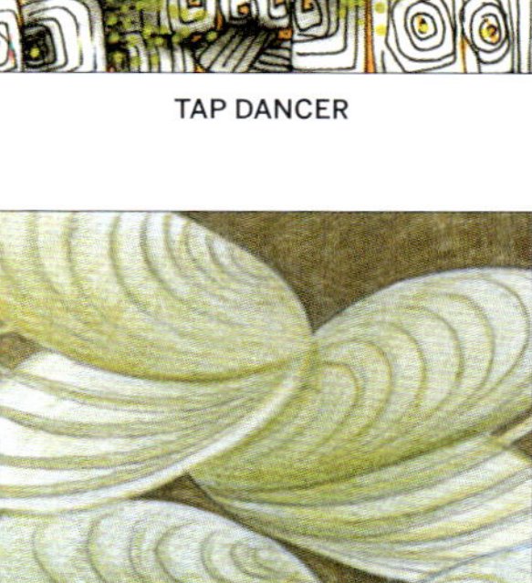

TAP DANCER

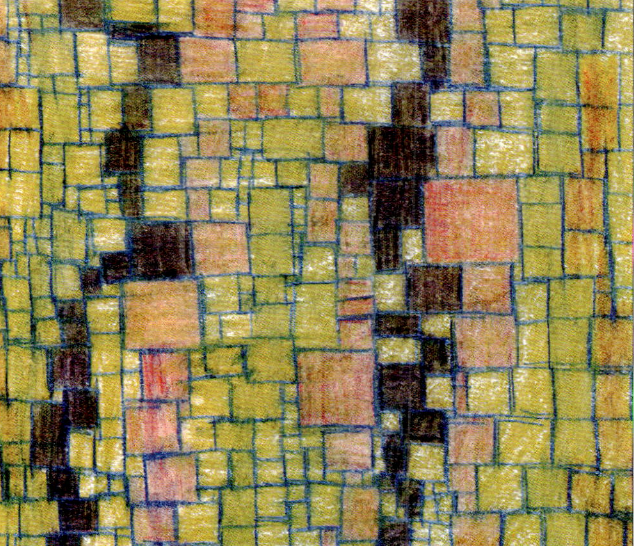

TAP DANCER

Solutions are compositionally and formally very different from one other. This can be said of most every solution in the sound project, because an emphasis is placed on personal interpretation.

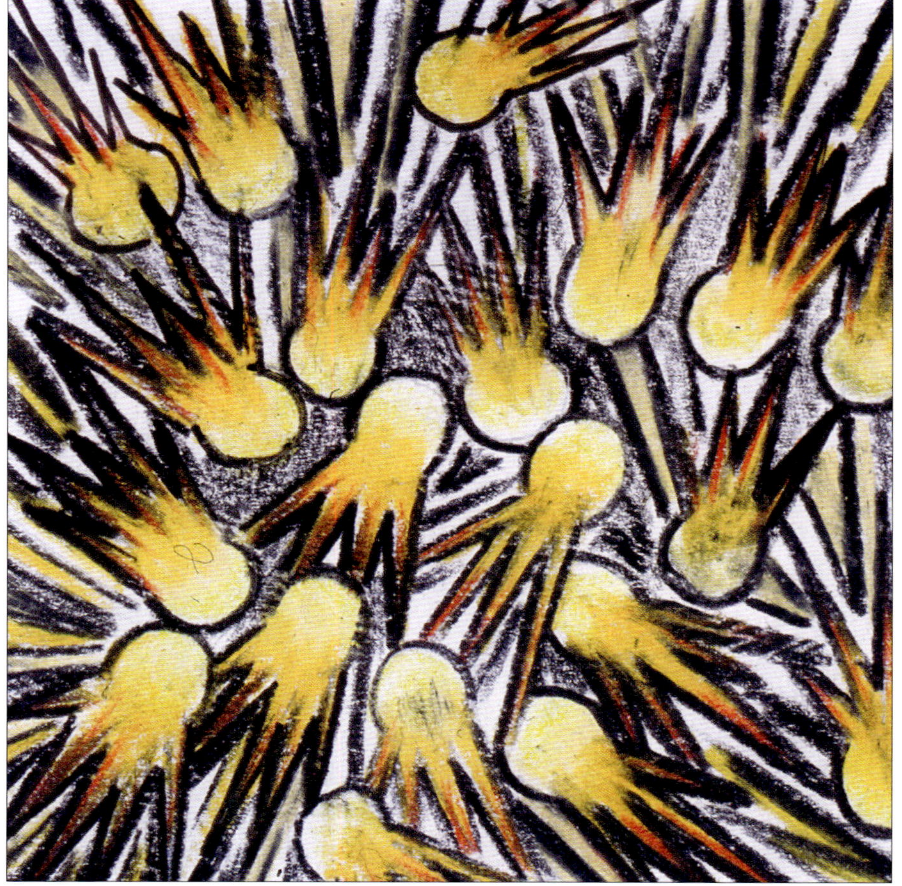
POPCORN POPPING

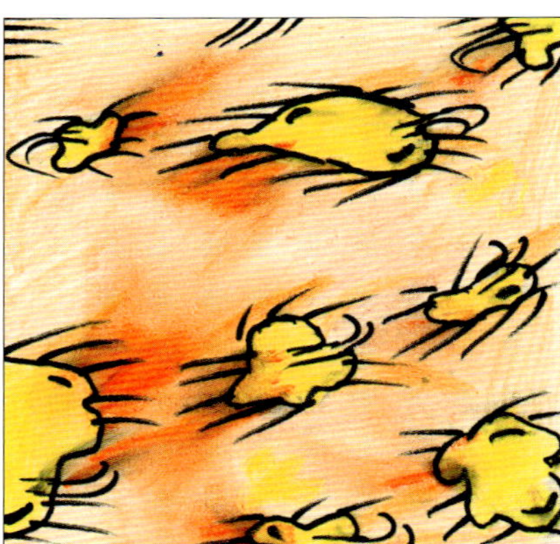
POPCORN POPPING

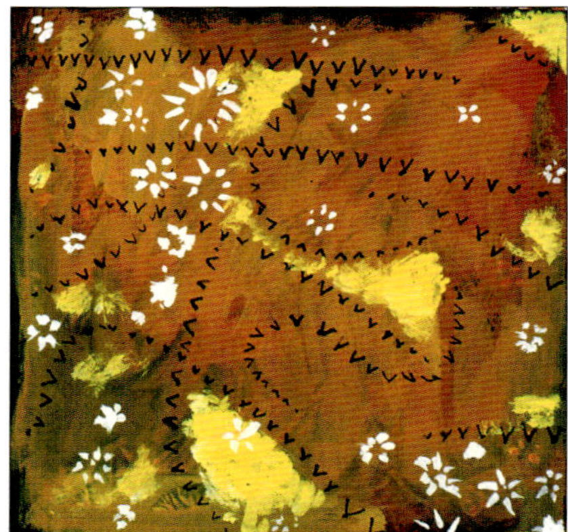
POPCORN POPPING

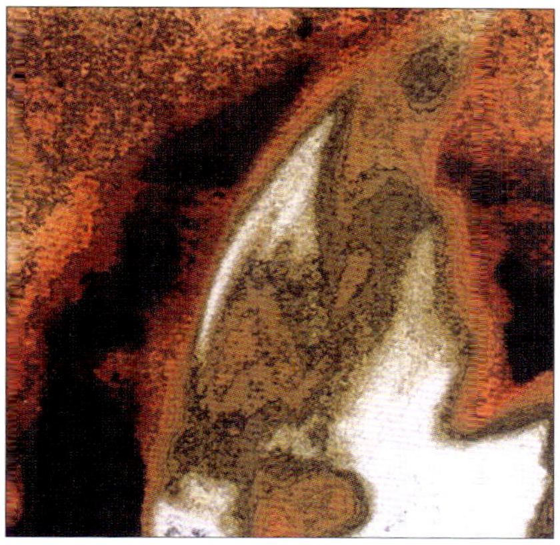

WAR

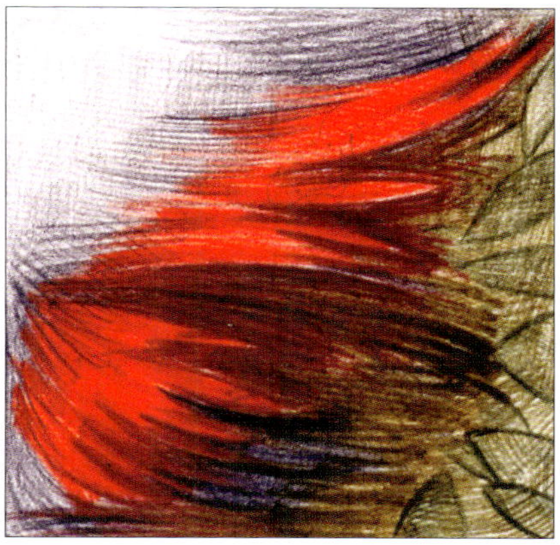

WAR

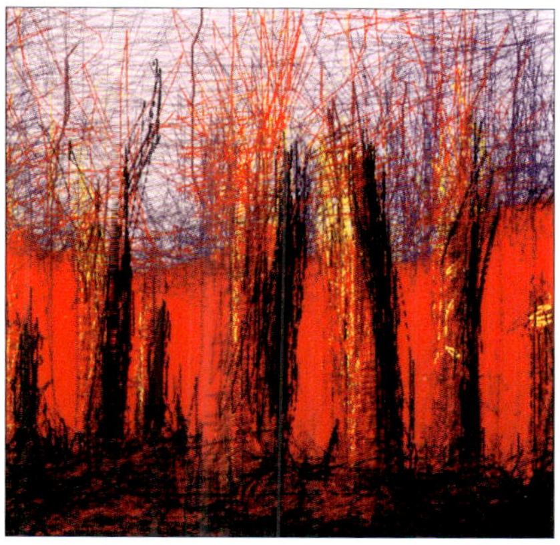

WAR

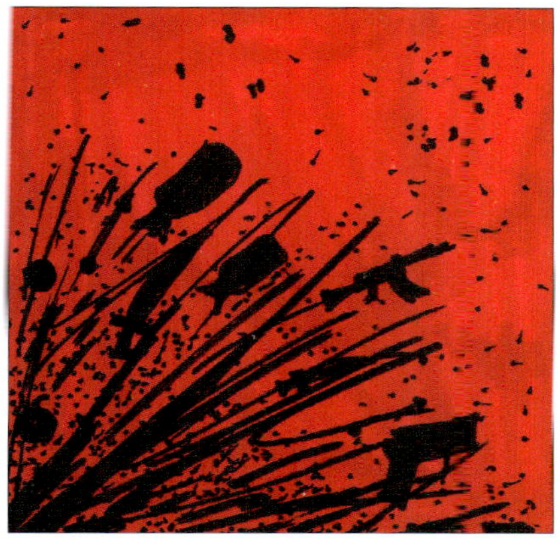

WAR

WAR

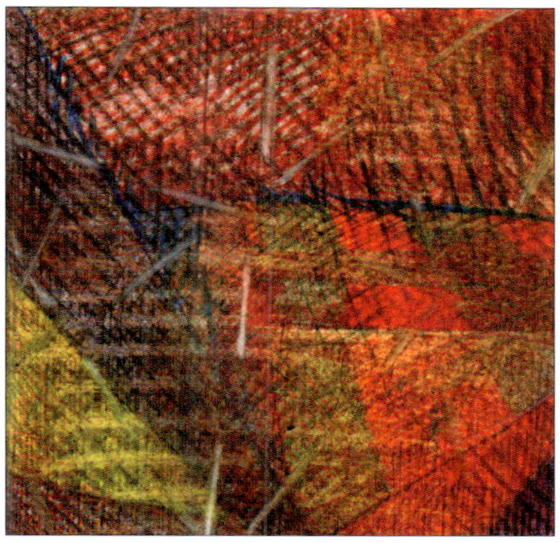

WAR

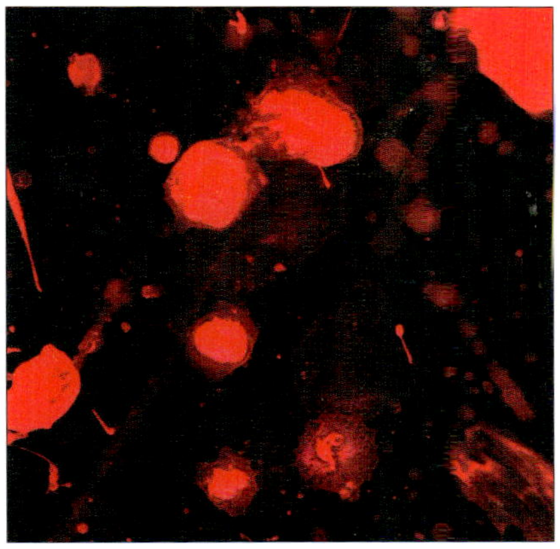

WAR

WAR

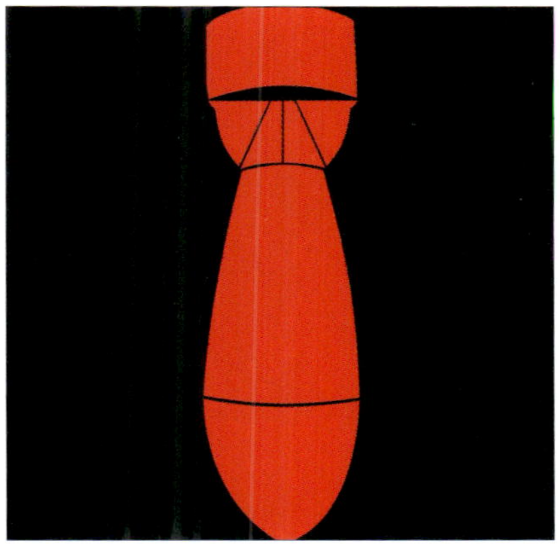

WAR

SOUND SOLUTIONS: POPCORN POPPING & WAR

In juxtaposing such divergent subjects as popcorn popping and war, oddly enough there are similarities to be found, such as the explosive activity of popcorn popping and the violent nature of war.

Figures 1 through 3, Popcorn Popping, use a palette of yellows and browns, which are indigenous to popcorn, while red and black dominate in figures 4 through 12, War.

Figures 1 through 3 also use representations of popcorn to create movement.

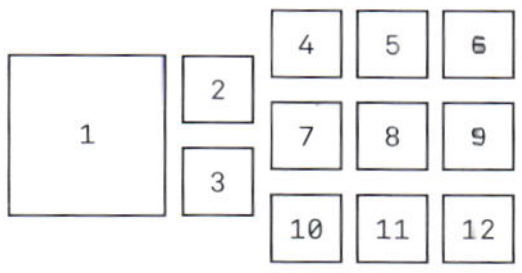

1. *Anne Landau*
2. *Natalia Campos*
3. *Jordan Winick*
4. *Deirdre Smith*
5. *Seungmin Chung*
6. *Francis Soriano*
7. *Jaehoon Park*
8. *Catalina Argomedo*
9. *Gregory Spuches*
10. *Yoonbin Lee*
11. *Blanda Eggenschwiler*
12. *Ryan Saks*

Figures 4 through 10 deal with the subject in a much more abstract way, while figures 11 and 12 use symbolic imagery to execute their concepts.

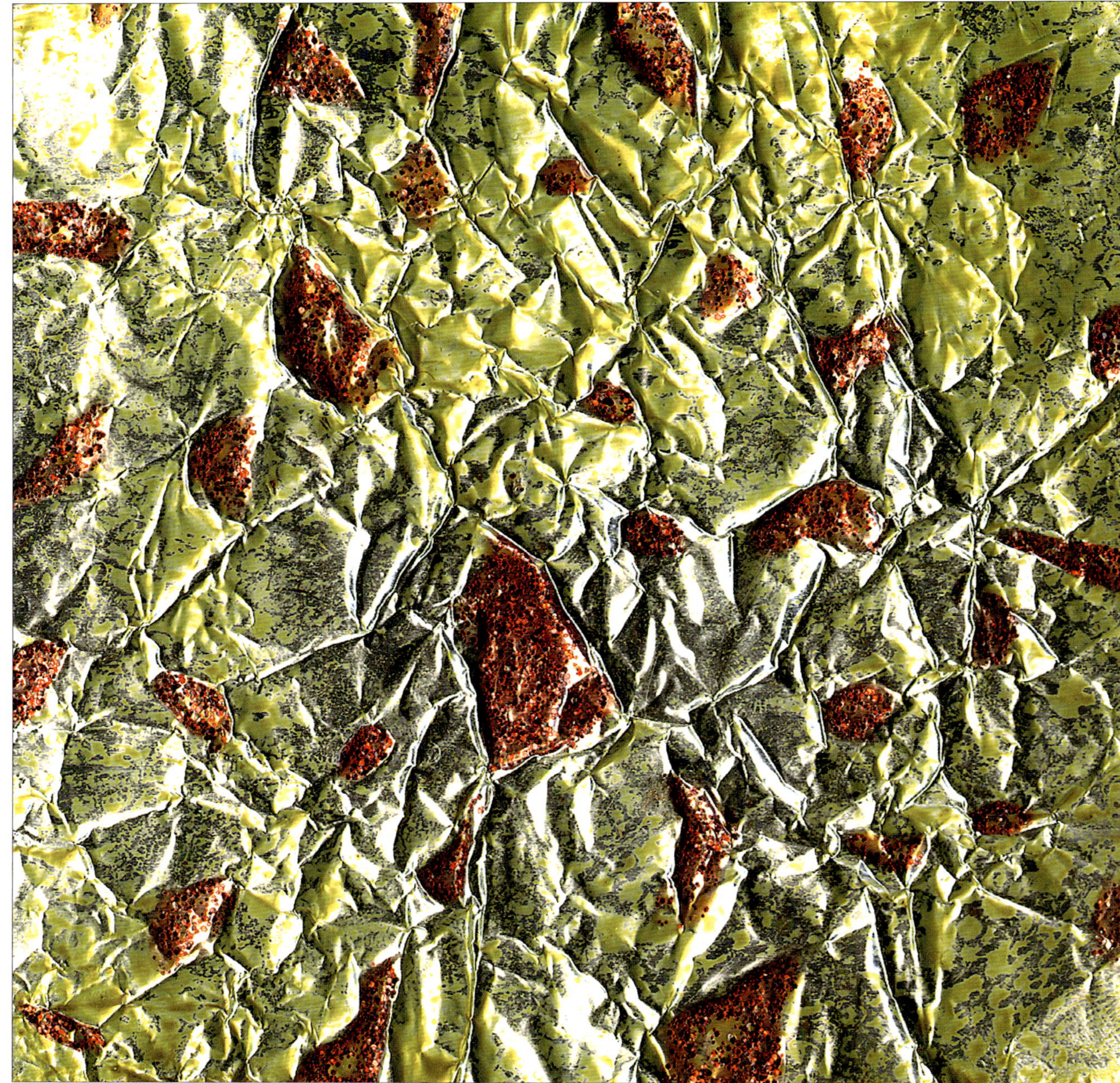

SHORT ORDER COOK

SOUND SOLUTIONS: SHORT ORDER COOK

The activity of a short order cook is accompanied with an array of sounds and movements that occur during the preparation of food.

Figure 1 uses crumpled tinfoil that is carefully painted in selected areas where various shapes have been created. The intensity of the sound is heightened by the reflective material.

Figures 2 through 7 are abstract in nature, referencing heat, activity, tension, noise, and movement.

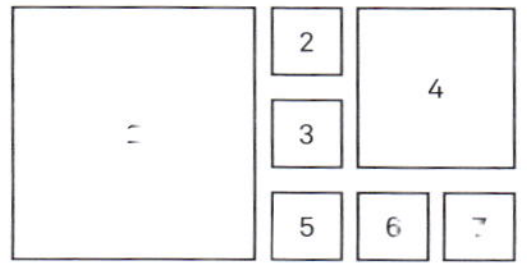

1. Hyeonkyeong Seo
2. Erika Yost
3. Jhonny Tufino
4. Gouhea Park
5. Jaeyeong Kim
6. John Kuhn
7. Seongmi Park

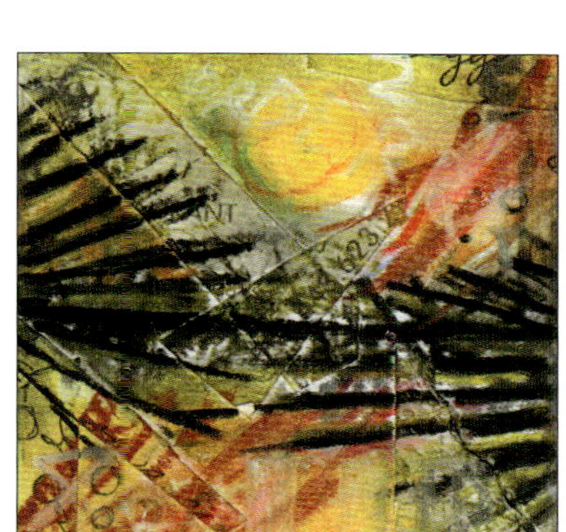

SHORT ORDER COOK

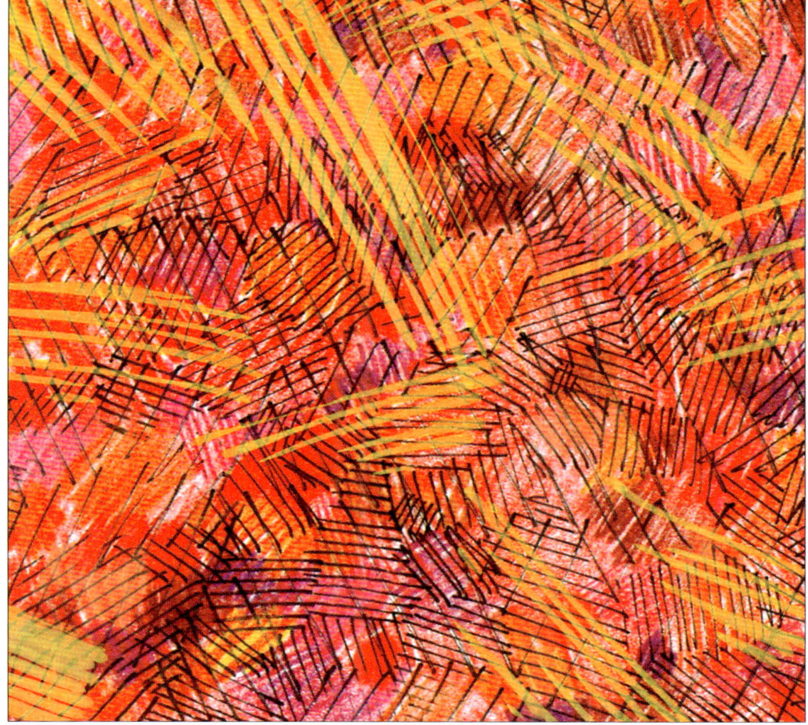

SHORT ORDER COOK

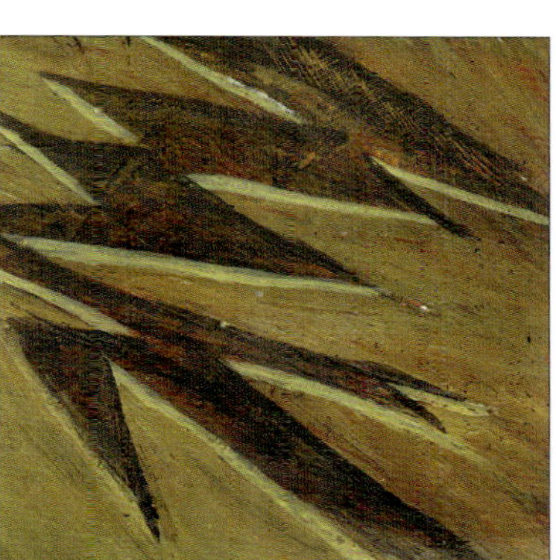

SHORT ORDER COOK

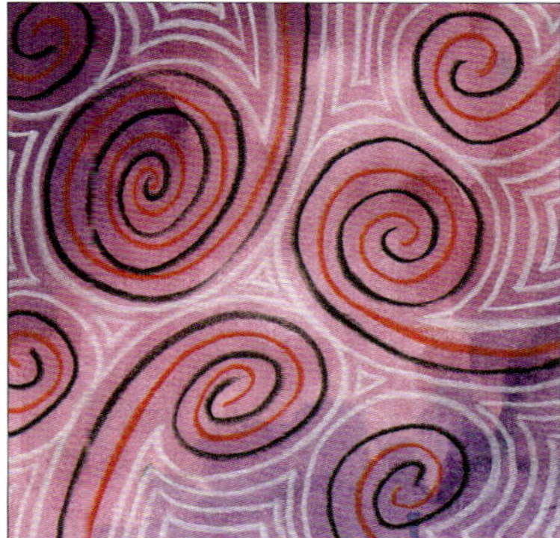

SHORT ORDER COOK

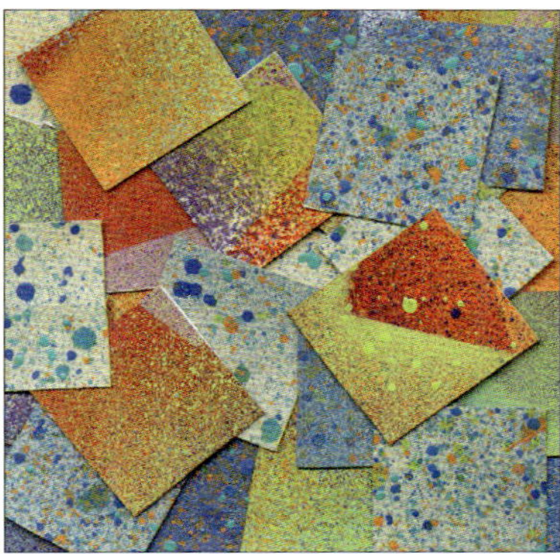

SHORT ORDER COOK

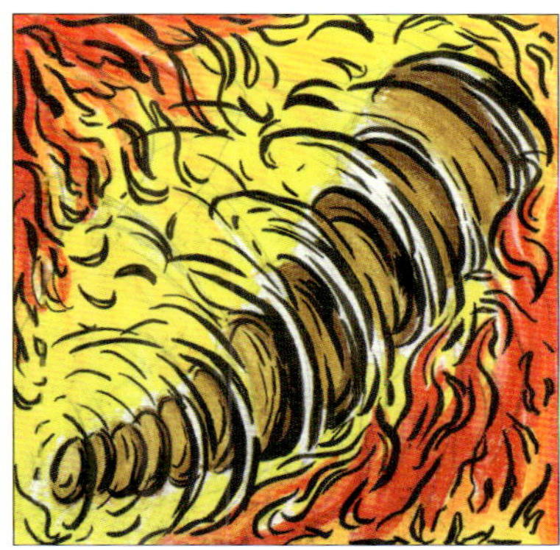

SHORT ORDER COOK

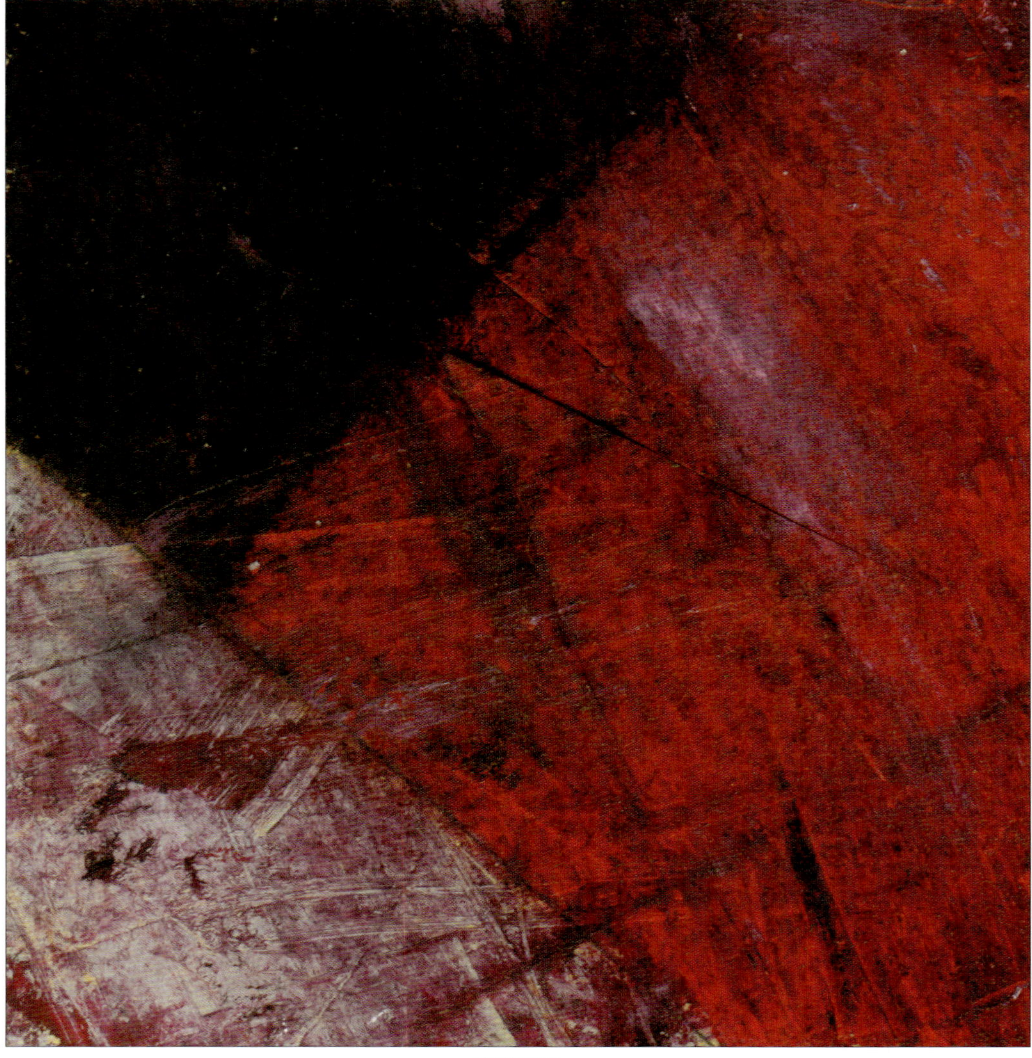
REJECTION

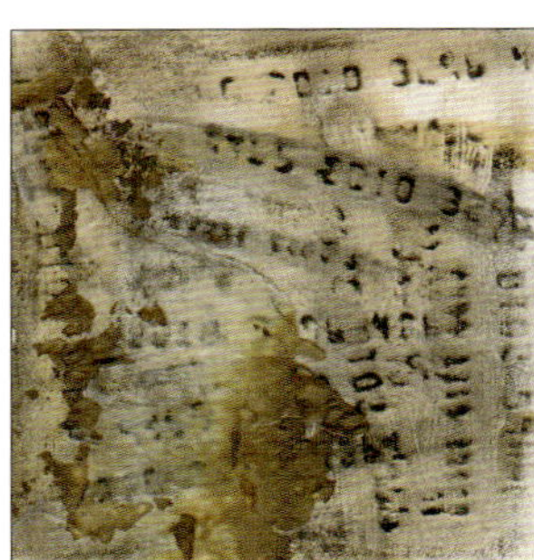
REJECTION

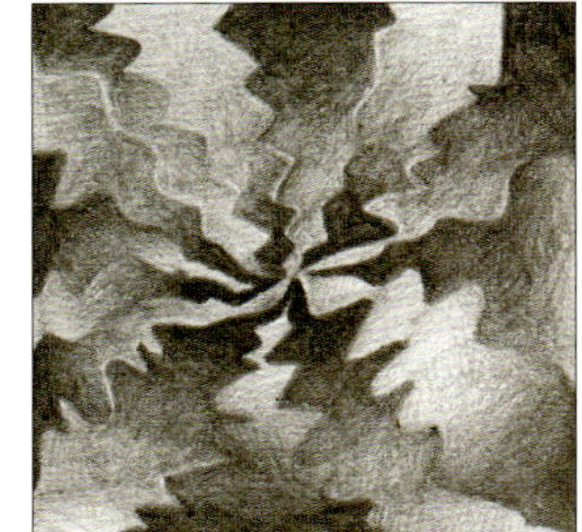
REJECTION

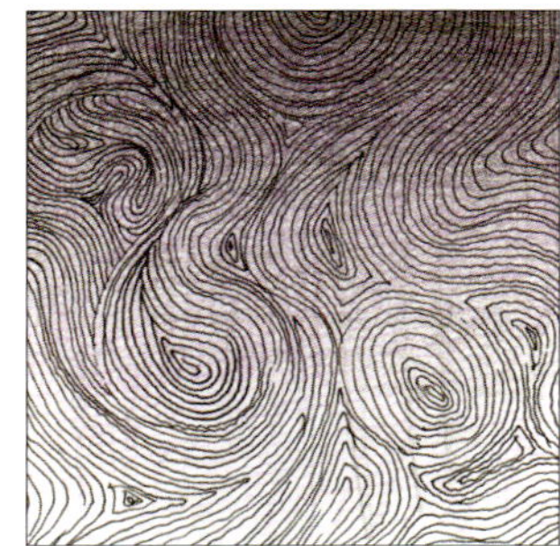
REJECTION

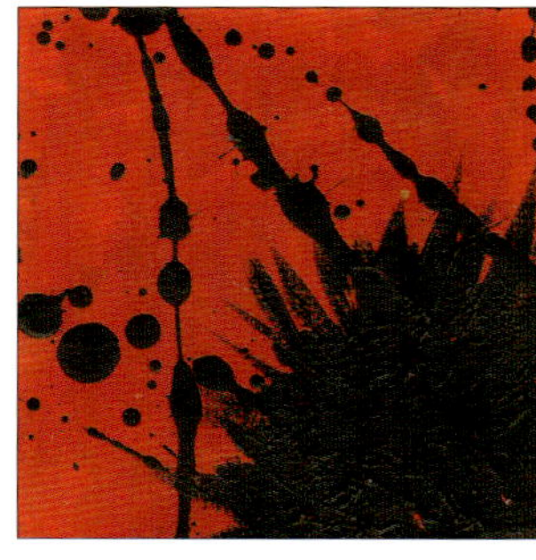
REJECTION

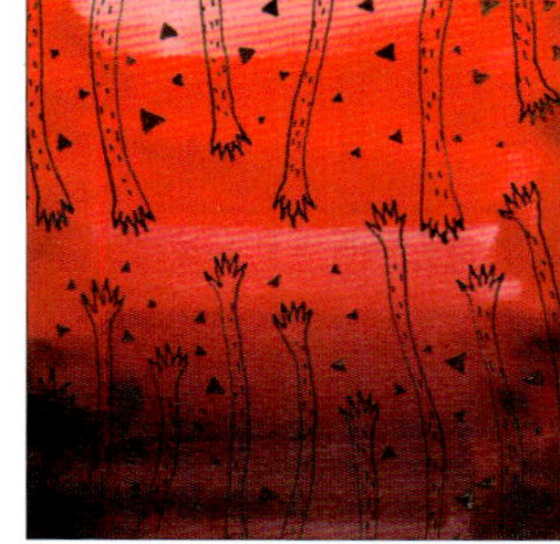
REJECTION

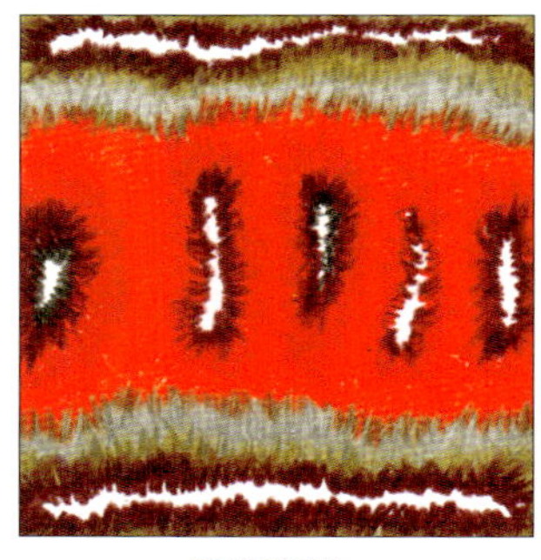
REJECTION

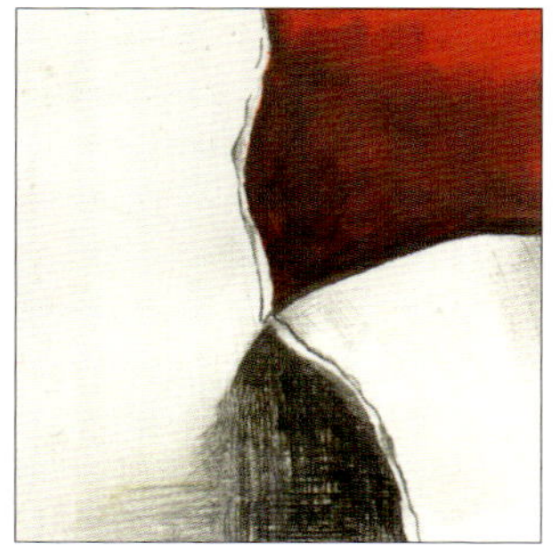
REJECTION

SOUND SOLUTIONS: REJECTION & GUILLOTINE

Rejection is the subject of figures 1 through 8. Here this inner, often emotionally heartfelt experience is not necessarily connected with an audible sound. Therefore, to infer this sound, one must appropriate a sensibility worthy of the subject. At the onset, invention is called for because of the lack of a clear starting point. Upon delving into the problem, and through a thorough investigation, corresponding imagery arises.

GUILLOTINE

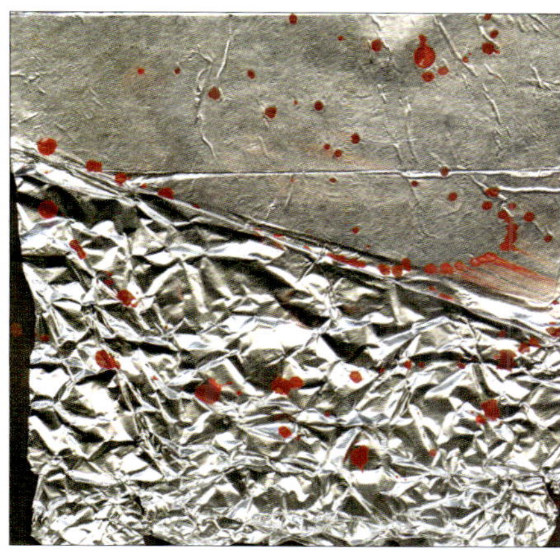

GUILLOTINE

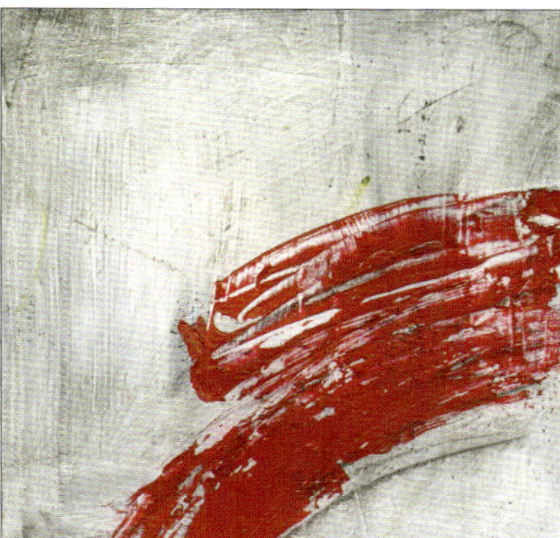

GUILLOTINE

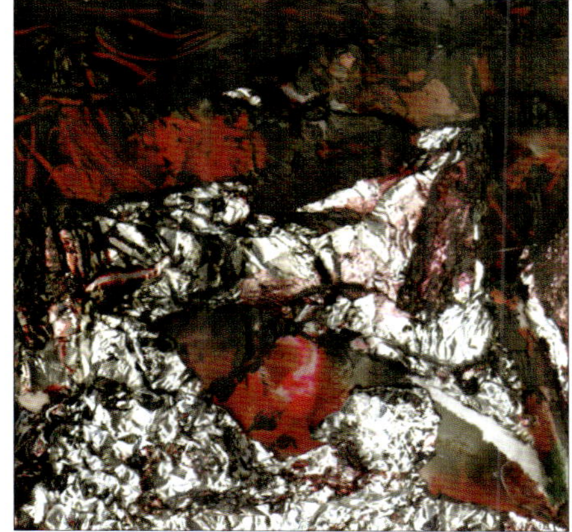

GUILLOTINE

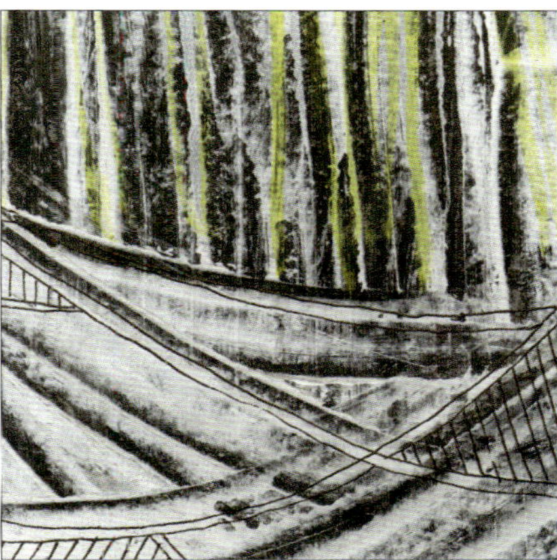

GUILLOTINE

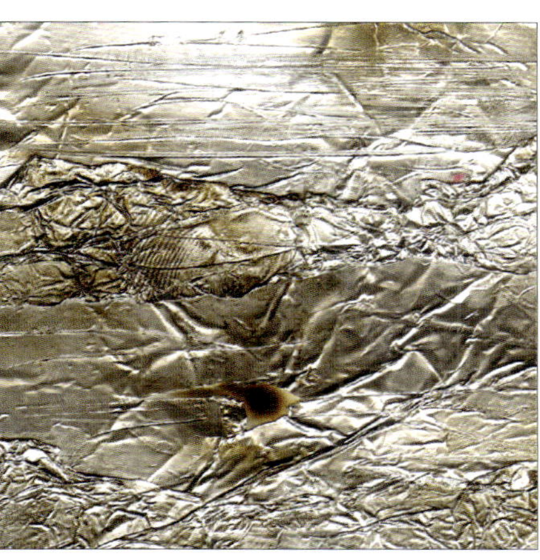

GUILLOTINE

1. *Margot Laborde*
2. *Angela Ham*
3. *Borim Kim*
4. *Seungjun Lee*
5. *Jane Goldman*
6. *Jiyun Moon*
7. *Estefania Ferrand*
8. *Hayoung Kim*
9. *Yeonwoo Jung*
10. *Sebit Min*
11. *Borim Kim*
12. *Alexandra Rosano*
13. *Elaine Park*
14. *Angela Ham*

Figure 8 works on both an abstract and metaphoric level. It is in fact an image of paper being torn.

Guillotine, which is depicted in figures 9 through 14, deals with the sound of the downward movement of a blade, coupled with the sound of decapitation.

Solutions 10, 12 and 14 incorporate tinfoil into their project.

To a degree, since one has not experienced a guillotine first hand, artistic license and invention are called for.

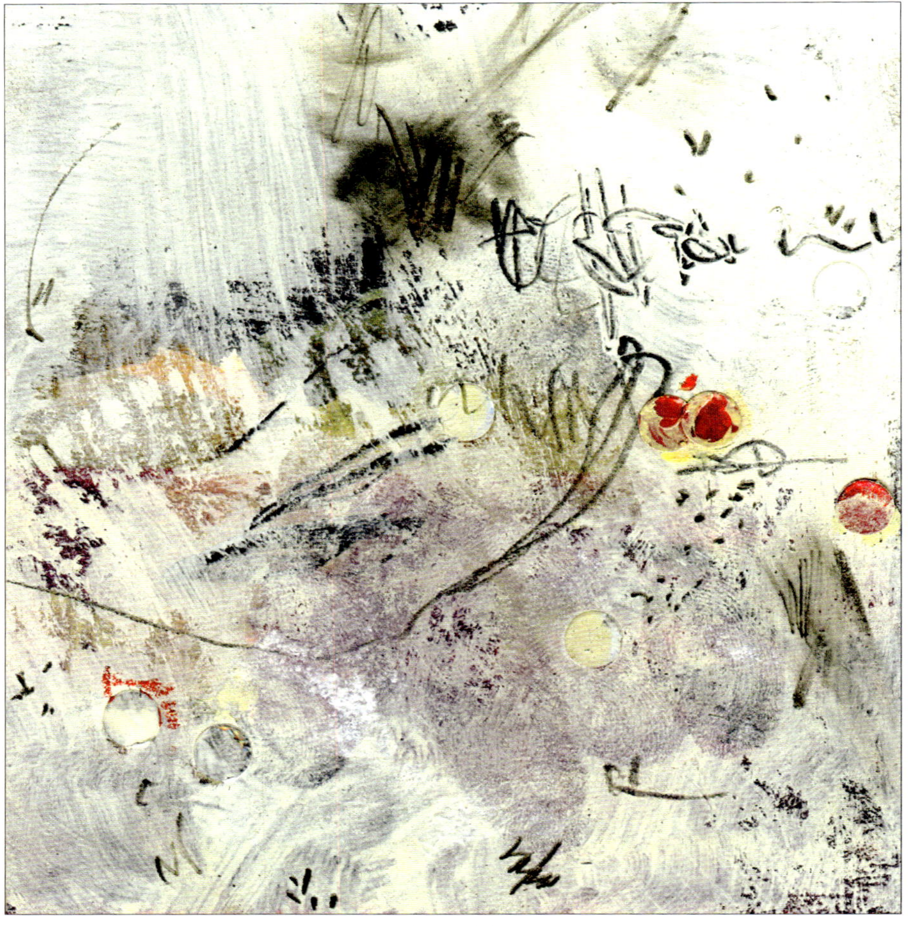

BUSY DINER

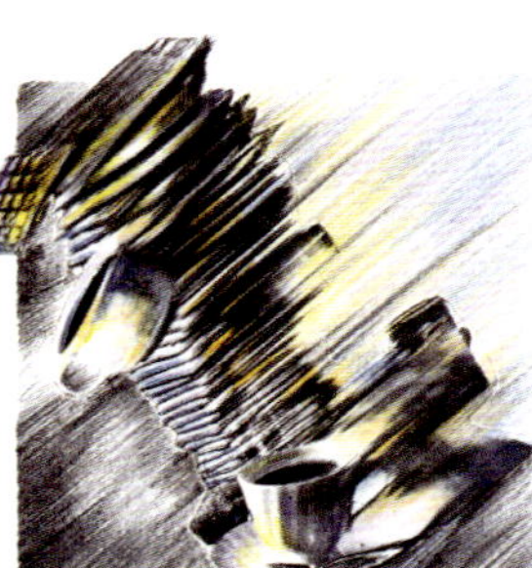

BUSY DINER

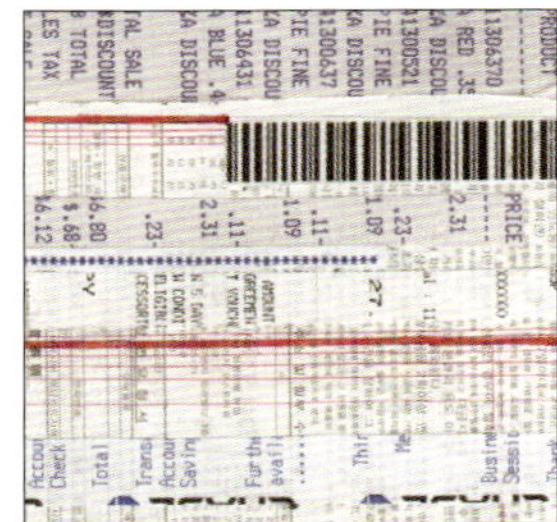

BUSY DINER

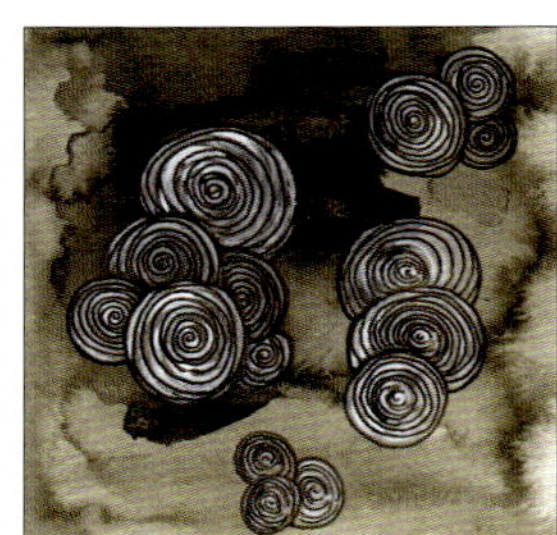

BUSY DINER

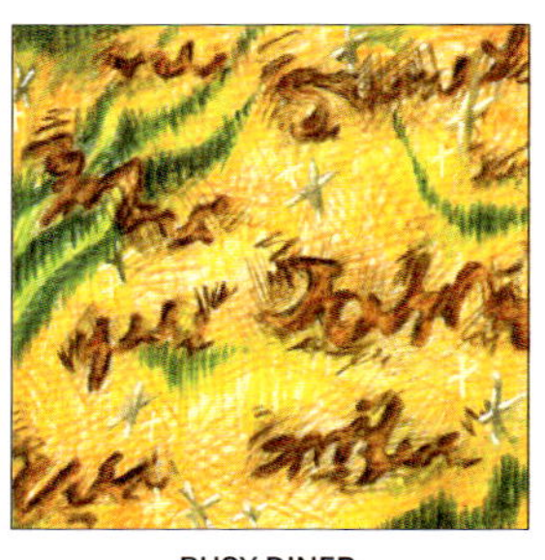

BUSY DINER

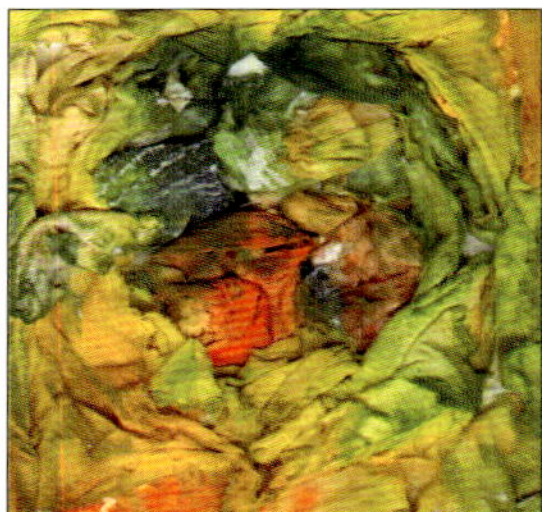

BUSY DINER

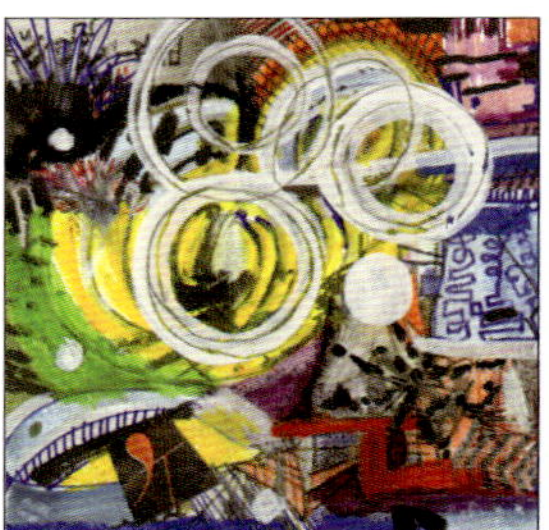

BUSY DINER

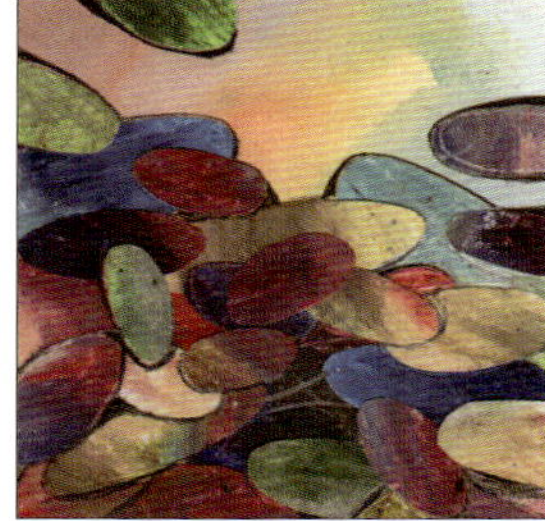

BUSY DINER

ECHO

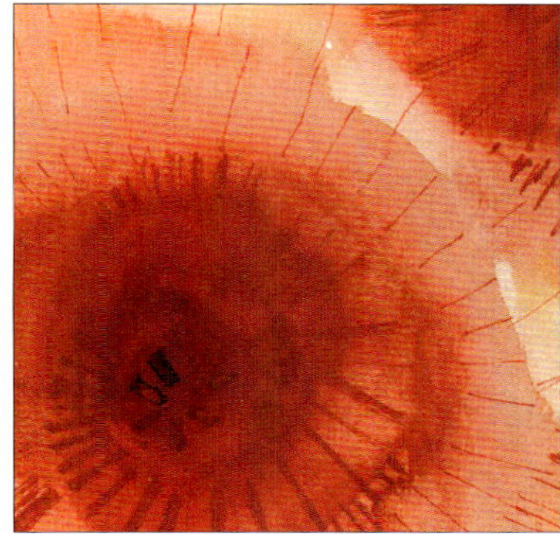

ECHO

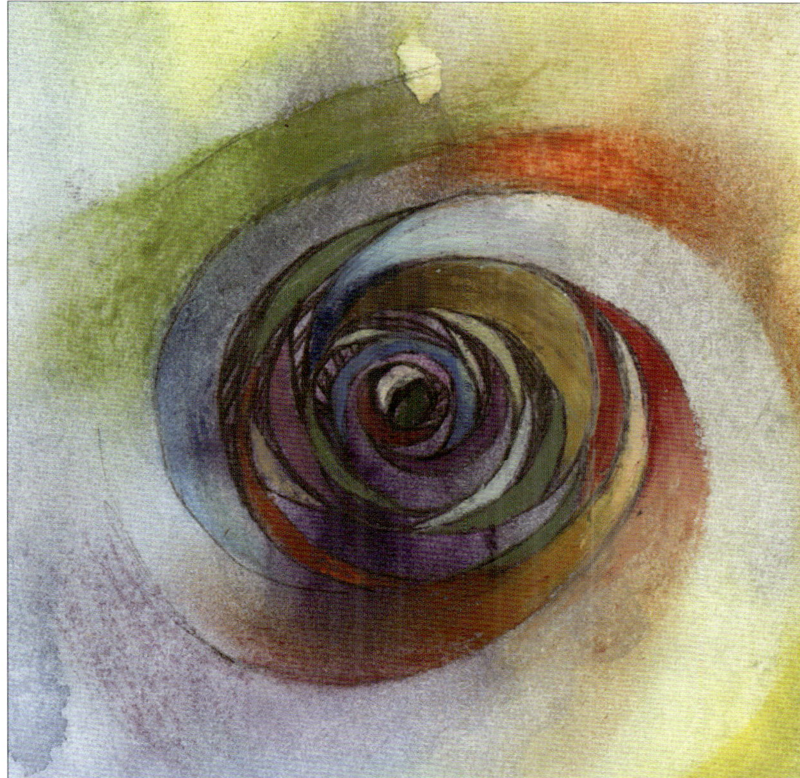

ECHO

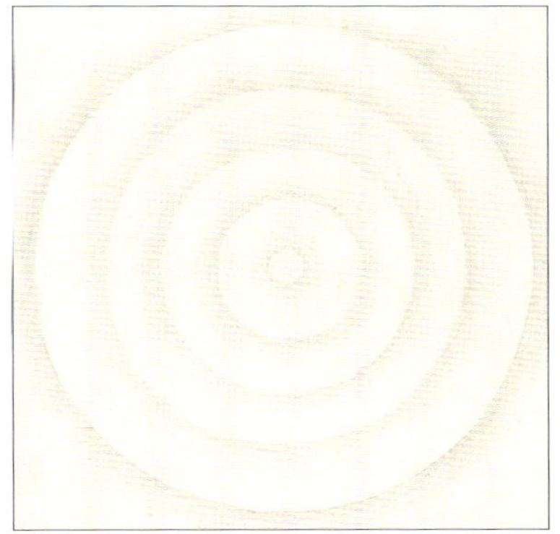

ECHO

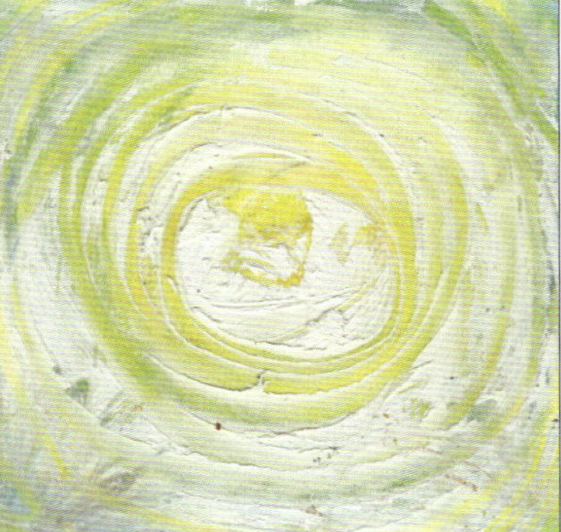

ECHO

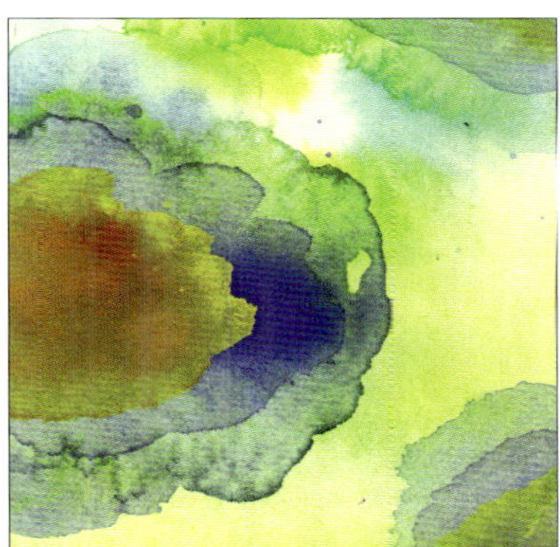

ECHO

SOUND SOLUTIONS: BUSY DINER & ECHO

Figures 1 through 8 depict a busy diner.

Figure 1, along with figures 4 through 8, deals with abstract interpretations of the cacophony of sound associated with a diner.

Figure 2 references objects such as plates, cups and saucers that are executed on the diagonal in an effort to denote movement.

Figure 3 is a typographic exploration that uses receipts, in a structured manner, to reference the activity associated with a diner.

1 2 3 4 5 6 7 8 9 10 11 12 13 14

1. *Yukyung Hwang*
2. *E. Shapiro*
3. *Minju Cho*
4. *Fanny Spång Artursson*
5. *Gina Shin*
6. *Jisoo Lee*
7. *Michele Demis*
8. *Jungeun Kwak*
9. *Hanbyul Lee*
10. *Hyojin Joo*
11. *Jungeun Kwak*
12. *Emily Pracher*
13. *Nicole Benson*
14. *Haeseung Joung*

Echo is depicted in figures 9 through 14, where the reverberation of the sound is shown in patterns that circumvent one another. Often sound is represented, ranging from loud to barely distinguishable. Movement emanating from a focal point is the key element in depicting this subject.

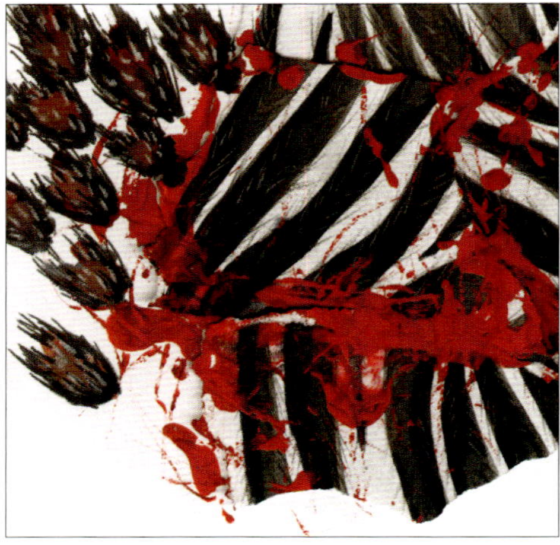
CONFRONTATION BETWEEN A LEOPARD AND A ZEBRA

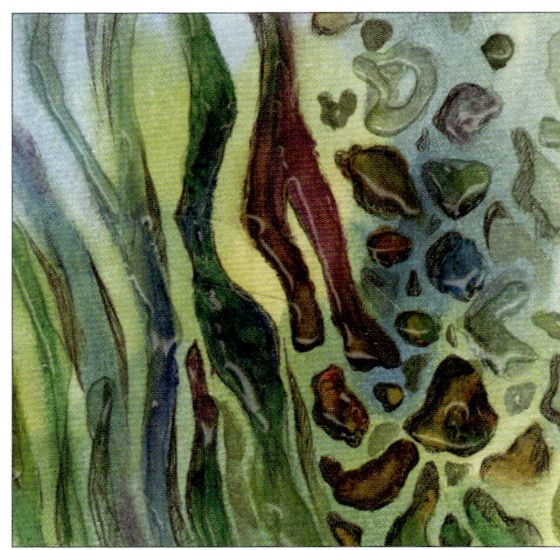
CONFRONTATION BETWEEN A LEOPARD AND A ZEBRA

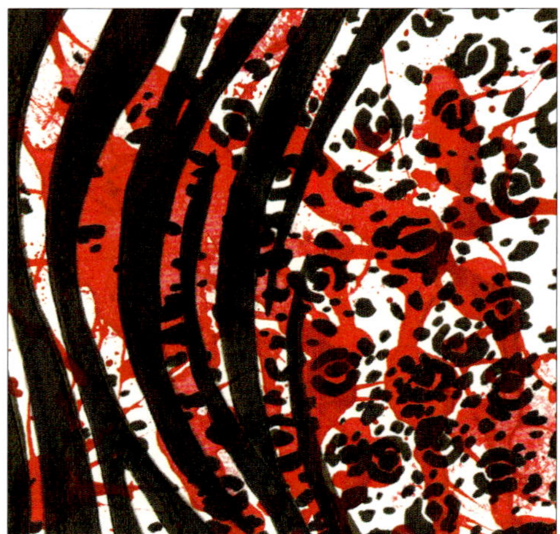
CONFRONTATION BETWEEN A LEOPARD AND A ZEBRA

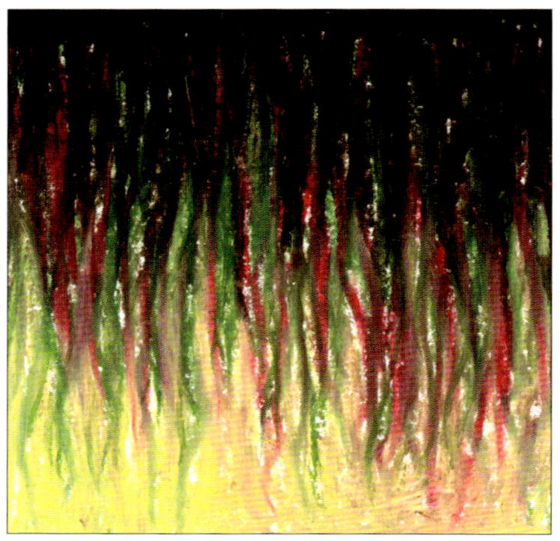
CONFRONTATION BETWEEN A LEOPARD AND A ZEBRA

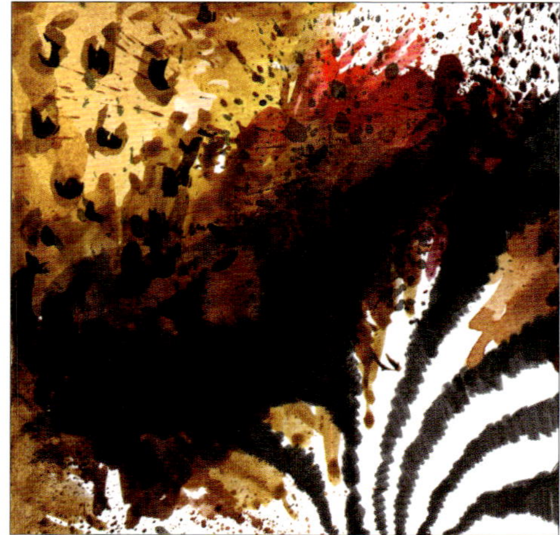
CONFRONTATION BETWEEN A LEOPARD AND A ZEBRA

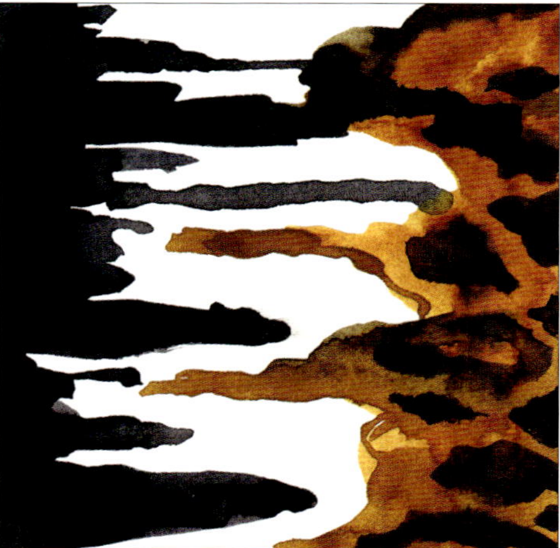
CONFRONTATION BETWEEN A LEOPARD AND A ZEBRA

SOUND SOLUTIONS: CONFRONTATION BETWEEN A LEOPARD AND A ZEBRA

The sound of conflict in one of nature's most violent encounters is depicted in figures 1 through 9.

For most solutions, graphic elements representing the interaction of the patterning of a leopard and a zebra are used to infer the sound of this confrontation.

Figure 7 functions more as a symbolic expression, where the zebra's eye is mirroring the leopard's spots.

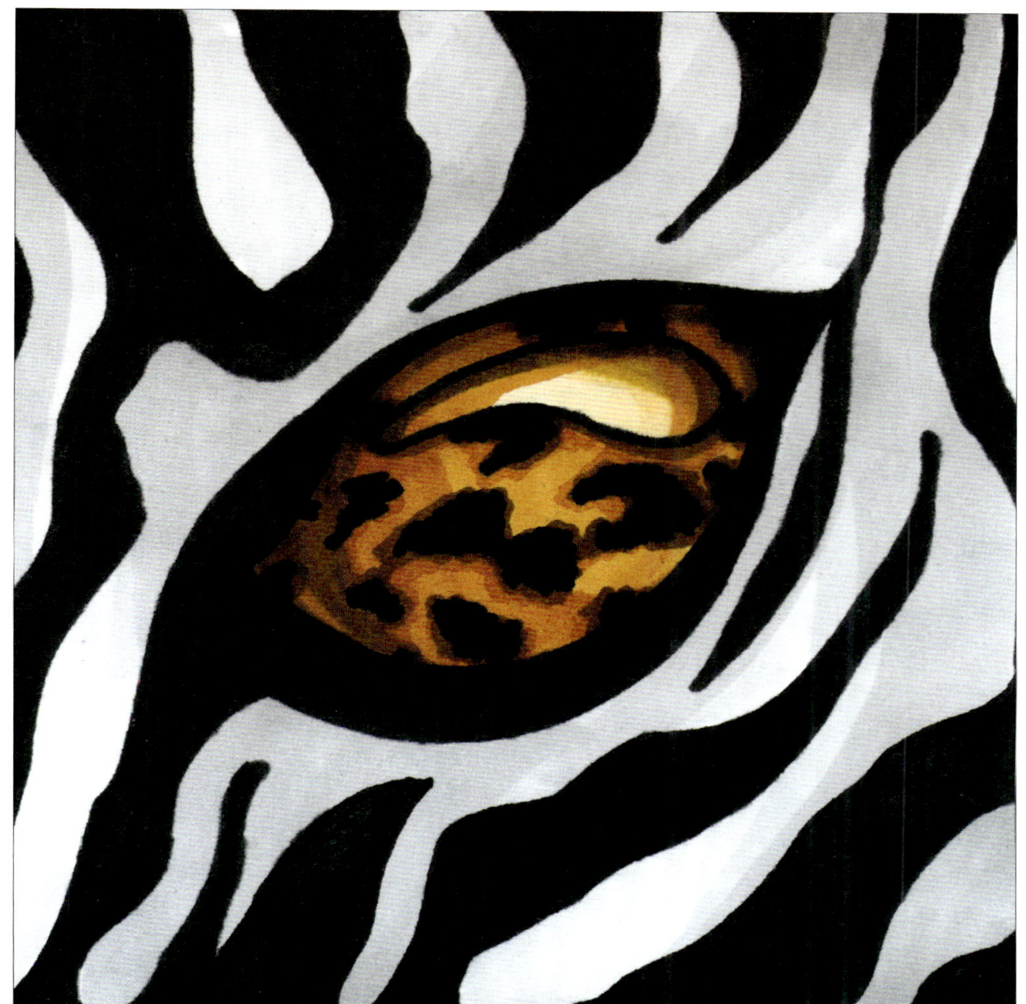

CONFRONTATION BETWEEN A LEOPARD AND A ZEBRA

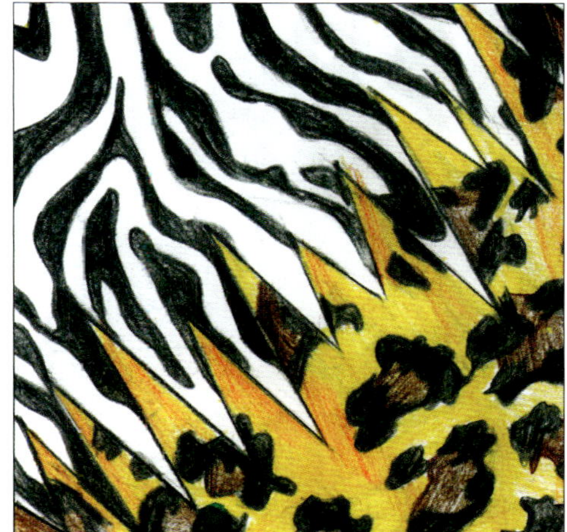

CONFRONTATION BETWEEN A LEOPARD AND A ZEBRA

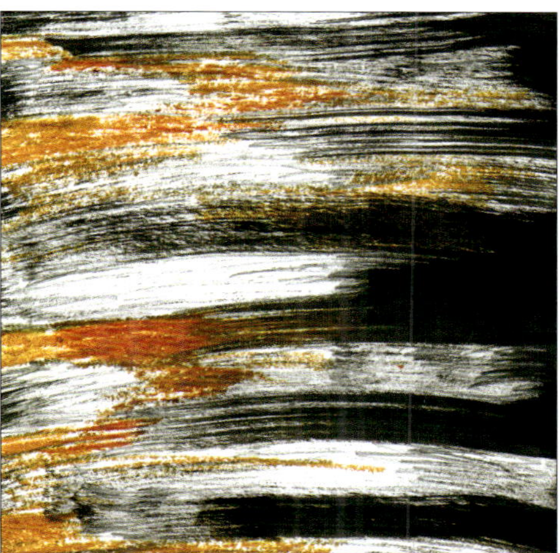

CONFRONTATION BETWEEN A LEOPARD AND A ZEBRA

1	2		7
3	4		
5	6	8	9

1. *Wei Tung Yeh*
2. *Jungeun Kwak*
3. *Bayard Morse*
4. *Sara Chaudhuri*

5–6. *Eunsung Do*

7. *Myungwon Seo*
8. *Yelin Seo*
9. *Woohyun Cho*

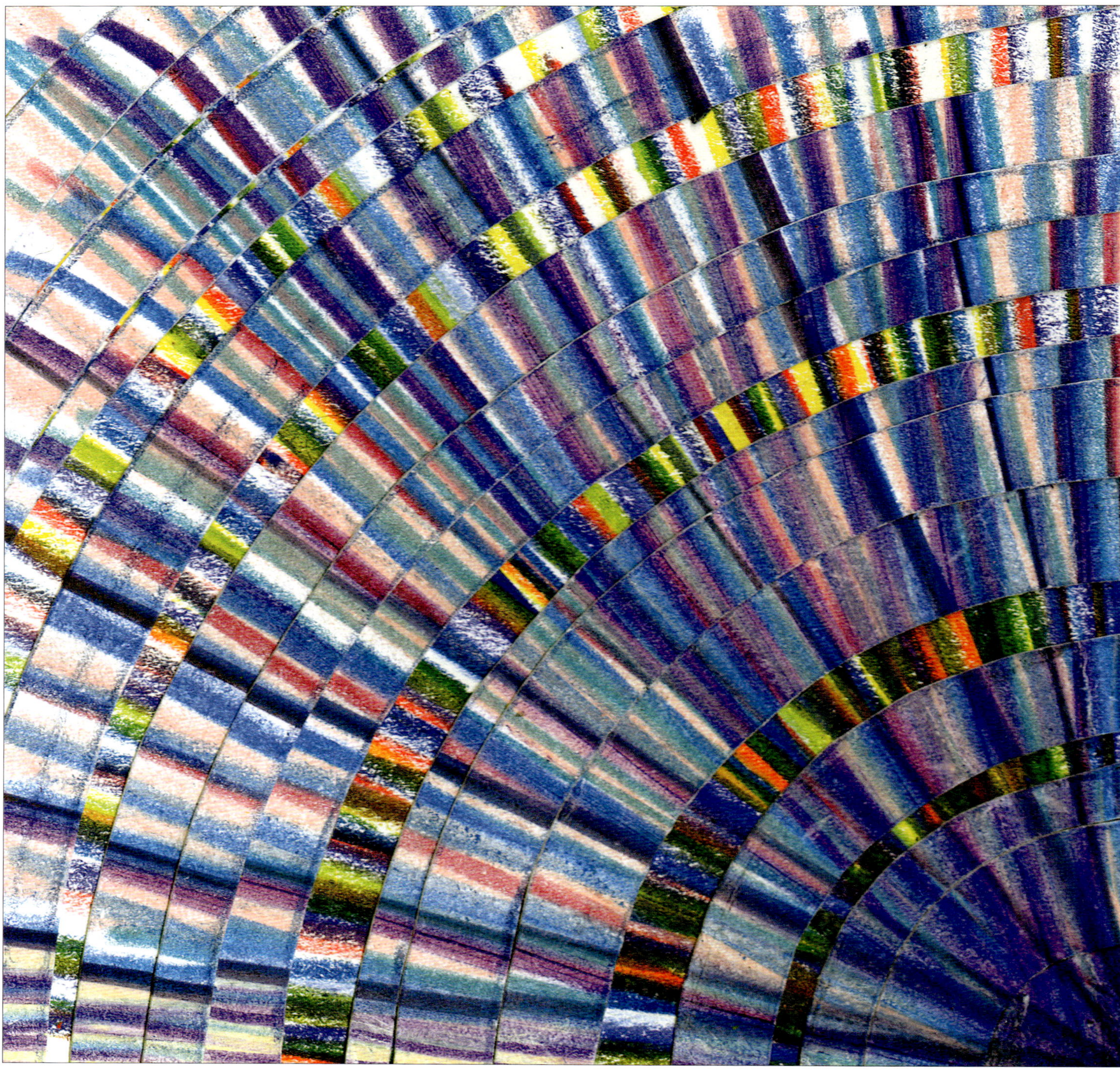

LOUD PERSON

SOUND SOLUTIONS: RANDOM

These seven solutions depict various subjects, yet the commonality is in the use of the color blue, which dominates each solution.

Certain colors are often associated with specific subjects, which can be influenced by social and cultural factors. By relying on one's more essential nature, which is not subject to learned constraints, almost any color can be appropriated.

Figure 1 expresses the sound of loudness in a rhythmic pattern that creates a sense of movement.

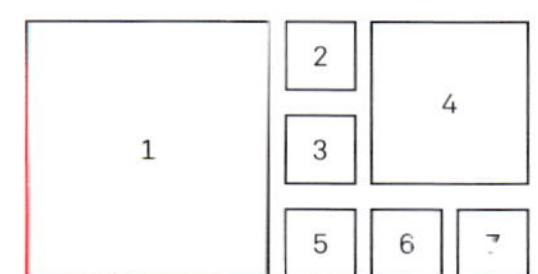
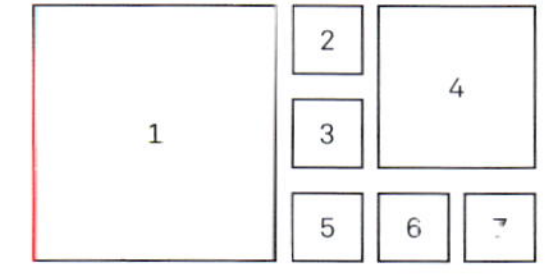

1. *Jeonghyeon Kim*
2. *Eunjung Yoo*
3. *Hyojeong Kim*
4. *Cheungyoon Kim*
5. *Yungui Sung*
6. *Jieun Jeon*
7. *Ariel Elias*

WHISTLING TEA KETTLE

GUILLOTINE

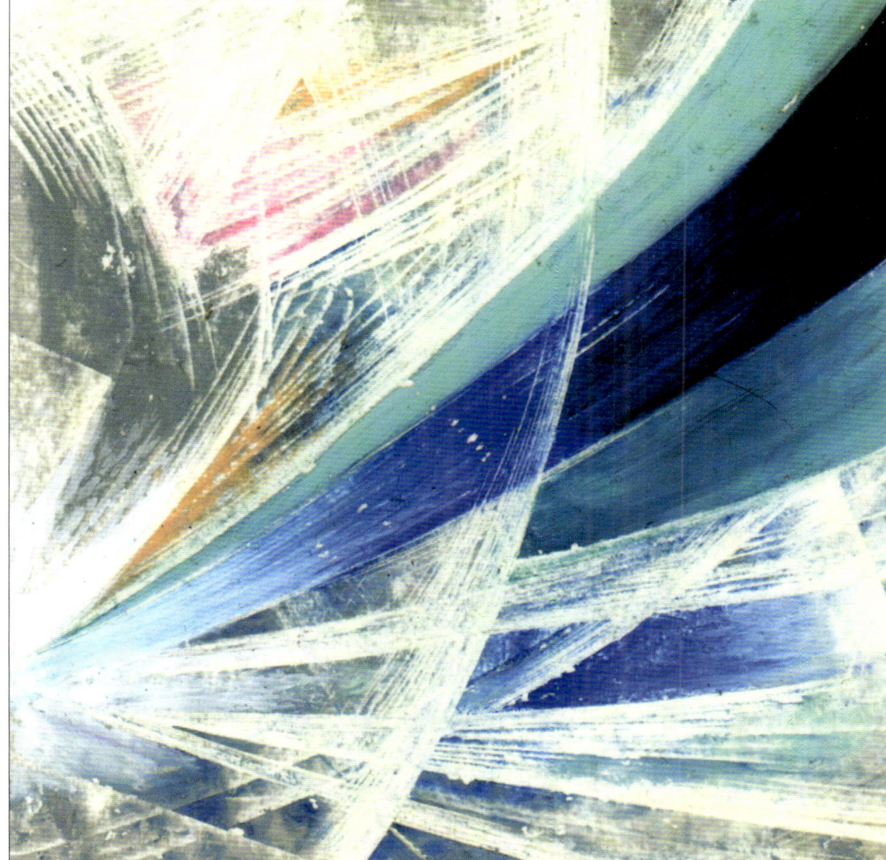

WHISTLING TEA KETTLE

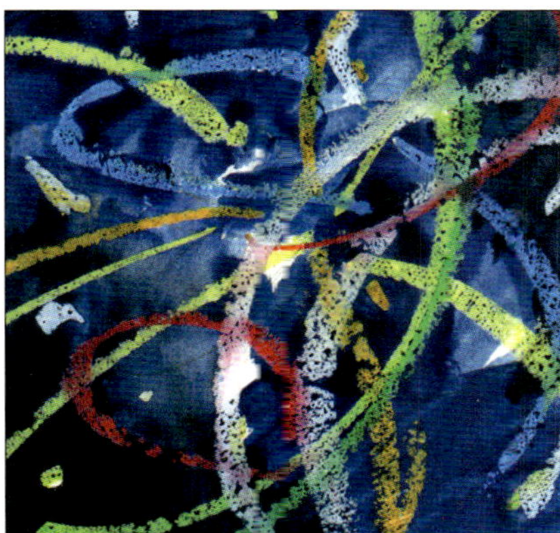

FIRECRACKERS

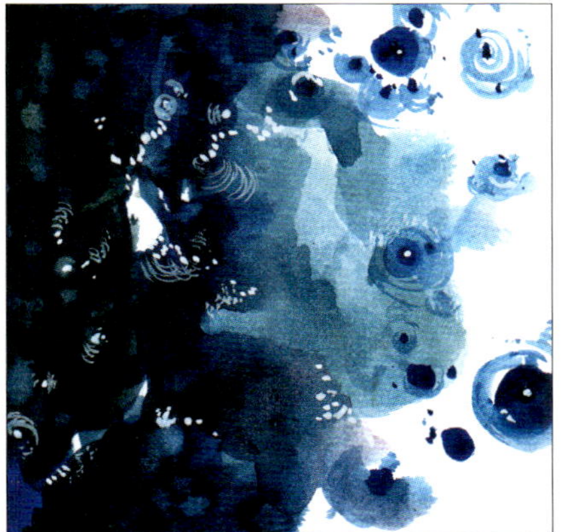

NERVOUS HABIT

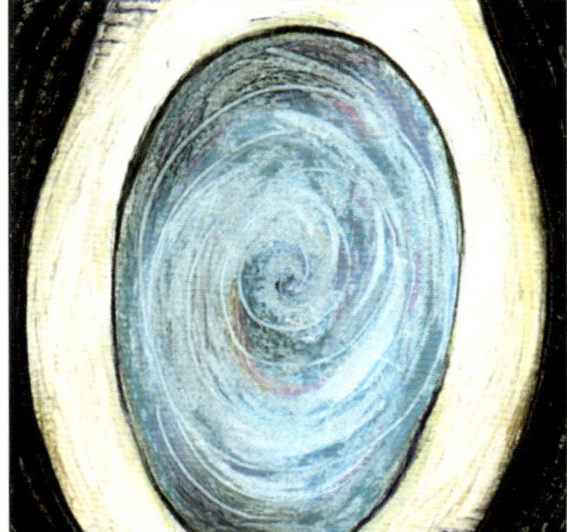

GARGLING

The diverse subjects in figures 2 through 7 use abstract elements to convey their intended messages.

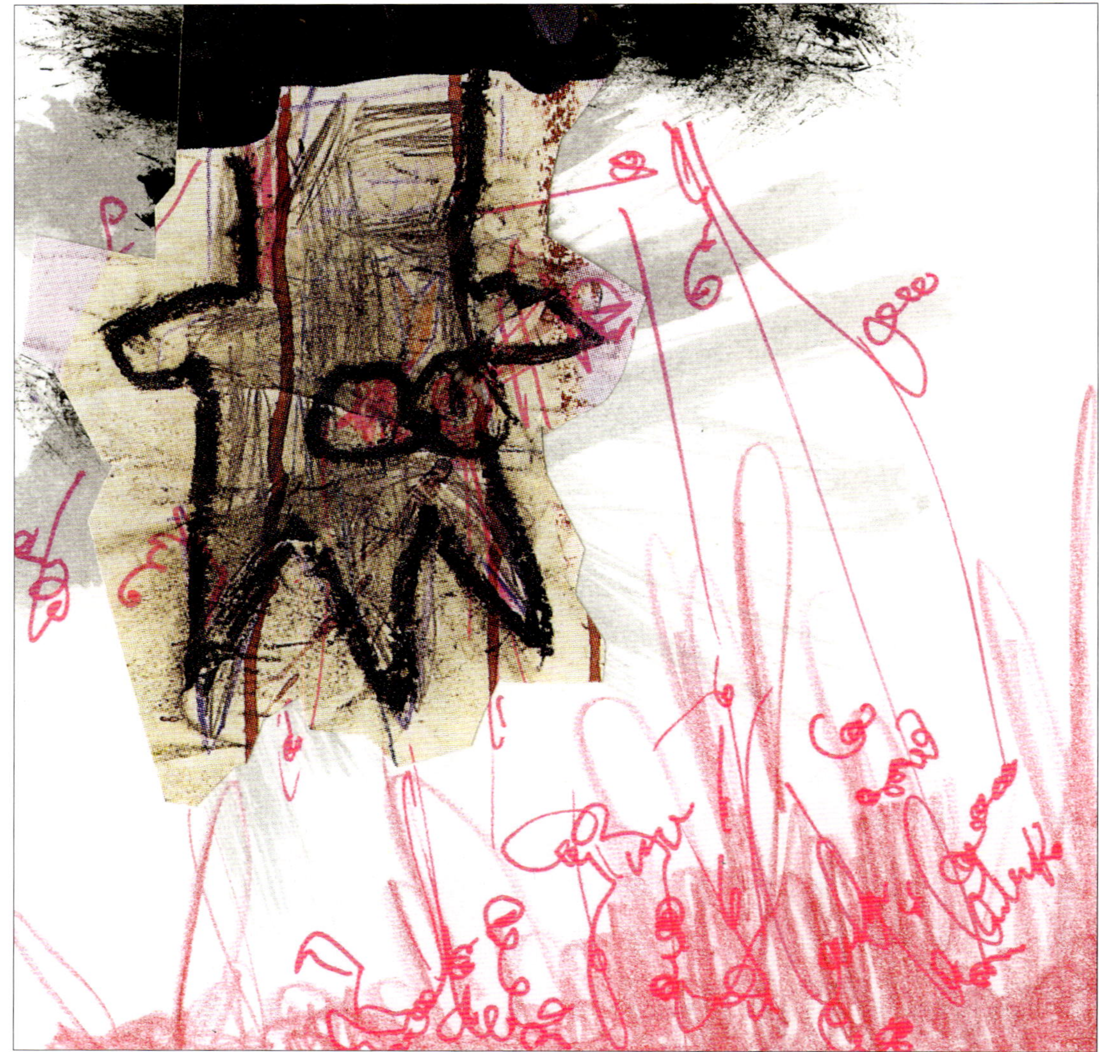

CONVERSATION BETWEEN A TUBA AND A FLUTE

SOUND SOLUTIONS: RANDOM

Figures 1 through 13 represent varied subjects, ranging from a conversation between a tuba and a flute, to the tranquility of nature, to waking up in the morning, to the pain of a toothache, to the turmoil of a rock concert, as well as other subjects.

This varied grouping of topics gives rise to an array of executional skills, ranging from naïveté to carefully structured solutions where the concept not only dictates the form, but at times, dictates the medium as well.

1. *Carla Martinez*
2. *M. Smith*
3. *Ruth Friedman*
4. *Okjeong Kim*
5. *Sejin Kim*
6. *Eunhye Kim*
7. *Seungmin Chung*
8. *David Fishman*
9. *Alejandra Sepúlveda*
10. *Jill Brody*
11. *Jongwoo Kim*
12. *Jungeun Kwak*
13. *Hyojin Joo*

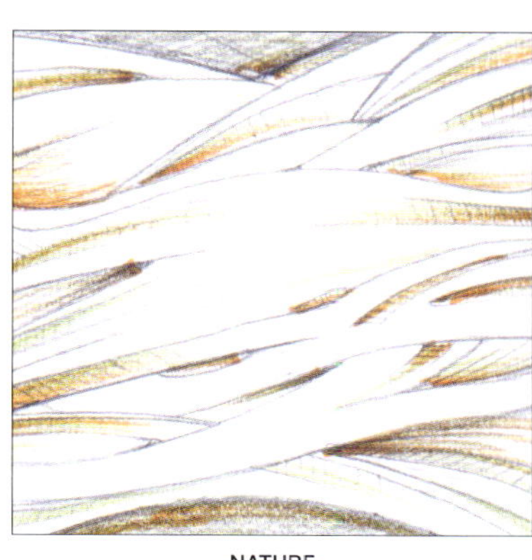
NATURE

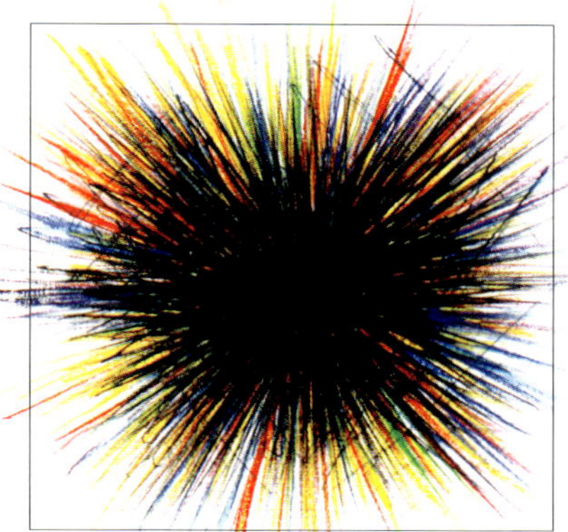
ROCK CONCERT

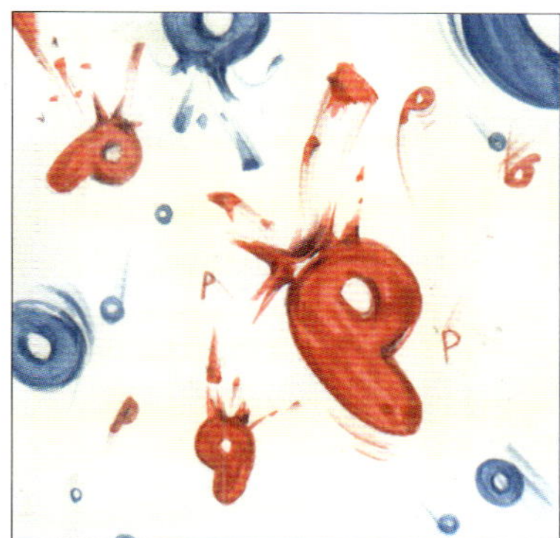
POPCORN POPPING

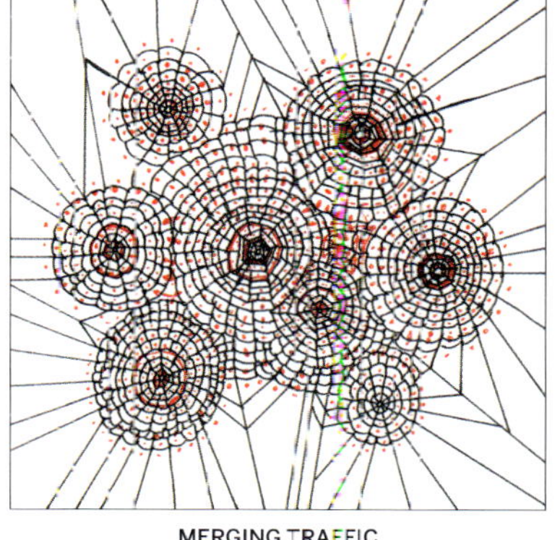
MERGING TRAFFIC

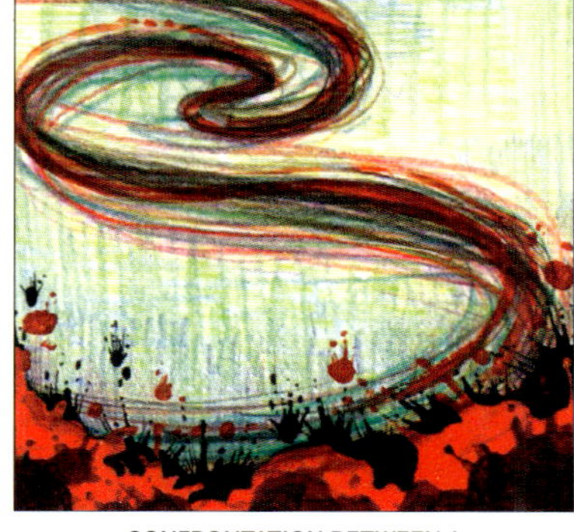
CONFRONTATION BETWEEN A LEOPARD AND A ZEBRA

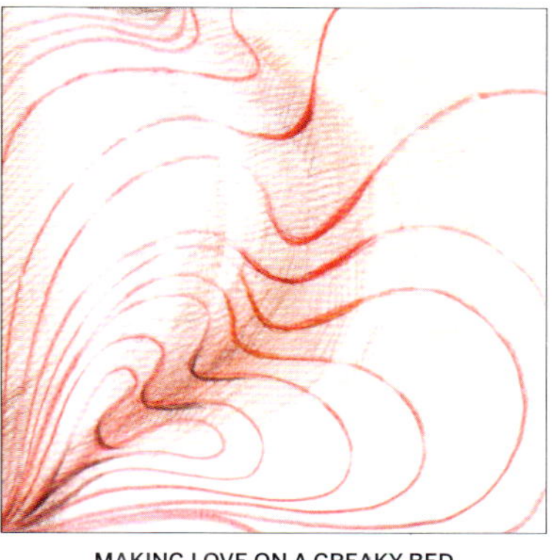
MAKING LOVE ON A CREAKY BED

WAKING UP

MISCOMMUNICATION

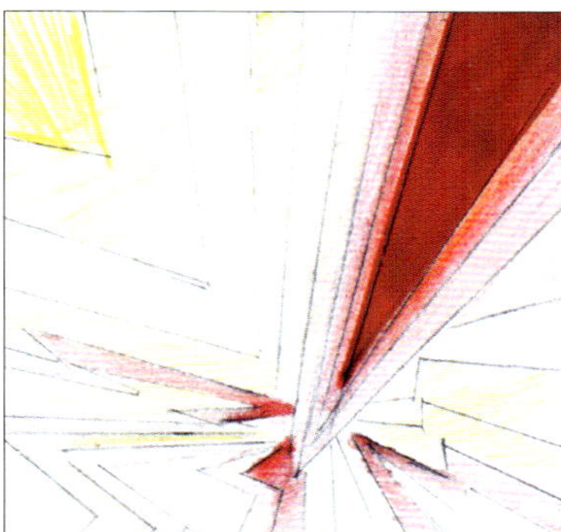
TOOTHACHE

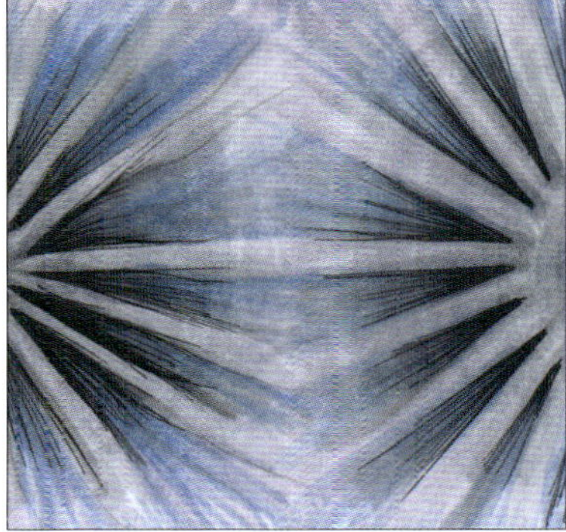
WINGS FLAPPING

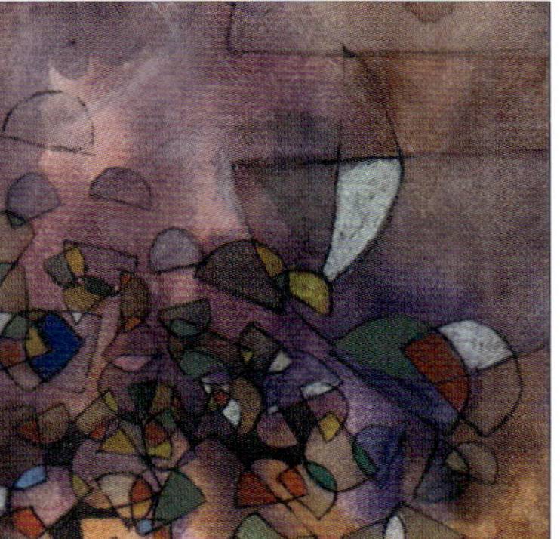
TAP DANCER

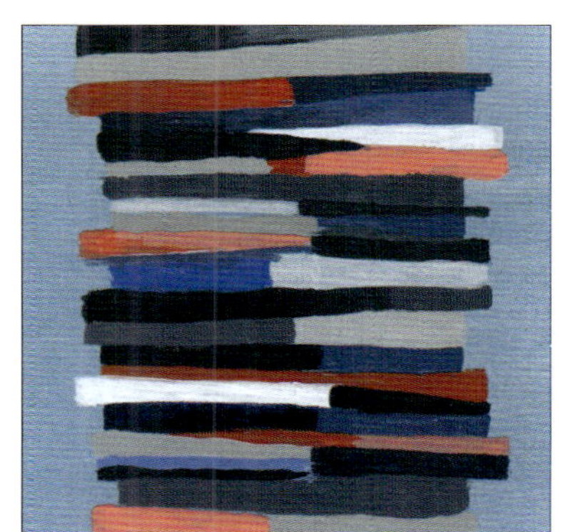
ZIPPER BEING ZIPPED

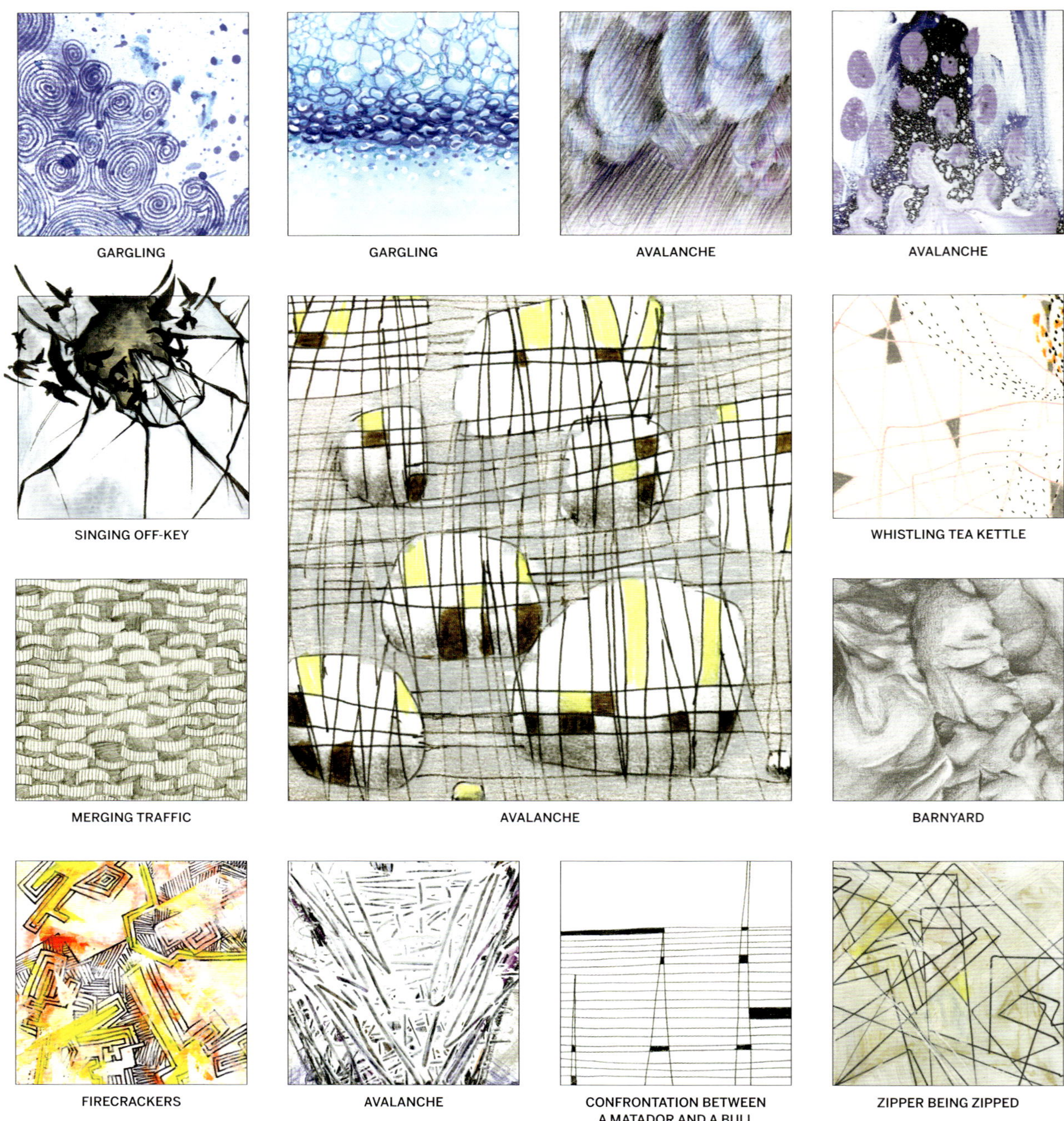

GARGLING

GARGLING

AVALANCHE

AVALANCHE

SINGING OFF-KEY

WHISTLING TEA KETTLE

MERGING TRAFFIC

AVALANCHE

BARNYARD

FIRECRACKERS

AVALANCHE

CONFRONTATION BETWEEN A MATADOR AND A BULL

ZIPPER BEING ZIPPED

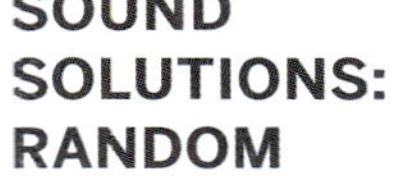

SOUND SOLUTIONS: RANDOM

All twenty-five of the following solutions cover a variety of subjects, along with those that have previously appeared in this chapter, and use form, shape, line, texture, space, and color to best evoke the character of a given sound.

Although abstraction is the overriding approach, some literal elements are utilized.

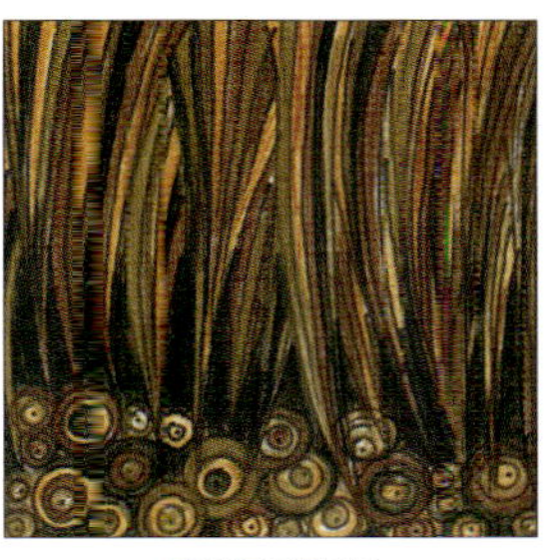

FRUSTRATION

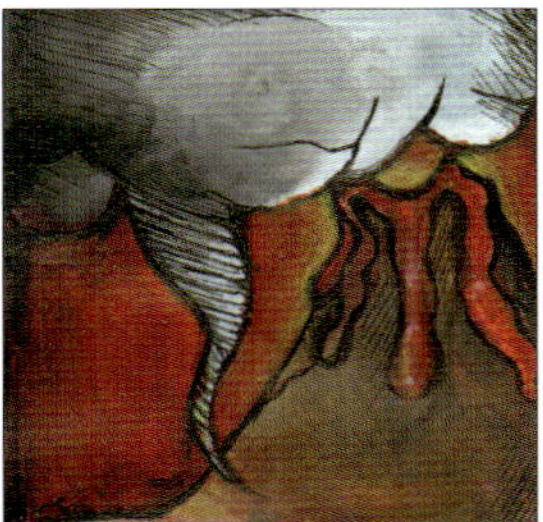

CONFRONTATION BETWEEN A MATADOR AND A BULL

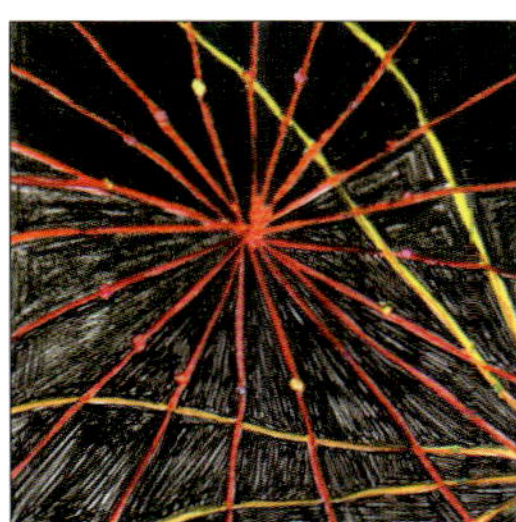

FIRECRACKERS

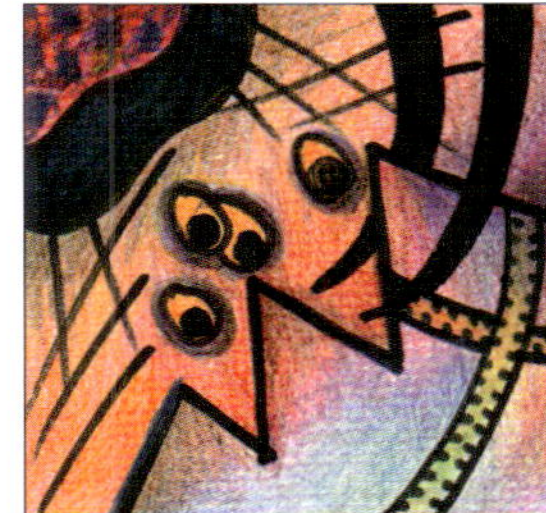

CONFRONTATION BETWEEN A MATADOR AND A BULL

GUILLOTINE

COCKFIGHT

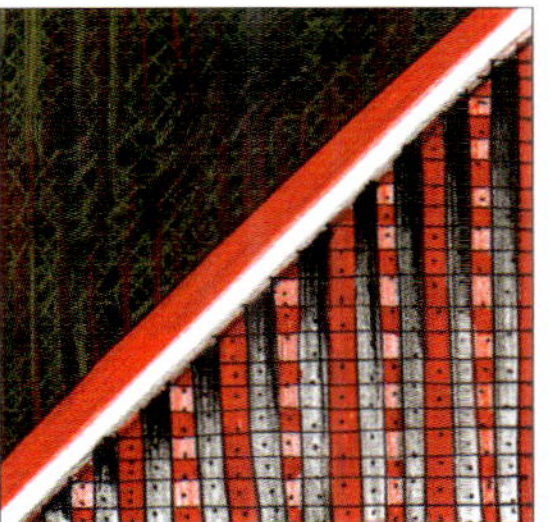

REJECTION

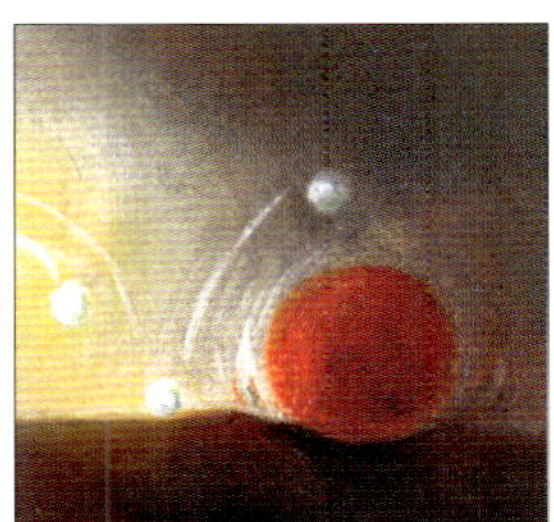

CONVERSATION BETWEEN A TUBA AND A FLUTE

OPENING A BOTTLE OR CAN OF BEER

BARNYARD

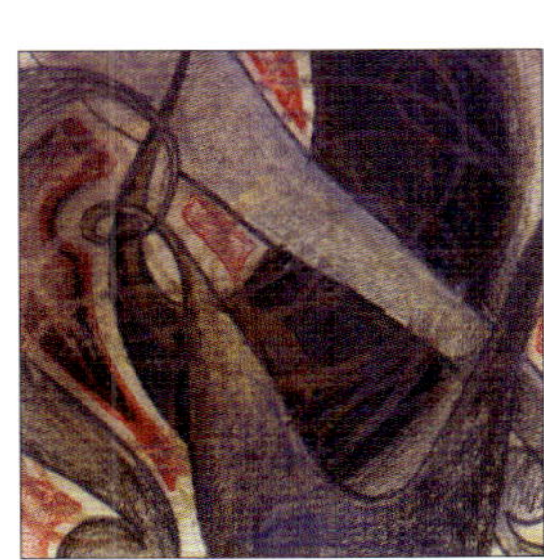

BUMBLEBEES MAKING LOVE

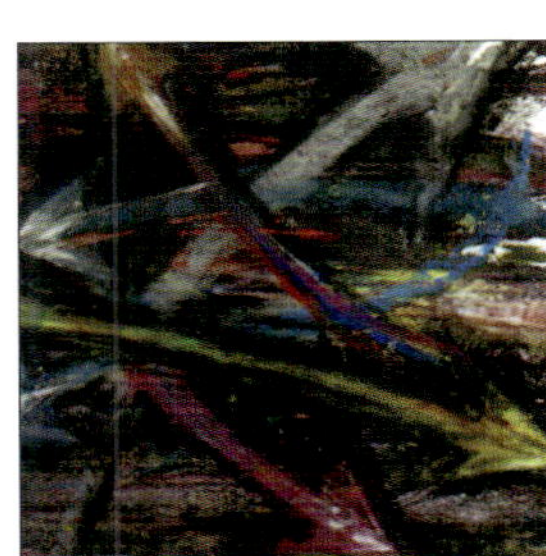

MISCOMMUNICATION

1. *Junewon Han*
2. *Yi Chen Tsai*
3. *Jinyoung Yoo*
4. *Heesang Lee*
5. *Mytran Dang*
6. *Yulsoo Sung*
7. *Gouhea Park*
8. *Yueh Lu*
9. *Nyoungha Chang*
10. *Donna Kwon*
11. *Juhee Lim*
12. *Yoejin Kim*
13. *Nicole Benson*
14. *Kristin Naranjo*
15. *Mytran Dang*
16. *Tess Lee*
17. *Max Kaplun*
18. *Juhee Lim*
19. *Maria Castellanos*
20. *Miyeon Kim*
21. *M. Takagi*
22. *Yueh Lu*
23. *Joo Kong*
24. *Judy Fine*
25. *Boram Chung*

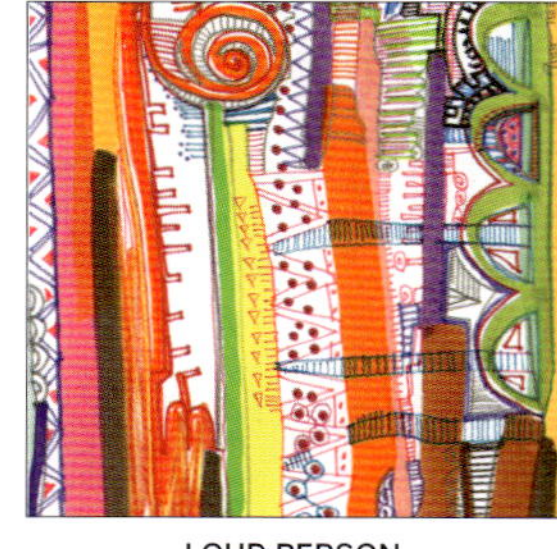

LOUD PERSON

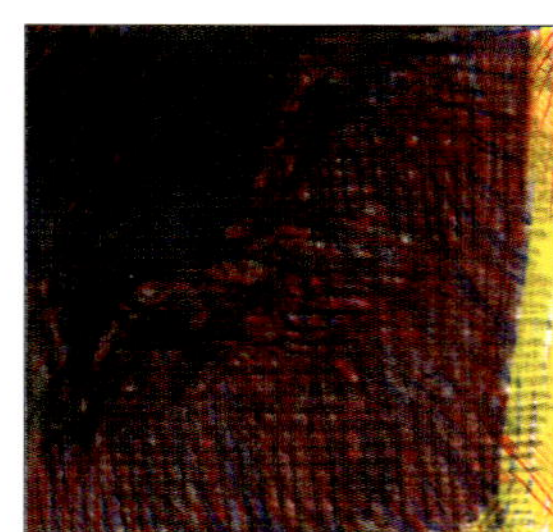

CONVERSATION BETWEEN A PICCOLO AND AN UPRIGHT BASS

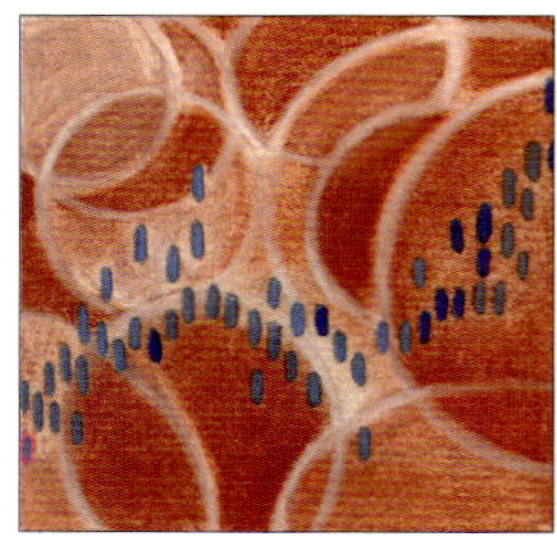

CONVERSATION BETWEEN A PICCOLO AND AN UPRIGHT BASS

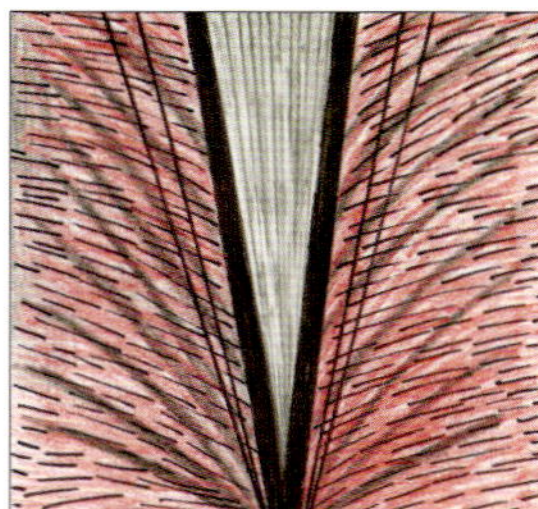

GUILLOTINE

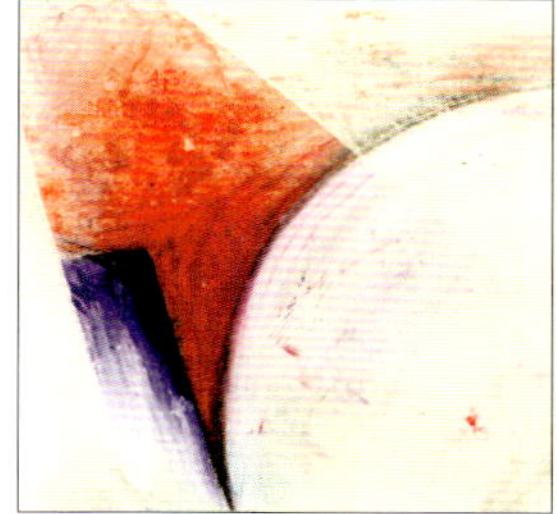

CASH REGISTER

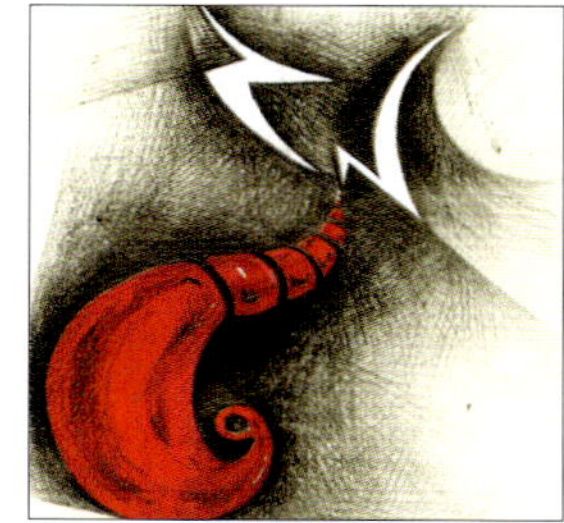

BEE STING

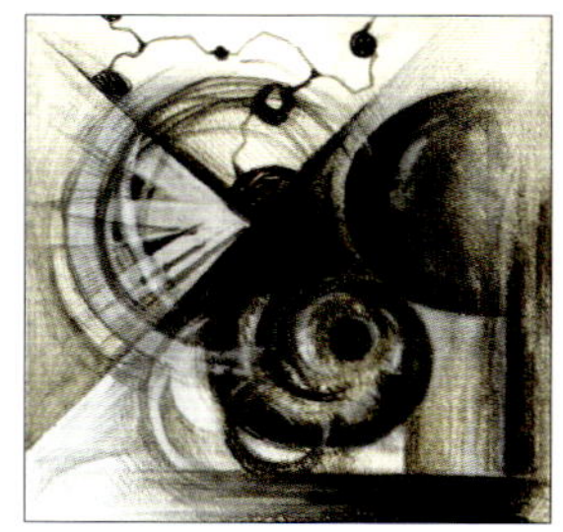

WAR

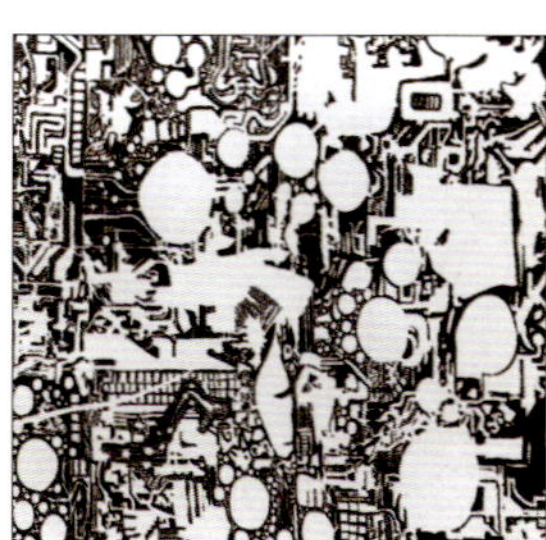

ROCK CONCERT

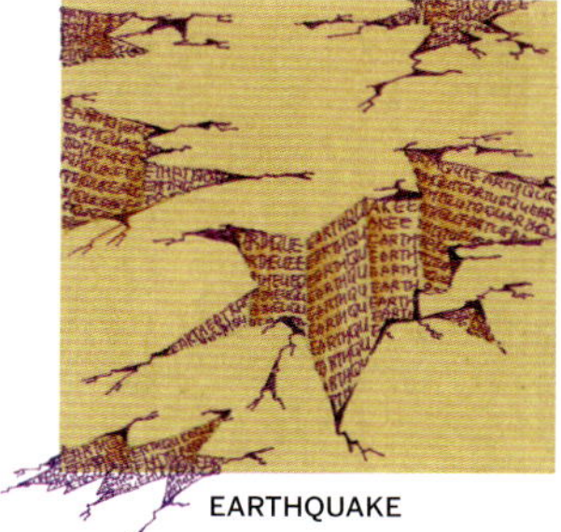

EARTHQUAKE

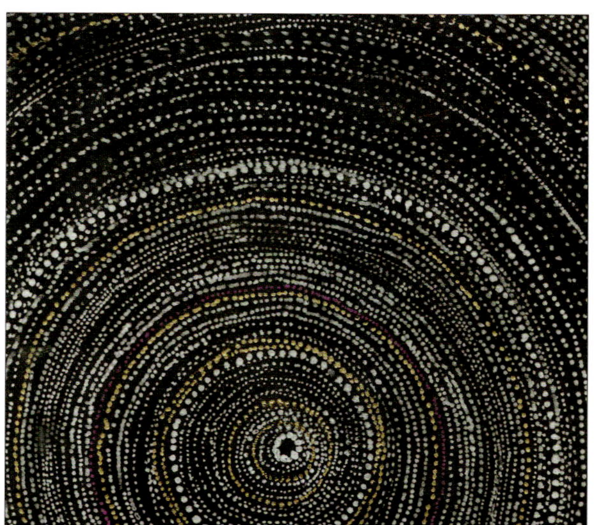

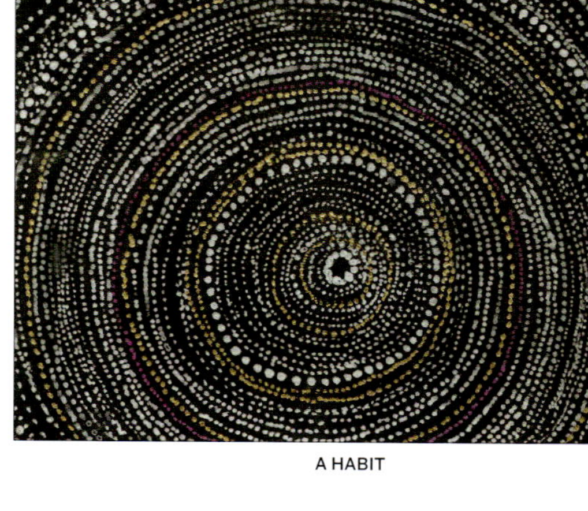

A HABIT

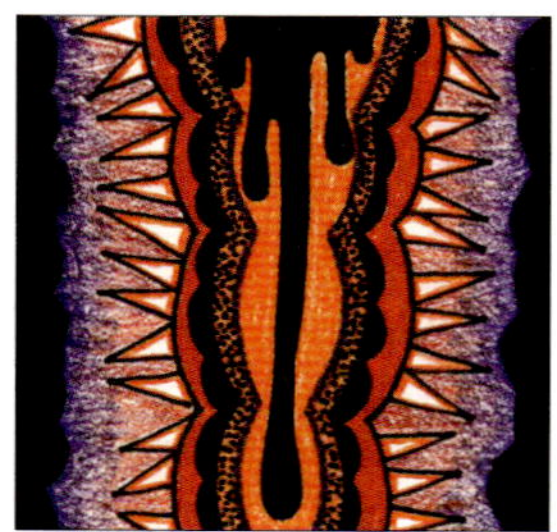

COCKFIGHT

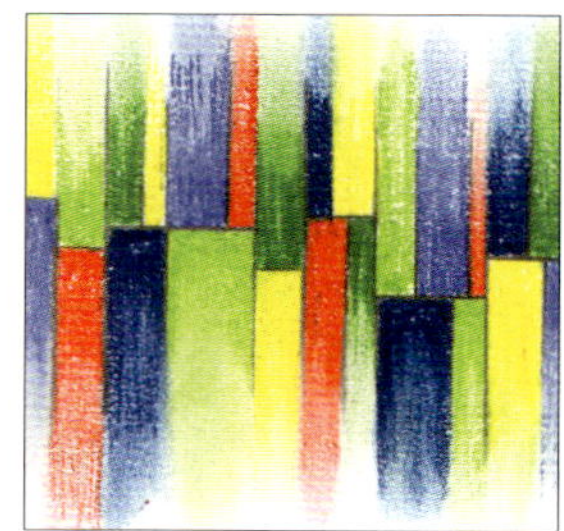

MERGING TRAFFIC

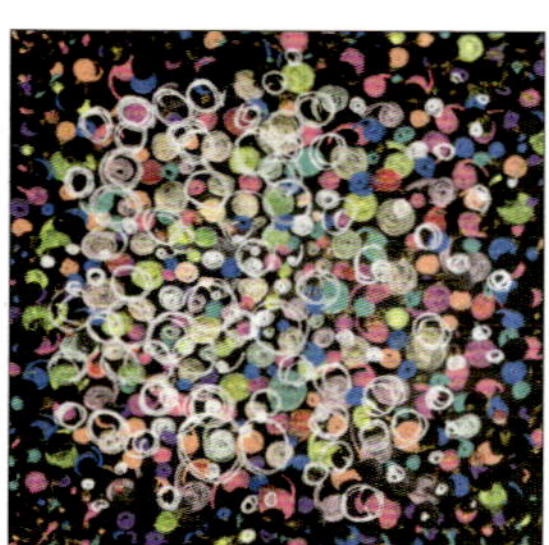

FIRECRACKERS

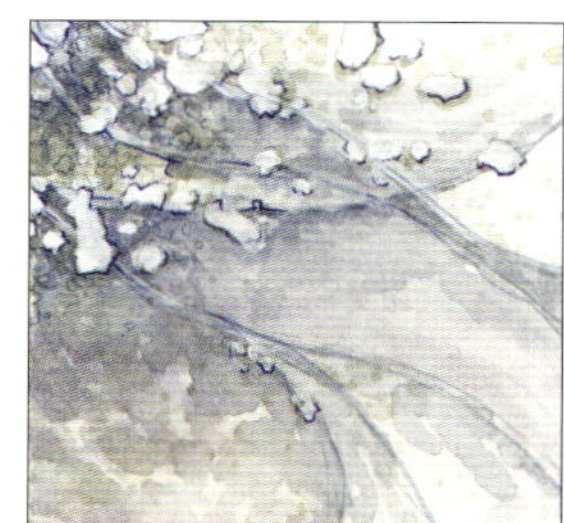

AVALANCHE

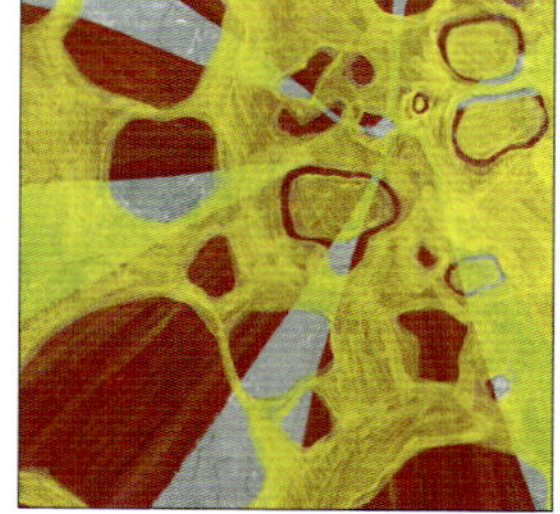

LOUD PERSON

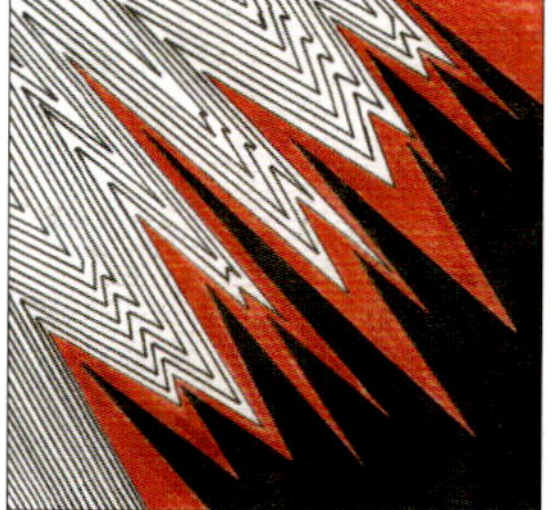

GUILLOTINE

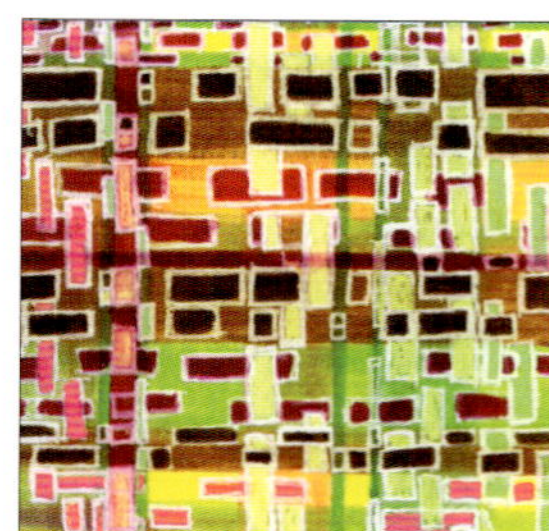

MERGING TRAFFIC

SOUND SOLUTIONS: RANDOM

This grouping of random subjects, as well as all the other solutions in this assignment, speak of the infinite ways of expressing form and color in problem solving, any of which has the ability to impact and define culture.

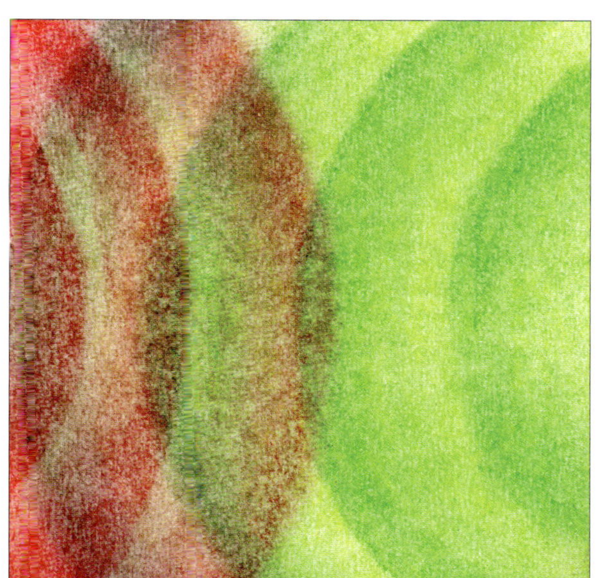

MISCOMMUNICATION

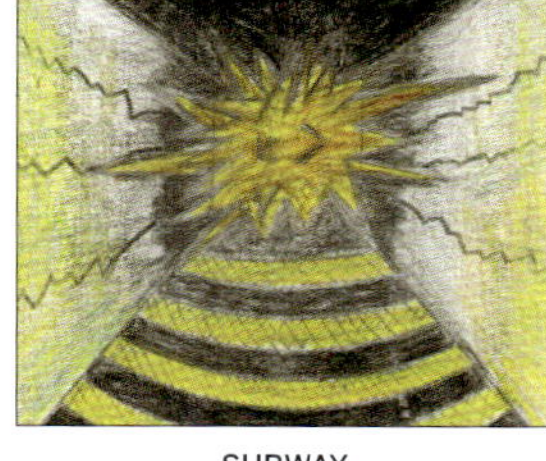

SUBWAY

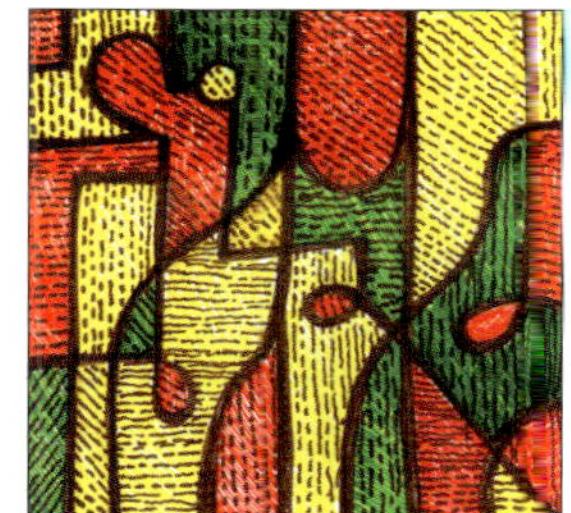

MERGING TRAFFIC

REJECTION

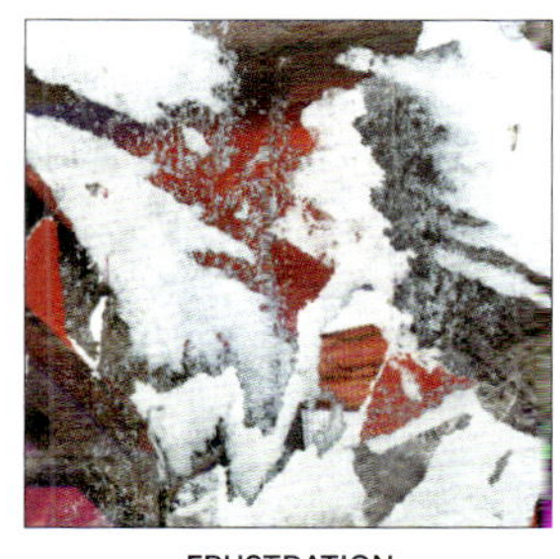

FRUSTRATION

LOUD PERSON

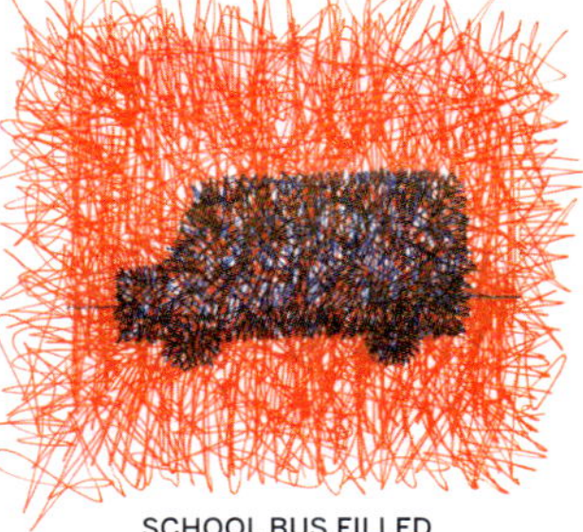

SCHOOL BUS FILLED WITH CHILDREN

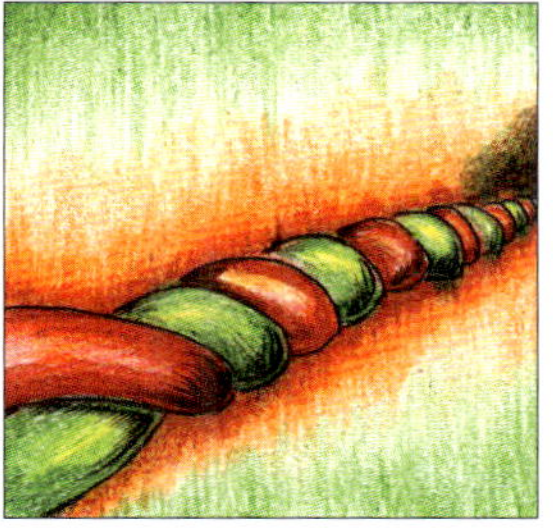

INDIGESTION

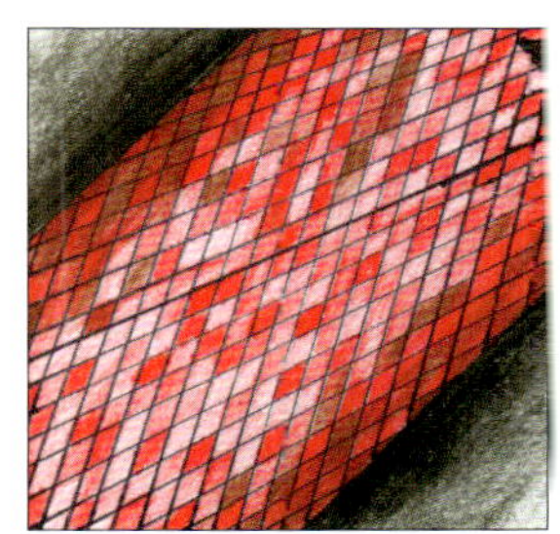

SUBWAY

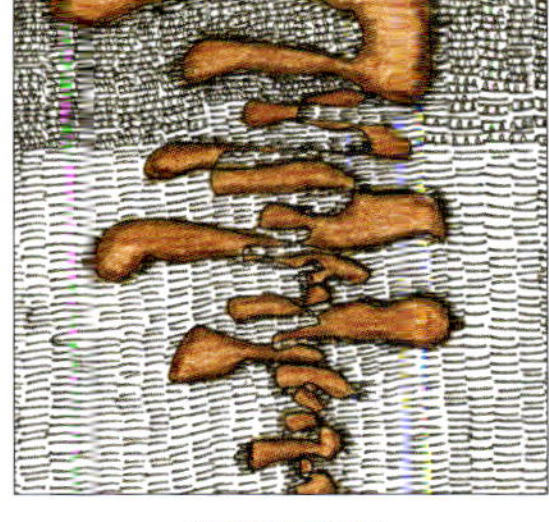

INDIGESTION

A HABIT

A HABIT

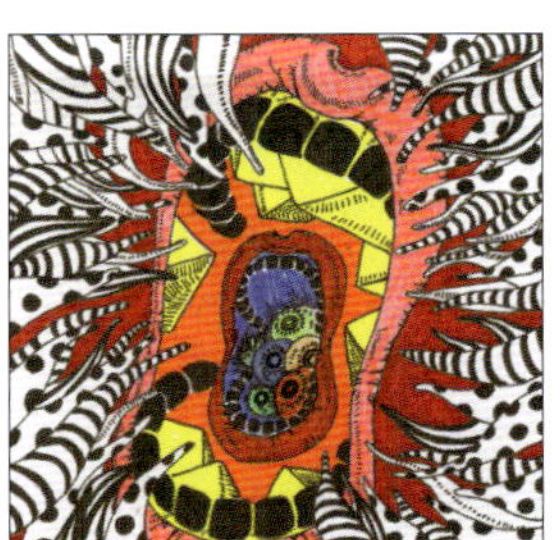

ROCK CONCERT

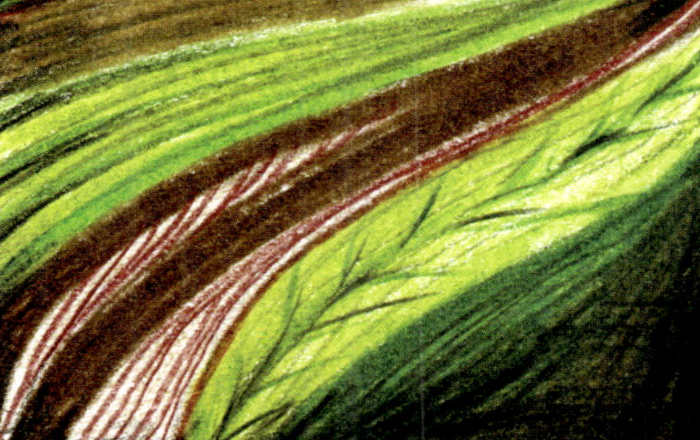

BARNYARD

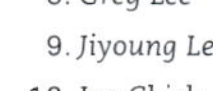

1. Yebyul Kim
2. Gregory Spuches
3. Leigh McCarron
4. Brent Philhower

5-7. Cheungyoon Kim

8. Greg Lee
9. Jiyoung Lee
10. Jen Chieh
11. Angela Ham
12. Brent Philhower
13. Yi Chen Tsai

14-15. Elaine Park

16. Connie Jun
17. Natasha Jacobs
18. Alan Tung
19. Brent Philhower
20. Sandra Woodruff
21. Kristin Naranjo

22-23. Aurelie Joly

24. Soomin Yoo
25. Carlos Acevedo
26. Melissa Arros

27-28. Gouhea Park

29. Jisu Park
30. Sira Kim
31. Dan Yang Yang

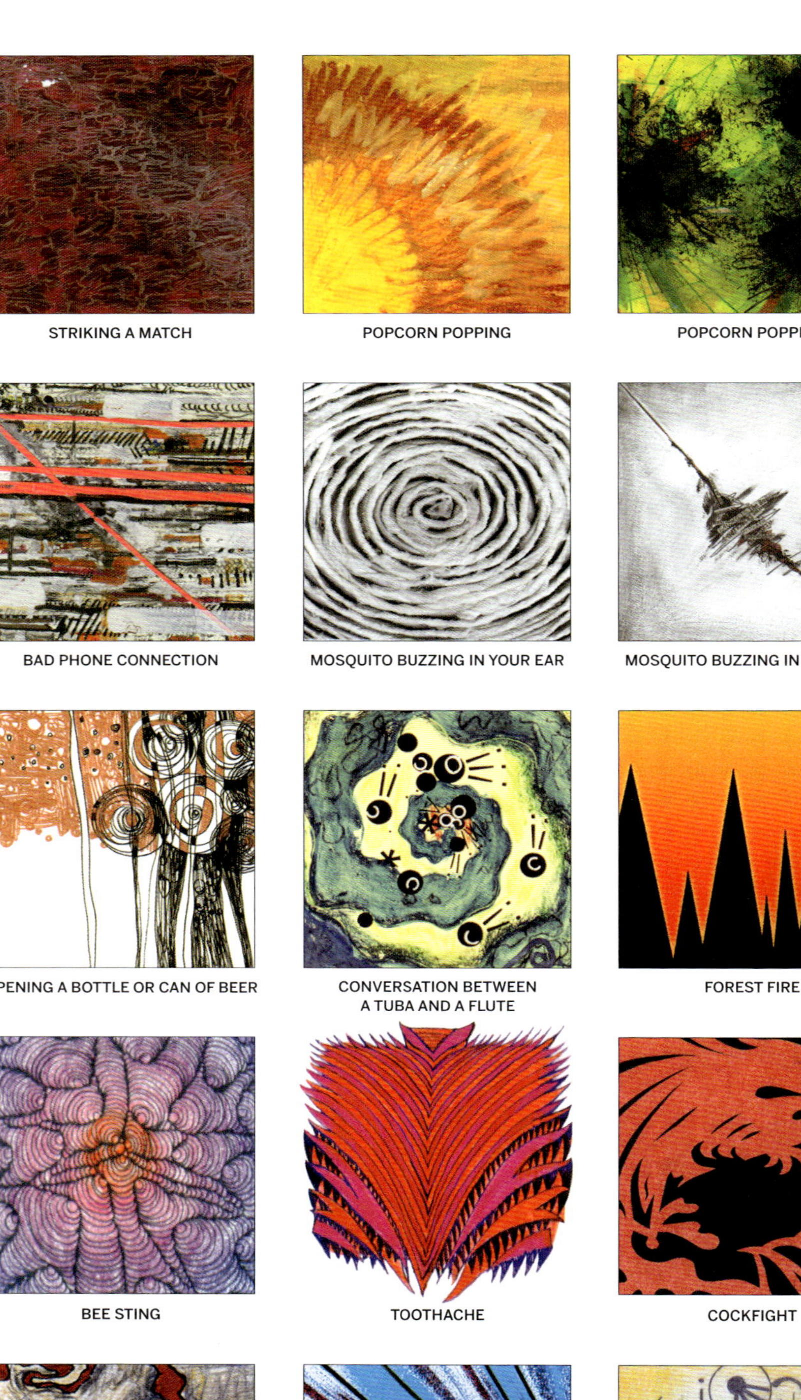

STRIKING A MATCH

POPCORN POPPING

POPCORN POPPING

CONFRONTATION BETWEEN A LEOPARD AND A ZEBRA

BAD PHONE CONNECTION

MOSQUITO BUZZING IN YOUR EAR

MOSQUITO BUZZING IN YOUR EAR

MOSQUITO BUZZING IN YOUR EAR

OPENING A BOTTLE OR CAN OF BEER

CONVERSATION BETWEEN A TUBA AND A FLUTE

FOREST FIRE

FOREST FIRE

BEE STING

TOOTHACHE

COCKFIGHT

FAULTY LIGHT BULB

WAR

WHISTLING TEA KETTLE

OPENING A BOTTLE OR CAN OF BEER

BEER DRINKING

SOUND SOLUTIONS: RANDOM

These random solutions are a compilation of new subjects coupled with topics that have already appeared in this chapter. Students who are put into conditions where invention is called upon are moved to establish their own vocabulary for solving visual communication problems.

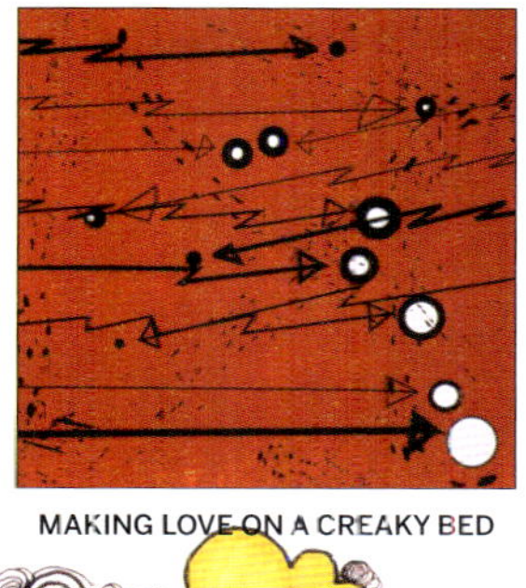

MAKING LOVE ON A CREAKY BED

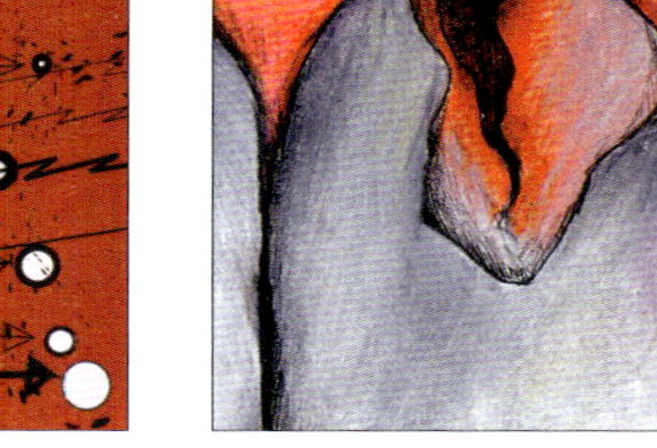

TOOTHACHE

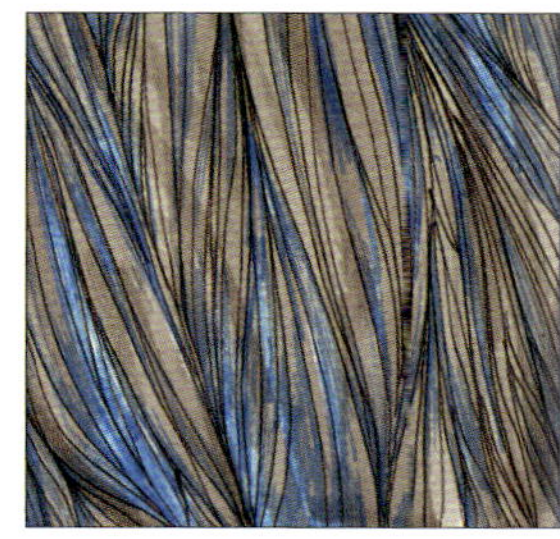

ELEVATOR MUSIC

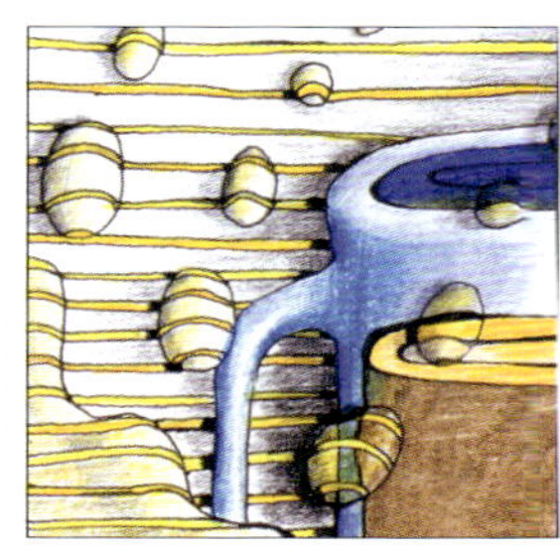

BEER DRINKING

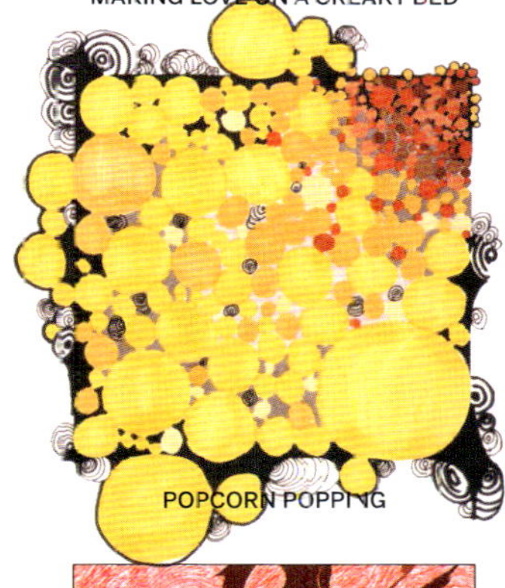

POPCORN POPPING

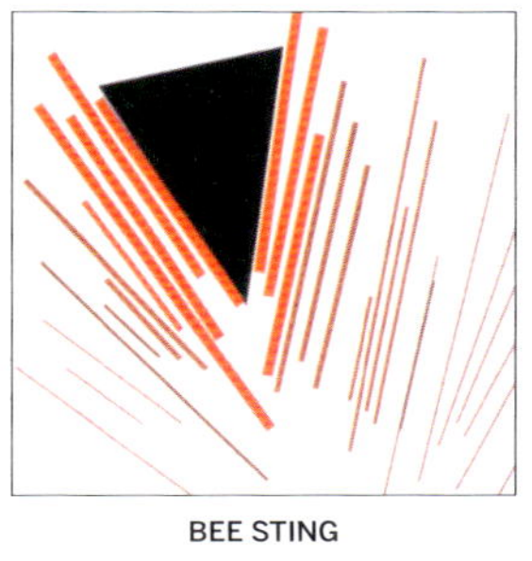

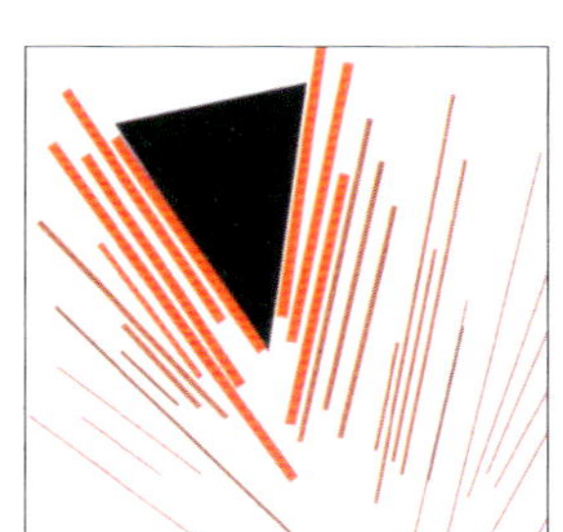

BEE STING

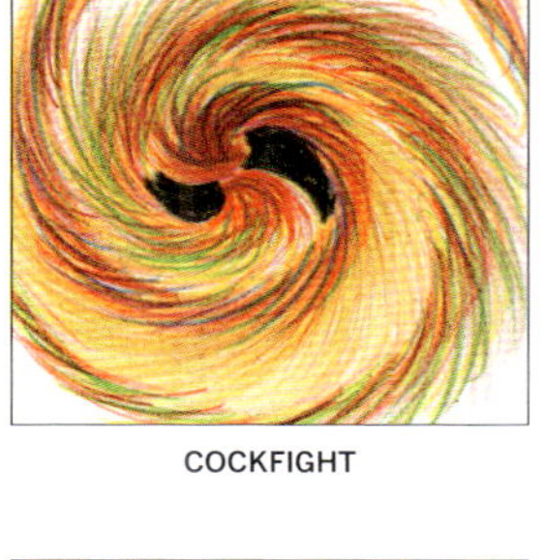

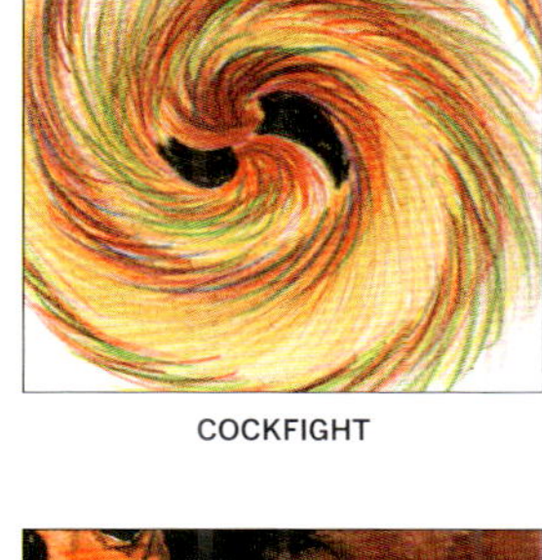

COCKFIGHT

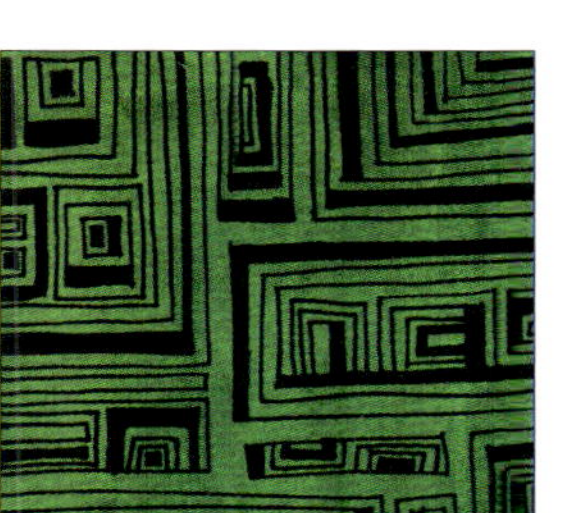

CASH REGISTER

COCKFIGHT

ECHO

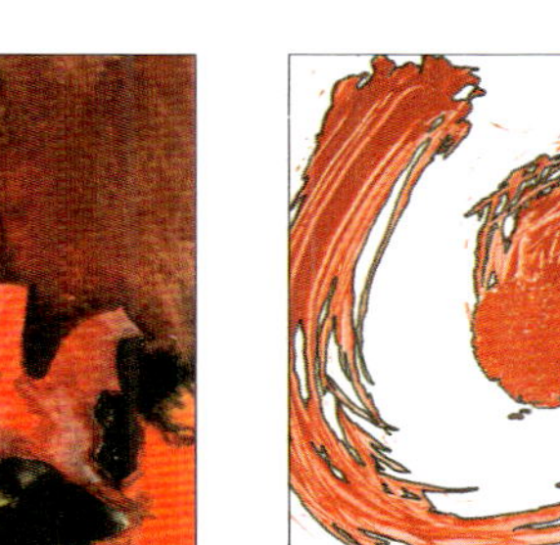

WAR

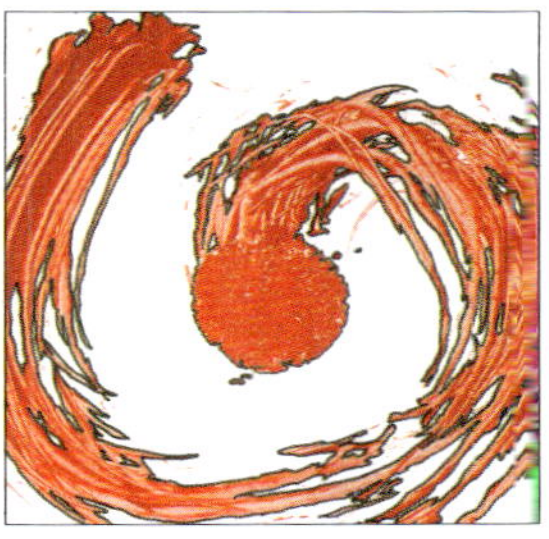

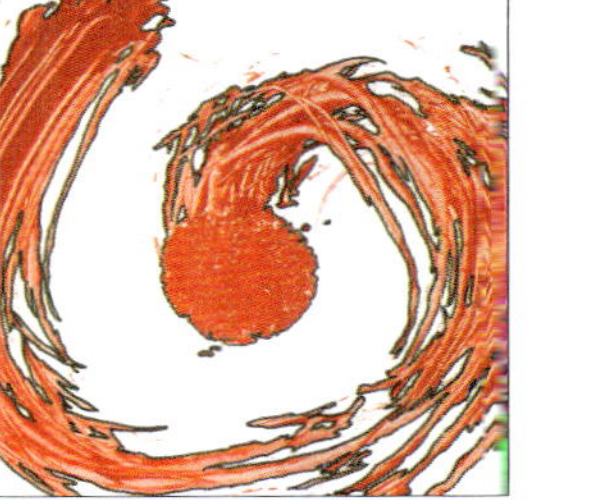

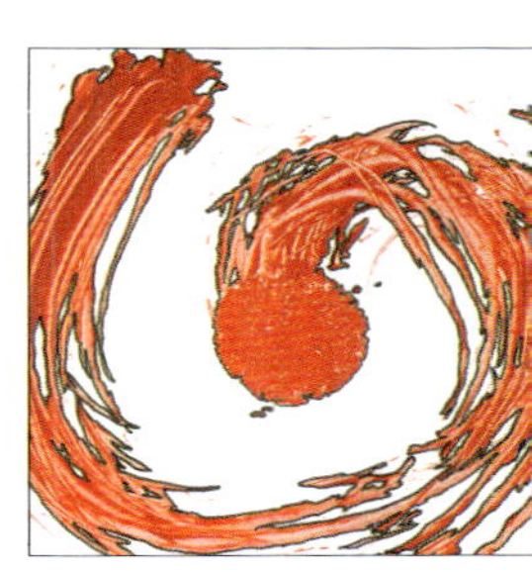

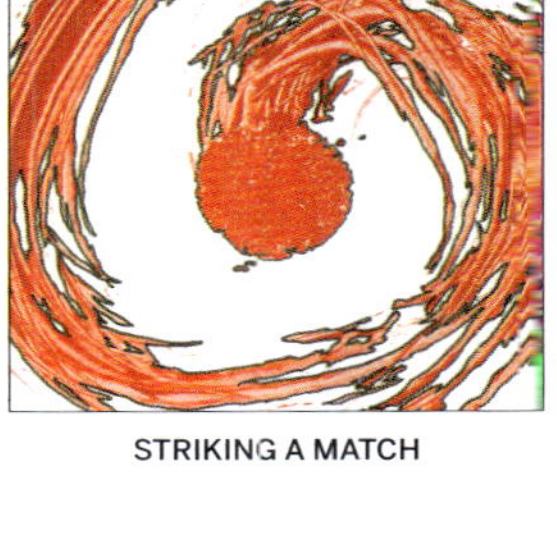

STRIKING A MATCH

LOUD PERSON

LOUD PERSON

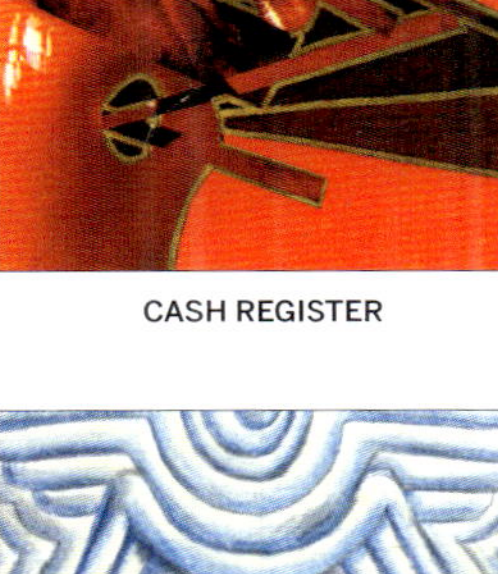

CASH REGISTER

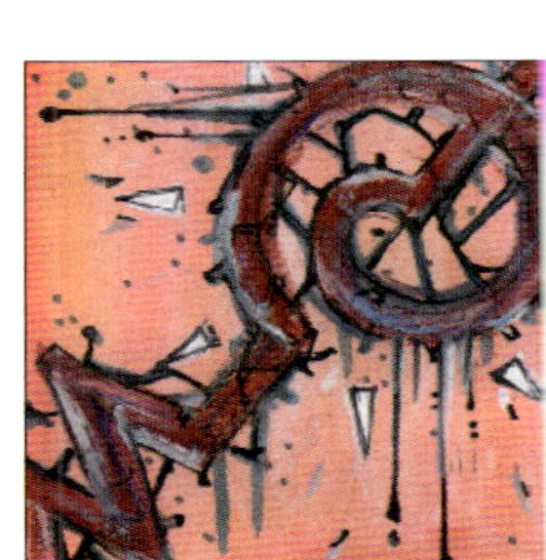

FRUSTRATION

ZIPPER BEING ZIPPED

FAULTY LIGHT BULB

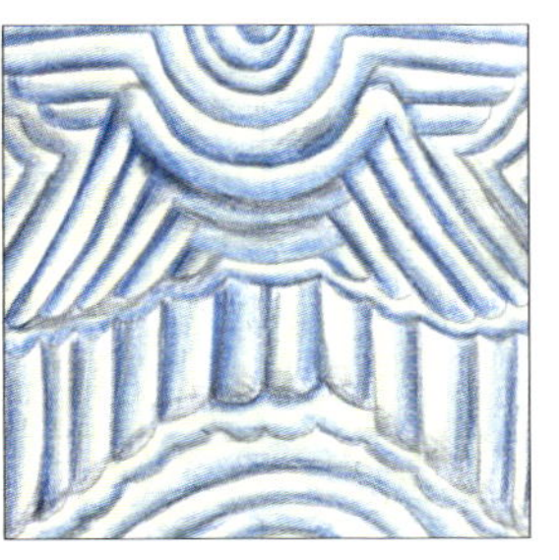

WINGS FLAPPING

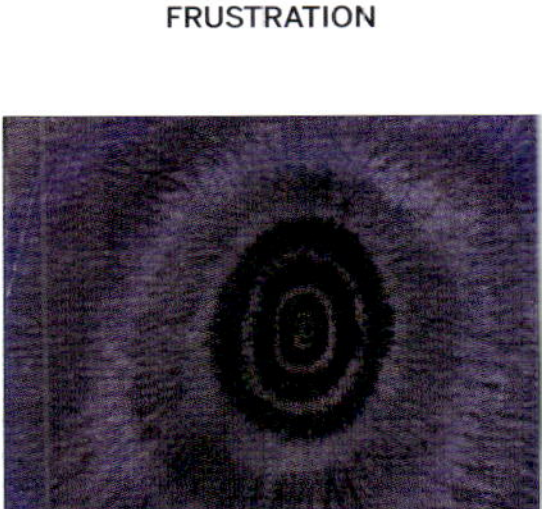

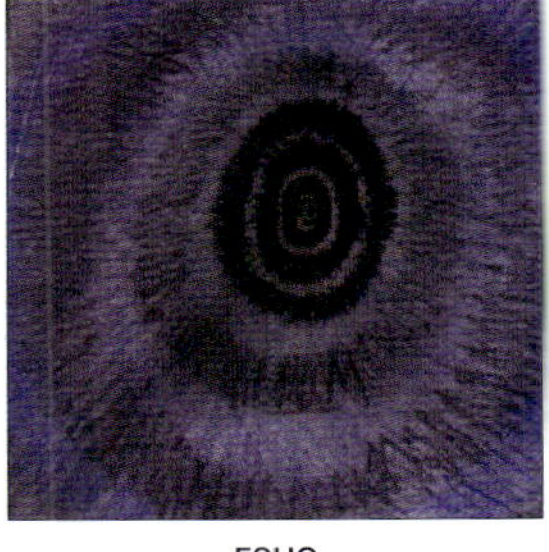

ECHO

1	2	3	4
5	6	7	8
9	10	11	12
13	14	15	16
17	18	19	20

21	22	23	24
25	26	27	28
29	30	31	32
33	34	35	36
37	38	39	40

1. *Da Yeon Roh*
2. *Jisoo Lee*
3. *Edward Yeung*
4–5. *Michele Demis*
6. *Youngsun Park*
7. *Dayoung Mun*
8. *Fanny Spång Artursson*
9. *Nataliya Hats*
10. *Judy Fine*
11. *Elliot Friedland*
12. *Jane Goldman*
13. *Jane Raskin*
14. *Jill Brody*
15. *Wei Lieh Lee*
16. *Olga Mezhibovskaya*
17. *Jean Kim*
18. *George Skoufas*
19. *Regina Kushnir*
20. *Francis Soriano*
21. *Deirdre Smith*
22. *Sandro Patella*
23. *Yoojin Lee*
24. *Alexia Leitich*
25. *Haejun Moon*
26. *M. Cross*
27. *Oscar Venagas*
28. *Alex Lieblein*
29. *Yoojin Lee*
30. *Jiyoon Jeong*
31. *Jungho Oh*
32. *Brian Lemus*
33. *Minhee Kim*
34. *Jamie Connell*
35. *Lisa Marie Gilardi*
36. *Samantha Raso*
37. *Jiyoon Jeong*
38. *Hyewon Shim*
39. *Alexia Leitich*
40. *Allan Weiss*

THOUGHTS ON THE CREATIVE PROCESS 4

When making aesthetic decisions, one needs to struggle with the given problem in a rightful way and trust something other than one's mind to effectively resolve the interaction between line, shape, form, space, scale, texture, and color.

"A LINE IS A DOT THAT WENT FOR A WALK."

PAUL KLEE'S FAMOUS QUOTE "A LINE IS A DOT THAT WENT FOR A WALK" IS TO BE USED AS A POINT OF DEPARTURE FOR CREATING INVENTIVE LINES BY GRAPHICALLY INTERPRETING THE EIGHTEEN TOPICS LISTED ON YOUR ASSIGNMENT SHEET. LINES MAY BE THICK, THIN, RIGID, BLURRED, BROKEN, CURVED OR ANGULAR TO EXPRESS THE QUALITIES AND CHARACTERISTICS OF THE SPECIFIC TOPICS. EXECUTE EACH SOLUTION WITHIN THE GIVEN SPACE UNLESS YOUR CONCEPT DICTATES OTHERWISE. THERE ARE NO LIMITATIONS ON THE USE OF COLOR OR MEDIUM.

ANXIOUS

EMBARRASSED

BIZARRE

EXHAUSTED

FRAGILE

SYSTEMATIC

LYRICAL

TURBULENT

NONSENSICAL

PSYCHOTIC

AMBIGUOUS

DISTRACTED

SENSUAL

SLOVEN

SPONTANEOUS

AGGRESSIVE

AWKWARD

INDECISIVE

PROBLEMS : SOLUTIONS SERIES

CREATED BY RICHARD WILDE / JUDITH WILDE, PRODUCED BY VISUAL ARTS PRESS, LTD. ART DIRECTORS: RICHARD WILDE / JUDITH WILDE

A LINE IS A DOT PROBLEM:

"A line is a dot that went for a walk" is a quote by Paul Klee, and the inspiration for this assignment. Use line as a point of departure to interpret the eighteen topics on the assignment sheet. Lines can vary greatly to express the character of the following subjects: anxious, embarrassed, bizarre, exhausted, fragile, systematic, lyrical, turbulent, nonsensical, psychotic, ambiguous, spontaneous, distracted, sloven, sensual, aggressive, awkward, and indecisive.

AIM:
"A line is a dot that went for a walk" suggests infinite possibilities. Given this directive, one can examine each subject and express its meaning within the parameters of a limited space. In dealing with these highly diverse topics an effort of experimentation is needed to find a formal equivalent for each subject.

SUGGESTIONS:
Keep in mind that the executions must be reduced to an expressive line. It is important to consider the background as an integral design element. Consider the use of color when making aesthetic and conceptual decisions to better define your solution, although, at times, black and white might serve as well.

SPECIFICATIONS:
There is no limitation on the use of color or medium. Execute each solution within the given space unless your concept dictates otherwise.

4

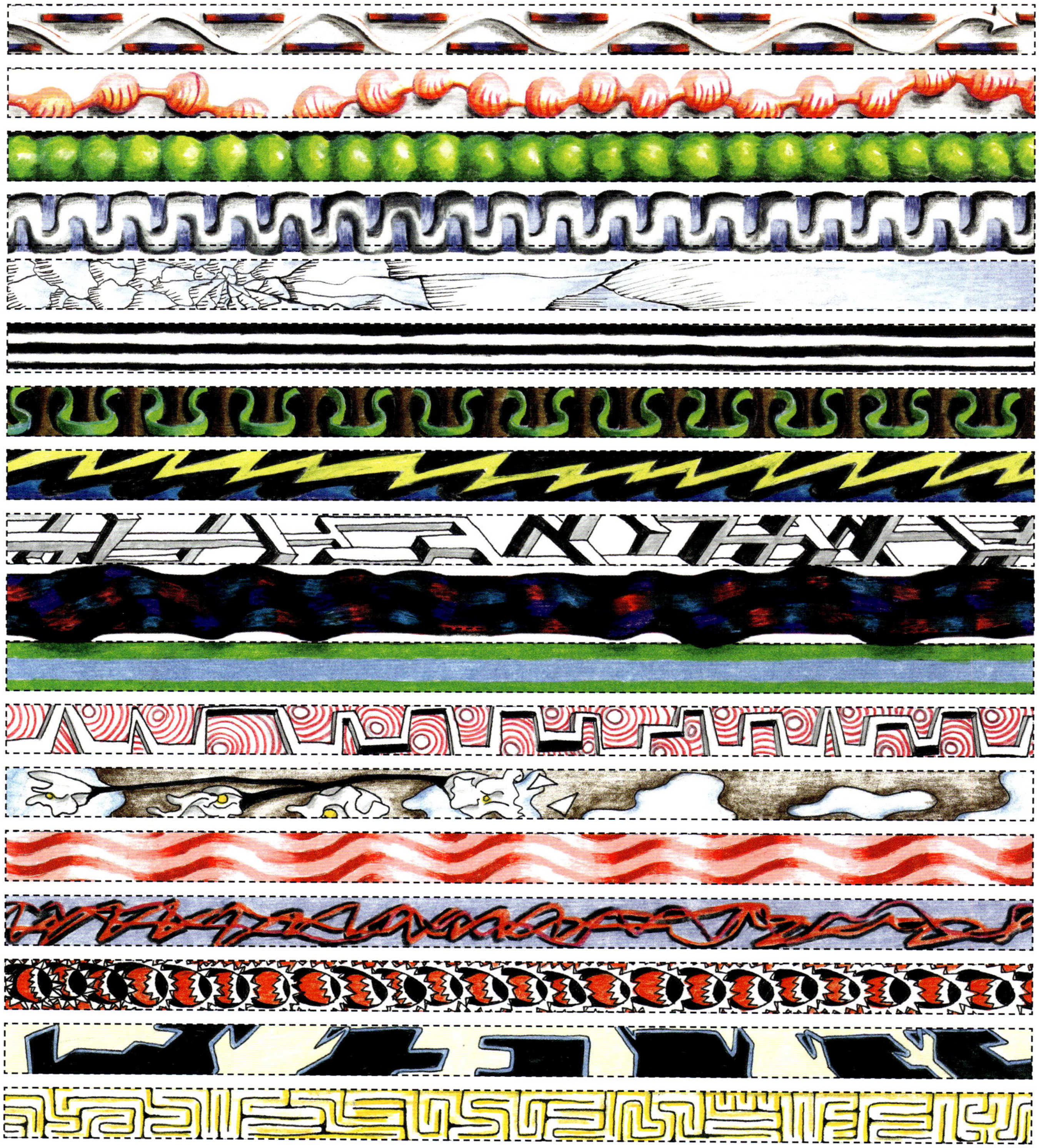

ANXIOUS

EMBARRASSED

BIZARRE

EXHAUSTED

FRAGILE

SYSTEMATIC

LYRICAL

TURBULENT

NONSENSICAL

PSYCHOTIC

AMBIGUOUS

DISTRACTED

SENSUAL

SLOVEN

SPONTANEOUS

AGGRESSIVE

AWKWARD

INDECISIVE

A LINE IS A DOT SOLUTIONS:

Figures 1 and 2 are examples of entire assignment sheets, executed by two different students. Although the intent is to focus on each individual line as an end in itself, the solutions contrast one another by their close proximity, which makes the entire assignment appear as an expression unto itself.

Figure 1 primarily uses abstraction, while figure 2 uses a more literal approach.

Most of the solutions for this project lie between these two approaches, with the majority leaning toward abstraction.

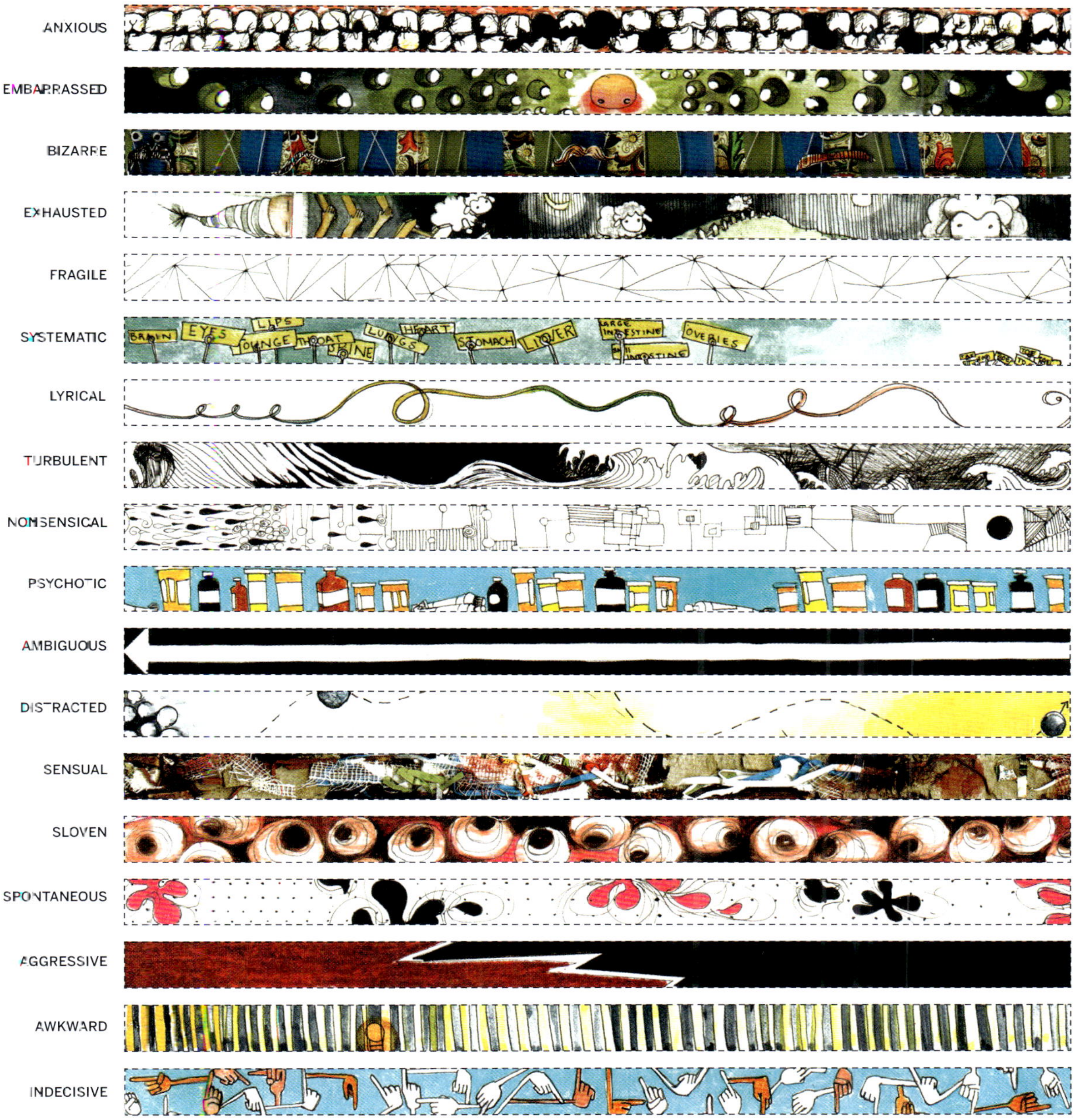

ANXIOUS
EMBARRASSED
BIZARRE
EXHAUSTED
FRAGILE
SYSTEMATIC
LYRICAL
TURBULENT
NONSENSICAL
PSYCHOTIC
AMBIGUOUS
DISTRACTED
SENSUAL
SLOVEN
SPONTANEOUS
AGGRESSIVE
AWKWARD
INDECISIVE

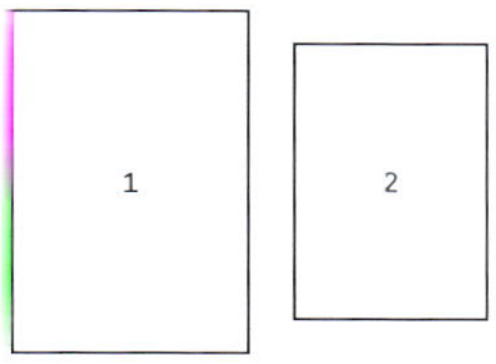

1
2

1. *Nathan Scruggs*
2. *Colette Nickola*

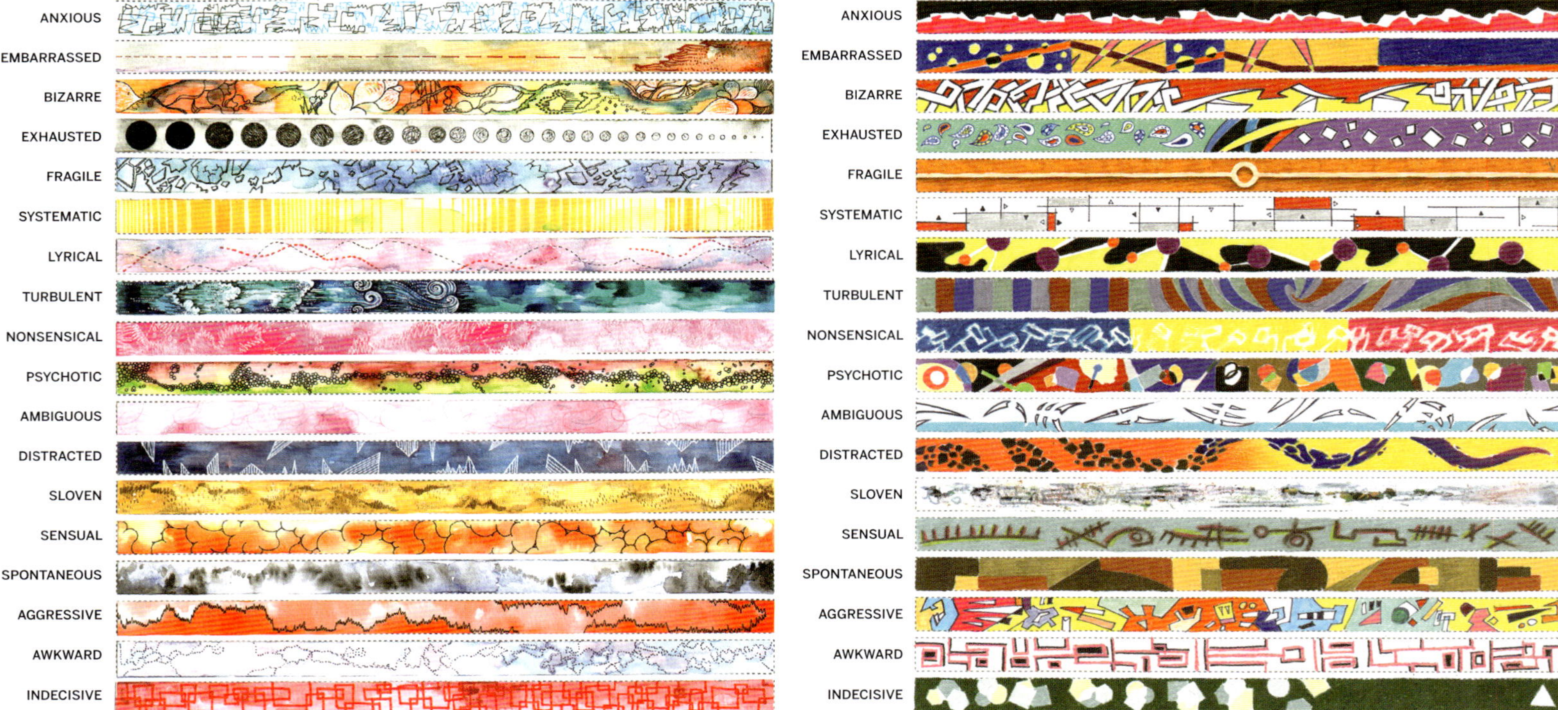
ANXIOUS
EMBARRASSED
BIZARRE
EXHAUSTED
FRAGILE
SYSTEMATIC
LYRICAL
TURBULENT
NONSENSICAL
PSYCHOTIC
AMBIGUOUS
DISTRACTED
SLOVEN
SENSUAL
SPONTANEOUS
AGGRESSIVE
AWKWARD
INDECISIVE
ANXIOUS
EMBARRASSED
BIZARRE
EXHAUSTED
FRAGILE
SYSTEMATIC
LYRICAL
TURBULENT
NONSENSICAL
PSYCHOTIC
AMBIGUOUS
DISTRACTED
SLOVEN
SENSUAL
SPONTANEOUS
AGGRESSIVE
AWKWARD
INDECISIVE

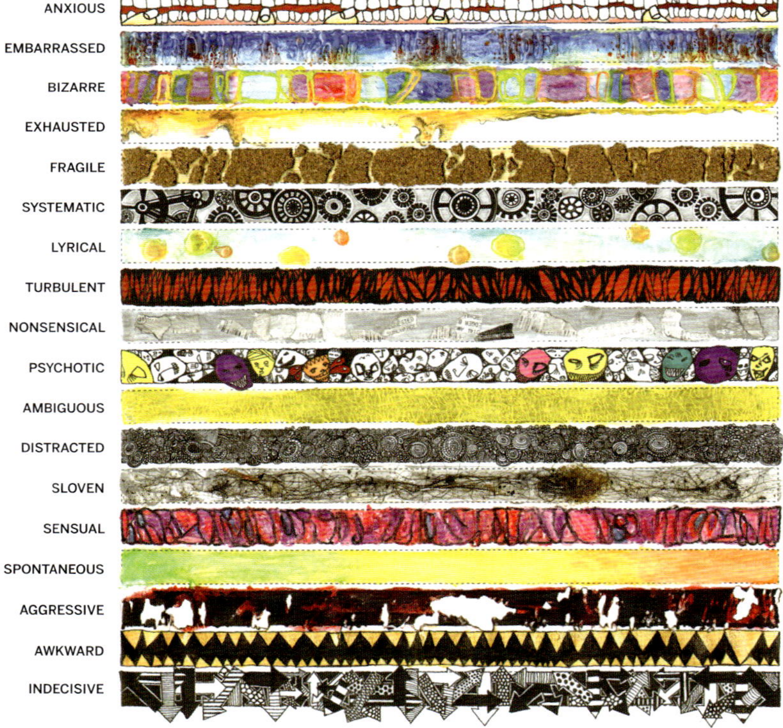
ANXIOUS
EMBARRASSED
BIZARRE
EXHAUSTED
FRAGILE
SYSTEMATIC
LYRICAL
TURBULENT
NONSENSICAL
PSYCHOTIC
AMBIGUOUS
DISTRACTED
SLOVEN
SENSUAL
SPONTANEOUS
AGGRESSIVE
AWKWARD
INDECISIVE

ANXIOUS
EMBARRASSED
BIZARRE
EXHAUSTED
FRAGILE
SYSTEMATIC
LYRICAL
TURBULENT
NONSENSICAL
PSYCHOTIC
AMBIGUOUS
DISTRACTED
SLOVEN
SENSUAL
SPONTANEOUS
AGGRESSIVE
AWKWARD
INDECISIVE

ANXIOUS

EMBARRASSED

BIZARRE

EXHAUSTED

FRAGILE

SYSTEMATIC

LYRICAL

TURBULENT

NONSENSICAL

PSYCHOTIC

AMBIGUOUS

DISTRACTED

SLOVEN

SENSUAL

SPONTANEOUS

AGGRESSIVE

AWKWARD

INDECISIVE

A LINE IS A DOT SOLUTIONS:

Figures 1 through 5 are examples of the assignment in its entirety. Viewed as single images, personal stylization becomes apparent.

Figure 1 expresses a softness that alludes to fantasy, while figure 2 is a more graphic interpretation in its reductive approach.

Figure 3 is highly textural, with a somber overtone, using both abstract and literal imagery.

Figure 4 ranges from graphic, to abstract, to the use of literal imagery.

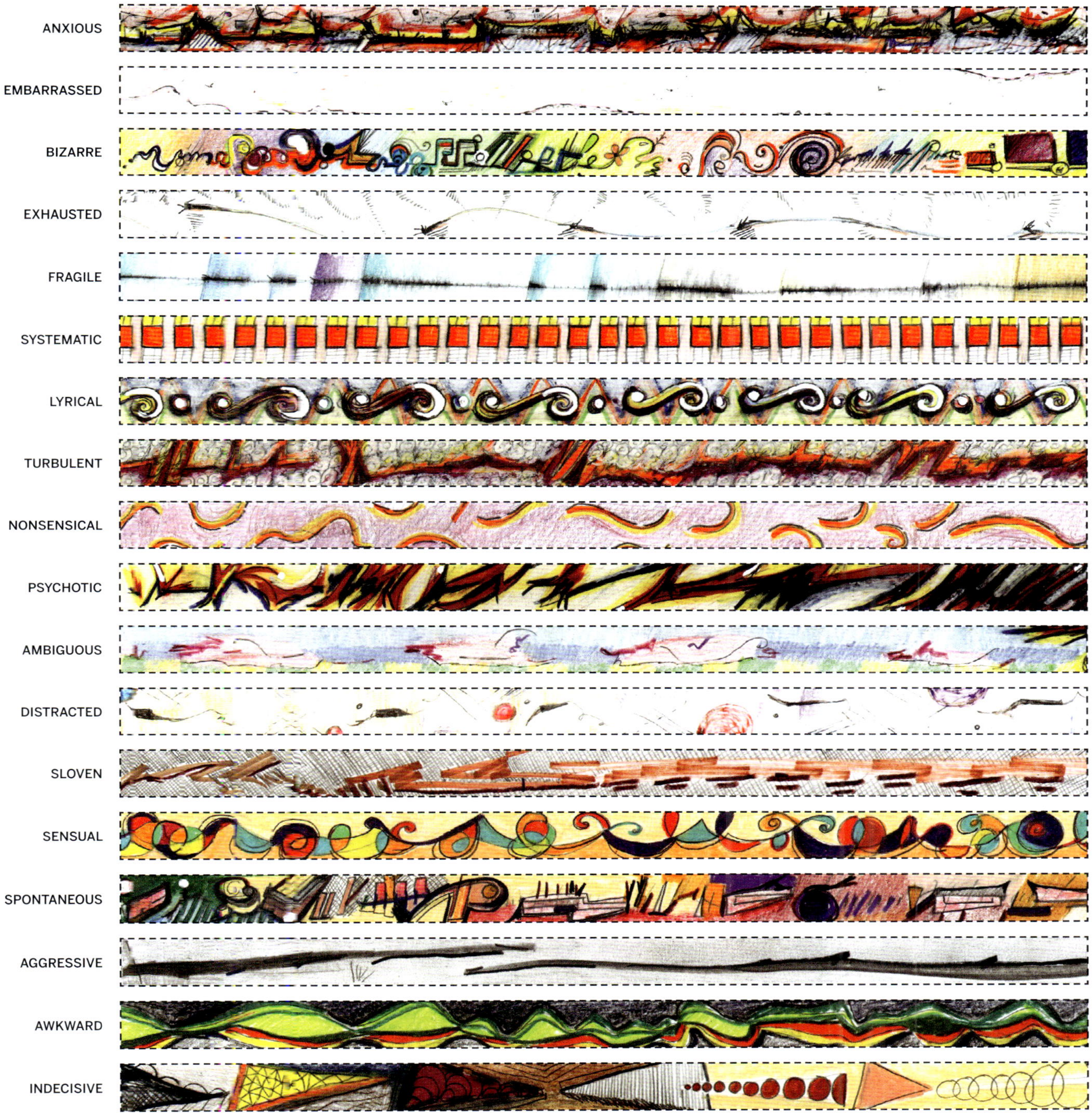

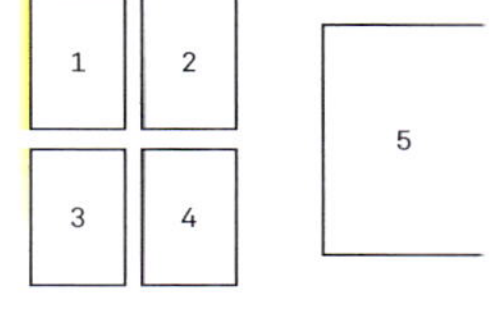

1. *Hannah Ahn*
2. *Fabricio Da Costa*
3. *Mikyung Kim*
4. *Jungeun Kwak*
5. *Michele Clark*

A sense of controlled spontaneity is expressed in figure 5, along with a comparatively consistent style in terms of shape, repetition, movement, color, and line.

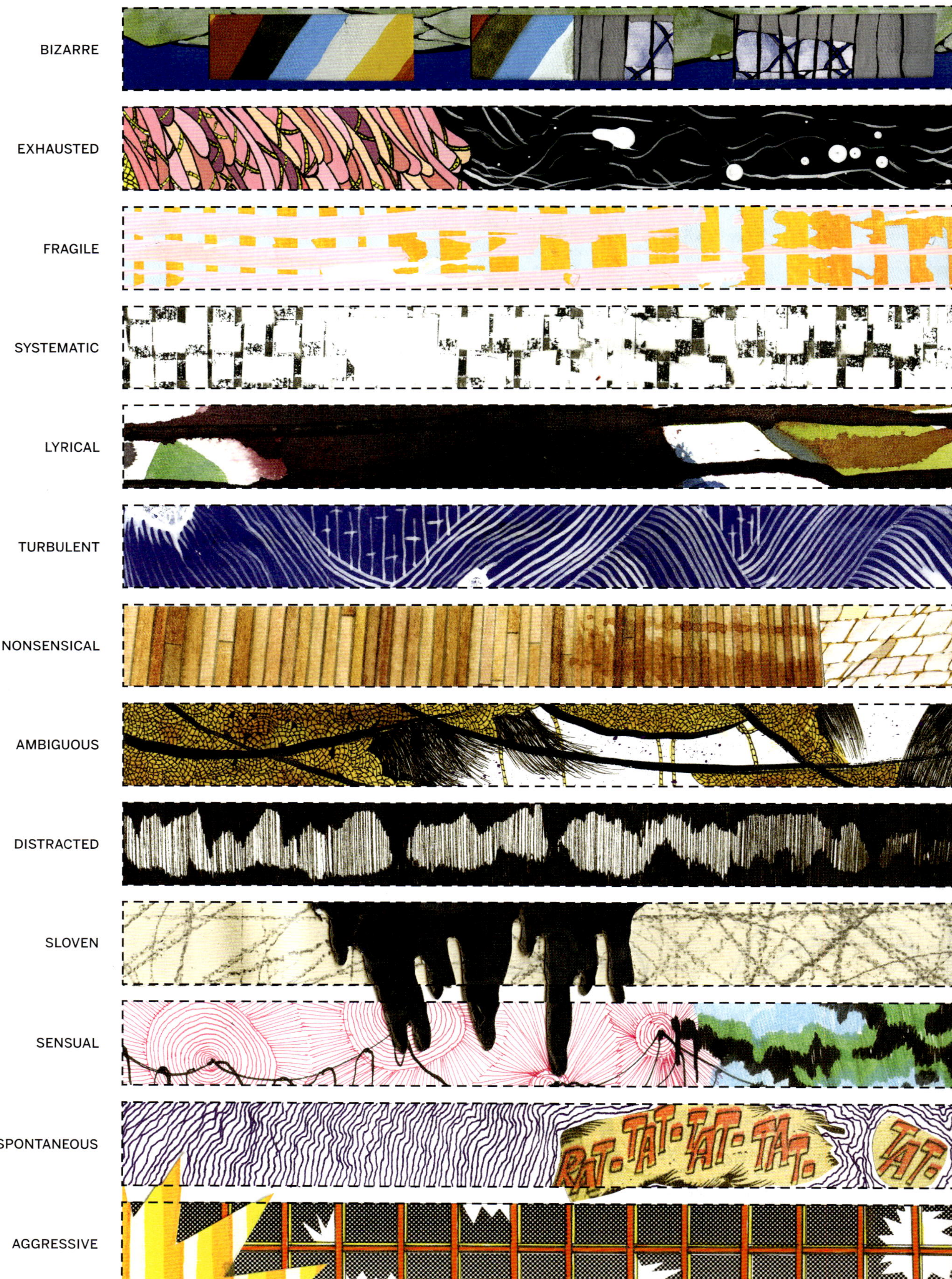
BIZARRE
EXHAUSTED
FRAGILE
SYSTEMATIC
LYRICAL
TURBULENT
NONSENSICAL
AMBIGUOUS
DISTRACTED
SLOVEN
SENSUAL
SPONTANEOUS
RAT-TAT-TAT-TAT.
TAT-
AGGRESSIVE

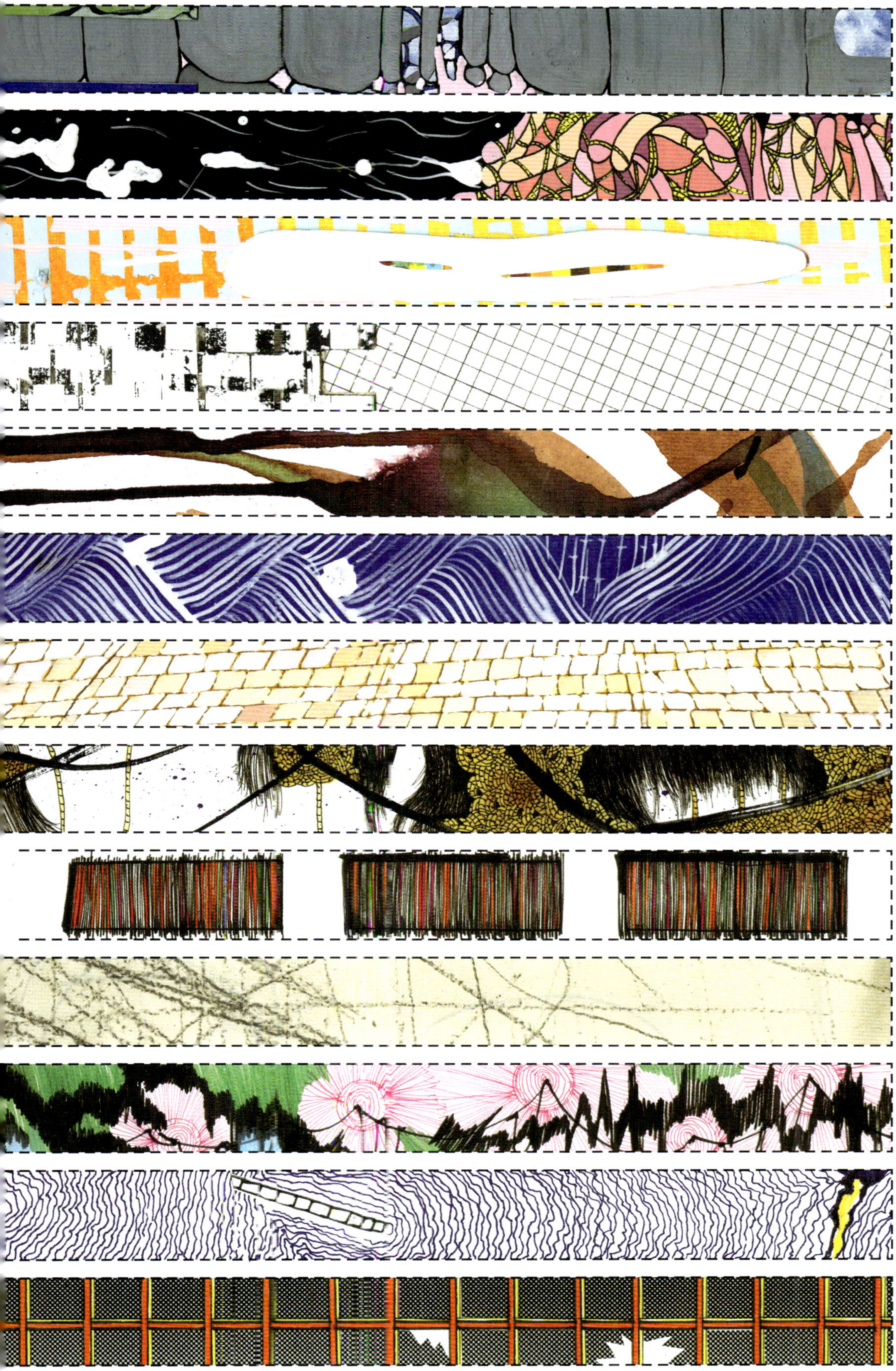

A LINE IS A DOT SOLUTIONS:

Figure 1 represents a highly personal abstract interpretation of each subject that incorporates various mediums including paint, pen and ink, and collage. The project expresses a consistency in terms of aesthetics.

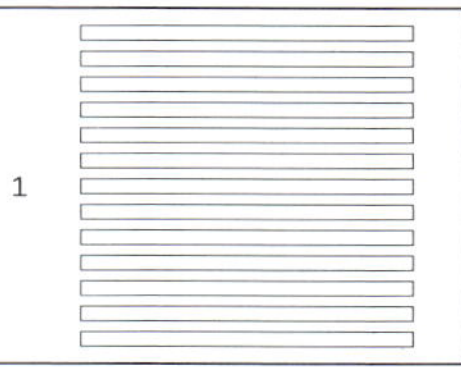

1. *Yueh Lu*

PSYCHOTIC

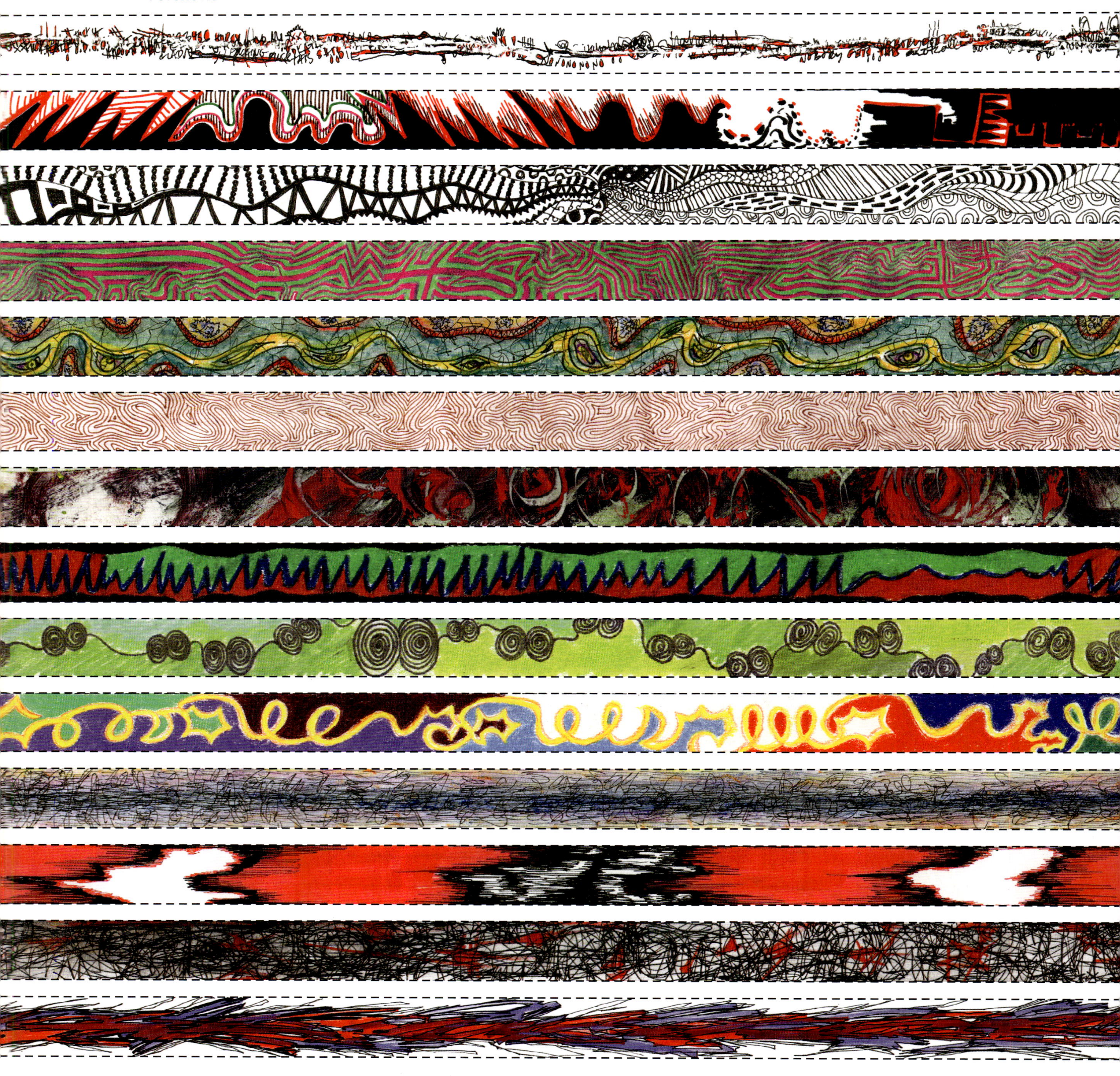

A LINE IS A DOT SOLUTIONS:

Figures 1 through 14 depict the subject psychotic, which has aspects of strange behavior, distorted thinking, and violence. The solutions range from anger, to a sense of mystery, to the dark side of the human condition.

Figures 15 through 21 and 22 through 27 are executed by two different students, whose color palettes differ in terms of vibrancy and muted earth tones.

Figure 24 takes the liberty of invading another solution to best express its concept.

EMBARRASSED

BIZARRE

EXHAUSTED

SYSTEMATIC

LYRICAL

TURBULENT

AMBIGUOUS

SLOVEN

NONSENSICAL

DISTRACTED

SLOVEN

SENSUAL

SPONTANEOUS

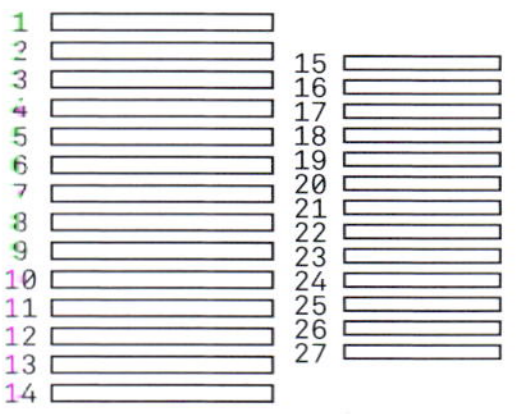

1. *Laura Scherling*
2. *Ying Chen*
3. *Jihye Hong*
4. *Renee Tranter*
5. *Sihan Zou*
6. *Caroline Provine*
7. *Jisoo Lee*
8. *Andre Alves Da Silva*
9. *Charles Beria*
10. *Daniella Parente*
11. *Sihan Zou*
12. *Neil Drossman*
13. *Hana Yoo*
14. *Yoonjin Lee*

15–21. *Deanne Nicpon*

22–27. *Leigh McCarron*

BIZARRE

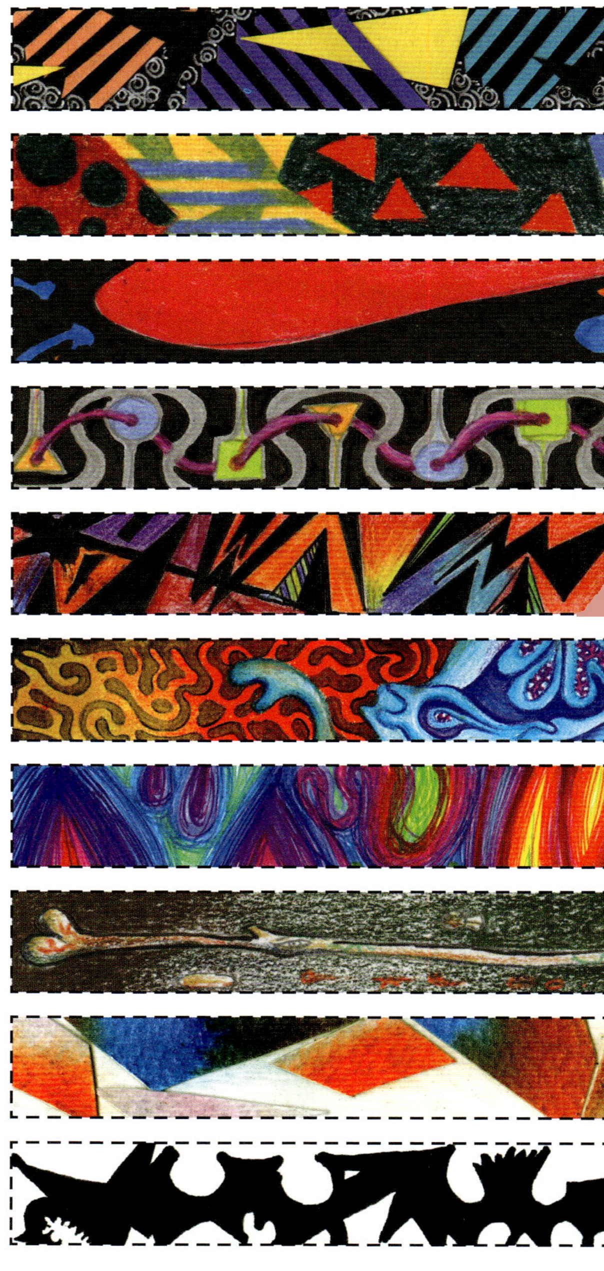

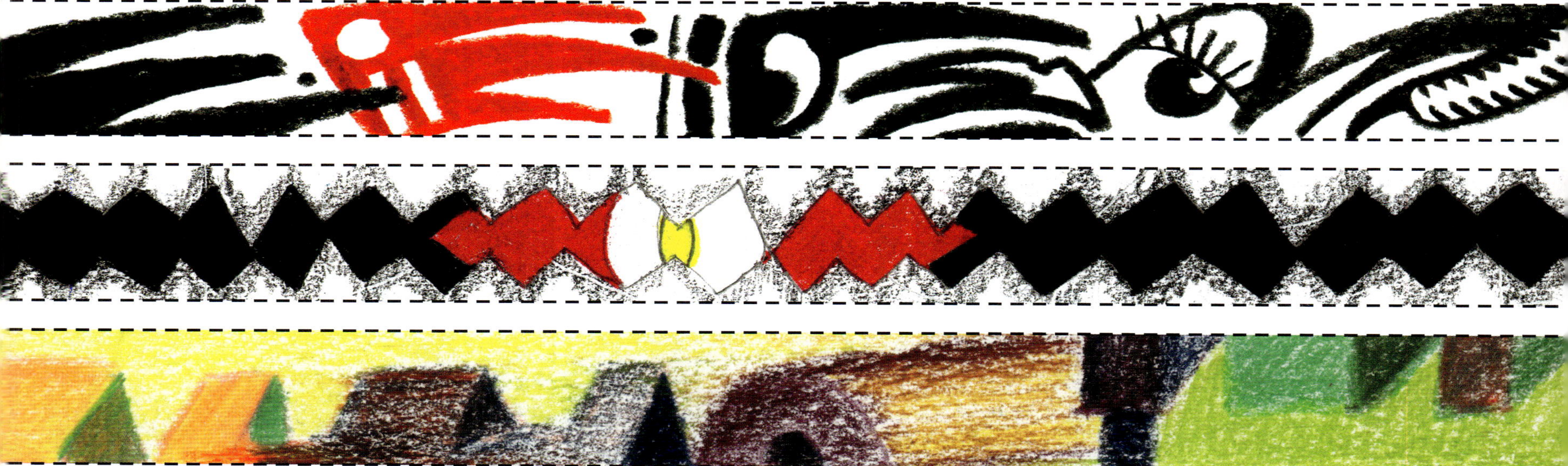

A LINE IS A DOT SOLUTIONS:

The subject bizarre, which has qualities of the unusual, the weird, the eccentric, and the fantastic, is dealt with in these thirteen solutions. For the most part, they draw from nonobjective imagery and range from reductive hard-edge graphic solutions to tonal textural imagery.

Given the subjectivity of the topic, what appears as bizarre for one, might be commonplace for another.

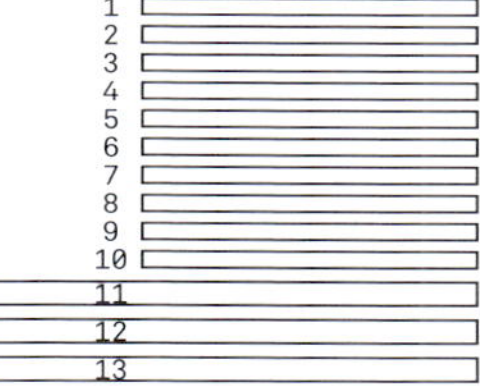

1. *Sunmin Chung*
2. *Andrea Ascoli*
3. *James Soto*
4. *Jennifer Swanson*
5. *Yelin Seo*
6. *Renee Tranter*
7. *Masha Vainblat*
8. *Tomantoules Salles*
9. *Dayeong Choi*
10. *Areum Park*
11. *Ricardo Osorio*
12. *Renata Braga*
13. *Heloisa Serqueira*

AGGRESSIVE

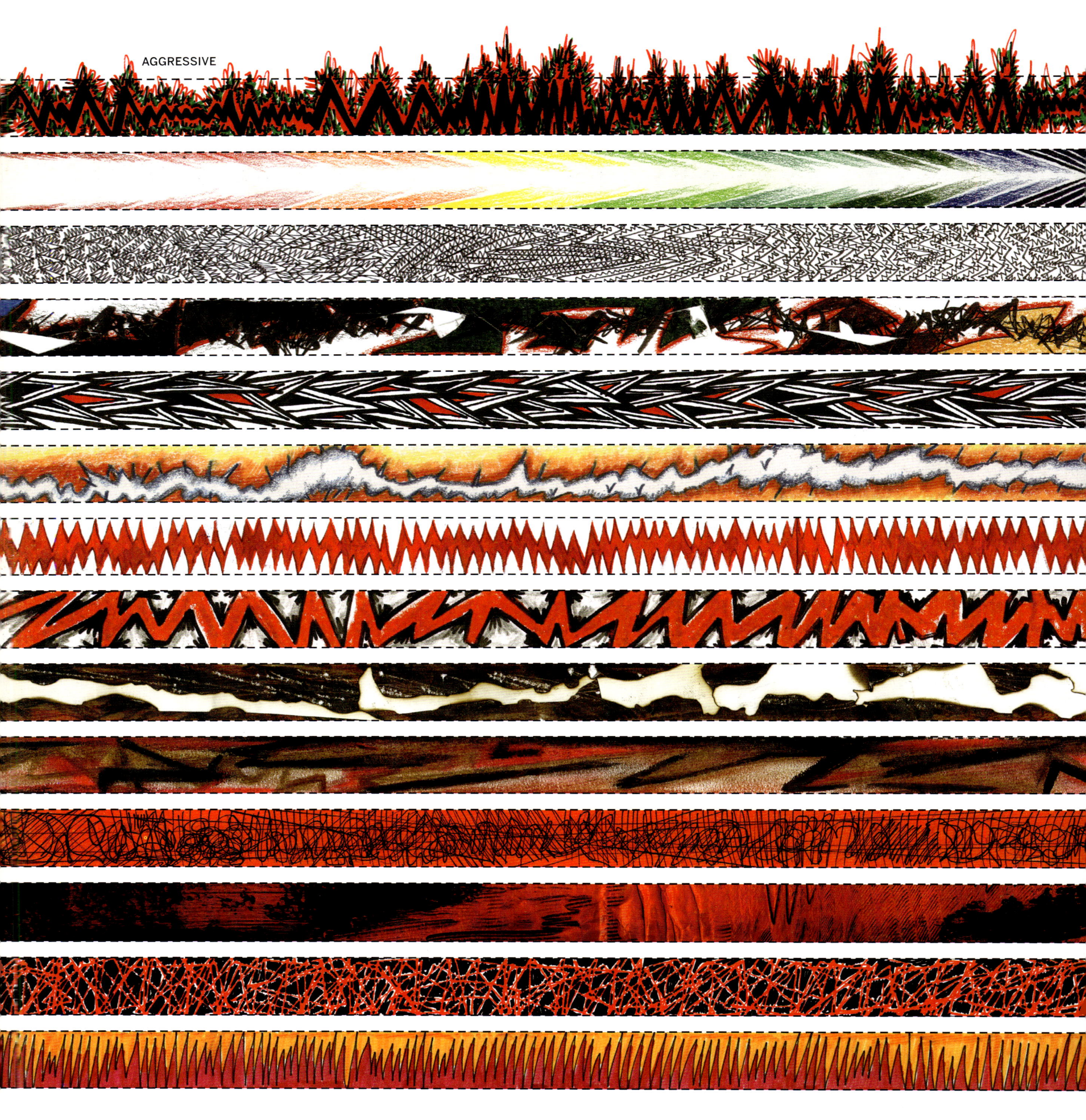

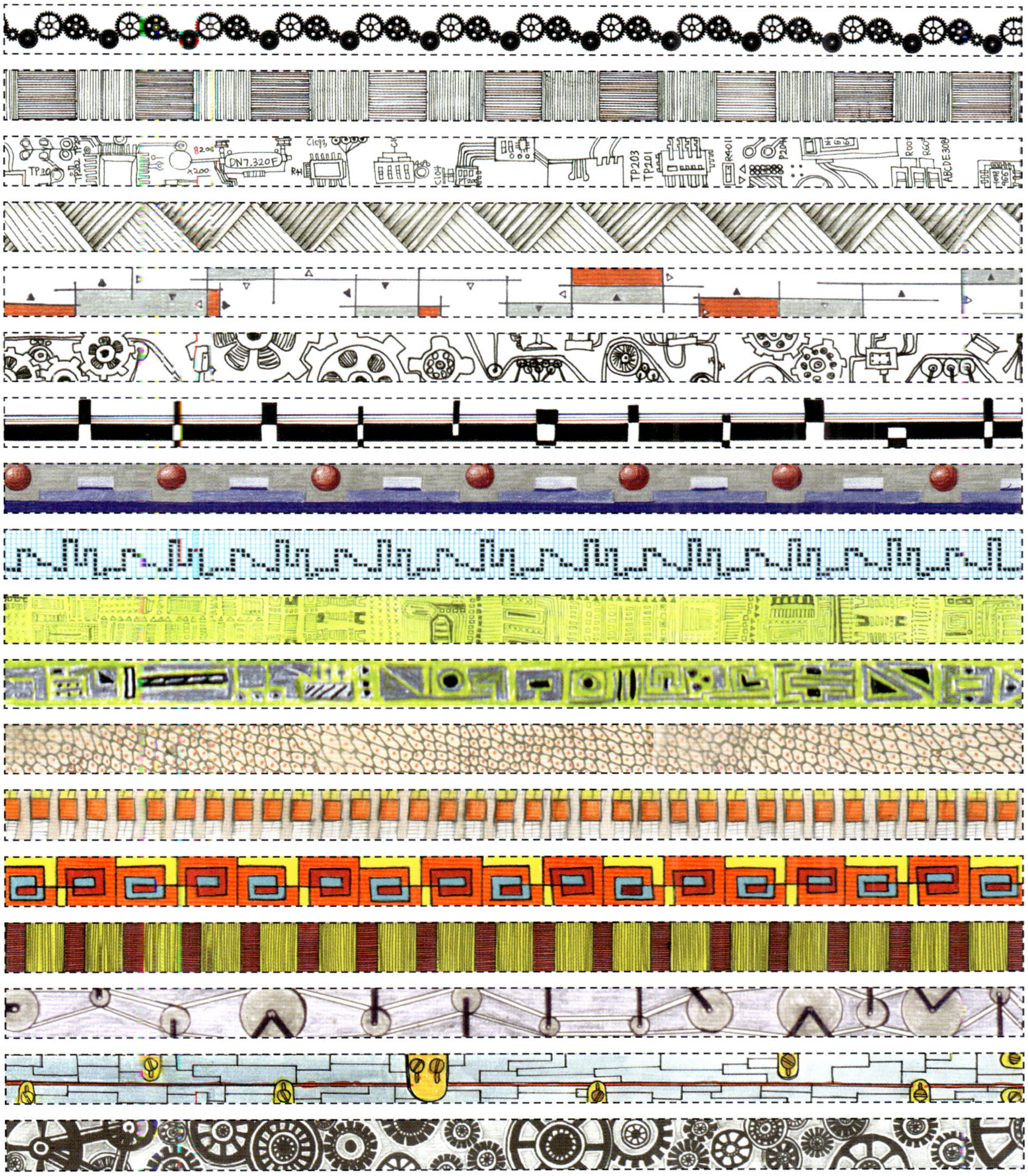

A LINE IS A DOT SOLUTIONS:

Aggressive is a subject with aspects of boldness, self-assertiveness and shades of hostility, depicted in figures 1 through 14. Most solutions have a forceful movement coupled with a quality of agitation, ranging from purely graphic to highly abstract. Red and black are often used as primary color choices.

Figures 15 through 32 depict systematic, which has methodical and mathematical attributes. Solutions range from a clear narrative of gears and graphs to abstract solutions. Patterning, sequencing, and repetition are often used in many of these executions.

SYSTEMATIC

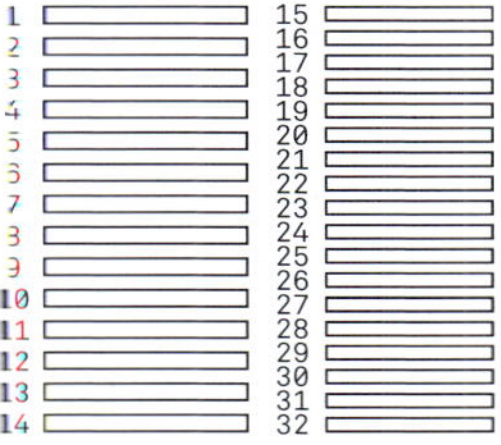

1. *Yin Chen*
2. *Daniel Chaves*
3. *Rachel Shin*
4. *Jil Brody*
5. *Gerald Soto*
6. *Jorge Sansone*
7. *Hana Yoo*
8. *Viktoriya Tsoy*
9. *Yelena Shokarova*
10. *Natalie Lobel*
11. *L. Y. Kim*
12. *Sunho Lee*
13. *Lindsay Franzoni*
14. *Youjung Choi*
15. *Jungho Oh*
16. *Jungheun Lee*
17. *Gina Shin*
18. *Janet Yeun*
19. *Fabricio Da Costa*
20. *Oscar Venagas*
21. *Michael MacKay*
22. *Jennifer Swanson*
23. *Eunhae Cho*
24. *Minju Cho*
25. *Jack Lin*
26. *Gwangyung Kim*
27. *Michele Clark*
28. *Youjung Choi*
29. *Flavia Castro*
30. *Martin Durkin*
31. *Hui Hong Liu*
32. *Mikyung Kim*

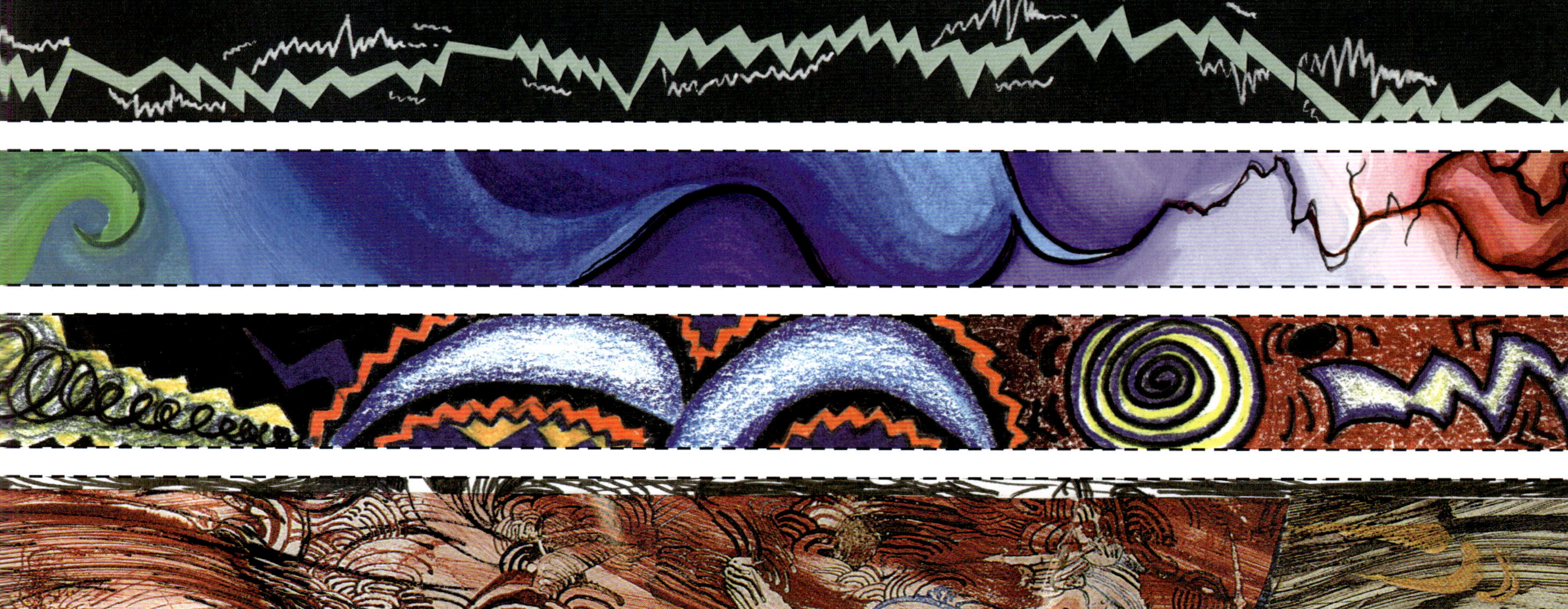

A LINE IS A DOT SOLUTIONS:

Turbulent, which infers energy, force, and chaotic movement, is depicted in figures 1 through 13.

Most of the solutions are abstract, except for figures 4 and 5, which depict seatbelts being fastened, pertaining to preparation for turbulence.

TURBULENT

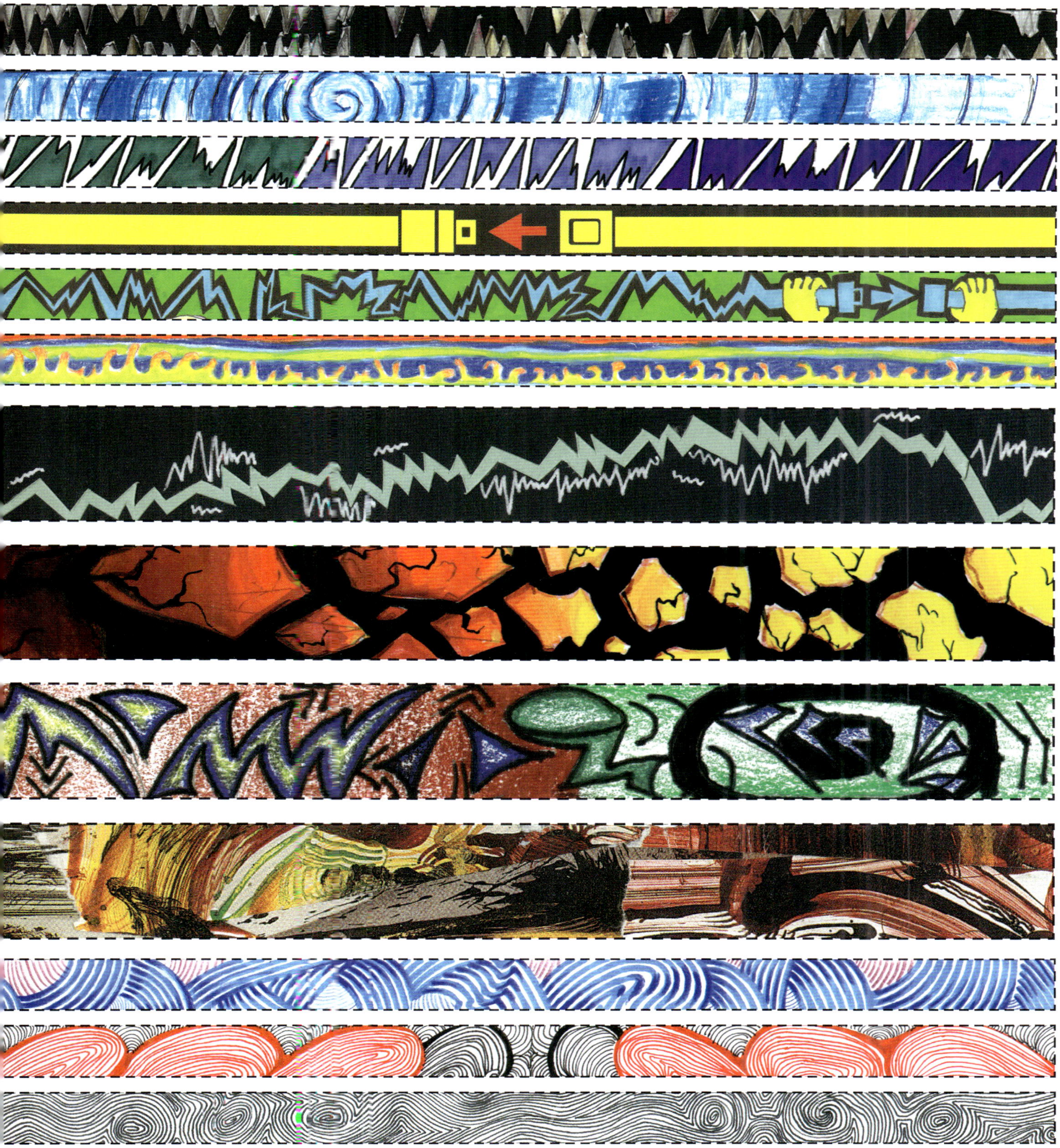

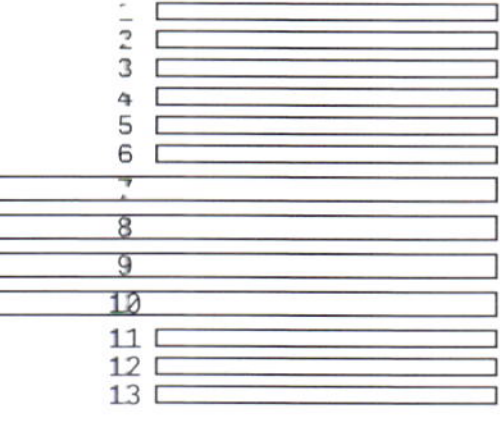

1. *Namhee Kim*
2. *Akil Grant*
3. *Ahrang Cho*
4. *Soojung Bae*
5. *Lindsay Kintgen*
6. *Soyun Lee*
7. *Sun Min Chung*
8. *Masha Vainblat*
9. *Ronaldo Carreiro de Melo*
10. *Jeein Lee*
11. *Sojung Lee*
12. *Qianyi Zhang*
13. *Rachel Shin*

EMBARRASSED

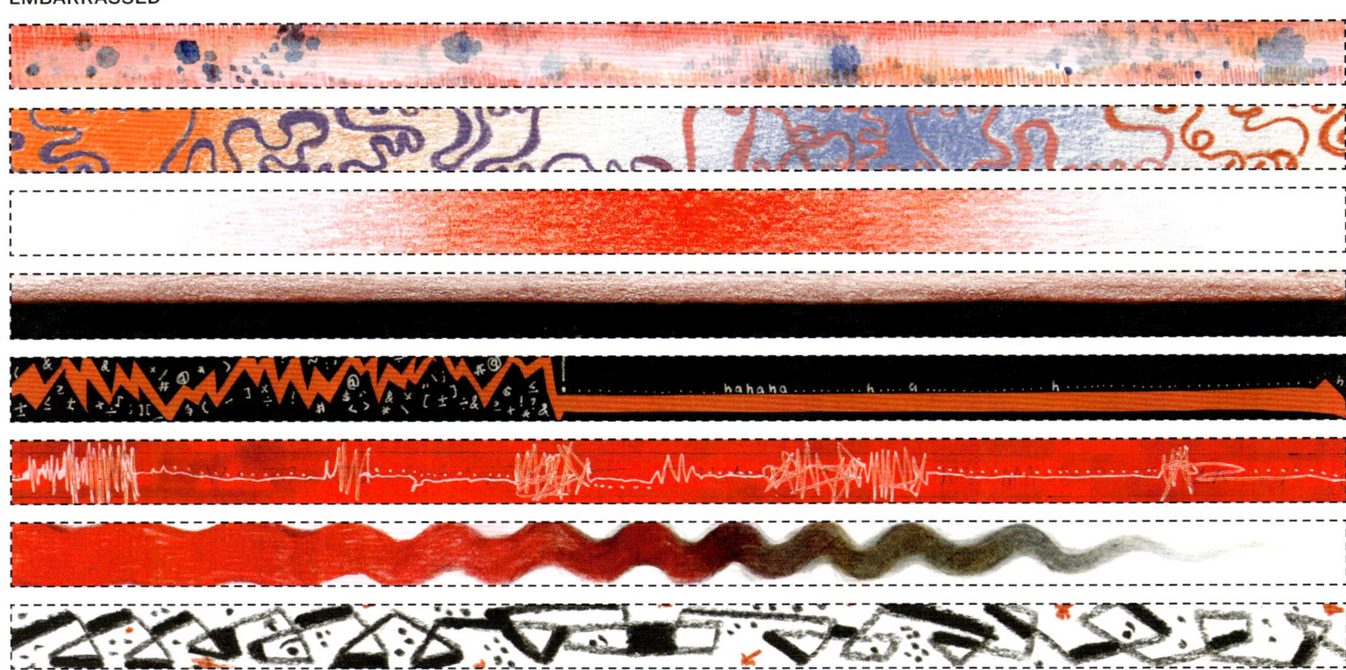

SENSUAL

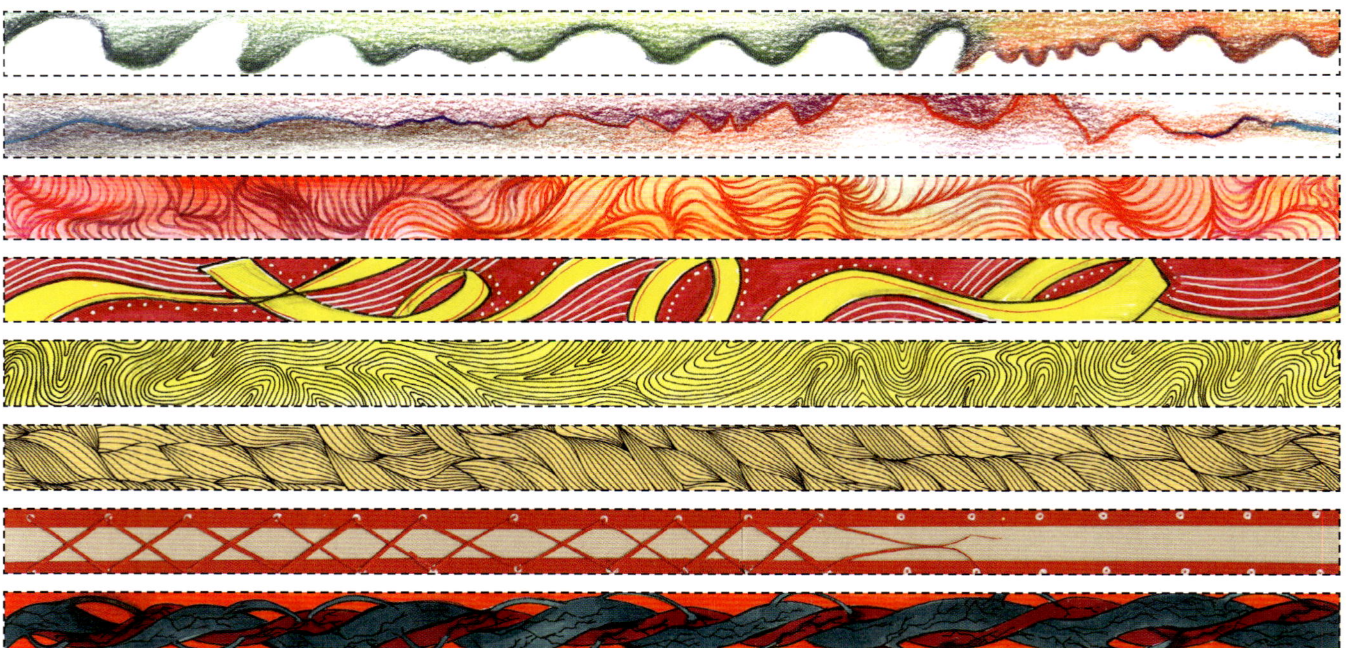

AMBIGUOUS

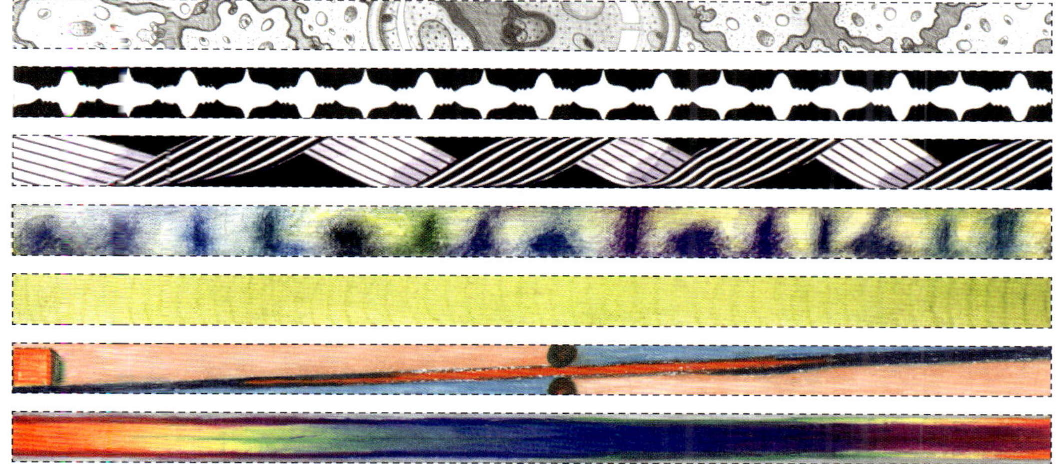

EXHAUSTED

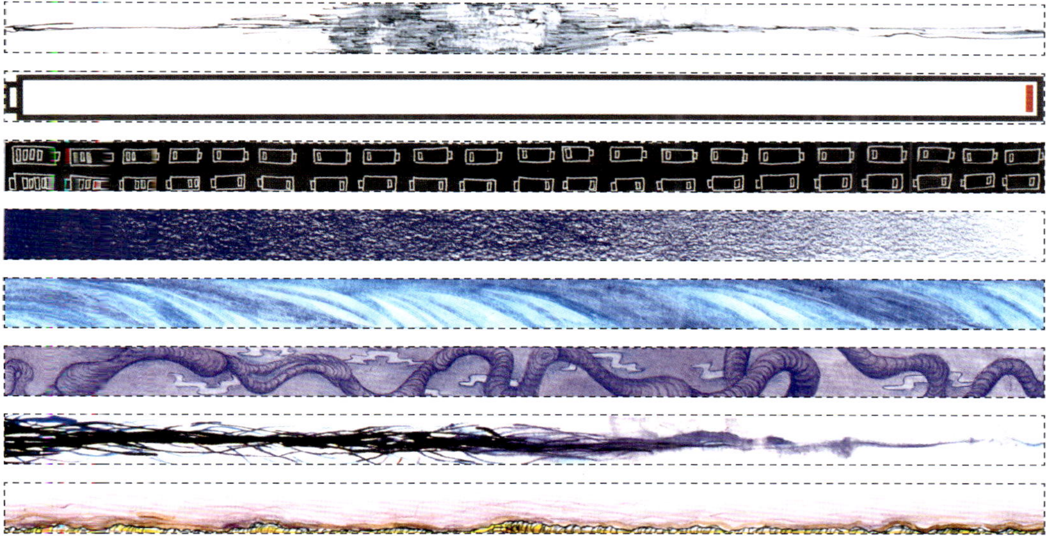

FRAGILE

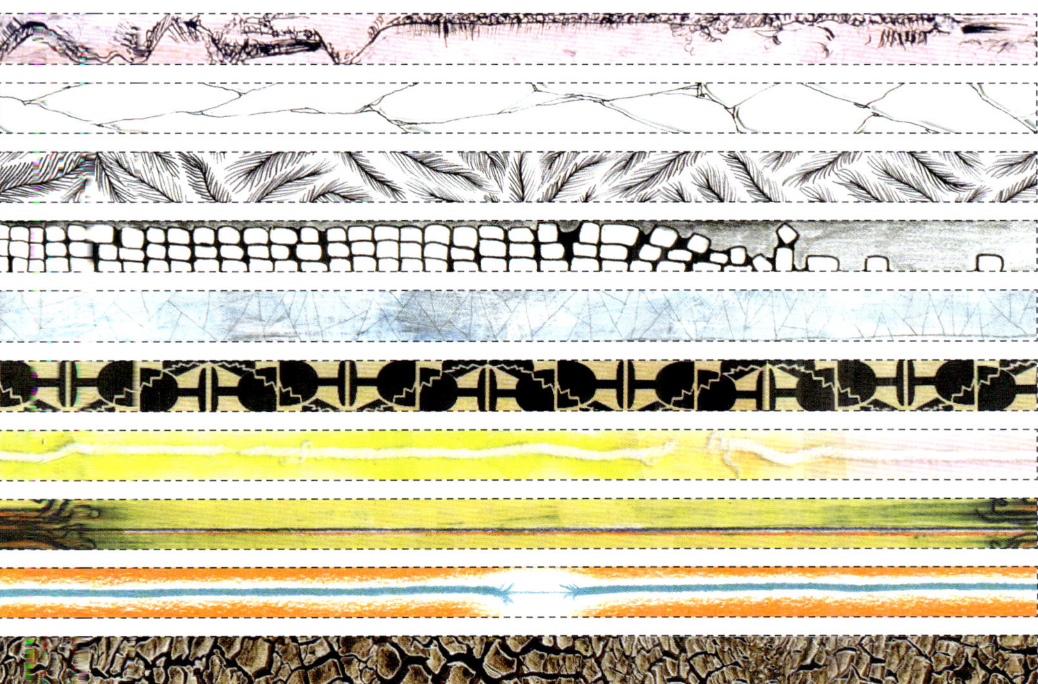

A LINE IS A DOT SOLUTIONS:

Figures 1 through 8 depict embarrassed. The color red is used to reference the act of blushing, yet each solution varies greatly concerning their approach to storytelling.

Sensual is the theme in figures 9 through 16, which for the most part utilize a flowing organic movement to capture a sense of passion and sexuality.

Figures 17 through 23 depict ambiguous, a subjective topic that can be interpreted from many points of view.

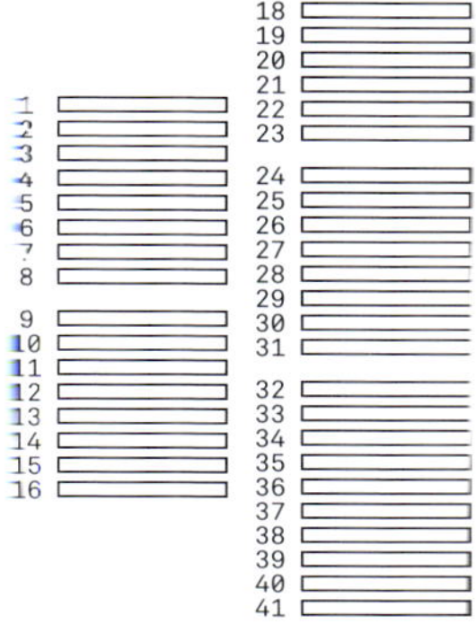

1. *Suwan Park*
2. *T. Salles*
3. *Steven Antholis*
4. *Jennifer Swanson*
5. *Sunmin Chung*
6. *Areum Park*
7. *Sojung Lee*
8. *Ricardo Osorio*
9. *Heloisa Serqueira*
10. *Claudio Barra*
11. *Jieun Kwak*
12. *Youjung Choi*
13. *Iy Kim*
14. *Enle Li*
15. *Sunmin Chung*
16. *Tae Yu*
17. *Brianna Hussey*
18. *Youngsun Park*
19. *Jiyeon Lee*
20. *Jungeun Kwak*
21. *Hyejin Ck*
22. *A. Pupim*
23. *J. Swanson*
24. *G. Kim*
25. *Mengya Wen*
26. *Minju Cho*
27. *Eduardo Varela*
28. *Lindsay Kirtgen*
29. *Renee Tranter*
30. *Jiyeon Lee*
31. *Aaron Nichols*
32. *A. Nebioto*
33. *Huihong Liu*
34. *Rachel Shin*
35. *Il Woo Kim*
36. *Yuna Lee*
37. *Evan Pokrandt*
38. *Ahrang Cho*
39. *T. Salles*
40. *O. Magalhaes*
41. *Y. Park*

Exhausted is the theme in figures 24 through 31. Solutions range from literal to abstract in their depiction of the depletion of energy.

Figures 32 through 41 deal with the subject, fragile. Solutions depict tenucus connections and fractured lines.

SPONTANEOUS

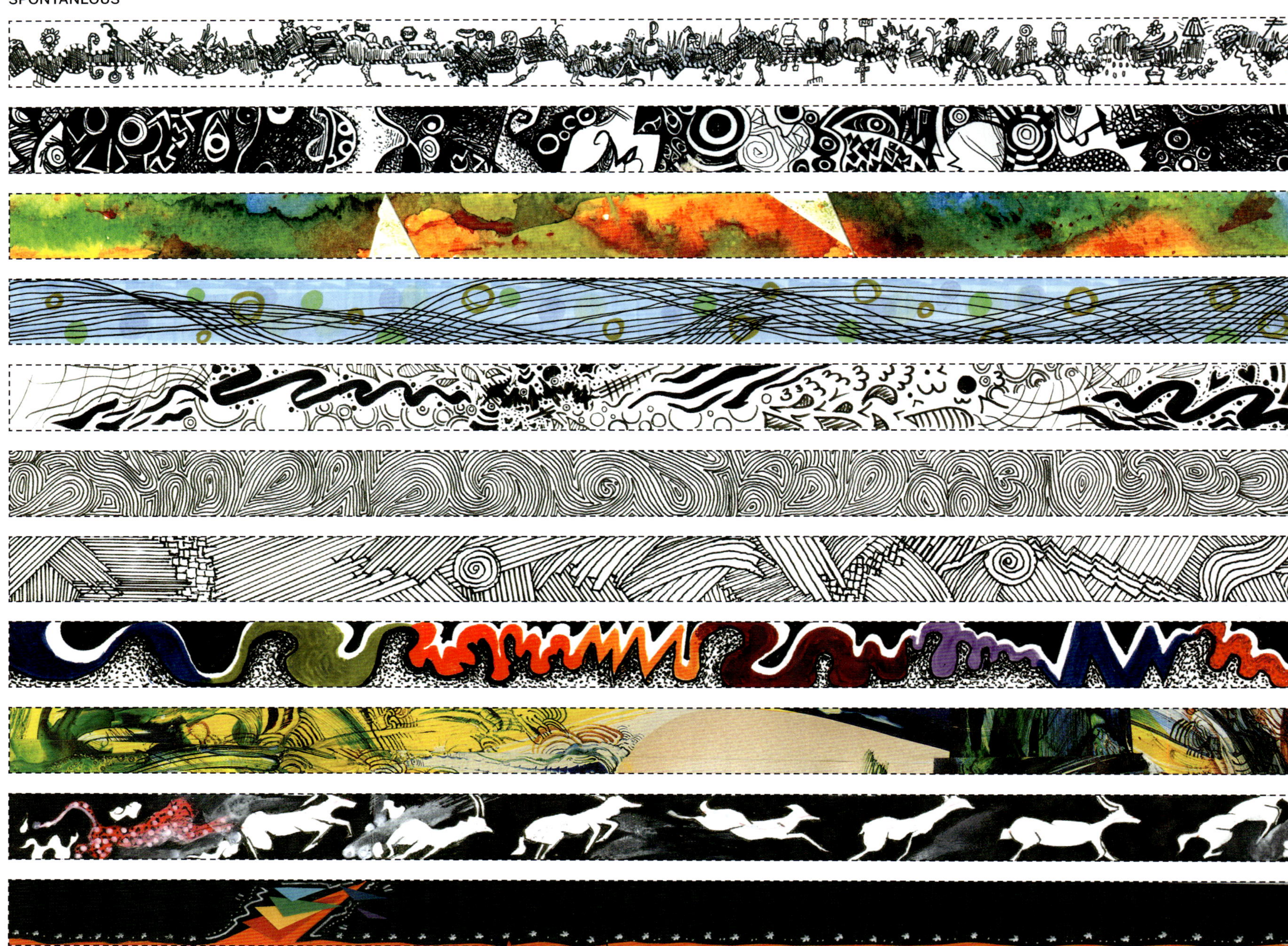

A LINE IS A DOT SOLUTIONS:

Figures 1 through 11 are depictions of the subject spontaneous. Many students approach this subject by doodling, which in turn leads them to a rhythm that dictates its next incarnation in an unpremeditated way resulting in a variety of personal solutions.

Figure 10 is a metaphoric depiction of a leopard attacking an antelope in an animated sequence.

Figure 11 uses abstraction as a form of storytelling, which can be interpreted as a spontaneous outburst in terms of the interruption of color on a black ground.

INDECISIVE

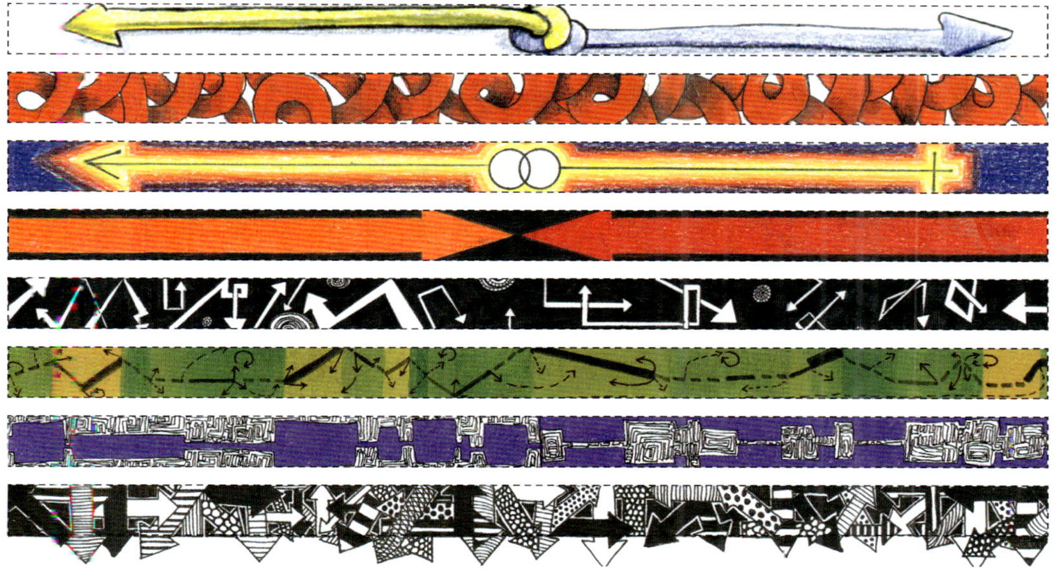

SLOVEN

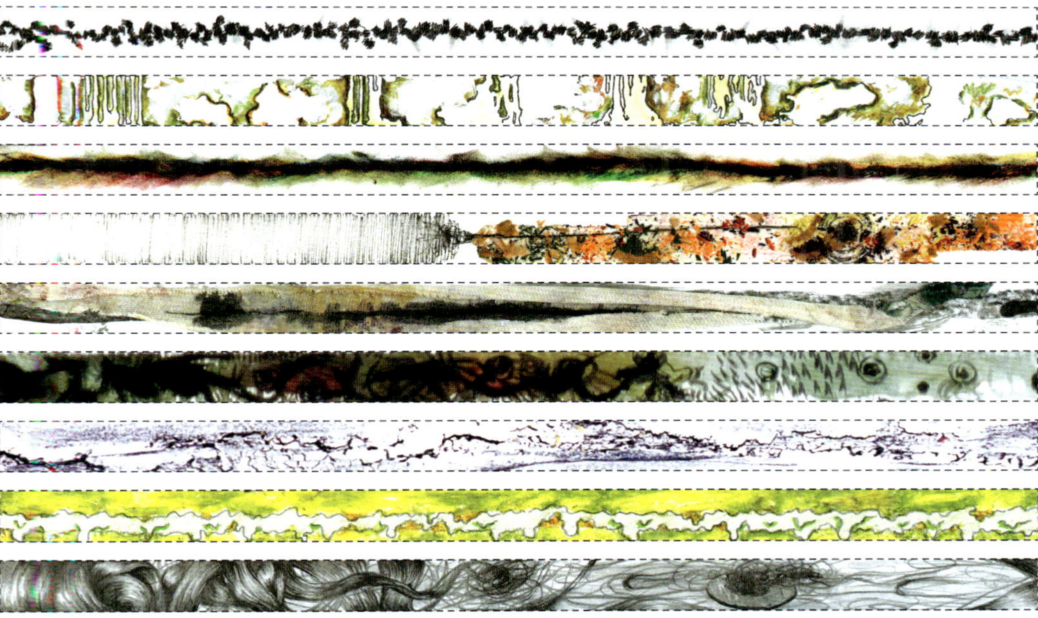

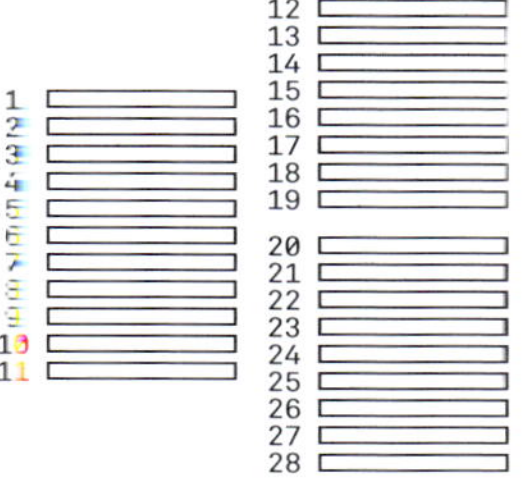

1. Laura Scherling
2. Renee Tranter
3. Dayeong Choi
4. Jiahui Guw
5. Allan Weiss
6. Eunhae Cho
7. Hiso Ide
8. Michael MacKay
9. Jeein Lee
10. Peng Cheng
11. Sunmin Chung
12. C. Hawthorne
13. Namhee Kim
14. F. Anapaulaf
15. Flavia Castro
16. Yelin Seo
17. S. Hyung Kim
18. J. Lee
19. Mikyung Kim
20. Jihye Hong
21. Sojung Lee
22. M. Jaramillo
23. Paola Fazzolari
24. Freddy Diaz
25. C. Lee
26. Y. Yoo
27. Jasmin Valcourt
28. Namhee Kim

Indecisive is the subject of figures 12 through 19. Most all solutions are literal, using arrows as a symbolic expression of movement.

Figures 20 through 28 deal with the subject sloven. These solutions describe messy and dirty qualities, yet given this unseemly subject, aesthetic value can be found in these interpretations.

AWKWARD

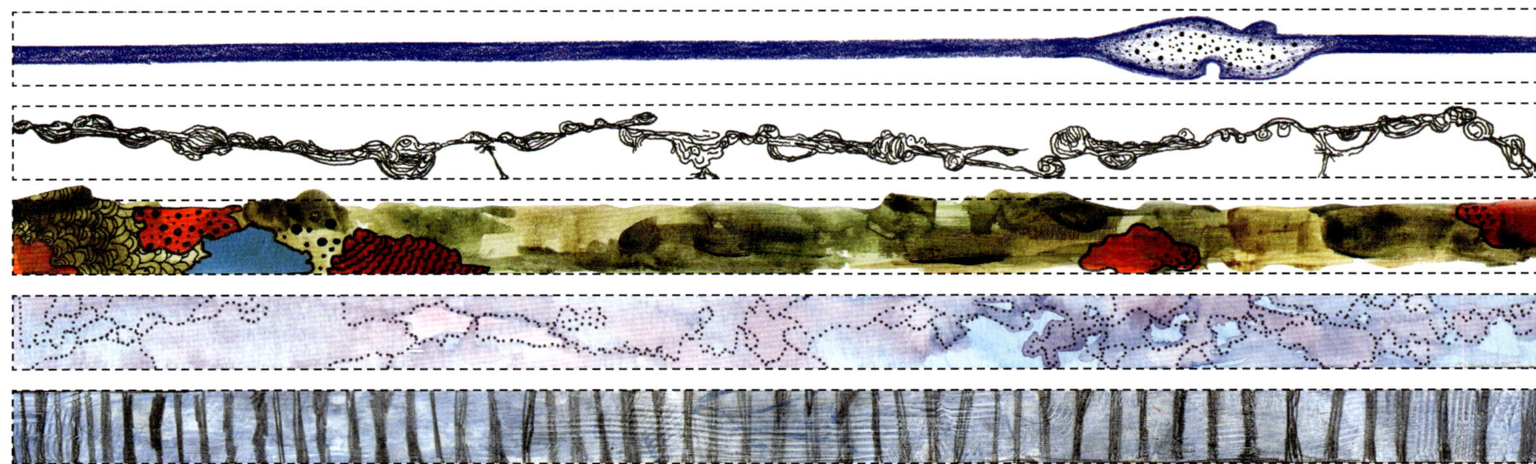

DISTRACTED

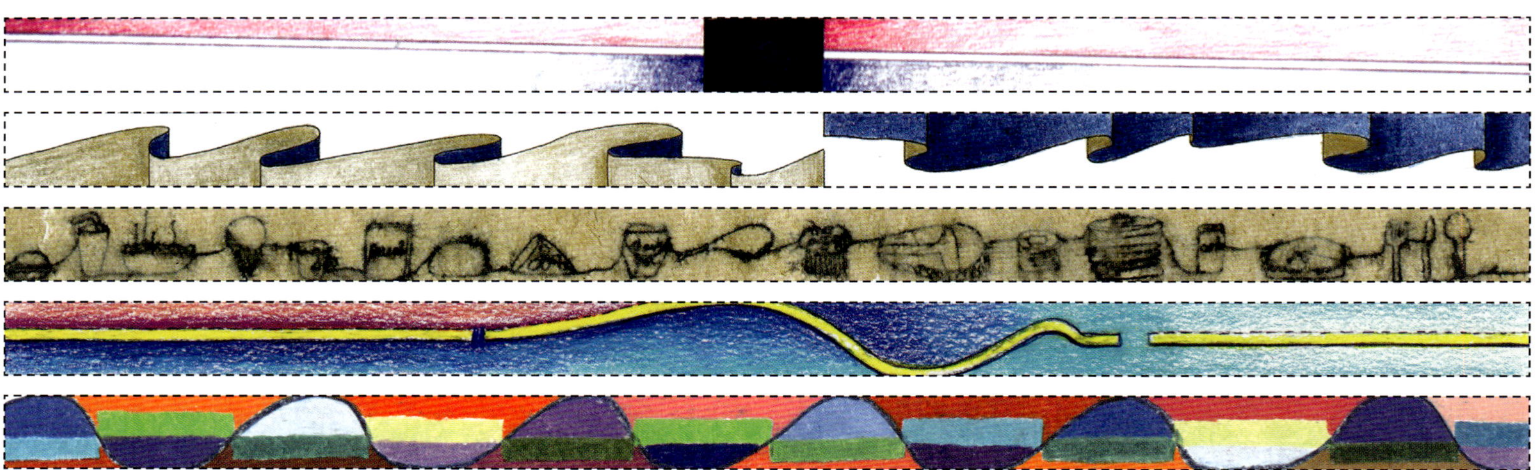

NONSENSICAL

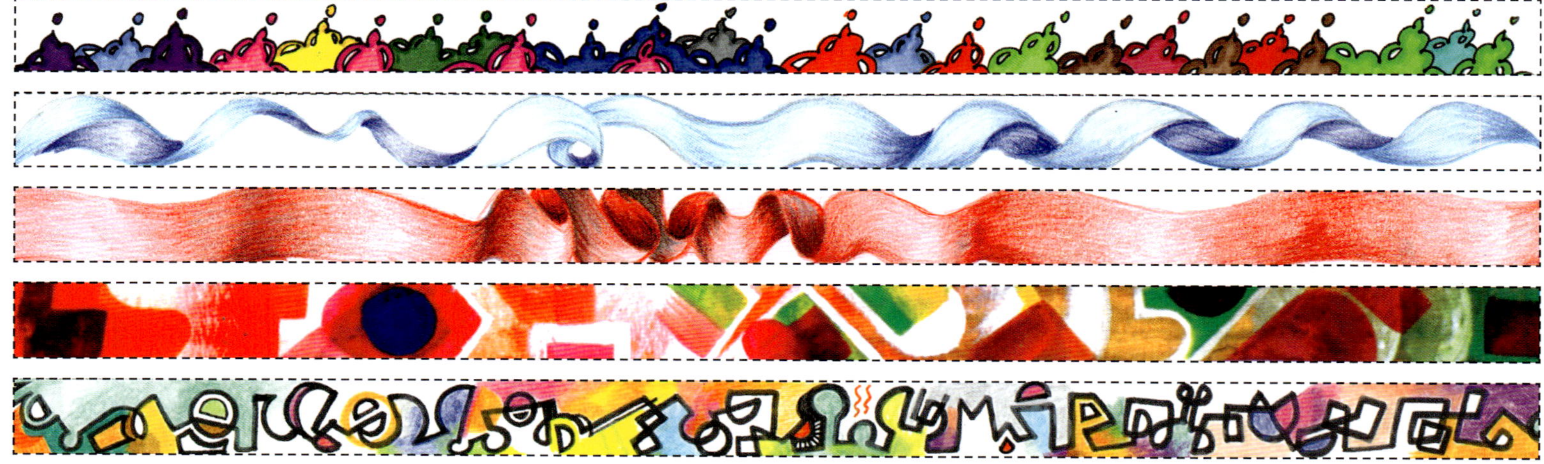

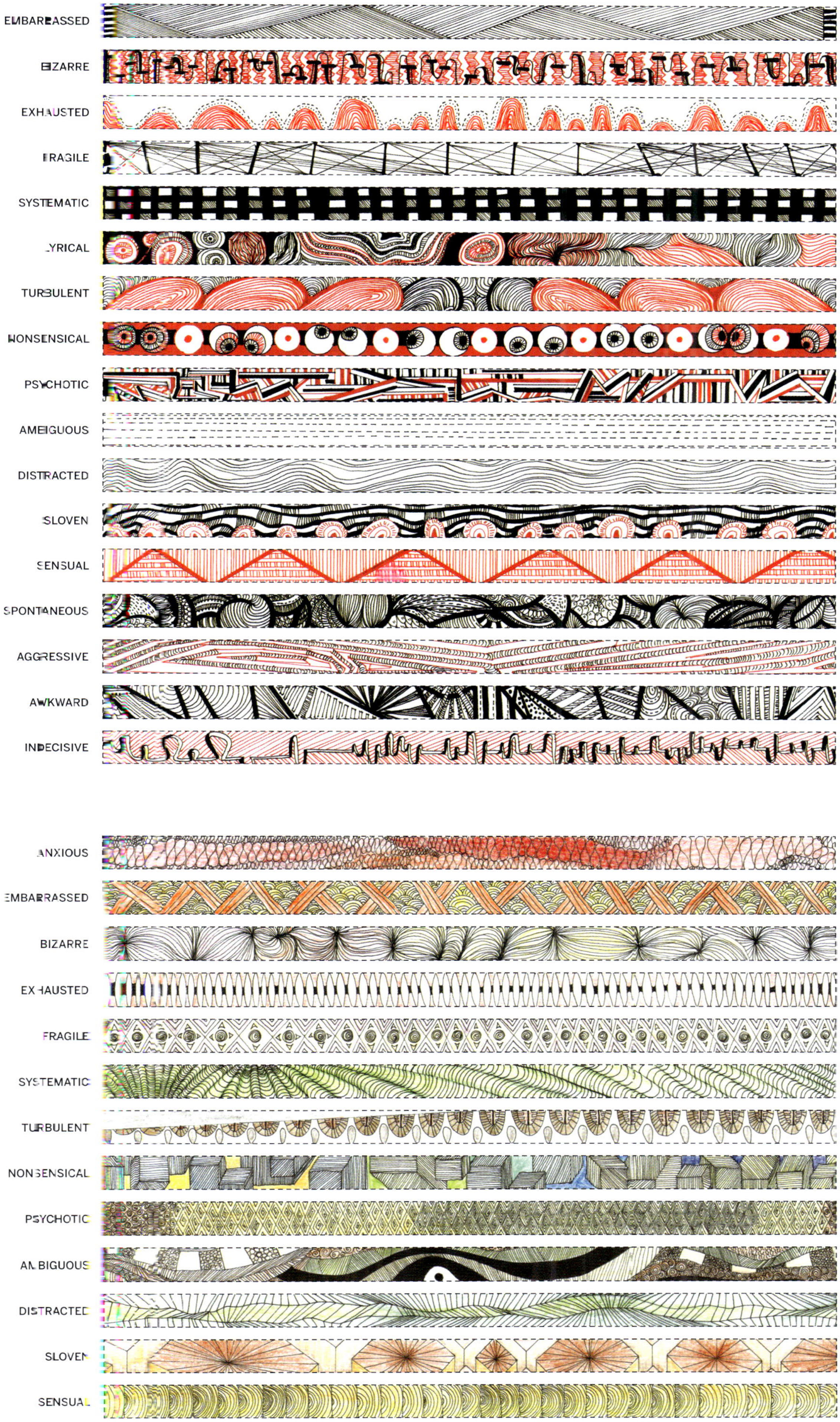

EMBARRASSED
BIZARRE
EXHAUSTED
FRAGILE
SYSTEMATIC
LYRICAL
TURBULENT
NONSENSICAL
PSYCHOTIC
AMBIGUOUS
DISTRACTED
SLOVEN
SENSUAL
SPONTANEOUS
AGGRESSIVE
AWKWARD
INDECISIVE

ANXIOUS
EMBARRASSED
BIZARRE
EXHAUSTED
FRAGILE
SYSTEMATIC
TURBULENT
NONSENSICAL
PSYCHOTIC
AMBIGUOUS
DISTRACTED
SLOVEN
SENSUAL

A LINE IS A DOT SOLUTIONS:

Awkward, depicted in figures 1 through 5, pertains to clumsy and ungraceful movement. What makes for a successful solution is when form and content merge.

Figures 6 through 10 depict distracted. These solutions reference interruption, diverted movement, or a change from one entity to another, which at times can be interpreted as a metaphor for daydreaming.

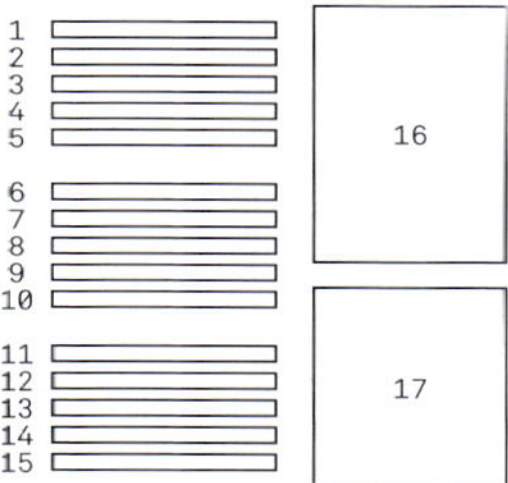

1. *Maria Jaramillo*
2. *Laura Scherling*
3. *C. Brand*
4. *Hannah Ahn*
5. *Yuna Lee*
6. *George Baier*
7. *Eunhae Cho*
8. *Megan Chong*
9. *F. Aravena*
10. *Carla Souza*
11. *V. Diego*
12. *Oscar Venegas*
13. *Oscar Venegas*
14. *A. Girard*
15. *Sojung Lee*
16. *Qianyi Zhang*
17. *Woohyun Cho*

Figures 11 through 15 depict nonsensical. Solutions reference geometric and amorphic shapes using a wide range of colors on a white ground.

Figures 16 and 17 both encompass multiple solutions executed by two different students where line, pattern, and texture dominate the vocabulary of form.

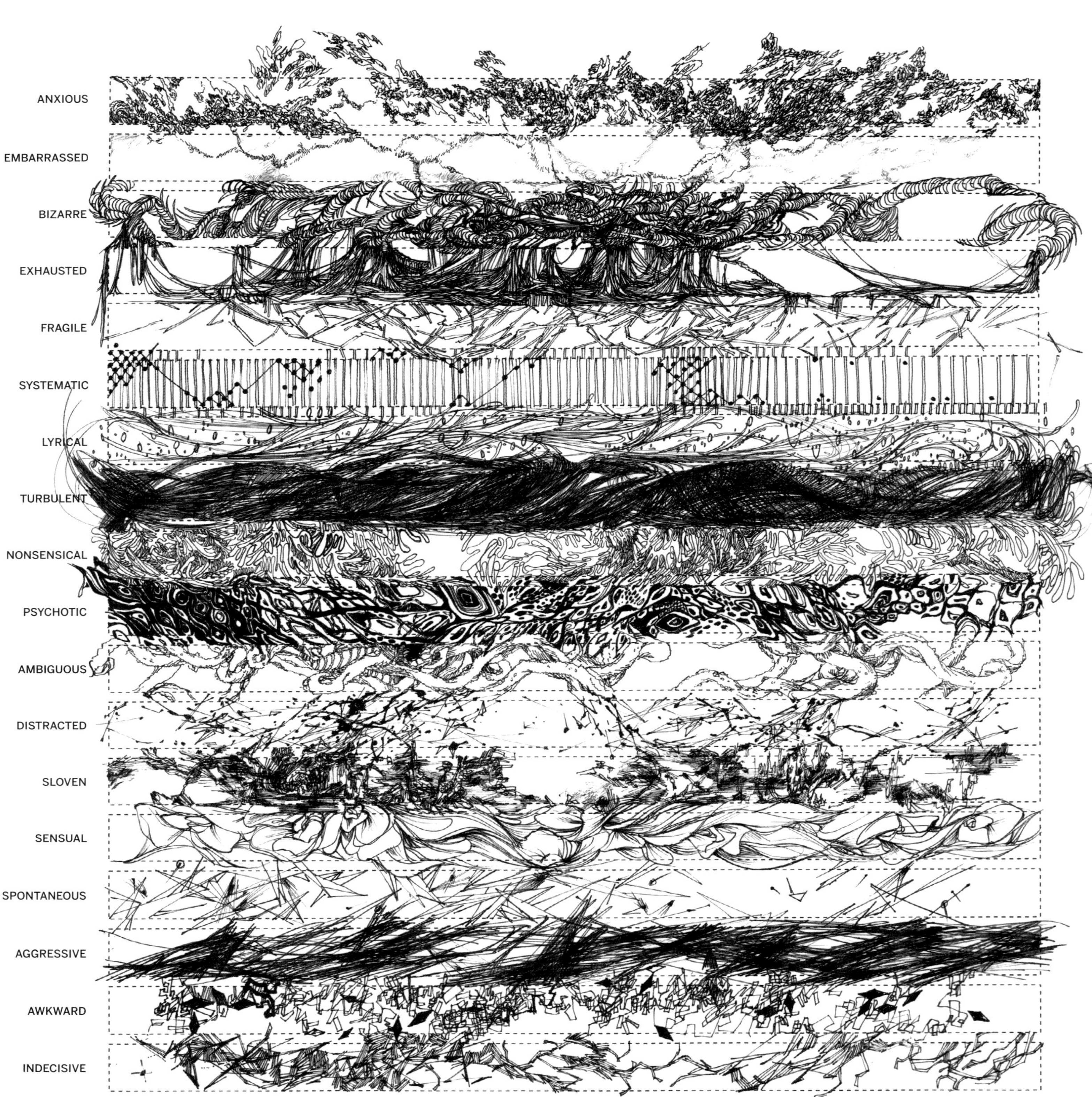
ANXIOUS
EMBARRASSED
BIZARRE
EXHAUSTED
FRAGILE
SYSTEMATIC
LYRICAL
TURBULENT
NONSENSICAL
PSYCHOTIC
AMBIGUOUS
DISTRACTED
SLOVEN
SENSUAL
SPONTANEOUS
AGGRESSIVE
AWKWARD
INDECISIVE

DISTRACTED

ANXIOUS

AGGRESSIVE

ANXIOUS

ANXIOUS

PSYCHOTIC

DISTRACTED

AGGRESSIVE

ANXIOUS

AGGRESSIVE

DISTRACTED

AWKWARD

FRAGILE

ANXIOUS

EMBARRASSED

BIZARRE

PSYCHOTIC

AMBIGUOUS

SLOVEN

A LINE IS A DOT SOLUTIONS:

Figure 1 is a black and white interpretation based solely on a spontaneous approach to the project. This highly personal version captures a quality of frenetic energy through the expressive use of line.

In contrast, figures 2 through 20 are, for the most part, carefully mannered solutions that utilize black and white exclusively, and through abstraction express the vast language of line.

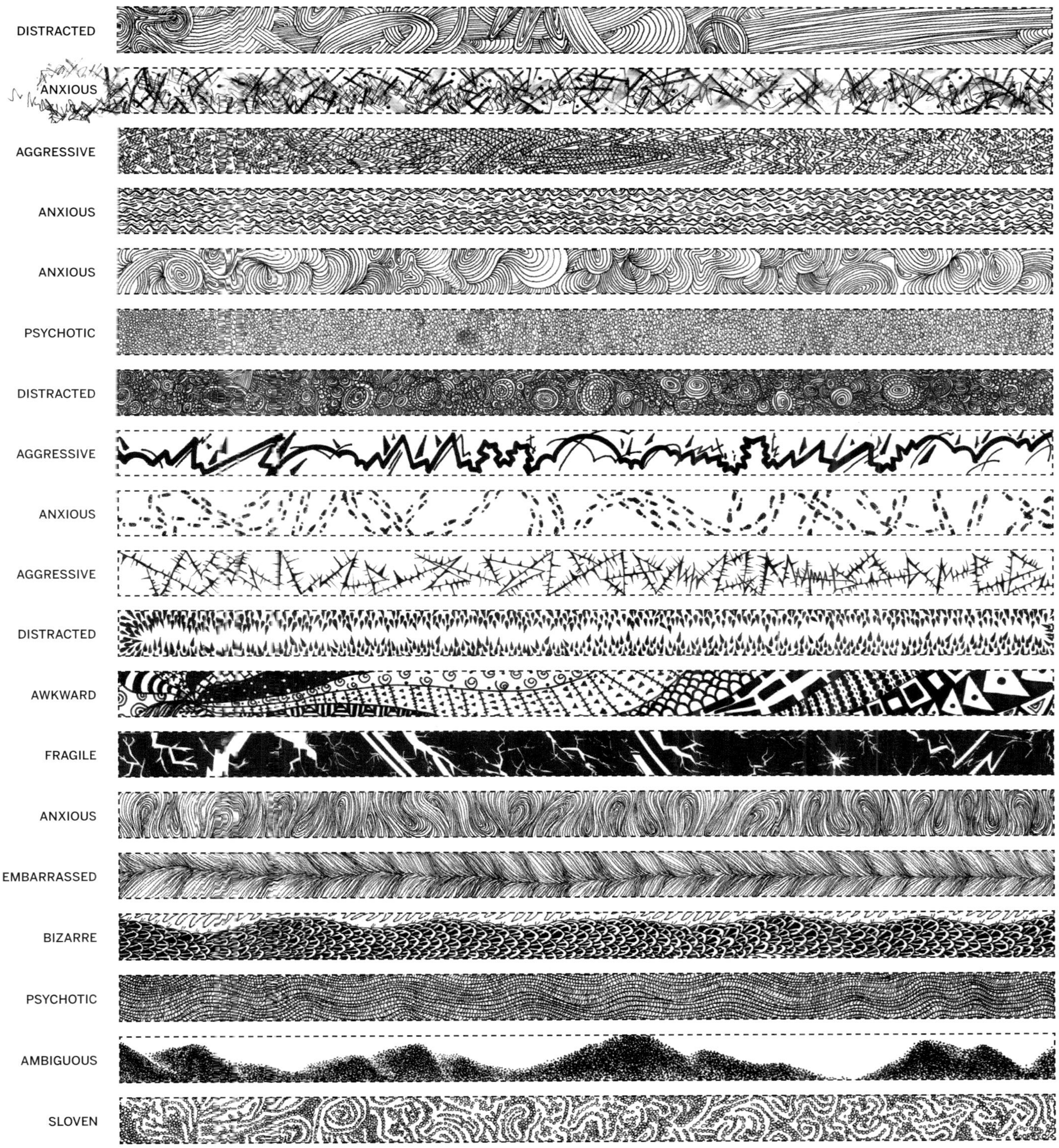

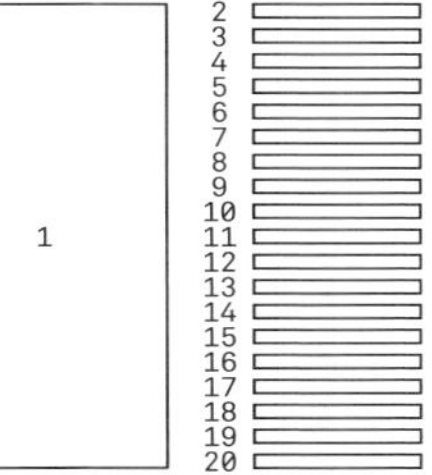

1. *Yu Kyung Hwang*
2. *Megan Calabro*
3. *Janet Yeun*
4-5. *Rachel Shin*
6. *Soojung Bae*
7. *Gina Shin*
8. *Miryung Kim*
9. *Minhee Lee*
10. *Jeonk Kim*
11. *Sujin Jung*
12. *Hana Yoo*
13. *Heejae Choi*
14. *Judith Landau*
15-20. *Bomi Kim*

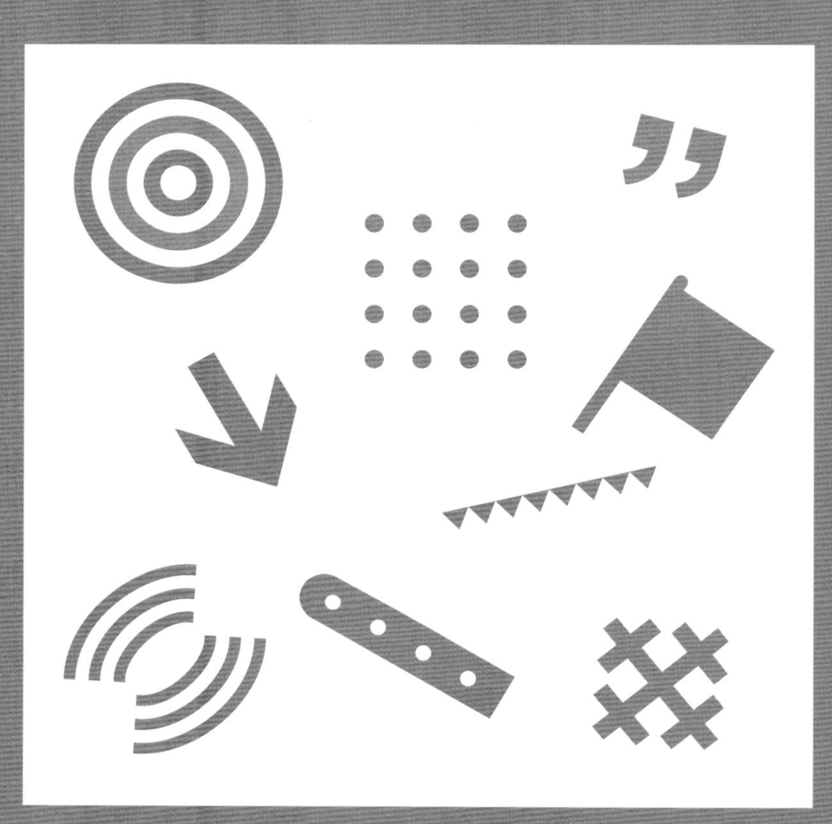

THOUGHTS ON THE CREATIVE PROCESS 5

Relying on cliché solutions is an habitual reaction
to problem solving that leads to predictable results.
Here one is dealing with the known, which is lacking
in terms of newness, energy, and spontaneity.
By reinterpreting time-worn images, one can revitalize
a prosaic idea and give it the power it once possessed.

NURSERY RHYME PROBLEM

IN THE AREAS INDICATED, DEPICT EACH PHRASE OF THE FOLLOWING NURSERY RHYMES BY CREATING IMAGES USING ONLY THE GIVEN SYMBOLS, PICTOGRAMS, DINGBATS, ICONS, AND ENGRAVINGS ON THE ACCOMPANYING SHEET. CONSIDER THE DESIGN PRINCIPLES THAT INCLUDE POSITIVE AND NEGATIVE RELATIONSHIPS AND THE PLACEMENT AND JUXTAPOSITION OF FORMS AS WELL AS CROPPING, OVERLAPPING, SCALE, TENSION, CONTRAST AND SPACE. USE BLACK AND WHITE UNLESS YOUR CONCEPT DICTATES OTHERWISE.

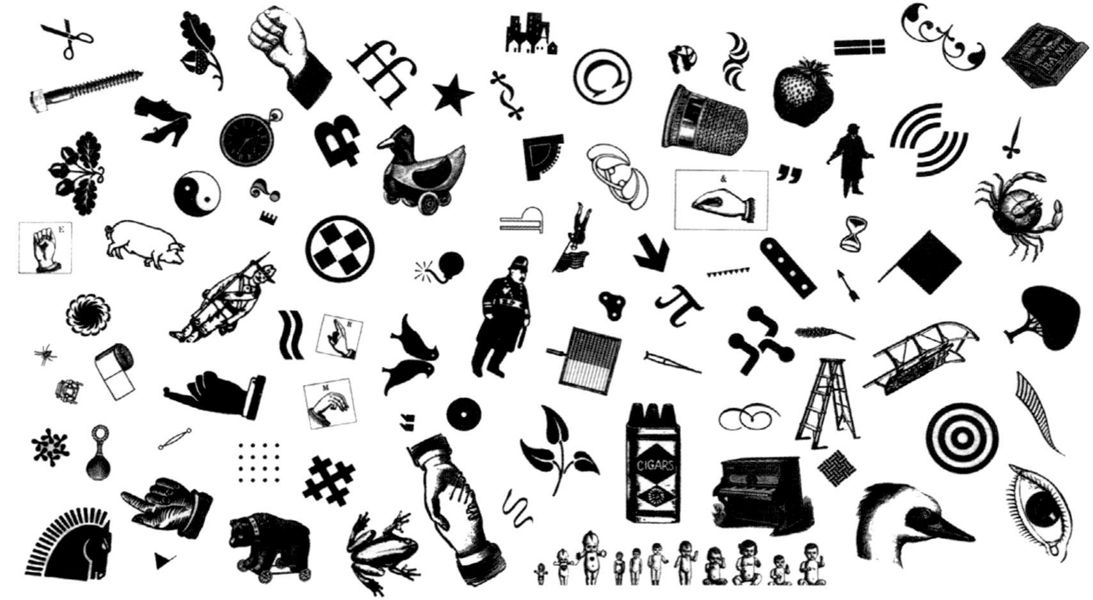

HEY DIDDLE DIDDLE! THE CAT AND THE FIDDLE,	THE COW JUMPED OVER THE MOON.	THE LITTLE DOG LAUGHED TO SEE SUCH SPORT,	AND THE DISH RAN AWAY WITH THE SPOON.
HUMPTY DUMPTY SAT ON A WALL,	HUMPTY DUMPTY HAD A GREAT FALL.	ALL THE KING'S HORSES AND ALL THE KING'S MEN	COULDN'T PUT HUMPTY TOGETHER AGAIN.
THERE WAS AN OLD WOMAN WHO LIVED IN A SHOE,	SHE HAD SO MANY CHILDREN SHE DIDN'T KNOW WHAT TO DO.	SHE GAVE THEM SOME BROTH WITHOUT ANY BREAD,	THEN WHIPPED THEM ALL SOUNDLY AND PUT THEM TO BED.

PROBLEMS : SOLUTIONS SERIES

CREATED BY RICHARD WILDE / JUDITH WILDE, PRODUCED BY VISUAL ARTS PRESS, LTD. ART DIRECTORS: RICHARD WILDE / JUDITH WILDE

NURSERY RHYME PROBLEM:

In the areas indicated on the assignment sheet, depict each phrase of the nursery rhymes "Hey Diddle Diddle," "Humpty Dumpty," and "The Old Woman Who Lived in a Shoe," by creating a narrative that expresses each rhyme using only the given dingbats, symbols, pictograms, and engravings that appear on the assignment sheet as your vocabulary of form.

AIM:
The aim is to manipulate, alter, and deconstruct the given graphic imagery to transcend its original meaning through the creation of the indicated narratives.

It is the limitation of the given visual vocabulary that puts one in a position to struggle to get past one's habitual approach to visual problem solving and embrace this graphic palette where one can play and invent new imagery.

Nursery rhymes often arise from folklore and many of the images, which include old engravings, have an historical context.

SUGGESTIONS:
Given the nonsensical nature of each of the nursery rhymes, one is urged to take liberties in personal interpretation and use the given imagery in an allegorical context. Although sequential interpretations are encouraged in terms of storytelling, it is also permissible to focus on individual frames in a non-linear manner, thus placing a greater demand on the viewer. Consider the design principles that include: positive and negative relationships, composition, the juxtapositioning of forms, cropping, overlapping, scale, tension, contrast, and space.

SPECIFICATIONS:
Use black and white to execute each solution.

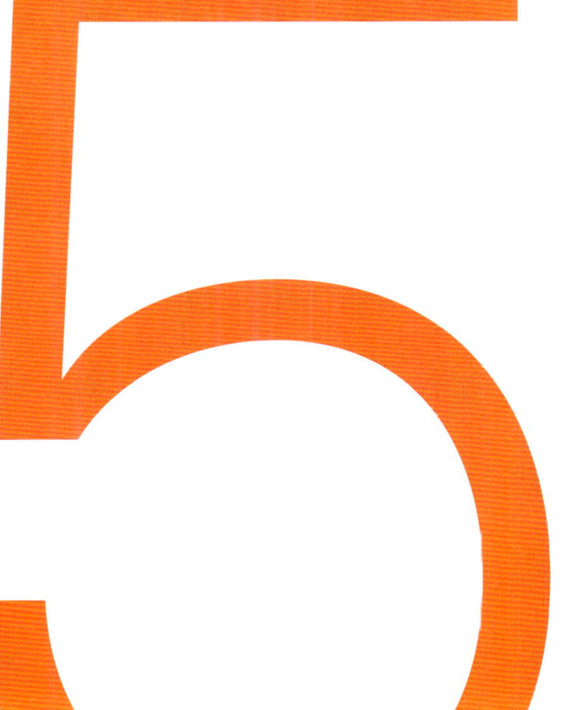

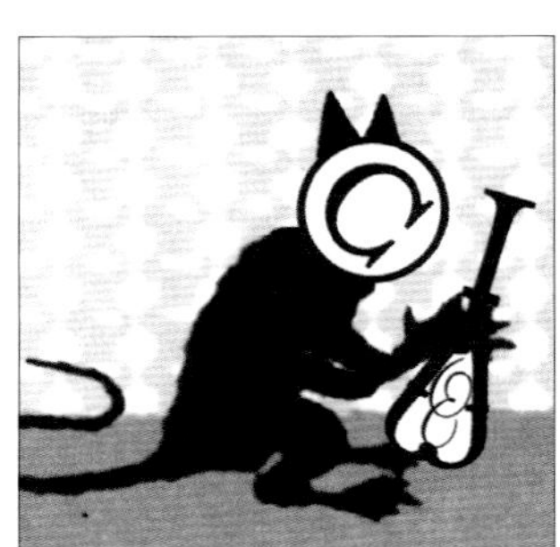
HEY DIDDLE DIDDLE! THE CAT AND THE FIDDLE,

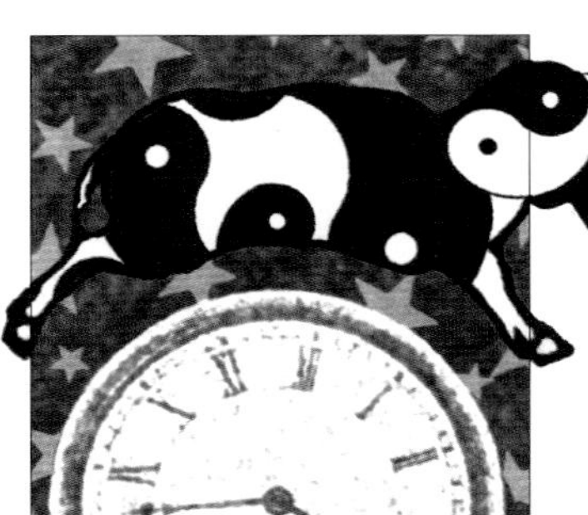
THE COW JUMPED OVER THE MOON.

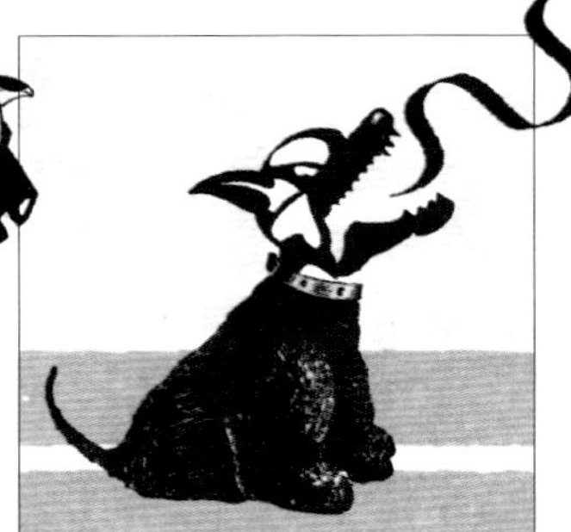
THE LITTLE DOG LAUGHED TO SEE SUCH SPORT,

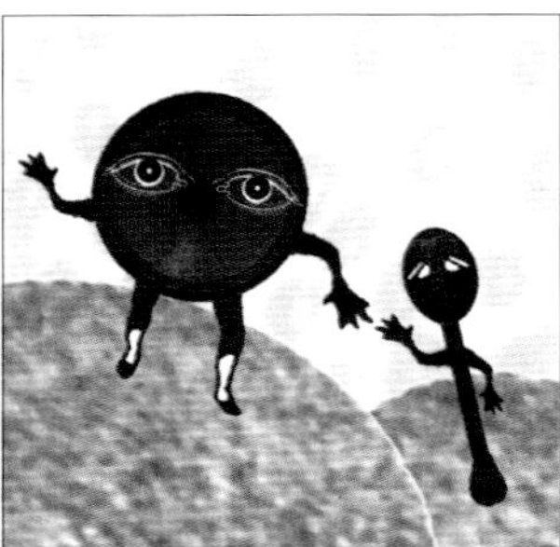
AND THE DISH RAN AWAY WITH THE SPOON.

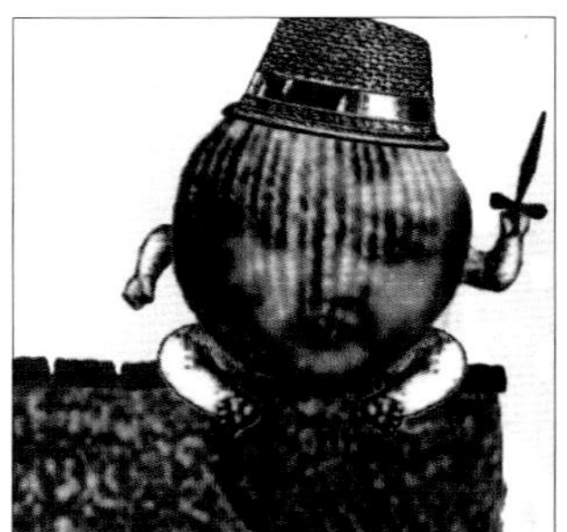
HUMPTY DUMPTY SAT ON A WALL,

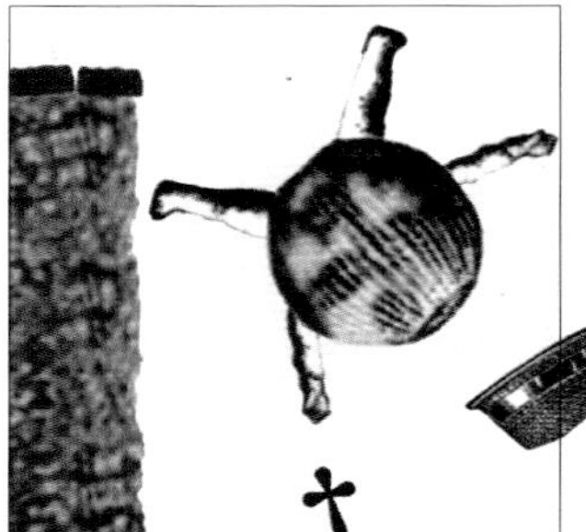
HUMPTY DUMPTY HAD A GREAT FALL.

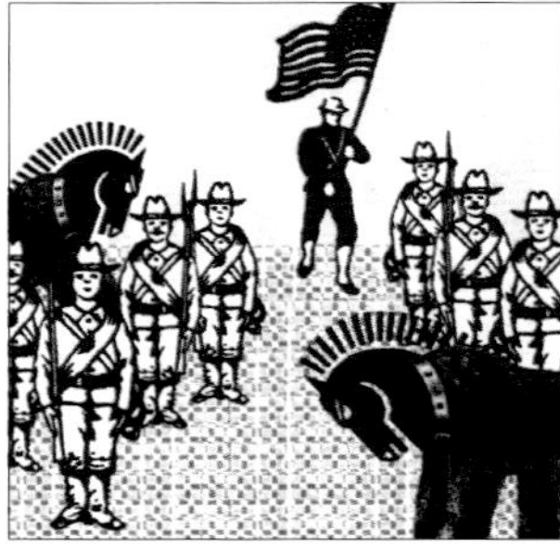
ALL THE KING'S HORSES AND ALL THE KING'S MEN

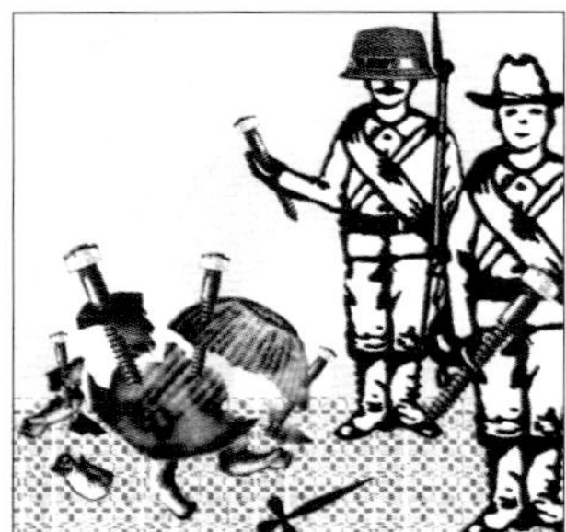
COULDN'T PUT HUMPTY TOGETHER AGAIN.

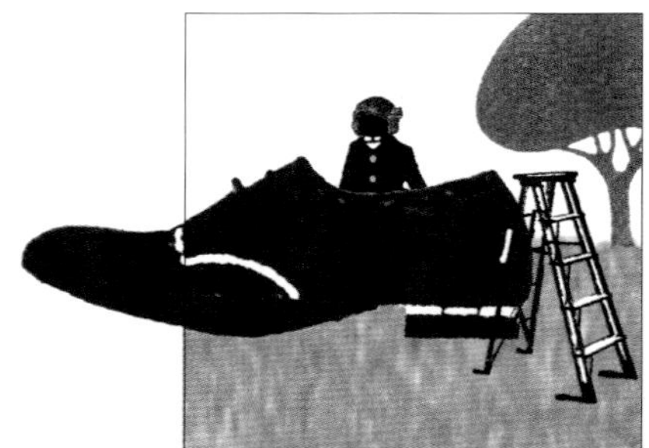
THERE WAS AN OLD WOMAN WHO LIVED IN A SHOE,

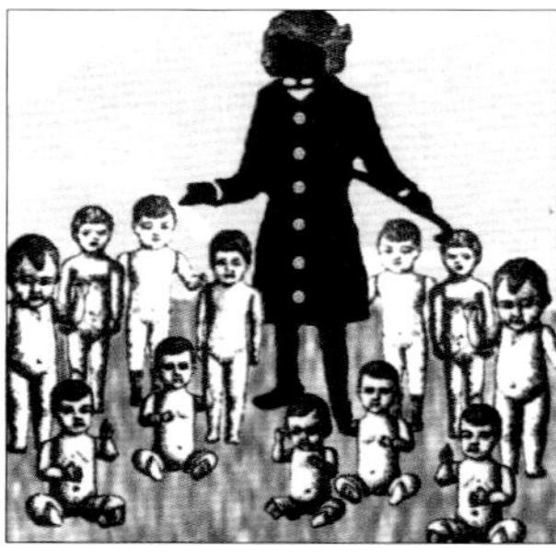
SHE HAD SO MANY CHILDREN SHE DIDN'T KNOW WHAT TO DO.

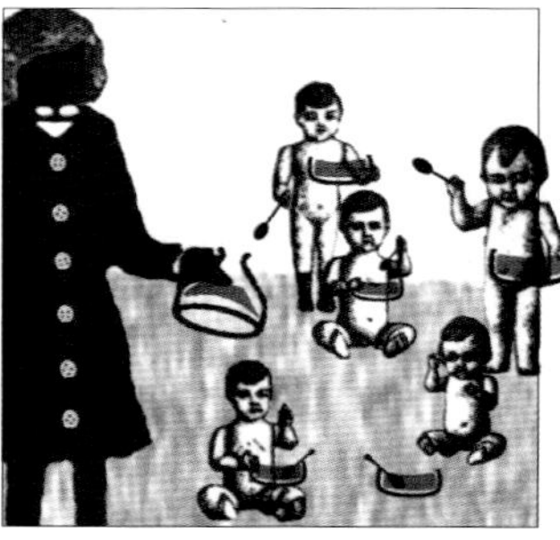
SHE GAVE THEM SOME BROTH WITHOUT ANY BREAD,

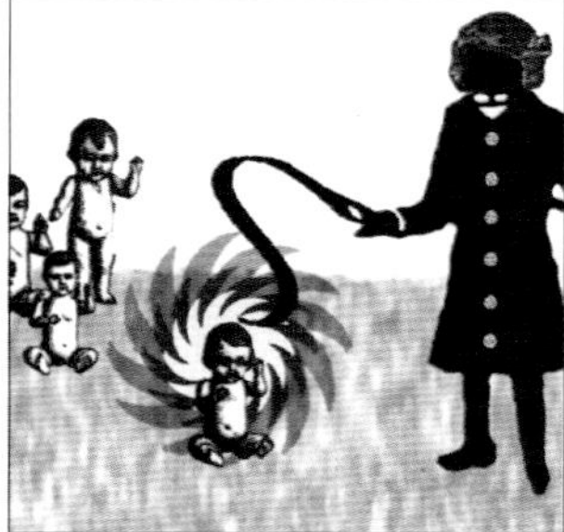
THEN WHIPPED THEM ALL SOUNDLY AND PUT THEM TO BED.

NURSERY RHYME SOLUTIONS:

Figure 1 represents all three solutions as they appear on the assignment sheet. Given the space, cropping, composition, ground, and the use of gray as a contrasting color, there is a consistency in the narrative of all three solutions, which takes on a new formal expression.

Figures 2 through 5 depict the rhyme "Hey Diddle Diddle" using primarily negative and positive relationships. This gives rise to a graphic stylization that could become one's personal image-making signature.

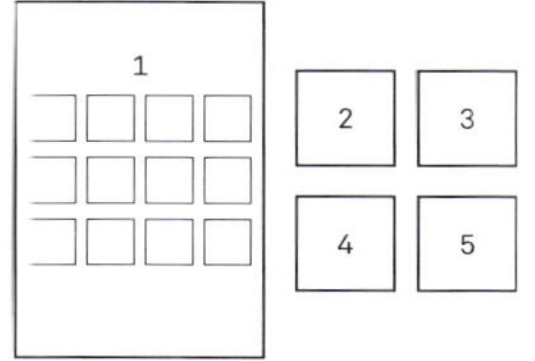

1 *Lindsay Kintgen*
2–5 *Tsai Khaung*

HEY DIDDLE DIDDLE! THE CAT AND THE FIDDLE,

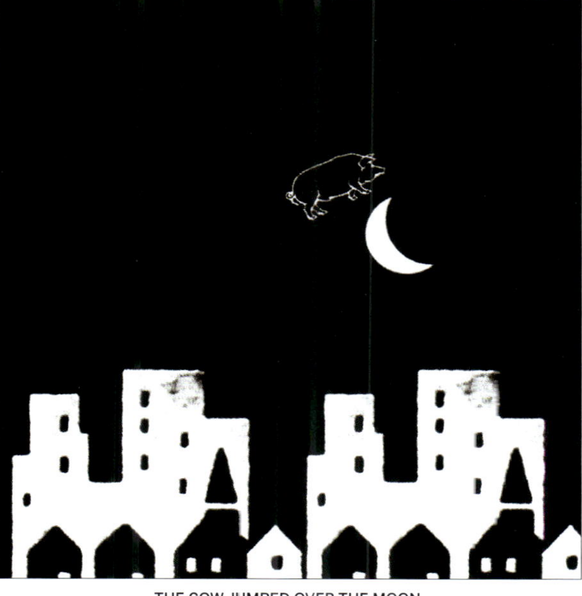

THE COW JUMPED OVER THE MOON.

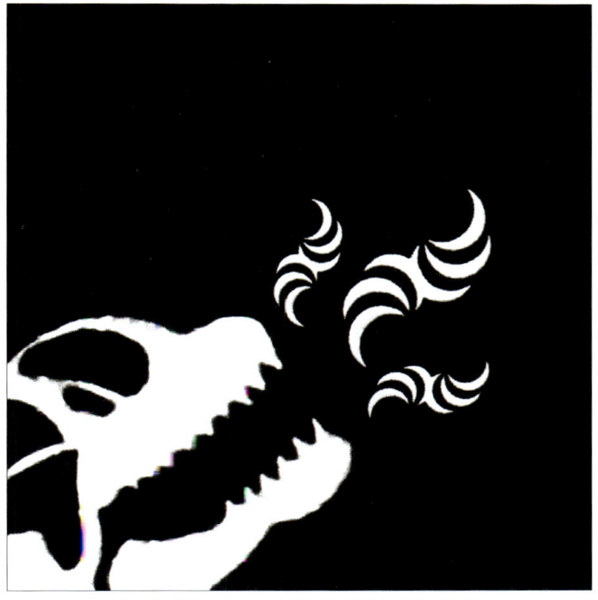

THE LITTLE DOG LAUGHED TO SEE SUCH SPORT,

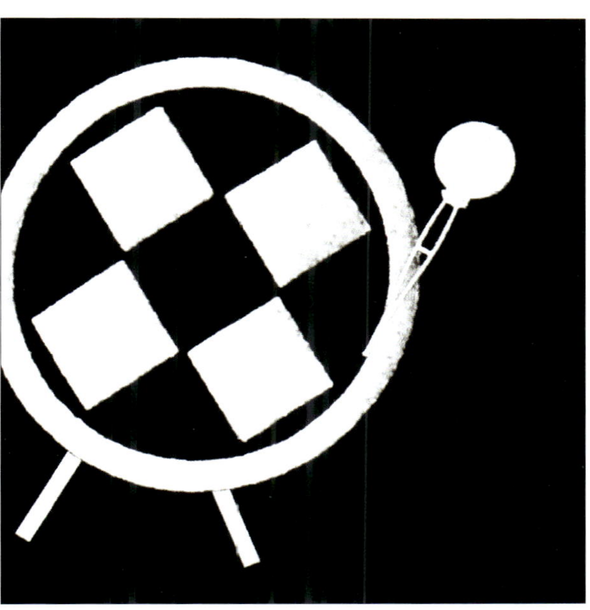

AND THE DISH RAN AWAY WITH THE SPOON.

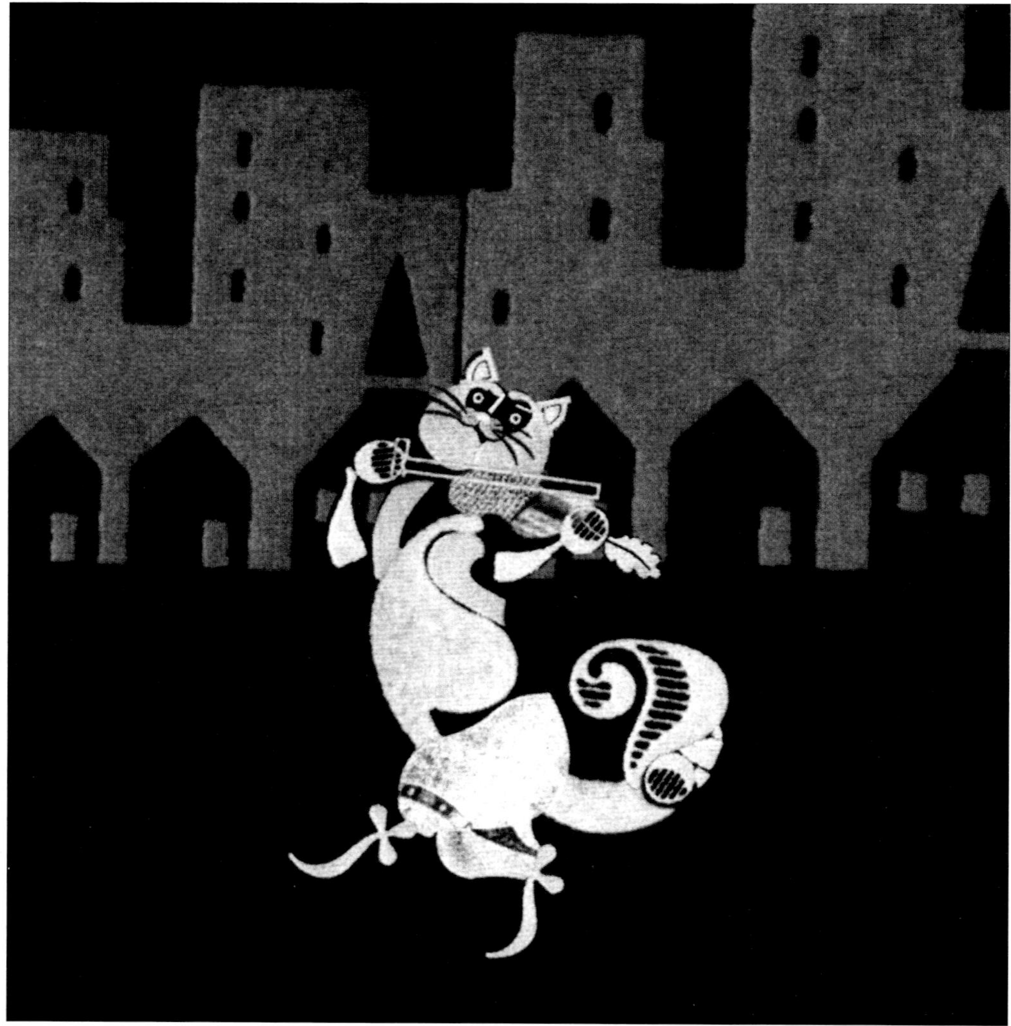

HEY DIDDLE DIDDLE! THE CAT AND THE FIDDLE,

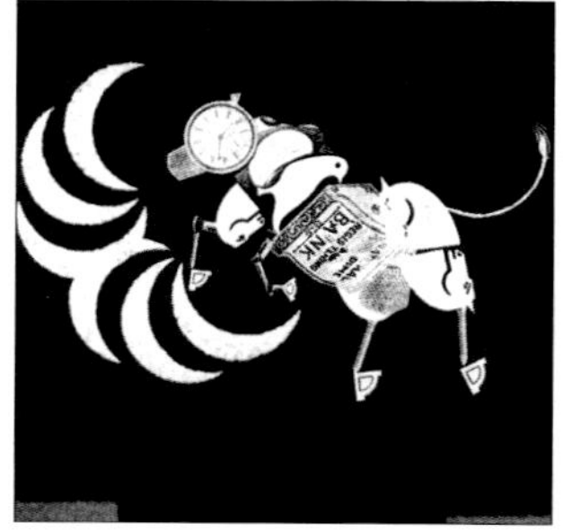

THE COW JUMPED OVER THE MOON.

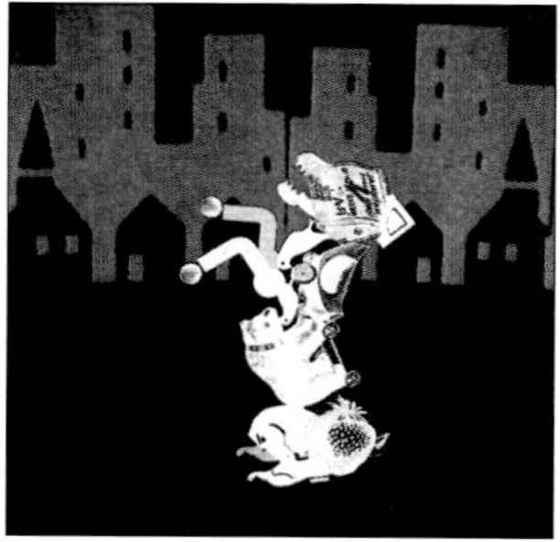

THE LITTLE DOG LAUGHED TO SEE SUCH SPORT,

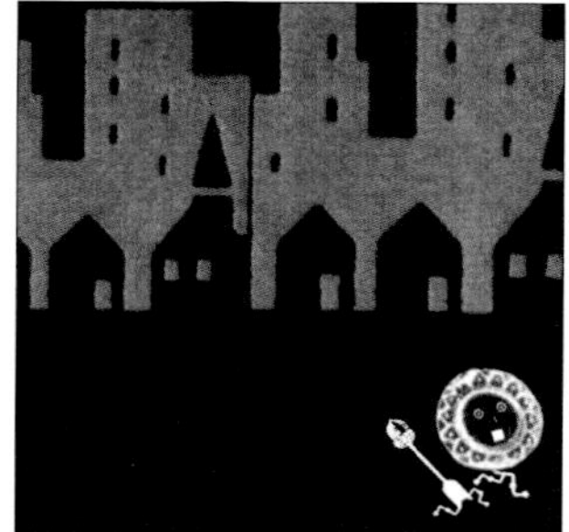

AND THE DISH RAN AWAY WITH THE SPOON.

NURSERY RHYME SOLUTIONS:

Figures 1 through 4 are interpretations of the rhyme "Hey Diddle Diddle," where the essential character in each frame is predominantly white, contrasted by a black and gray ground, giving each frame a distinct focal point.

Figures 5 through 20 represent four different interpretations of "Hey Diddle Diddle" that reference four distinct executions in terms of the selection and manipulation of form, space, shape, and composition.

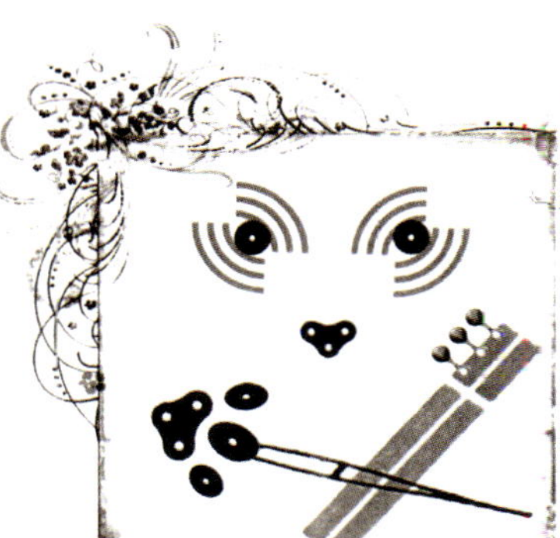
HEY DIDDLE DIDDLE! THE CAT AND THE FIDDLE,

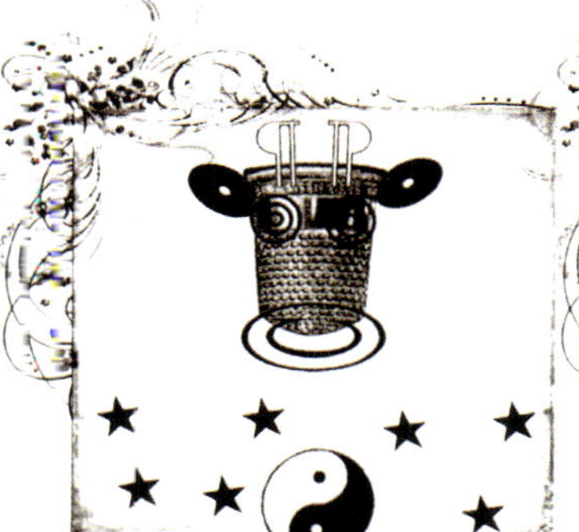
THE COW JUMPED OVER THE MOON.

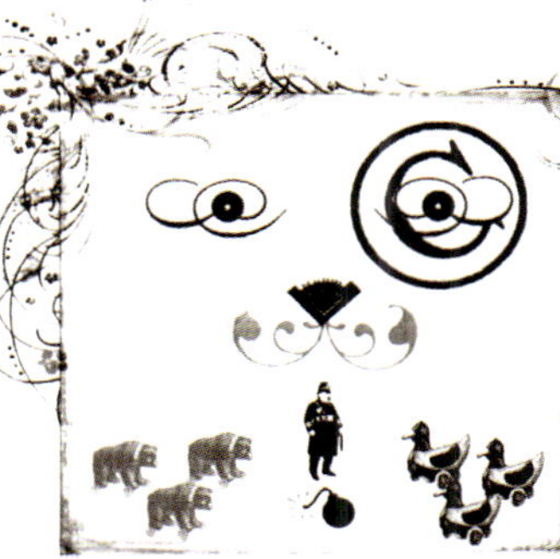
THE LITTLE DOG LAUGHED TO SEE SUCH SPORT,

AND THE DISH RAN AWAY WITH THE SPOON.

HEY DIDDLE DIDDLE! THE CAT AND THE FIDDLE,

THE COW JUMPED OVER THE MOON.

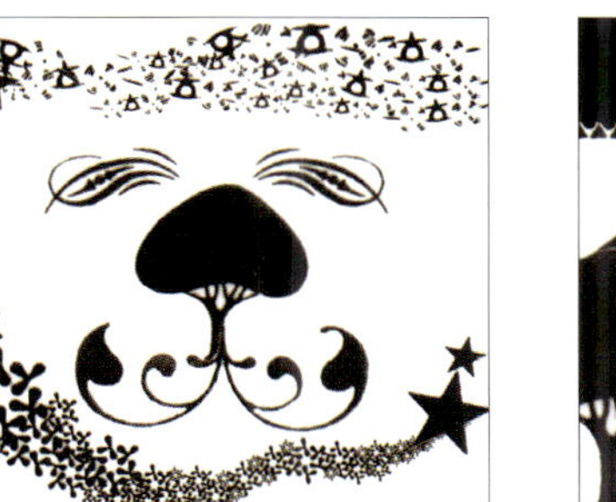
THE LITTLE DOG LAUGHED TO SEE SUCH SPORT,

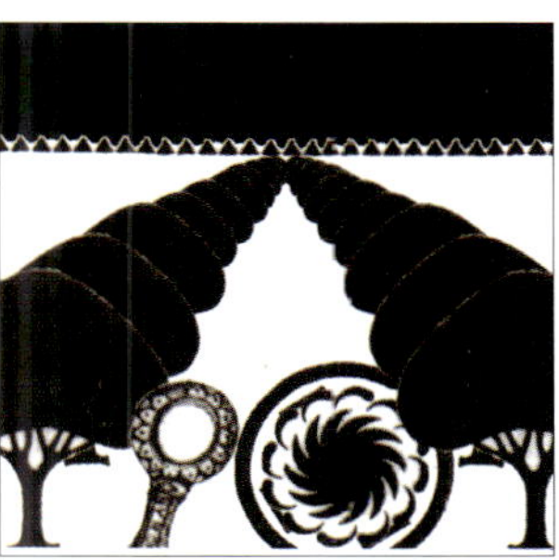
AND THE DISH RAN AWAY WITH THE SPOON.

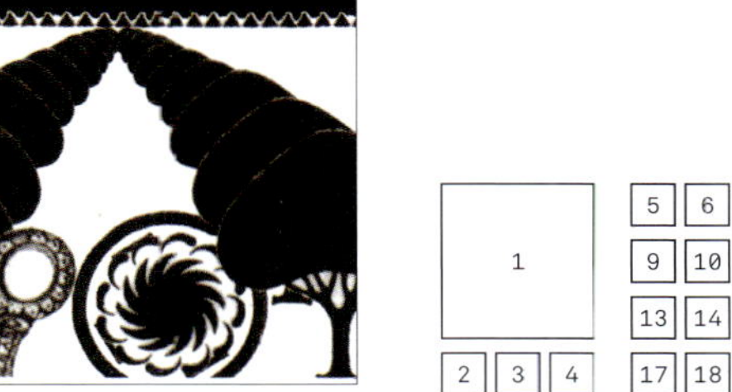

1–4. *Minhyun Chun*
5–8. *Sungho Kim*
9–12. *Minkyung Kang*
13–16. *Brandon Ruschmann*
17–20. *Young Park*

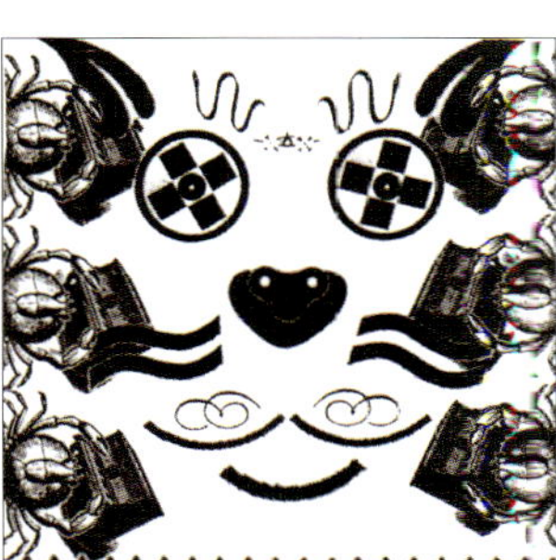
HEY DIDDLE DIDDLE! THE CAT AND THE FIDDLE,

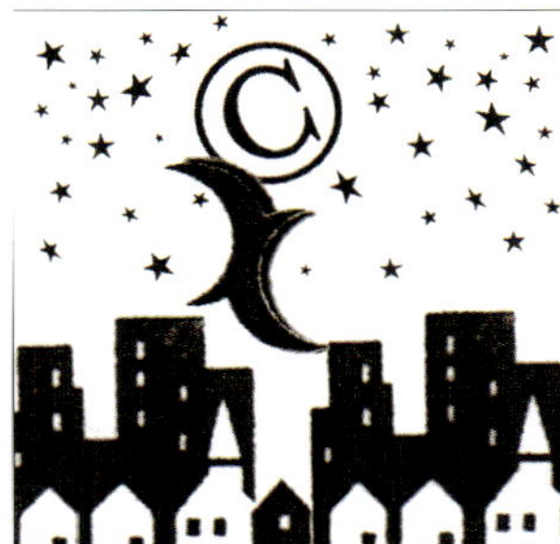
THE COW JUMPED OVER THE MOON.

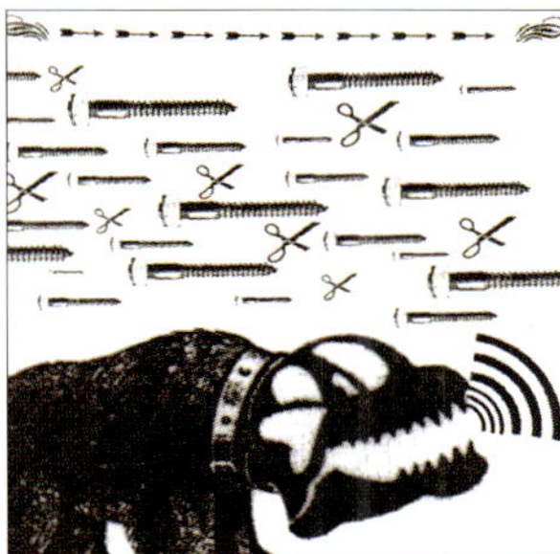
THE LITTLE DOG LAUGHED TO SEE SUCH SPORT,

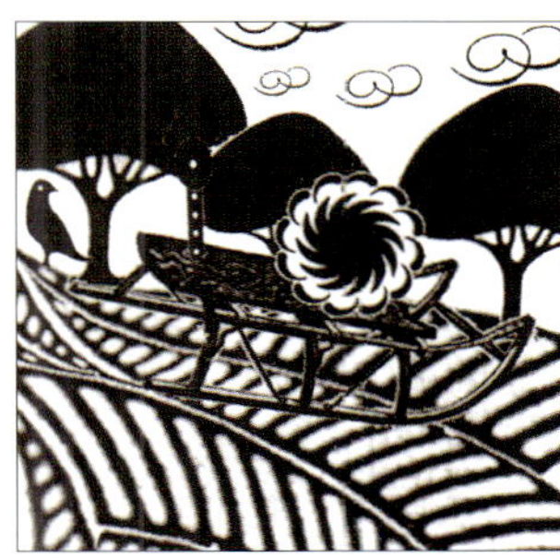
AND THE DISH RAN AWAY WITH THE SPOON.

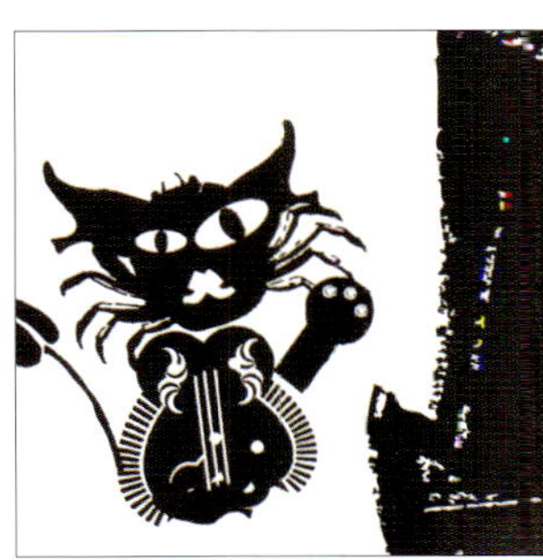
HEY DIDDLE DIDDLE! THE CAT AND THE FIDDLE,

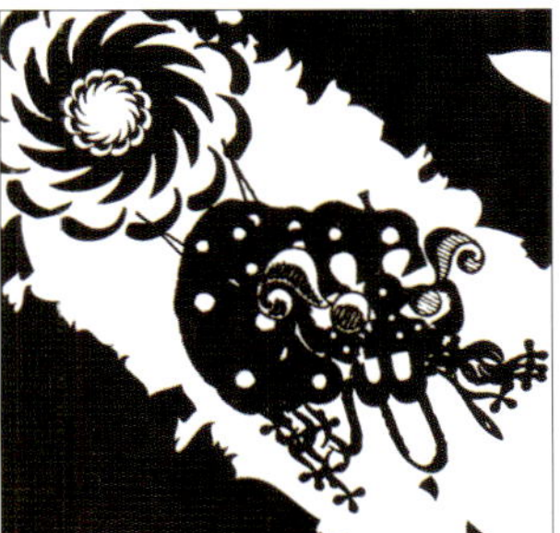
THE COW JUMPED OVER THE MOON.

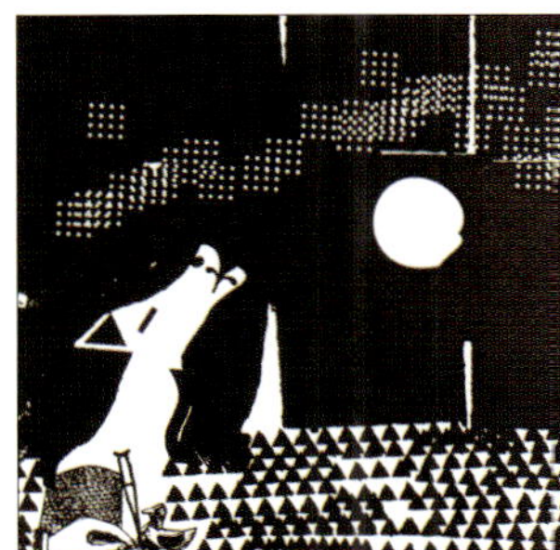
THE LITTLE DOG LAUGHED TO SEE SUCH SPORT,

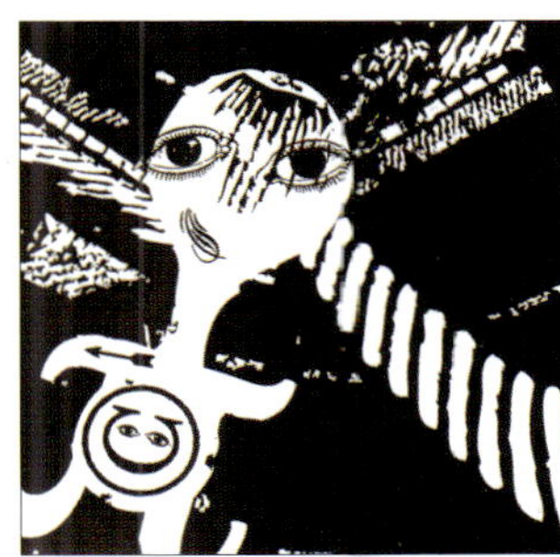
AND THE DISH RAN AWAY WITH THE SPOON.

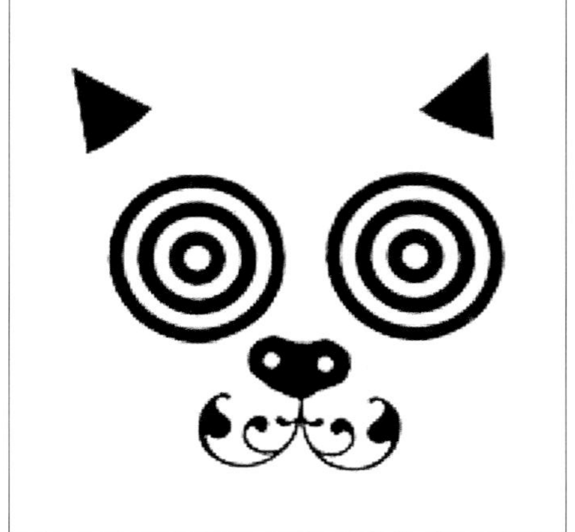
HEY DIDDLE DIDDLE! THE CAT AND THE FIDDLE,

HEY DIDDLE DIDDLE! THE CAT AND THE FIDDLE,

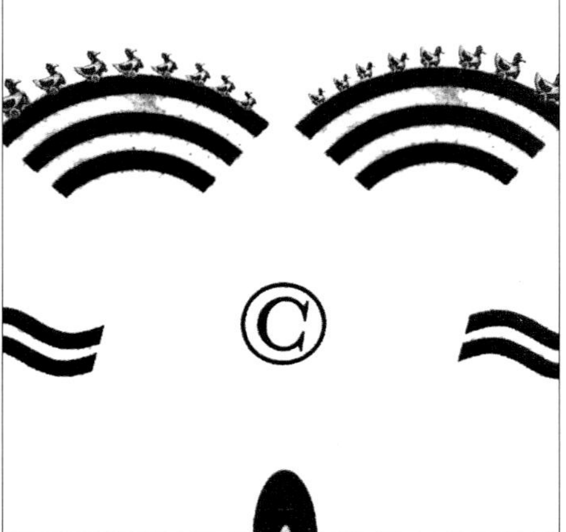
HEY DIDDLE DIDDLE! THE CAT AND THE FIDDLE,

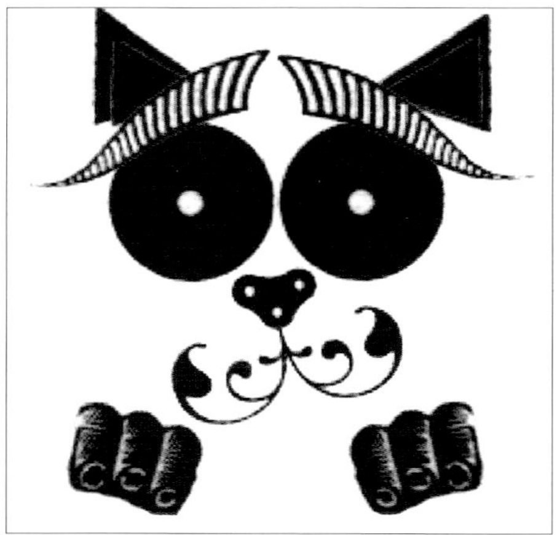
HEY DIDDLE DIDDLE! THE CAT AND THE FIDDLE,

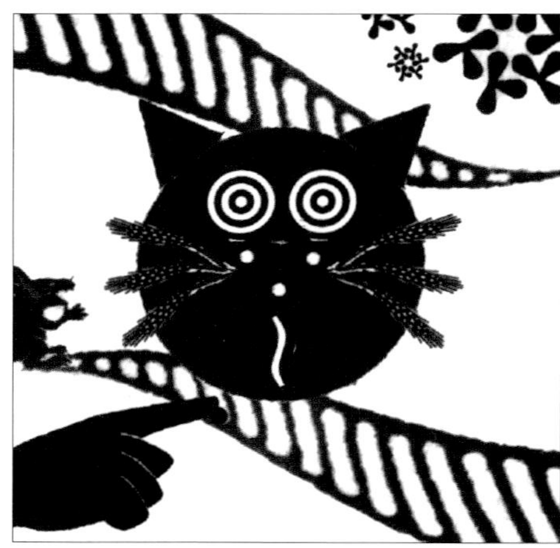
HEY DIDDLE DIDDLE! THE CAT AND THE FIDDLE,

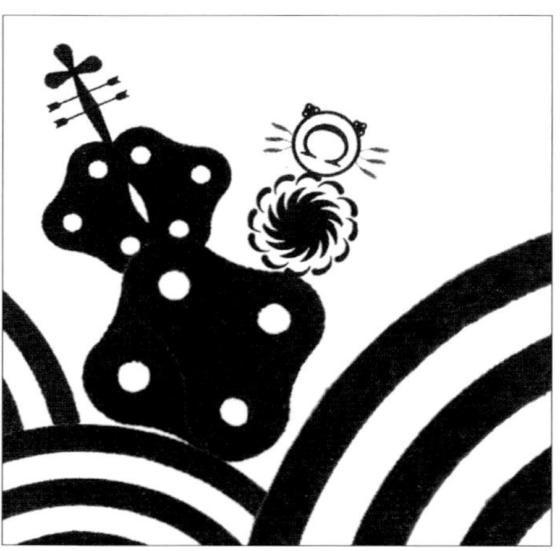
HEY DIDDLE DIDDLE! THE CAT AND THE FIDDLE,

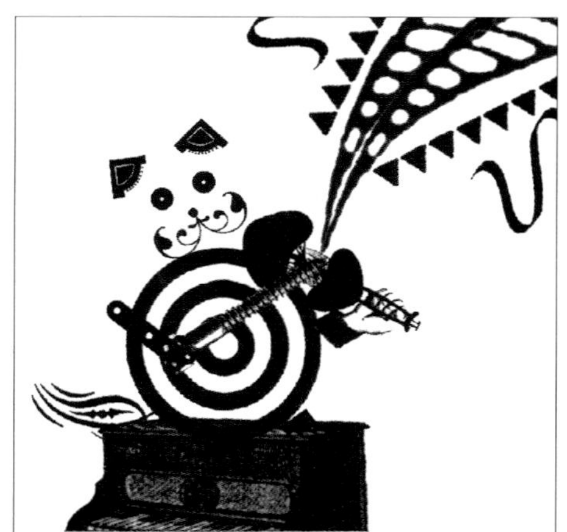
HEY DIDDLE DIDDLE! THE CAT AND THE FIDDLE,

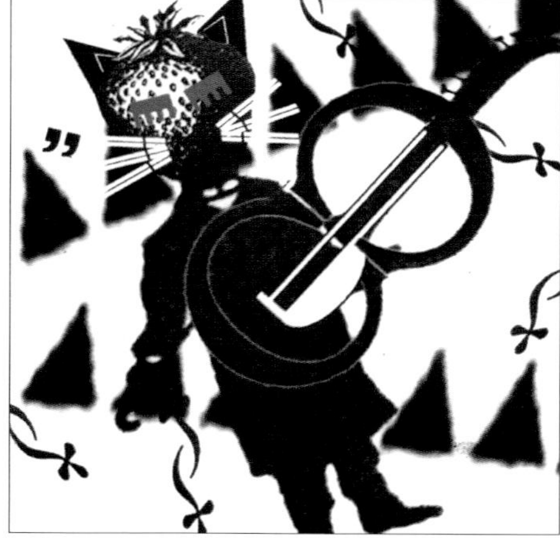
HEY DIDDLE DIDDLE! THE CAT AND THE FIDDLE,

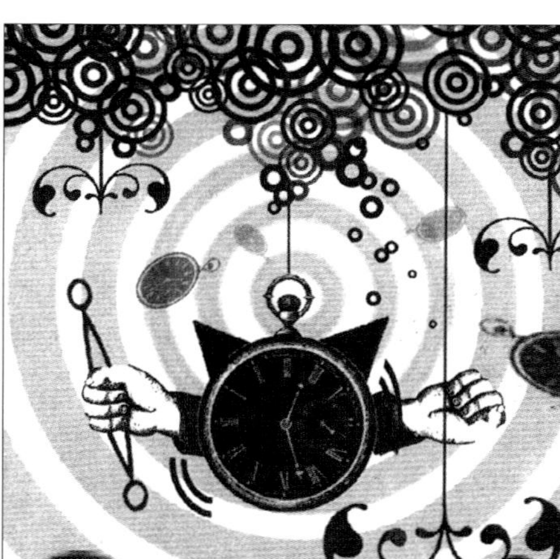
HEY DIDDLE DIDDLE! THE CAT AND THE FIDDLE,

NURSERY RHYME SOLUTIONS:

Figures 1 through 9 represent the first line in the rhyme "Hey Diddle Diddle," depicting a cat and, in some instances, a cat and a fiddle.

Figures 10 through 18 depict the second line in the rhyme, "The cow jumped over the moon." Solutions range from typographic, to abstract, to literal interpretations

As in many of these solutions throughout this chapter, the viewer is challenged to complete the message.

1. *Seungjoo F. Lee*
2. *Candice Lee*
3. *Jeonghyun Ahn*
4. *Rhonny Tufino*
5. *Kyle Chaille*
6. *Jocelyn Tsaih*
7. *Sunmin Chung*
8. *Mae Choi*
9. *Jungeun Kwak*
10. *Woohyun Cho*
11. *Alison Bitton*
12. *Kyle Chaille*
13. *Daeun Ko*
14. *Kyla Kim*
15. *Kristen Sorace*
16. *Steve Choi*
17. *Shay Inbar*
18. *Sunmin Chung*

THE COW JUMPED OVER THE MOON.

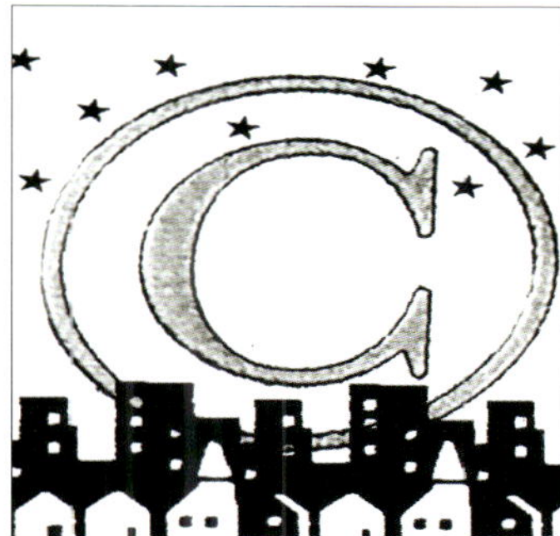

THE COW JUMPED OVER THE MOON.

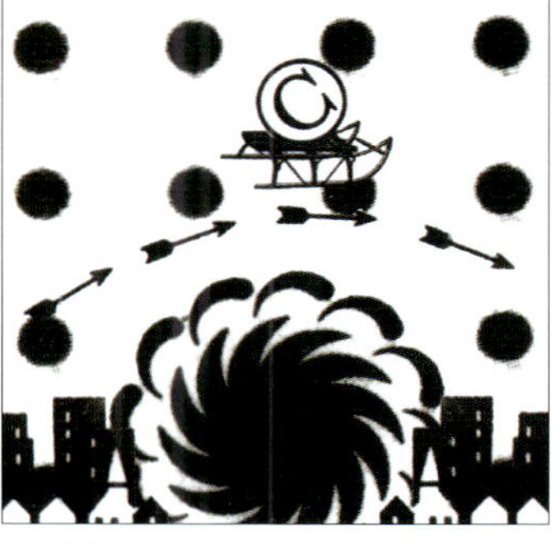

THE COW JUMPED OVER THE MOON.

THE COW JUMPED OVER THE MOON.

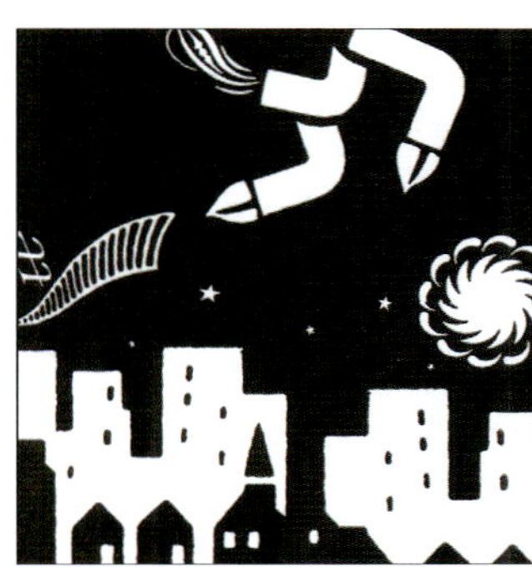

THE COW JUMPED OVER THE MOON.

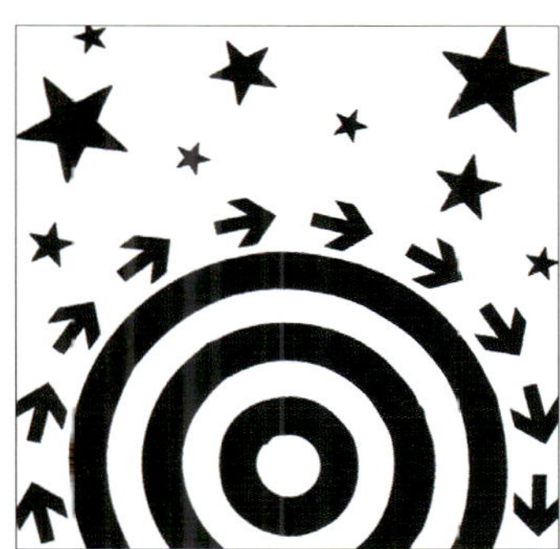

THE COW JUMPED OVER THE MOON.

THE COW JUMPED OVER THE MOON.

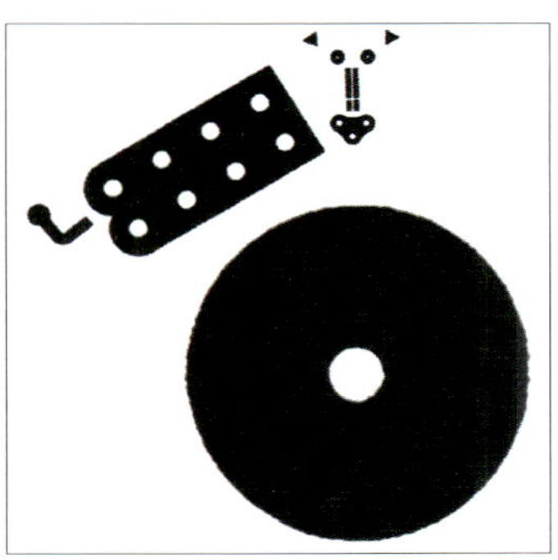

THE COW JUMPED OVER THE MOON.

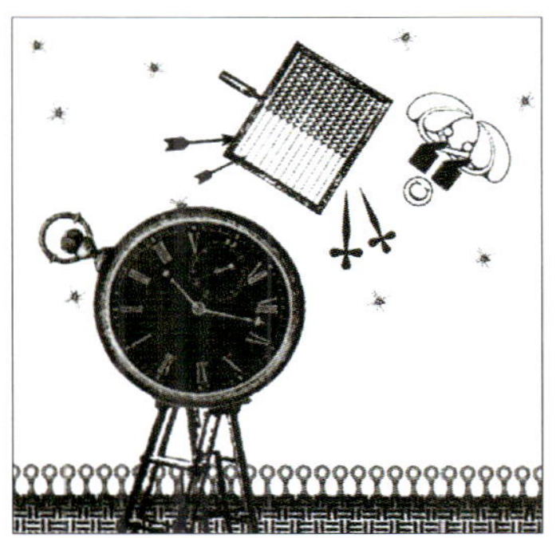

THE COW JUMPED OVER THE MOON.

THE LITTLE DOG LAUGHED TO SEE SUCH SPORT,

THE LITTLE DOG LAUGHED TO SEE SUCH SPORT,

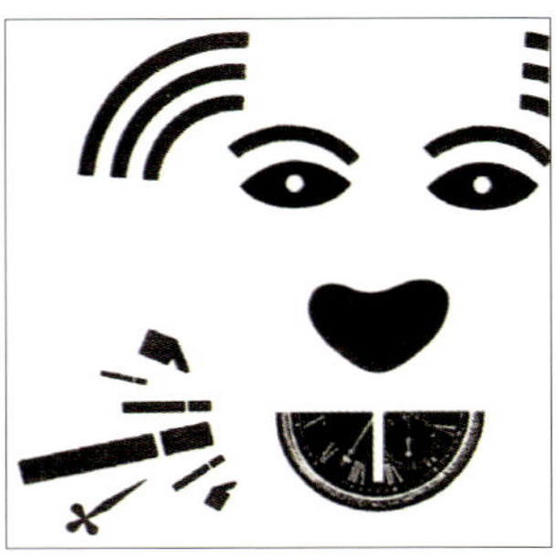
THE LITTLE DOG LAUGHED TO SEE SUCH SPORT,

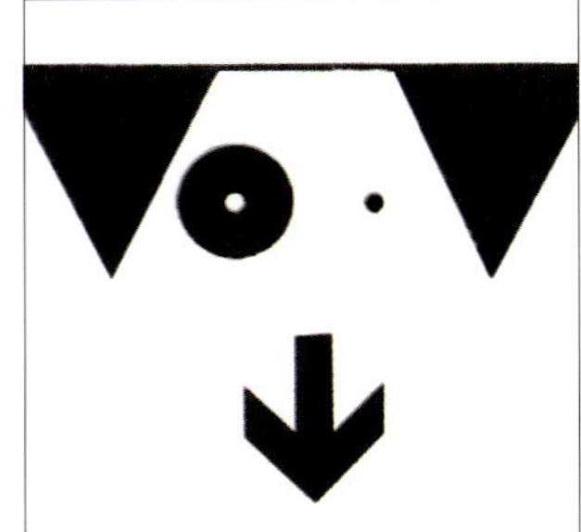
THE LITTLE DOG LAUGHED TO SEE SUCH SPORT,

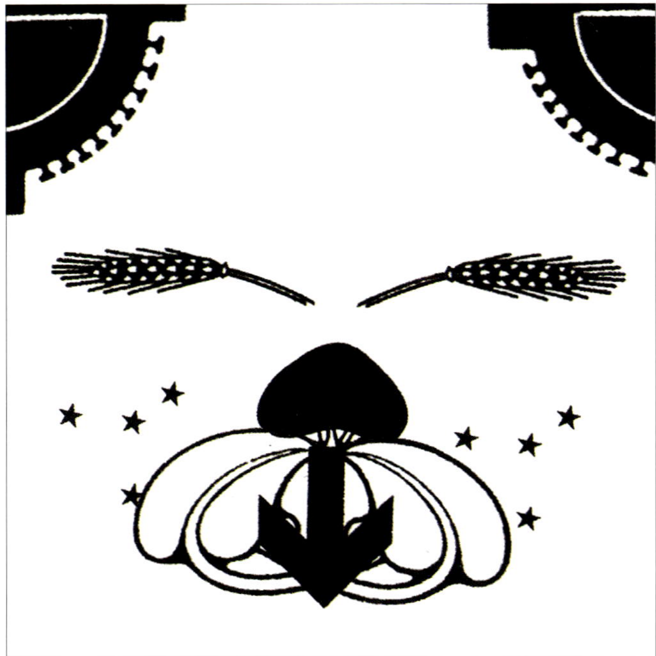
THE LITTLE DOG LAUGHED TO SEE SUCH SPORT,

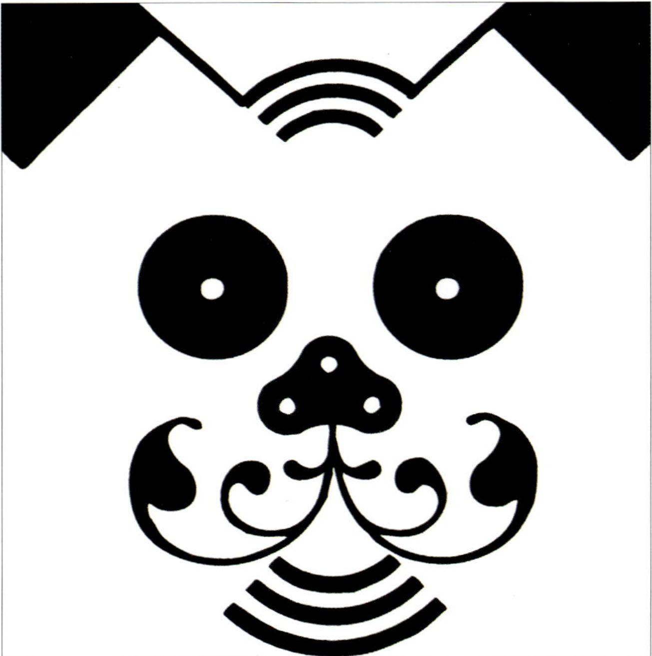
THE LITTLE DOG LAUGHED TO SEE SUCH SPORT,

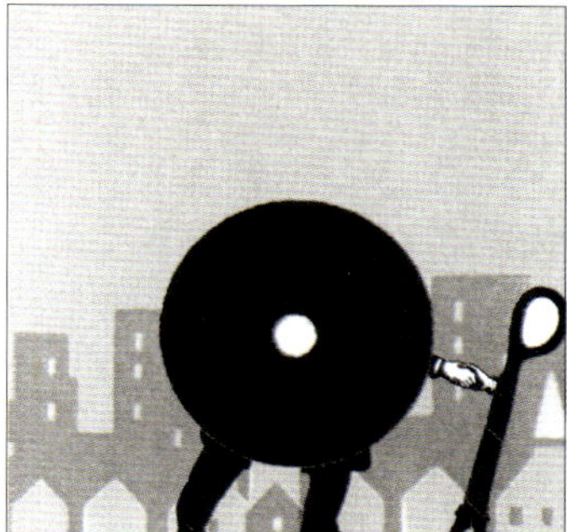
AND THE DISH RAN AWAY WITH THE SPOON.

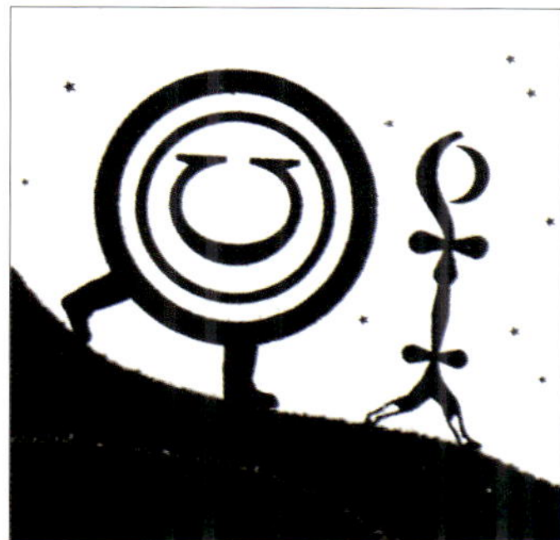
AND THE DISH RAN AWAY WITH THE SPOON.

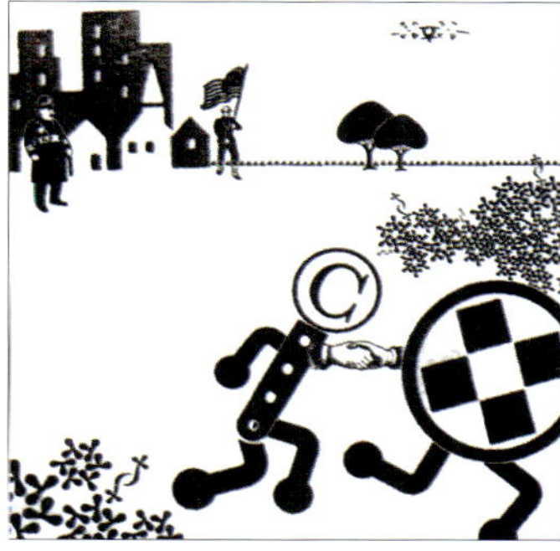
AND THE DISH RAN AWAY WITH THE SPOON.

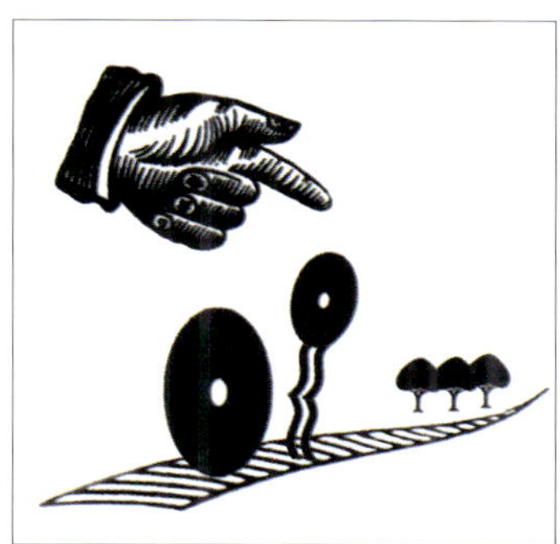
AND THE DISH RAN AWAY WITH THE SPOON.

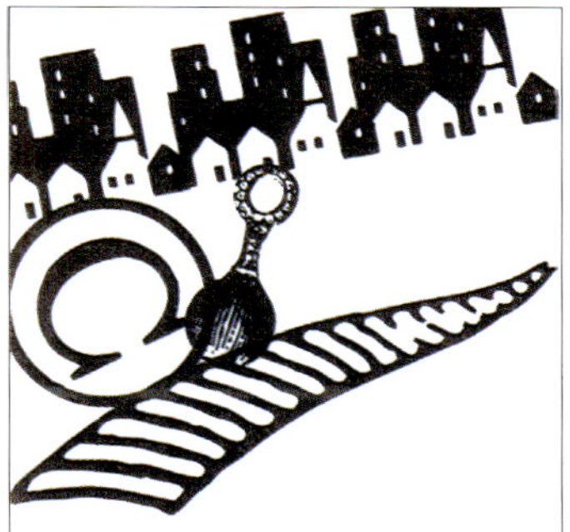
AND THE DISH RAN AWAY WITH THE SPOON.

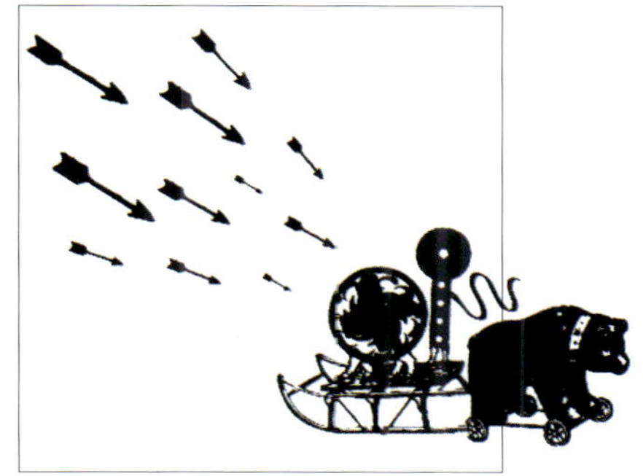
AND THE DISH RAN AWAY WITH THE SPOON.

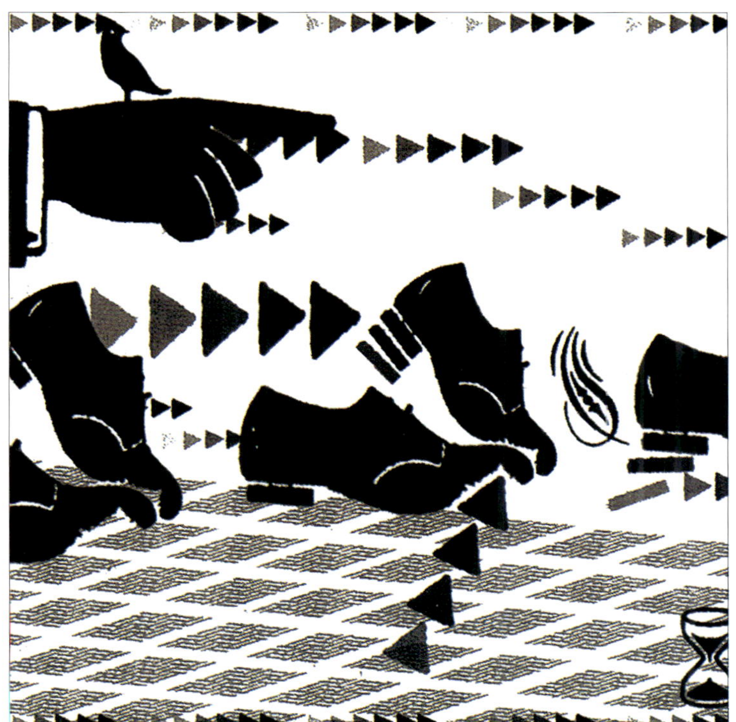
AND THE DISH RAN AWAY WITH THE SPOON.

NURSERY RHYME SOLUTIONS:

Figures 1 through 6 are depictions of the third line, "The little dog laughed to see such sport," using various combinations of the given vocabulary to create a laughing dog's face.

Figures 7 through 13 depict the final line of the rhyme, "And the dish ran away with the spoon." The images range from static to having a sense of movement.

Most all of the solutions are marked by the absurdity of the rhyme.

1. *Jihyun Park*
2. *Minkyung Kang*
3. *Kevin Harris*
4. *Alyssa Leary*
5. *Min Yoon*
6. *Kristen Sorace*
7. *Candice Lee*
8. *Steve Choi*
9. *Hanmyung Song*
10. *Heather Seksinsky*
11. *Kristen Sorace*
12. *June Hong*
13. *Jungeun Kwak*

HUMPTY DUMPTY SAT ON A WALL,

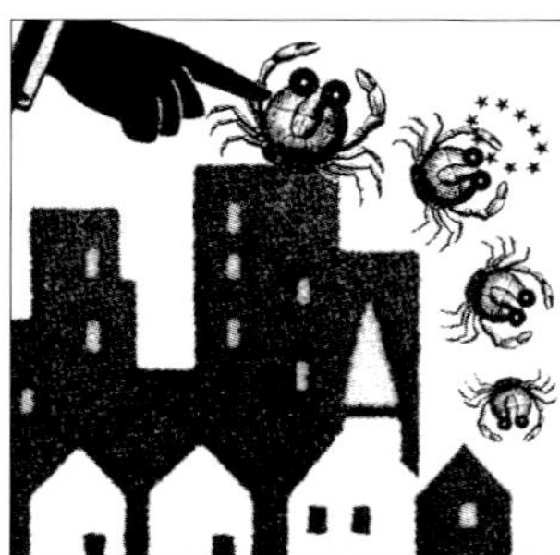

HUMPTY DUMPTY HAD A GREAT FALL.

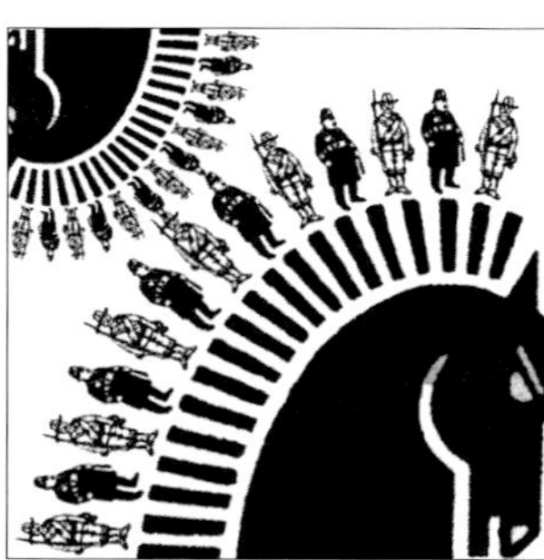

ALL THE KING'S HORSES AND
ALL THE KING'S MEN

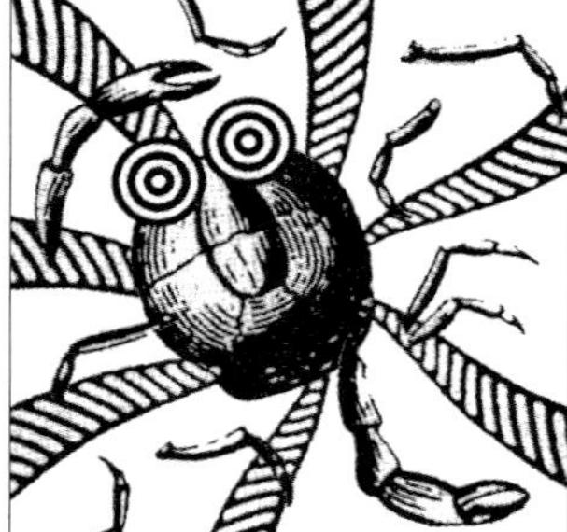

COULDN'T PUT HUMPTY
TOGETHER AGAIN.

NURSERY RHYME SOLUTIONS:

Figures 1 through 4 represent the rhyme "Humpty Dumpty," where liberties are taken in the depiction of Humpty Dumpty as a crab with a human face.

Figures 5 through 20 represent four separate interpretations of the "Humpty Dumpty" rhyme. All solutions are done on a white ground and rely heavily on patterning, cropping, texture, and spatial considerations.

In these solutions Humpty Dumpty is represented as a baby doll, a thimble, a crab wearing a high hat, and a duck.

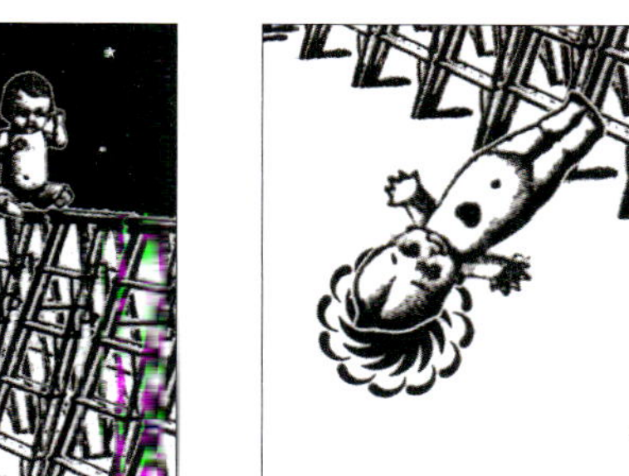
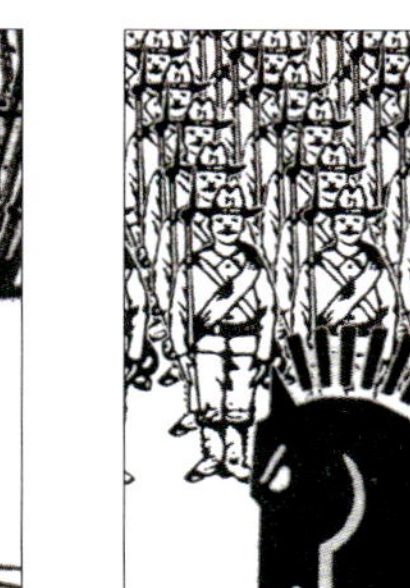
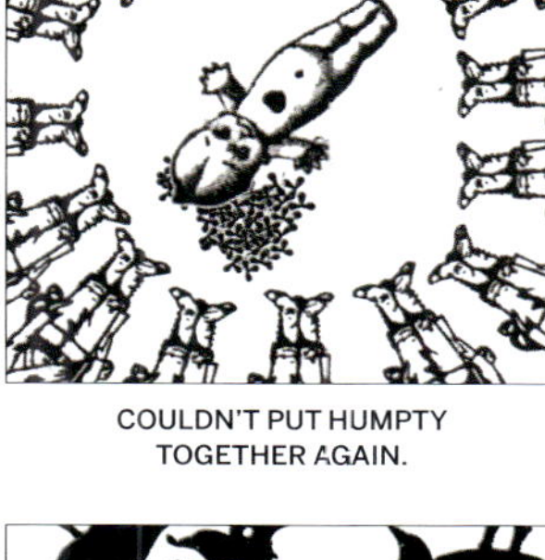

HUMPTY DUMPTY SAT ON A WALL,

HUMPTY DUMPTY HAD A GREAT FALL.

ALL THE KING'S HORSES AND ALL THE KING'S MEN

COULDN'T PUT HUMPTY TOGETHER AGAIN.

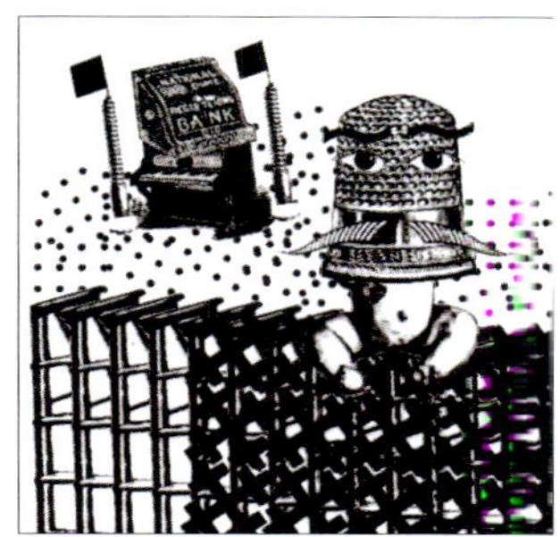
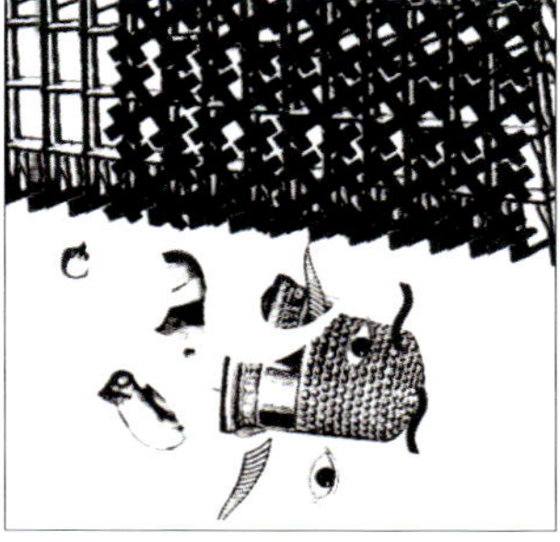
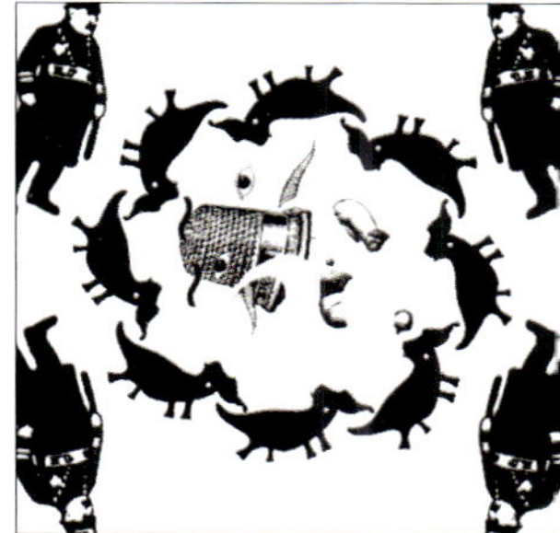
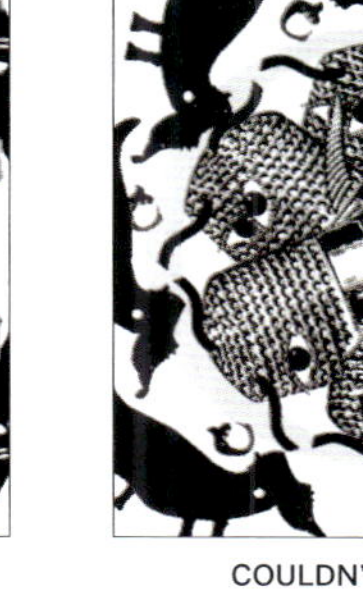

HUMPTY DUMPTY SAT ON A WALL,

HUMPTY DUMPTY HAD A GREAT FALL.

ALL THE KING'S HORSES AND ALL THE KING'S MEN

COULDN'T PUT HUMPTY TOGETHER AGAIN.

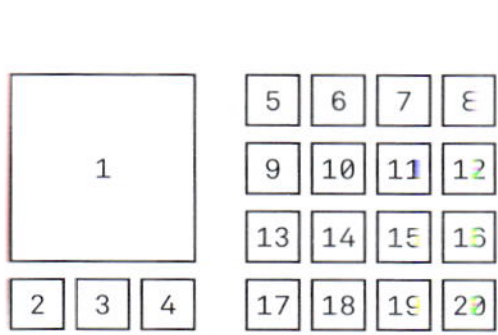

1-4. *Borana Kim*
5-8. *Hanmyung Song*
9-12. *Kejun Liu*
13-16. *Elaine Park*
17-20. *Youngmi Jung*

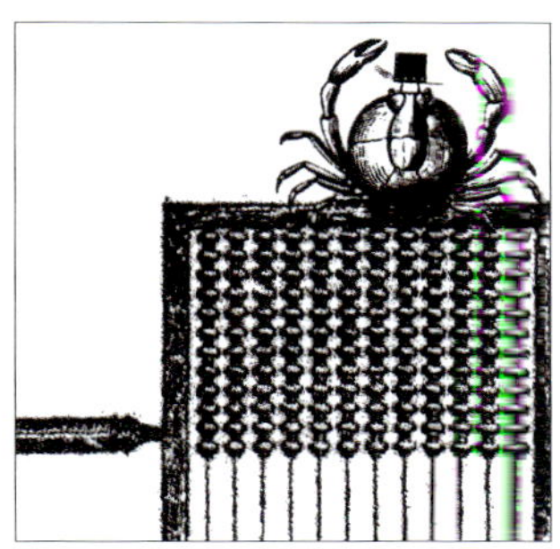
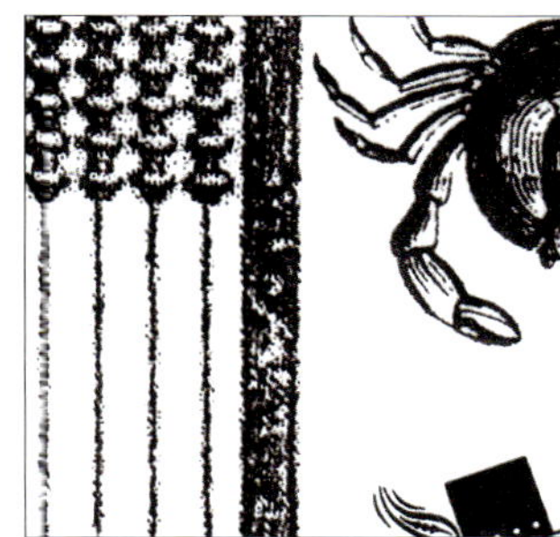
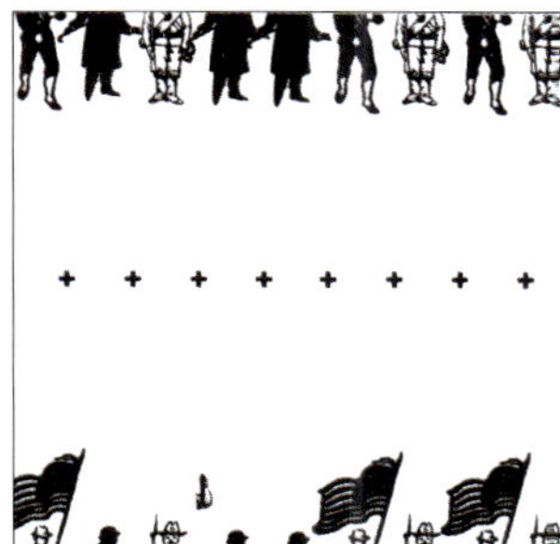
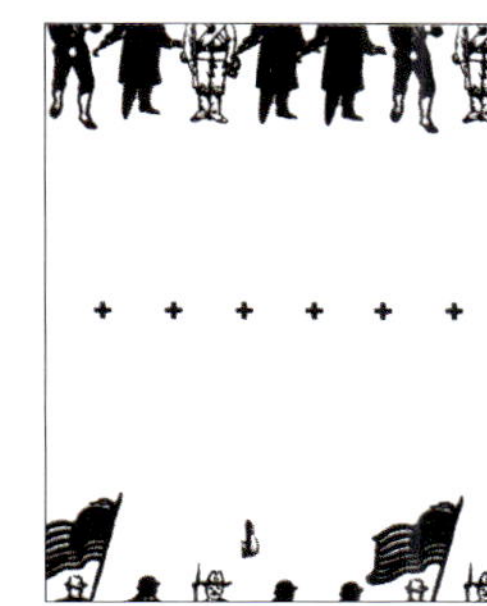
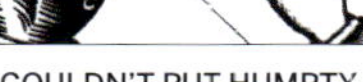

HUMPTY DUMPTY SAT ON A WALL

HUMPTY DUMPTY HAD A GREAT FALL.

ALL THE KING'S HORSES AND ALL THE KING'S MEN

COULDN'T PUT HUMPTY TOGETHER AGAIN.

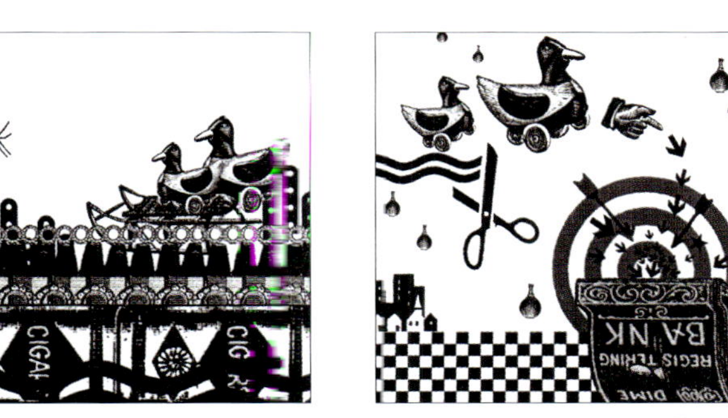
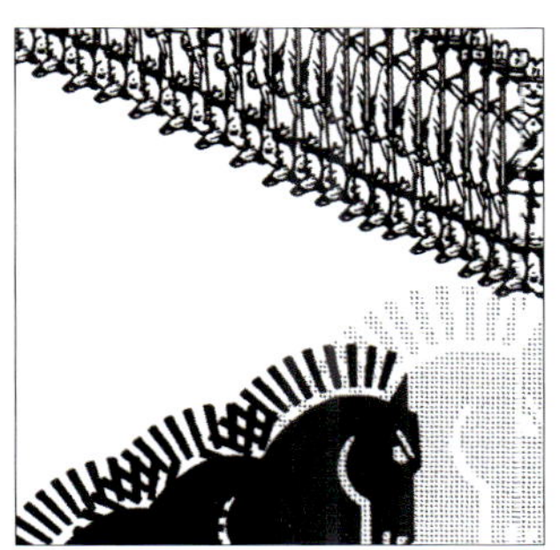
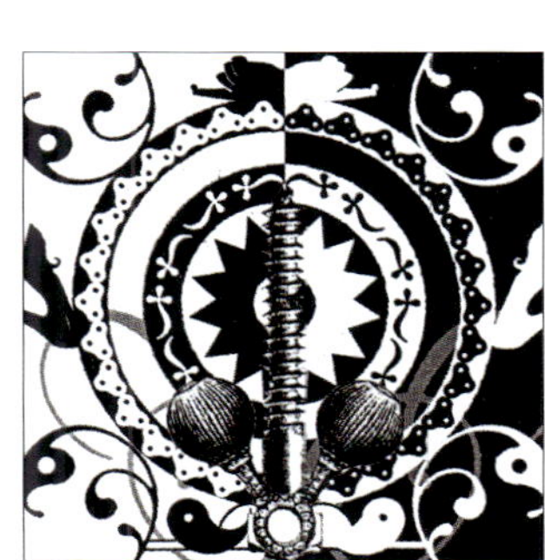
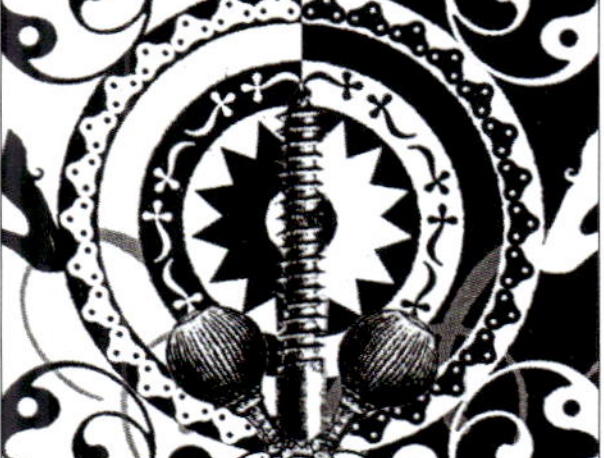

HUMPTY DUMPTY SAT ON A WALL,

HUMPTY DUMPTY HAD A GREAT FALL.

ALL THE KING'S HORSES AND ALL THE KING'S MEN

COULDN'T PUT HUMPTY TOGETHER AGAIN.

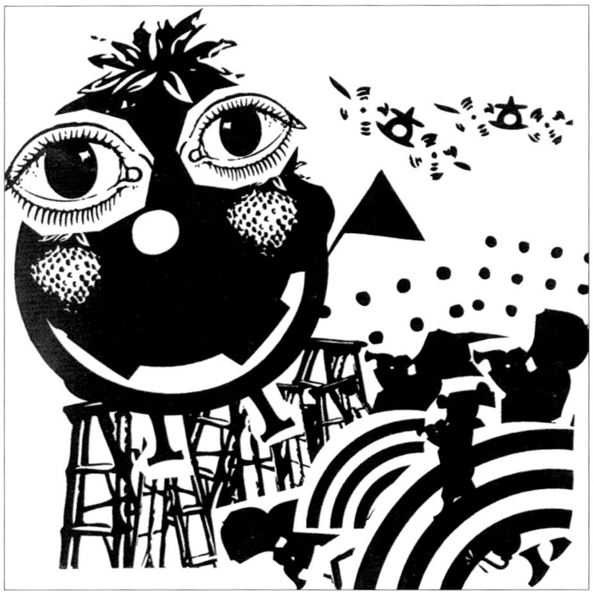

HUMPTY DUMPTY SAT ON A WALL,

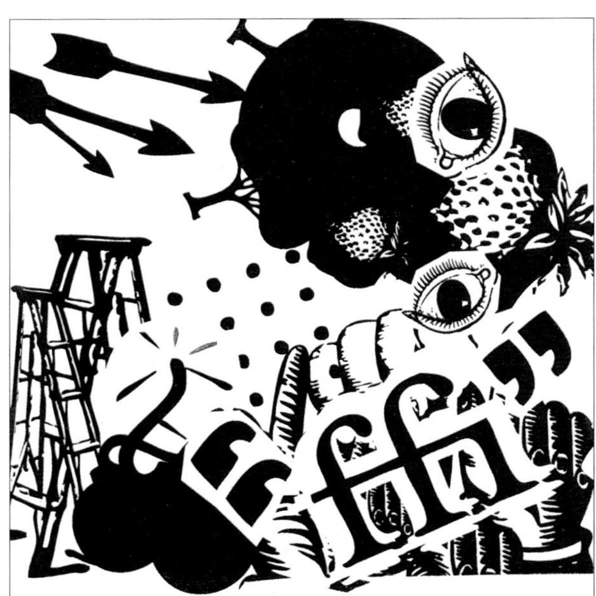

HUMPTY DUMPTY HAD A GREAT FALL.

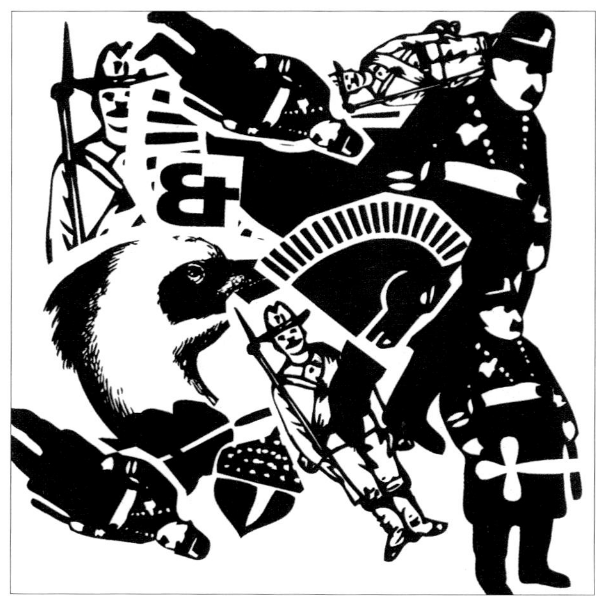

ALL THE KING'S HORSES AND ALL THE KING'S MEN

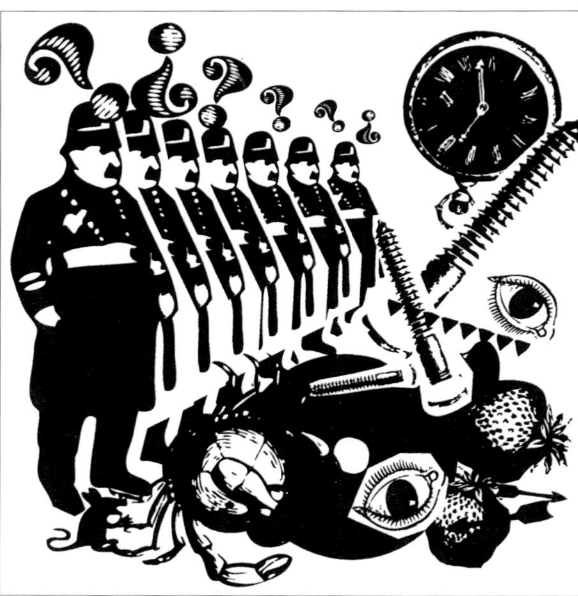

COULDN'T PUT HUMPTY TOGETHER AGAIN.

HUMPTY DUMPTY SAT ON A WALL,

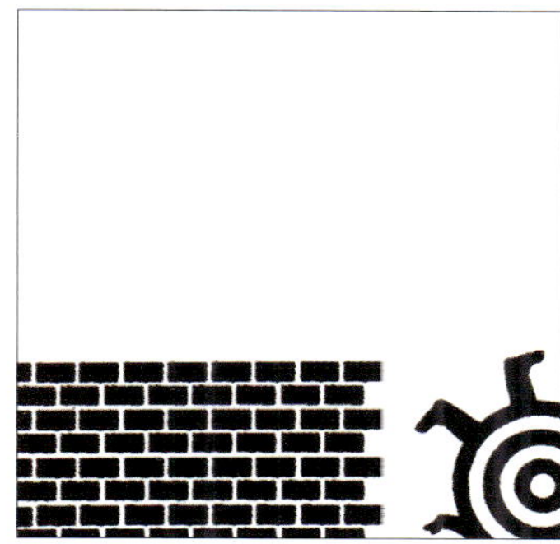

HUMPTY DUMPTY HAD A GREAT FALL.

HUMPTY DUMPTY SAT ON A WALL,

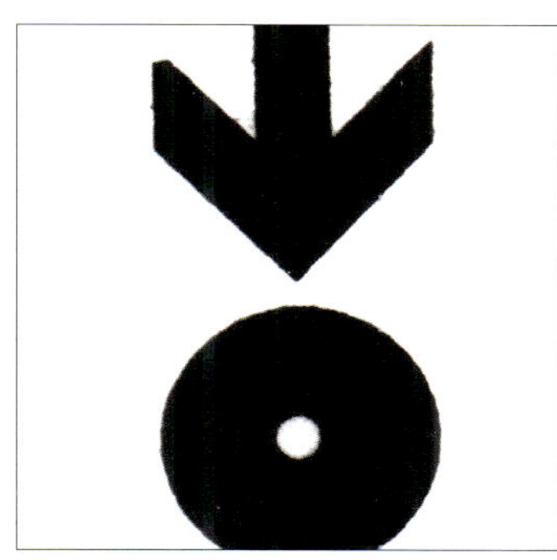

HUMPTY DUMPTY HAD A GREAT FALL.

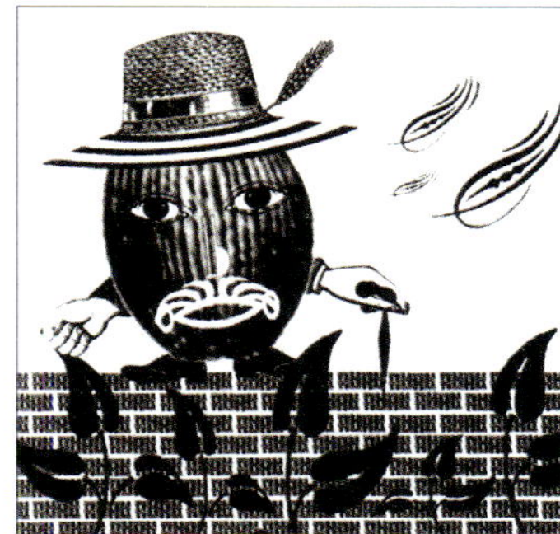

HUMPTY DUMPTY SAT ON A WALL,

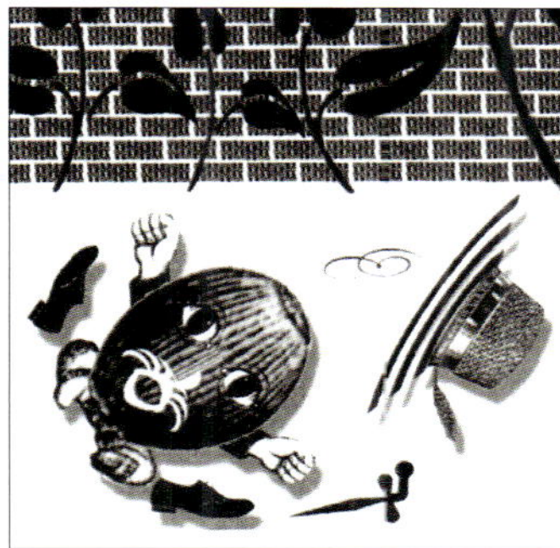

HUMPTY DUMPTY HAD A GREAT FALL.

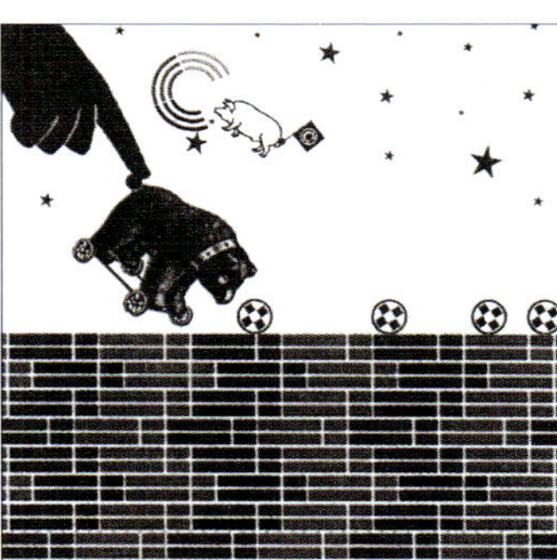

HUMPTY DUMPTY SAT ON A WALL,

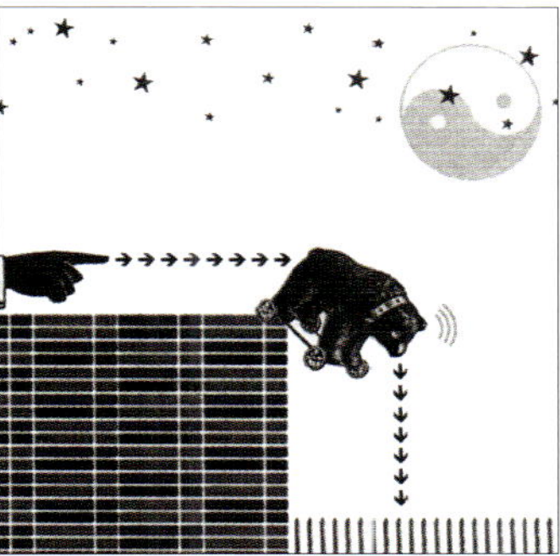

HUMPTY DUMPTY HAD A GREAT FALL.

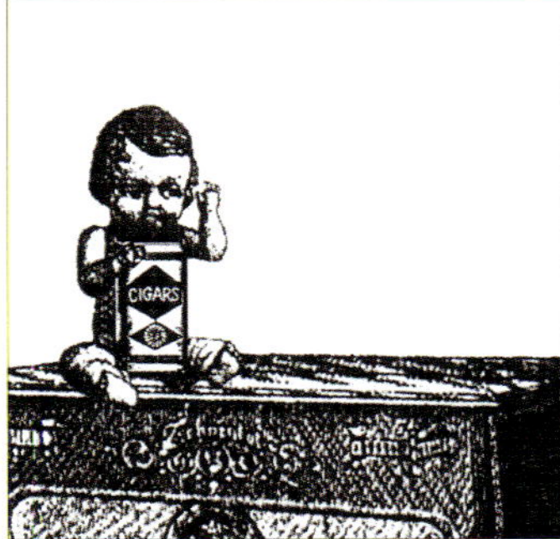

HUMPTY DUMPTY SAT ON A WALL,

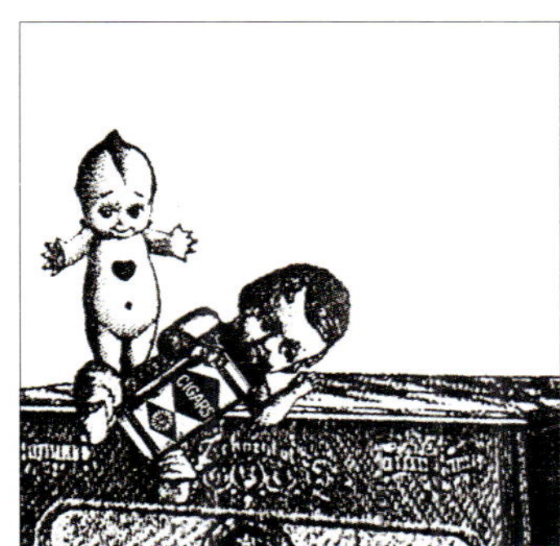

HUMPTY DUMPTY HAD A GREAT FALL.

NURSERY RHYME SOLUTIONS:

Figures 1 through 4 are highly personal interpretations of the "Humpty Dumpty" rhyme, where seemingly abstract configurations become comprehensible with the support of the text. The compositions are investigations of overlapping elements, scale, space, cropping, and diminishing size, all executed in a playful manner, while staying true to the given narrative.

Figures 5 through 14 represent the first two lines of the rhyme, where Humpty Dumpty is sitting on a wall and then subsequently falls. Solutions range from symbolic to literal.

1	2
3	4

5	6
7	8
9	10
11	12
13	14

1–4. *Nova Pan*
5–6. *Alexandra Benet*
7–8. *Kyle Chaille*
9–10. *Jaeyoon Song*
11–12. *Jeonghyun Ahn*
13–14. *Hyung Suh*

Figures 11 through 14 give a personal explanation of Humpty Dumpty's fall.

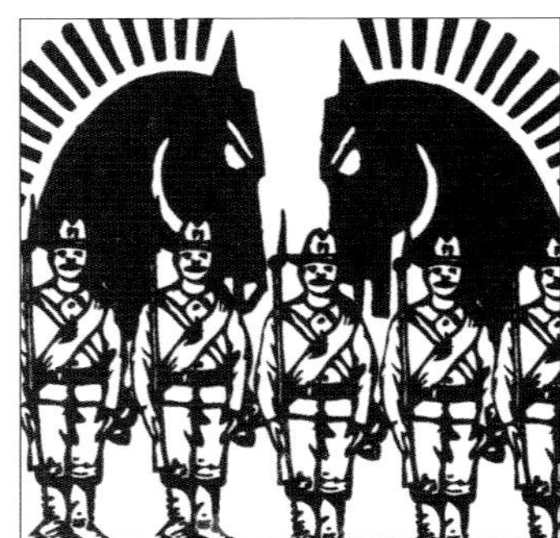

ALL THE KING'S HORSES AND ALL THE KING'S MEN

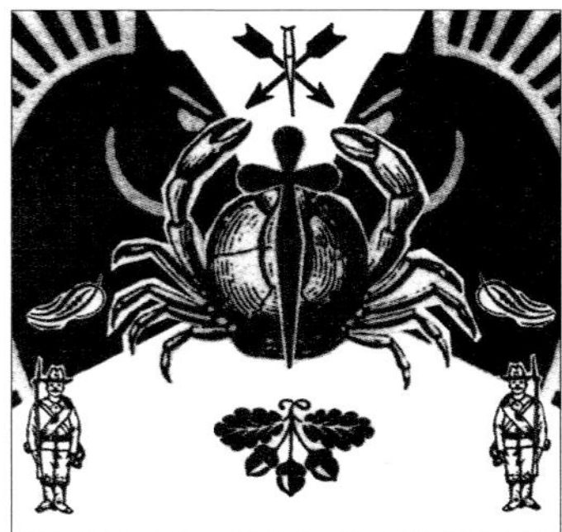

ALL THE KING'S HORSES AND ALL THE KING'S MEN

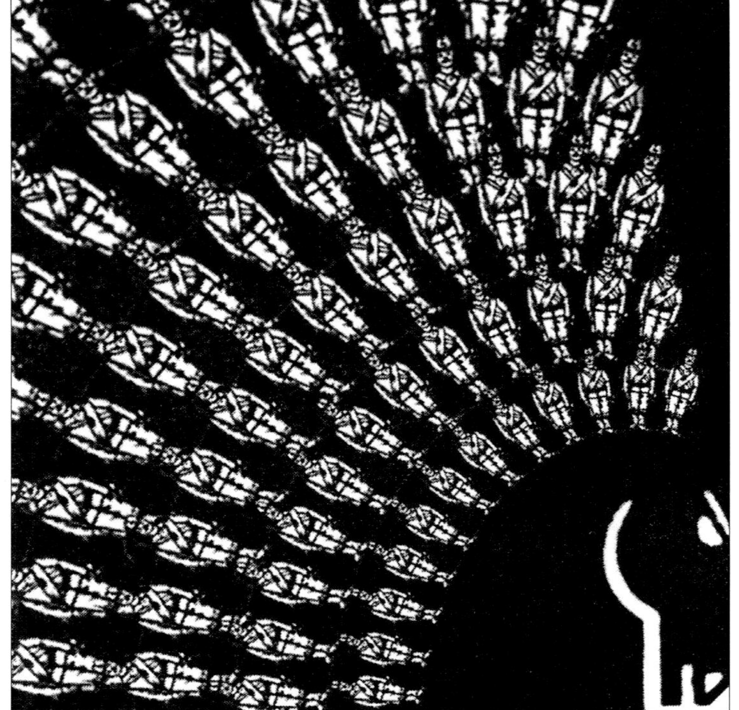

ALL THE KING'S HORSES AND ALL THE KING'S MEN

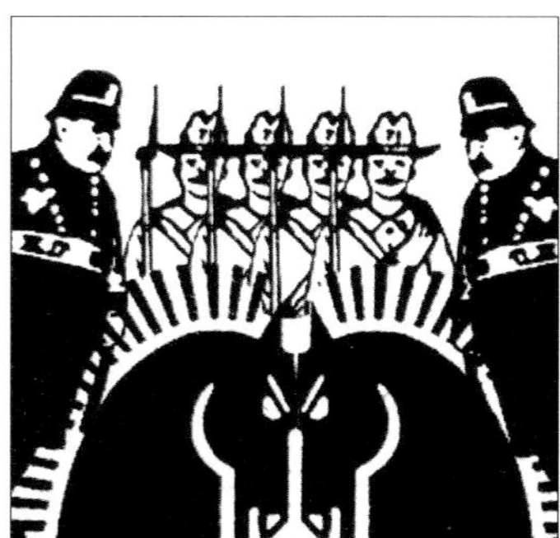

ALL THE KING'S HORSES AND ALL THE KING'S MEN

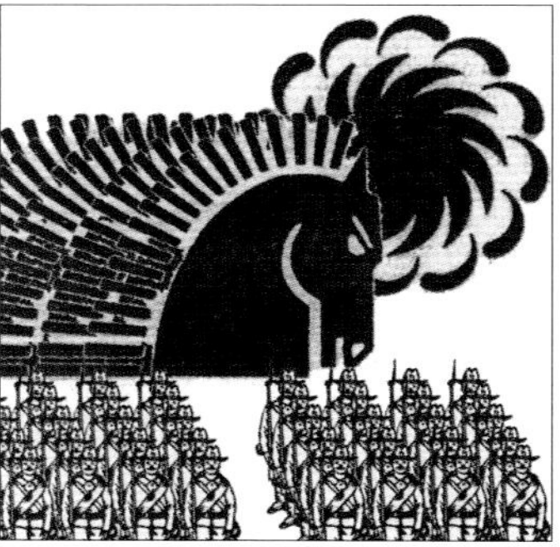

ALL THE KING'S HORSES AND ALL THE KING'S MEN

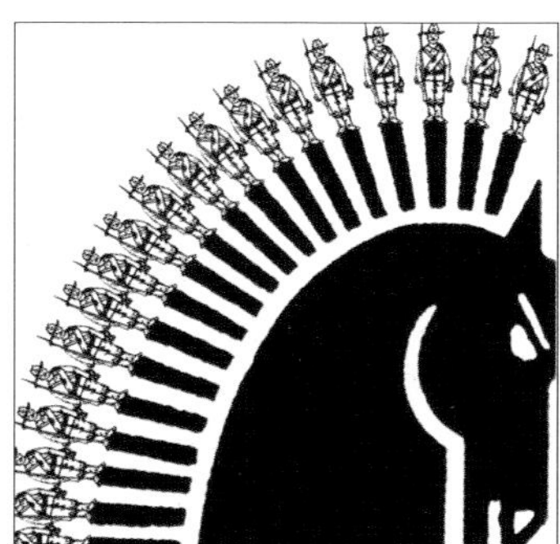

ALL THE KING'S HORSES AND ALL THE KING'S MEN

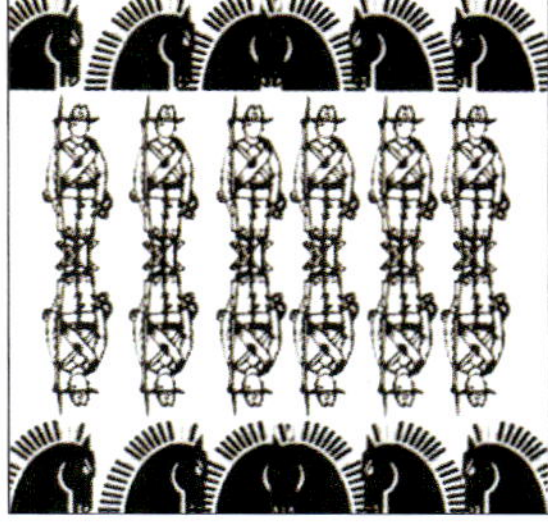
ALL THE KING'S HORSES AND ALL THE KING'S MEN

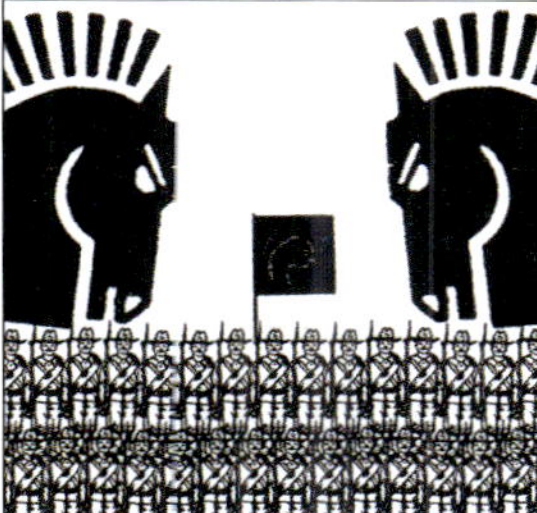
ALL THE KING'S HORSES AND ALL THE KING'S MEN

ALL THE KING'S HORSES AND ALL THE KING'S MEN

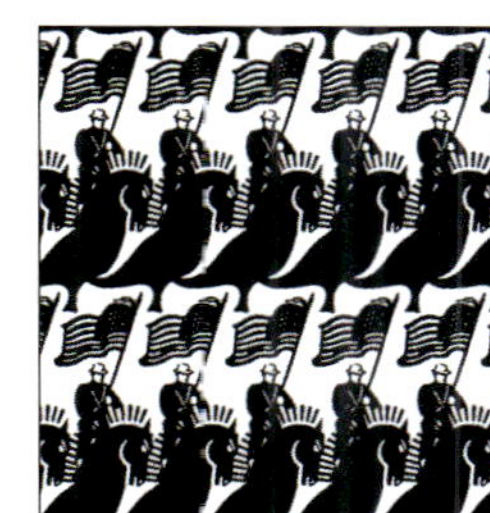
ALL THE KING'S HORSES AND ALL THE KING'S MEN

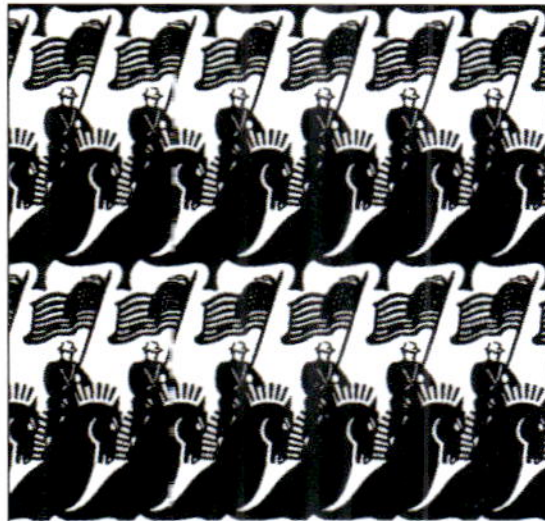
ALL THE KING'S HORSES AND ALL THE KING'S MEN

ALL THE KING'S HORSES AND ALL THE KING'S MEN

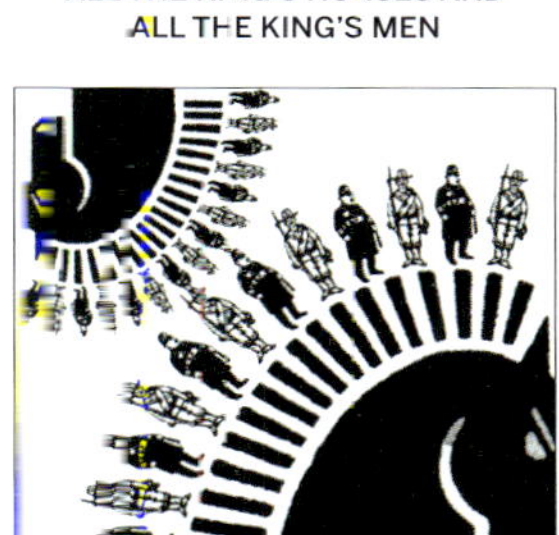
ALL THE KING'S HORSES AND ALL THE KING'S MEN

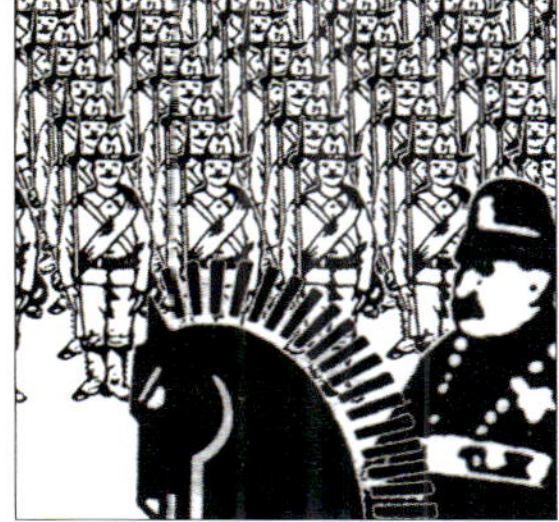
ALL THE KING'S HORSES AND ALL THE KING'S MEN

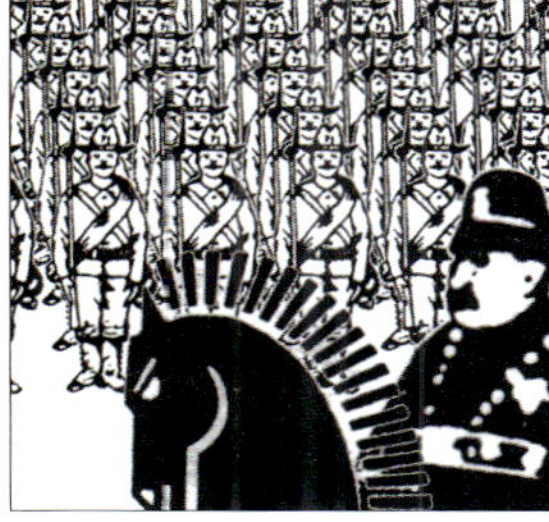
ALL THE KING'S HORSES AND ALL THE KING'S MEN

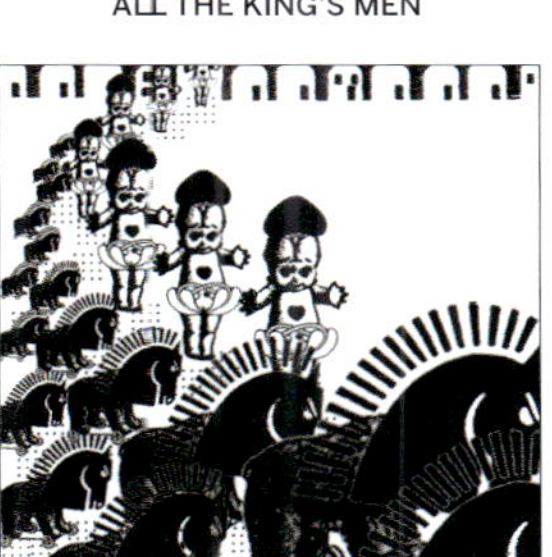
ALL THE KING'S HORSES AND ALL THE KING'S MEN

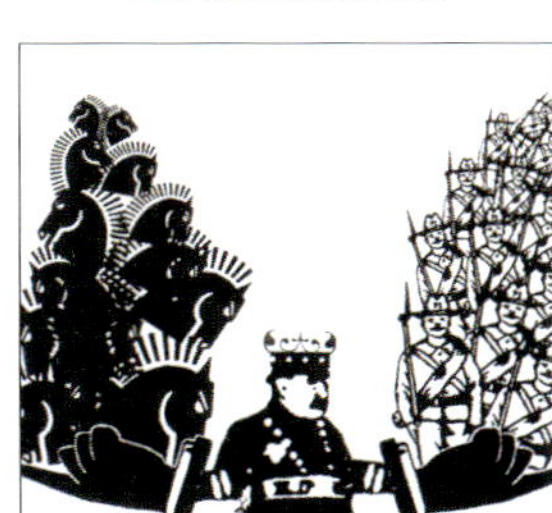
ALL THE KING'S HORSES AND ALL THE KING'S MEN

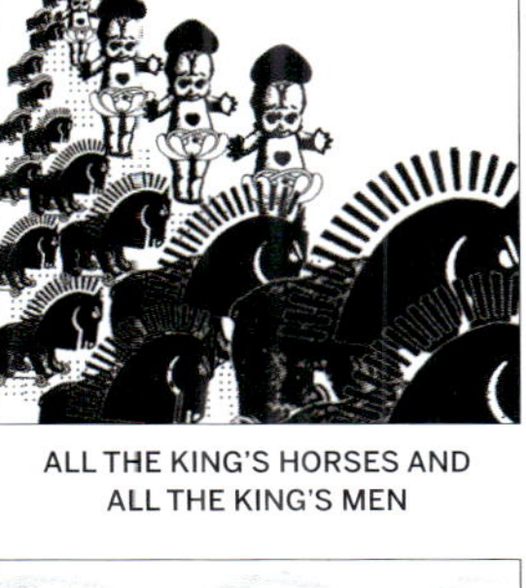
ALL THE KING'S HORSES AND ALL THE KING'S MEN

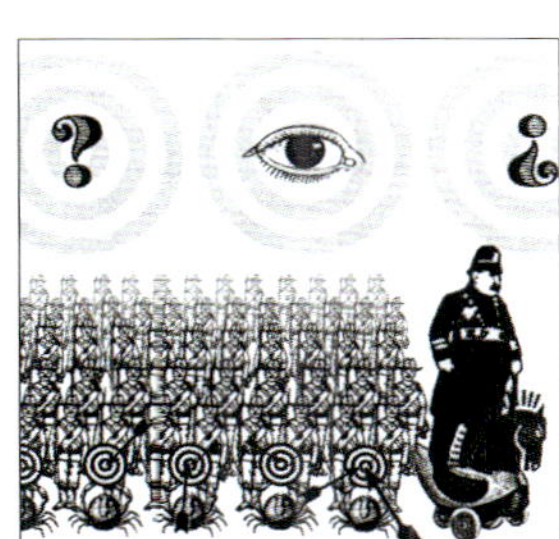
ALL THE KING'S HORSES AND ALL THE KING'S MEN

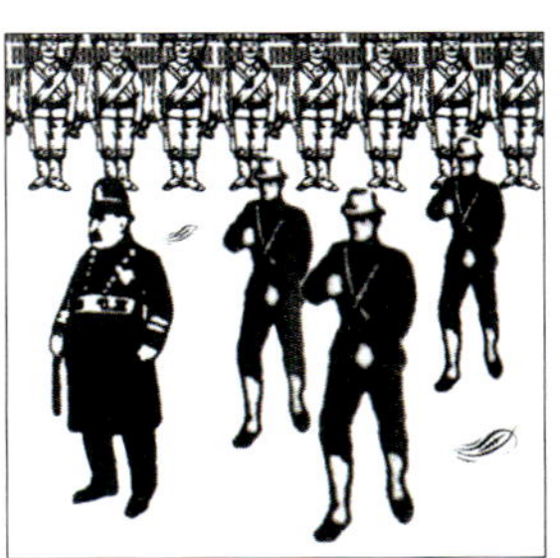
ALL THE KING'S HORSES AND ALL THE KING'S MEN

ALL THE KING'S HORSES AND ALL THE KING'S MEN

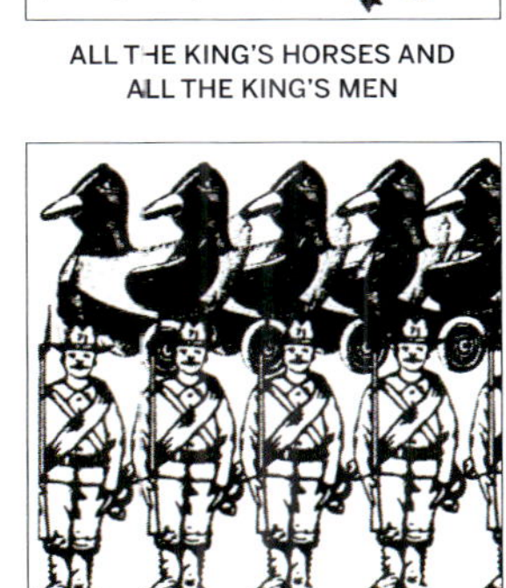
ALL THE KING'S HORSES AND ALL THE KING'S MEN

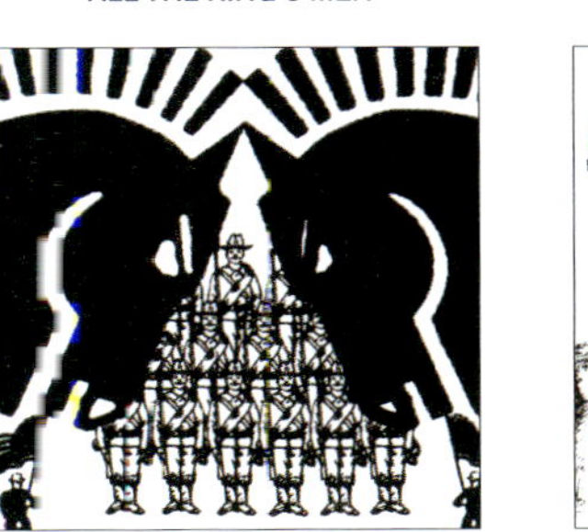
ALL THE KING'S HORSES AND ALL THE KING'S MEN

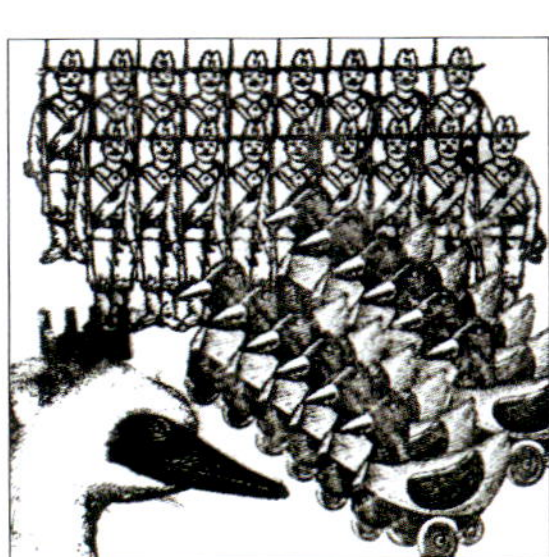
ALL THE KING'S HORSES AND ALL THE KING'S MEN

NURSERY RHYME SOLUTIONS:

Solutions 1 through 24 represent the third line of the "Humpty Dumpty" nursery rhyme. They vary in terms of the depiction of the king's men and horses, as well as the implementation of symmetry, asymmetry, pattern, scale, and space.

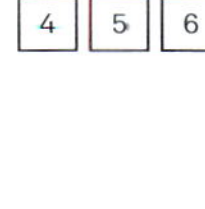

1. *Carrie Lam*
2. *Chris Brown*
3. *Gunyoung Park*
4. *Caroline Tak*
5. *Rochelle Jiang*
6. *Kyungmo Yang*
7. *Heesang Lee*
8. *Junghyun Ko*
9. *Enle Li*
10. *Kevin Harris*
11. *Heejae Choi*
12. *Haejin Chang*
13. *Borana Kim*
14. *Jeongyun Kim*
15. *Hanmyung Song*
16. *Chris Hawthorne*
17. *Nada Shin*
18. *Jackson Park*
19. *Chanju Yu*
20. *Jaeyoon Song*
21. *Jeonghyun Ahn*
22. *Sunyoung Yoon*
23. *Jaeyeon Lee*
24. *Maria Lotuffo*

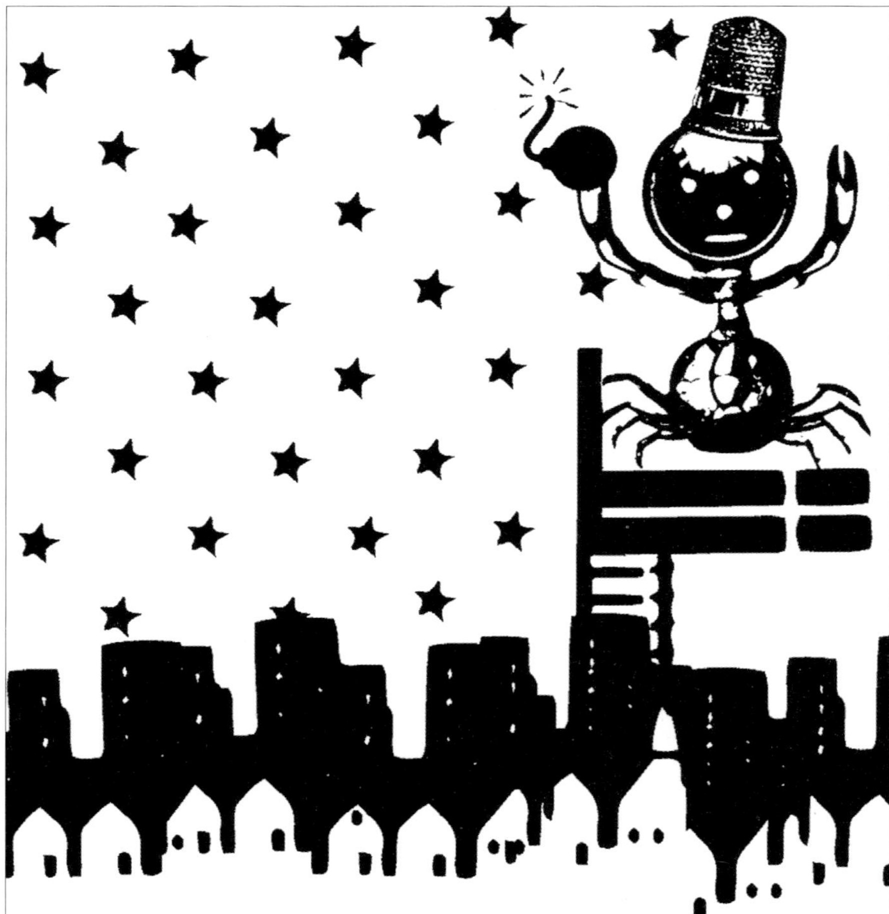

HUMPTY DUMPTY SAT ON A WALL,

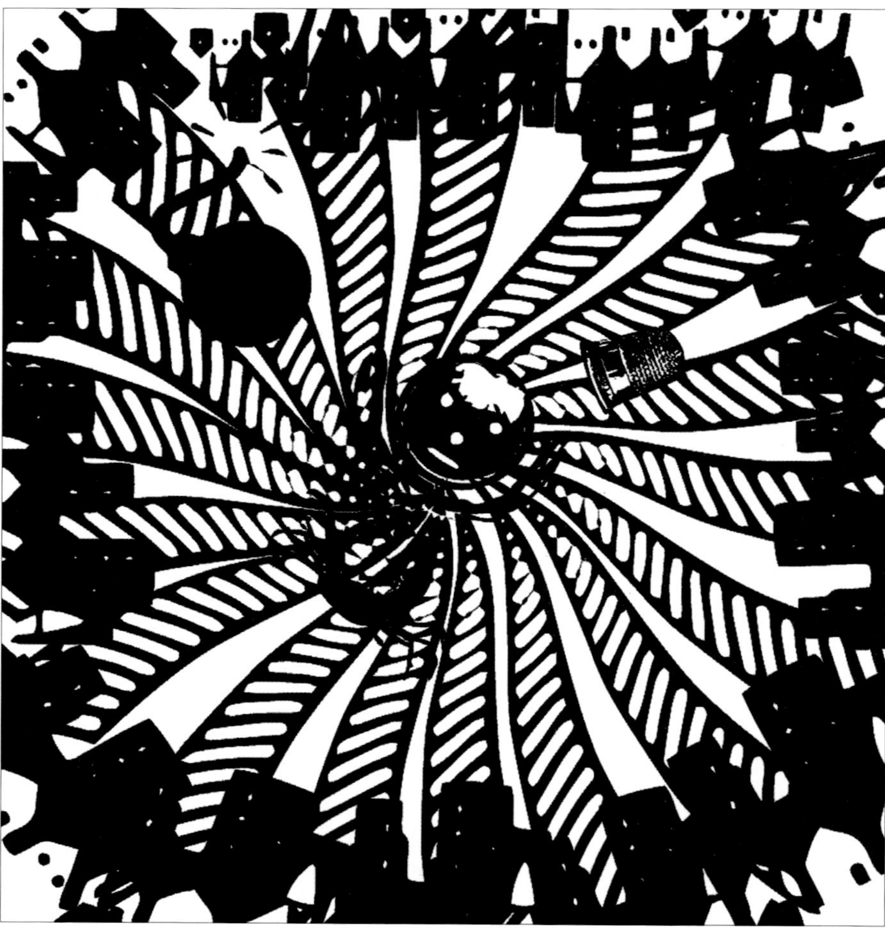

HUMPTY DUMPTY HAD A GREAT FALL.

NURSERY RHYME SOLUTIONS:

Figures 1 and 2 depict the first two lines of the rhyme, turning Humpty Dumpty into an allegorical figure who subsequently falls into a dizzying space.

Figures 3 through 8 represent the last two lines of the "Humpty Dumpty" rhyme, where figures 5 through 8 are depictions of an inability to put Humpty Dumpty together again.

ALL THE KING'S HORSES AND ALL THE KING'S MEN

COULDN'T PUT HUMPTY TOGETHER AGAIN.

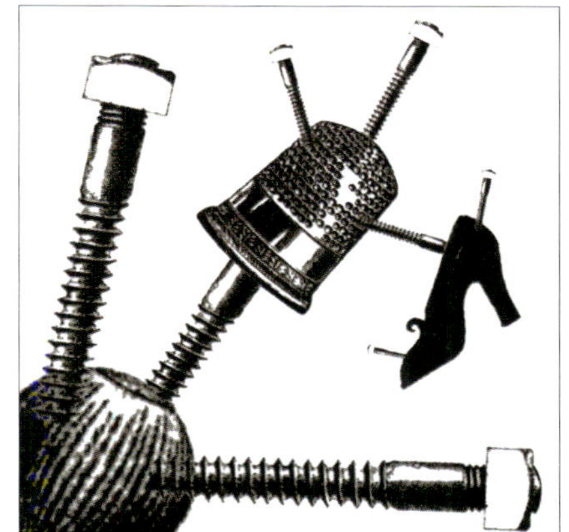

COULDN'T PUT HUMPTY TOGETHER AGAIN.

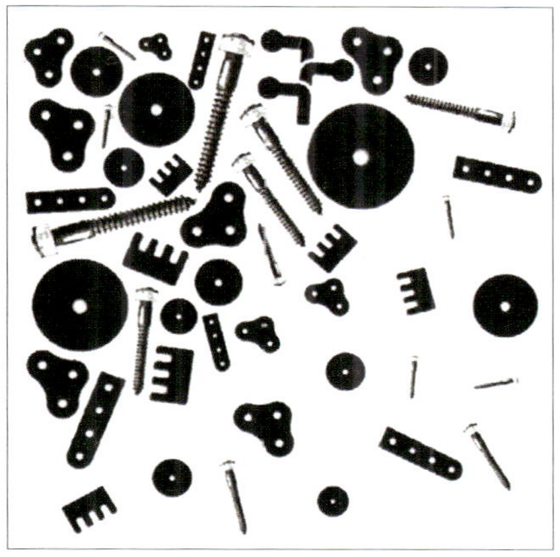

COULDN'T PUT HUMPTY TOGETHER AGAIN.

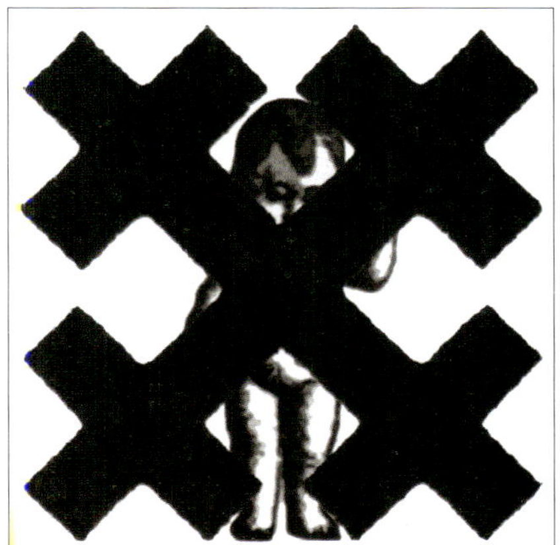

COULDN'T PUT HUMPTY TOGETHER AGAIN.

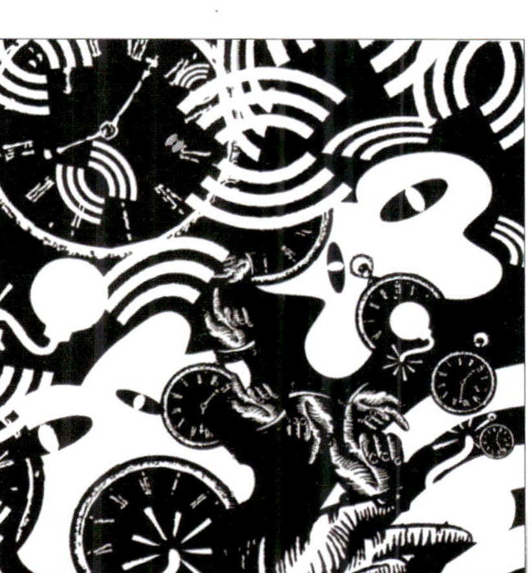

COULDN'T PUT HUMPTY TOGETHER AGAIN.

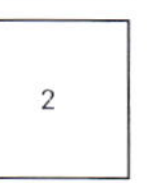

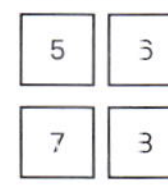

1–2. *June Hong*
3–4. *Seoungjun Lee*
5. *Brent Philhower*
6. *Duekhyun Kim*
7. *Youngyun Yang*
8. *Young Park*

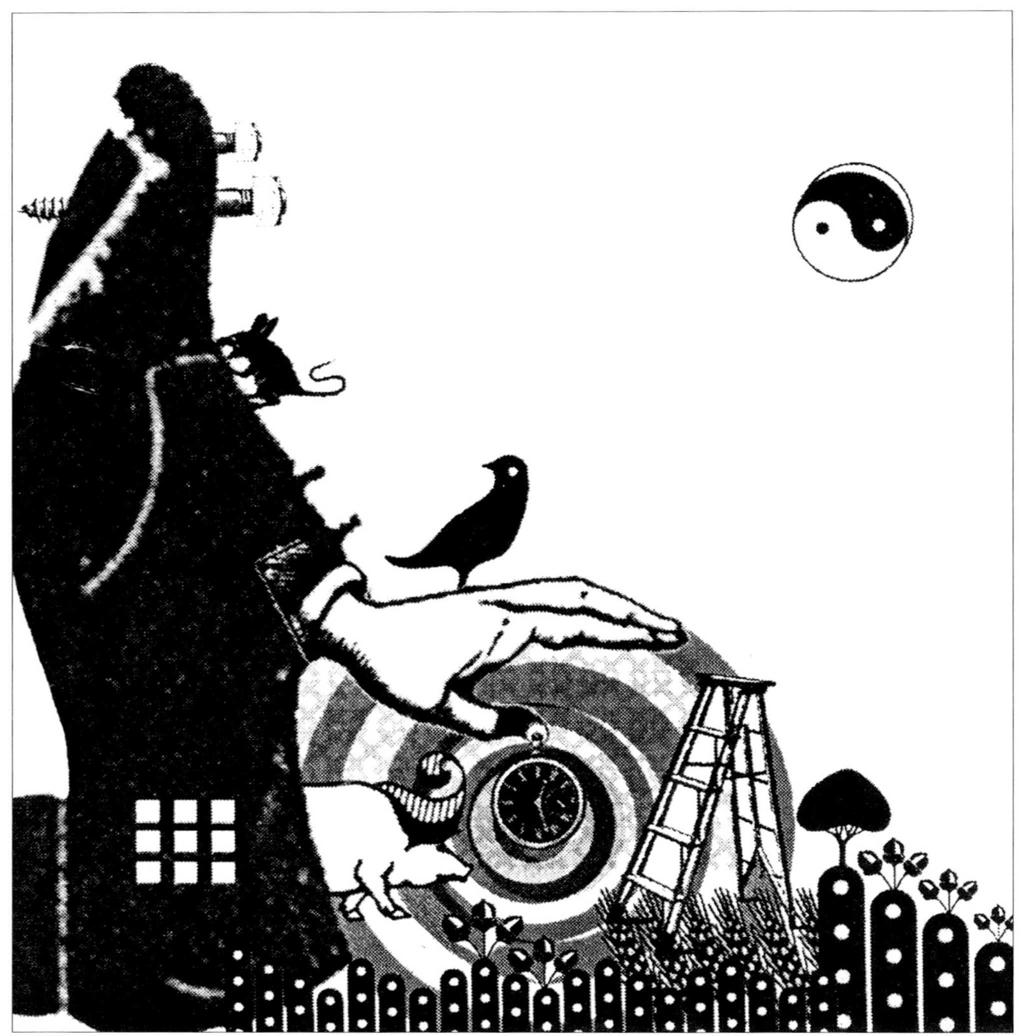

THERE WAS AN OLD WOMAN WHO LIVED IN A SHOE,

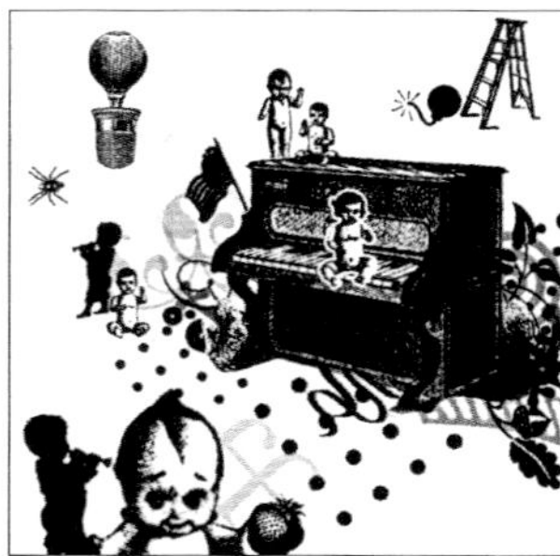

SHE HAD SO MANY CHILDREN SHE DIDN'T KNOW WHAT TO DO.

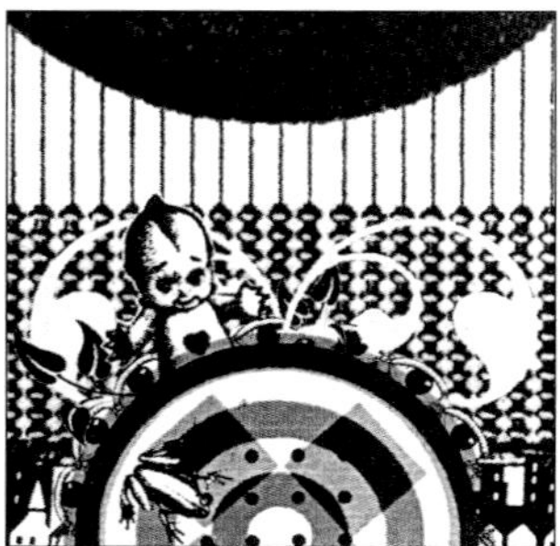

SHE GAVE THEM SOME BROTH WITHOUT ANY BREAD.

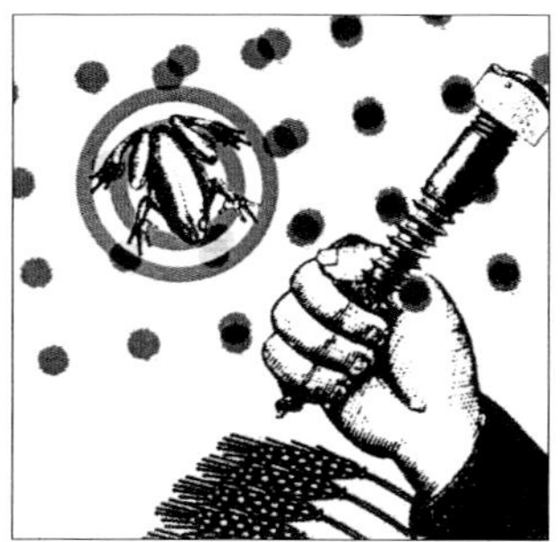

THEN WHIPPED THEM ALL SOUNDLY, AND PUT THEM TO BED.

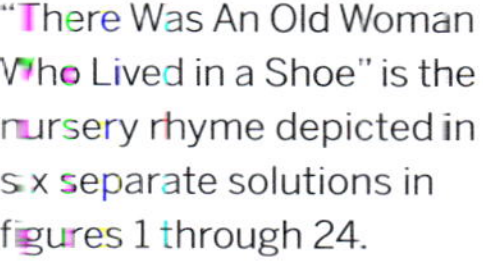

NURSERY RHYME SOLUTIONS:

"There Was An Old Woman Who Lived in a Shoe" is the nursery rhyme depicted in six separate solutions in figures 1 through 24.

The old woman living in the shoe is variously portrayed as a large hand, a strange bird, and a crab. The shoe is often shown as a shoe, but also, as a cash register and a thimble.

As in most nursery rhymes, fantasy is an important element that allows one the opportunity to suspend disbelief. Hence, the solutions range from narrative to symbolic, to allegorical imagery.

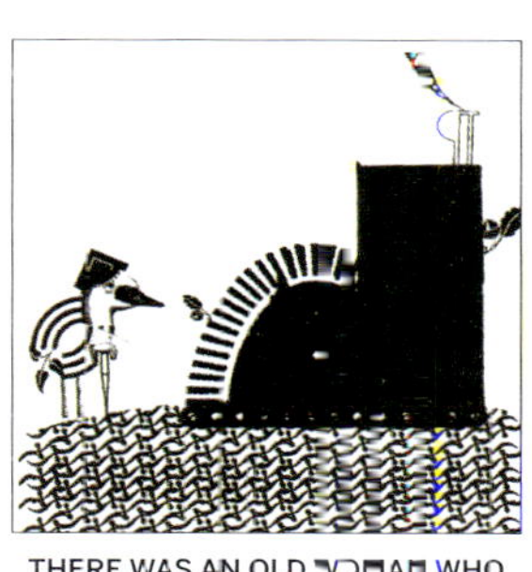

THERE WAS AN OLD WOMAN WHO LIVED IN A SHOE.

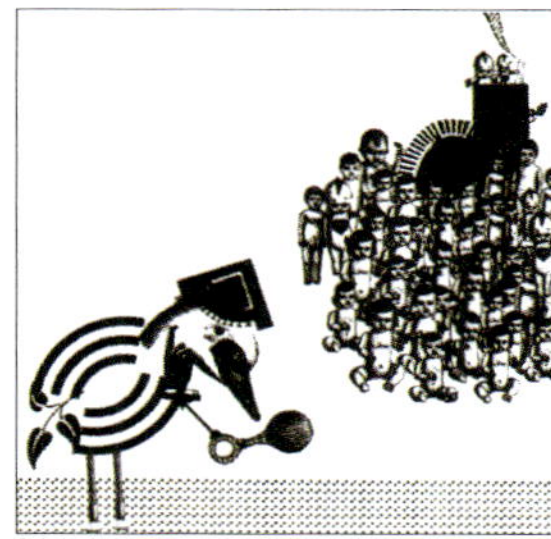

SHE HAD SO MANY CHILDREN SHE DIDN'T KNOW WHAT TO DO.

SHE GAVE THEM SOME BROTH WITHOUT ANY BREAD,

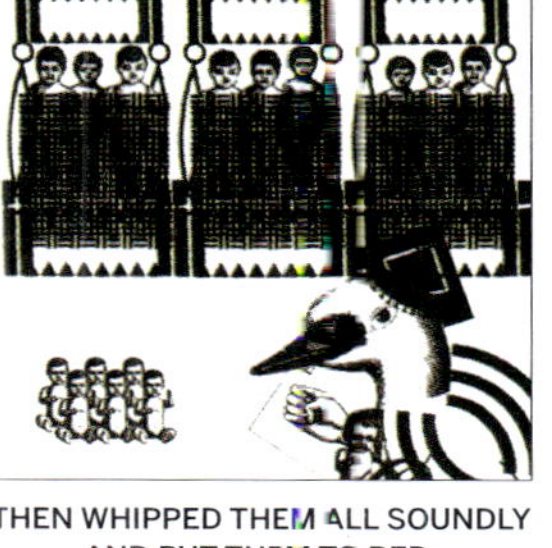

THEN WHIPPED THEM ALL SOUNDLY AND PUT THEM TO BED.

THERE WAS AN OLD WOMAN WHO LIVED IN A SHOE.

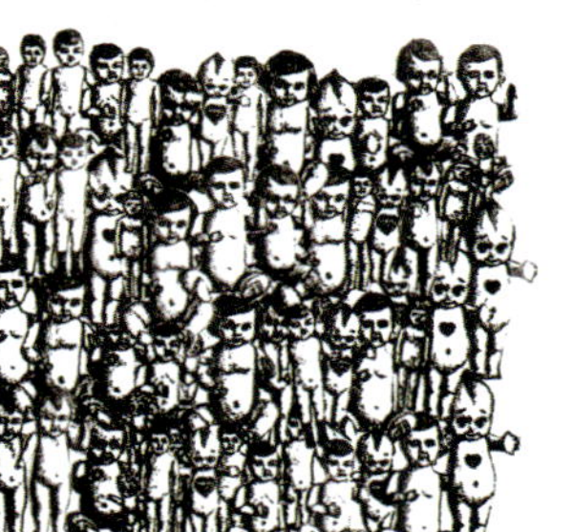

SHE HAD SO MANY CHILDREN SHE DIDN'T KNOW WHAT TO DO.

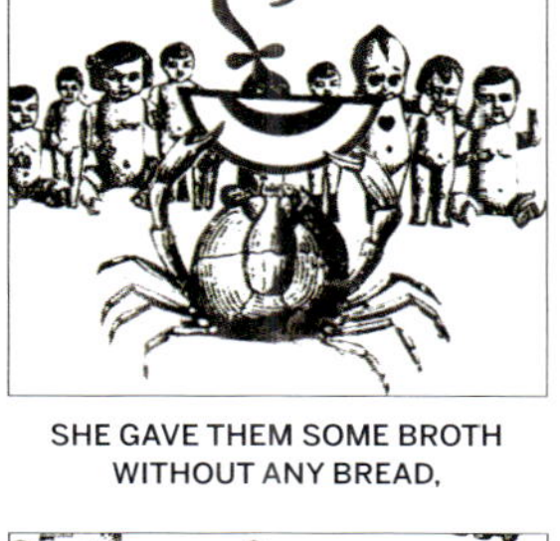

SHE GAVE THEM SOME BROTH WITHOUT ANY BREAD,

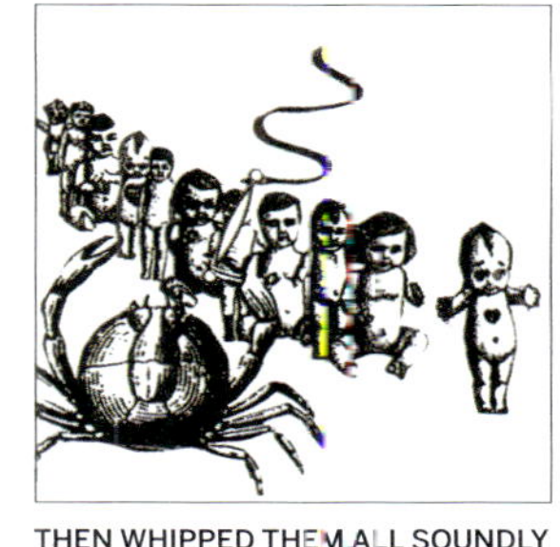

THEN WHIPPED THEM ALL SOUNDLY AND PUT THEM TO BED.

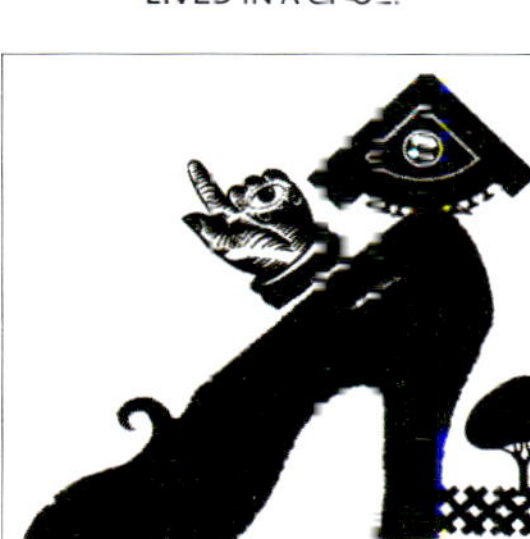

THERE WAS AN OLD WOMAN WHO LIVED IN A SHOE.

SHE HAD SO MANY CHILDREN SHE DIDN'T KNOW WHAT TO DO.

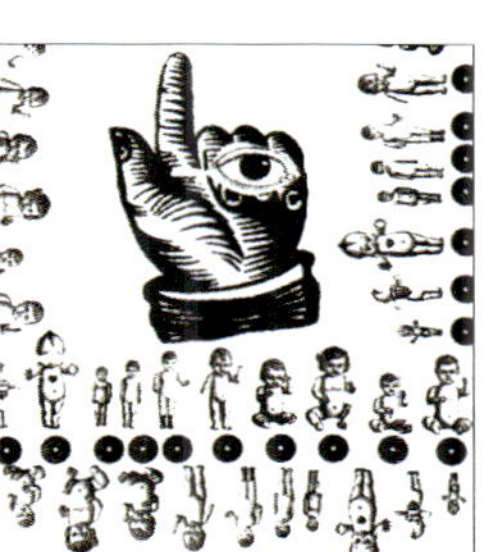

SHE GAVE THEM SOME BROTH WITHOUT ANY BREAD,

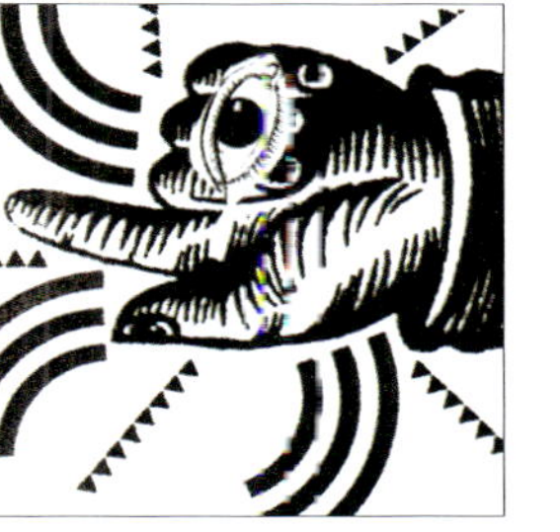

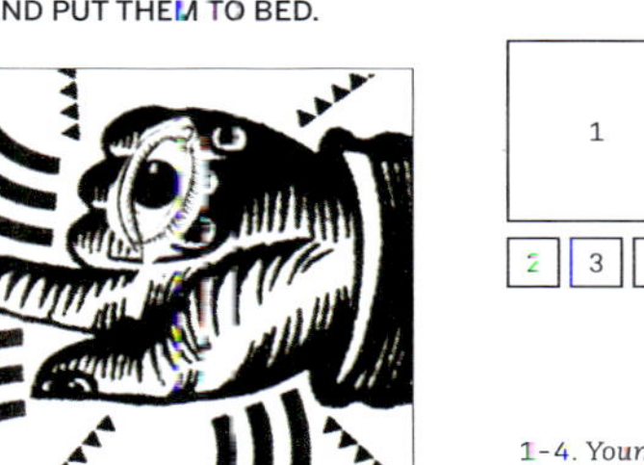

THEN WHIPPED THEM ALL SOUNDLY AND PUT THEM TO BED.

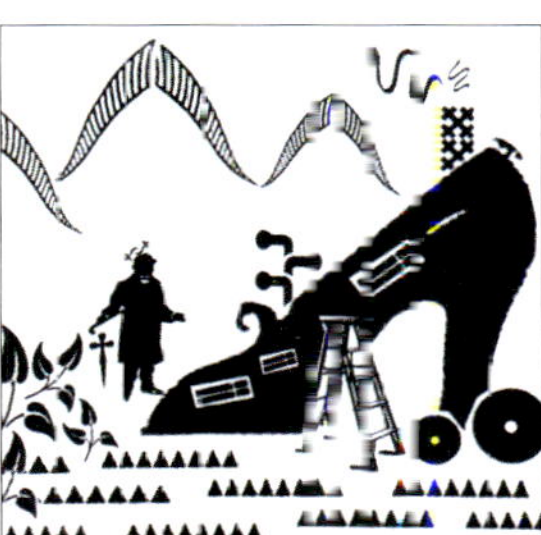

THERE WAS AN OLD WOMAN WHO LIVED IN A SHOE.

SHE HAD SO MANY CHILDREN SHE DIDN'T KNOW WHAT TO DO.

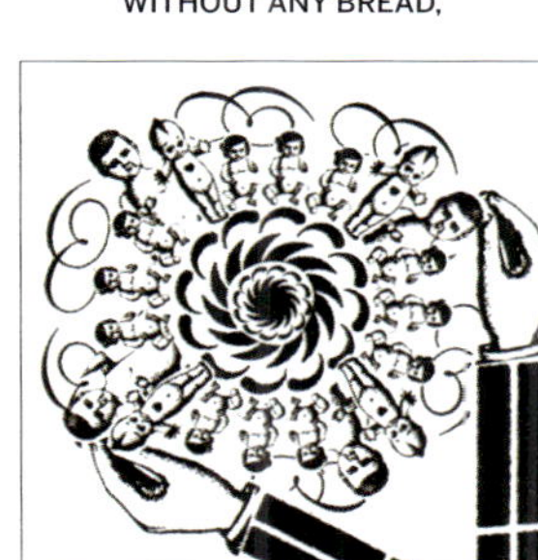

SHE GAVE THEM SOME BROTH WITHOUT ANY BREAD,

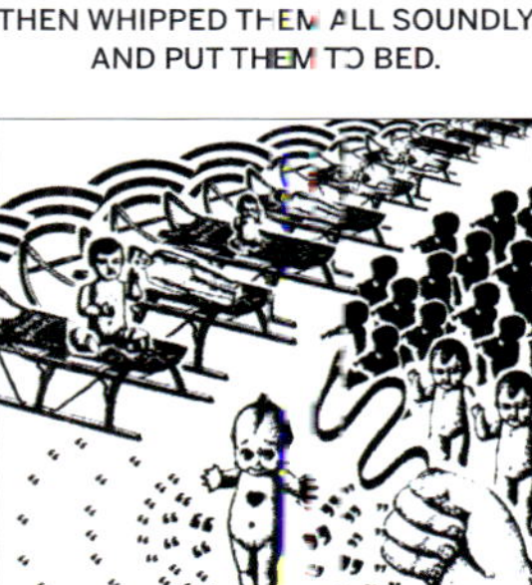

THEN WHIPPED THEM ALL SOUNDLY AND PUT THEM TO BED.

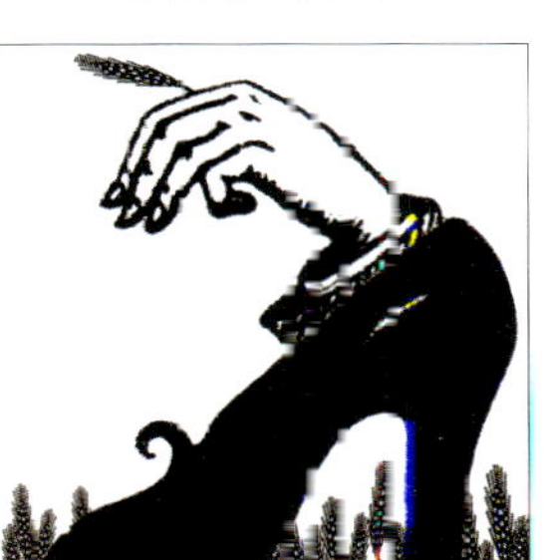

THERE WAS AN OLD WOMAN WHO LIVED IN A SHOE.

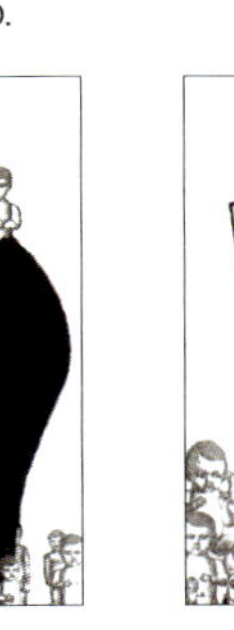

SHE HAD SO MANY CHILDREN SHE DIDN'T KNOW WHAT TO DO.

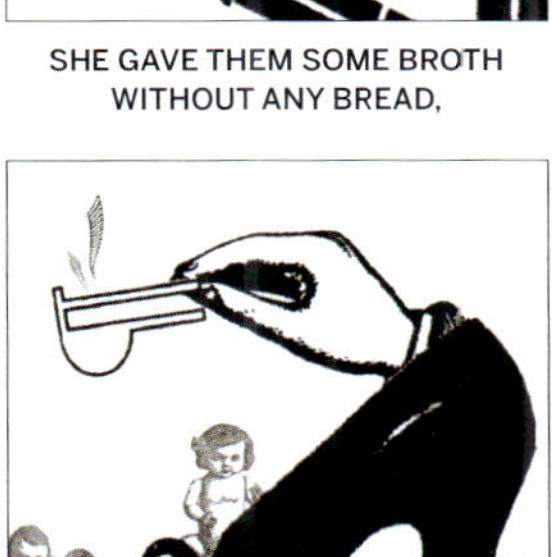

SHE GAVE THEM SOME BROTH WITHOUT ANY BREAD,

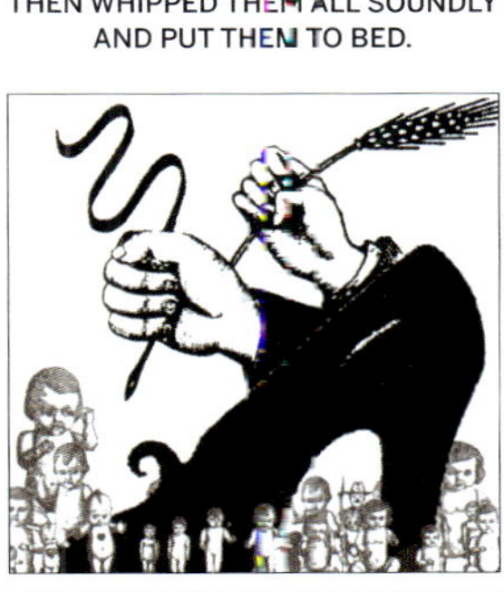

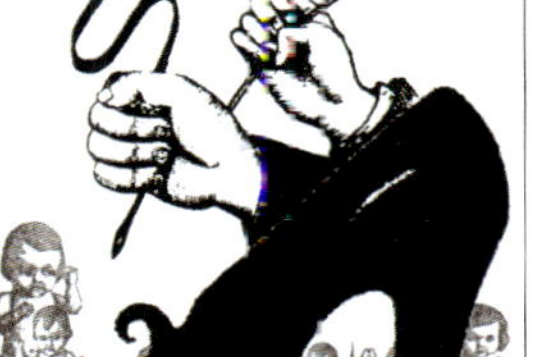

THEN WHIPPED THEM ALL SOUNDLY AND PUT THEM TO BED.

1–4. Youngmi Jung
5–8. Sunmin Chung
9–12. Emily Bertone
13–16. Erika Yost
17–20. Miseong Park
21–24. Steve Choi

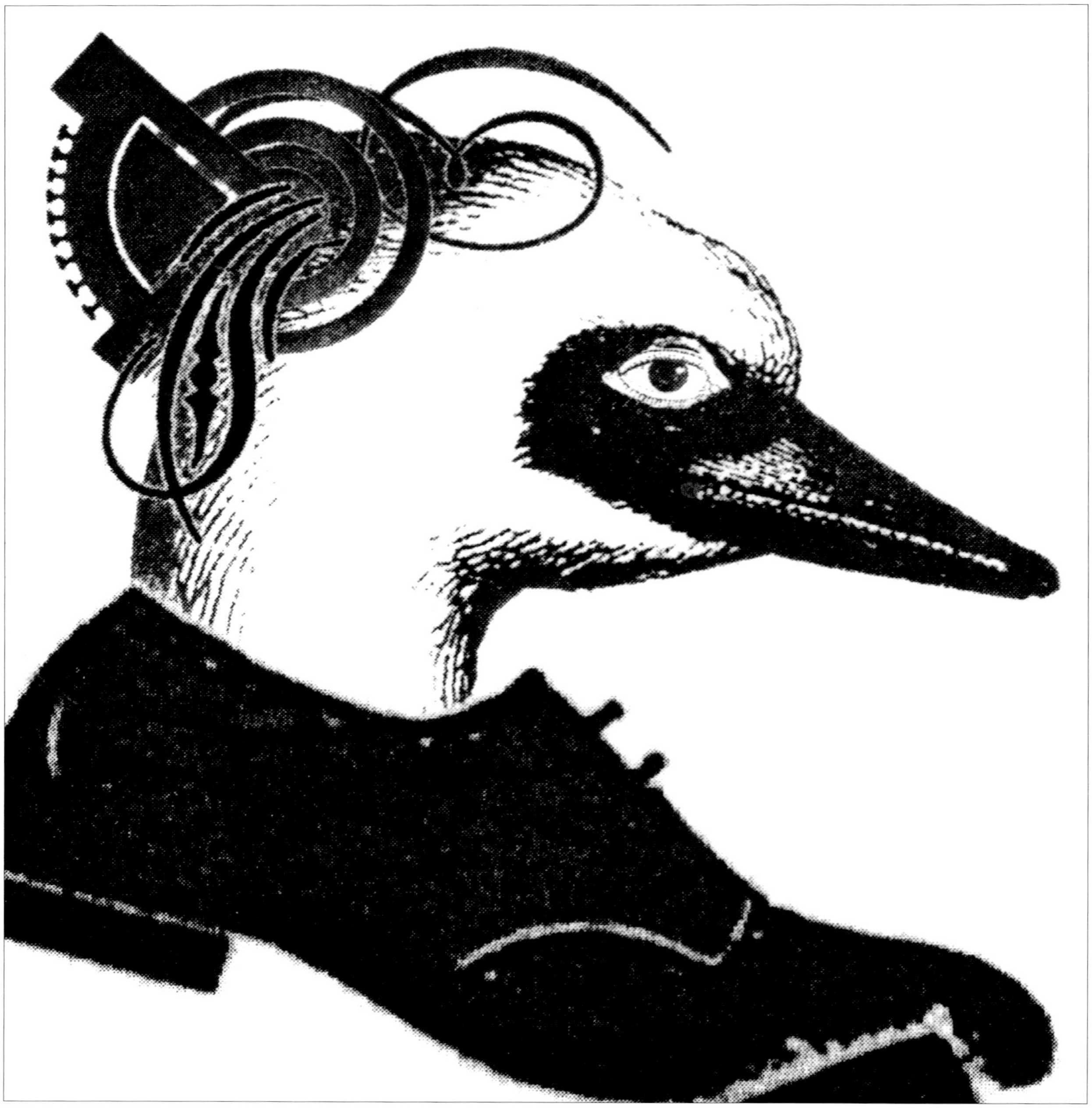

THERE WAS AN OLD WOMAN WHO LIVED IN A SHOE,

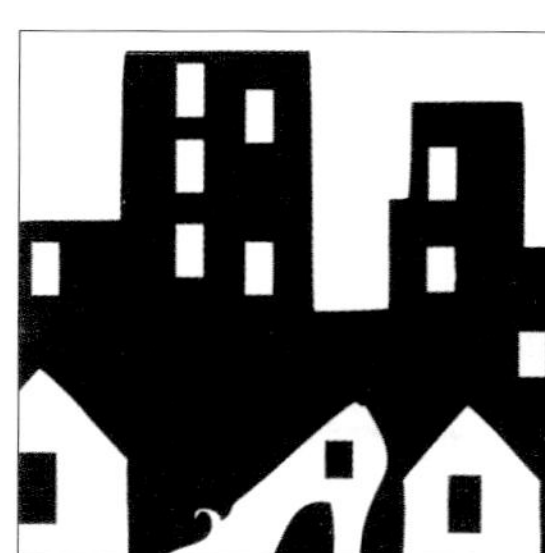

THERE WAS AN OLD WOMAN WHO LIVED IN A SHOE,

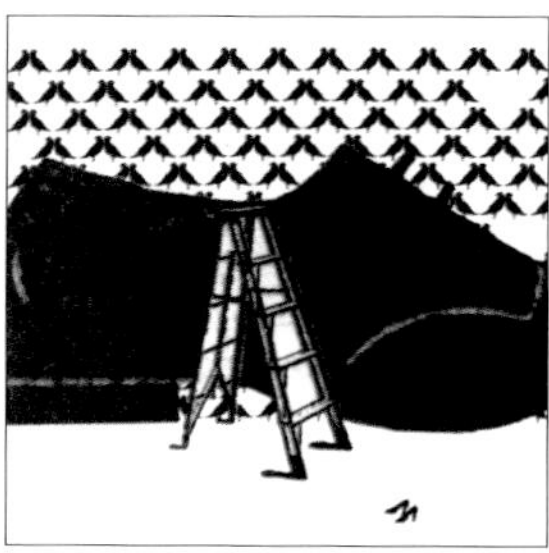

THERE WAS AN OLD WOMAN WHO LIVED IN A SHOE,

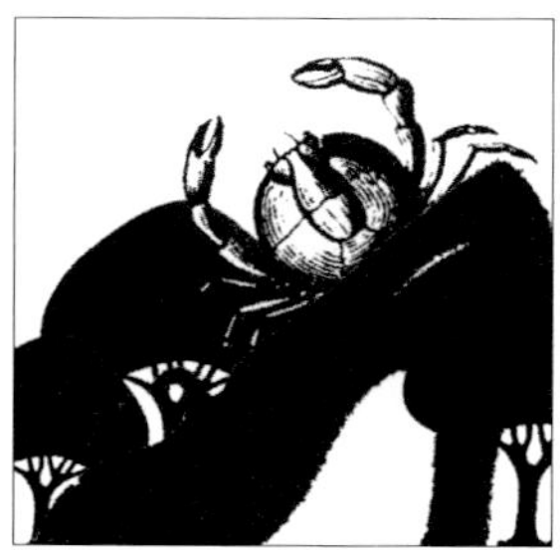

THERE WAS AN OLD WOMAN WHO LIVED IN A SHOE,

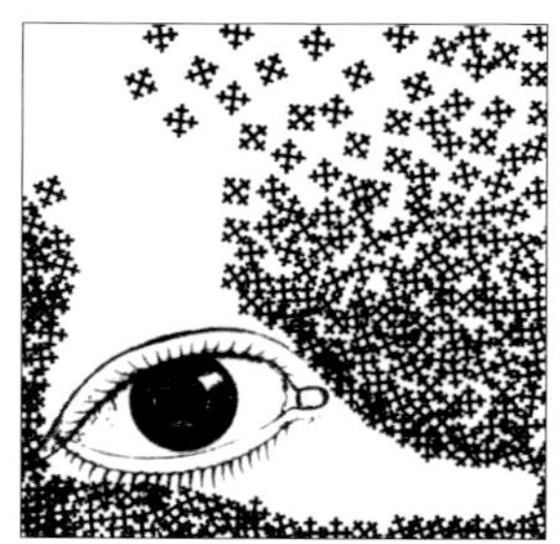

THERE WAS AN OLD WOMAN WHO LIVED IN A SHOE,

NURSERY RHYME SOLUTIONS:

Figures 1 through 5 represent five different interpretations of the line "There was an old woman who lived in a shoe", which utilize different spatial compositions.

Figures 6 through 15 all deal with the line "She had so many children she didn't know what to do." Here the sense of congestion and overcrowding are the overriding formal considerations.

Figure 11 humorously highlights the "old woman's" ability to propagate, while at the same time conveying congestion. In all these solutions exaggeration in terms of numbers is utilized to heighten the visual impact.

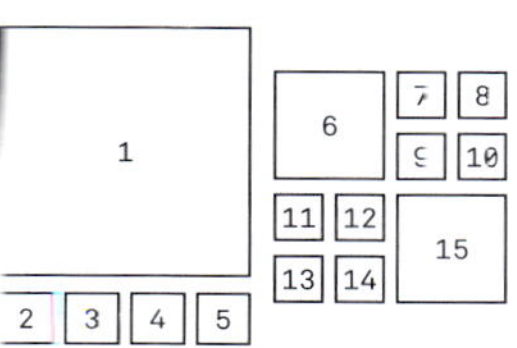

1. Heesang Lee
2. Holly Trotta
3. Josselin Altere
4. Gin Chen
5. Jihyun Park
6. Elaine Park
7. Kyung Hwang
8. Borana Kim
9. Rochelle Jiang
10. Jeonghyun Ahn
11. Duekhyun Kim
12. Jacob Rowe
13. Yuri Byun
14. Youngmi Jung
15. Misuk Suh

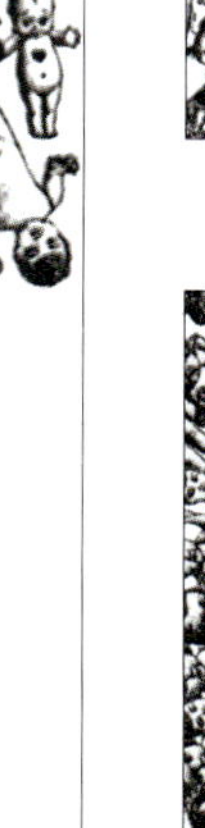

SHE HAD SO MANY CHILDREN SHE DIDN'T KNOW WHAT TO DO.

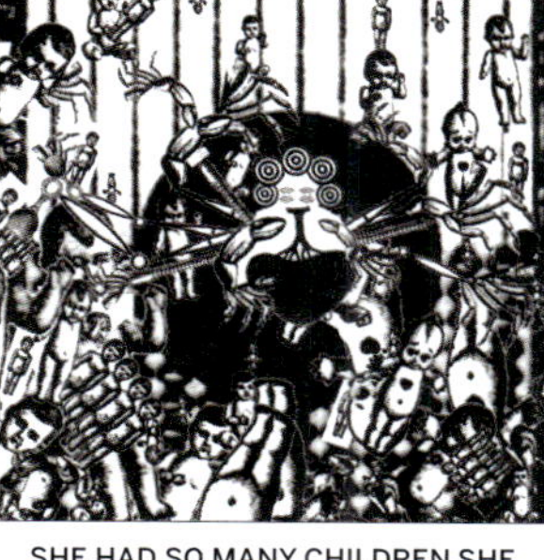

SHE HAD SO MANY CHILDREN SHE DIDN'T KNOW WHAT TO DO.

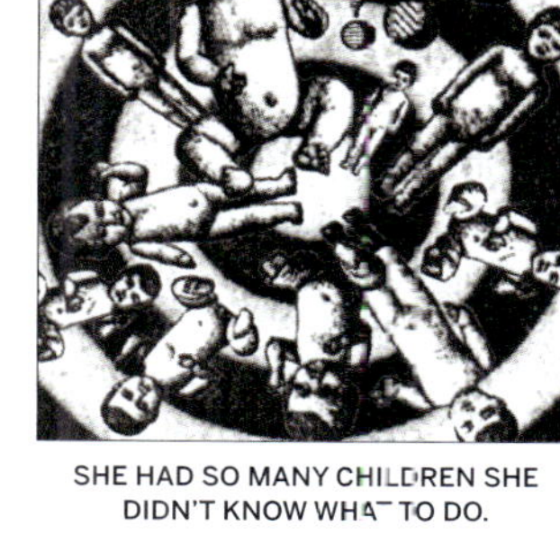

SHE HAD SO MANY CHILDREN SHE DIDN'T KNOW WHAT TO DO.

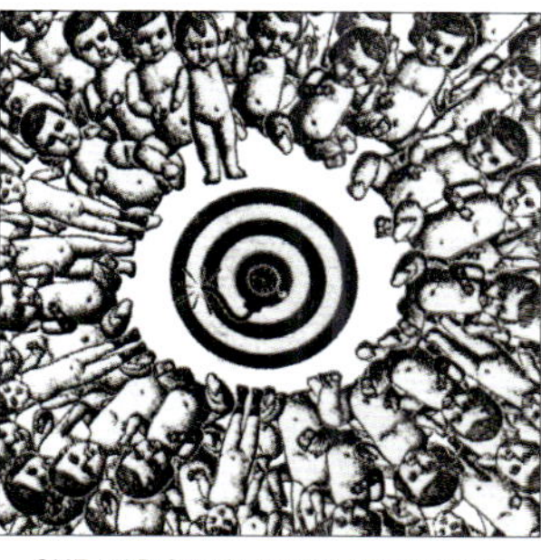

SHE HAD SO MANY CHILDREN SHE DIDN'T KNOW WHAT TO DO.

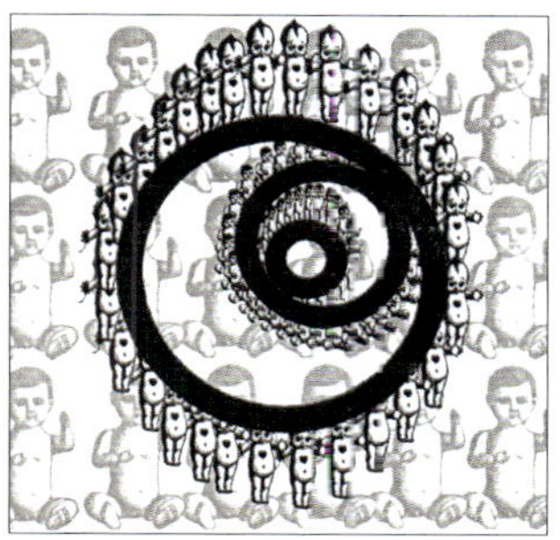

SHE HAD SO MANY CHILDREN SHE DIDN'T KNOW WHAT TO DO.

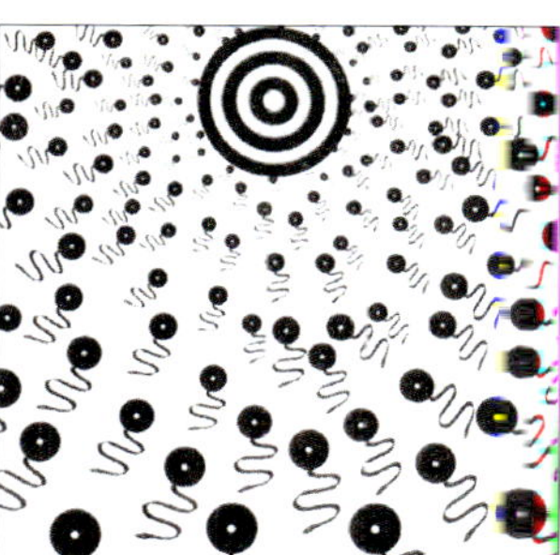

SHE HAD SO MANY CHILDREN SHE DIDN'T KNOW WHAT TO DO.

SHE HAD SO MANY CHILDREN SHE DIDN'T KNOW WHAT TO DO.

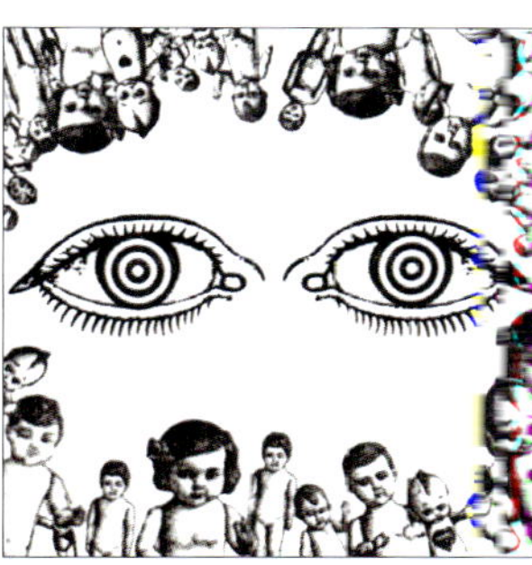

SHE HAD SO MANY CHILDREN SHE DIDN'T KNOW WHAT TO DO.

SHE HAD SO MANY CHILDREN SHE DIDN'T KNOW WHAT TO DO.

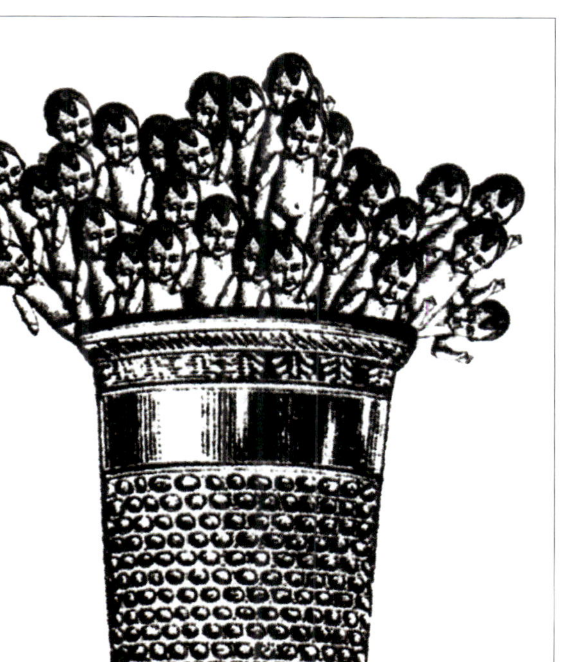

SHE HAD SO MANY CHILDREN SHE DIDN'T KNOW WHAT TO DO.

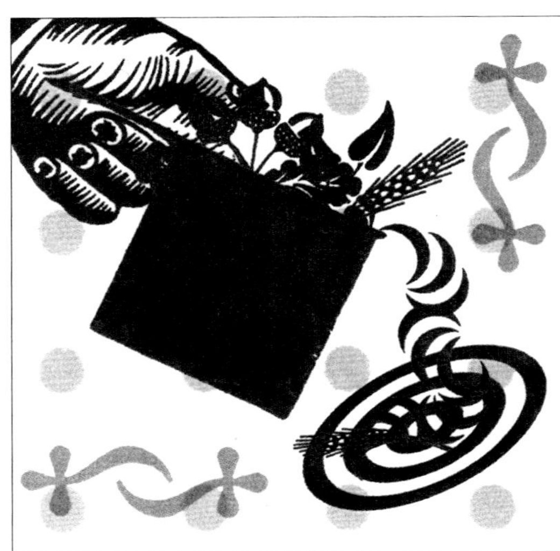

SHE GAVE THEM SOME BROTH
WITHOUT ANY BREAD,

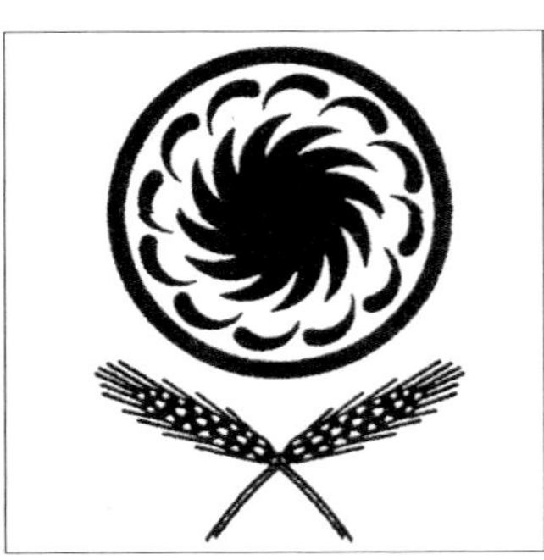

SHE GAVE THEM SOME BROTH
WITHOUT ANY BREAD,

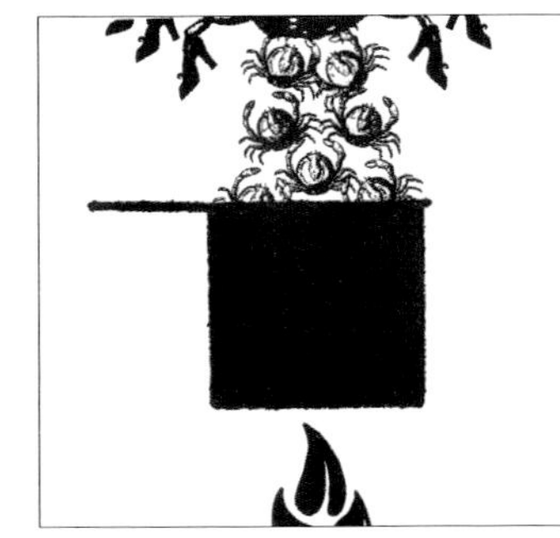

SHE GAVE THEM SOME BROTH
WITHOUT ANY BREAD,

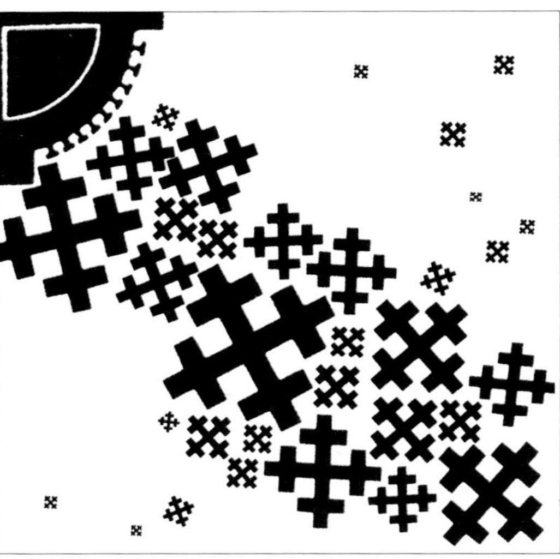

SHE GAVE THEM SOME BROTH
WITHOUT ANY BREAD,

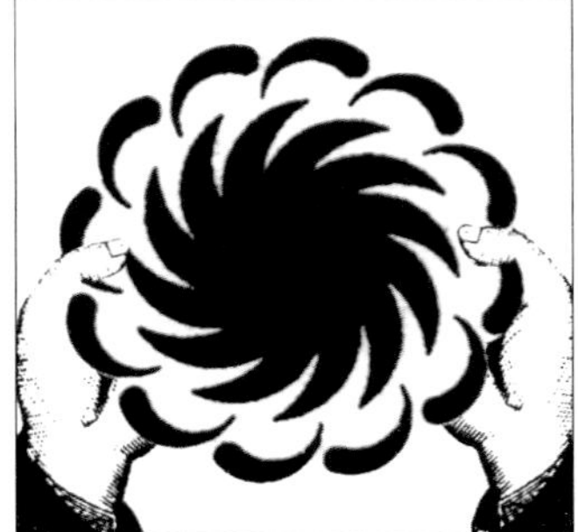

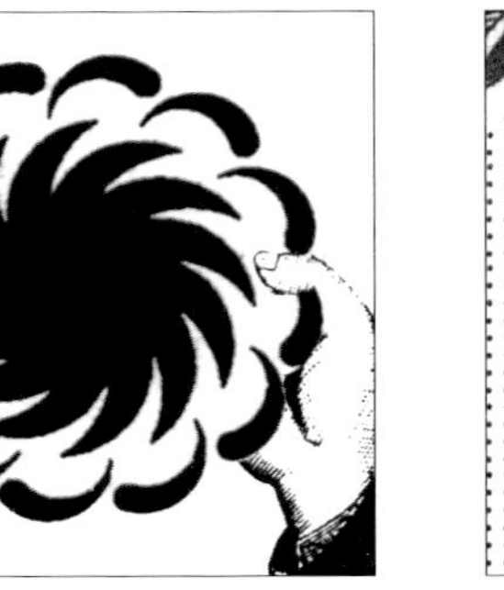

SHE GAVE THEM SOME BROTH
WITHOUT ANY BREAD,

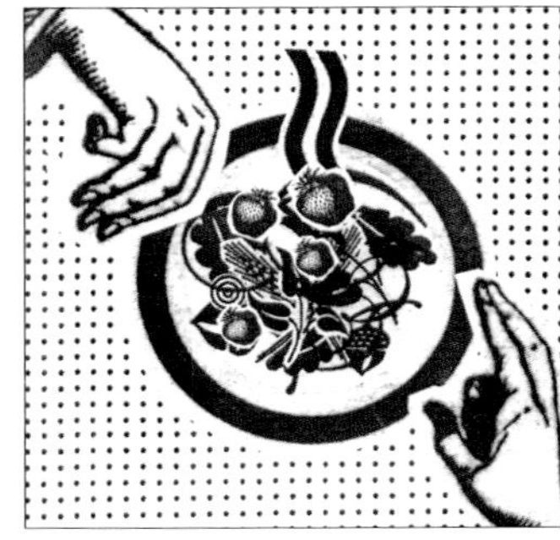

SHE GAVE THEM SOME BROTH
WITHOUT ANY BREAD,

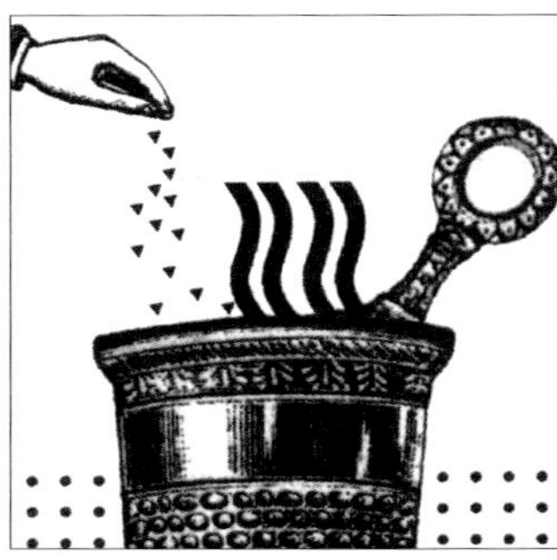

SHE GAVE THEM SOME BROTH
WITHOUT ANY BREAD,

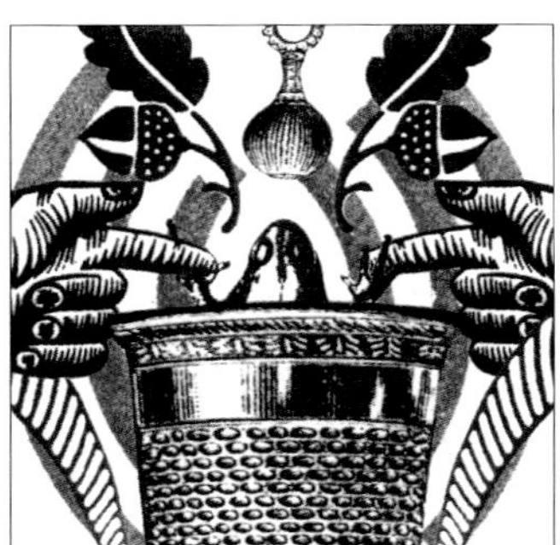

SHE GAVE THEM SOME BROTH
WITHOUT ANY BREAD,

THEN WHIPPED THEM ALL SOUNDLY AND PUT THEM TO BED.

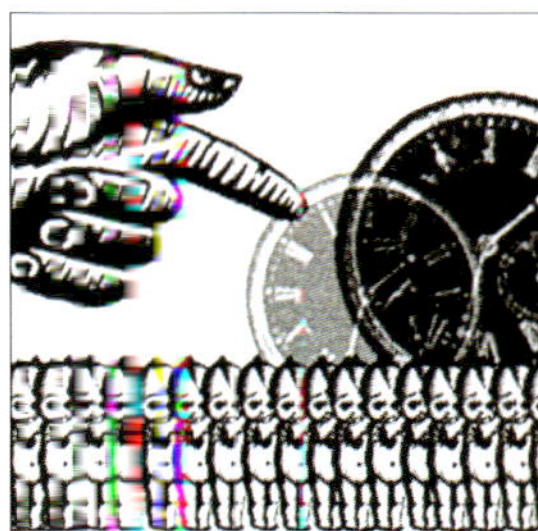

THEN WHIPPED THEM ALL SOUNDLY AND PUT THEM TO BED.

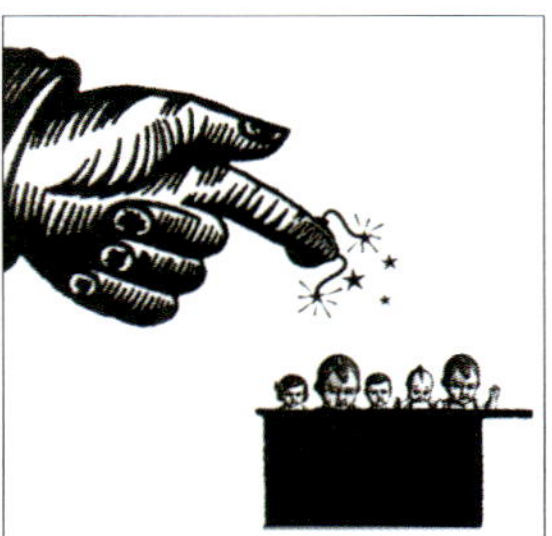

THEN WHIPPED THEM ALL SOUNDLY AND PUT THEM TO BED.

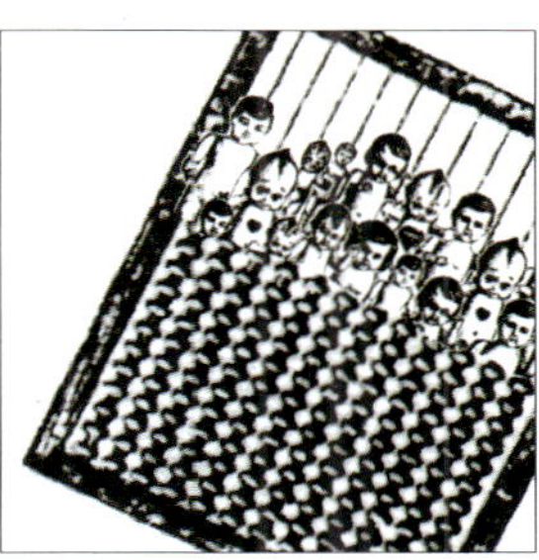

THEN WHIPPED THEM ALL SOUNDLY AND PUT THEM TO BED.

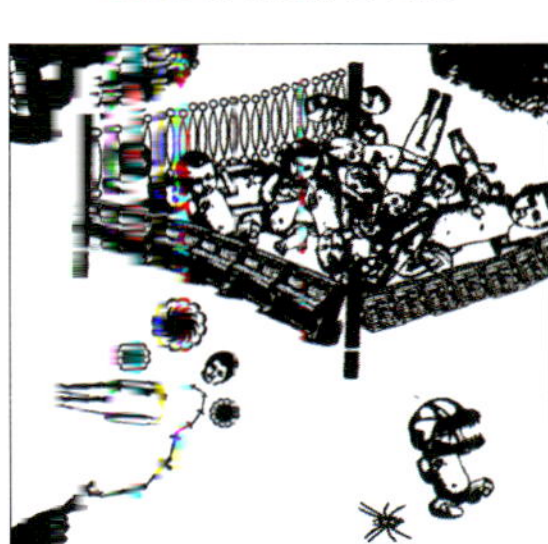

THEN WHIPPED THEM ALL SOUNDLY AND PUT THEM TO BED.

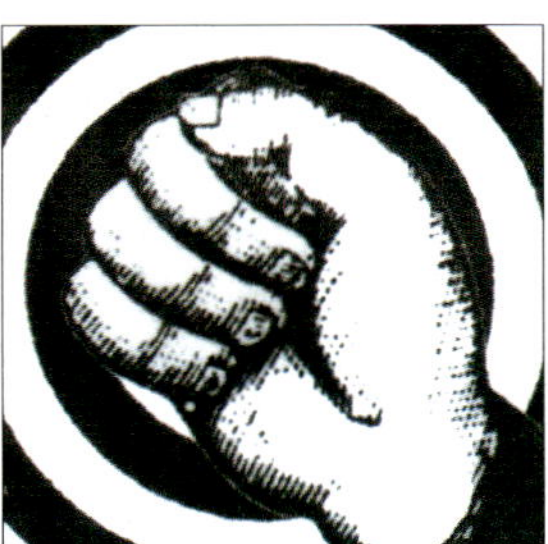

THEN WHIPPED THEM ALL SOUNDLY AND PUT THEM TO BED.

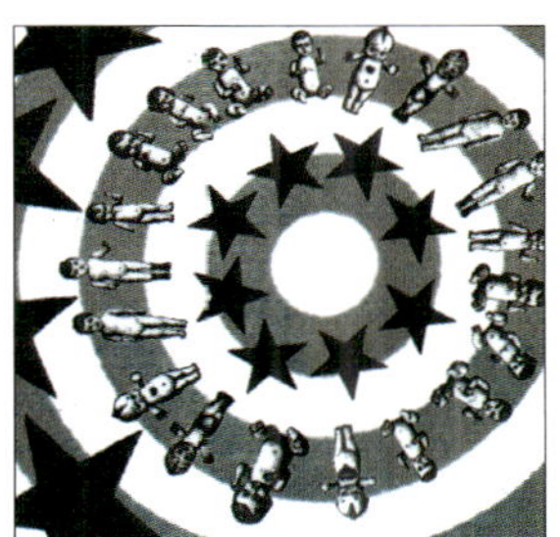

THEN WHIPPED THEM ALL SOUNDLY AND PUT THEM TO BED.

NURSERY RHYME SOLUTIONS:

"She gave them some broth without any bread" is depicted in figures 1 through 8. The activities of cooking, feeding, pouring, and serving are addressed in these solutions.

Figures 9 through 15 use the design principle of scale to create an ominous scenario in their interpretation of the last line, "Then whipped them all soundly and put them to bed." In figure 9, the old woman is portrayed as a robotic machine, lifting and placing each child into bed.

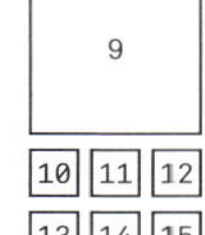

1 Youjung Choi
2 Soyun Lee
3 Joo Leng Lucien Ng
4 Jacob Rowe
5 Fnu Herry
6 Aurelie Joly
7 Sooim Heo
8 Jahye Chai
9 Kyung Hwang
10 Caroline Tak
11 Seoseung Kim
12 Alexandra Barron
13 Young Park
14 Maxwell Beucler
15 Sujin Jung

THOUGHTS ON THE CREATIVE PROCESS 6

Creative problem solving encompasses risk taking and the ability to dare. Fear of failure, the inability to begin, and playing it safe keeps one from moving in the direction of openness, where one's innate creativity lies.

TYPOGRAPHIC PORTRAITS

USING YOUR WHOLE NAME, PART OF YOUR NAME, YOUR NICKNAME, OR YOUR INITIALS, CREATE A TYPOGRAPHIC PORTRAIT FOR EACH SUBJECT INDICATED BELOW. DEPICT YOUR NAME IN THE GIVEN AREAS TAKING INTO CONSIDERATION THE STYLE, WEIGHT, SIZE OF TYPEFACE, THE USE OF UPPER OR LOWERCASE CHARACTERS, AS WELL AS THE SPACE BETWEEN EACH LETTER. FORMAL CONSIDERATIONS SHOULD INCLUDE: CROPPING, TOUCHING, OVERLAPPING, INTERSECTING AND PENETRATING OF ELEMENTS. USE EITHER BLACK AND WHITE OR COLOR TO EXECUTE YOUR SOLUTIONS.

MY NAME IS

AND I WORK ON AN ASSEMBLY LINE

MY NAME IS

AND I'M AN OPTOMETRIST

MY NAME IS

AND I'M A PARASITE

MY NAME IS

AND I'M A LIBRARIAN

MY NAME IS

AND I'M AN INSOMNIAC

MY NAME IS

AND I'M A BUTTERFLY COLLECTOR

MY NAME IS

AND I'M A CAKE DECORATOR

MY NAME IS

AND I'M A PROFESSIONAL RACE CAR DRIVER

MY NAME IS

AND I'M A CHAIN SMOKER

MY NAME IS

AND I WAS PABLO PICASSO IN A PAST LIFE

MY NAME IS

AND I'M A POSTAL WORKER

MY NAME IS

AND I'M AN EXPERT VIDEO GAME PLAYER

PROBLEMS : SOLUTIONS SERIES

CREATED BY RICHARD WILDE / JUDITH WILDE, PRODUCED BY VISUAL ARTS PRESS, LTD. ART DIRECTORS: RICHARD WILDE / JUDITH WILDE

TYPOGRAPHIC PORTRAIT PROBLEM:

Create typographic portraits by using your whole name, part of your name, your nickname or your initials to describe the twelve subjects indicated on the assignment sheet.

Each solution must be executed considering: choice of typeface, style, size, weight, the use of upper and lowercase characters, as well as the space between each letter.

AIM:
The aim of this project is to use typography as an end in itself, minimizing supporting imagery.

SUGGESTIONS:
Formal considerations should be taken into account including: cropping, touching, overlapping, intersecting, and penetration of elements. If you create your own typeface, pay close attention to the proportions of each character. Also, grappling with the nuances of each subject and taking on the persona of the character will move you toward a place where new ideas arise.

SPECIFICATIONS:
Use black and white or color to execute each solution.

NOTE:
The assignment sheet shown represents twelve of the subjects. However, there are twenty-four subjects reviewed in this chapter.

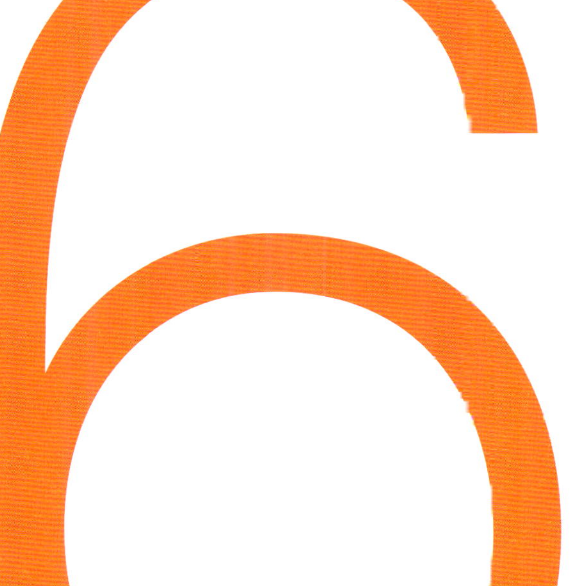

MY NAME IS

BOMI

AND I'M OBSESSIVE COMPULSIVE

MY NAME IS

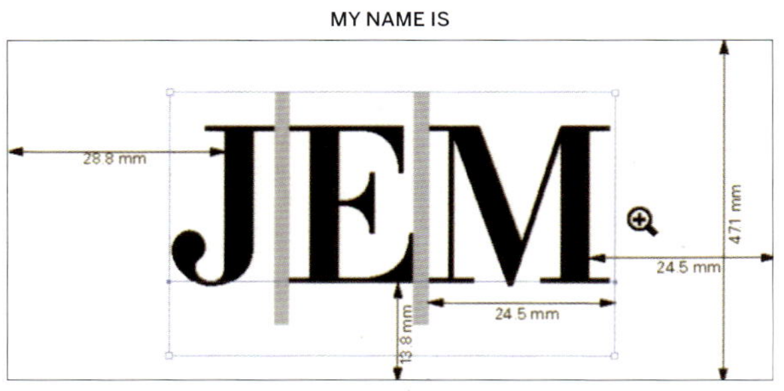

AND I'M OBSESSIVE COMPULSIVE

MY NAME IS

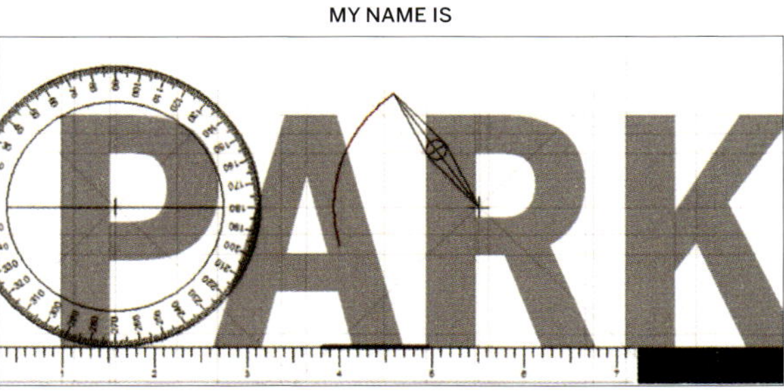

AND I'M OBSESSIVE COMPULSIVE

MY NAME IS

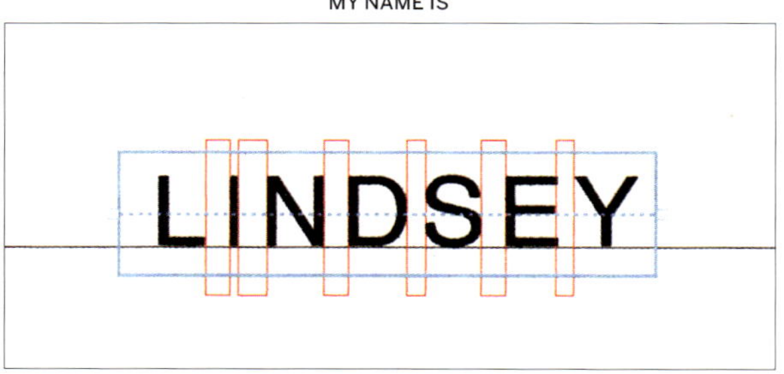

AND I'M OBSESSIVE COMPULSIVE

MY NAME IS

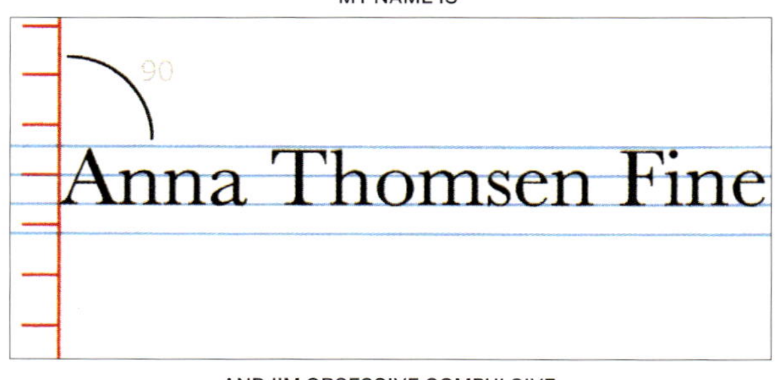

AND I'M OBSESSIVE COMPULSIVE

TYPOGRAPHIC PORTRAIT SOLUTIONS:

Figures 1 through 13 depict the subject of obsessive-compulsive behavior. Solutions range from illustrating the rigidity of exactness to the complexity of repetitious behavior and being at the mercy of uncontrolled impulses.

MY NAME IS

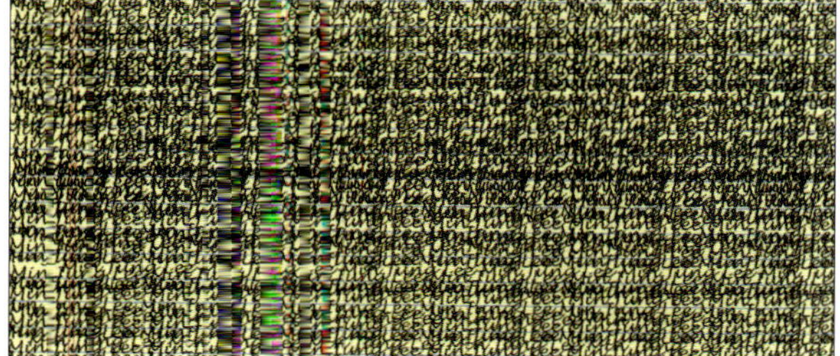

AND I'M OBSESSIVE COMPULSIVE

MY NAME IS

AND I'M OBSESSIVE COMPULSIVE

MY NAME IS

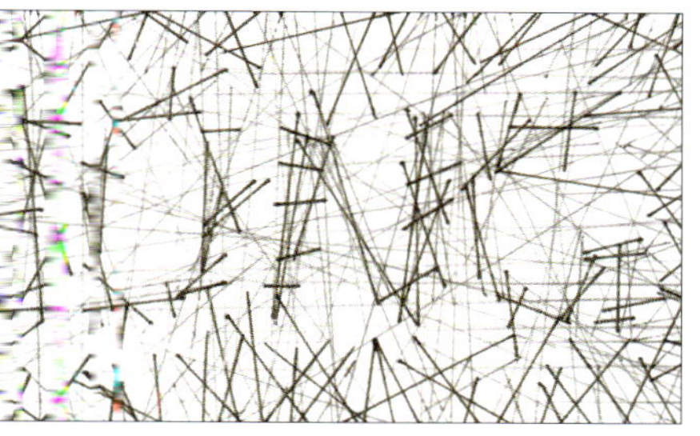

AND I'M OBSESSIVE COMPULSIVE

MY NAME IS

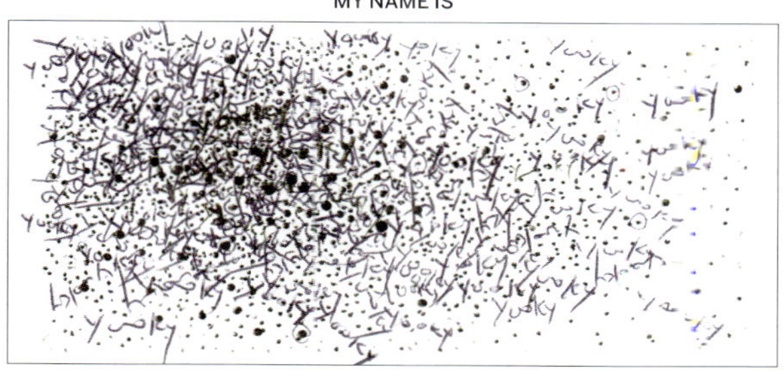

AND I'M OBSESSIVE COMPULSIVE

MY NAME IS

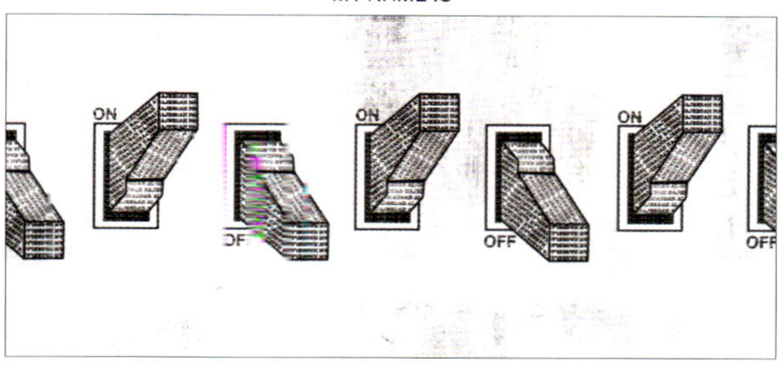

AND I'M OBSESSIVE COMPULSIVE

MY NAME IS

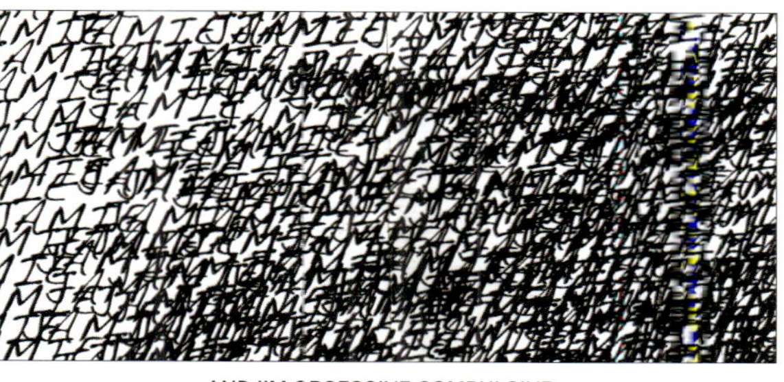

AND I'M OBSESSIVE COMPULSIVE

MY NAME IS

AND I'M OBSESSIVE COMPULSIVE

MY NAME IS

AND I'M OBSESSIVE COMPULSIVE

1. Bomi Jo
2. Jieun Moon
3. Haehyun Park
4. Lindsey Kelly
5. Anna Fine
6. Minjung Lee
7. Jinkyung Myung
8. Hongjoon Jang
9. Yookyung Kim
10. Najeebah Al Ghadban
11. Jamie Connell
12. Jiyoung Byun
13. Jeonghyun Ahn

MY NAME IS

AND I WORK ON AN ASSEMBLY LINE

MY NAME IS

AND I WORK ON AN ASSEMBLY LINE

MY NAME IS

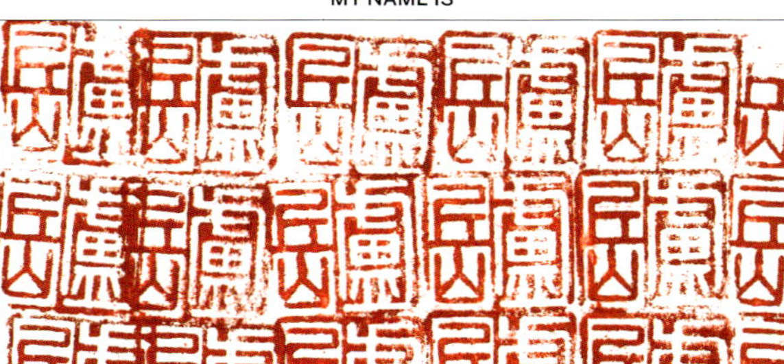

AND I WORK ON AN ASSEMBLY LINE

MY NAME IS

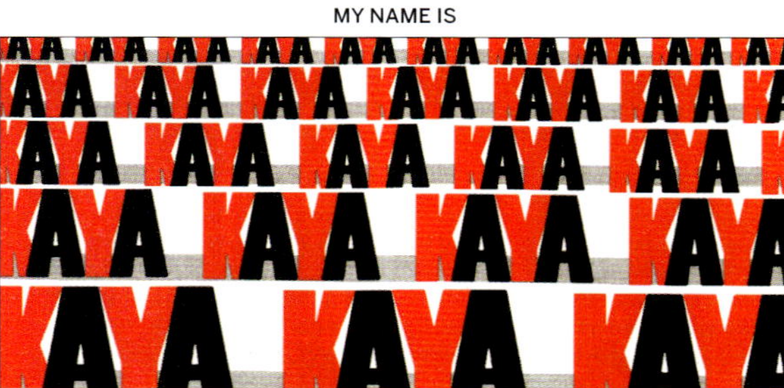

AND I WORK ON AN ASSEMBLY LINE

MY NAME IS

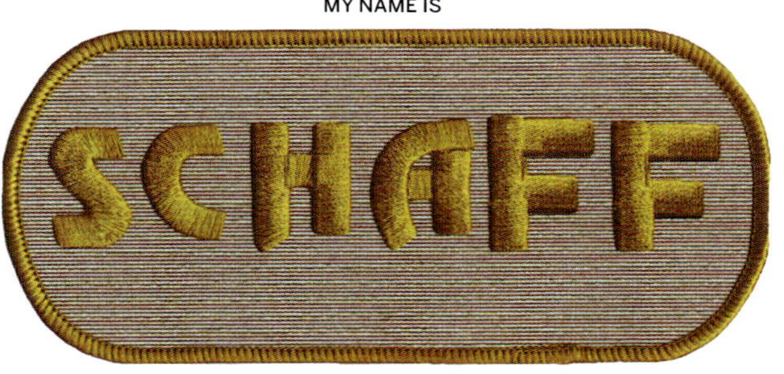

AND I WORK ON AN ASSEMBLY LINE

MY NAME IS

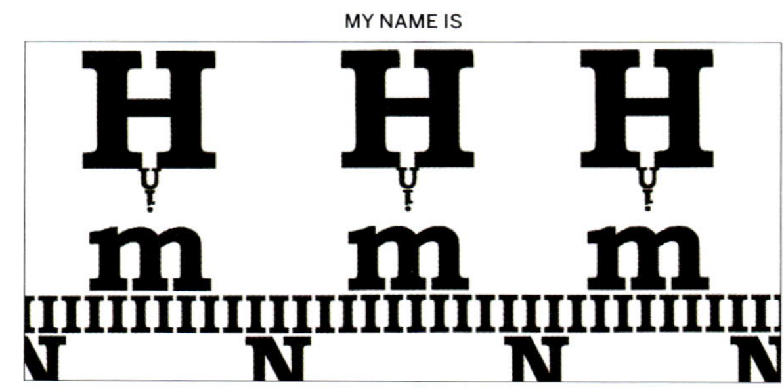

AND I WORK ON AN ASSEMBLY LINE

MY NAME IS

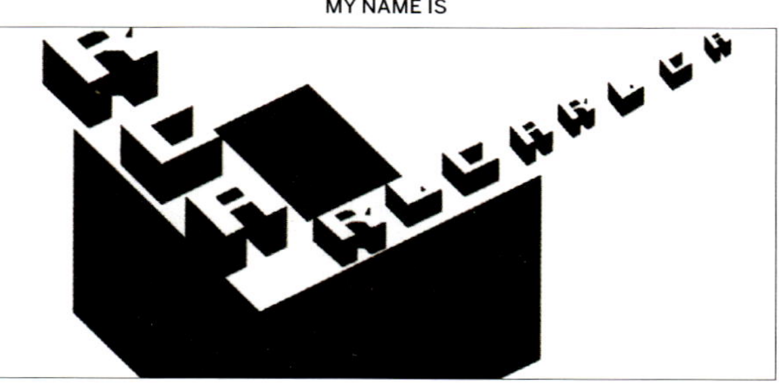

AND I WORK ON AN ASSEMBLY LINE

TYPOGRAPHIC PORTRAIT SOLUTIONS:

Figures 1 through 7 depict working on an assembly line, with imagery that deals with complexity and repetition, to conceptual interpretations.

Figures 8 through 15 focus on the subject of being lost. Conceptually driven solutions and letterforms are combined with literal imagery to express the intended message.

MY NAME IS

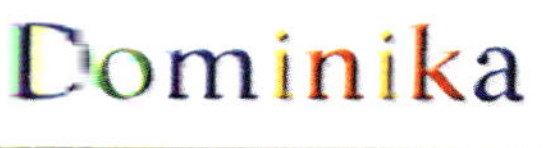

AND I'M LOST

MY NAME IS

BOOKAHORALH
EHAJPOLPLNCA
LAPLJAMPRDPT
LNARPOLKAFAT
SANDWICHDEPI
BURGERADLLZ
POLLAJAMIEFU

BELLS JAM
BOOK JAM E
BURGER ORAL
FAT POLKA
HAT SANDWICH

AND I'M LOST

MY NAME IS

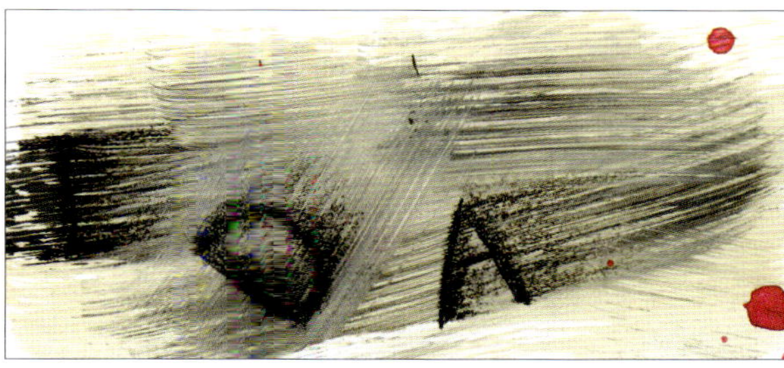

AND I'M LOST

MY NAME IS

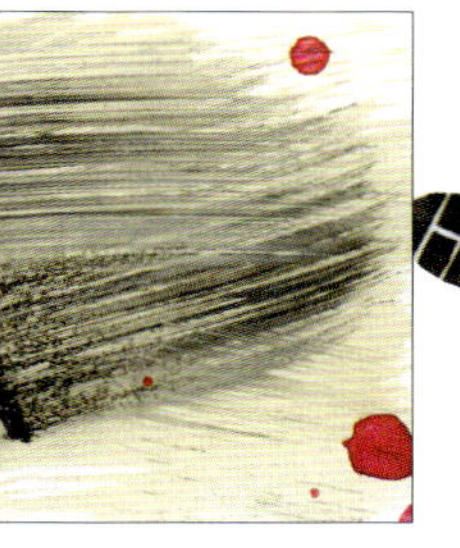

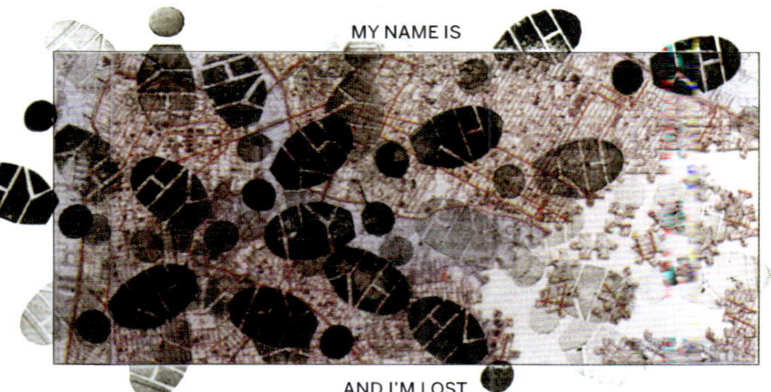

AND I'M LOST

MY NAME IS

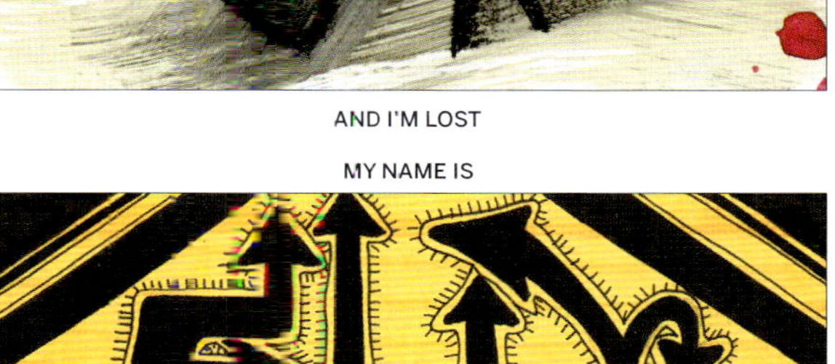

AND I'M LOST

MY NAME IS

AND I'M LOST

MY NAME IS

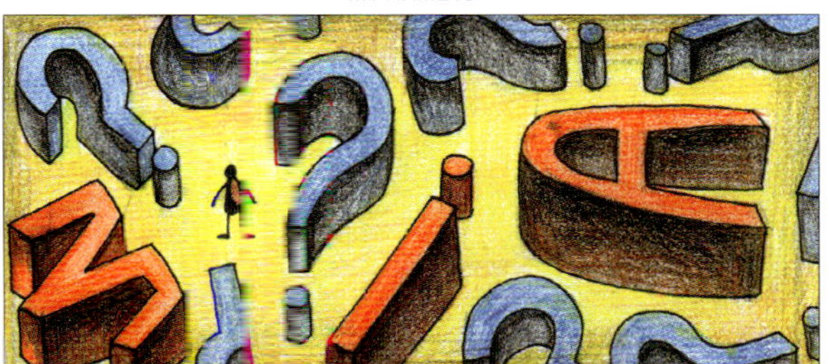

AND I'M LOST

MY NAME IS

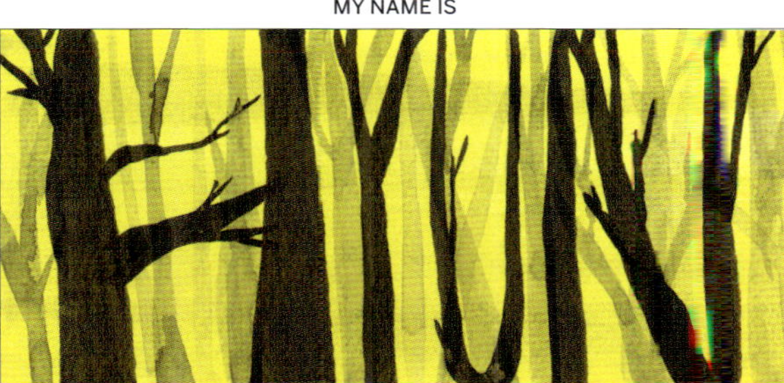

AND I'M LOST

1. Junghee Yoon
2. Eunjung Yoo
3. Yueh Lu
4. Kaya Ono
5. Andrew Schaff
6. Huimin Lee
7. Carlo Cabigao
8. Dominika Kramerova
9. Jamie Kakleas
10. Dain An
11. Hyo Han
12. Hye Ok Row
13. Brent Philhower
14. Seongmi Park
15. Hyunjung Hwang

MY NAME IS

AND I'M A CRIME SCENE INVESTIGATOR

MY NAME IS

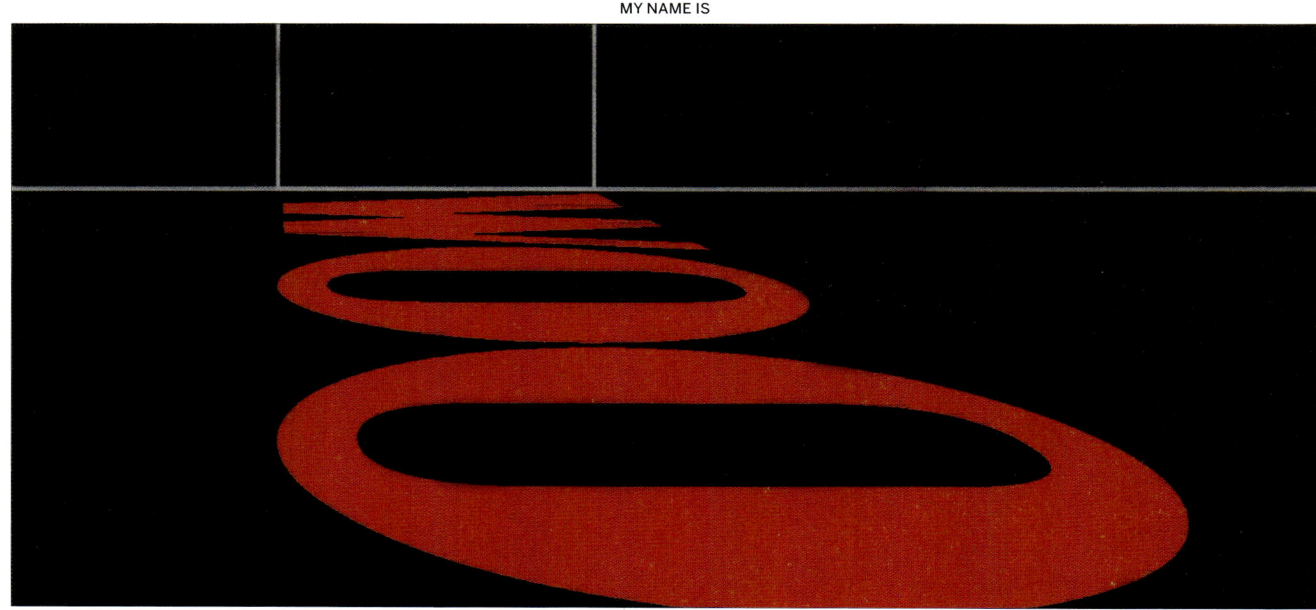

AND I'M A CRIME SCENE INVESTIGATOR

TYPOGRAPHIC PORTRAIT SOLUTIONS:

Figures 1 through 8 represent the mystery and drama associated with crime scene investigation.

Figure 1 is an emotional depiction, while figure 2 is a classically rendered interpretation. Most all solutions in the typographic portrait project fall between these two sensibilities.

The imagery in figures 3 through 8 varies greatly in terms of interpretation of procedures and techniques related to crime scene investigation.

MY NAME IS

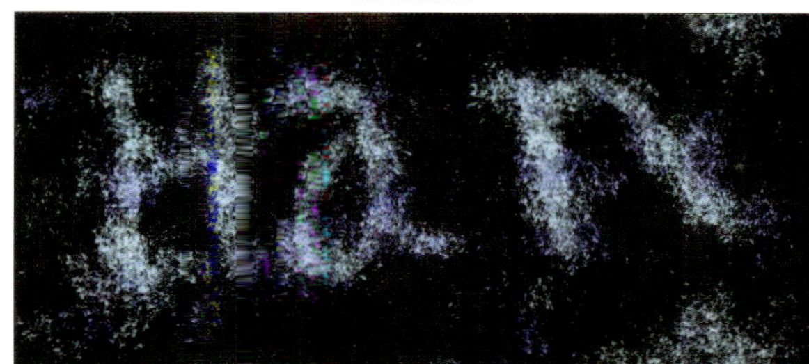

AND I'M A CRIME SCENE INVESTIGATOR

MY NAME IS

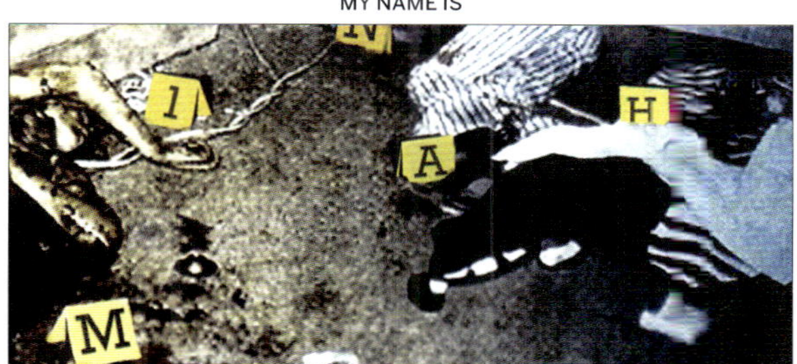

AND I'M A CRIME SCENE INVESTIGATOR

MY NAME IS

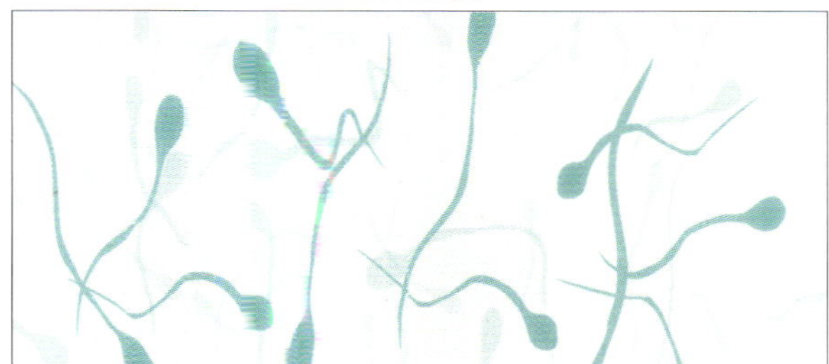

AND I'M A CRIME SCENE INVESTIGATOR

MY NAME IS

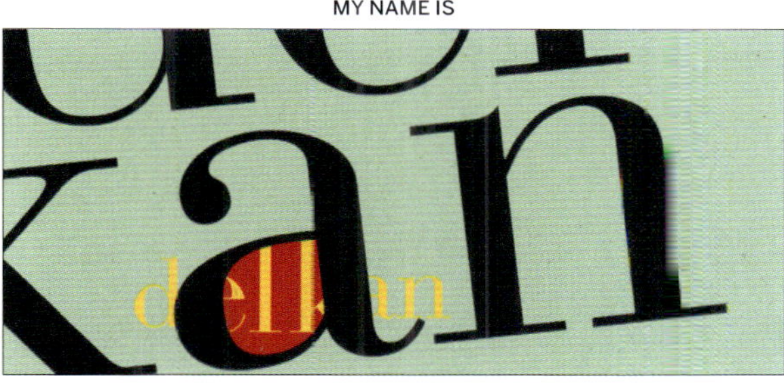

AND I'M A CRIME SCENE INVESTIGATOR

MY NAME IS

AND I'M A CRIME SCENE INVESTIGATOR

MY NAME IS

AND I'M A CRIME SCENE INVESTIGATOR

1. *Chris Foxx*
2. *Woosung Lee*
3. *Myungsong Han*
4. *Minah Kim*
5. *Kyle Chaille*
6. *Pablo Delkan*
7. *Hyo Han*
8. *Minkyung Kang*

MY NAME IS

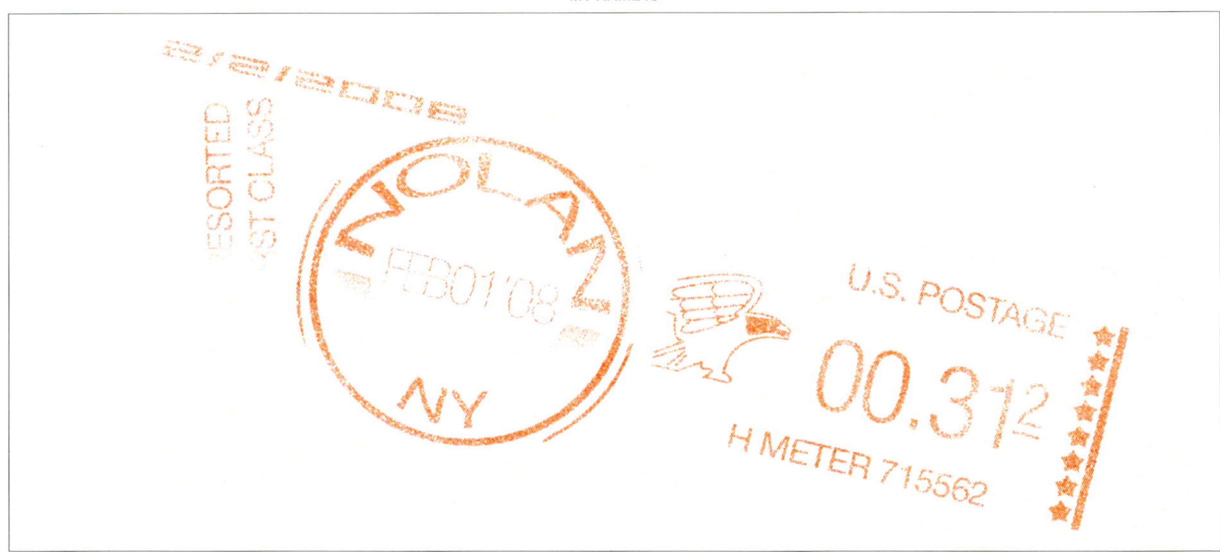

AND I'M A POSTAL WORKER

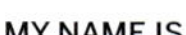

MY NAME IS

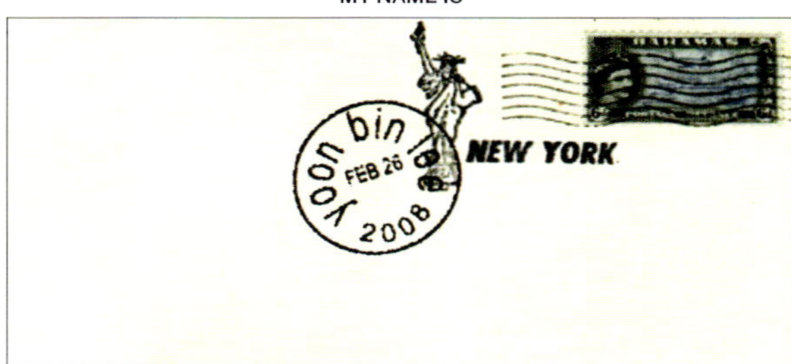

AND I'M A POSTAL WORKER

MY NAME IS

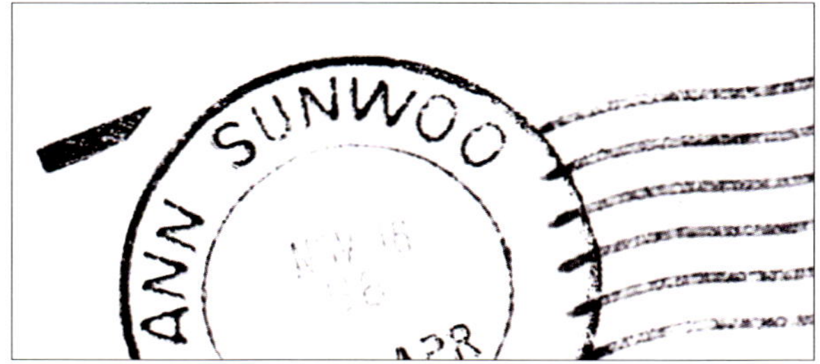

AND I'M A POSTAL WORKER

MY NAME IS

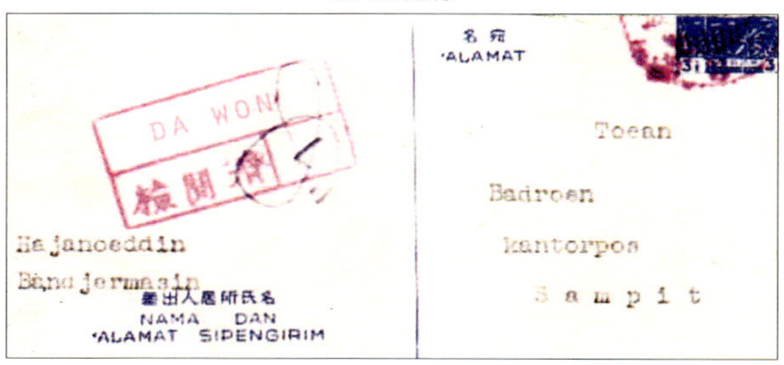

AND I'M A POSTAL WORKER

MY NAME IS

AND I'M A POSTAL WORKER

MY NAME IS

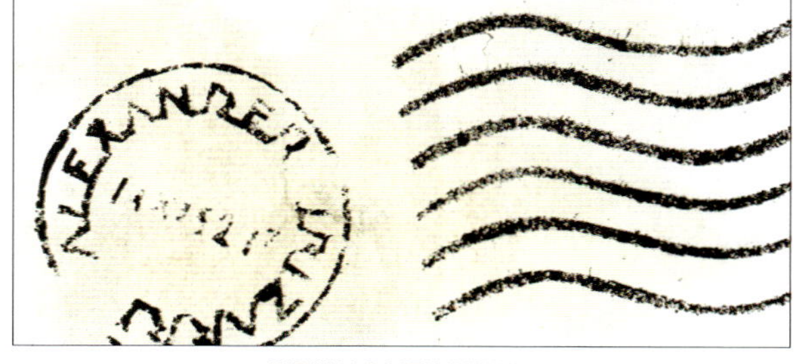

AND I'M A POSTAL WORKER

MY NAME IS

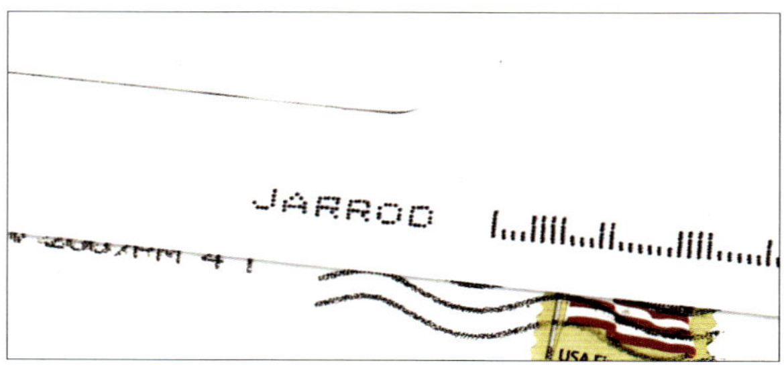

AND I'M A POSTAL WORKER

TYPOGRAPHIC PORTRAIT SOLUTIONS:

Figures 1 through 7, which represent postal workers, and figures 8 through 15, which represent librarians, all use indigenous thematic typography associated with these two professions. The cancellation marks differ from one another in terms of scale, color, texture, and cropping, while the images for librarian include rubber stamps, handwriting, and typewriter type, which set the stage for an array of executions that capture the historical activity of the library.

MY NAME IS

AND I'M A LIBRARIAN

MY NAME IS

AND I'M A LIBRARIAN

MY NAME IS

AND I'M A LIBRARIAN

MY NAME IS

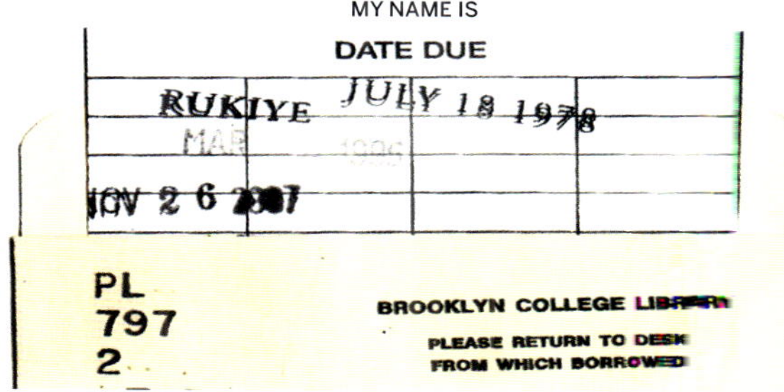

AND I'M A LIBRARIAN

MY NAME IS

AND I'M A LIBRARIAN

MY NAME IS

AND I'M A LIBRARIAN

MY NAME IS

AND I'M A LIBRARIAN

MY NAME IS

AND I'M A LIBRARIAN

1. *Nolan Constantino*
2. *Yoon Bin Lee*
3. *Ann Sunwoo*
4. *Dawon Chung*
5. *Colette Nickola*
6. *Alexander Irizarry*
7. *Jarrod Barretto*
8. *Irene Fernandez*
9. *Matthew Klein*
10. *Chelsea Cumings*
11. *Hollis Maloney*
12. *Sara Berks*
13. *Rukiye Sahin*
14. *Michael Lubrano*
15. *Natalie Mertz*

MY NAME IS

AND I'VE BEEN ON A DIET SINCE 2002

MY NAME IS

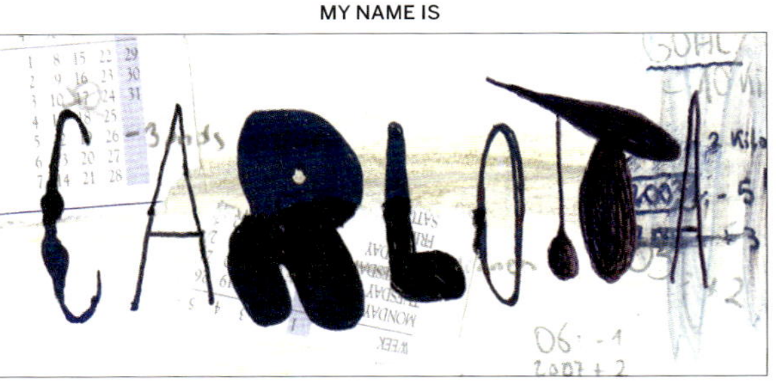

AND I'VE BEEN ON A DIET SINCE 2002

MY NAME IS

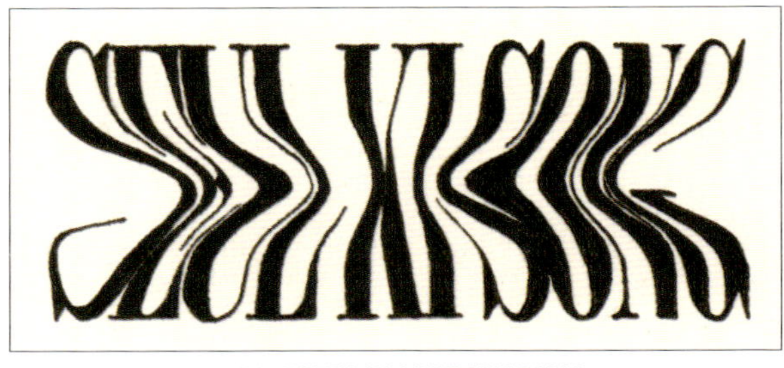

AND I'VE BEEN ON A DIET SINCE 2002

MY NAME IS

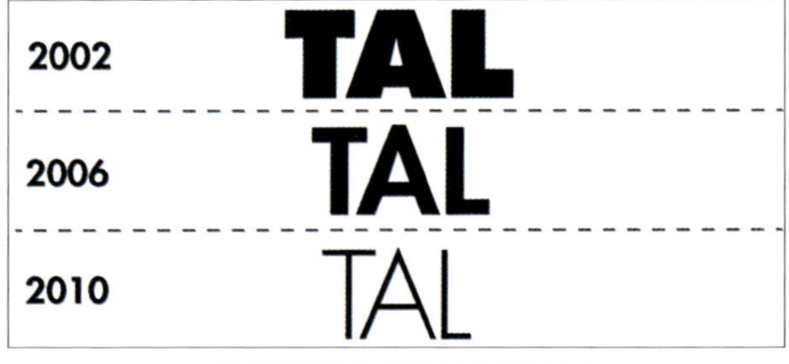

AND I'VE BEEN ON A DIET SINCE 2002

MY NAME IS

shin, hin, in,

AND I'VE BEEN ON A DIET SINCE 2002

TYPOGRAPHIC PORTRAIT SOLUTIONS:

Figures 1 through 11 deal with the subject of weight loss. The concepts range from diminishing size, exaggeration, and fluctuation of weight through the use of hand-drawn characters, to computer-generated solutions, to collage imagery. Humor is an underlying theme for many of these solutions.

MY NAME IS

MY NAME IS

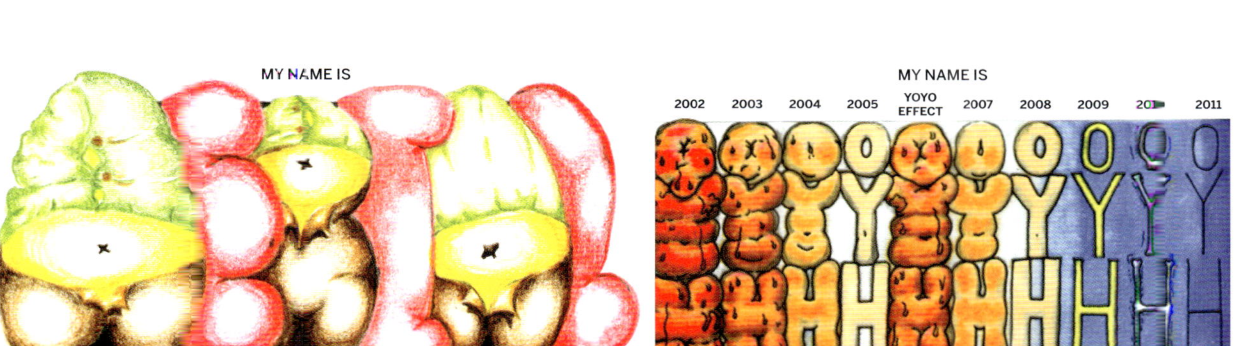

AND I'VE BEEN ON A DIET SINCE 2002

AND I'VE BEEN ON A DIET SINCE 2002

MY NAME IS

MY NAME IS

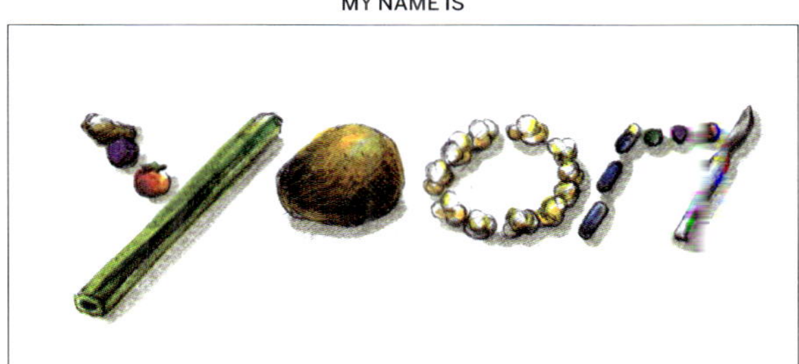

AND I'VE BEEN ON A DIET SINCE 2002

AND I'VE BEEN ON A DIET SINCE 2002

MY NAME IS

MY NAME IS

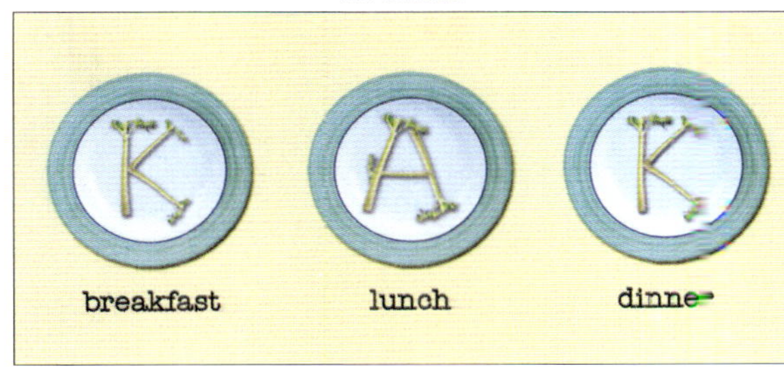

AND I'VE BEEN ON A DIET SINCE 2002

AND I'VE BEEN ON A DIET SINCE 2002

1. *Eunji Kim*
2. *Carlotta Merzari*
3. *Seulki Son*
4. *Tal Shu*
5. *Minjin Shin*
6. *Aerial Chen*
7. *Hyo Han*
8. *Joseph Hollier*
9. *Yoonsook Jee*
10. *Mihee Choi*
11. *Jamie Kakleas*

MY NAME IS

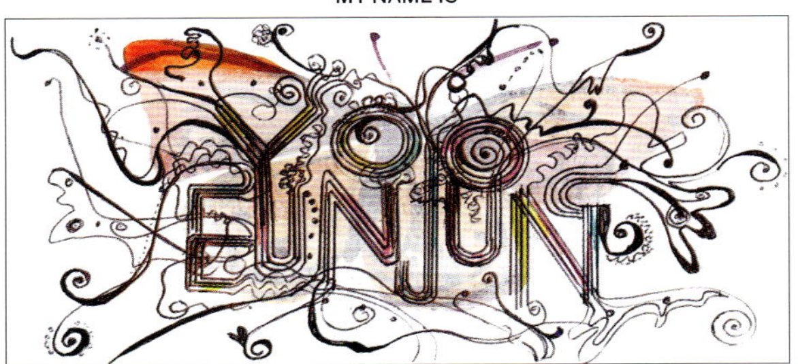

AND I'M A BUTTERFLY COLLECTOR

MY NAME IS

AND I'M A BUTTERFLY COLLECTOR

MY NAME IS

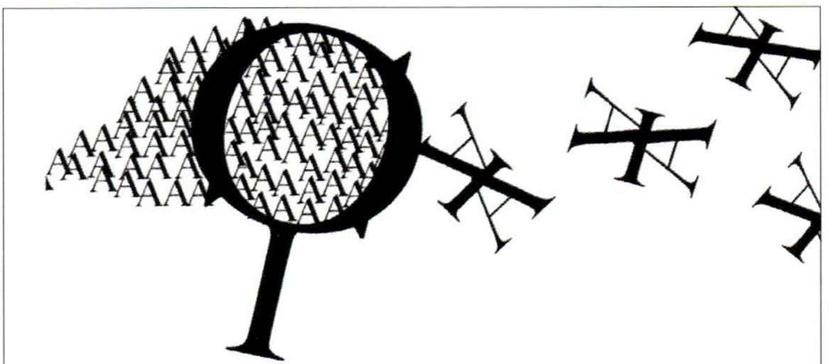

AND I'M A BUTTERFLY COLLECTOR

MY NAME IS

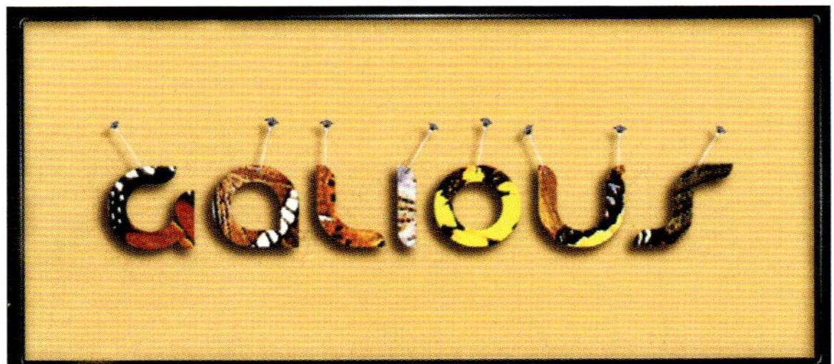

AND I'M A BUTTERFLY COLLECTOR

MY NAME IS

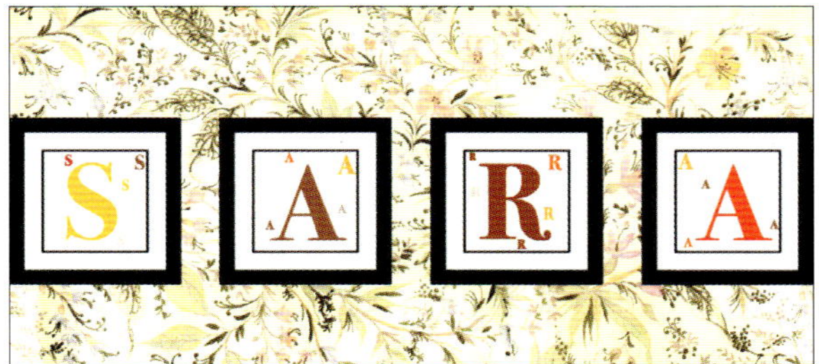

AND I'M A BUTTERFLY COLLECTOR

MY NAME IS

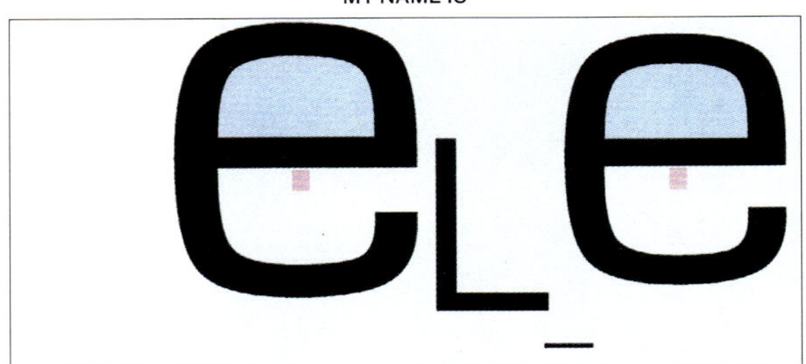

AND I'M AN INSOMNIAC

MY NAME IS

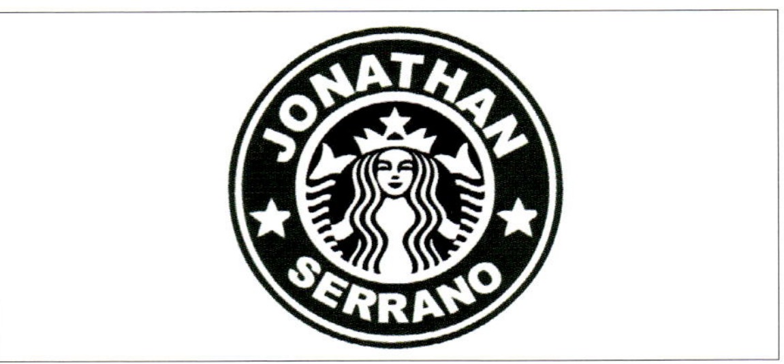

AND I'M AN INSOMNIAC

MY NAME IS

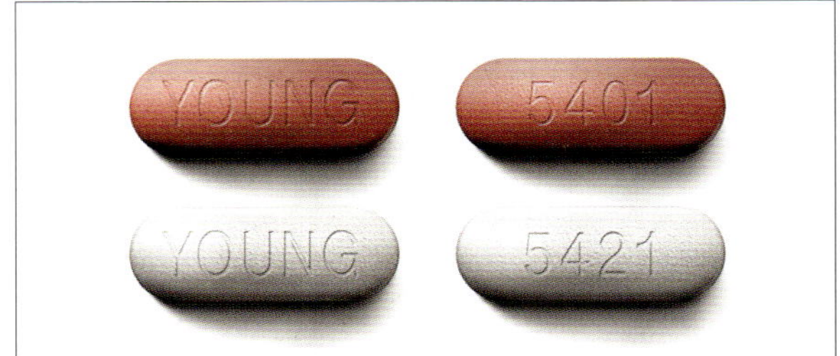

AND I'M AN INSOMNIAC

MY NAME IS

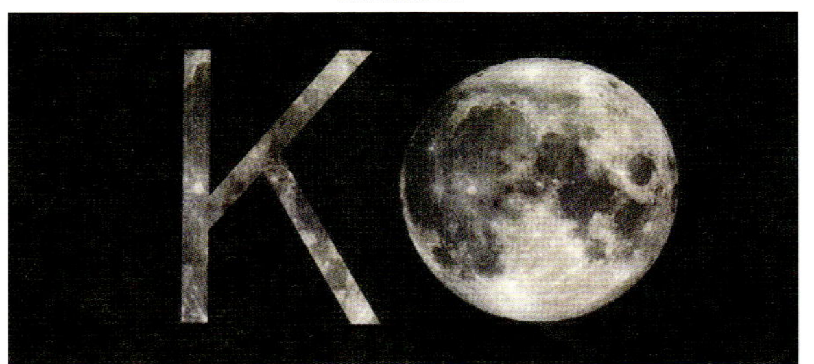

AND I'M AN INSOMNIAC

MY NAME IS

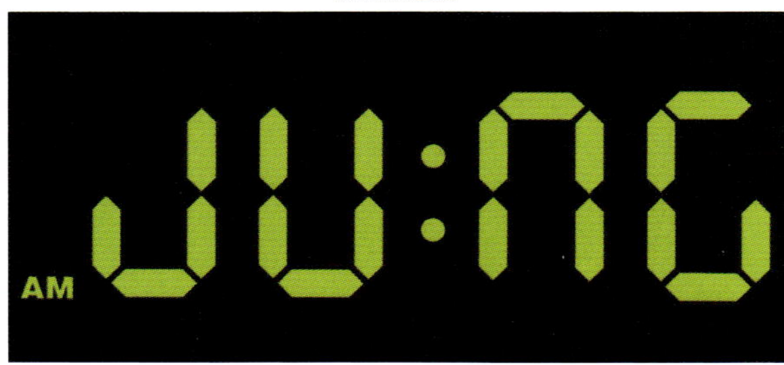

AND I'M AN INSOMNIAC

TYPOGRAPHIC PORTRAIT SOLUTIONS:

Figures 1 through 5 address the subject of being a butterfly collector. Figure 1 is a formal investigation that deals with movement by combining abstract elements and literal imagery. Figures 2, 4 and 5 use the butterfly specimen display by substituting letterforms to represent butterflies. Figure 3 is a depiction of the activity of catching butterflies.

Figures 6 through 10 deal with insomnia. Solutions range from depicting the event in figures 6, 9 and 10, to figure 7, which refers to a possible cause and figure 8 which references a remedy.

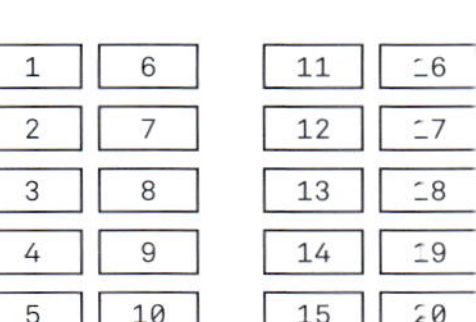

1. *Eunjung Yoo*
2. *Kaya Ono*
3. *Jessica Scro*
4. *Janghyun Cho*
5. *Sara Berks*
6. *Huimin Lee*
7. *Jon Serrano*
8. *Yasmin Malki*
9. *Daisy Lee*
10. *Jaesung Jung*
11. *Jamie Kahleas*
12. *Joey Cofone*
13. *Stephanie Tin*
14. *V. Gorbunova*
15. *Kim Capers*
16. *Sara Berks*
17. *Eunhae Cho*
18. *Kirstin Huber*
19. *Inyoung Kim*
20. *Misun Youn*

In figures 11 through 15 one is required to invent their own subject for a past life. Solutions include: an alien, Robocop, which upon closer observation spells out the name Joey, a Lego builder, a hopscotch champion, and a cave woman.

Figures 16 through 20 represent an optometrist. Most of the solutions are seen through a magnification lens except figure 18, which deals with a color-blindness test.

MY NAME IS

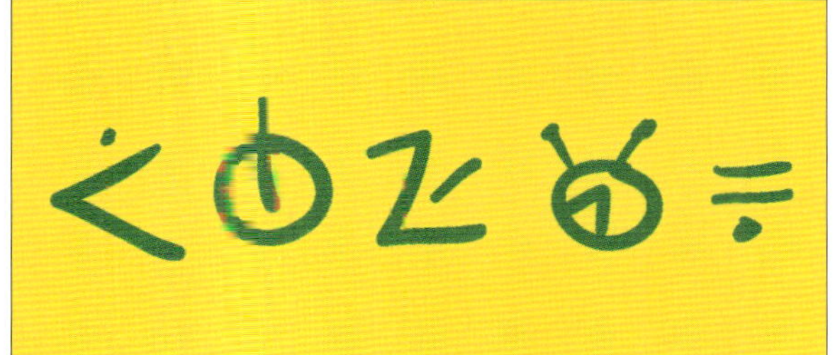

AND I WAS AN ALIEN IN MY PAST LIFE

MY NAME IS

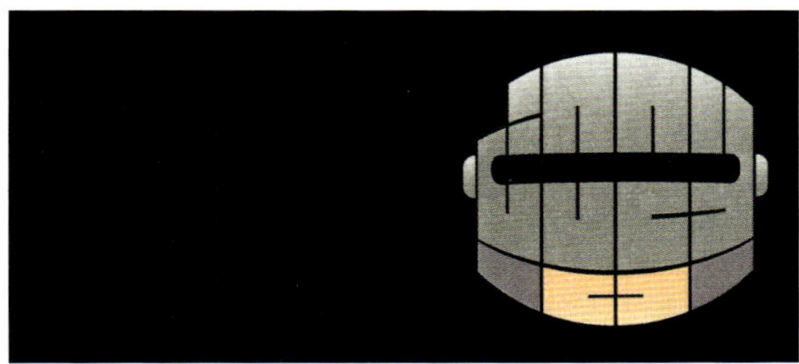

AND I WAS ROBOCOP IN MY PAST LIFE

MY NAME IS

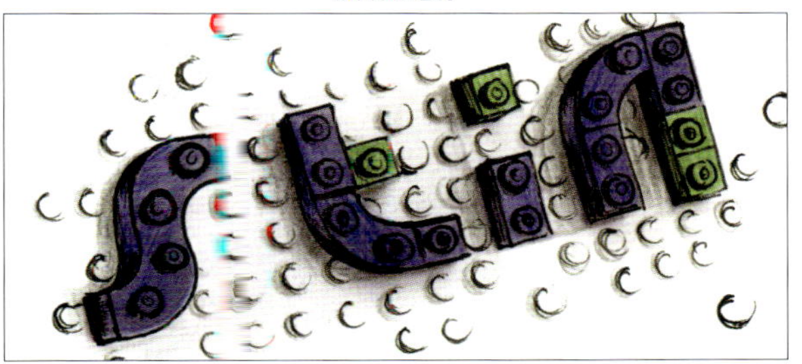

AND I WAS A LEGO BUILDER IN MY PAST LIFE

MY NAME IS

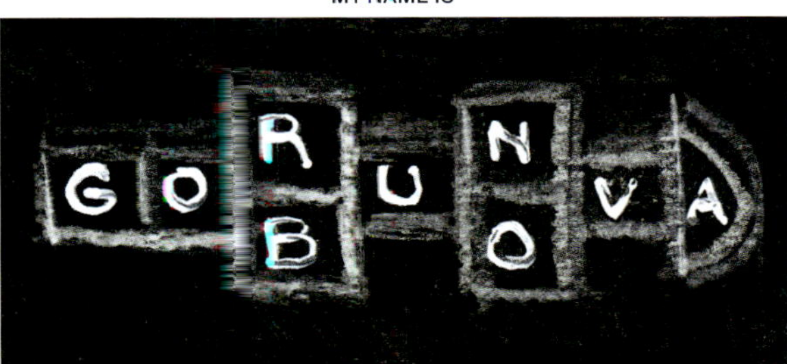

AND I WAS A HOPSCOTCH CHAMPION IN MY PAST LIFE

MY NAME IS

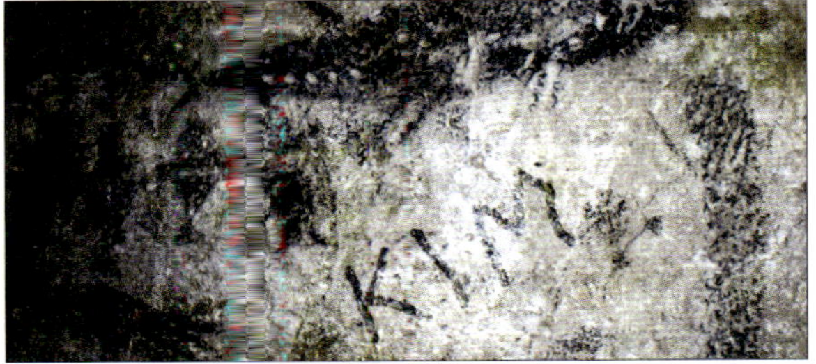

AND I WAS A CAVE WOMAN IN MY PAST LIFE

MY NAME IS

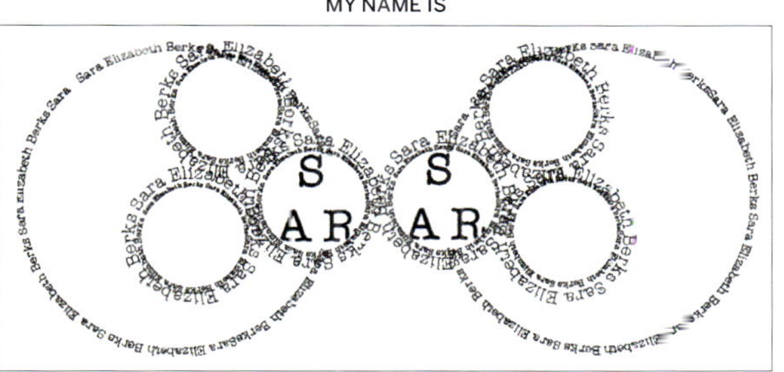

AND I'M AN OPTOMETRIST

MY NAME IS

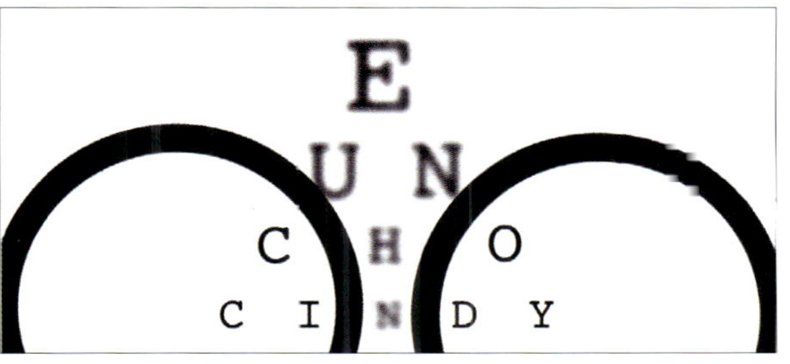

AND I'M AN OPTOMETRIST

MY NAME IS

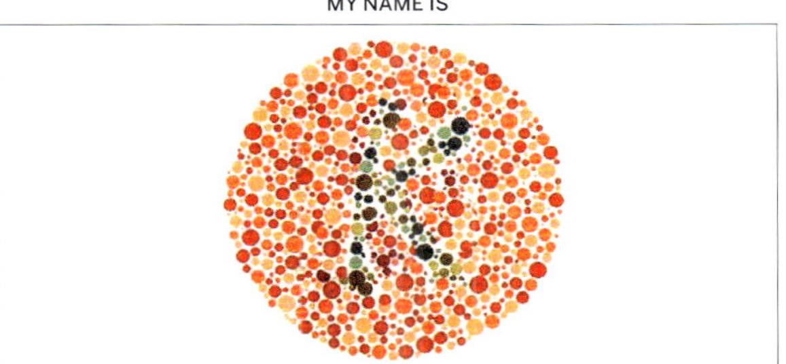

AND I'M AN OPTOMETRIST

MY NAME IS

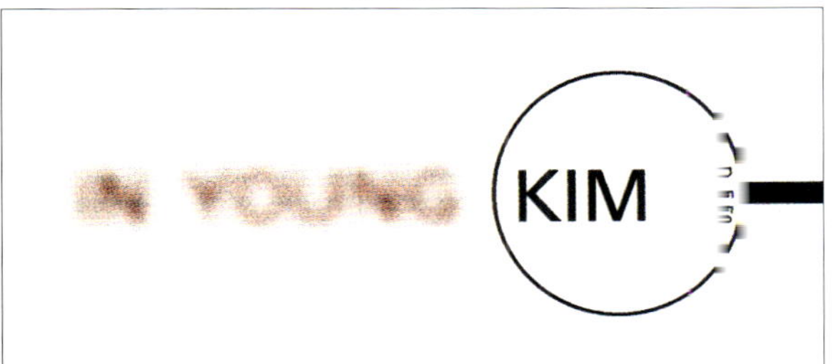

AND I'M AN OPTOMETRIST

MY NAME IS

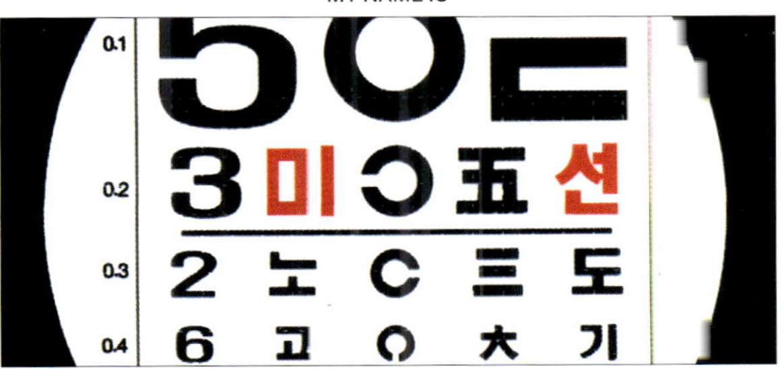

AND I'M AN OPTOMETRIST

MY NAME IS

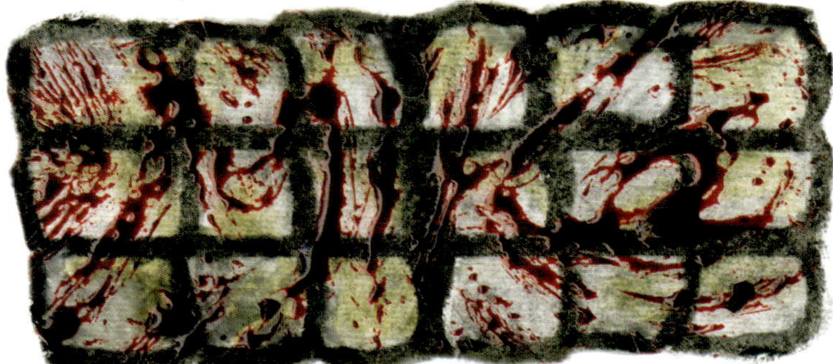

AND I HAVE SEASONAL AFFECTIVE DISORDER (SAD)

MY NAME IS

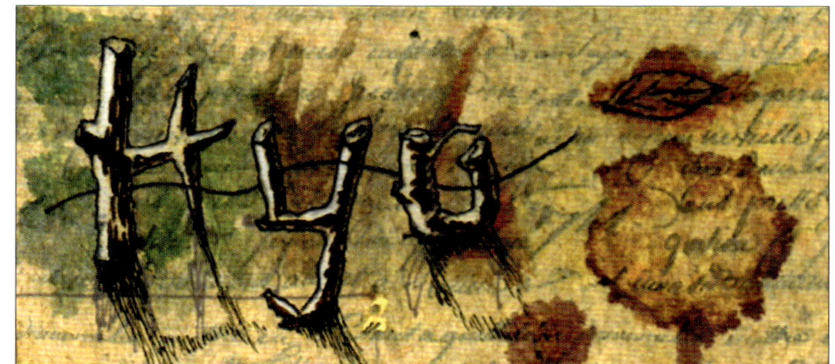

AND I HAVE SEASONAL AFFECTIVE DISORDER (SAD)

MY NAME IS

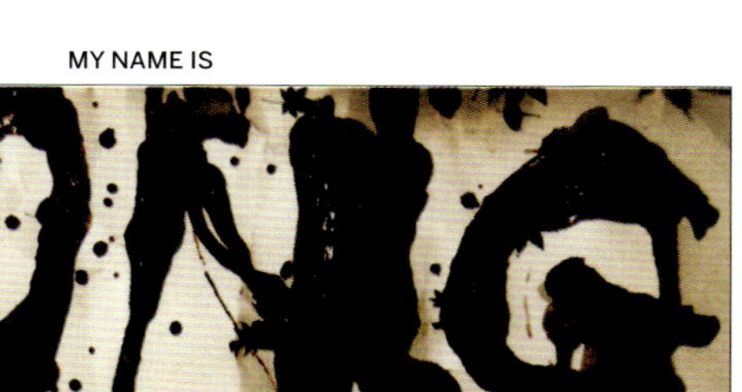

AND I HAVE SEASONAL AFFECTIVE DISORDER (SAD)

MY NAME IS

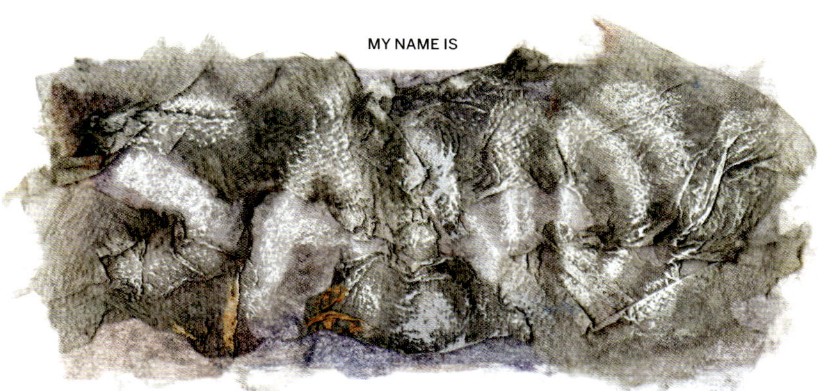

AND I HAVE SEASONAL AFFECTIVE DISORDER (SAD)

MY NAME IS

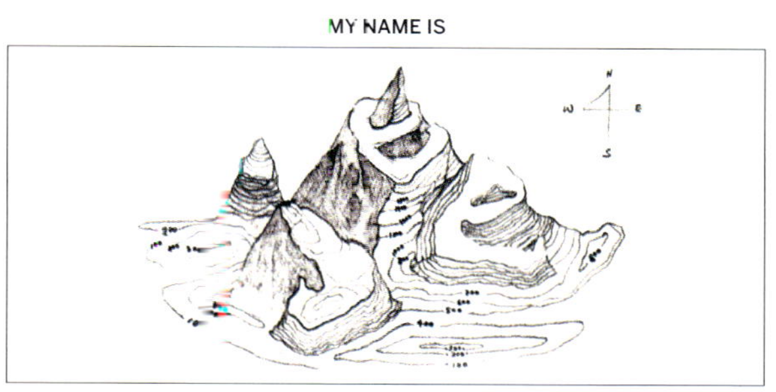

AND I'M A MAP MAKER

MY NAME IS

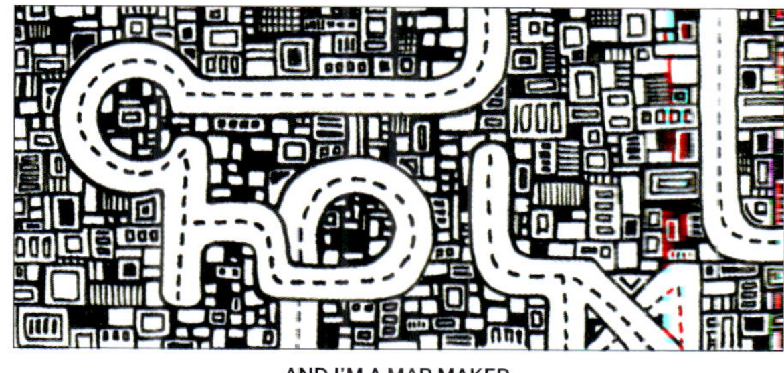

AND I'M A MAP MAKER

MY NAME IS

AND I'M A MAP MAKER

MY NAME IS

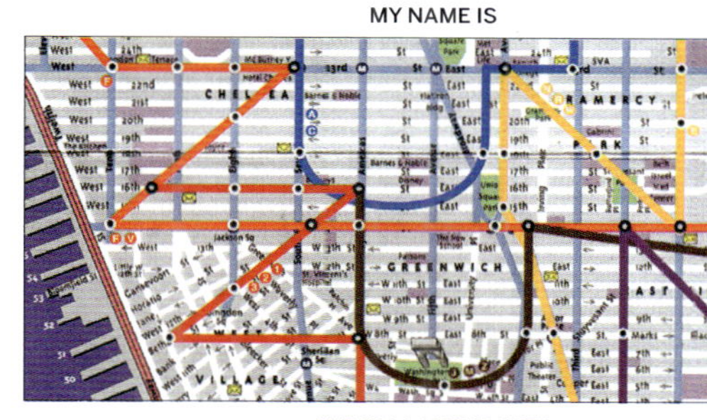

AND I'M A MAP MAKER

MY NAME IS

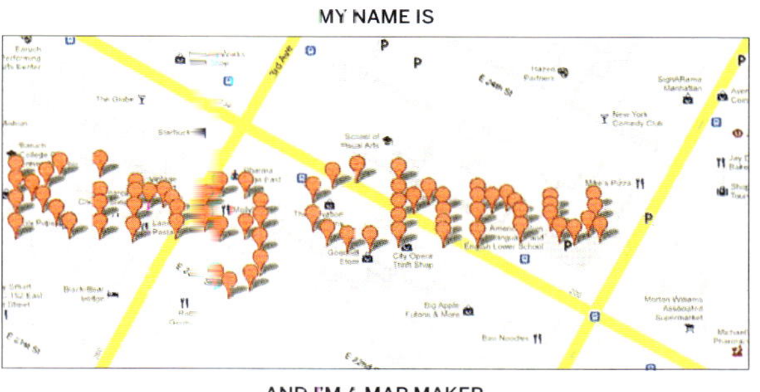

AND I'M A MAP MAKER

MY NAME IS

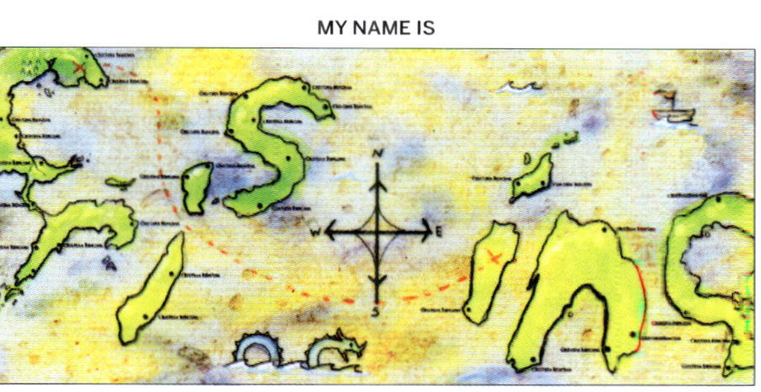

AND I'M A MAP MAKER

MY NAME IS

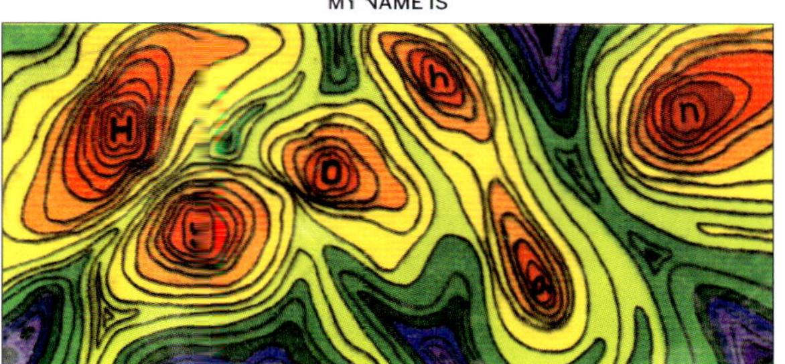

AND I'M A MAP MAKER

MY NAME IS

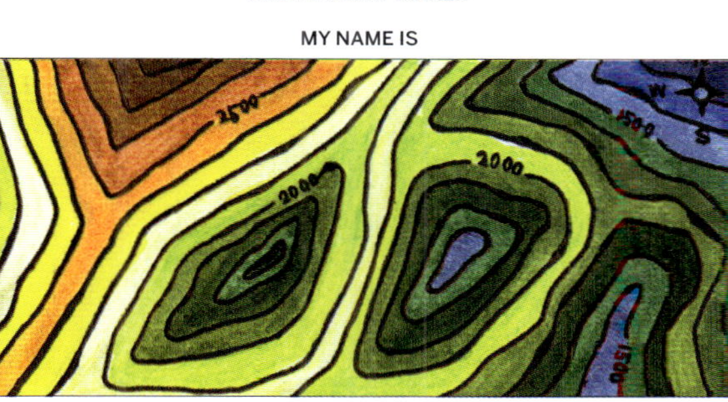

AND I'M A MAP MAKER

MY NAME IS

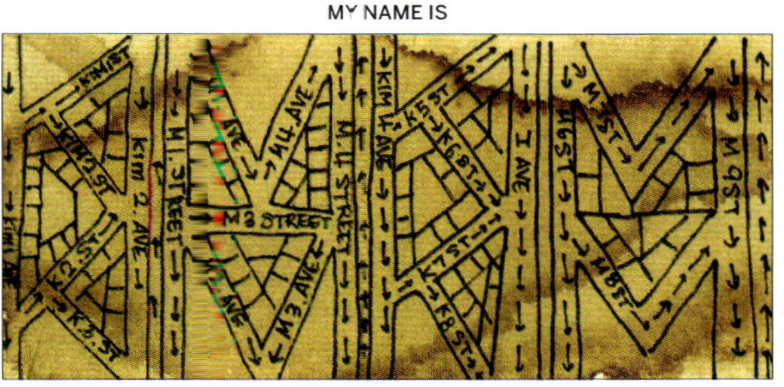

AND I'M A MAP MAKER

MY NAME IS

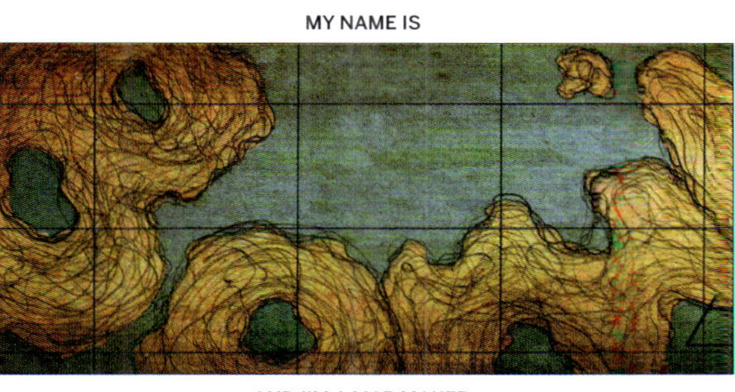

AND I'M A MAP MAKER

TYPOGRAPHIC PORTRAIT SOLUTIONS:

Figures 1 through 4 are expressions of Seasonal Affective Disorder (SAD), which is a type of depression that occurs usually in the winter. These emotionally driven solutions address the anguish of this depressive disorder.

The subject of map making is expressed in figures 5 through 14. Topology is a recurring theme, as is the reconfiguring of traditional maps using an array of executions.

1	2		5	6
3	4		7	8
			9	10
			11	12
			13	14

1. *Michael DeFelice*
2. *Hyo Han*
3. *Seokmin Hong*
4. *Sandra Woodruff*
5. *Jeeyoung Hwang*
6. *Minhee Choi*
7. *Yi Chieh Jen*
8. *Jung Tien Chang*
9. *King Chun Wong*
10. *Cristina Bencina*
11. *Hyo Han*
12. *Younsook Jee*
13. *Seonghye Kim*
14. *Bomi Jo*

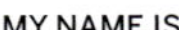

MY NAME IS

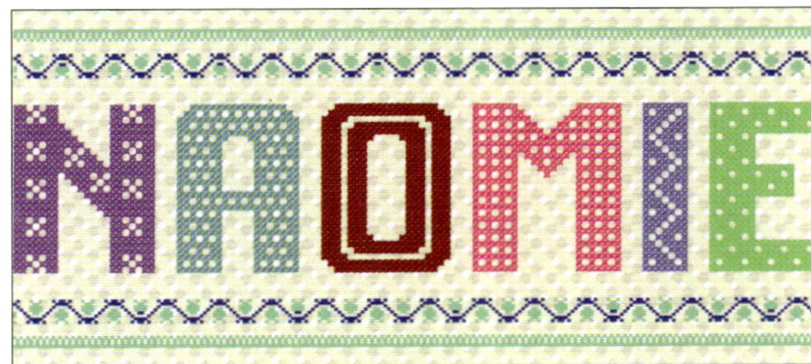

AND I DO NEEDLEPOINT

MY NAME IS

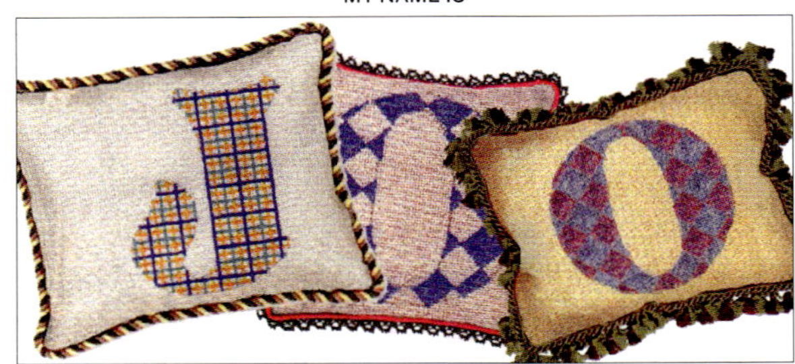

AND I DO NEEDLEPOINT

MY NAME IS

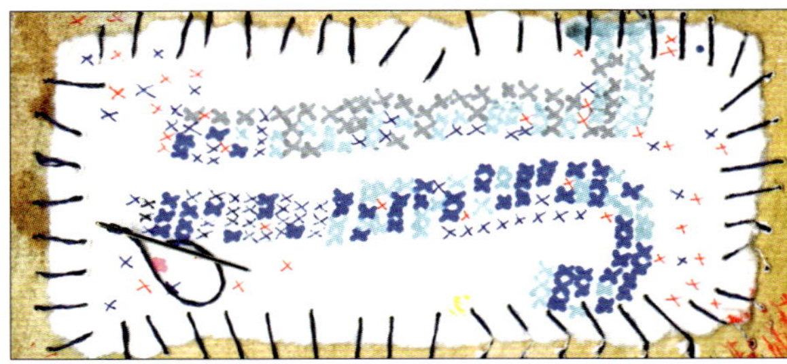

AND I DO NEEDLEPOINT

MY NAME IS

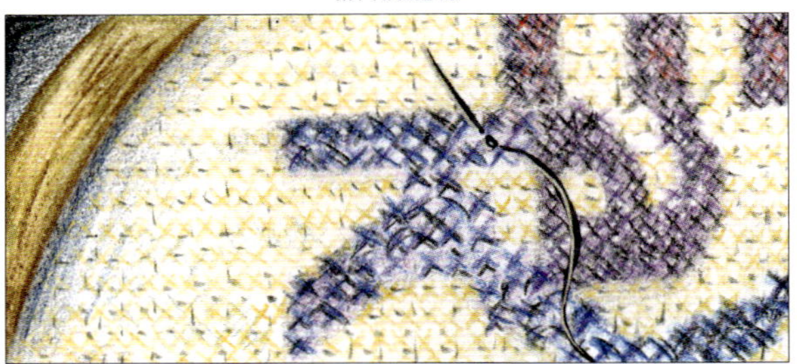

AND I DO NEEDLEPOINT

MY NAME IS

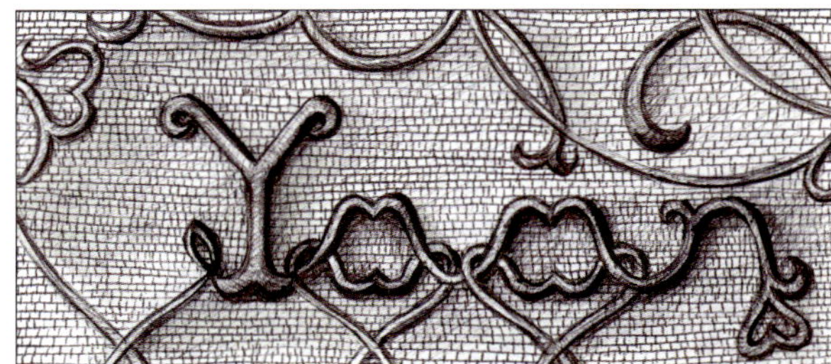

AND I DO NEEDLEPOINT

MY NAME IS

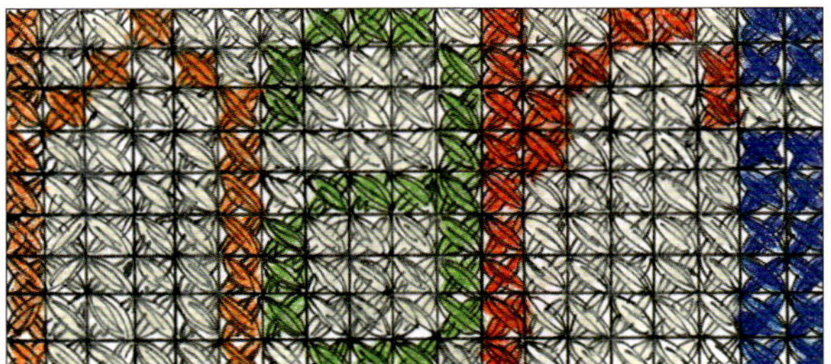

AND I DO NEEDLEPOINT

MY NAME IS

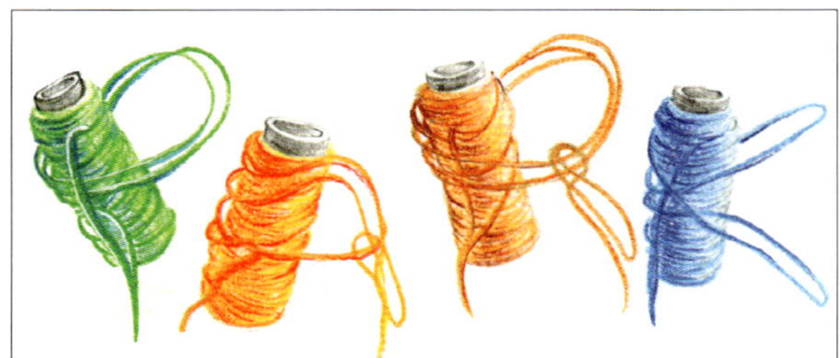

AND I DO NEEDLEPOINT

MY NAME IS

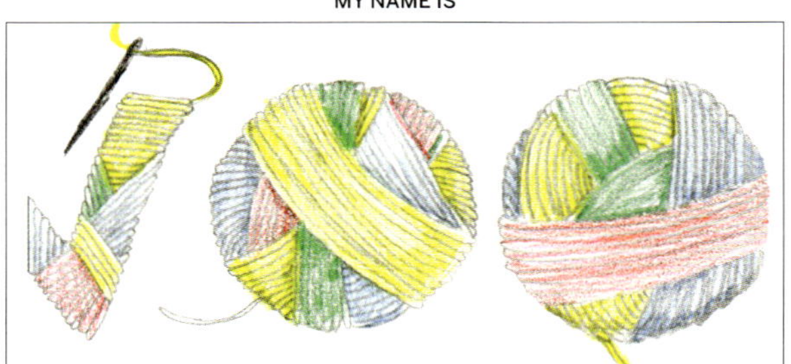

AND I DO NEEDLEPOINT

MY NAME IS

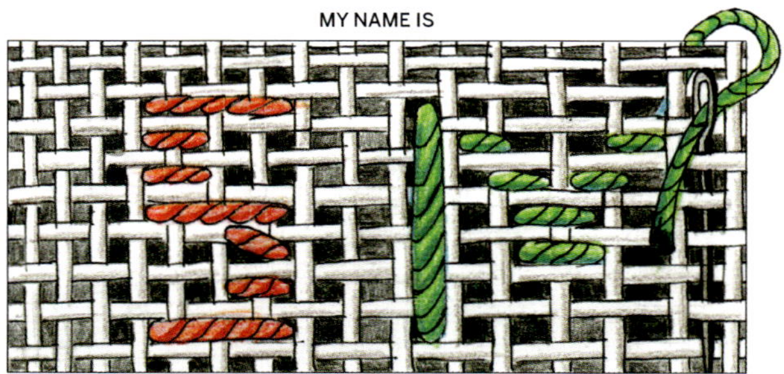

AND I DO NEEDLEPOINT

MY NAME IS

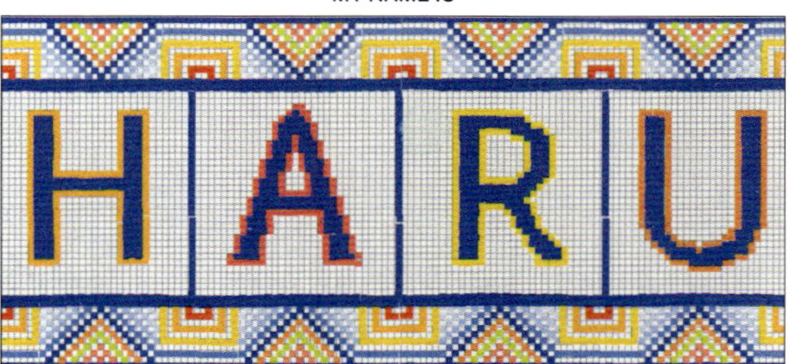

AND I DO NEEDLEPOINT

TYPOGRAPHIC PORTRAIT SOLUTIONS:

Needlepoint, which is a type of embroidery using yarns of either cotton, wool or silk that is stitched through an open weave or canvas mesh, is the subject depicted in the following images.

Solutions address either the materials, the process, or the results of doing needlepoint.

The gridlike pattern of a needlepoint canvas is used to represent the underpinnings of many of the solutions.

MY NAME IS

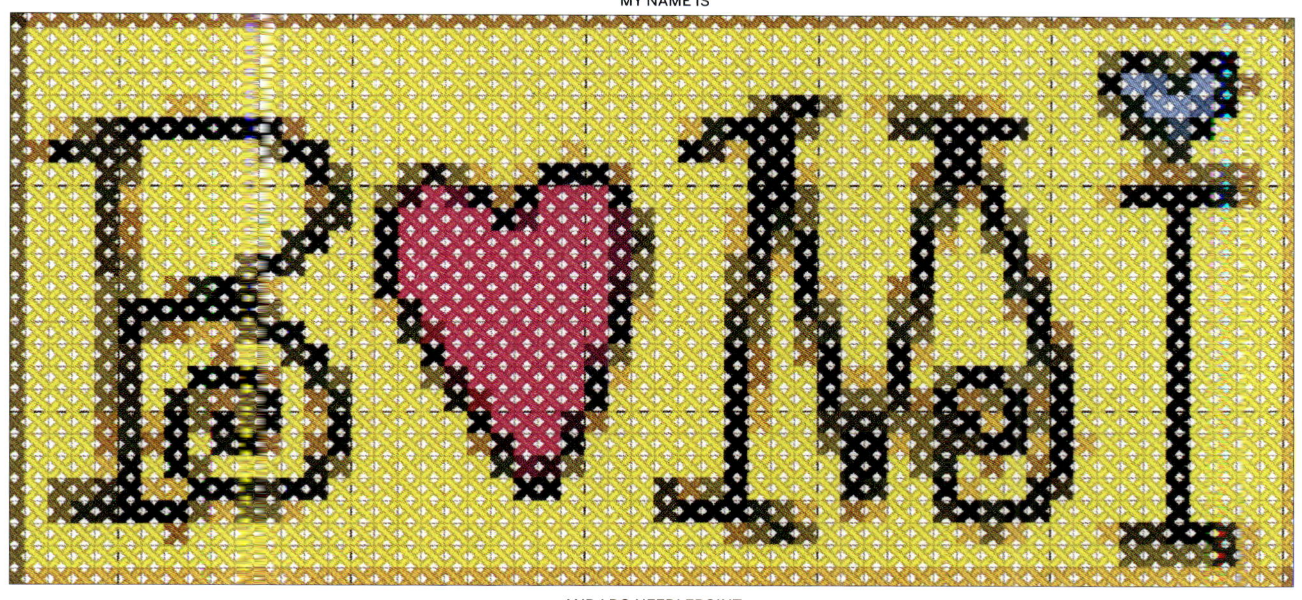

AND I DO NEEDLEPOINT

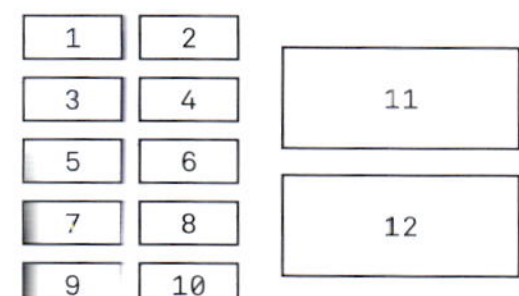

1. *Naomie Ross*
2. *Joo Kong*
3. *Jennifer Lee*
4. *Kay Kim*
5. *Younsook Jee*
6. *Nari Park*
7. *Jaewon Park*
8. *Woosung Lee*
9. *Seongmi Park*
10. *Haruyo Kaneko*
11. *Bomi Jo*
12. *Somyi Yang*

MY NAME IS

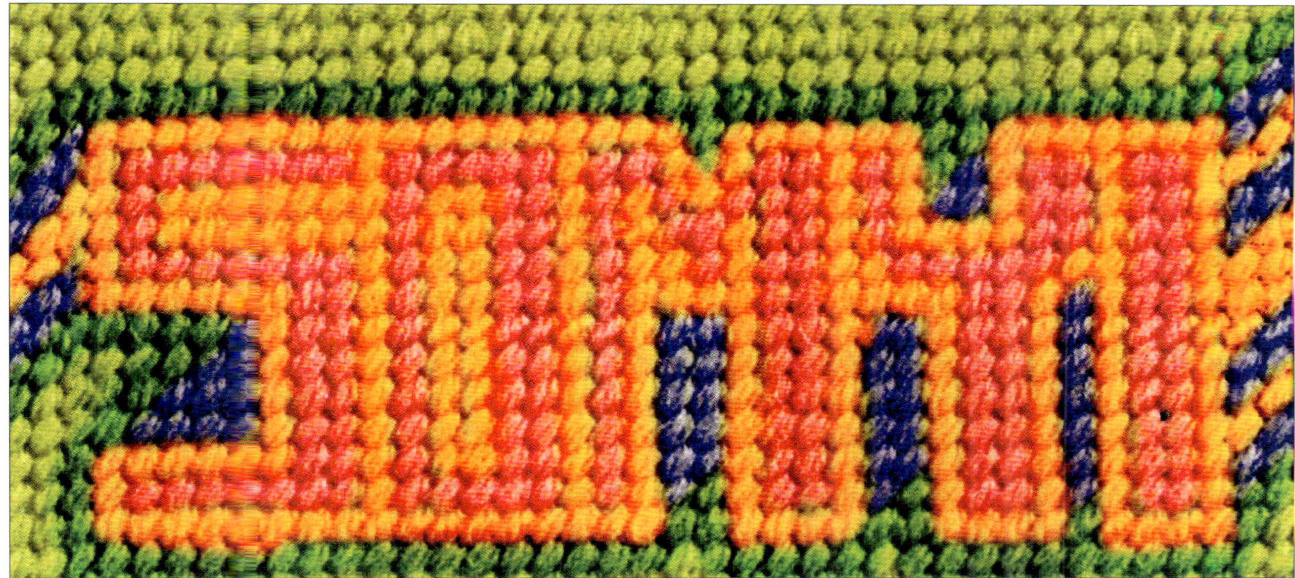

AND I DO NEEDLEPOINT

MY NAME IS

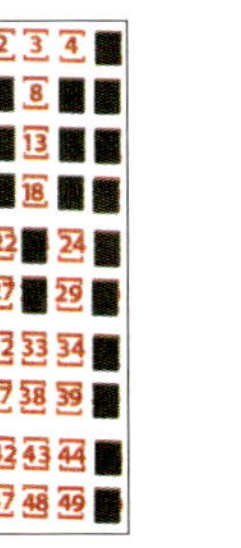

AND I WON THE LOTTERY

MY NAME IS

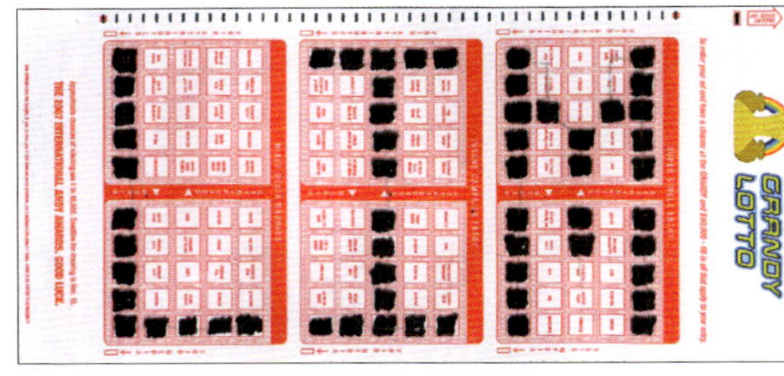

AND I WON THE LOTTERY

MY NAME IS

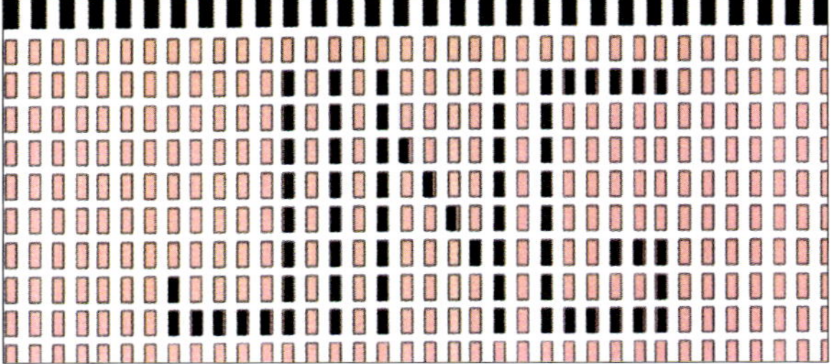

AND I WON THE LOTTERY

MY NAME IS

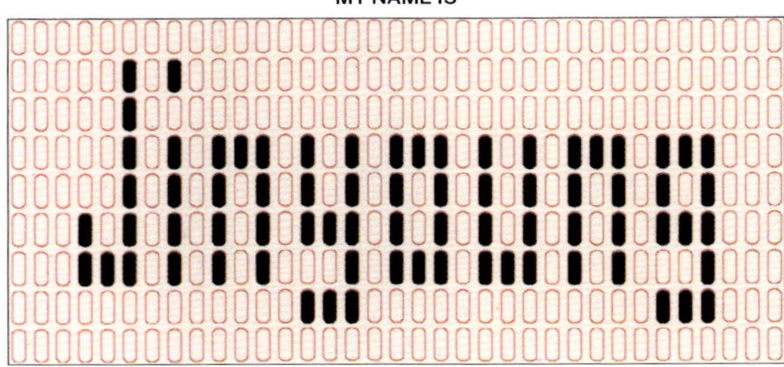

AND I WON THE LOTTERY

MY NAME IS

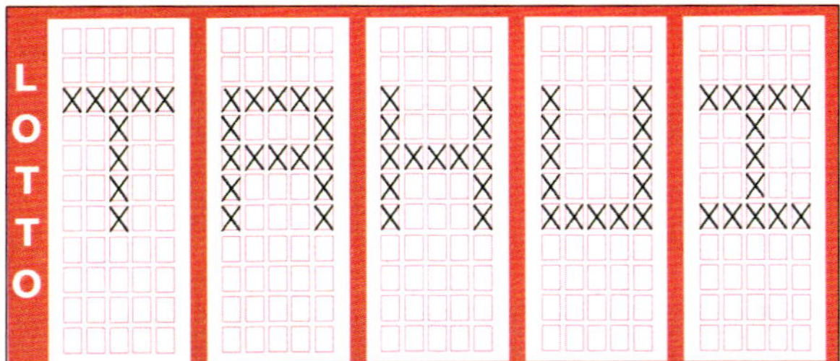

AND I WON THE LOTTERY

MY NAME IS

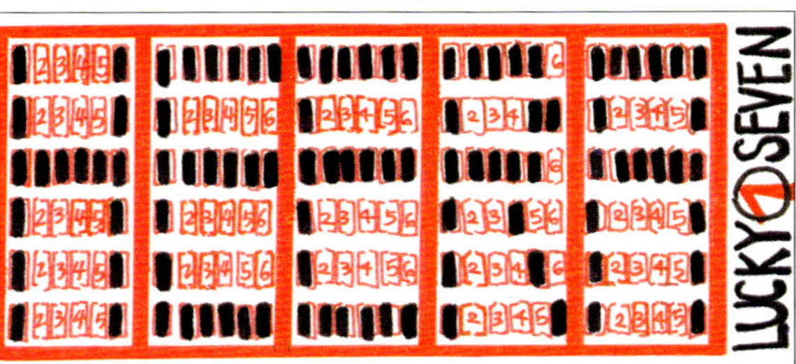

AND I WON THE LOTTERY

MY NAME IS

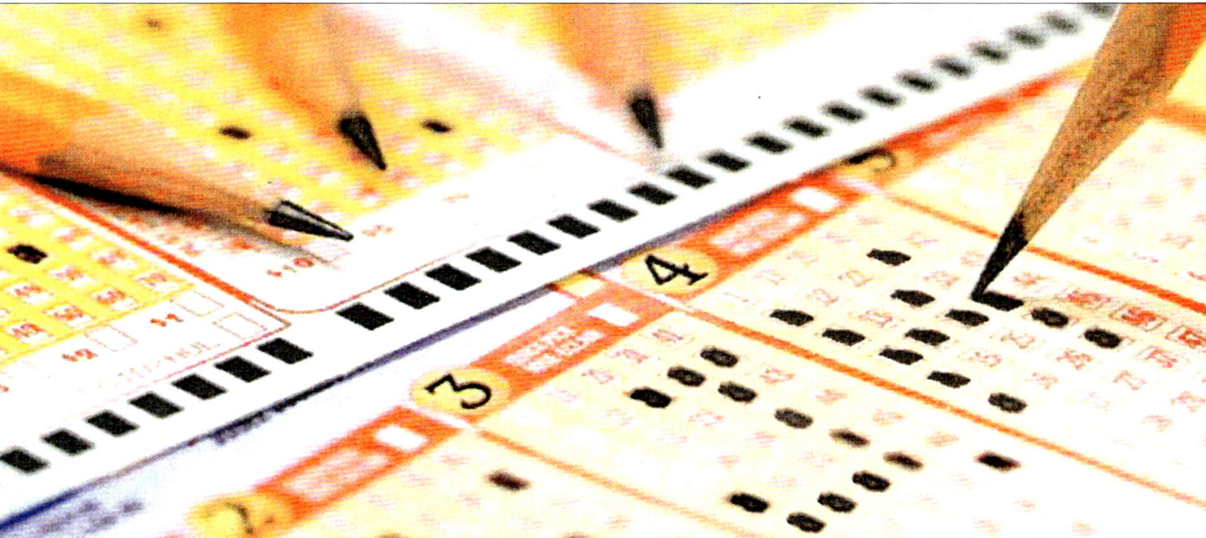

AND I WON THE LOTTERY

MY NAME IS

AND I WON THE LOTTERY

MY NAME IS

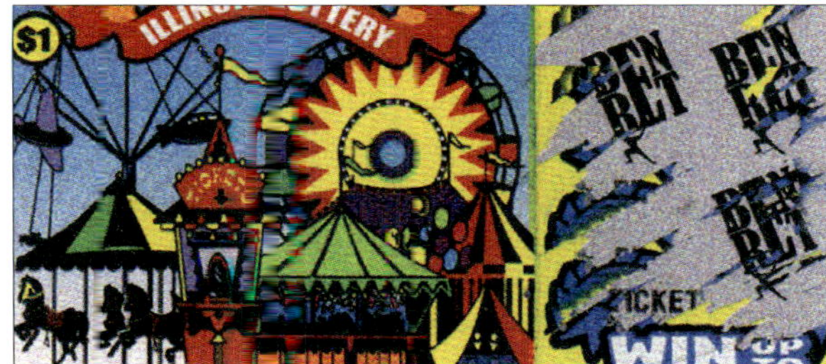

AND I WON THE LOTTERY

MY NAME IS

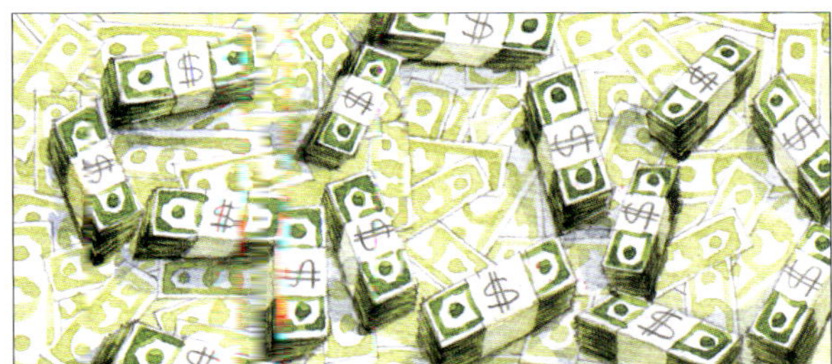

AND I WON THE LOTTERY

MY NAME IS

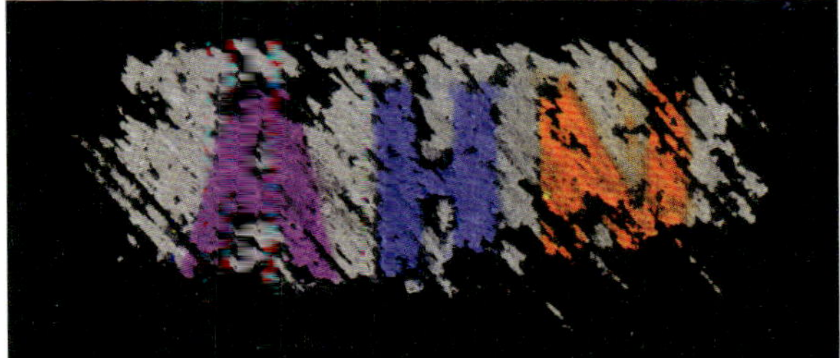

AND I WON THE LOTTERY

MY NAME IS

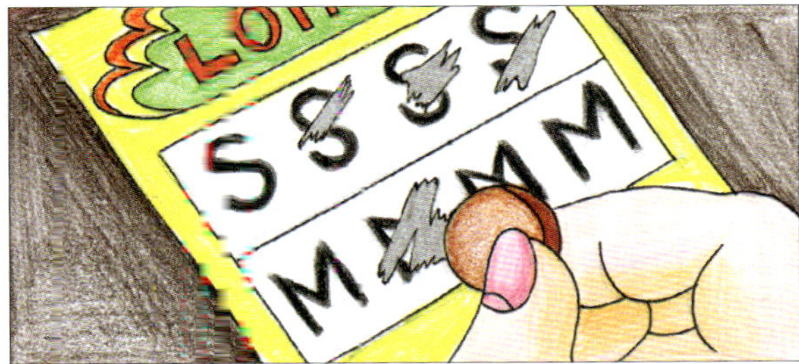

AND I WON THE LOTTERY

MY NAME IS

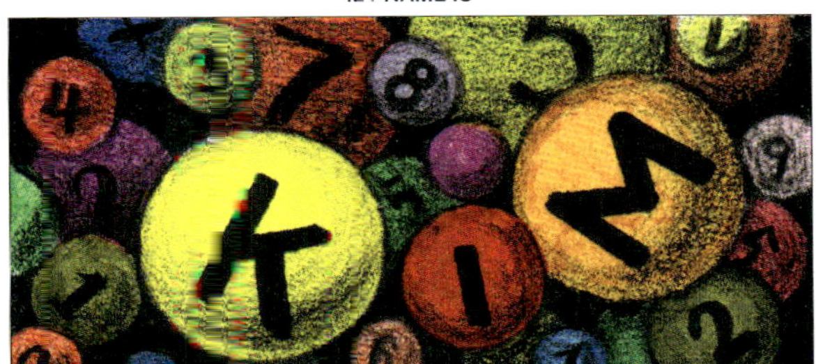

AND I WON THE LOTTERY

MY NAME IS

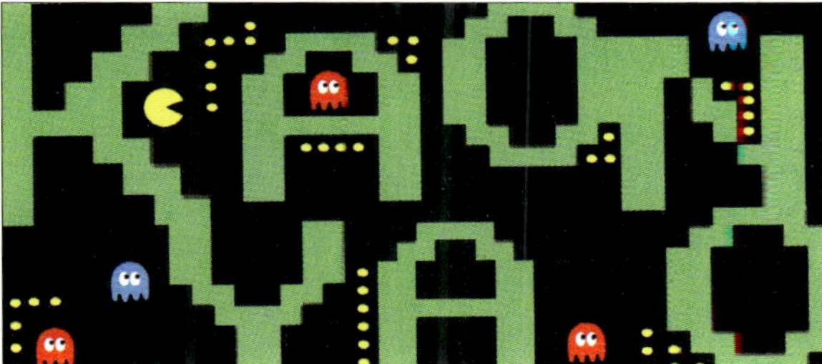

AND I'M AN EXPERT VIDEO GAME PLAYER

MY NAME IS

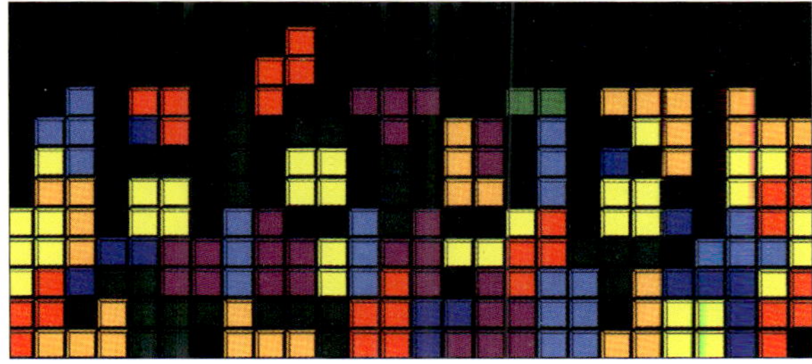

AND I'M AN EXPERT VIDEO GAME PLAYER

MY NAME IS

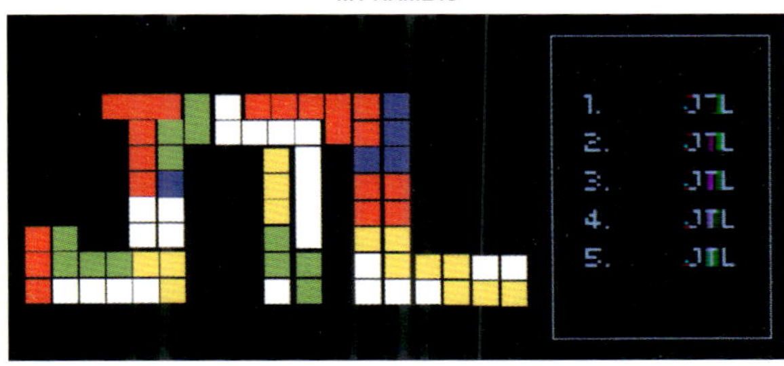

AND I'M AN EXPERT VIDEO GAME PLAYER

MY NAME IS

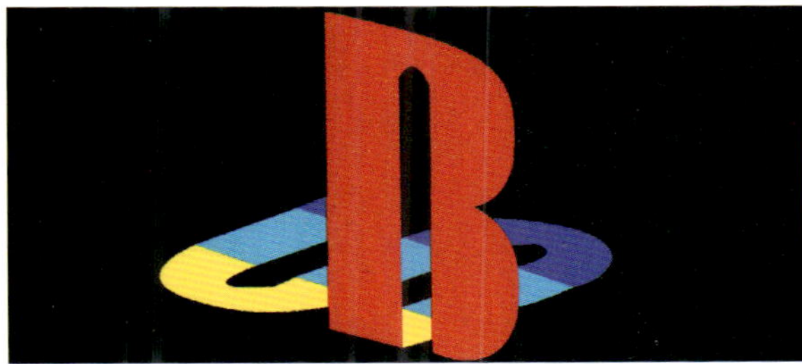

AND I'M AN EXPERT VIDEO GAME PLAYER

MY NAME IS

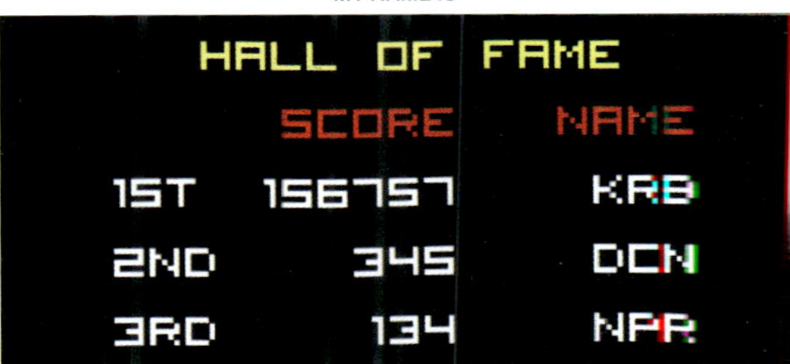

AND I'M AN EXPERT VIDEO GAME PLAYER

MY NAME IS

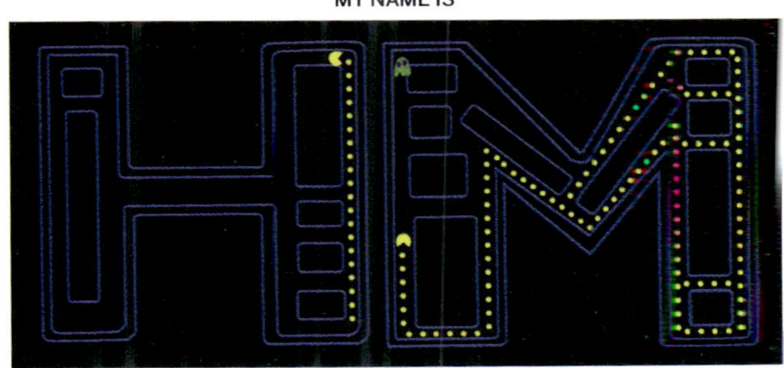

AND I'M AN EXPERT VIDEO GAME PLAYER

TYPOGRAPHIC PORTRAIT SOLUTIONS:

Figures 1 through 7 are personal interpretations of winning the lottery, in all of which a lottery ticket functions as the ground where the name is penciled in, while in figures 8 through 13, other imagery associated with the lottery is used.

Figures 14 through 19 are solutions that represent being an expert video game player. Inspiration for most solutions is taken from various aspects of the genre of computer games.

1. *Kim Capers*
2. *Duri Lim*
3. *Yumi Kunz*
4. *Jinyoung Yoo*
5. *Tahui Lee*
6. *Heera Kim*
7. *Joo King*
8. *Mihee Choi*
9. *Brent Philhower*
10. *Soomin Yoo*
11. *Jeonghyun Ahn*
12. *Seongmi Park*
13. *Seonghye Kim*
14. *Kaya Ono*
15. *Saehoon Park*
16. *Jennie Lou*
17. *Sara Berks*
18. *Kevin Banker*
19. *Hollis Maloney*

MY NAME IS

EUNJUNG

AND I WAS POPULAR IN MY PAST LIFE

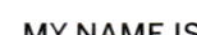

MY NAME IS

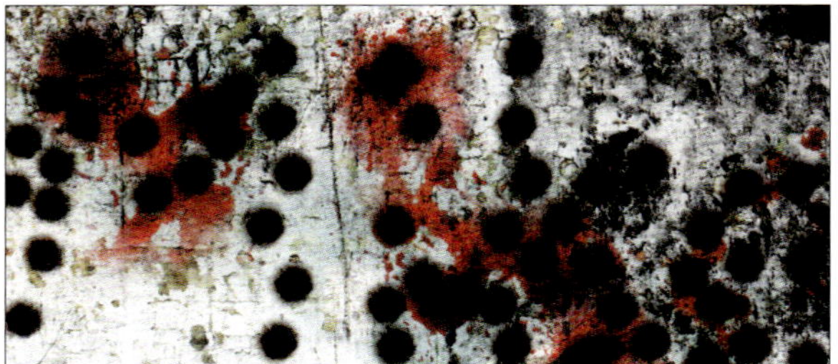

AND I'M A POSTAL WORKER

MY NAME IS

AND I'M A LIBRARIAN

MY NAME IS

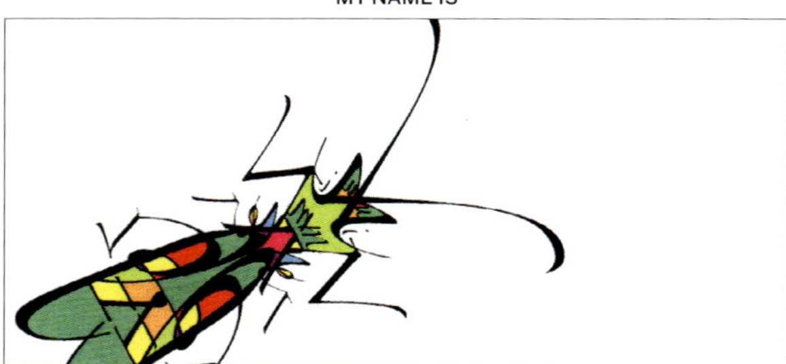

AND I'M A PARASITE

MY NAME IS

araBerkSaraBer

AND I'M A CHAIN SMOKER

MY NAME IS

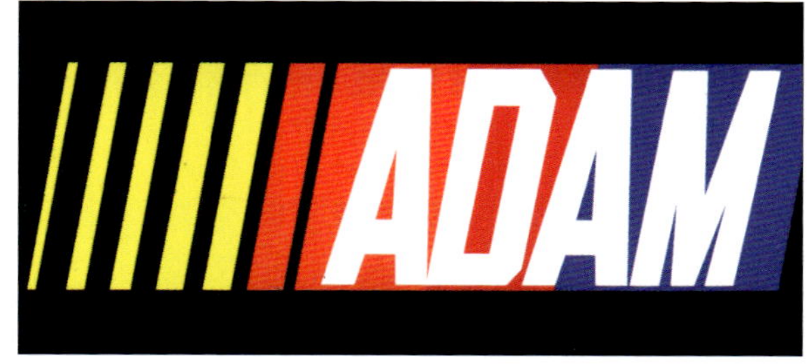

AND I'M A PROFESSIONAL RACE CAR DRIVER

MY NAME IS

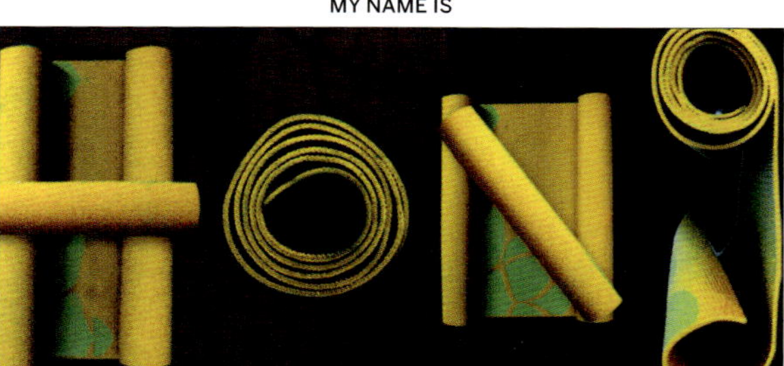

AND I DO YOGA

TYPOGRAPHIC PORTRAIT SOLUTIONS:

Figures 1 through 17 represent a variety of subjects, including: parasite, chain smoker, racecar driver, yoga enthusiast, preschool teacher, cross dresser, and other subjects that have previously appeared in this chapter.

MY NAME IS

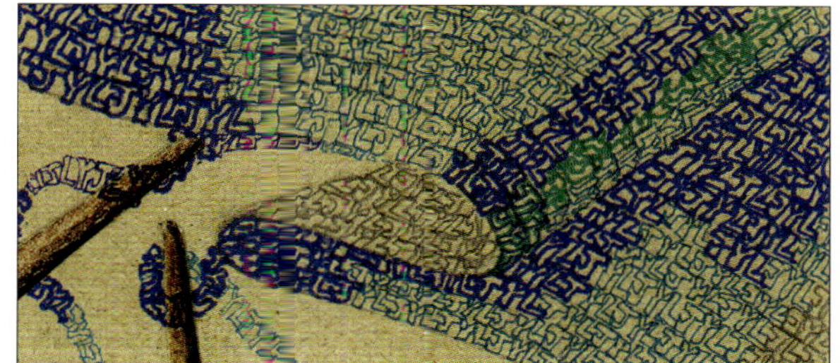

AND I DO NEEDLEPOINT

MY NAME IS

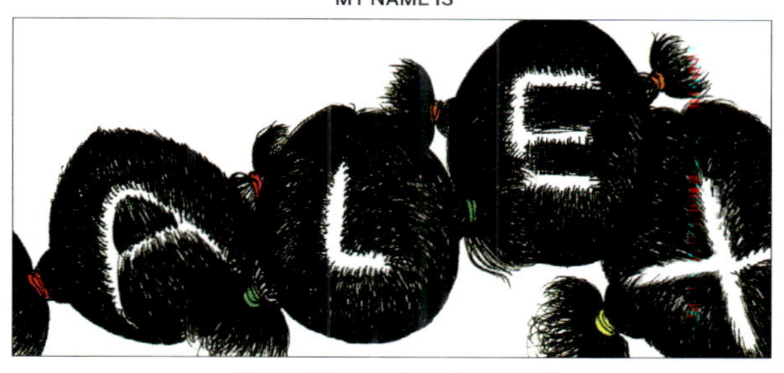

AND I'M A PRESCHOOL TEACHER

MY NAME IS

AND I'M A LIBRARIAN

MY NAME IS

AND I DO NEEDLEPOINT

MY NAME IS

Lauraiisha Proviiiidence
Lauraiisha Proviiiidence
Lauraiisha Proviiiidence
Lauraiisha Proviiiidence

AND I'M OBSESSIVE COMPULSIVE

MY NAME IS

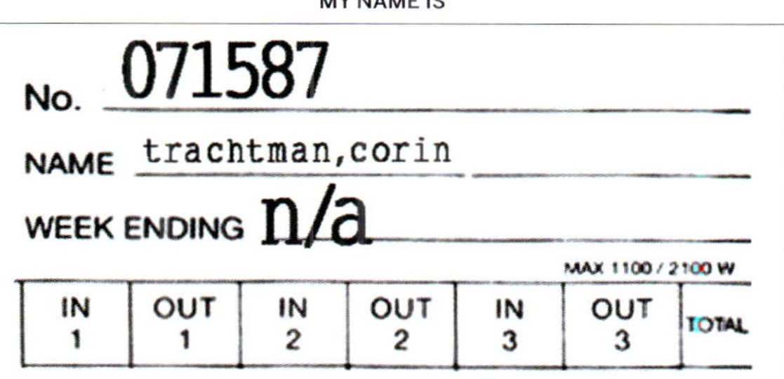

AND I WORK ON AN ASSEMBLY LINE

MY NAME IS

HMS

AND I'M A CROSS DRESSER

MY NAME IS

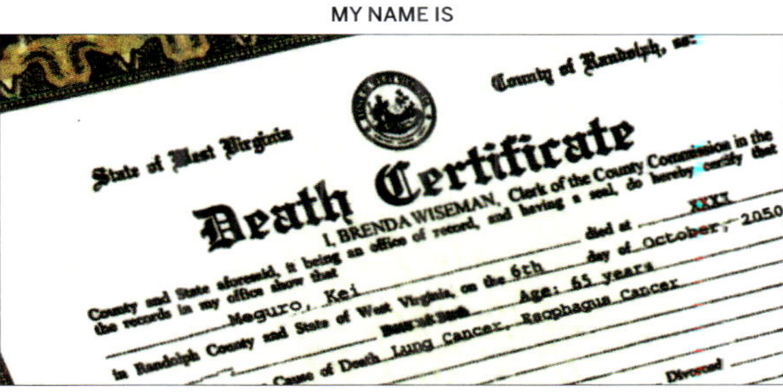

AND I'M A CRIME SCENE INVESTIGATOR

MY NAME IS

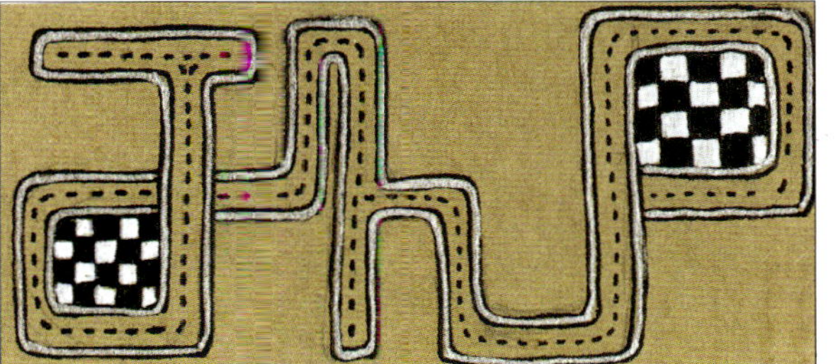

AND I'M A PROFESSIONAL RACE CAR DRIVER

MY NAME IS

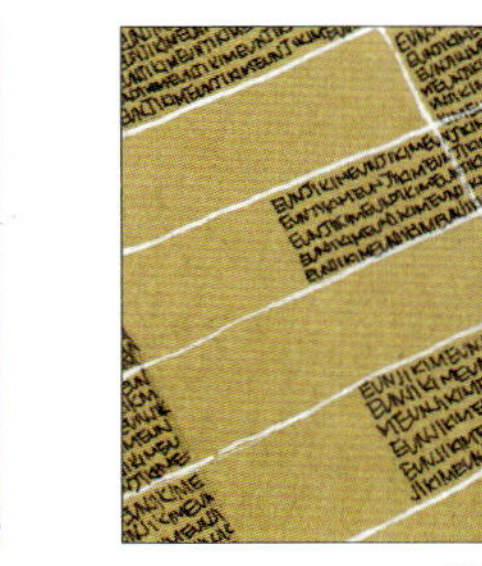

AND I'M OBSESSIVE COMPULSIVE

1. Eunjung Kim
2. Michael Milyavsky
3. Adam Kostman
4. Huimin Lee
5. Sara Berks
6. Adam Augustine
7. Seokmin Hong
8. Jiyoung Lee
9. Luree Lee
10. Lauraisha Providence
11. Heather Seksinsky
12. Jihyun Park
13. Alex Lu
14. Seokmin Hong
15. Corin Trachtman
16. Kei Meguro
17. Eunji Kim

THOUGHTS ON THE CREATIVE PROCESS 7

Remember it's a process. Research. Ponder. Digest.

"HEY TAXI!"

USE A TAXICAB AS A VEHICLE TO EXPRESS THE FOLLOWING SUBJECTS THAT ARE PREVALENT IN NEW YORK CITY. IN THE SPACES PROVIDED BELOW USE THE YELLOW AND BLACK CHECKERED TAXICAB IN ITS ENTIRETY, OR IN PART. ALSO CONSIDER: THE OFF DUTY SIGN, CHECKERED MOTIF, MEDALLION, CAB DRIVER I.D., METER, RATE CHART THAT APPEARS ON THE OUTER DOOR OF THE TAXI, OBJECTS HANGING FROM THE REAR VIEW MIRROR, LICENSE PLATE, ETC. TO BEST EXPRESS YOUR CONCEPTS CONSIDER COMBINING DESIGN PRINCIPLES THAT INCLUDE: SCALE, CONTRAST, PATTERN, RHYTHM, SHAPE, TEXTURE, COLOR, LINE, OVERLAPPING, PERSPECTIVE, CROPPING, NEGATIVE/POSITIVE RELATIONSHIPS AND COMPOSITION.

TRAFFIC JAM OR OVERCROWDING

NOISE OR HOSTILITY

POLLUTION

CONSUMERISM

DIVERSITY

HOMELESSNESS

PROBLEMS : SOLUTIONS SERIES

CREATED BY RICHARD WILDE / JUDITH WILDE, PRODUCED BY VISUAL ARTS PRESS, LTD. ART DIRECTORS: RICHARD WILDE / JUDITH WILDE

HEY TAXI PROBLEM:

Use a taxicab as a vehicle to express the following subjects that are prevalent in New York City that include: traffic jam or overcrowding, noise or hostility, pollution, consumerism, diversity and homelessness.

AIM:
The idea of taking an item and either deconstructing it, repeating it, or altering it, while at the same time maintaining its integrity and adhering to a consistent color palette might at the onset seem restricting. Yet, this very limitation creates the conditions that give rise to an array of executions. Limiting one's palette, coupled with specific subjects of investigation, helps focus one's thinking. When a visual vocabulary of forms is established the stage is set to play and experiment. The more specific the vocabulary the clearer one's journey is.

SUGGESTIONS:
One's visual vocabulary of forms should consist of the characteristics of a New York City taxicab. Images to consider are: the black and yellow checkerboard motif, the off-duty sign, medallion, driver ID, the meter, rate chart, objects hanging from the rear view mirror, and the license plate. To best express one's concept consider: scale, contrast, patterning, rhythm, line, perspective, overlapping, shape, texture, and cropping while also considering composition as it pertains to negative and positive relationships, which represents the formal design principles that are the underpinnings of one's solution.

SPECIFICATIONS:
Execute your solutions in the given areas on the assignment sheet. Color is limited to black and yellow, unless concept dictates otherwise. The color yellow can range from cadmium yellow to a yellow-orange. There are no restrictions on medium. Literal, abstract and metaphoric explorations are suggested modes of expression.

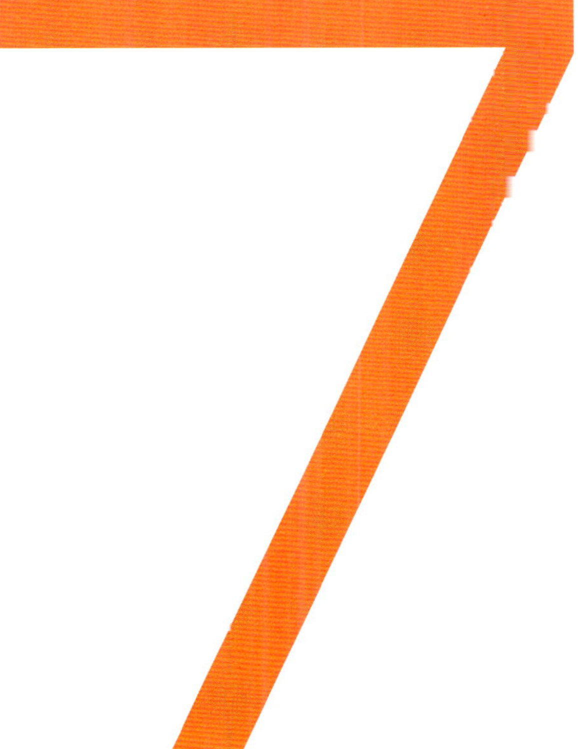

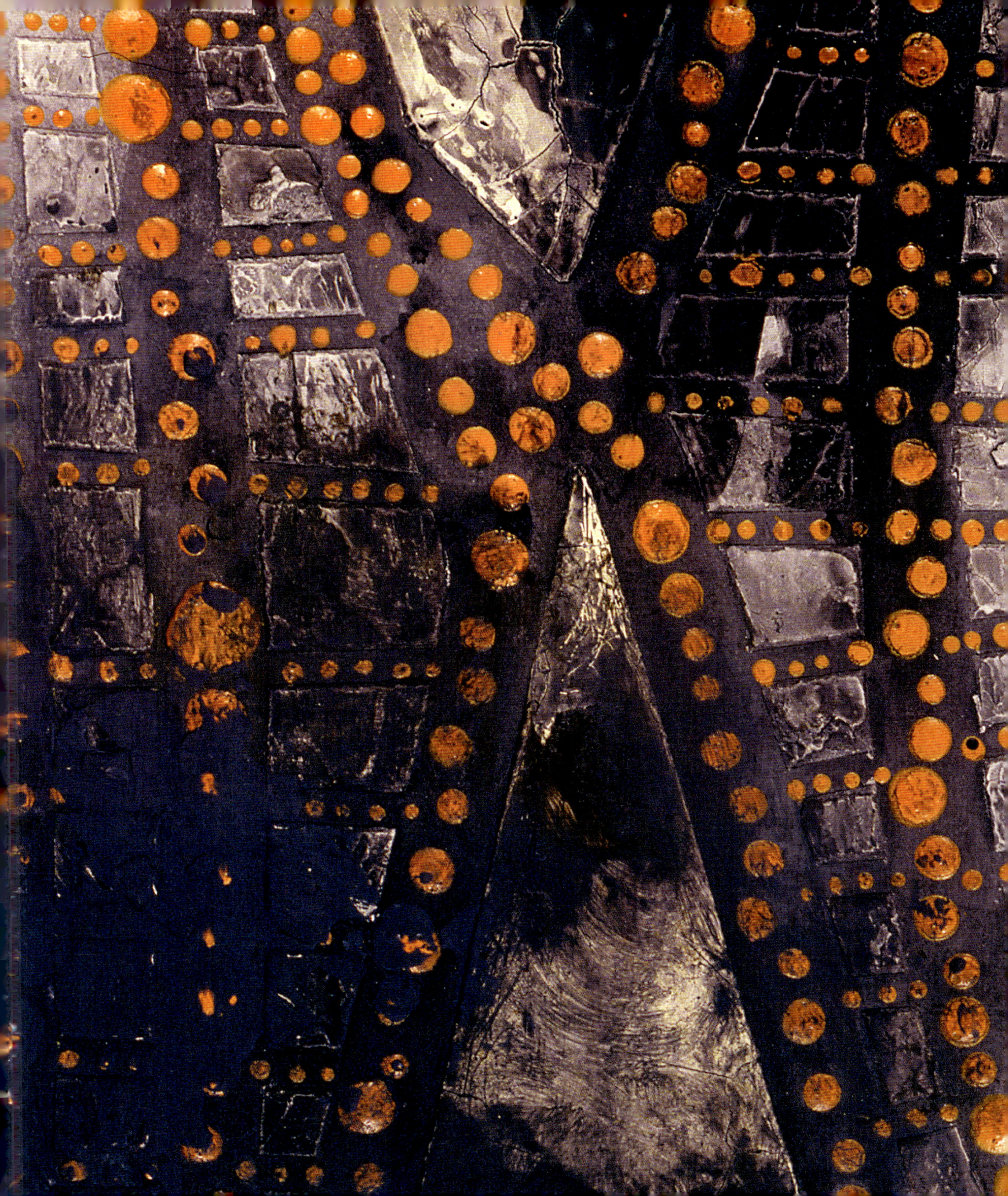

HEY TAXI SOLUTIONS:

Figure 1 is an abstract solution using tinfoil and paint to depict the subject of a traffic jam.

Figure 2 is one student's solution to the project, which uses a personal vocabulary of forms that reference a taxicab, yet goes beyond the given limitation on color to best communicate the concepts. As in many of the other projects, students who do not abide by the limitations risk failure or possible success, as per this example.

"HEY TAXI!"

USE A TAXICAB AS A VEHICLE TO EXPRESS THE FOLLOWING SUBJECTS THAT ARE PREVALENT IN NEW YORK CITY. IN THE SPACES PROVIDED BELOW USE THE YELLOW AND BLACK CHECKERED TAXICAB IN ITS ENTIRETY, OR IN PART. ALSO CONSIDER: THE OFF DUTY SIGN, CHECKERED MOTIF, MEDALLION, CAB DRIVER I.D., METER, RATE CHART THAT APPEARS ON THE OUTER DOOR OF THE TAXI, OBJECTS HANGING FROM THE REAR VIEW MIRROR, LICENSE PLATE, ETC. TO BEST EXPRESS YOUR CONCEPTS CONSIDER COMBINING DESIGN PRINCIPLES THAT INCLUDE: SCALE, CONTRAST, PATTERN, RHYTHM, SHAPE, TEXTURE, COLOR, LINE, OVERLAPPING, PERSPECTIVE, CROPPING, NEGATIVE/POSITIVE RELATIONSHIPS AND COMPOSITION.

TRAFFIC JAM OR OVERCROWDING

NOISE OR HOSTILITY

POLLUTION

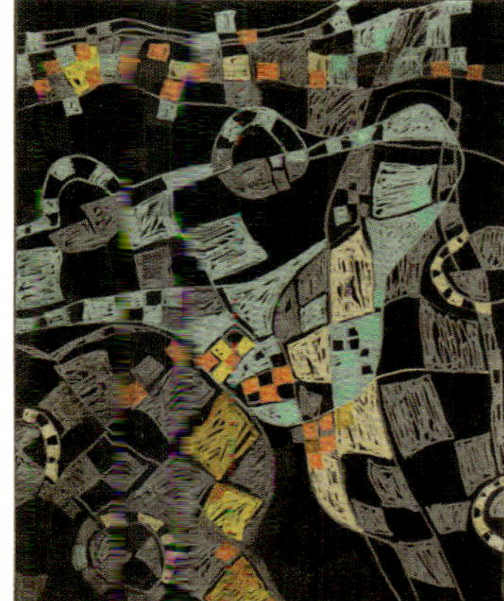

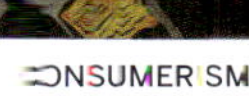

CONSUMERISM

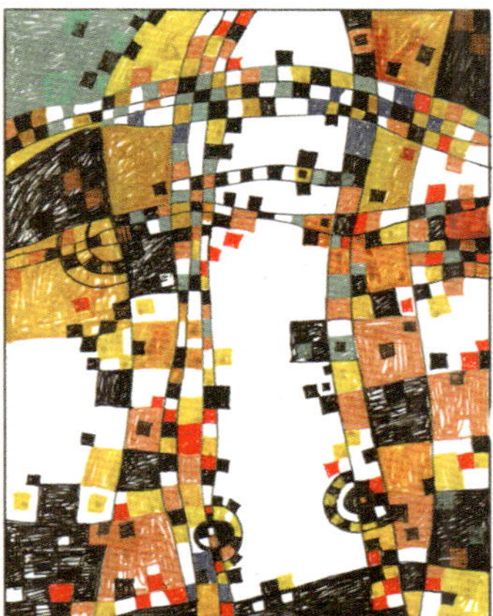

DIVERSITY

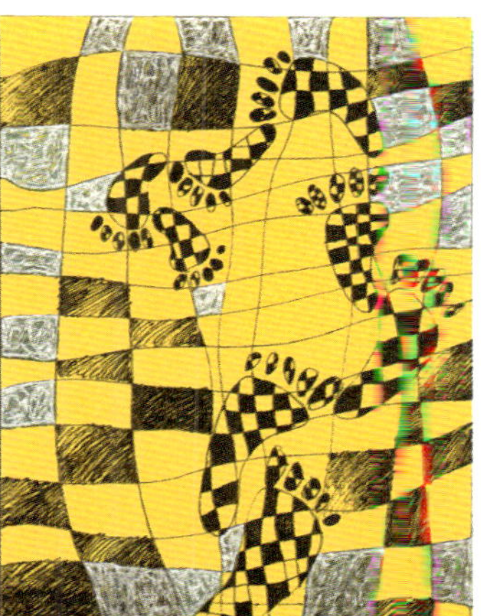

HOMELESSNESS

PROBLEMS : SOLUTIONS SERIES

CREATED BY RICHARD WILDE / JUDITH WILDE. PRODUCED BY VISUAL ARTS PRESS, LTD. ART DIRECTORS: RICHARD WILDE / JUDITH WILDE

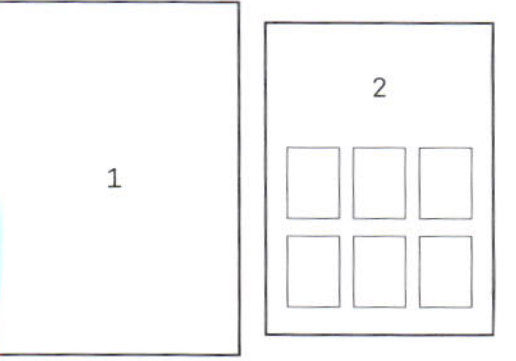

1. *Matt Ryan*
2. *Nataliya Hats*

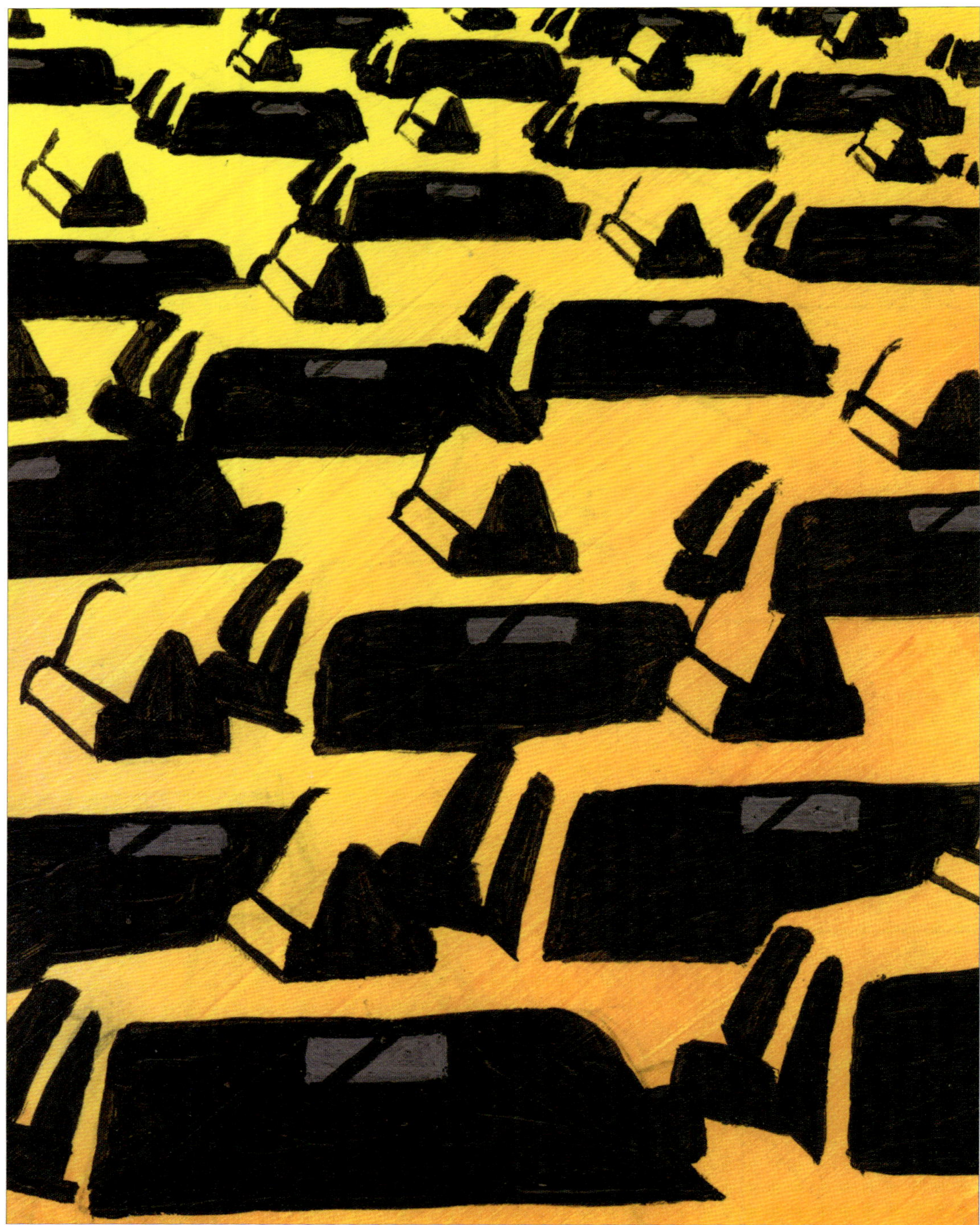

TRAFFIC JAM OR OVERCROWDING

HEY TAXI SOLUTIONS:

Figures 1 through 11 express a traffic jam or overcrowding.

Figure 1 is a reductive solution using negative and positive shapes coupled with perspective to graphically interpret a sea of taxicabs. Given the limited amount of information that is used to describe a taxicab, the viewer is challenged as in many other solutions to discern the narrative.

Figures 2 through 11 range from abstract to literal to symbolic depictions.

Figure 4 uses as a metaphor sperm heading toward the taxicab symbol, which represents an egg.

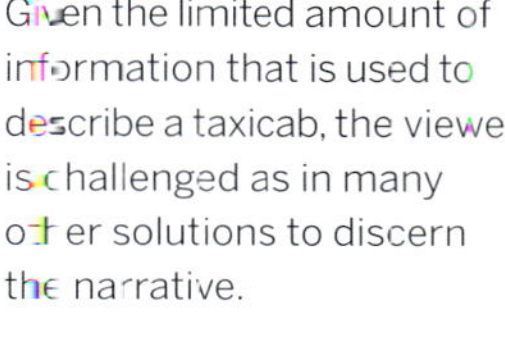

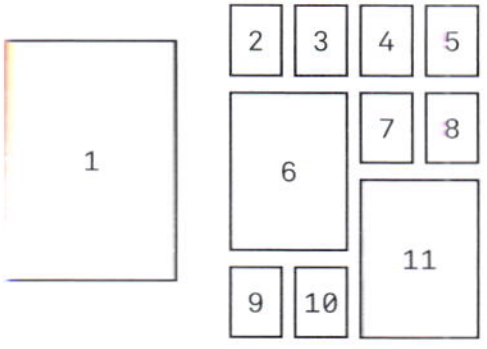

1 2 3 4 5 6 7 8 9 10 11

1. *Sunyoung Koo*
2. *Chris Mohr*
3. *Youngbum Kim*
4. *Hyungkyu Choi*
5. *Matt Schoch*
6. *Nancy Balsamello*
7. *S.S. Kim*
8. *Hyo Han*
9. *M. Choi*
10. *Wei Lieh Lee*
11. *Charles Russo*

Figure 6 represents a map of lower Manhattan, where repetition of form is used to express the concept.

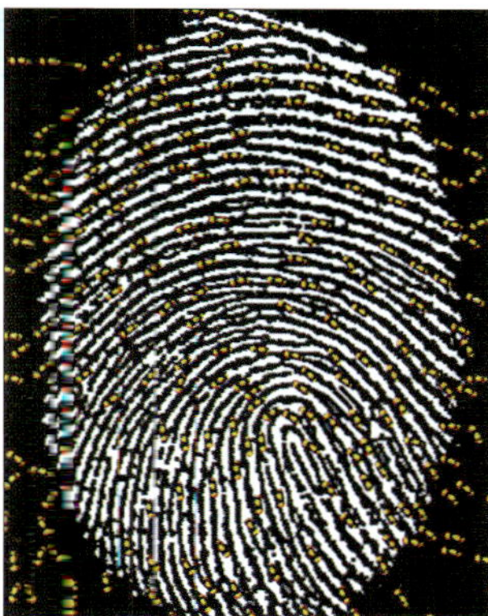

TRAFFIC JAM OR OVERCROWDING

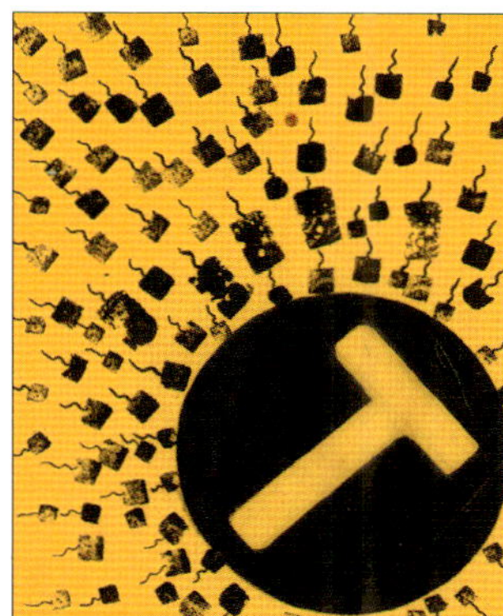

TRAFFIC JAM OR OVERCROWDING

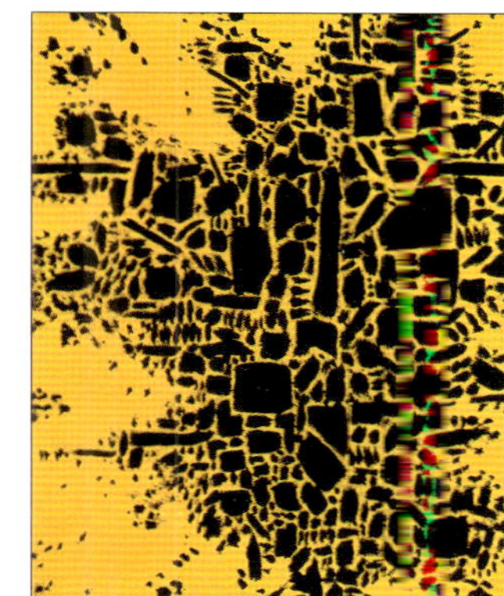

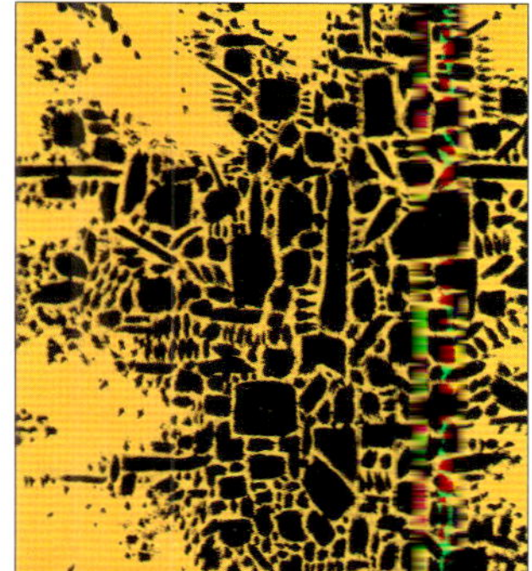

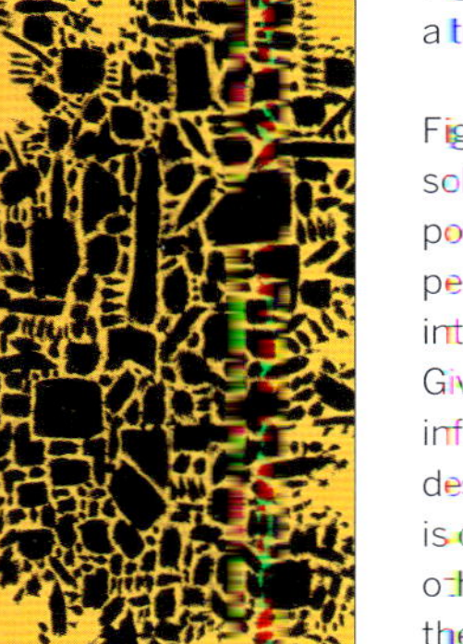

TRAFFIC JAM OR OVERCROWDING

TRAFFIC JAM OR OVERCROWDING

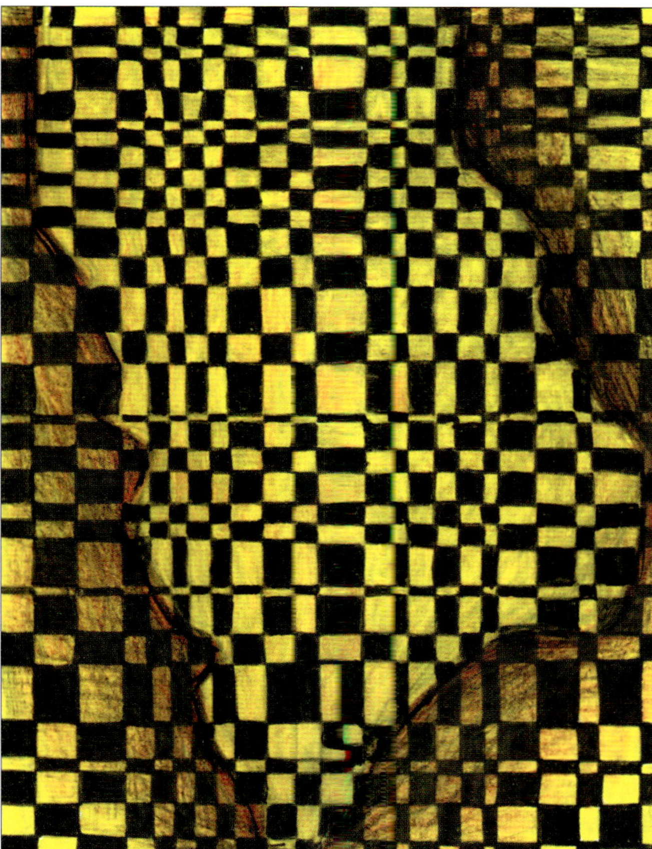

TRAFFIC JAM OR OVERCROWDING

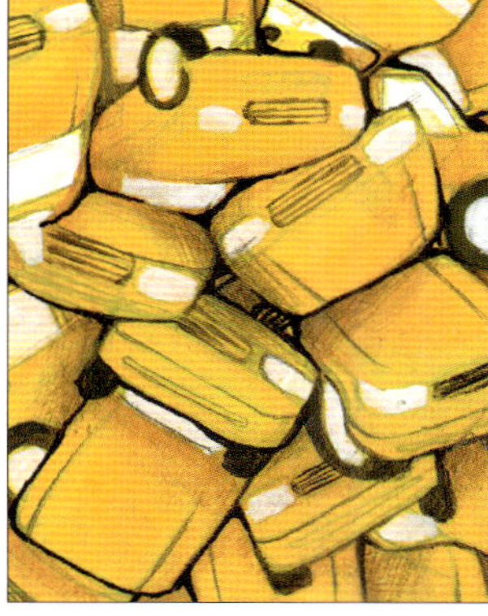

TRAFFIC JAM OR OVERCROWDING

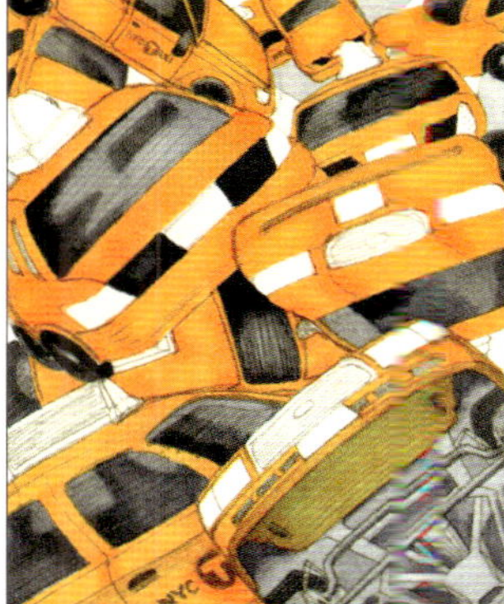

TRAFFIC JAM OR OVERCROWDING

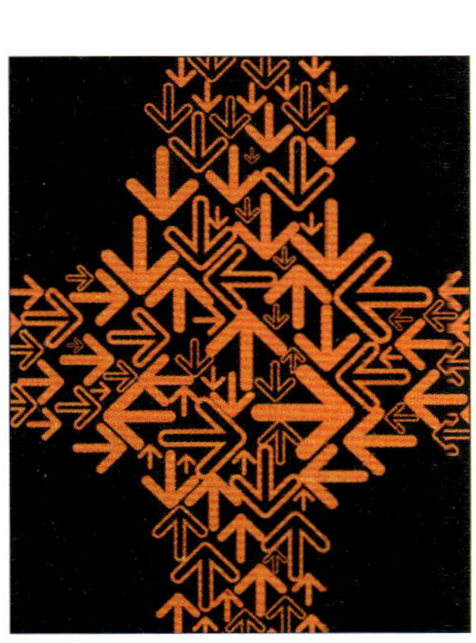

TRAFFIC JAM OR OVERCROWDING

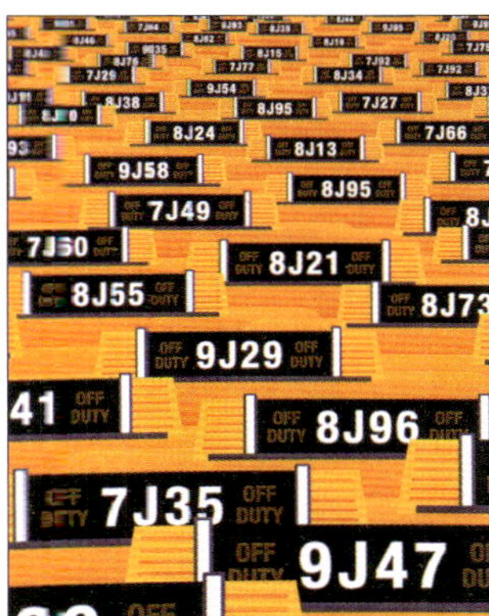

TRAFFIC JAM OR OVERCROWDING

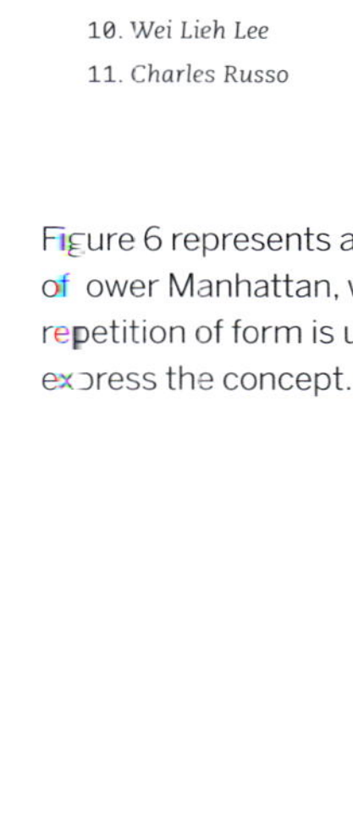

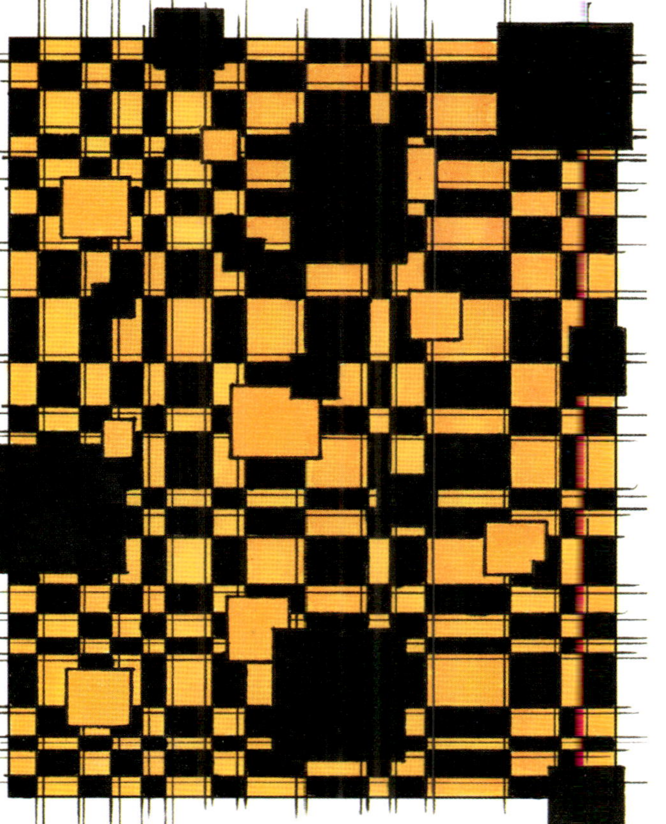

TRAFFIC JAM OR OVERCROWDING

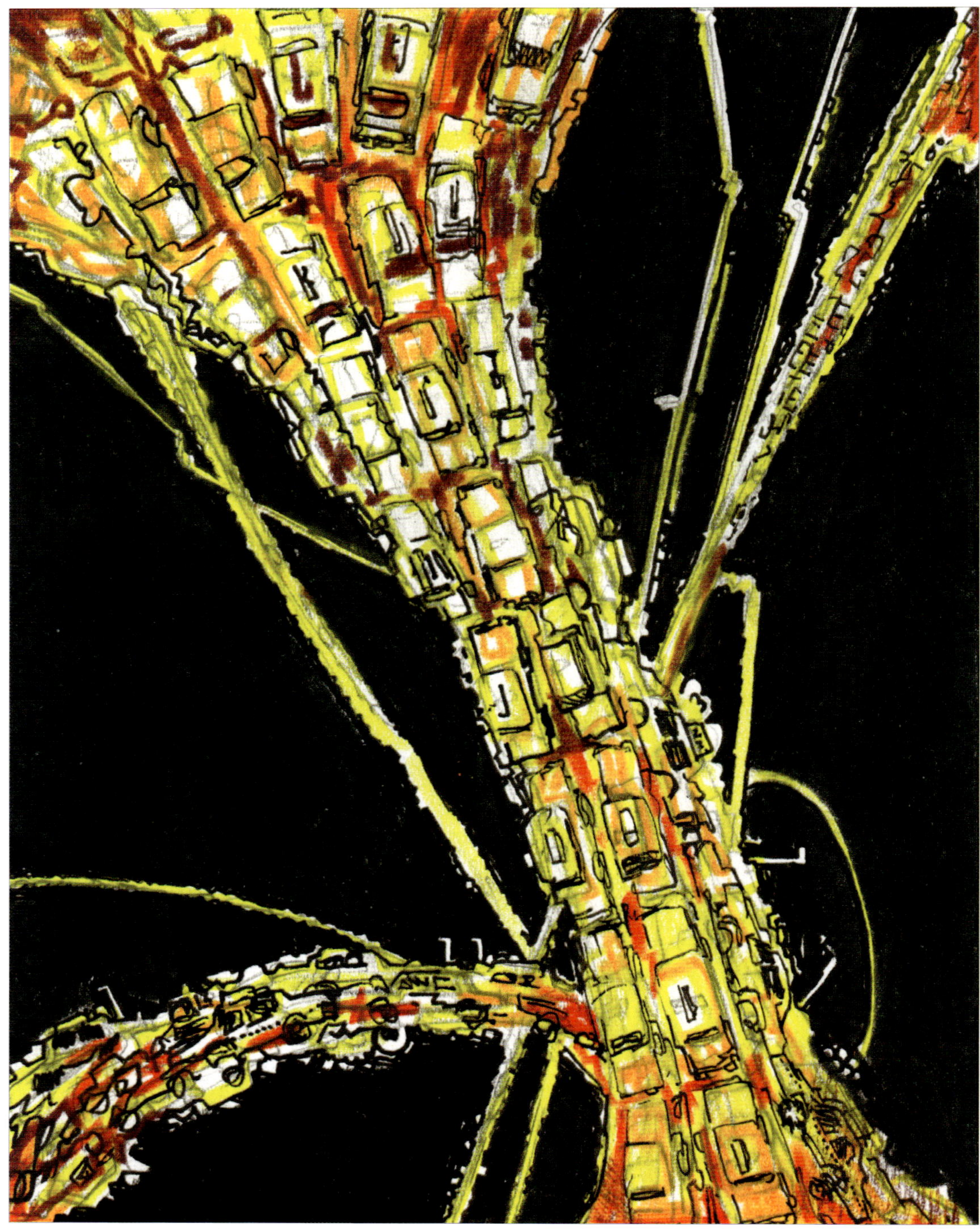

TRAFFIC JAM OR OVERCROWDING

HEY TAXI SOLUTIONS:

Figure 1 is a dynamic composition on a black ground that dramatizes a sense of overcrowding and congestion.

Figures 2 and 3 are executed as traditional illustrations.

In figures 4 through 7 and 9, patterning, texture, and repetition are the dominant elements in each solution.

Figure 8 offers a futuristic interpretation with a stylized robotic car.

TRAFFIC JAM OR OVERCROWDING

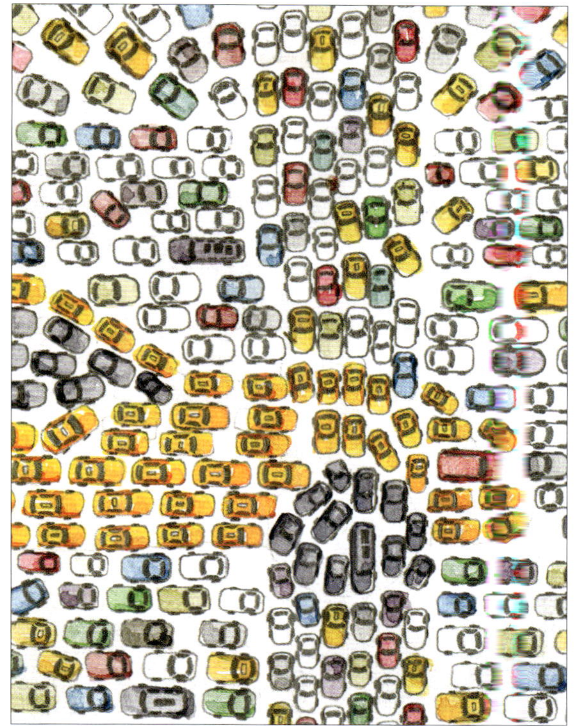

TRAFFIC JAM OR OVERCROWDING

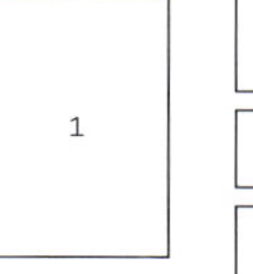

1. Eric Ku
2. S. Kim
3. Soomin Yoo
4. Daniel Cantada
5. Dahyee Hoh
6. Chelsea Cumings
7. Raisa Ivanikova
8. Jaekwang Kim
9. Yesul Kim

TRAFFIC JAM OR OVERCROWDING

TRAFFIC JAM OR OVERCROWDING

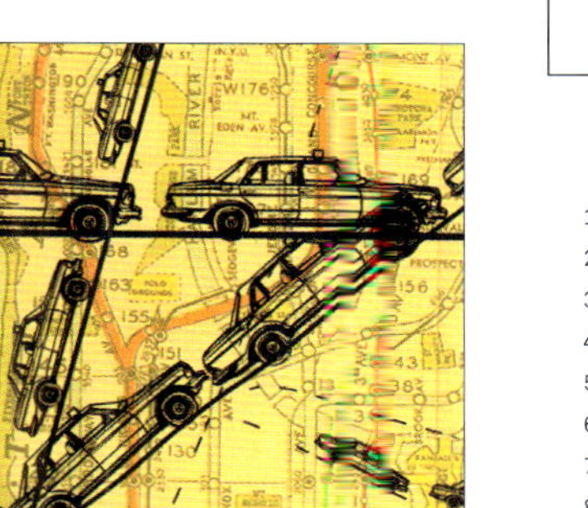

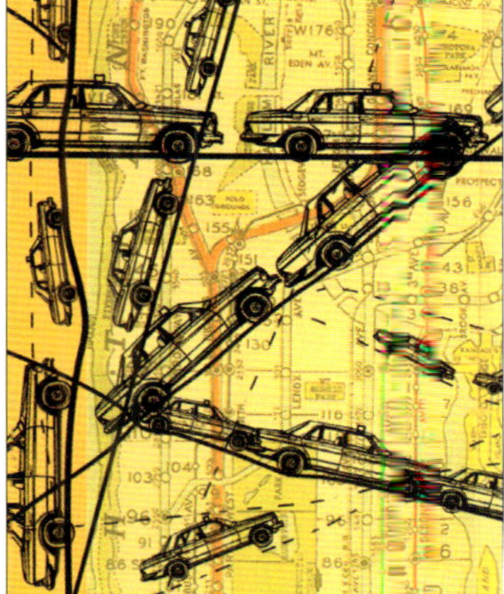

TRAFFIC JAM OR OVERCROWDING

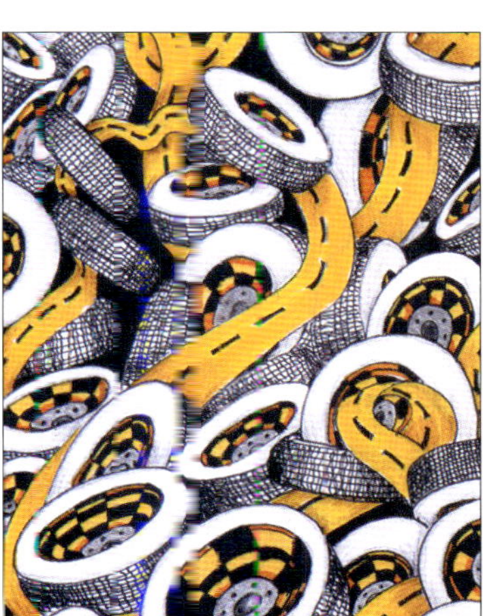

TRAFFIC JAM OR OVERCROWDING

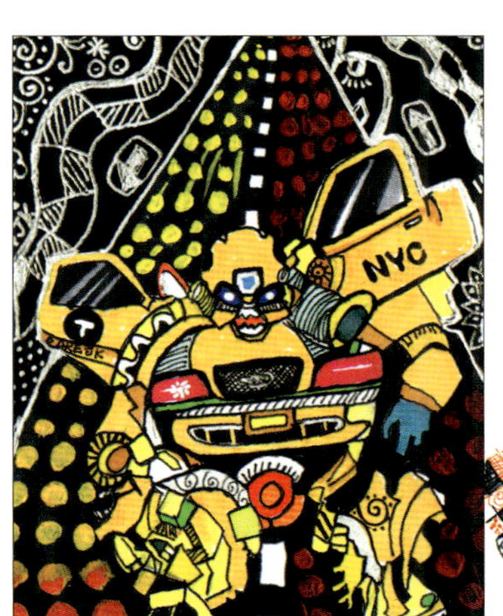

TRAFFIC JAM OR OVERCROWDING

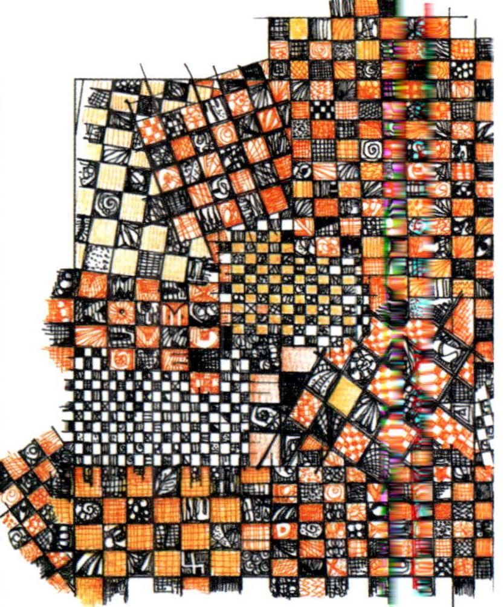

TRAFFIC JAM OR OVERCROWDING

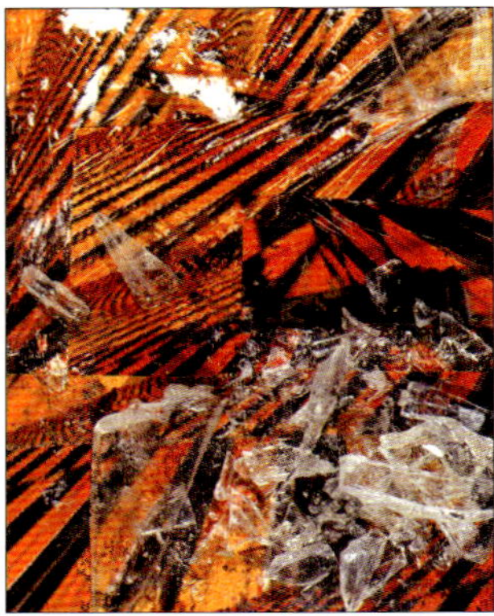
NOISE OR HOSTILITY

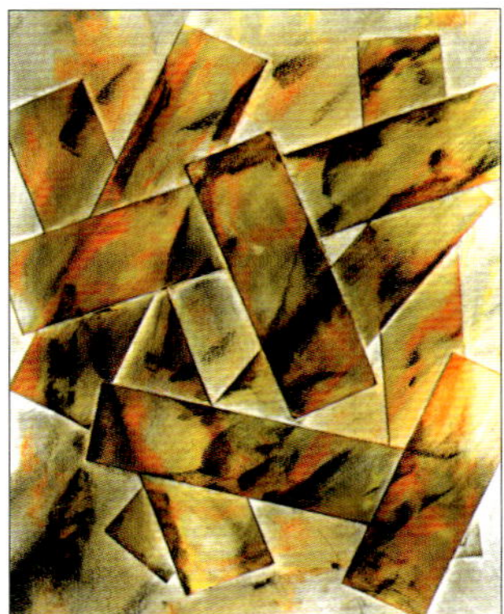
NOISE OR HOSTILITY

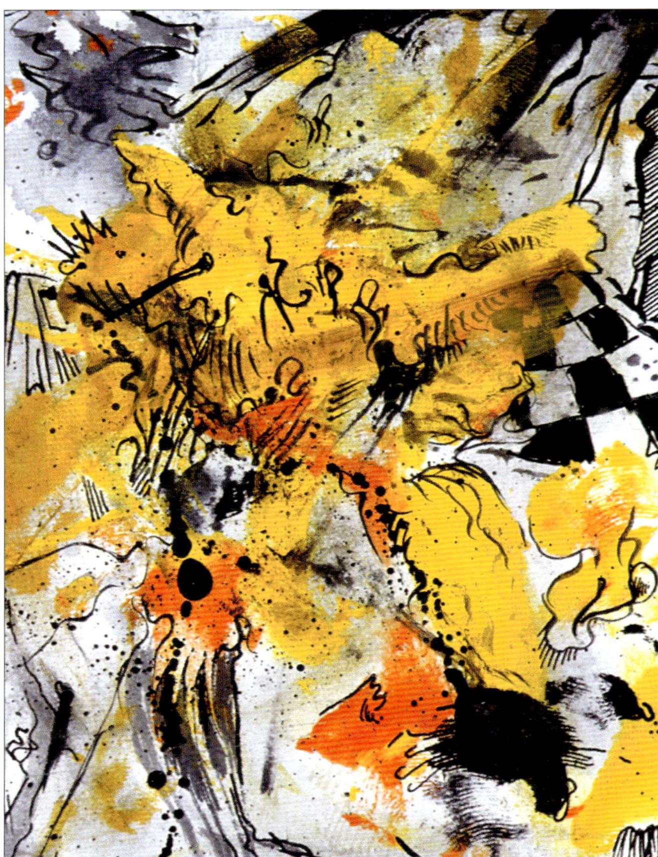
NOISE OR HOSTILITY

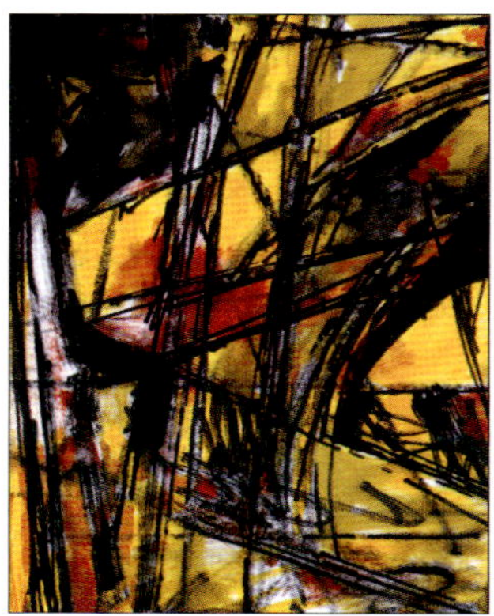
NOISE OR HOSTILITY

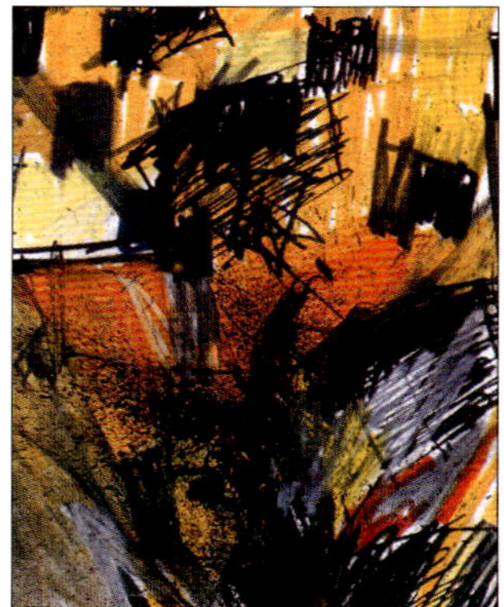
NOISE OR HOSTILITY

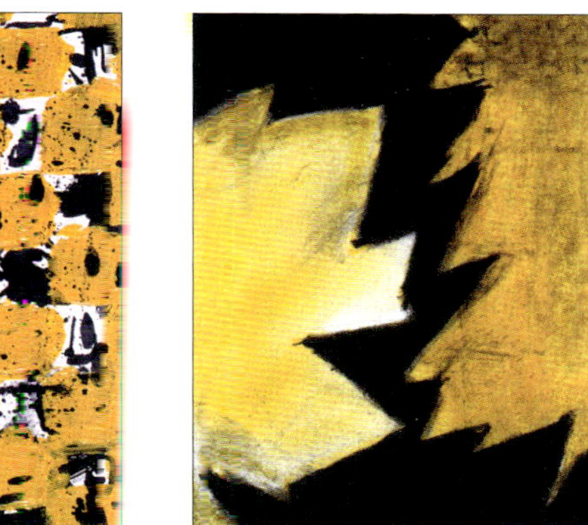

NOISE OR HOSTILITY

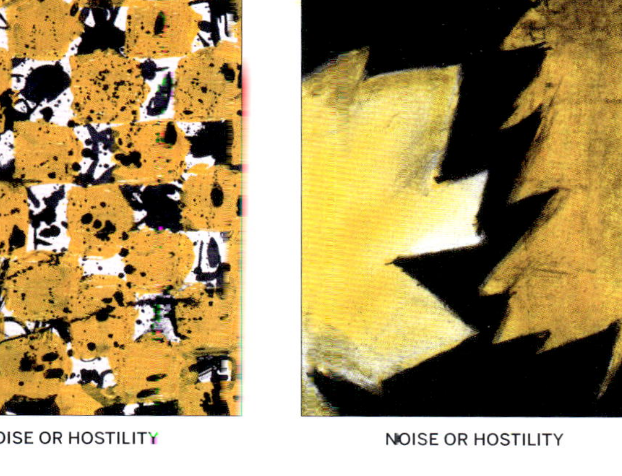

NOISE OR HOSTILITY

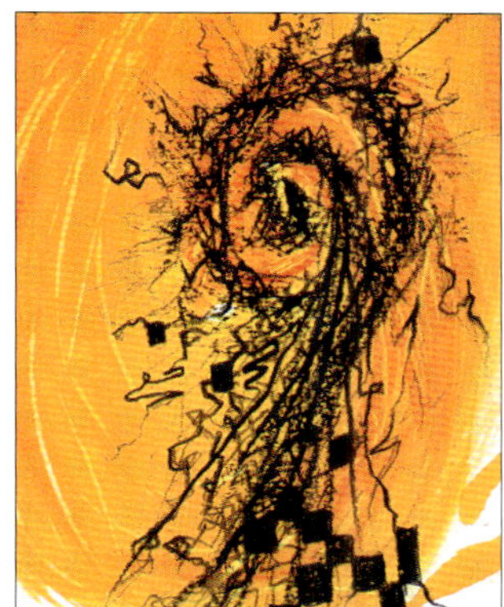

NOISE OR HOSTILITY

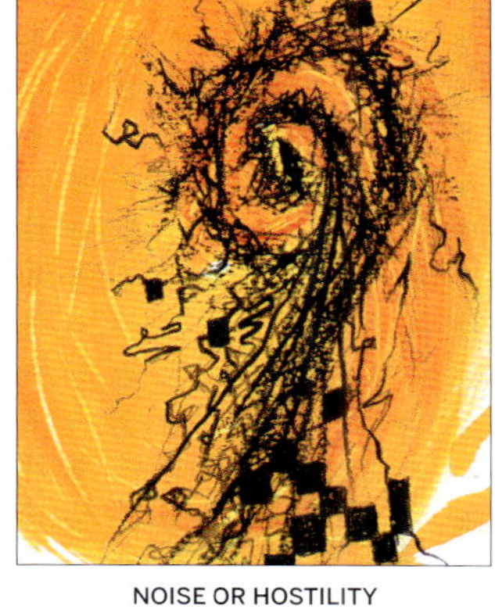

NOISE OR HOSTILITY

NOISE OR HOSTILITY

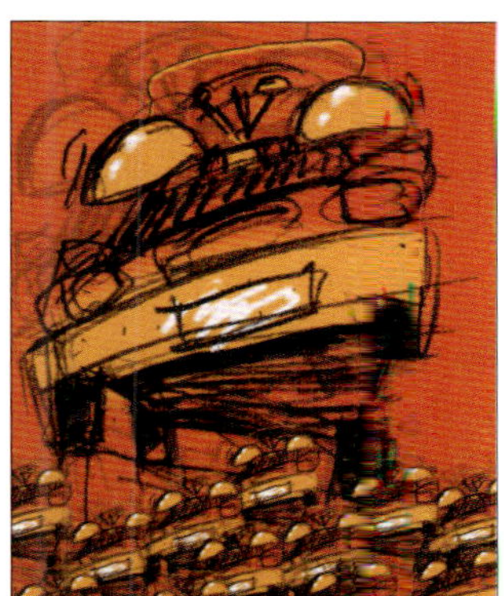

NOISE OR HOSTILITY

NOISE OR HOSTILITY

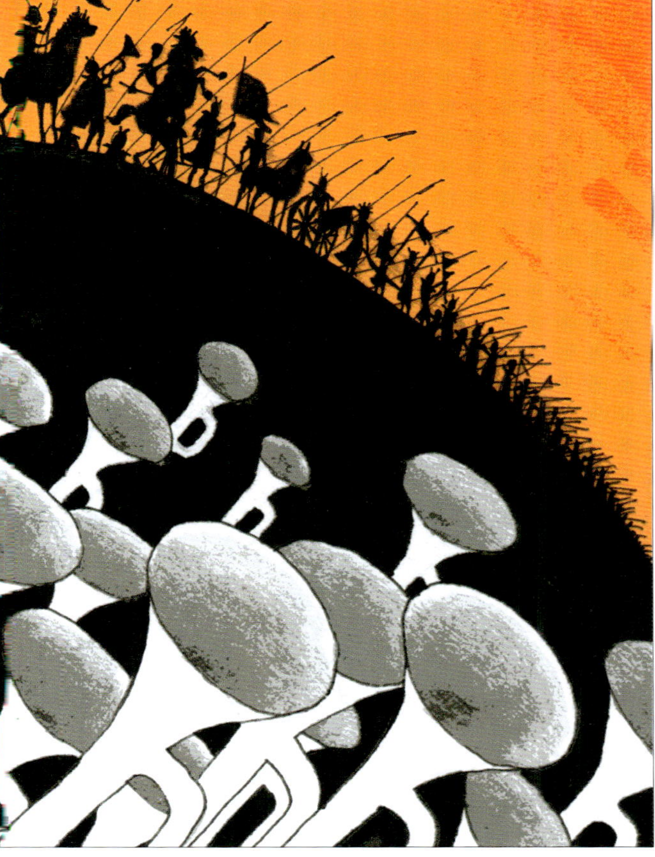

NOISE OR HOSTILITY

NOISE OR HOSTILITY

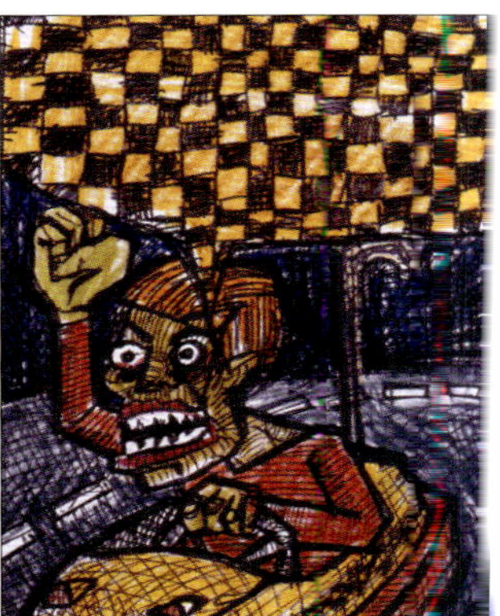

NOISE OR HOSTILITY

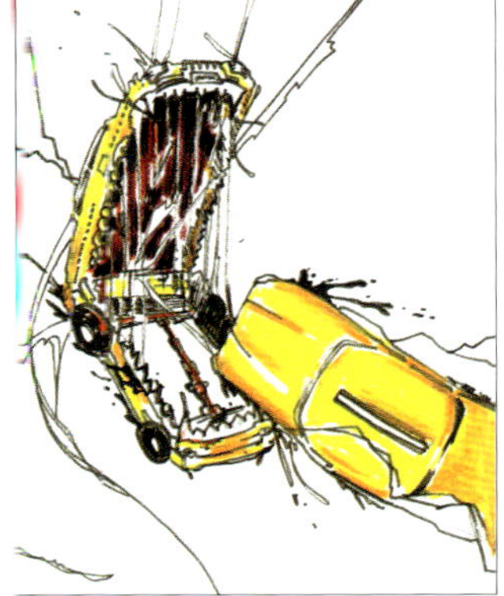

NOISE OR HOSTILITY

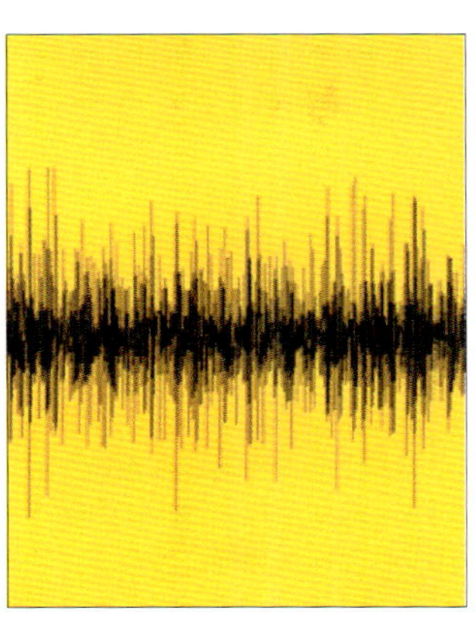

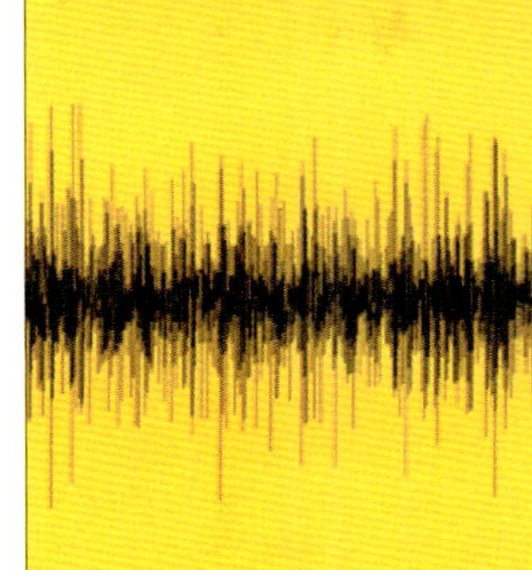

NOISE OR HOSTILITY

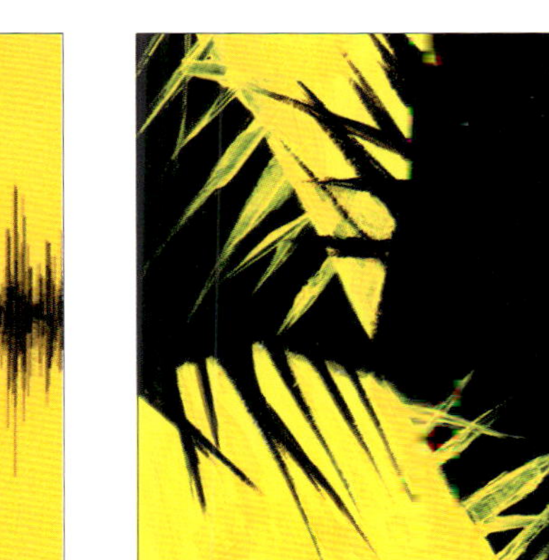

NOISE OR HOSTILITY

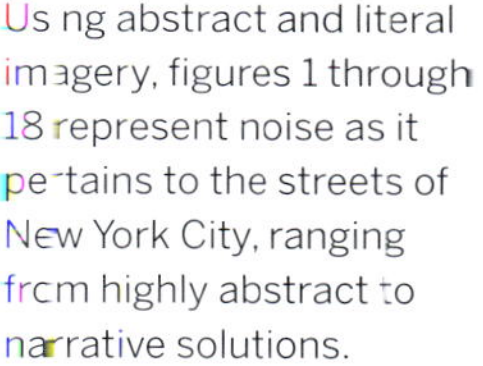

HEY TAXI SOLUTIONS:

Using abstract and literal imagery, figures 1 through 18 represent noise as it pertains to the streets of New York City, ranging from highly abstract to narrative solutions.

Figures 15 and 16 deal with hostility and road rage, using literal exaggerated imagery. All 18 solutions share a quality of agitation and angst.

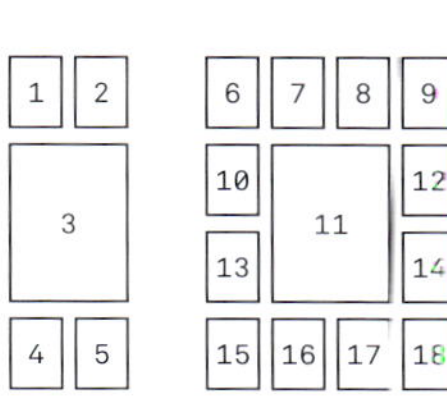

1. *Felice Simon*
2. *Ryan Sacks*
3. *Aaron Nichols*
4. *J. Kim*
5. *Felice Simon*
6. *Kiera Lewis*
7. *Patricia Han*
8. *Caroline Kim*
9. *Deukgyu Lee*
10. *Elaine Georgeou*
11. *Daewook Do*
12. *Miae Choi*
13. *Deaeun Kim*
14. *Jinkyung Myung*
15. *David Fishman*
16. *Eric Ku*
17. *Christian Arichabala*
18. *Joyce Chen*

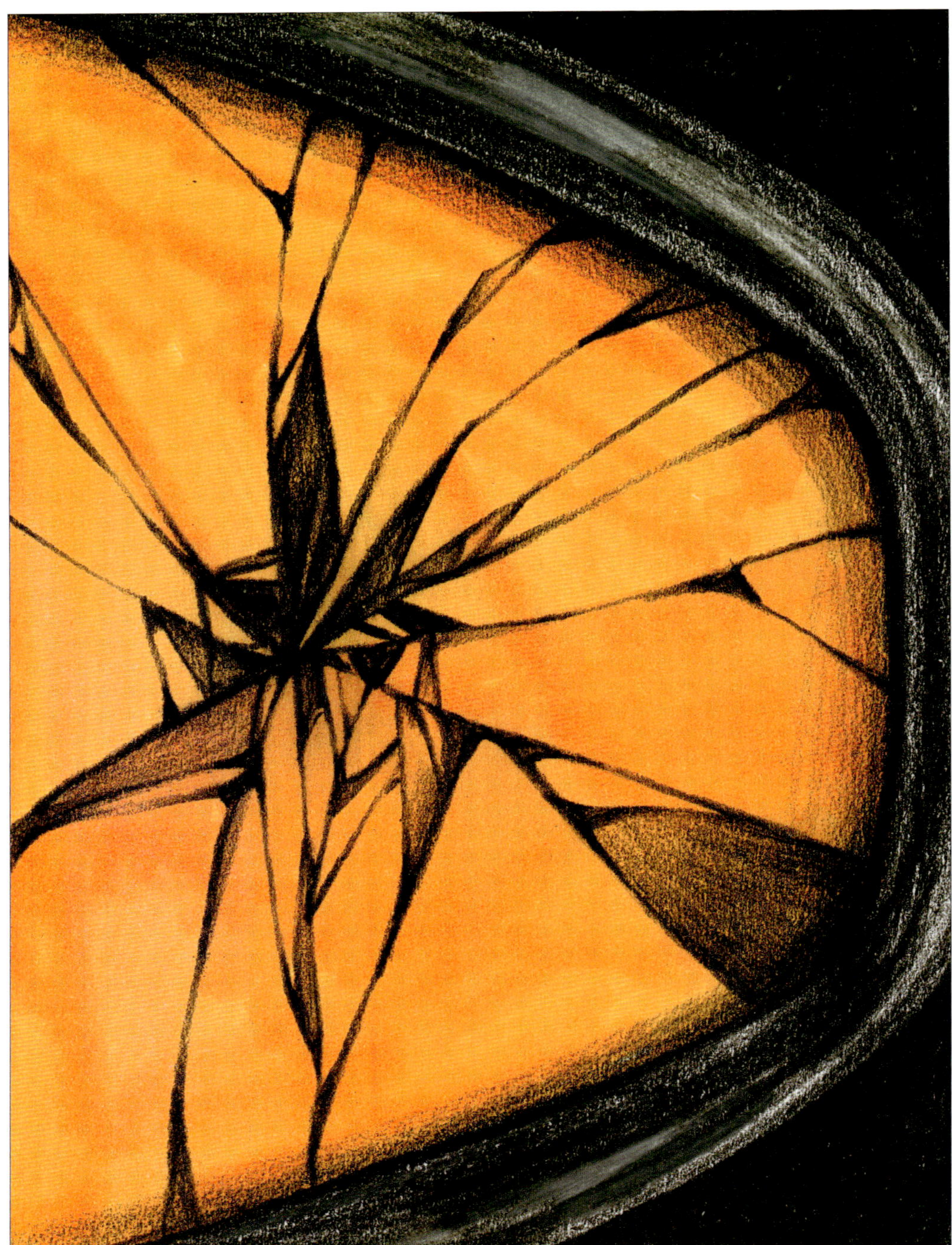

NOISE OR HOSTILITY

NOISE OR HOSTILITY

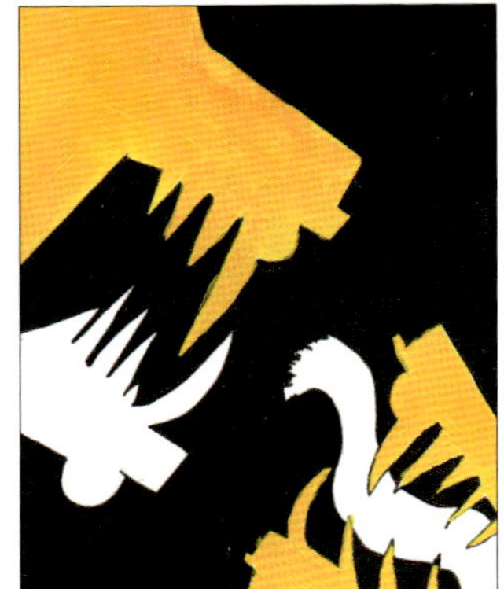

NOISE OR HOSTILITY

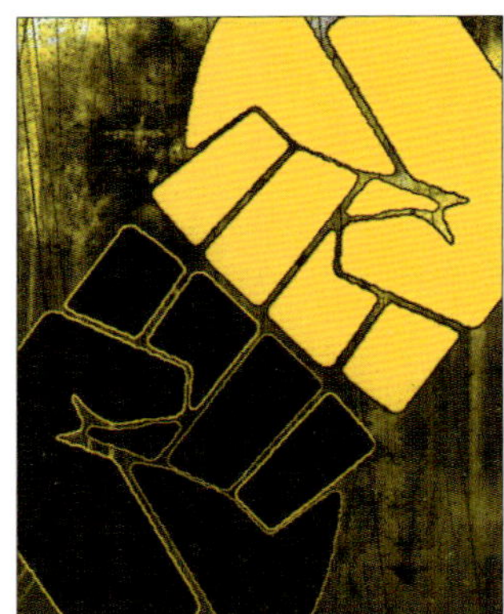

NOISE OR HOSTILITY

HEY TAXI SOLUTIONS:

Figures 1 through 4 depict hostility and road rage. Images include a broken side-view mirror, naïvely drawn weapons, anthrophomorphic warring cars, and the tension between two fists.

Figure 5 is a reimagined tire tread that depicts animals in combat.

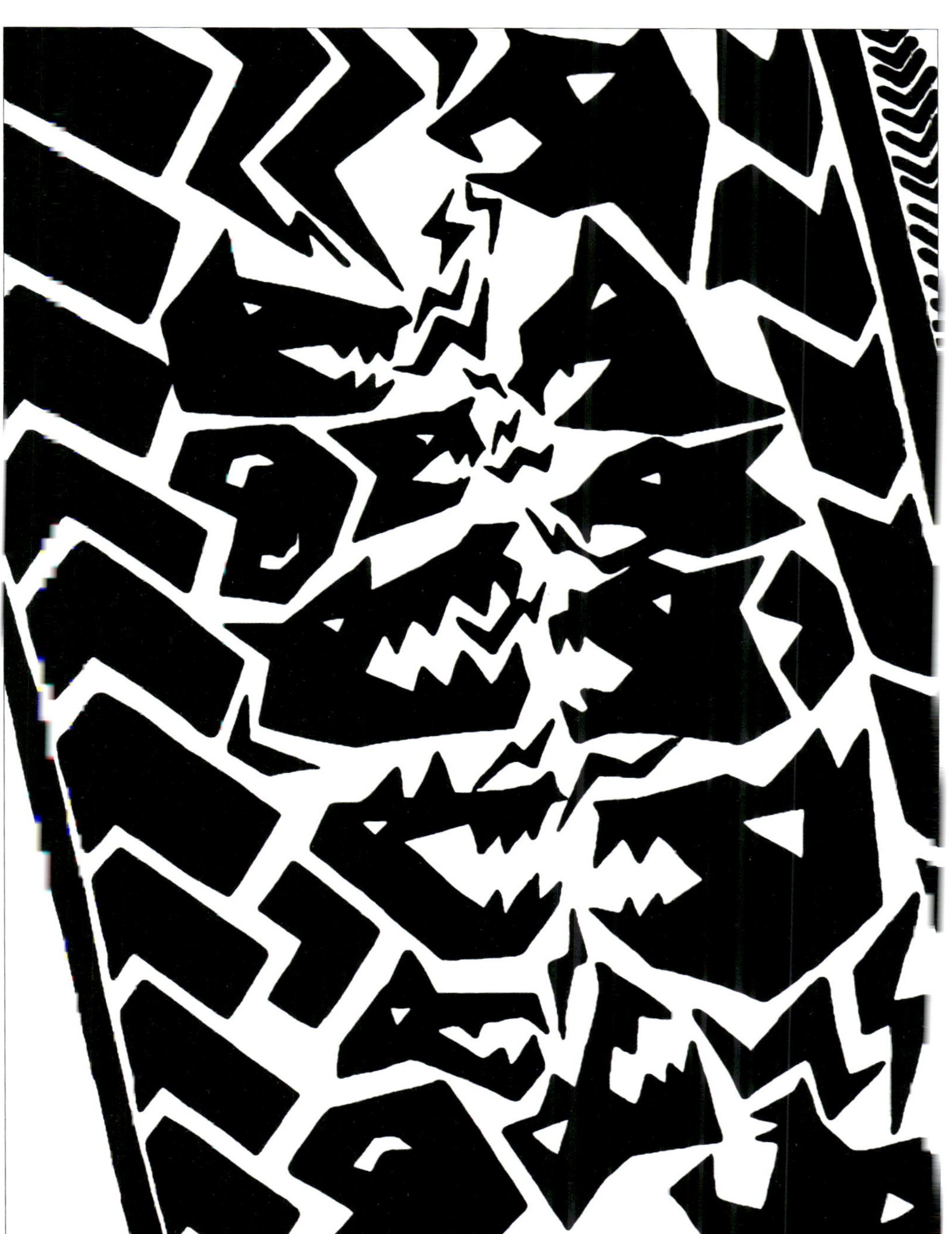

NOISE OR HOSTILITY

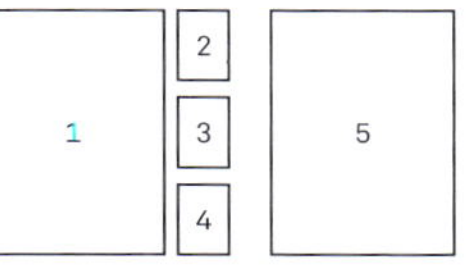

1. *Minjung Lee*
2. *Robert Tepper*
3. *Melanie Teppich*
4. *Eric Perez*
5. *Ji Min Nam*

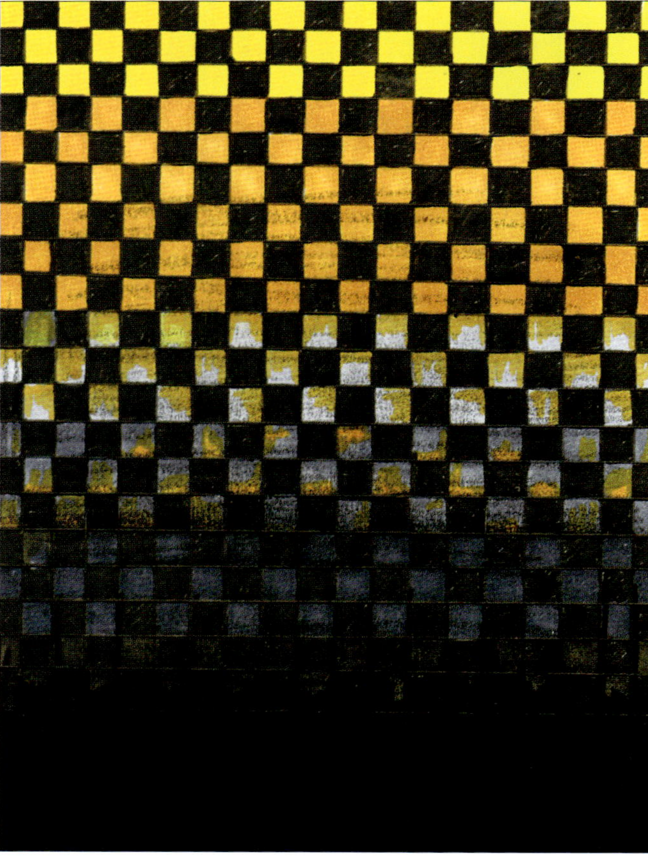

POLLUTION

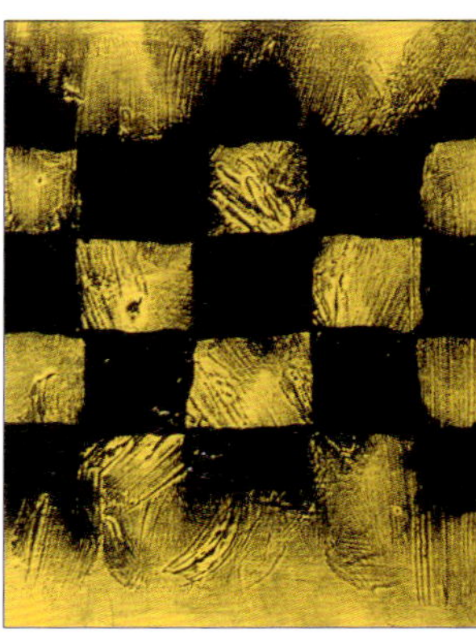

POLLUTION

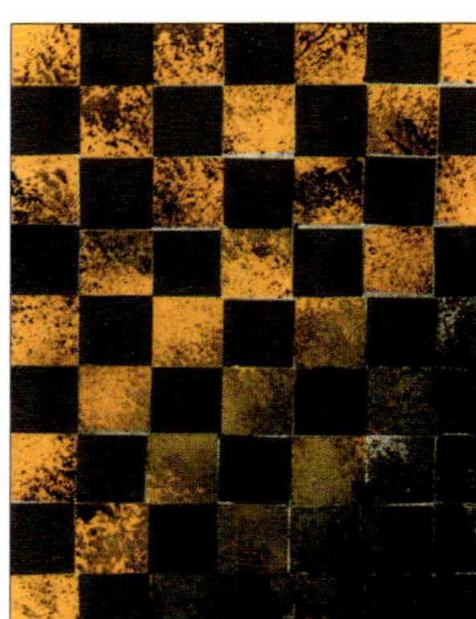

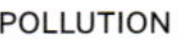

POLLUTION

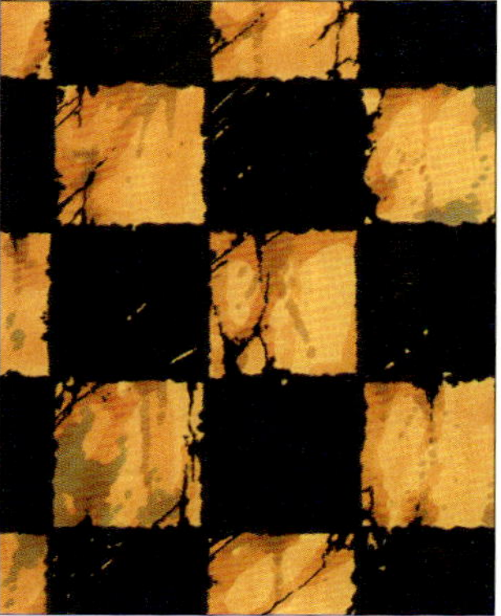

POLLUTION

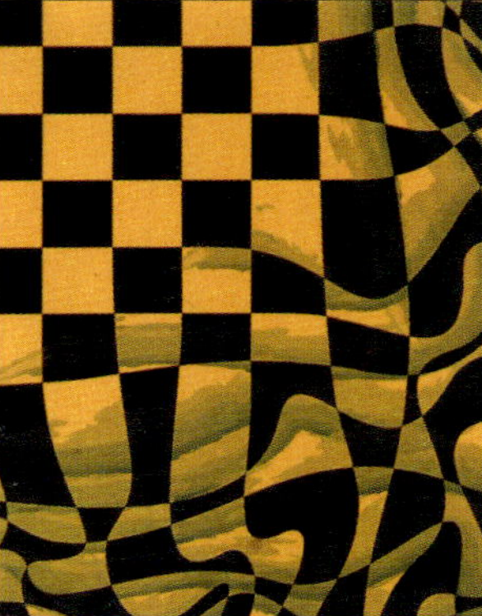

POLLUTION

HEY TAXI SOLUTIONS:

Pollution is the subject in figures 1 through 15, specifically pertaining to automobile exhaust.

Figures 1 through 5 are abstract interpretations of how pollution impacts corrosively on the environment.

Figures 6 through 9 use smokestacks as a metaphor for tailpipe exhaust.

Figure 10 uses the black squares from the checkered pattern of the taxi to represent exhaust.

Figures 11 through 15 are different scenarios depicting the effects of air pollution on humanity.

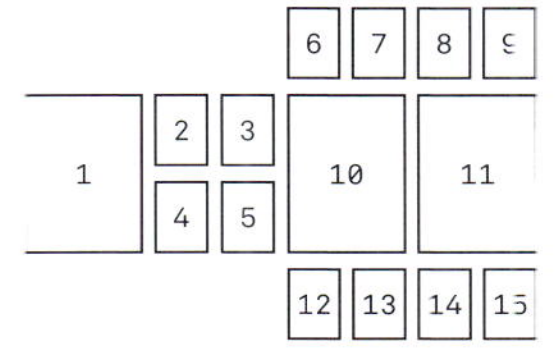

1. Inyoung Kim
2. Jecheol Kim
3. Haehyun Park
4. Rebecca Williams
5. Wei Lieh Lee
6. Sammy Kang
7. Ivan Simin
8. Benjamin Jura
9. Jennie Lou
10. Ivan Simin
11. Daewook Do
12. Hyungkyu Choi
13. Jayoung Jung
14. Roza Khamitovis
15. Guerim Lee

POLLUTION

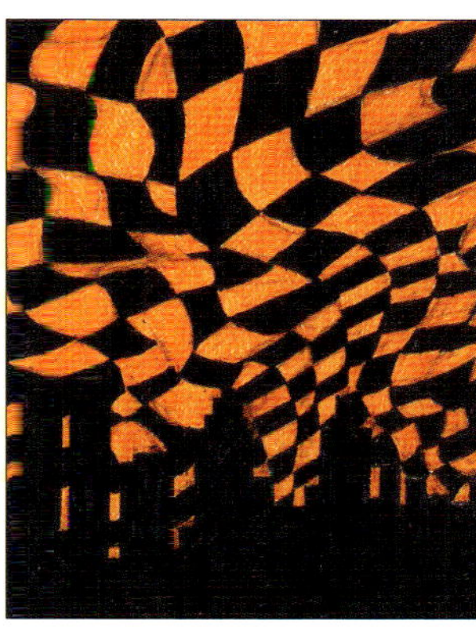

POLLUTION

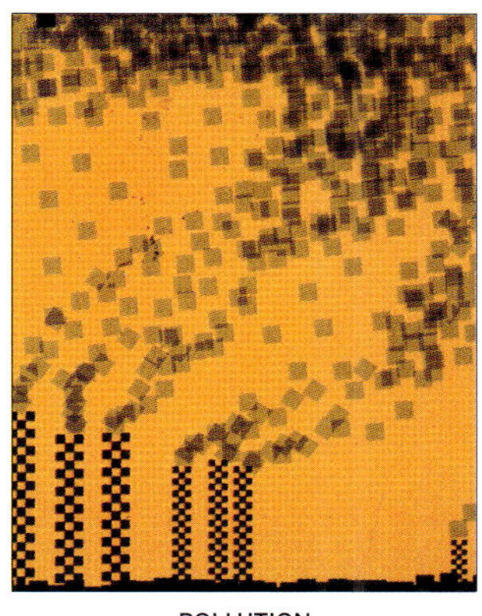

POLLUTION

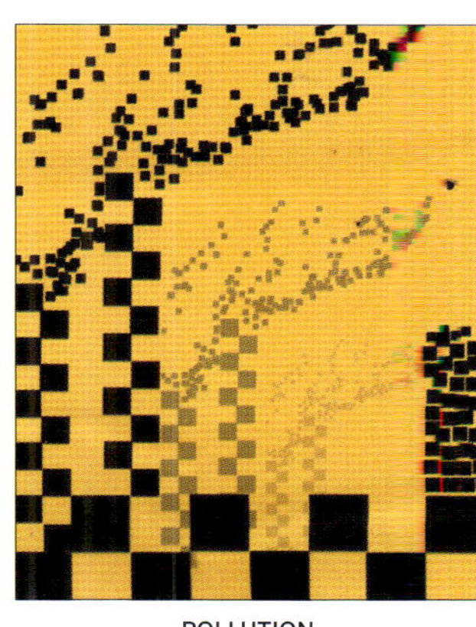

POLLUTION

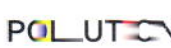

POLLUTION

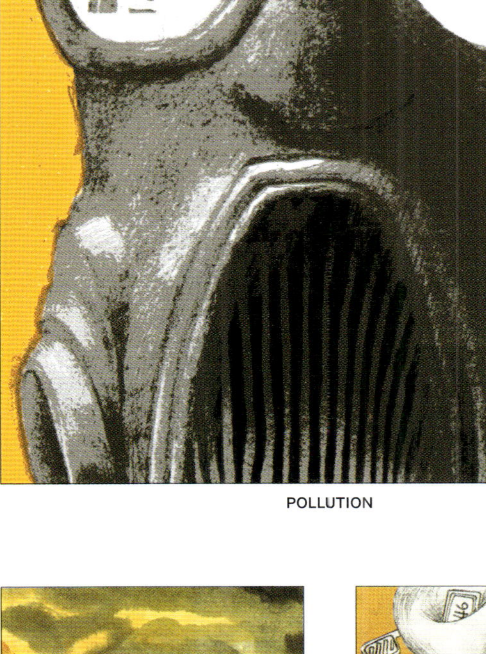

POLLUTION

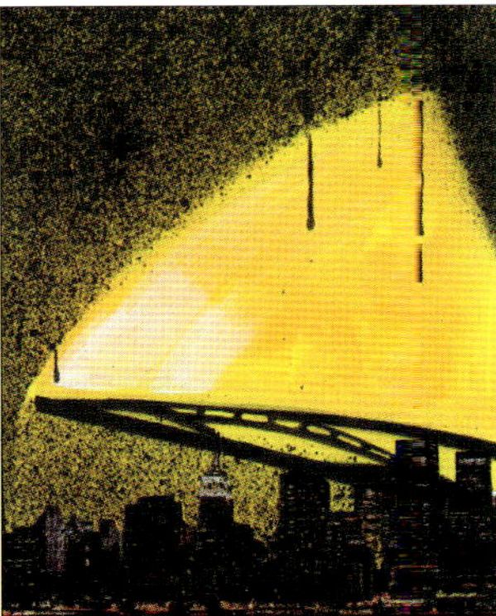

POLLUTION

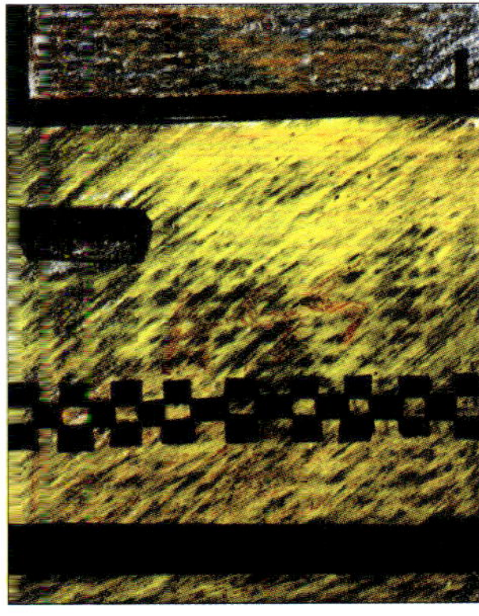

POLLUTION

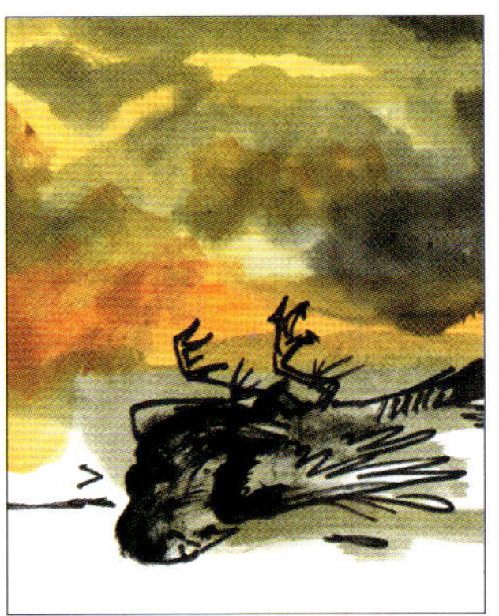

POLLUTION

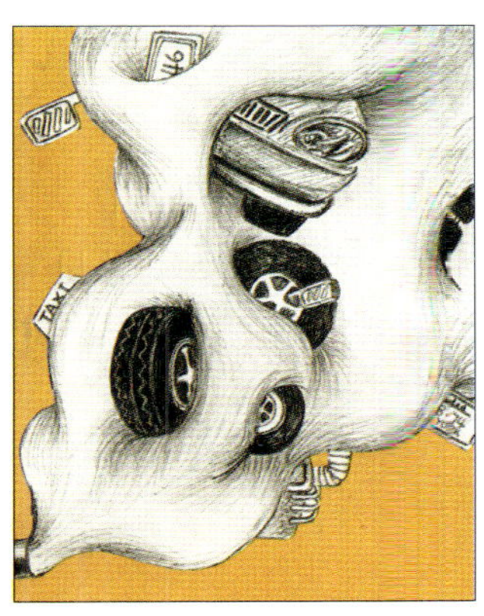

POLLUTION

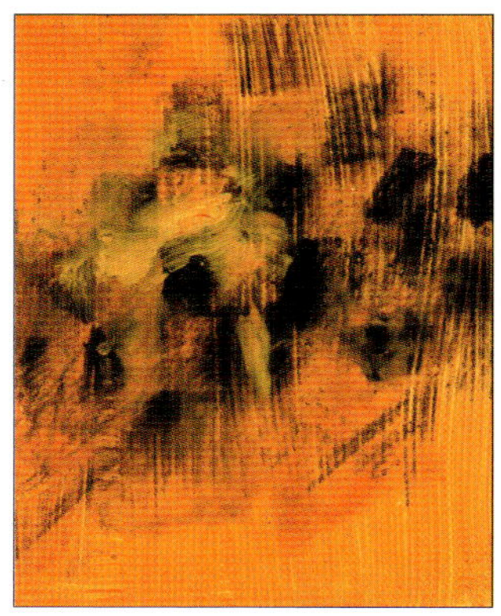

POLLUTION

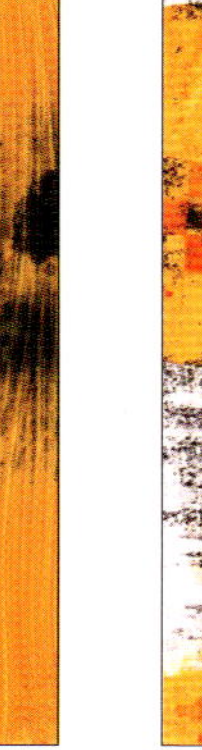

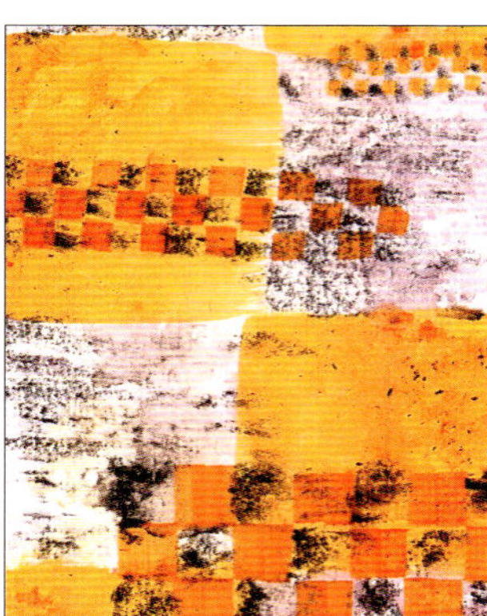

POLLUTION

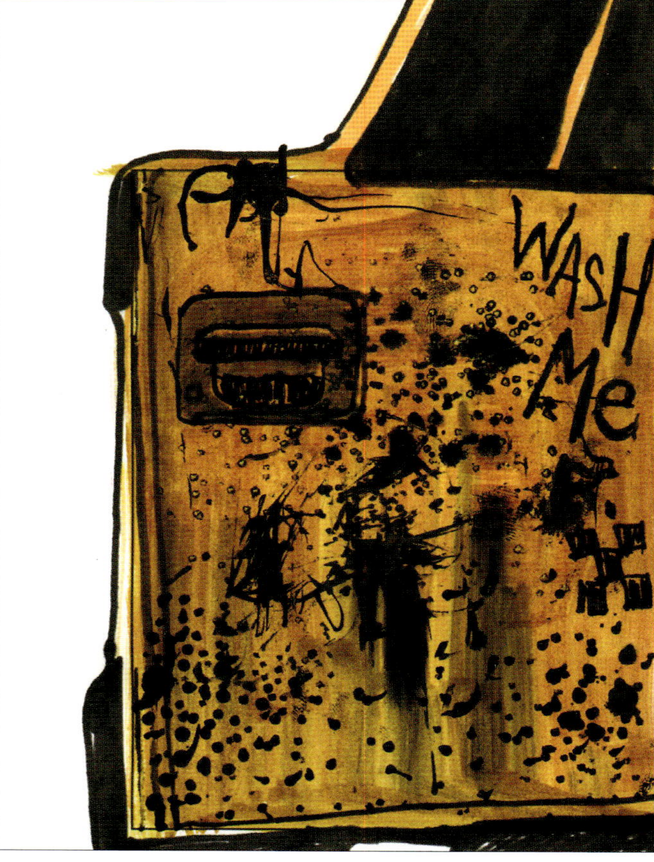

POLLUTION

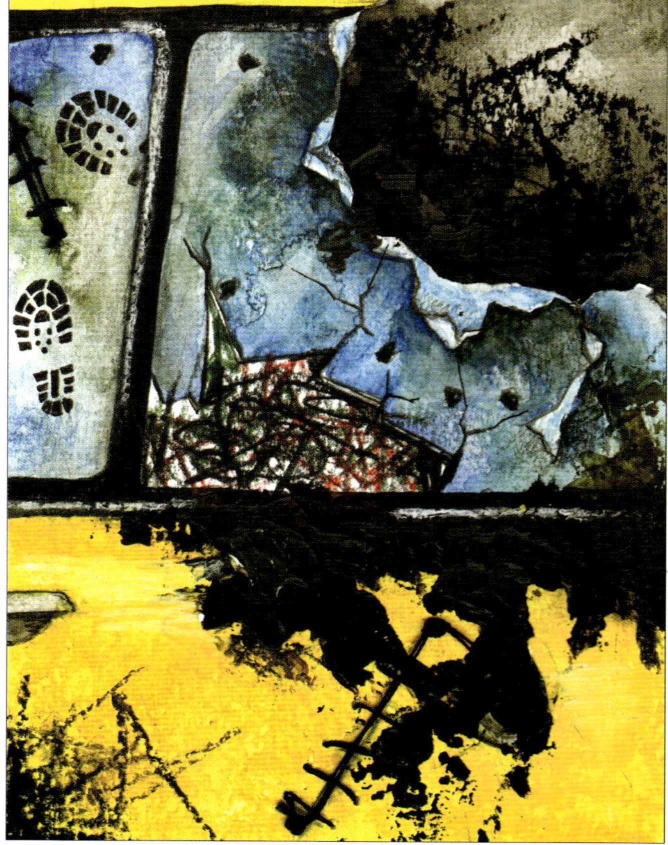

POLLUTION

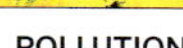

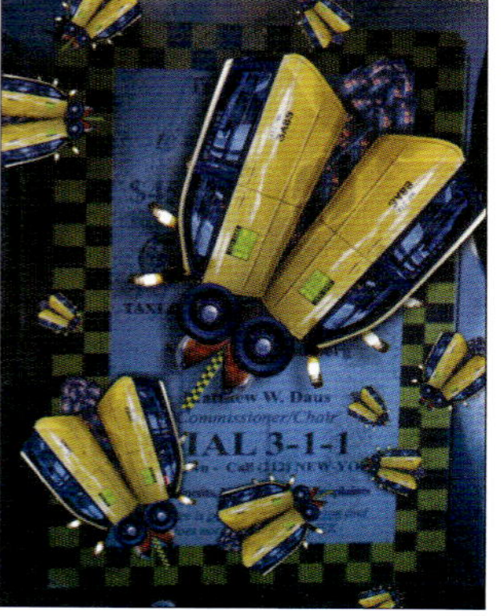

POLLUTION

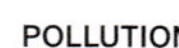

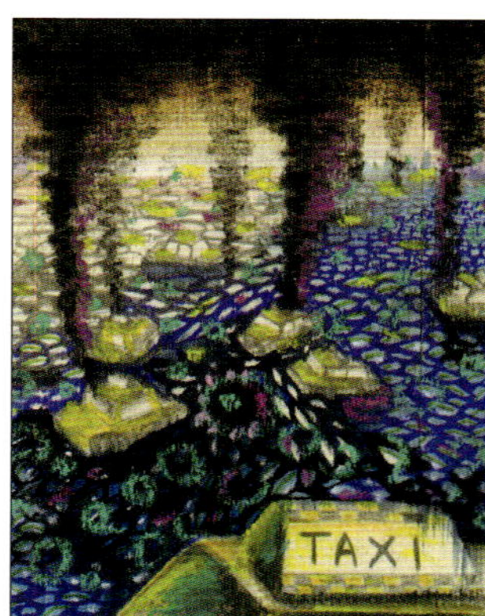

POLLUTION

HEY TAXI SOLUTIONS:

The following images include both abstract and narrative solutions that address a polluted metropolitan environment and the implied negative effect of taxicabs spewing carbon monoxide into the air.

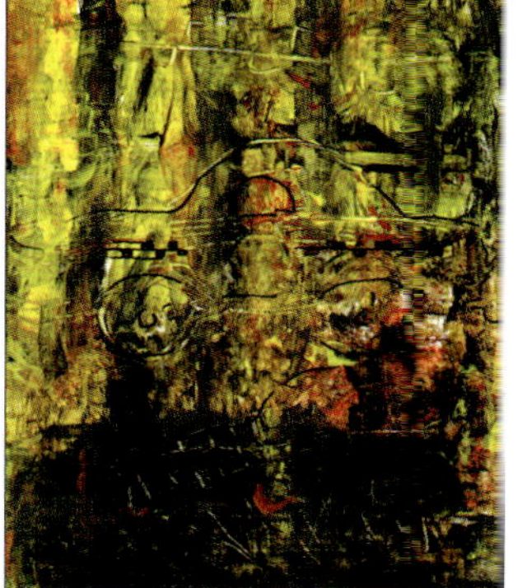

POLLUTION

POLLUTION

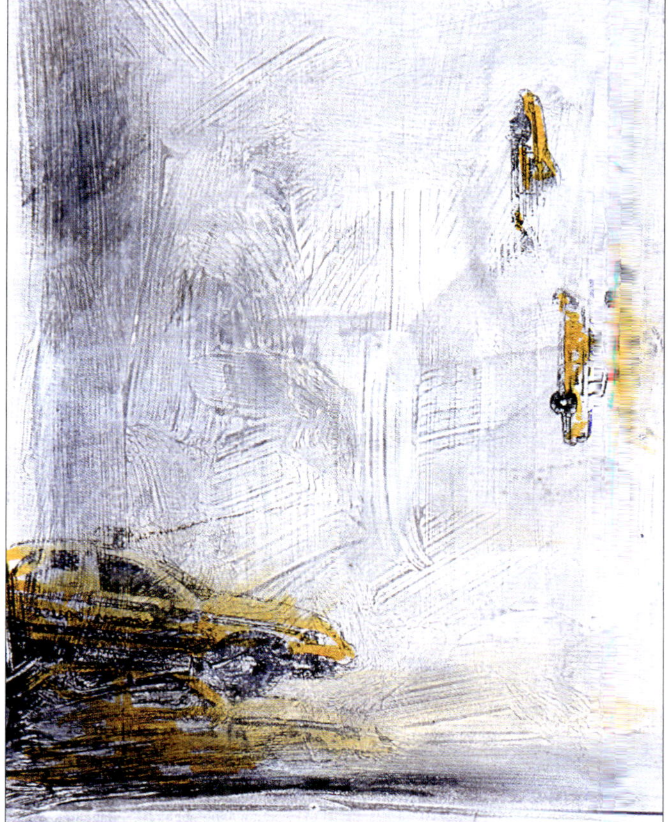

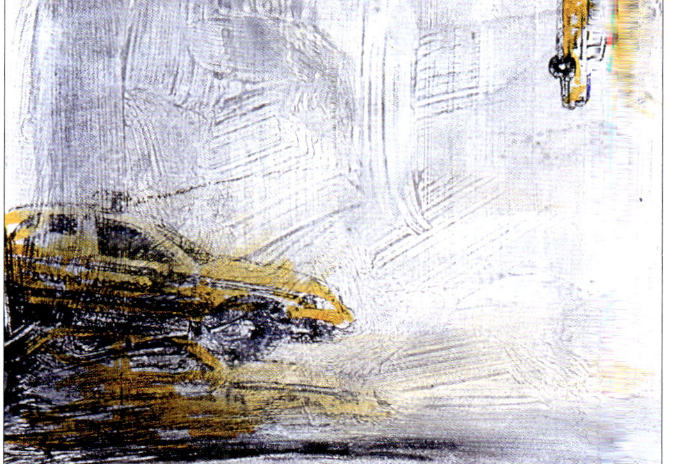

POLLUTION

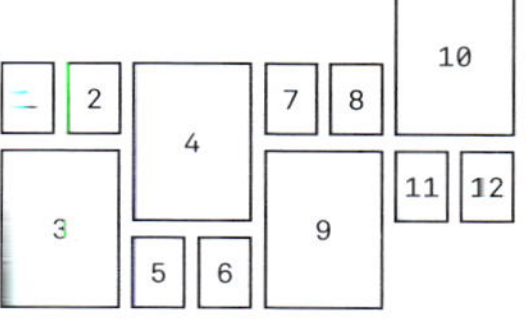

1. *Andrea Preston*
2. *Tai Hua Wang*
3. *Max Kaplun*
4. *Hana Yoo*
5. *Sean Hannon*
6. *Jiyoung Lee*
7. *Jennifer Villas*
8. *Jungheun Lee*
9. *Jamus Marquette*
10. *Misuk Suh*
11. *Michael Mejia*
12. *Aaron Nichols*

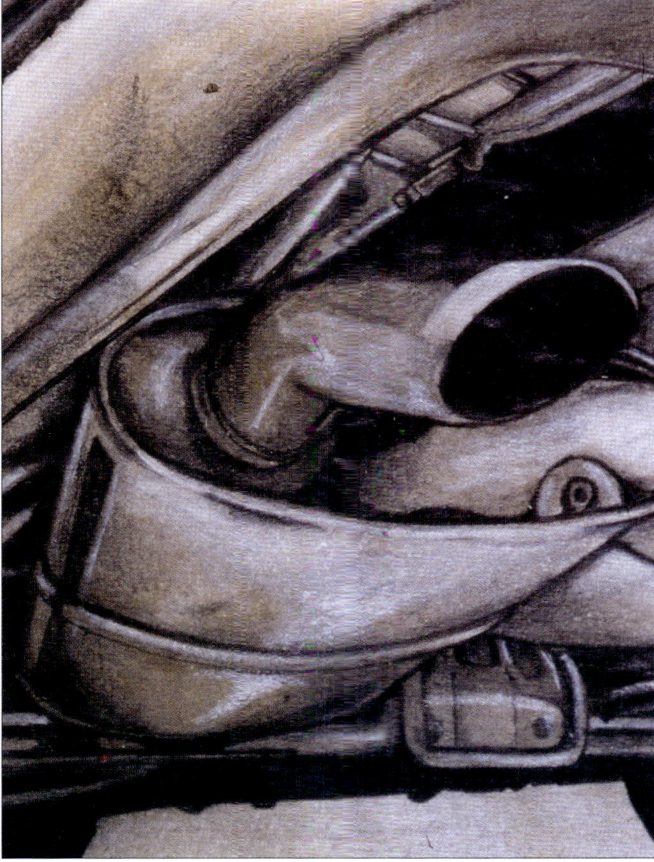

POLLUTION

POLLUTION

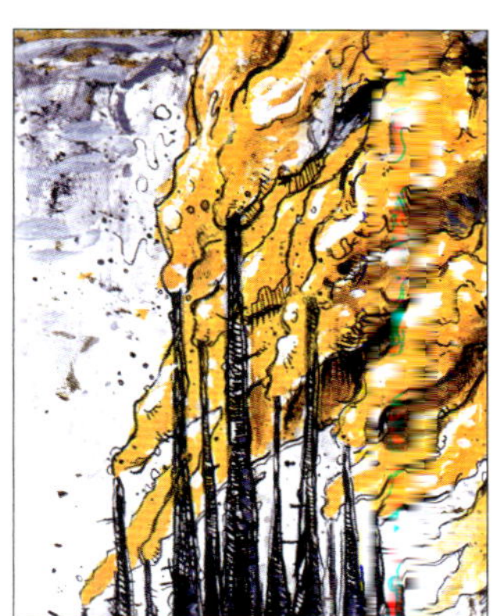

POLLUTION

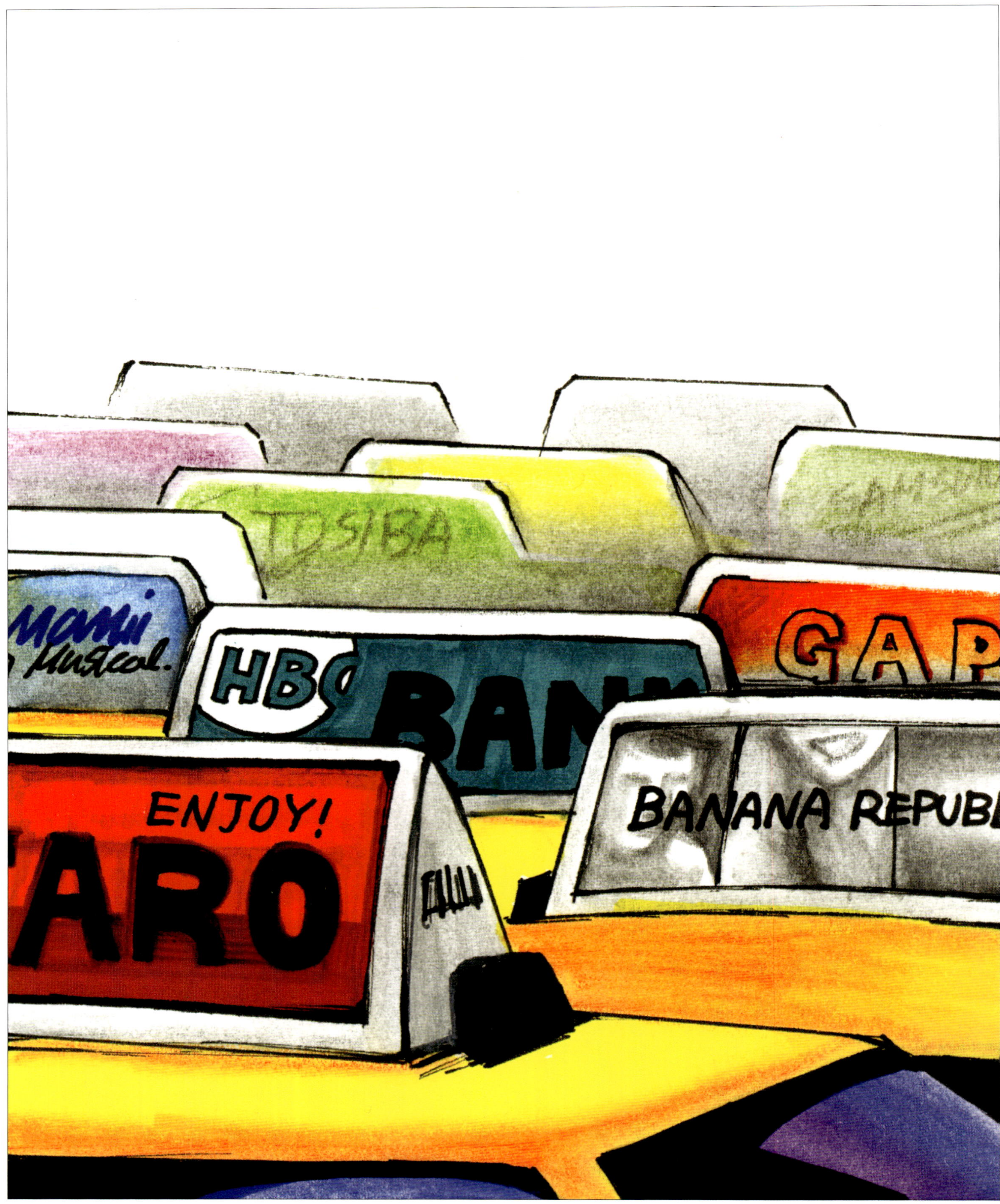

CONSUMERISM

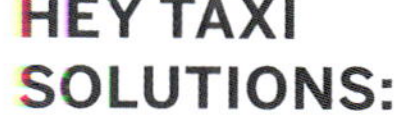

HEY TAXI SOLUTIONS:

Figures 1 through 11 deal with consumerism, reflecting a wide range of attitudes.

Figure 1 depicts a sea of advertising as it appears on the tops of taxicabs.

Figures 2 and 3 use the barcode pattern as a point of departure to reference consumerism.

Figures 4 and 5 are abstract interpretations, while figure 6 commercializes the checkered motif, which is synonymous with New York City taxicabs.

Figure 7 portrays porters with bowed heads lining a red carpet, which elevates the activity of riding in a taxicab to an elite status.

CONSUMERISM

CONSUMERISM

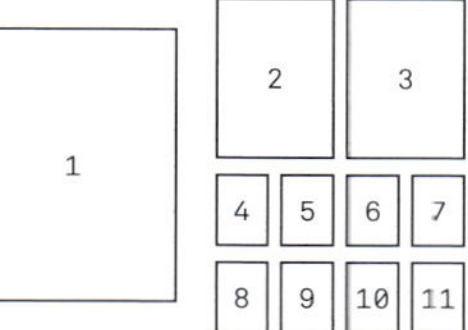

1. *Eunjoung Park*
2. *Hyosook Kang*
3. *Kiljae Kim*
4. *Miry Shin*
5. *J. Lee*
6. *Kelly Schultz*
7. *J. Choo*
8. *Wei Lieh Lee*
9. *Alison Rubenstein*
10. *Katharine Dwyer*
11. *Jarwon Shin*

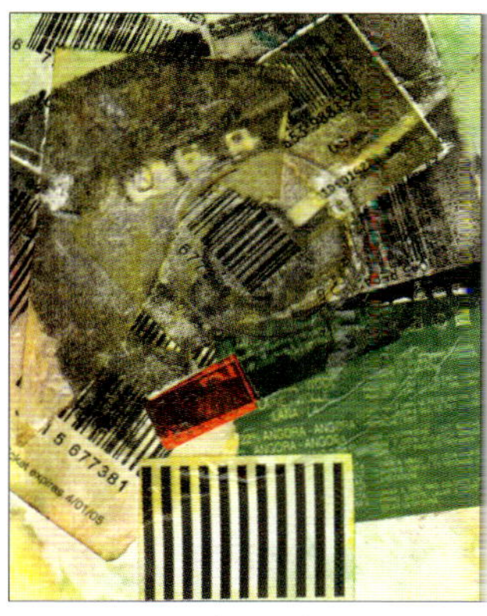

CONSUMERISM

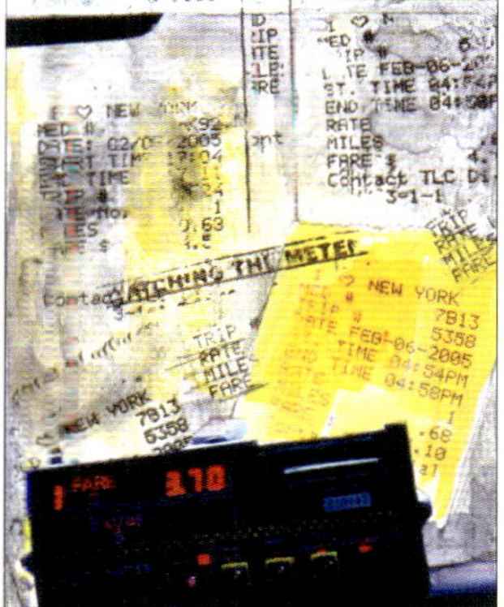

CONSUMERISM

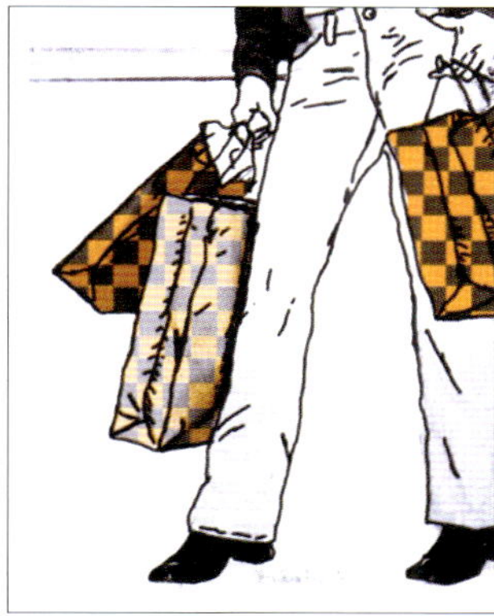

CONSUMERISM

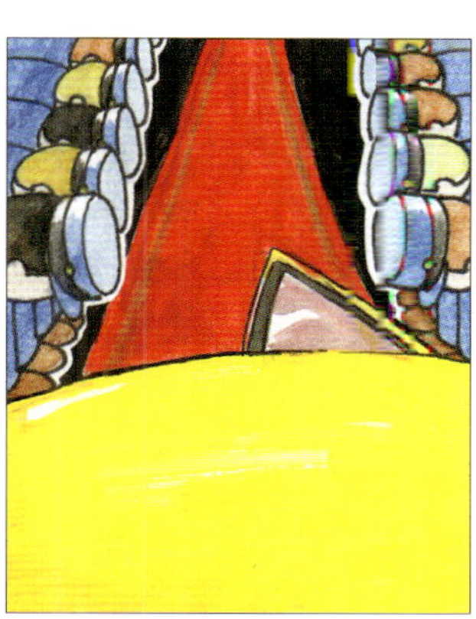

CONSUMERISM

Figure 8 utilizes negative and positive shapes in the depiction of hands hailing a taxi.

Figure 9 uses George Washington and Andrew Jackson as passengers. Their images have been taken from U.S. currency, hence the connection to consumerism.

The meter shown in figure 10 addresses the high cost of travel, while figure 11 is a personal interpretation of a futuristic taxicab.

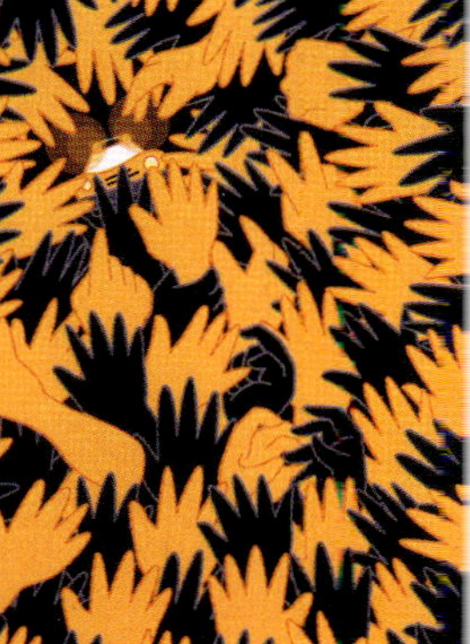

CONSUMERISM

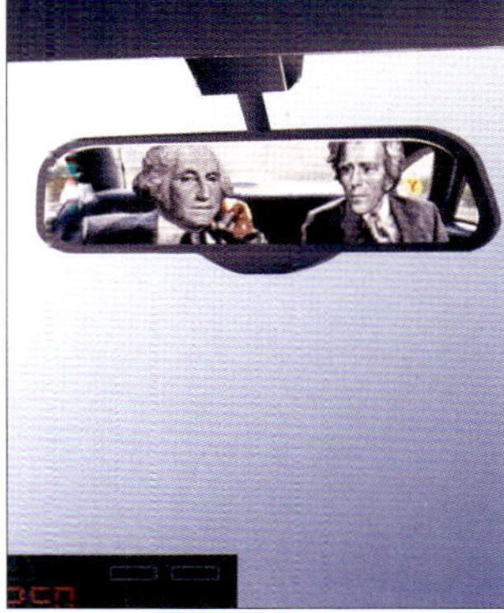

CONSUMERISM

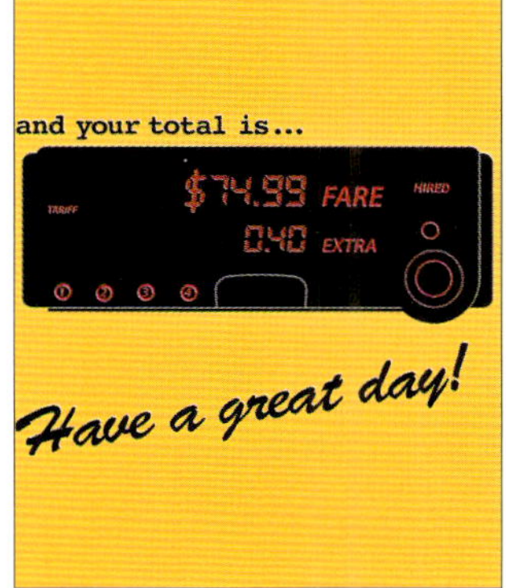

CONSUMERISM

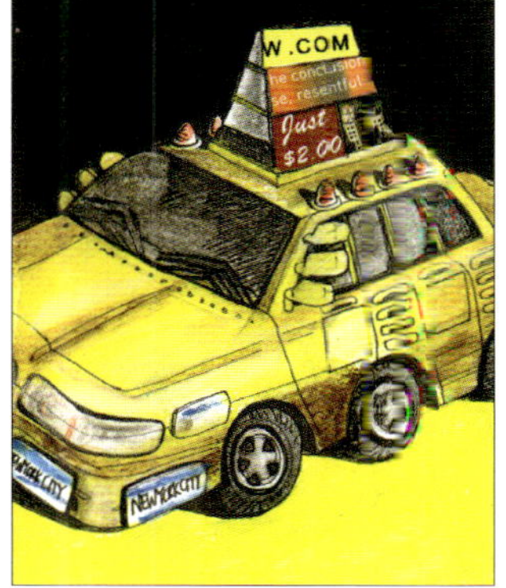

CONSUMERISM

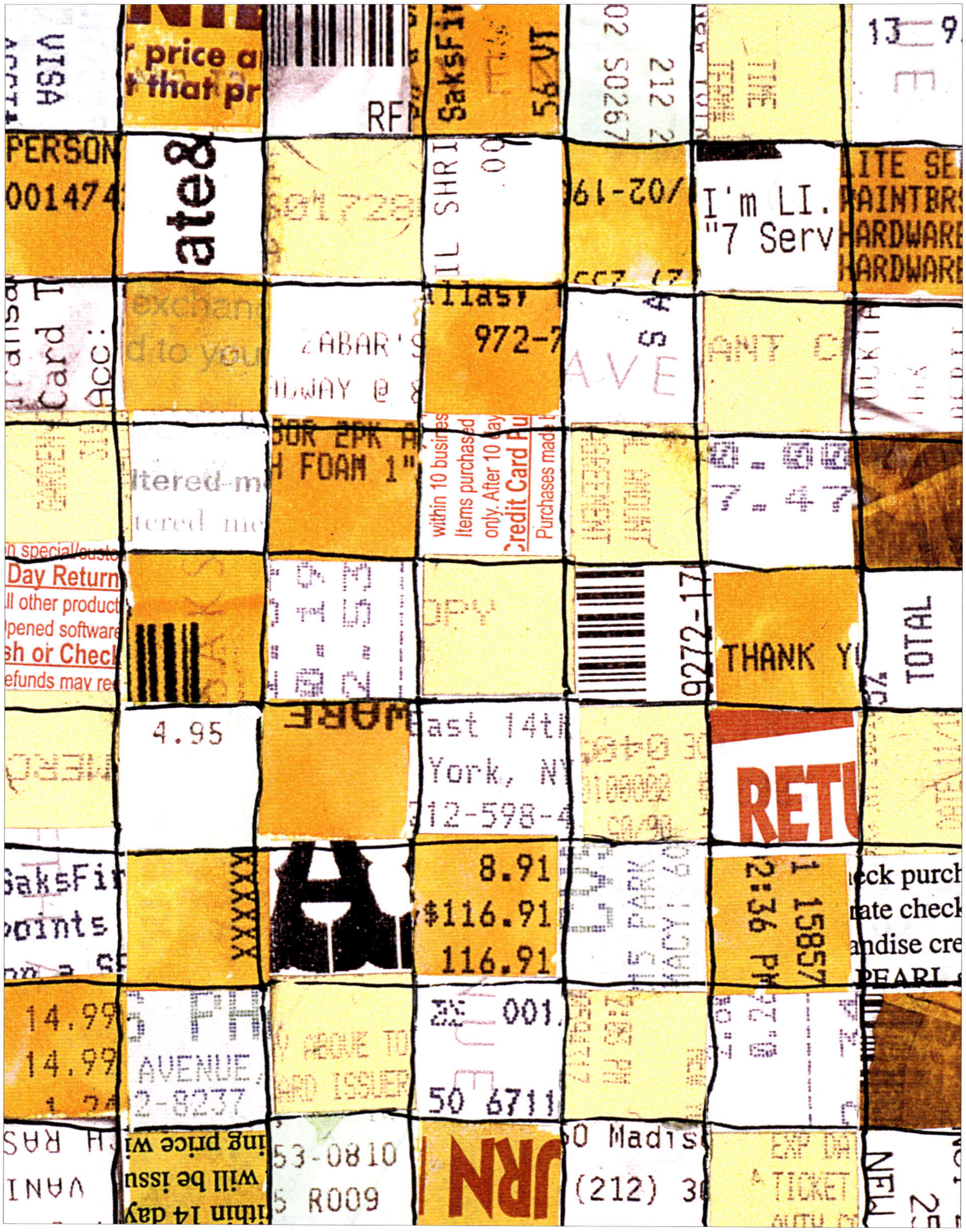

CONSUMERISM

HEY TAXI SOLUTIONS:

Consumerism is the theme of figure 1, a typographic collage set into a checkerboard motif using receipts and other ephemera pertaining to purchasing goods and services.

Figures 2 through 7 look at the subject of diversity, which can have many interpretations in the context of a taxicab environment.

Figure 2 depicts iconography referencing the image found on the side of a taxicab.

Figure 3 addresses a humorous juxtaposition of diverse cultures sharing a ride.

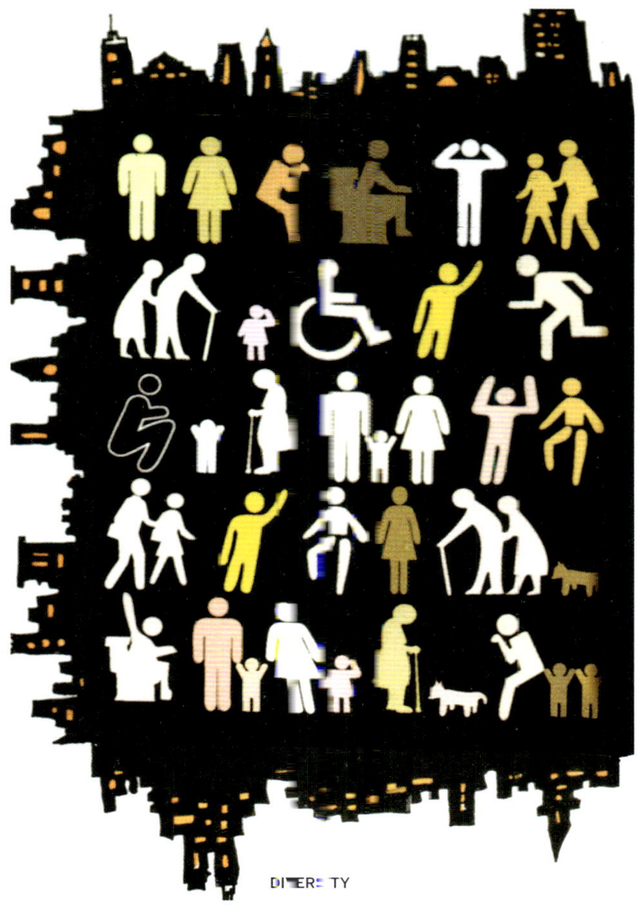

DIVERSITY

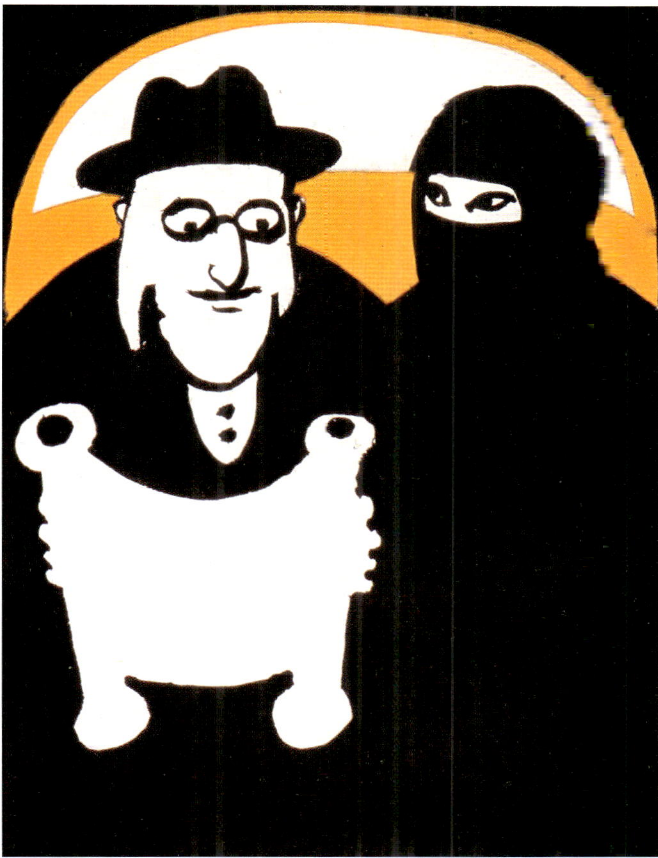

DIVERSITY

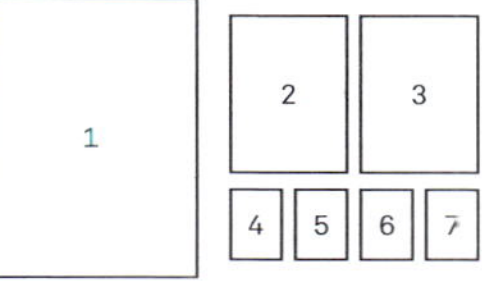

1. *Lindsay Josal*
2. *Jihee Yoon*
3. *Neil Drossman*
4. *Yoonsook Jee*
5. *Robin Birnbaum*
6. *Eunhae Lee*
7. *Youngji Kim*

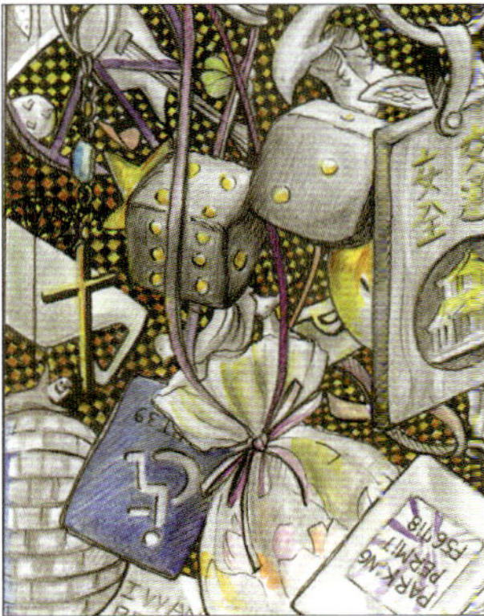

DIVERSITY

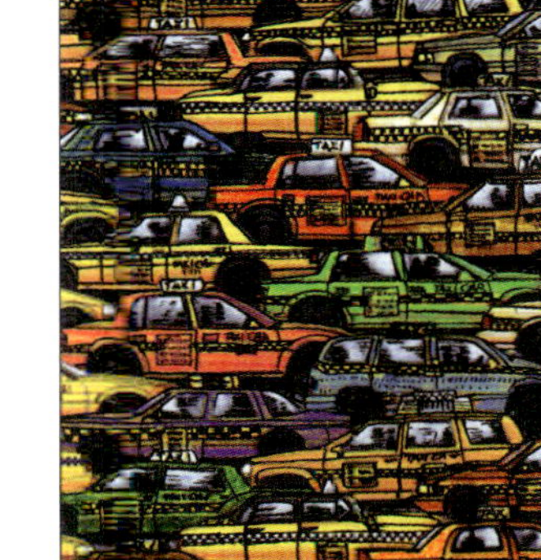

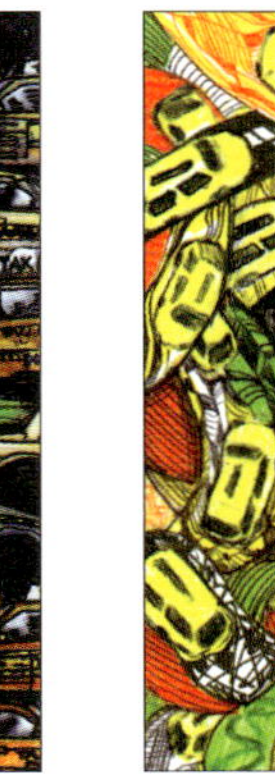

DIVERSITY

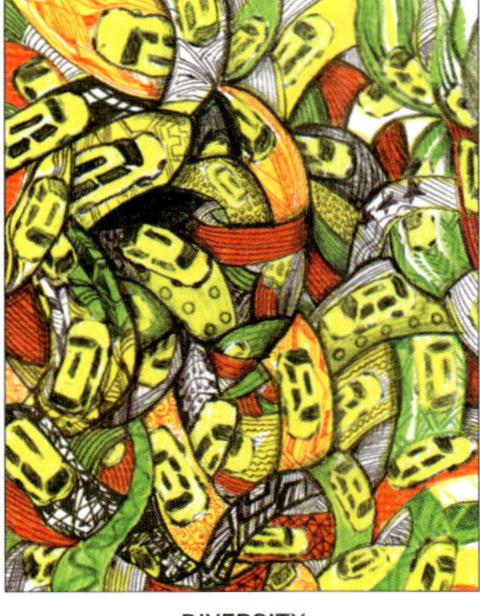

DIVERSITY

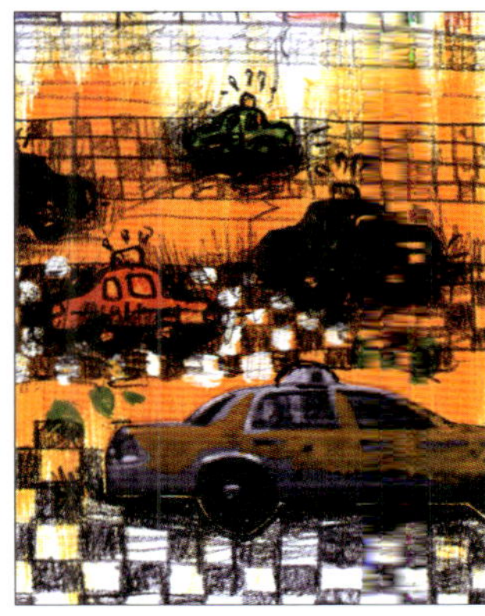

DIVERSITY

Figure 4 depicts objects that are often suspended from the rear-view mirror.

Figures 5 through 7 use multiple taxicabs to address aspects of diversity.

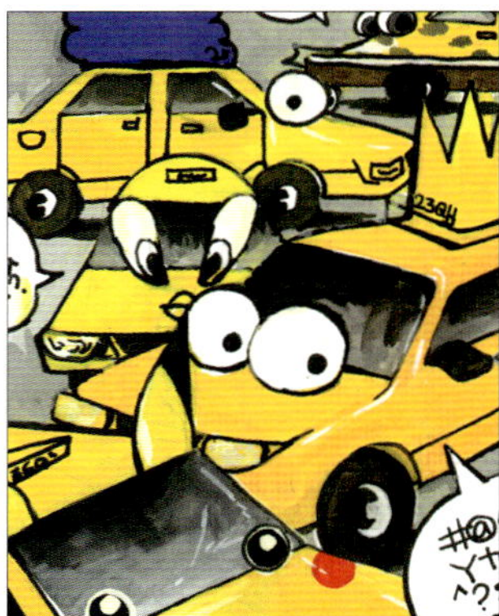
DIVERSITY

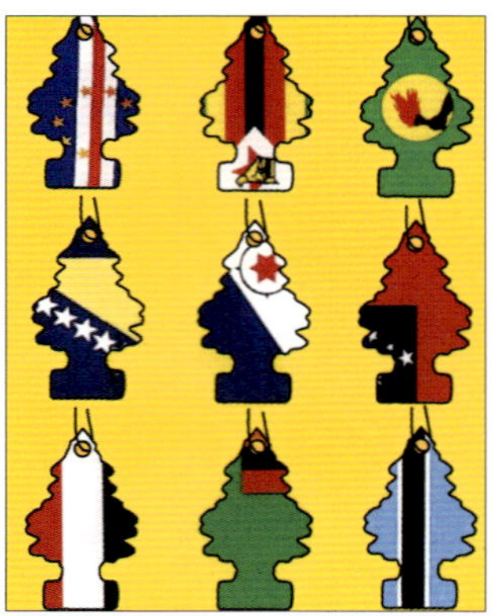
DIVERSITY

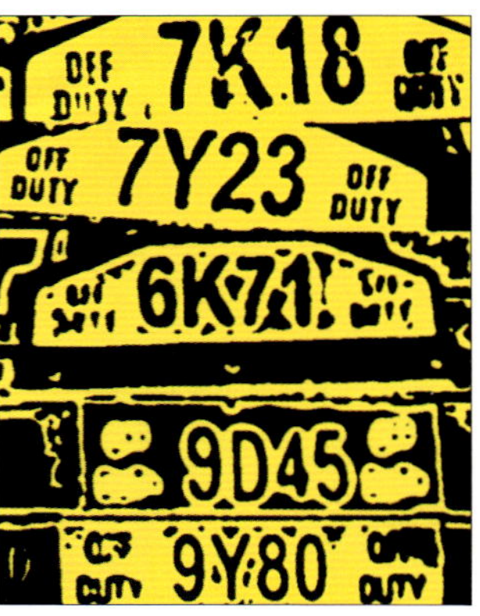

DIVERSITY

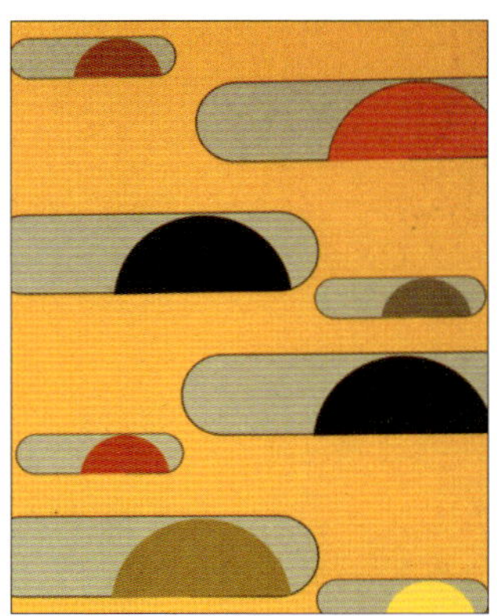
DIVERSITY

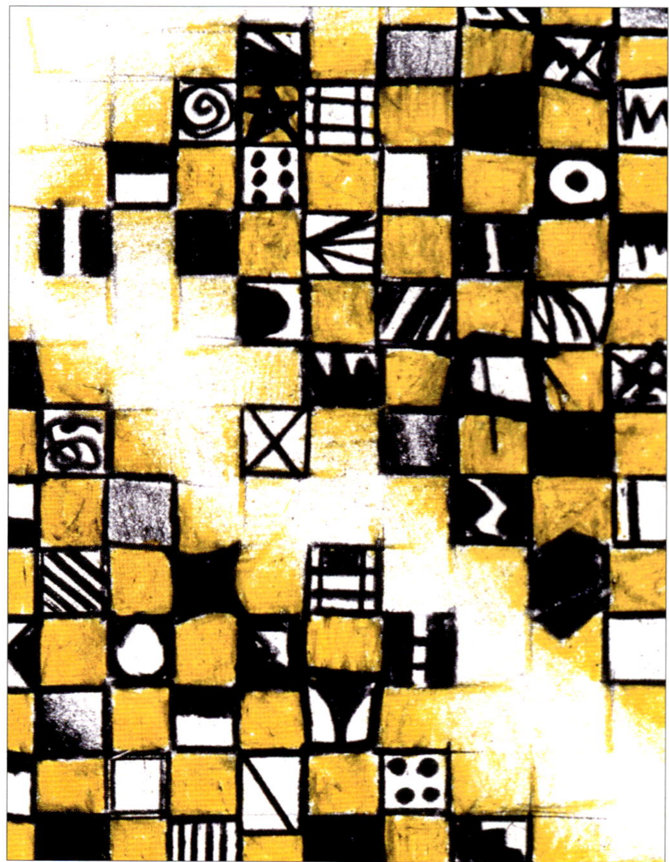
DIVERSITY

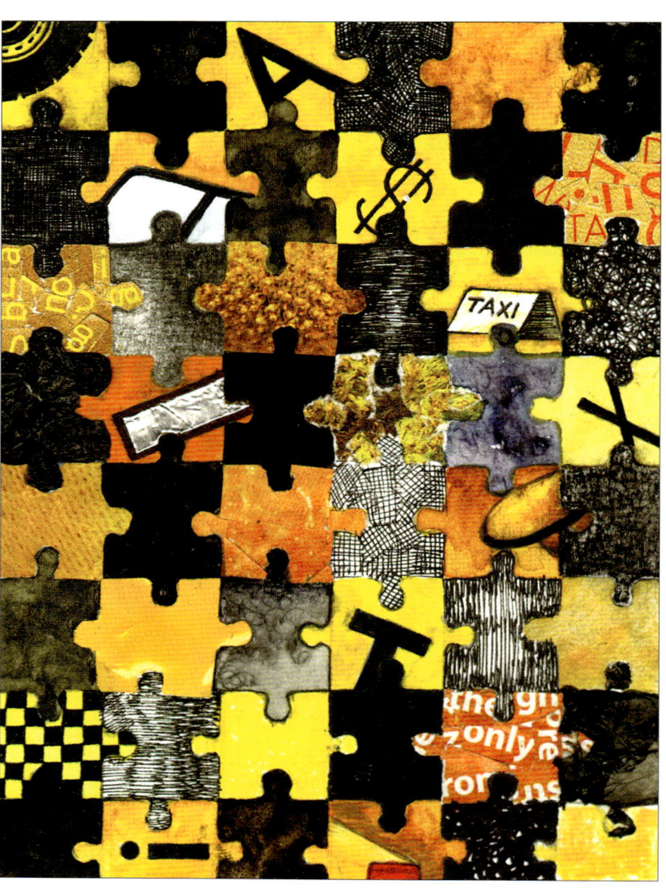

DIVERSITY

HEY TAXI SOLUTIONS:

Figures 1 through 4 deal with literal narratives of diversity through an array of subjects.

Figure 4 is a reductive solution of the top of heads as viewed by a taxi driver in the rear-view mirror.

The remaining figures, 5 through 12, are all abstract interpretations that utilize the checkerboard pattern to varying degrees.

DIVERSITY

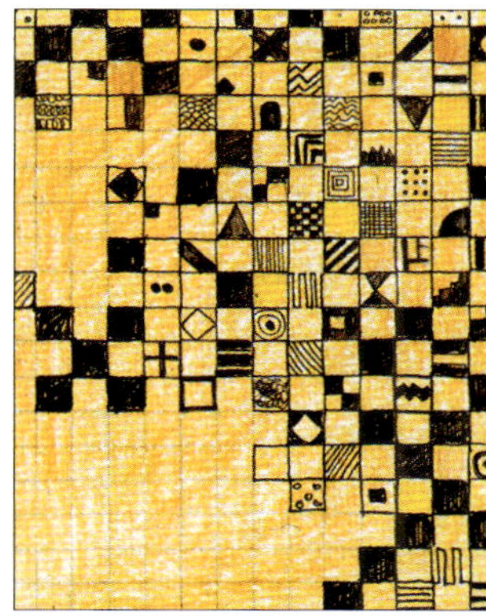

DIVERSITY

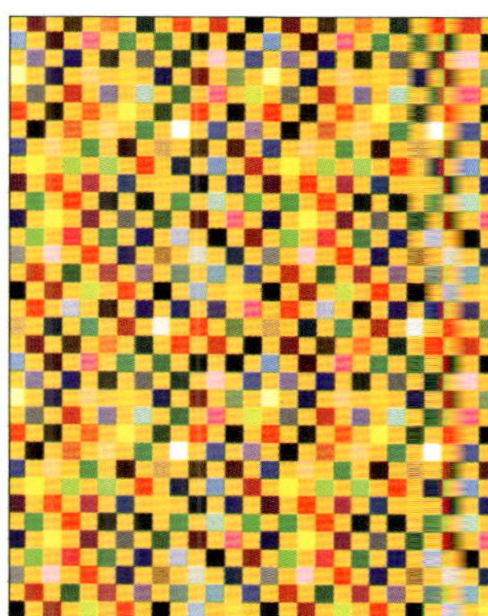

DIVERSITY

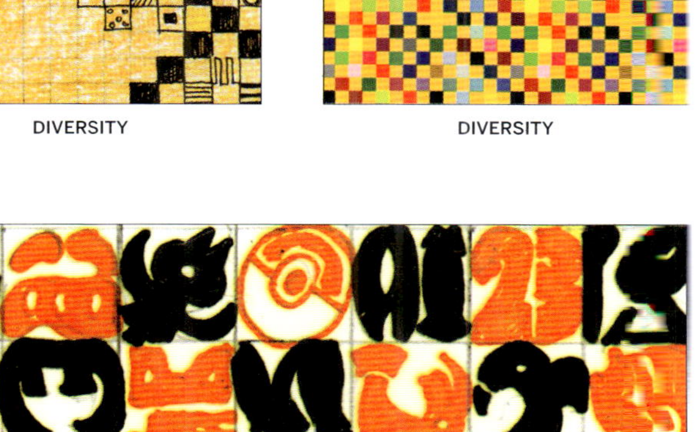

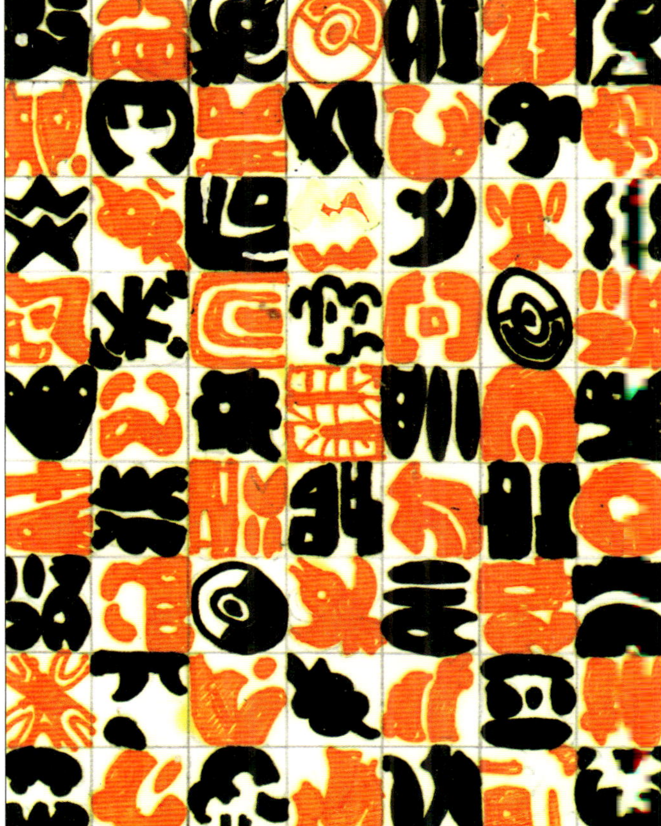

DIVERSITY

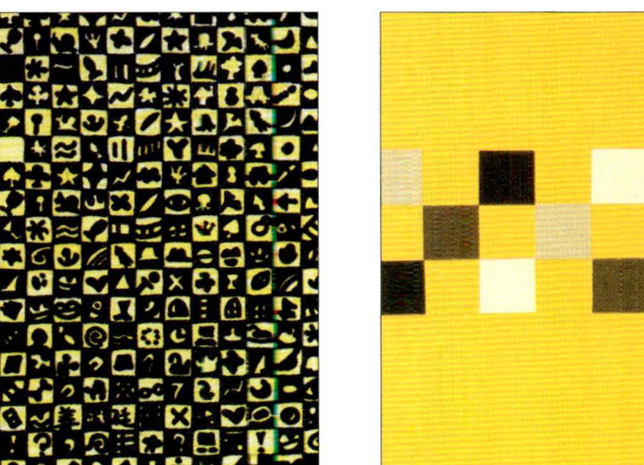

DIVERSITY

DIVERSITY

1. *Hyunhwa Lee*
2. *Annie Chan*
3. *Quek Jing Cheng*
4. *Michael Gonzalez*
5. *Robert Marchhart*
6. *Hana Yoo*
7. *Kristina Romeo*
8. *Christopher Brand*
9. *Michael Debout*
10. *Minjung Kang*
11. *P. Livingston*
12. *Gaon Kim*

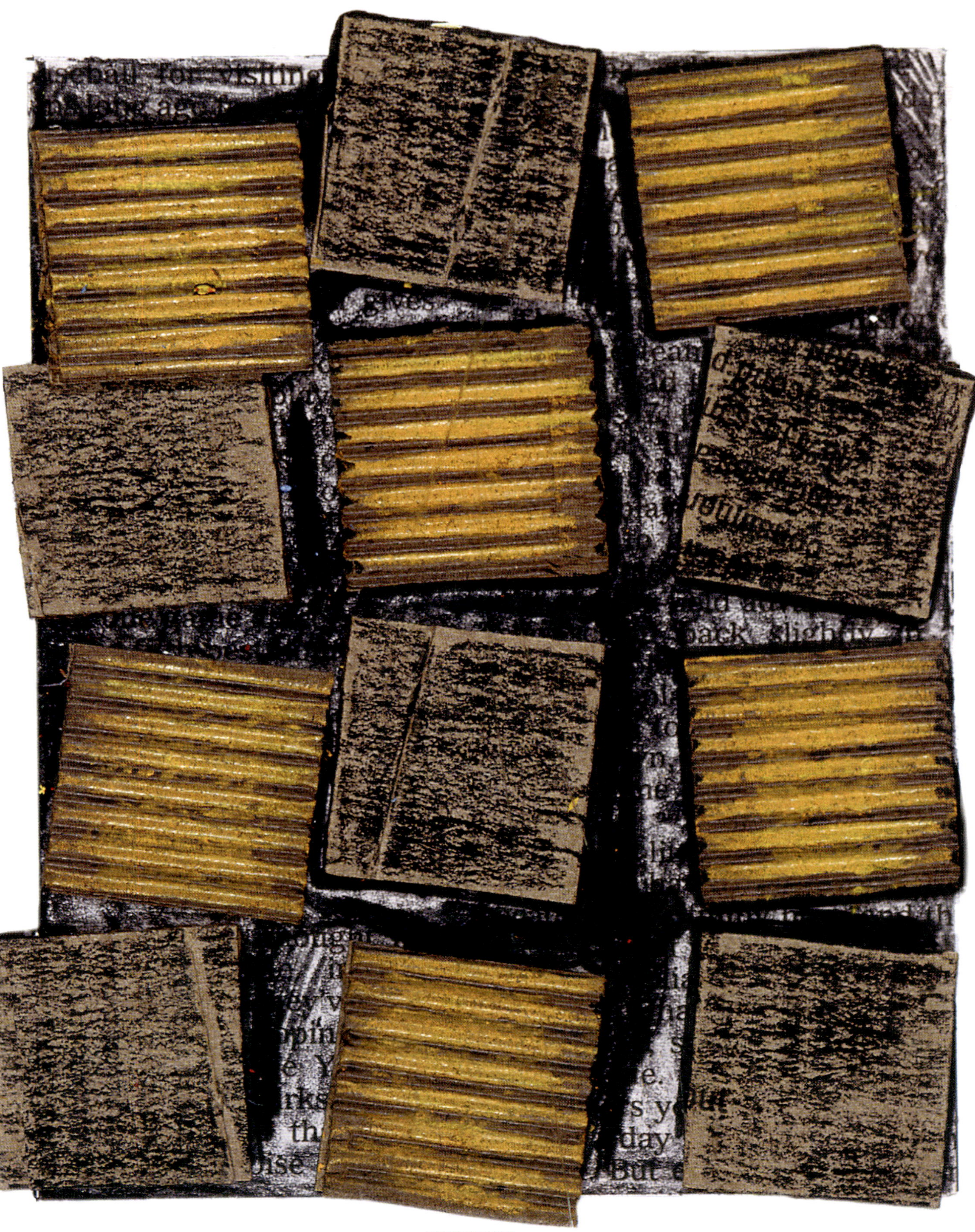

HOMELESSNESS

HEY TAXI SOLUTIONS:

Figures 1 through 6 deal with the complex issue of homelessness.

Figure 1 depicts a corregated cardboard structure that the homeless often use for a living space, designed in a checkerboard configuration.

Figure 2 is a taxicab by day and a homeless living space by night.

Figures 3 through 6 are abstract interpretations that reference imagery pertaining to living on the street.

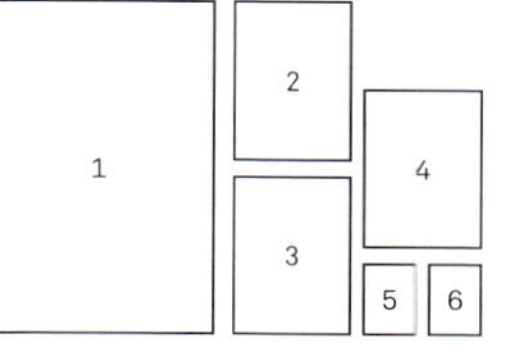

1. *Jessica White*
2. *Tai Hua Wang*
3. *Hana Yoo*
4. *Alicia Rodriguez*
5. *Hyesoo Lim*
6. *Dale James-Charles*

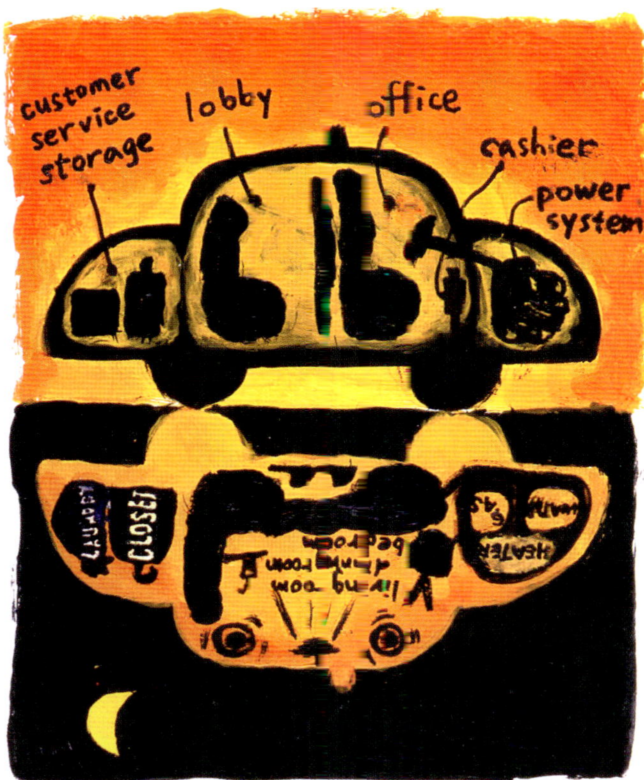

HOMELESSNESS

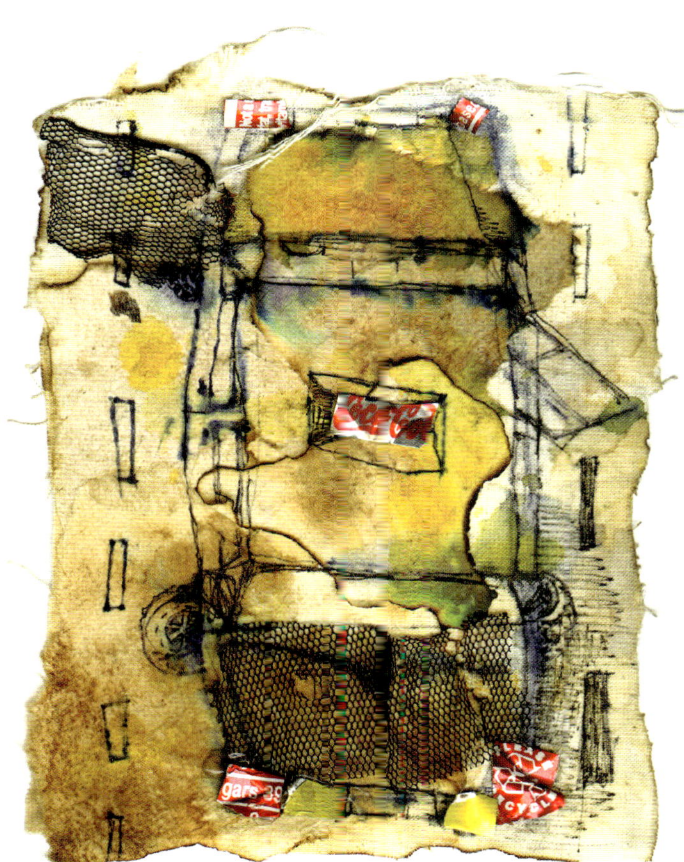

HOMELESSNESS

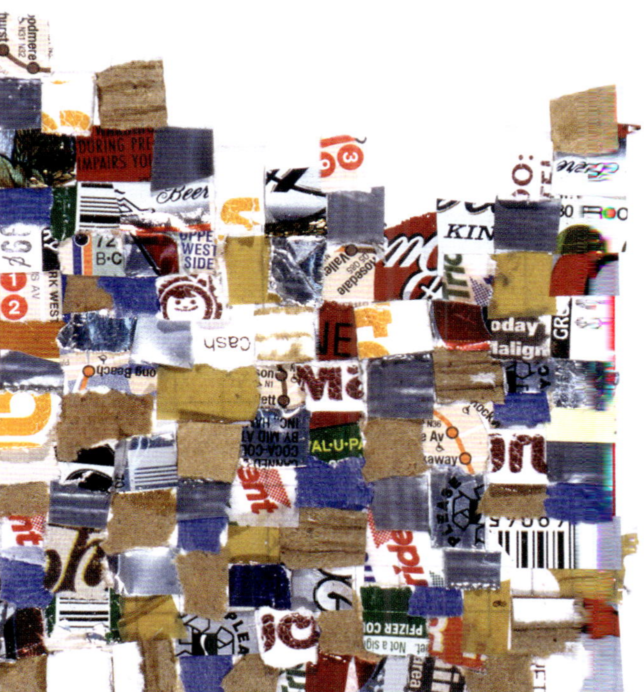

HOMELESSNESS

HOMELESSNESS

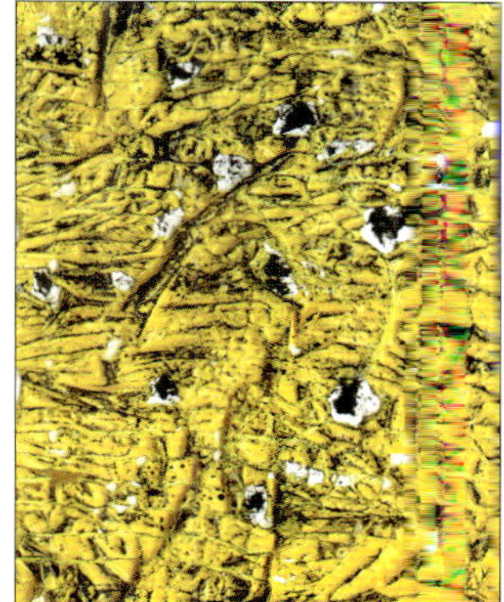

HOMELESSNESS

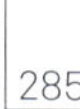

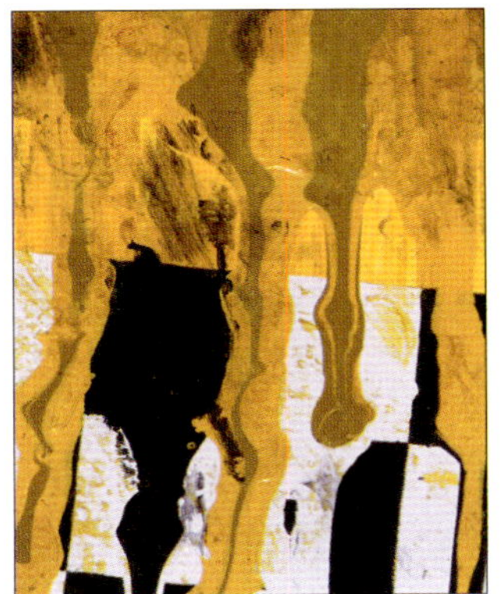
HOMELESSNESS

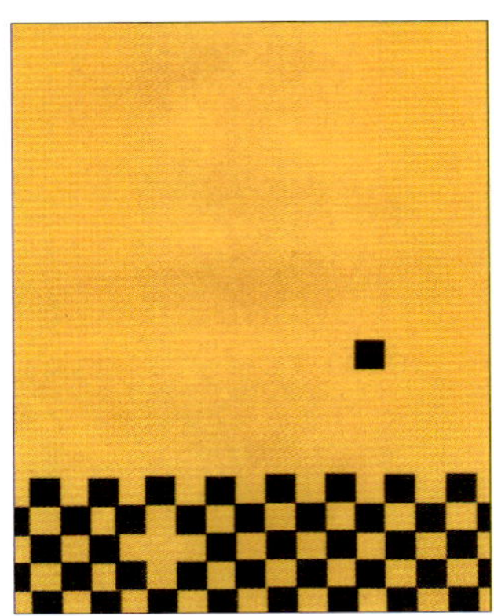
HOMELESSNESS

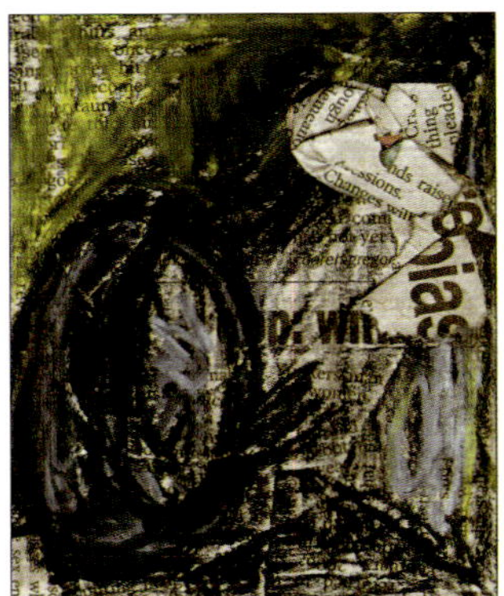
HOMELESSNESS

HOMELESSNESS

HOMELESSNESS

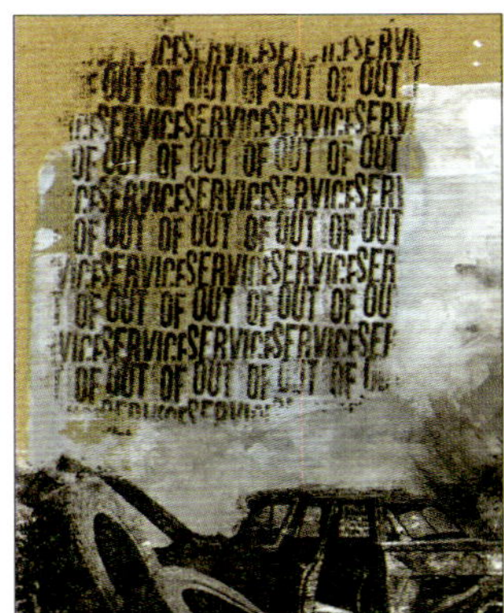
HOMELESSNESS

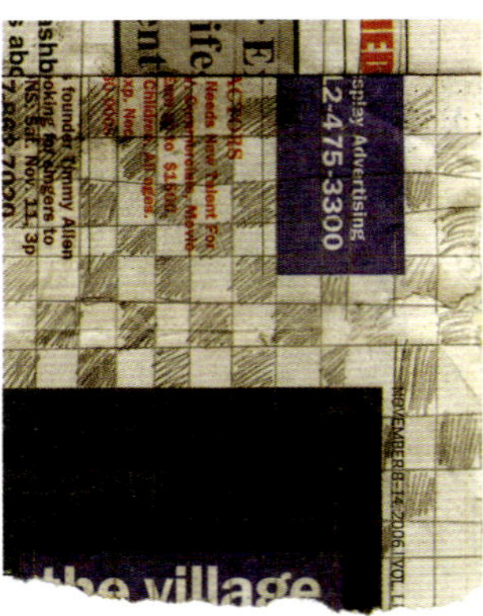
HOMELESSNESS

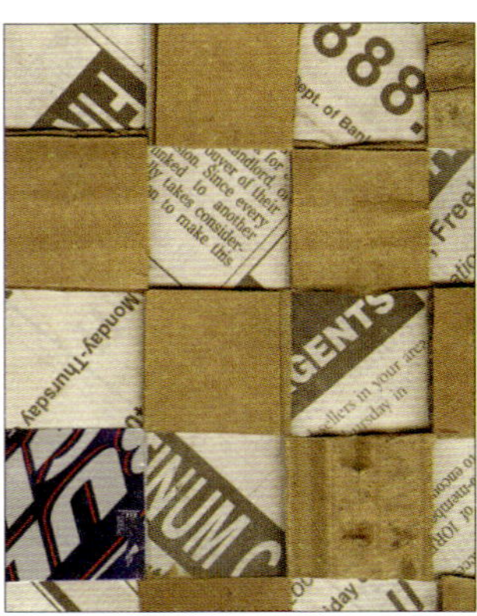
HOMELESSNESS

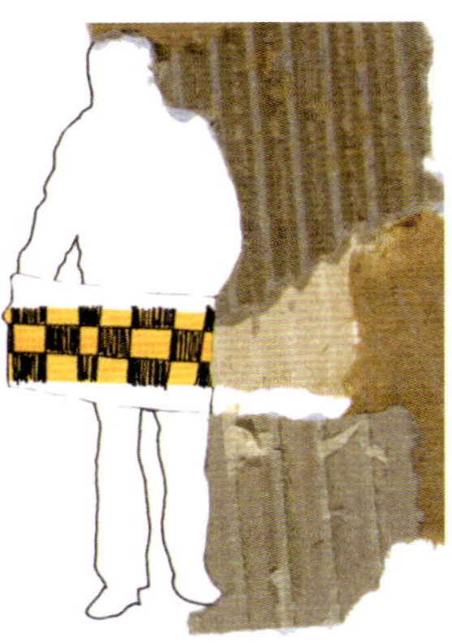
HOMELESSNESS

HEY TAXI SOLUTIONS:

Figures 1, 3, and 6 through 9 are highly personal abstract investigations into form, pattern, and texture, referencing homelessness.

Figures 2 and 4 symbolize a homeless person as one who is at the fringe of society.

Figure 5 is done in the iconography of a road sign, which illustrates an activity to earn money by the homeless.

Figures 10 through 15 show one student's personal journey in solving the six subjects on the assignment sheet. Here, a voice begins to emerge in terms of form, composition, texture, line, space, and limited use of color.

NOISE OR HOSTILITY

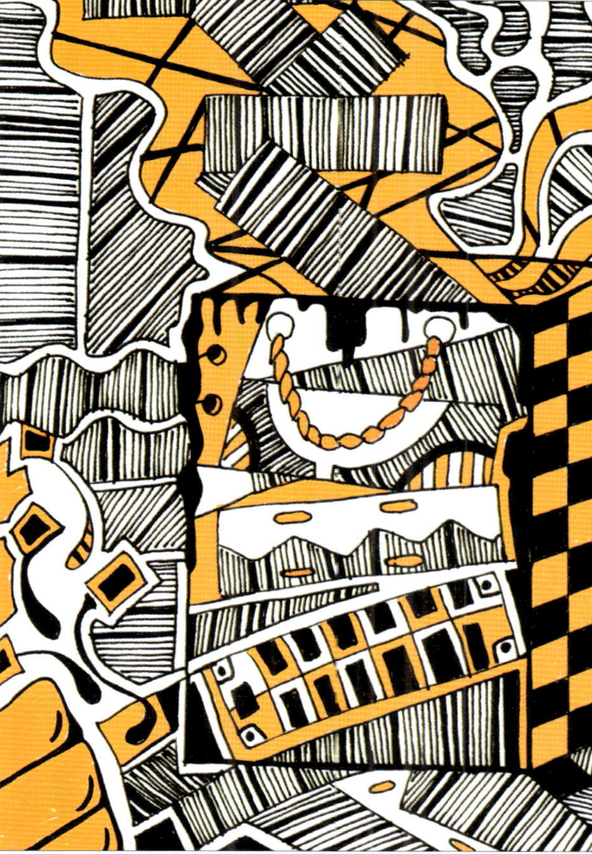

CONSUMERISM

TRAFFIC JAM OR OVERCROWDING

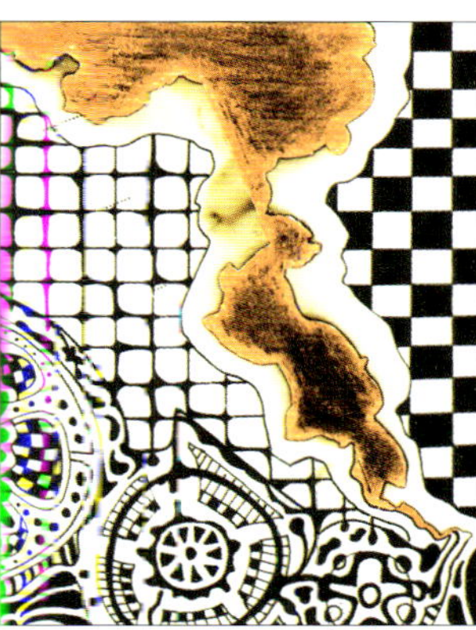

POLLUTION

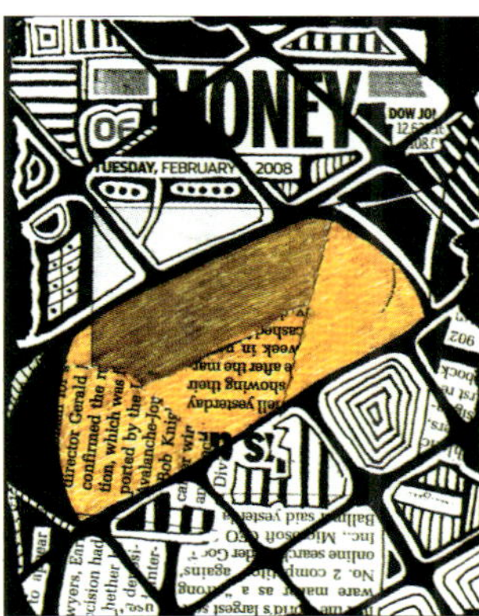

HOMELESSNESS

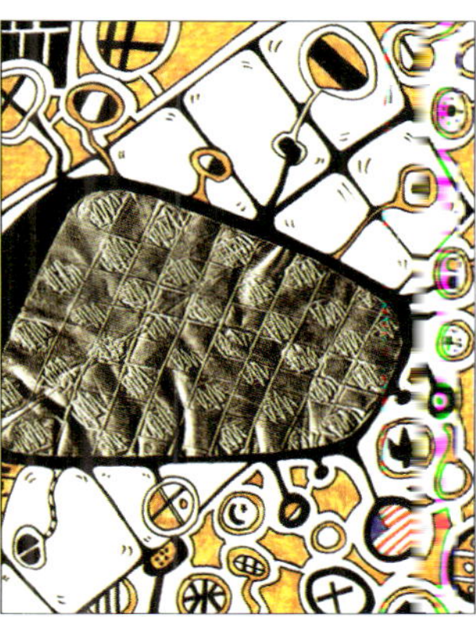

DIVERSITY

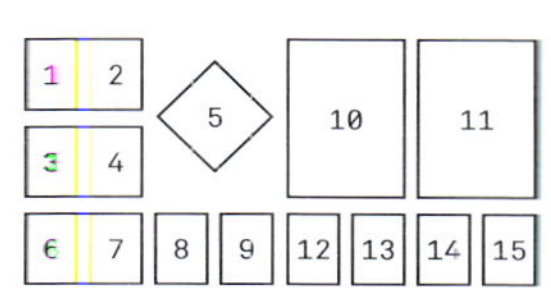

1. *Matt Ryan*
2. *Maya Cata*
3. *M. Lee*
4. *Hannah Song*
5. *Jennifer Laga*
6. *Christopher Mills*
7. *John O'Callaghan*
8. *Michael Bebout*
9. *June Lim*

10–15. *Fnu Herry*

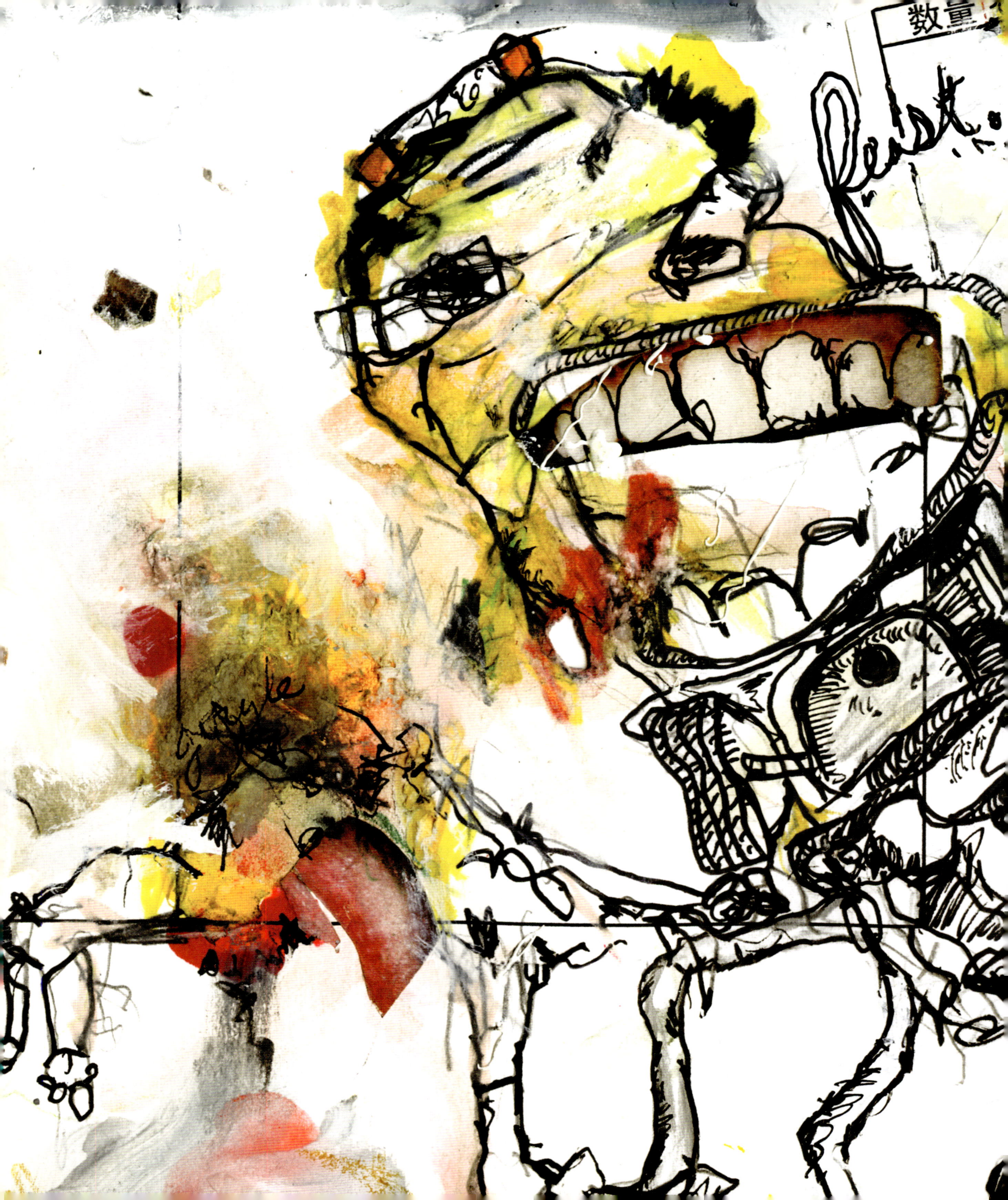
数量
feast.

HEY TAXI SOLUTIONS:

Figure 1 is a highly personal, spontaneously drawn and collaged image that expresses consumerism. The word feast, which appears in the upper right-hand corner, expresses the act of overconsumption, referencing food.

Figures 2 through 7, created by one student, are in direct contrast to figure 1, in that they are carefully rendered images. Yet, the connection between the two is that they are both highly abstract and much is left to individual interpretation.

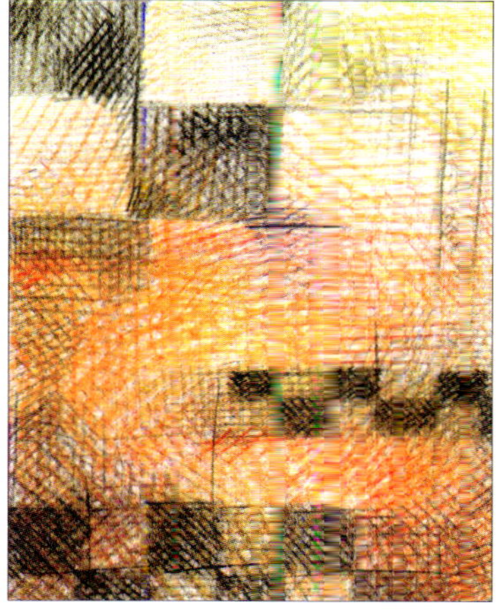
TRAFFIC JAM OR OVERCROWDING

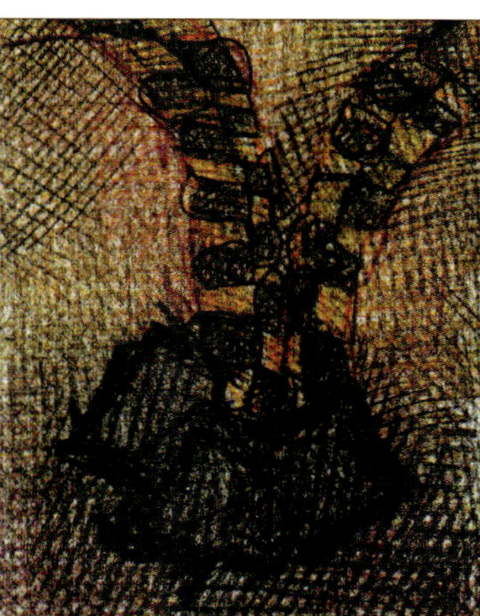
NOISE OR HOSTILITY

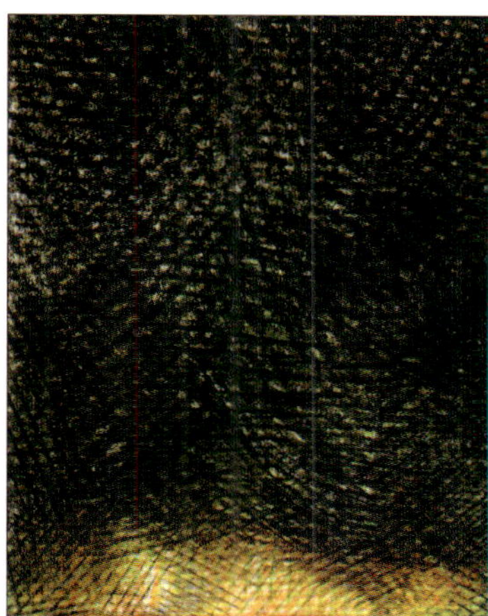
POLLUTION

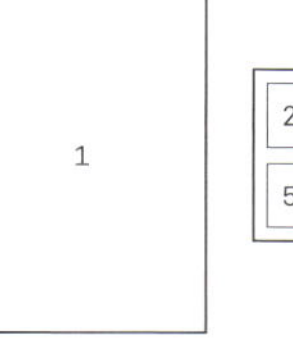

1. Kyle Fetzer
2–7. Gregory Spuches

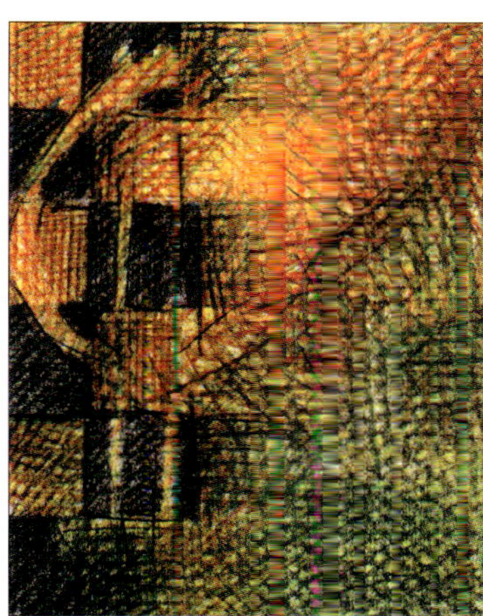
CONSUMERISM

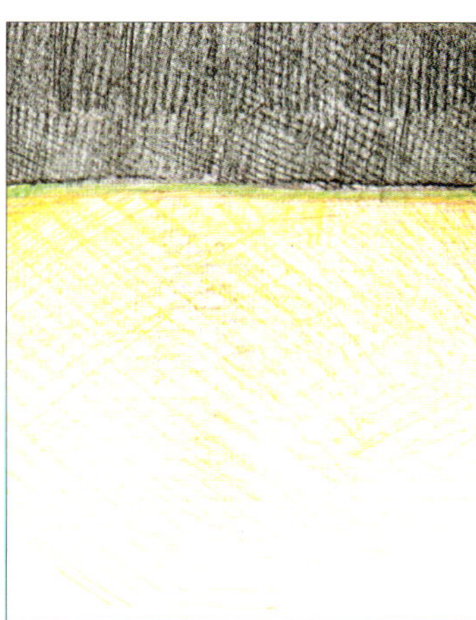
DIVERSITY

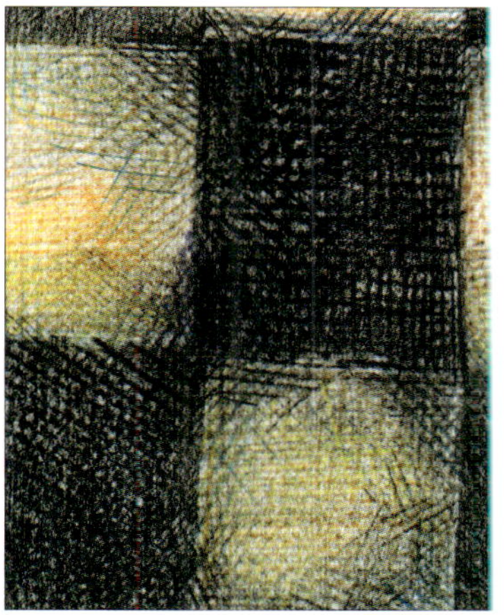
HOMELESSNESS

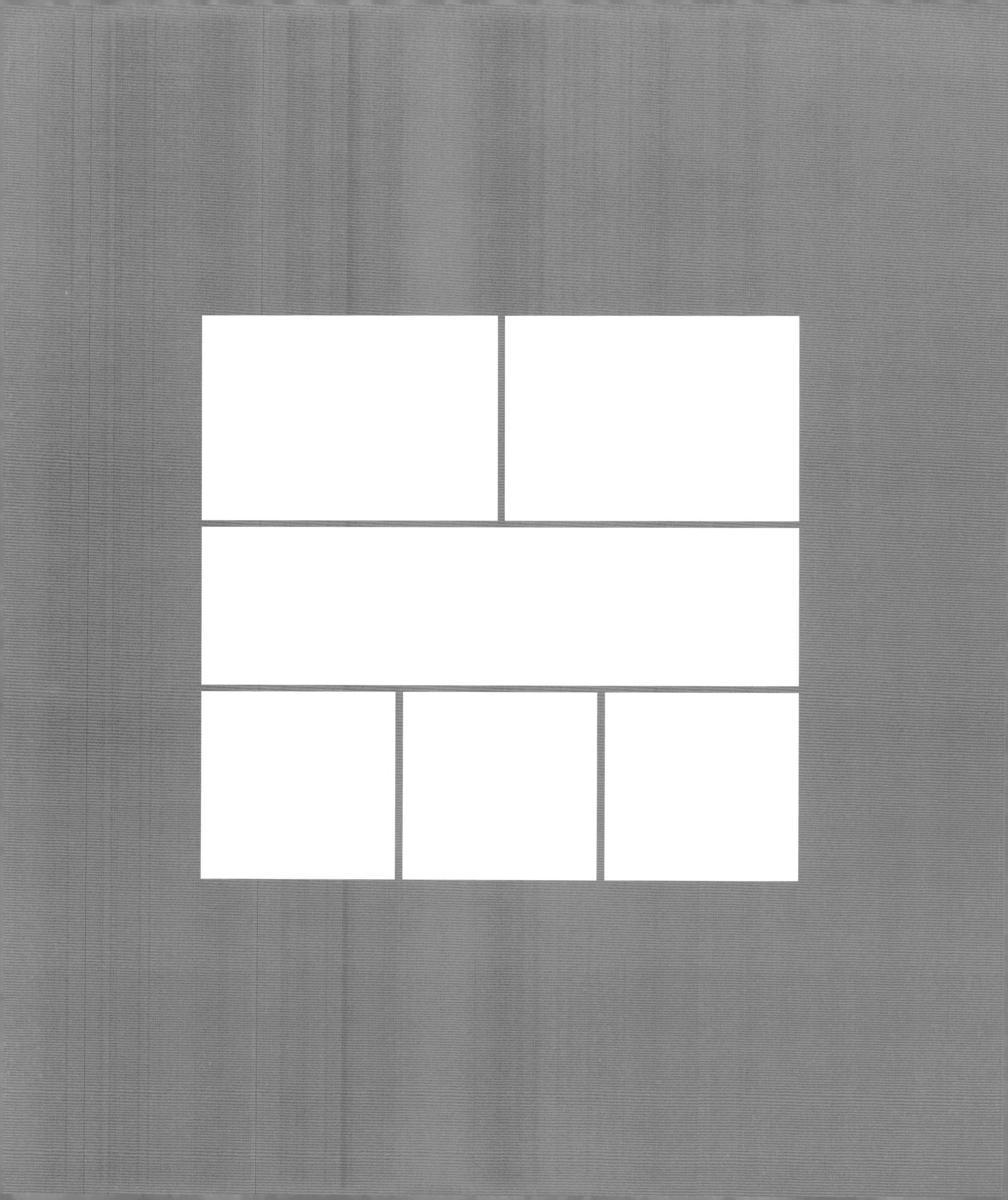

THOUGHTS ON THE CREATIVE PROCESS 8

When one begins a project, no matter what state one finds oneself in, it is necessary simply to begin to work, to doodle, to play. This often sets the conditions for a quieter place in oneself to emerge, which connects one directly to the problem at hand. Often, creativity is a state that moves one toward relaxation. The practice of meditation can help in creating this state.

CLOUDS

"WHEN YOU LOOK AT A STAINED WALL, OR ONE BUILT OF MANGLED STONES, YOU MIGHT FIND A RESEMBLANCE TO LANDSCAPES, WITH MOUNTAINS, RIVERS, ROCKS, TREES, WIDE VALLEYS AND HILLS IN VARIED ARRANGEMENTS; OR YOU MAY SEE BATTLES AND MEN IN ACTION OR STRANGE FACES AND COSTUMES – AN ENDLESS VARIETY."

LEONARDO DA VINCI

Stare at each of the following cloud formations for as long as necessary until a specific area of that very picture suggests an identifiable image. Define the area that you have selected by enhancing the image for readability by darkening, lightening, or outlining it. In the small rectangle beneath each cloud formation, clearly describe your discovery. The key to the assignment lies in being open to the state of suggestibility.

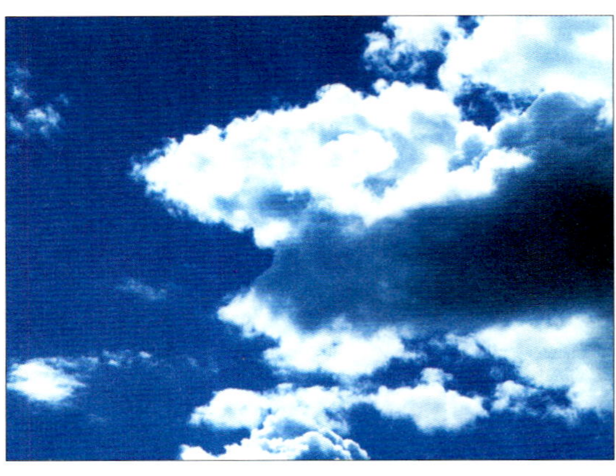

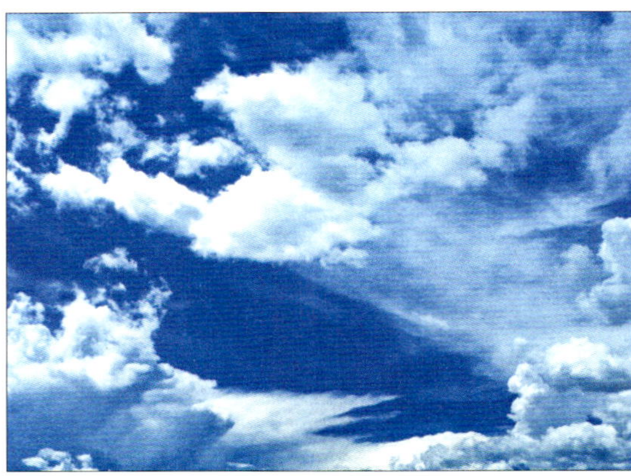

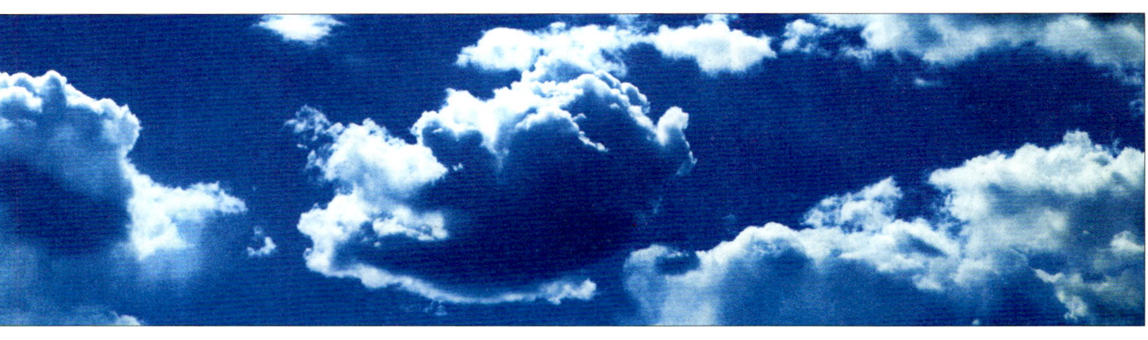

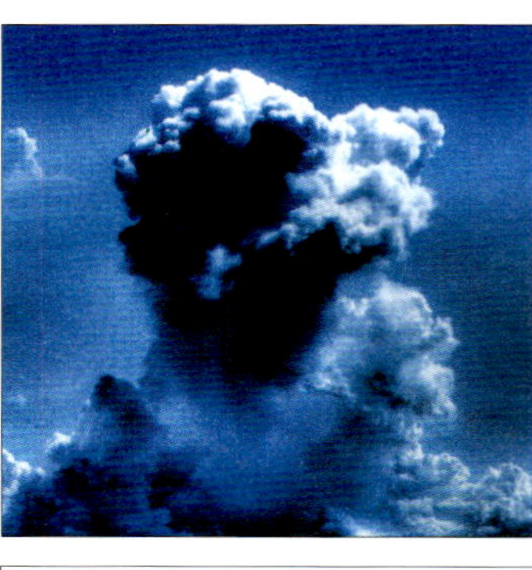

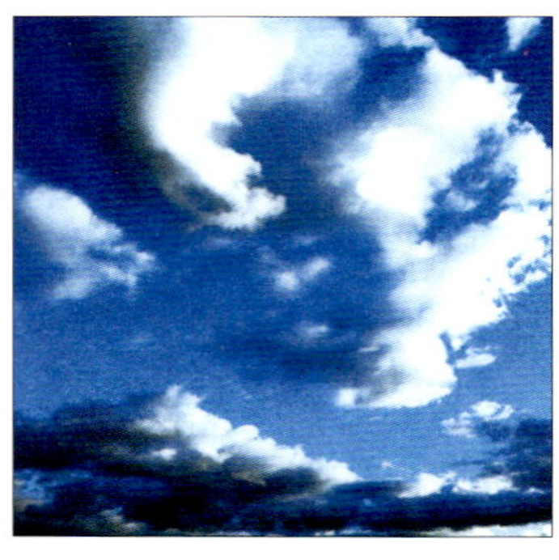

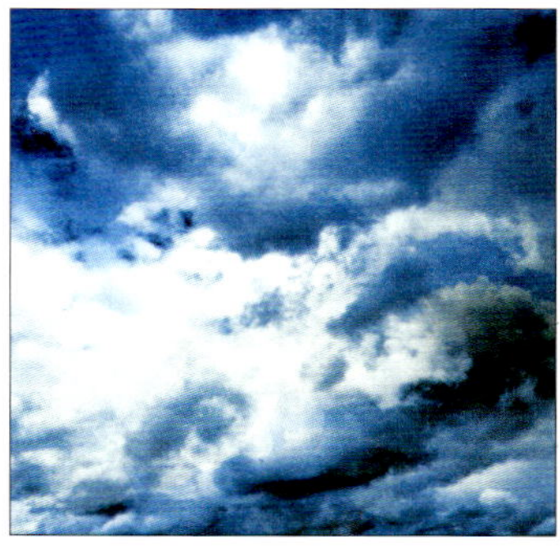

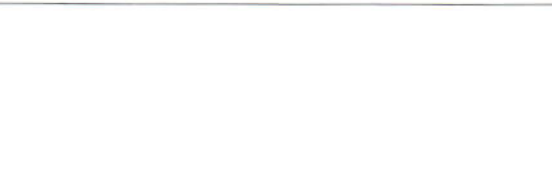

PROBLEMS : SOLUTIONS SERIES

CREATED BY RICHARD WILDE / JUDITH WILDE, PRODUCED BY VISUAL ARTS PRESS, LTD. ART DIRECTORS: RICHARD WILDE / JUDITH WILDE

CLOUD PROBLEM:

Gaze at each of the following cloud formations for as long as necessary until a recognizable image appears. At times, a single image may appear, or multiple images may appear. Define the images you've discovered by outlining, darkening, or lightening them to create greater contrast, and develop a clear narrative for each of the six cloud formations on the assignment sheet.

AIM:
The aim is to move from one's everyday reactive state to a more responsive state that encourages new impressions to arise

SUGGESTIONS:
For this assignment, contrast is an important consideration that helps in defining an image. Also, the attention to detail impacts on the development of one's imagery. Carefully consider the intricacies of the cloud formations as well as the negative space between the clouds.

By allowing oneself to get lost in the clouds, it is possible for unexpected imagery to arise.

This assignment aligns one with the experiences of childhood and re-establishes the innate ability to look at one thing and see another. In moving away from one's habitual reactions and inertia to a freer state, surprisingly a subtle inner shift occurs, where seeing is possible and recognizable narratives appear.

Many artists struggle to recapture the ability to reconnect to this childlike way of seeing. It is an inner state, an essential connection to oneself that minimizes mechanical thinking and allows new impressions to arise.

The act of shifting from the known to the unknown is where the secret of personal expression lies. This is a phenomenon that must be experienced and deepened so as to allow oneself to gain access to uncharted territory.

The struggle is to simply reconnect to this state, which is our birthright. Pablo Picasso said, "All children are artists. The problem is how to remain an artist once one grows up."

SPECIFICATIONS:
Use black ink. Color or white ink may be included only if concept dictates.

NOTE:
The assignment sheet shown represents six cloud formations; however, there are ten cloud formations reviewed in this chapter.

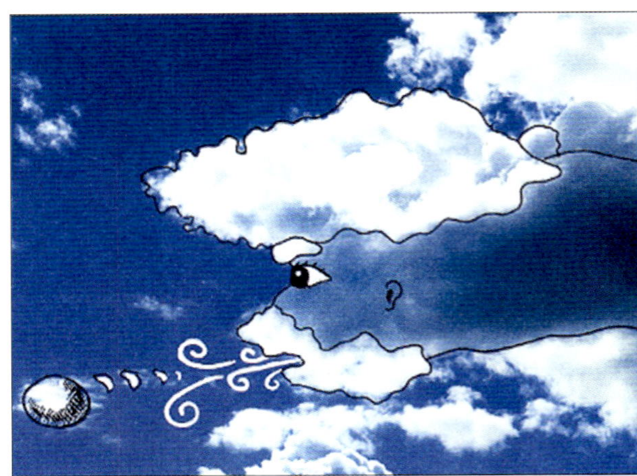

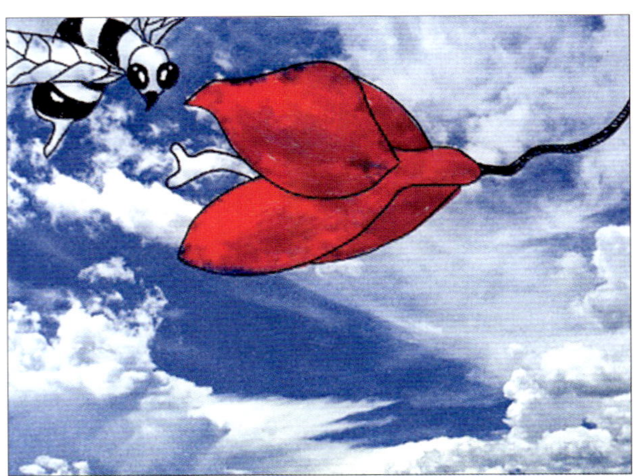

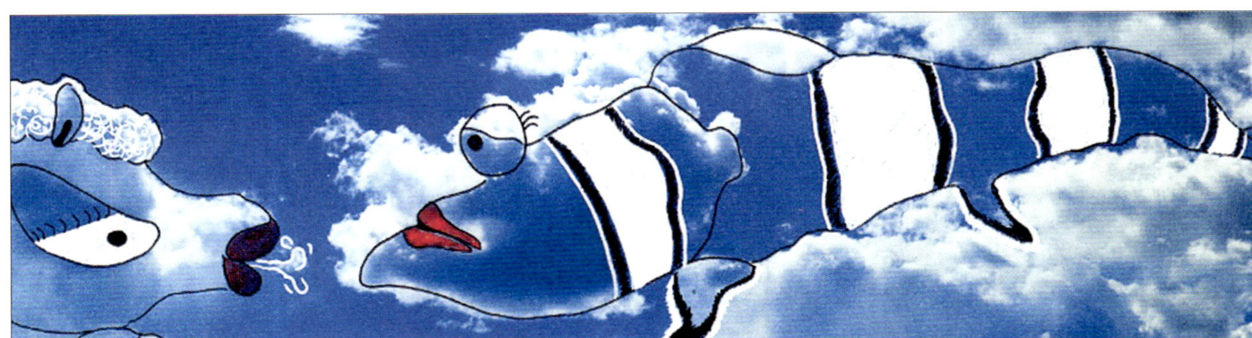

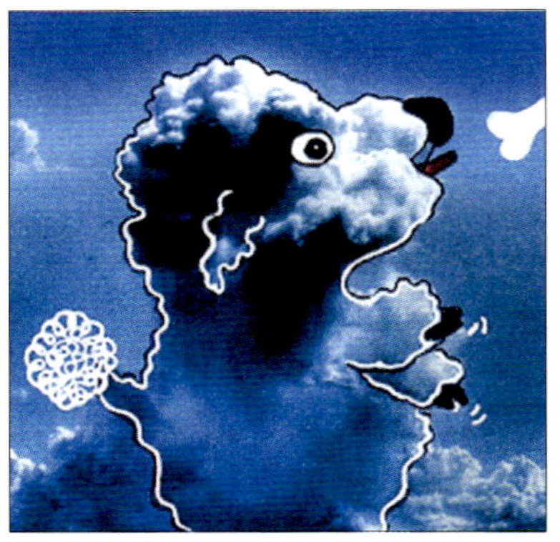

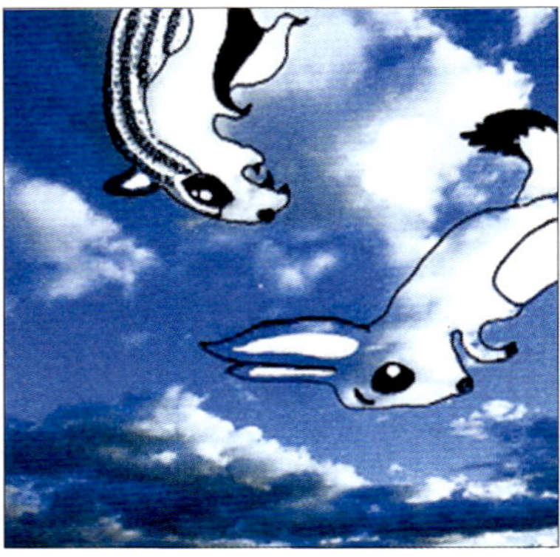

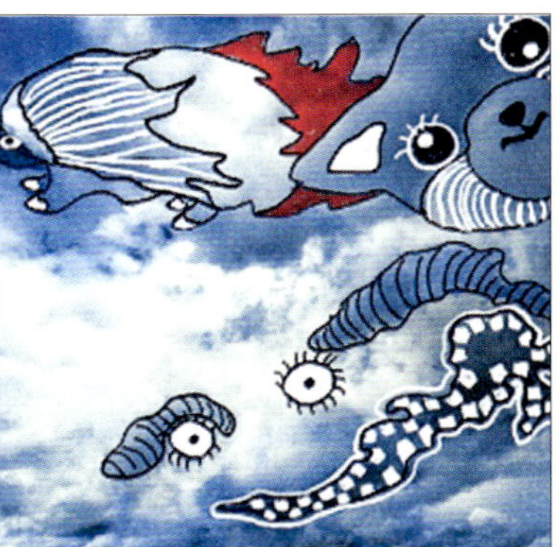

CLOUD SOLUTIONS:

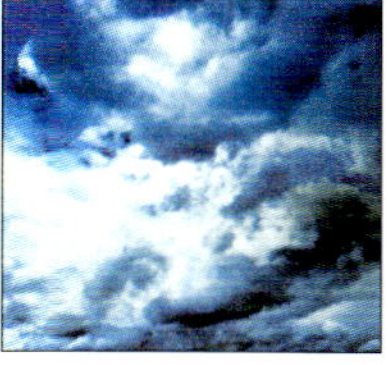

Figure 1 is an example of one student's solution to the six cloud formations, and conveys an emerging voice that is both playful and humorous. Color was used in a sparing yet effective way.

Figures 2 through 7 are examples of the same cloud formation as indicated above. It is evident that what each person sees varies greatly.

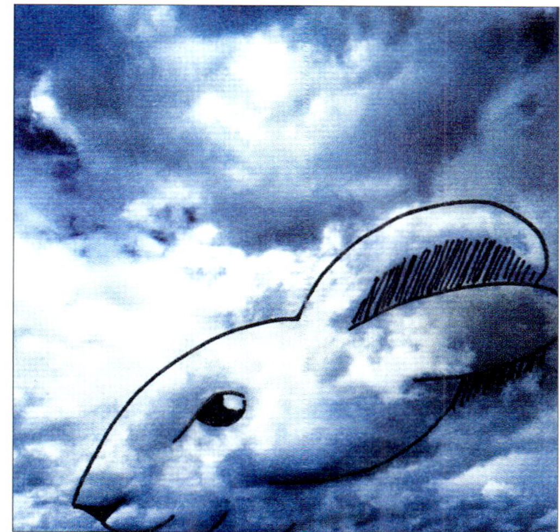

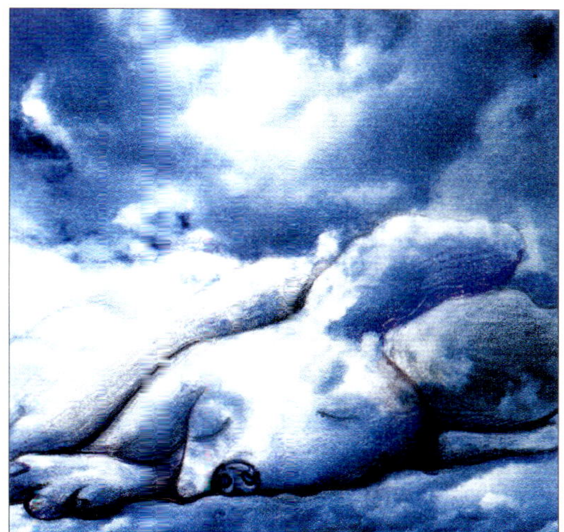

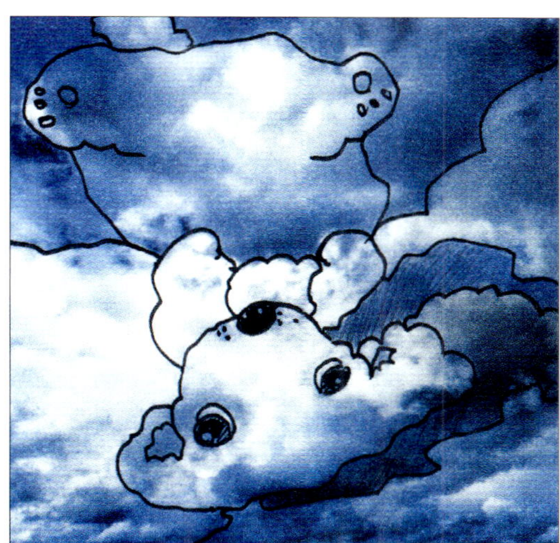

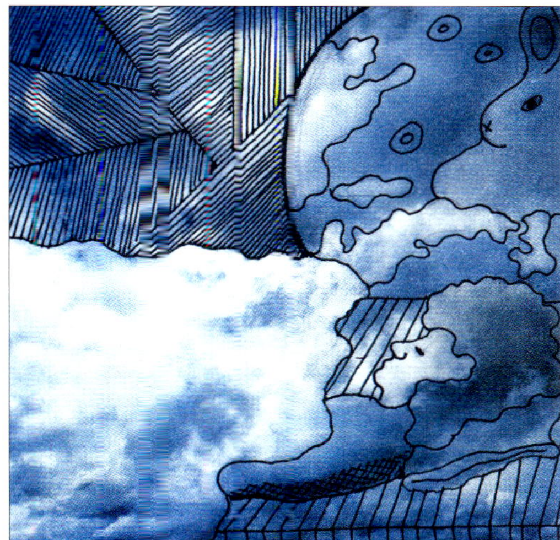

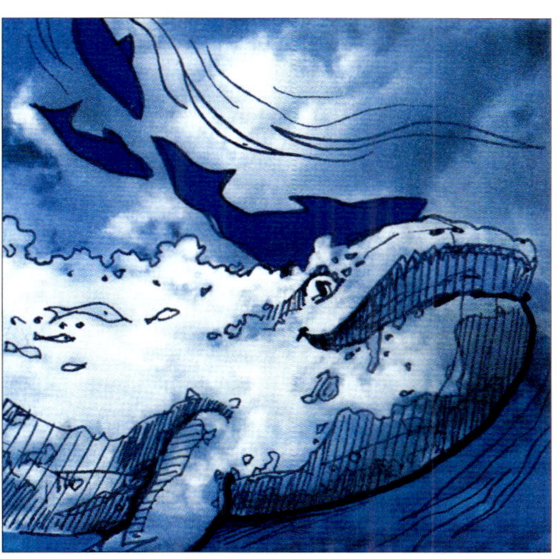

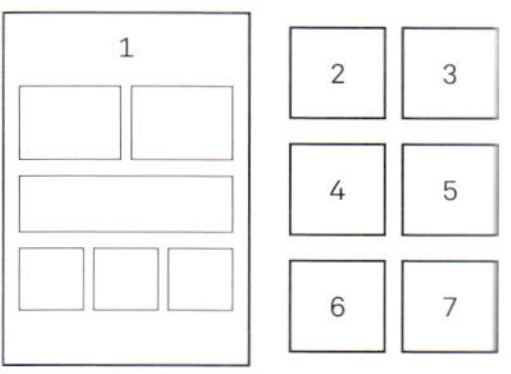

1. *Yoonhee Kim*
2. *Myung Song*
3. *Estefania Soin*
4. *Jaewon Park*
5. *Motoko Ishii*
6. *Kaneko Haryo*
7. *Yuki Murata*

Here, the possibilities of the assignment become apparent: where one person sees two swimmers, another sees a rabbit, while another sees a dog, and so on.

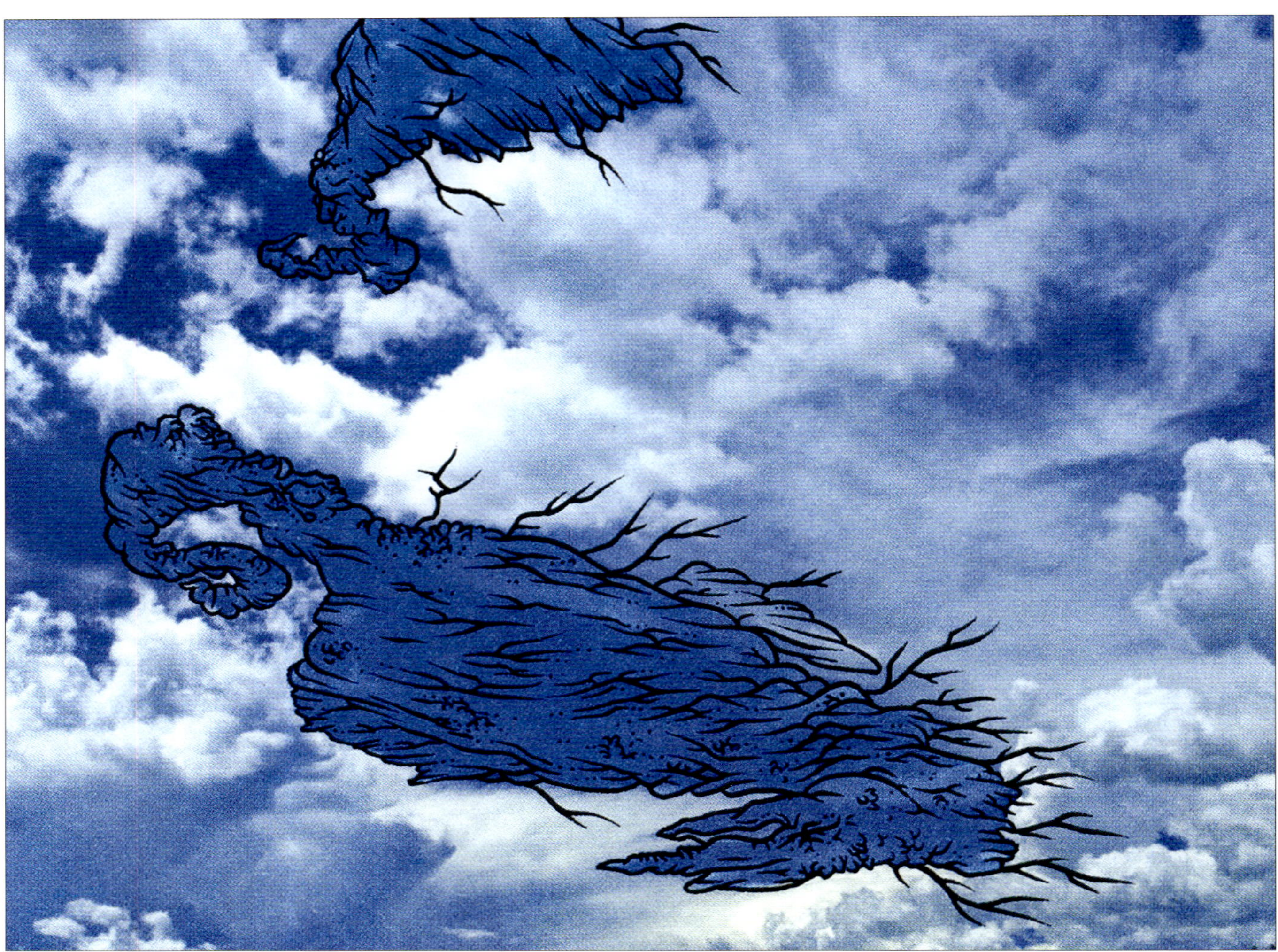

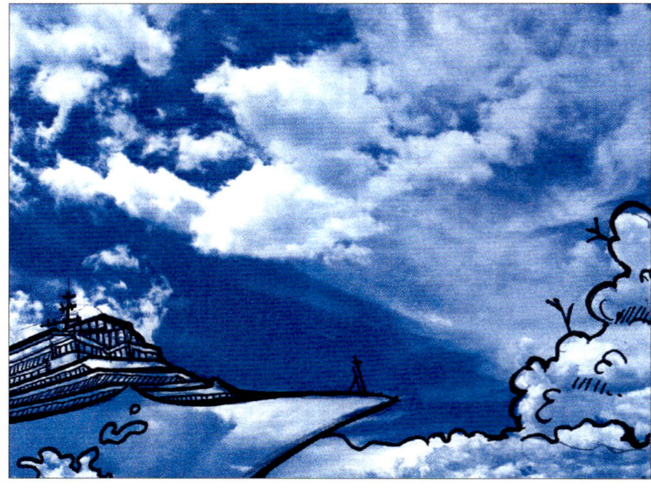

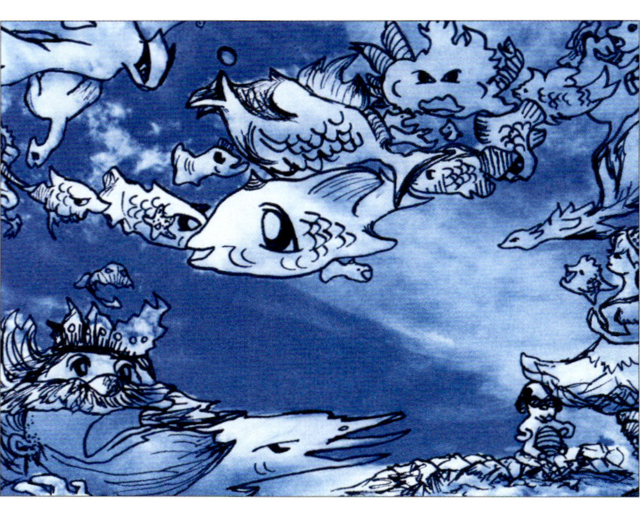

CLOUD SOLUTIONS:

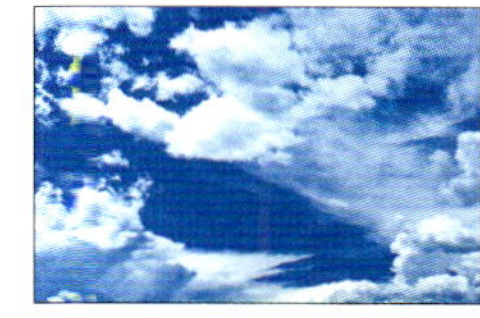

Figures 1 through 6 are variations of the same cloud formation.

Although the intent of the assignment is to address the given cloud formation as an integral element of the image, for certain solutions, liberties were taken where embellishments were added to better actualize the narrative.

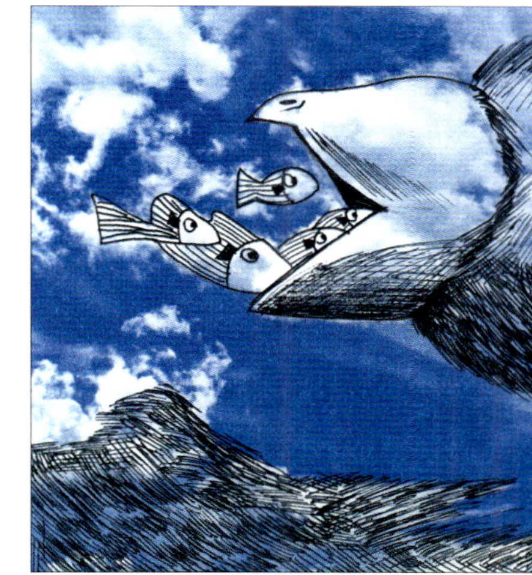

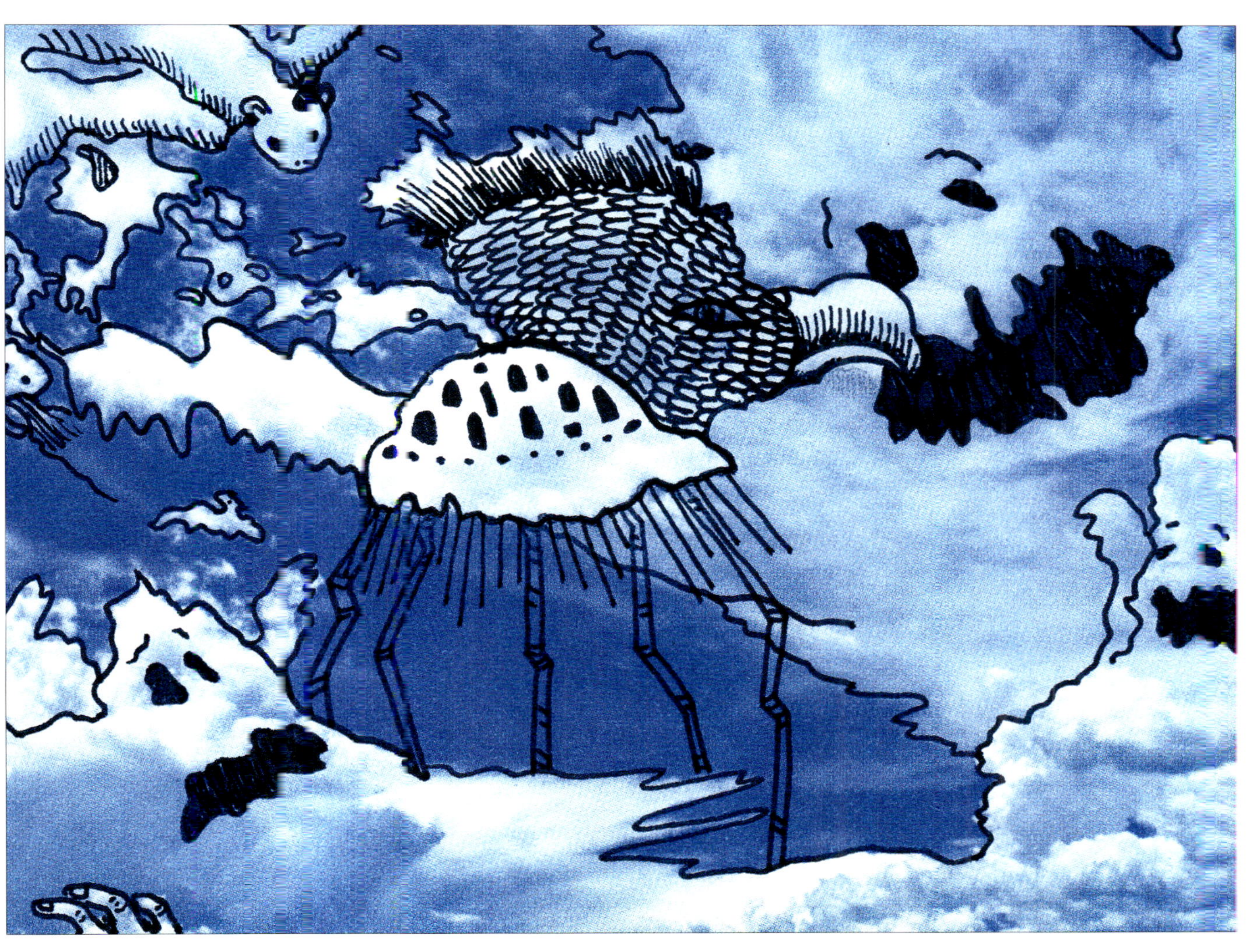

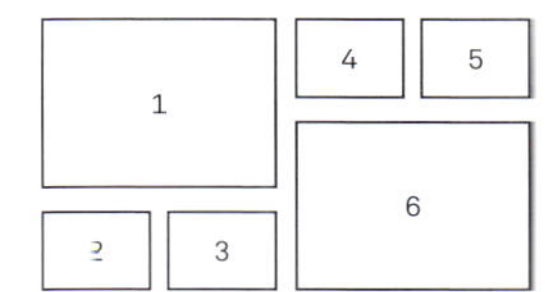

1. *Chris Wright*
2. *Xing Pei Wang*
3. *Ariele Villanueva*
4. *Kyung-A Na*
5. *Seongmi Park*
6. *Hyejin Hong*

Figure 6, for example, deals with fantasy. Certain dictates of the clouds were interpreted as ghosts and monsters, while the central image was created with the addition of legs that were drawn regardless of the cloud formation. Here, artistic license was taken.

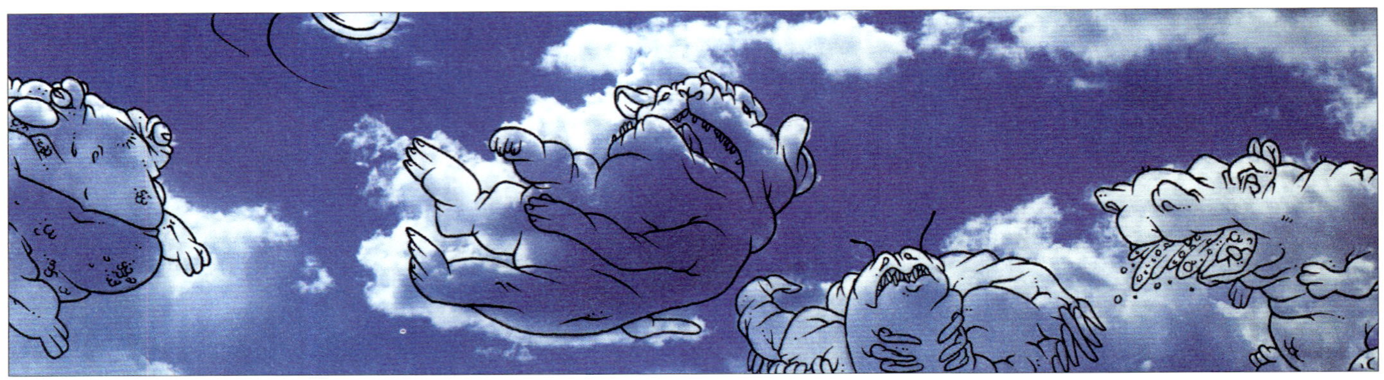

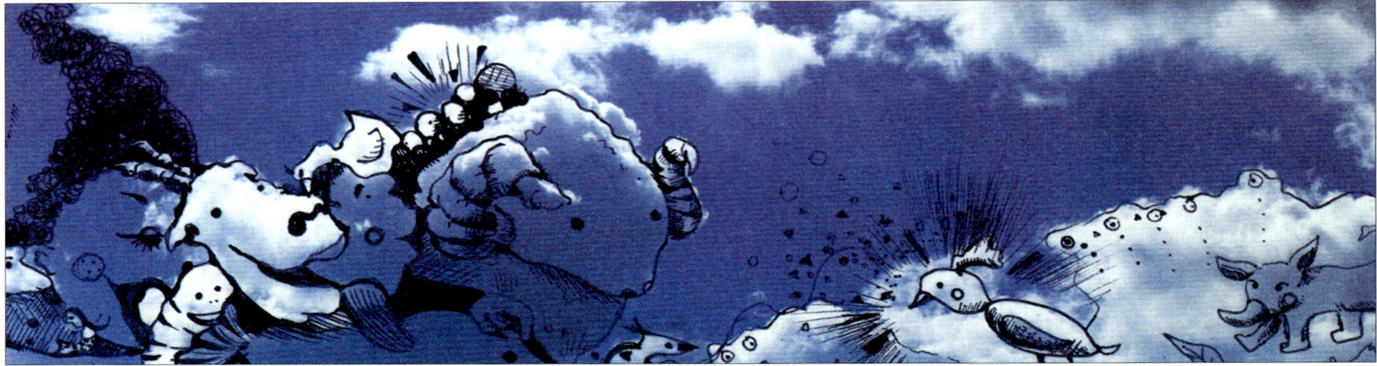

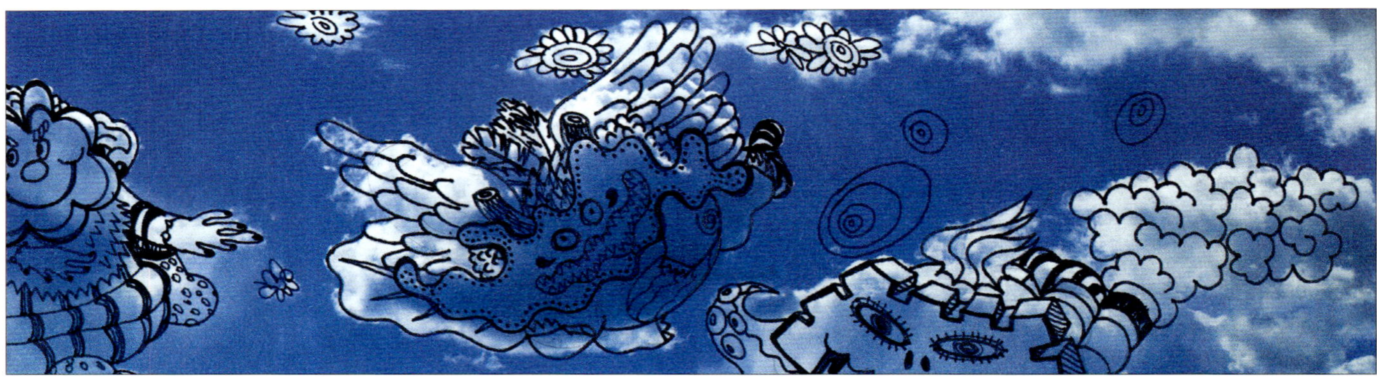

CLOUD SOLUTIONS:

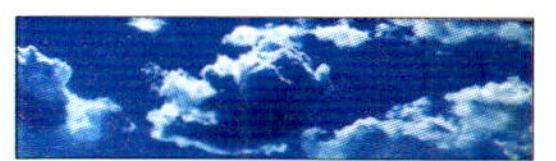

These six solutions offer various subjects, each depicting a world that includes an array of imaginative characters.

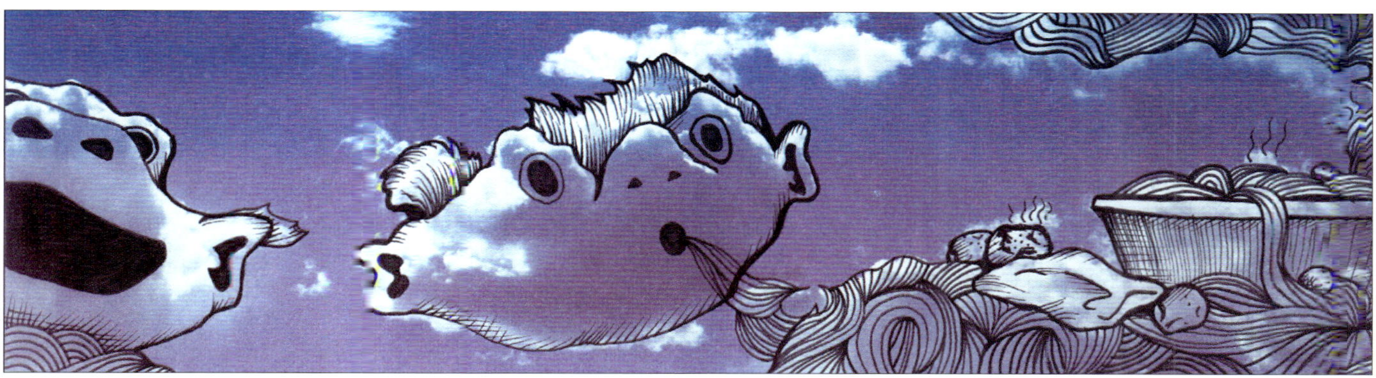

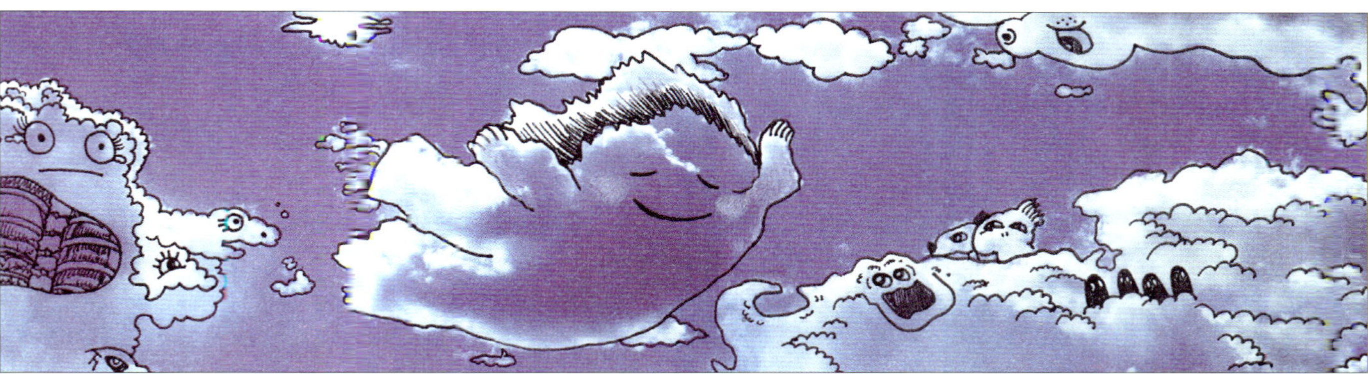

1	4
2	5
3	6

1. *Chris Wright*
2. *Baekhyeon Jung*
3. *Seolhee Cho*
4. *Jocelyn Tsaih*
5. *Hyejin Hong*
6. *Joo Kong*

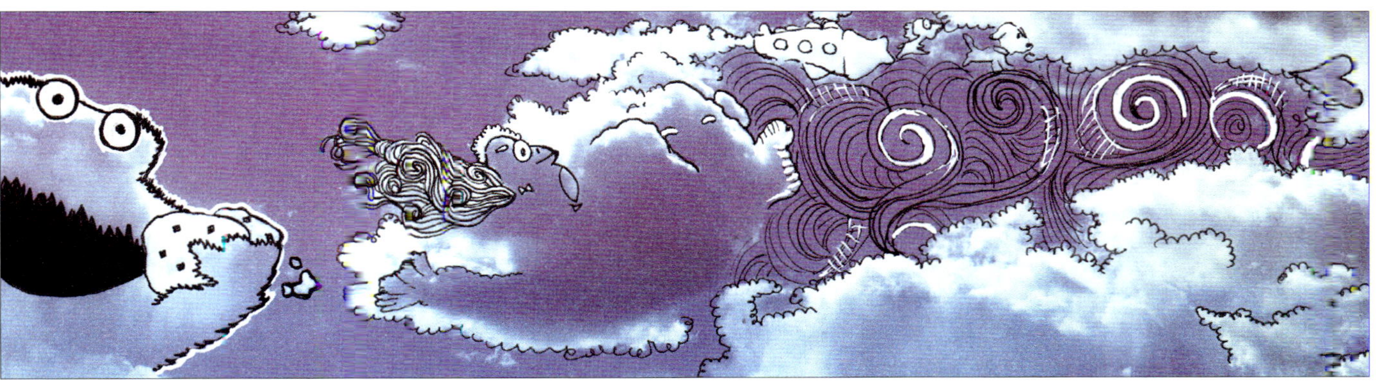

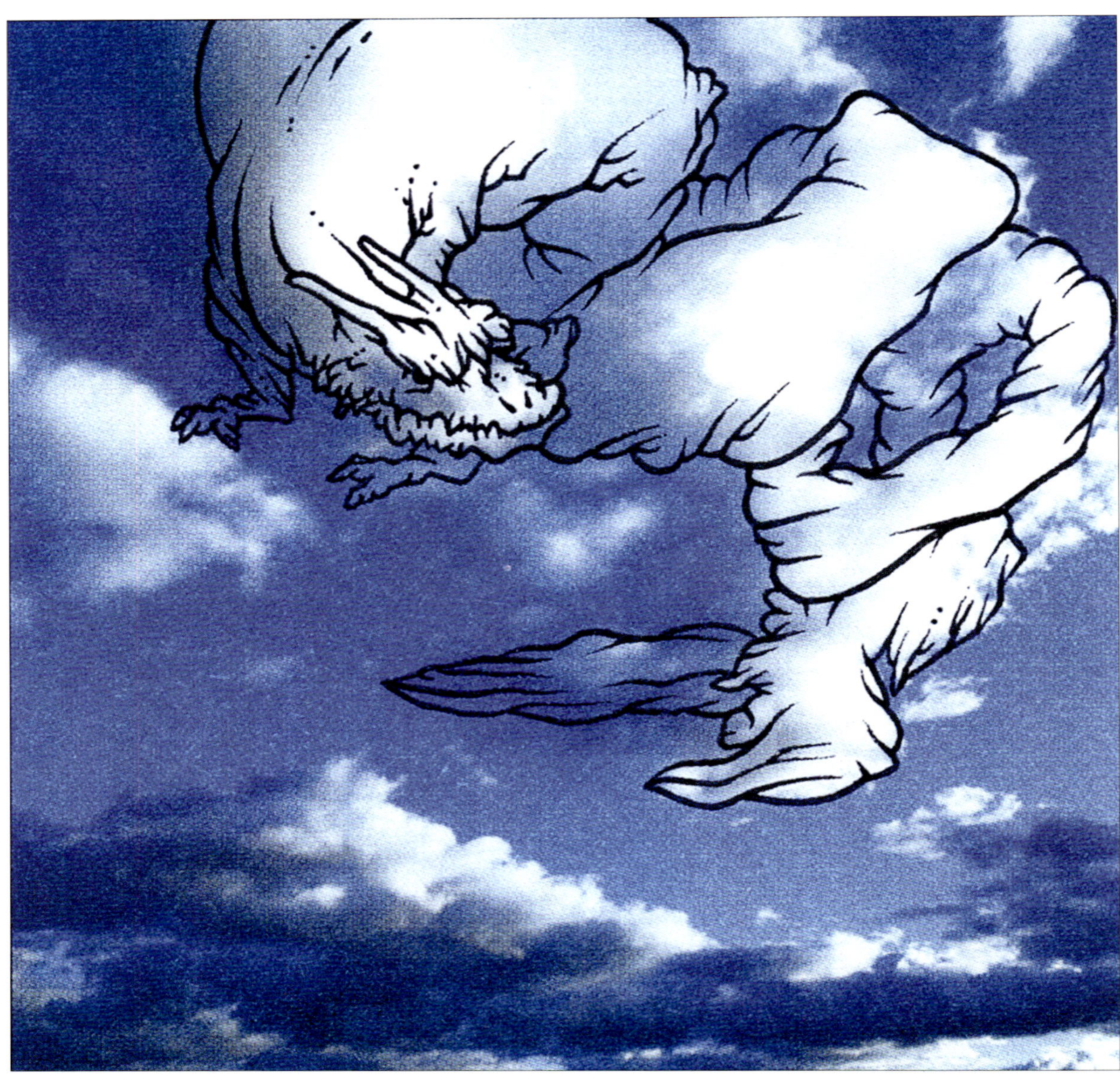

CLOUD SOLUTIONS:

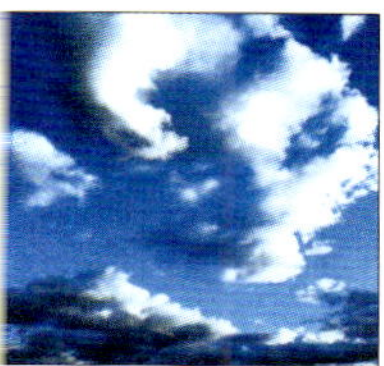

These investigations deal with mythical and surrealistic imagery, each articulating volume, form, line, and space in its own way.

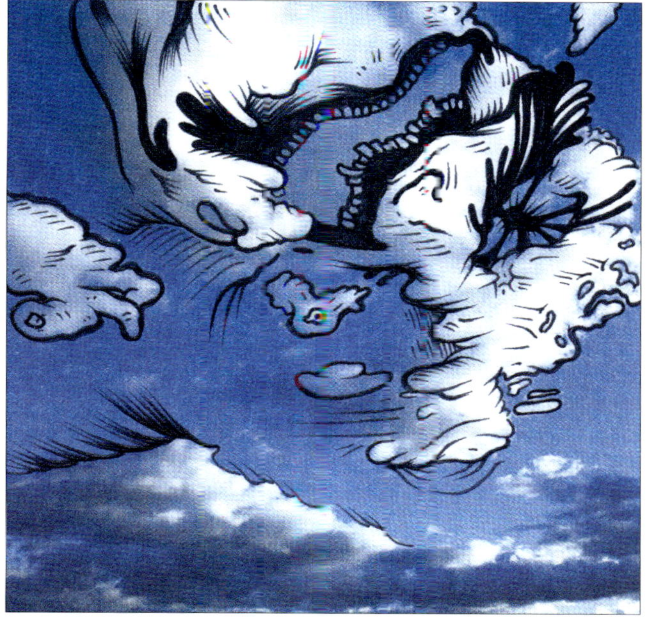

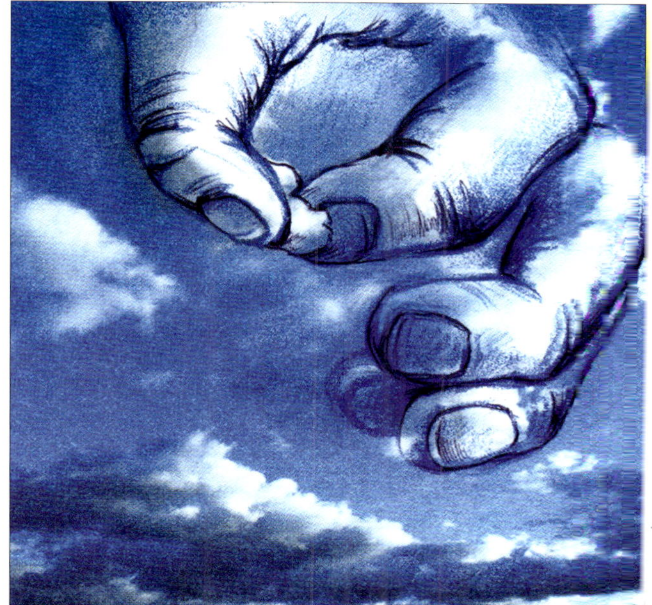

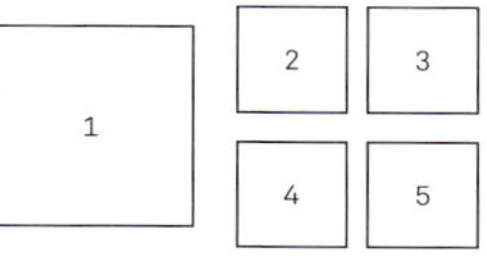

1. *Chris Wright*
2. *Sam Ba*
3. *Jaewon Park*
4. *Kyle Chaille*
5. *Myeongjin Shin*

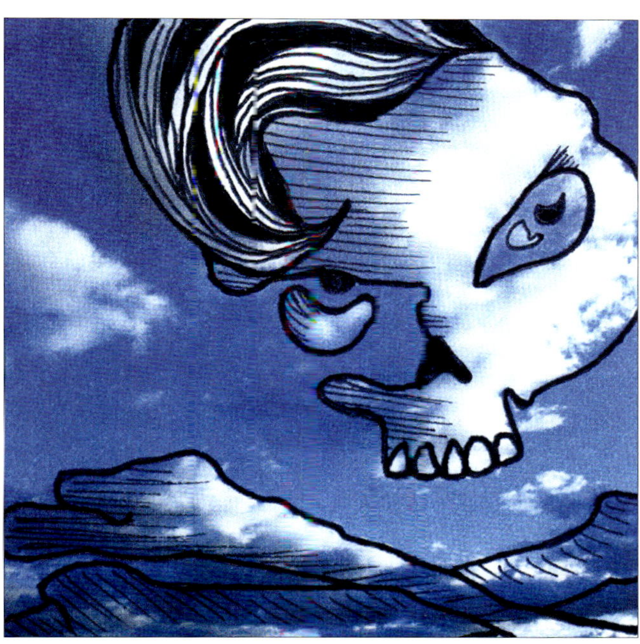

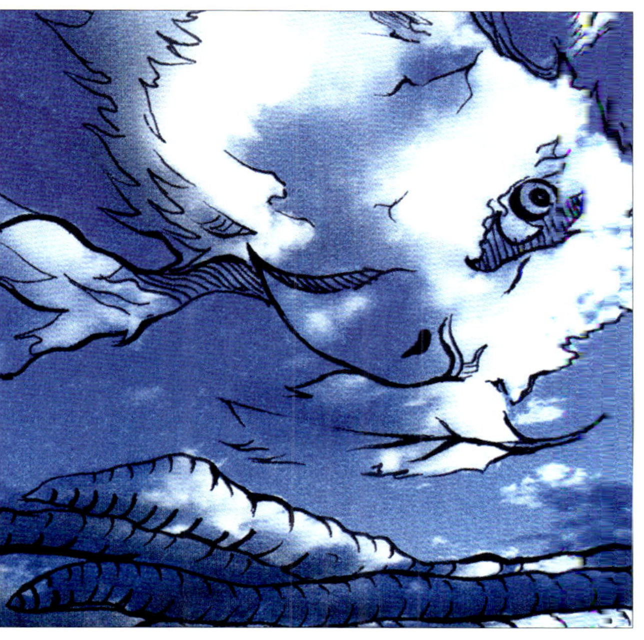

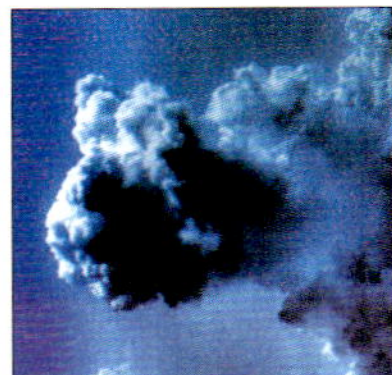

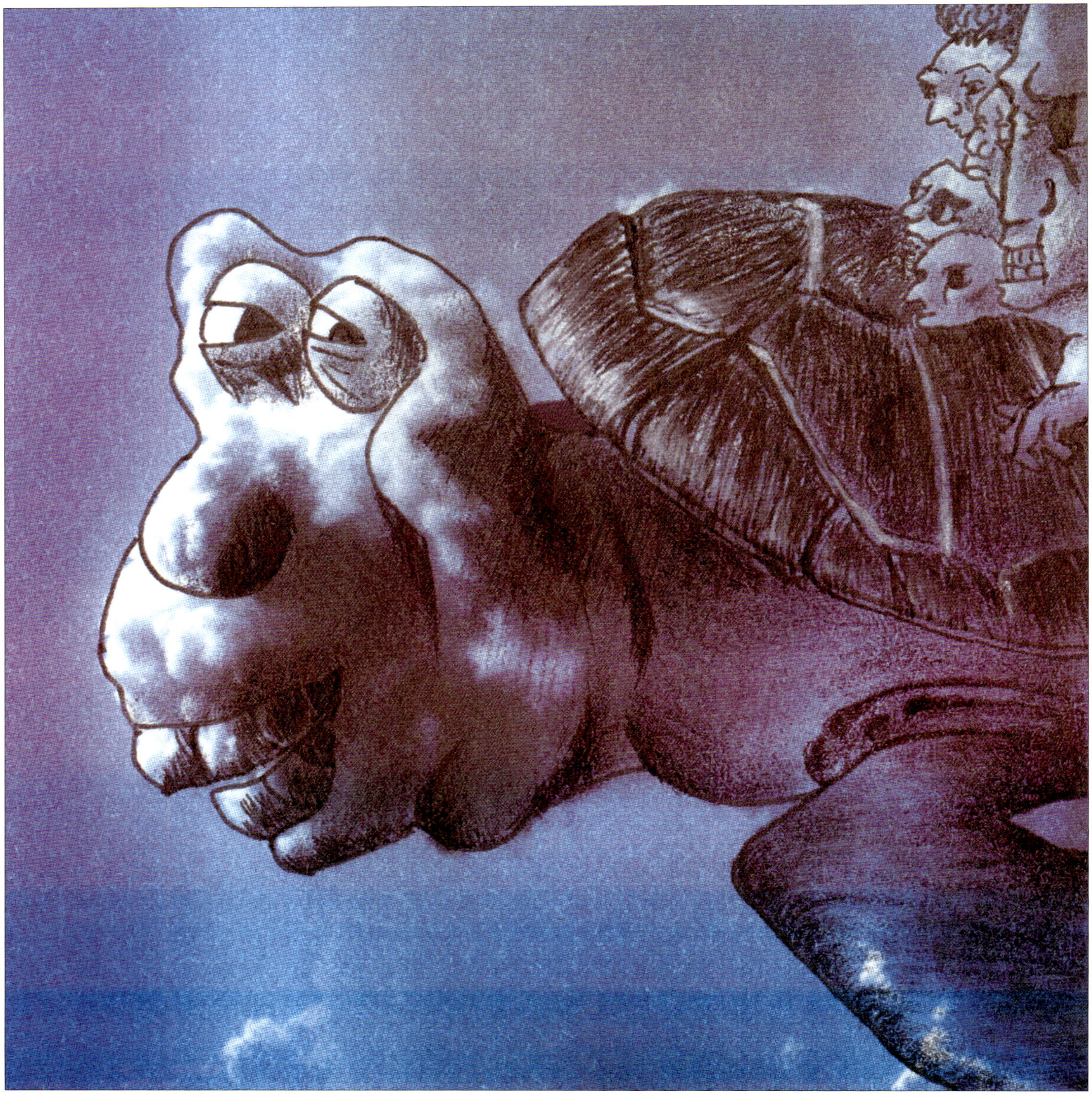

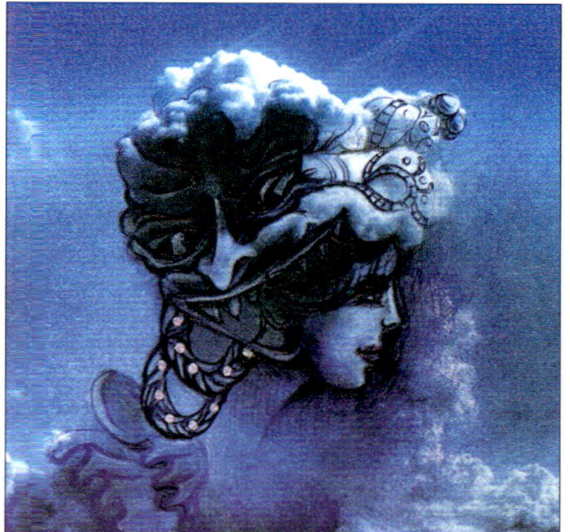

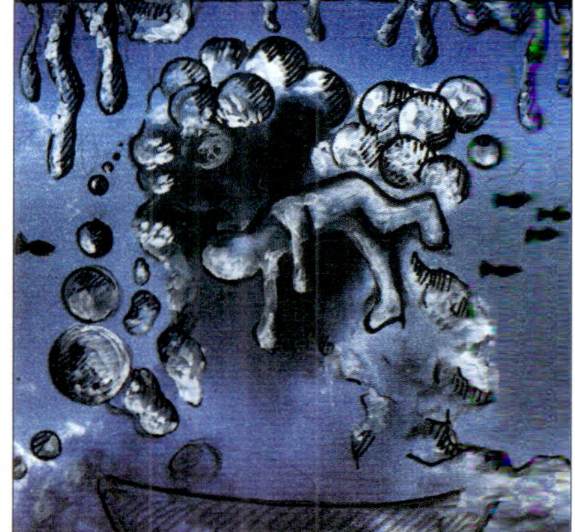

CLOUD SOLUTIONS:

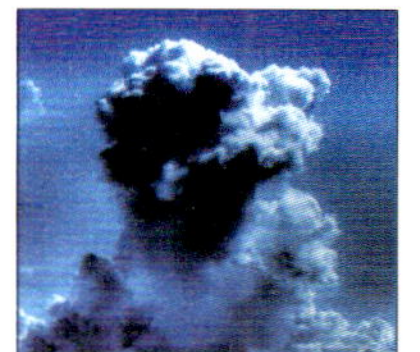

One's search must begin by allowing the intricacies of the given cloud formation to suggest imagery.

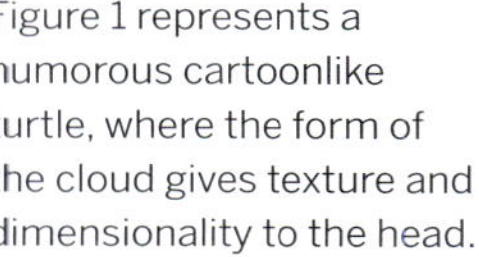

Figure 1 represents a humorous cartoonlike turtle, where the form of the cloud gives texture and dimensionality to the head.

The range of solutions shown demonstrates the infinite possibilities, ranging from a woman's profile, to Mozart, to broccoli, to a bear and its cub.

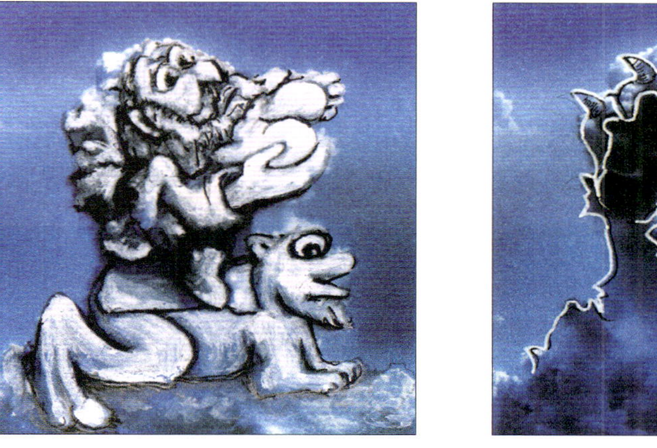

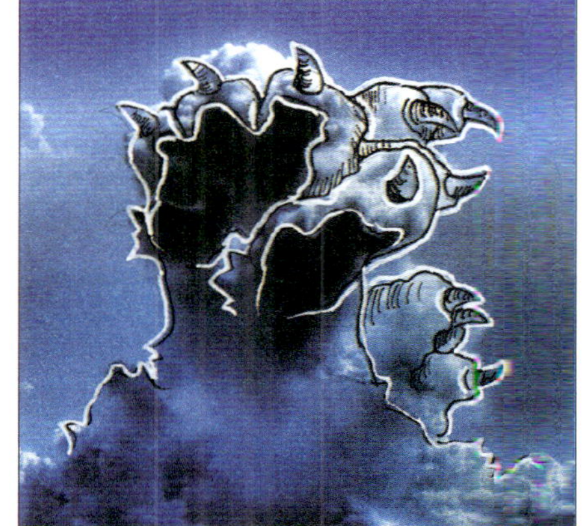

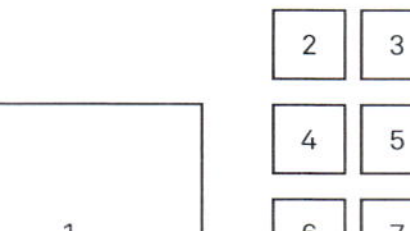

1. *Hoyun Son*
2. *Jaewon Park*
3. *Sanghyun Lee*
4. *Saebom Bae*
5. *Maxine Taylor*
6. *Seongmi Park*
7. *Daeun Ko*
8. *Joo Kong*
9. *Hyunsoo Nam*

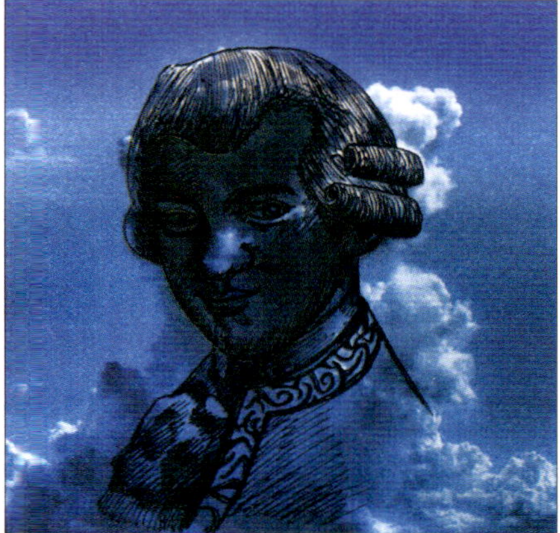

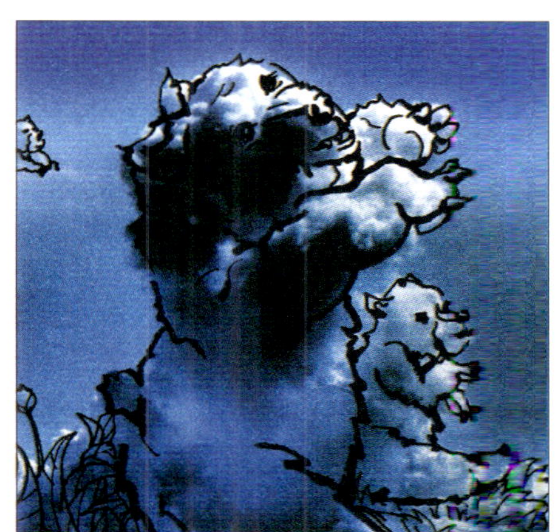

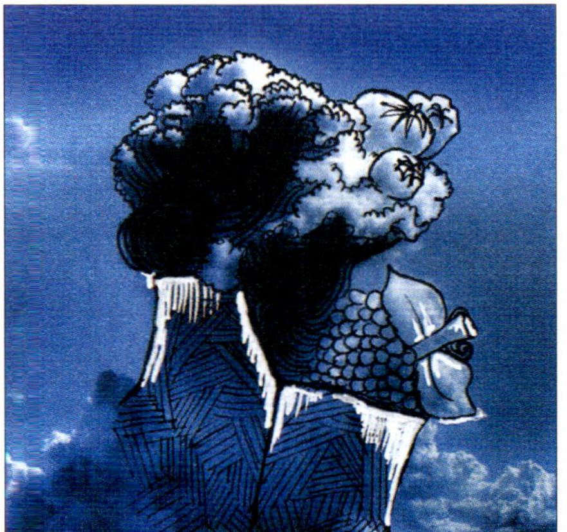

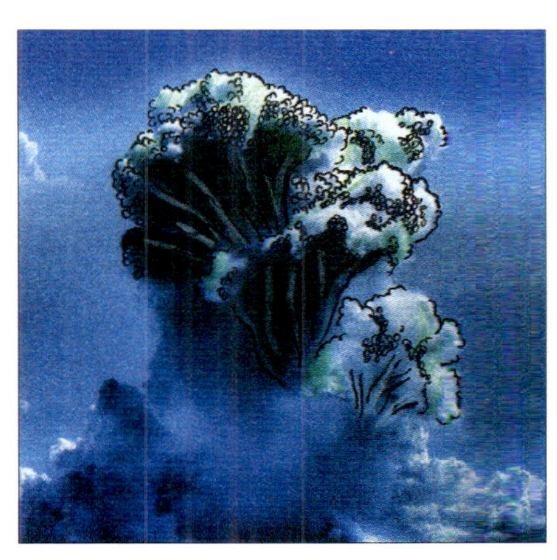

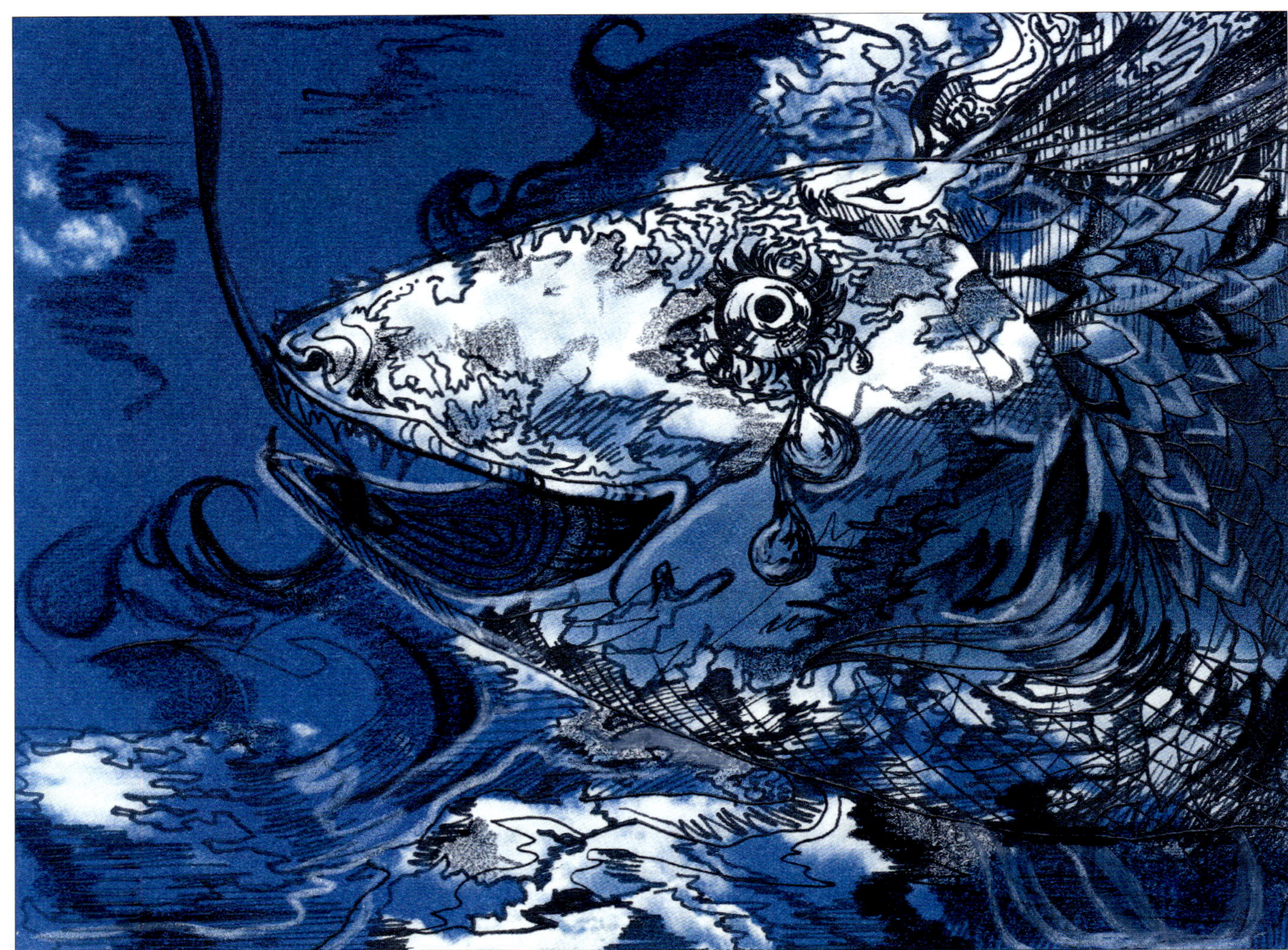

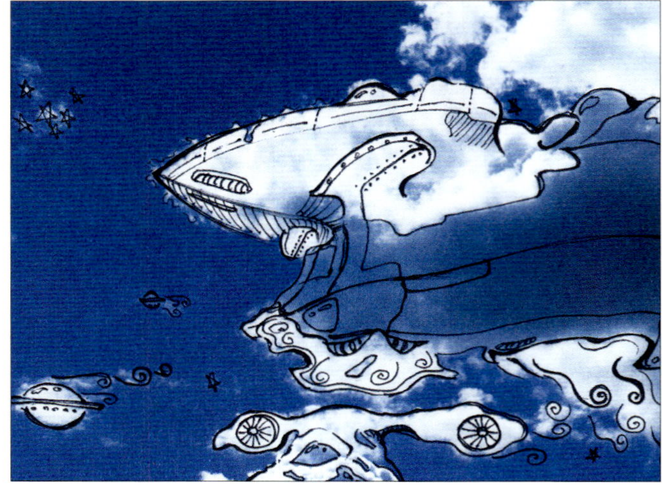

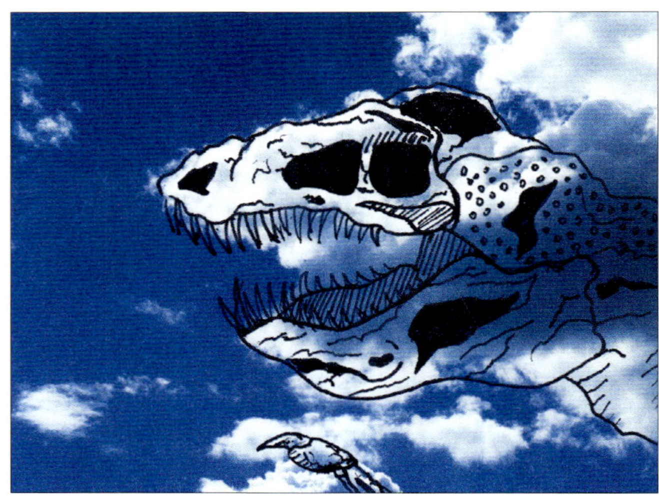

CLOUD SOLUTIONS:

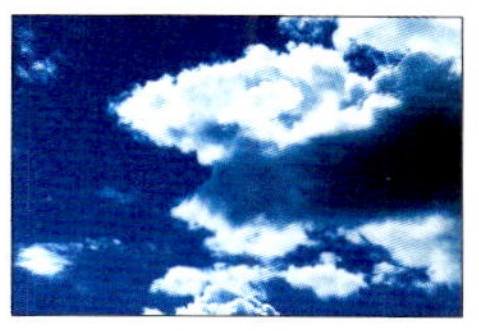

These solutions followed the dictates of the clouds. Yet, in figure 6, this was only partially addressed, for at times a greater emphasis was placed on drawing skills to create an image beyond what the cloud formations provided.

Although the image has merit, by not risking deeper investigation into the intricacies of the cloud formation, an opportunity for further discovery was lost.

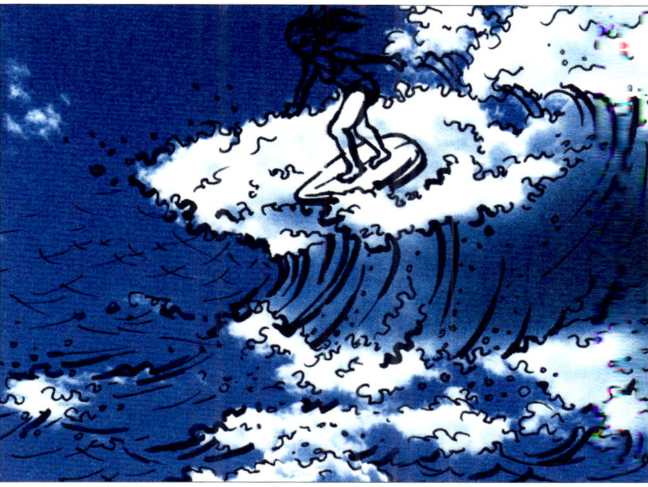

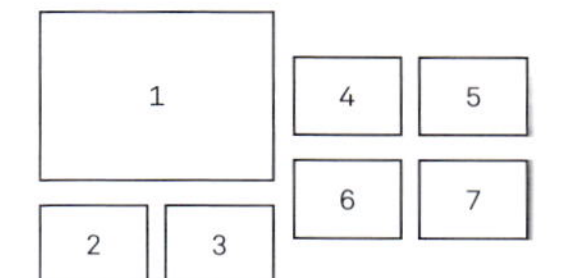

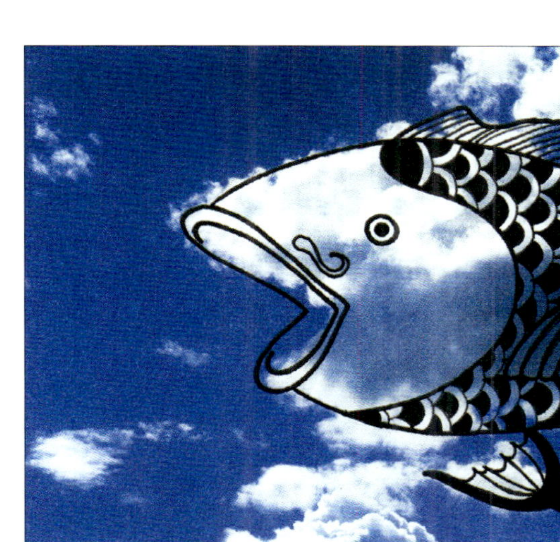

1. *Jumi Yoon*
2. *Myeongjin Shin*
3. *Sungjae Park*
4. *Seolhee Cho*
5. *Daeun Ko*
6. *Myung Song*
7. *Yoojung Kang*

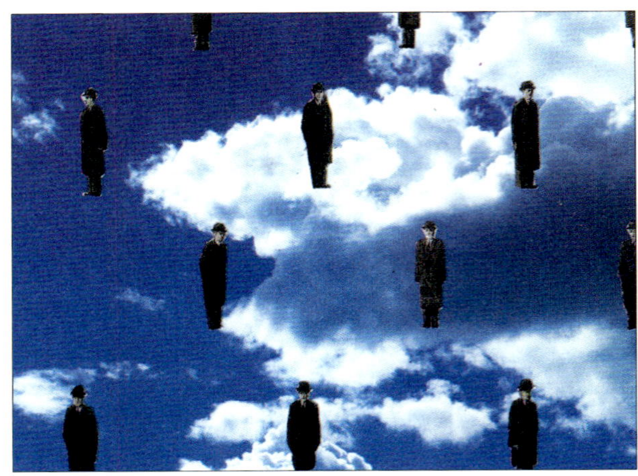

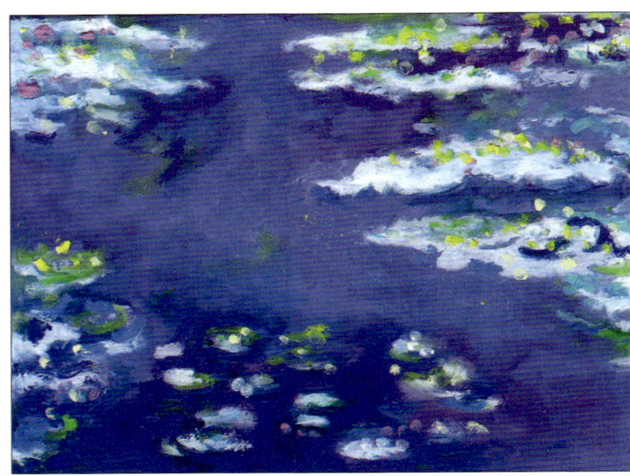

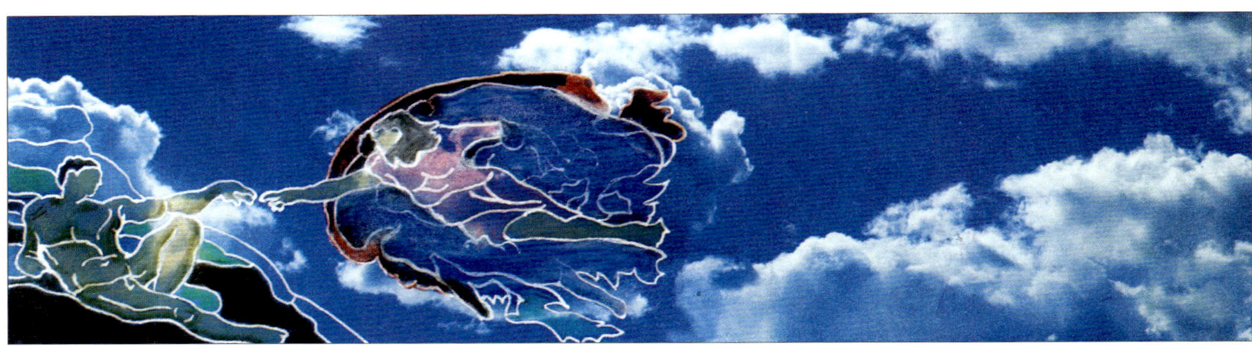

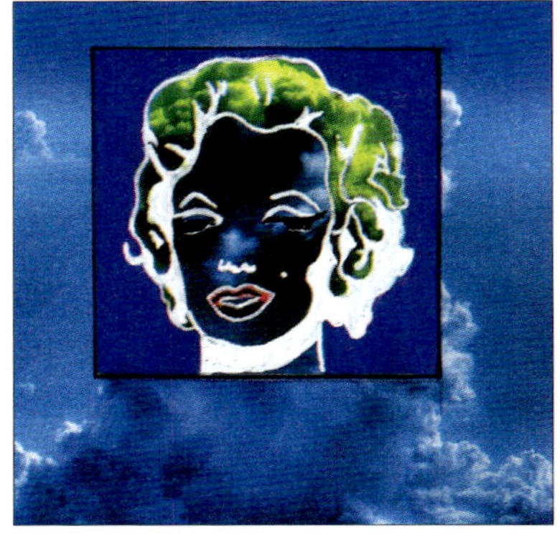

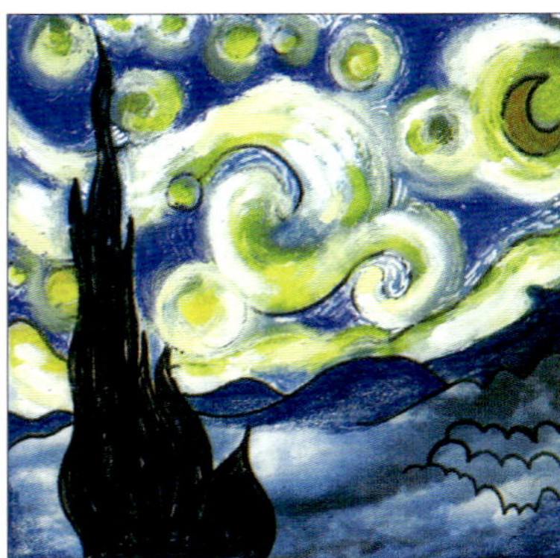

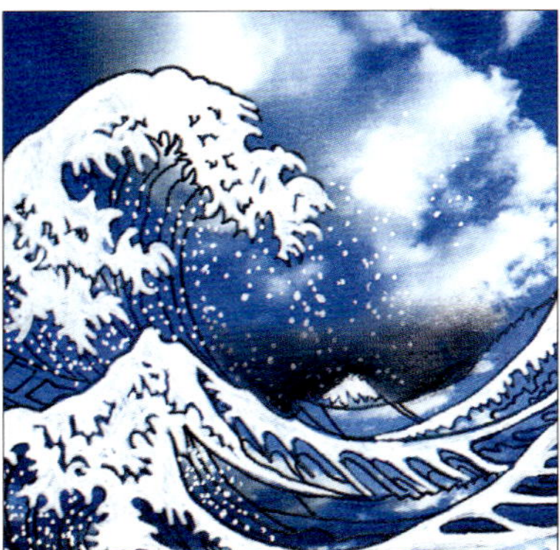

CLOUD SOLUTIONS:

Figure 1 represents one student's interpretation of this project in its entirety, which is a deviation from the specifications of the given assignment.

The student depicted the work of different artists for each cloud, which is a separate challenge to undertake. The artists represented are Magritte, Monet, Michelangelo, Warhol, Van Gogh, and Hokusai.

Figures 2, 5 and 6 are the same cloud formations. Figures 5 and 6 have been rotated 90 degrees to allow further exploration of the imagery.

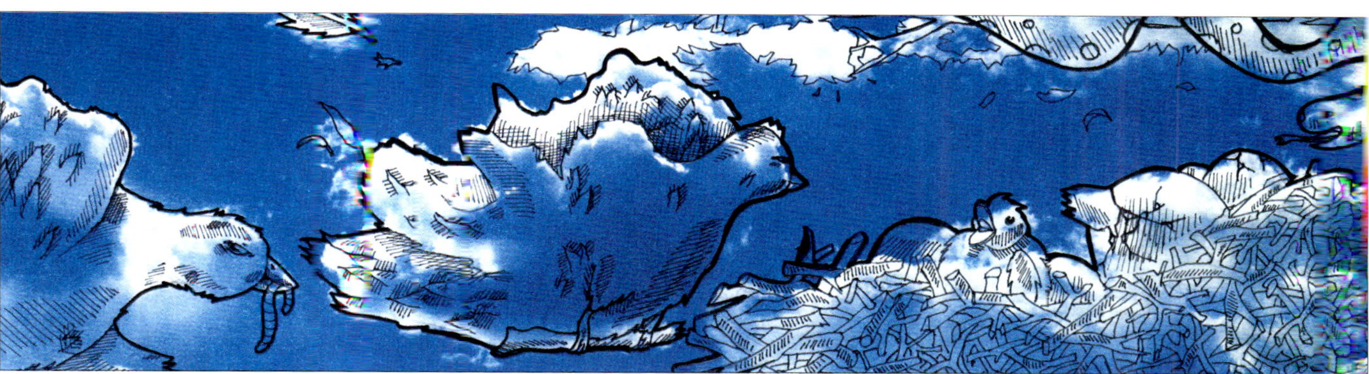

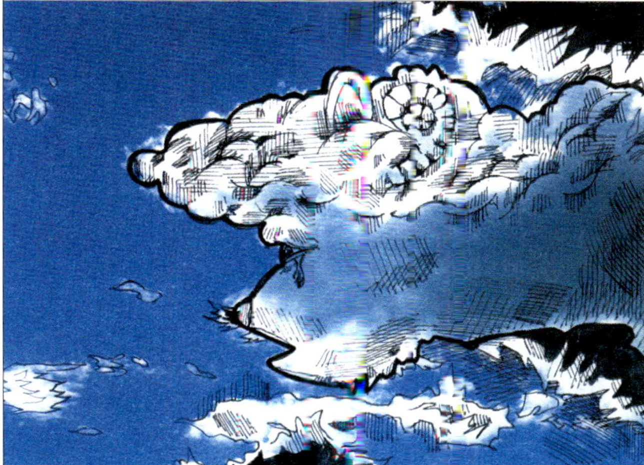

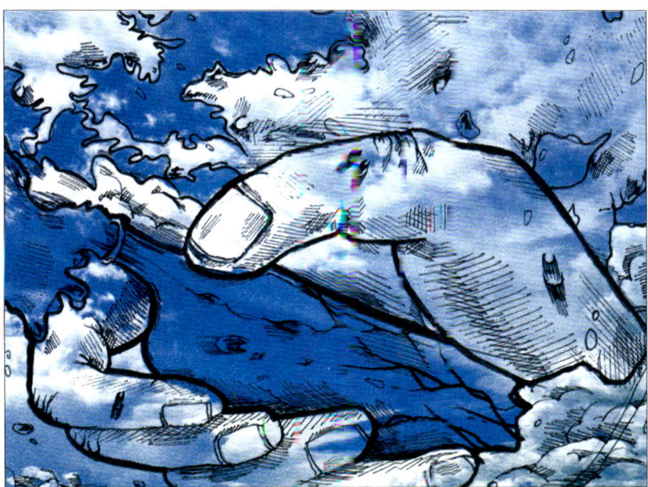

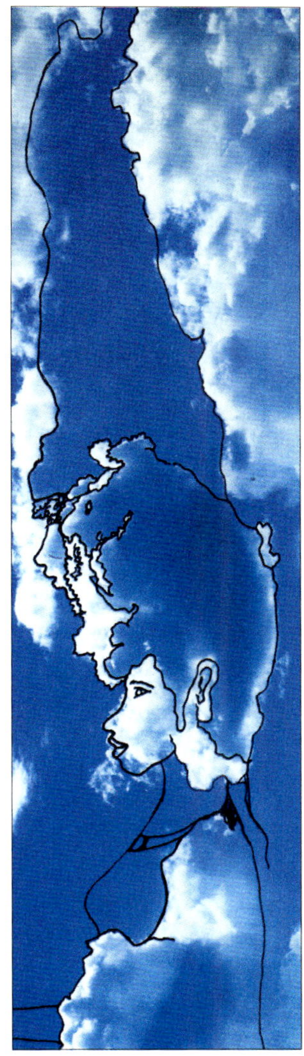

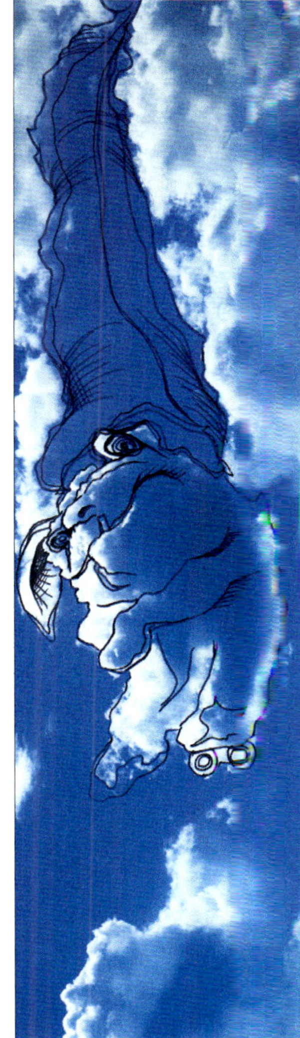

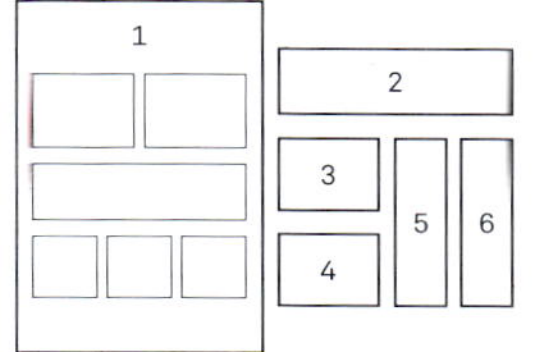

1. *Yoonha Chung*
2–4. *Seolhee Cho*
5. *Saebom Bae*
6. *Ella Kang*

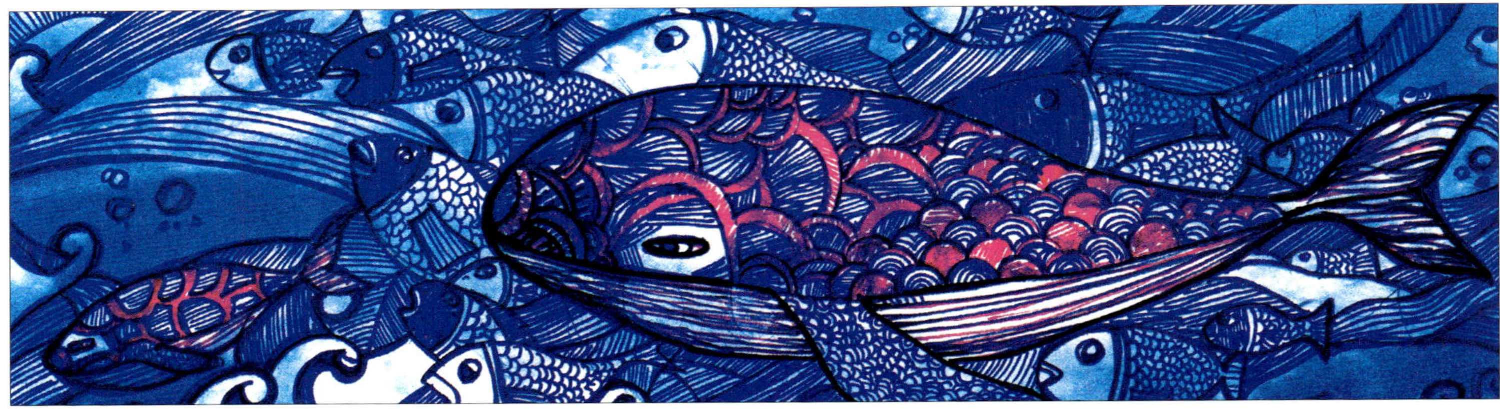

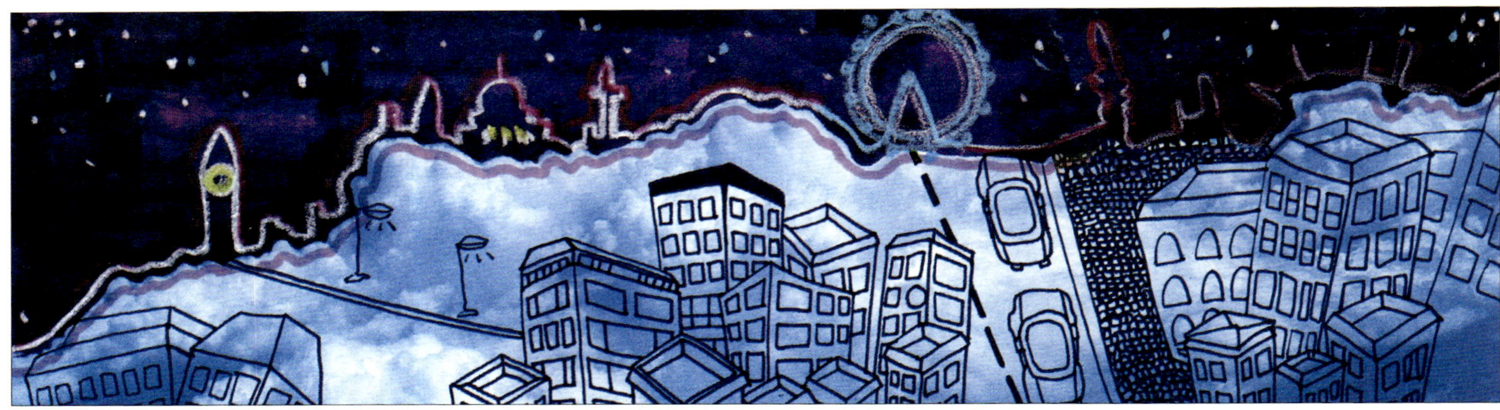

CLOUD SOLUTIONS:

Various themes are expressed within the exaggerated horizontal format, which lends itself to landscape and seascape imaginings.

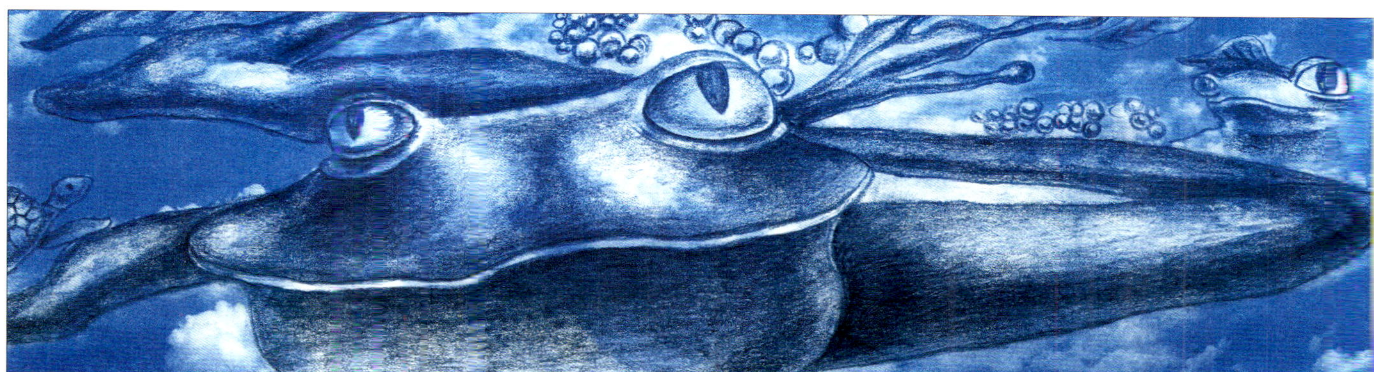

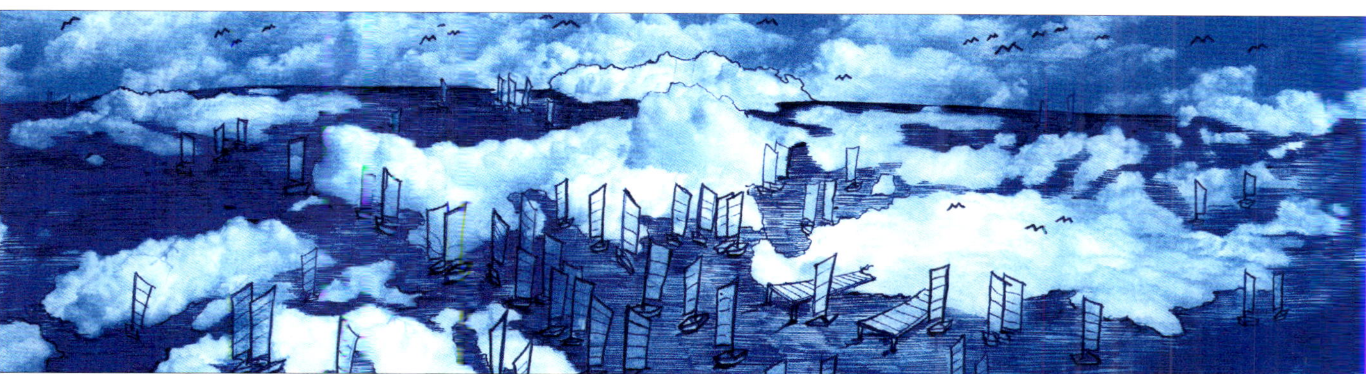

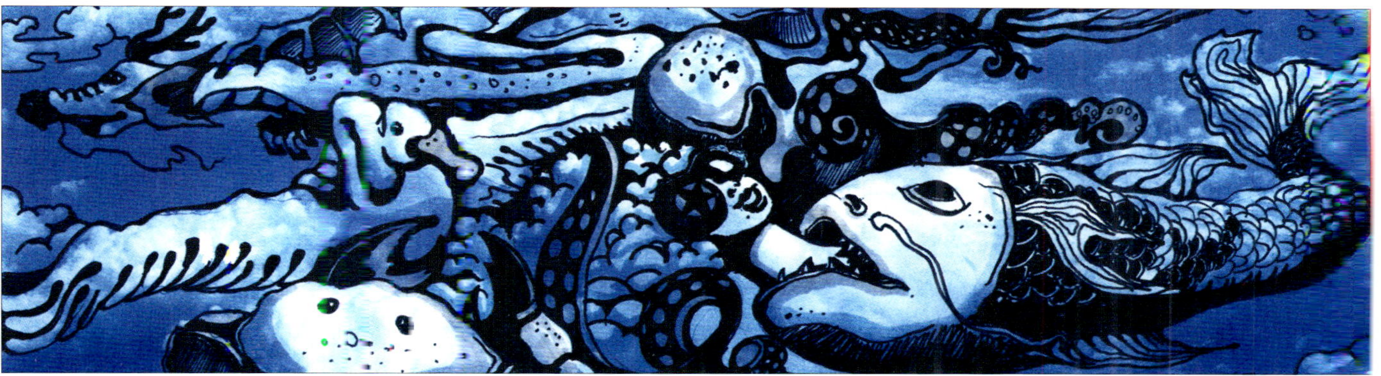

1. Youngwook Choi
2. Jaehyuk Choi
3. Youngjin Lee
4. Yeonwoo Jung
5. Dongyoung Kim

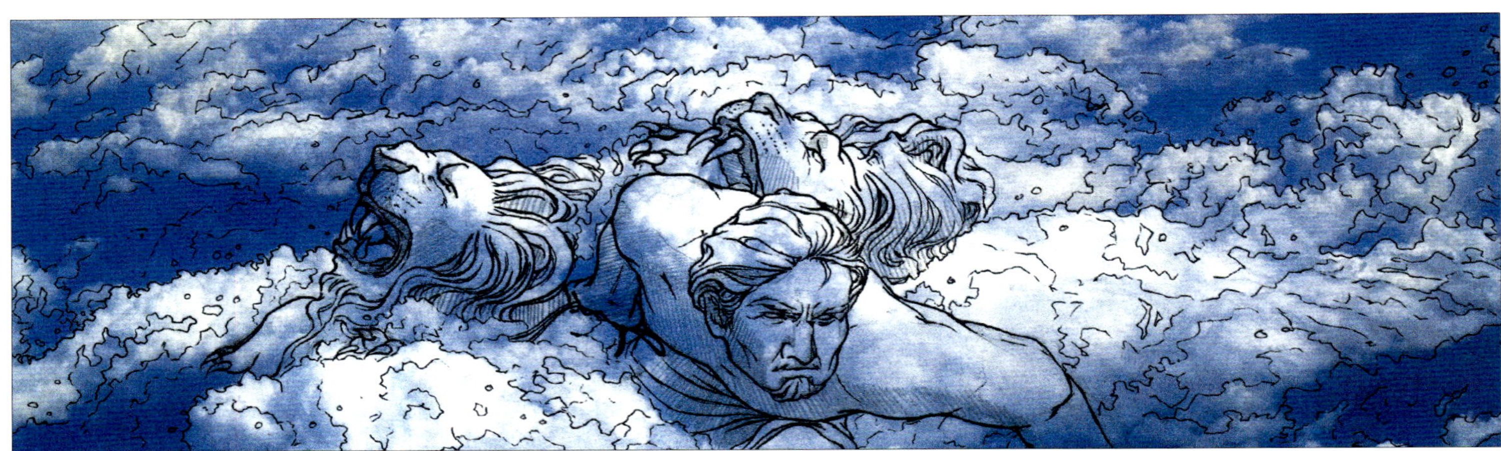

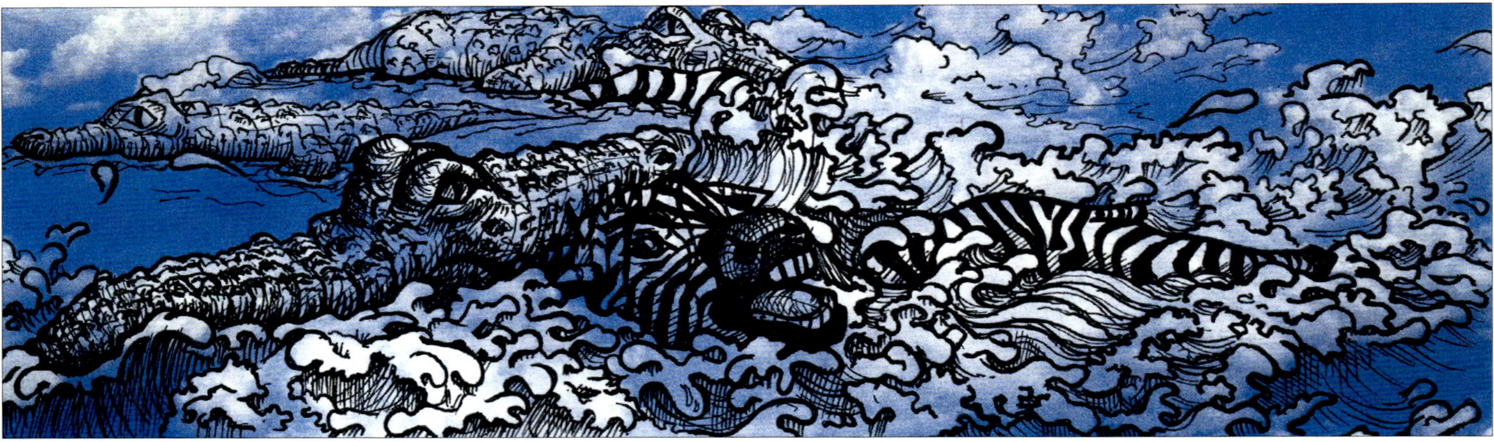

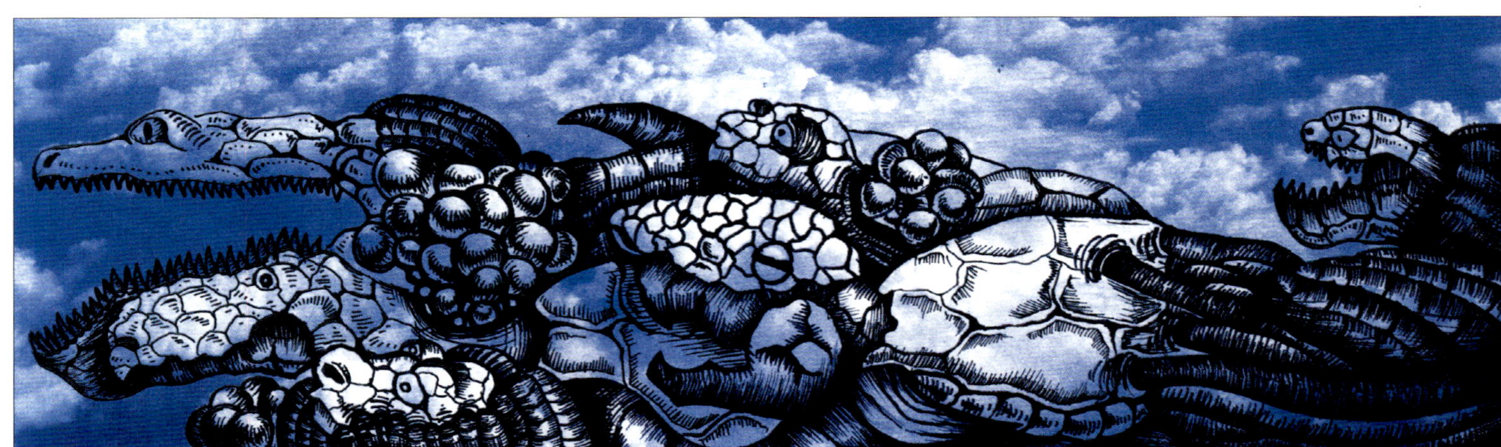

CLOUD SOLUTIONS:

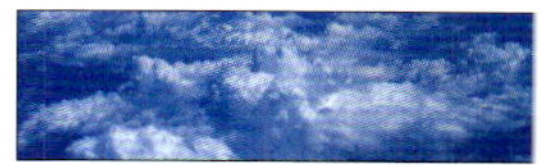

Figure 1 closely adheres to the delineation of the cloud in a heroic comic book-like interpretation.

Figure 2 portrays survival of the fittest, while figure 3 depicts frightening imagery.

Figures 4 through 6 show animals in a changing world, alluding to the melting of the polar ice caps.

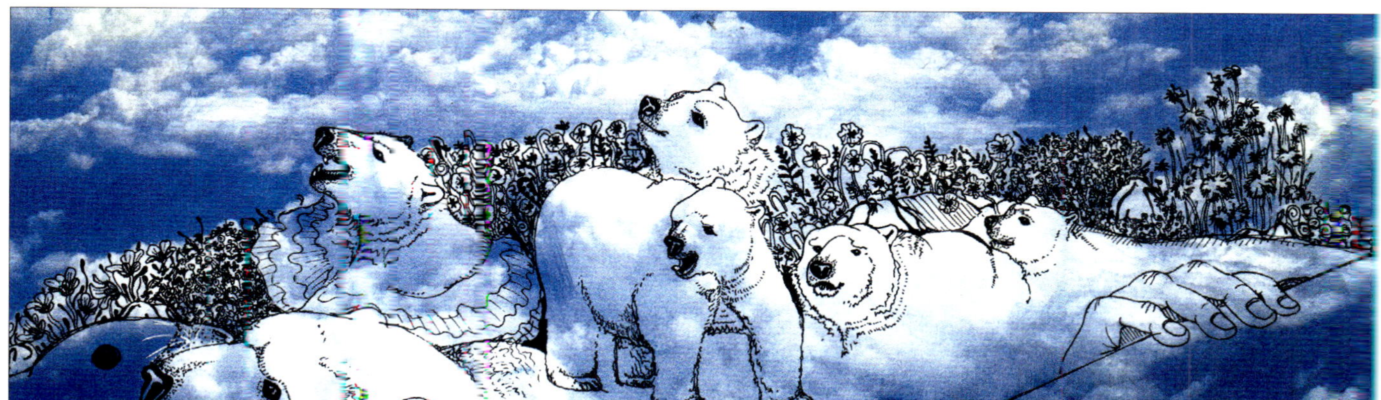

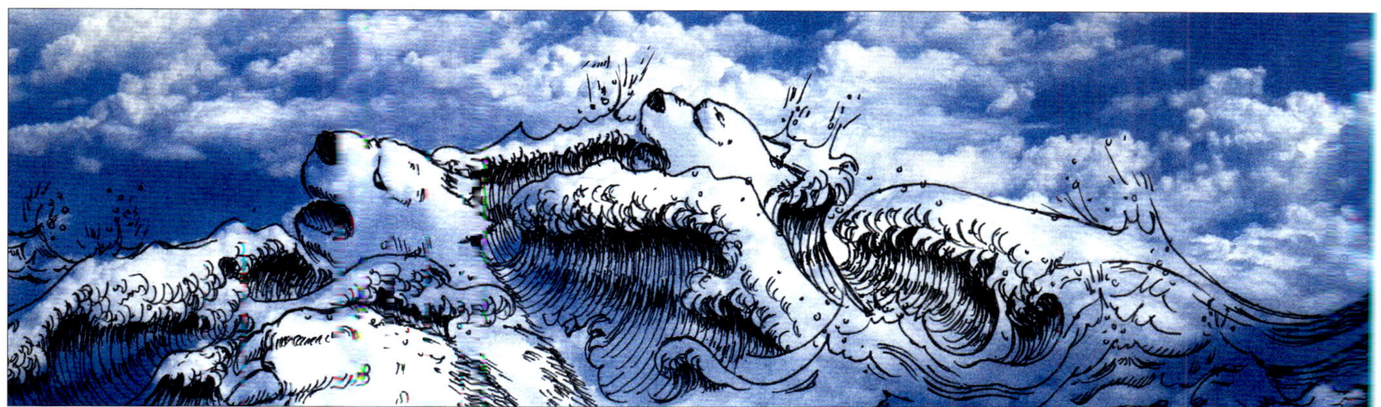

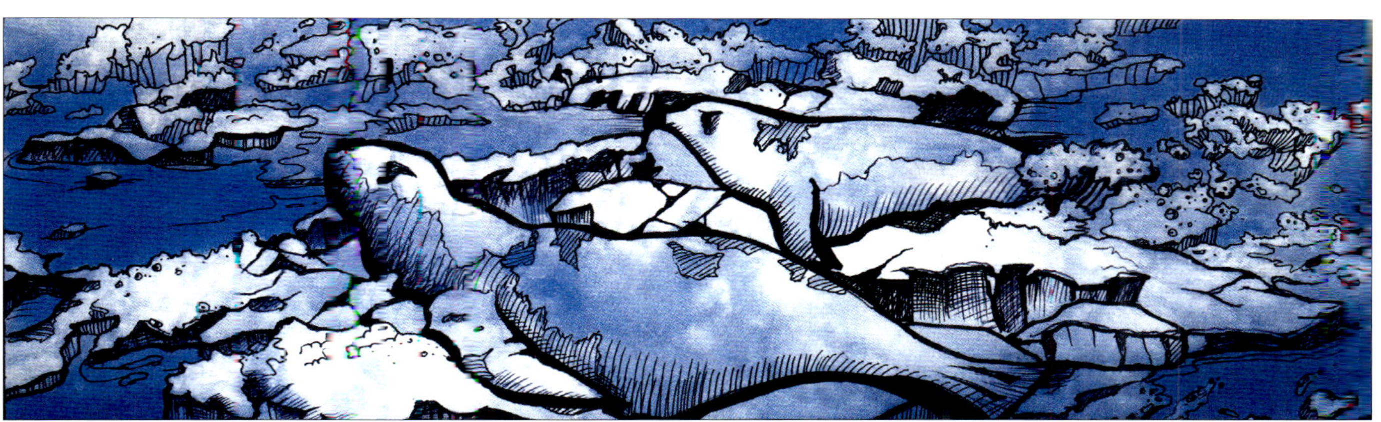

1	4
2	5
3	6

1. *Bomi Kim*
2. *Sungmin Ro*
3. *Hao Yen Chuang*
4. *Dong Shon*
5. *Ji Soo Kim*
6. *Minhwa Kang*

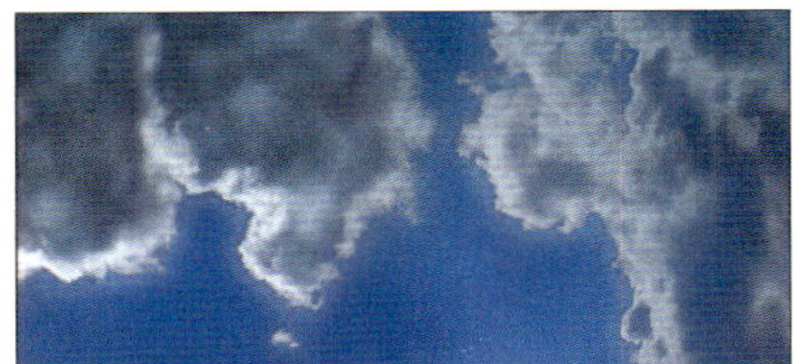

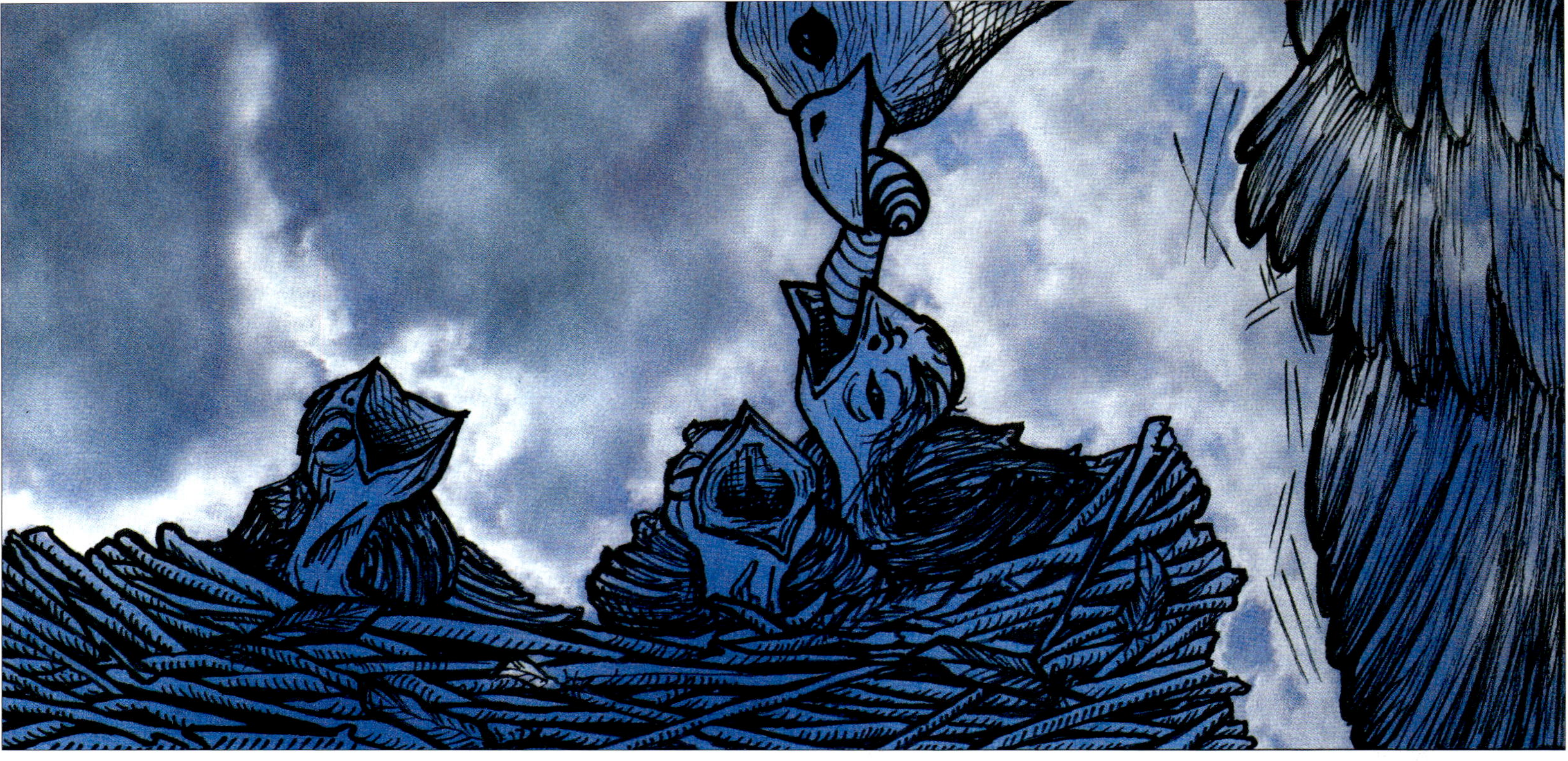

CLOUD SOLUTIONS:

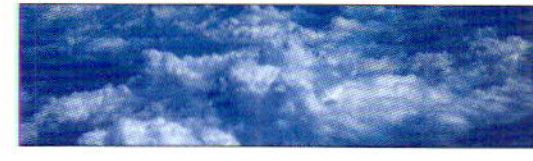

Figure 1 deals with the negative space between the clouds and, in this particular solution, the clouds function as clouds.

Figure 2 deals with an imaginative exploration of creatures that live in an aquatic world, while figures 3 through 5 deal with images that reference storybook-like narratives.

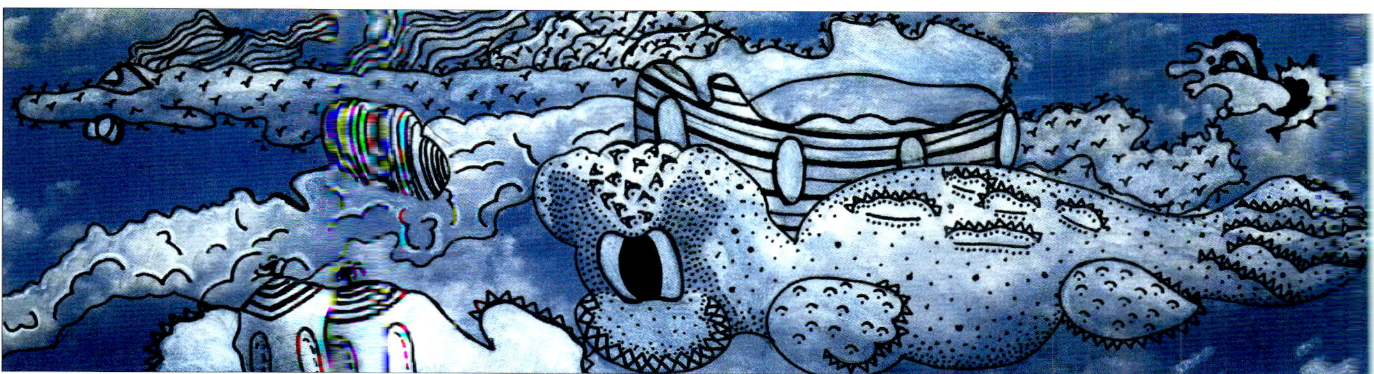

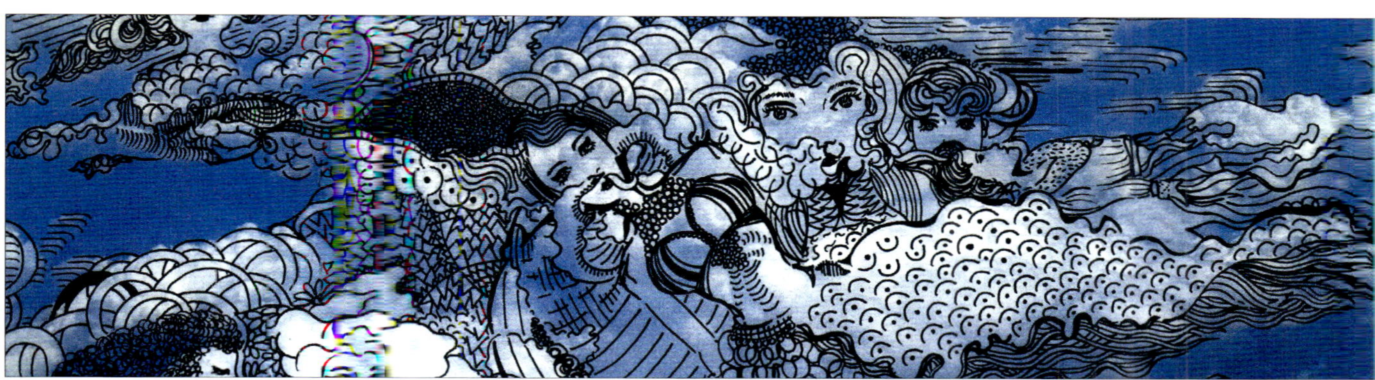

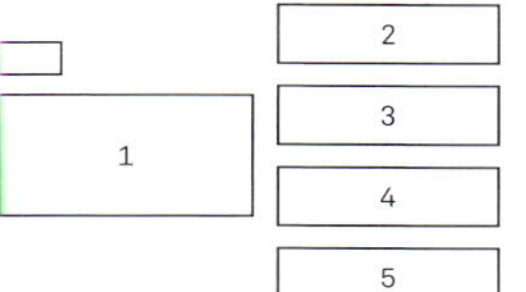

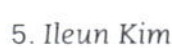

1. *Sungmin Ro*
2. *Maria Alvarez*
3. *Xinyi Lin*
4. *Yoomee Kwak*
5. *Ileun Kim*

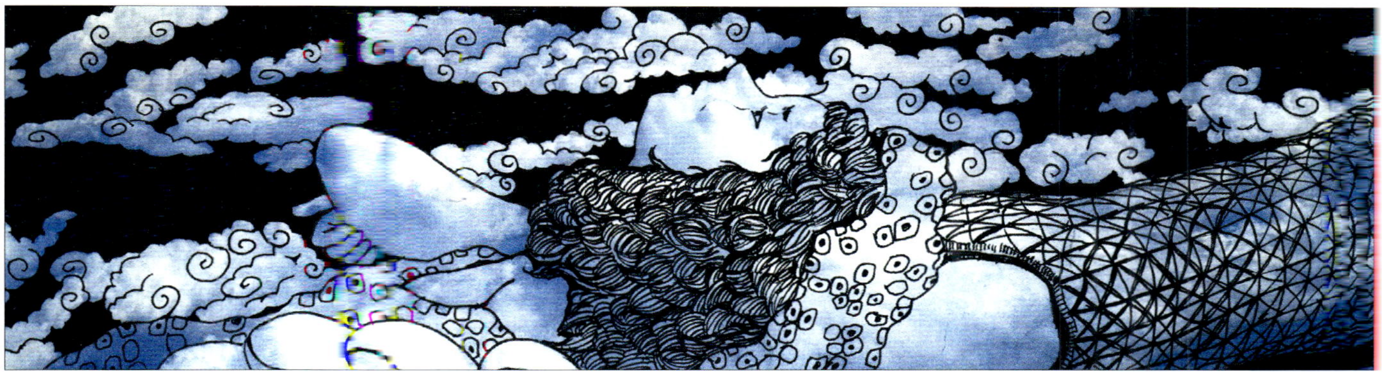

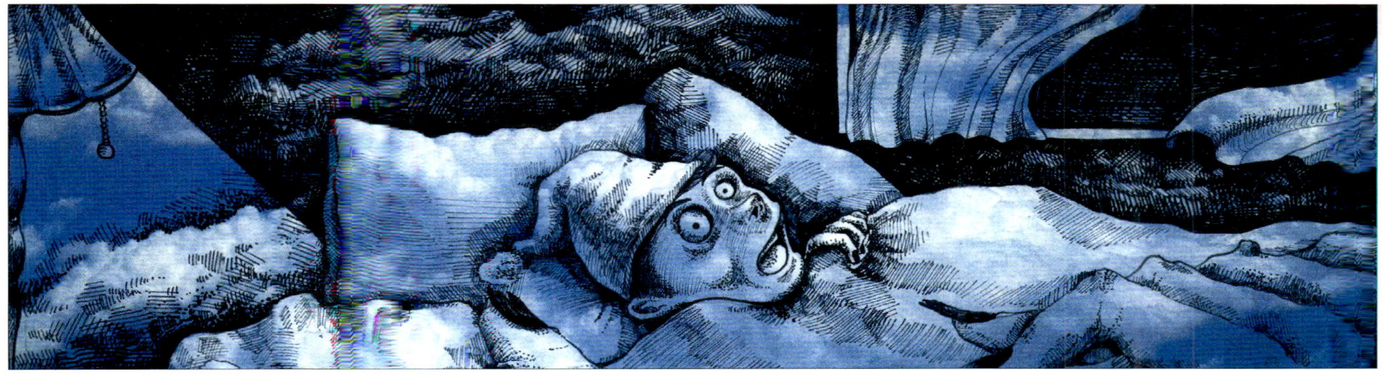

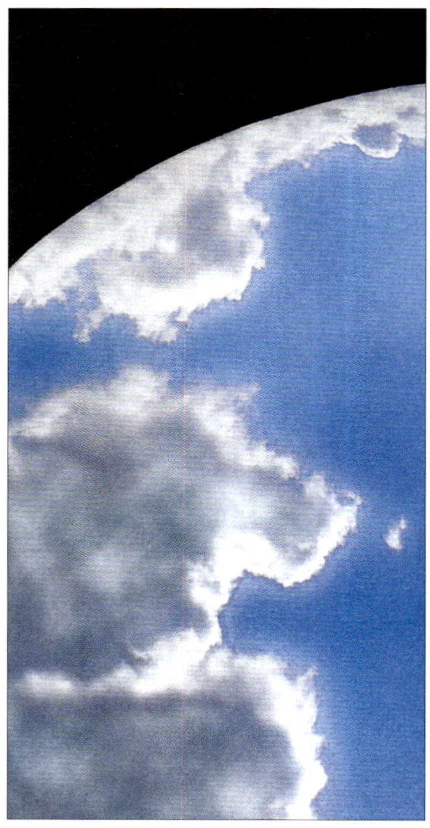

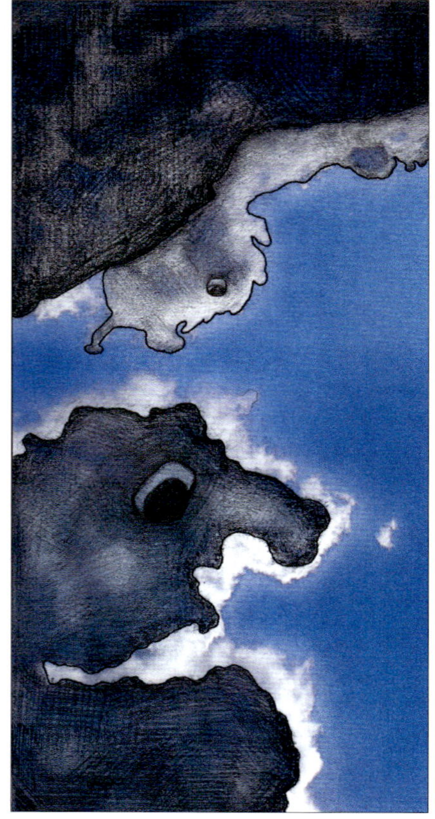

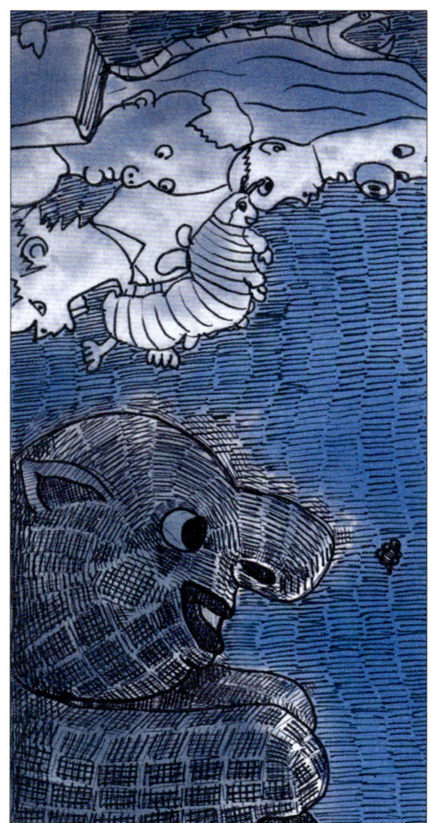

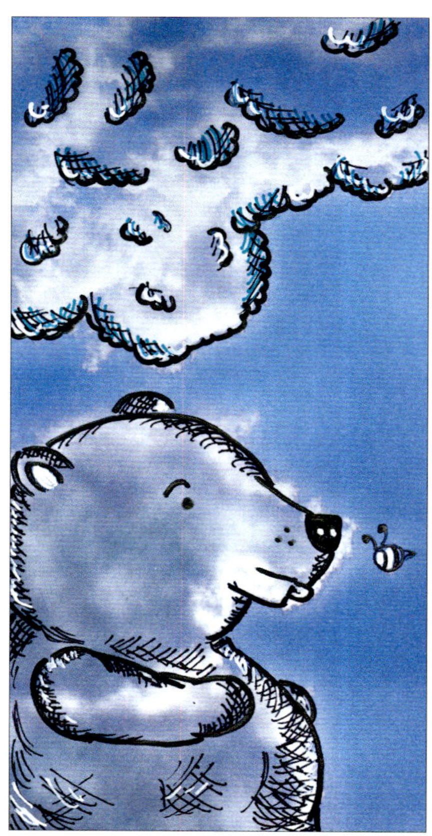

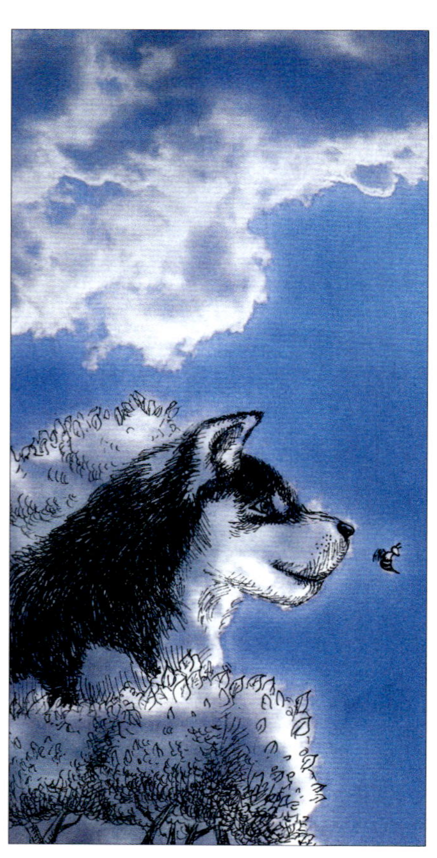

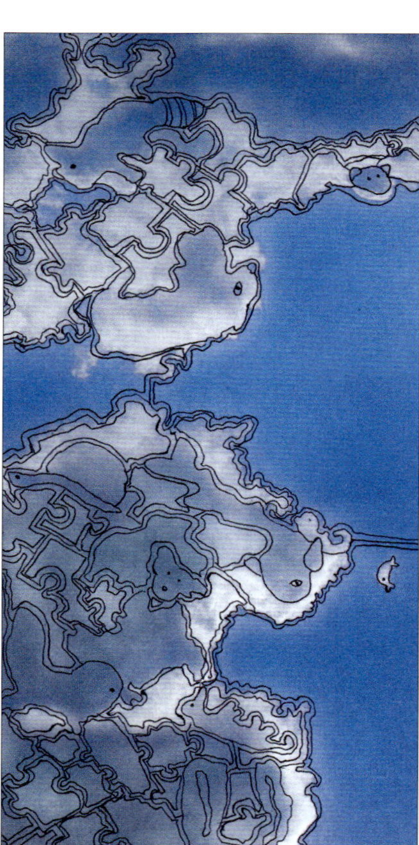

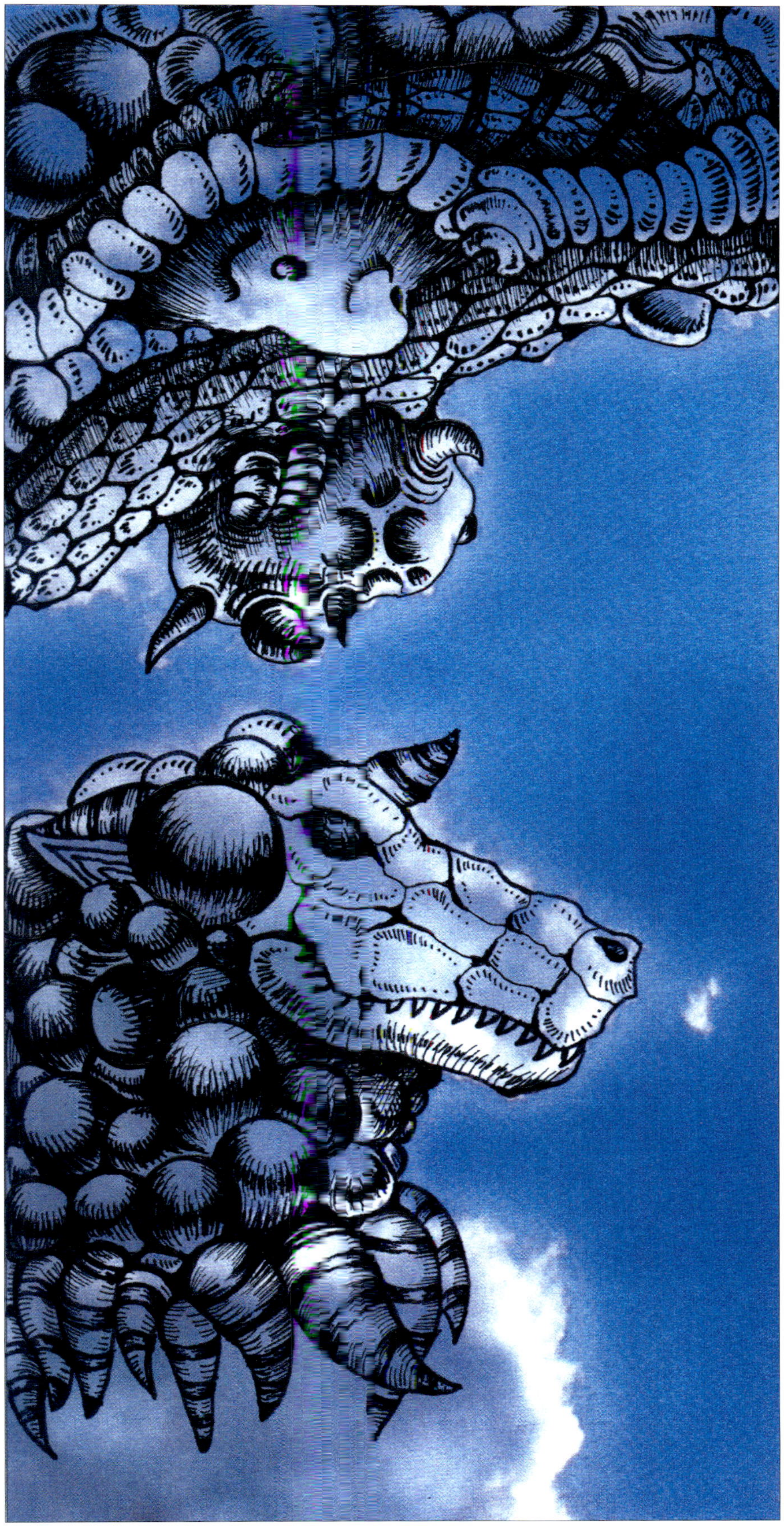

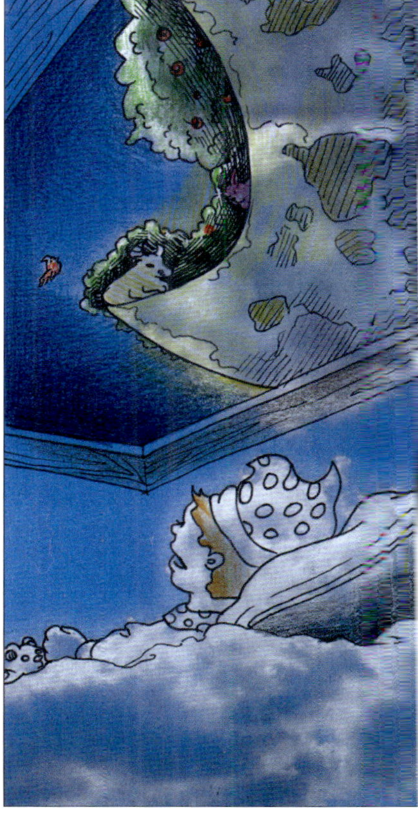

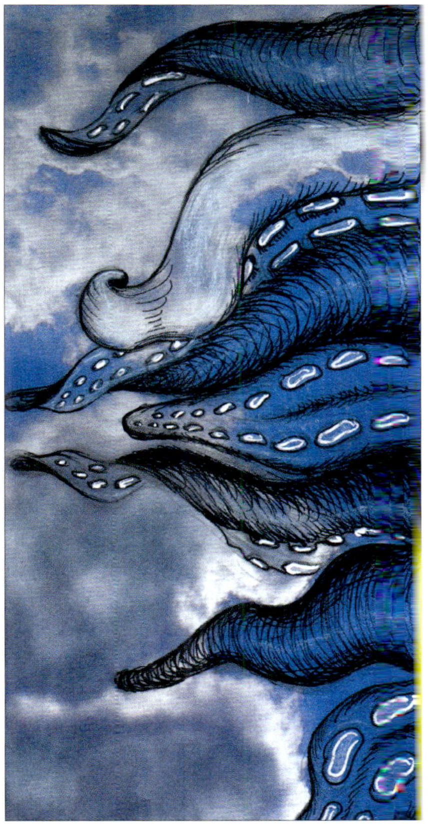

CLOUD SOLUTIONS:

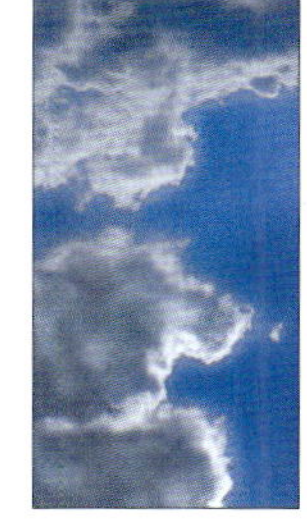

Figure 1 is a minimalistic approach that adds one shape to create a view of the planet earth where the clouds and sky become land masses and oceans.

Figures 2 and 3 portray an array of humorous characters.

In figures 4 and 5 a small insect engages the characters depicted.

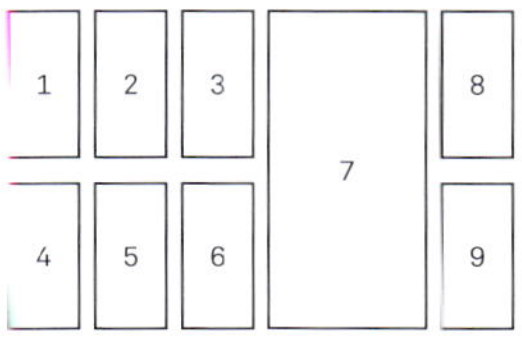

1. *Yijun Zhu*
2. *Injoon Jung*
3. *Joohyun Park*
4. *Josephine Tan*
5. *Swan Lee*
6. *Yurn Kim*
7. *Hao Yen Chuang*
8. *Jisoo Lee*
9. *Masha Vainblat*

Figure 6 is an aerial view of a map, but upon closer inspection, ten animals appear.

In figure 7, through the exploration of patterning, various images emerge.

In figure 8 the cloud has been rotated 180 degrees for a clearer representation of a sleeping child's dream.

Figure 9 deals primarily with the negative space, in the depiction of the tentacles of an octopus.

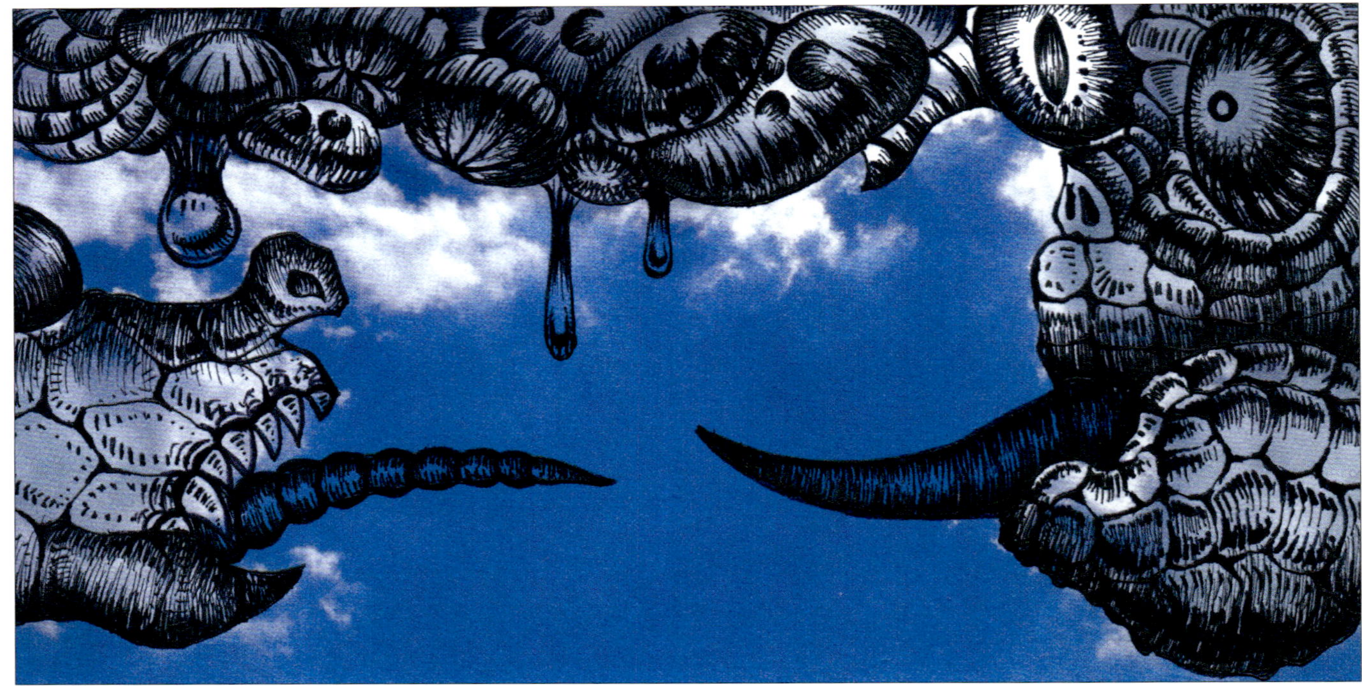

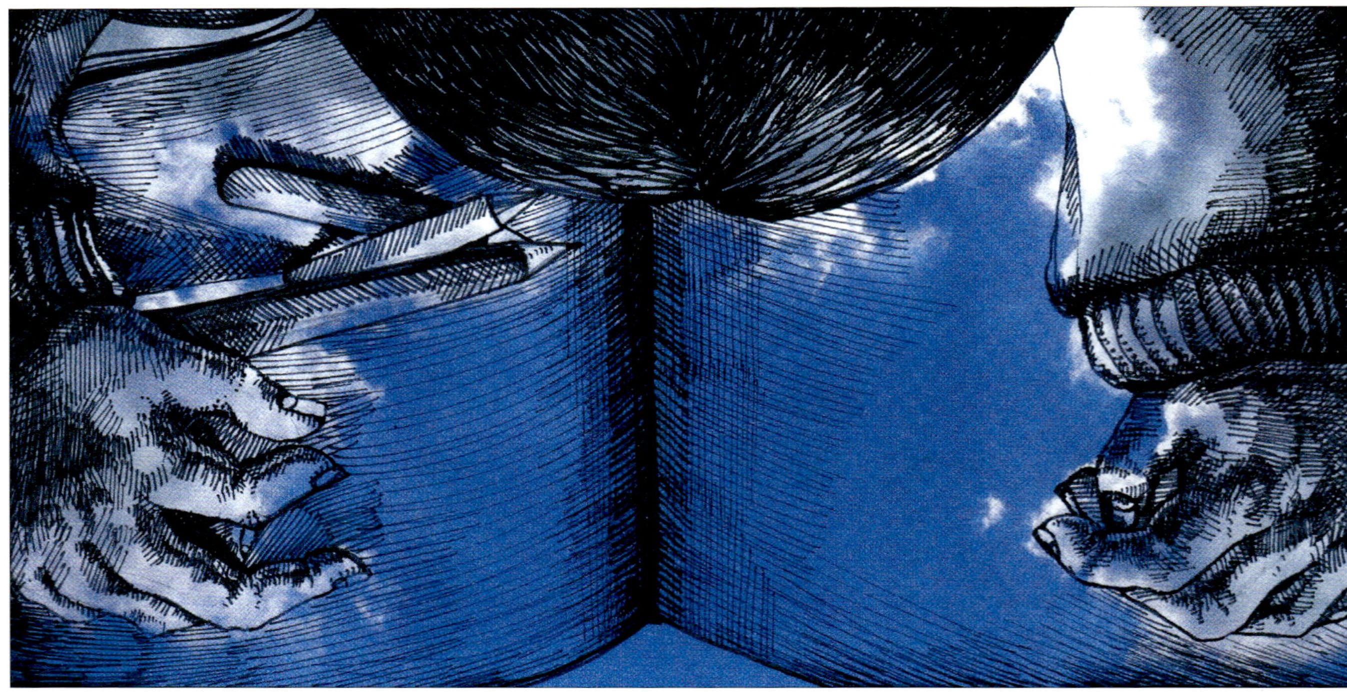

CLOUD SOLUTIONS:

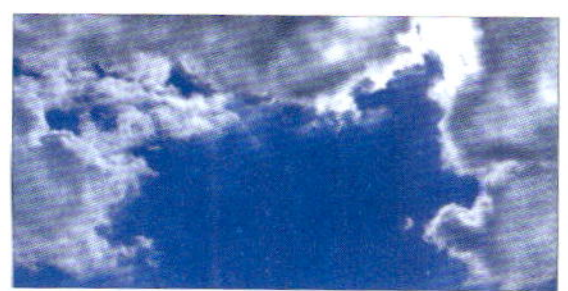

Figure 1 shows two monsters glaring at each other.

Figures 2 through 6 take liberties in developing imagery in the negative space of the sky.

Figure 4 interprets the cloud as hair, while adding facial features in the negative space to further enhance the image.

In figure 5 several animals are depicted in a circus ring by using both the clouds and the negative space between them.

1. *Hao Yen Chuang*
2. *Ileun Kim*
3. *Youngjin Lee*
4. *Angela Song*
5. *Carlos Cisterna*
6. *Sunho Lee*
7. *Michael Sierra*

An aerial view is the focal point in figure 6, where a cat is looking up from the bottom of a hole, while figure 7 portrays a crab.

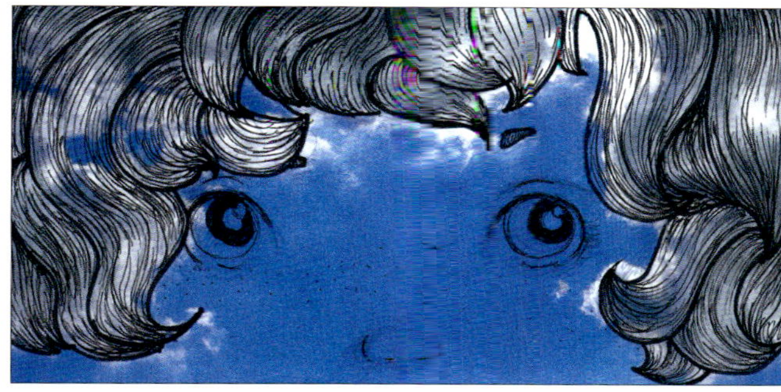

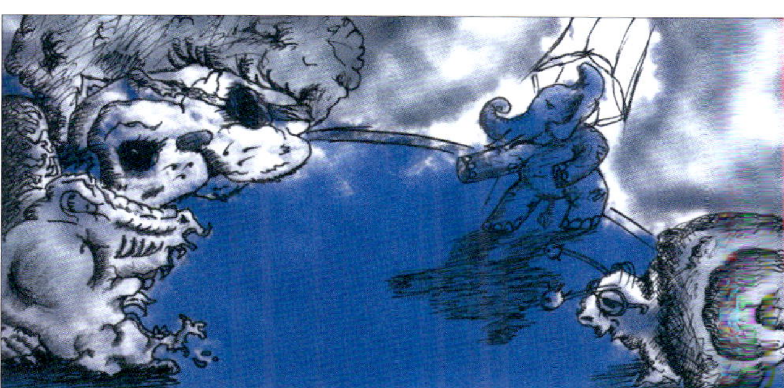

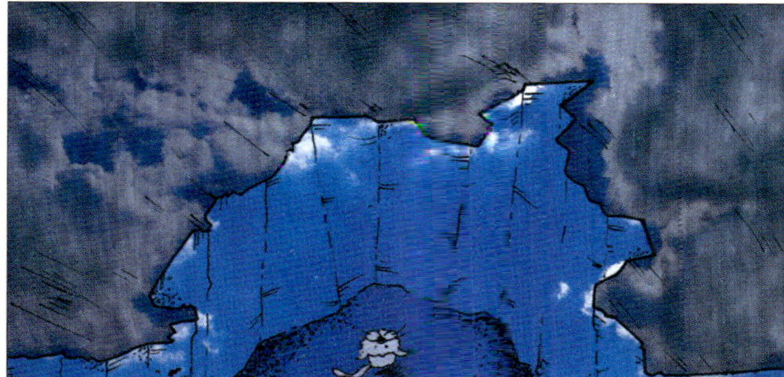

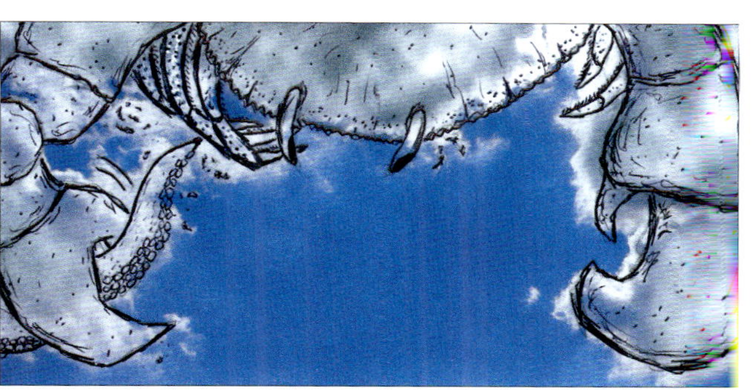

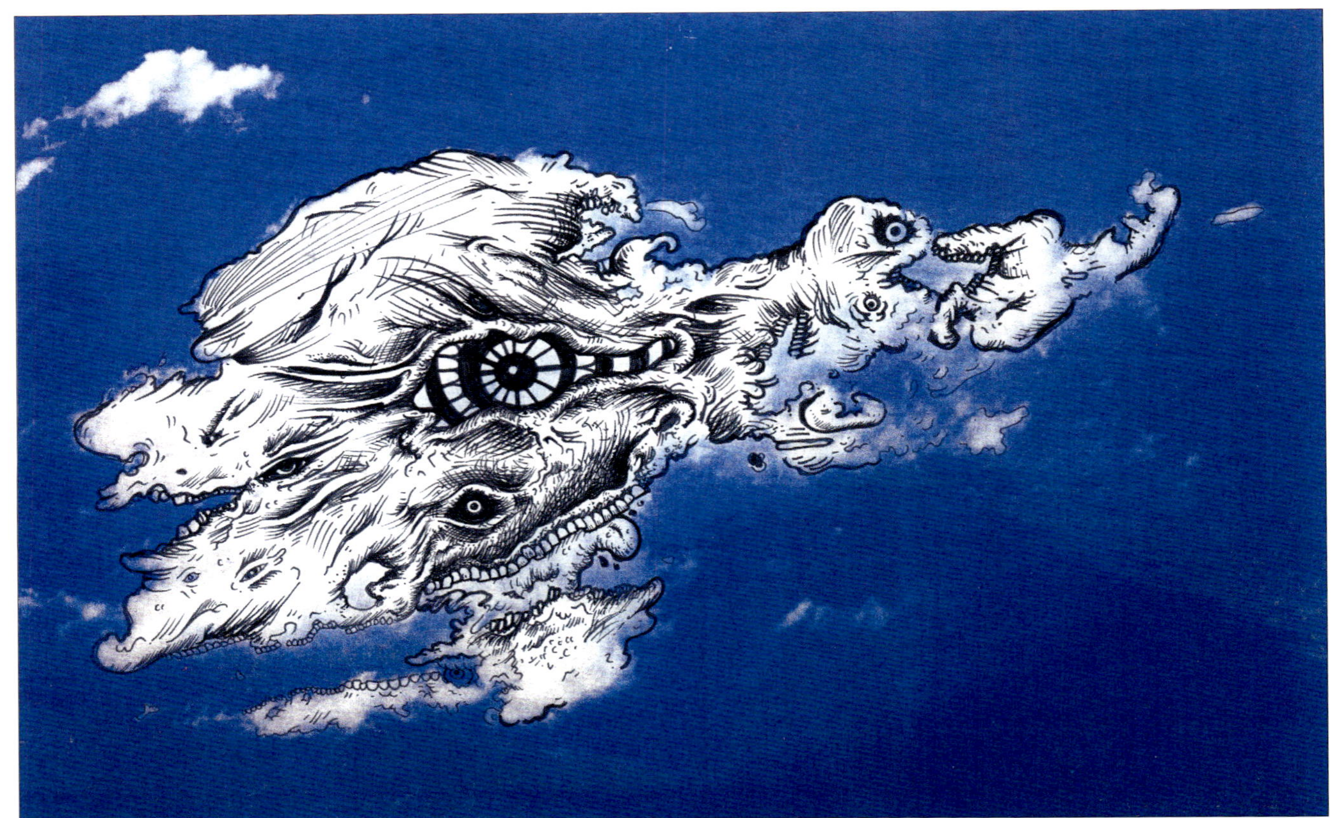

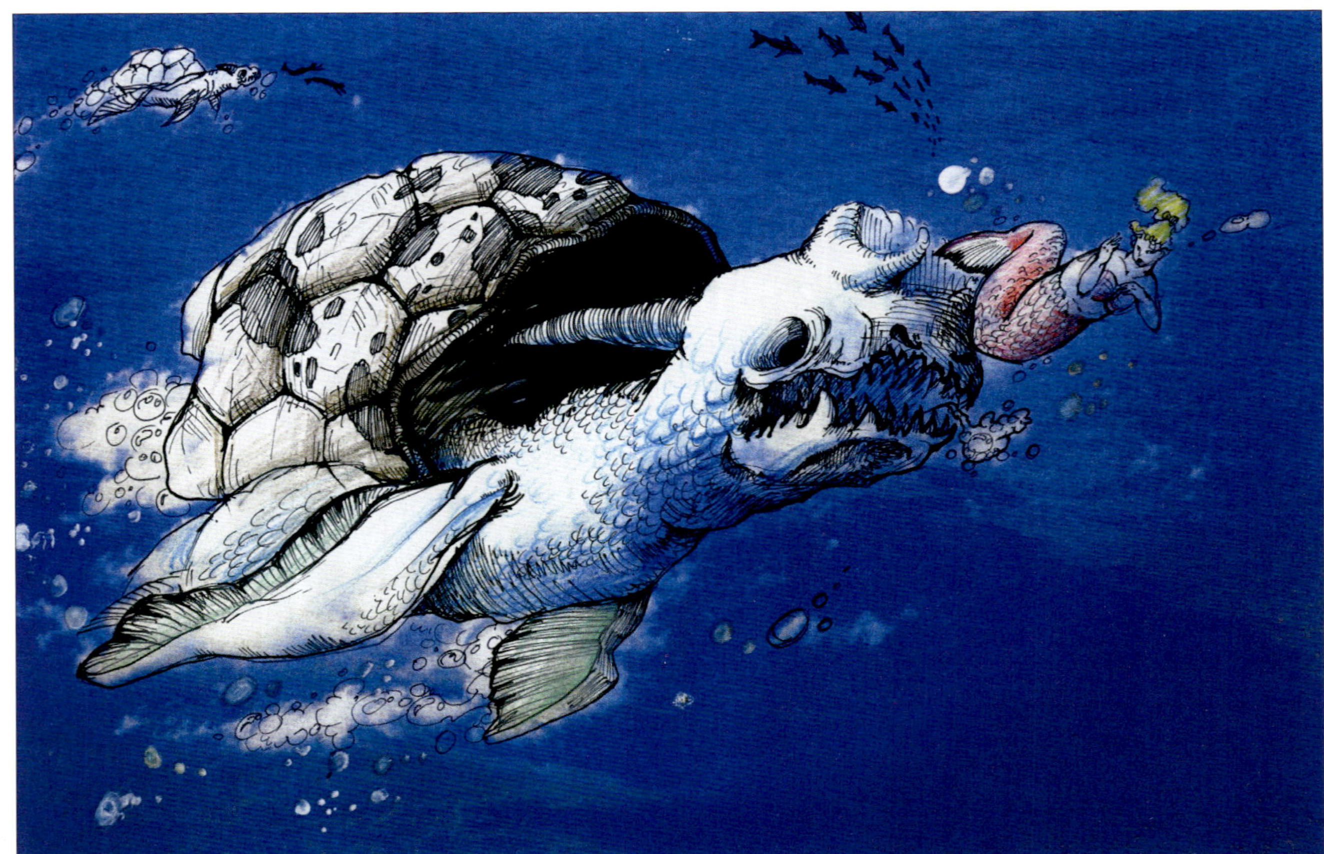

CLOUD SOLUTIONS:

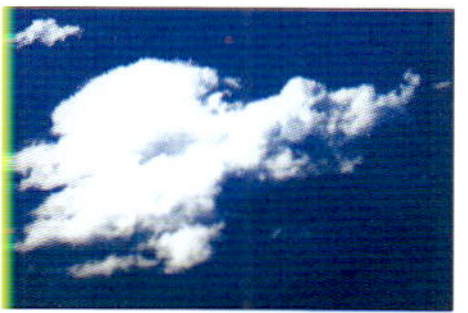

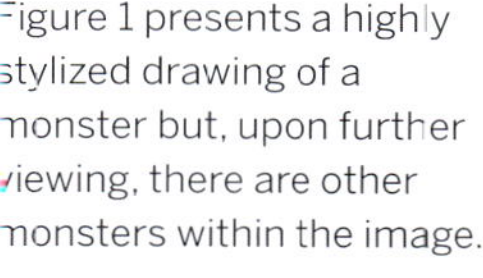

Figure 1 presents a highly stylized drawing of a monster but, upon further viewing, there are other monsters within the image.

Figure 2 maintains the cloud's integrity while using every aspect of it to develop a clear narrative of an imaginary sea-turtle monster chasing a mermaid.

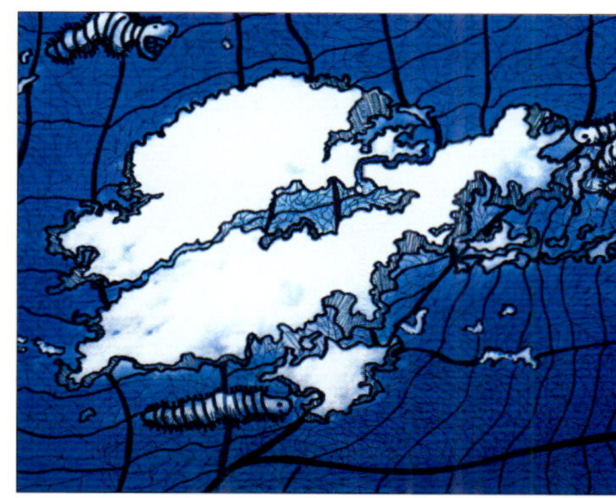

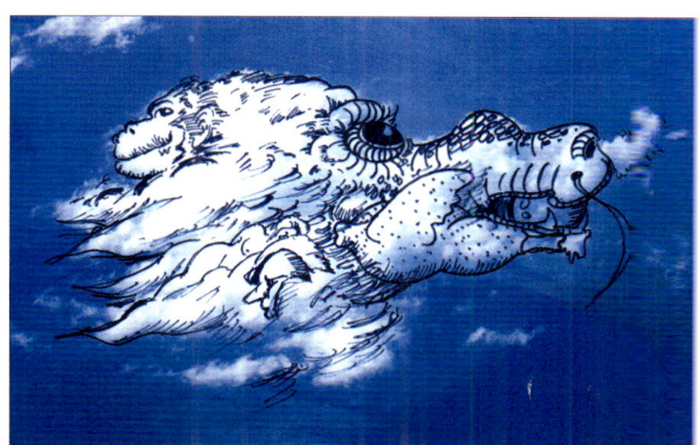

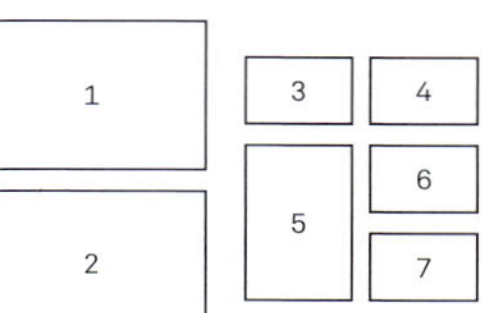

1. *Sam Ba*
2. *Heejung Kim*
3. *C. Malherios*
4. *Cheng Wen Fung*
5. *Minju Kang*
6. *Manho Park*
7. *Yasmin Malki*

Figure 3 offers a personal interpretation of the images, which at times did not follow the dictates of the cloud formation, while figure 4 depicts caterpillars devouring a leaf. The white areas of the cloud now represent the areas that have been eaten.

Figure 5 is the same cloud formation rotated 90 degrees clockwise to create a goat.

Figure 6 composes a dragon from various recognizable forms, while figure 7 depicts the cloud as cotton candy.

THOUGHTS ON THE CREATIVE PROCESS 9

Wonder is a higher state of consciousness that leads to questioning. The state of questioning is the definitive tool for being creative. Creativity is ultimately about the art of questioning.

NOTEBOOK PROBLEM:

THE STANDARD PAGE IN A NOTEBOOK IS A SHEET OF WHITE PAPER, PRINTED WITH HORIZONTAL BLUE LINES AND A VERTICAL RED DOUBLE LINED MARGIN (SEE SAMPLE). UTILIZING THE BASIC ELEMENTS OF THE NOTEBOOK PAGE, CREATE A PERSONALITY FOR 20 DIFFERENT CHILDREN IN A GRADE-SCHOOL CLASS. EACH PERSONALITY THAT YOU CREATE SHOULD REFLECT EMOTIONAL, PSYCHOLOGICAL, PHYSICAL CHARACTERISTICS AND DEVELOPMENTAL TRAITS. IN REDESIGNING THE NOTEBOOK PAGE, YOU CAN ALTER THE SPACE BETWEEN THE LINES, INCREASE OR DECREASE THE THICKNESS OF THE LINES OR CHANGE THE DIRECTION OF THE LINES. THE ONLY LIMITATION IS THAT YOU MAINTAIN THE INTEGRITY OF THE NOTEBOOK PAGE. EXECUTE YOUR SOLUTIONS IN THE TWENTY RECTANGLES BELOW. USING THE LARGE RECTANGLE AT THE TOP OF THE ASSIGNMENT SHEET, CREATE A PERSONALITY FOR THE TEACHER OF THE CLASS.

Sample

PROBLEMS : SOLUTIONS SERIES

CREATED BY RICHARD WILDE / JUDITH WILDE, PRODUCED BY VISUAL ARTS PRESS, LTD. ART DIRECTORS: RICHARD WILDE / JUDITH WILDE

NOTEBOOK PROBLEM:

A standard notebook page has rows of horizontal blue lines, and two vertical red lines on the left-hand side indicating the margin. Use these linear elements to depict the emotional or physical characteristics of pupils in a grade-school classroom, as well as the personality of the teacher, in the given areas on the assignment sheet. Note that the assignment sheet stands for a classroom, with the larger rectangle positioned at the top to represent the teacher.

AIM:
The intent of this project is to move away from literal image-making and stretch one's creative endurance through the use of a limited palette, while maintaining the integrity of the notebook page to infer one's intended message. Successful solutions bypass representational drawing skills and rely on a purely graphic idiom. These seemingly abstract solutions demand the participation of the viewer to complete the message.

SUGGESTIONS:
To best express your subjects deconstruct the notebook page by: altering the spaces between the lines; changing the width of the lines; reconfiguring the direction of the lines; or overlapping the lines. The only limitation is that one must to some degree maintain the integrity of the notebook page. The problem concerns itself with finding new ways of interpreting various subjects, therefore it is most helpful to begin by writing a list of at least thirty possible characteristics and edit accordingly.

SPECIFICATIONS:
The use of red and blue ink lines on a white ground is suggested, however, other colors may be added if your concept dictates. Titles should appear beneath each solution.

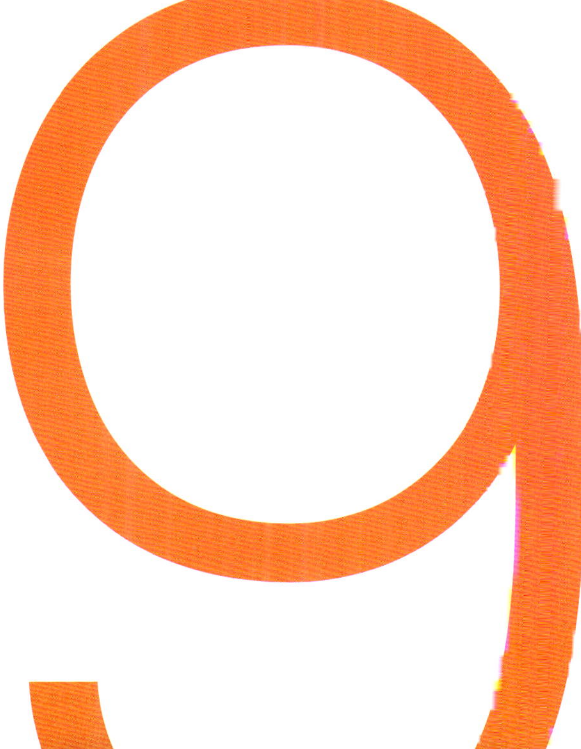

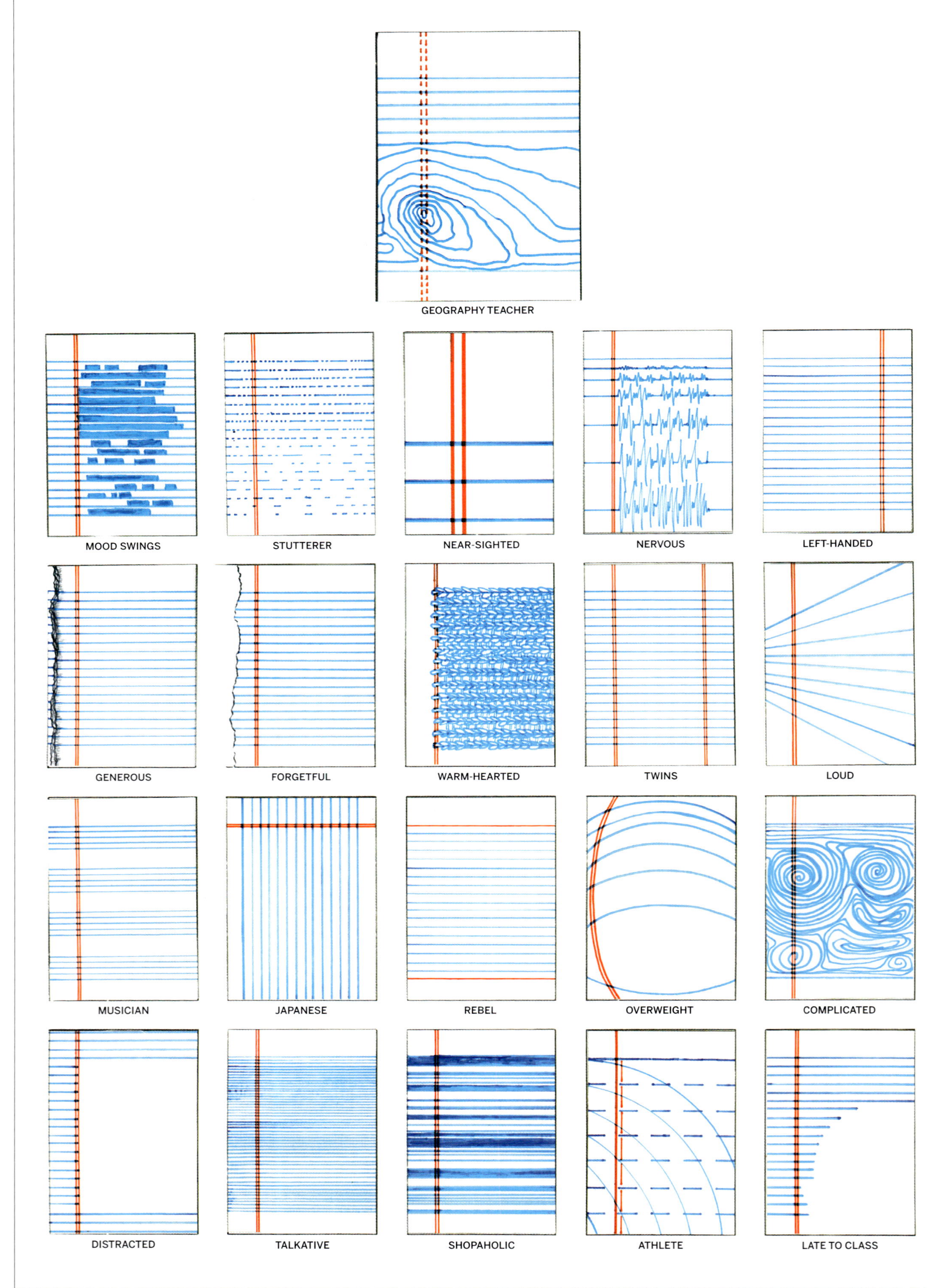
GEOGRAPHY TEACHER
MOOD SWINGS
STUTTERER
NEAR-SIGHTED
NERVOUS
LEFT-HANDED
GENEROUS
FORGETFUL
WARM-HEARTED
TWINS
LOUD
MUSICIAN
JAPANESE
REBEL
OVERWEIGHT
COMPLICATED
DISTRACTED
TALKATIVE
SHOPAHOLIC
ATHLETE
LATE TO CLASS

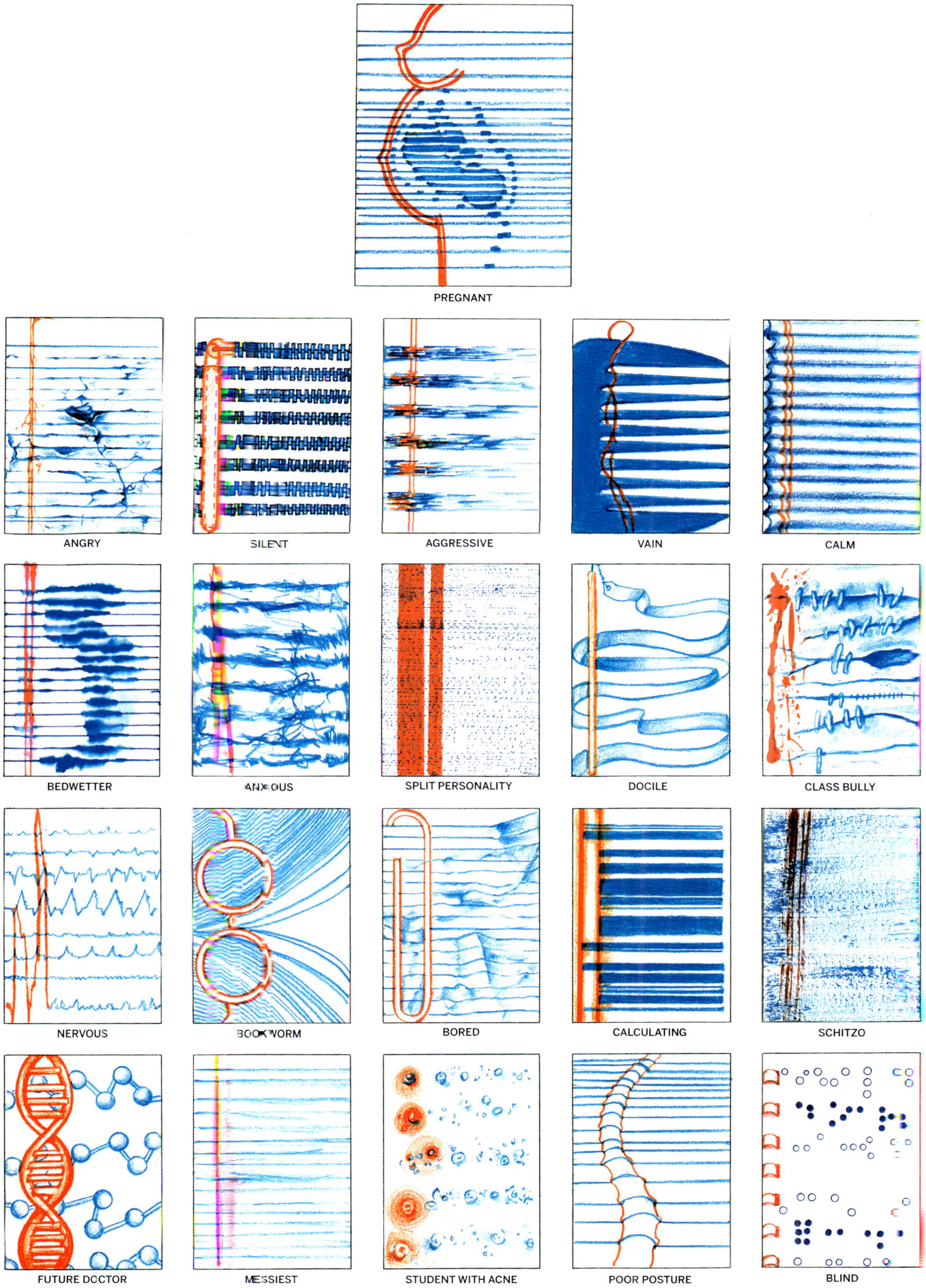

PREGNANT

ANGRY | SILENT | AGGRESSIVE | VAIN | CALM

BEDWETTER | ANXIOUS | SPLIT PERSONALITY | DOCILE | CLASS BULLY

NERVOUS | BOOKWORM | BORED | CALCULATING | SCHITZO

FUTURE DOCTOR | MESSIEST | STUDENT WITH ACNE | POOR POSTURE | BLIND

NOTEBOOK SOLUTIONS:

Figure 1 represents an entire project, where the dictates of the assignment were carefully followed.

Figure 2 uses narrative as well as inferred imagery to execute the project.

Although figure 2 has merit, it is figure 1 that adhered more closely to the given parameters.

Most solutions in this chapter fall somewhere between these two approaches.

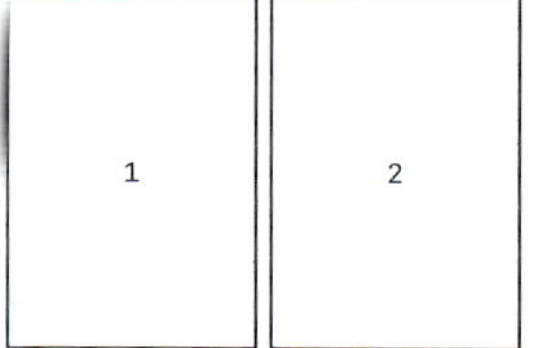

1. *Yoojin Young*
2. *Nami Mo*

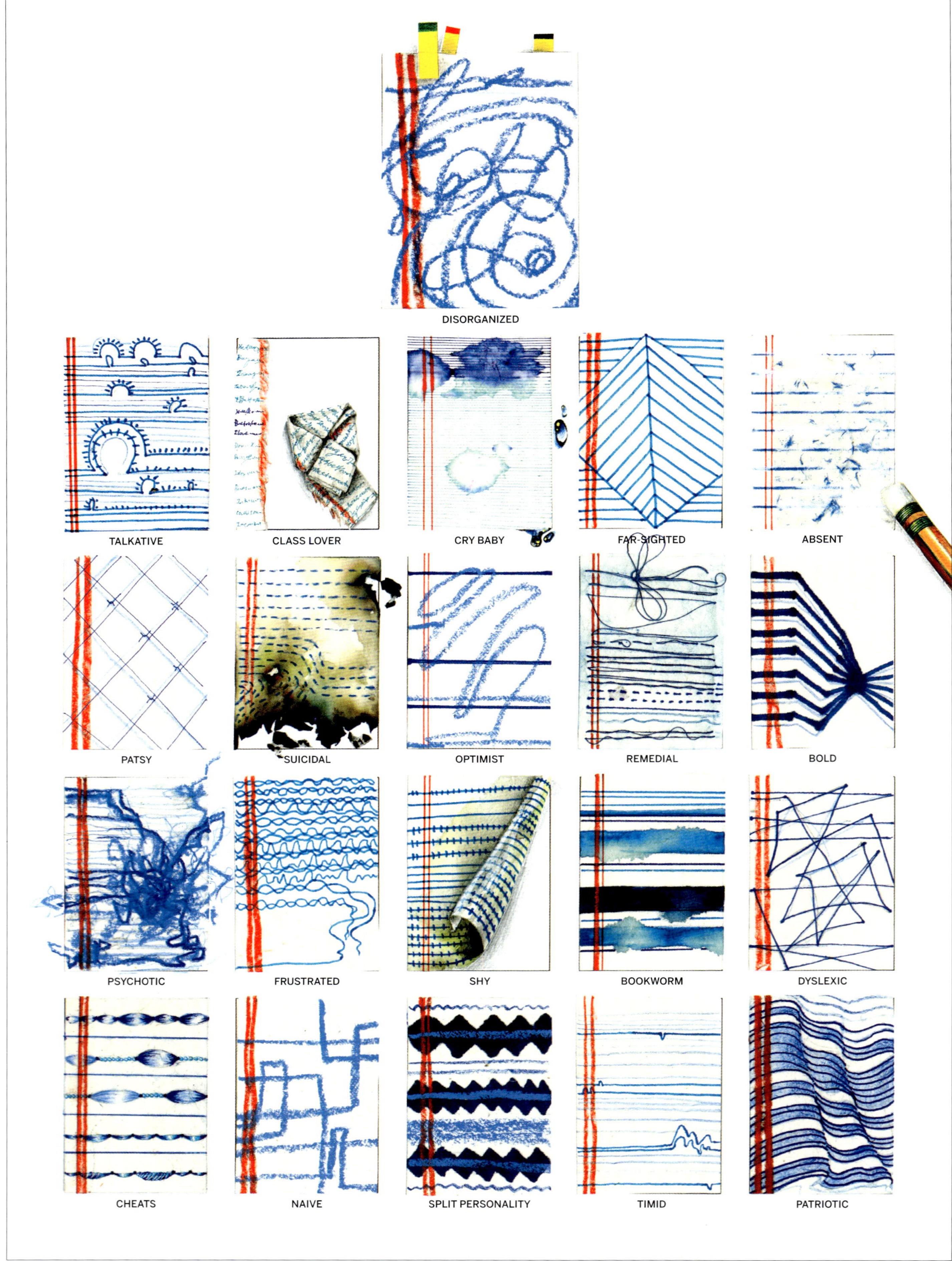
DISORGANIZED
TALKATIVE
CLASS LOVER
CRY BABY
FAR-SIGHTED
ABSENT
PATSY
SUICIDAL
OPTIMIST
REMEDIAL
BOLD
PSYCHOTIC
FRUSTRATED
SHY
BOOKWORM
DYSLEXIC
CHEATS
NAIVE
SPLIT PERSONALITY
TIMID
PATRIOTIC

NOTEBOOK SOLUTIONS:

Figure 1 represents a personal interpretation of the entire assignment, where solutions range from abstract to literal imagery.

Figures 2 through 5 are enlarged solutions from the same assignment that utilize dimensionality, typography, burnt paper, and erased imagery to maximize the visual impact of each subject. Tinting the page yellow and incorporating shadows adds a warm element against the starkness of the notebook page.

SKY

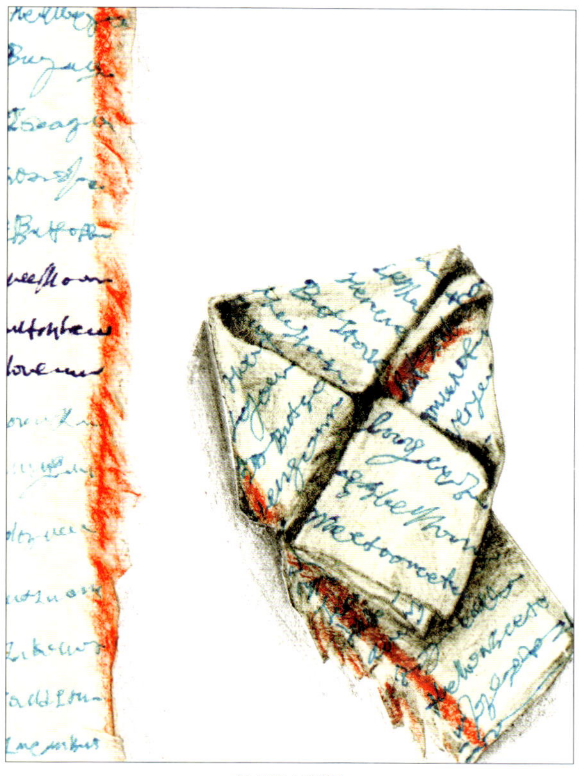
CLASS LOVER

SUICIDAL

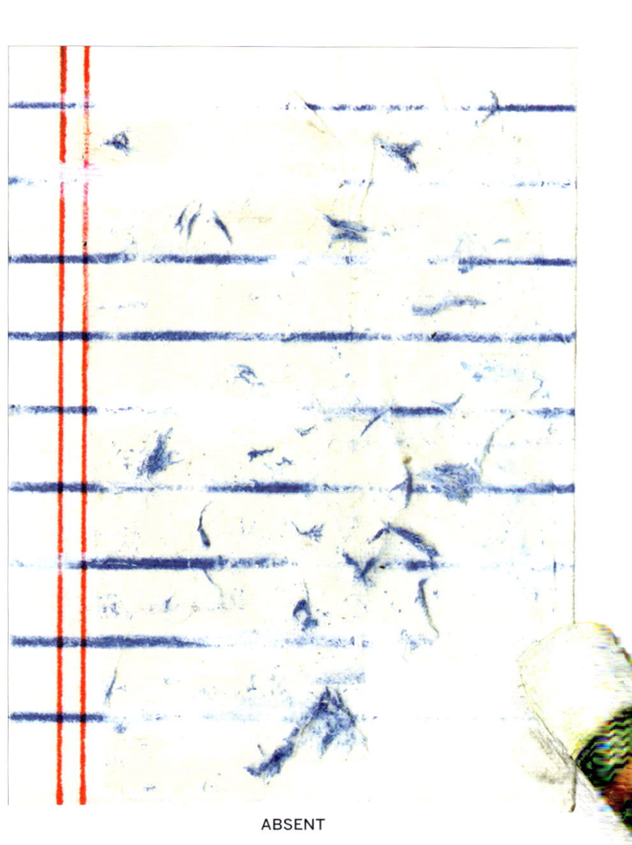
ABSENT

1	2	3
	4	5

1–5. *Jiyoung Lee*

CHEWS GUM INCESSANTLY

STRONG AND BOASTFUL

A GIRL WITH LARGE BREASTS

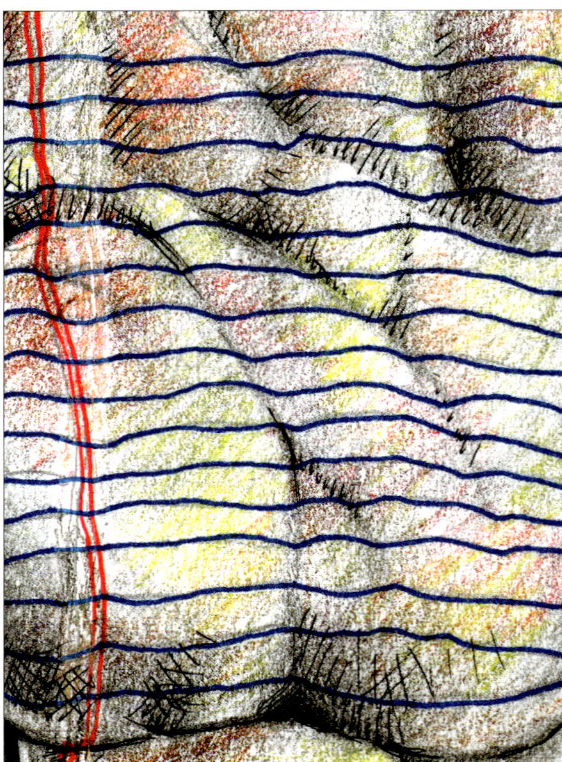

FORGETS NOTEBOOK (WRITES ON HAND)

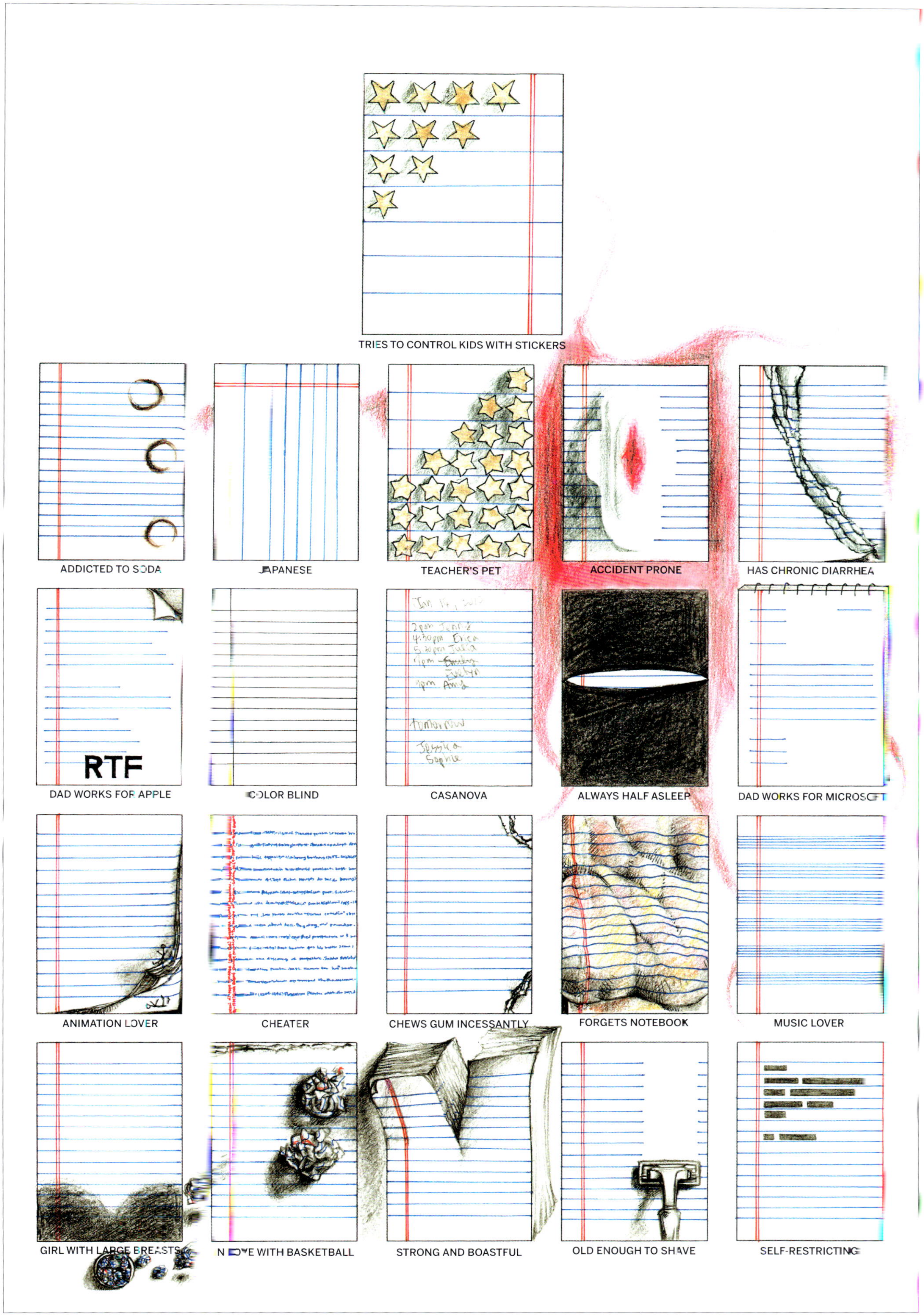

TRIES TO CONTROL KIDS WITH STICKERS

ADDICTED TO SODA

JAPANESE

TEACHER'S PET

ACCIDENT PRONE

HAS CHRONIC DIARRHEA

RTF

DAD WORKS FOR APPLE

COLOR BLIND

CASANOVA

ALWAYS HALF ASLEEP

DAD WORKS FOR MICROSOFT

ANIMATION LOVER

CHEATER

CHEWS GUM INCESSANTLY

FORGETS NOTEBOOK

MUSIC LOVER

GIRL WITH LARGE BREASTS

IN LOVE WITH BASKETBALL

STRONG AND BOASTFUL

OLD ENOUGH TO SHAVE

SELF-RESTRICTING

NOTEBOOK SOLUTIONS:

Figures 1 through 4 address storytelling with a sense of humor, from ripping the corners of the notebook page so as to wrap up chewed gum, to using a ream of notebook paper similar to a telephone directory and tearing it as an act of strength, to casting the shadow of breasts of an early developer over the notebook page, to the palm of a hand that is used in lieu of a notebook.

Figure 5 represents an assignment of twenty-one solutions that range from a suggestion of the subject to clearly defined narratives.

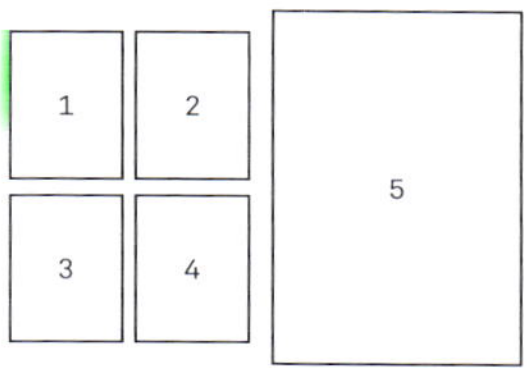

1	2	5
3	4	

1–5. *Jarwon Shin*

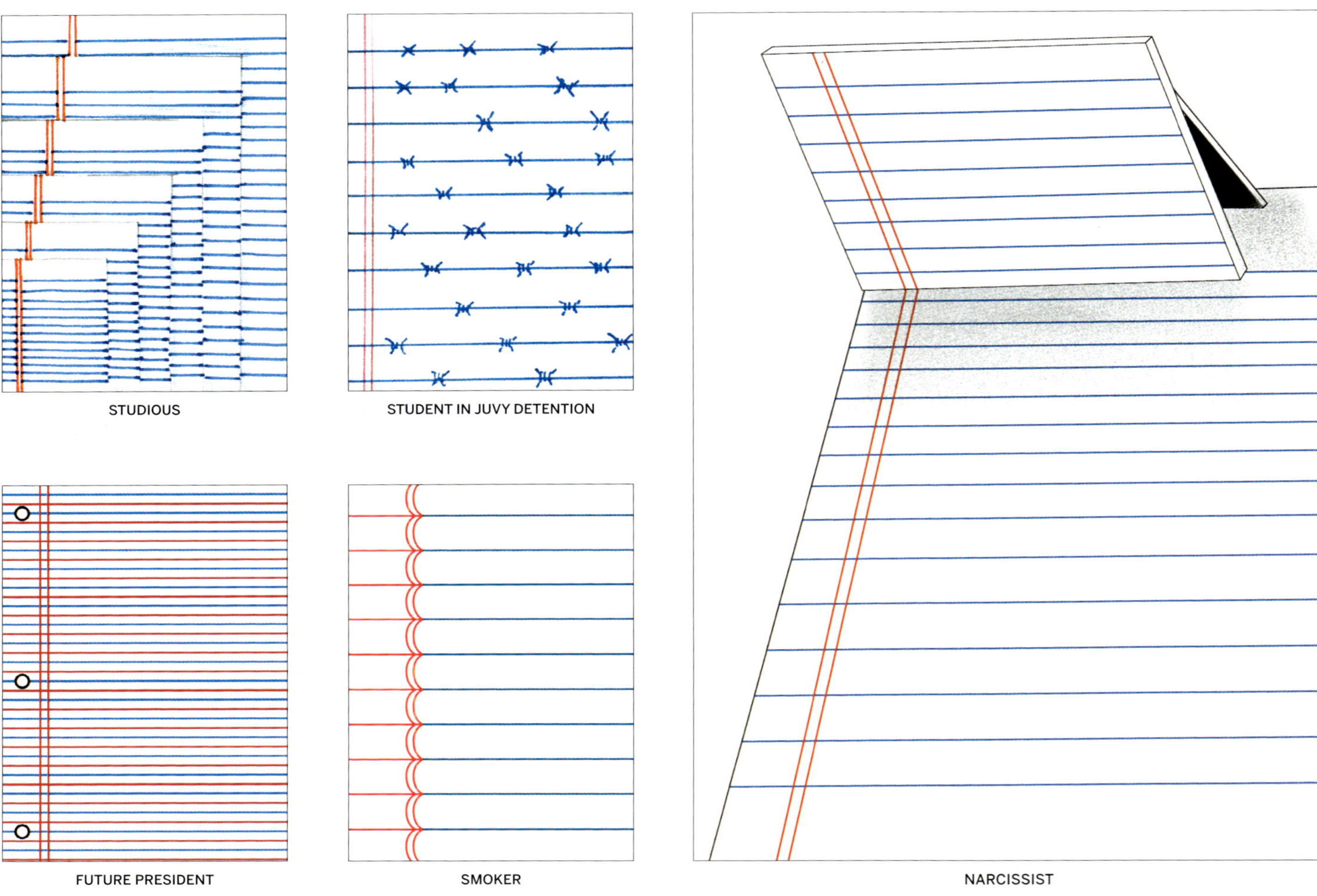

STUDIOUS

STUDENT IN JUVY DETENTION

FUTURE PRESIDENT

SMOKER

NARCISSIST

NOTEBOOK SOLUTIONS:

Figures 1 through 11 represent an array of characteristics that utilize various executional approaches including: duplication, referencing definable objects, as well as notebook pages that are ripped, folded, curled, and burnt.

In figure 6, which depicts "trouble maker," one of its missing pages appears above it as a crumpled ball of paper, presumably being tossed at another student.

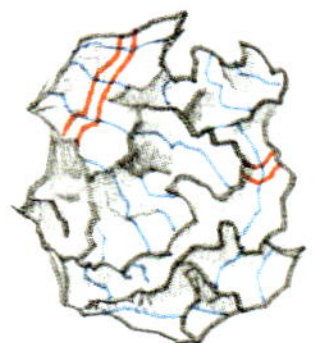

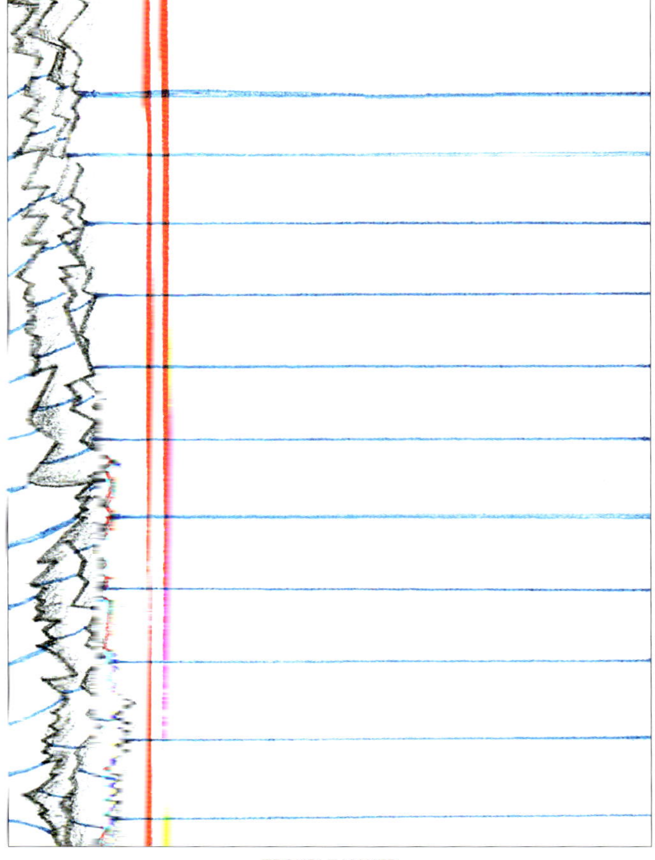

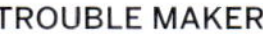

TROUBLE MAKER

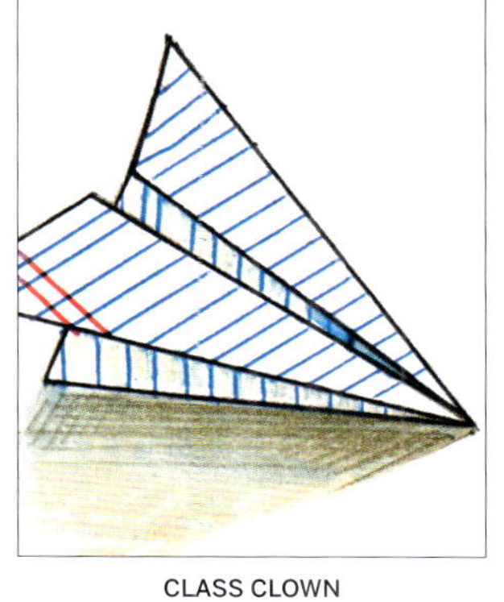

CLASS CLOWN

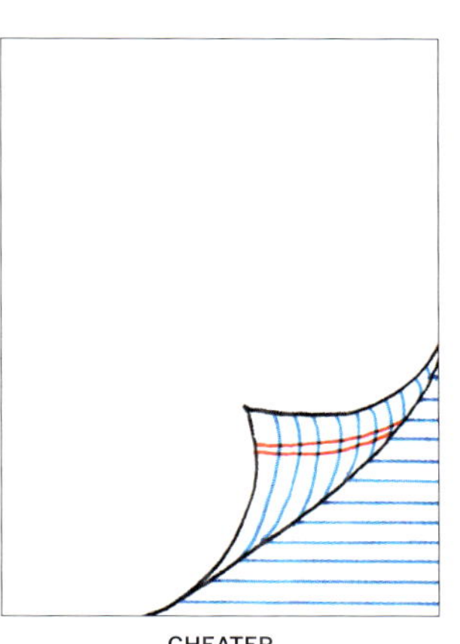

CHEATER

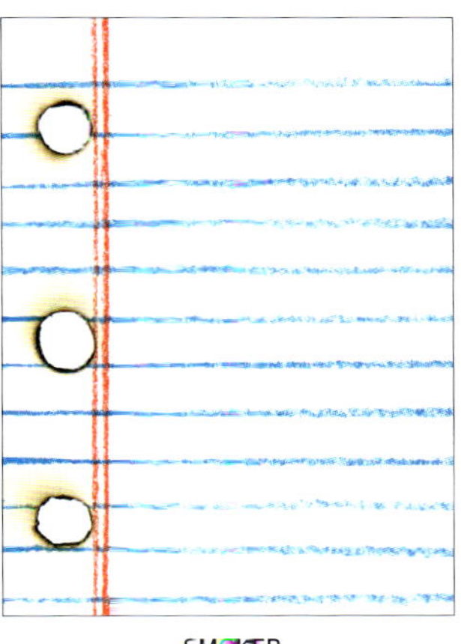

SMOKER

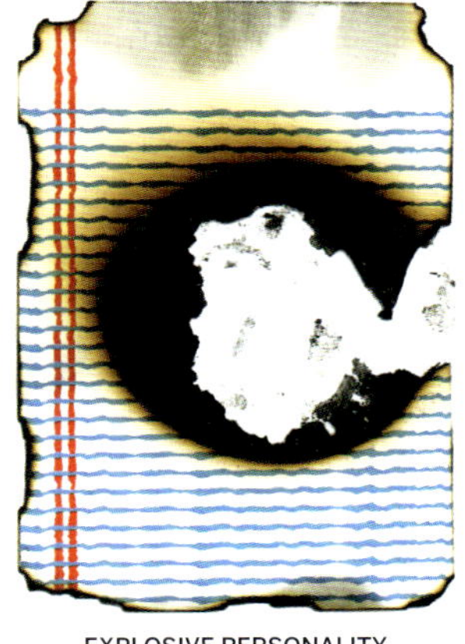

EXPLOSIVE PERSONALITY

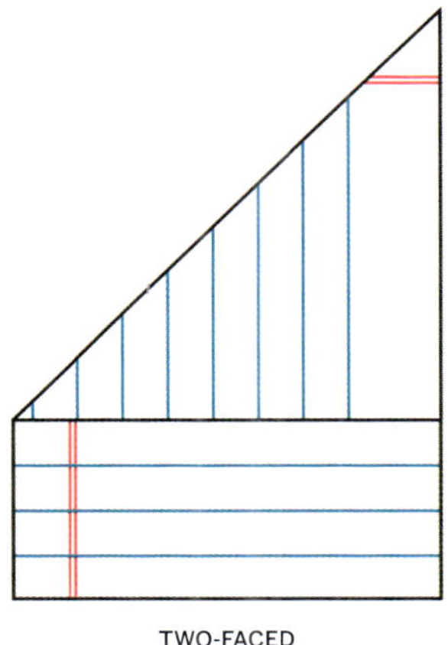

TWO-FACED

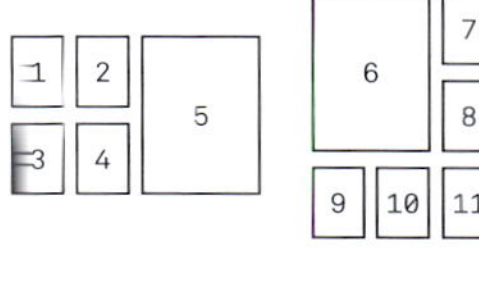

1. *Yuhan Wang*
2. *Danielle De Biasio*
3. *Rachel Ake*
4. *Joowon Ahn*
5. *Aemin Shim*
6. *June Hong*
7. *Lynne Yun*
8. *June Hong*
9. *Alyssa Leary*
10. *Louis Rivera*
11. *Yongjoon Cho*

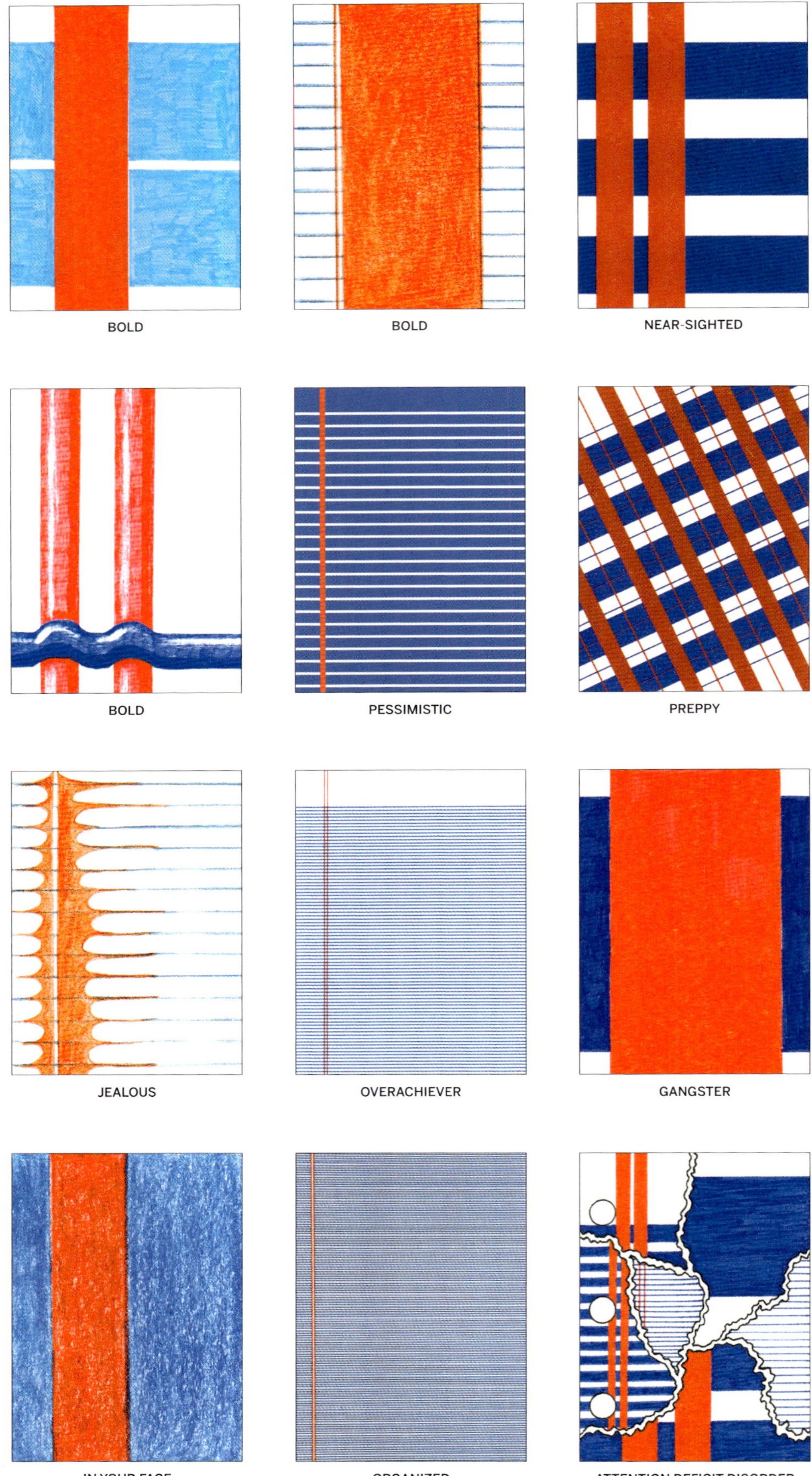

BOLD

BOLD

NEAR-SIGHTED

BOLD

PESSIMISTIC

PREPPY

JEALOUS

OVERACHIEVER

GANGSTER

IN YOUR FACE

ORGANIZED

ATTENTION DEFICIT DISORDER

NOTEBOOK SOLUTIONS:

Figures 1 through 12 are primarily interpretations that utilize scale and the expansion of the width of the red and blue lines to convey a wide range of subjects that necessitate the use of bold graphic imagery. Yet, in figures 8 and 11, the opposite is done to depict subjects that require an abundance of lines positioned in close proximity to one another.

Figures 13 through 15 are emotionally drawn lines that represent different interpretations of psychotic disorders.

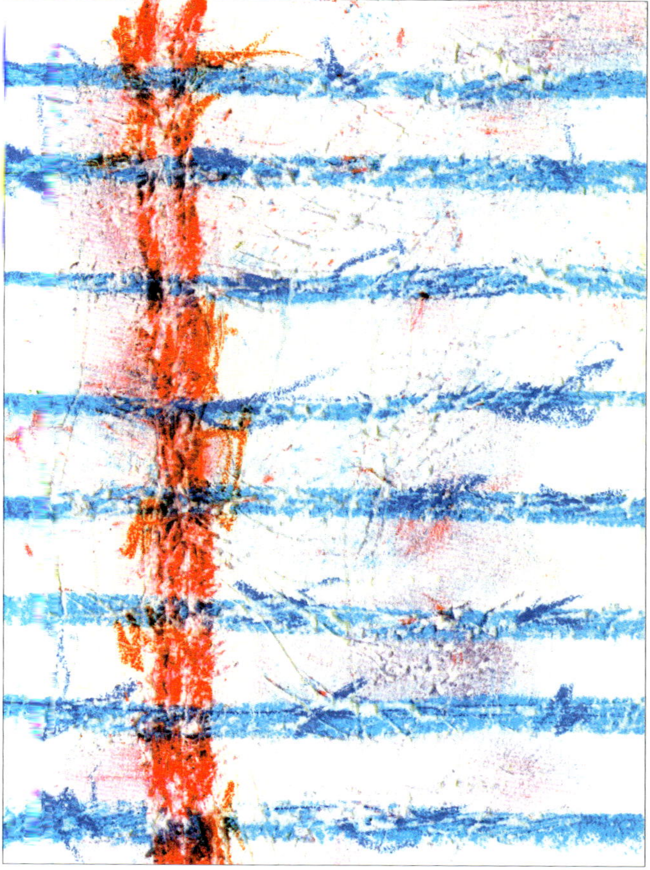

PSYCHOTIC

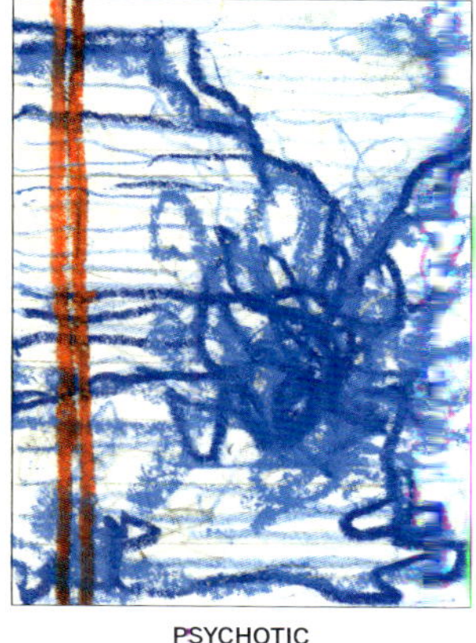

PSYCHOTIC

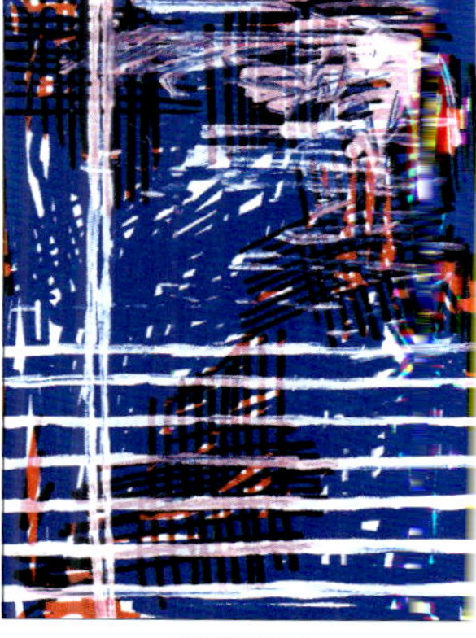

PSYCHOTIC

1 2 3 | 13 14 15
4 5 6
7 8 9 | 16 17 18
10 11 12

1. *Stephanie Macchione*
2. *Minhee Kim*
3. *Jason Gargano*
4. *Hyo Han*
5. *Michael Gonzales*
6. *Gyuwon Park*
7. *Minhee Kim*
8. *Kimberly Pasqualetto*
9. *Kirsten Karkanen*
10. *Wei Zu Chen*
11. *Daisy Roberts*
12. *Kirsten Karkanen*
13. *Sangwook Kim*
14. *Jiyoung Lee*
15. *Junghee Yoo*
16. *Kelly Shami*
17. *Jiyoung Lee*
18. *Chris Mohr*

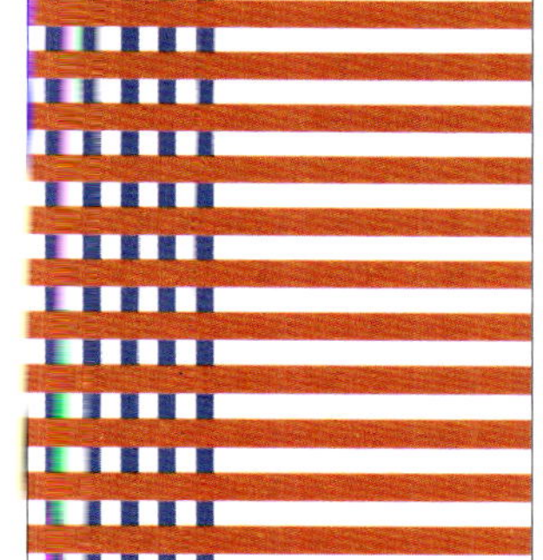

PATRIOTIC

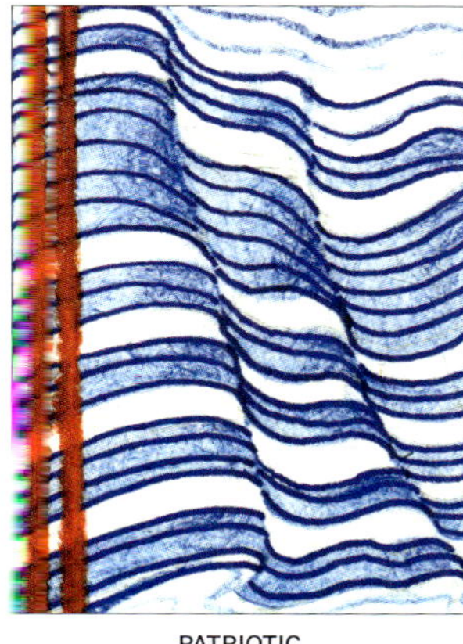

PATRIOTIC

PATRIOTIC

Figures 16 through 18 are a range of American flags used as a metaphor for patriotism.

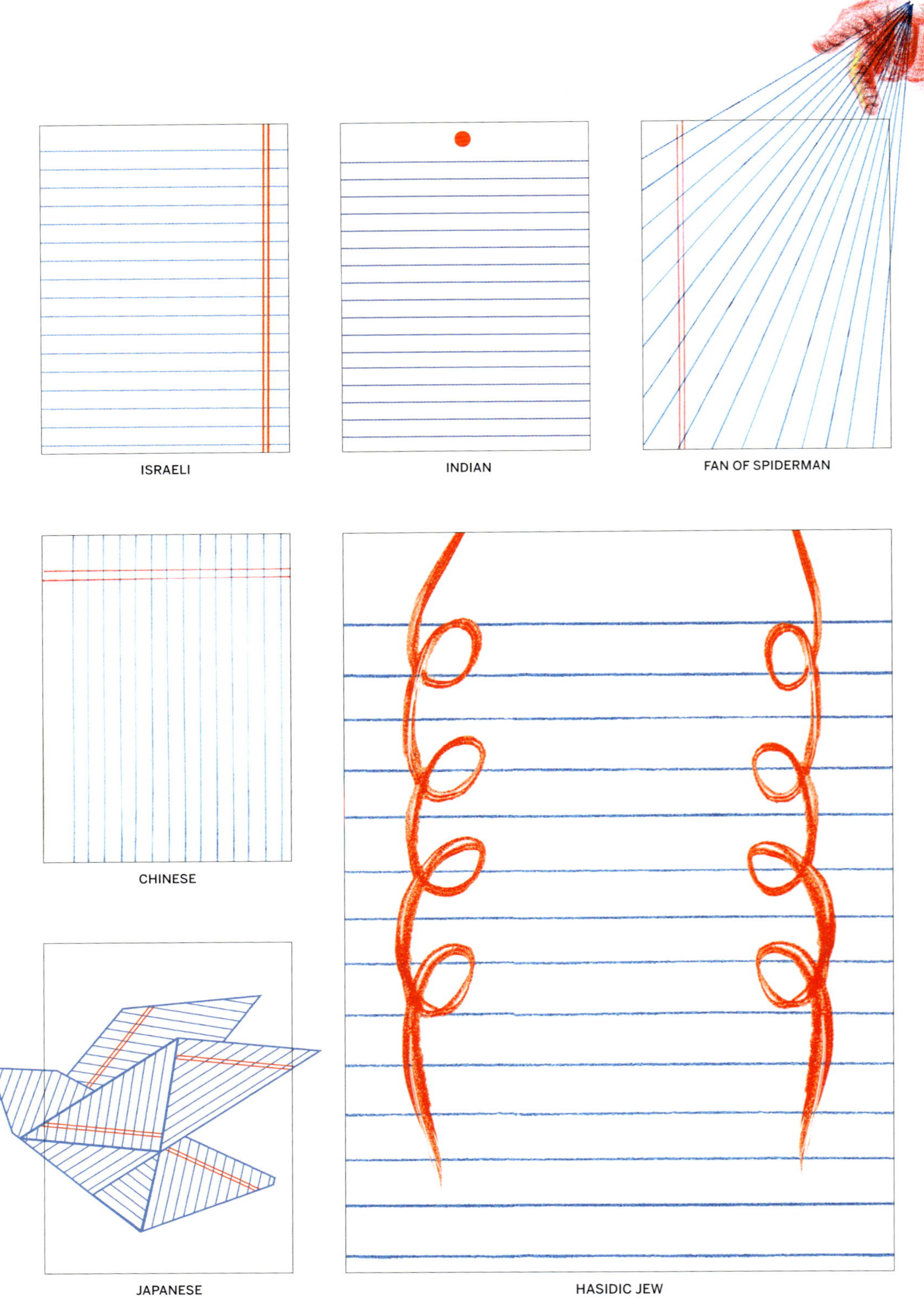
ISRAELI
INDIAN
FAN OF SPIDERMAN
CHINESE
JAPANESE
HASIDIC JEW

STAR WARS FAN

NOTEBOOK SOLUTIONS:

Figures 1, 2 and 4 through 6 are expressions of different nationalities and religions, referencing the direction in which a language is written, as well as cultural characteristics.

Figures 3 and 7 represent movie enthusiasts, whose solutions incorporate literal imagery and dimensionality that references movie titles.

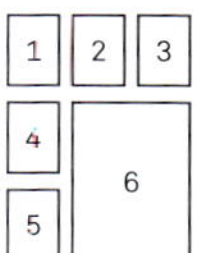

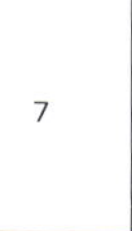

1. *Lyanne Dubon*
2. *Jonas Christiansen*
3. *Yuri Byun*
4. *Kelly McGreen*
5. *Sofie Rostad*
6. *Rebecca Lim*
7. *Blanda Eggenschwiler*

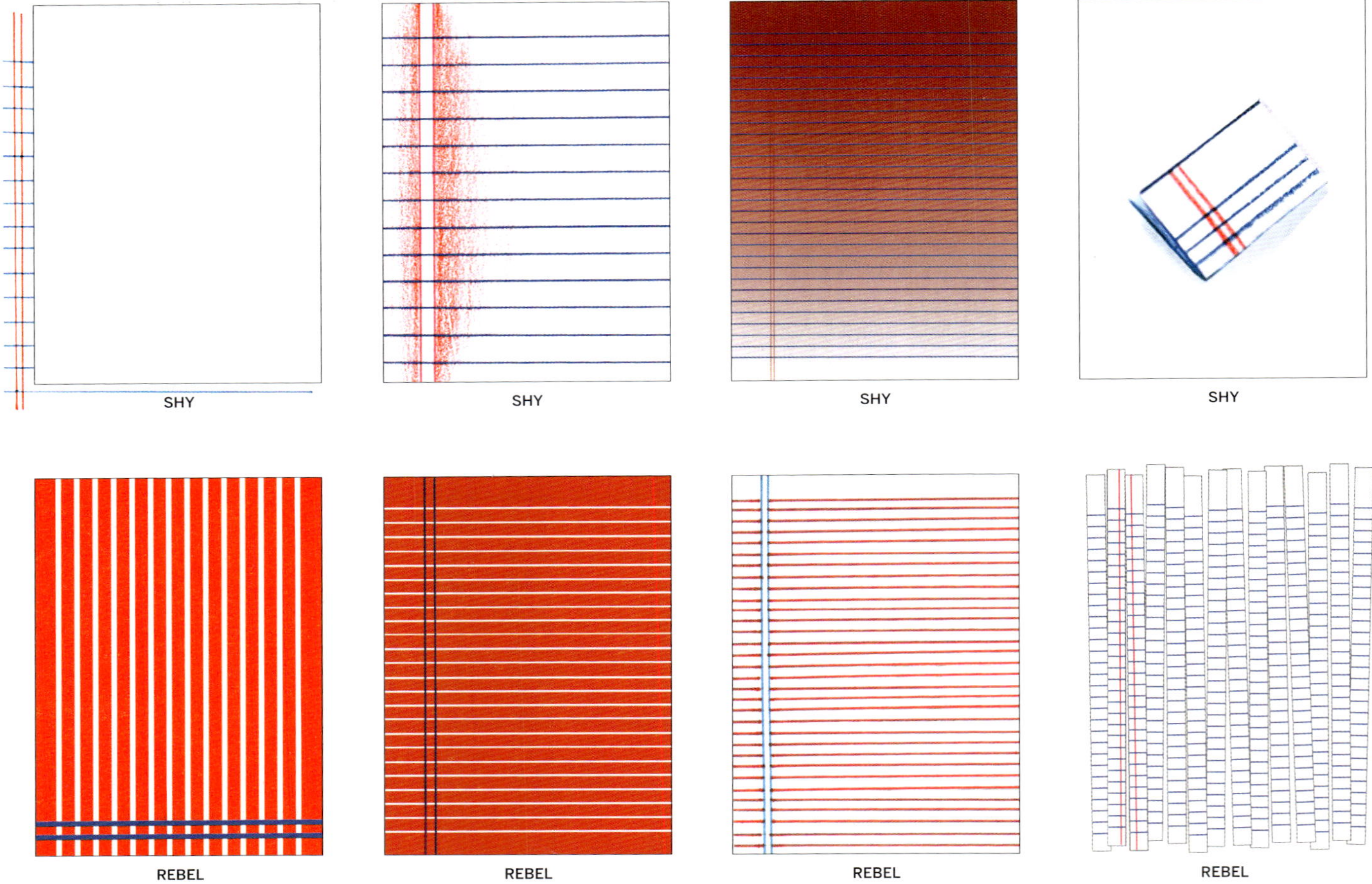
SHY
SHY
SHY
SHY
REBEL
REBEL
REBEL
REBEL

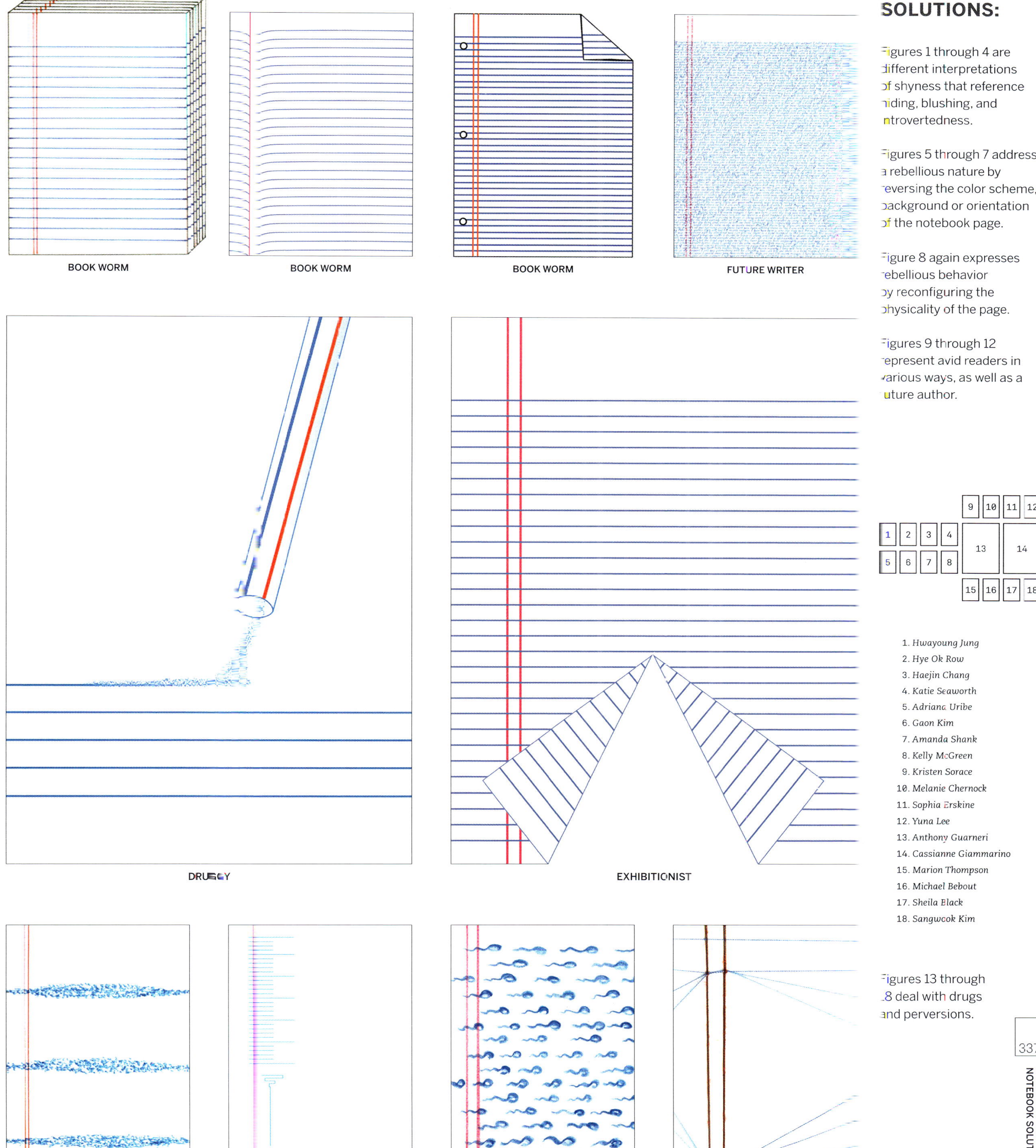

BOOK WORM — BOOK WORM — BOOK WORM — FUTURE WRITER

DRUGGY — EXHIBITIONIST

DRUGGY — DRUG ADDICT — PERVERT — PERVERT

NOTEBOOK SOLUTIONS:

Figures 1 through 4 are different interpretations of shyness that reference hiding, blushing, and introvertedness.

Figures 5 through 7 address a rebellious nature by reversing the color scheme, background or orientation of the notebook page.

Figure 8 again expresses rebellious behavior by reconfiguring the physicality of the page.

Figures 9 through 12 represent avid readers in various ways, as well as a future author.

1. *Hwayoung Jung*
2. *Hye Ok Row*
3. *Haejin Chang*
4. *Katie Seaworth*
5. *Adriana Uribe*
6. *Gaon Kim*
7. *Amanda Shank*
8. *Kelly McGreen*
9. *Kristen Sorace*
10. *Melanie Chernock*
11. *Sophia Erskine*
12. *Yuna Lee*
13. *Anthony Guarneri*
14. *Cassianne Giammarino*
15. *Marion Thompson*
16. *Michael Bebout*
17. *Sheila Black*
18. *Sangwcok Kim*

Figures 13 through 18 deal with drugs and perversions.

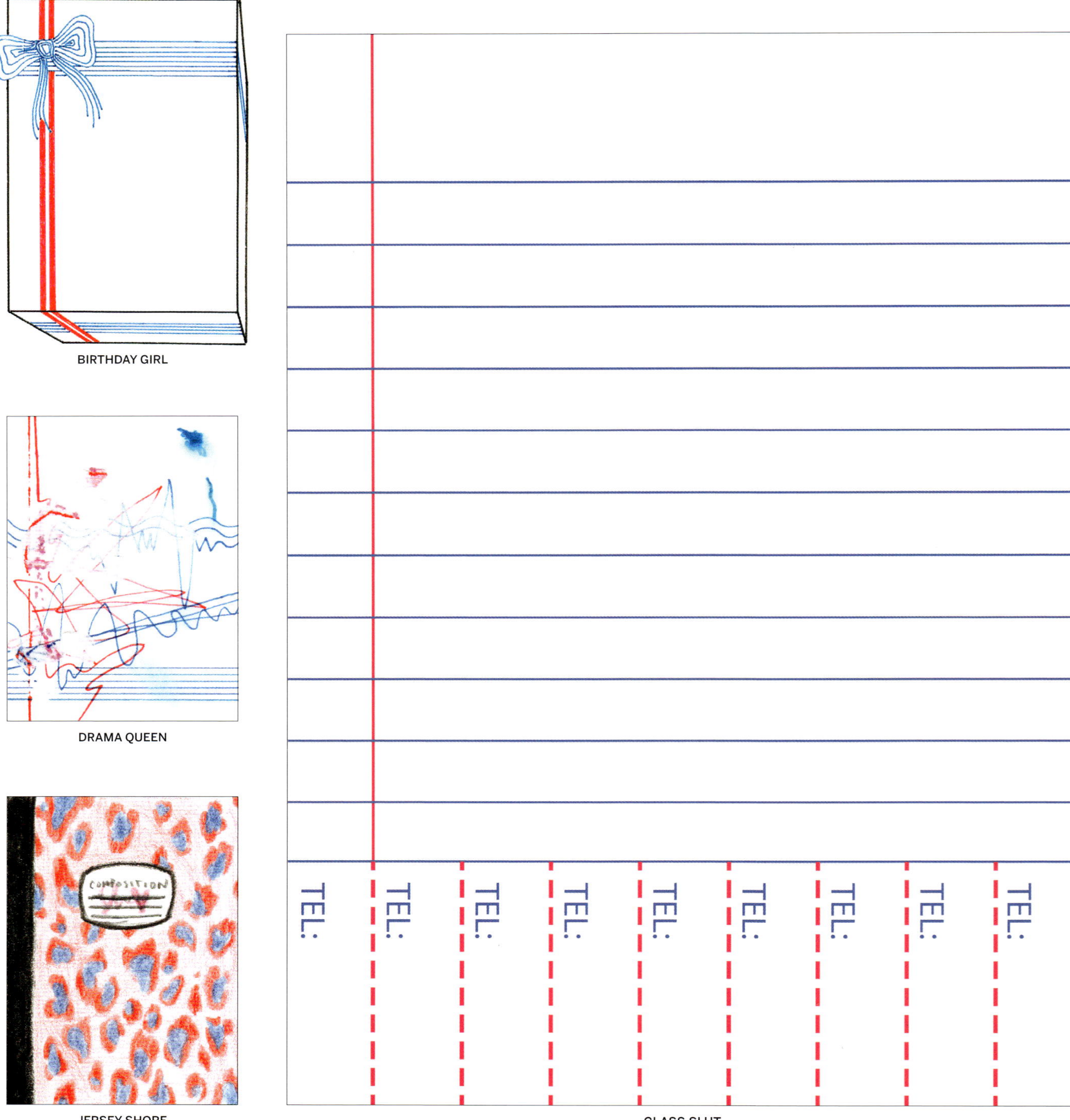

BIRTHDAY GIRL

DRAMA QUEEN

JERSEY SHORE

CLASS SLUT

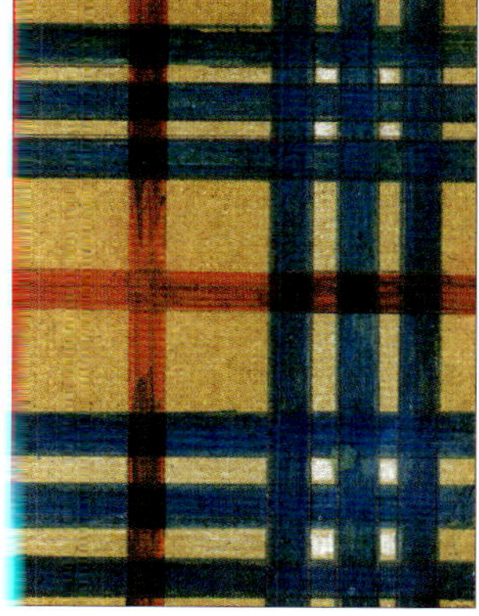
RICH BITCH

DIVA

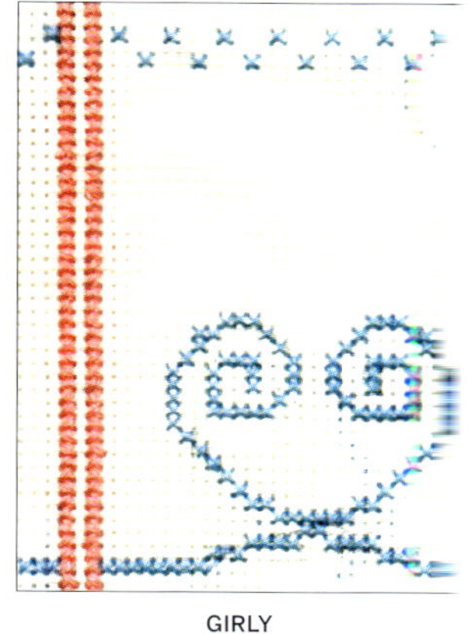
GIRLY

NOTEBOOK SOLUTIONS:

Figures 1 through 13 address various perceptions of female pubescent behaviors, ranging from girly and goody two shoes to slutty.

Figures 6 through 10 use a variety of mediums including glitter, cloth, embroidery, beads, lace, and other fabrics to exaggerate their concepts.

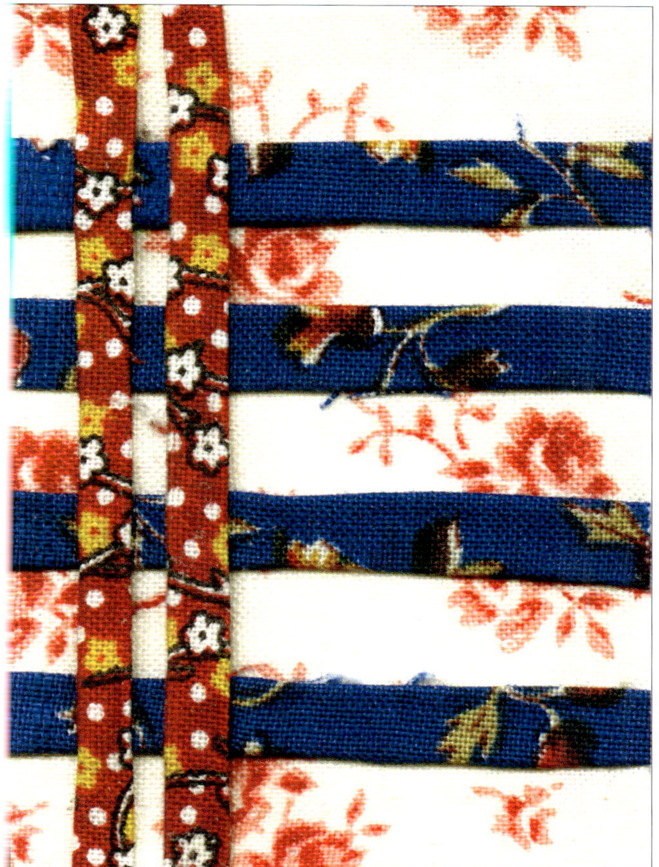
GIRLY

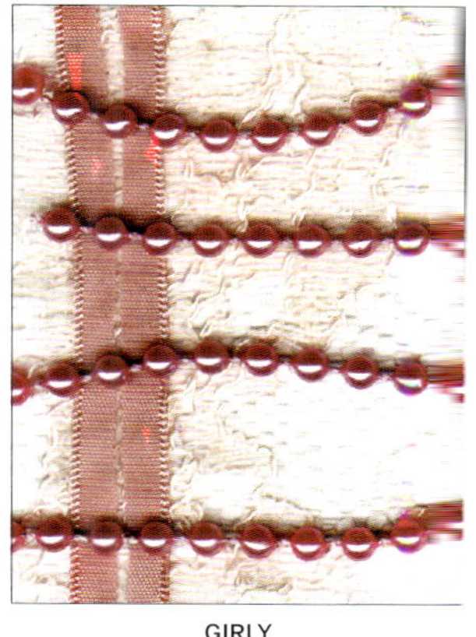
GIRLY

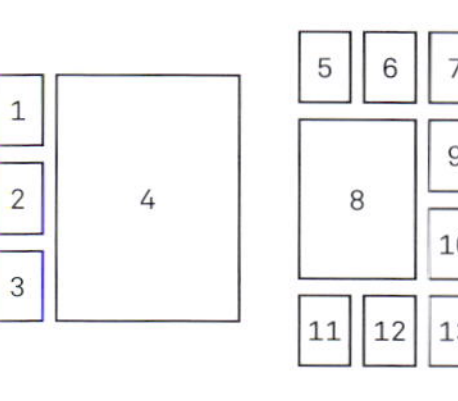

1. *Yuri Byun*
2. *Sunyoung Koo*
3. *Julia Kim*
4. *Kimberly Fulcher*
5. *April Sharp*
6. *Sarah Macreading*
7. *Erin Kim*
8. *Nari Park*
9. *Samantha Zahabian*
10. *Sarah Macreading*
11. *Angela Han*
12. *Holly Jarrett*
13. *Raci Merigime*

CLASS FLIRT

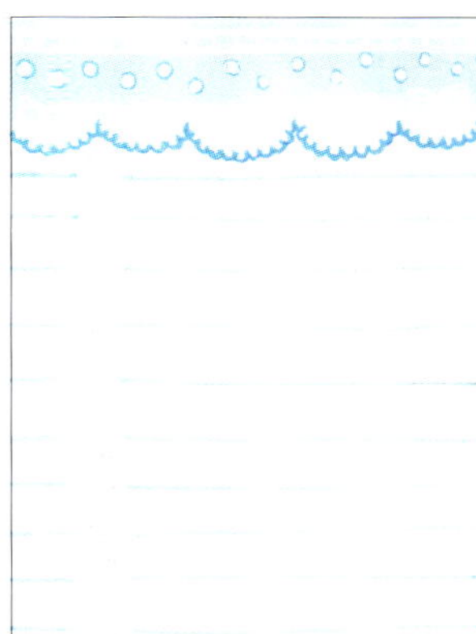
THE PRINCESS

THE "LOLITA"

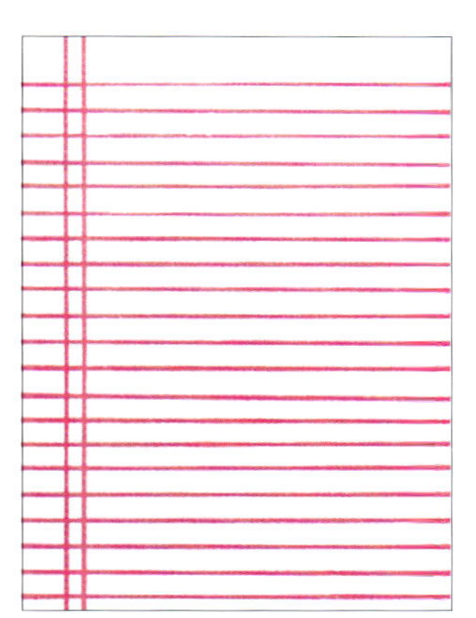
THE BARBIE

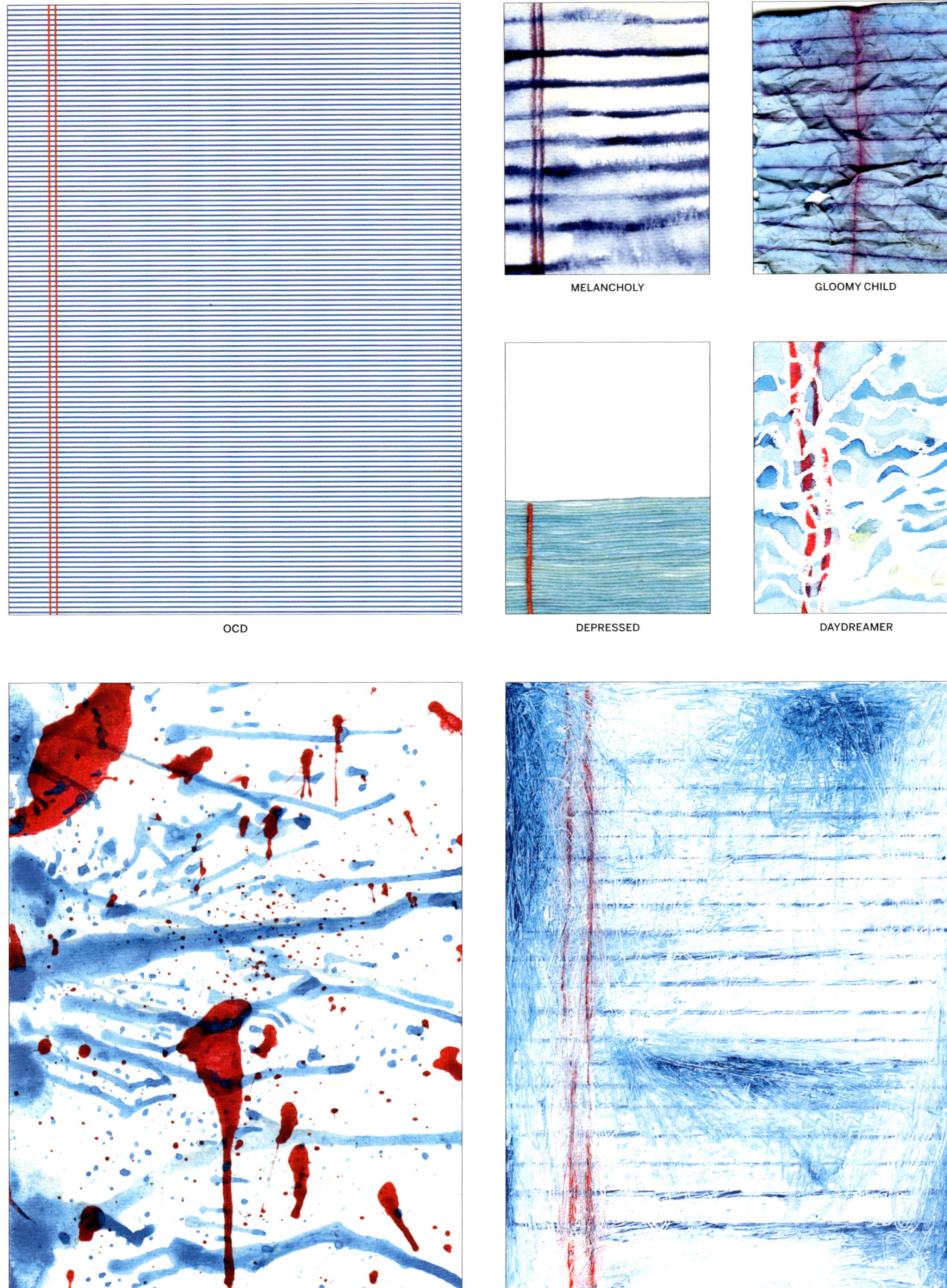

OCD

MELANCHOLY

GLOOMY CHILD

DEPRESSED

DAYDREAMER

IMPULSIVE

MELANCHOLY

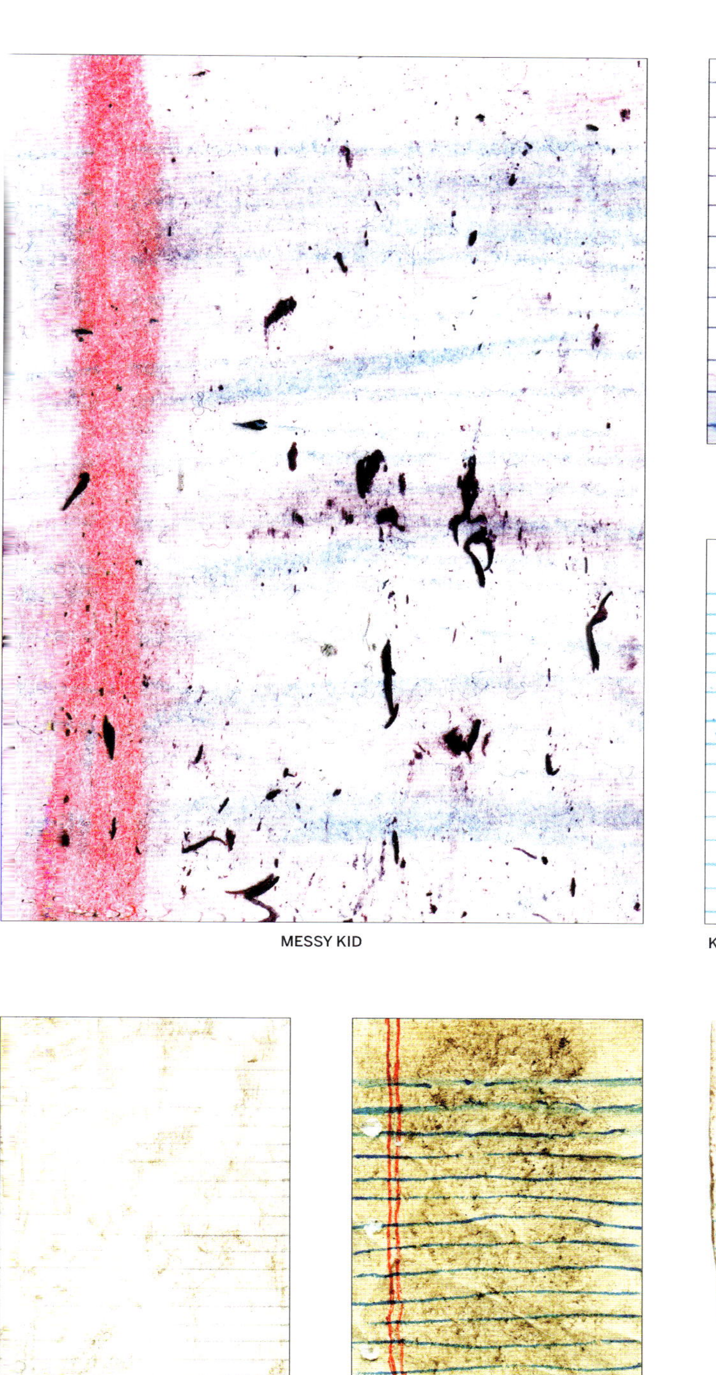

MESSY KID

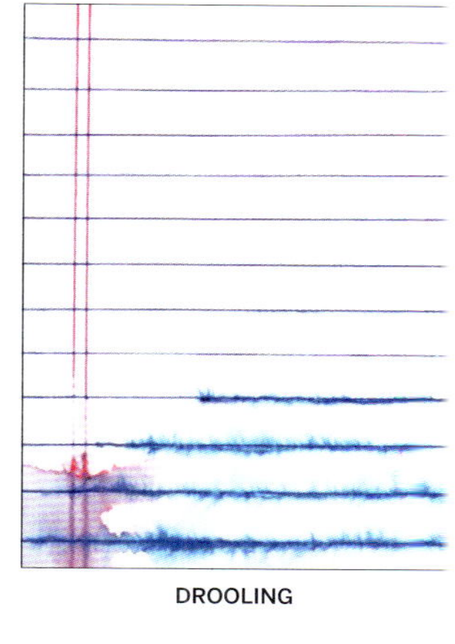

DROOLING

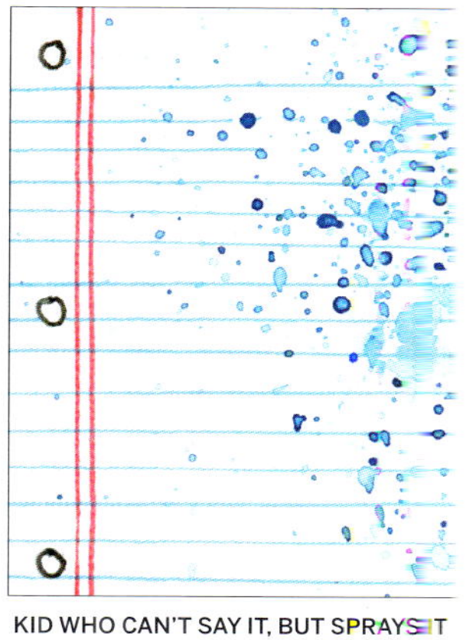

KID WHO CAN'T SAY IT, BUT SPRAYS IT

NOTEBOOK SOLUTIONS:

Figures 1 through 7 deal with psychological manifestations including: compulsive behavior, depression, and inattentiveness.

Figure 4 uses closely positioned colored strands of cord to create a modulated pattern that infers sadness.

Figure 6 is spontaneously executed imagery, but misses on one of the assignment's demands of maintaining some semblance of the notebook page.

Figures 8 through 16 deal with hygienic issues. Figure 10 uses the technique of splattered ink, which captures the intent of the subject.

POOR HYGIENE

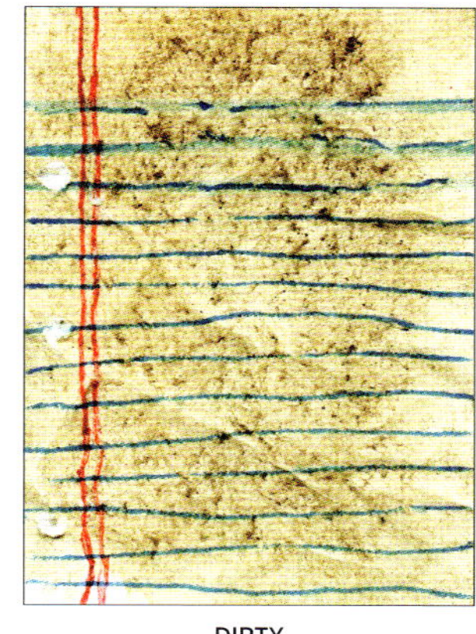

DIRTY

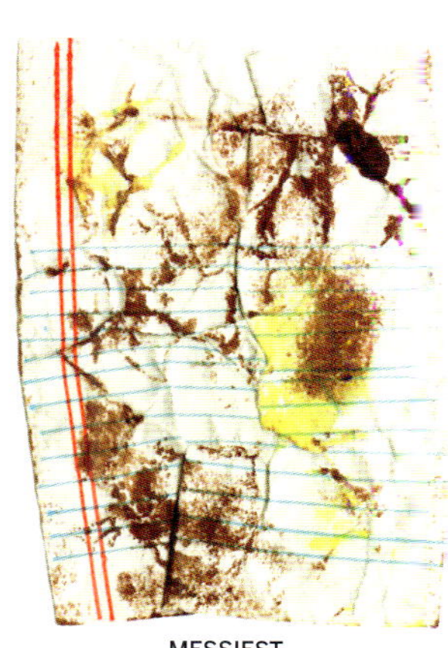

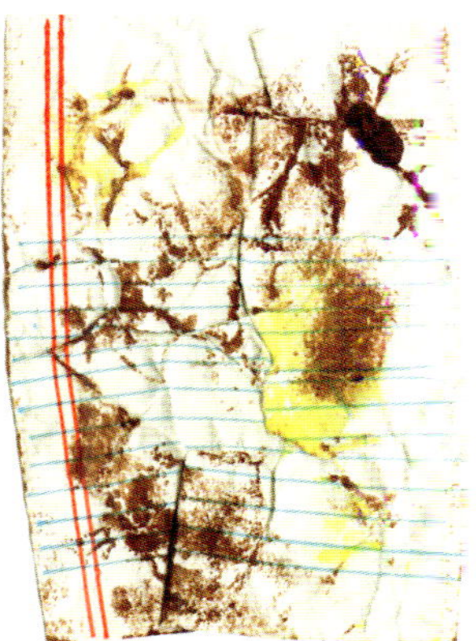

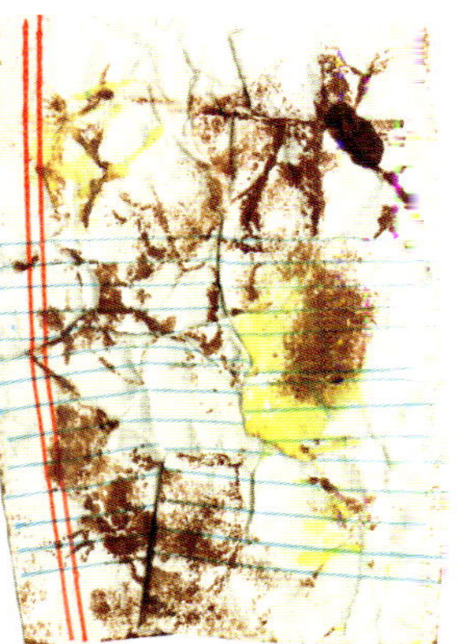

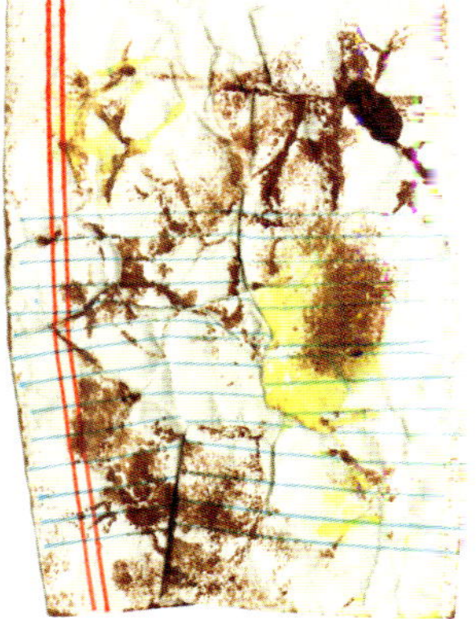

MESSIEST

1. *Joshua Cohen*
2. *Joohae Lee*
3. *Hyunjung Ra*
4. *Yoonha Chang*
5. *Ahyoung Moon*
6. *Heesang Lee*
7. *Yi Wun Lu*
8. *Diane Wilder*
9. *Minkyung Kang*
10. *Lauren Ahn*
11. *Mary Di Lillo*
12. *Louis Rivera*
13. *Soobin Jeon*
14. *James Yankowsky*
15. *Yi Wun Lu*
16. *Joonmo Kang*

FILTHY

CLASS SLOB

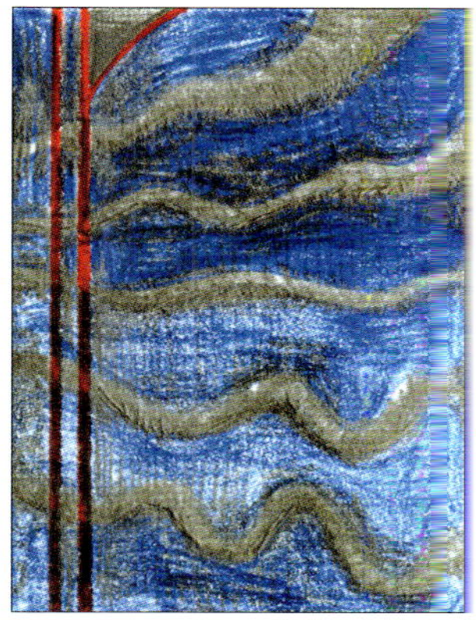

SMELLY

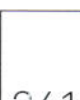

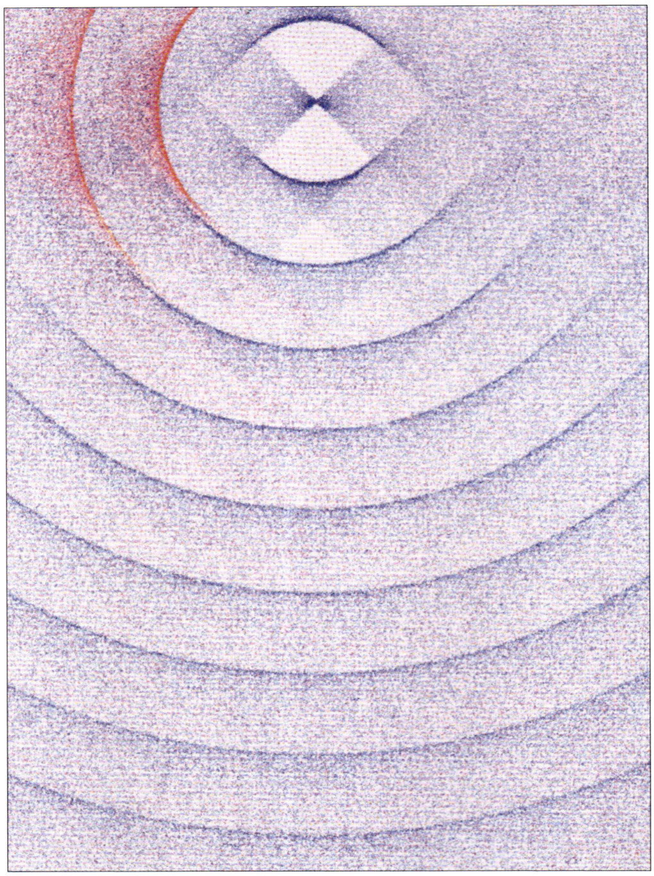
AUTISTIC

DAYDREAMER

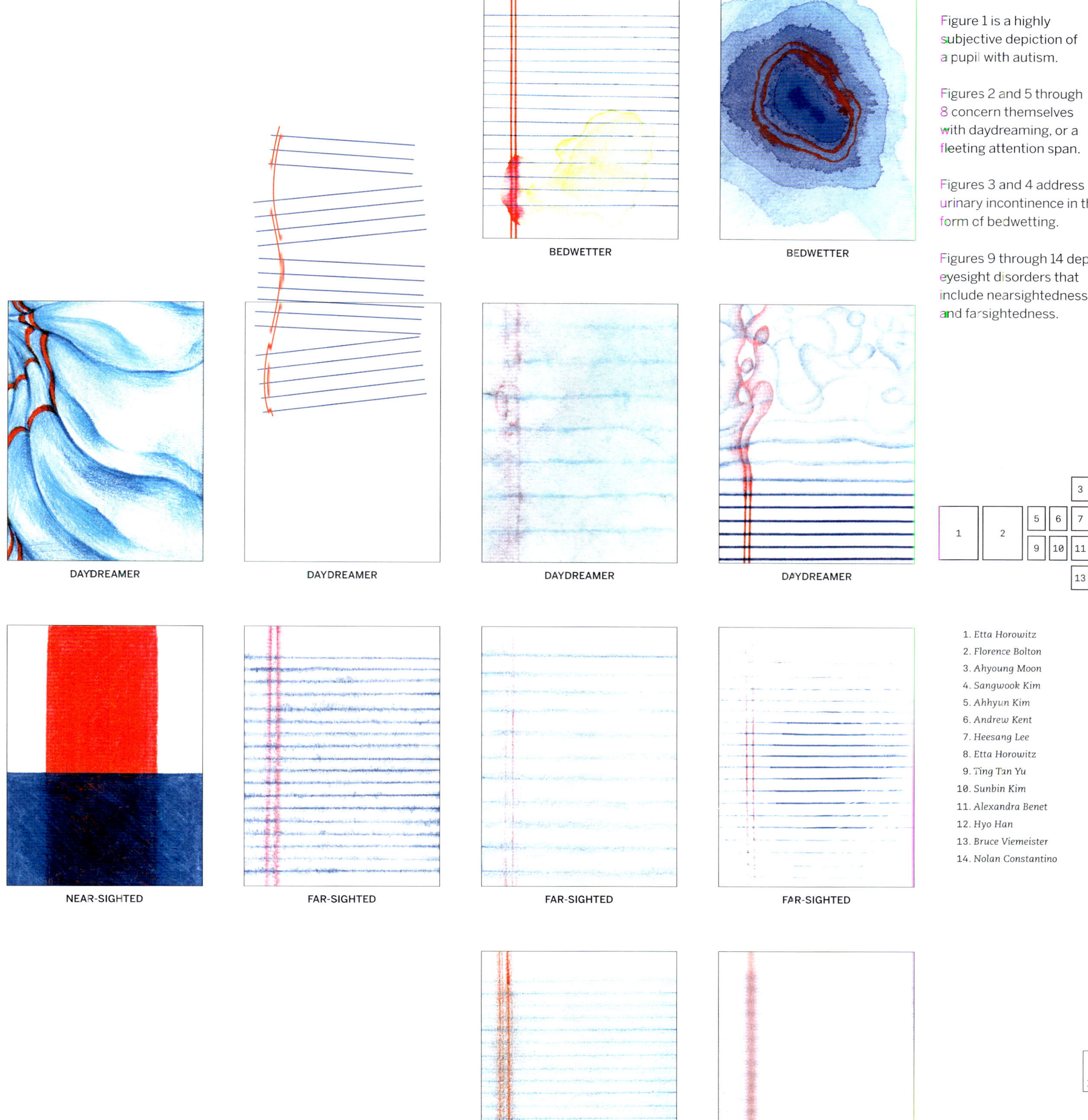

NOTEBOOK SOLUTIONS:

Figure 1 is a highly subjective depiction of a pupil with autism.

Figures 2 and 5 through 8 concern themselves with daydreaming, or a fleeting attention span.

Figures 3 and 4 address urinary incontinence in the form of bedwetting.

Figures 9 through 14 depict eyesight disorders that include nearsightedness and farsightedness.

1. *Etta Horowitz*
2. *Florence Bolton*
3. *Ahyoung Moon*
4. *Sangwook Kim*
5. *Ahhyun Kim*
6. *Andrew Kent*
7. *Heesang Lee*
8. *Etta Horowitz*
9. *Ting Tan Yu*
10. *Sunbin Kim*
11. *Alexandra Benet*
12. *Hyo Han*
13. *Bruce Viemeister*
14. *Nolan Constantino*

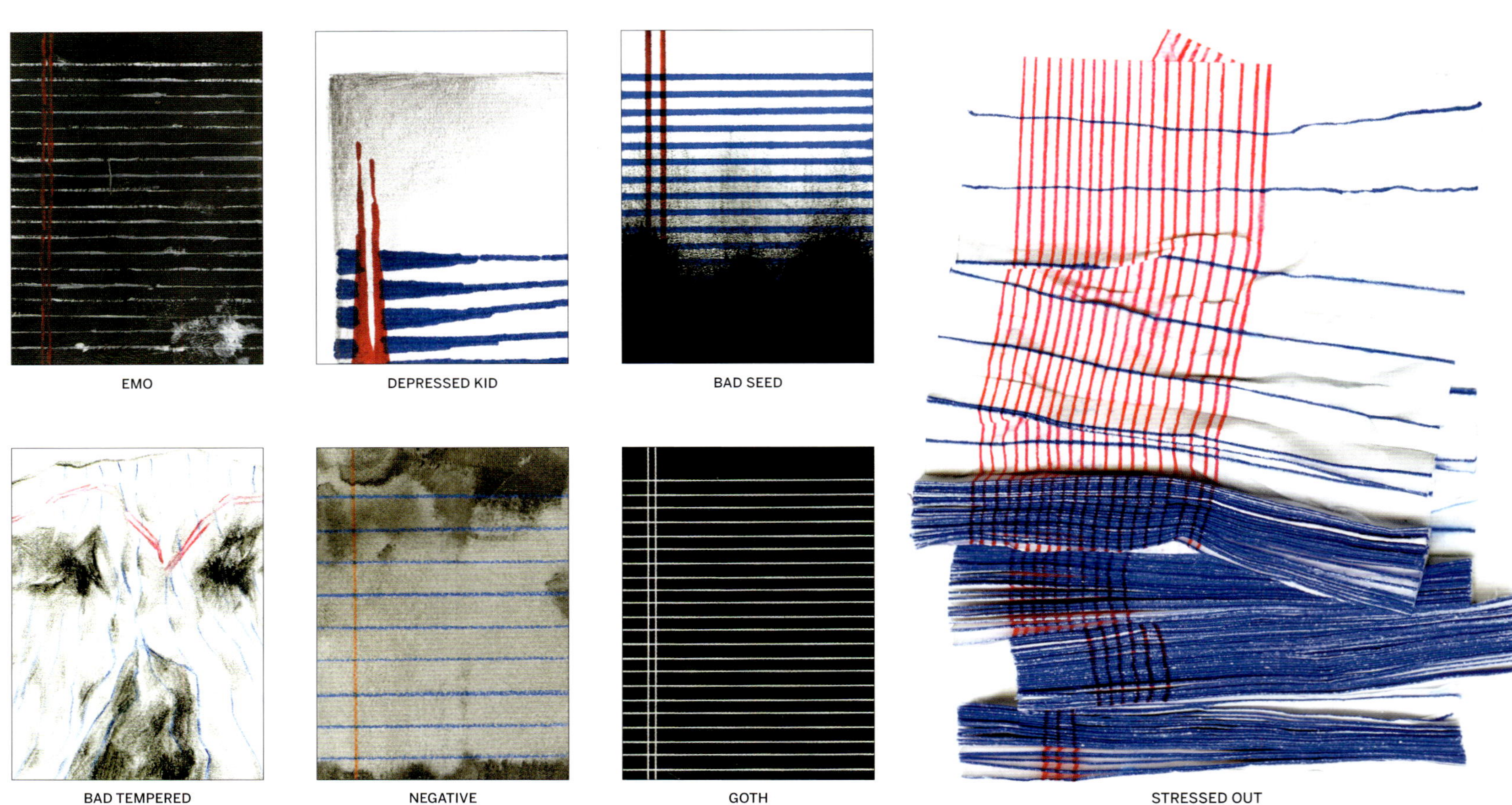

EMO

DEPRESSED KID

BAD SEED

BAD TEMPERED

NEGATIVE

GOTH

STRESSED OUT

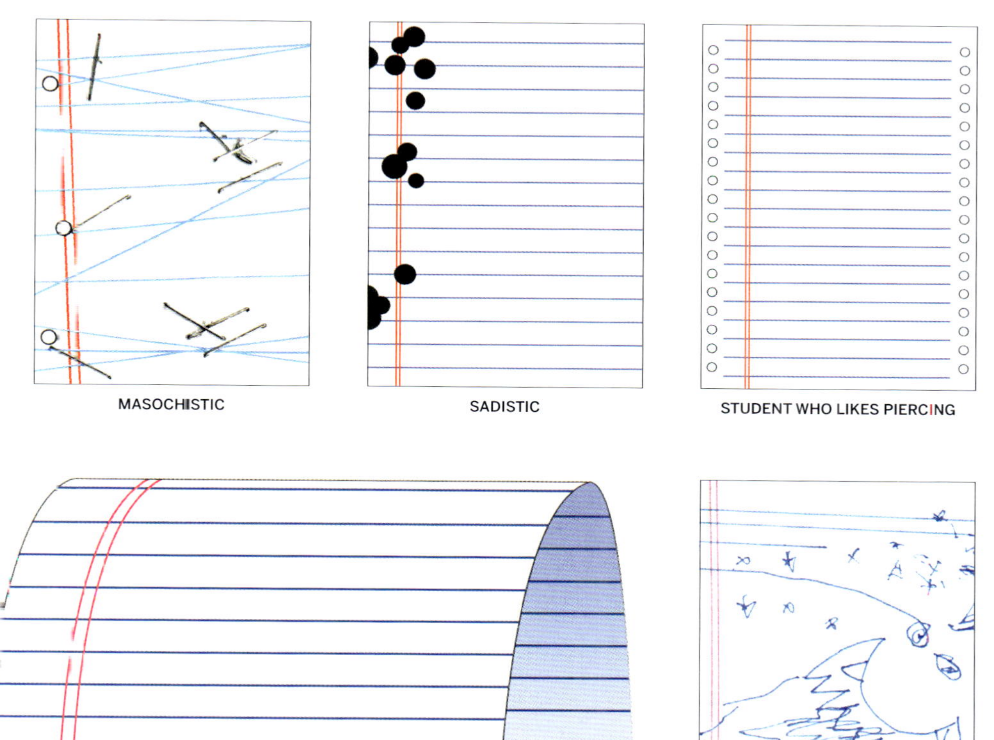

MASOCHISTIC

SADISTIC

STUDENT WHO LIKES PIERCING

THE NARCOLEPTIC

A.D.D.

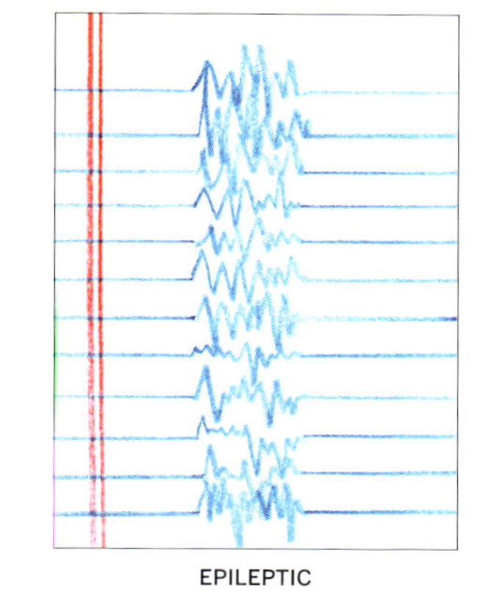

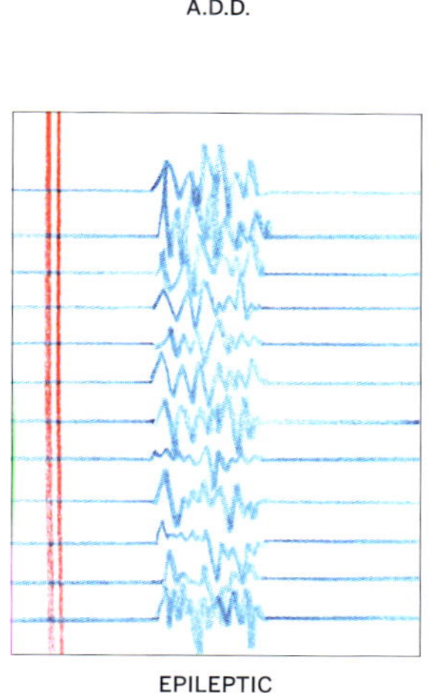

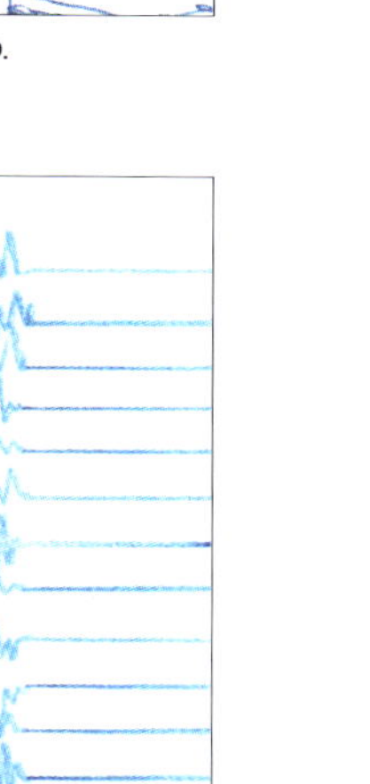

EPILEPTIC

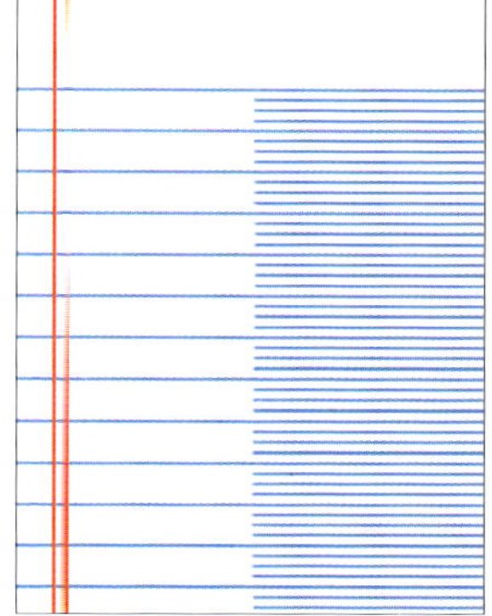

BIPOLAR

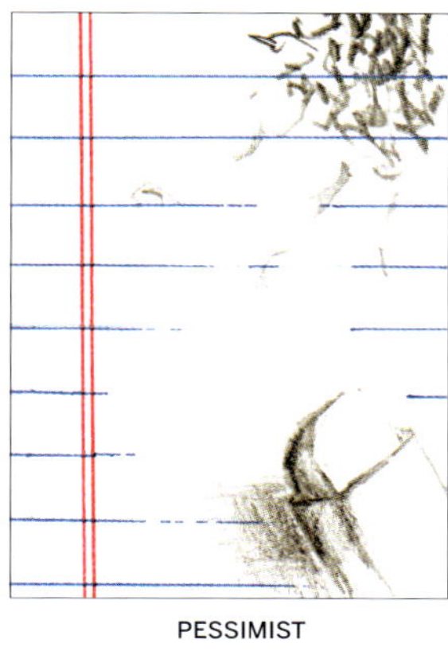

PESSIMIST

AICHMOPHOBIA

NOTEBOOK SOLUTIONS:

Figures 1 through 6 delve into the rebellious and negative nature of various personalities, ranging from Goth to depressed.

Figure 7 uses folded paper to visualize the intensity of pressure.

Figures 8 through 10 deal with rebellious attitudes, resulting in body piercings and self-mutilation.

Figures 11 through 15 deal with physical, psychological, and emotional disorders.

Figure 16 represents a fear of sharp or pointed objects.

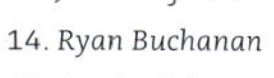

1. *Myung Song*
2. *Rebecca Lievert*
3. *James Yankowsky*
4. *Hyeyoon Park*
5. *Brian Anderson*
6. *Reggie Dankwa*
7. *Hyun Jung Ra*
8. *Renina Powell*
9. *Sandra Woodruff*
10. *Jim Sarfati*
11. *Christopher Rogers*
12. *Jesse Smith*
13. *Joshua Pforsich*
14. *Ryan Buchanan*
15. *Aemin Shim*
16. *Sujin Jung*

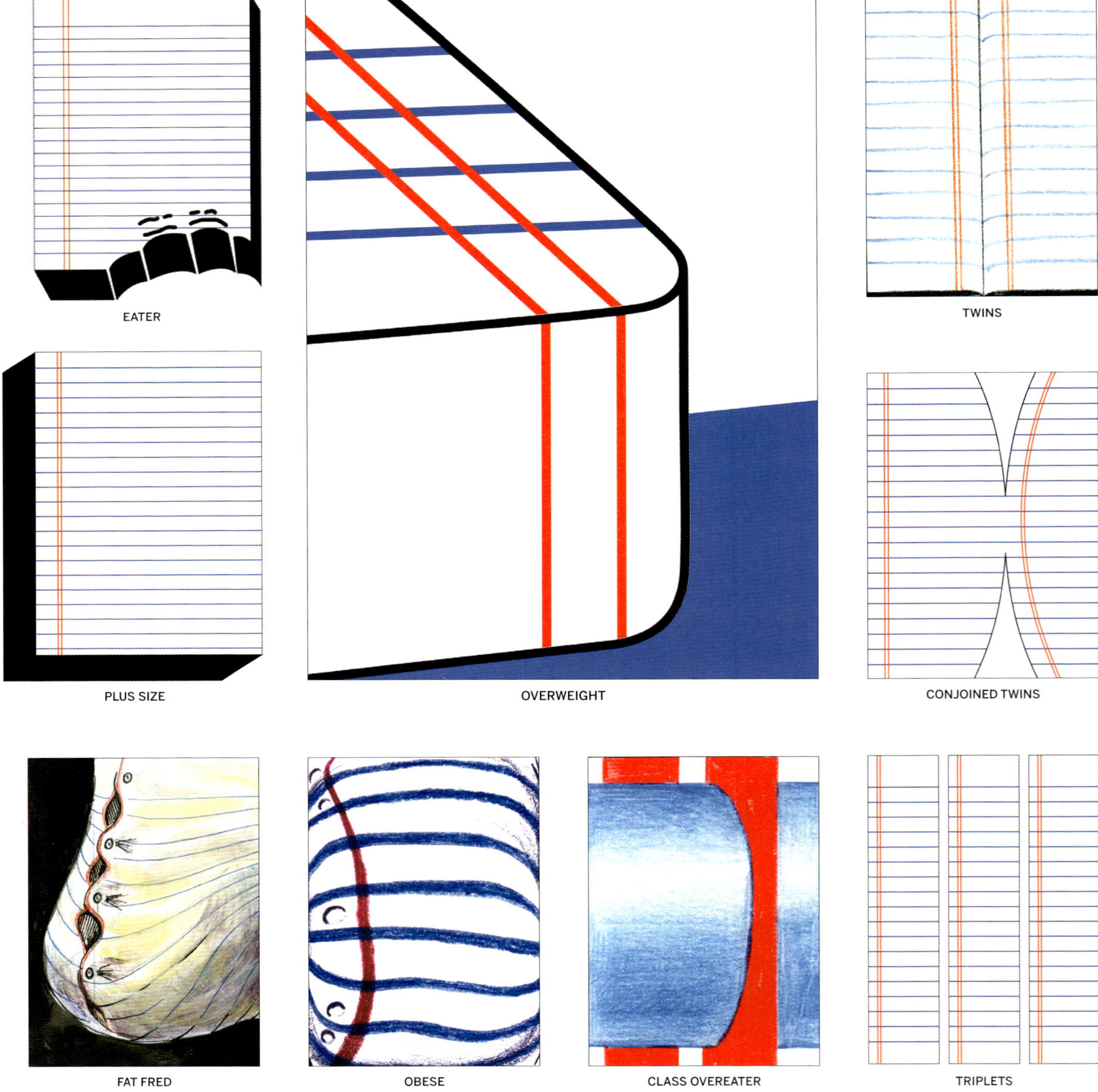

EATER

PLUS SIZE

OVERWEIGHT

TWINS

CONJOINED TWINS

FAT FRED

OBESE

CLASS OVEREATER

TRIPLETS

NOTEBOOK SOLUTIONS:

Obesity and eating disorders are addressed in figures 1 through 6, with literal and inferred solutions to represent being overweight.

Figures 7 through 9 address multiple births.

Figures 10 through 16 represent pupils with an interest in various athletic activities.

Figure 12 is a metaphoric representation of competitiveness, which is synonymous with sports. It depicts the chart used in sporting events to show the process of elimination that results in a champion.

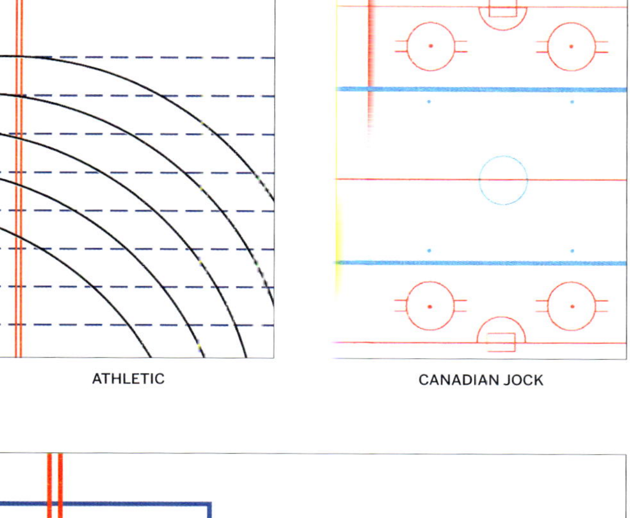

ATHLETIC

CANADIAN JOCK

IN LOVE WITH BASKETBALL

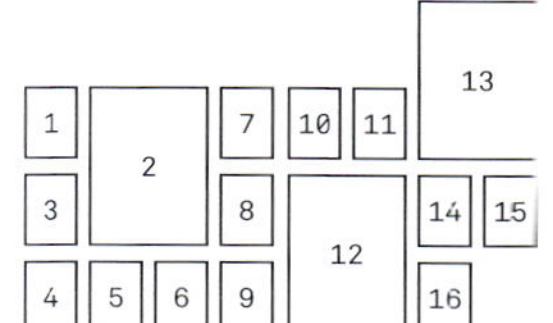

1. *Kate Lee*
2. *Quekjing Cheng*
3. *Yoojung Kang*
4. *John Kuhn*
5. *Daisy Lee*
6. *Yasmin Malki*
7. *Carrie Manson*
8. *Hannah Ahn*
9. *Angela Han*
10. *Yoojin Young*
11. *Kyle Chaille*
12. *Hwayoung Jung*
13. *Jarwon Shin*
14. *Aemin Shim*
15. *Andrew Teoh*
16. *Alyssa Leary*

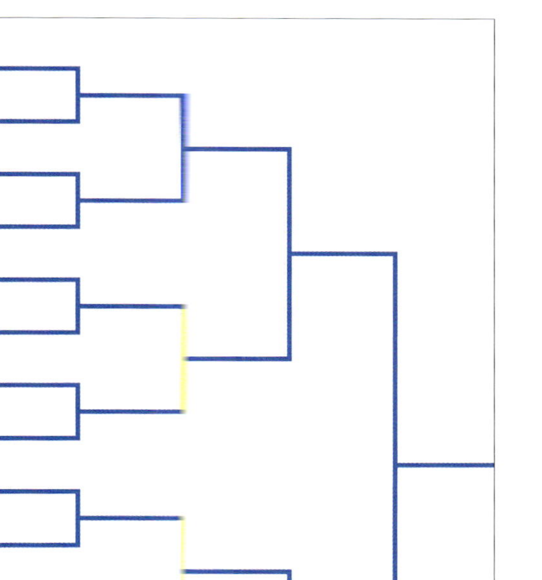

COMPETITIVE

SWIMMER

FUTURE NFL PLAYER

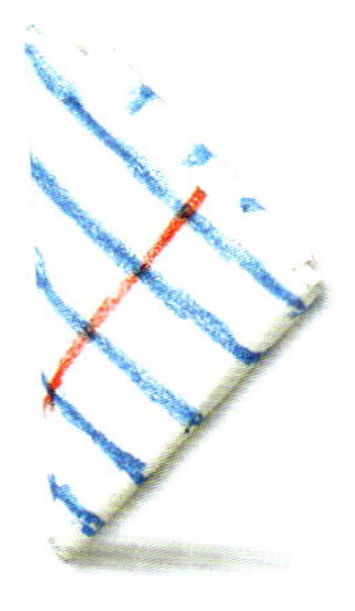

JOCK

Figure 13 shows crumpled notebook paper simulating basketballs, to be played with by tossing them into a wastebasket.

Figure 16 represents a triangular football, created from a folded notebook page, to be used in a game where one student tries to flick the paper football through the "goalposts" of his opponent's fingers.

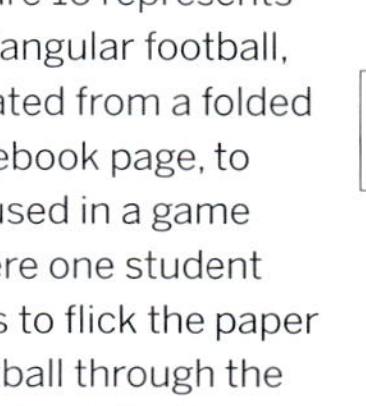

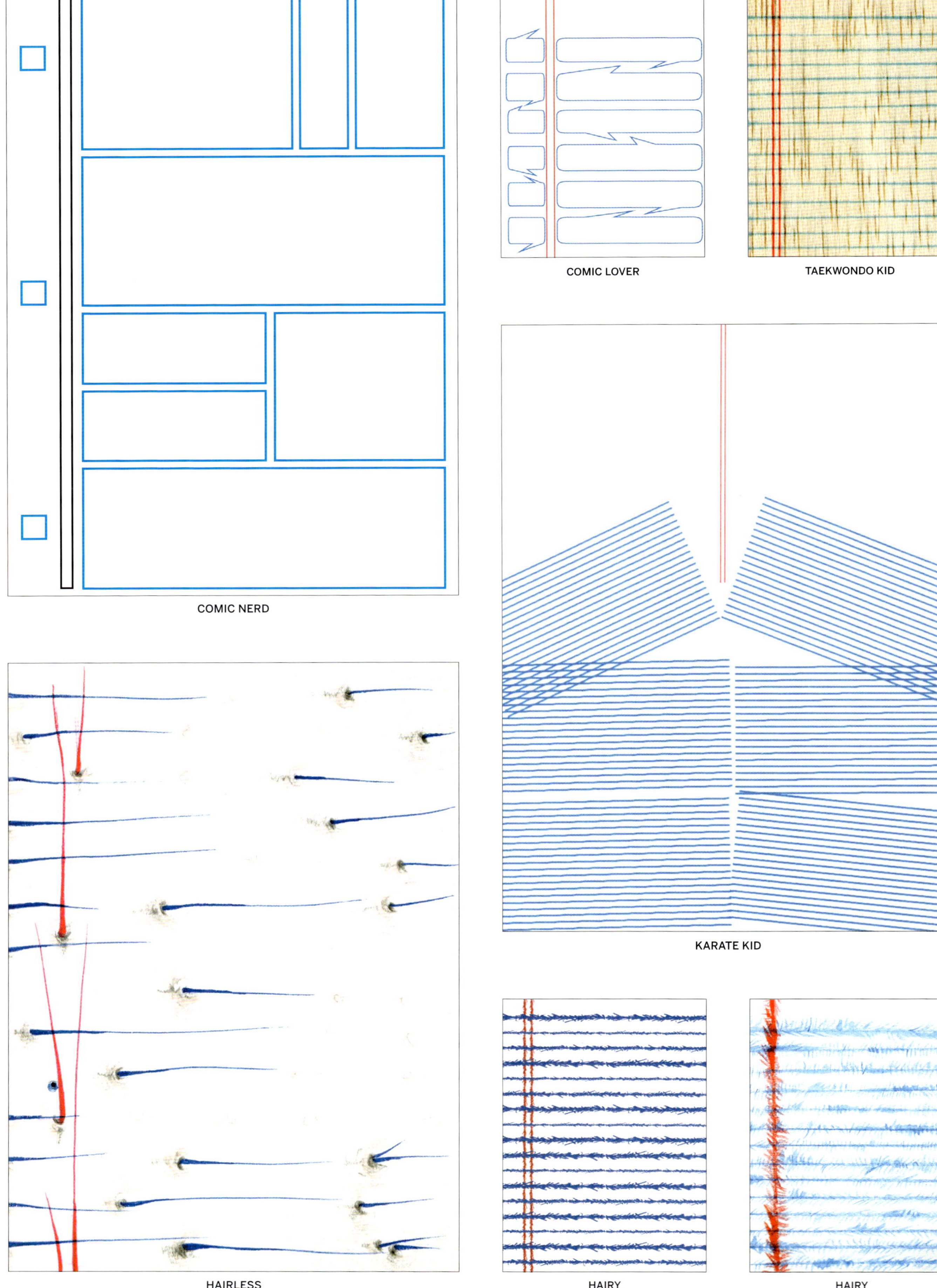

COMIC NERD

COMIC LOVER

TAEKWONDO KID

KARATE KID

HAIRLESS

HAIRY

HAIRY

NOTEBOOK SOLUTIONS:

Figures 1 and 2 denote comic book enthusiasts.

The martial arts are the subject of figures 3 and 4.

Figures 5 through 7 deal with a range of baldness to hairiness.

Figure 8 uses humor in the depiction of a descendant of Moses.

Figures 9 through 12 represent aspects of the most industrious and brilliant students.

The creative faction of future artists is explored in figures 13 through 16.

1. *Louis Rivera*
2. *Daeun Ko*
3. *Hyunji Kim*
4. *Max Kaplun*
5. *Jaewon Park*
6. *Kelly Shami*
7. *Amy Churchwell*
8. *Janghyun Cho*
9. *S. Song*
10. *Yasmin Malki*
11. *Hea Eun Han*
12. *A. Im*
13. *Jihyun Park*
14. *Sarah Macreading*
15. *Samantha Zahabian*
16. *Amanat Dugal*

MOSES' DESCENDANT

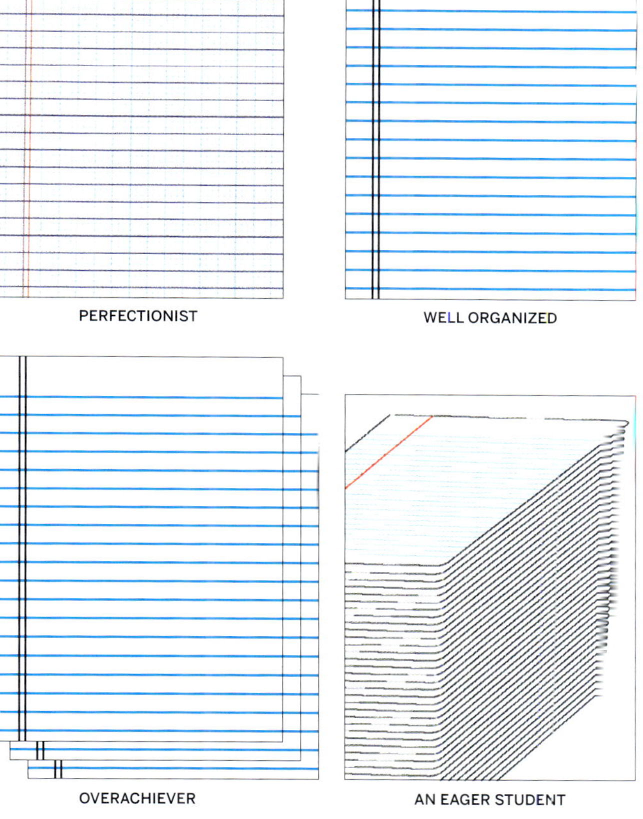

PERFECTIONIST

WELL ORGANIZED

OVERACHIEVER

AN EAGER STUDENT

ARTIST

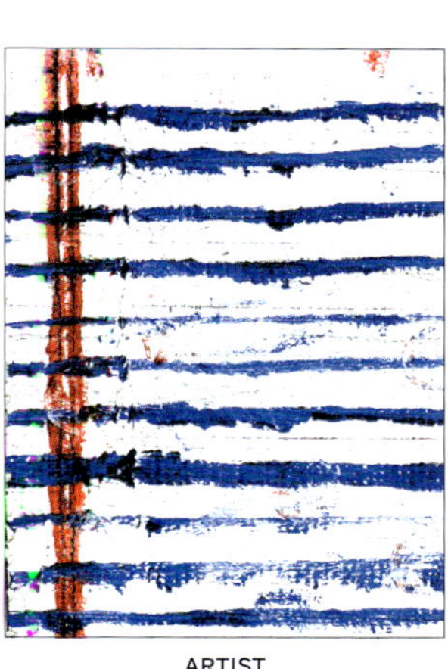

ARTIST

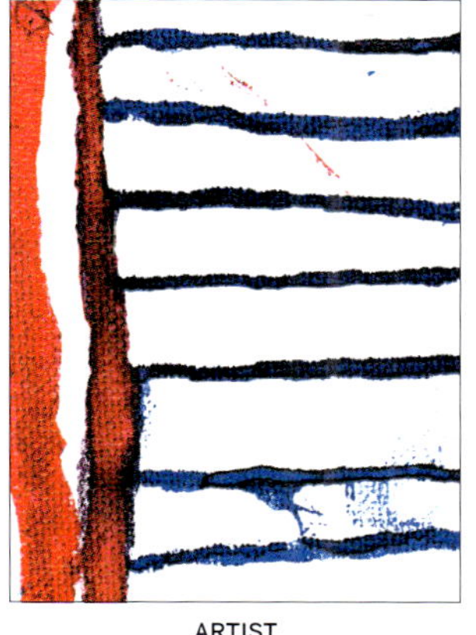

ARTIST

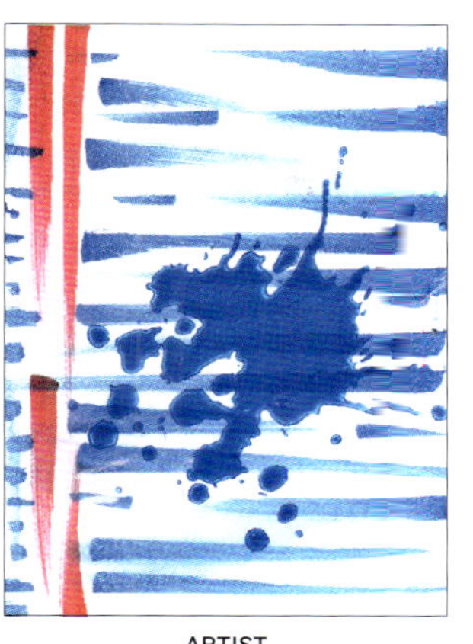

ARTIST

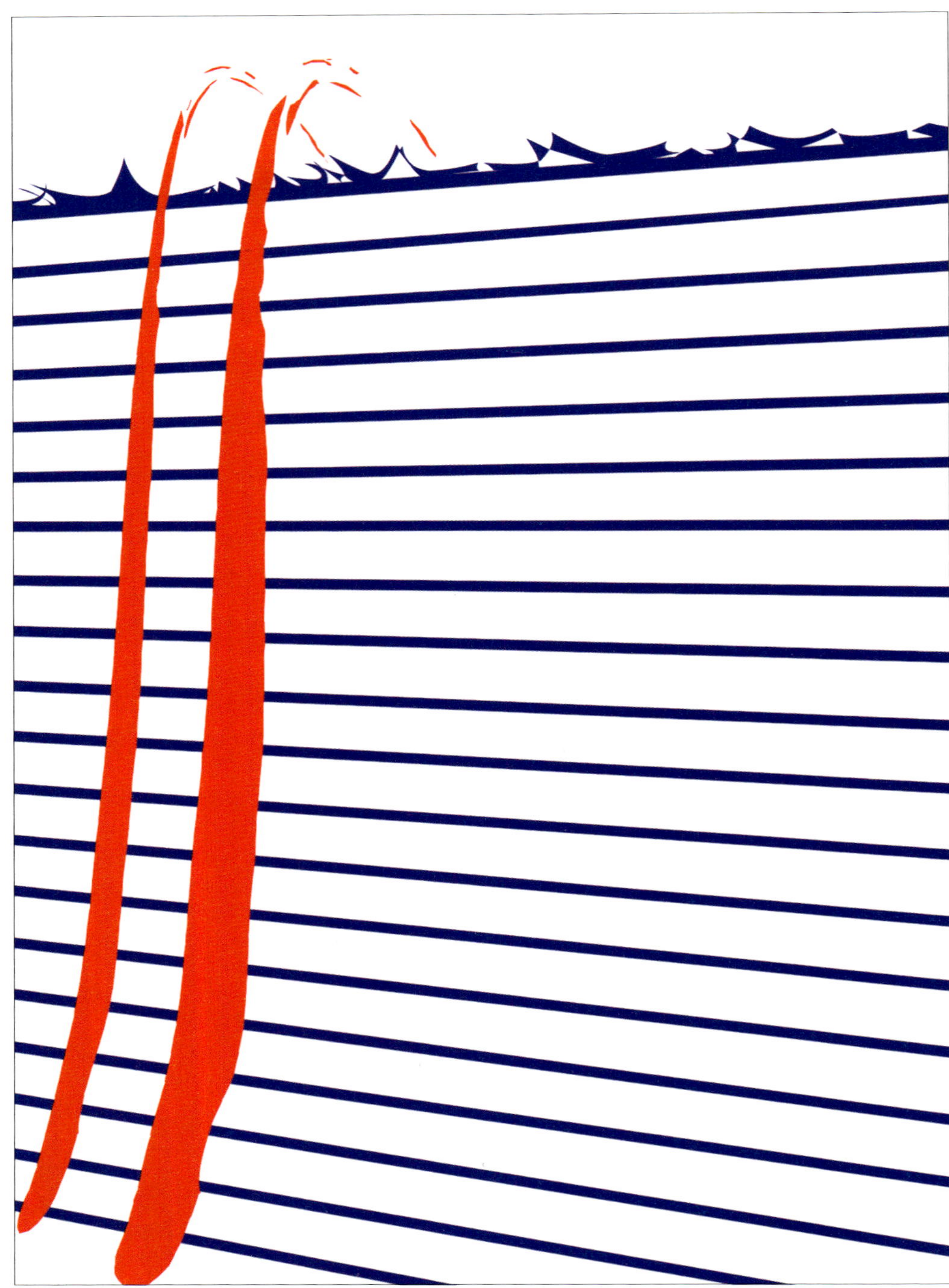

ILLEGAL IMMIGRANT

NOTEBOOK SOLUTIONS:

Figure 1 deals with the issue of immigration, while figures 2 through 4 are New York City related subjects.

Figure 4 depicts a portion of a New York City map that addresses the fact that Broadway runs through the city on a diagonal.

Figures 5 through 7 are various subjects that have incorporated the color black either as part of a notebook page, or as a background to dramatize the concepts.

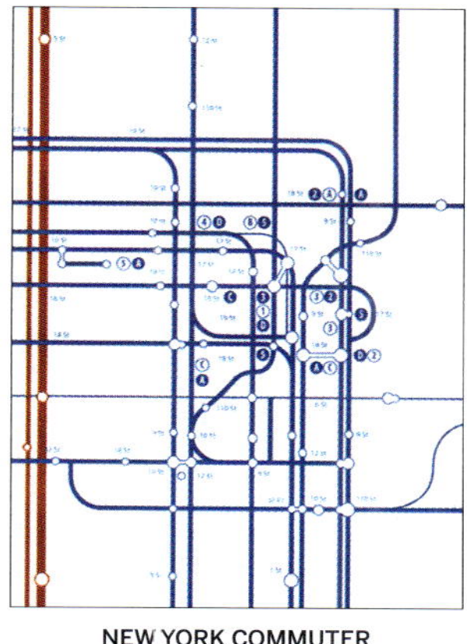

NEW YORK COMMUTER

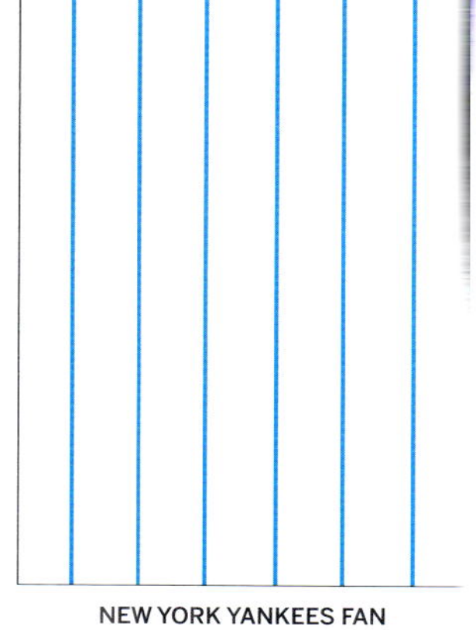

NEW YORK YANKEES FAN

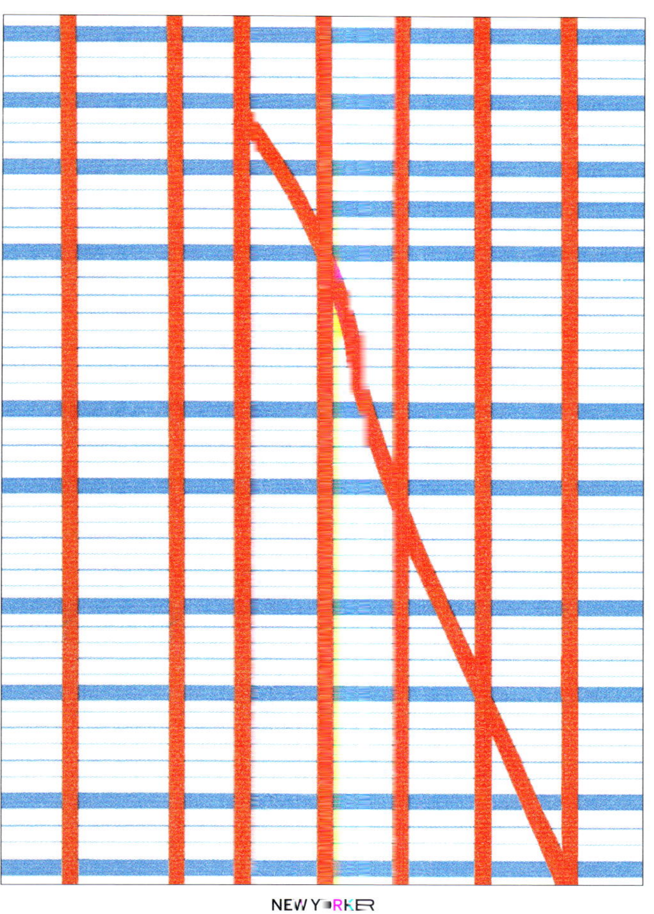

NEW YORKER

HYPOCRITICAL

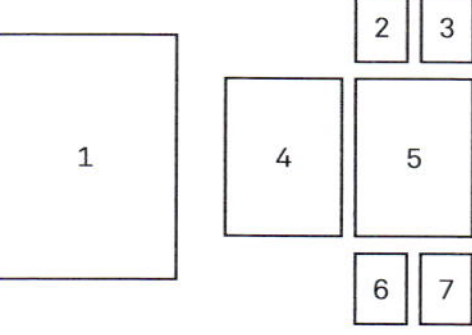

1. *Nolan Constantino*
2. *Liron Ashkenazi*
3. *Jiwon Kim*
4. *Kyle Chaille*
5. *King Chun Wong*
6. *Kelly Shami*
7. *Daisy Roberts*

TECH SAVVY

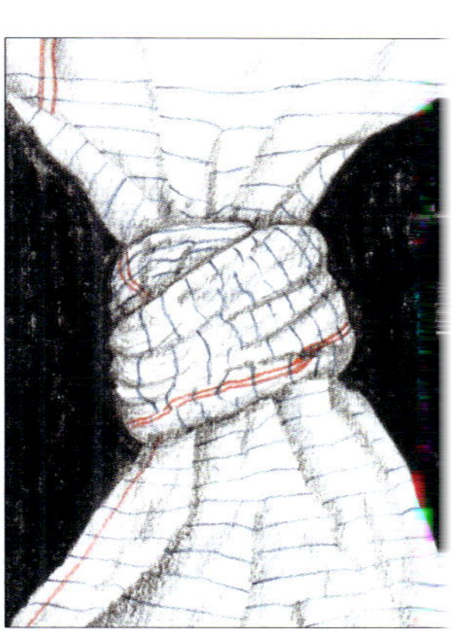

FRUSTRATED

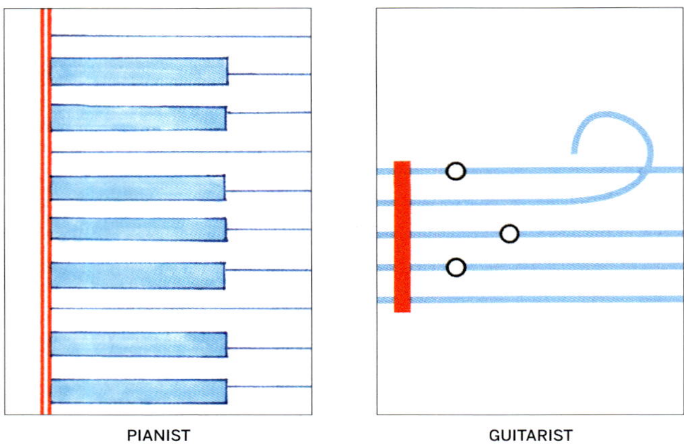

PIANIST

GUITARIST

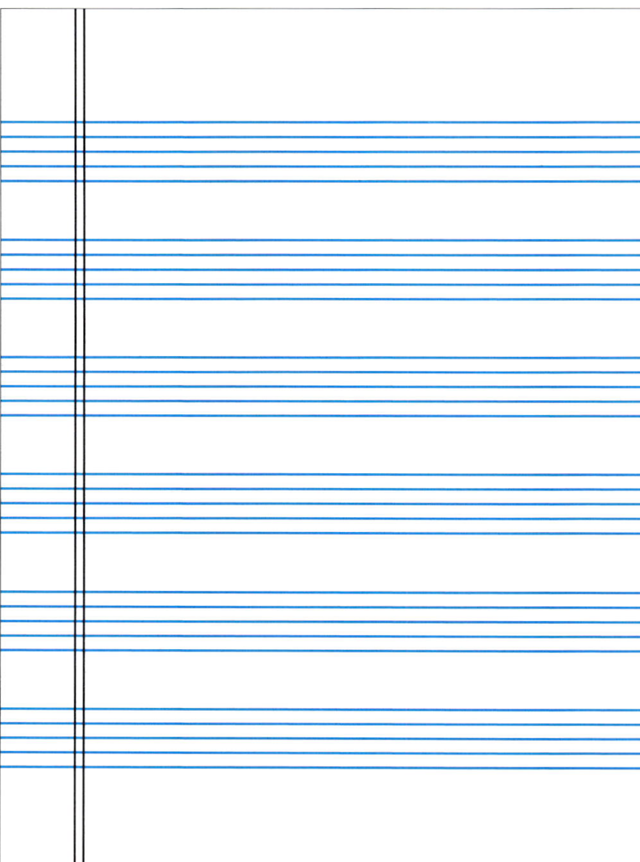

FUTURE COMPOSER

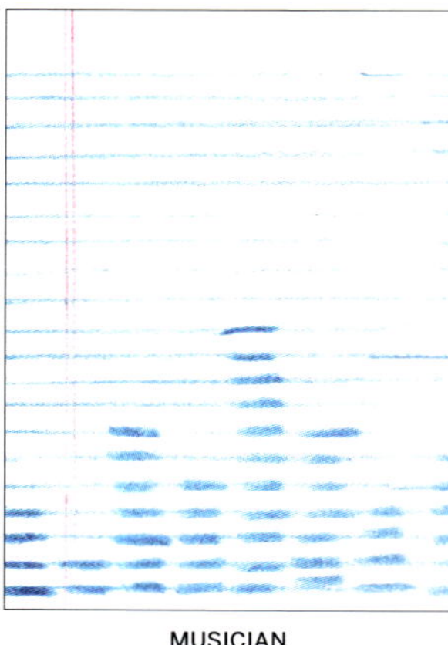

MUSICIAN

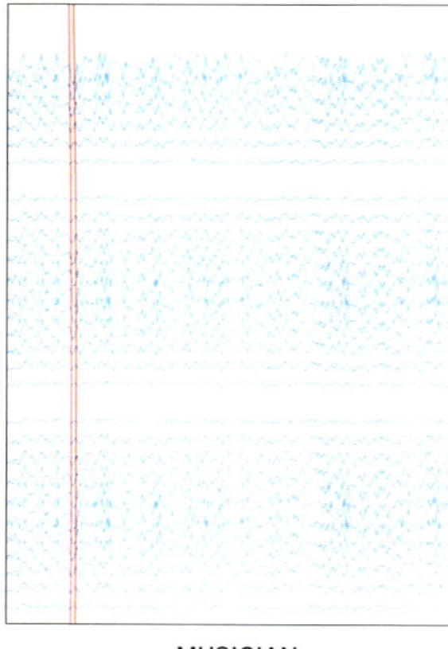

MUSICIAN

NOTEBOOK SOLUTIONS:

Figures 1 through 5 concern themselves with pupils who have an affinity toward music, ranging from clear narratives to minimalistic executions.

Figures 6 through 18 depict the future professions of students.

FUTURE ILLUSIONIST

FUTURE ESCAPE ARTIST

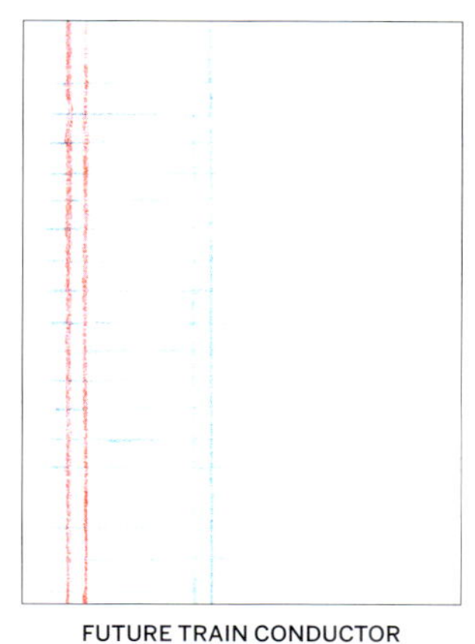

FUTURE TRAIN CONDUCTOR

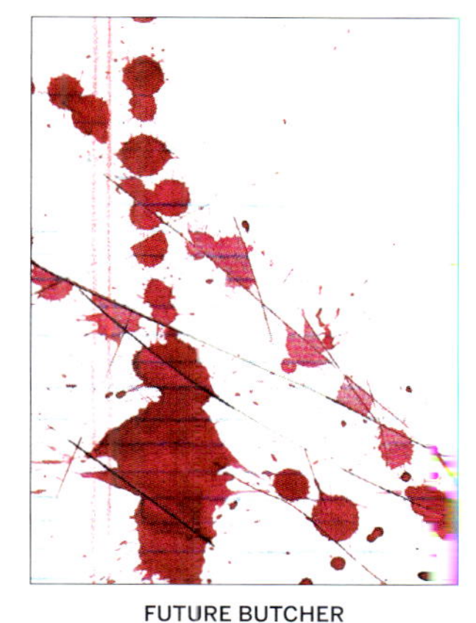

FUTURE BUTCHER

FUTURE TAILOR

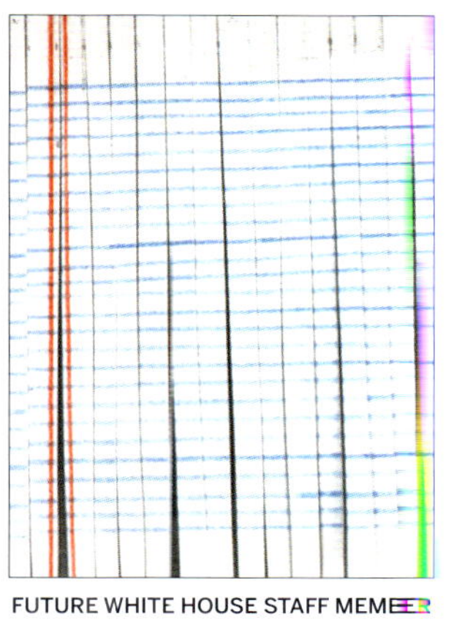

FUTURE WHITE HOUSE STAFF MEMBER

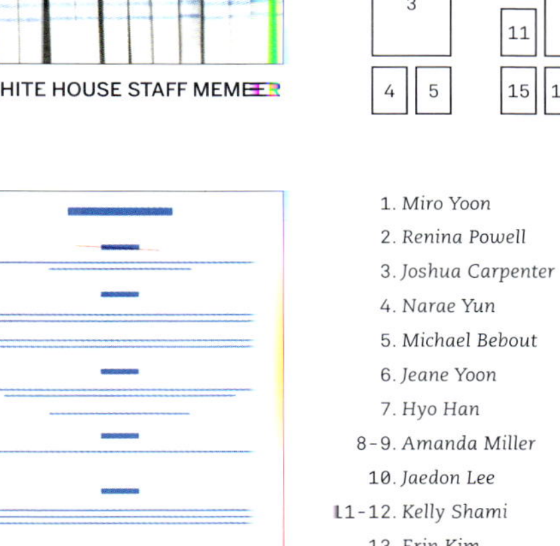

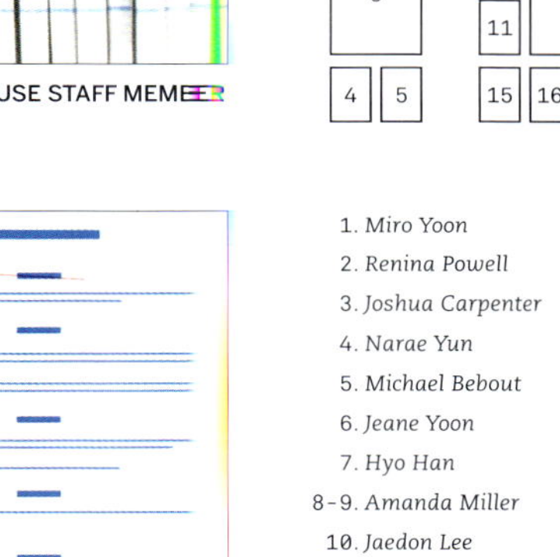

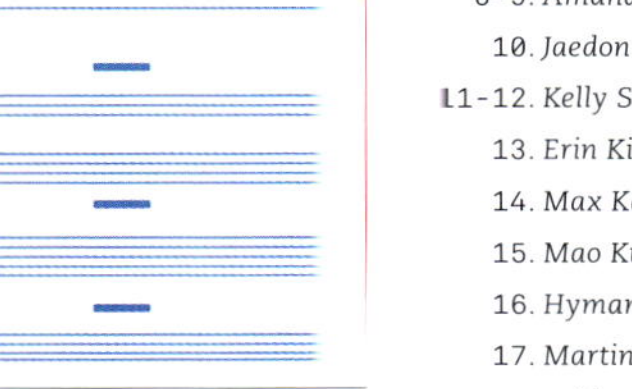

FUTURE ENVIRONMENTALIST

FUTURE ARCHITECT

FUTURE ACTOR

1. Miro Yoon
2. Renina Powell
3. Joshua Carpenter
4. Narae Yun
5. Michael Bebout
6. Jeane Yoon
7. Hyo Han
8–9. Amanda Miller
10. Jaedon Lee
11–12. Kelly Shami
13. Erin Kim
14. Max Kaplun
15. Mao Kudo
16. Hyman Richter
17. Martin Gross
18. Michael Zucker

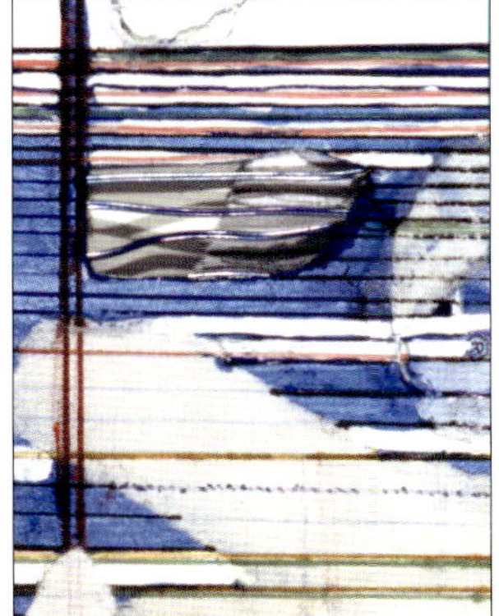

FUTURE ABSTRACT ARTIST

FUTURE GEORGIA O' KEEFFE

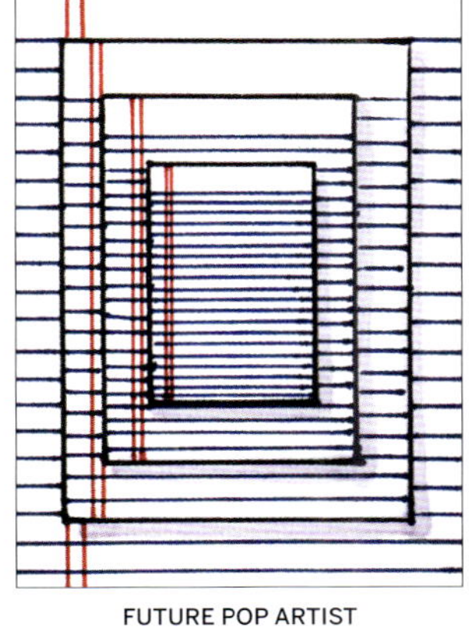

FUTURE POP ARTIST

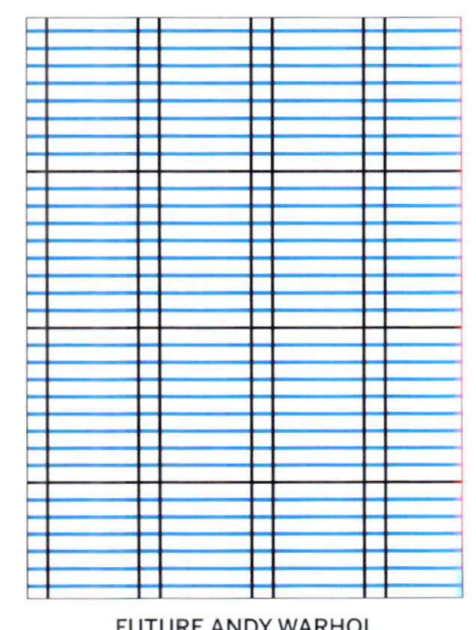

FUTURE ANDY WARHOL

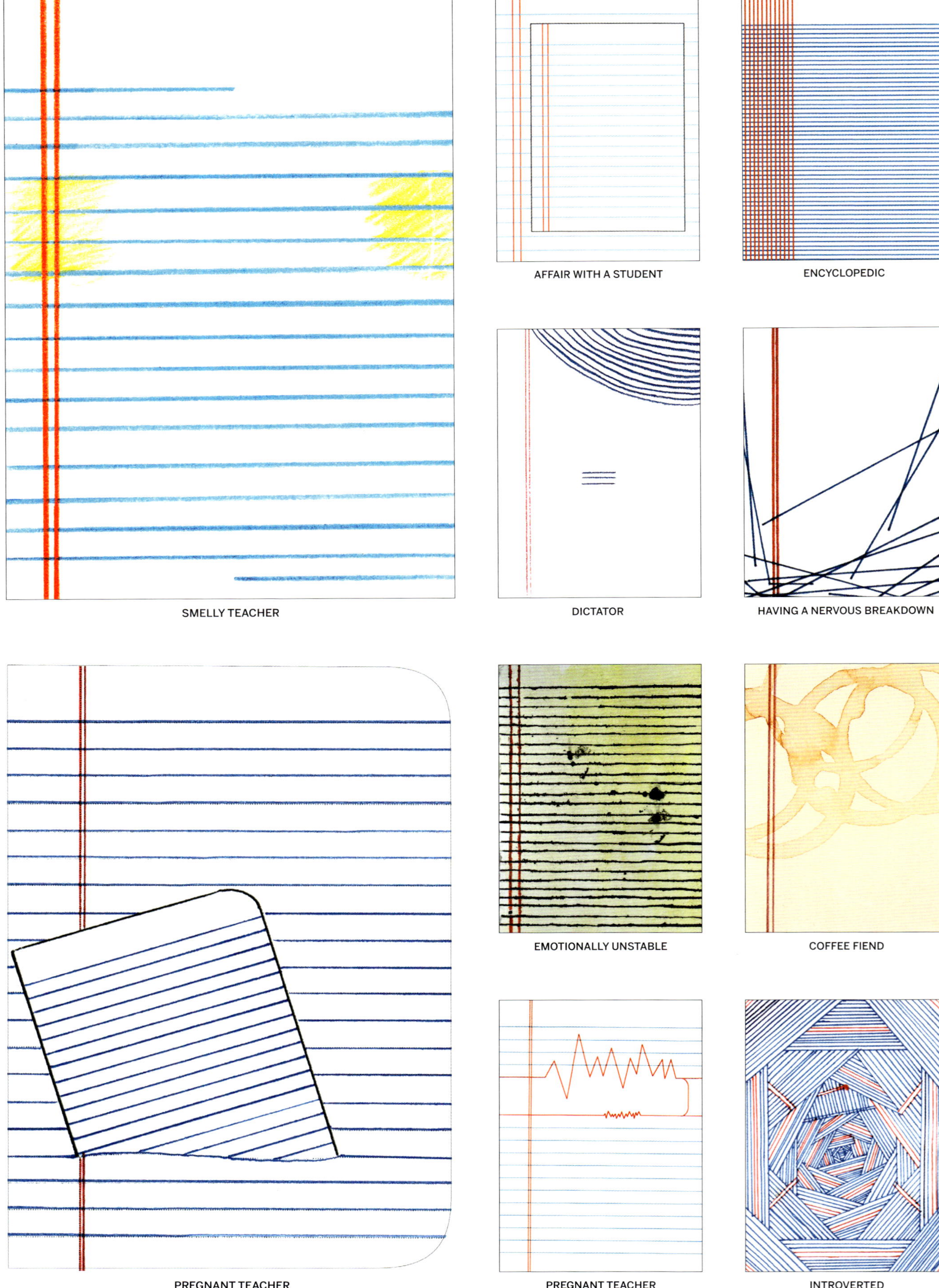
SMELLY TEACHER

AFFAIR WITH A STUDENT

ENCYCLOPEDIC

DICTATOR

HAVING A NERVOUS BREAKDOWN

PREGNANT TEACHER

EMOTIONALLY UNSTABLE

COFFEE FIEND

PREGNANT TEACHER

INTROVERTED

NOTEBOOK SOLUTIONS:

At the top of the printed notebook assignment sheet is a larger rectangle that represents the teacher.

Figures 1 through 10 are depictions of elementary school teachers exhibiting physical, emotional and intellectual characteristics that as a grouping makes a social statement as to how teachers are perceived.

Random subjects are depicted in figures 11 through 19.

Figures 14 and 15, Eco Friendly and Homeless, use cardboard as both a medium and a ground to execute two very different ideas.

CLASS BULLY

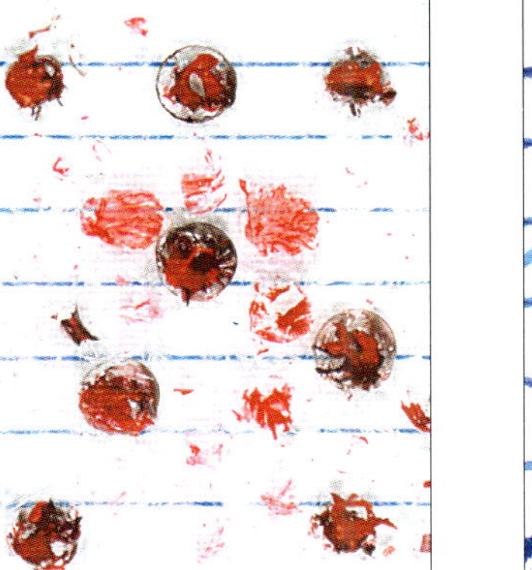

BAD CASE OF ACNE

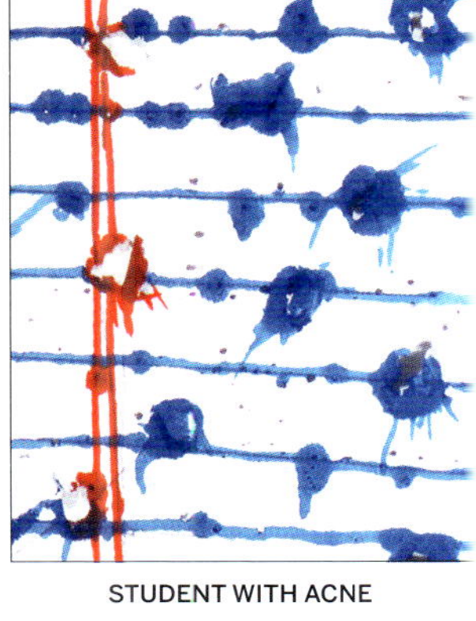

STUDENT WITH ACNE

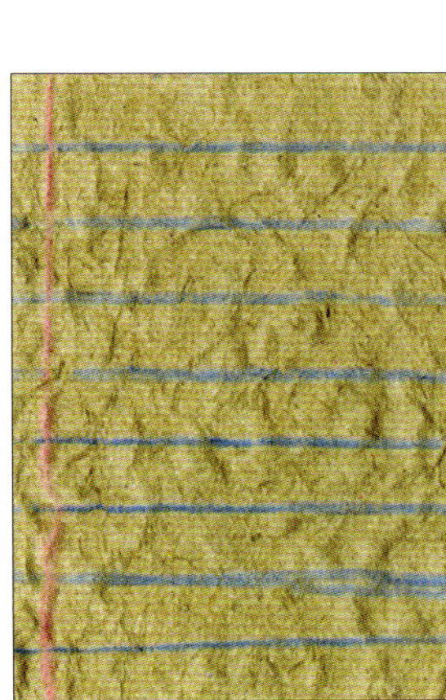

ECO FRIENDLY

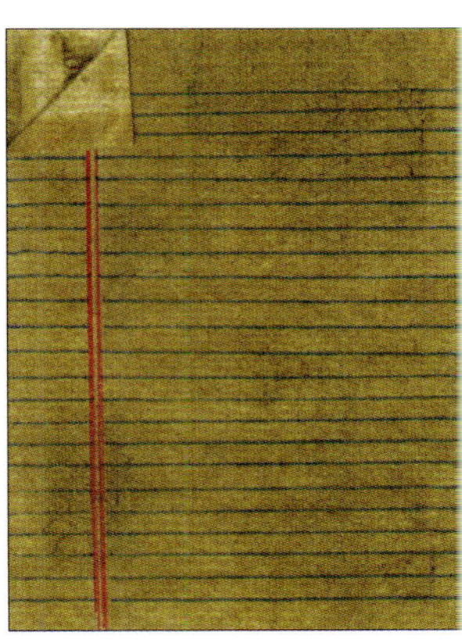

HOMELESS

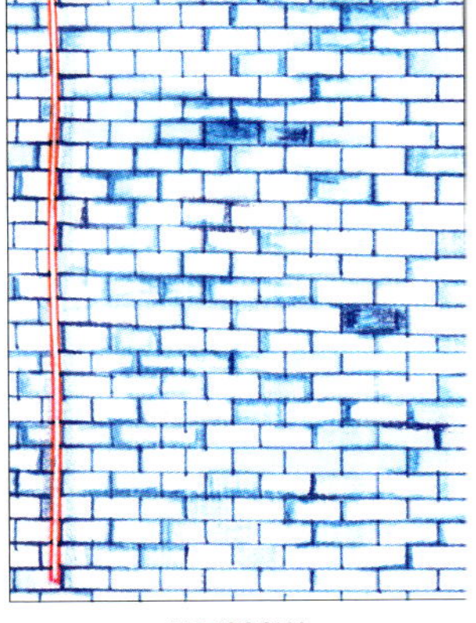

ANTISOCIAL

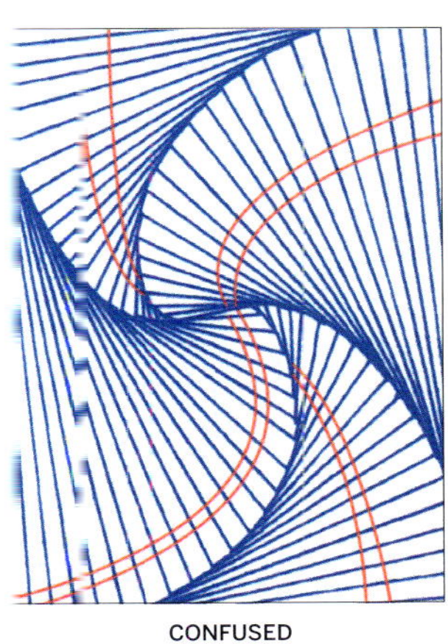

CONFUSED

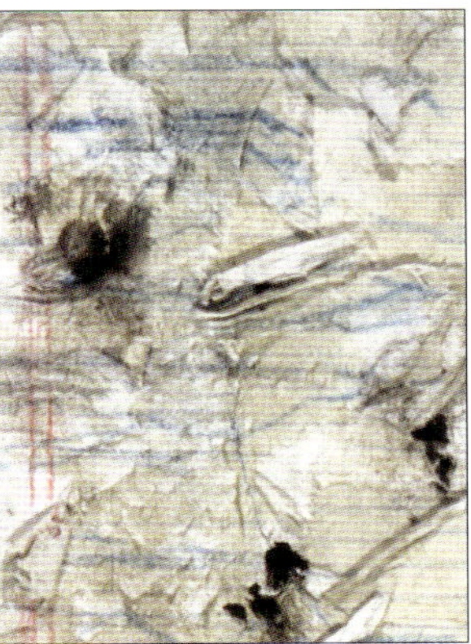

IRRITATED

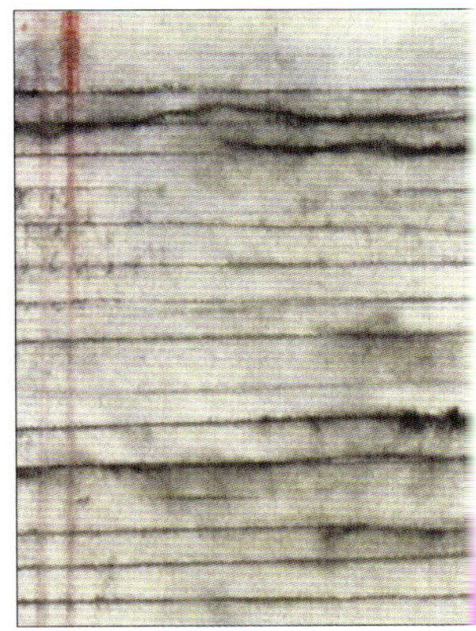

DEPRESSED

1	2	3	11	12	13
	4	5		14	15
6	7	8	16	17	18	19
	9	10			

1. *Joseph Cofone*
2. *Jasmin Valcourt*
3. *Joyce Chen*
4. *Paul Devejian*
5. *Toby Fox*
6. *Miry Shin*
7. *Andrew Colletie*
8. *Lisa Rosel*
9. *King Chun Wong*
10. *Namhee Kim*
11. *Nami Mo*
12. *Heejin Sang*
13. *Shiyeon Kim*
14. *Marie Graboso*

15–16. *Namhee Kim*

17. *Stephen Cho*

18–19. *Mao Kudo*

Figures 18 and 19 for the most part have obliterated the red and blue lines of the notebook page and primarily used values of gray to exaggerate the negative aspects of their subjects.

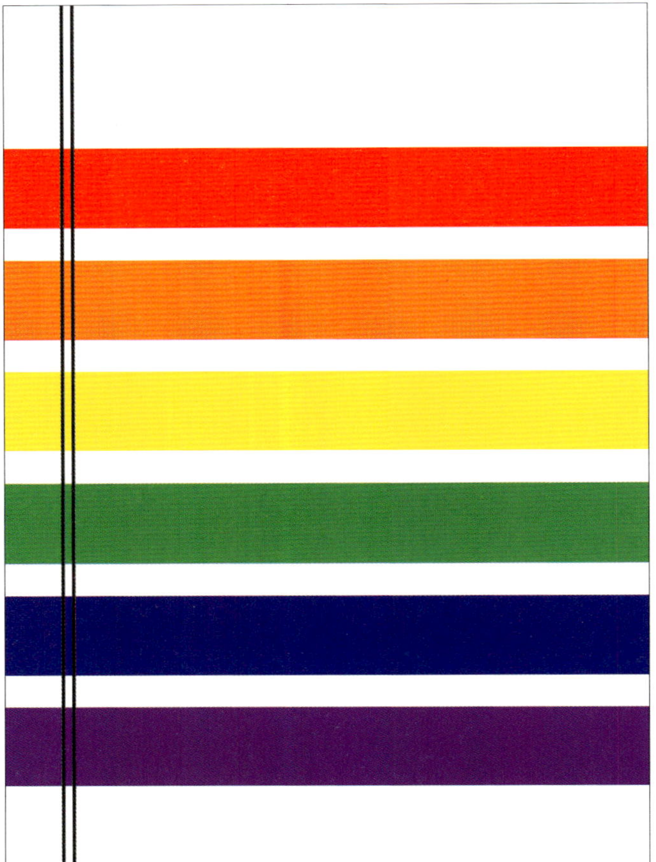
OPENLY GAY

CLOSET GAY

NOTEBOOK SOLUTIONS:

Figures 1 and 2 deal with sexual orientation, while figures 3 and 4 deal with political preferences.

Figures 5 through 14 depict personality opposites and class lovers.

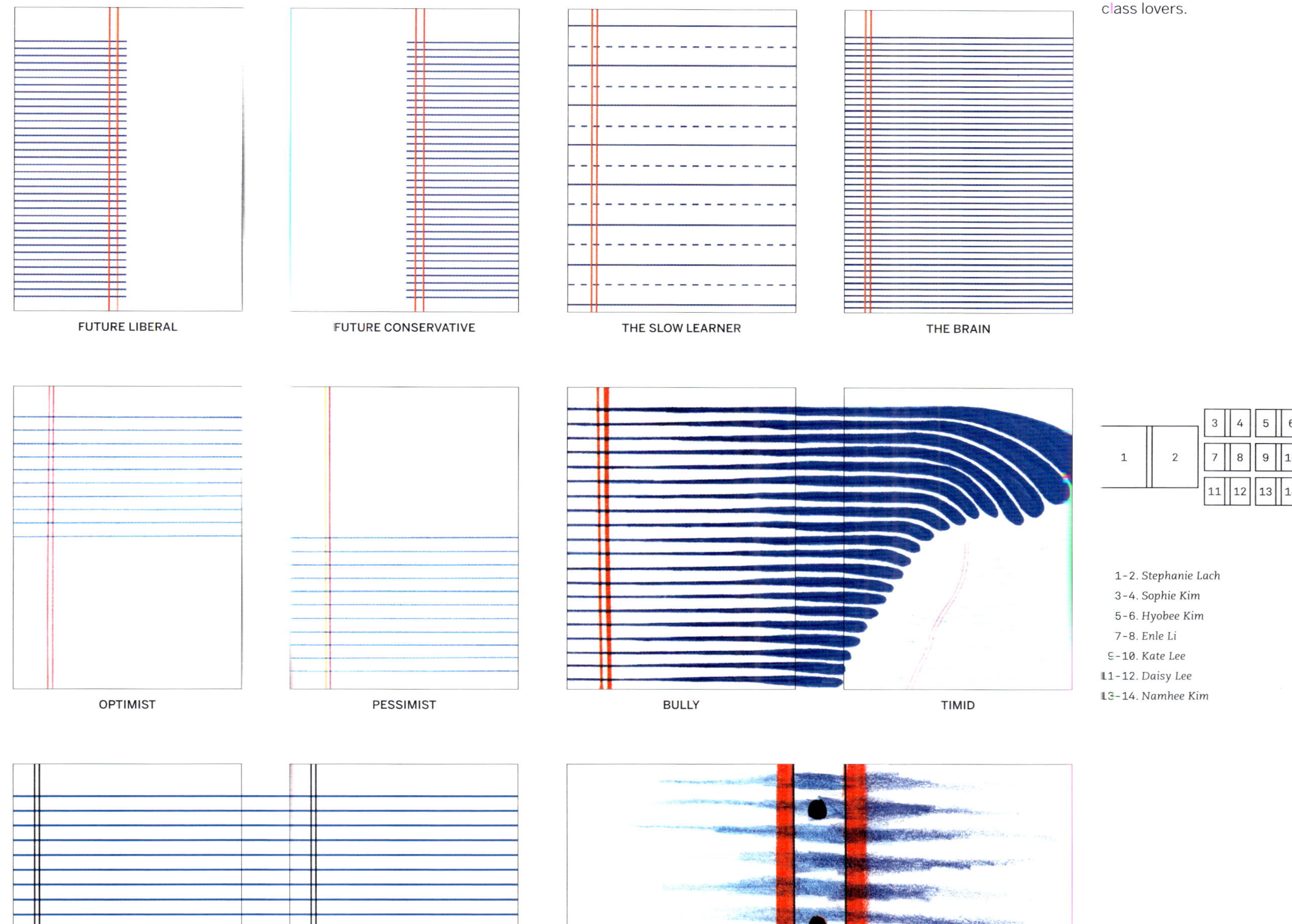

FUTURE LIBERAL

FUTURE CONSERVATIVE

THE SLOW LEARNER

THE BRAIN

OPTIMIST

PESSIMIST

BULLY

TIMID

1–2. Stephanie Lach
3–4. Sophie Kim
5–6. Hyobee Kim
7–8. Enle Li
9–10. Kate Lee
11–12. Daisy Lee
13–14. Namhee Kim

CLASS LOVERS

CLASS LOVERS

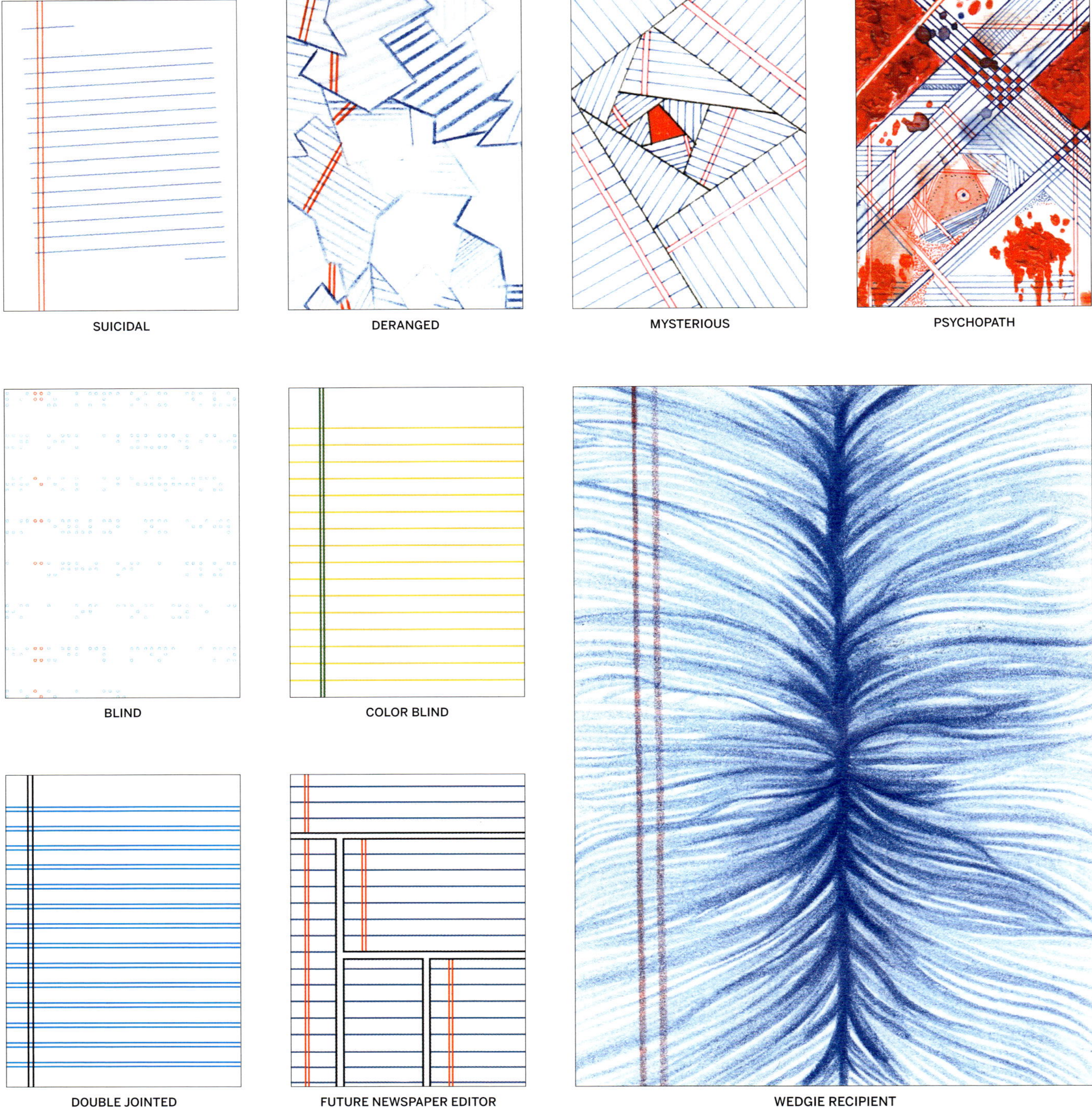

SUICIDAL

DERANGED

MYSTERIOUS

PSYCHOPATH

BLIND

COLOR BLIND

DOUBLE JOINTED

FUTURE NEWSPAPER EDITOR

WEDGIE RECIPIENT

IMPATIENT KID

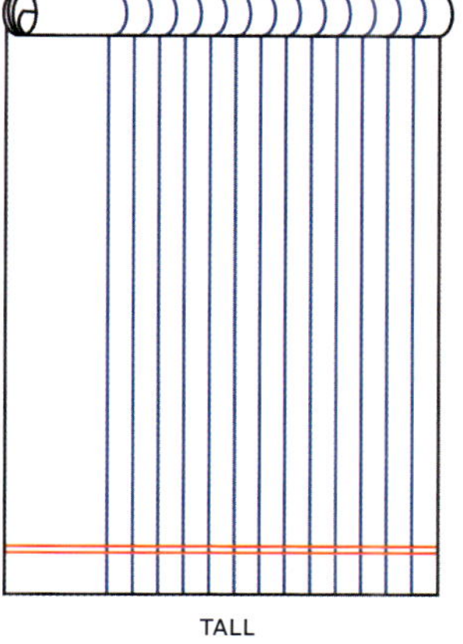
TALL

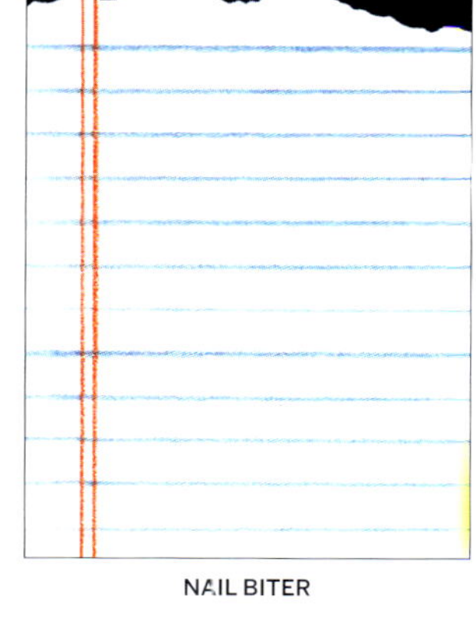
NAIL BITER

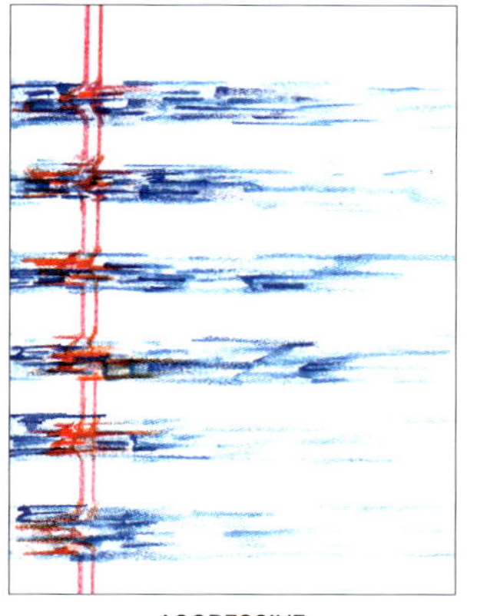
AGGRESSIVE

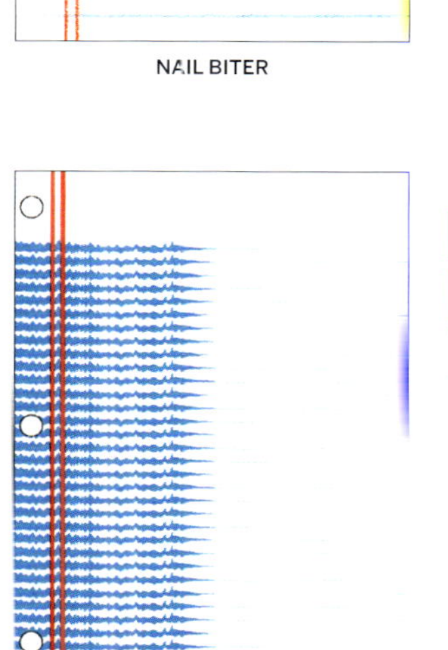

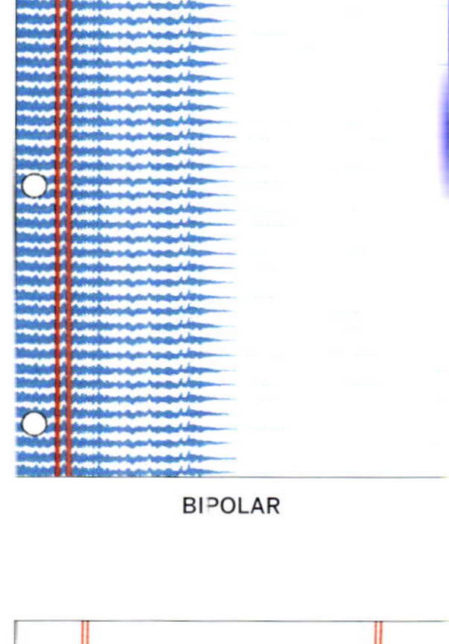
BIPOLAR

LEFT-HANDED

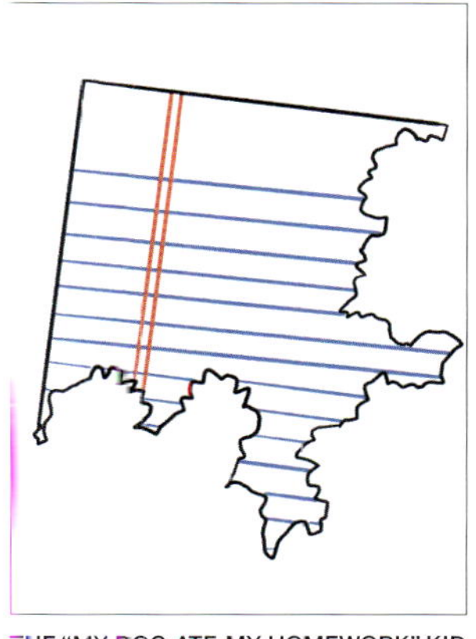
THE "MY-DOG-ATE-MY-HOMEWORK" KID

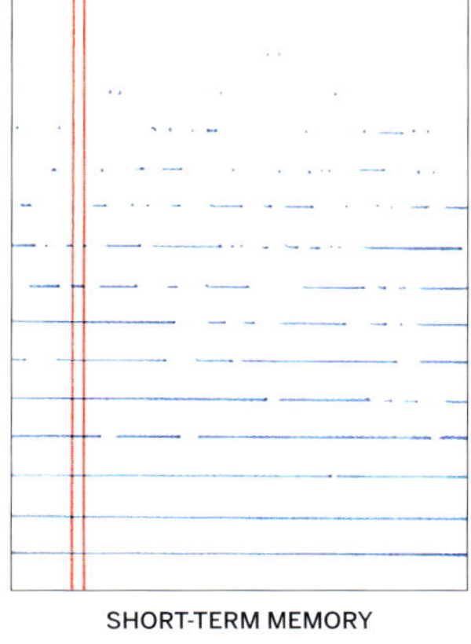
SHORT-TERM MEMORY

AMBIDEXTROUS

NOTEBOOK SOLUTIONS:

Figures 1 through 18 represent various traits of grade-school children. It should be noted that most of these solutions, as well as many others shown in this chapter, address adult behavior. These solutions point to the fact that childhood offers a clear indication of and lays the foundation for all the habits, traits, and inclinations that will define one's adult personality.

Figures 3 and 4 use overlapping forms that diminish in size, alluding to an inner journey. Yet, while one solution points to intrigue, the other expresses a disturbing disorder.

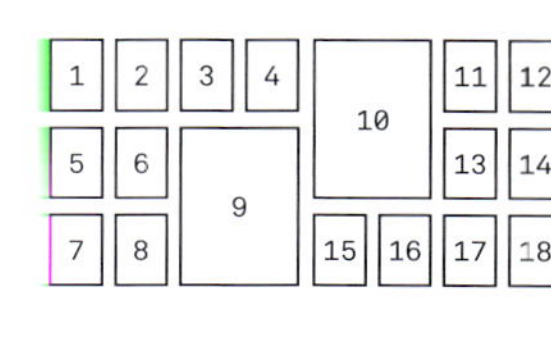

1. *Nova Pan*
2. *Michael Wang*
3. *Enle Li*
4. *Namhee Kim*
5. *A. Im*
6. *Andreina Carrillo*
7. *Namhee Kim*
8. *Hwayoung Jung*
9. *Tal Shub*
10. *Christopher Cohen*
11. *Daseul Ahn*
12. *Yoojung Kang*
13. *Nami Mo*
14. *Minhee Choi*
15. *Minhee Choi*
16. *Rebecca Lim*
17. *Hwayoung Jung*
18. *Haein Kim*

Figure 15 depicts an issue that left-handed students face in having a tendency to smear their writing.

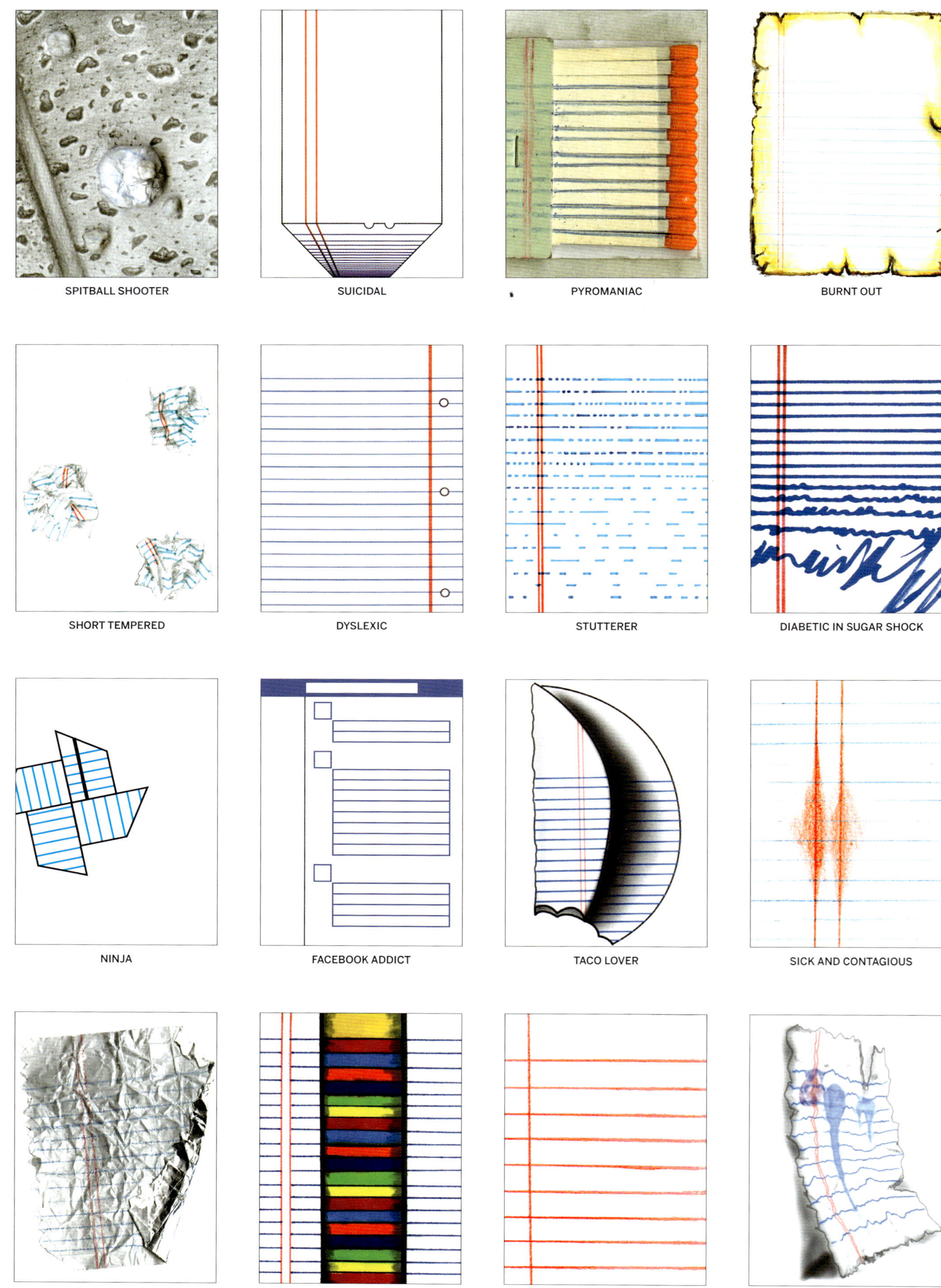

SPITBALL SHOOTER

SUICIDAL

PYROMANIAC

BURNT OUT

SHORT TEMPERED

DYSLEXIC

STUTTERER

DIABETIC IN SUGAR SHOCK

NINJA

FACEBOOK ADDICT

TACO LOVER

SICK AND CONTAGIOUS

THE GUM CHEWER

CLOSETED GAY

REPUBLICAN

CRY BABY

NOTEBOOK SOLUTIONS:

Figures 1 through 26 represent a variety of characteristics through media including colored pencil, crayon, pen and ink, fabric, and computer-generated imagery.

Figures 17 through 22 are emotionally driven interpretations.

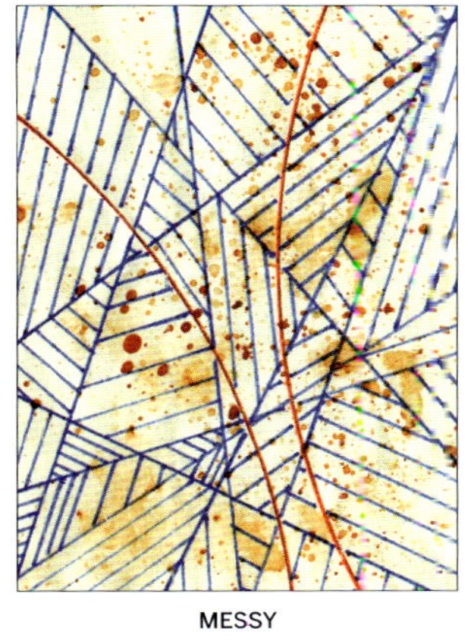

MESSY

SMELLIEST

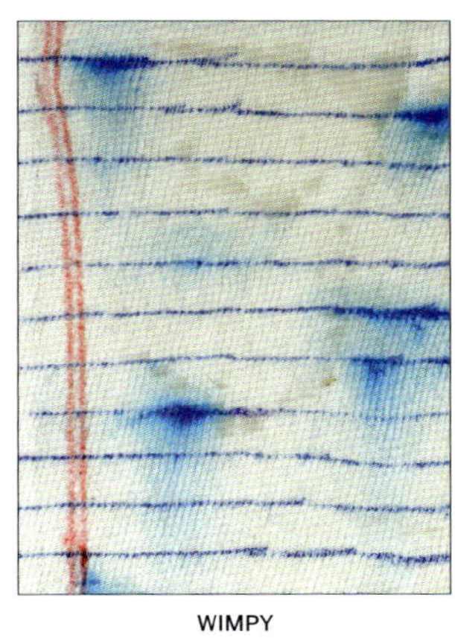

WIMPY

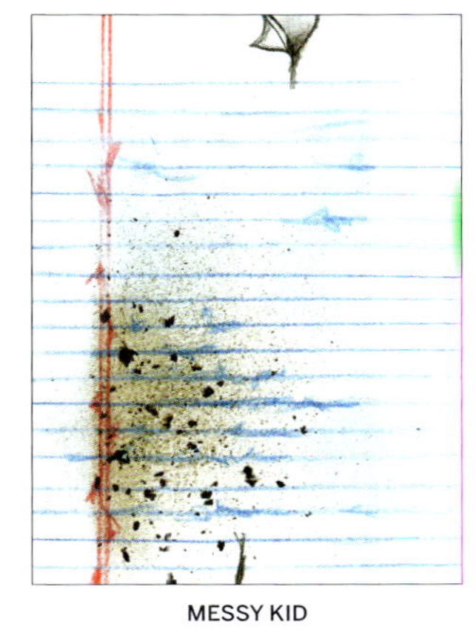

MESSY KID

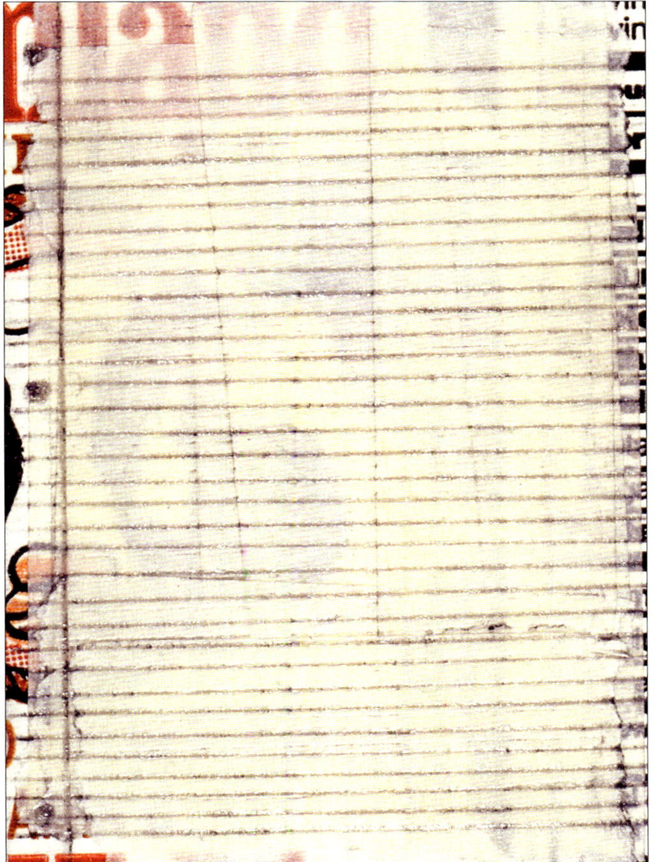

EARTHY

WILD

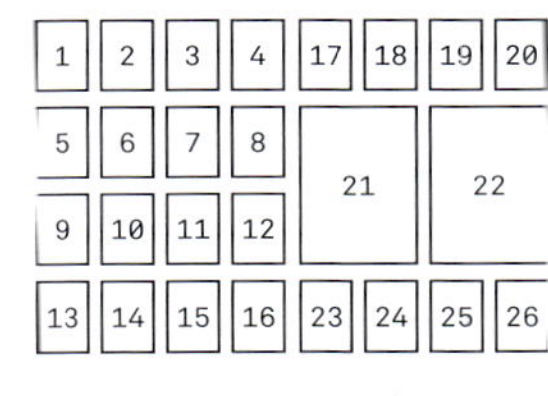

1. Alison Eng
2. Sangwook Kim
3. Ashley Soliman
4. Chris Givoelle
5. Danielle Lee
6. Jeannie Park
7. Yoojin Young
8. Daisy Roberts
9. Yookyung Hwang
10. Dalhae Lee
11. Stephen Cho
12. Maya Kaplun
13. Ashley Soliman
14. Brianna DiFelice
15. Brian Anderson
16. Stephen Cho
17. Catherine Small
18. Seola Jo
19. Camilo De Galofre
20. Trudy Chinwing
21. Carla Martinez
22. Myung Song
23. Jeannie Hong
24. Hyejin Yoon
25. Sungjune Park
26. Miro Yoon

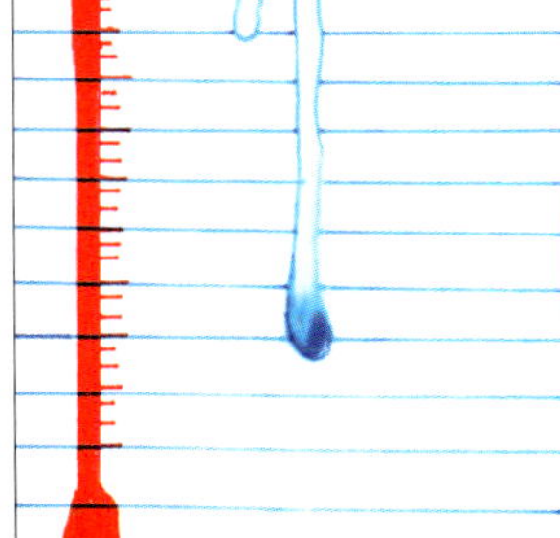

RUNNING NOSE

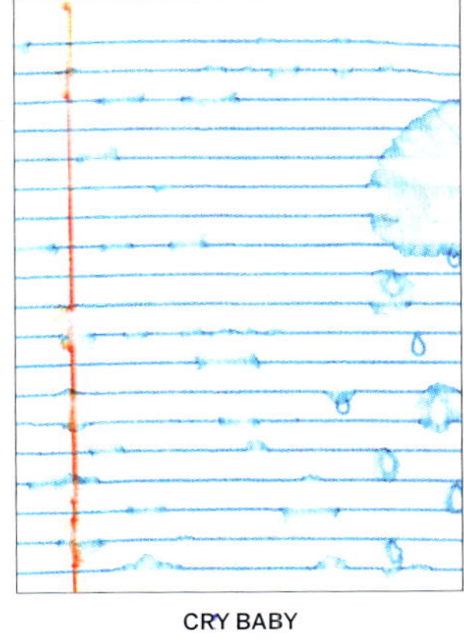

CRY BABY

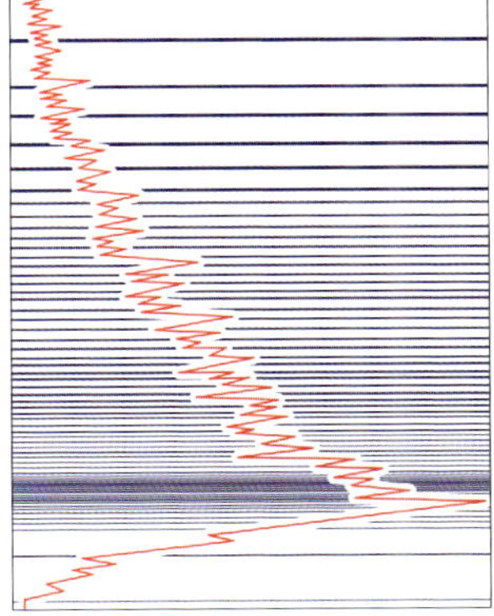

STUDENT HAVING AN ORGASM

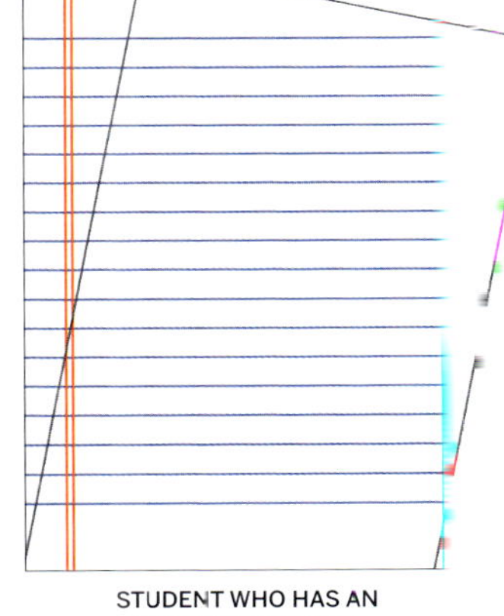

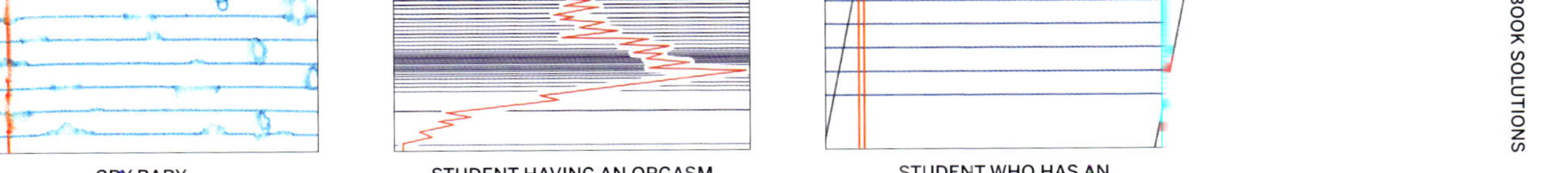

STUDENT WHO HAS AN IMAGINARY FRIEND

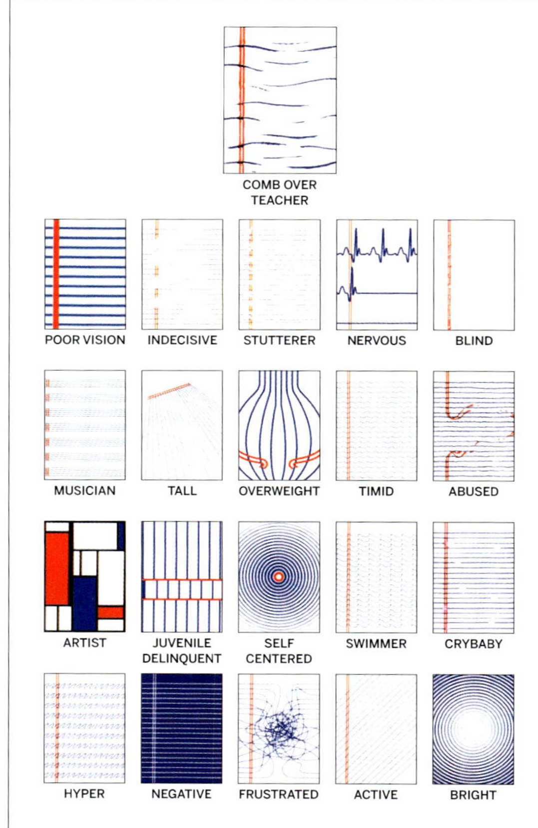
COMB OVER TEACHER
POOR VISION
INDECISIVE
STUTTERER
NERVOUS
BLIND
MUSICIAN
TALL
OVERWEIGHT
TIMID
ABUSED
ARTIST
JUVENILE DELINQUENT
SELF CENTERED
SWIMMER
CRYBABY
HYPER
NEGATIVE
FRUSTRATED
ACTIVE
BRIGHT

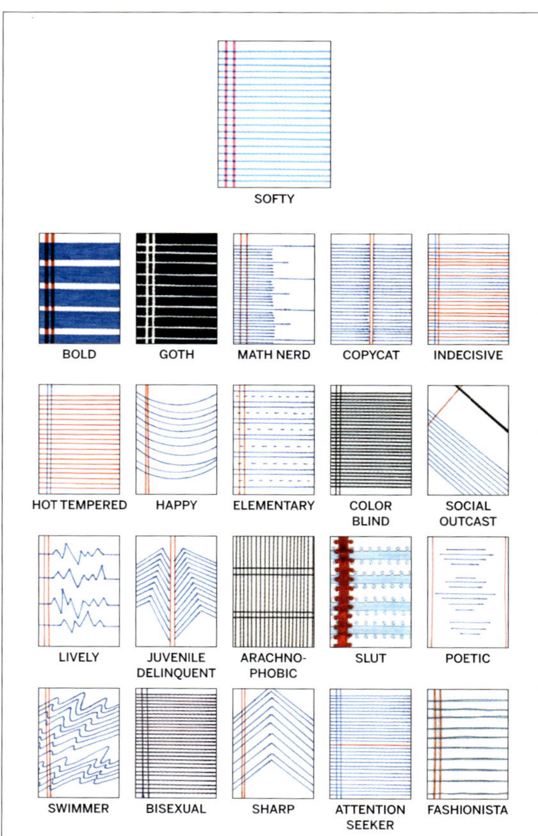
SOFTY
BOLD
GOTH
MATH NERD
COPYCAT
INDECISIVE
HOT TEMPERED
HAPPY
ELEMENTARY
COLOR BLIND
SOCIAL OUTCAST
LIVELY
JUVENILE DELINQUENT
ARACHNO-PHOBIC
SLUT
POETIC
SWIMMER
BISEXUAL
SHARP
ATTENTION SEEKER
FASHIONISTA

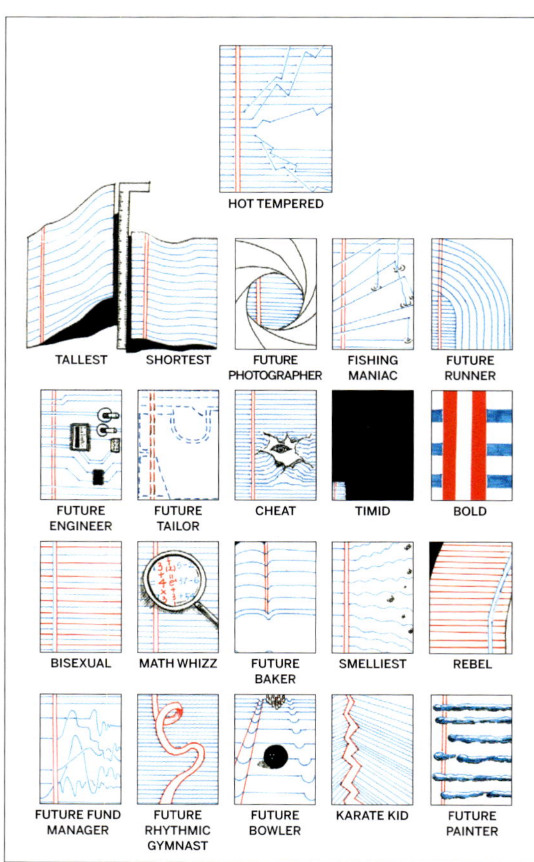
HOT TEMPERED
TALLEST
SHORTEST
FUTURE PHOTOGRAPHER
FISHING MANIAC
FUTURE RUNNER
FUTURE ENGINEER
FUTURE TAILOR
CHEAT
TIMID
BOLD
BISEXUAL
MATH WHIZZ
FUTURE BAKER
SMELLIEST
REBEL
FUTURE FUND MANAGER
FUTURE RHYTHMIC GYMNAST
FUTURE BOWLER
KARATE KID
FUTURE PAINTER

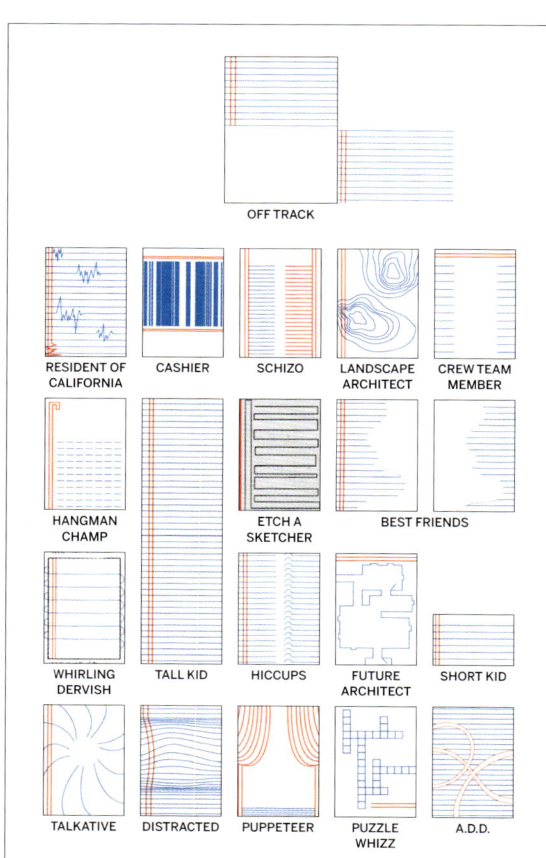
OFF TRACK
RESIDENT OF CALIFORNIA
CASHIER
SCHIZO
LANDSCAPE ARCHITECT
CREW TEAM MEMBER
HANGMAN CHAMP
ETCH A SKETCHER
BEST FRIENDS
WHIRLING DERVISH
TALL KID
HICCUPS
FUTURE ARCHITECT
SHORT KID
TALKATIVE
DISTRACTED
PUPPETEER
PUZZLE WHIZZ
A.D.D.

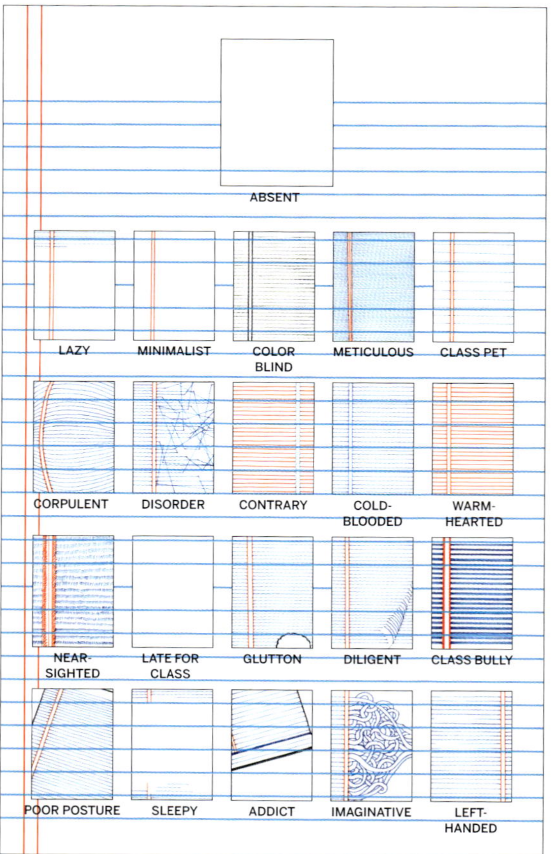
ABSENT
LAZY
MINIMALIST
COLOR BLIND
METICULOUS
CLASS PET
CORPULENT
DISORDER
CONTRARY
COLD-BLOODED
WARM-HEARTED
NEAR-SIGHTED
LATE FOR CLASS
GLUTTON
DILIGENT
CLASS BULLY
POOR POSTURE
SLEEPY
ADDICT
IMAGINATIVE
LEFT-HANDED

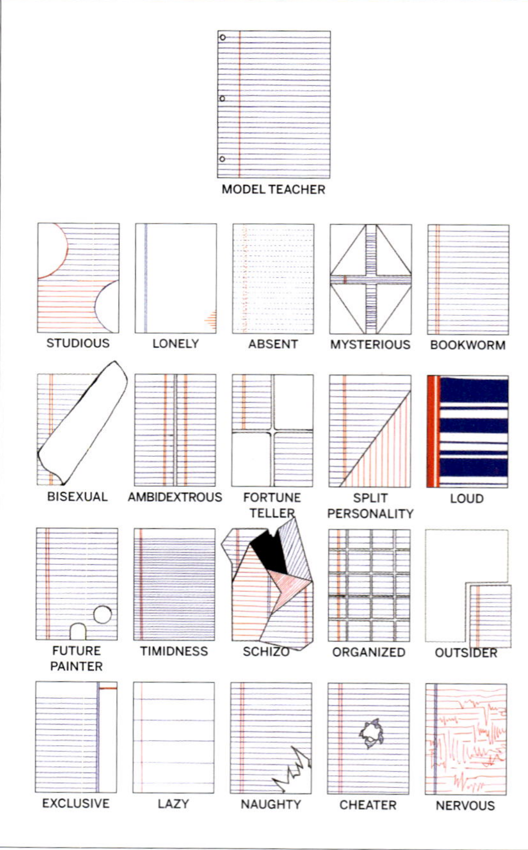
MODEL TEACHER
STUDIOUS
LONELY
ABSENT
MYSTERIOUS
BOOKWORM
BISEXUAL
AMBIDEXTROUS
FORTUNE TELLER
SPLIT PERSONALITY
LOUD
FUTURE PAINTER
TIMIDNESS
SCHIZO
ORGANIZED
OUTSIDER
EXCLUSIVE
LAZY
NAUGHTY
CHEATER
NERVOUS

NOTEBOOK SOLUTIONS:

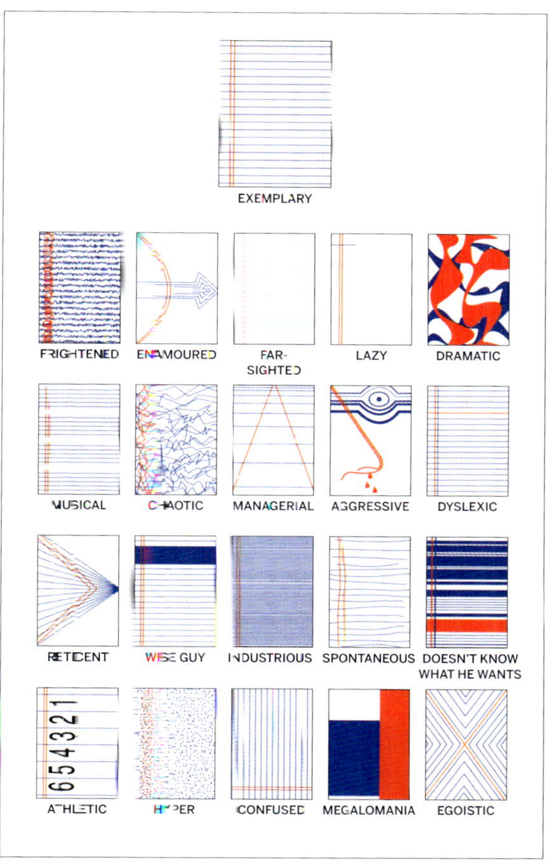

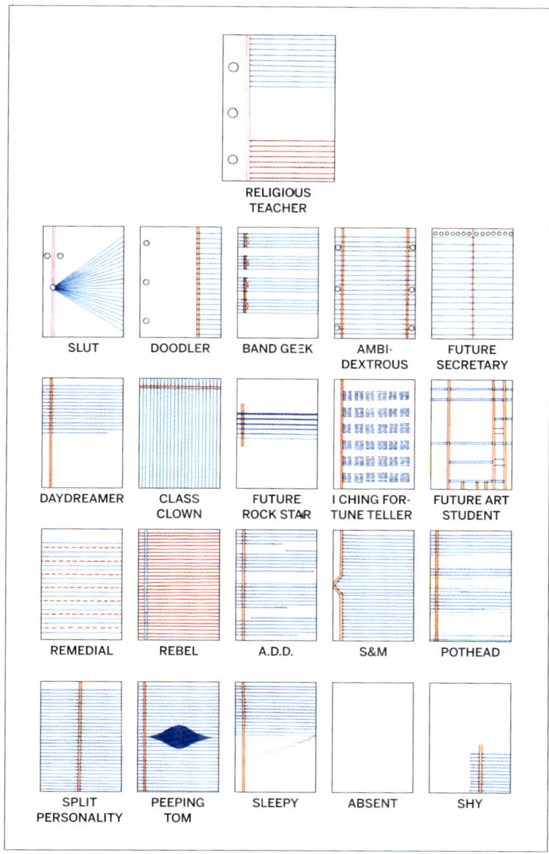

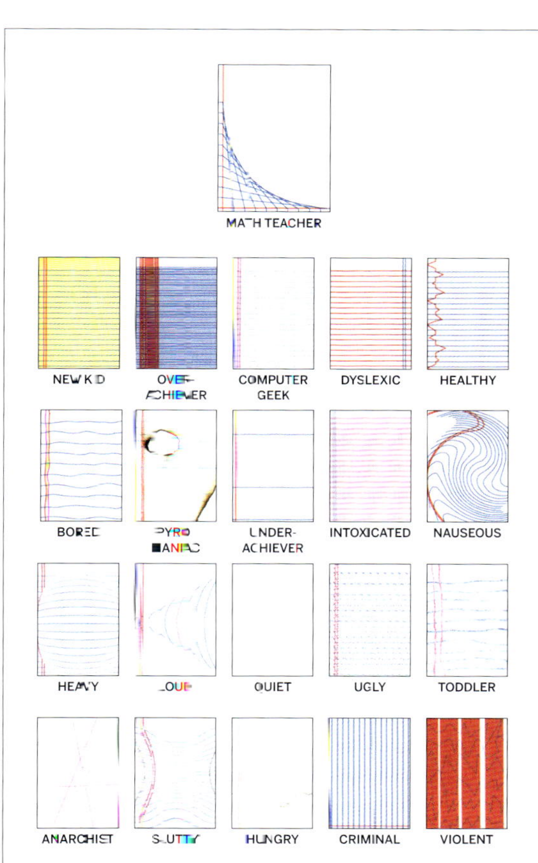

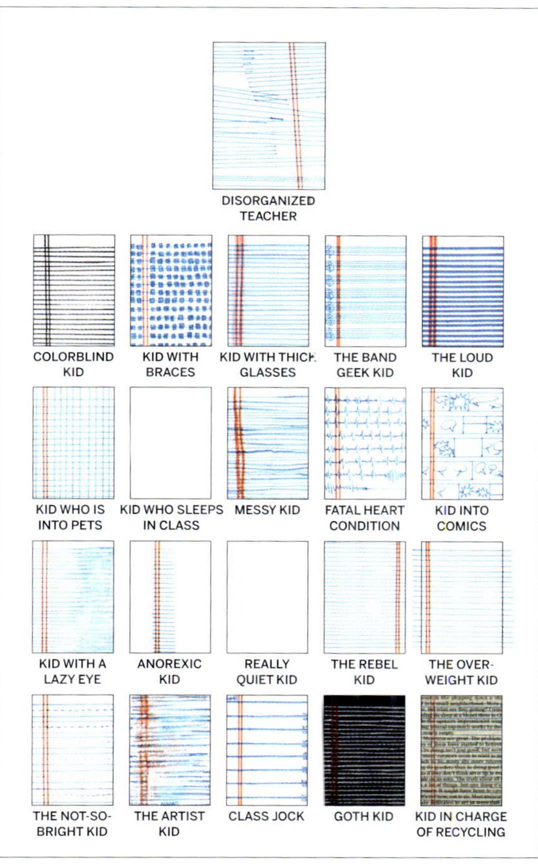

Figures 1 through 10 are examples of the entire assignment sheet.

In this assignment, students often select the same subjects, but execute their solutions from different perspectives, in terms of concepts, choice of medium, and techniques.

The majority of the solutions suggest their intended meaning. For these solutions the viewer is invited to distill the message, which makes for an ideal situation between the audience and the artwork.

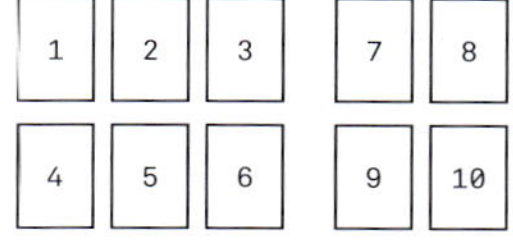

1. A. Kwak
2. Kimberly Yau
3. Jaedon Yoo
4. F. Skater
5. Eric Ku
6. Yeon Hur
7. Carsen Berkel
8. Amanda Shank
9. Jon Cowley
10. Erika Bettencourt

At times, some solutions are too literal and lack interest for the viewer, while at other times, solutions are too subjective, rendering them noncommunicative. To successfully solve this assignment, finding a balance between these two problems is where the challenge presents itself.

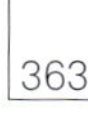

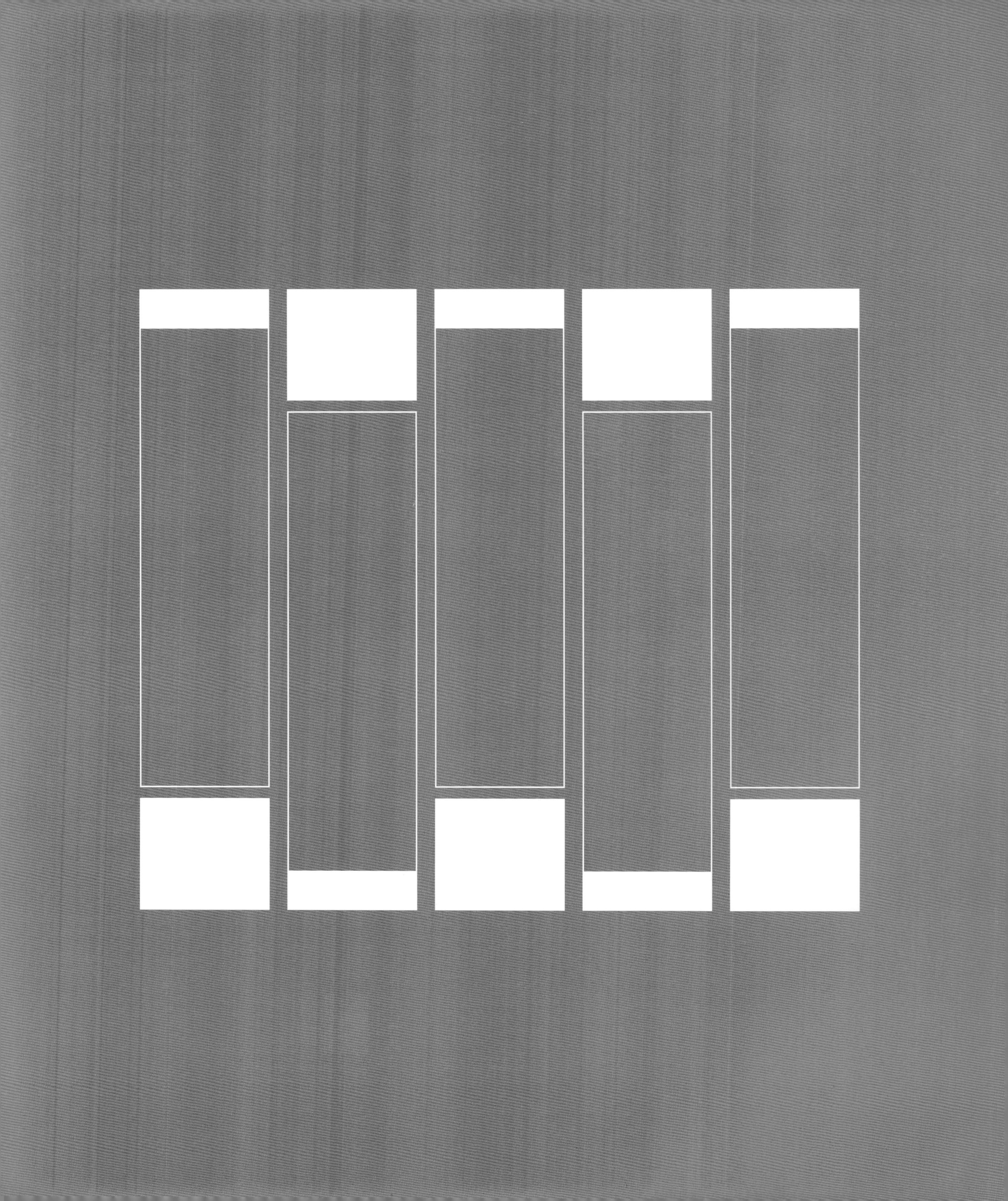

THOUGHTS ON THE CREATIVE PROCESS 10

Problem solving is always a struggle. The question is how to embrace this very struggle? How to maintain it? How to be fed by the process? This is the arena we all need to play in; not only to solve the problem at hand, but to nurture one's inner sense of wonder.

T Y P O G R A P H I C D I A R Y

Using only type as a graphic vocabulary, create a typographic diary in the seven designated grids. Type should be used expressively, legibly or illegibly, in color or in black and white, or both, to express as meaningfully as possible the events that occur during your day that you deem worthy of depicting in your diary. Consider structuring each day in terms of: the hierarchy of events, time of occurrence, and overall pacing of the entire week. Formal considerations should include overlapping, cropping, composition, touching, scale, intersecting and penetrating of elements. In the areas that are indicated below each day, write the specific intent of each typographic message.

SUNDAY	MONDAY	TUESDAY	WEDNESDAY

P R O B L E M S : S O L U T I O N S S E R I E S

CREATED BY RICHARD WILDE / JUDITH WILDE, PRODUCED BY VISUAL ARTS PRESS, LTD. ART DIRECTORS: RICHARD WILDE / JUDITH WILDE

THURSDAY FRIDAY SATURDAY

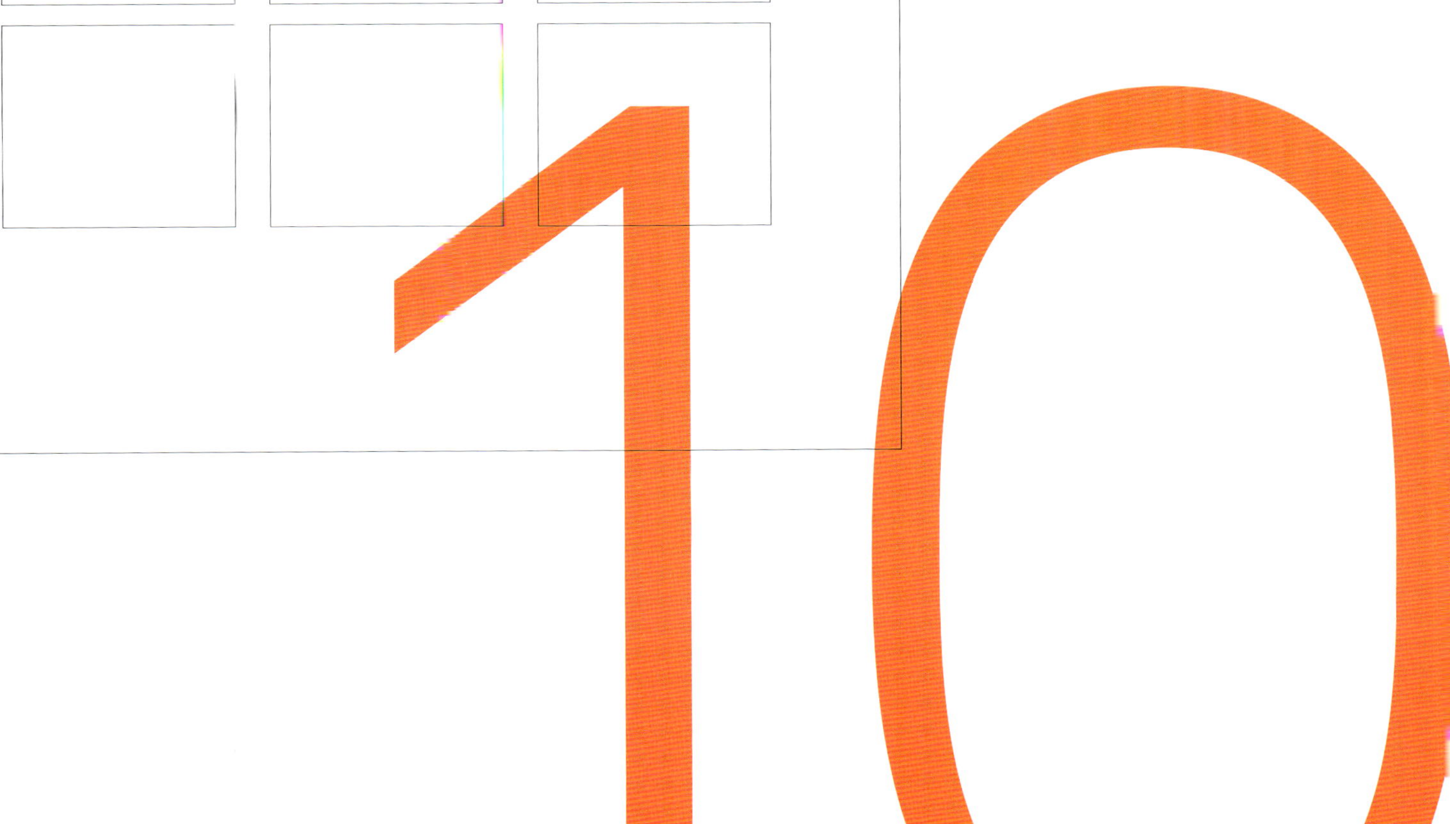

TYPOGRAPHIC DIARY PROBLEM:

Make a diary entry each day in the given areas on the assignment sheet. Use typography to express your message.

An additional demand is made on one's problem-solving capabilities by adhering to the given elongated vertical rectangles. One can use this constraint to one's advantage, for the very shape of the rectangle gives rise to dramatic compositions.

AIM:
This project is about storytelling. For the most part, it has to do with taking mundane information and expressing it in a memorable way. The intent of this project is to use typography, in an effort to develop one's voice in this specific idiom. The written content must support the visual explorations.

SUGGESTIONS:
The first step in solving this problem is to create a solution that touches one's self in a meaningful way, which can be used as a measure of effectiveness.

This process of creating art will enable one to trust one's essential nature and therefore bypass habitual reactions to problem solving.

Although computer technology offers numerous fonts to select from, it is the hand-drawn solutions that give one a greater range of possibilities in terms of personal expression.

SPECIFICATIONS:
Using typography as a form of expression, create an entry that describes a day's activity, or a moment of that day, or a memorable event of that day in the areas indicated.

There are no limitations on color or medium. The only specification is that you must use typography.

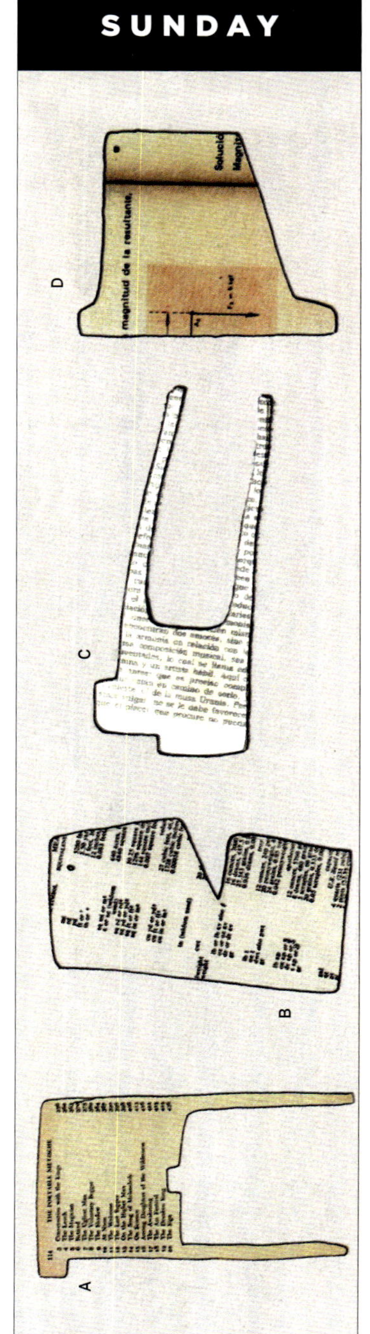

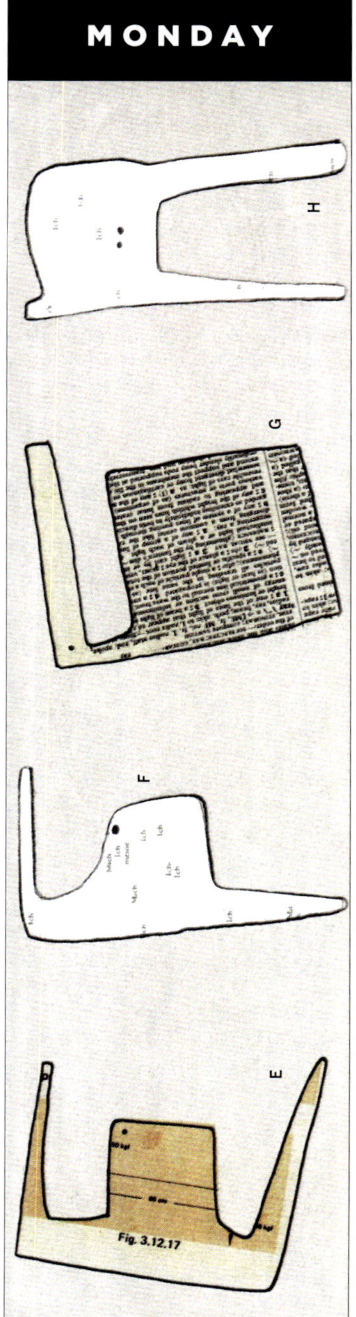

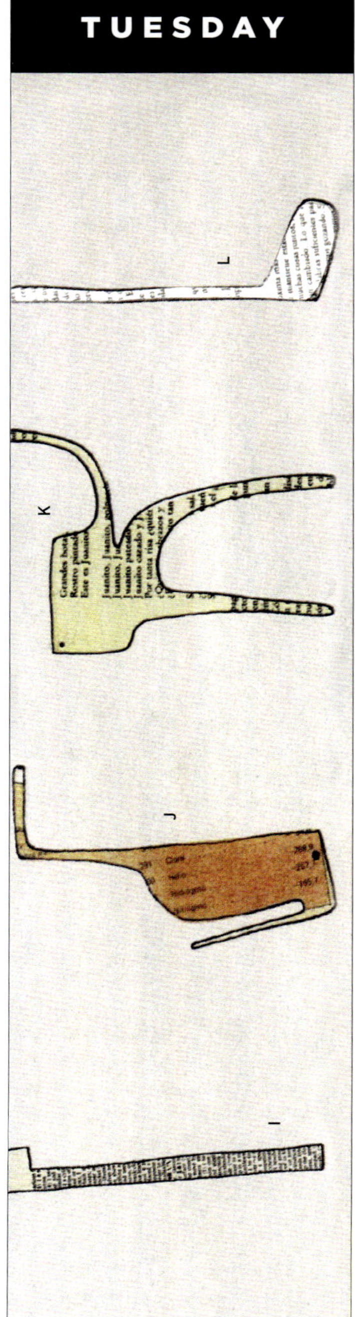

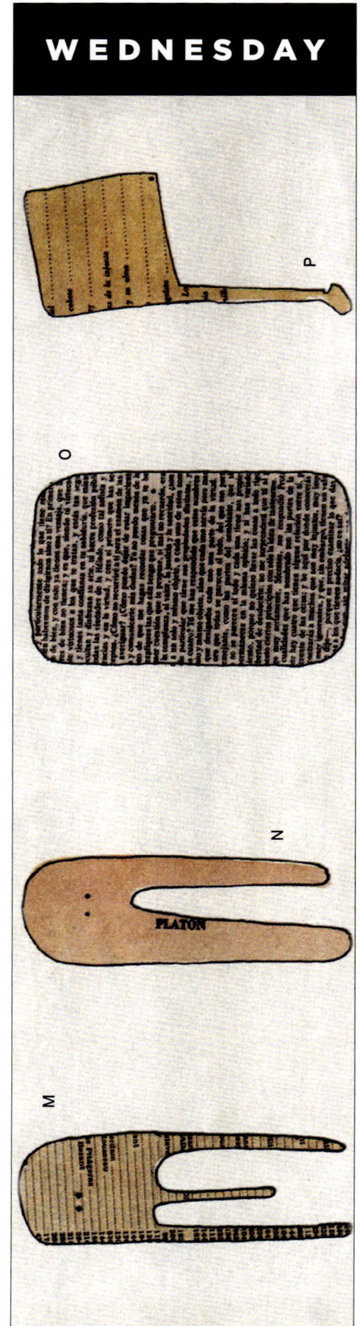

por una combinación difere
más graves y terribles que
que tienen el origen preced
posiciones secundarias se fo
La carne I los nervios nace
las fibras a causa de la anal
sangre que se coagula al se
carne proviene una sustanci
ne a los huesos y a alime
recubre la médula. En fin,

te, (144) son el asiento de las
ueden atacarnos; las más num
ntemente indicado, y es cuan
man contra el orden natural y
create de la sangre;
gia de naturaleza, y la causa
ararse de las fibras. De los n
viscosa y grasa, que sirve pa
tar e incrementar la envolve
través del espesor de los hue

orque en la corte celestial está
y banquete que les espera, av
ima más elevada de la bóveda
tenidos siempre en equilibri
n sin esfuerzo; my otros cami
pesa sobre el carro inclinado
sujetado por su cochero. Ent
y sostiene una terrible lucha. L
cuando han subido a lo más a
bóveda celeste y se fijan sobr

terrada la envidia. Cuando
an por un camino escarpa-
Uranos. Los carros de los
or sus corceles dóciles al
con dificultad, own el
le arrastra hacia la tierra,
es es cuando el alma sufre
almas de los que se llaman
del Uranos, se elevan por

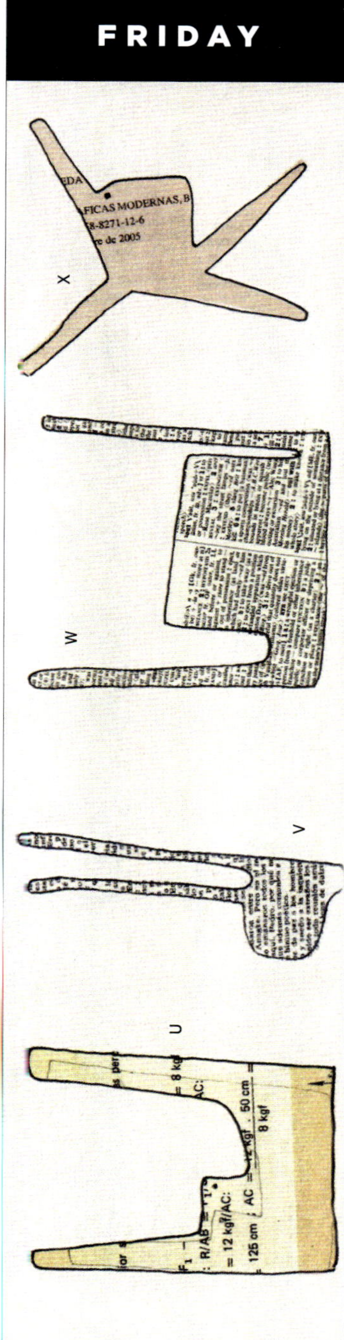

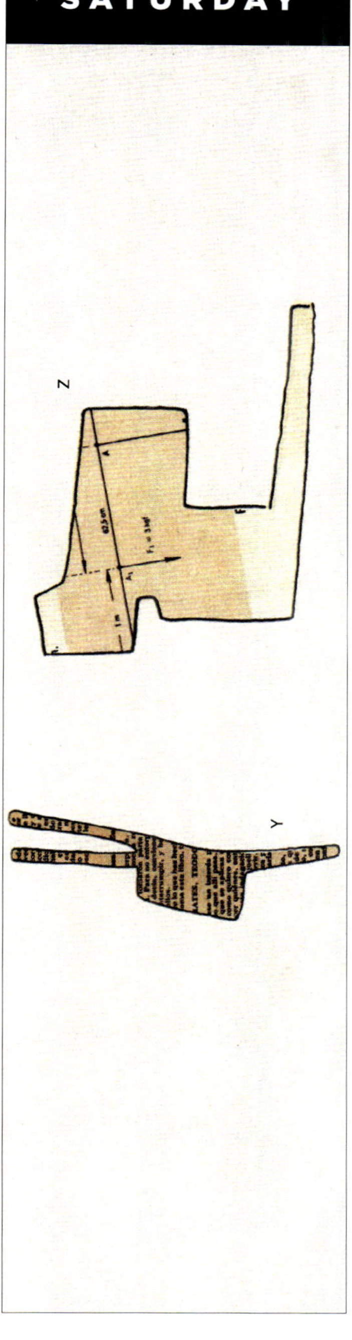

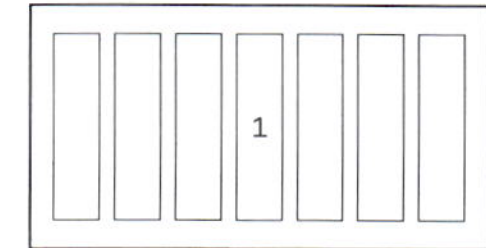

TYPOGRAPHIC DIARY SOLUTIONS:

In this solution a highly personal hand-drawn vocabulary of linear letter-forms was created as an alphabet, from A to Z.

The written explanation for each solution functions as a design element. The adherence to a limited muted palette enhances the overall impression.

Unlike the following solutions that appear in this chapter, this student gave herself a task to create an alphabet, to express her love of type.

Although this was not the intent of the project, new discoveries should always be encouraged.

1. *Karen Montero*

SUNDAY

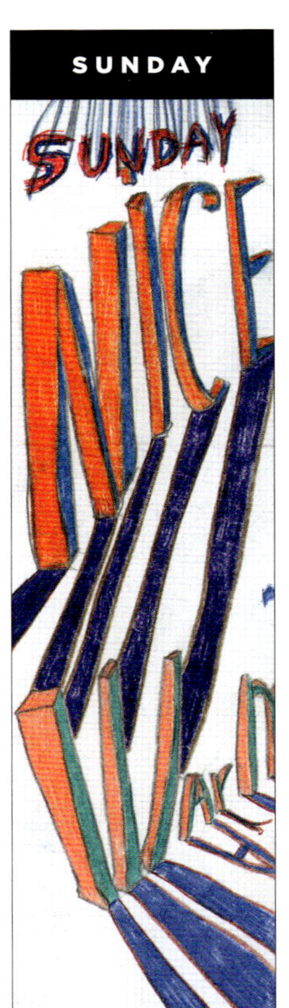

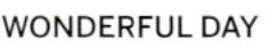

WONDERFUL DAY

MONDAY

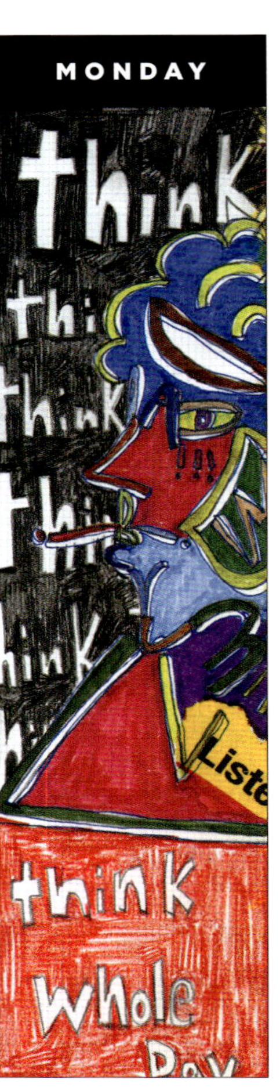

TOO MUCH HOMEWORK

TUESDAY

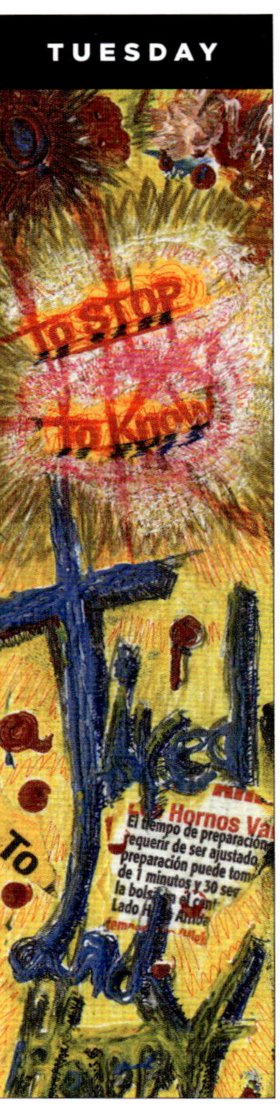

SLEEPING IS AN UNPRODUCTIVE ACTIVITY FOR ME

FRIDAY

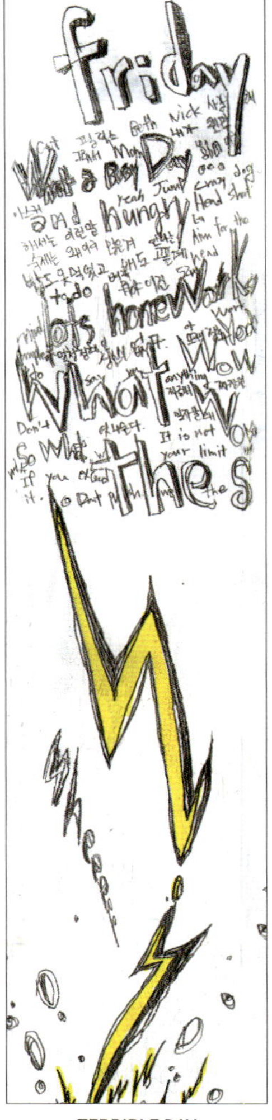

TERRIBLE DAY

THURSDAY

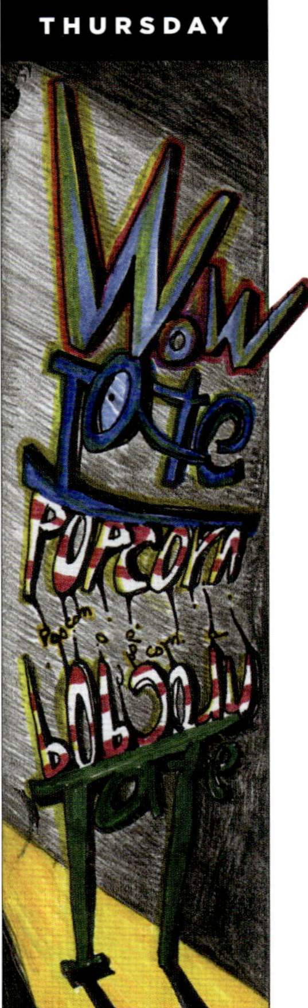

YUM YUM DAY

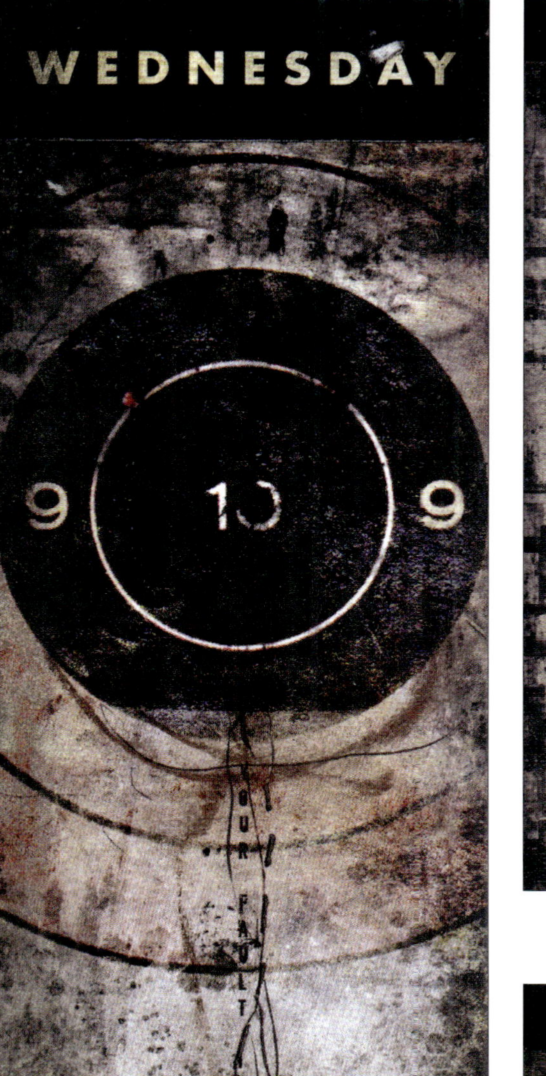

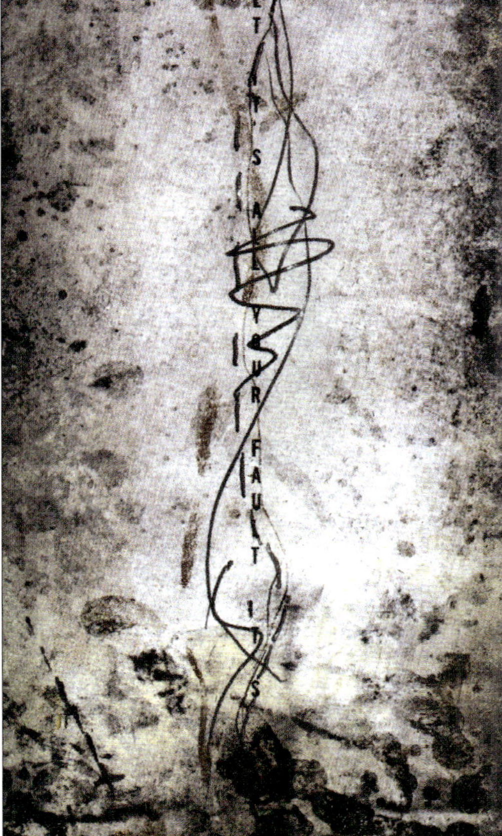

I'M AT MY WIT'S END

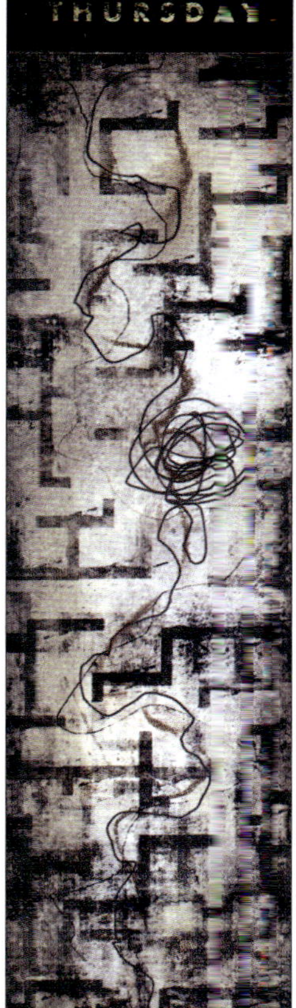

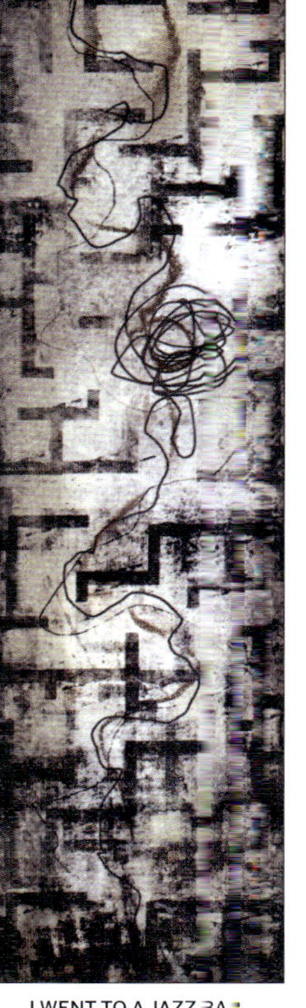

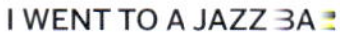

I WENT TO A JAZZ BAR

TYPOGRAPHIC DIARY SOLUTIONS:

Two different attitudes are established on this and the facing page.

Figures 1 through 5 rely on personally drawn characters supported by primary colors, while figures 6 through 10 rely on texture, atmosphere and a muted color palette to create an ominous gestalt.

1 2 3 4 5 6 7 8 9 10

1–5. *Sanggun Park*
6–10. *Thomas Shim*

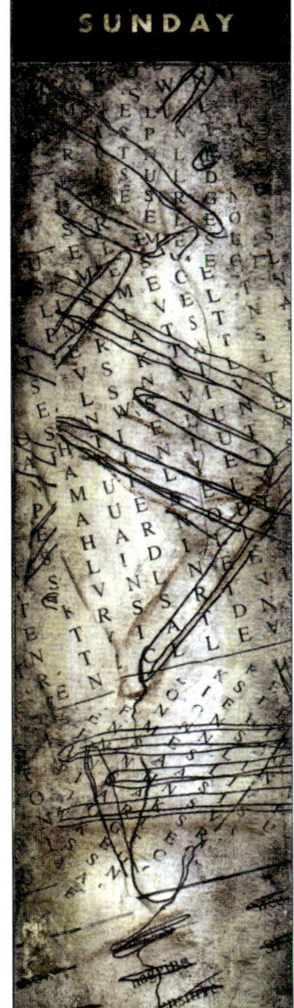

COMPLICATED

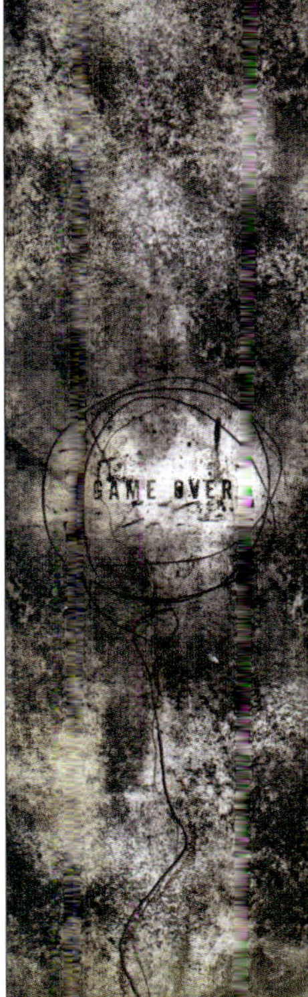

DIZZY

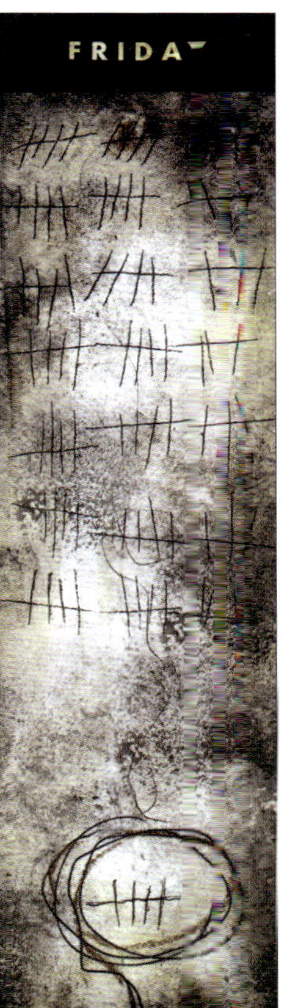

EXAMINING MY LIFE

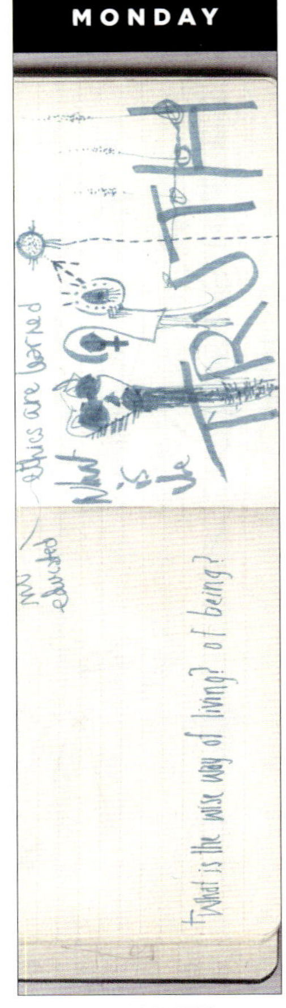

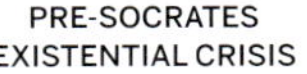
PRE-SOCRATES
EXISTENTIAL CRISIS

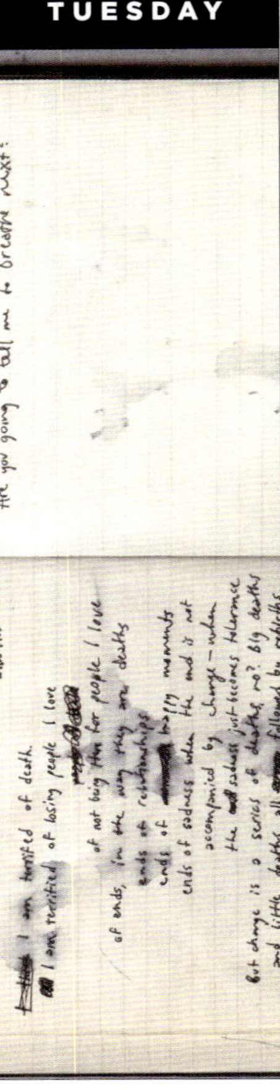

FOUND OUT SOMEONE'S
CANCER HAS SPREAD

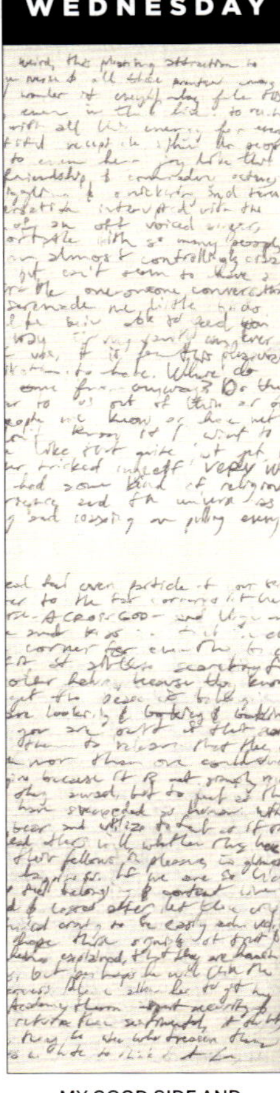

MY GOOD SIDE AND
EVIL SIDE ARE FIGHTING

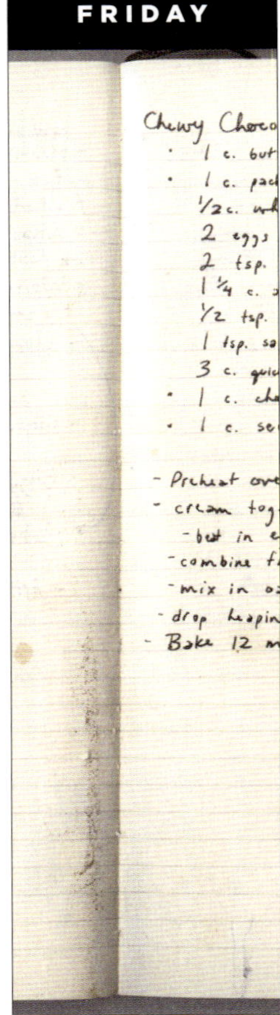

BAKED COOKIES

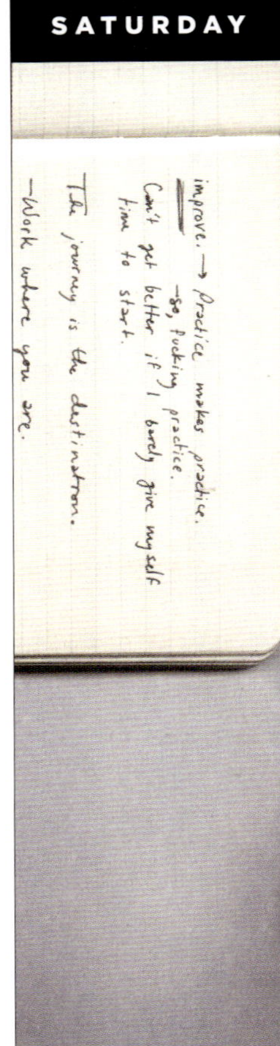

LATE RESOLUTIONS

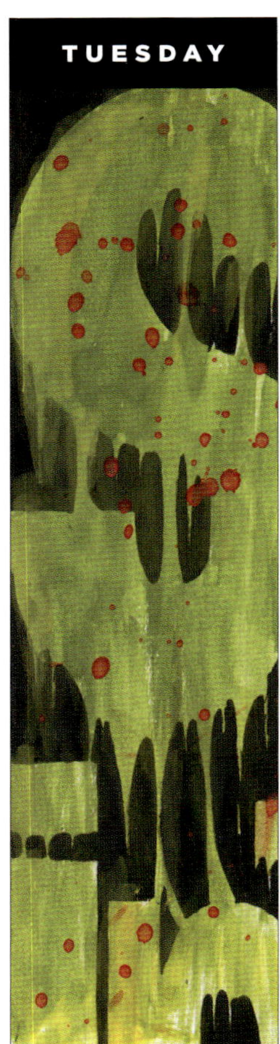

MY COLD FROM
THE PREVIOUS WEEK TURNED
INTO A SINUS INFECTION

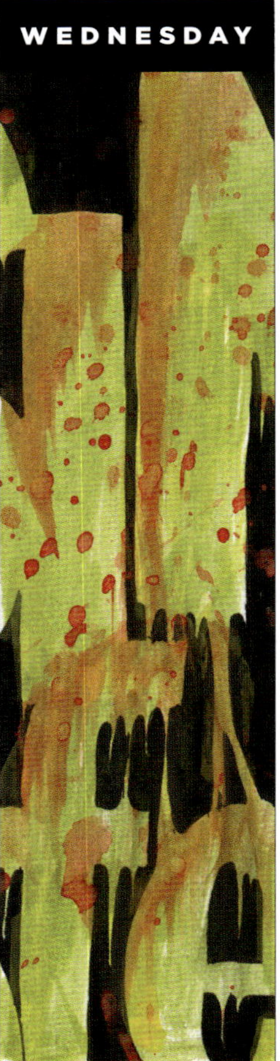

WEDNESDAY WAS
PARTICULARLY BAD, THANKS
TO THE NOSEBLEEDS

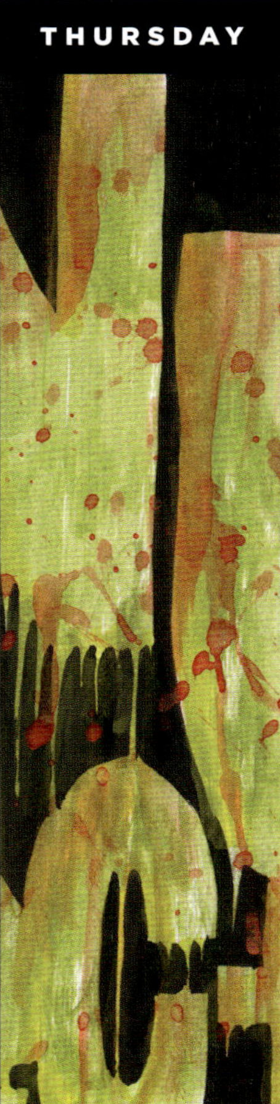

STILL FELT
DISGUSTING

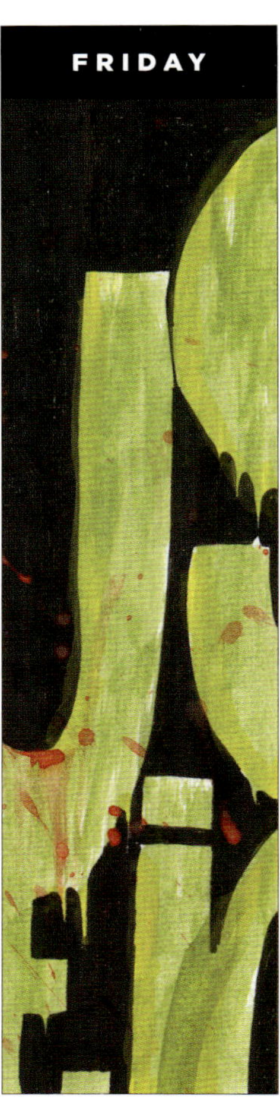

STARTED TAKING
ANTIBIOTICS,
STILL SOME BLOOD

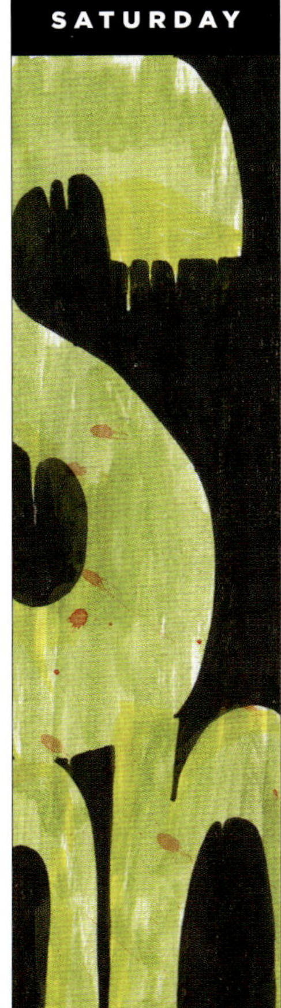

GETTING BETTER,
BUT STILL NOT "GOOD"

TYPOGRAPHIC DIARY SOLUTIONS:

These solutions created by three different students represent distinct points of view, ranging from storytelling in figures 1 through 5, using body copy primarily as form in figures 6 through 10 to represent a sinus infection that dominated the entire week, to figures 11 through 14, a study of various activities that exhibit a range of executions, emotionally dictated by a specific moment of each day.

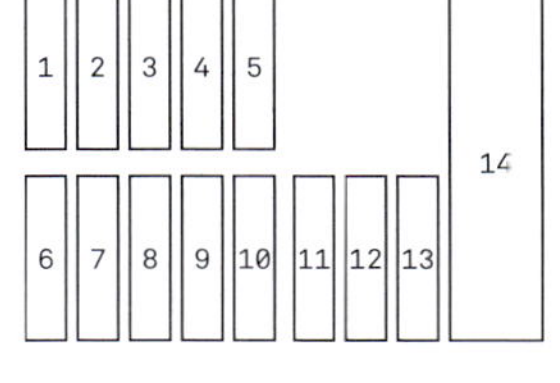

1-5. Rachel Wheeler
6-10. Lucas Kalina
11-14. Sandra Woodruff

FRIDAY

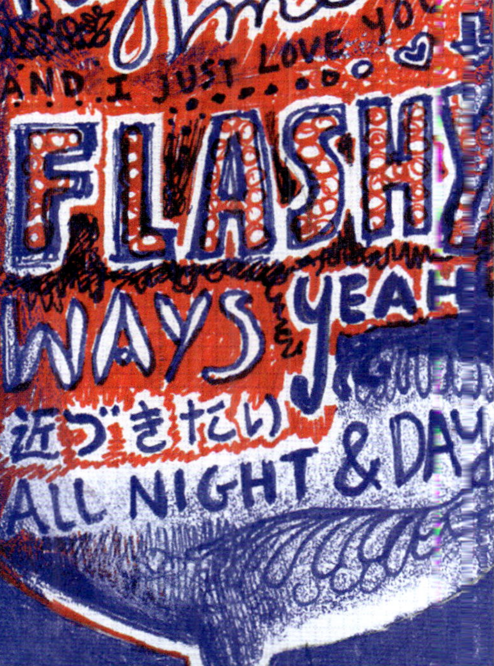

3 HOURS OF KARAOKE

SUNDAY

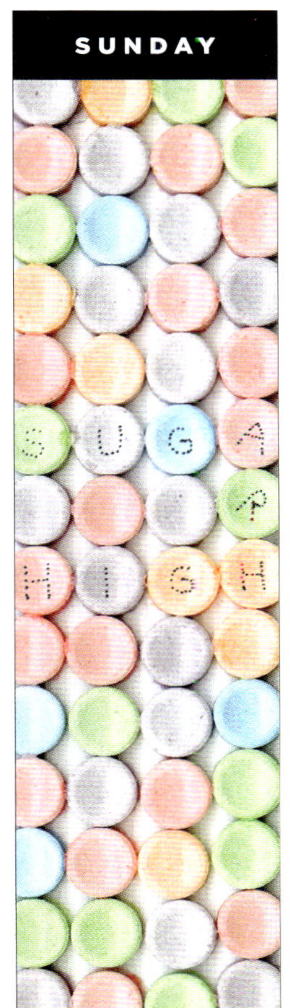

HAD A SUGAR HIGH

MONDAY

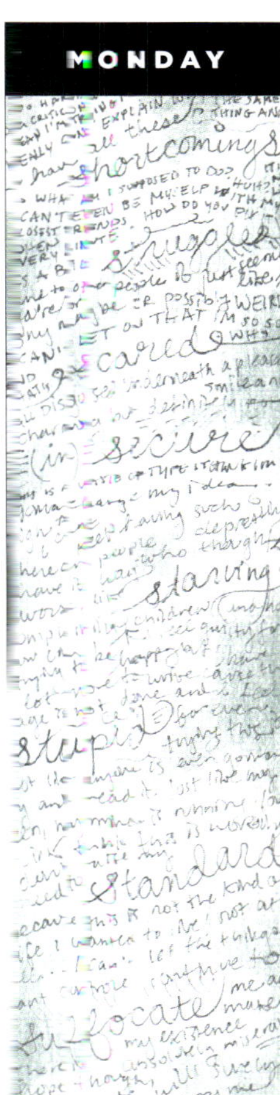

REFLECTED ON LIFE

THURSDAY

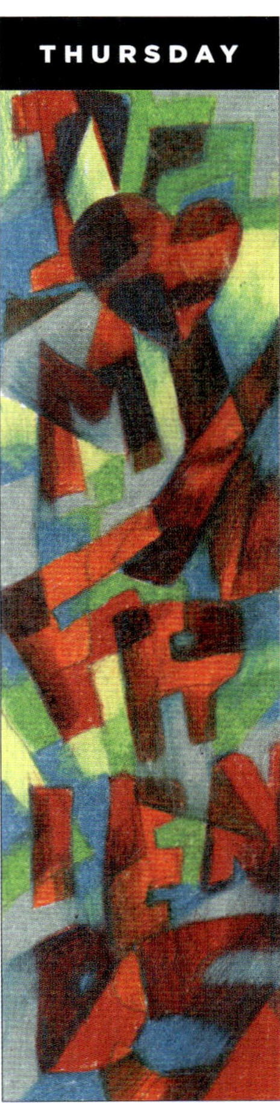

FRIENDS FROM MY HOMETOWN VISITED

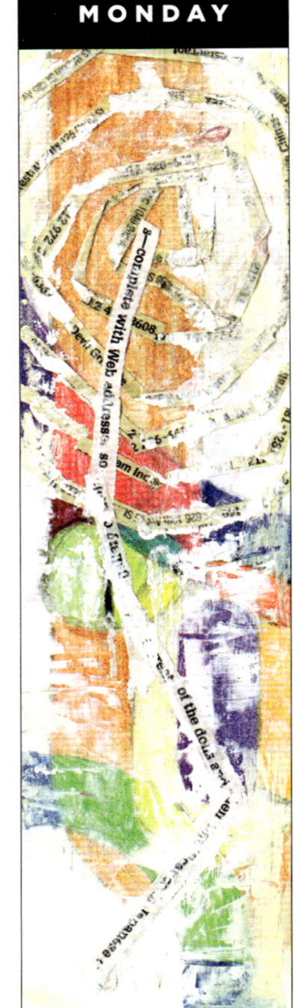

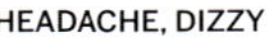

HEADACHE, DIZZY

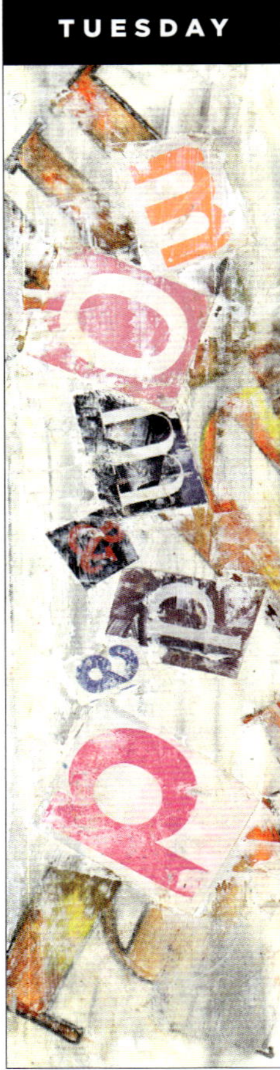

MY MOM & DAD CAME TO NY

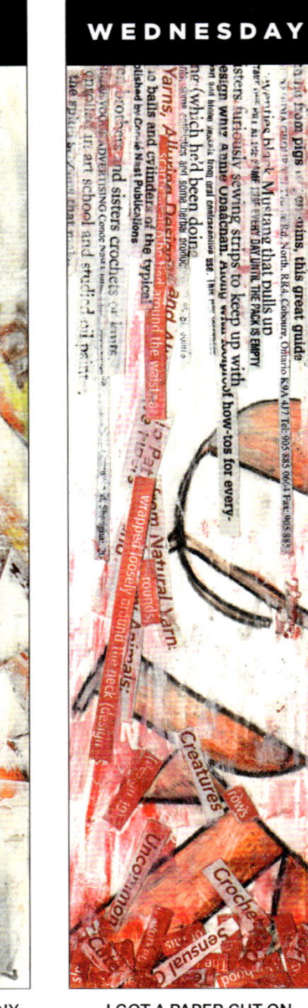

I GOT A PAPER CUT ON MY FINGER AND BLED ON MY WORK

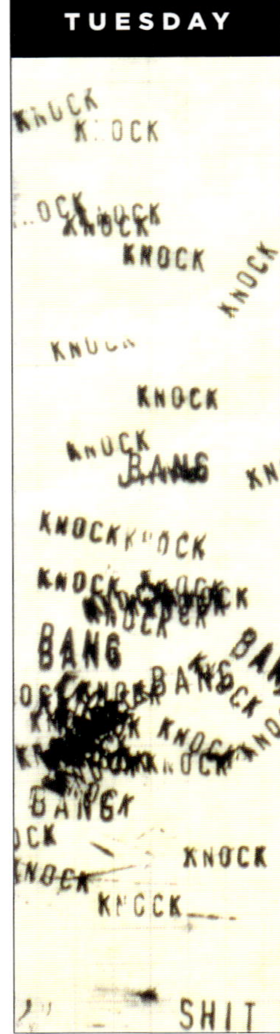

I GOT LOCKED OUT OF MY HOUSE

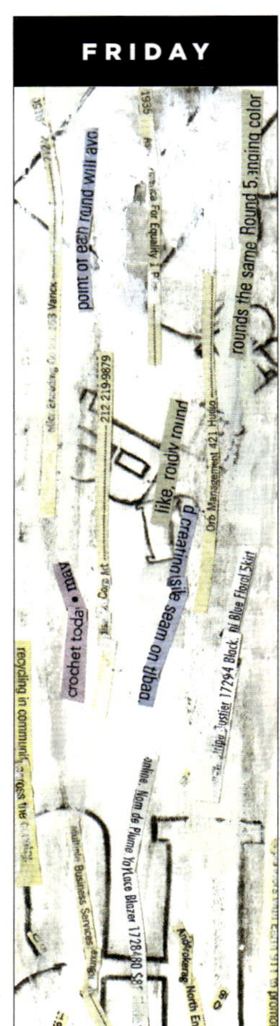

RAINING ALL DAY

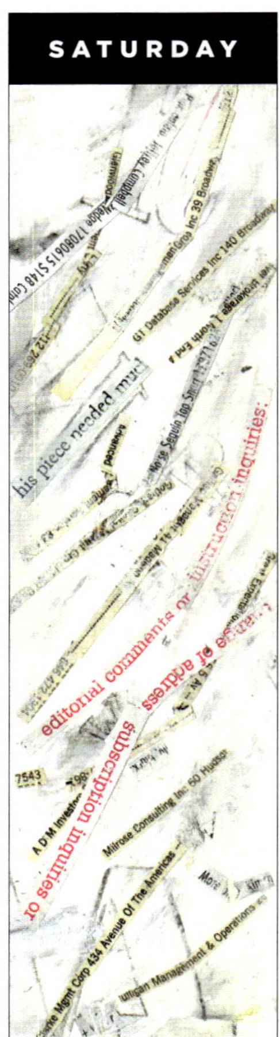

RAINY AND WINDY

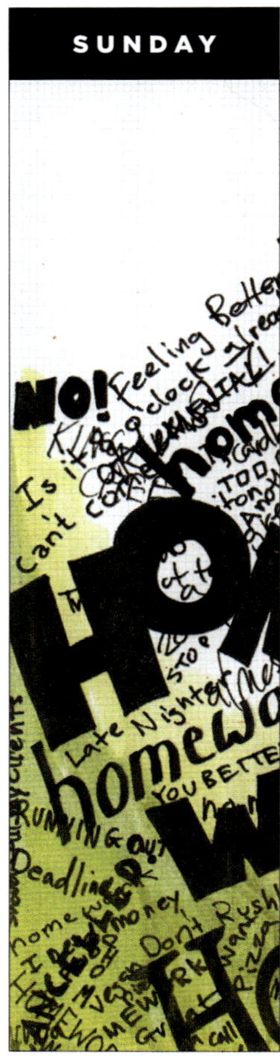

MY SINUS ISSUE STARTED TO REALLY IMPROVE

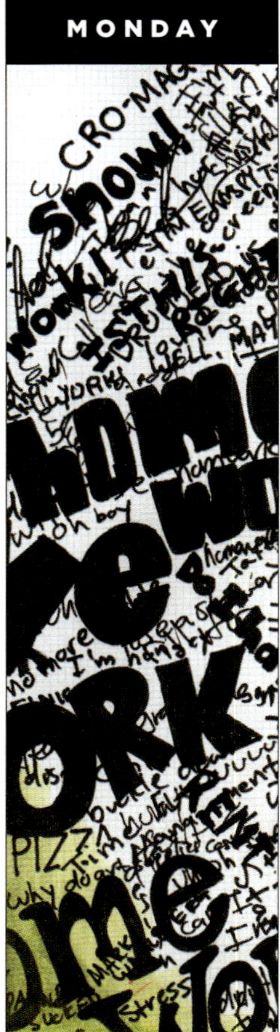

I HAVEN'T STARTED HOMEWORK. DISTRACTIONS WERE PLENTIFUL.

THURSDAY

FAUX OR FALSE. PONDERED ALL THE LIES, BETRAYALS

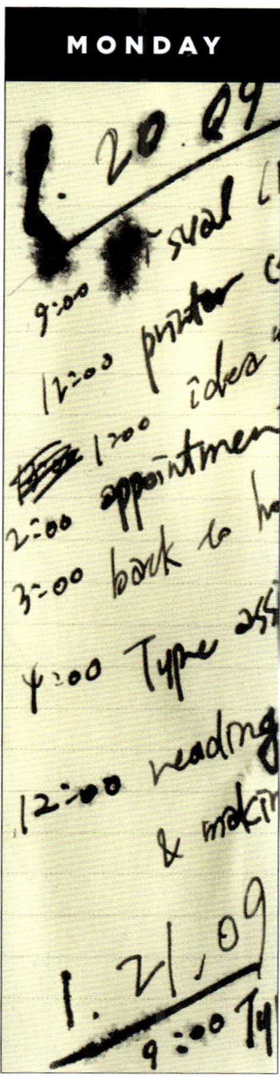

I PLAN MY WEEK'S SCHEDULE EVERY MONDAY

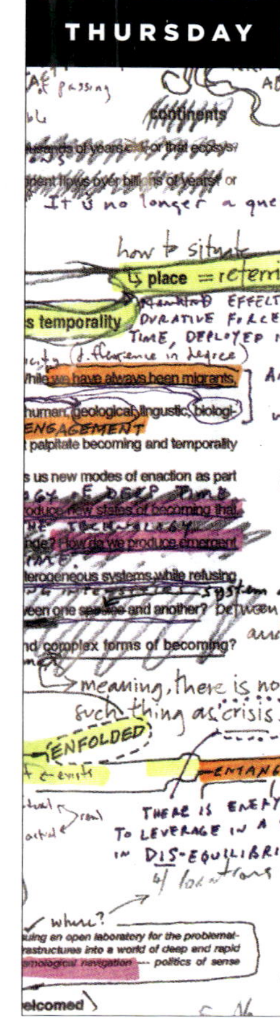

OVER-THINKING

CONFUSED

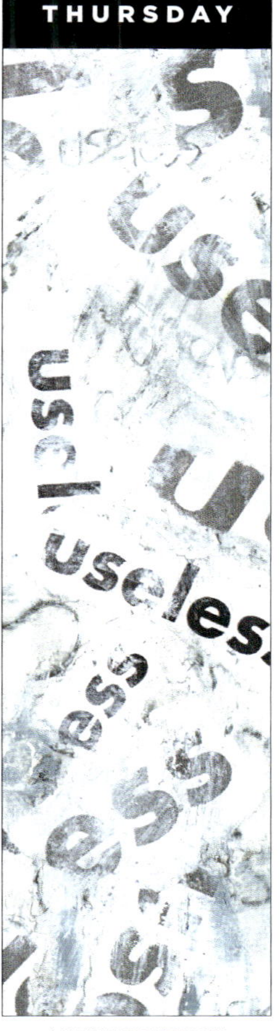

I HAVE NO PURPOSE

TYPOGRAPHIC DIARY SOLUTIONS:

The medium of collage, rubber stamps, and hand-drawn characters are the primary palette in figures 1 through 6, while in solutions 7 and 8 hand-drawn type is used to heighten a narrative message.

Figures 9 through 13 reflect images that at first glance seem haphazard and randomly composed, but on further viewing reflect highly personal sensibilities.

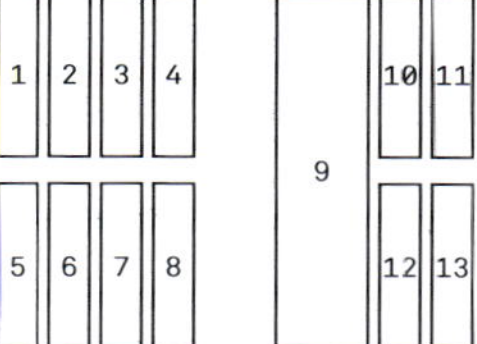

1–3. *Minji Hong*
4. *Helen Yentus*
5–6. *Minji Hong*
7–8. *L. Kalina*
9. *Becca Kalande*
10. *Yoonjoo Lee*
11. *Sasha Safir-Temple*
12–13. *A Ran Yeo*

SUNDAY

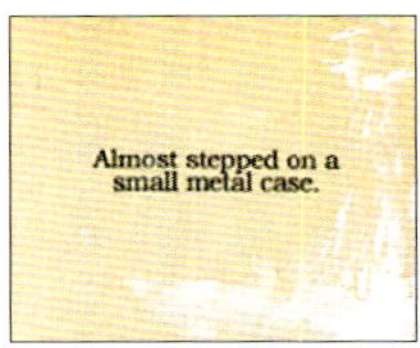

MONDAY

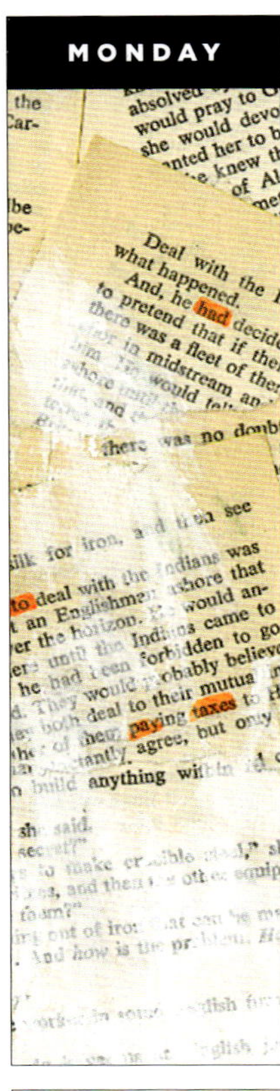

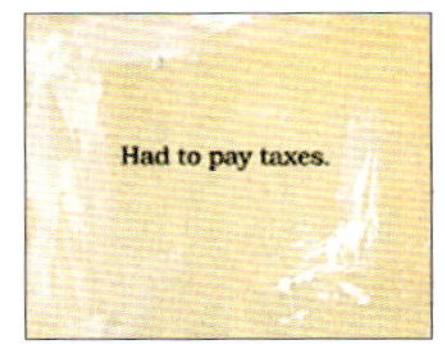

TUESDAY

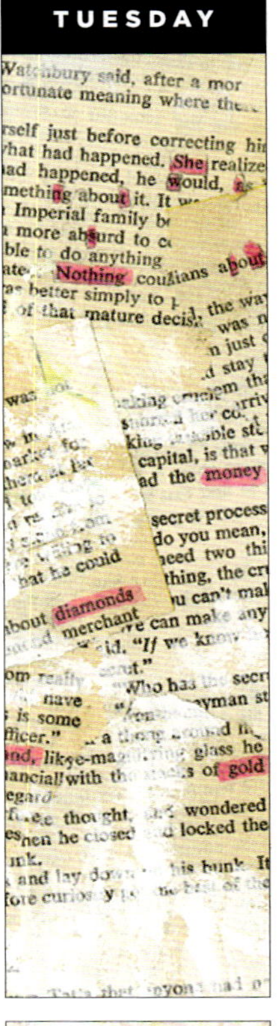

She wants nothing but money, diamonds and gold.

WEDNESDAY

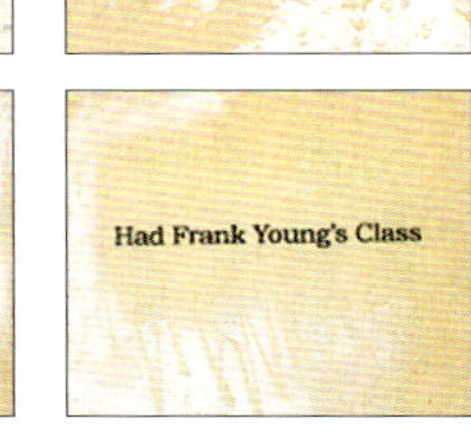

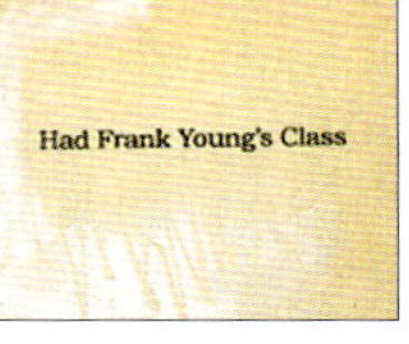

THURSDAY

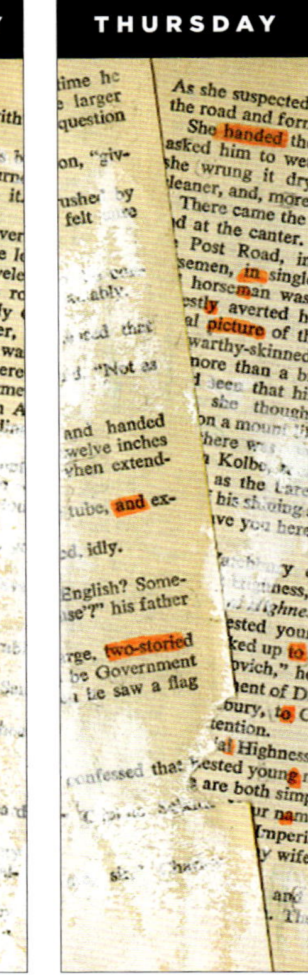

Handed in my picture and two stories to Olga

FRIDAY

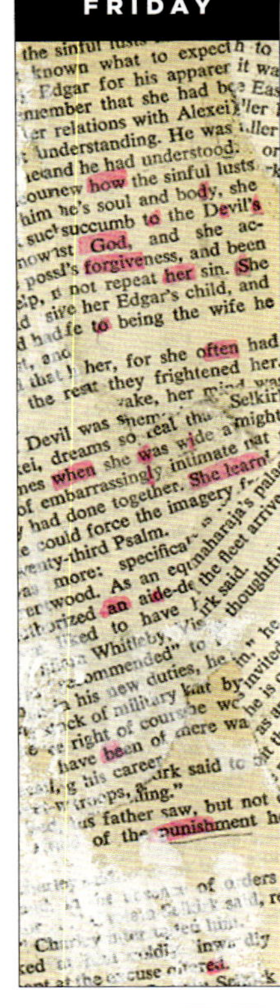

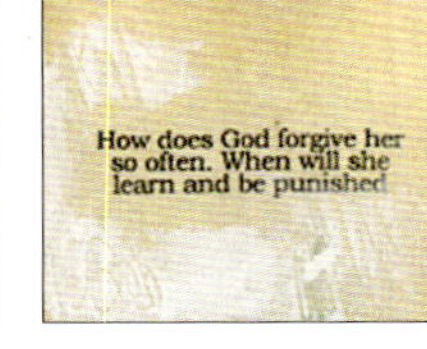

SATURDAY

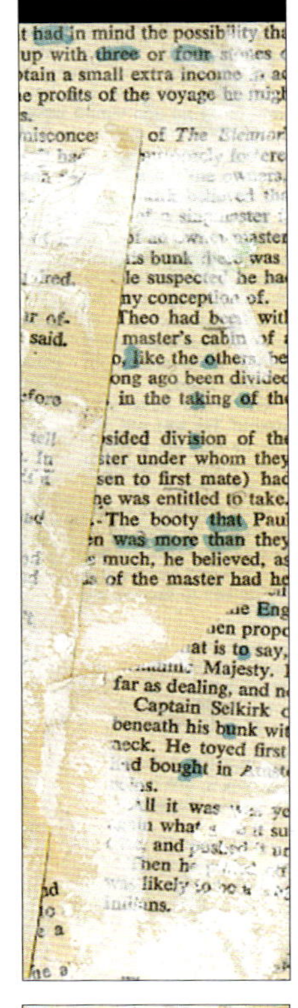

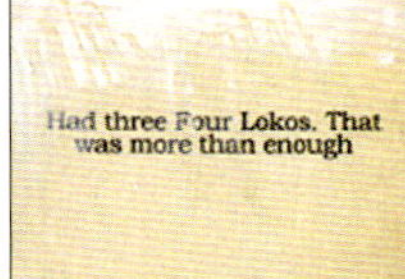

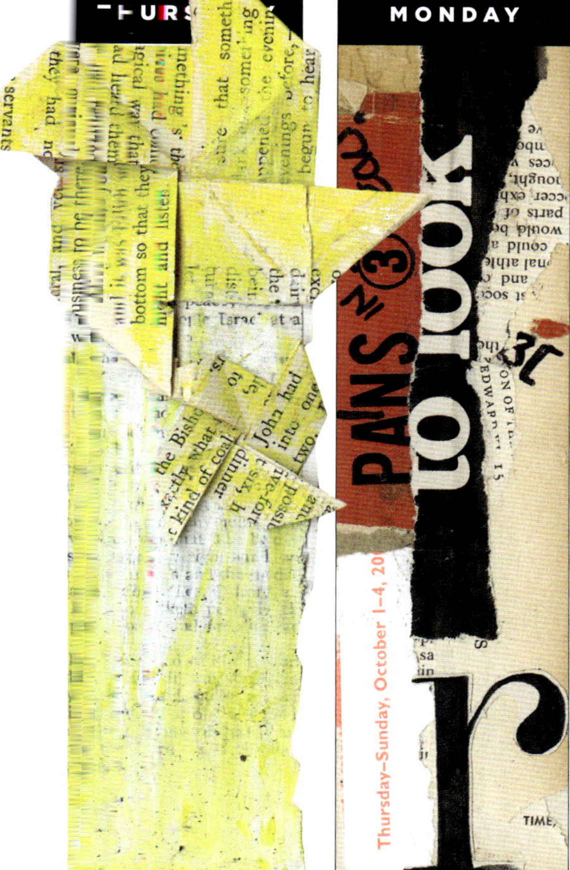

SO HAPPY, MY TEACHER LIKED MY IDEA

HAD A DIFFICULT DAY

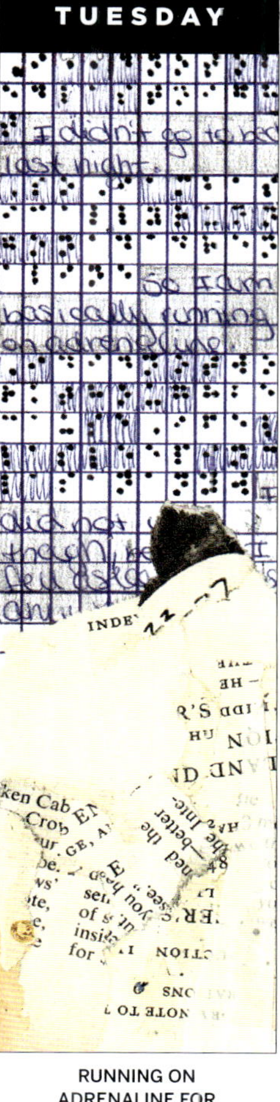

RUNNING ON ADRENALINE FOR HALF THE DAY

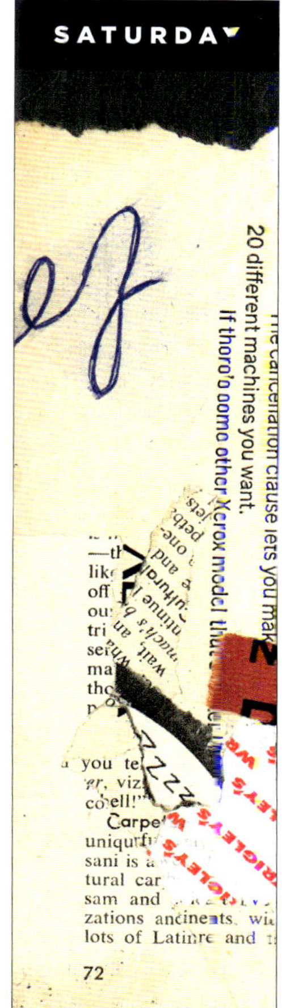

FELL ASLEEP IN CLASS

TYPOGRAPHIC DIARY SOLUTIONS:

These solutions are executed using the medium of collage. The highlighted words and letters in figure 1 reveal the content of each day. Figures 2 through 9 are highly personal solutions relying on pattern and texture to enhance each solution.

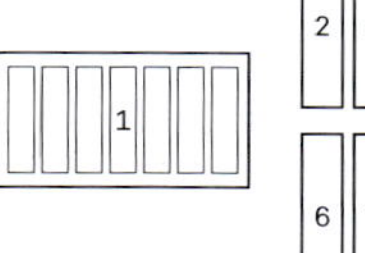
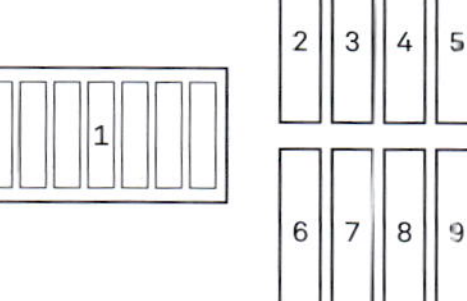

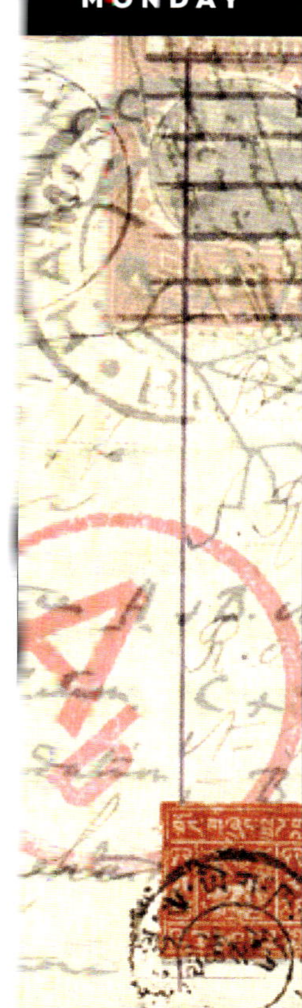

SENT A LETTER

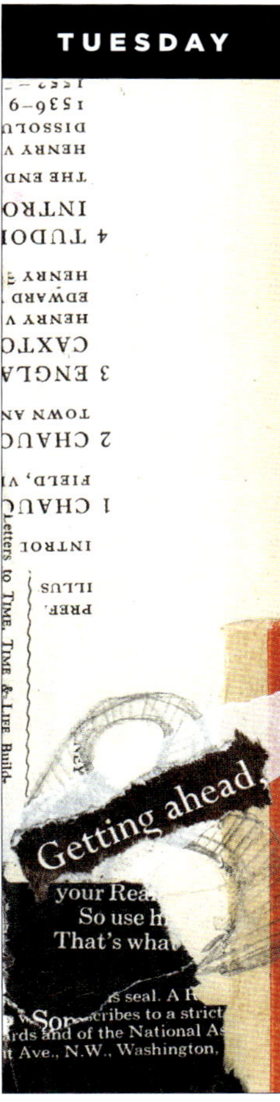

WORKING HARD

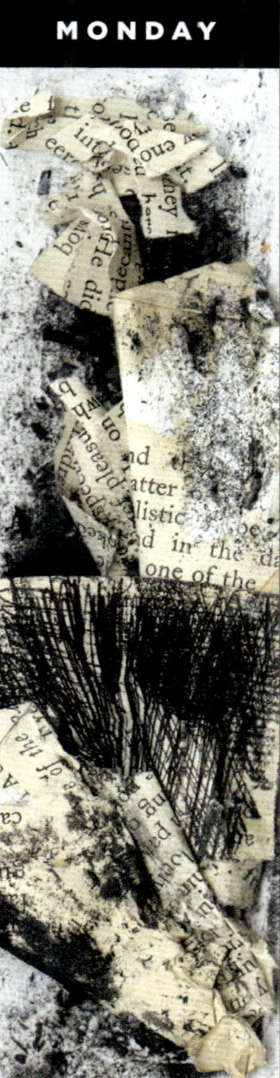

HAD A TERRIBLE NIGHT'S SLEEP AND WAS MOODY ALL DAY

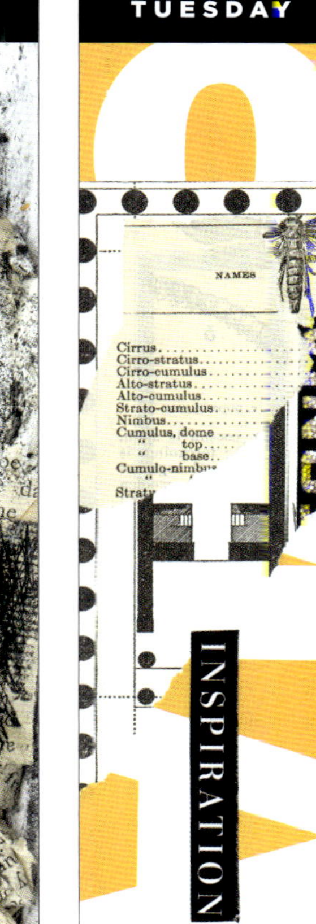

I WENT TO A MUSEUM FOR INSPIRATION AND SAW WONDERFUL WORK BY FAMOUS ARTISTS

1. *Tal Midyan*
2. *Jessie Gang*
3–5. *Anna Fine*
6. *Kyunyoung Oh*
7. *Anna Fine*
8. *Jessie Gang*
9. *Antonina Badagoff*

WEDNESDAY

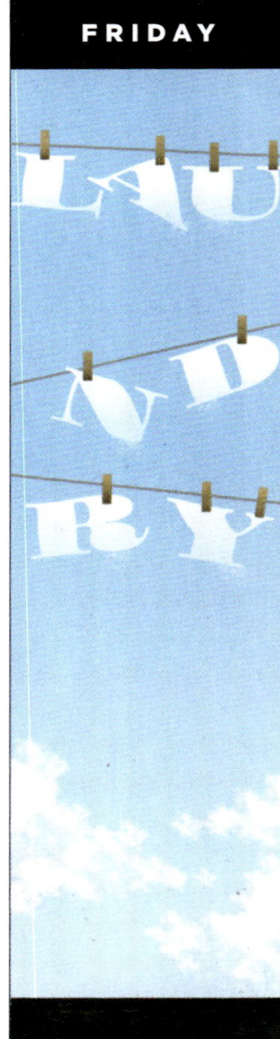

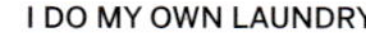

I DO MY OWN LAUNDRY

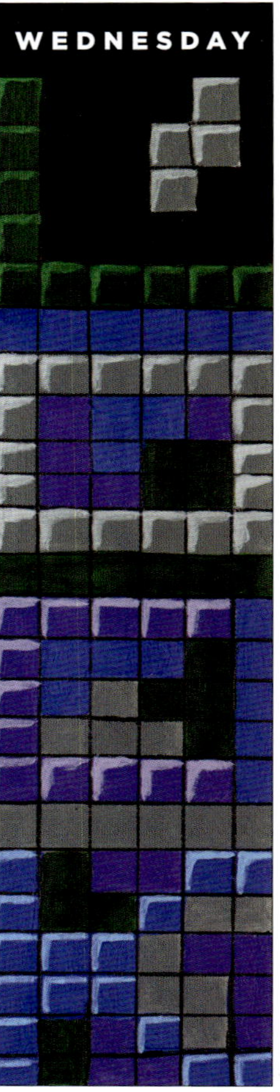

I AM LOCKED INSIDE MYSELF,
I CAN'T BE FREE.

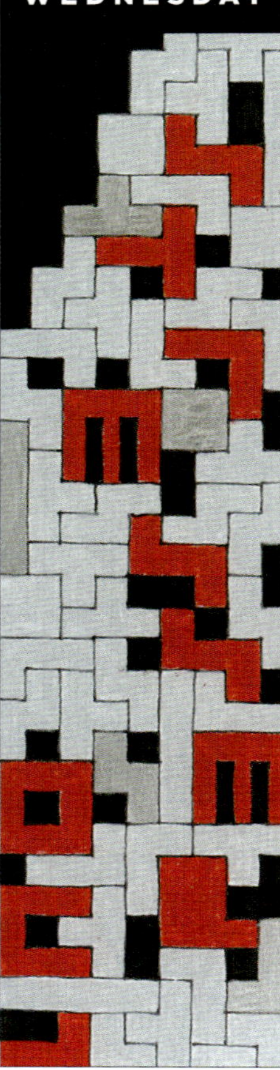

THE TOUGHEST DAY OF
MY WEEK

FURNITURE SHOPPING

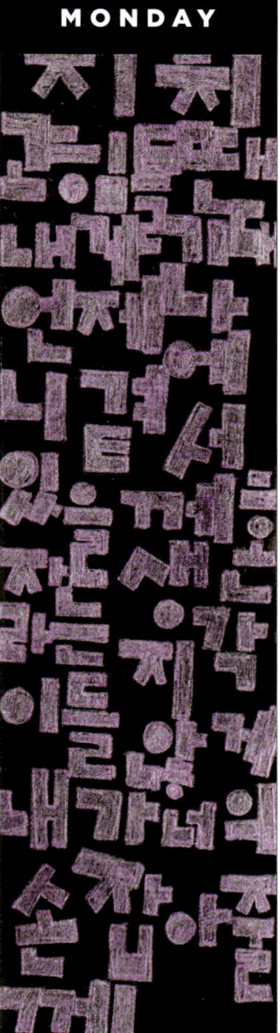

STRESSING

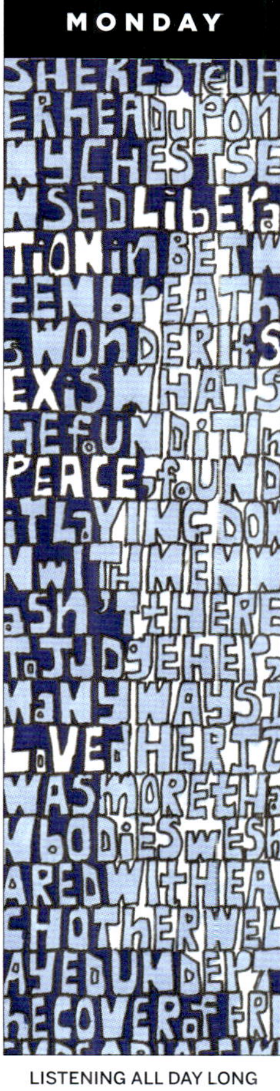

LISTENING ALL DAY LONG

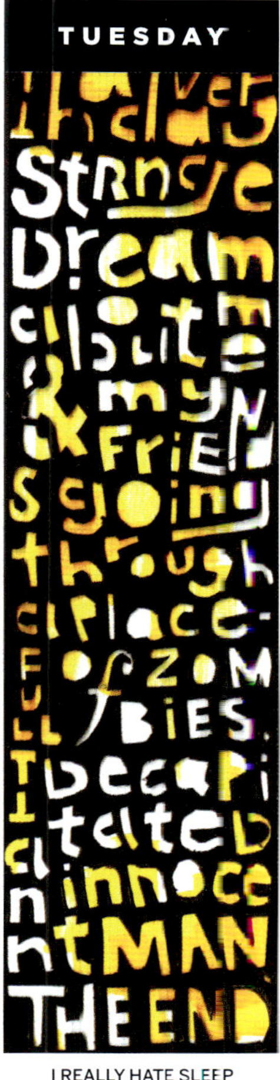

I REALLY HATE SLEEP

TYPOGRAPHIC DIARY SOLUTIONS:

Although the emphasis of the problem was to move one away from computer-generated images, at times the computer was permitted if the concept necessitated its use.

Figures 1 and 4 are computer-generated images.

Figures 2 and 3 based their solutions on a grid pattern, but hand drew their solutions.

Figure 4 spells out the word IKEA. At the same time, this solution reflects a floor plan.

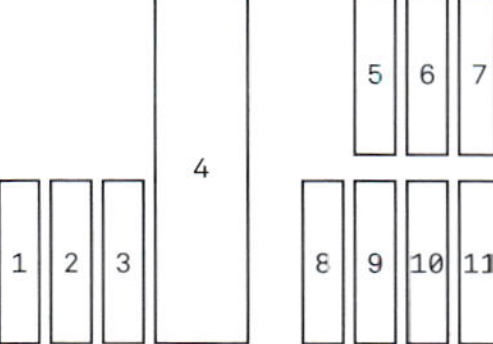

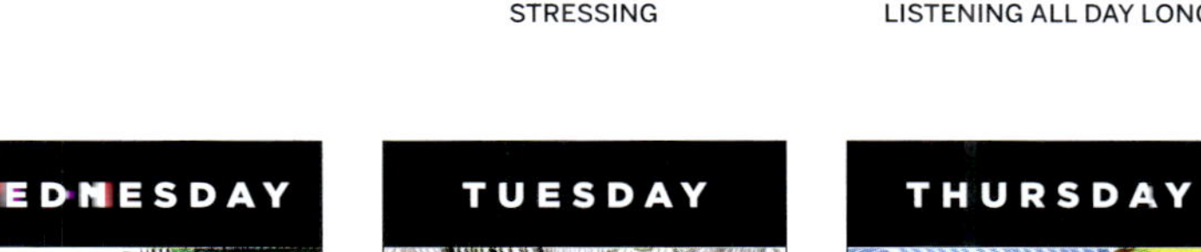

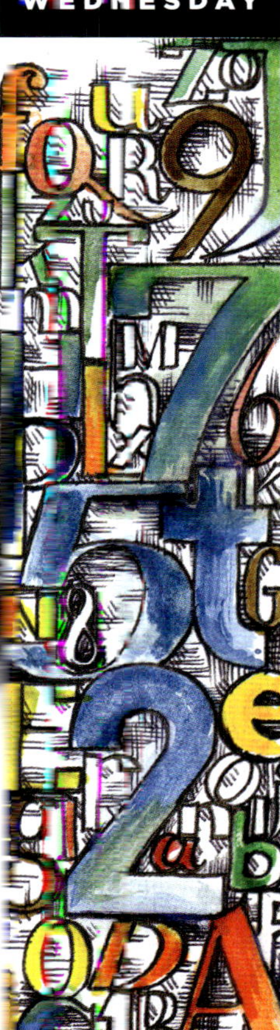

I ATTENDED A LECTURE ON SYNESTHESIA. I DIDN'T KNOW THERE WAS A NAME FOR SUCH A THING.

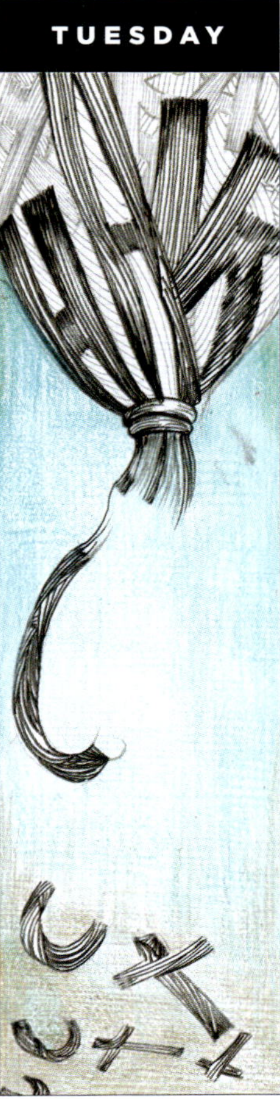

I HAD MY HAIR CUT

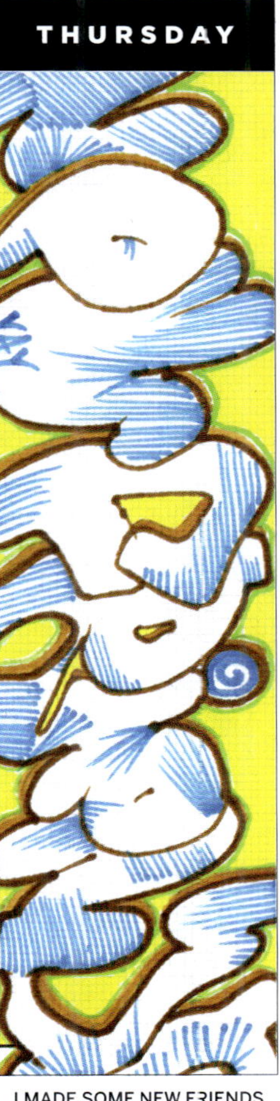

I MADE SOME NEW FRIENDS TODAY

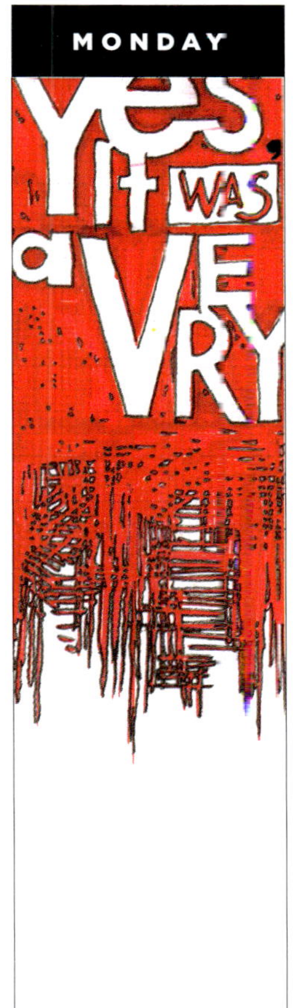

I WASTED AN ENTIRE DAY

1. *Yoonyoung Choi*
2. *Kyungsun Hong*
3. *Yoojung Kang*
4. *Dominika Kramerova*
5. *Helen Park*
6. *Tanka Machinko*

7–8. *Hayun Moon*

9. *Jaewon Park*
10. *Jack Winthrop*
11. *Hayun Moon*

Figures 5 through 11 use hand-drawn imagery in a somewhat spontaneous way. Certain solutions focus on typographic complexity that functions as a texture unto itself, while heightening the communication value.

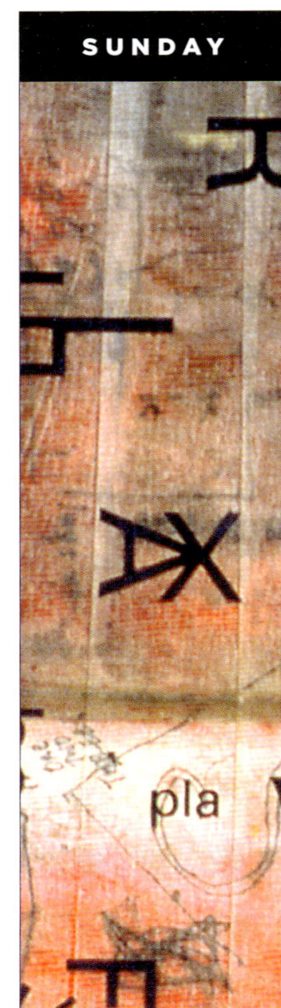

I HAD LOTS OF ENCOUNTERS ALL DAY LONG

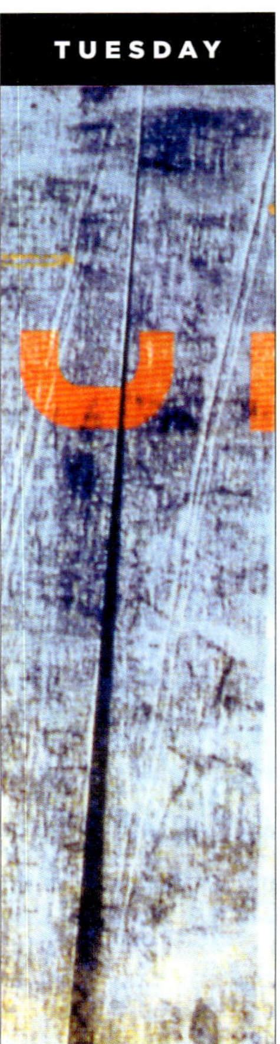

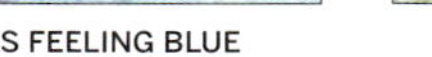

I WAS FEELING BLUE

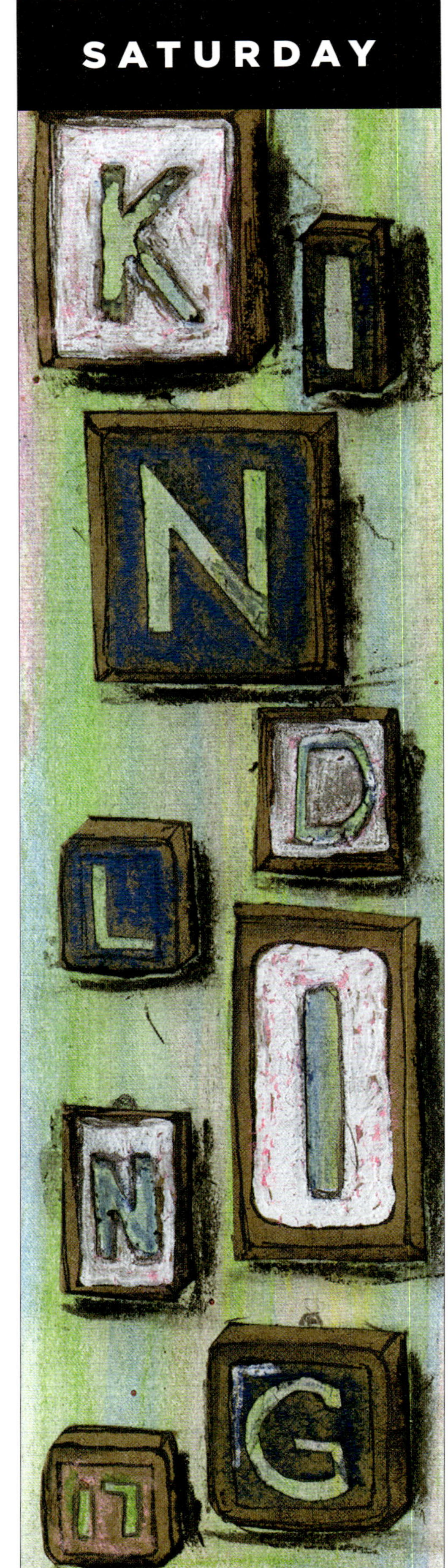

I WENT TO THE JONATHAN JENNE GALLERY TO SEE THE WORK OF MY FAVORITE ARTIST, JAMES JEAN.

TYPOGRAPHIC DIARY SOLUTIONS:

Figures 1 and 2 are highly personal abstractions, while figure 3 references an art exhibition.

In figures 4 through 12, collage is the medium used, where at times body copy functions as an integral textural element.

Qualities of agitation, motion, intricacy, and rawness are reflected in these solutions.

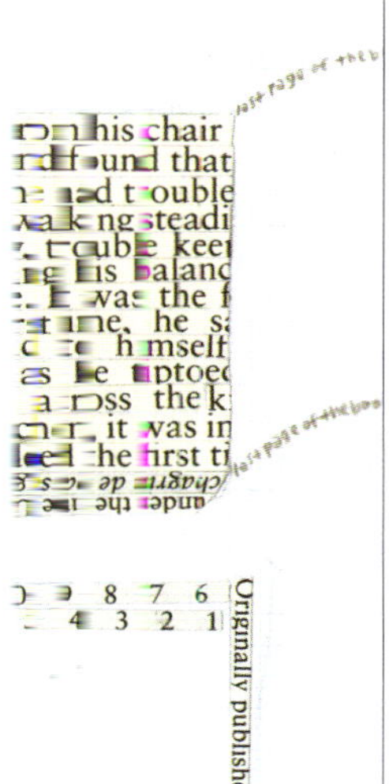

STARTED READING FRANÇOISE SAGAN'S NOVEL "A FLEETING SORROW"

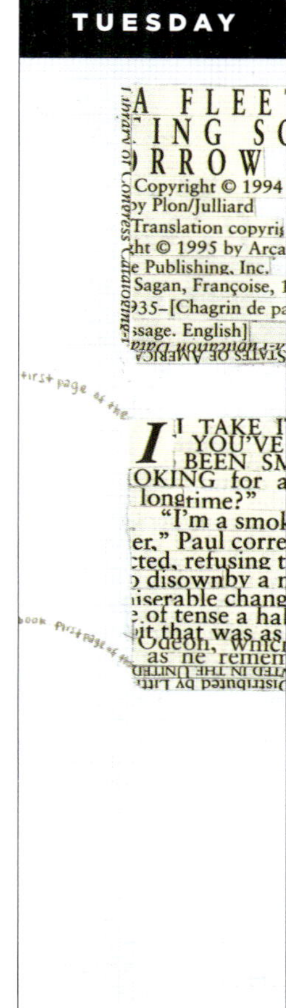

FINISHED READING FRANÇOISE SAGAN'S NOVEL "UN CHAGRIN DE PASSAGE". TRÈS TRÈS BIEN!

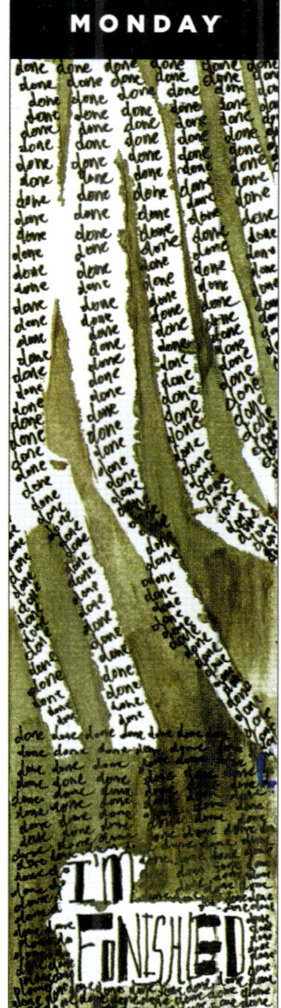

DONE WORKING

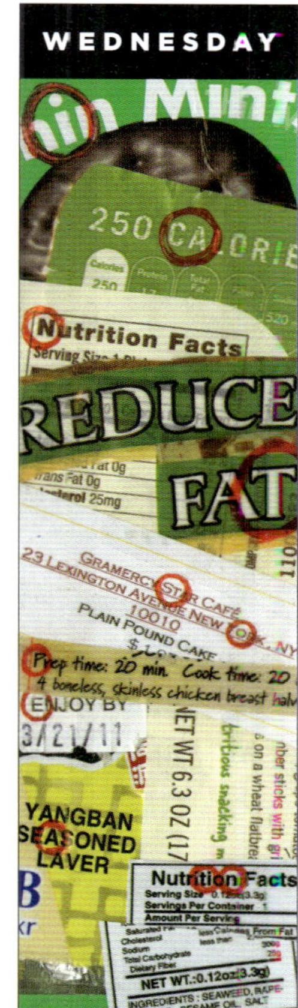

I CAN'T STOP EATING

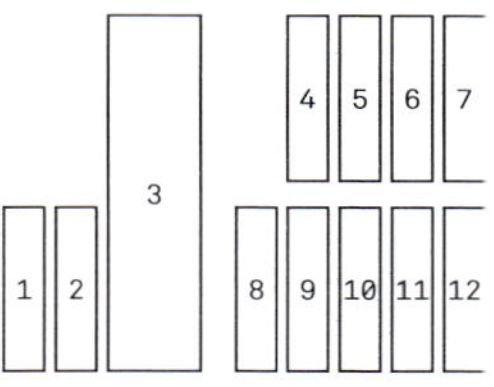

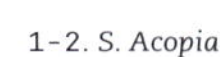

1–2. *S. Acopian*
3. *Enoi Tsao*
4–5. *Sebit Min*
6. *Connor Fitzgerald*
7. *Kyungsuk Jin*
8–9. *Hye Ok Row*
10–12. *Sulah Kim*

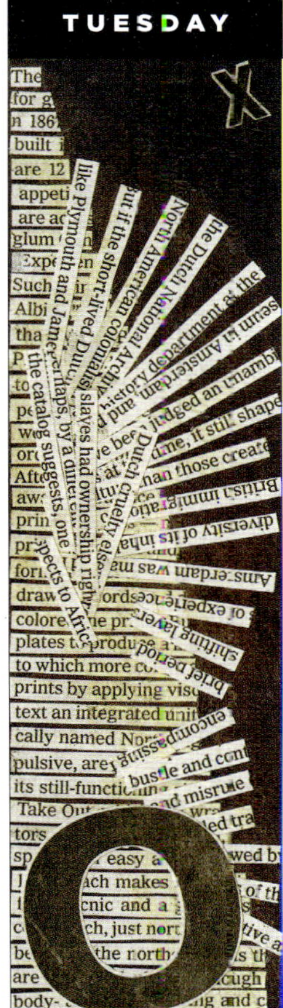

MY GOOD SIDE AND EVIL SIDE ARE FIGHTING! (GOOD SIDE WINS)

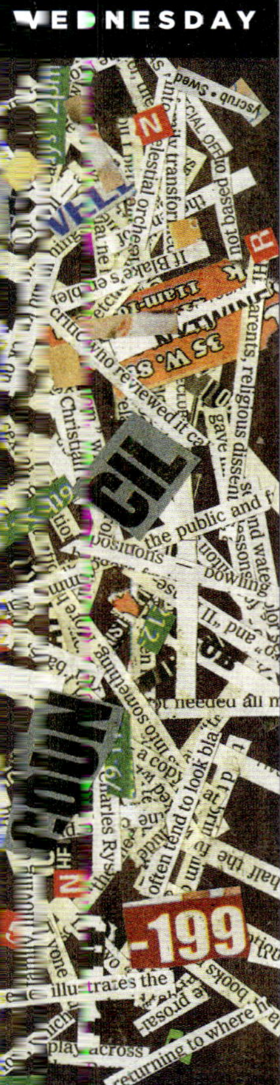

ALL MY IDEAS AND THOUGHTS ARE MESSED UP

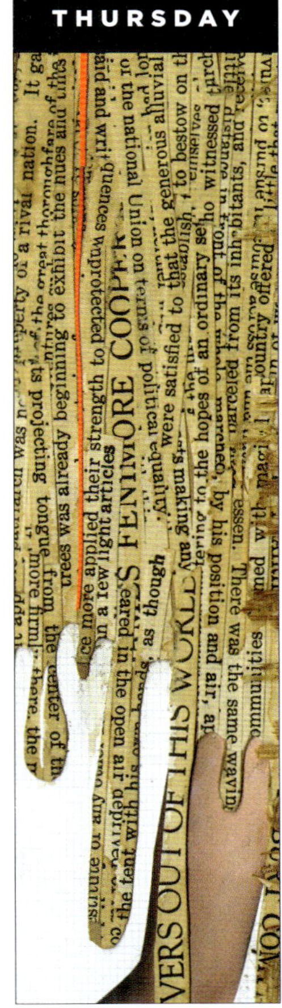

DIZZY, OVERWHELMED

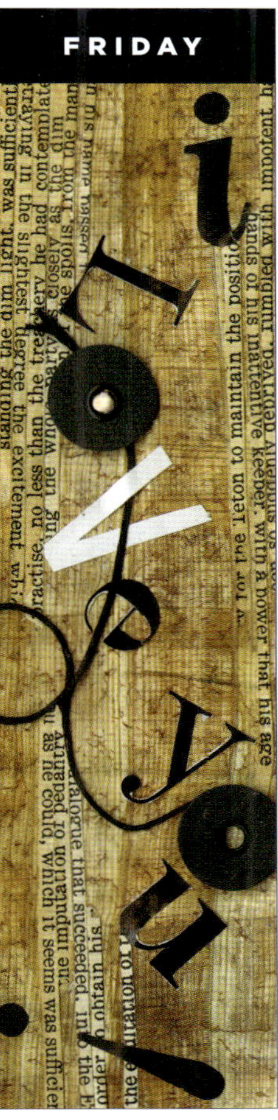

A COMMON WORD IS HARD TO EXPRESS

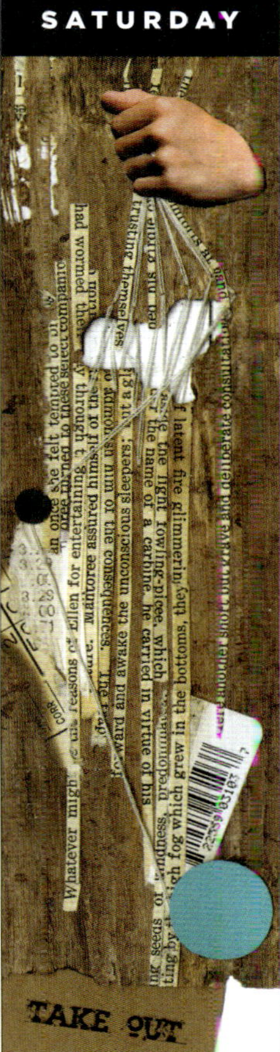

WENT SHOPPING

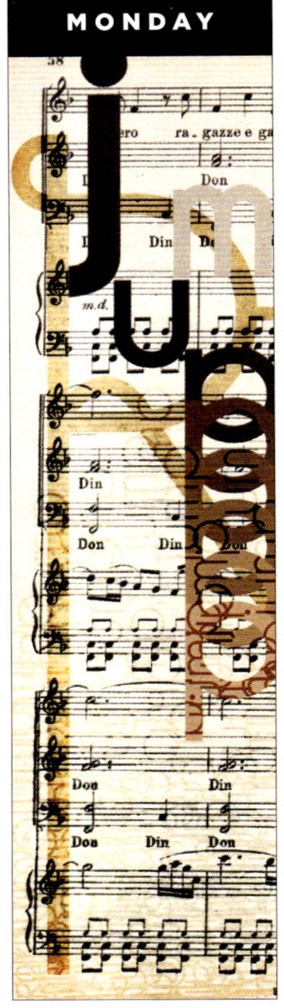

I WAS EXCITED BECAUSE TODAY WAS THE FIRST DAY OF THIS WEEK

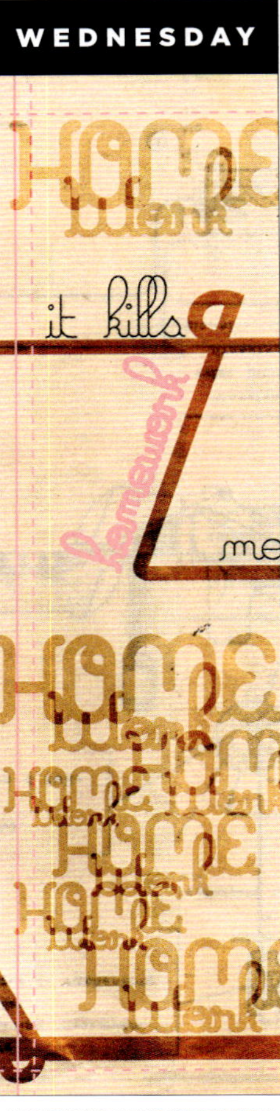

HOMEWORK WAS STRESSFUL

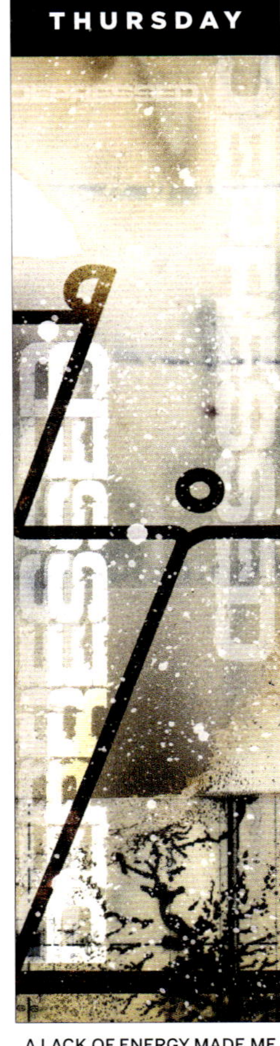

A LACK OF ENERGY MADE ME DEPRESSED

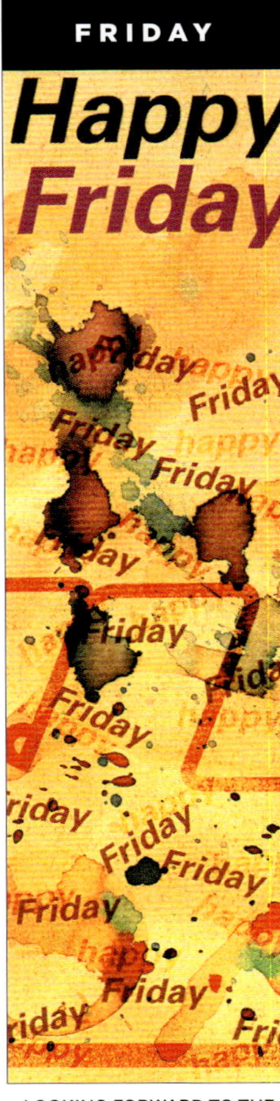

LOOKING FORWARD TO THE WEEKEND

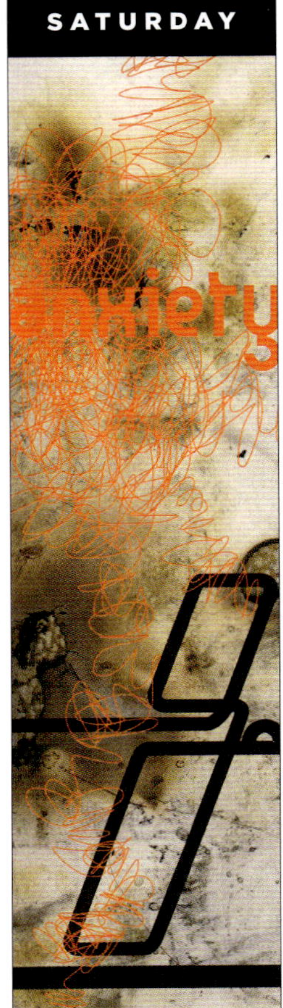

MY ANXIETY THAT I MIGHT NOT GET AN "A" MADE IT IMPOSSIBLE TO FALL ASLEEP

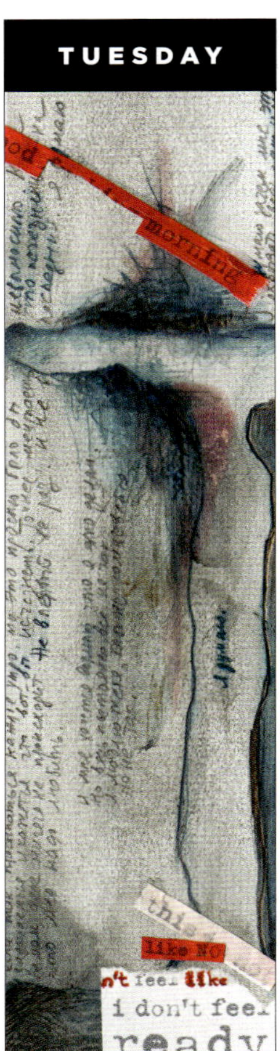

FIRST DAY OF CLASS

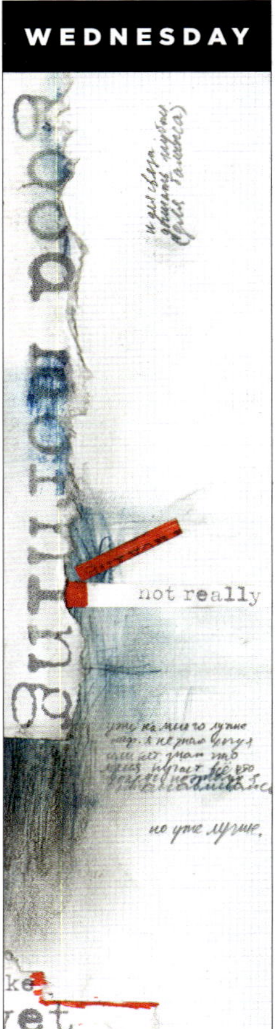

SECOND DAY OF CLASS

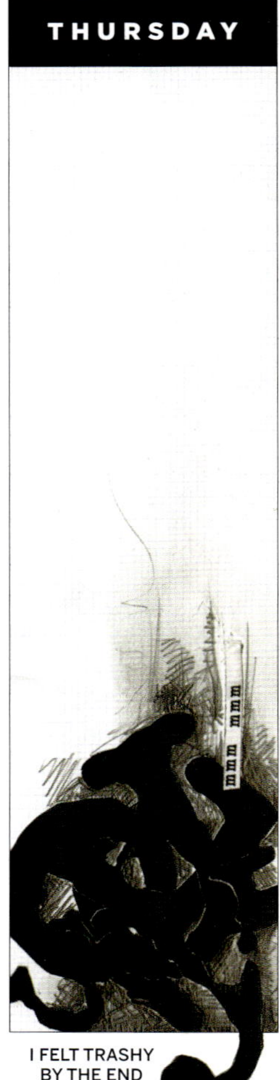

I FELT TRASHY BY THE END OF THE DAY

I HAD THE WORST DAY IN DRAWING CLASS

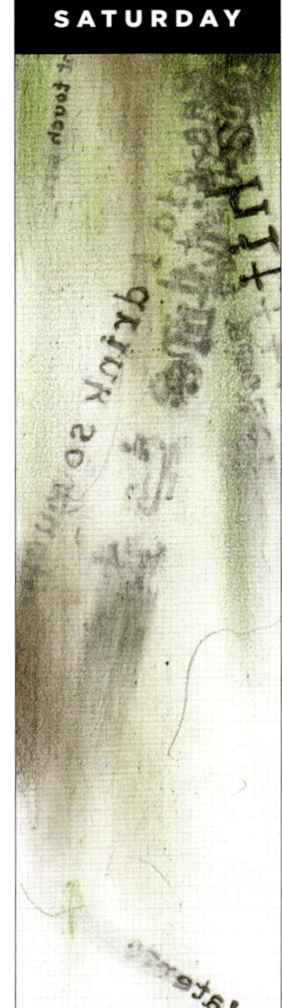

ANOTHER HANGOVER

SUNDAY

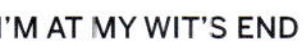

I'M AT MY WIT'S END

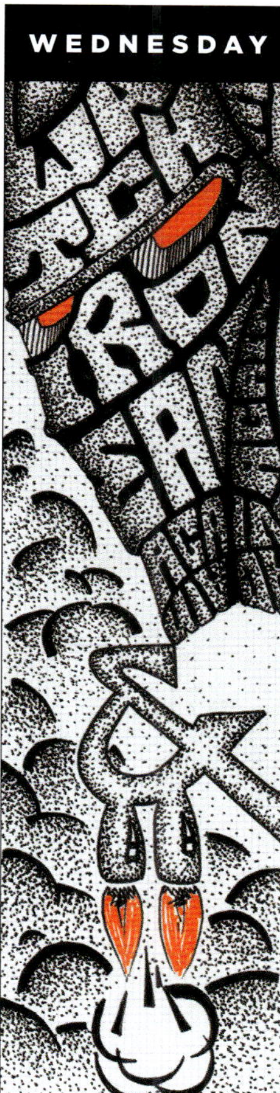

I WISH I WAS IRONMAN

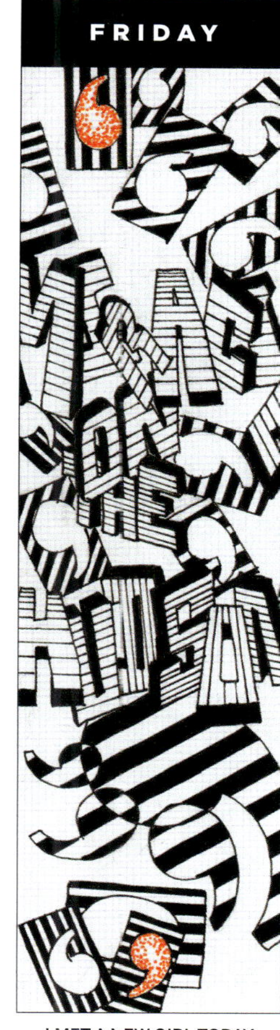

I MET A NEW GIRL TODAY

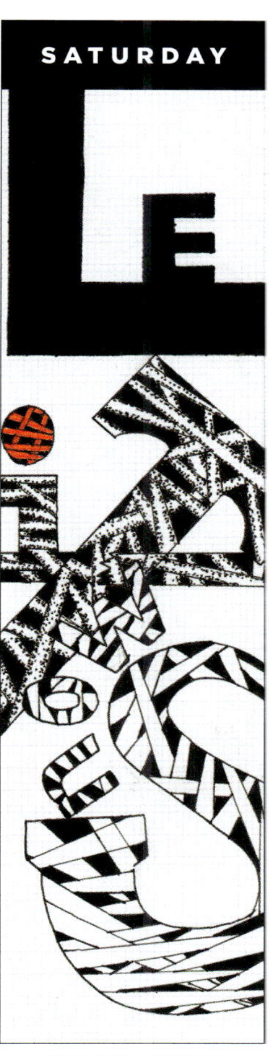

IT SNOWED TODAY.
THINGS ARE EVEN WORSE

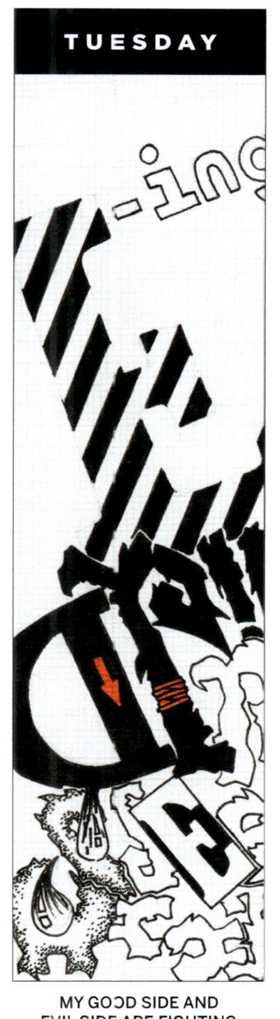

MY GOOD SIDE AND
EVIL SIDE ARE FIGHTING

TYPOGRAPHIC DIARY SOLUTIONS:

Figures 1 through 5, 6 through 10, and 12 through 15 represent the emergence of three distinct stylistic directions toward problem solving.

Figure 11 depicts a complex structure of habitual recurring thoughts to symbolize this everyday occurrence in the form of a monolith, much like the Tower of Babel. This image, like many others that appear in this chapter, is a portrait of humanity.

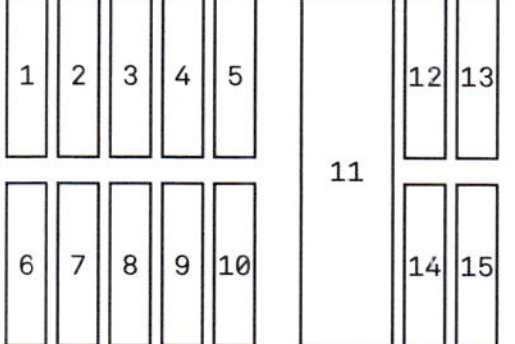

1–5. *Mee Jang*
6–10. *Roza Gazarian*
11. *David Freiman*
12–15. *Shuang Wan*

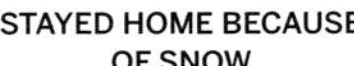

MONDAY

STAYED HOME BECAUSE OF SNOW

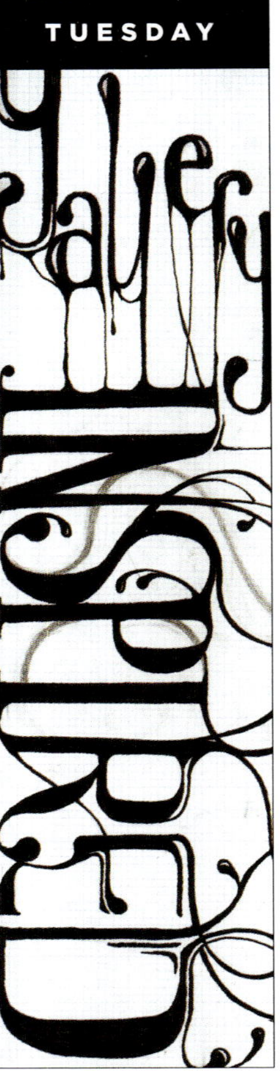

GOING TO A GALLERY INSPIRED ME

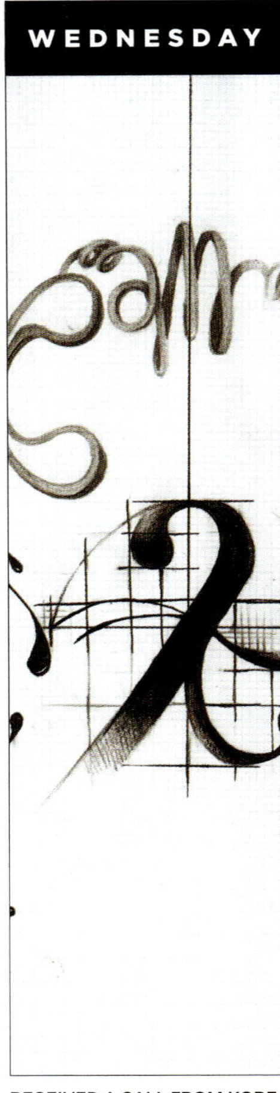

RECEIVED A CALL FROM KOREA

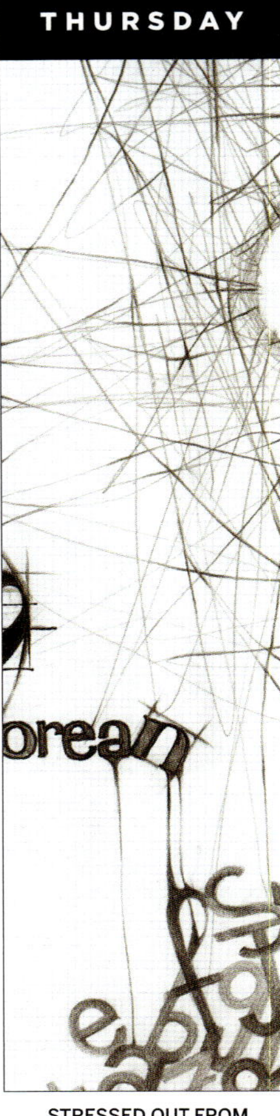

STRESSED OUT FROM STUDYING ENGLISH

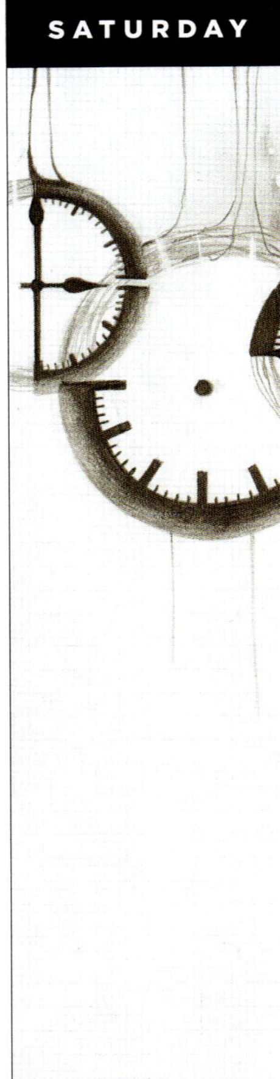

BUSY ALL DAY AND NIGHT

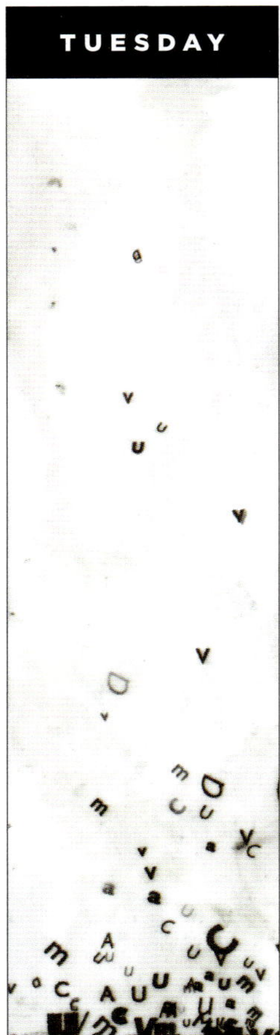

CLEANED UP MY ROOM

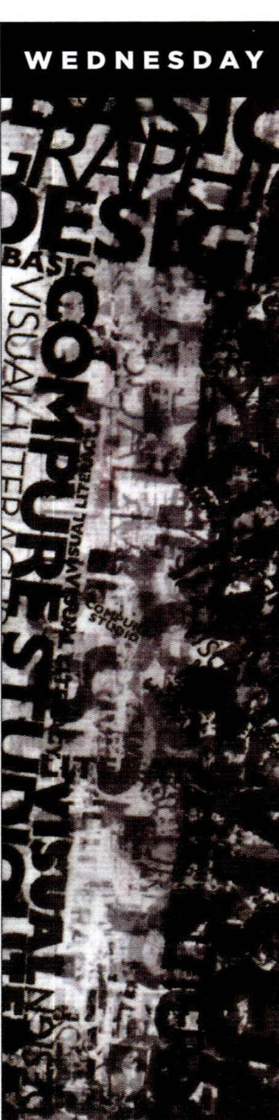

STRESSED OUT. TOO MANY THINGS TO DO

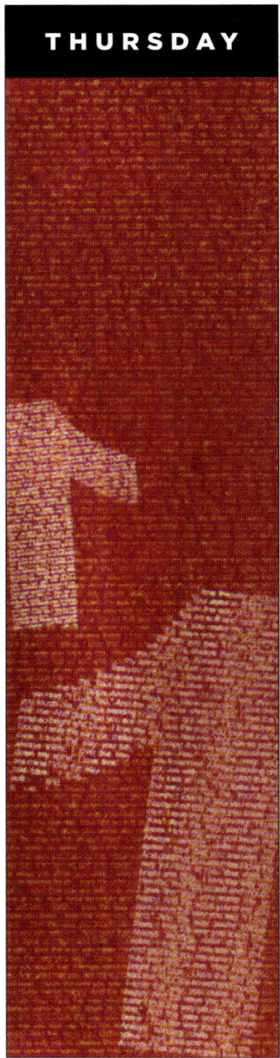

TODAY IS OUR FIRST ANNIVERSARY

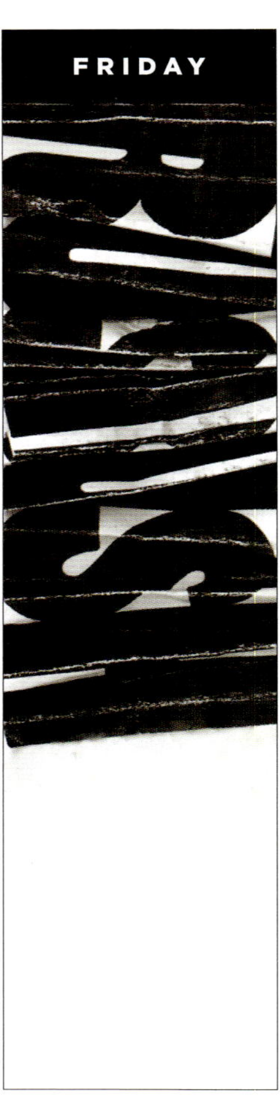

I AM IN A RUSH

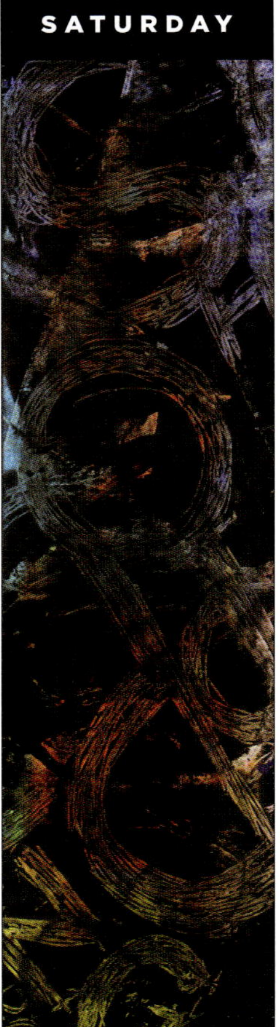

EXPERIMENTED WITH OIL PAINT

TYPOGRAPHIC DIARY SOLUTIONS:

Figures 1 through 5 are hand-drawn explorations.

Figures 6 through 10 approach the problem more emotionally, except for figure 8, which is computer generated.

Figures 11 through 13 use literal imagery to support the playful attitude of the concept.

Figure 14 contrasts typefaces to represent a moment of pondering.

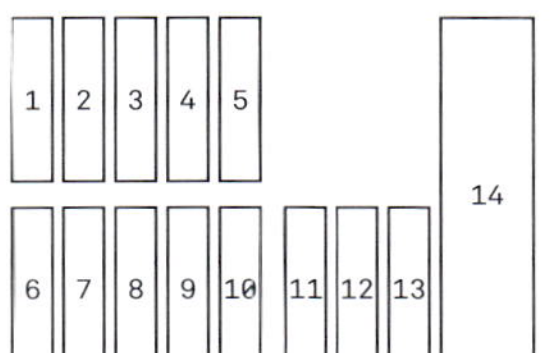

1–5. *Eunji Kim*
6–10. *Miry Shin*
11–13. *Maria Sanoja*
14. *Rheesa Persaud*

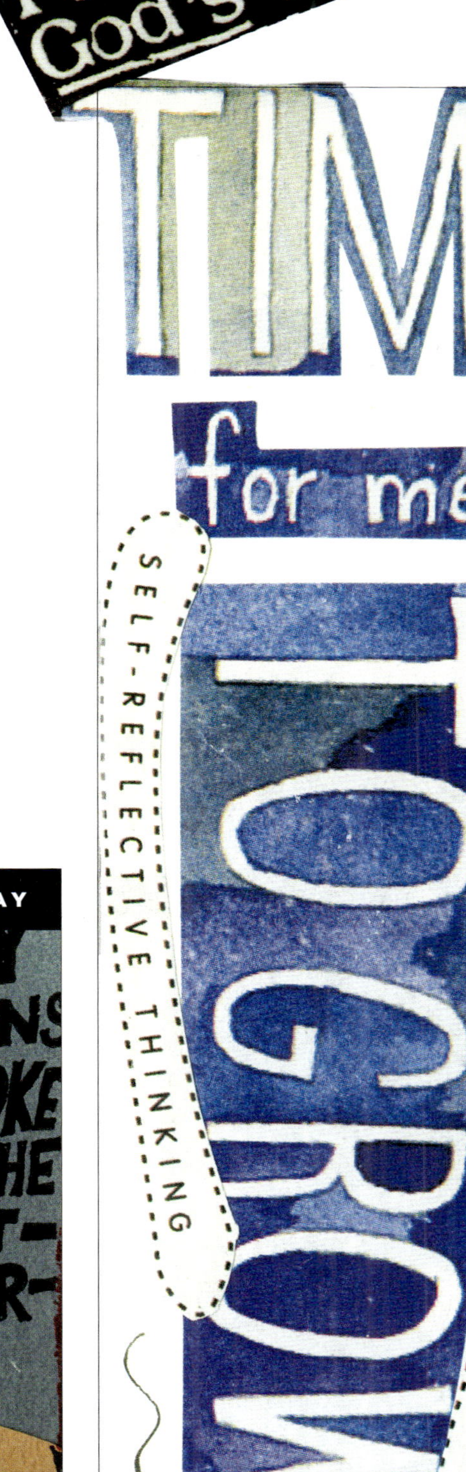

FIRST CLASS NEW RESOLUTIONS

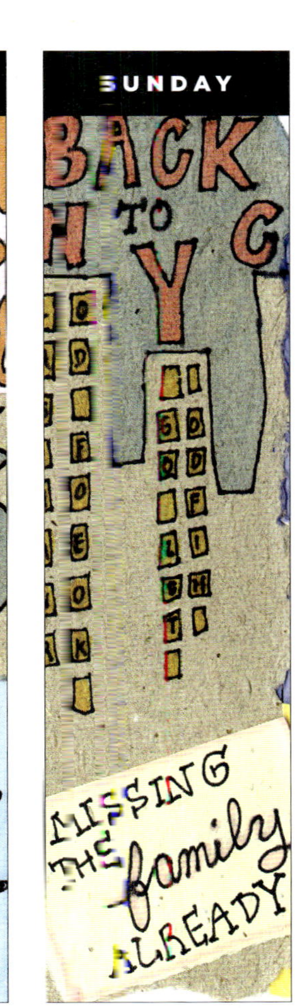

GOT DAD'S FAVORITE COFFEE BLEND

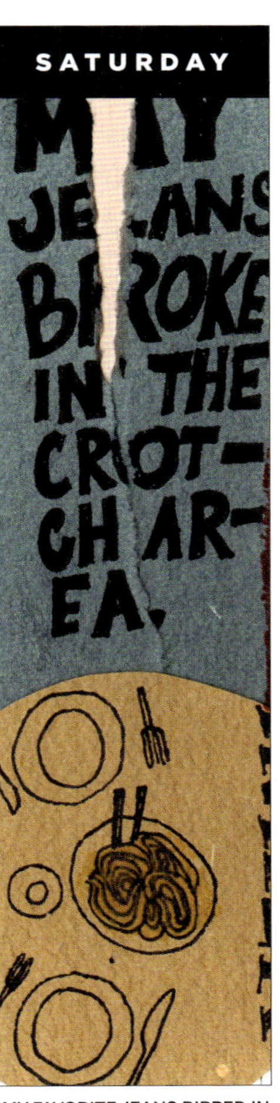

BACK IN THE CITY, LOTS OF HOMEWORK, I ALREADY MISS MY FAMILY.

MY FAVORITE JEANS RIPPED IN THE CROTCH AT A FAMILY DINNER

THURSDAY

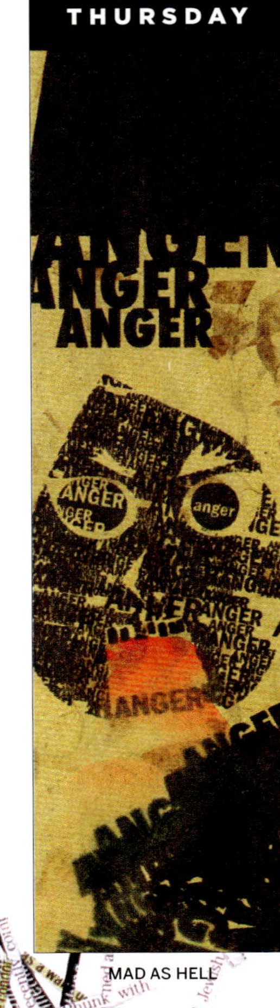

MAD AS HELL

TUESDAY

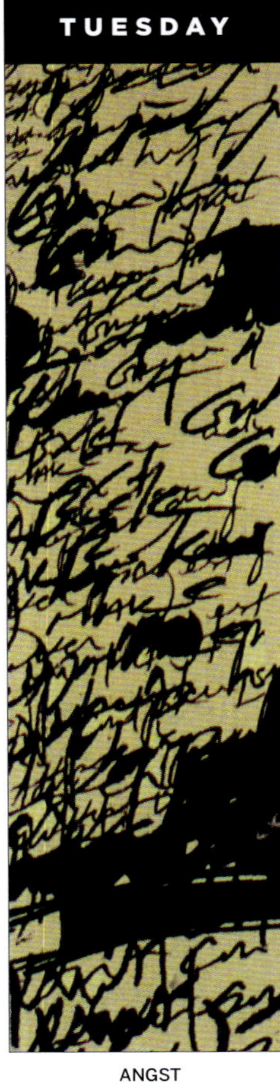

ANGST

FRIDAY

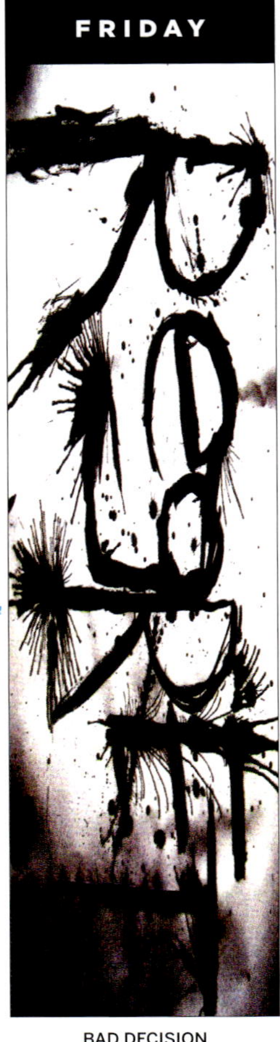

BAD DECISION

THURSDAY

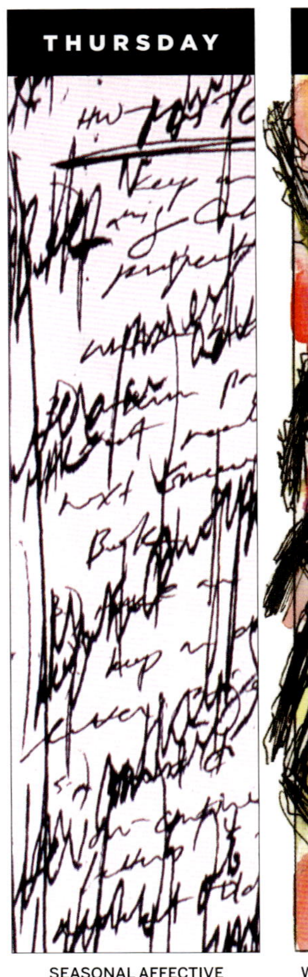

SEASONAL AFFECTIVE DISORDER

THURSDAY

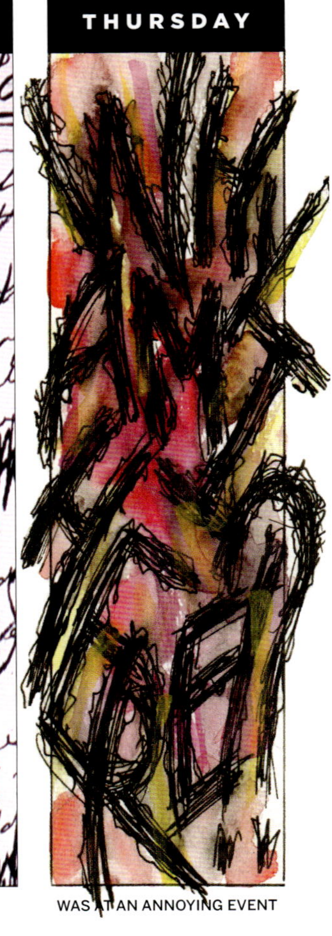

WAS AT AN ANNOYING EVENT

WEDNESDAY

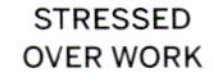

STRESSED OVER WORK

WEDNESDAY

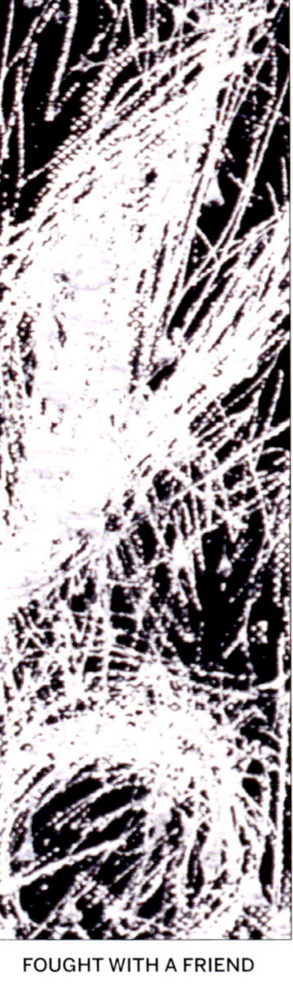

FOUGHT WITH A FRIEND

TUESDAY

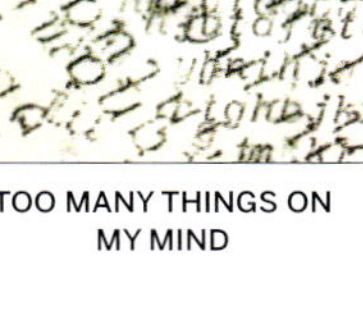

TOO MANY THINGS ON MY MIND

THURSDAY

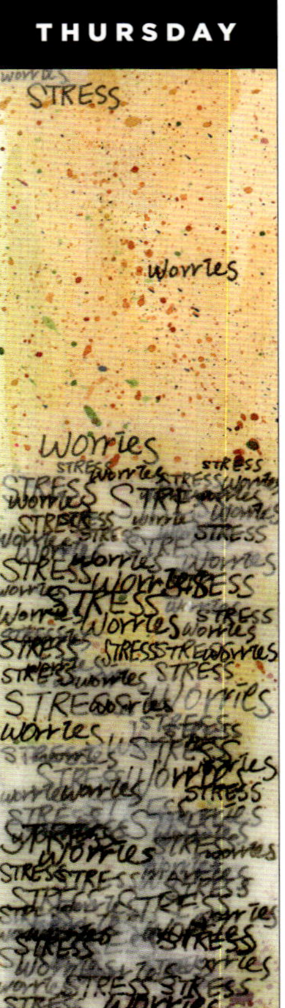

60% STRESS

WEDNESDAY

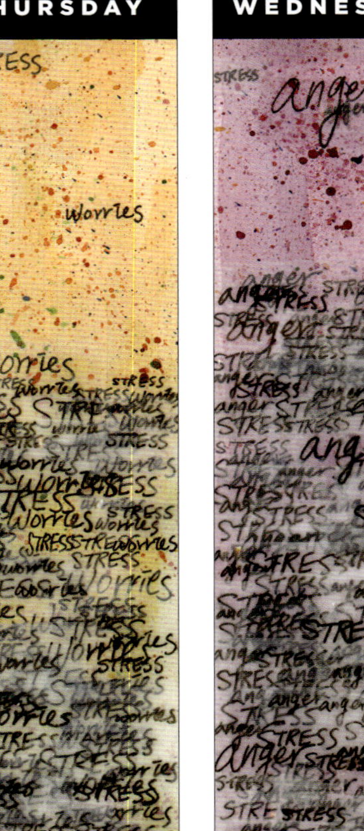

75% STRESS

WEDNESDAY

I WENT TO A VINTAGE SHOP

WEDNESDAY

SNOWING THE WHOLE DAY IN NEW YORK CITY

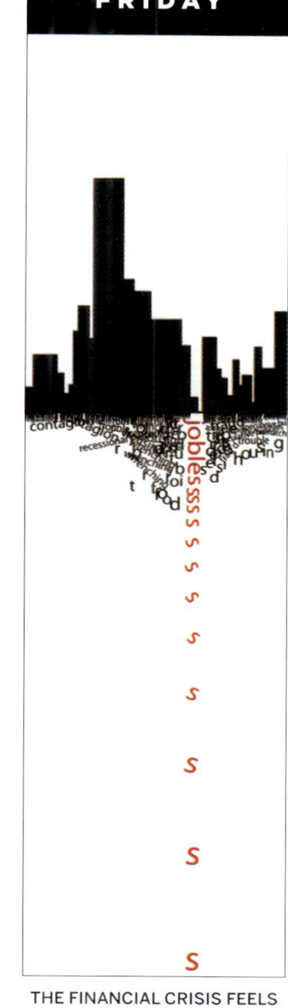

THE FINANCIAL CRISIS FEELS LIKE NEW YORK IS BLEEDING

SATURDAY

tic
tok
tic
tok
tic
tok
tic
tok
tic
tok
tic
tok
tic
tok
tic
tok
tic
tok
tic
tok
tic
tok
tic
tok
tic

I TOOK THE PROFICIENCY EXAM. I WAS RUSHED FOR TIME

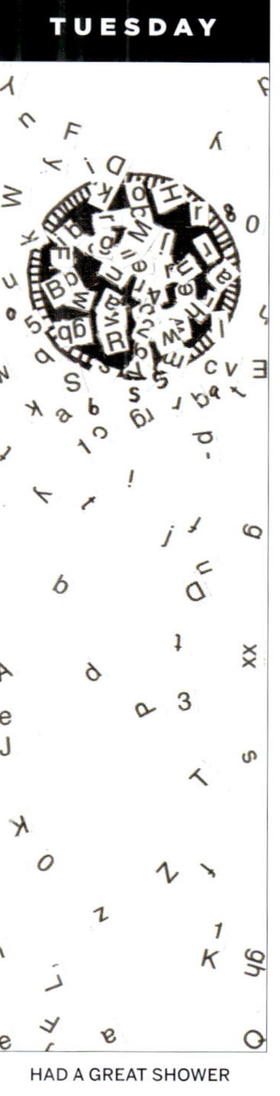

HAD A GREAT SHOWER

TYPOGRAPHIC DIARY SOLUTIONS:

Figures 1 through 10 are expressions of anguish. All these solutions have the common denominator of being spontaneously drawn, which represents an emotional response to the project. For many, the handwritten word is first viewed for its formal impact and secondly, for comprehending the narrative.

Figure 11 spells out the word "vintage," where artistic license is taken with the letter "N" and the letter "A."

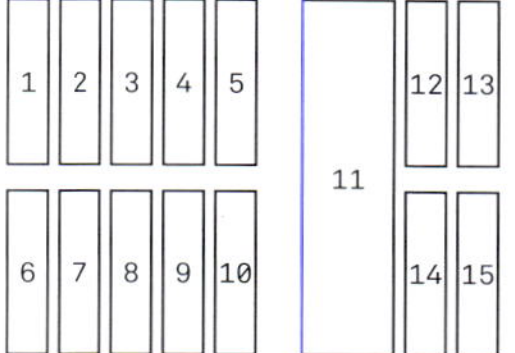

1. *Jimin Nam*
2. *Mao Kudo*
3. *David Mannion*
4. *Mao Kudo*
5. *Alexandra Stikeleather*
6. *Suhyun Kim*
7. *Kayoung Lee*
8. *Zia Frank*

9–10. *Soomin Yoo*

11. *Soyoon Lee*
12. *Andrea Espinosa*
13. *Wanqin Nong*
14. *Minjee Cho*
15. *Y. Kim*

Figures 12 through 14 use computer-generated typography and figure 15 uses collage, all expressing personal narratives.

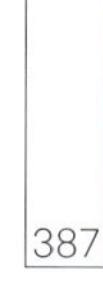

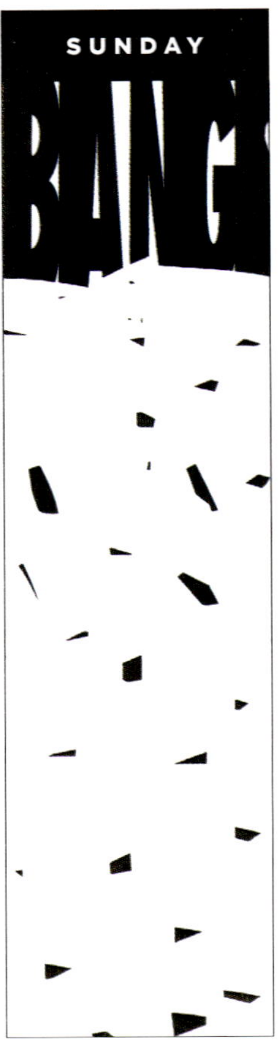

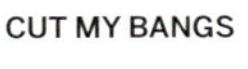

CUT MY BANGS

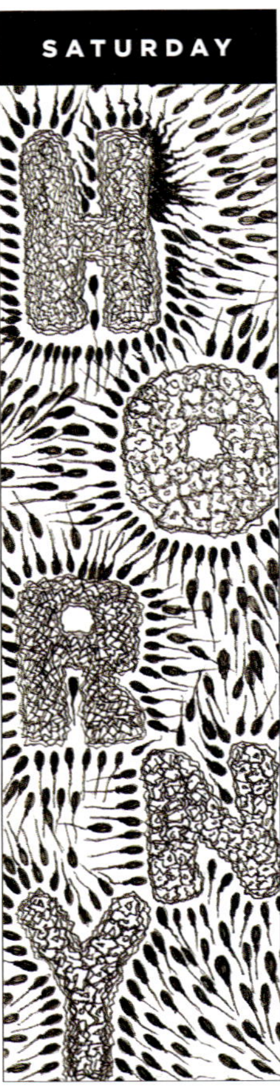

FELT A LITTLE BIT HORNY TODAY

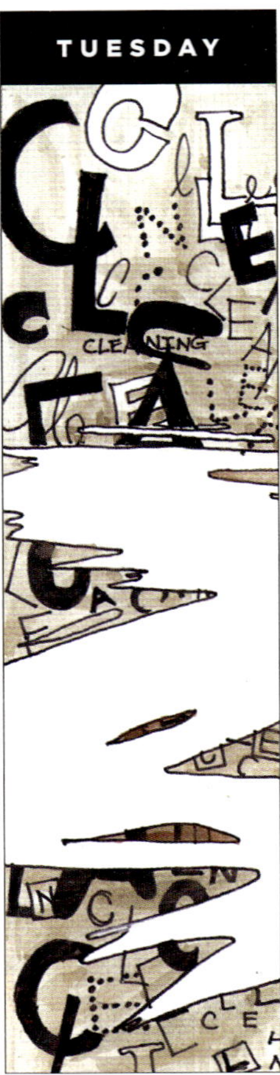

CLEANED MY ROOM

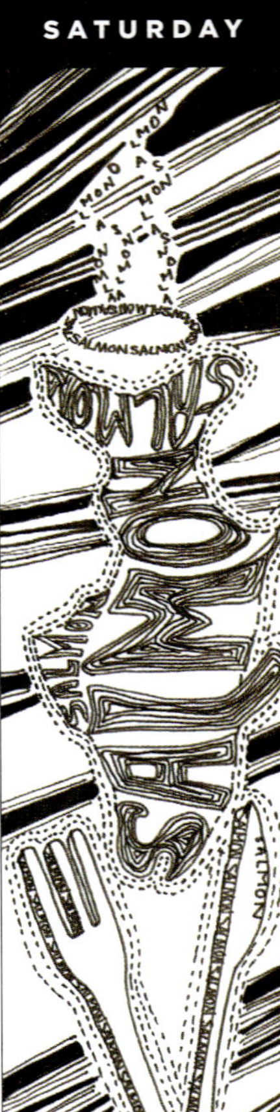

I ATE SALMON

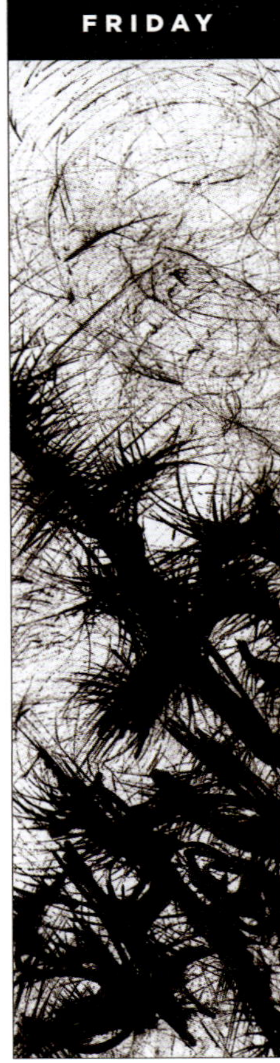

LISTENED TO MUSIC

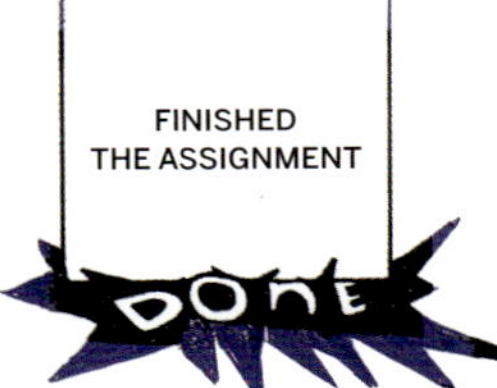

WAS IN A BAD MOOD FOR MOST OF THE DAY

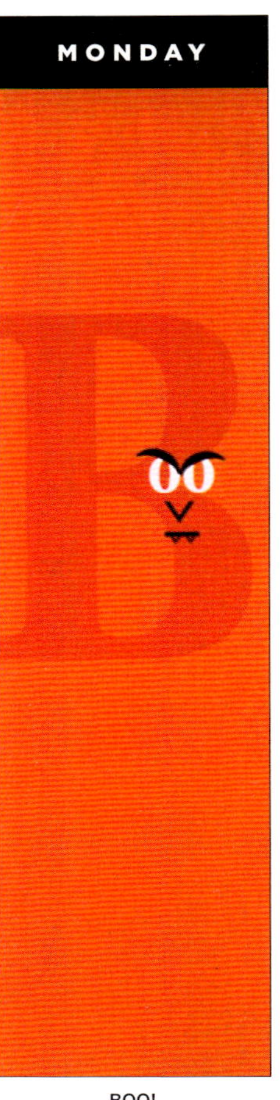

BOO!
HAPPY HALLOWEEN

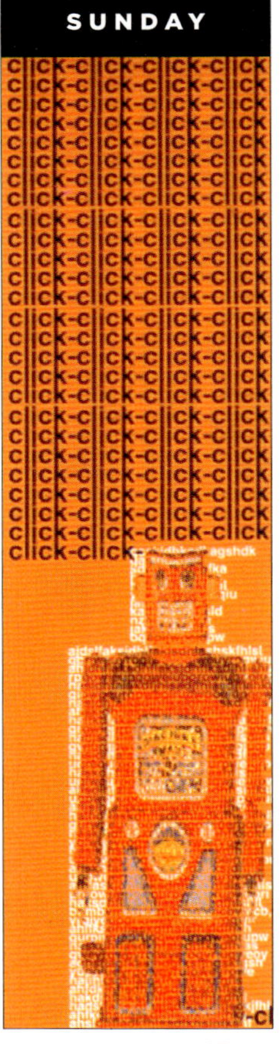

I FELT LIKE A ROBOT, CLICKING THE MOUSE ALL DAY

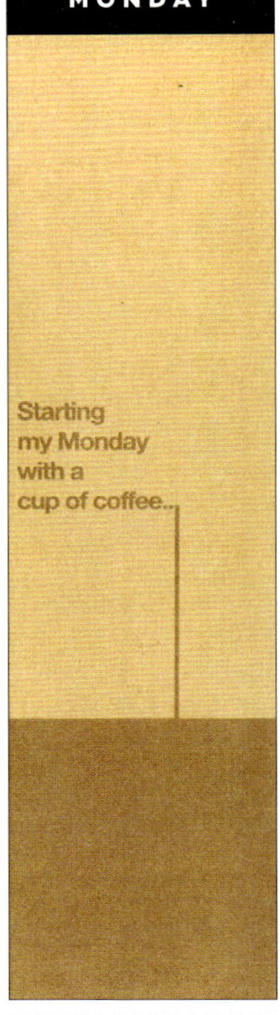

HAPPY MONDAY! BLOODSHOT EYES, STARTED MY CLASS WITH COFFEE.

MY BOYFRIEND CAME TO VISIT

I GO TO CHURCH AND PRAY ON SUNDAY

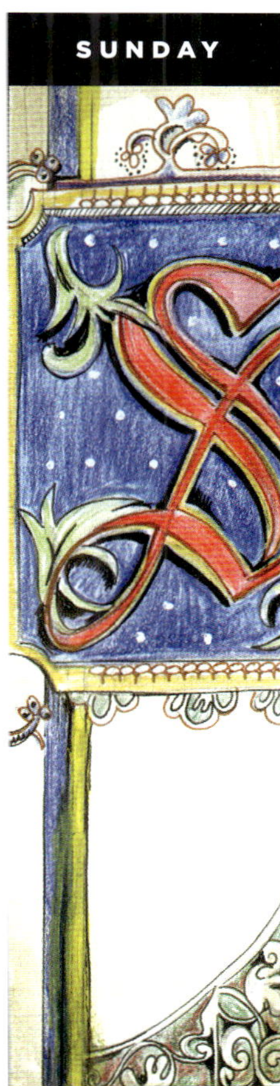

WENT TO CHURCH

TYPOGRAPHIC DIARY SOLUTIONS:

Figures 1 through 6 are various solutions, ranging from spontaneous to more deliberate. The principle of space is imaginatively used in many of the compositions.

Figures 7 through 10 are computer generated and adhere to a more structured and gridlike underpinning.

In both figures 6 and 11, the given format of the assignment is transformed into an exclamation mark inferring "completion" and "innuendo" respectively.

Figures 12 and 13 represent two different interpretations of the same theme, using collage and colored pencils to depict aspects of religious beliefs.

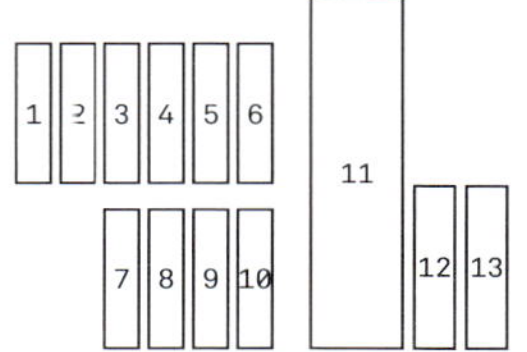

1. *Soyoon Lee*
2. *Min Choi*
3. *Hyunhwa Lee*
4. *Hye Ram Jeon*
5. *Dohee Kim*
6. *S. Kim*
7. *Francis Soriano*
8. *Meaghan Tirandola*
9. *Natasha Jen*
10. *Somang Kim*
11. *Nicole Benson*
12. *Hye Ok Row*
13. *Christina Choi*

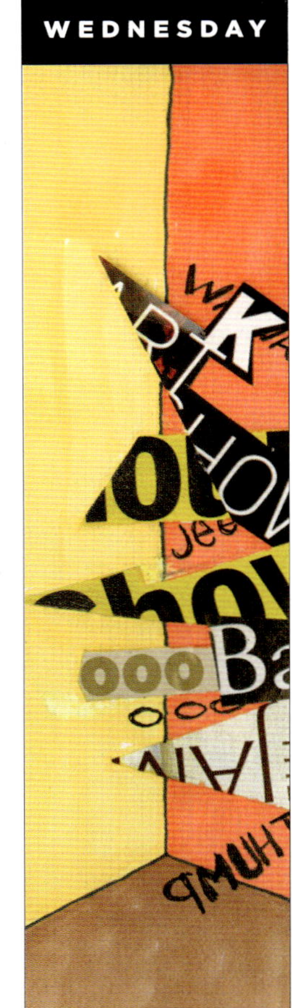

NEIGHBORS WON'T STOP PLAYING MUSIC

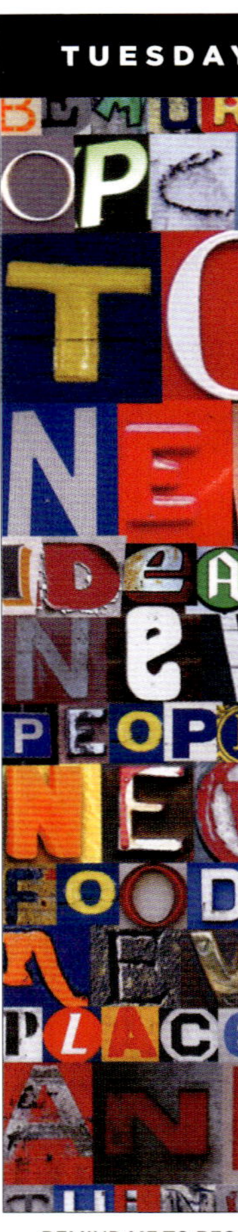

REMIND ME TO REOPEN MY MIND

GETTING LOST IN MY ORANGE PROJECT

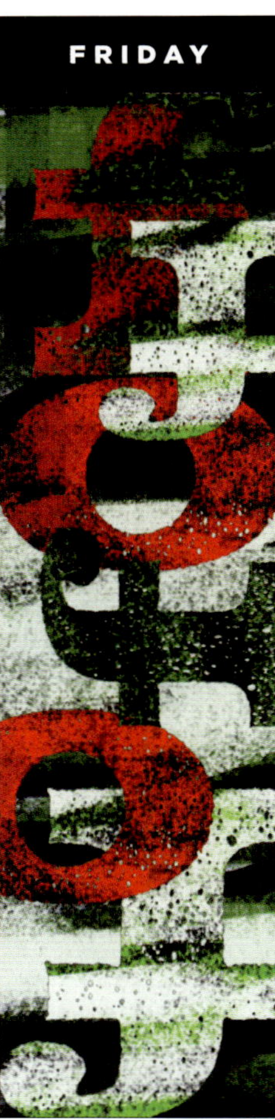

FINALLY HAD A DAY OFF

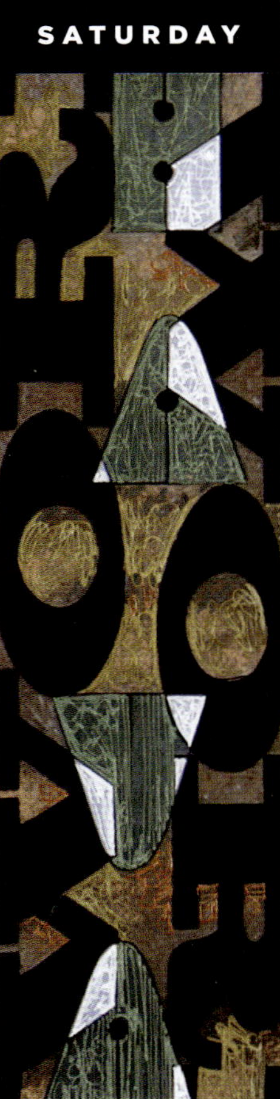

WORK, WORK, WORK

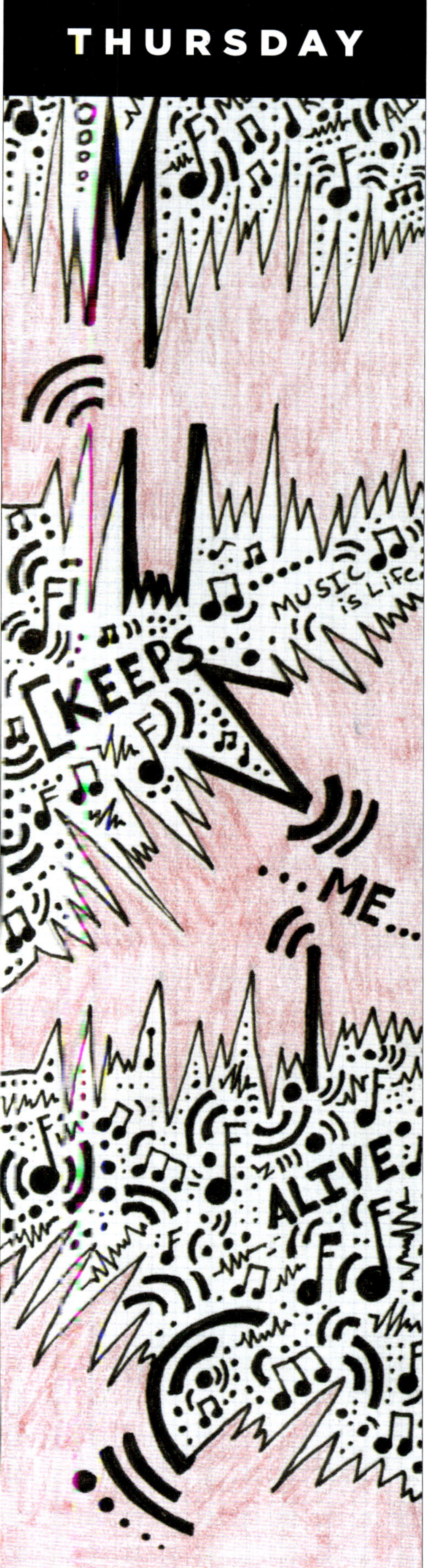

I DOWNLOADED MUSIC FOR MOST OF THE DAY. HIP HOP MAKES ME SO HAPPY.

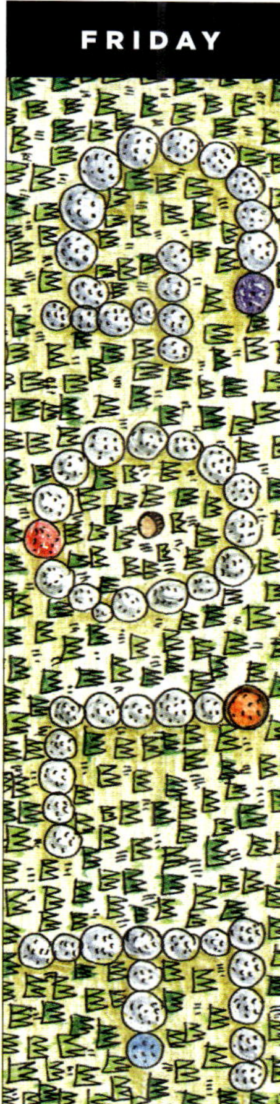

SHOT AN 83

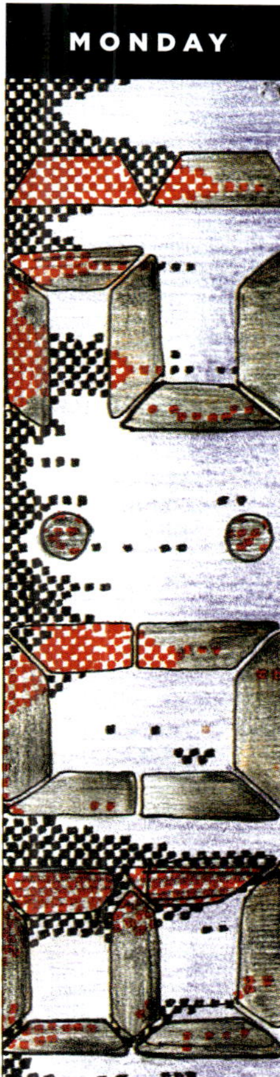

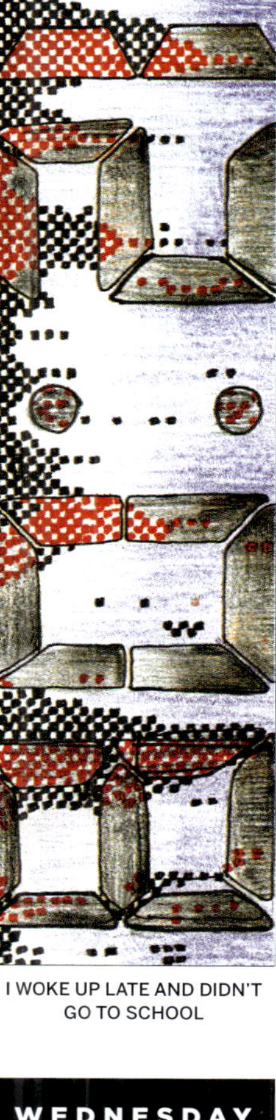

I WOKE UP LATE AND DIDN'T GO TO SCHOOL

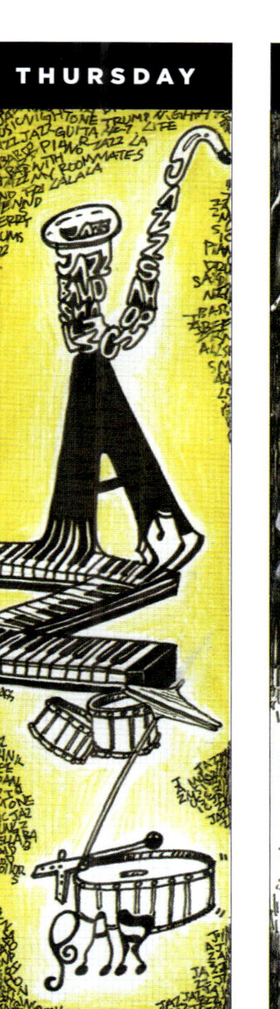

WENT TO A JAZZ BAR

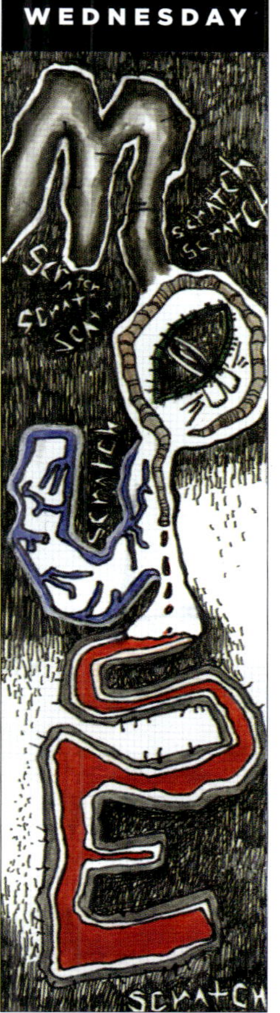

I HEARD A MOUSE

TYPOGRAPHIC DIARY SOLUTIONS:

Figure 1 expresses noise in a lighthearted way.

Figure 2 utilizes numerous typefaces to reinforce the concept of being open to the new.

Figure 3 deals with layering as a way of capturing frenetic energy.

Figures 4 and 5 depict the interaction of negative and positive shapes to dramatize the complexity of life.

Figures 6 through 10 encompass a playful approach supported by narrative elements.

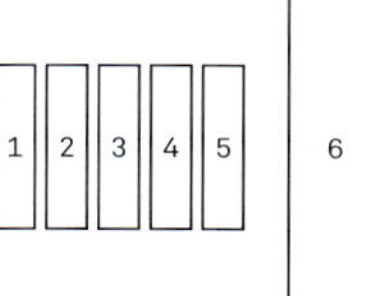

1. *Michael Murphy*
2. *Joshua Carpenter*
3-5. *Nataliya Hats*
6. *Brent Philhower*
7-8. *Anna Kim*
9-10. *Myungjin Kyung*

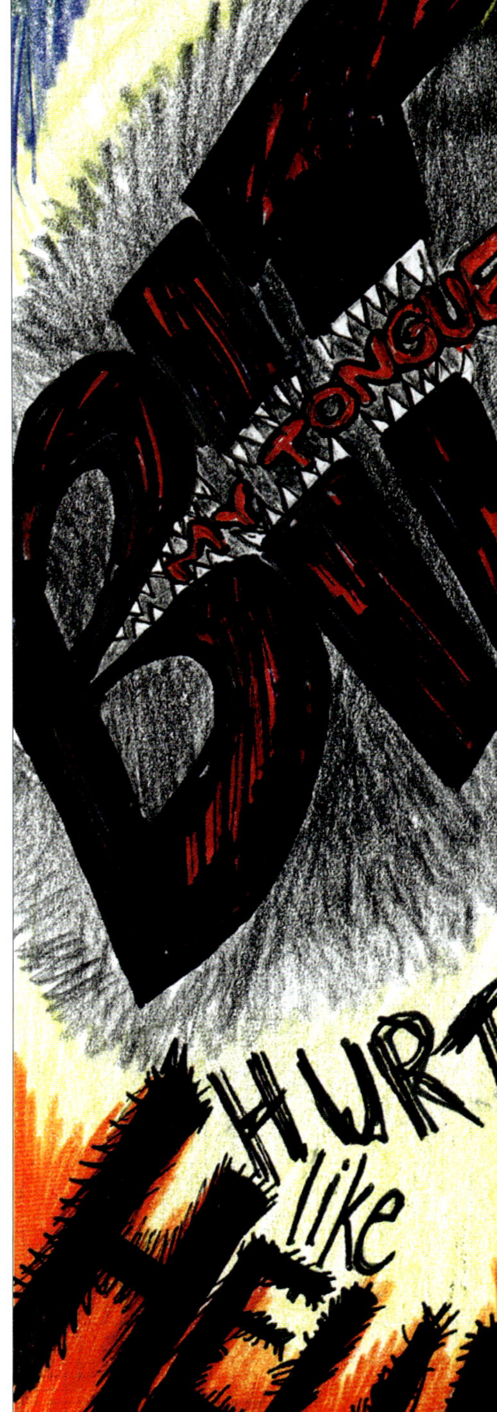

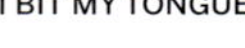
I BIT MY TONGUE

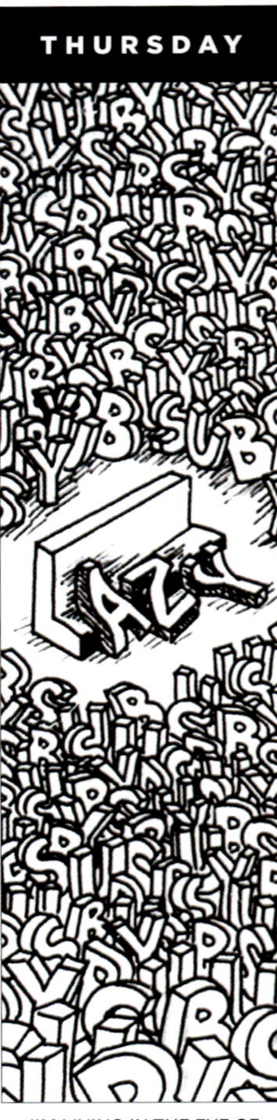

I'M LIVING IN THE EYE OF A STORM

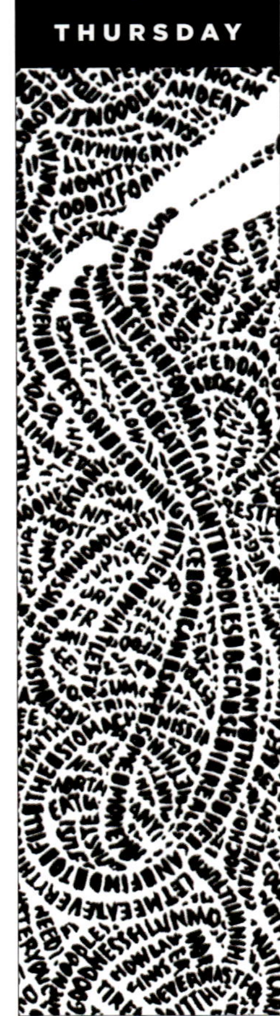

INSTANT NOODLES ALL DAY LONG

VISITED THE QUEENS LIBRARY

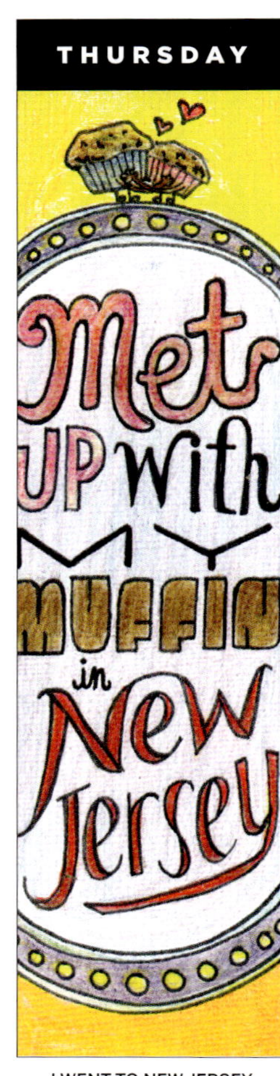

I WENT TO NEW JERSEY

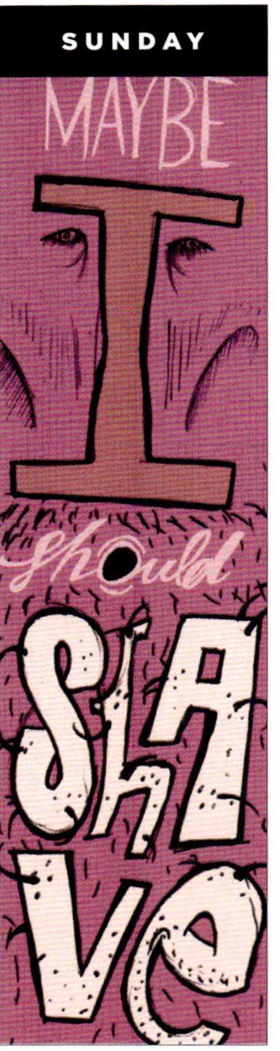

I FEEL HAIRY,
MAYBE I SHOULD SHAVE

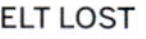

FELT LOST

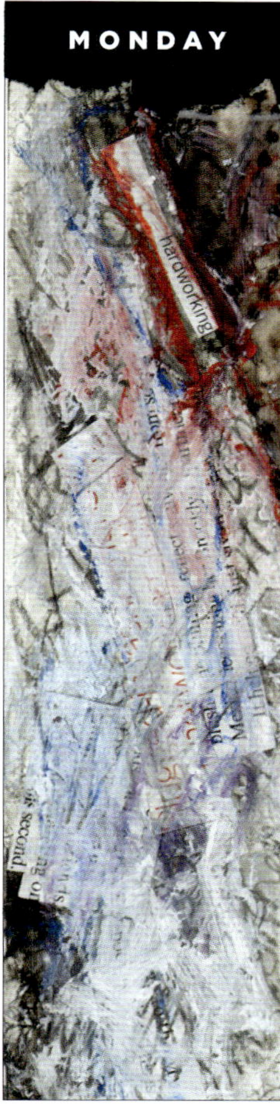

WORKING VERY HARD ON AN ASSIGNMENT

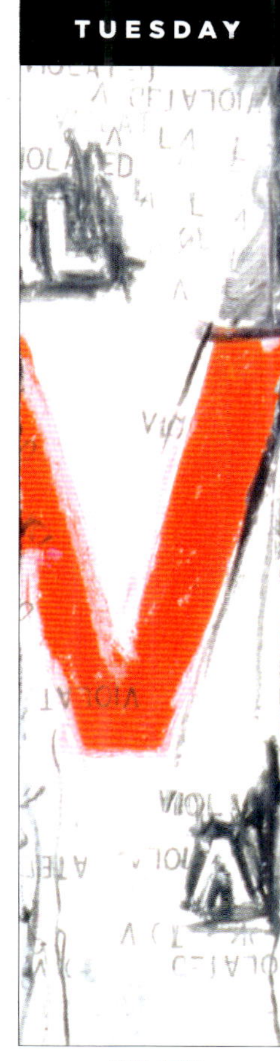

VIOLATED

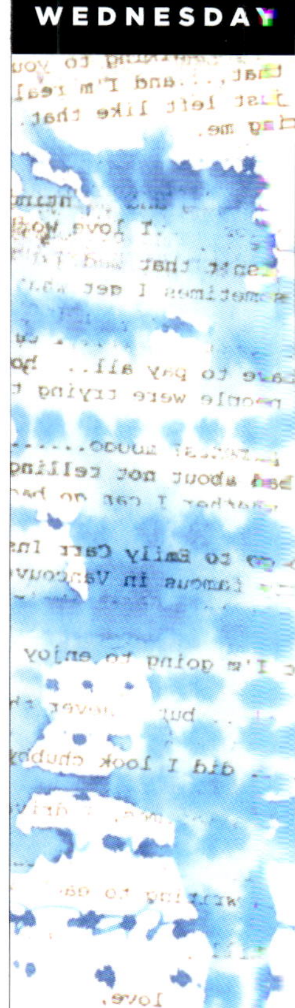

I BOUGHT A FISH TODAY

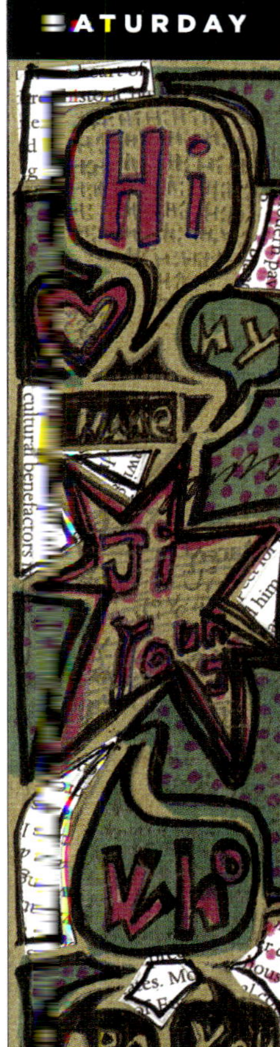

I MET A NEW FRIEND

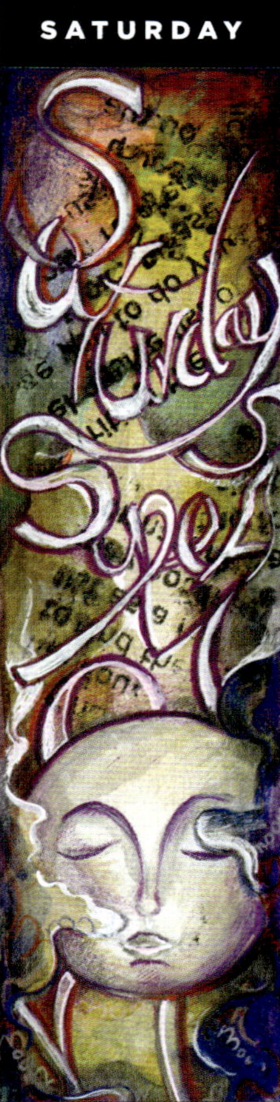

SATURDAY'S SUPER MOON (THE MOON WAS CLOSER TO EARTH THAN IT HAS BEEN IN 18 YEARS)

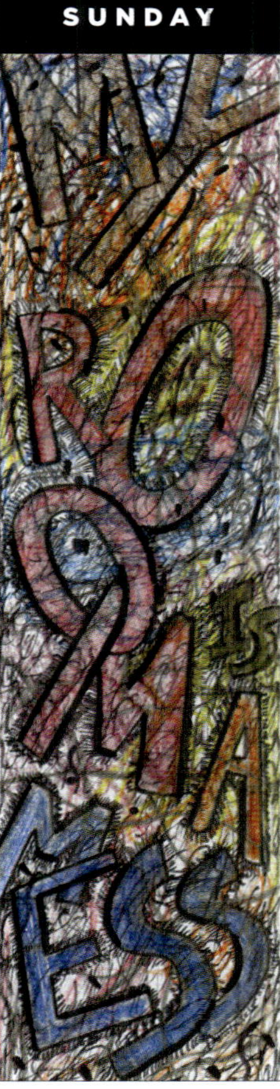

MY ROOM IS SO MESSY. I SHOULD PROBABLY CLEAN IT SOON

TYPOGRAPHIC DIARY SOLUTIONS:

Figure 1 uses dramatically drawn typography to enact the painful moment of biting one's tongue.

Figure 2 uses typography anthropomorphically, while figure 3 uses hand-drawn typography to create a pattern that simulates the act of eating noodles, where chopsticks appear in the negative space.

Figures 4, 5, 6 and 12 use literal imagery, while figures 7 through 11 and 13 are abstract interpretations that place a greater demand on the viewer's attention.

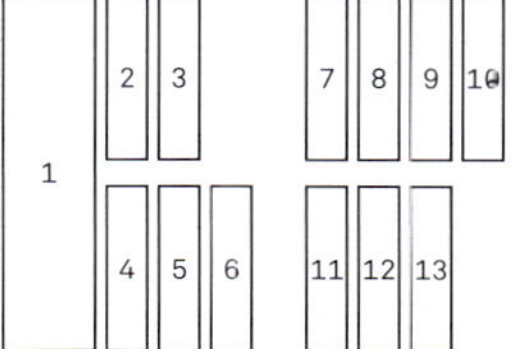

1. *Raisa Serrano*
2–3. *Wei Lieh Lee*
4–5. *Emily Matsuno*
6. *Pablo Delcan*
7. *J. Welho*
8. *Borim Kim*
9. *Nicole Caputo*
10. *Jieun Cho*
11. *Jiyoung Lee*
12. *Jaewon Park*
13. *Brent Philhower*

MONDAY

WANNA BE INVISIBLE FROM THIS WORLD

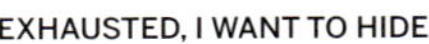

EXHAUSTED, I WANT TO HIDE

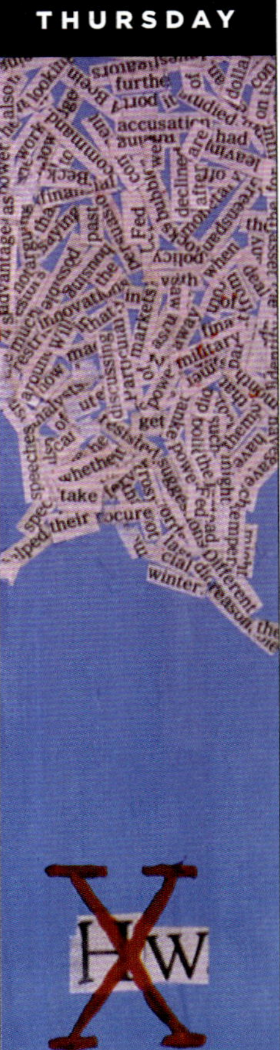

COULD NOT DO MY HOME-WORK BECAUSE MY PARENTS WERE ARGUING

CLUBBING

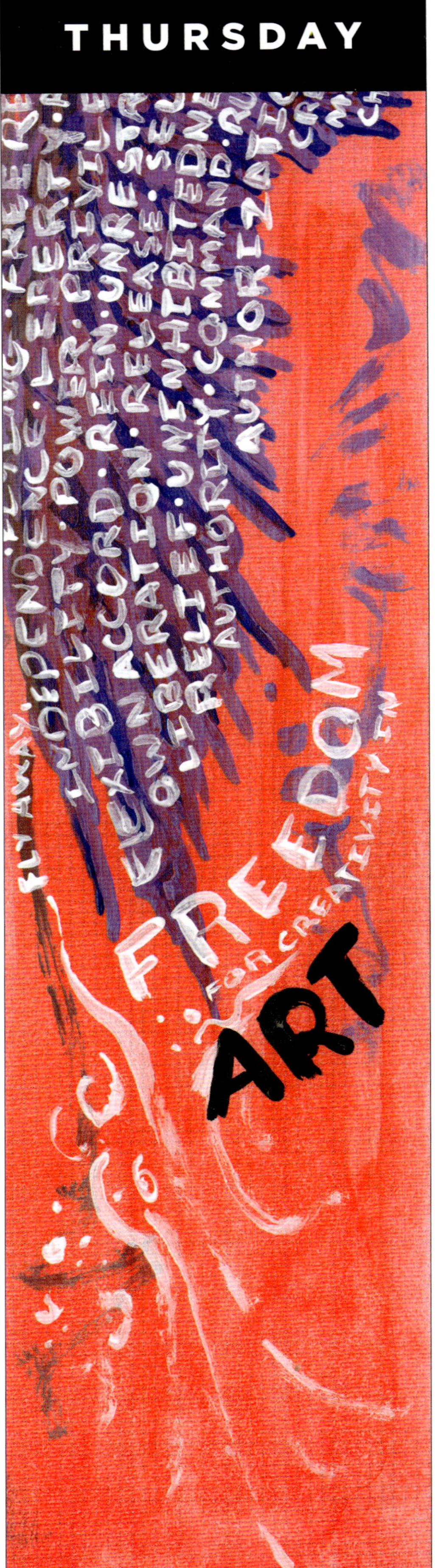

I AM ENJOYING FREEDOM OF EXPRESSION

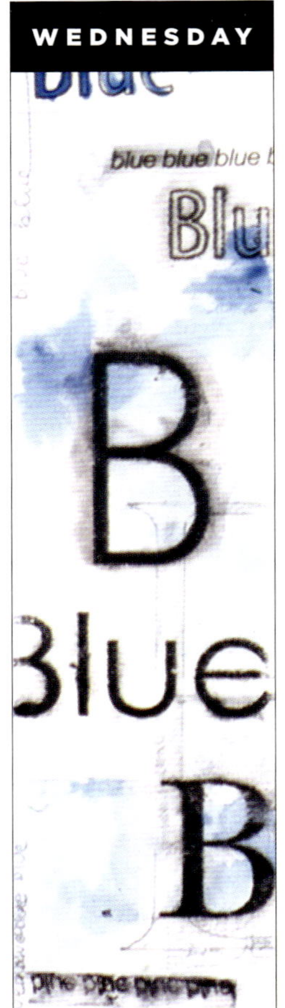

BLUE ALL DAY

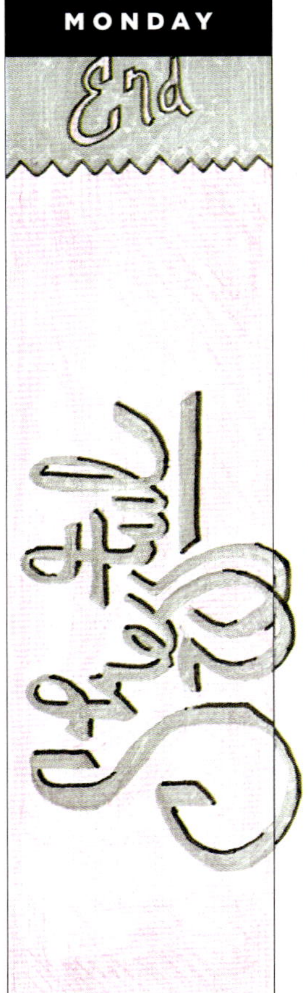

LONG DAY

TUESDAY

I DIDN'T HAVE PATIENCE

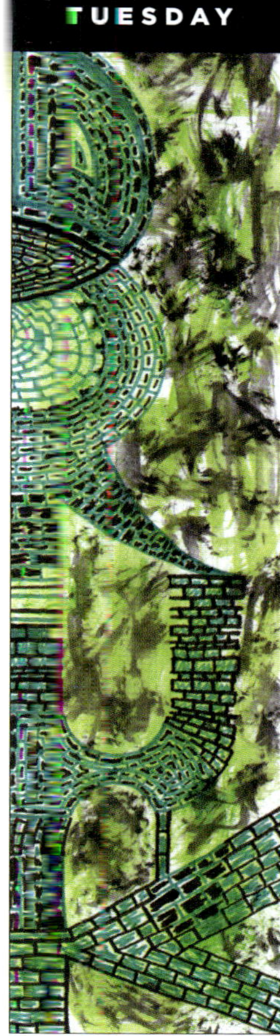

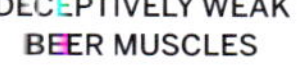

DECEPTIVELY WEAK BEER MUSCLES

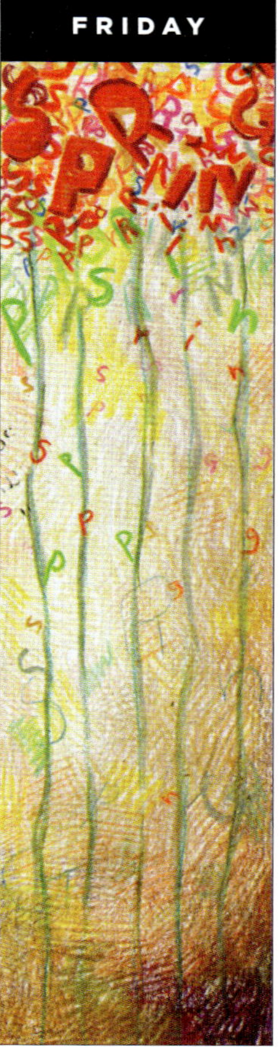

I SMELL SPRING

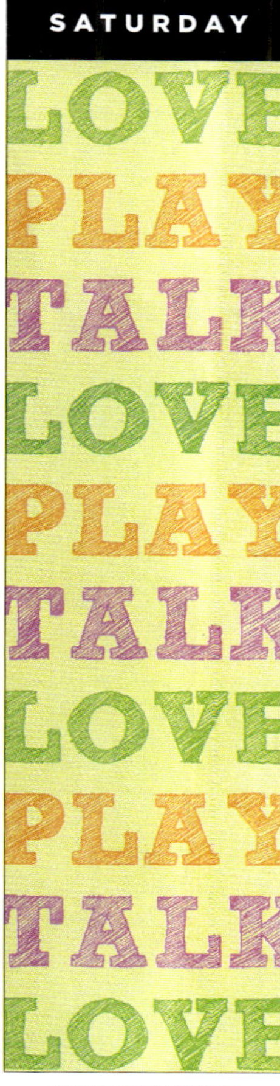

I HAVE A BOYFRIEND

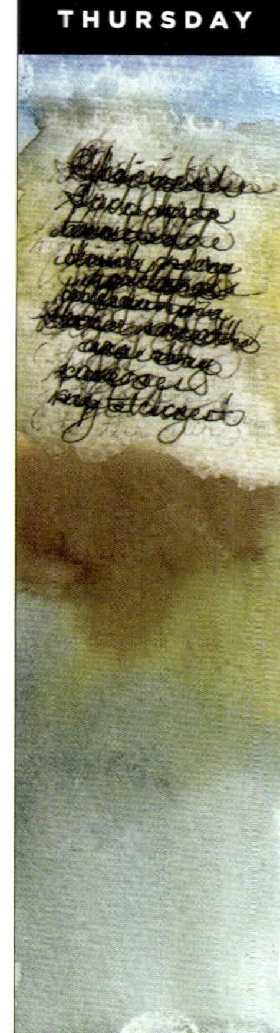

TAKING THE TIME TO PROCESS MY THOUGHTS

TYPOGRAPHIC DIARY SOLUTIONS:

These solutions represent a diversity of attitudes and styles for solving this assignment, ranging from emotionally driven executions to conceptually oriented approaches.

Figures 13 and 14, which were executed by the same student, express late-night eating and endless homework, but what is noteworthy is how one day visually runs into the next.

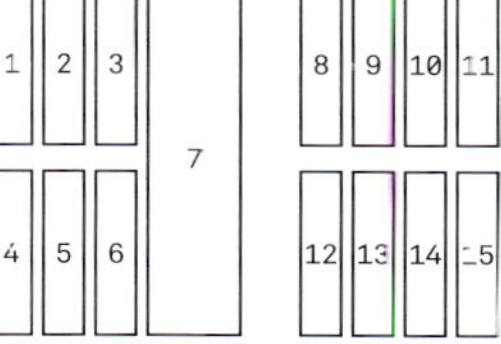

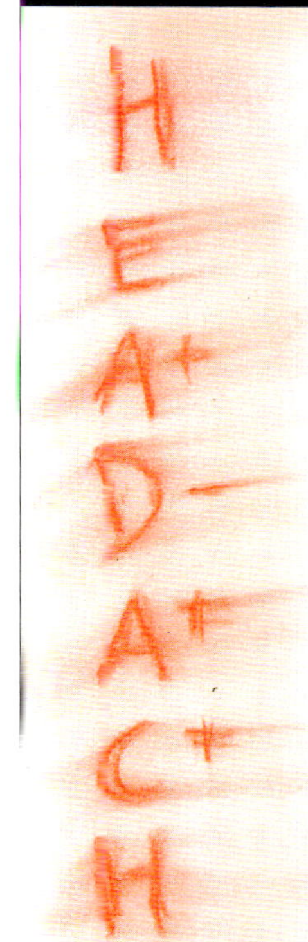

ASSIGNMENT AFTER ASSIGNMENT CAUSED MY HEAD TO ACHE

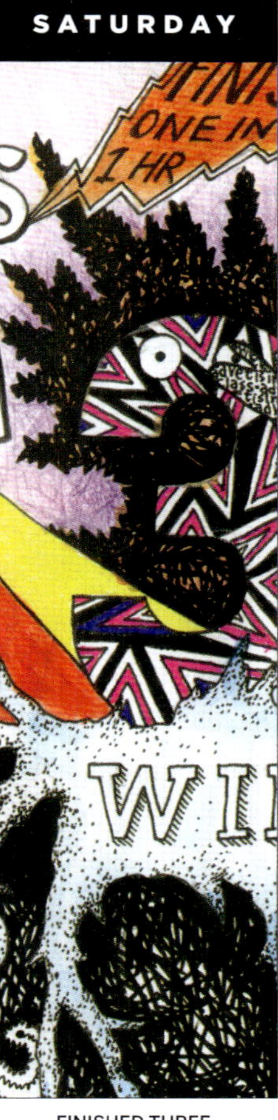

FINISHED THREE ASSIGNMENTS IN ONE HOUR

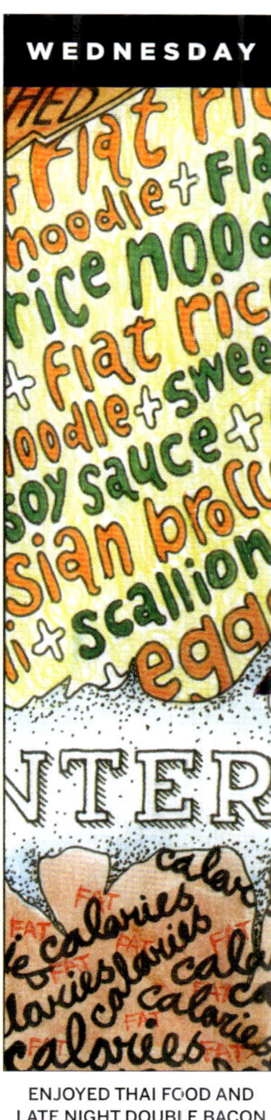

ENJOYED THAI FOOD AND LATE NIGHT DOUBLE BACON CHEESE PIZZA

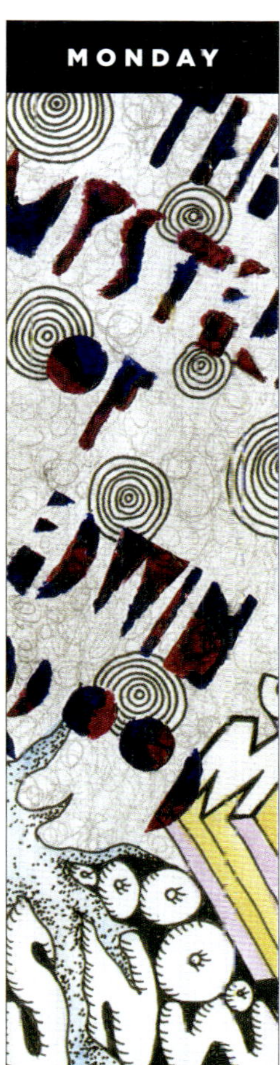

SAW A BROADWAY SHOW

1. *Jiah Min*
2. *Kate Cerigo*
3. *Youngji Kim*
4. *Jill Brody*
5. *Alexander Cook*
6. *Yoejin Kim*
7. *Chris Foxx*
8. *David Freiman*
9. *Jaewon Park*
10. *Lynn Yun*
11. *Vera Gorbunova*
12. *Nicole Martino*

13–15. *Mei Chun Lin*

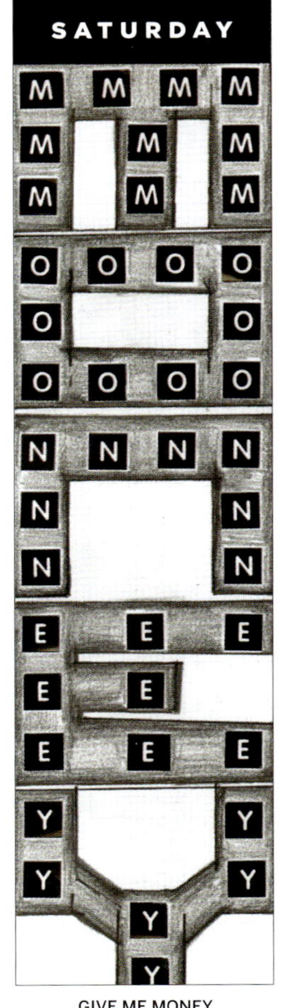

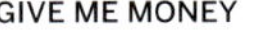

GIVE ME MONEY

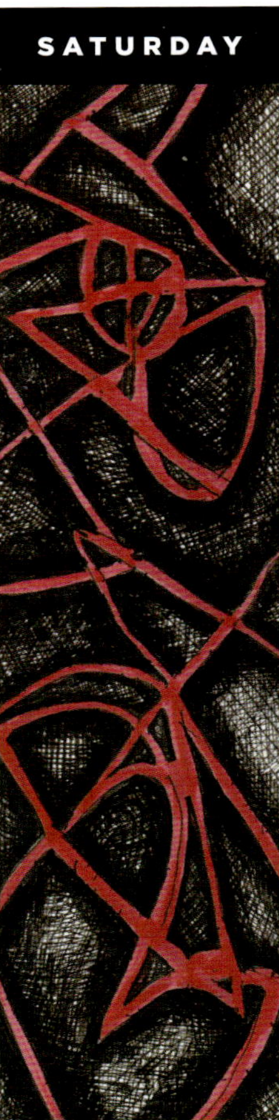

BIRTHDAY PARTY

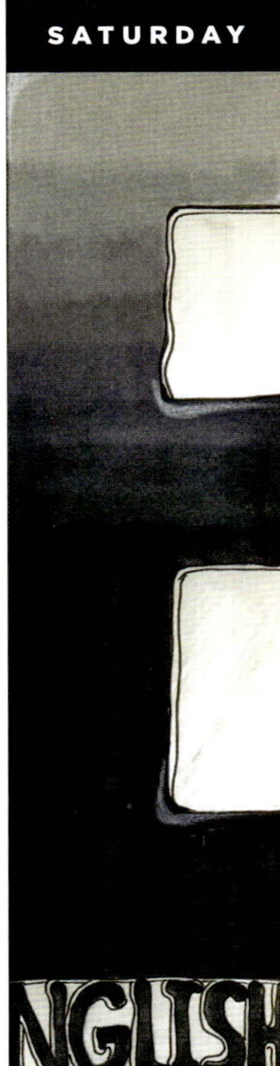

PRESSURE OF TAKING AN ENGLISH TEST

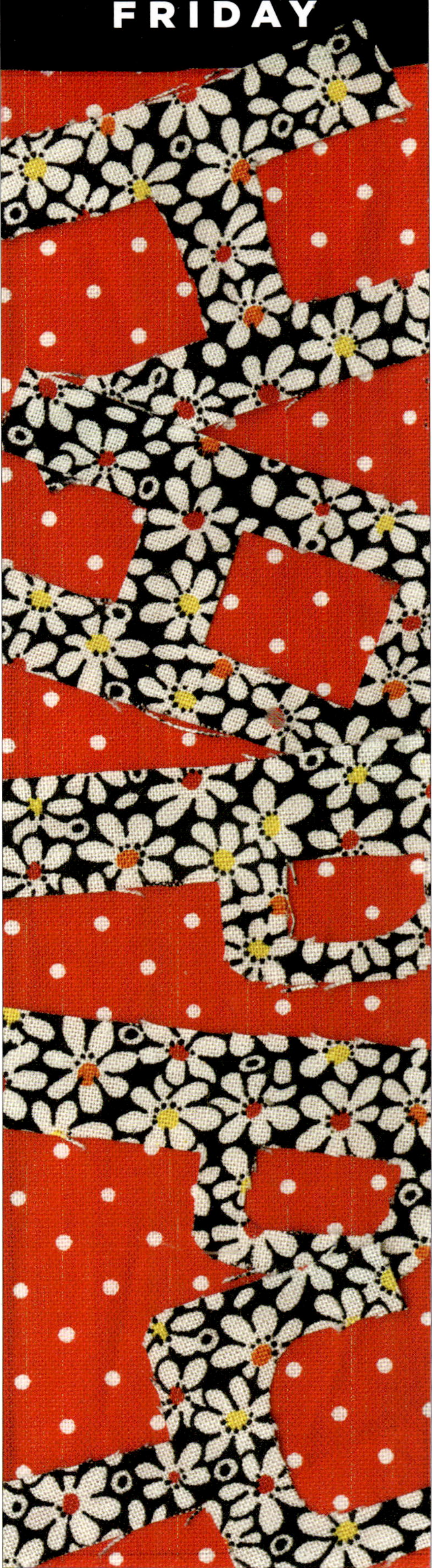

I HAD A GREAT TIME WITH MY FRIENDS

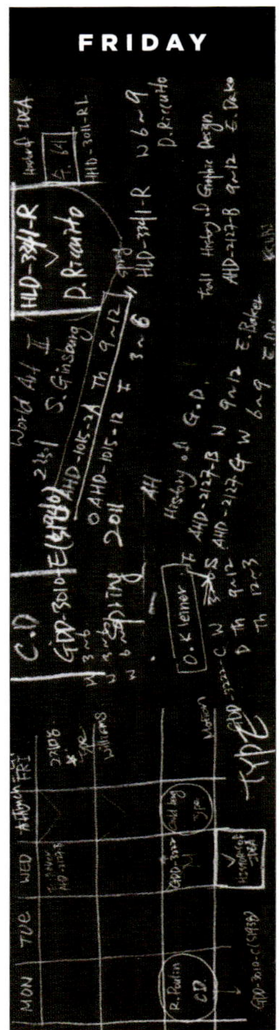

REGISTRATION FOR SCHOOL WAS COMPLICATED

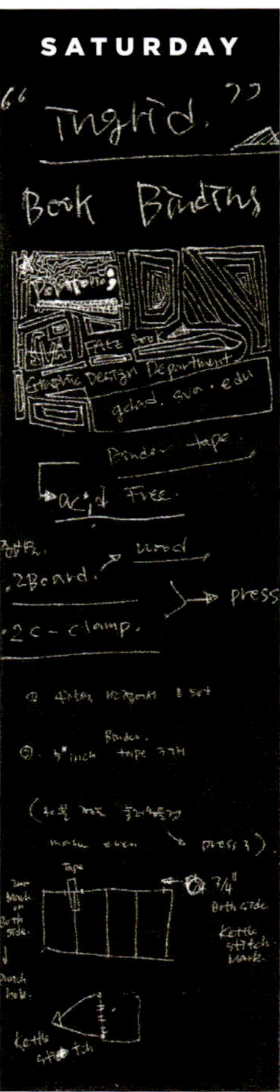

BOOK BINDING CLASS ON SATURDAY WAS INTENSE

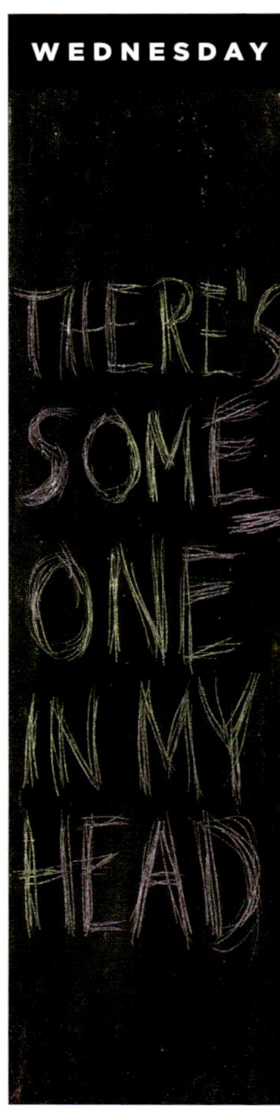

BUT IT'S NOT ME

WEDNESDAY

73% —

HOMEWORK

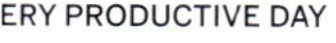

VERY PRODUCTIVE DAY

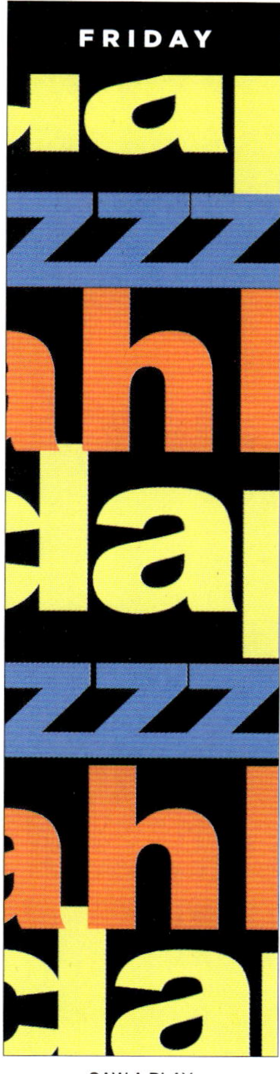

SAW A PLAY

I WAS AWAKE FOR ONLY FIVE HOURS, NOT PRODUCTIVE AT ALL.

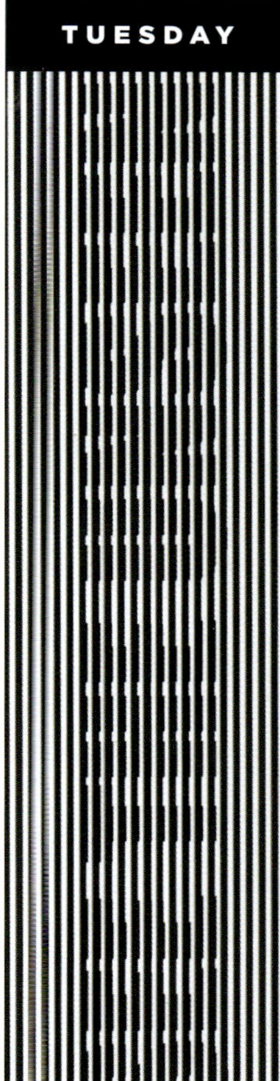

THE PROJECT WAS TO FIND SOMETHING CREATIVE AS A DESIGNER

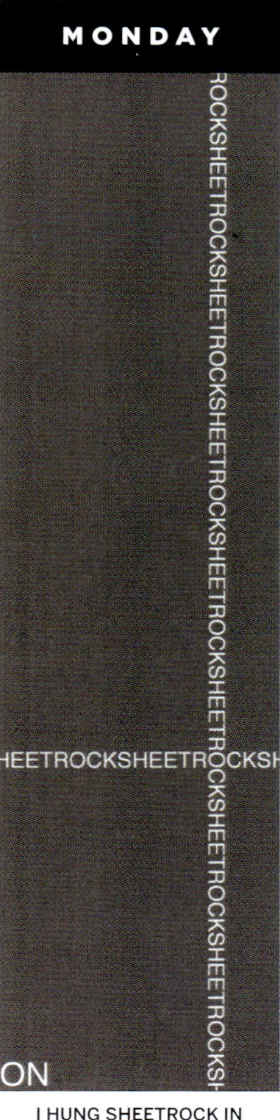

I HUNG SHEETROCK IN MY BATHROOM

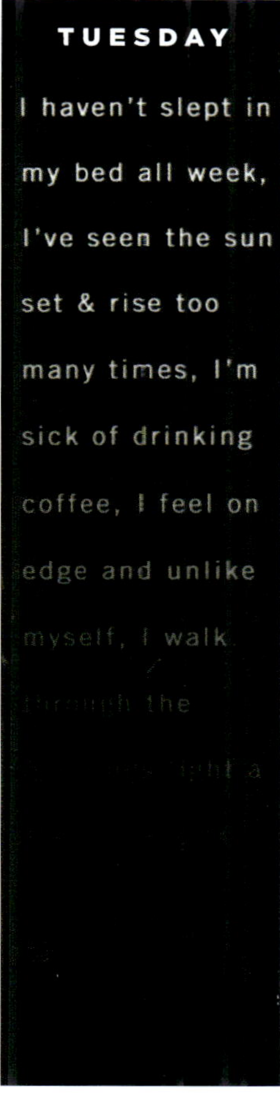

HAVEN'T SLEPT, FEEL LIKE A SHADOW OF MYSELF

TYPOGRAPHIC DIARY SOLUTIONS:

Figures 1 through 7 are comprised of hand-drawn and collage solutions that are contrasted by figures 8 through 13, which are computer generated.

Figures 8 through 10 approach a gridlike design in a lighthearted way.

For this assignment, all approaches are of equal value to the development of an artist. However, in this assignment, creating projects by hand was the directive.

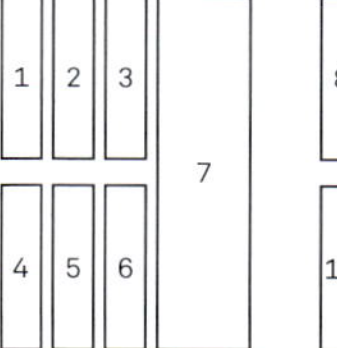

1. *Jiyoon Yeom*
2. *Andrew Lee*
3. *Myeongjin Shin*
4. *Hyunkyu Choi*
5. *Yoondeok Jang*
6. *P. Santos*
7. *Yuki Murata*
8. *Nari Park*
9. *A. Conway*
10. *Hannah Song*
11. *Duesung Byun*
12. *Bruce Viemeister*
13. *Rachel Willey*

SUNDAY

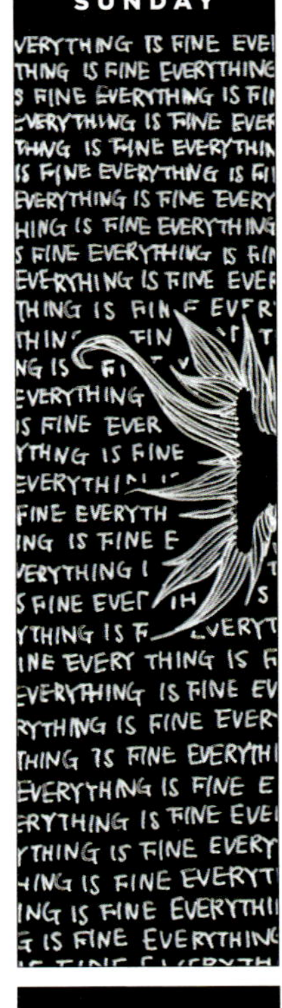

MONDAY

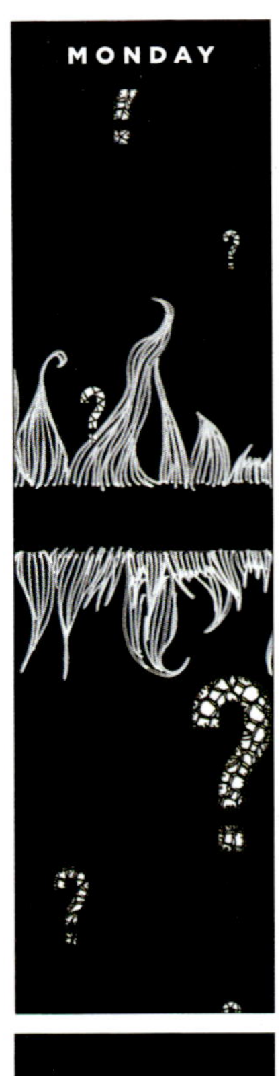

TUESDAY

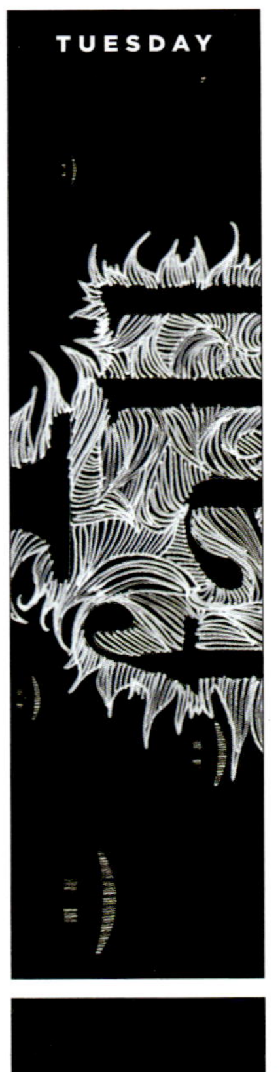

WEDNESDAY

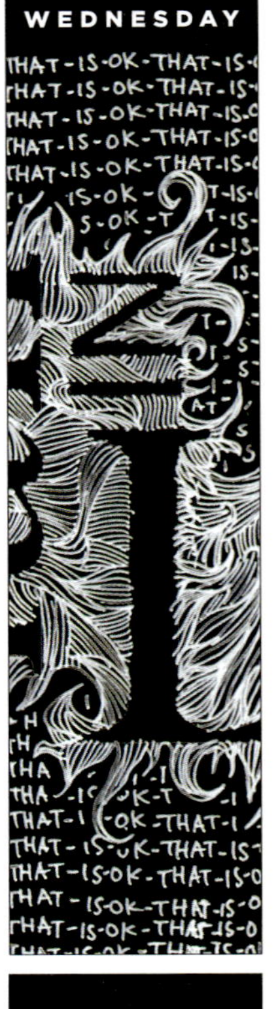

THURSDAY

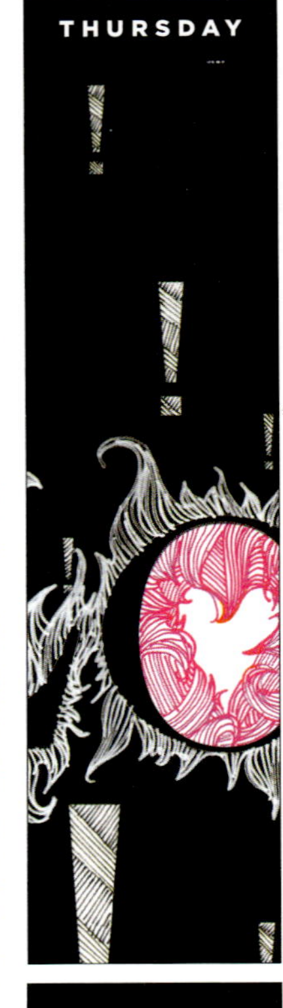

FRIDAY

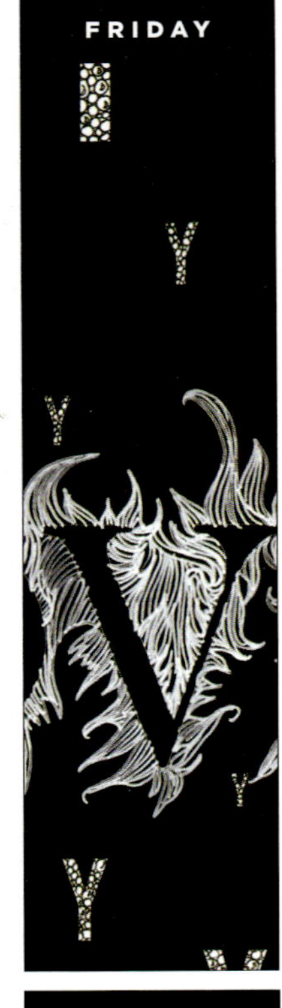

SATURDAY

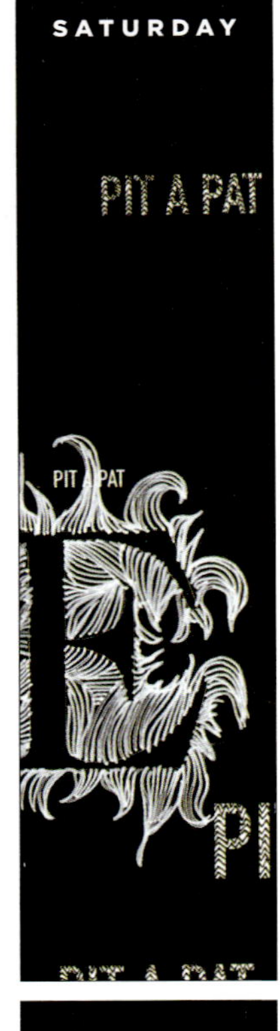

EVERYTHING IS FINE

I WONDER WHAT HE IS DOING NOW

I AM HAPPY ALL DAY LONG

I AM MORE TOLERANT

HE IS THE INSPIRATION OF MY WORK

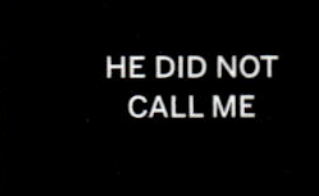

HE DID NOT CALL ME

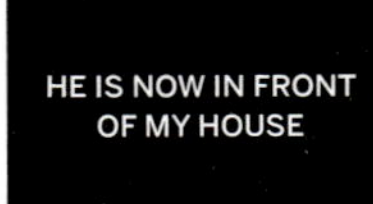

HE IS NOW IN FRONT OF MY HOUSE

SUNDAY

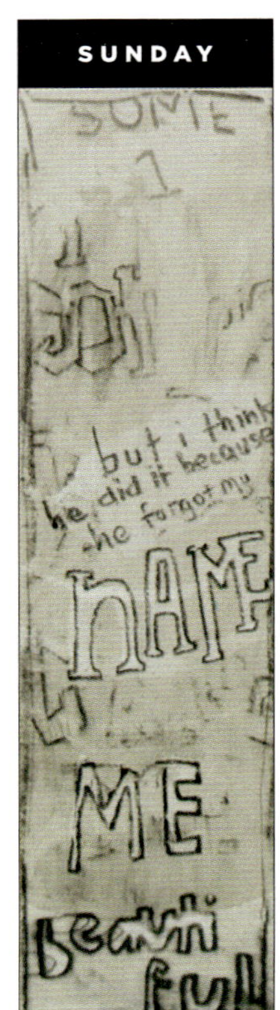

MONDAY

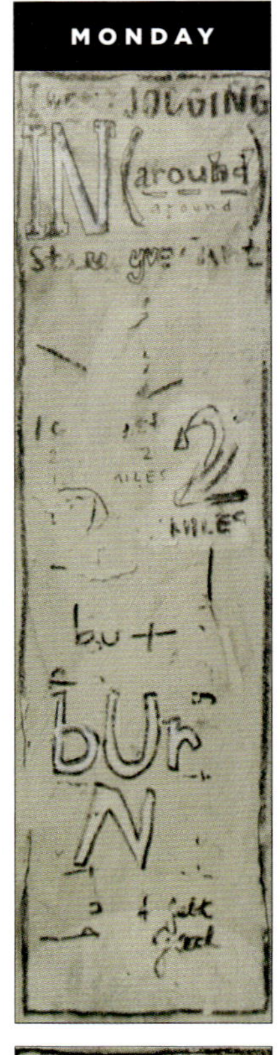

TUESDAY

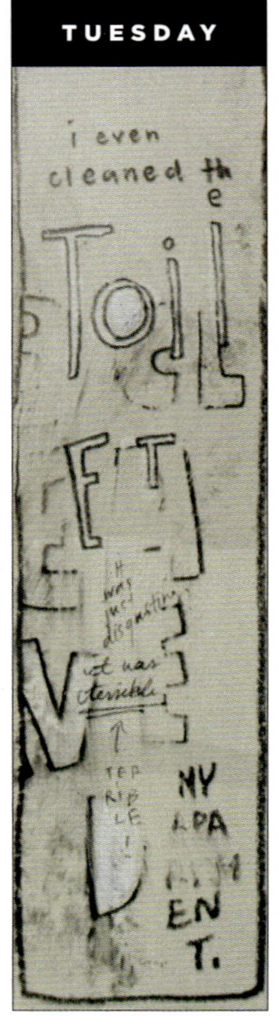

WEDNESDAY

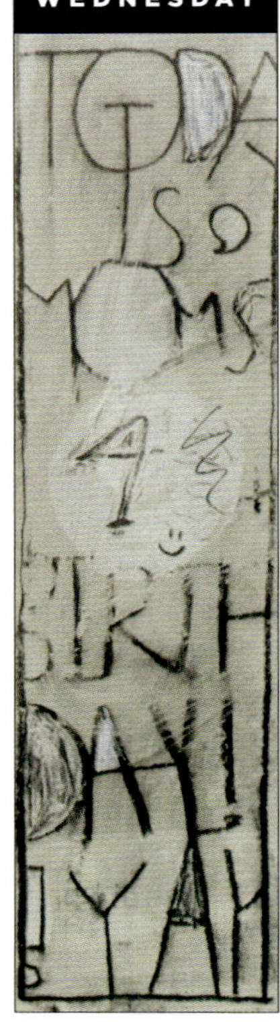

THURSDAY

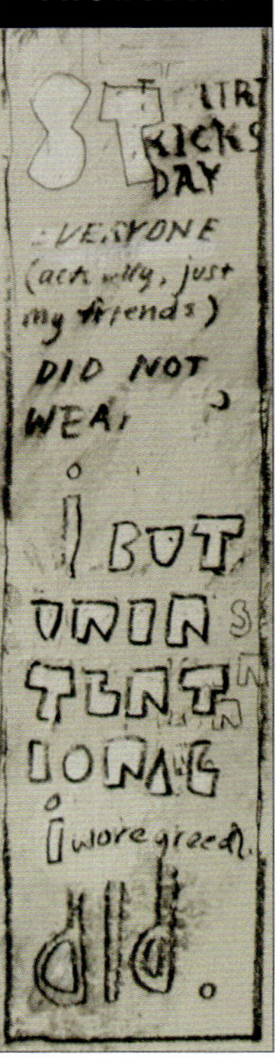

FRIDAY

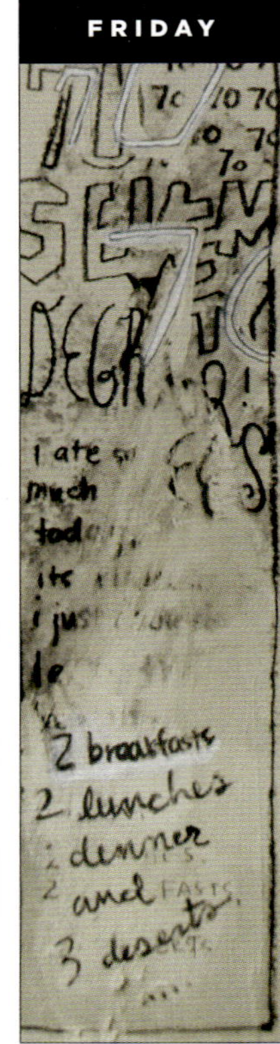

SATURDAY

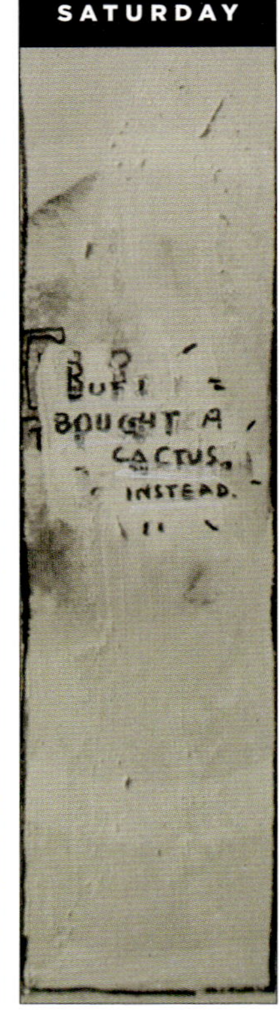

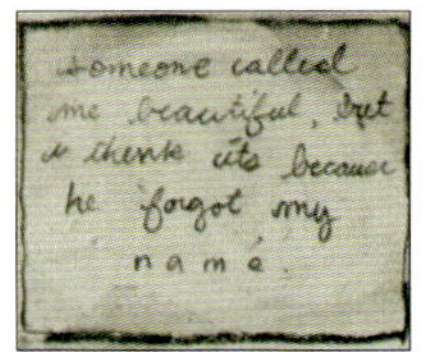

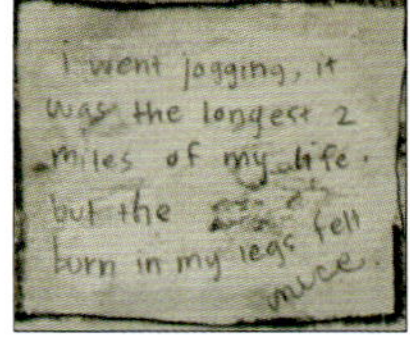

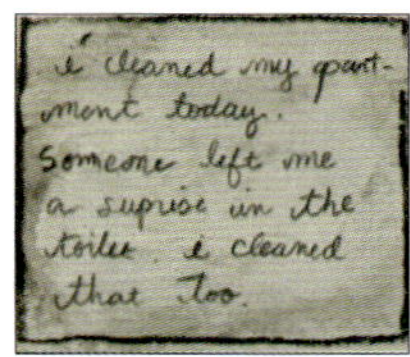

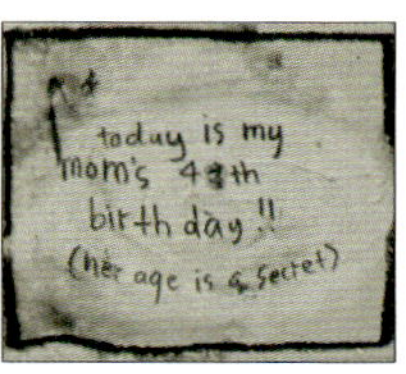

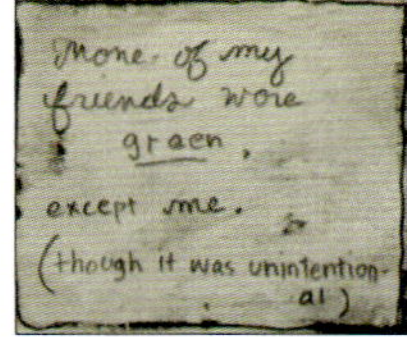

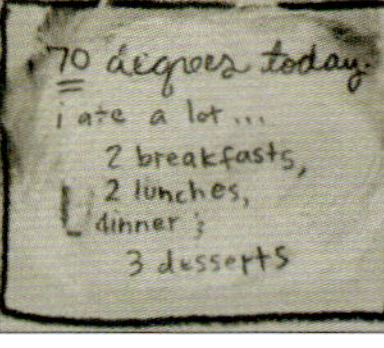

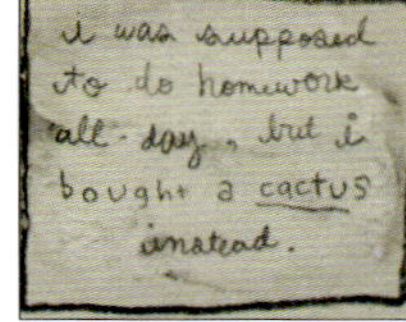

TYPOGRAPHIC DIARY SOLUTIONS:

Figures 1 through 4 represent four projects that have been done in their entirety, each with their own separate approach, where the explanation areas on the assignment sheet have become an integral part of the overall image.

To balance the problem of finding one's voice while at the same time communicating the intended message is always a struggle, and the challenges undertaken in the typographic diary assignment and in the other projects that appear in this book are the building blocks toward this goal.

SUNDAY	MONDAY	TUESDAY	WEDNESDAY	THURSDAY	FRIDAY	SATURDAY
DYNASTY SUPERMARKET 68 ELIZABETH ST. N.Y.C. N.Y.10013 212-966-4943 THANK YOU 04-02-2000 SAT #1 GROCERY 1 10.00 F GROCERY 1 0.65 F GROCERY 1 1.08 F GROCERY 1 1.08 F GROCERY 1 1.48 F GROCERY 1 5.88 F GROCERY 1 1.39 F SUBTL 21.56 TOTAL 21.56 CATEND 22.06 CHANGE 0.50 ITEM 7 # 5 3146 17:12TM		03-28-00 25 3.24 01 2 3 06-3	PEARL PAINT 107 EAST 23 STREET NEW YORK NY 10010 03/29/00 FINE ART 2.07 FINE ART 3.43 .76 FINE ART 3.04 SUBTTL 8.54 5 DISC SUBTTL 7.69 TAX .70 TOTAL 8.39 CASH 20.39 CHANGE 12.00 6 #ITEMS CLERK B 3088 (212) 592-2179	OTHER MUSIC 15 EAST 4TH STREET NEW YORK NY 10003	NEW YORK LINE SUPERMARKET INC 202 MOTT INC TEL:212-941-6601 03/31/00 1:56PM DEPT02 $2.19 DEPT02 $0.60 DEPT02 $0.60 DEPT02 $0.89 DEPT02 $3.29 ITEMS 5@ CASH $7.57	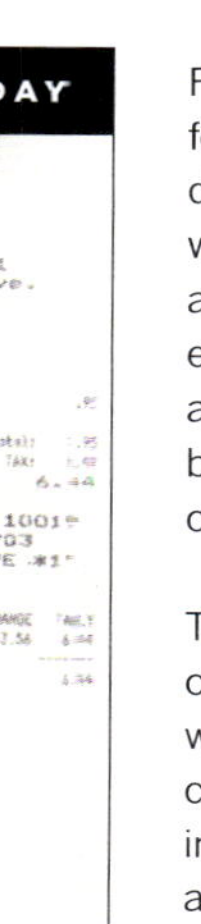 RANCH #1 585 6th Ave. TOTAL: New York, NY 10011 212 271-7703 "YA GOTTA HAVE 'EM"

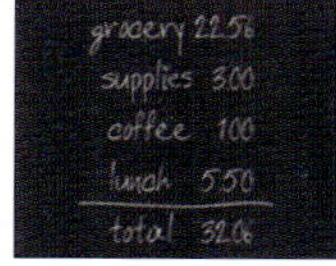

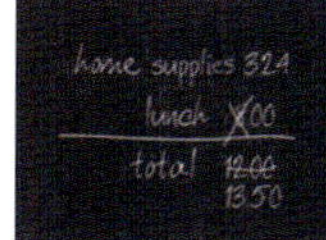
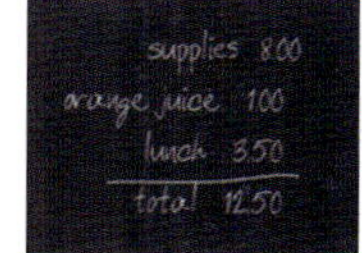
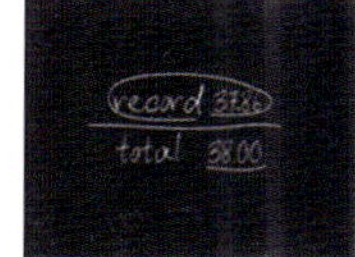
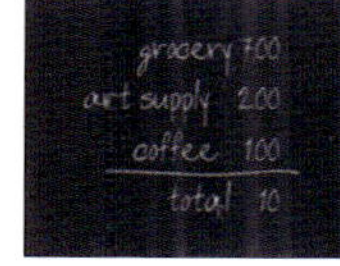
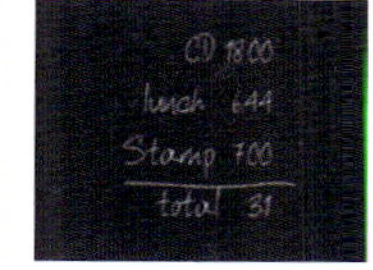

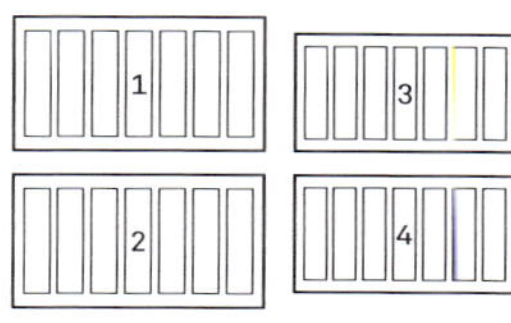
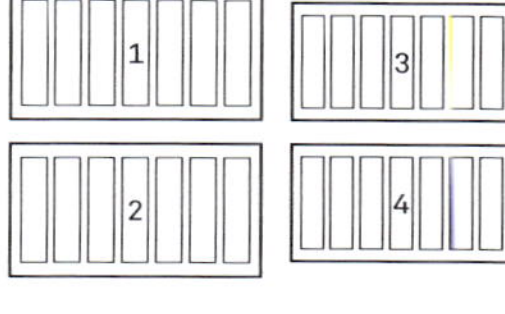

SUNDAY	MONDAY	TUESDAY	WEDNESDAY	THURSDAY	FRIDAY	SATURDAY

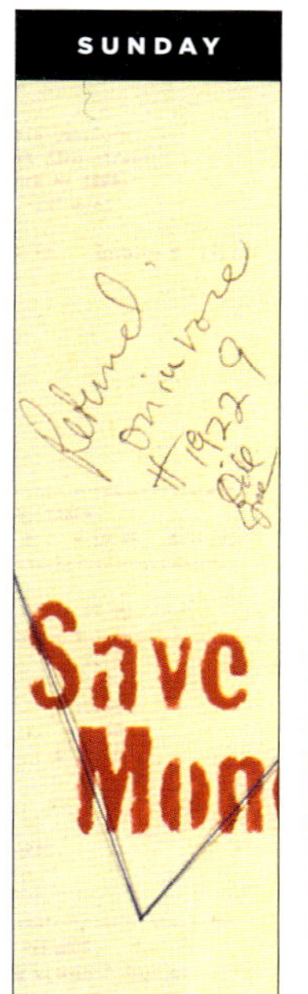

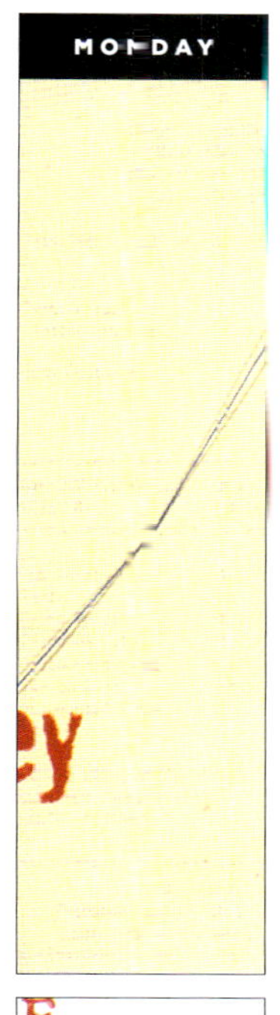
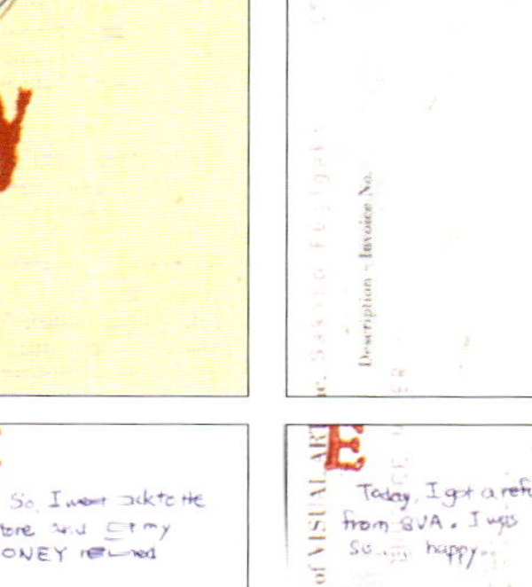
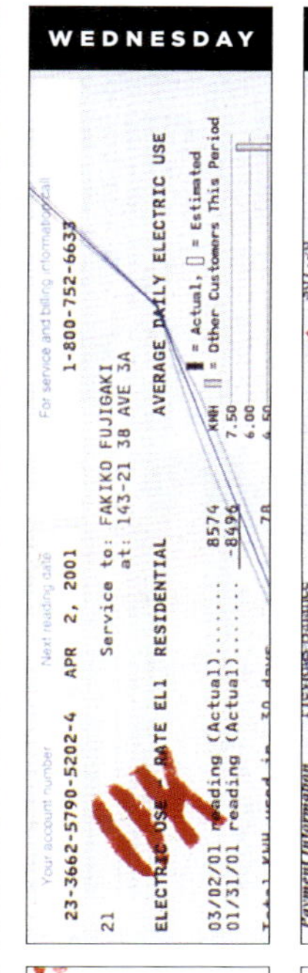

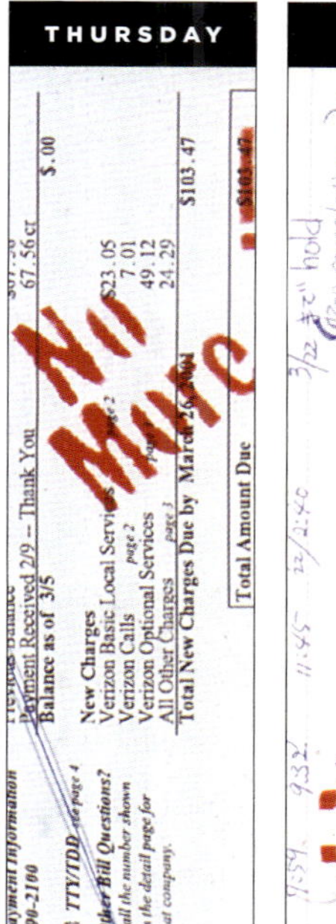

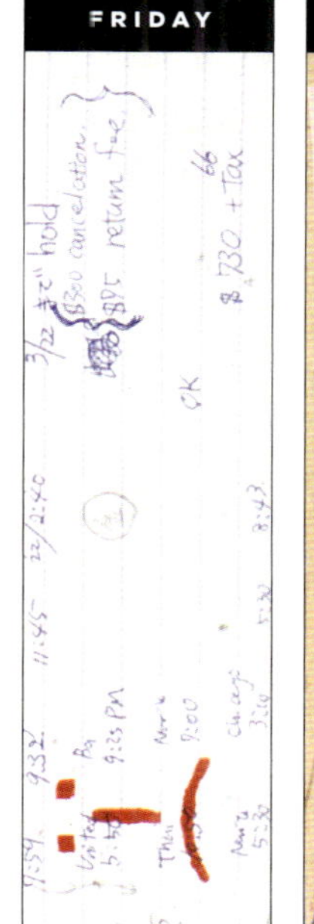

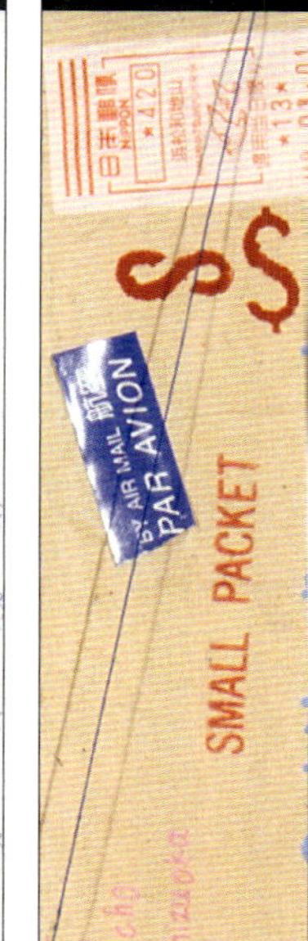

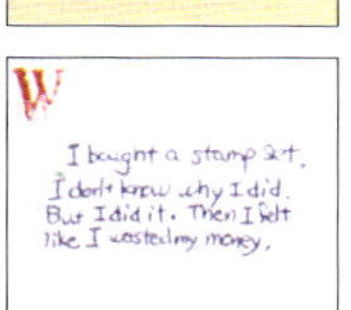

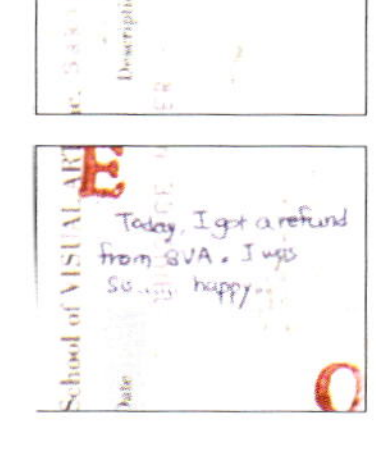

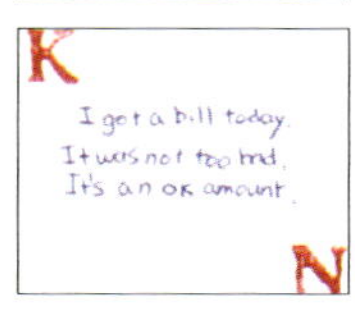

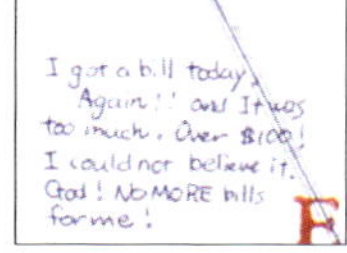

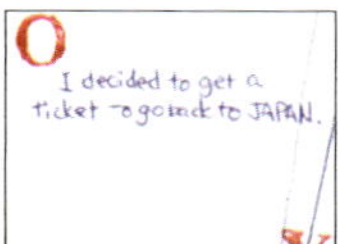

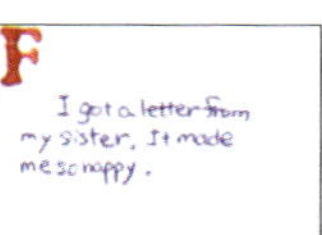

1. *Mijung Park*
2. *Elaine Park*
3. *Sakuma Gaku*
4. *Sakiko Fujigaki*

THOUGHTS ON THE CREATIVE PROCESS 11

Creative problem solving needs the condition of priority. High priority means carrying a question with you all the time. This state of being inquisitive is a condition that is necessary for ideas to magically appear.

EGO

THE HUMAN PSYCHE IS A VERY COMPLEX ORGANISM WHERE EACH INDIVIDUAL IS UNIQUE UNTO THEMSELVES. IN ADDITION, OUR GOALS CONTINUALLY CHANGE THROUGHOUT OUR LIVES AS DO OUR ASPIRATIONS. WITH THIS IN MIND, IN THE AREAS INDICATED, VISUALLY EXPRESS THE FOUR FOLLOWING EQUATIONS.

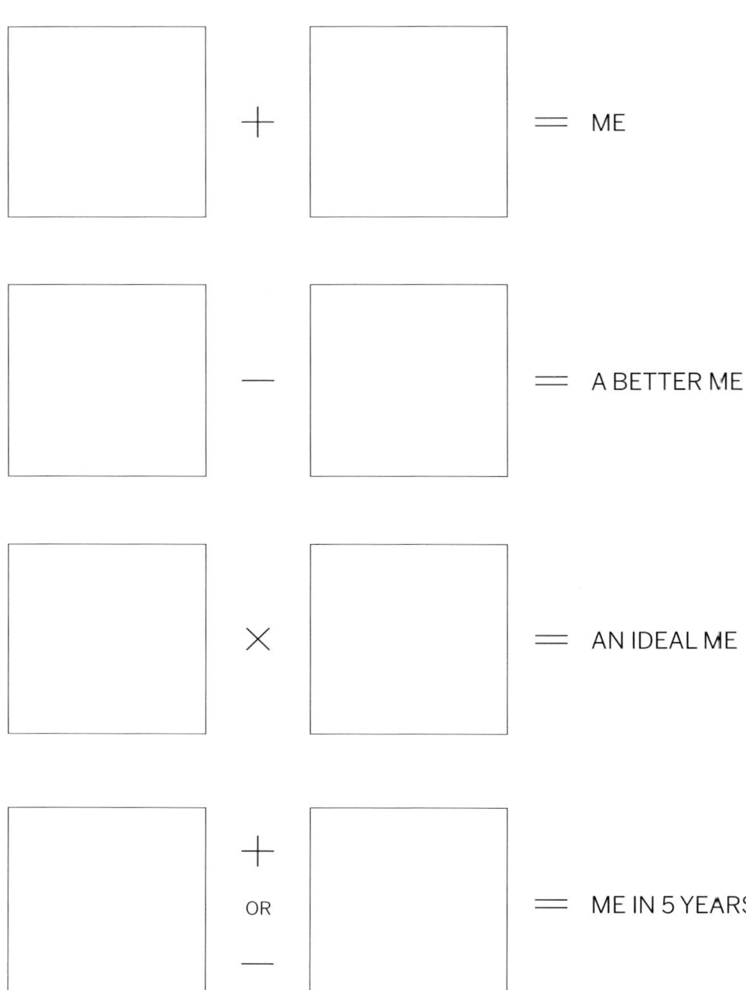

In the rectangular area below, create an equation using mathematical symbols such as: [+ ,- x ,÷, âV, ⋕, ⋕, =, ff, ⋕] to best depict a defining aspect of your personality.

PROBLEMS : SOLUTIONS SERIES

CREATED BY RICHARD WILDE / JUDITH WILDE, PRODUCED BY VISUAL ARTS PRESS, LTD. ART DIRECTORS: RICHARD WILDE / JUDITH WILDE

11

EGO PROBLEM:

In the eight squares on the assignment sheet create a self-portrait based on mathematical equations. In the first equation describe two aspects of your personality that make you who you are. In the second equation depict what aspect you would eliminate to improve yourself. In the third equation describe what would make you an ideal person by multiplying specific aspects about yourself. In the fourth equation either add or subtract an aspect of your personality to identify where you see yourself in five years. In the rectangle at the bottom of the page, create an equation that defines you using mathematical functions, which can range from the nonsensical to the real.

AIM:
This project allows one the opportunity to touch a truth in oneself and then find the best means of executing that truth, using either a narrative, metaphoric, abstract, or symbolic approach.

SUGGESTIONS:
Hold the question of who you are in the form of a two-part equation to see what arises. The greater the priority of the question, the greater the possibility that original solutions will arise. In this way, you will not be imposing your will, but creating an opportunity, where solutions can present themselves.

SPECIFICATIONS:
There are no limitations on color or medium.

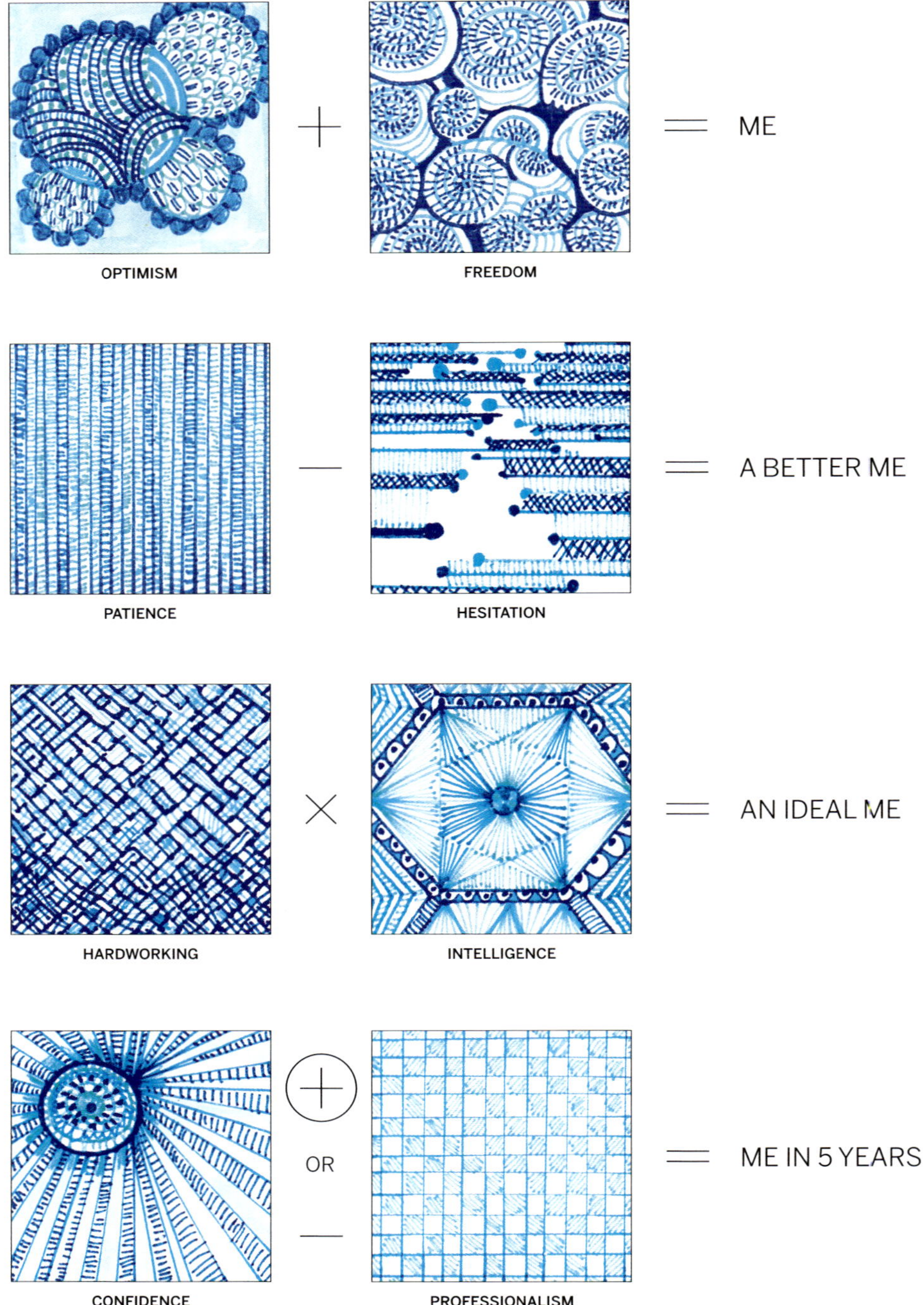

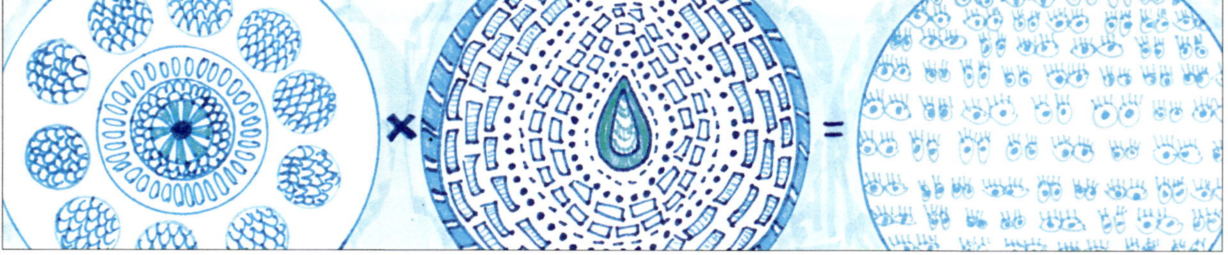

CURIOSITY COURAGE EXPLORATION

EGO SOLUTIONS:

Figure 1 is an entire assignment that uses abstraction to communicate the intended messages. Here, titles are useful in understanding the meaning.

In direct contrast, figures 2 and 3 exhibit a narrative approach that incorporates metaphoric imagery.

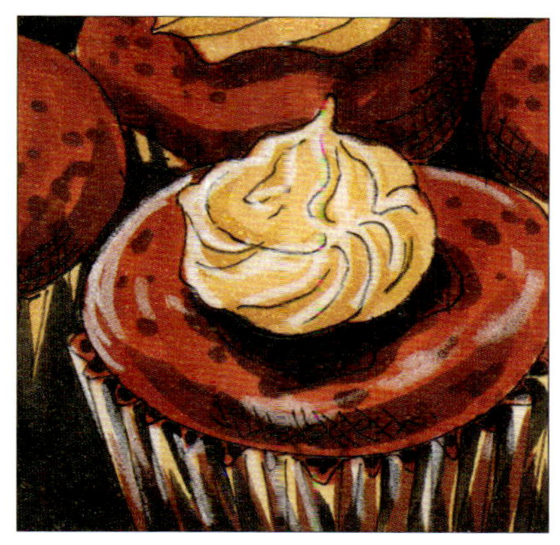

SIMPLE MINDED
(EVERYTHING IS CHOCOLATE FLAVORED)

+

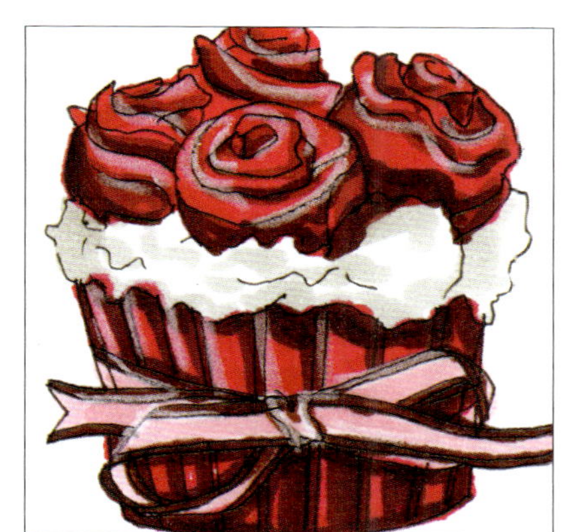

SPECIAL (I RATHER THINK RED VELVET CUPCAKES ARE SPECIAL)

= ME

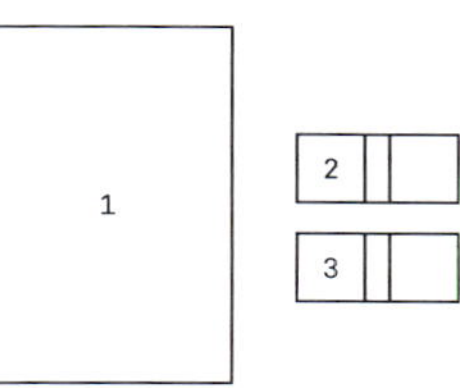

1. *Qianyi Zhang*
2–3. *Lynne Yun*

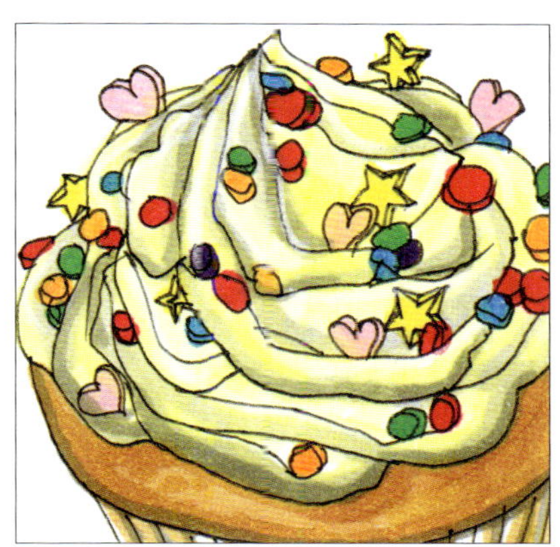

DIVERSITY (RAINBOW SPRINKLES)

×

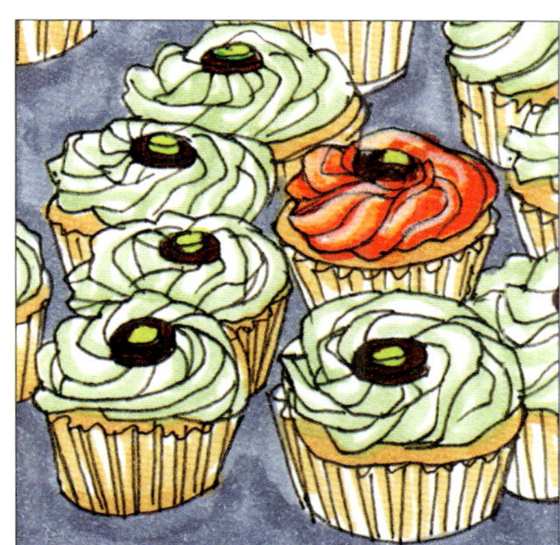

INDIVIDUALISTIC

= AN IDEAL ME

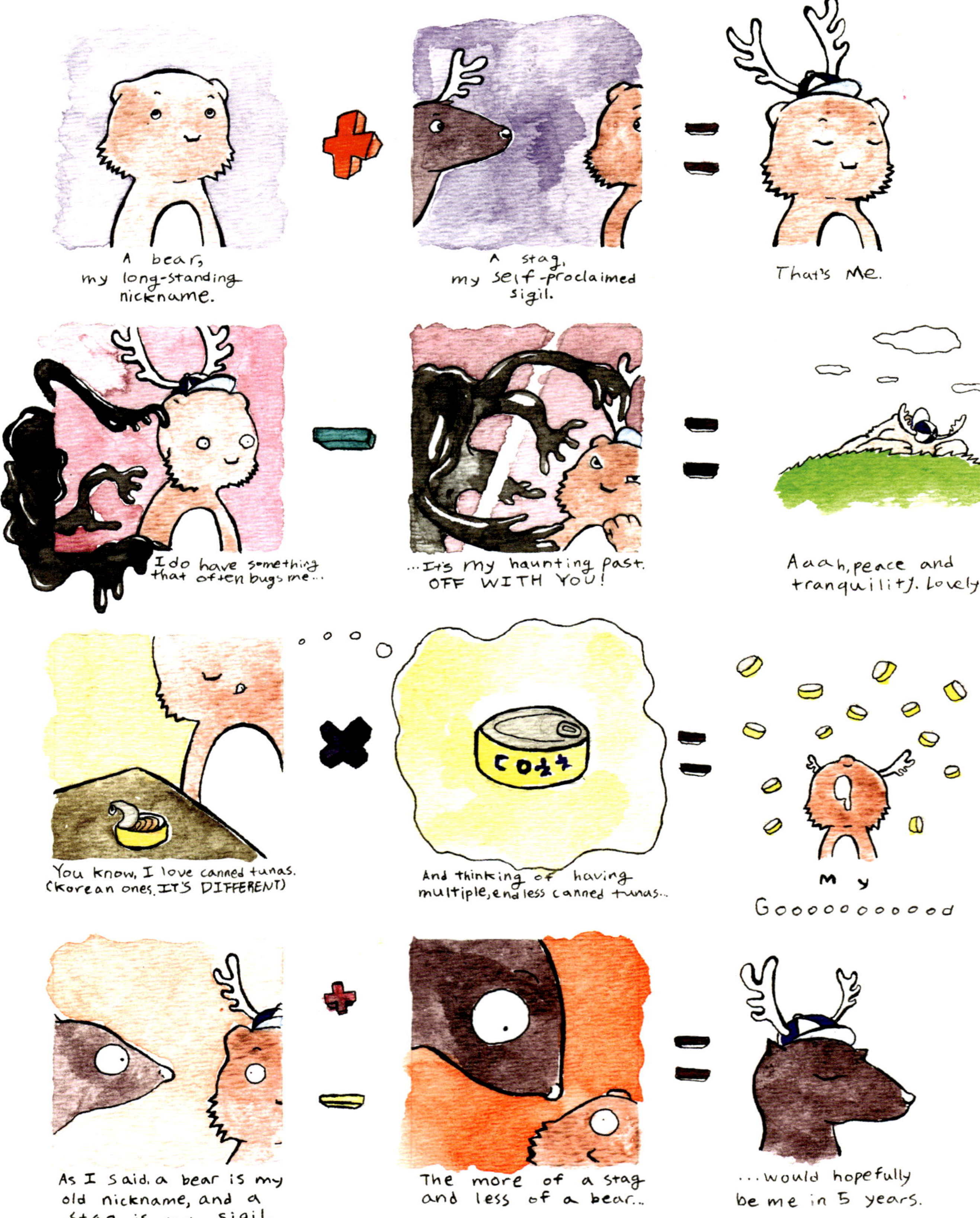
A bear,
my long-standing
nickname.
A stag,
my self-proclaimed
sigil.
That's Me.
I do have something
that often bugs me...
...It's my haunting past.
OFF WITH YOU!
Aaah, peace and
tranquility. Lovely.
You know, I love canned tunas.
(Korean ones. IT'S DIFFERENT)
And thinking of having
multiple, endless canned tunas...
My
Goooooooooood
As I said, a bear is my
old nickname, and a
stag is my sigil.
The more of a stag
and less of a bear...
...would hopefully
be me in 5 years.

EGO SOLUTIONS:

Both figures 1 and 2 are thematic solutions that utilize pen and ink, watercolor, collage, and mixed media to express their ideas.

In figure 1 the equations were redrawn in a personal style using an animal in a humorous narrative to represent himself.

Figure 2 uses highly personal imagery to represent an array of issues.

= ME
CAREFUL OBSERVATION + BRILLIANCE

= A BETTER ME
DARK SIDE - PANIC

= AN IDEAL ME
THINK (BEFORE YOU ACT) X FREEDOM

OR

= ME IN 5 YEARS
MOST SUCCESSFUL DESIGNER + TRAVELING ALL OVER THE WORLD

1 2

1. *Sungmin Ryu*
2. *Jinyi Roh*

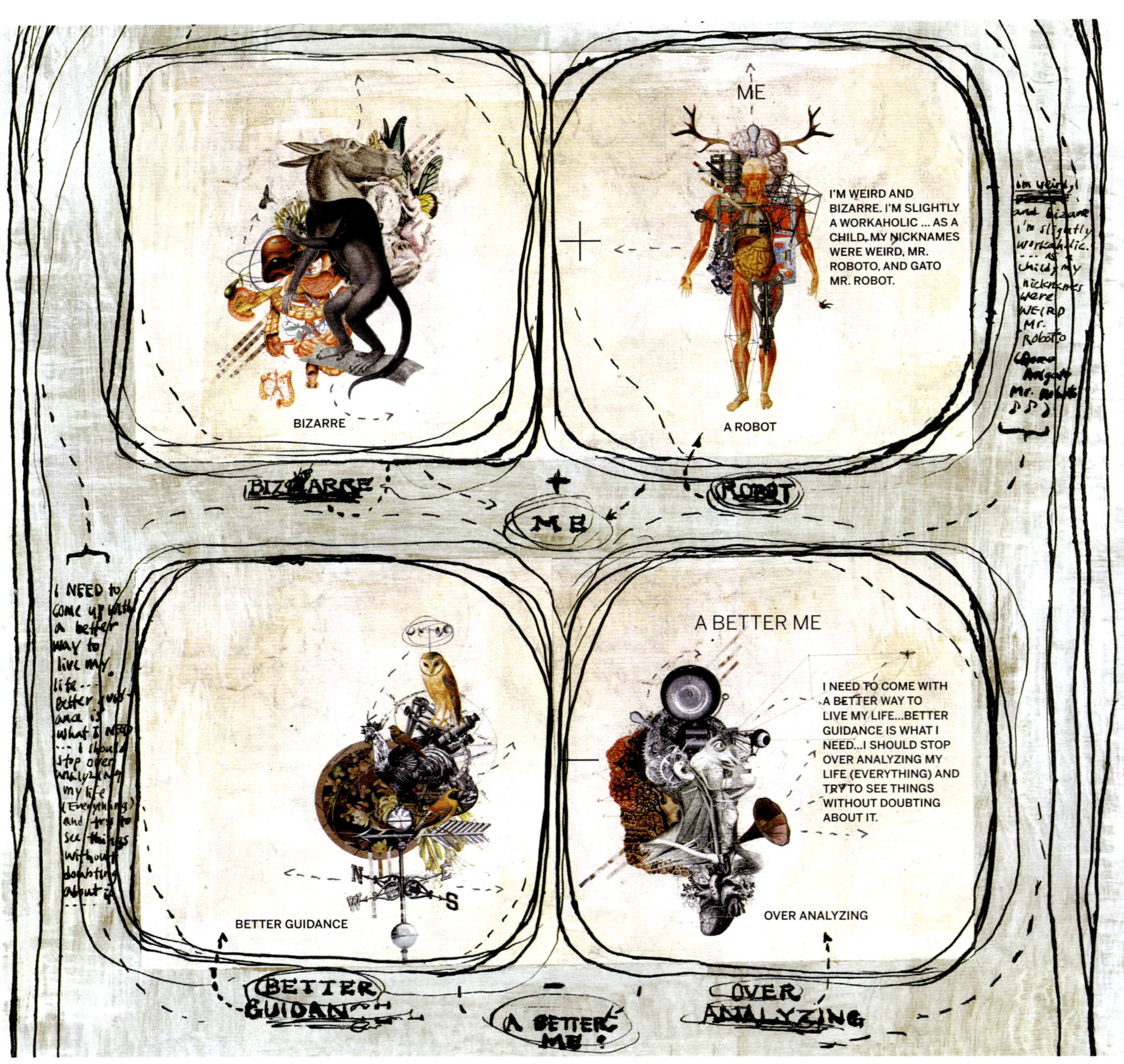
ME
I'M WEIRD AND BIZARRE. I'M SLIGHTLY A WORKAHOLIC ... AS A CHILD, MY NICKNAMES WERE WEIRD, MR. ROBOTO, AND GATO MR. ROBOT.
BIZARRE
A ROBOT
BIZARRE
ME
ROBOT
A BETTER ME
I NEED TO COME WITH A BETTER WAY TO LIVE MY LIFE...BETTER GUIDANCE IS WHAT I NEED...I SHOULD STOP OVER ANALYZING MY LIFE (EVERYTHING) AND TRY TO SEE THINGS WITHOUT DOUBTING ABOUT IT.
BETTER GUIDANCE
OVER ANALYZING
BETTER GUIDANCE
A BETTER ME!
OVER ANALYZING

EGO SOLUTIONS:

Figures 1 and 2 took liberties in reconfiguring the entire assignment sheet, using collage imagery supported by the addition of text to help clarify the complex subject matter.

This is an example of risk taking where the end result transcended the project in a most inventive way.

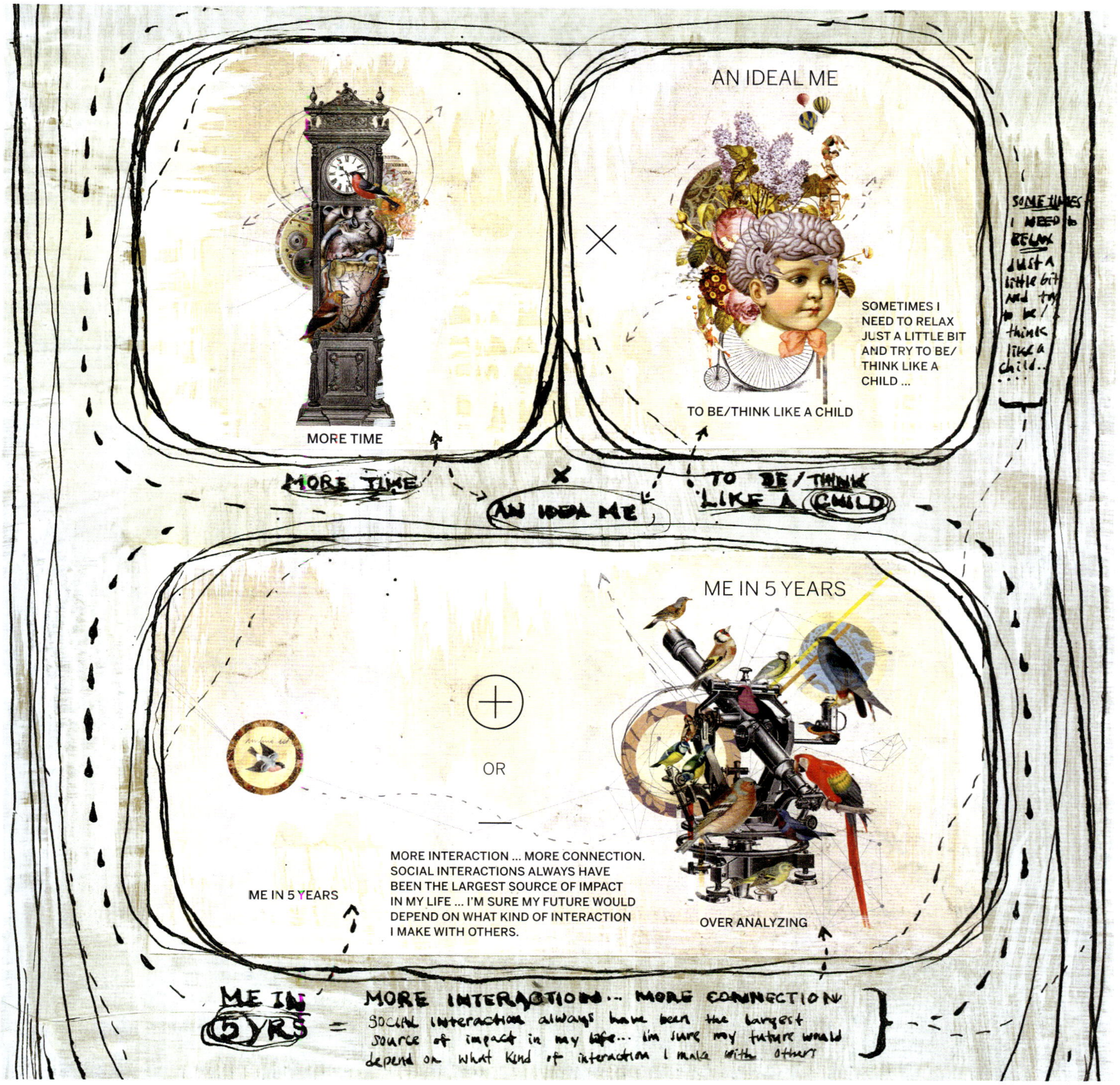

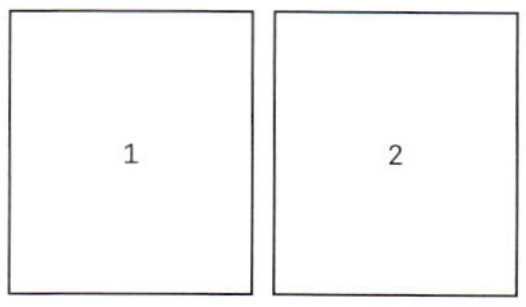

AN IDEAL ME

SOMETIMES I NEED TO RELAX JUST A LITTLE BIT AND TRY TO BE/ THINK LIKE A CHILD ...

MORE TIME

TO BE/THINK LIKE A CHILD

ME IN 5 YEARS

OR

MORE INTERACTION ... MORE CONNECTION. SOCIAL INTERACTIONS ALWAYS HAVE BEEN THE LARGEST SOURCE OF IMPACT IN MY LIFE ... I'M SURE MY FUTURE WOULD DEPEND ON WHAT KIND OF INTERACTION I MAKE WITH OTHERS.

ME IN 5 YEARS

OVER ANALYZING

1 2

1–2. *Thomas Shim*

THE PROCESS

EGO SOLUTIONS

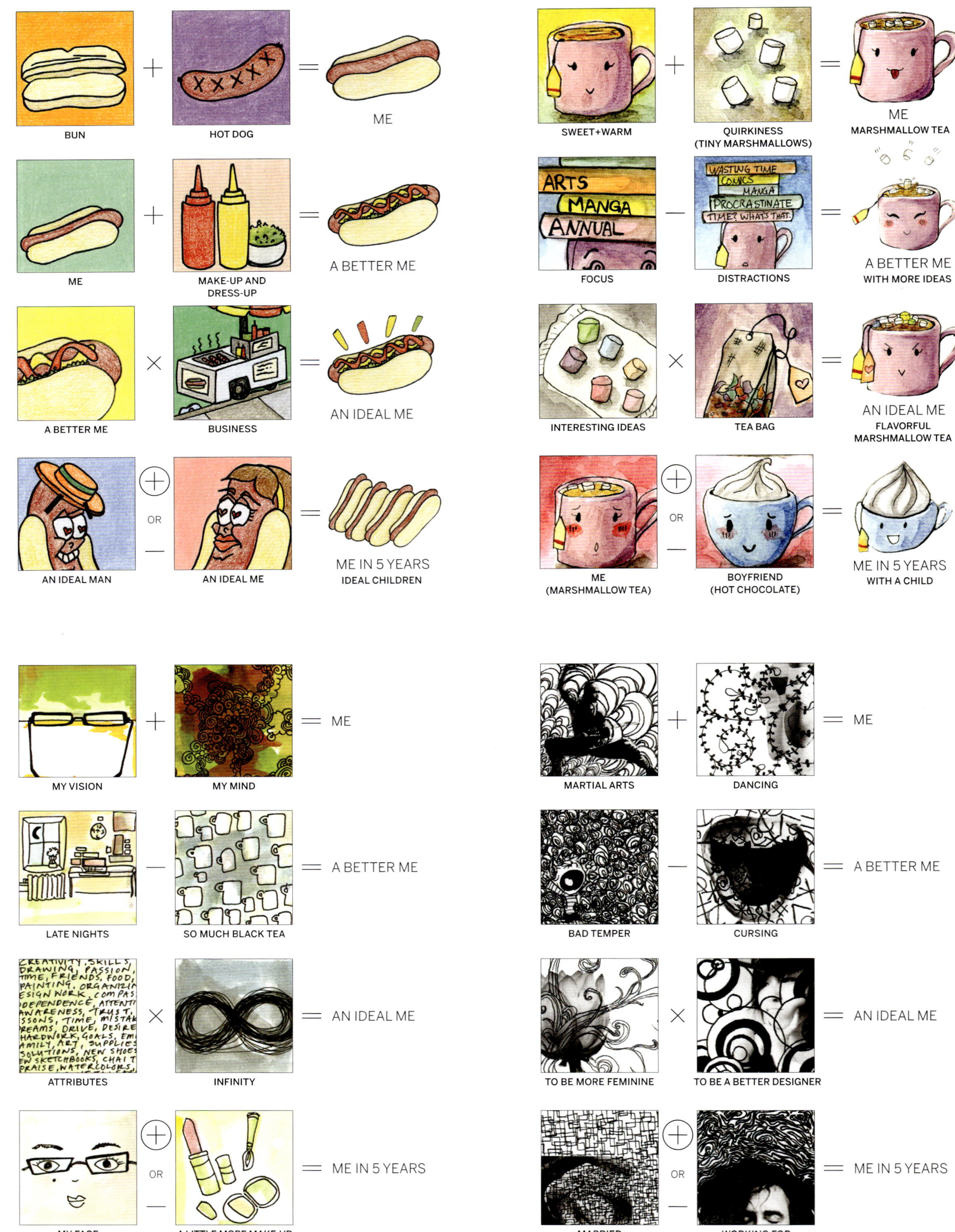

EGO SOLUTIONS:

Figures 1, 2, 3 and 4 represent the entire assignment, ranging from metaphoric to literal to abstract solutions.

Figures 5 through 7 use a rabbit as a metaphor to illustrate each idea.

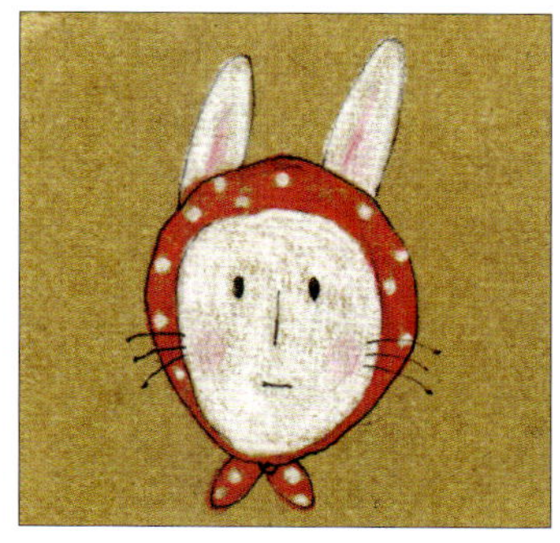
ME

+

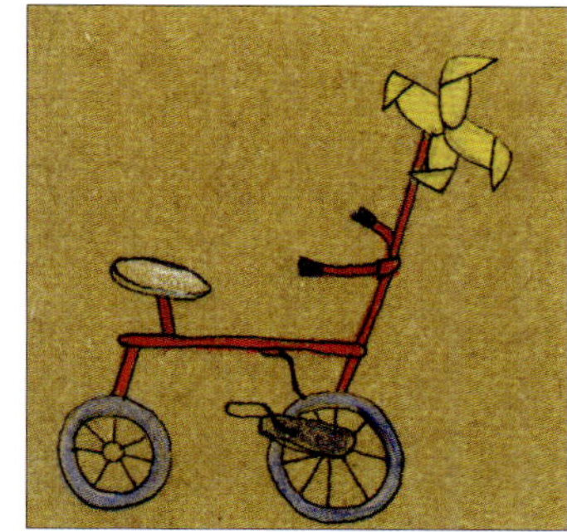
PLAYFULNESS

= ME

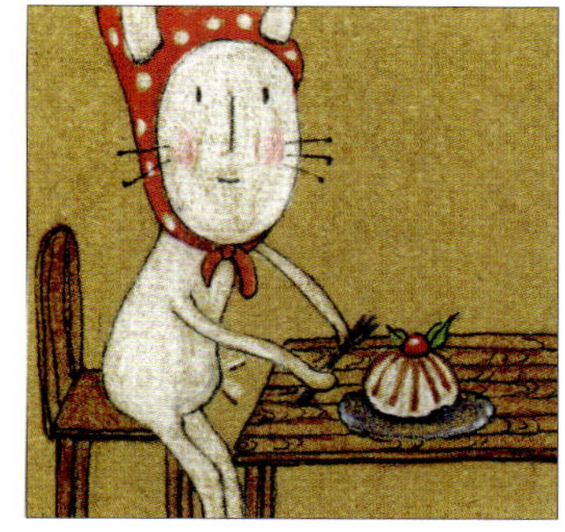

ME

−

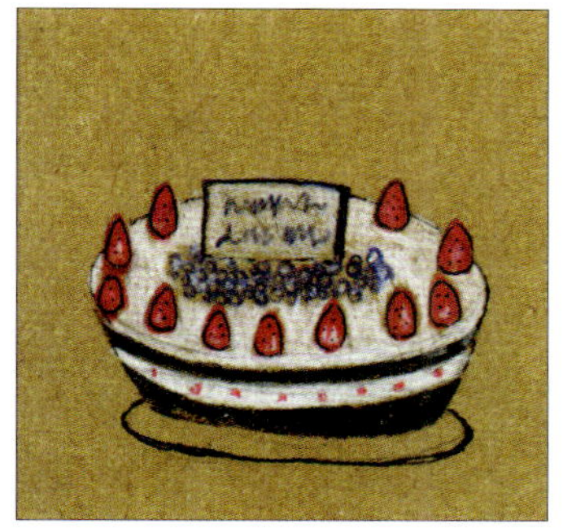
INDULGING

= A BETTER ME

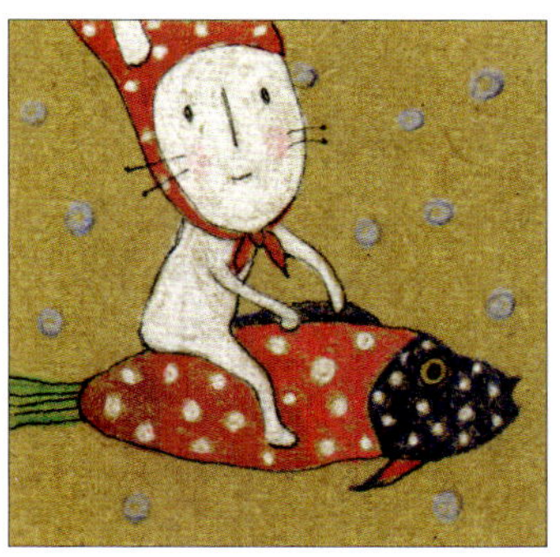
DREAMING

×

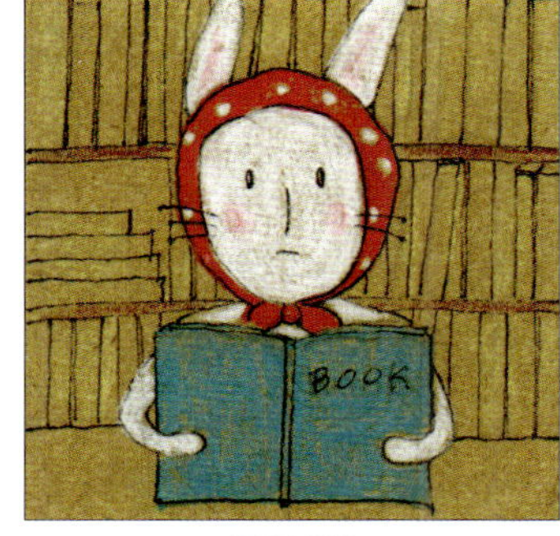

STUDYING

= AN IDEAL ME

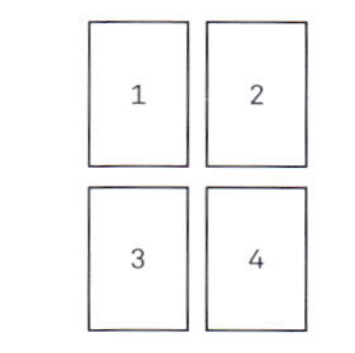

1. *Heera Kim*
2. *Alyssa Colina*
3. *Erica Knauss*
4. *Young Kim*

5–7. *Jeonghyung Ahn*

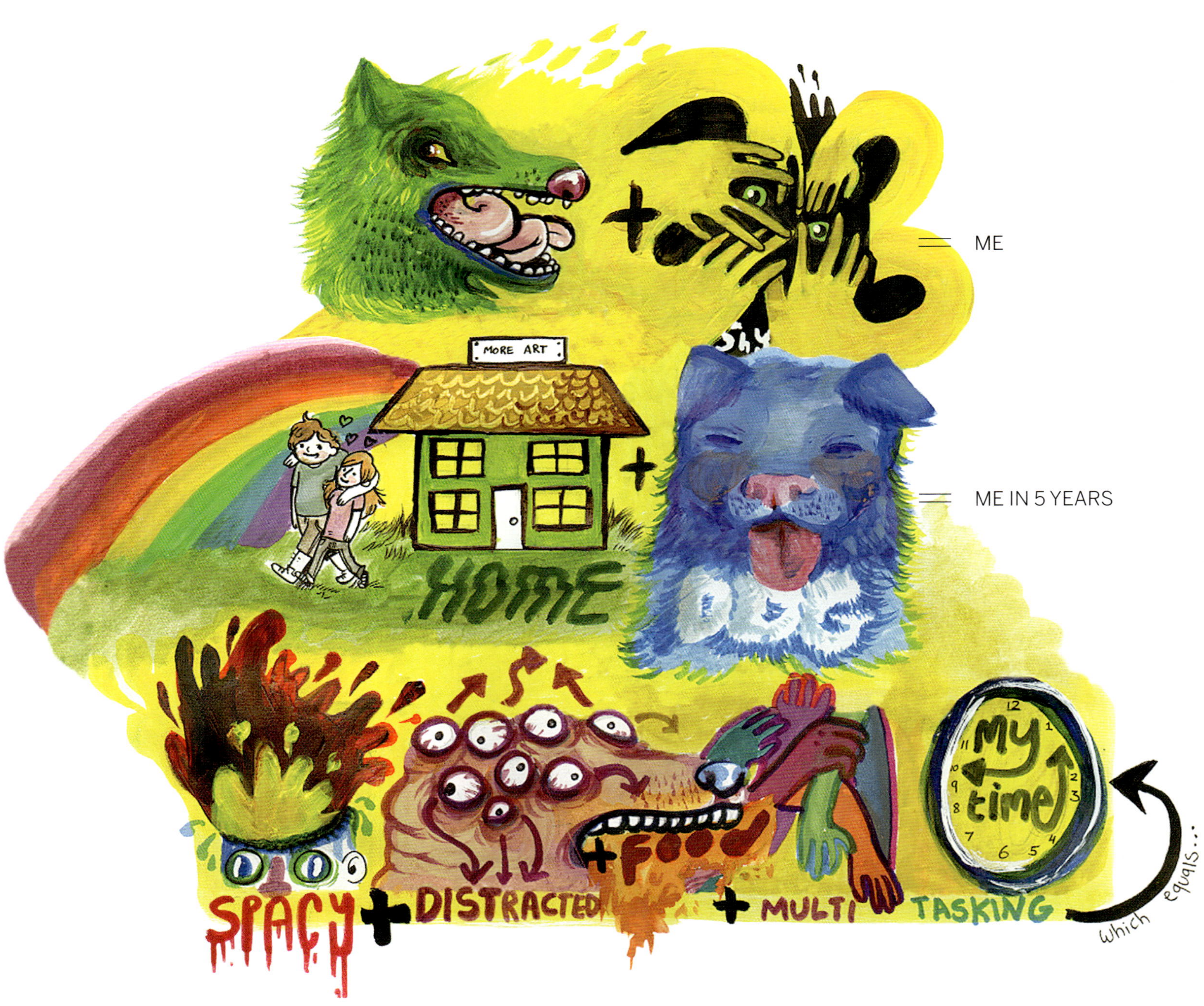
ME
MORE ART
HOME
ME IN 5 YEARS
SPACY + DISTRACTED + food + MULTI TASKING
My time
which equals...

BRAIN + BODY = ME

DREAMING + ACHIEVEMENT = ME

NATURAL FACE + PLASTIC SURGERY = ME

INTENSITY + SHORT TEMPER = ME

HEART + MIND = ME

EGO SOLUTIONS:

Figure 1 uses a literal painterly approach including titles in the imagery for a clearer narrative, supported at times by exaggeration.

Figures 2 through 6 are examples of the plus sign equation. Solutions include illustrated narratives to symbolic representations.

All executions are done with colored markers, except for figure 3, which uses collage along with pen and ink.

1. *Amy Churchwell*
2. *Daewook Do*
3. *Daisy Millard*
4. *Soyeon Lee*
5. *Yasmin Malki*
6. *Pablo Delkan*

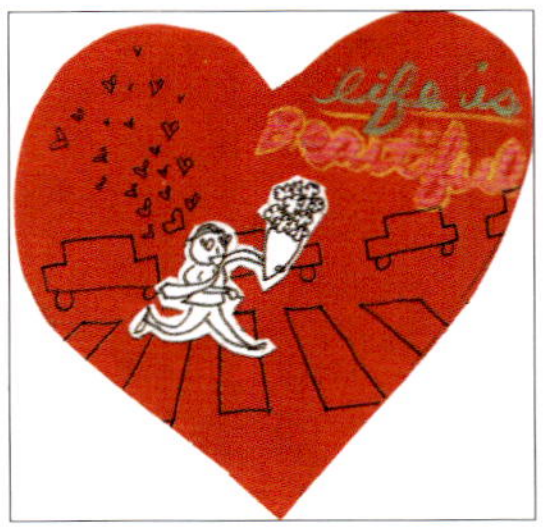

DAD 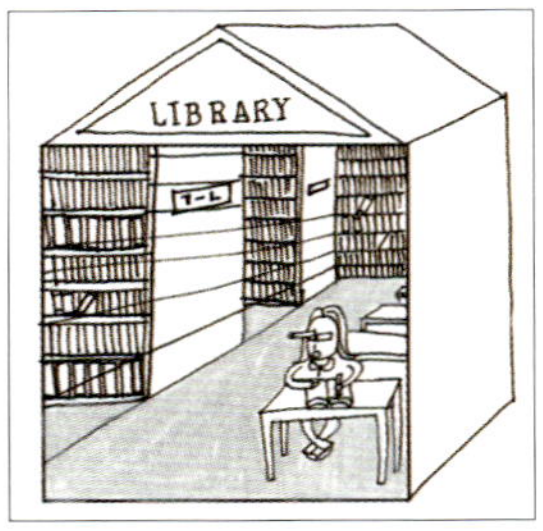 + MOM = ME

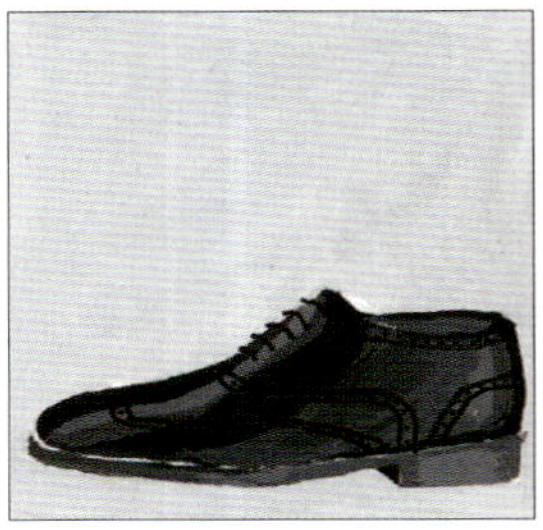

DAD 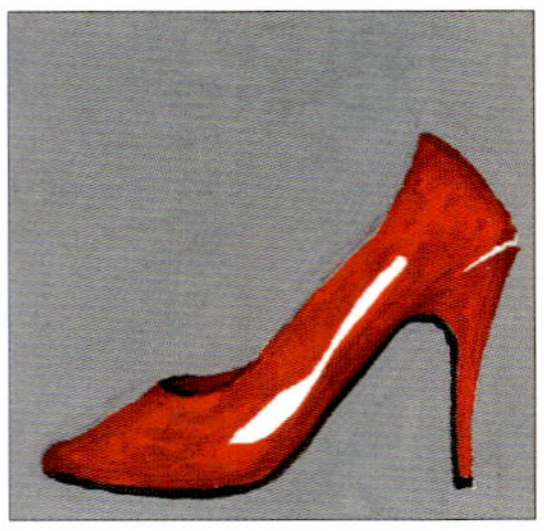 + MOM = ME

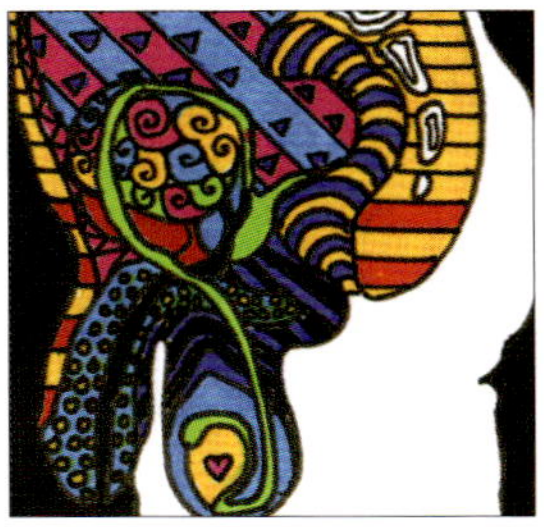

DAD 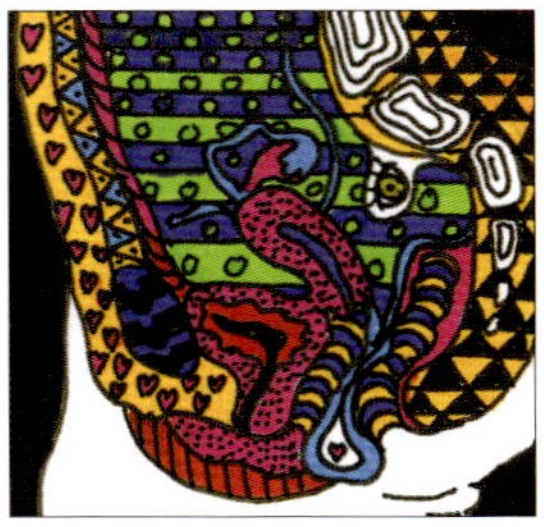 + MOM = ME

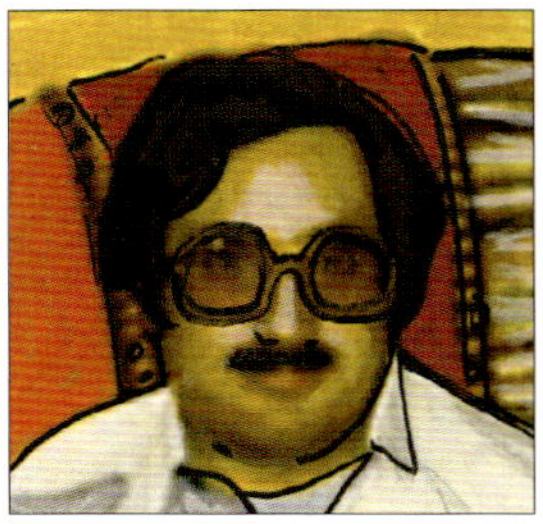

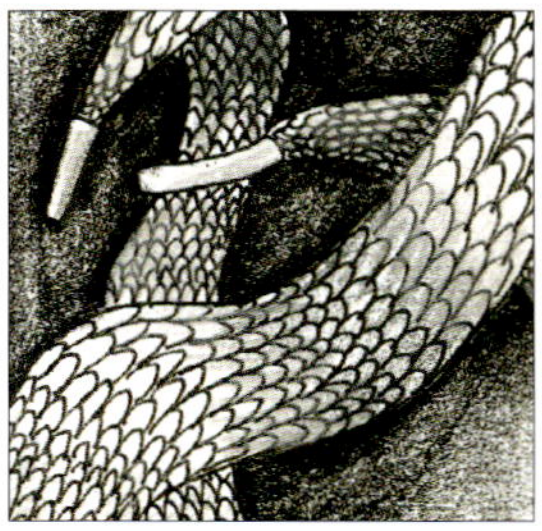

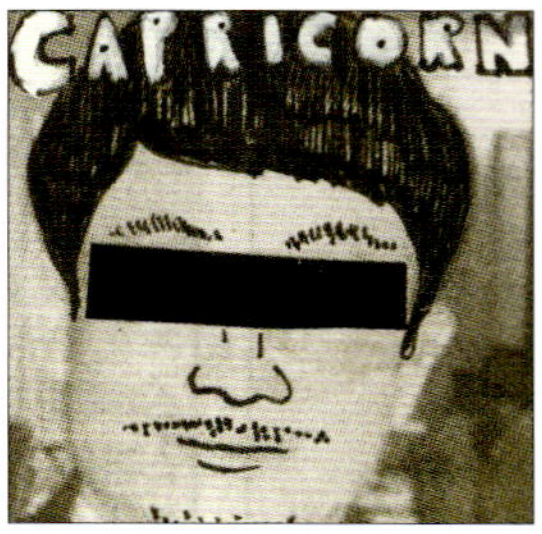

DAD 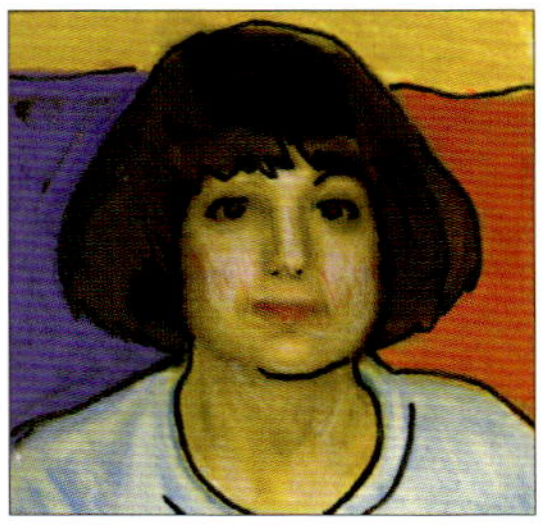 + MOM = ME

DAD 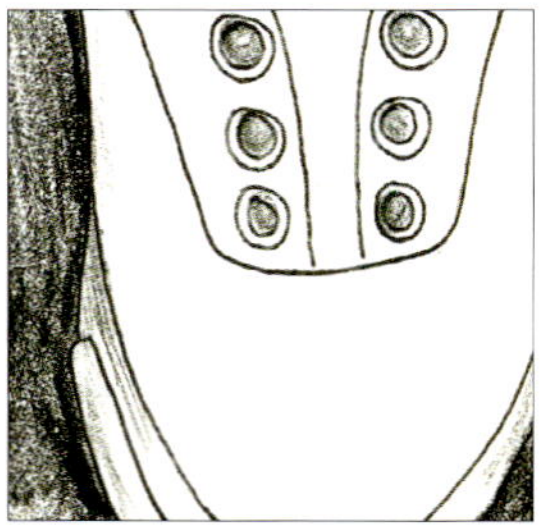 + MOM = ME

DAD
CONSERVATIVE DAD / MONEY MAKER
+
MOM 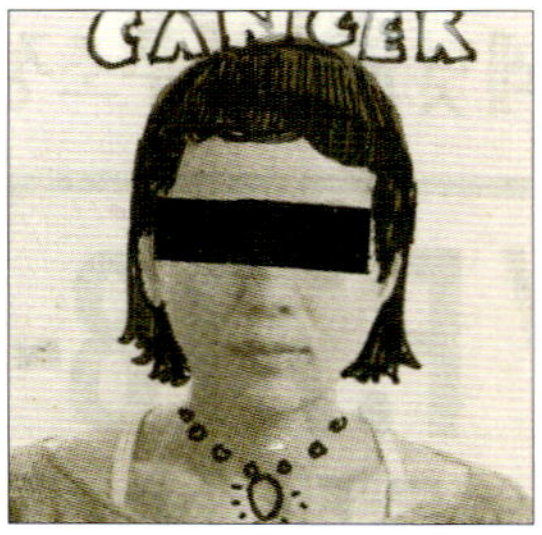
SHOPAHOLIC MOM / THE SPENDER
=
ME
GEMINI, SOMEWHAT CONSERVATIVE, SOMEWHAT OF A SPENDER, THE ONLY "ARTIST" IN FAMILY.

EGO SOLUTIONS:

Figures 1 through 6 are depictions of the plus sign equation that represent parents to reference the student's conception and birth.

Figures 7 and 8 deal with the minus sign equation, using two distinctly different problem-solving modes of expression.

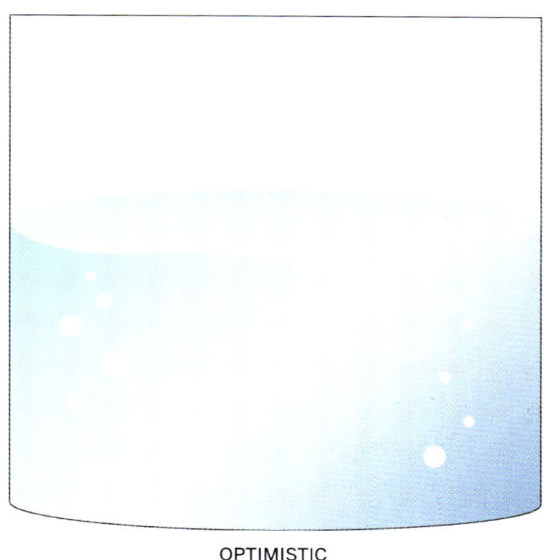

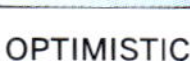

OPTIMISTIC

—

PESSIMISTIC

═ ME

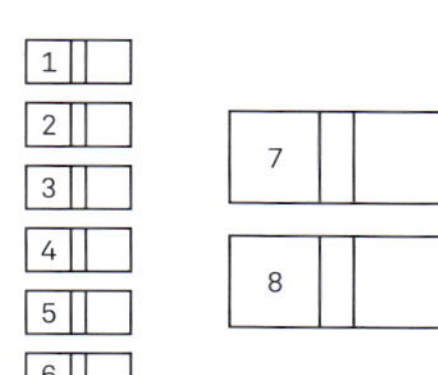

1. *Hyun Chae*
2. *Yulsoo Sung*
3. *Alex Morel*
4. *Rachel Willey*
5. *Minkjung Kang*
6. *Tahui Lee*
7. *Morimoto Yukiyo*
8. *Yesul Kim*

ME

—

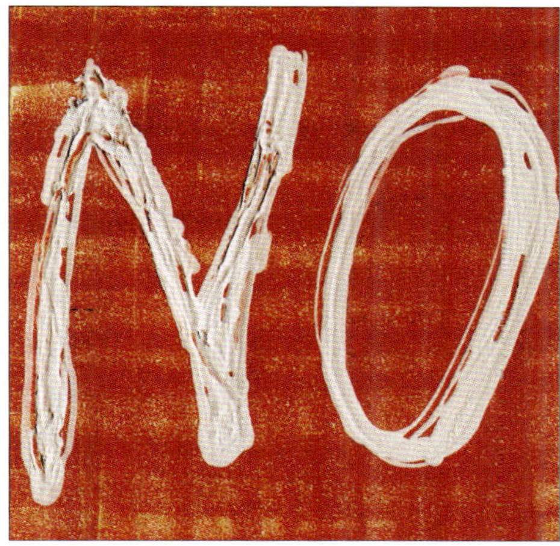

BARRIERS

═ AN IDEAL ME

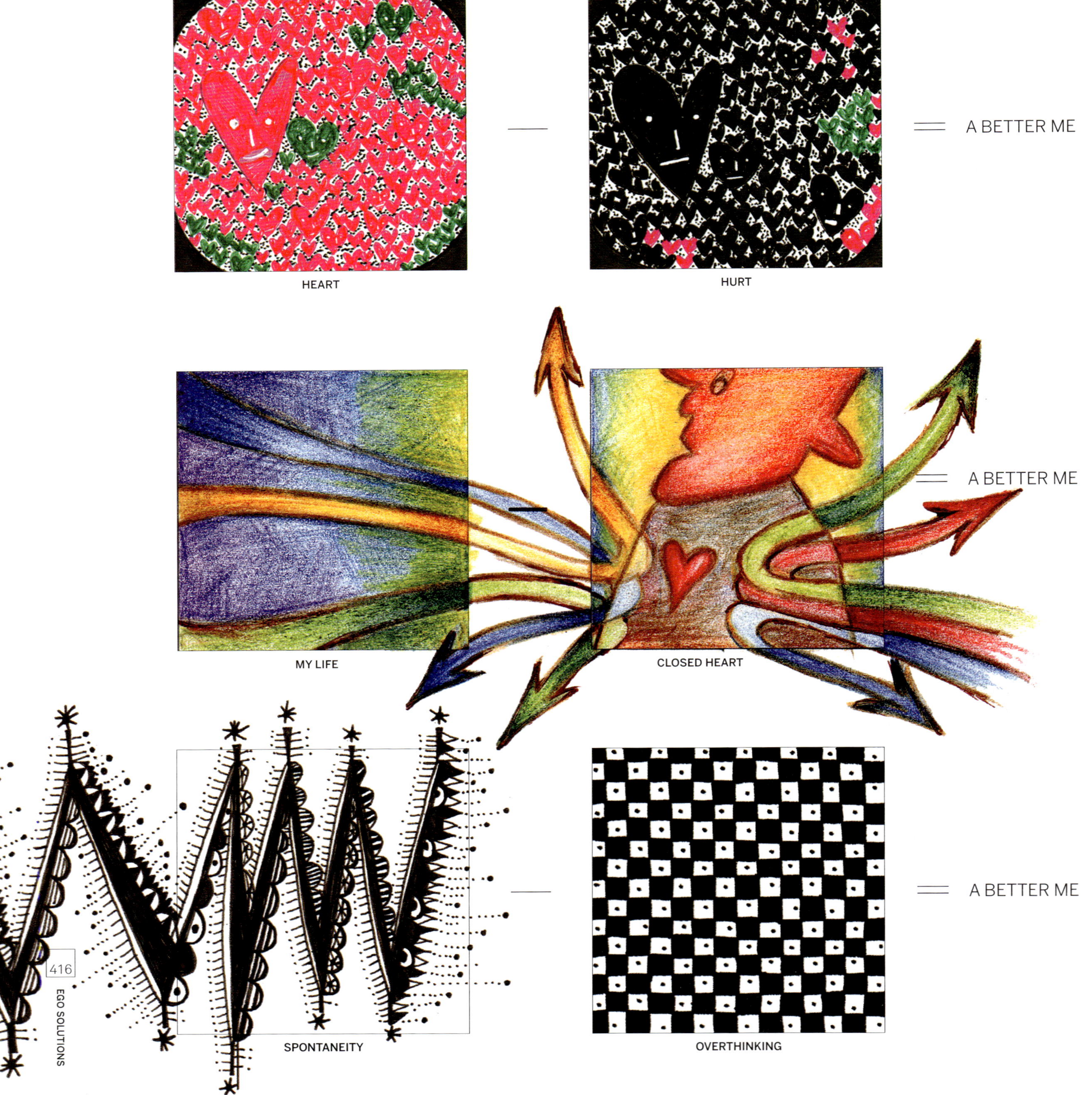
HEART
—
HURT
= A BETTER ME
MY LIFE
—
CLOSED HEART
= A BETTER ME
SPONTANEITY
—
OVERTHINKING
= A BETTER ME

EGO SOLUTIONS:

Figures 1 through 7 deal with the minus sign equation.

Figure 1 depicts a person who is both loving and vulnerable. Color is used to heighten the concept.

Figure 2 represents the opposite of figure 1, where the subtraction is of a closed-hearted person who wishes for love.

In figure 3, one's spontaneous nature is hampered by one's regimented state of being.

In figures 4 through 7 students eliminate constraints, habits, stress, and distractions to create "A Better Me."

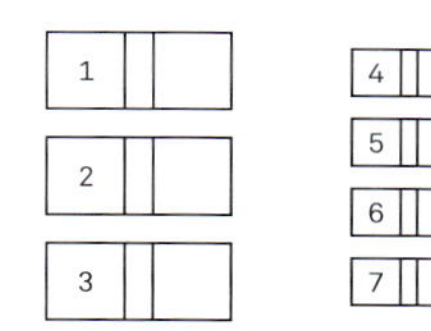

1. *Narae Lee*
2. *Anna Kim*
3. *Jiwon Kim*
4. *Stephanie Tin*
5. *Etta Horowitz*
6. *Kelly Shami*
7. *June Lim*

MY PERSONALITY — 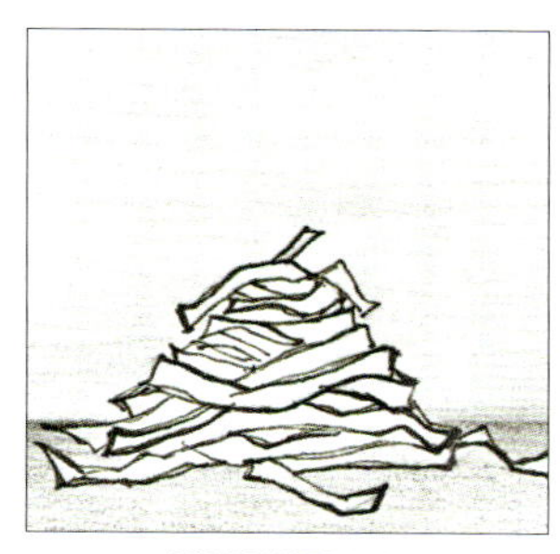 MY CONSTRAINT = A BETTER ME

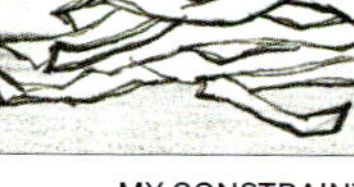

ME — 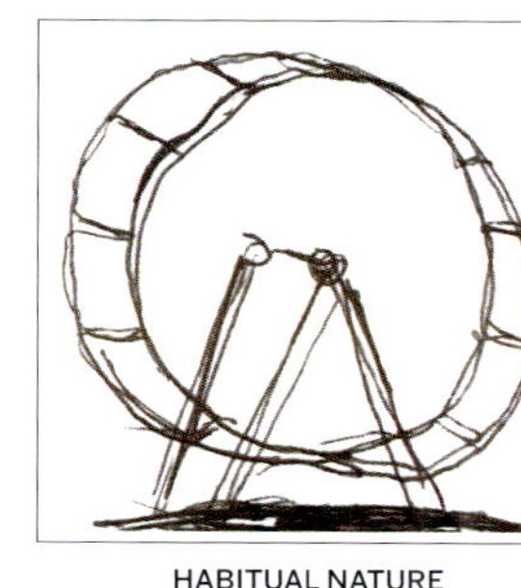 HABITUAL NATURE = A BETTER ME

MY LIFE — 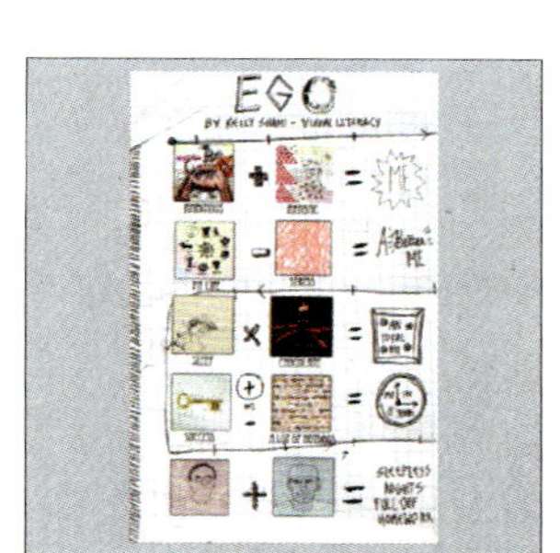
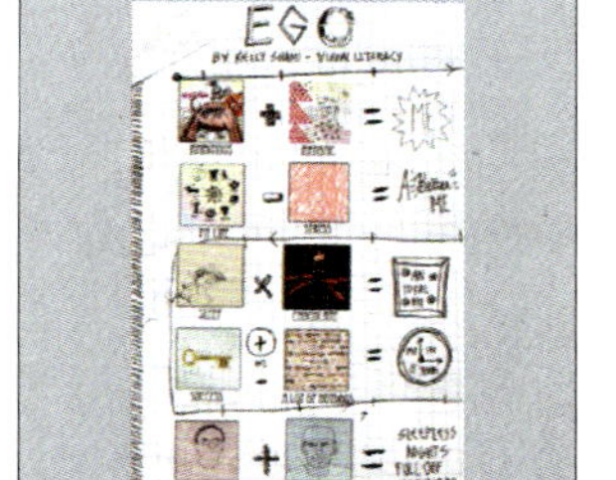

STRESS = A BETTER ME

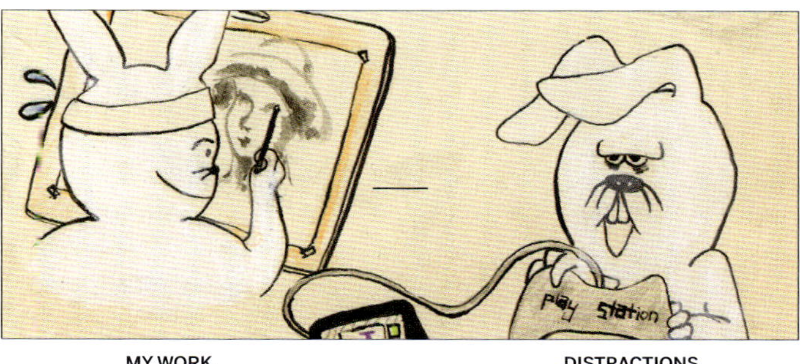

MY WORK — DISTRACTIONS = A BETTER ME

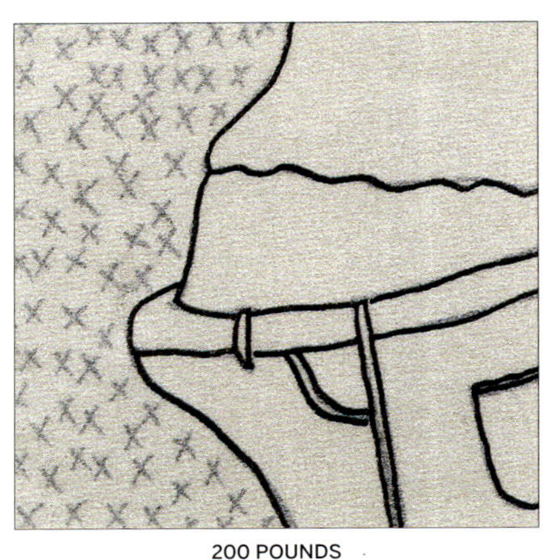

200 POUNDS

—

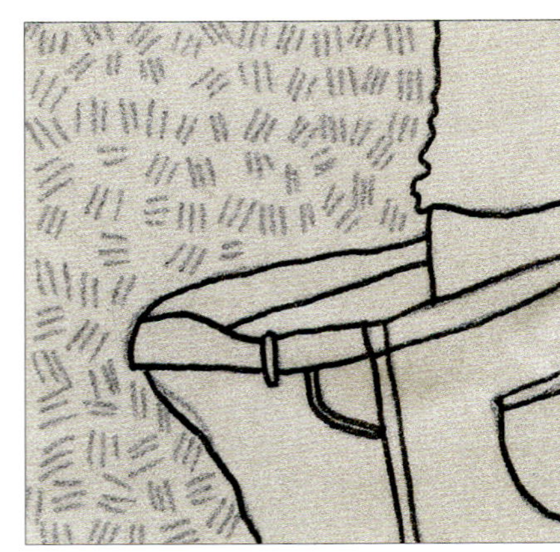

40 POUNDS

= A BETTER ME

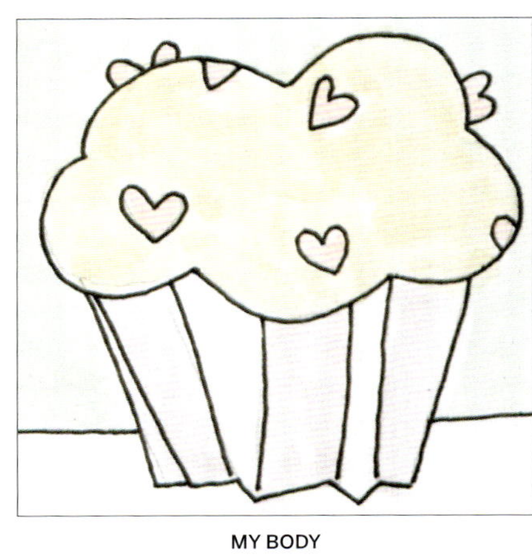

MY BODY

—

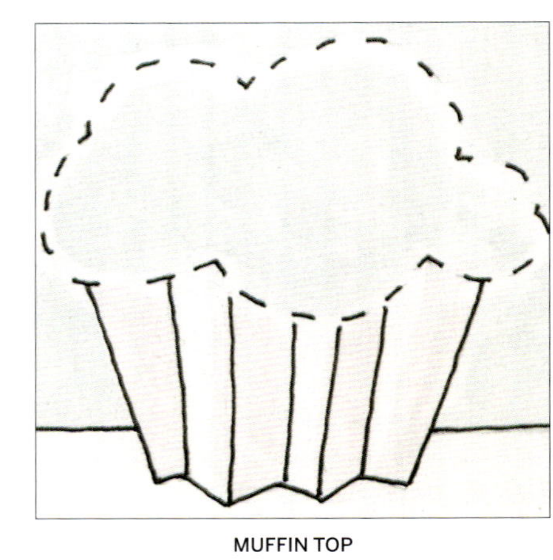

MUFFIN TOP

= A BETTER ME

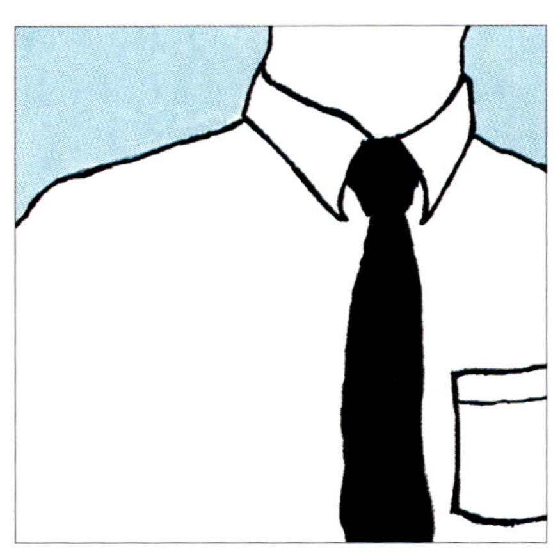

MY LIFE

—

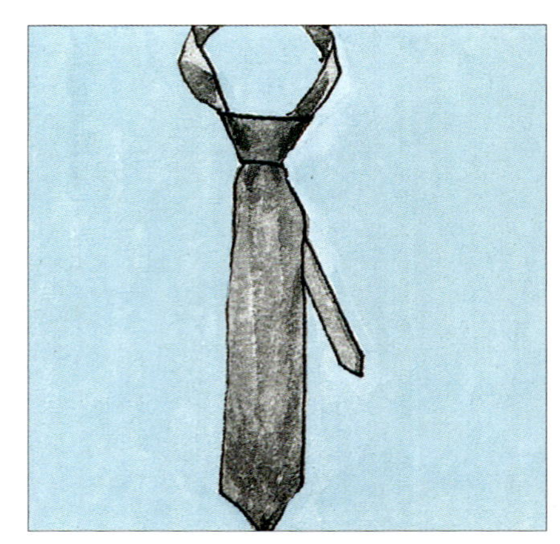

SOCIAL EXPECTATIONS

= A BETTER ME

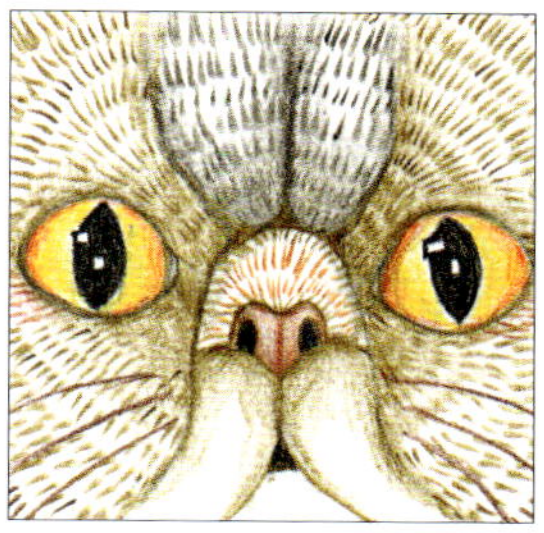

EGO SOLUTIONS:

Figures 1 and 2 deal with weight loss, while figure 3 deals with nonconformity.

Figures 4 through 9 also deal with subtraction in a range of subjects using pictorial, typographic, and symbolic imagery, where many solutions exhibit a sense of humor.

In figure 8, whose subject is coffee drinking, a face is created by using coffee-related objects.

PASSIVE — AGGRESSIVE = A BETTER ME

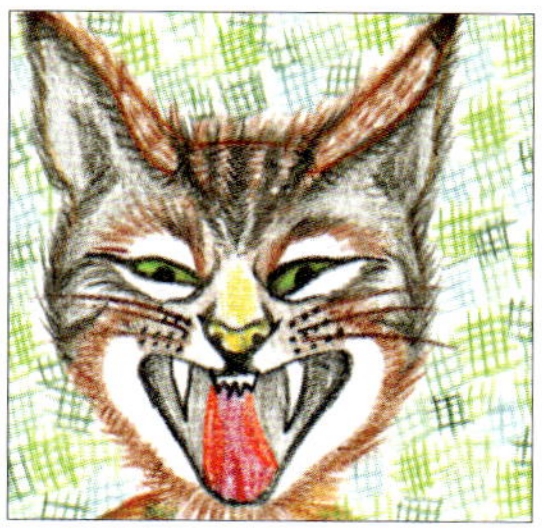

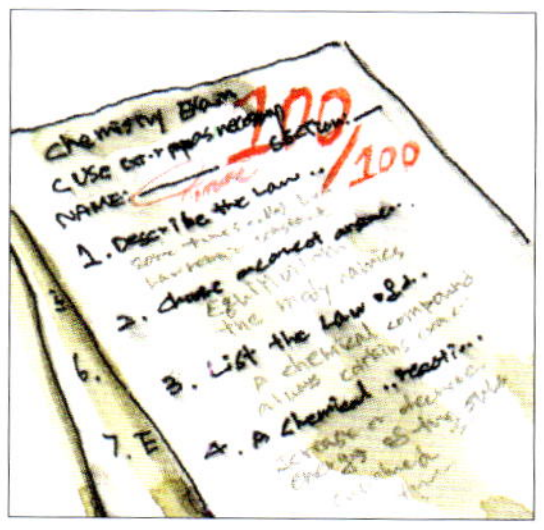

MY ABILITIES — FORGETFULNESS = A BETTER ME

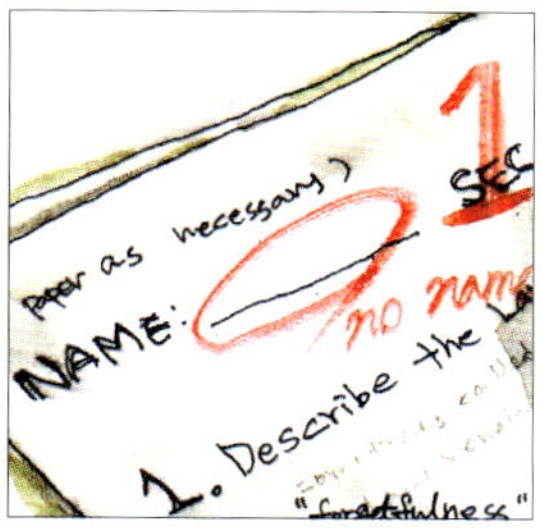

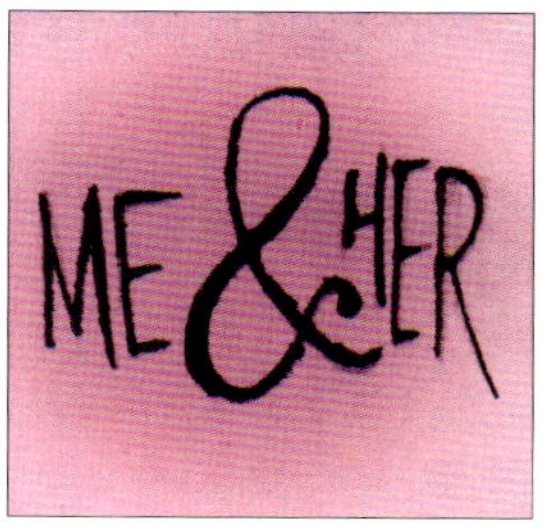

US — HER = A BETTER ME

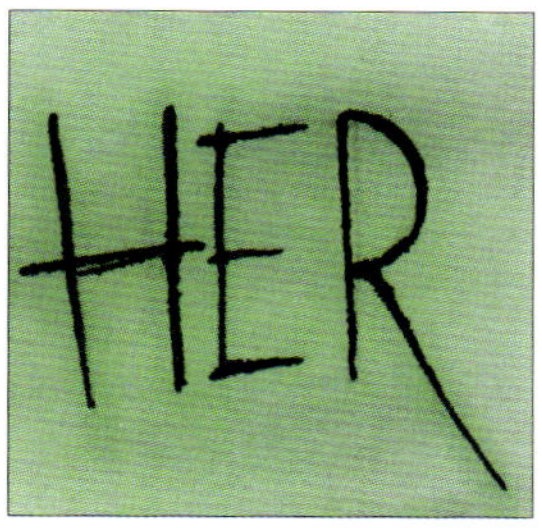

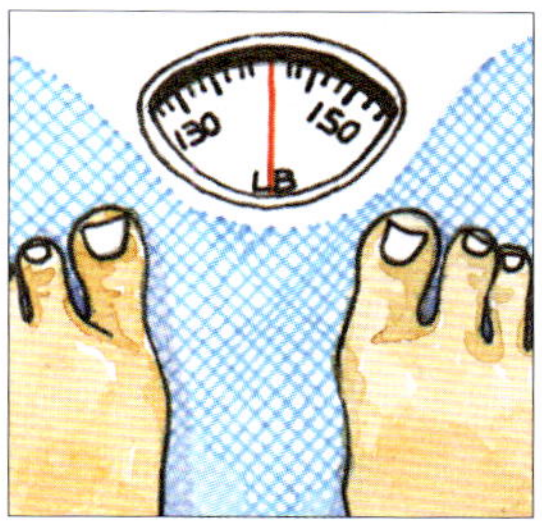

140 LBS — 120 LBS = A BETTER ME

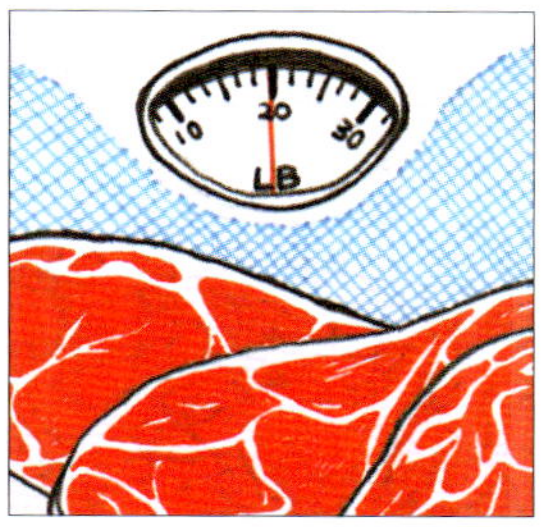

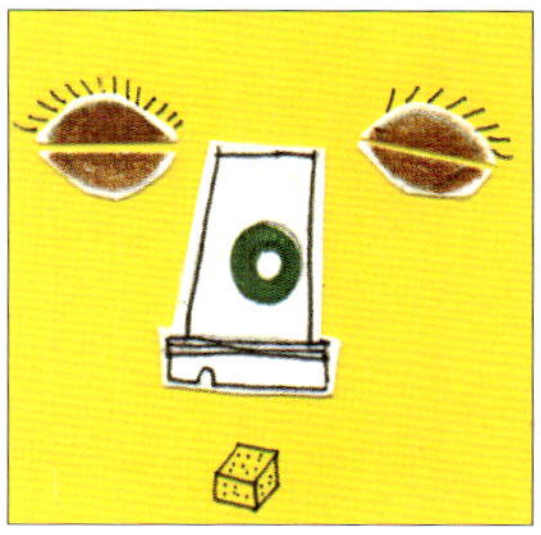

COFFEE FACE — COFFEE = A BETTER ME

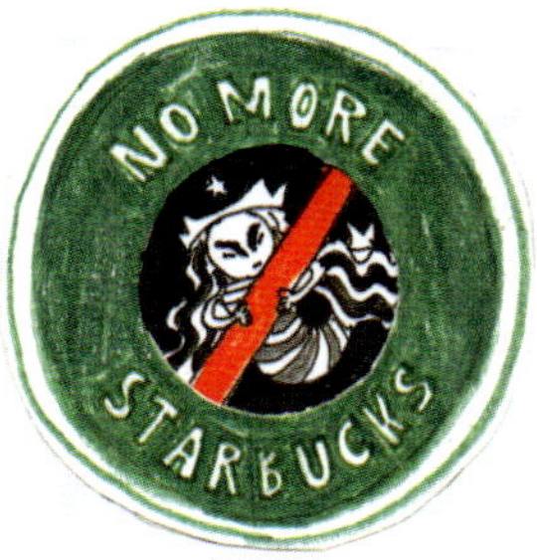

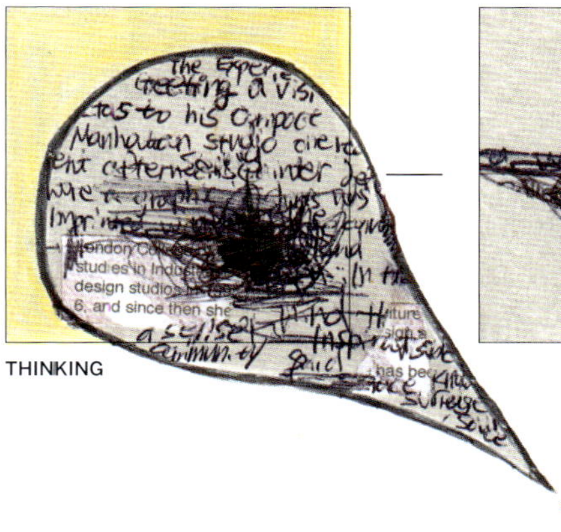

THINKING — FRUSTRATION = A BETTER ME

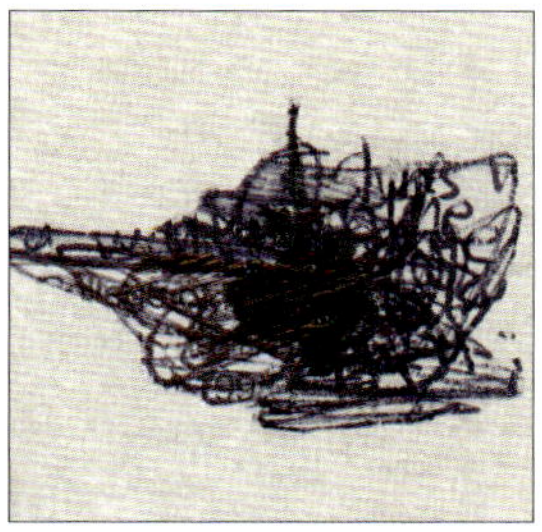

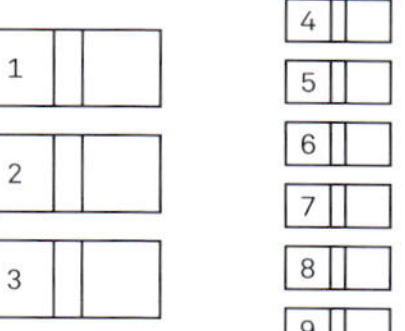

1. *Seyoung Park*
2. *Elaine Park*
3. *Yulsoo Sung*
4. *Jiyoon Yeom*
5. *Mee Jang*
6. *Pablo Delkan*
7. *Soomin Yoo*
8. *Hyun Chae*
9. *Youjin Kim*

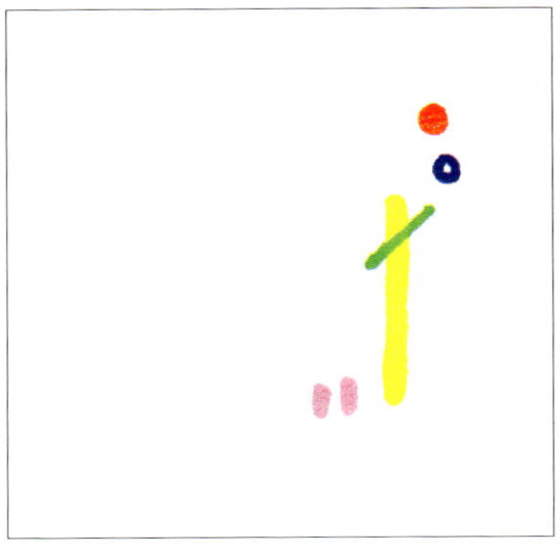

MY CURRENT CREATIVITY 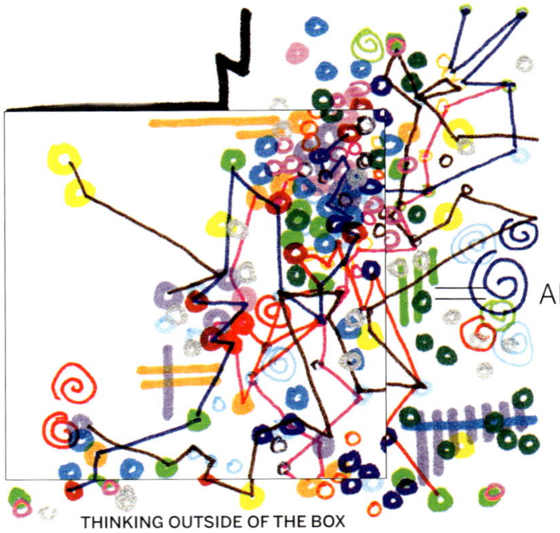 × THINKING OUTSIDE OF THE BOX = AN IDEAL ME

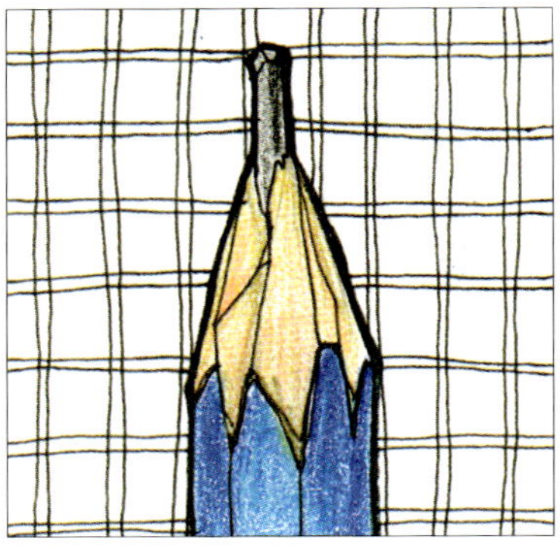

ONE DIMENSIONAL 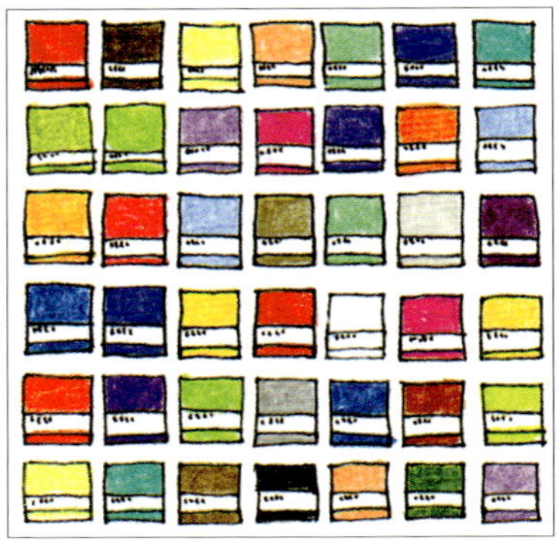 × POSSIBILITIES 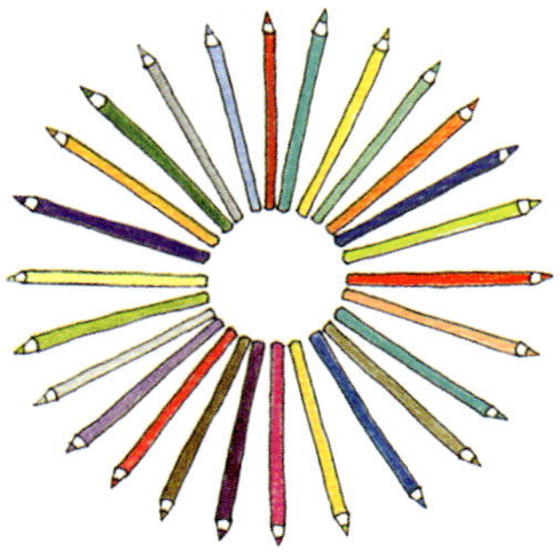 = AN IDEAL ME

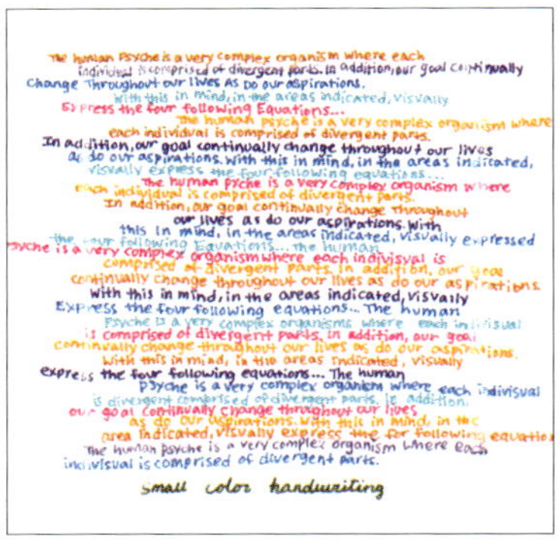

SMALL COLORED INK HANDWRITING 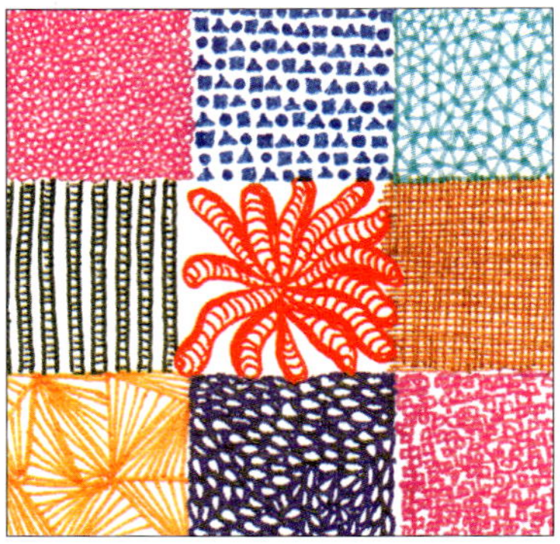 × SMALL COLOR PATTERNS = AN IDEAL ME

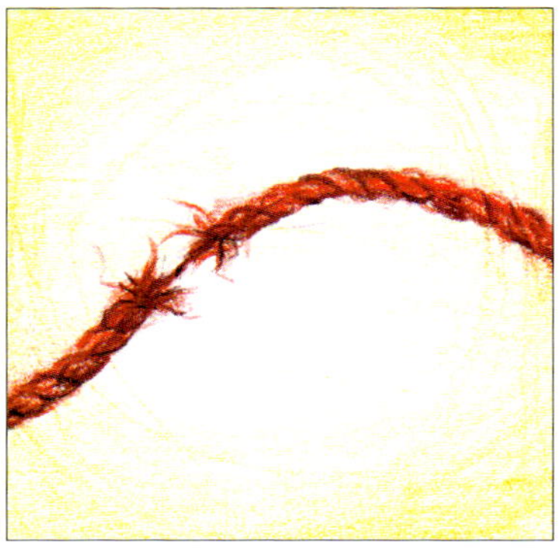

OUTGROWING RESTRICTIONS ×

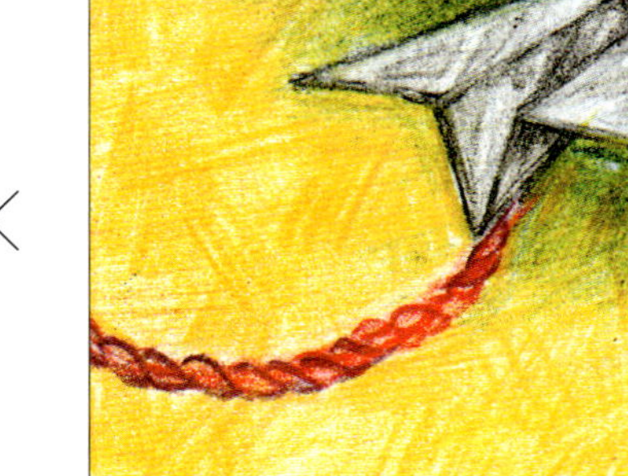

FREEDOM = AN IDEAL ME

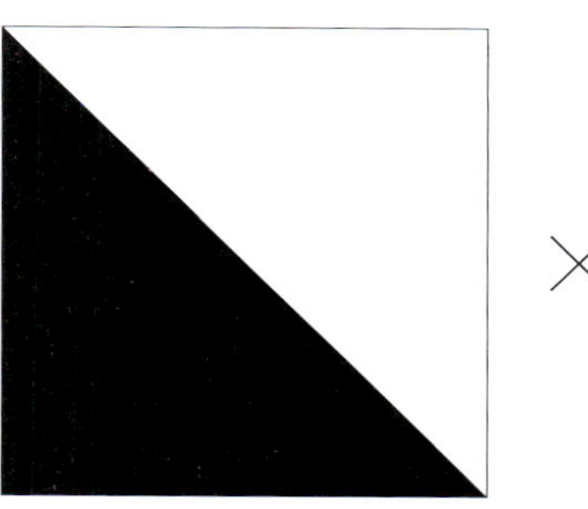

TENDENCY TO SEE THINGS IN ABSOLUTES

×

ABILITY TO SEE "THE GRAY"

= AN IDEAL ME

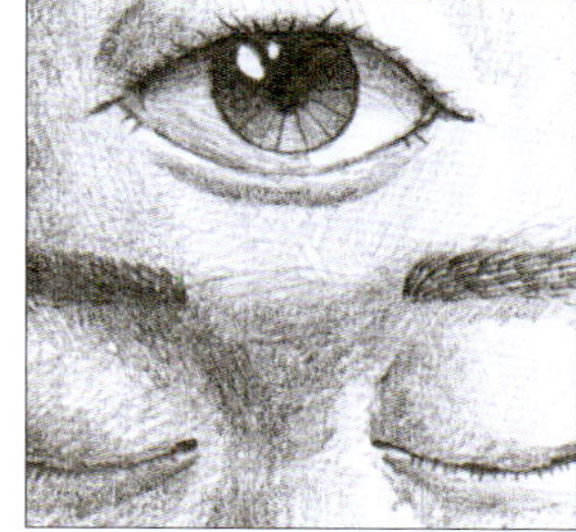

EYE OF WISDOM

×

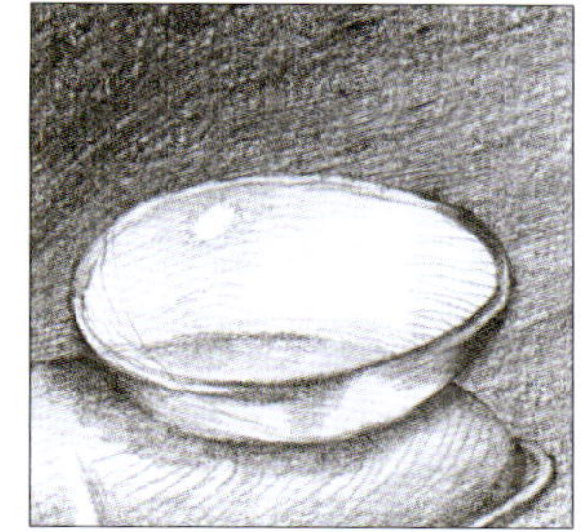

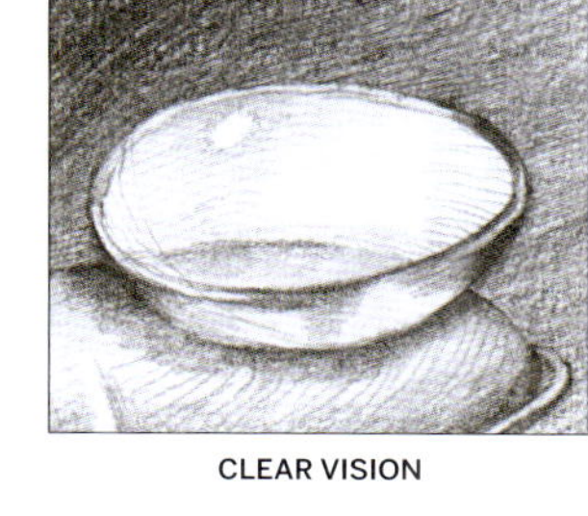

CLEAR VISION

= AN IDEAL ME

ME

×

OPPORTUNITY

= AN IDEAL ME

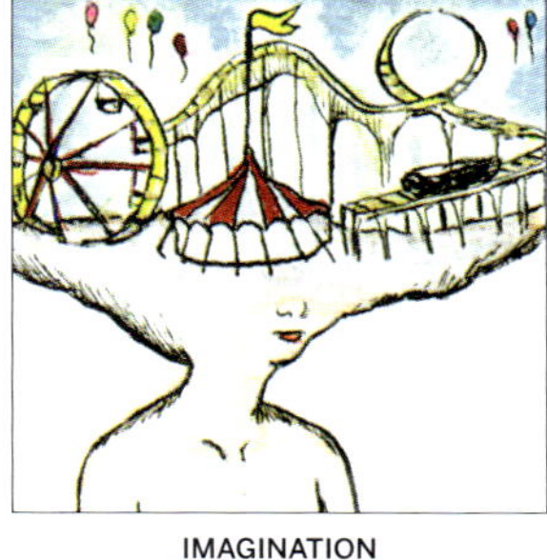

IMAGINATION

×

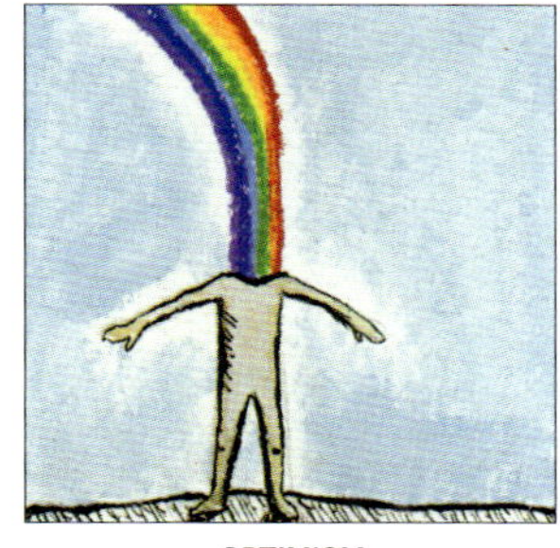

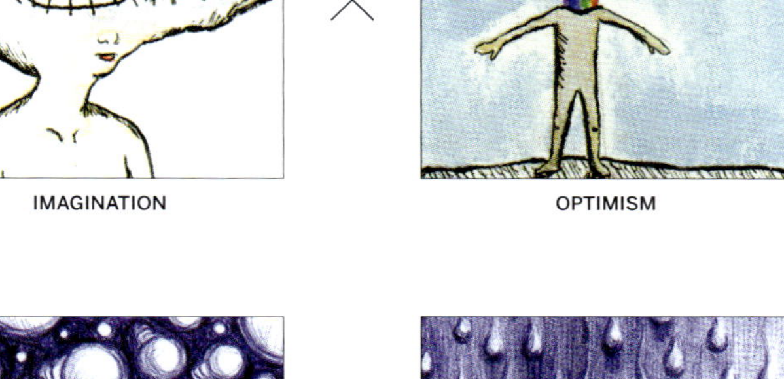

OPTIMISM

= AN IDEAL ME

IDEAS

×

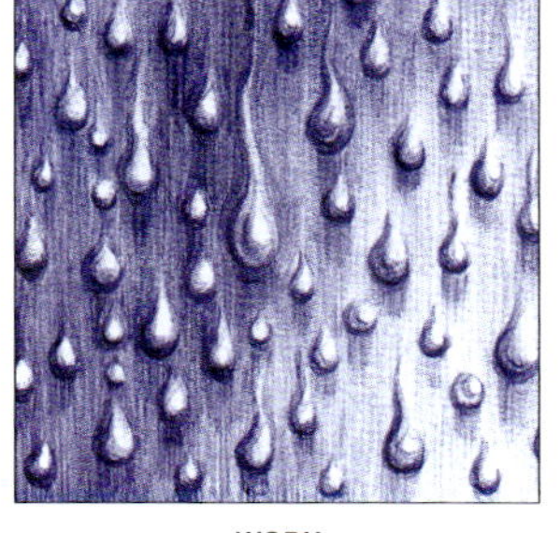

WORK

= AN IDEAL ME

EGO SOLUTIONS:

Figures 1 through 9 depict the multiplication equation, resulting in perfection.

Figure 3 references idiosyncratic aspects that are highly personal.

Figures 1 through 4 and 8 use a varied color palette to enhance their solutions, while figures 5 through 7 and 9 use a more monochromatic approach.

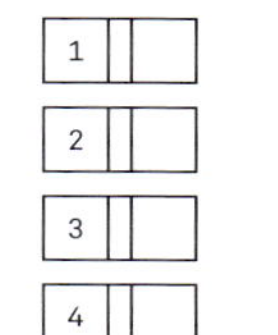

1. *Sunah Lee*
2. *Youngmi Jung*
3. *Jenna Kim*
4. *Anna Kim*
5. *Elizabeth Vautour*
6. *Daewook Do*
7. *Jieun Moon*
8. *Yasmin Malki*
9. *Younsook Jee*

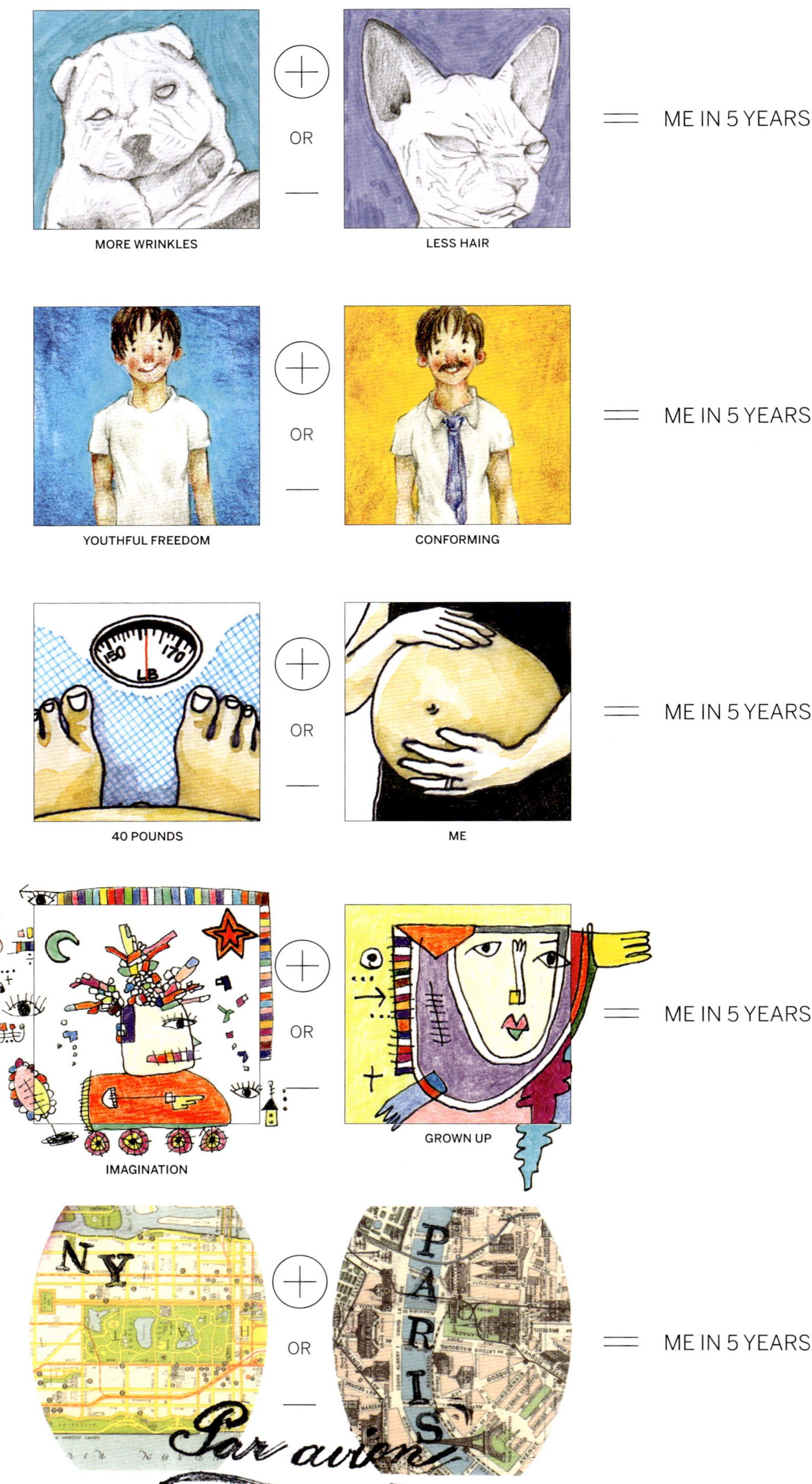
OR
MORE WRINKLES
LESS HAIR
ME IN 5 YEARS
OR
YOUTHFUL FREEDOM
CONFORMING
ME IN 5 YEARS
150
170
LB
OR
40 POUNDS
ME
ME IN 5 YEARS
OR
IMAGINATION
GROWN UP
ME IN 5 YEARS
NY
PARIS
OR
Par avion
ME IN 5 YEARS

EGO SOLUTIONS:

Figures 1 through 9 are depictions of the plus or minus sign that equals how one envisions oneself in five years.

In every case, students chose to add an aspect as opposed to subtracting one.

Solutions range from bodily changes, to emotionally growing up, to living on two continents, to issues of maturity, family, working in the USA, and to becoming a superstar.

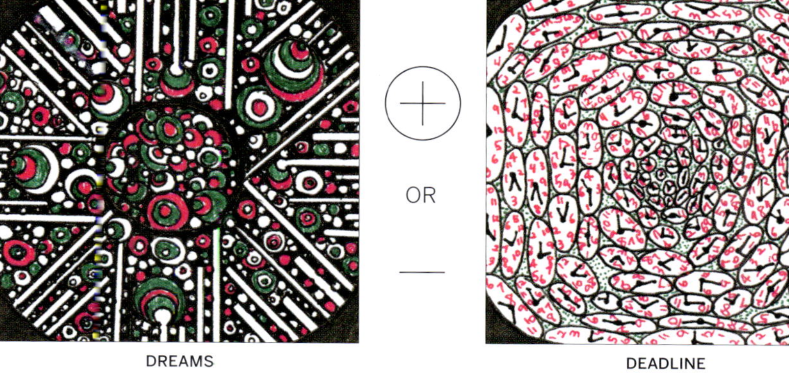

DREAMS + OR − DEADLINE = AN IDEAL ME

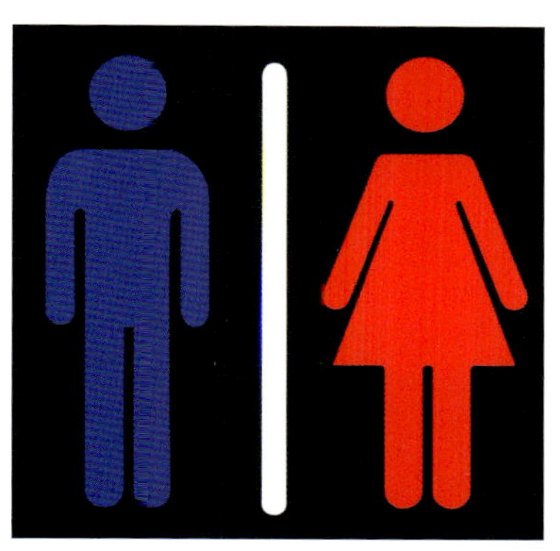

APART

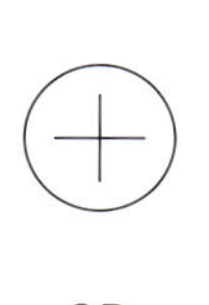

OR

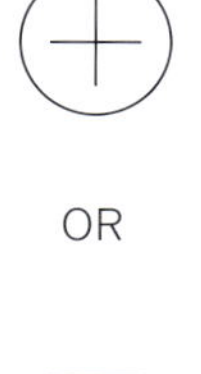

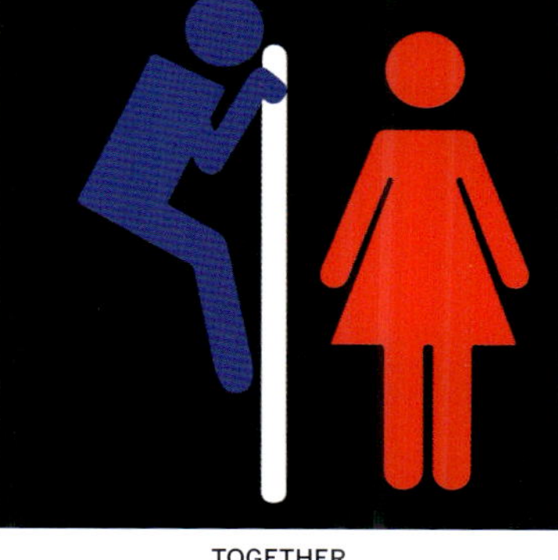

TOGETHER

=

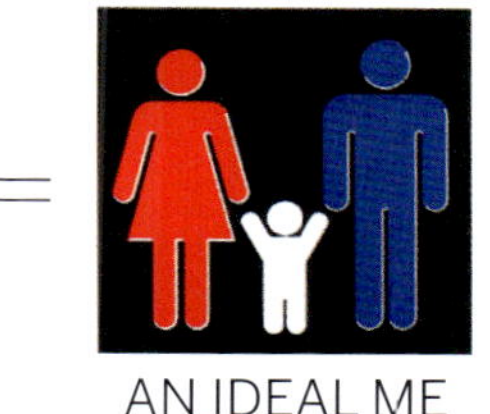

AN IDEAL ME

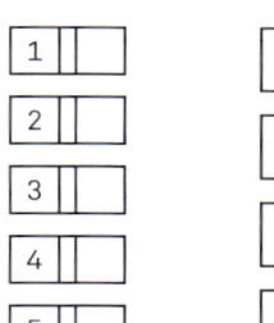

1. *Daewook Do*
2. *Chris Wright*
3. *Soomin Yoo*
4. *Soyeon Kim*
5. *Julia Coelho*
6. *Narae Lee*
7. *Heewon Cho*
8. *Younsook Jee*
9. *Seongmi Park*

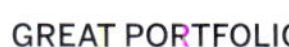

GREAT PORTFOLIO

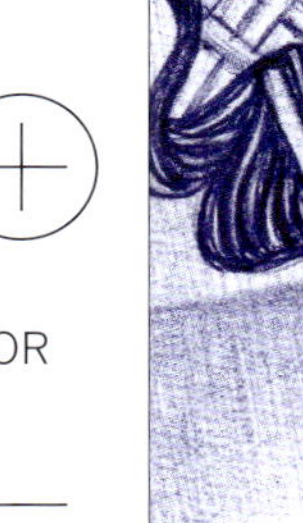

OR

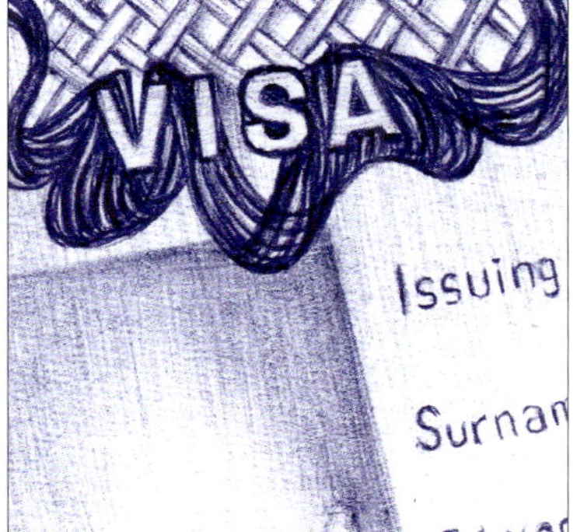

PERMANENT VISA

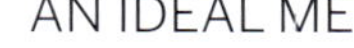

= AN IDEAL ME

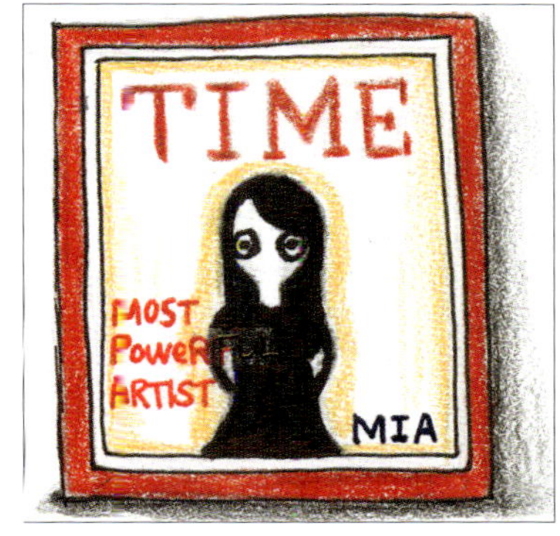

FORTUNE

+ OR −

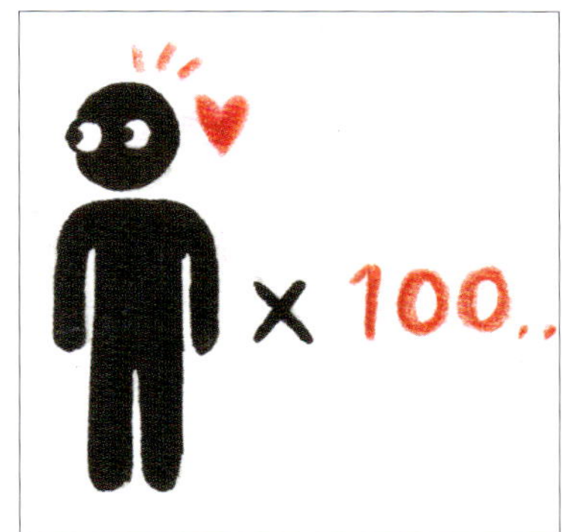

FAME

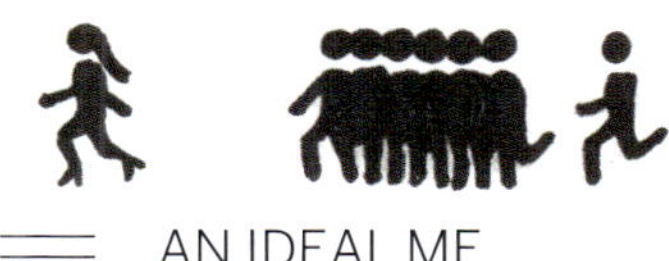

= AN IDEAL ME

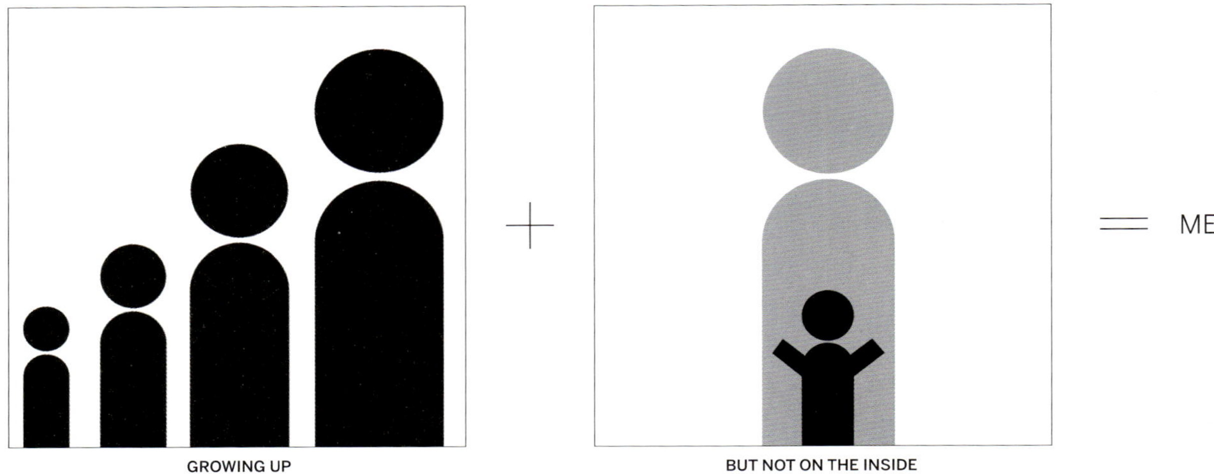

GROWING UP

BUT NOT ON THE INSIDE

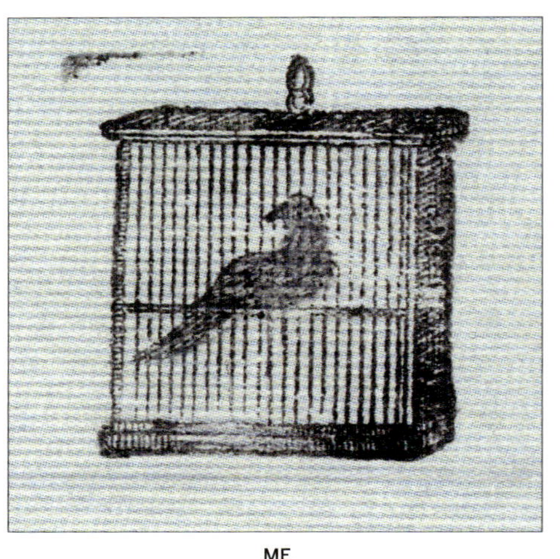

ME

—

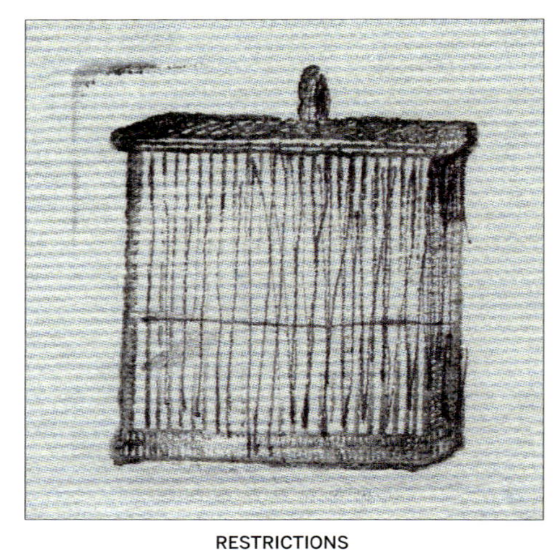

RESTRICTIONS

= A BETTER ME

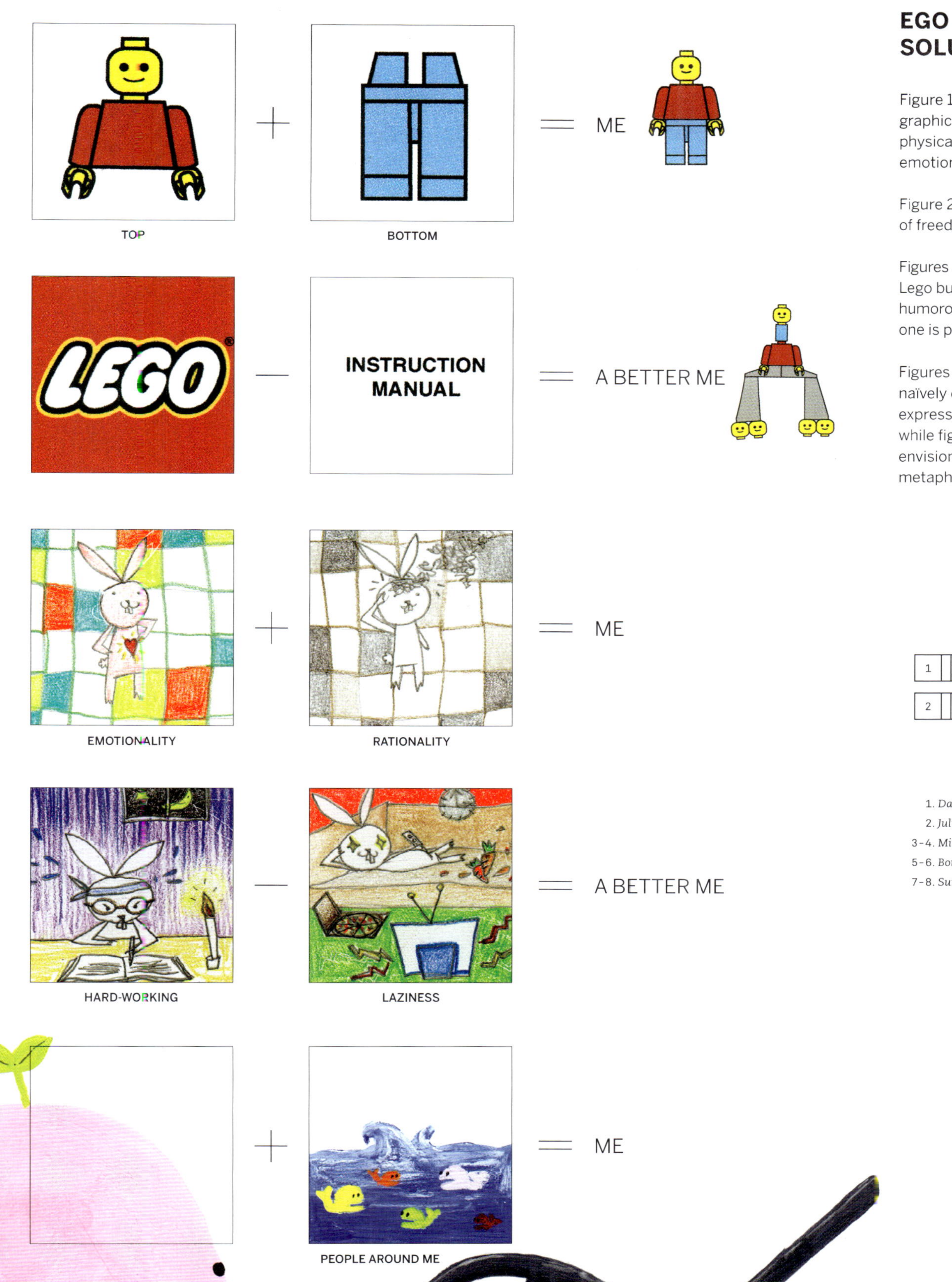

EGO SOLUTIONS:

Figure 1 uses a simplified graphic image to illustrate physical growth without emotional development.

Figure 2 is an illustration of freedom.

Figures 3 and 4 depict using Lego building blocks to humorously formulate how one is put together.

Figures 5 and 6 use a naïvely drawn rabbit to express one's concept, while figures 7 and 8 envision a whale, as a metaphoric solution.

1. *David Petrucco*
2. *Julia Coelho*
3–4. *Minjoon Lee*
5–6. *Borim Kim*
7–8. *Sunmin Chung*

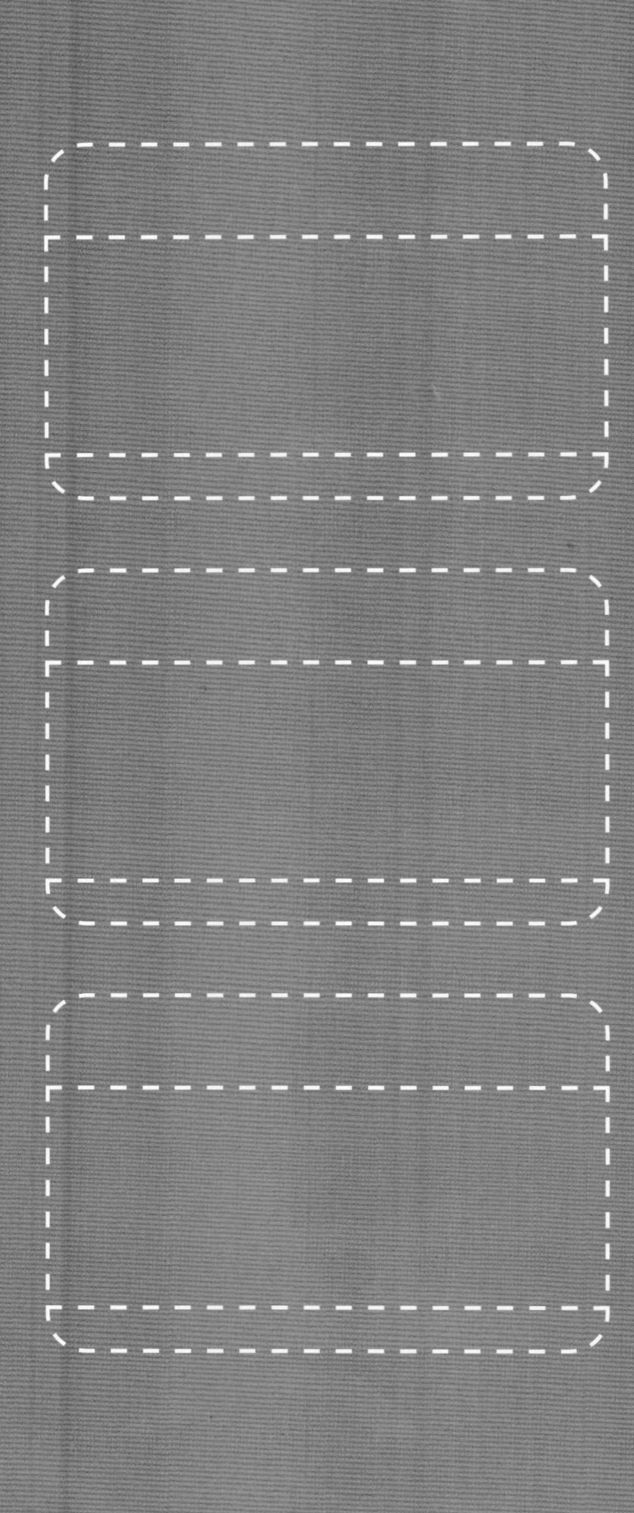

THOUGHTS ON THE CREATIVE PROCESS 12

Looking for a formula will keep you from getting there.

"HELLO
my name is
________"

HELLO MY NAME IS________________, IS A COMMONLY USED STICK-ON NAMETAG TO IDENTIFY PEOPLE ATTENDING A CONFERENCE OR A LARGE GATHERING. USING THE STICK-ON NAMETAG AS A POINT OF DEPARTURE, SELECT A SUBJECT THAT REPRESENTS YOURSELF, OR AN ASPECT OF YOUR PERSONALITY. INTERPRET IT IN THE FOLLOWING THREE WAYS:

1. USE THE TOP NAMETAG TO TYPOGRAPHICALLY DEPICT YOURSELF BY SELECTING OR CREATING A TYPEFACE THAT BEST REPRESENTS YOUR SUBJECT. CAREFULLY CONSIDER: CHOICE OF TYPEFACE(S), USE OF UPPER AND/OR LOWERCASE, LETTER SPACING, TOUCHING, OVERLAPPING, NEGATIVE/POSITIVE RELATIONSHIPS, SIZE OF TYPE IN RELATION TO THE GIVEN AREA, CROPPING, COLOR, ETC.

2. USE THE MIDDLE NAMETAG TO CREATE AN ABSTRACT SOLUTION TO BEST REPRESENT YOURSELF BY INFERRING OR SUGGESTING THE INTENDED MESSAGE.

3. USE THE BOTTOM NAMETAG TO CREATE AN IMAGE THAT IS CONCEPTUALLY DRIVEN THAT COULD BE EITHER LITERAL, SYMBOLIC, OR METAPHORIC, WHICH AGAIN REPRESENTS YOURSELF. USE EITHER THE SAME ASPECT OF YOUR PERSONALITY, OR YOUR NAME FOR ALL THREE SOLUTIONS. OR SELECT A DIFFERENT ASPECT FOR EACH SOLUTION. IN SHORT, THE FIRST SOLUTION IS TYPOGRAPHIC, THE SECOND IS ABSTRACT AND THE THIRD IS AN IDENTIFIABLE IMAGE.

HELLO
my name is

HELLO
my name is

HELLO
my name is

PROBLEMS : SOLUTIONS SERIES

CREATED BY RICHARD WILDE / JUDITH WILDE, PRODUCED BY VISUAL ARTS PRESS, LTD. ART DIRECTORS: RICHARD WILDE / JUDITH WILDE

HELLO MY NAME IS PROBLEM:

Describe aspects of yourself using the three nametags on the given assignment sheet. In the top nametag create a typographic solution; use the center nametag to create an abstract solution and the bottom nametag to create an identifiable image. You may select a single aspect, or three different aspects of your personality.

AIM:
This project is an opportunity to be inventive in different genres. It expands one's creative problem-solving abilities to view a subject, or subjects from different perspectives.

SUGGESTIONS:
It is helpful to be honest about whatever qualities of your personality you wish to portray. Your solutions will have a better chance of resonating to yourself and others.

SPECIFICATIONS:
There is no limitation on medium or color.

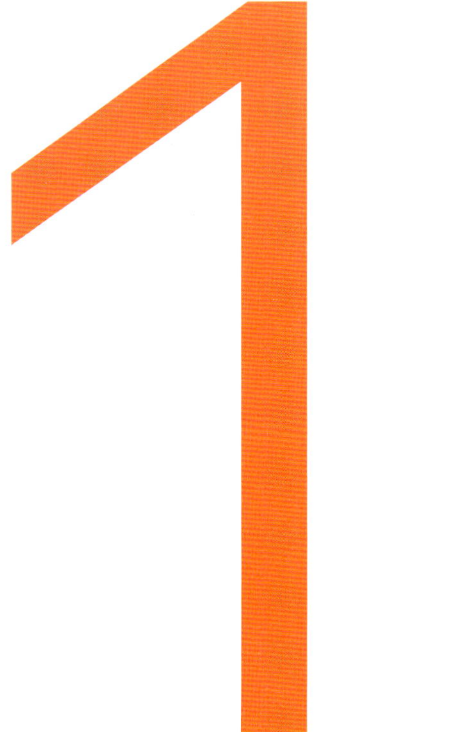

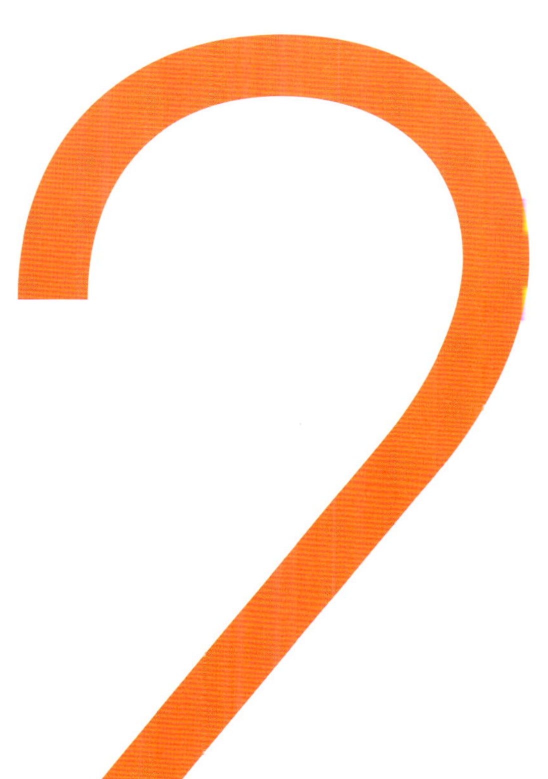

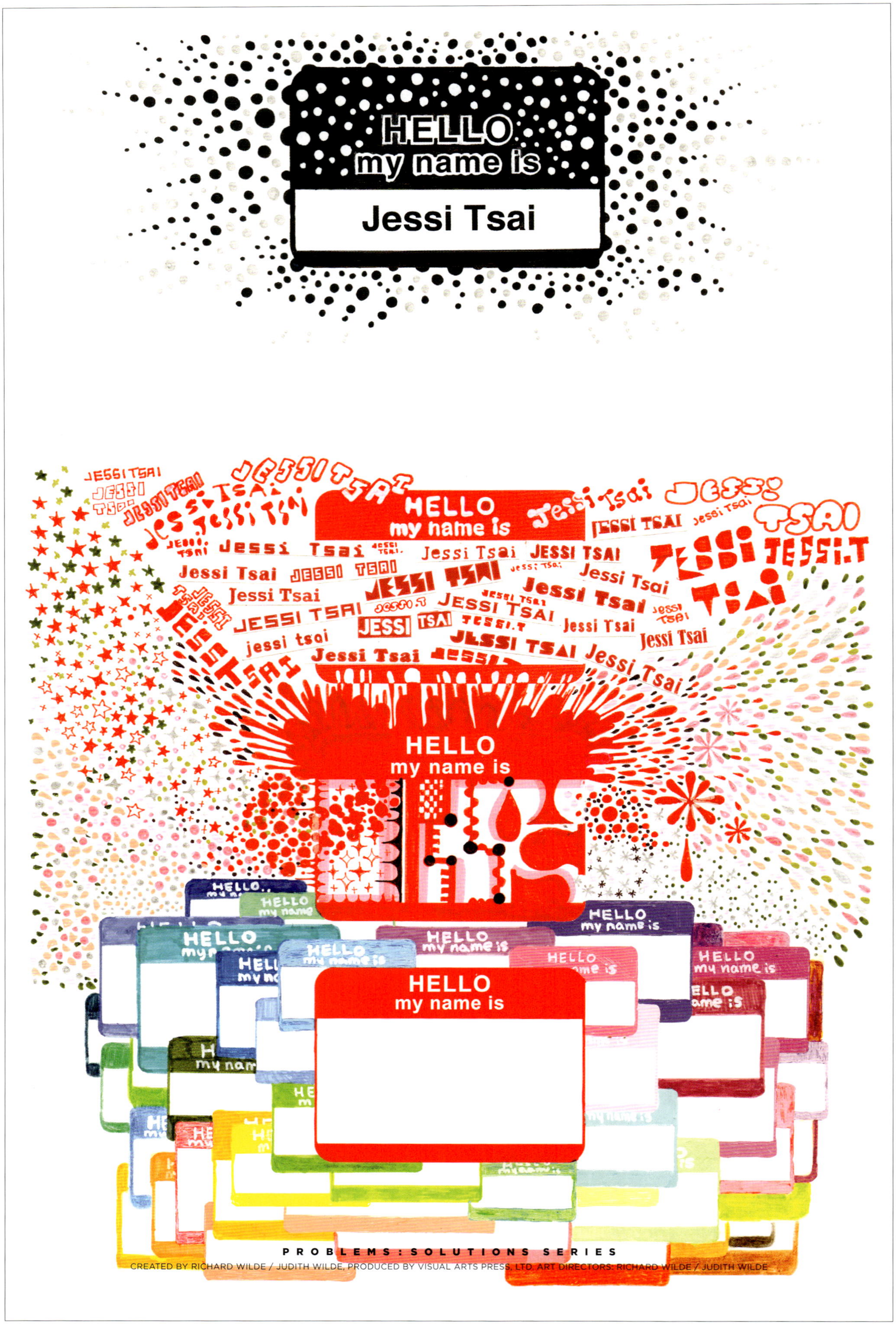

HELLO
my name is
Jessi Tsai

HELLO
my name is

HELLO
my name is

HELLO
my name is

PROBLEMS:SOLUTIONS SERIES

CREATED BY RICHARD WILDE / JUDITH WILDE, PRODUCED BY VISUAL ARTS PRESS, LTD. ART DIRECTORS: RICHARD WILDE / JUDITH WILDE

HELLO MY NAME IS SOLUTIONS:

In figure 1 liberty was taken in solving the assignment, which functions as a personal expression.

In figures 2 through 4, all solutions are depictions of obsessive-compulsive behavior, executed as typographic, literal, and abstract interpretations.

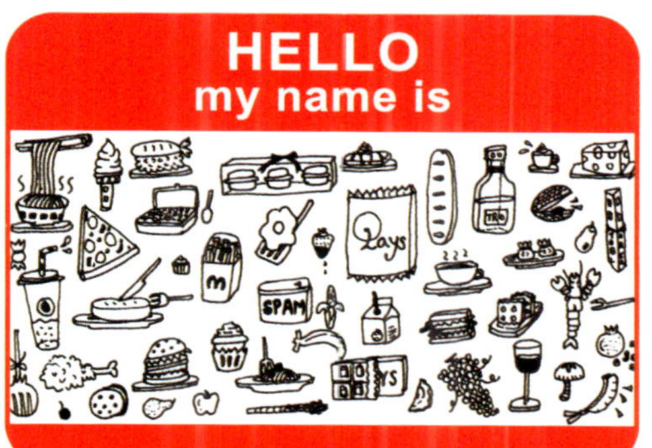

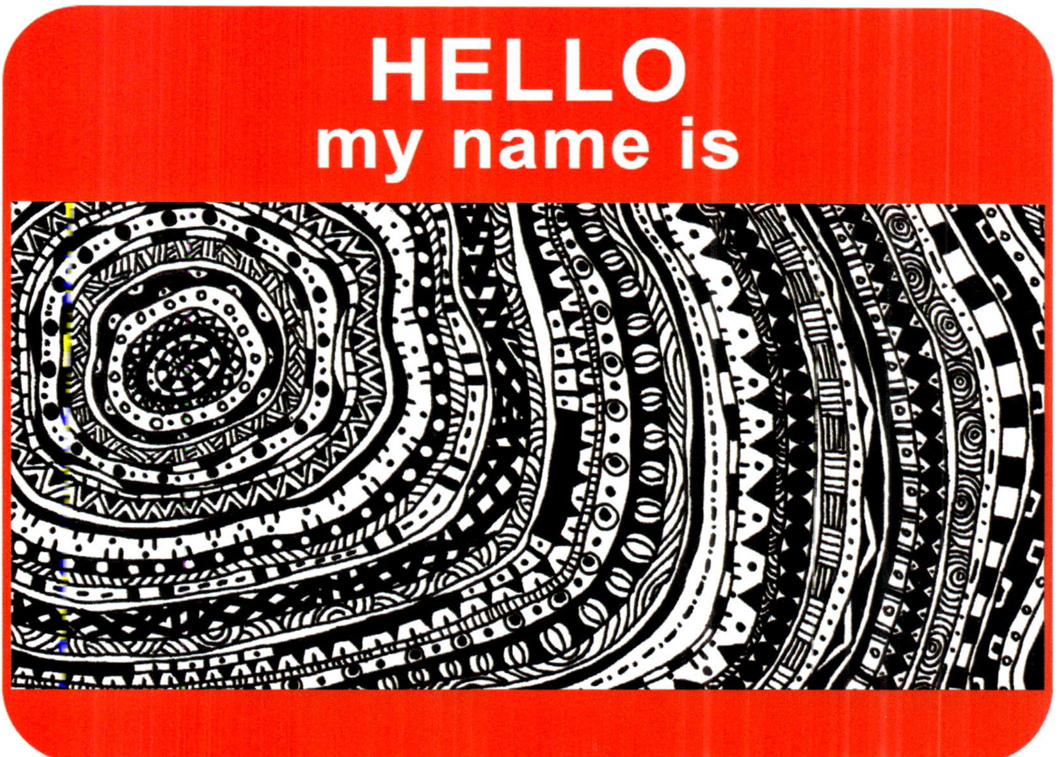

1 2 3 4

1. *Yi Chen Tsai*
2–4. *Sunmin Chung*

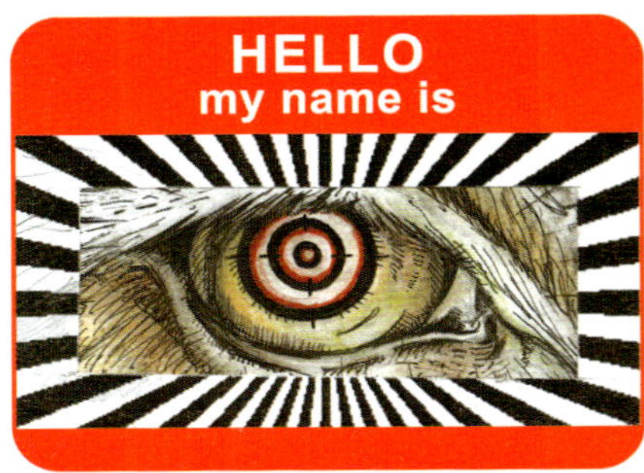
HELLO
my name is

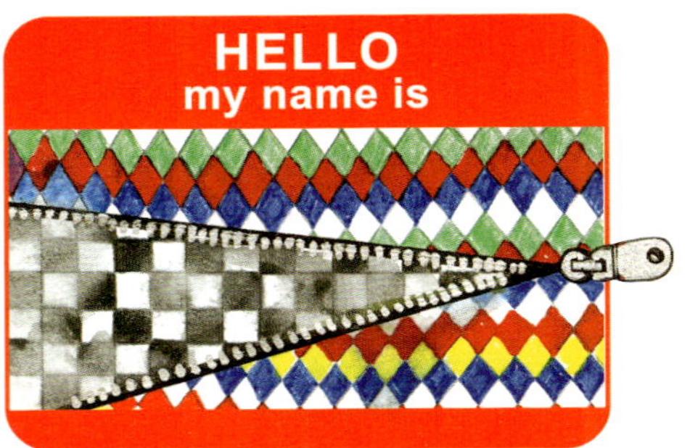
HELLO
my name is

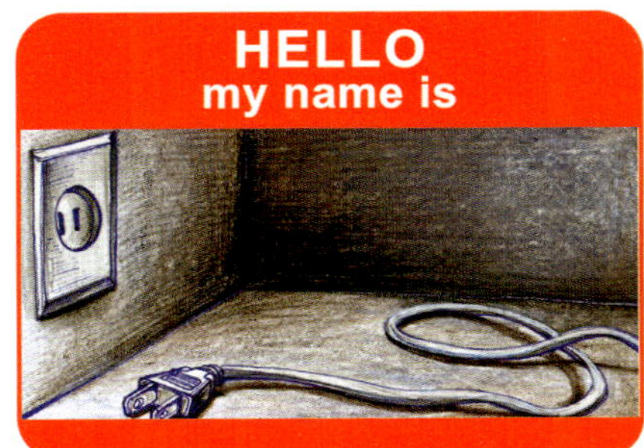
HELLO
my name is

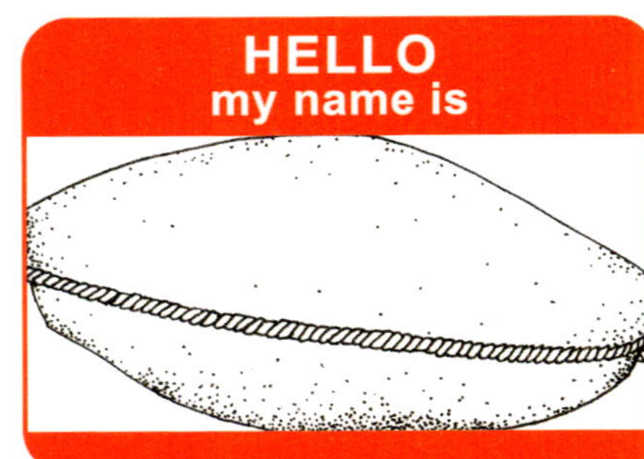
HELLO
my name is

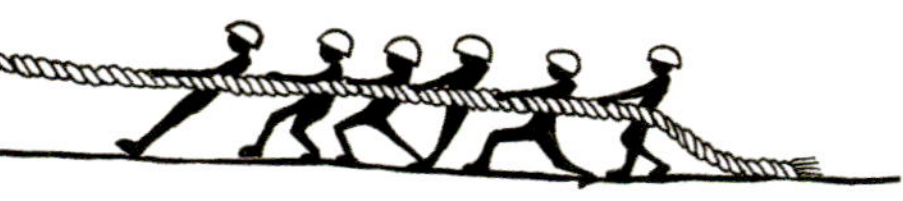

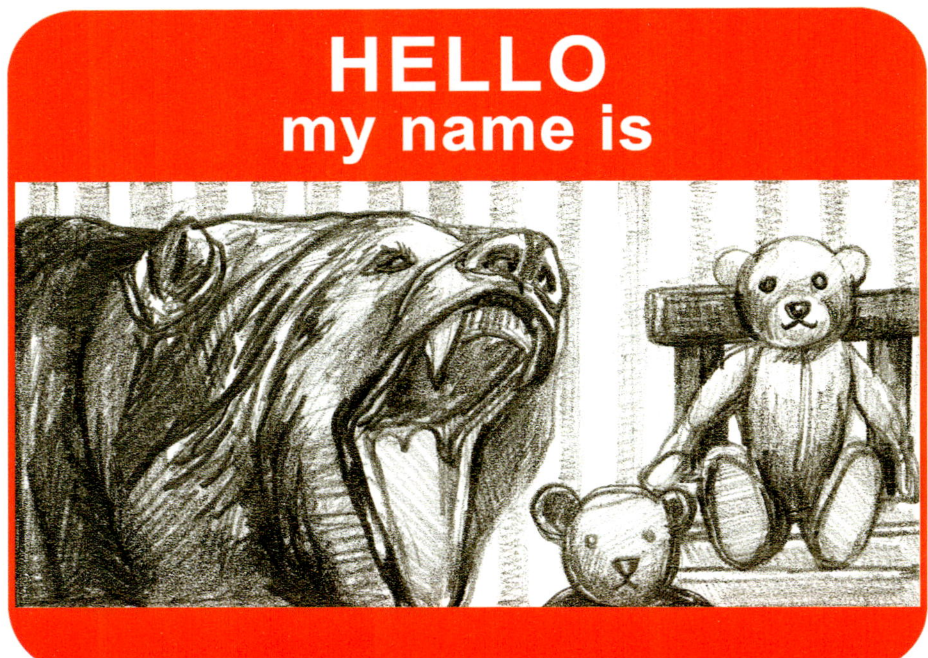
HELLO
my name is

HELLO MY NAME IS SOLUTIONS:

Figure 1 deals with a focused attention, while figure 2 expresses a false front.

Figure 3 grapples with exhaustion, while figure 4 demonstrates a struggle beyond all odds.

Figure 5 depicts passive-aggressive behavior.

Figure 6 humorously illustrates "an iron fist in a velvet glove." Upon closer viewing, one sees Superman's cape worn beneath the rabbit costume.

HELLO
my name is

HELLO!

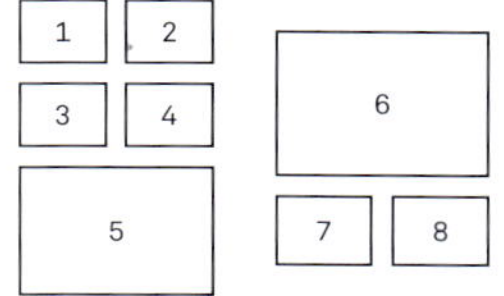

1. *Dayoung Mun*
2. *Sehee Lee*
3. *Jaewon Park*
4. *Sunho Lee*
5. *Sohyun Park*
6. *Jina Lee*
7. *Suan Lee*
8. *Tyler Comrie*

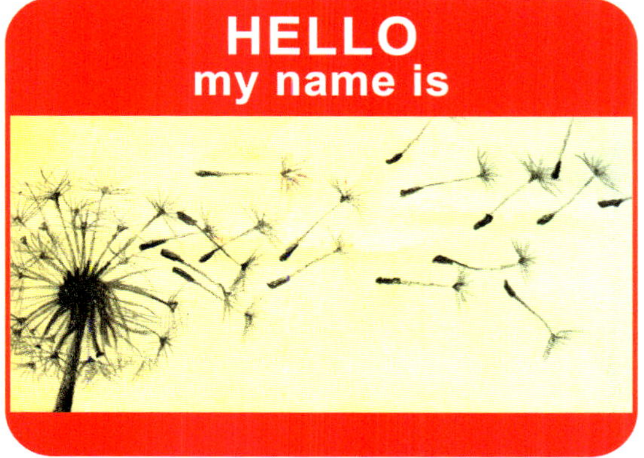

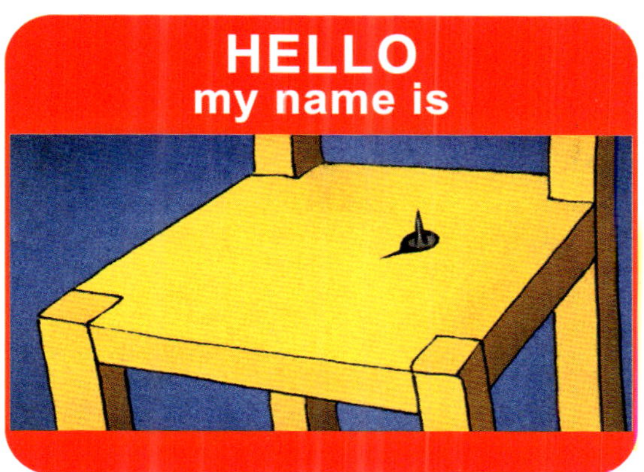

Figure 7 depicts the wishful act of blowing away the seeds of a dandelion.

Figure 8 deals with the impulse to be a practical joker.

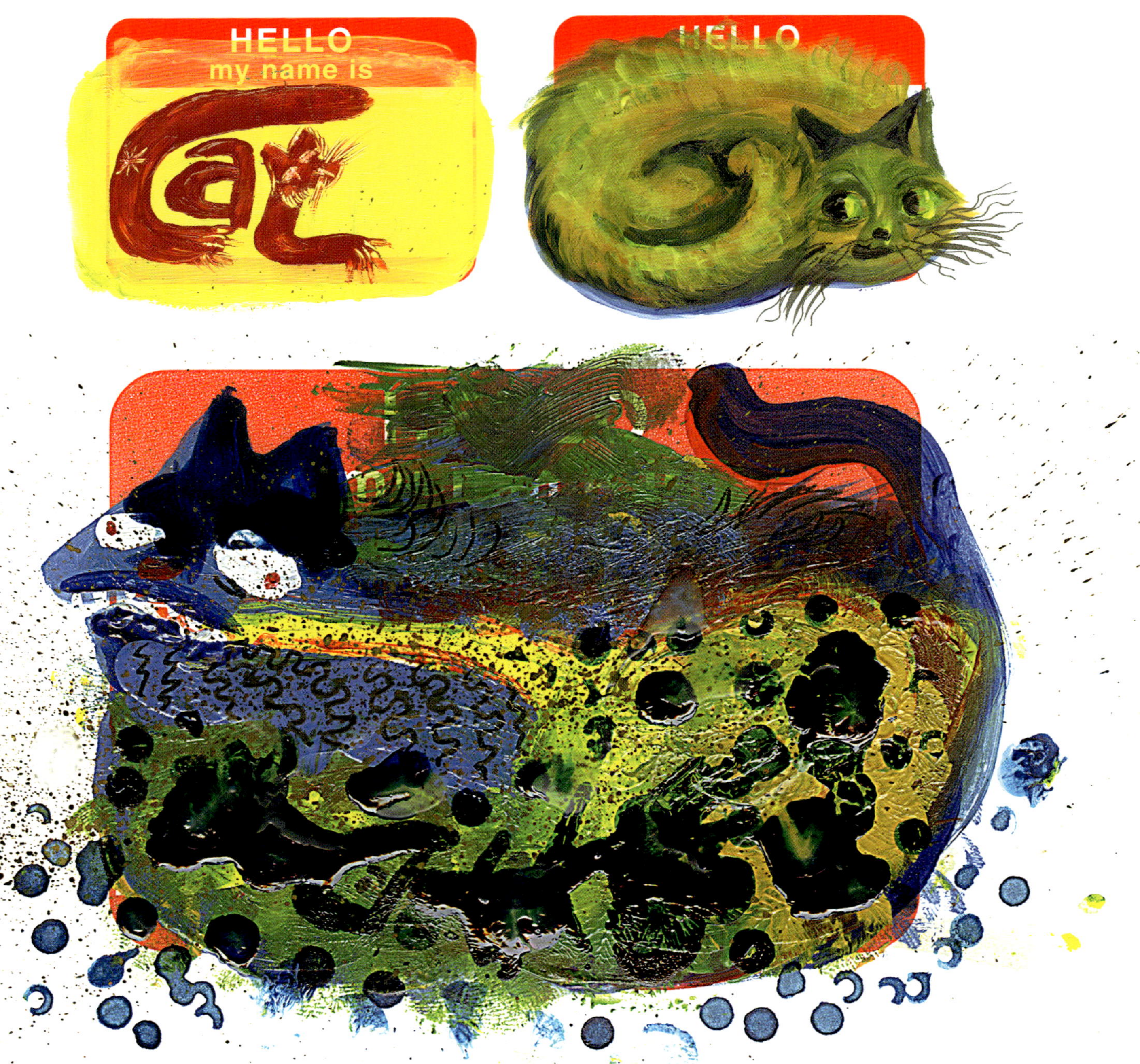
HELLO
my name is
Cat
HELLO

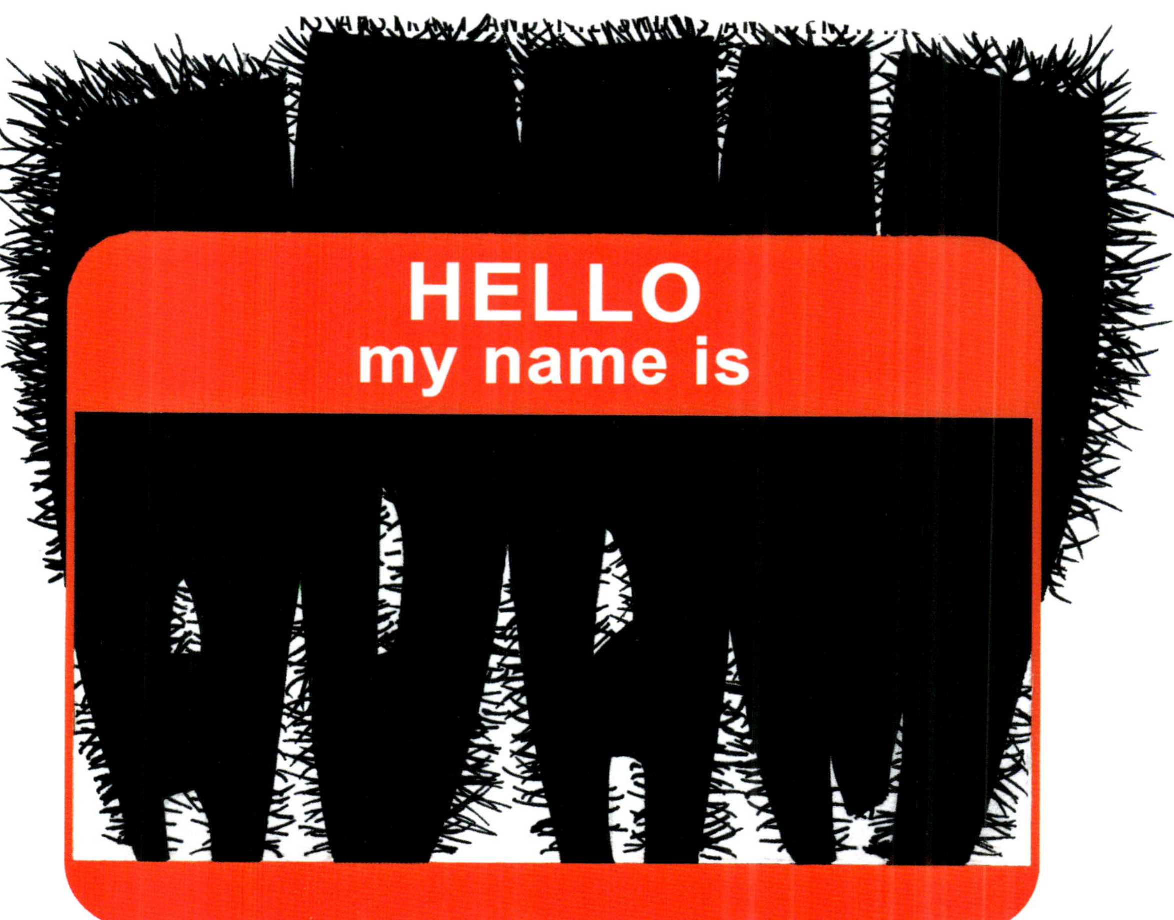

HELLO MY NAME IS SOLUTIONS:

Figures 1 through 3 use the nickname "Cat" to express various personality traits; spontaneity, being cuddily, and easily excitable behaviors.

Figures 4 through 8 address specific narratives using typography. Solutions exhibit an array of traits, including hairiness, emotionally complex, techno-wizardry, gloominess, and despondency.

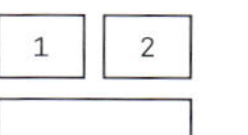

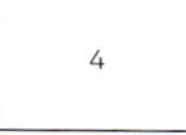

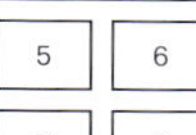

1–3. Amy Churchwell
4. Adam Augustine
5. Jeonghyun Ahn
6. Miseong Park
7. Soyeon Kim
8. Nayoung Kim

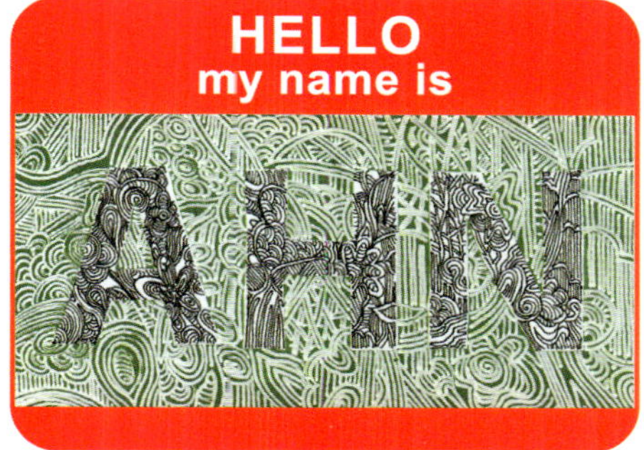

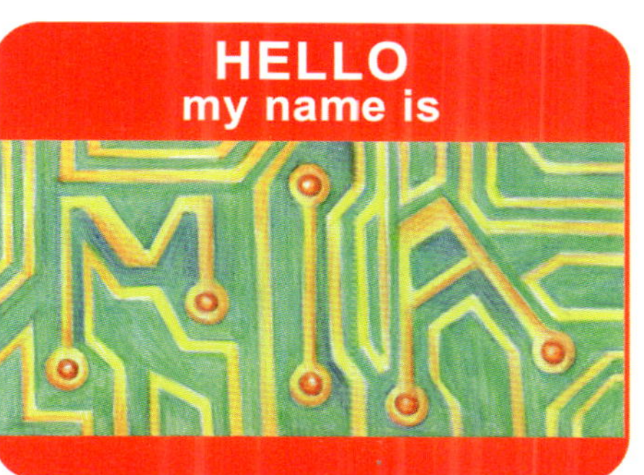

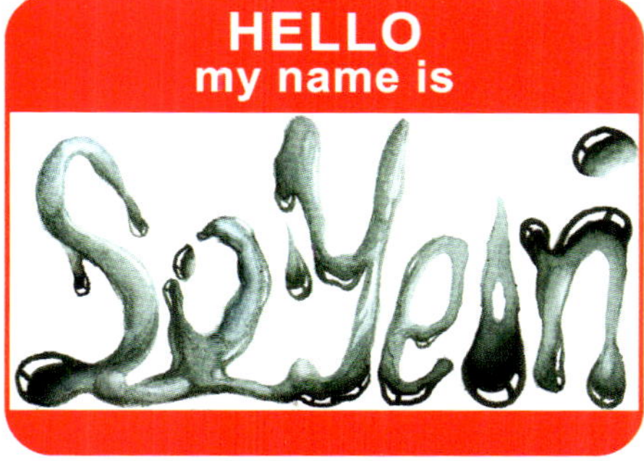

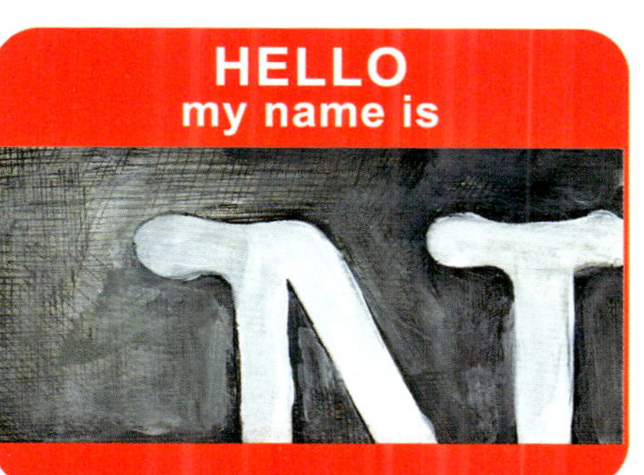

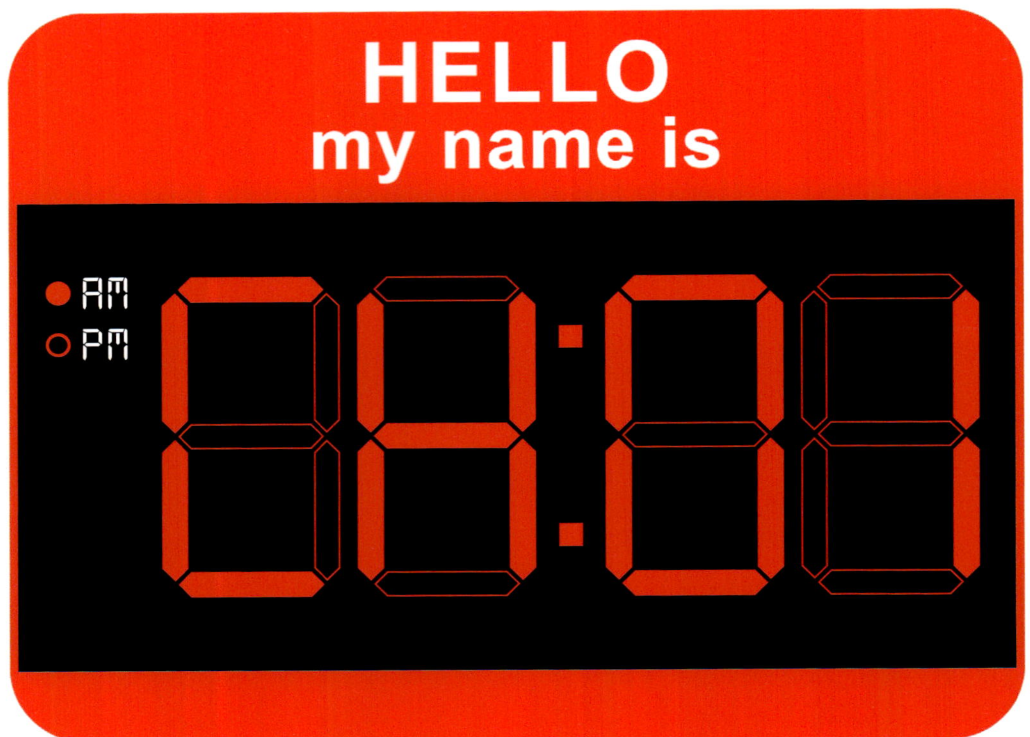
HELLO
my name is
AM
PM

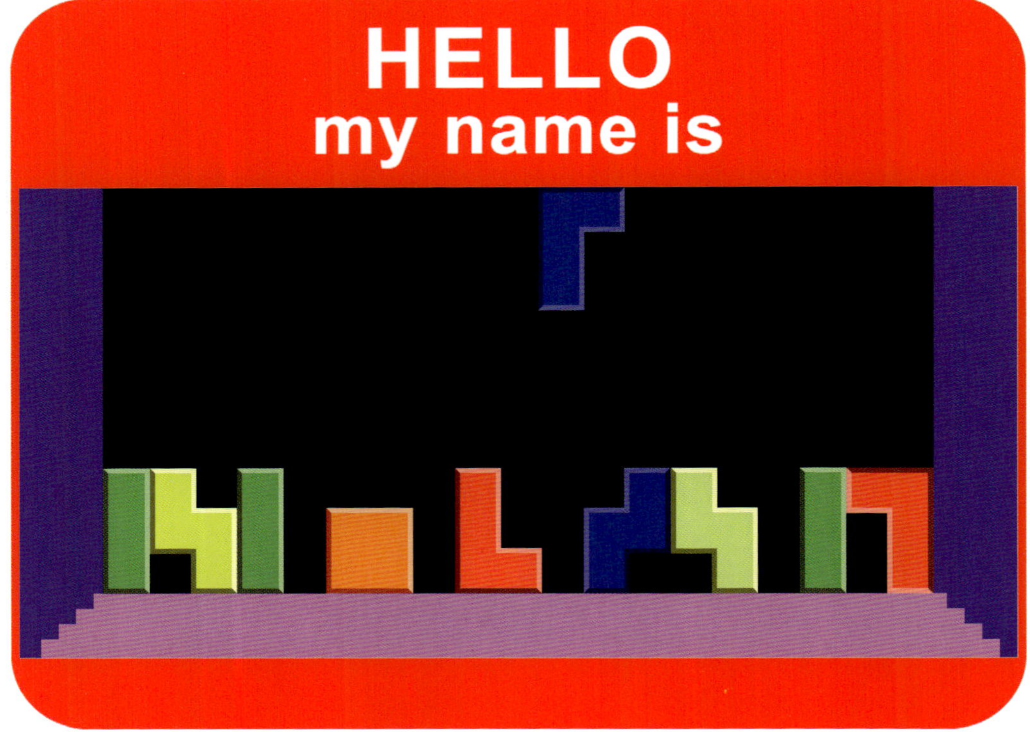
HELLO
my name is

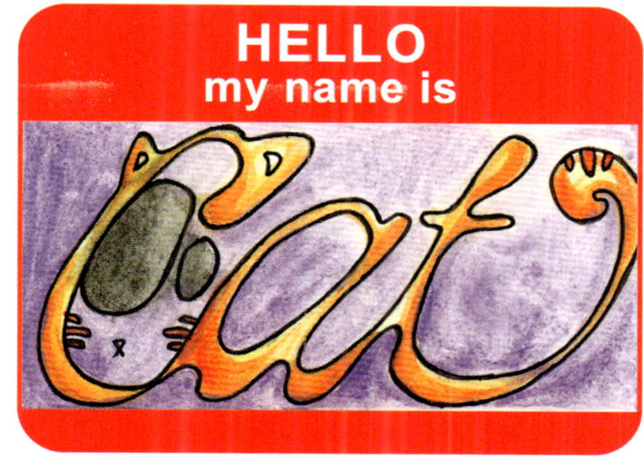

HELLO MY NAME IS SOLUTIONS:

Figures 1 through 10 are typographic solutions.

Figure 1 uses the face of an alarm clock to express insomnia, while figure 2 uses a computerized game spelling out the name Nolan to illustrate strategic behavior.

Figure 3 uses line as pattern to create letterforms that spell Josephine, expressing a fascination with the color pink.

Figure 4 uses the nickname Cat, combining illustration and typography.

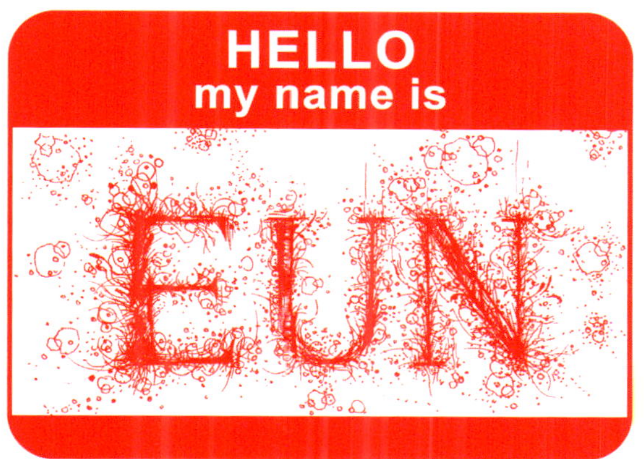

Figure 5 uses the initials MG to depict laziness using the metaphor of a creased blanket.

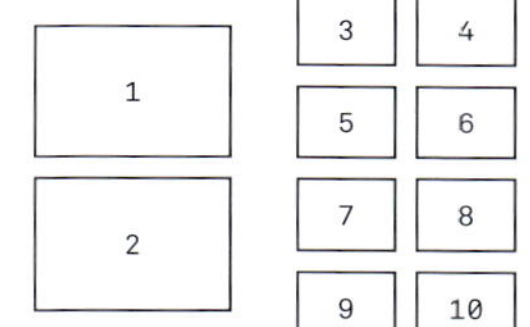

1. Sugin Choi
2. Nolan Constantino
3. Josephine Tan
4. Catherine Lee
5. Yi Hsuan Yu
6. Eunyoung Chung
7. Mohmed Zakria Tebbal
8. Hyungkyu Choi
9. Joshua Fiebig
10. Min Choi

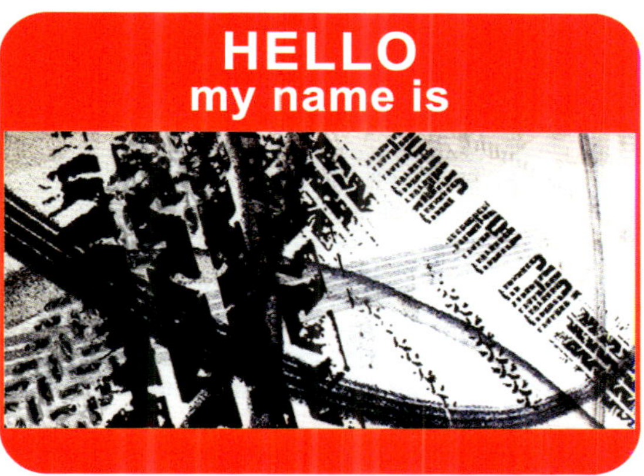

Figure 6 illustrates an allergic reaction, while figure 7 deals with religious beliefs.

Figure 8 depicts a persona relationship with speed as it pertains to cars.

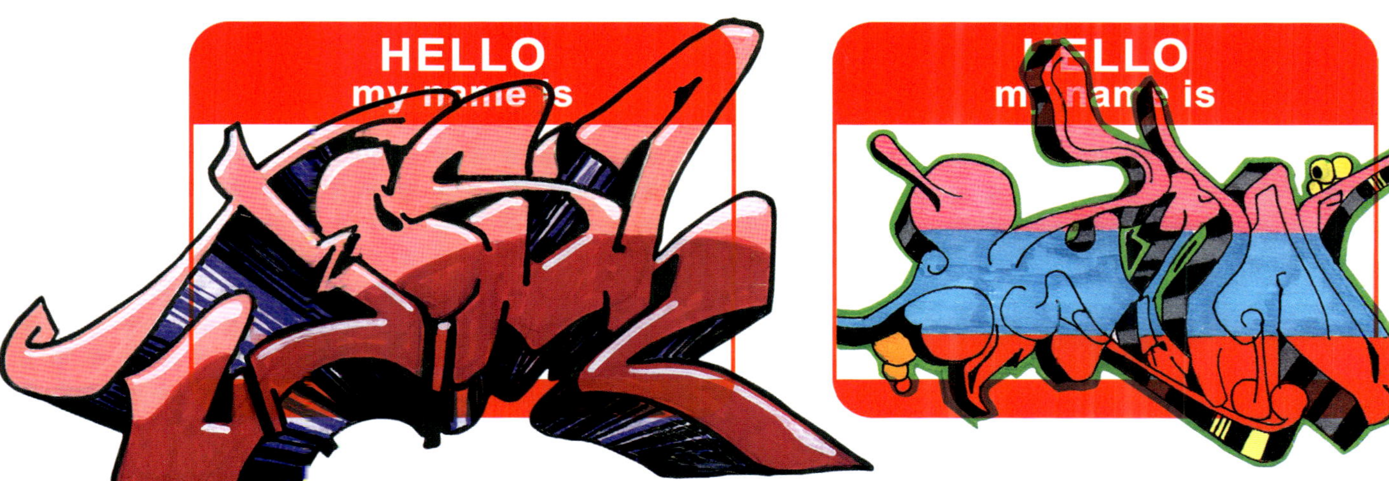

Figures 9 and 10 explore the genre of graffiti to express rebellious behavior.

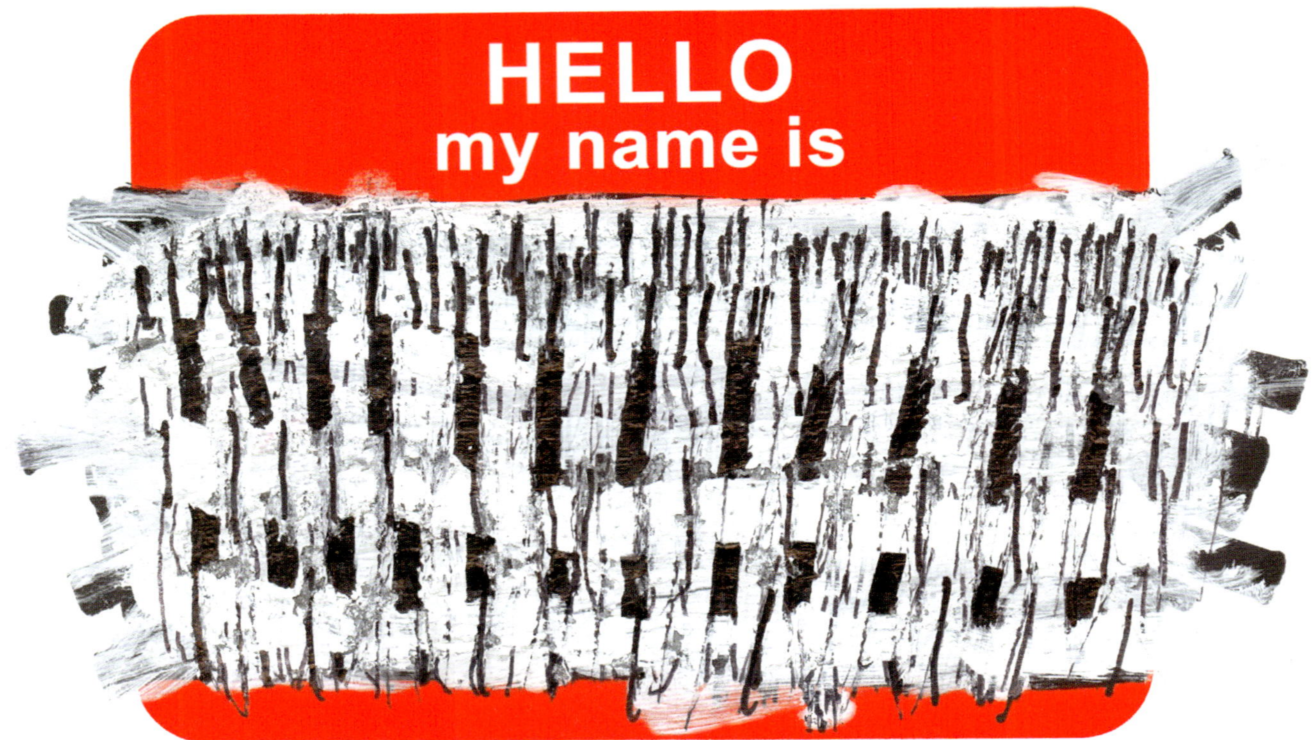
HELLO
my name is

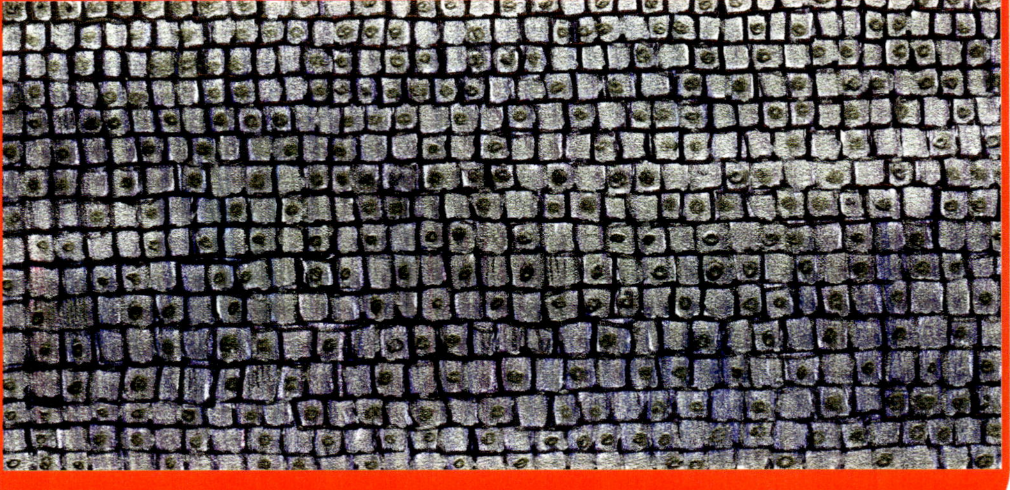
HELLO
my name is

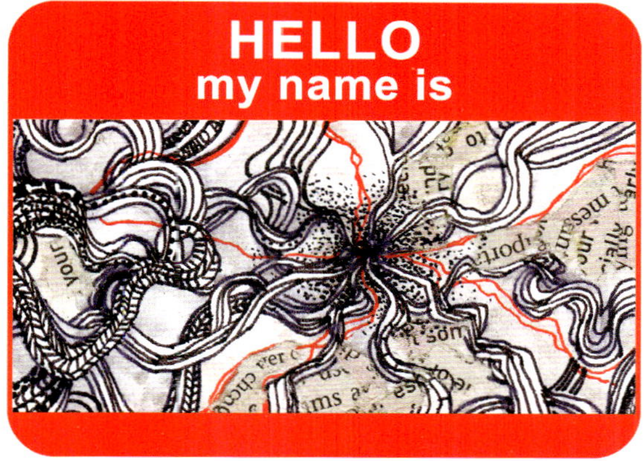

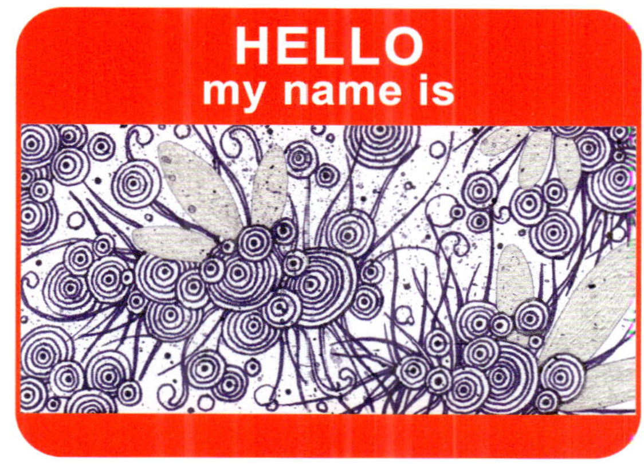

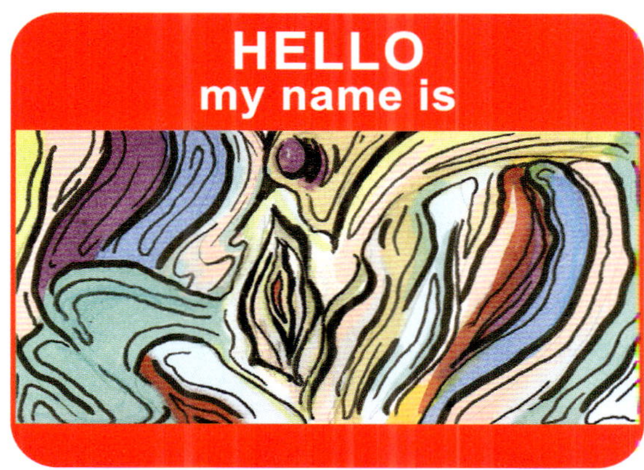

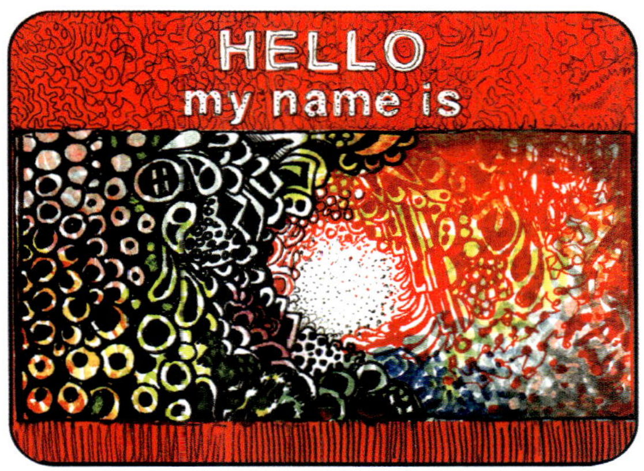

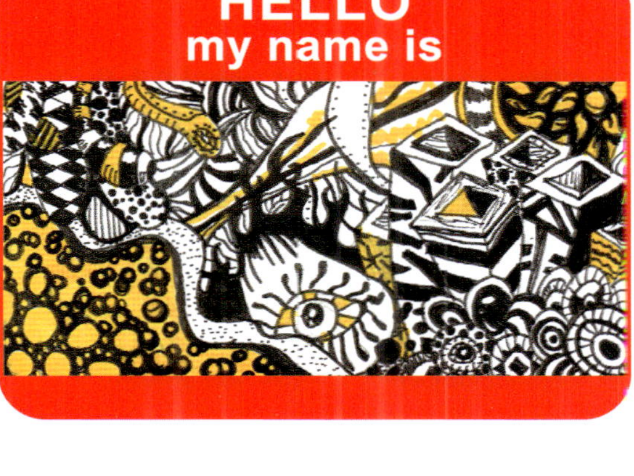

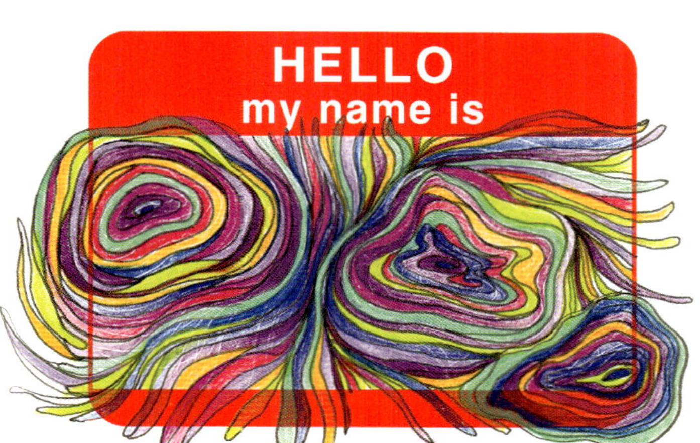

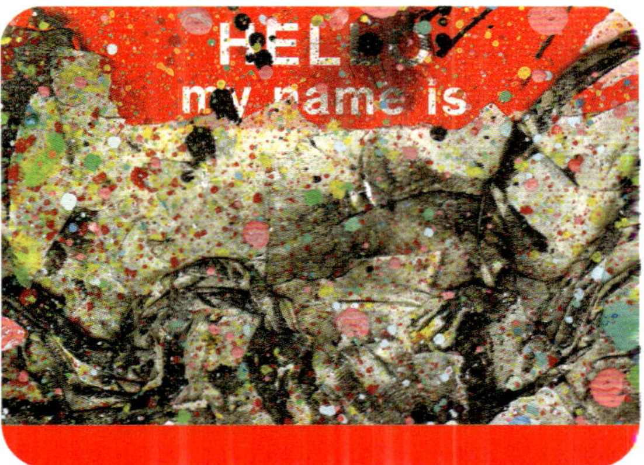

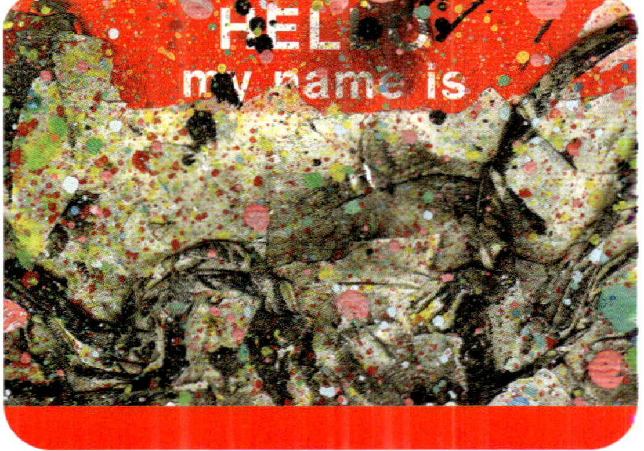

HELLO MY NAME IS SOLUTIONS:

Figures 1 through 10 are highly subjective abstract solutions.

Figure 1 uses an emotionally drawn image to express neurotic behavior.

Figure 2 uses an obsessively drawn image to express the concept of being soulless.

Figure 3 alludes to the mystery of an unknown adventure.

Figure 4 depicts a love of the decorative in a purple world.

In figure 5 the modus operandi is breaking out of a confined world to exhibit expressive behavior.

1	3	4
	5	6
2	7	8
	9	10

1. *Casey Conchinha*
2. *Suwan Park*
3. *Eungyoung Cho*
4. *Soomin Yeo*
5. *Myungsong Han*
6. *Soojin Jung*
7. *Sandra Woodruff*
8. *Pedro Dos Santos*
9. *Borim Kim*
10. *Jieun Choi*

Figure 6 is an expression of one's femininity.

Figure 7 depicts the condition of agoraphobia, which is the fear of closed-in spaces.

Figure 8 illustrates a strange and complex world where one feels insecure.

Figure 9 uses the interaction of colorful forms to depict the complexities of life, coupled with its richness.

Figure 10 uses splattered paint to illustrate a messy, slovenly nature.

HELLO
my name is

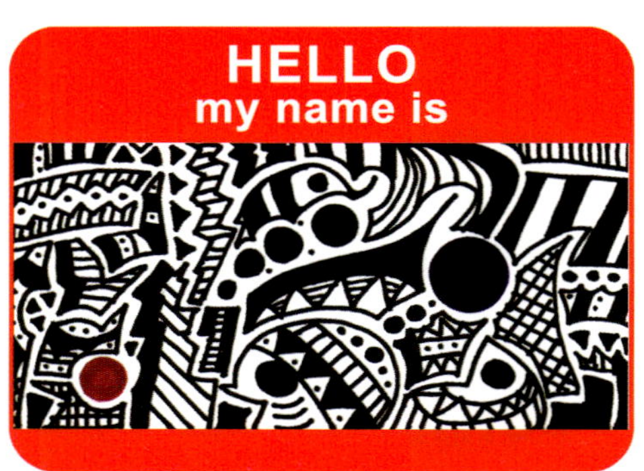
HELLO
my name is

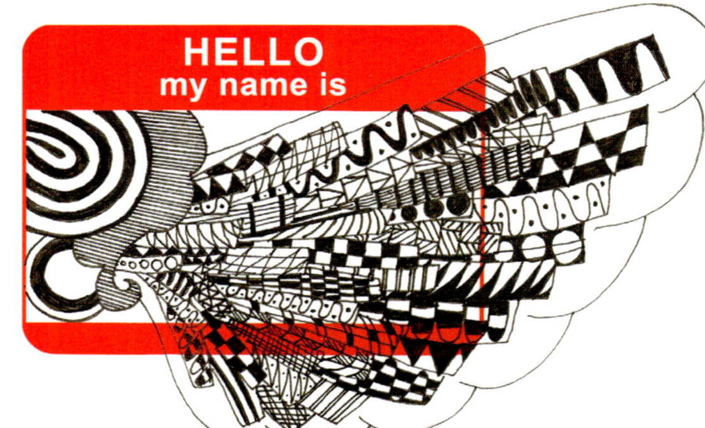
HELLO
my name is

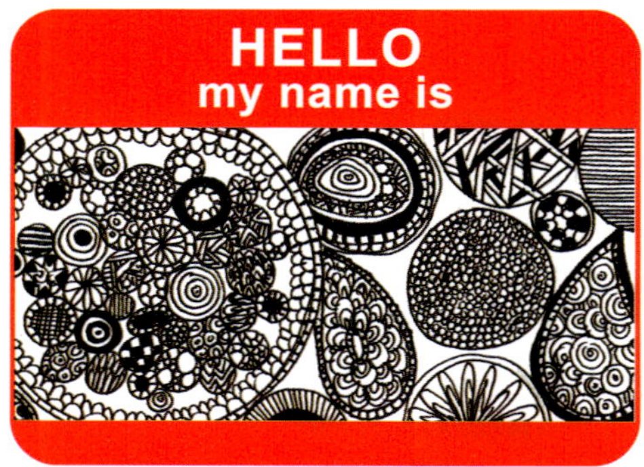
HELLO
my name is

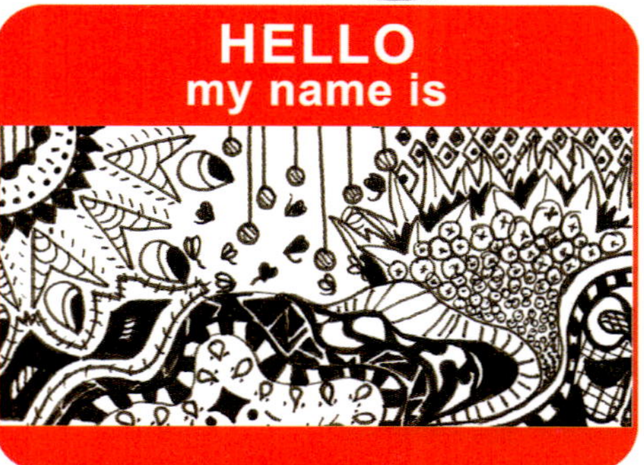
HELLO
my name is

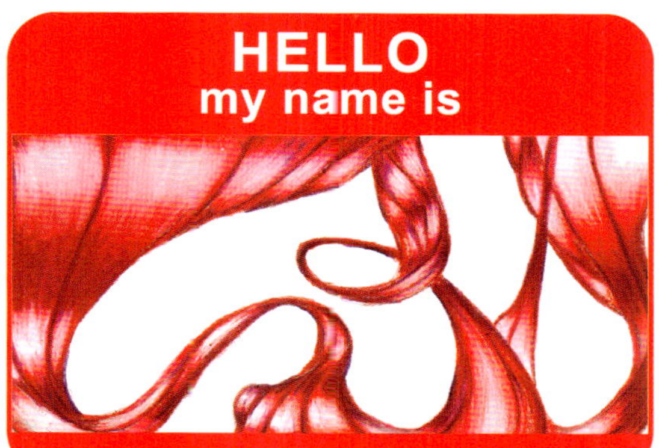

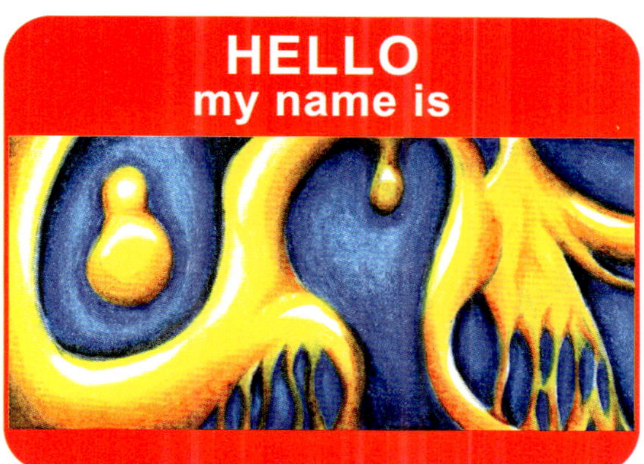

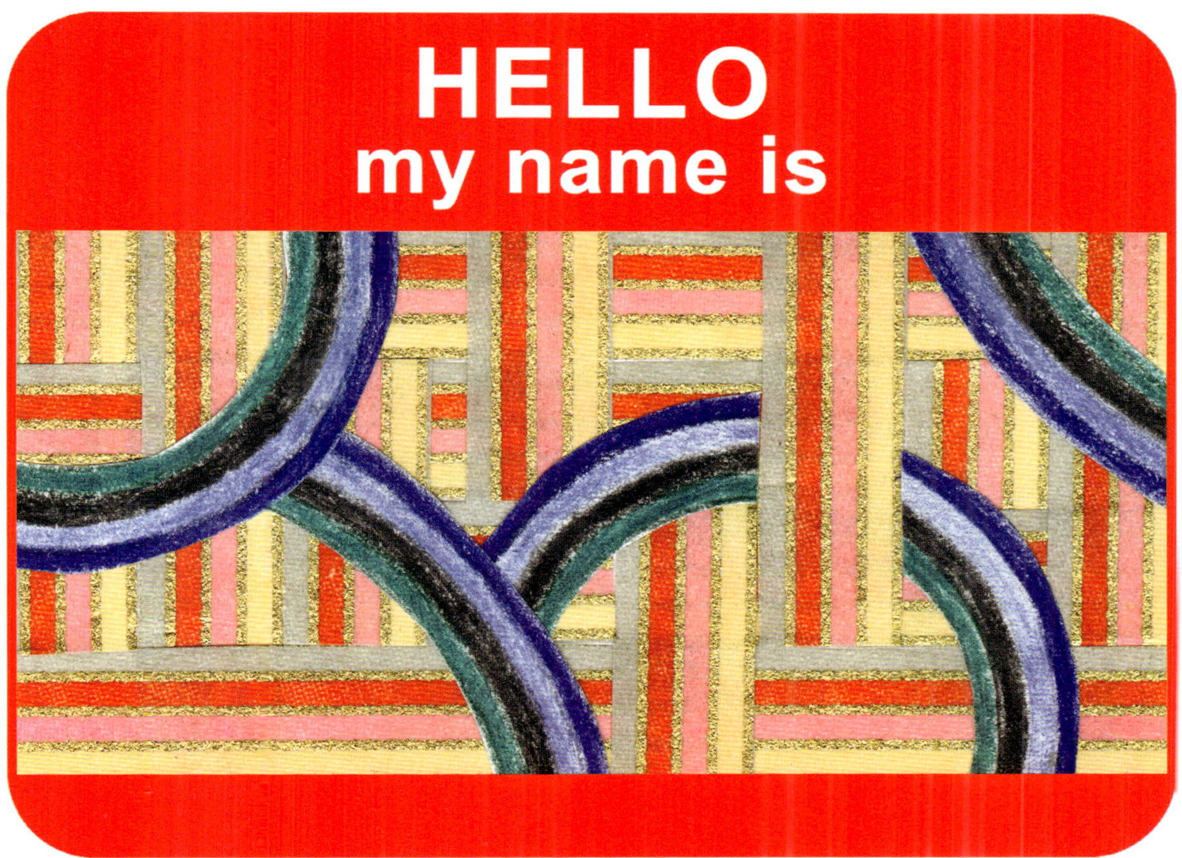

HELLO MY NAME IS SOLUTIONS:

Figures 1 through 8 are a continuation of the abstract directive of the assignment.

Figures 1 through 5 are executed in a spontaneous manner, where speed is depicted in figure 1.

Solutions in figures 2 through 5 restricted their palette to black and white with the common denominator of doodling.

In figure 2 line and flat areas are utilized in the creation of a decorative composition that expresses playfulness.

1		6	7
2	3	8	
4	5		

1. *Mihee Choi*
2. *Michelle Wao*
3. *Jaeyoon Song*
4. *Danielle Han*
5. *N. Scott*
6. *Jiyoon Byun*
7. *Kirt Small*
8. *S. Kim*

In figure 5, doodles infer literal imagery, depicting a world of fantasy in an abstract solution.

Figures 6 through 8 are carefully mannered solutions, where figure 8 uses geometric shapes of contrasting colors to depict conflicting personalities.

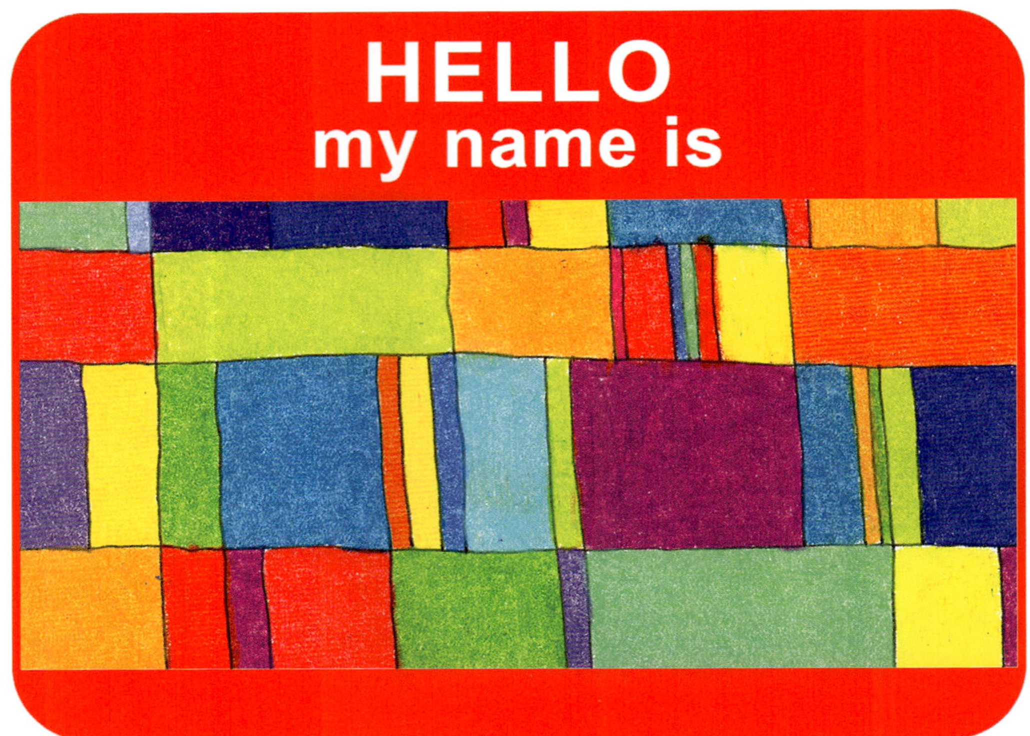
HELLO
my name is

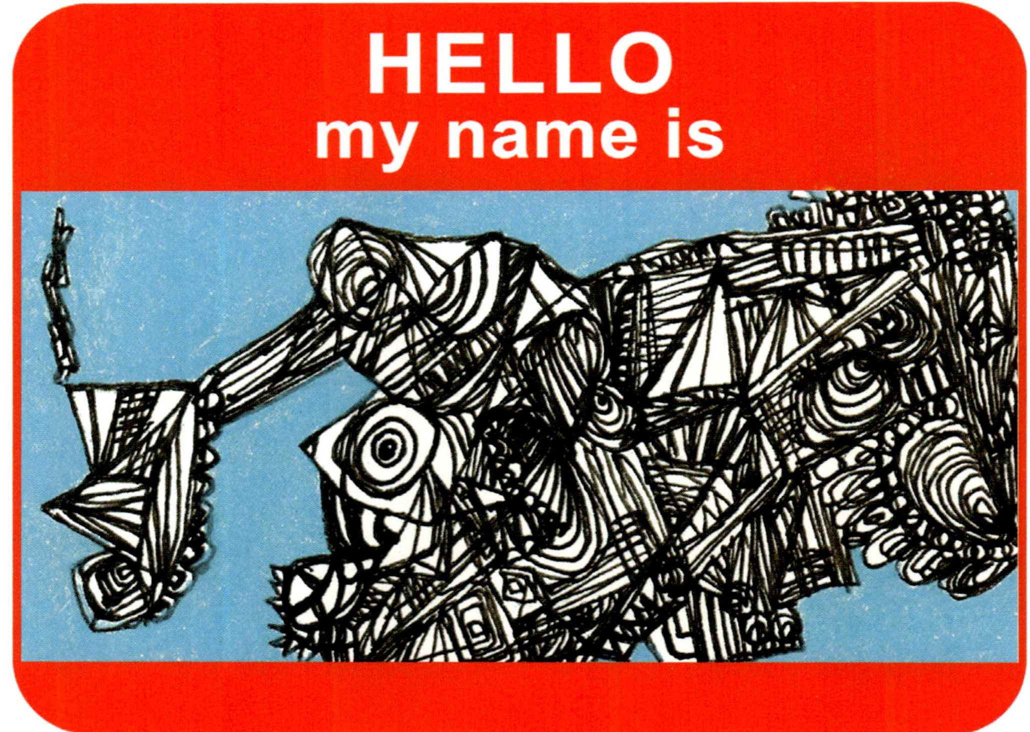
HELLO
my name is

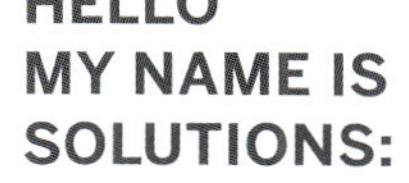

HELLO MY NAME IS SOLUTIONS:

In the following solutions, abstraction merges with literal imagery.

Figure 1 is a colorful solution that alludes to one's vibrant nature.

Figure 2 is a seemingly abstract solution, yet upon closer investigation a figure with its arm extended, tipping its hat, while riding a monster becomes visible. The intent was to create a metaphor for heroism.

Figure 3 illustrates joyfulness, while figures 4 and 6 express the state of moodiness depicted through multiple expressions.

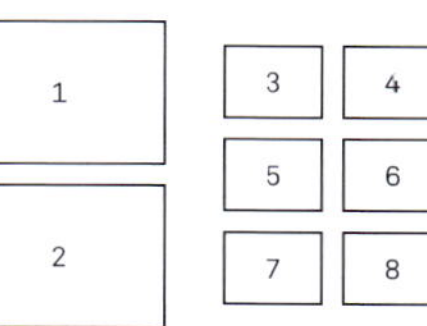

1. *Connie Jun*
2. *Heayoung Cho*
3. *Jae Kwang 'Rare JK' Kim*
4. *Nam Gyeong Kim*
5. *Daseul Ryu*
6. *Kyle Fetzer*
7. *Joung Soo Kim*
8. *Jiwon Kim*

Figure 5 depicts sensitivity, which lends itself to various organic interpretations.

Figures 7 and 8 are both expressions of passionate states, ranging from a sense of containment to an explosive nature.

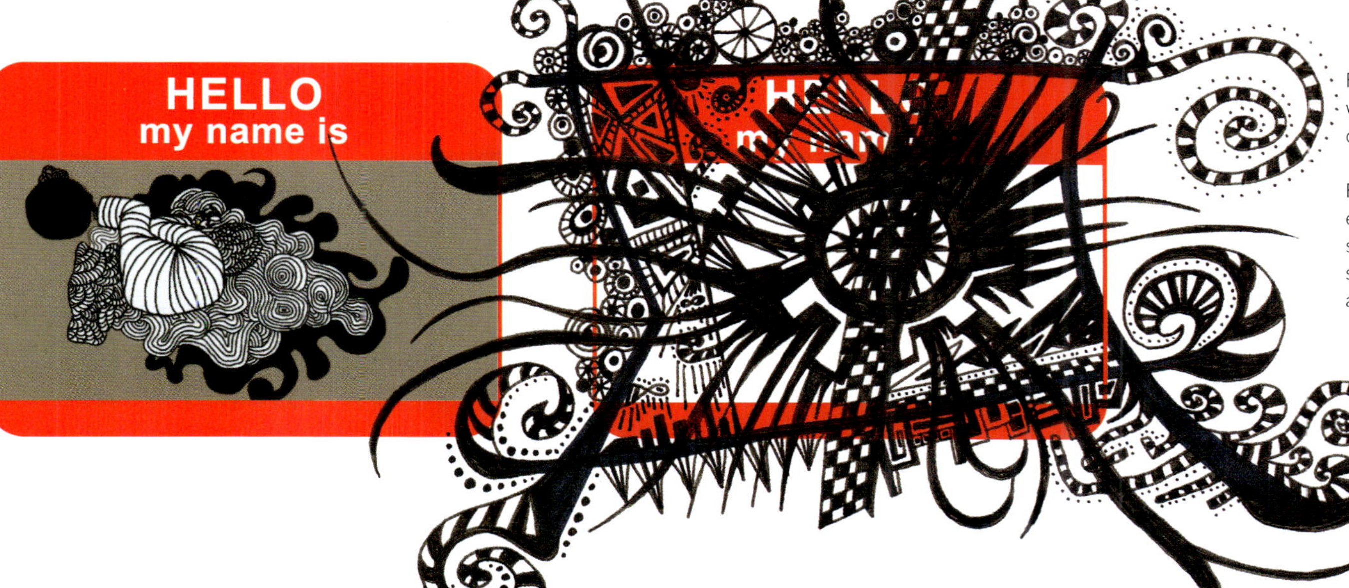

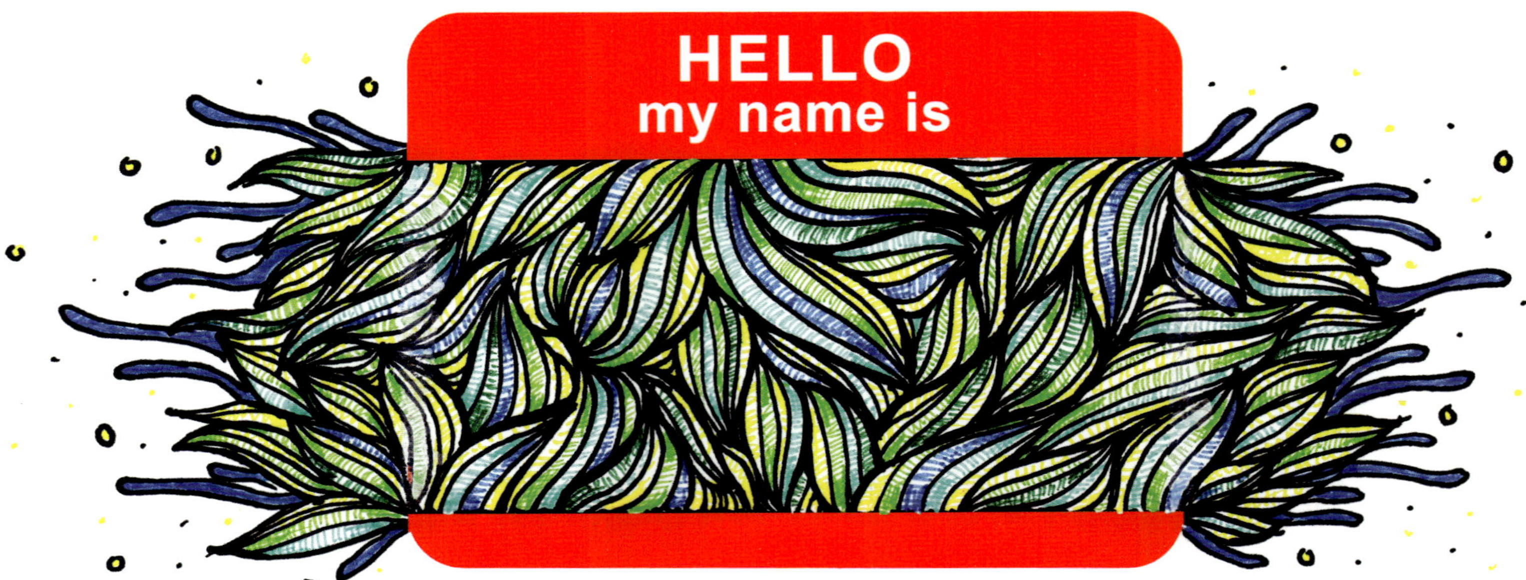
HELLO
my name is

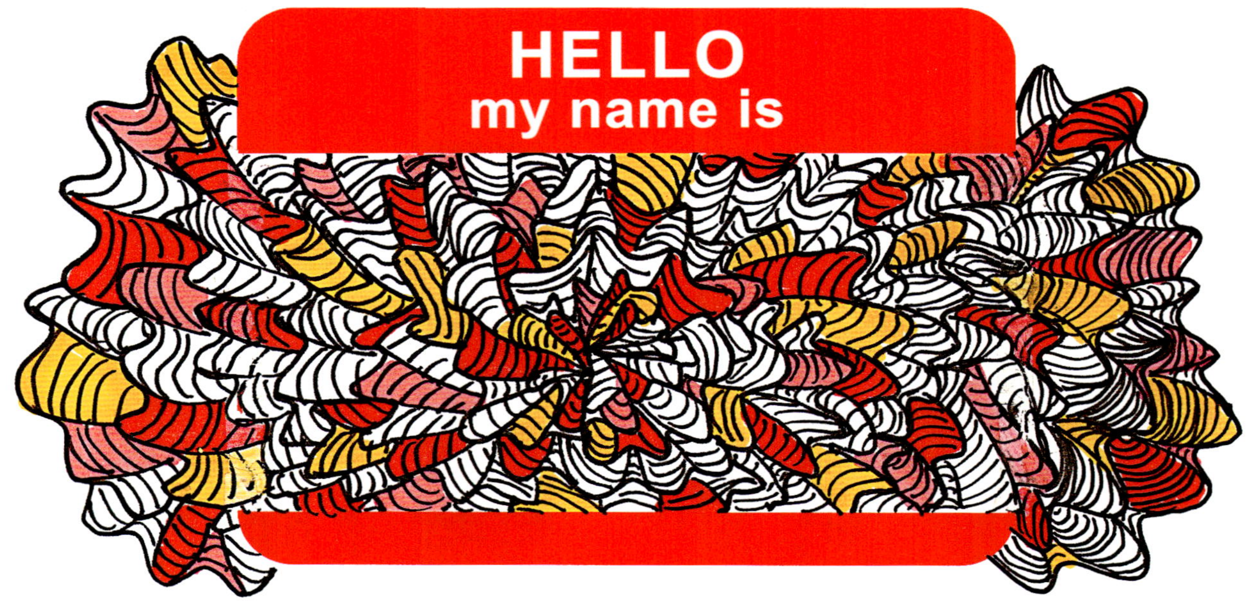
HELLO
my name is

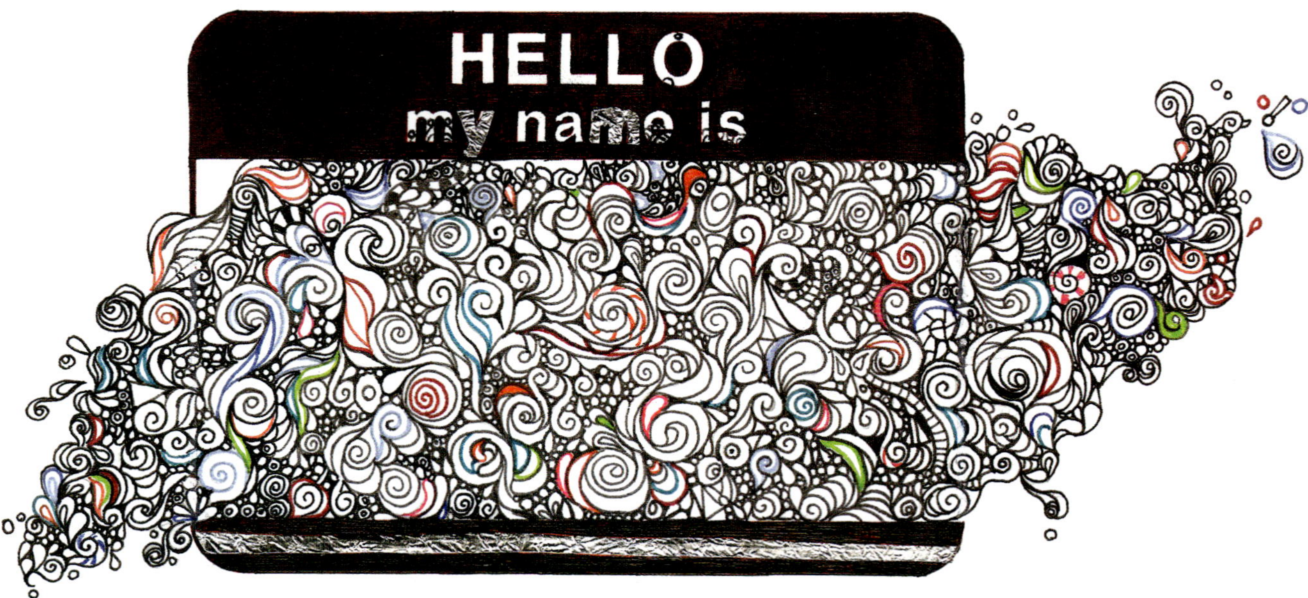
HELLO
my name is

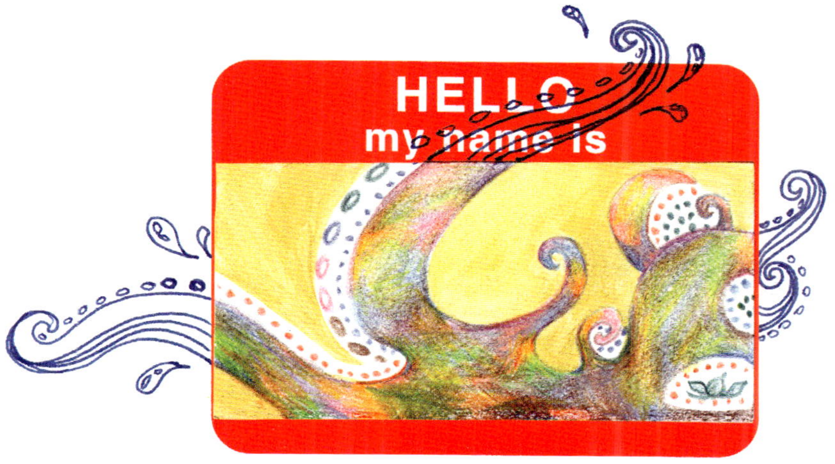

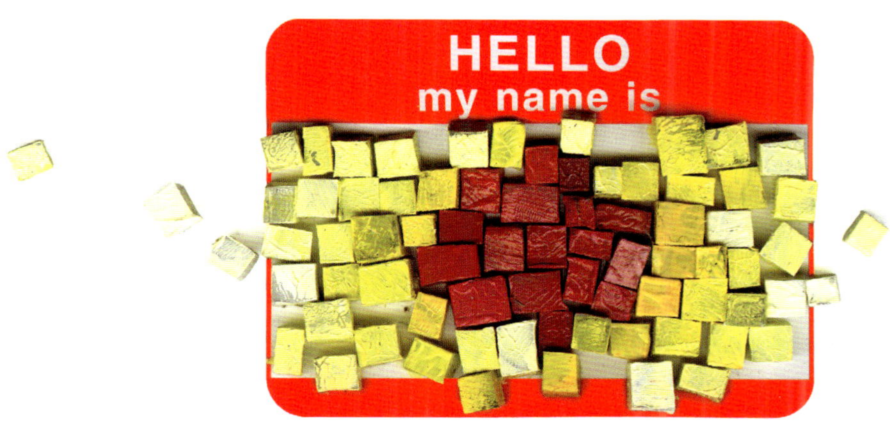

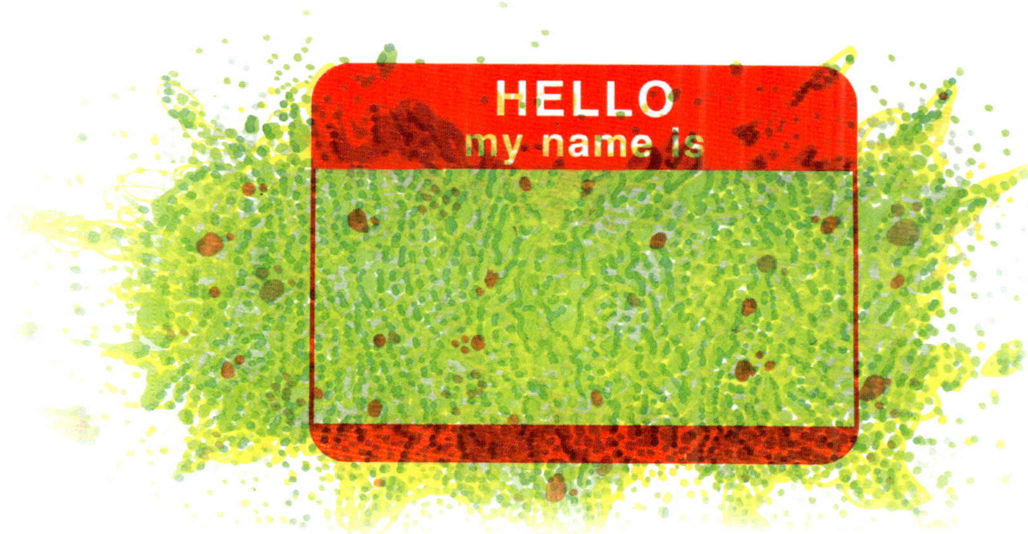

HELLO MY NAME IS SOLUTIONS:

Figures 1 through 6 deal with abstraction. All six solutions, as well as others in this chapter, did not follow the directions to execute each solution within the given area, but went outside of the rectangle to further embellish their ideas. It is here, where one risks breaking the rules, that has its place in innovative image-making.

Figure 1 depicts a playful exuberant state utilizing an intertwining mannered execution, while figure 2 infers vivaciousness where the imagery emanates from a central focal point.

1	4
2	5
3	6

1. *Alexandra Stikeleather*
2. *Alexandra Barron*
3. *Minjung Suh*
4. *Jiyoung Lee*
5. *Yuji Seo*
6. *Robert Collum*

Figure 3 is an array of circular doodles denoting an explorative nature.

Figure 4 uses a decorative octopus to express creativity.

Figure 5 uses red and yellow dimensional square shapes in its depiction of warm-heartedness.

Figure 6 appears totally abstract, yet, with the addition of its intended message, which is drunkenness, the image becomes a clear narrative.

HELLO
my name is

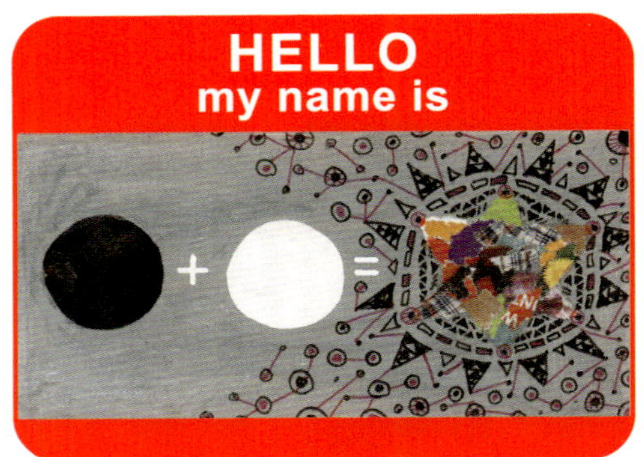

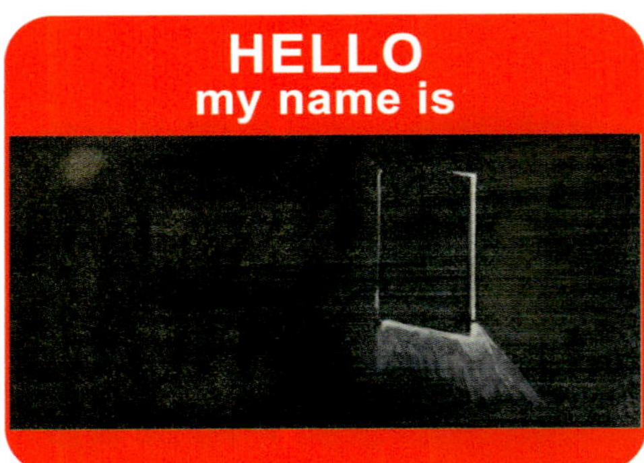

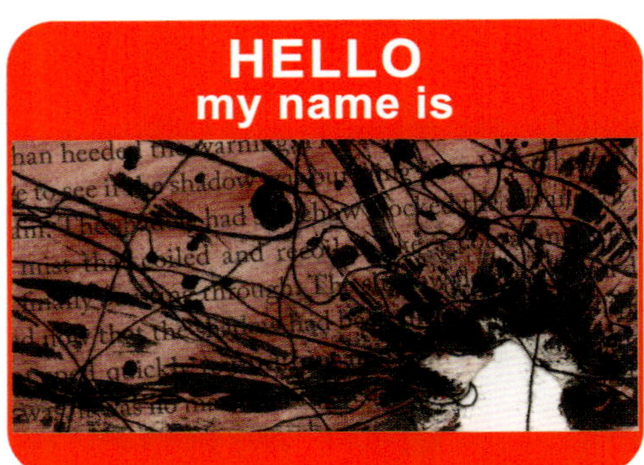

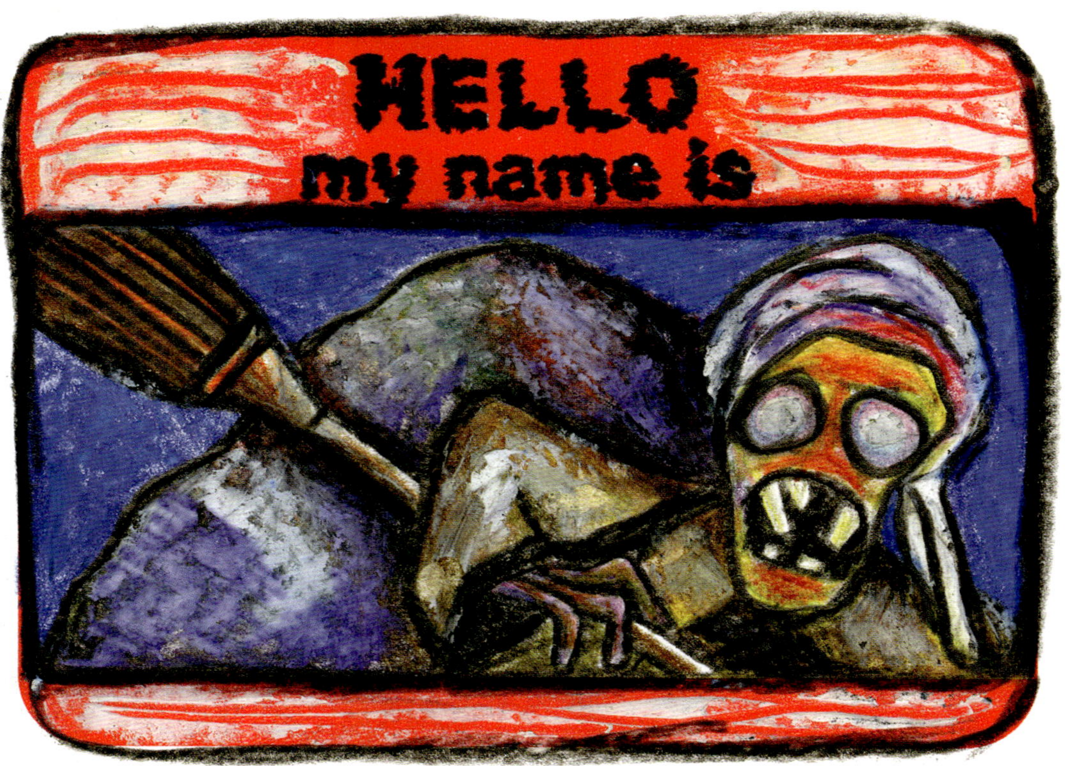

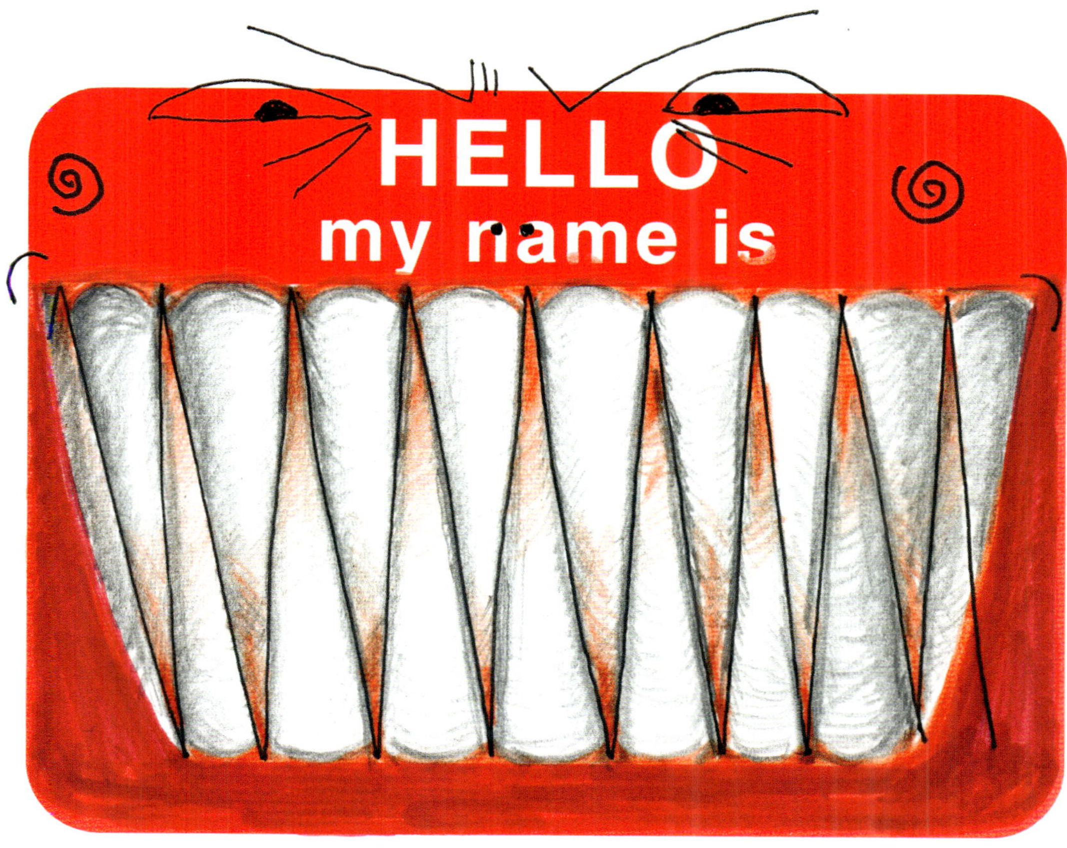

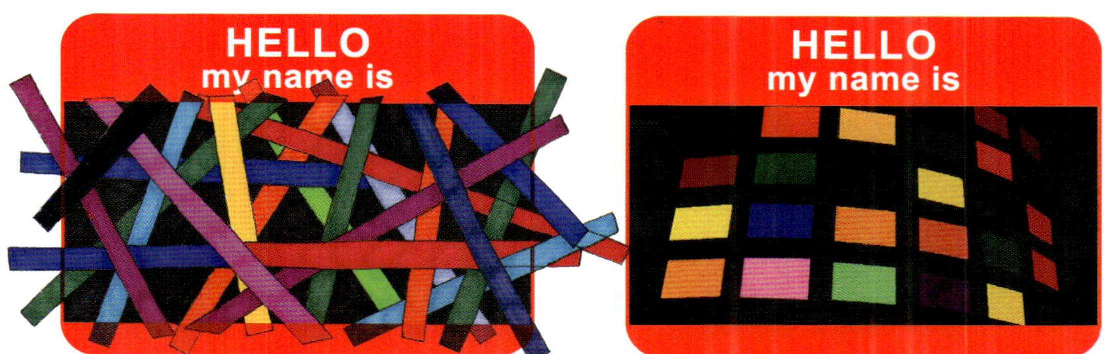

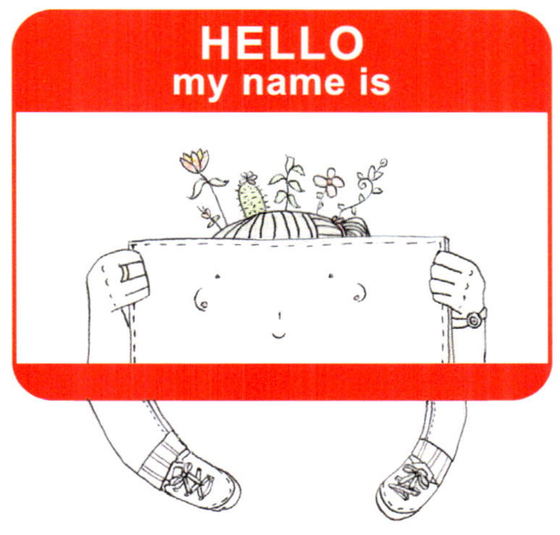

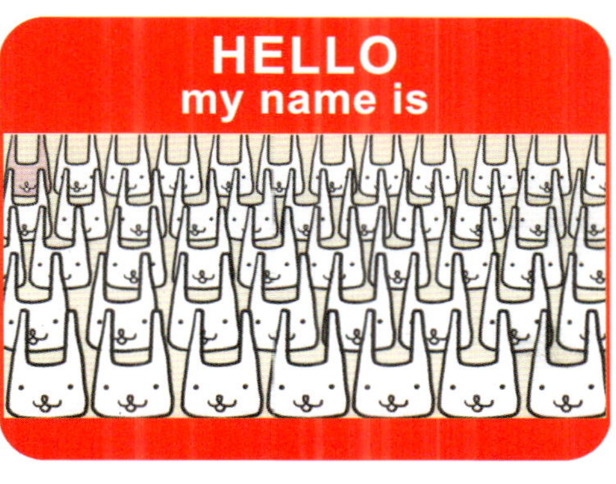

HELLO MY NAME IS SOLUTIONS:

A more literal approach to problem solving is used in figures 1 through 10. Here, storytelling is a quicker study than the abstract solutions. Yet, the interest of each solution lies in the underlying composition, supported by color, shape, line, texture, patterning, volume, cropping, contrast, space, and scale.

Figure 1 represents a change of mood, and in figure 2 a black and a white circle express a formatted equation that results in an image of unpredictability.

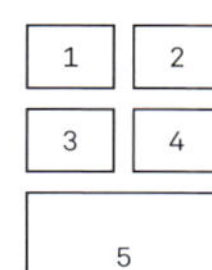

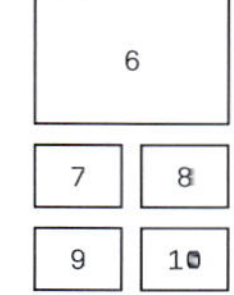

1. *Yukyung Hwang*
2. *Sophie Kim*
3. *Motoko Ishii*
4. *Lindsay Kintgen*
5. *Maya Kaplun*
6. *S. Kim*
7. *Ege Dalaman*
8. *Youngyoun Kim*
9. *Elaine Park*
10. *Mengya Wen*

Figure 3 describes the halation of light emanating from behind a door that is slightly ajar, alluding to the unknown, while figure 4 suggests mystery.

Through the depiction of a witch in figure 5, mean intentions are inferred.

Using the image of exaggerated teeth, figure 6 expresses devilish behavior.

In figure 7, confusion is graphically executed by overlapping colorful shapes.

Figure 8 uses the metaphor of a disco-ball to reference partying.

Figures 9 and 10 address shyness through hiding.

HELLO
my name is

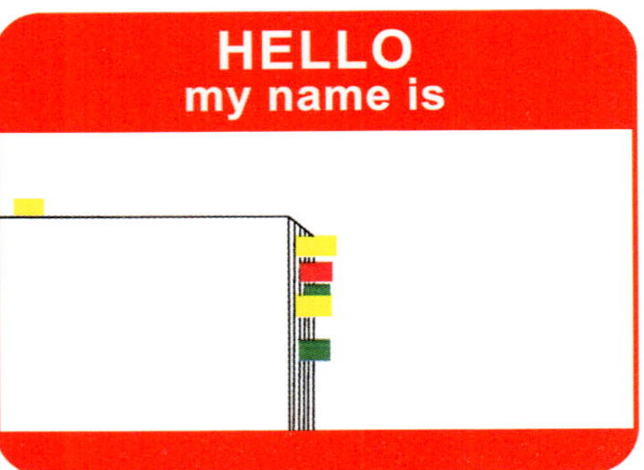
HELLO
my name is

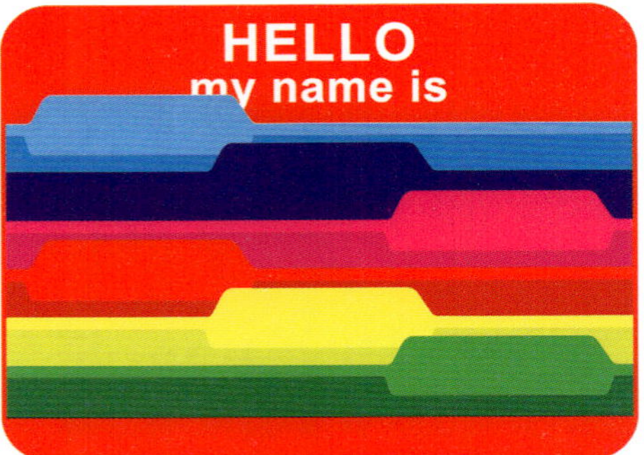
HELLO
my name is

HELLO MY NAME IS SOLUTIONS:

In these mostly literal solutions, figure 1 is a symbolic expression of energy.

Figures 2 and 3 reference organizational skills. All three solutions are executed using flat graphic imagery.

Exhaustion is expressed in figure 4, where an eye is part of an amorphic blob, as if it were a living entity.

Figure 5 depicts being hopelessly romantic, by juxtaposing two red raspberries against a field of gray.

Figures 6 through 9 are various interpretations of shyness.

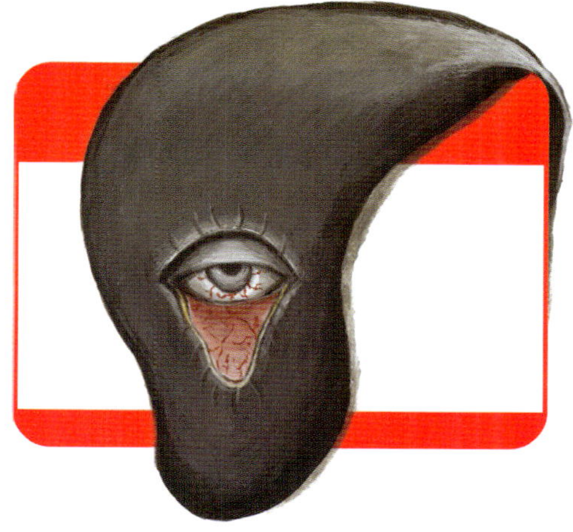

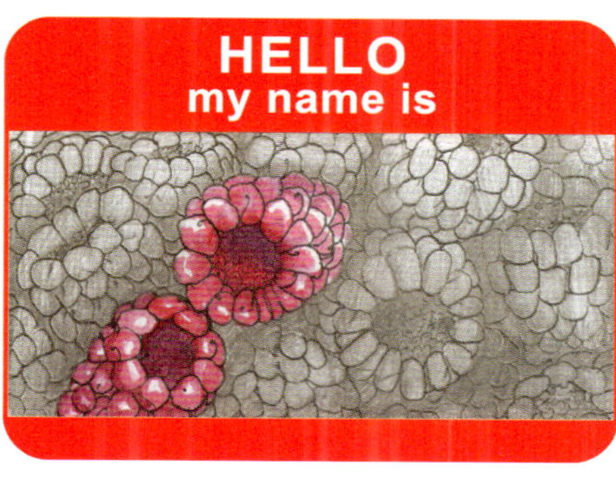

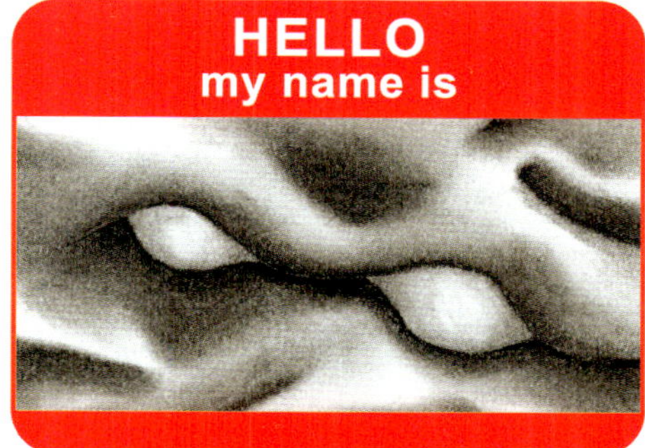

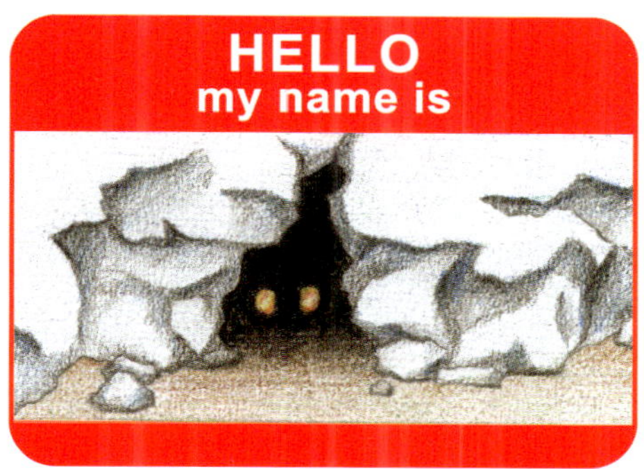

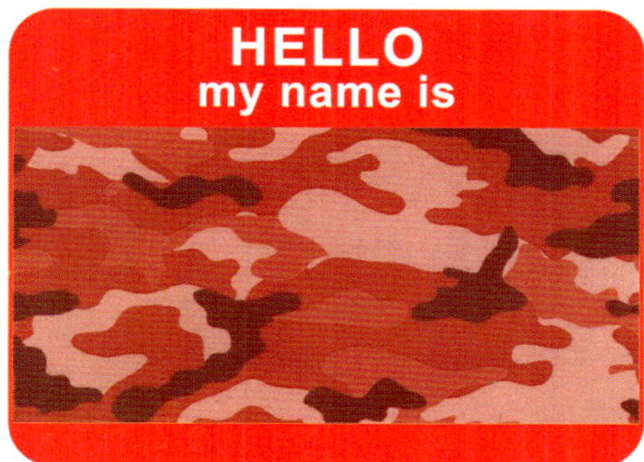

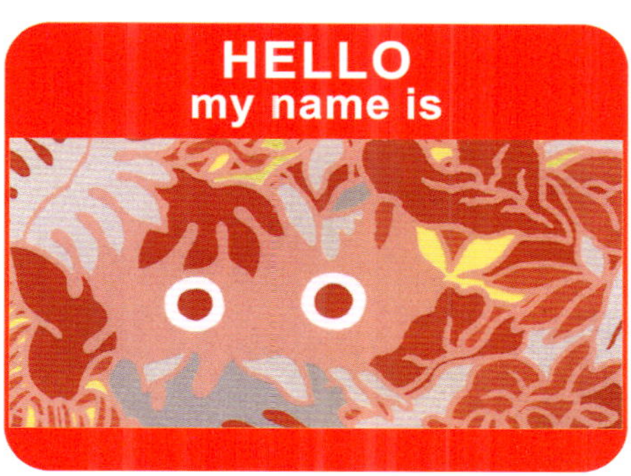

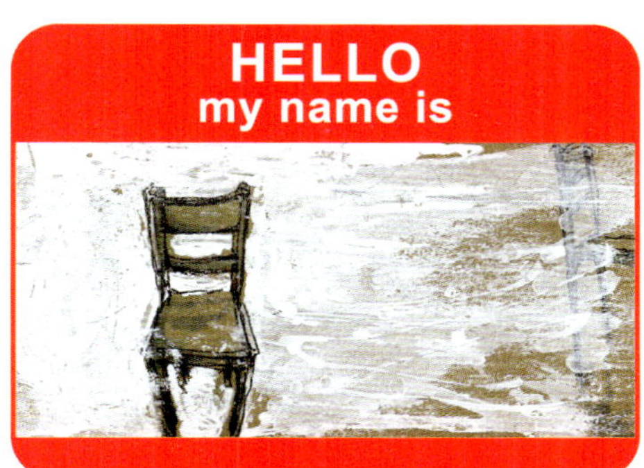

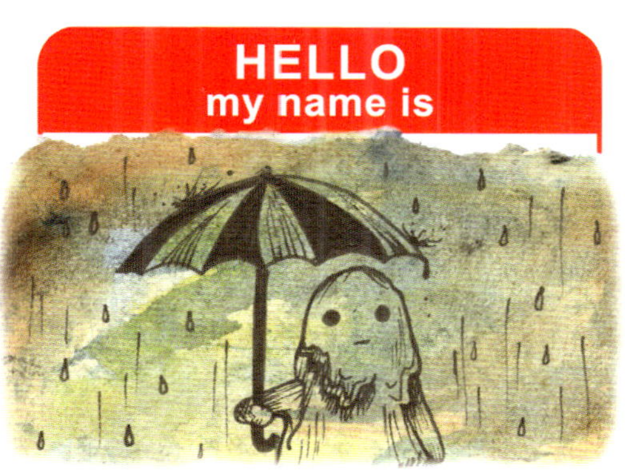

1. *Yonghwa Choi*
2. *Namgyeong Kim*
3. *Tal Shub*
4. *Heejae Choi*
5. *Sandra Woodruff*

6–7. *A. Tung*

8–9. *Sojung Lee*

10. *Diao Shurong*
11. *Jocelyn Tsaih*

Figure 10 uses a chair as a metaphor for loneliness, while figure 11 depicts a gloomy scenario in expressing melancholia.

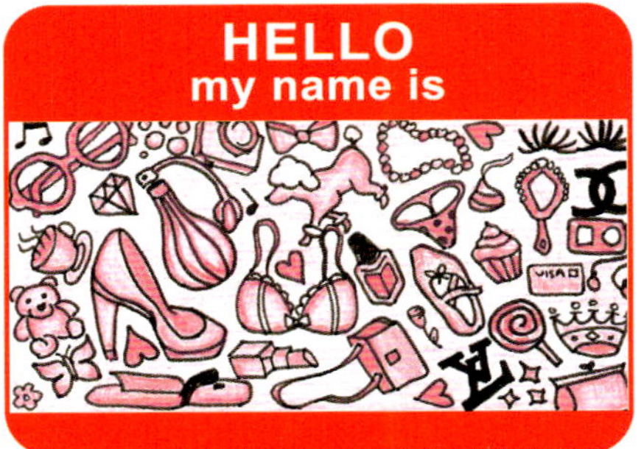
HELLO
my name is

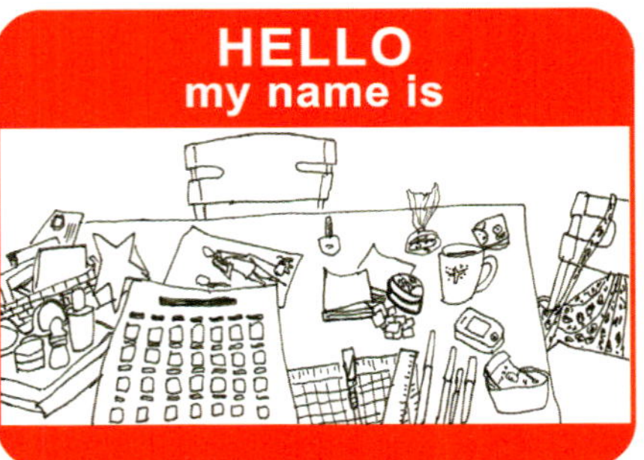
HELLO
my name is

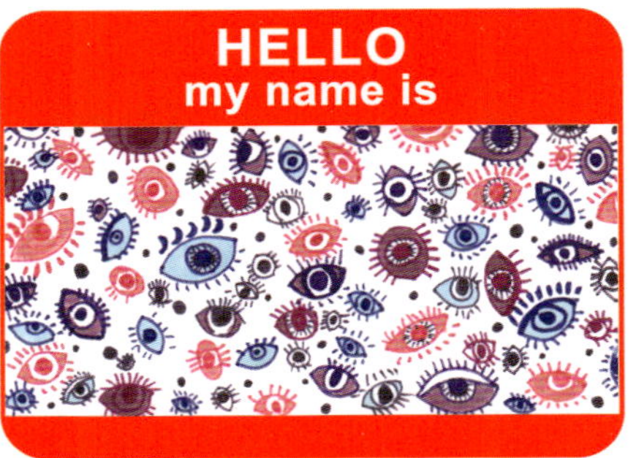
HELLO
my name is

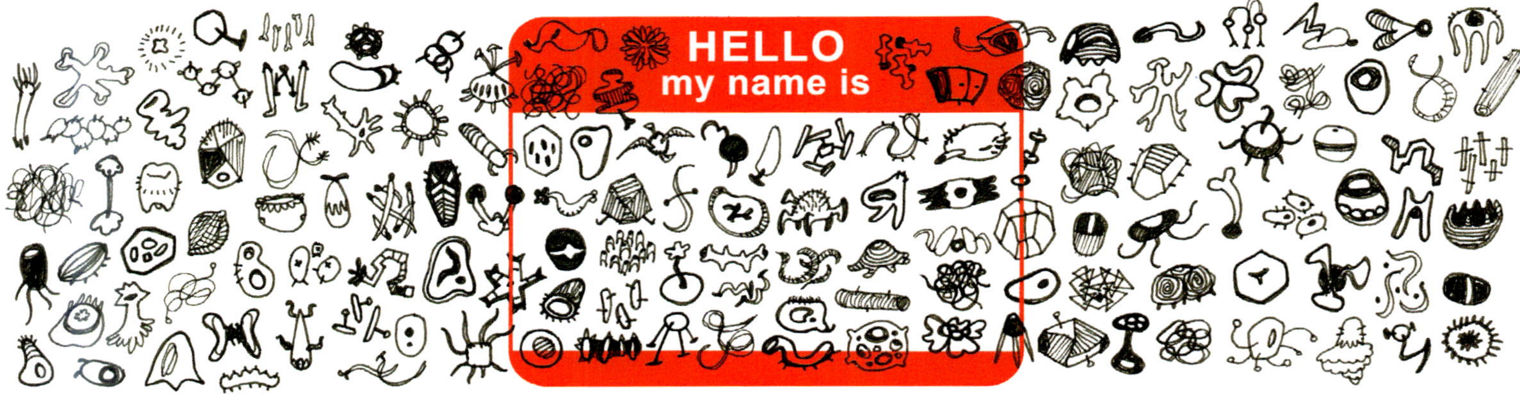
HELLO
my name is

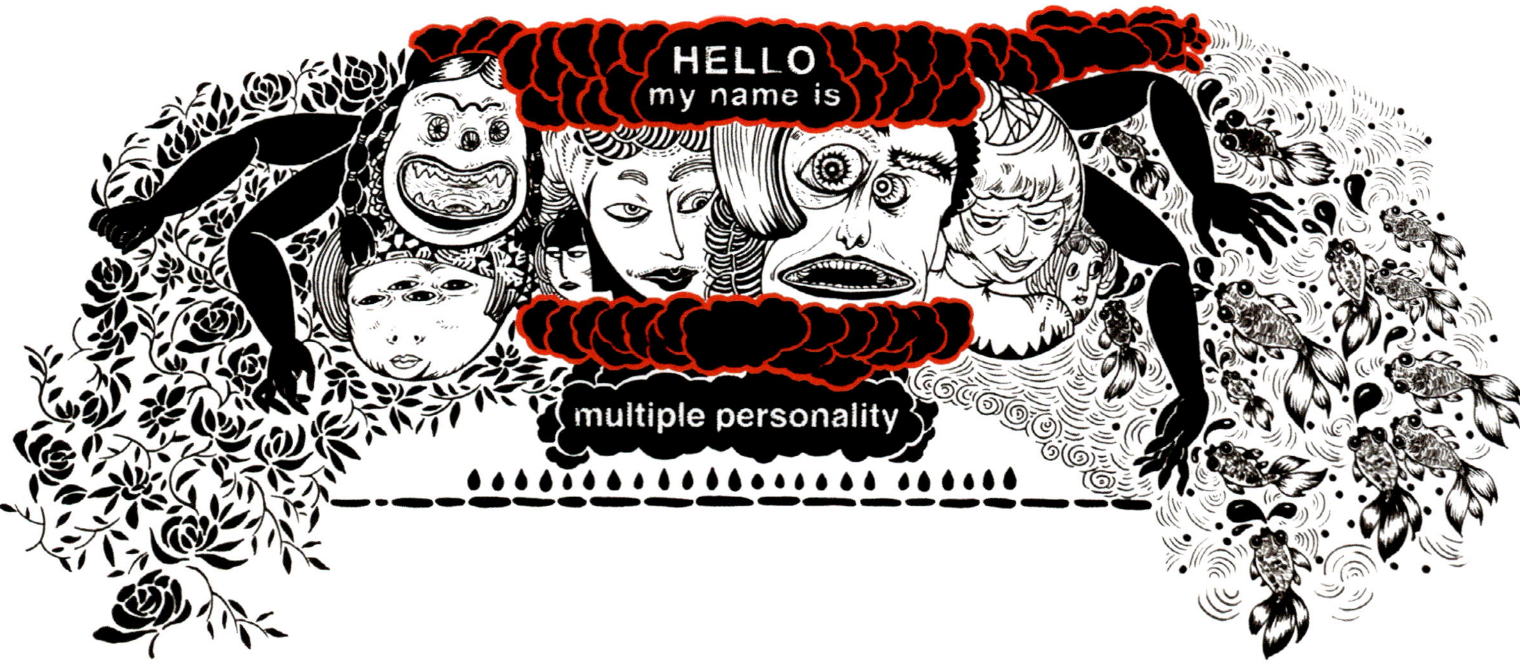
HELLO
my name is
multiple personality

HELLO MY NAME IS SOLUTIONS:

Obsessive-compulsive behavior, insomnia, and multiple personalities are the themes in figures 1 through 5.

Figures 6 and 8 both deal with determination, while figures 7 and 9 address gluttony.

Figure 10 is a metaphor for mood swings.

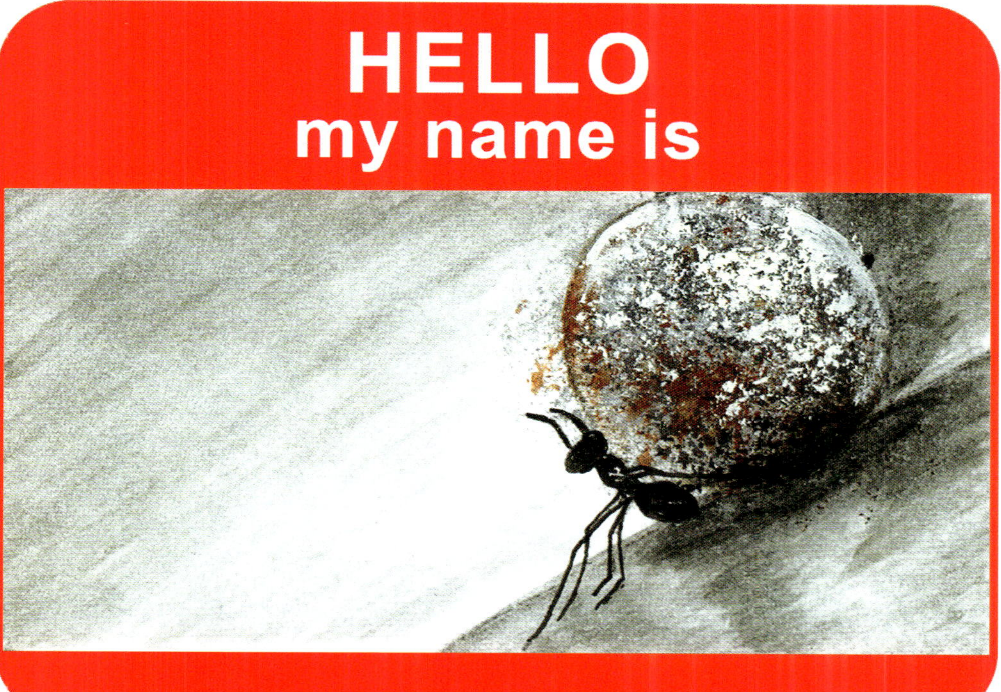

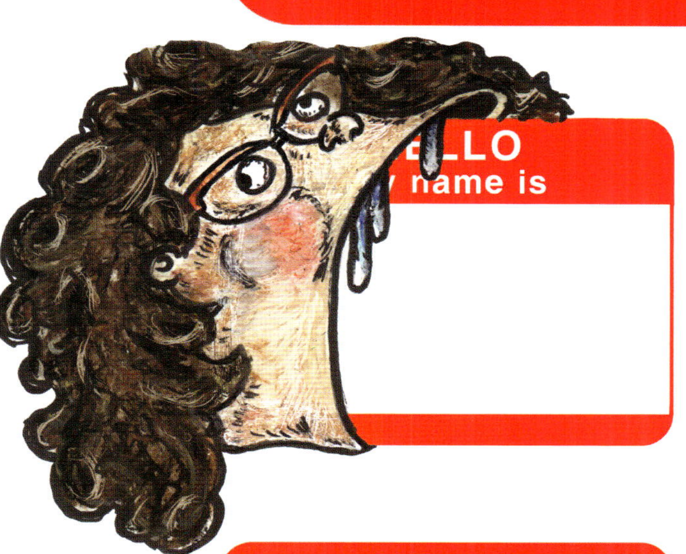

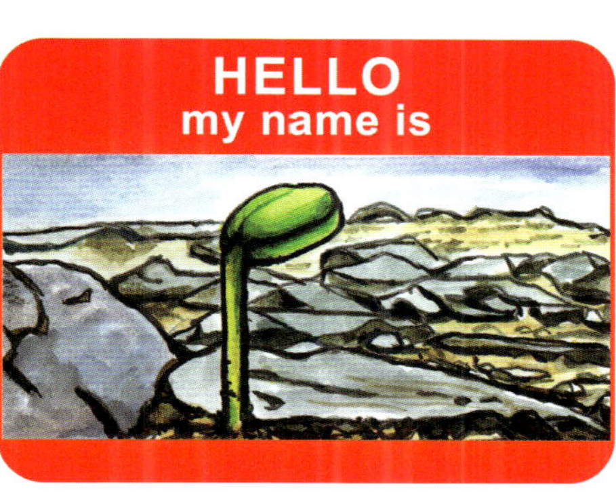

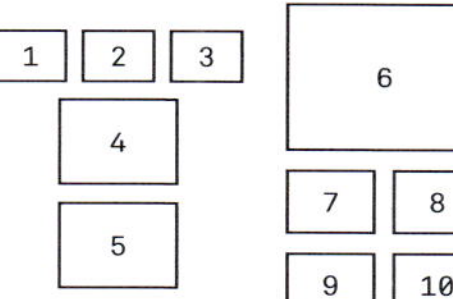

1. *Jiyoon Byun*
2. *Soobin Park*
3. *Qianyi Zhang*
4. *Alex Cook*
5. *Danyang Yang*
6. *Holly Trotta*
7. *Larissa Stephens*
8. *Haruyo Kaneko*
9. *Hwayyoung Jung*
10. *Kathryn Lewis*

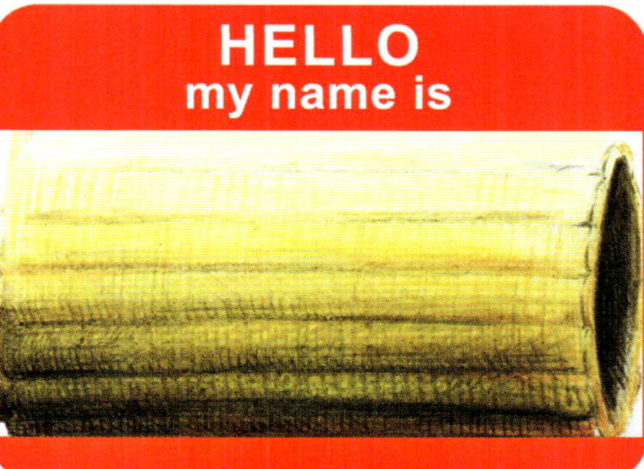

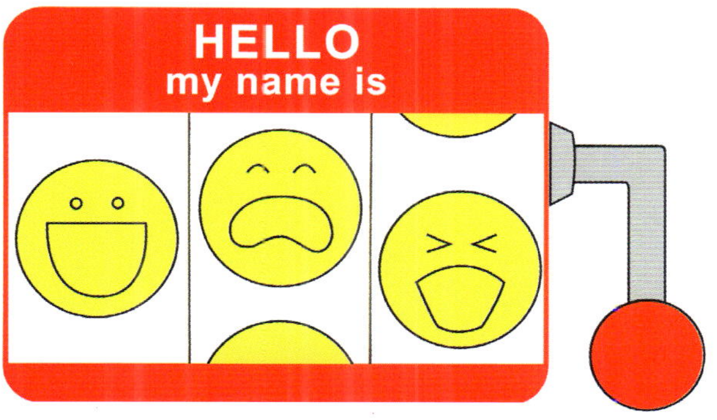

THOUGHTS ON THE CREATIVE PROCESS 13

By questioning, which puts one into the unknown, by playing around with the spirit and enthusiasm of a child, by being patient and not forcing the issue of imposing your will, solutions have a way, when you least expect them, to simply present themselves.

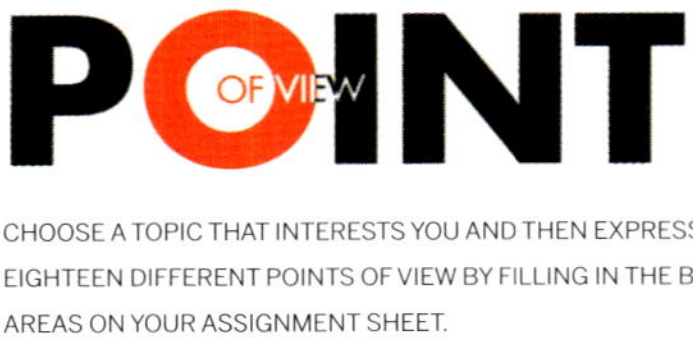

CHOOSE A TOPIC THAT INTERESTS YOU AND THEN EXPRESS IT FROM EIGHTEEN DIFFERENT POINTS OF VIEW BY FILLING IN THE BLANK AREAS ON YOUR ASSIGNMENT SHEET.

SAMPLE SOLUTION: TOPIC **CIGARETTE**
A **CIGARETTE** FROM THE POINT OF VIEW OF **A FOREST** IS **DESTRUCTION**
A **CIGARETTE** FROM THE POINT OF VIEW OF **A DOCTOR** IS **CANCER**
A **CIGARETTE** FROM THE POINT OF VIEW OF **TEETH** IS **YELLOW**

AFTER COMPLETING THE EIGHTEEN WRITTEN POINTS OF VIEW, CHOOSE THE MOST INTERESTING SIX SOLUTIONS AND REWRITE THEM IN THE GIVEN AREAS AND THEN GRAPHICALLY VISUALIZE THE FINAL WORD BY INFERRING OR SUGGESTING ITS INTENDED MEANING. THERE ARE NO LIMITATIONS ON THE USE OF COLOR OR MEDIUM.

BRAINSTORMING AREA:

A ________ FROM THE POINT OF VIEW OF ________ IS ________.
A ________ FROM THE POINT OF VIEW OF ________ IS ________.
A ________ FROM THE POINT OF VIEW OF ________ IS ________.
A ________ FROM THE POINT OF VIEW OF ________ IS ________.
A ________ FROM THE POINT OF VIEW OF ________ IS ________.
A ________ FROM THE POINT OF VIEW OF ________ IS ________.
A ________ FROM THE POINT OF VIEW OF ________ IS ________.
A ________ FROM THE POINT OF VIEW OF ________ IS ________.
A ________ FROM THE POINT OF VIEW OF ________ IS ________.
A ________ FROM THE POINT OF VIEW OF ________ IS ________.
A ________ FROM THE POINT OF VIEW OF ________ IS ________.
A ________ FROM THE POINT OF VIEW OF ________ IS ________.
A ________ FROM THE POINT OF VIEW OF ________ IS ________.
A ________ FROM THE POINT OF VIEW OF ________ IS ________.
A ________ FROM THE POINT OF VIEW OF ________ IS ________.
A ________ FROM THE POINT OF VIEW OF ________ IS ________.
A ________ FROM THE POINT OF VIEW OF ________ IS ________.

A __________ FROM THE POINT OF VIEW OF __________ IS

A __________ FROM THE POINT OF VIEW OF __________ IS

A __________ FROM THE POINT OF VIEW OF __________ IS

A __________ FROM THE POINT OF VIEW OF __________ IS

P R O B L E M S : S O L U T I O N S   S E R I E S

CREATED BY RICHARD WILDE / JUDITH WILDE, PRODUCED BY VISUAL ARTS PRESS, LTD. ART DIRECTORS: RICHARD WILDE / JUDITH WILDE

A ________ FROM THE POINT OF VIEW OF ________ IS

A ________ FROM THE POINT OF VIEW OF ________ IS

13

POINT OF VIEW PROBLEM:

Select a subject that interests you and express it from eighteen points of view in the brainstorming area on the assignment sheet.

For example, topic: **Cigarette**

A **cigarette** from the point of view of **a 1940s movie star** is **image**

A **cigarette** from the point of view of **parents** is **rebellion**

A **cigarette** from the point of view of **creativity** is **blowing a smoke ring**

A **cigarette** from the point of view of **a tobacco company** is **billions of dollars**

After completing the list of the eighteen brainstorming solutions, select six and graphically interpret the final word in the given areas. Include **the title**, **the point of view** and **the conclusion** on the assignment sheet as indicated.

AIM:
The Point of View project gives one the opportunity to approach visual problem solving in a more methodical, conceptual, thought-provoking way. Making the effort to see subjects from different vantage points opens one to the process of self-generating new ideas.

SUGGESTIONS:
One should infer or imply the intended meaning, so that the viewer can complete the message. Be careful not to include too much, or too little information.

SPECIFICATIONS:
There are no limitations on color or medium. Make sure to complete the brainstorming area in its entirety before beginning the visual portion of the project.

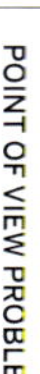

TIME FROM THE POINT OF VIEW OF **A BREAK-UP** IS

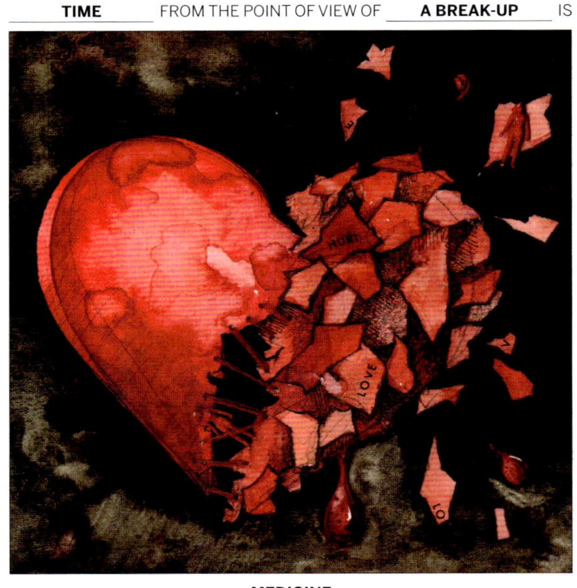

MEDICINE

TIME FROM THE POINT OF VIEW OF **SKIN** IS

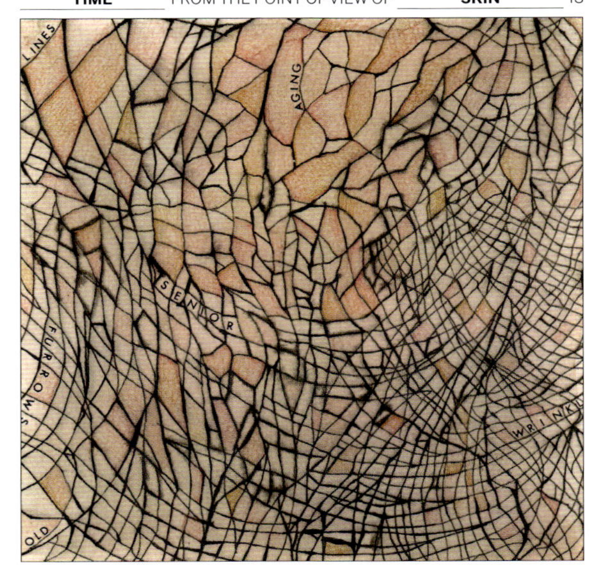

AGING

BEAUTY FROM THE POINT OF VIEW OF **A PEDOPHILE** IS

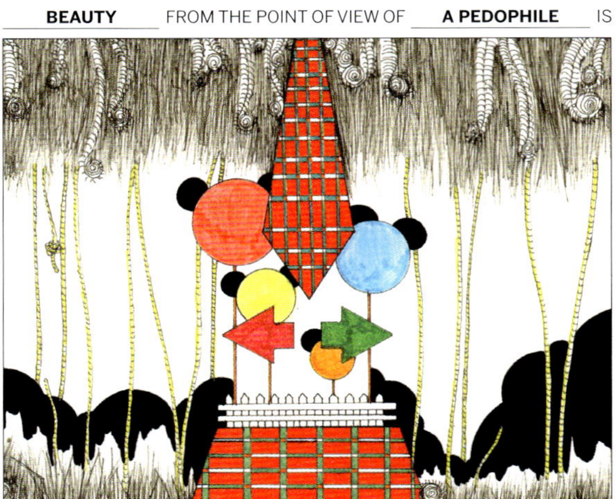

A CHILD

BEAUTY FROM THE POINT OF VIEW OF **A CHRISTIAN** IS

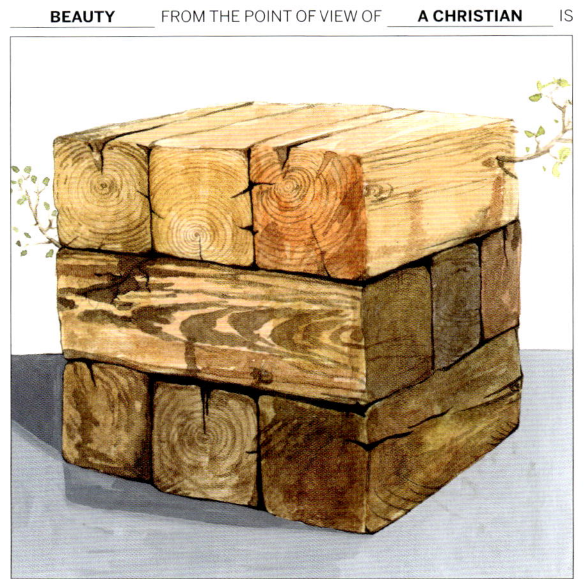

LIFE AFTER DEATH

THE NYC SUBWAY FROM THE POINT OF VIEW OF **A HOMELESS PERSON** IS

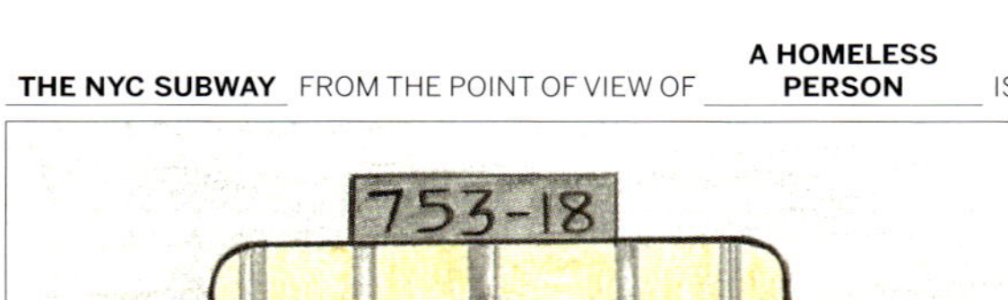

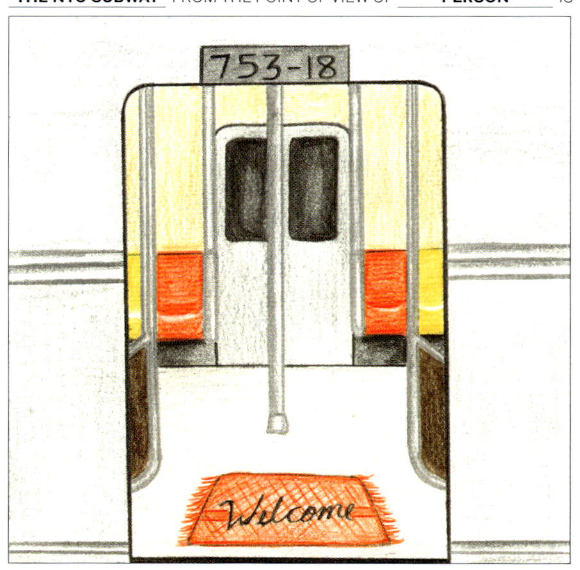

HOME

THE NYC SUBWAY FROM THE POINT OF VIEW OF **A CHILD** IS

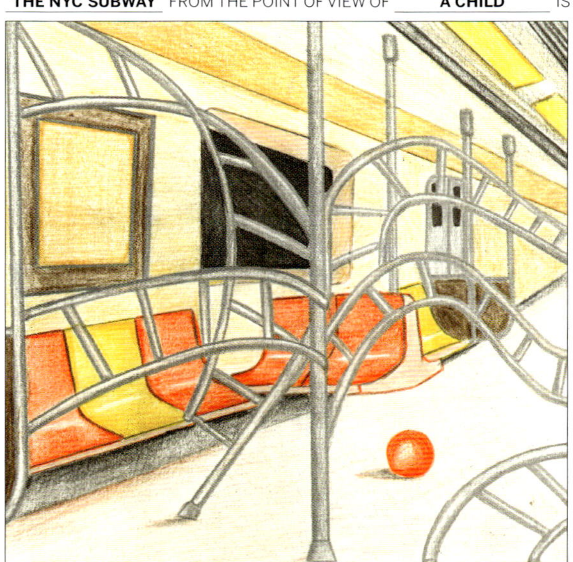

A PLAYGROUND

POINT OF VIEW SOLUTIONS:

Figures 1 and 2, 3 and 4, and 5 and 6 are groupings of two solutions each, that deal with the subjects time, beauty, and the New York City subway respectively.

Figure 3 references Nabokov's book, *Lolita*, in which an older man falls in love with a teenager.

Figures 7 through 12 represent an entire project of six solutions using a fish as the subject.

A FISH FROM THE POINT OF VIEW OF **A CHILD** IS

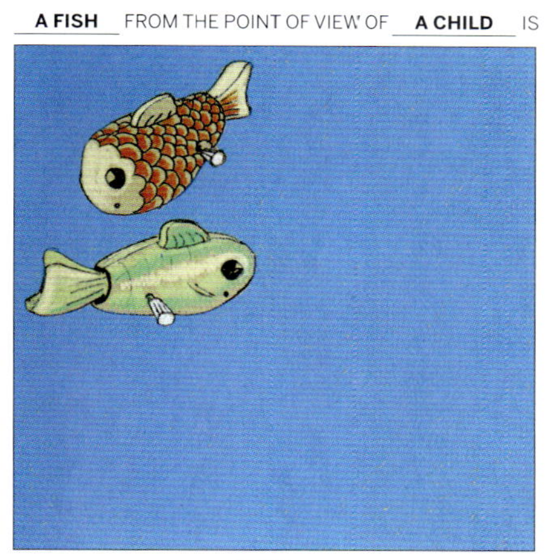

A TOY

A FISH FROM THE POINT OF VIEW OF **A CAT** IS

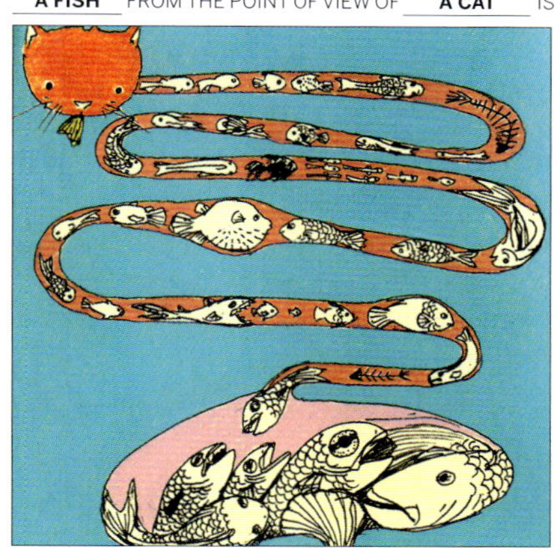

DINNER

A FISH FROM THE POINT OF VIEW OF **A TOILET BOWL** IS

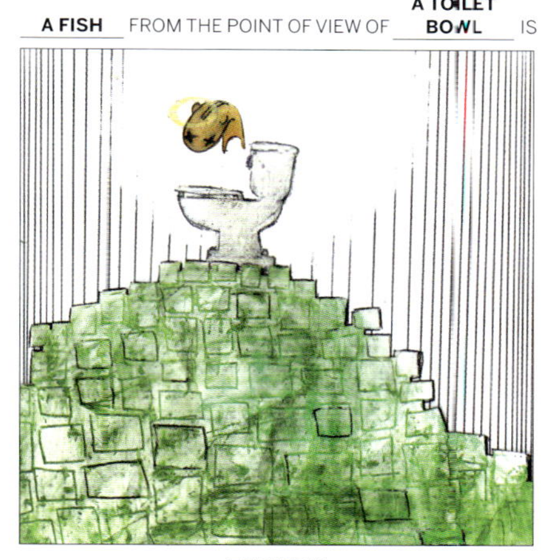

A FUNERAL

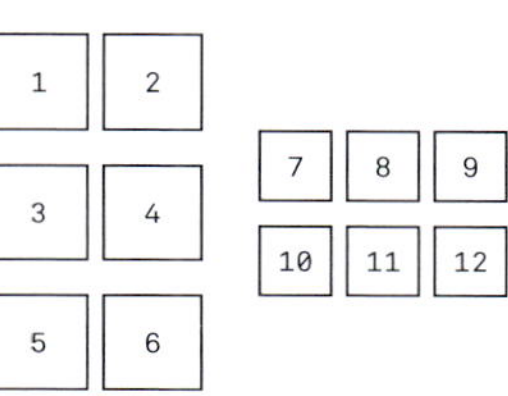

A FISH FROM THE POINT OF VIEW OF **A FLOOR** IS

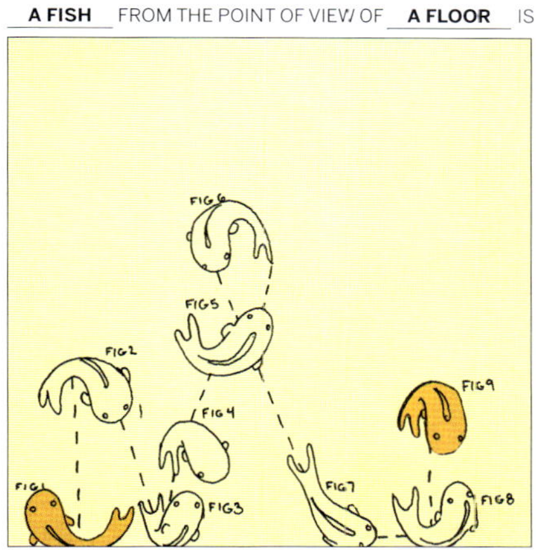

FIGURES 1 THROUGH 9

A FISH FROM THE POINT OF VIEW OF **MY FATHER** IS

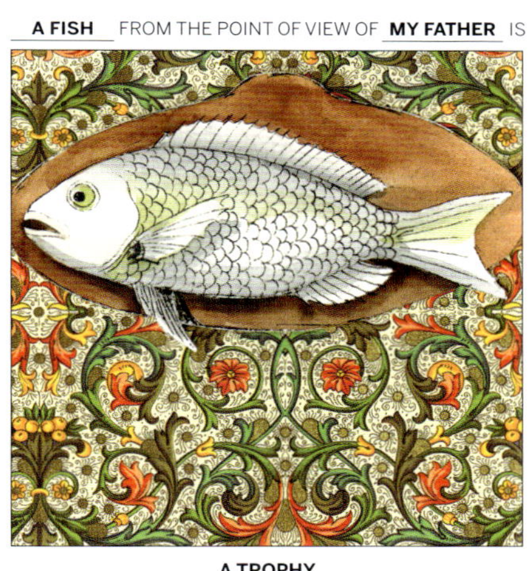

A TROPHY

A FISH FROM THE POINT OF VIEW OF **A CHEF** IS

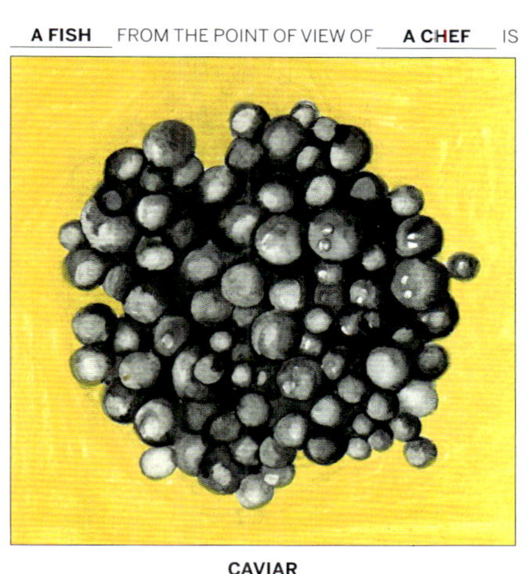

CAVIAR

1–2. *Hana Yoo*
3–4. *Yueh Lu*
5–6. *Maria Jaramillo*
7–12. *Colette Nickola*

A CAN OPENER FROM THE POINT OF VIEW OF **A CAT** IS

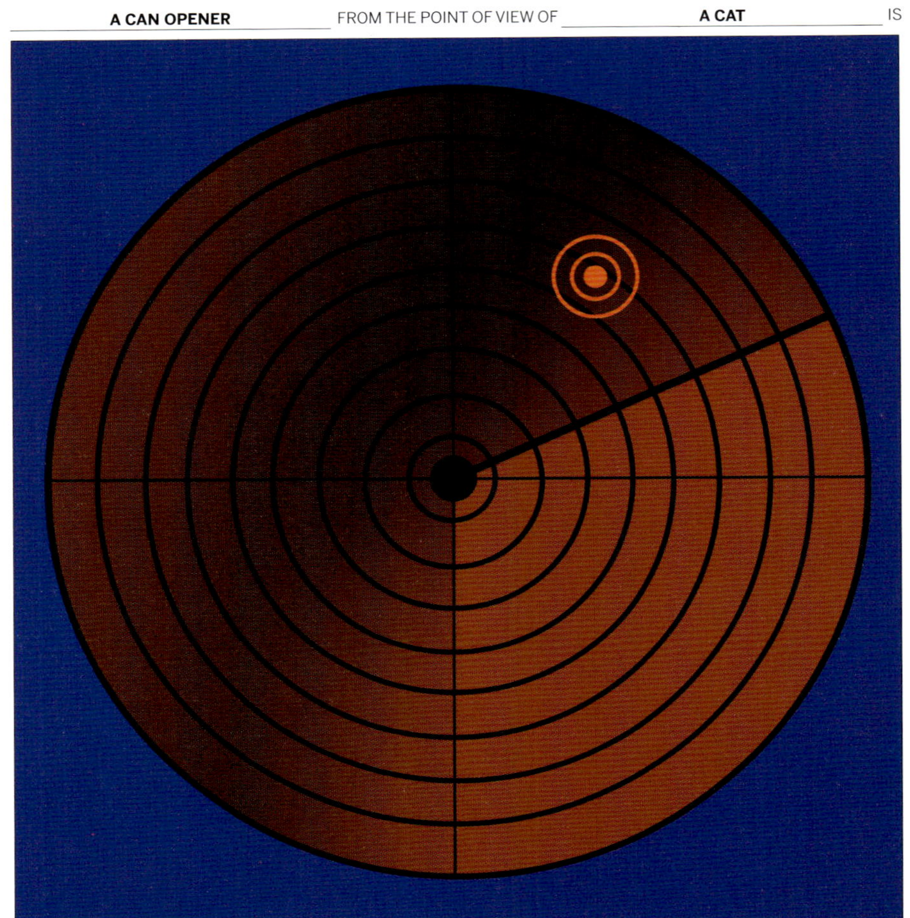

BEHAVORIAL CONDITIONING

ANXIETY FROM THE POINT OF VIEW OF **A MEXICAN RESTAURANT CUSTOMER** IS

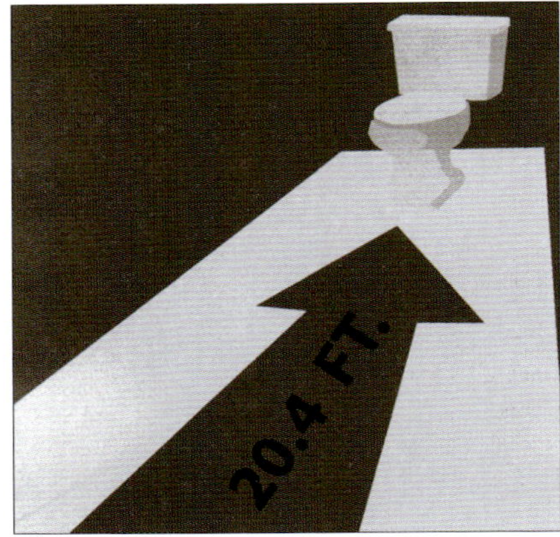

THE DISTANCE TO A TOILET

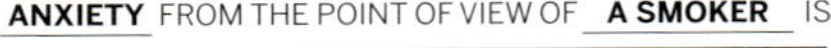

ANXIETY FROM THE POINT OF VIEW OF **A SMOKER** IS

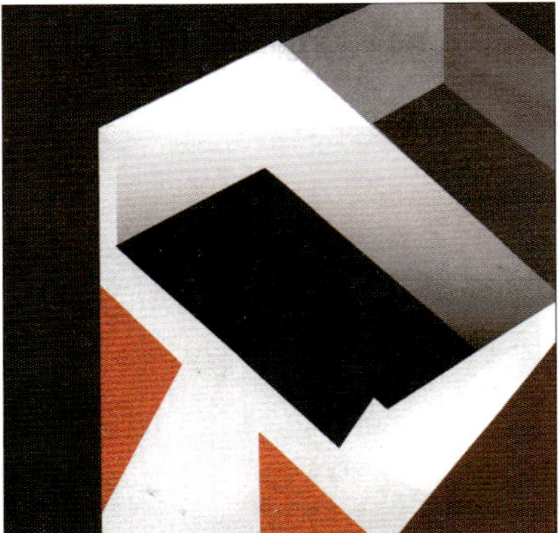

RUNNING OUT OF CIGARETTES

A LEAF FROM THE POINT OF VIEW OF A 2ND GRADER IS

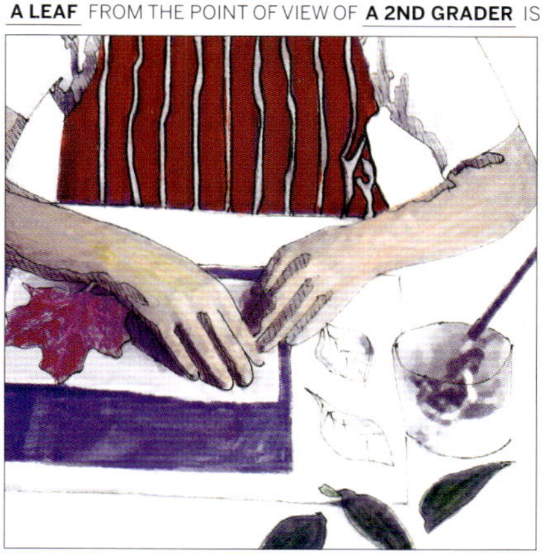

AN ART PROJECT

A LEAF FROM THE POINT OF VIEW OF A FOREST ANIMAL IS

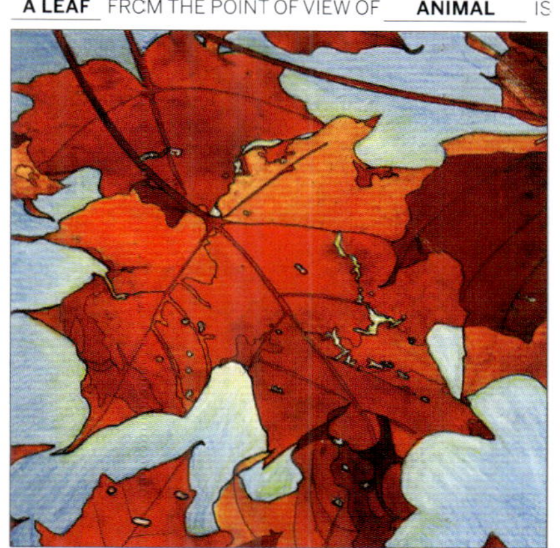

WELCOME SHADE FROM THE SUN

POINT OF VIEW SOLUTIONS:

The subjects of eyeglasses in figures 1 through 3, a cat in figures 4 and 5, and leaves in figures 6 through 10 represent different groupings of executions in terms of style and technique.

Eyeglasses deals with humorous stylized characterizations, while the subject of cats uses a limited palette of primarily red and black, depicting closely cropped images to dramatize the concept of being afraid.

A CAT FROM THE POINT OF VIEW OF A MOUSE IS

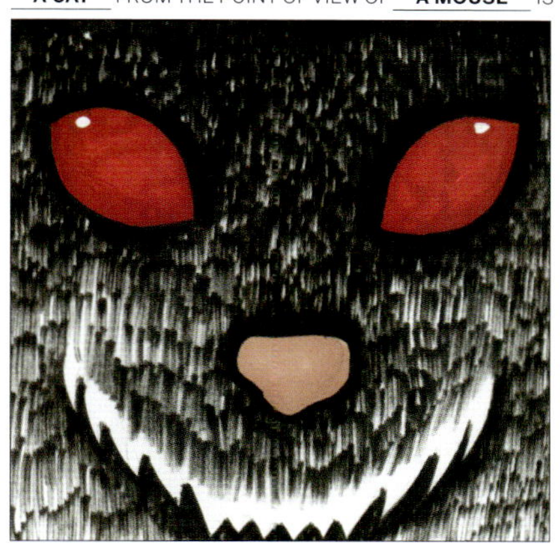

GREAT DANGER

A CAT FROM THE POINT OF VIEW OF A MOUSE IS

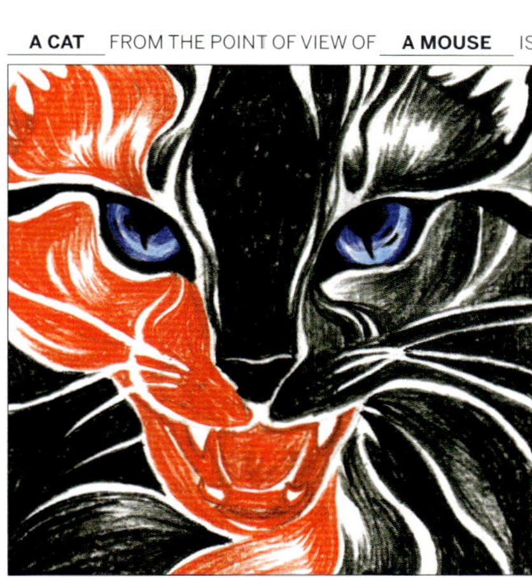

TERRIFYING BEYOND IMAGINATION

A LEAF FROM THE POINT OF VIEW OF A CATERPILLAR IS

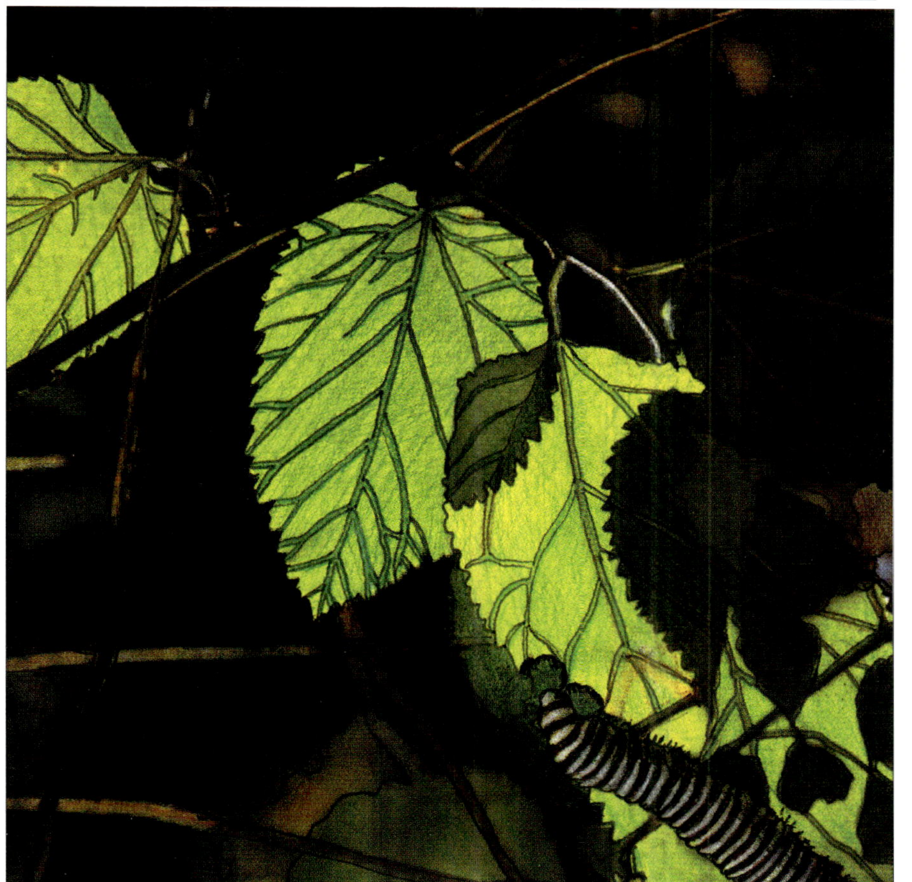

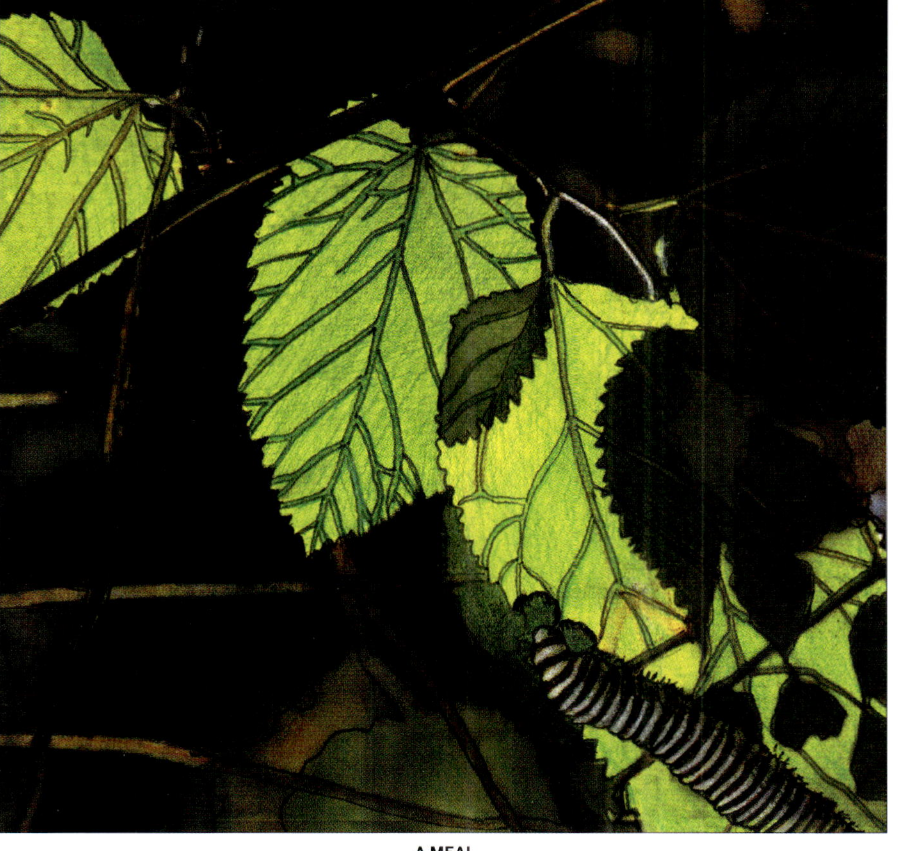

A MEAL

1	2, 3	4, 5	6, 7, 8, 9, 10

1–3. *Thomas Shim*
4. *Rachelle Bowers*
5. *Lynne Yun*
6–10. *Robin Birnbaum*

Leaves are depicted through the technique of drawing with color pencils, ink and paint on photographs, resulting in highly stylized imagery.

A LEAF FROM THE POINT OF VIEW OF A WATER LILY IS

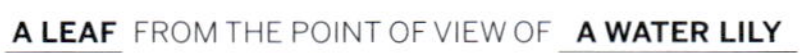

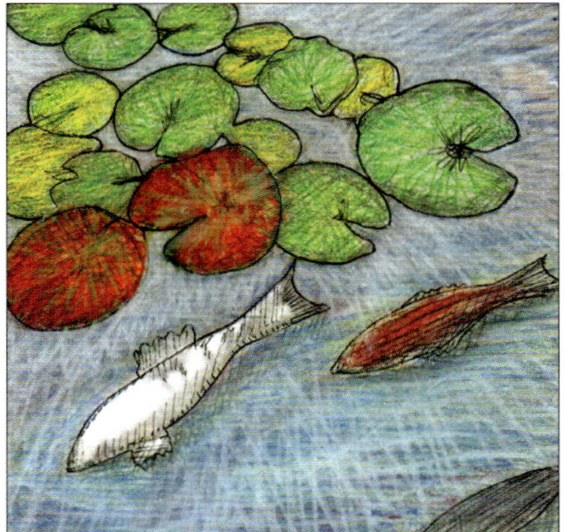

FLOATING

A LEAF FROM THE POINT OF VIEW OF AN ARCHEOLOGIST IS

A FOSSIL

SHOES FROM THE POINT OF VIEW OF **A DOG** ARE

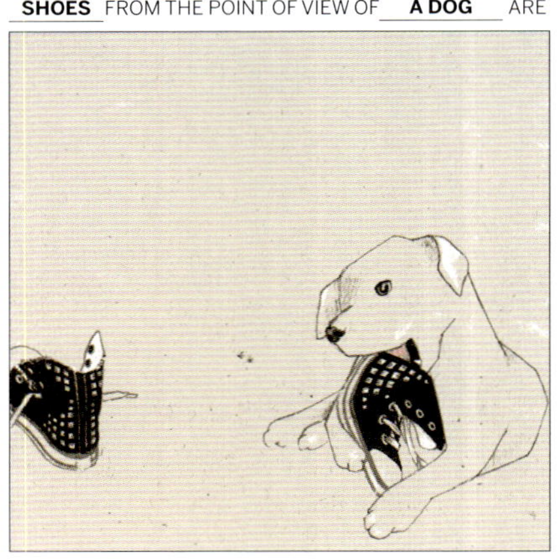

A CHEW TOY

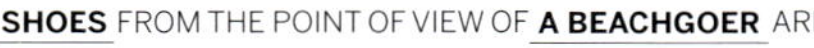

SHOES FROM THE POINT OF VIEW OF **A BEACHGOER** ARE

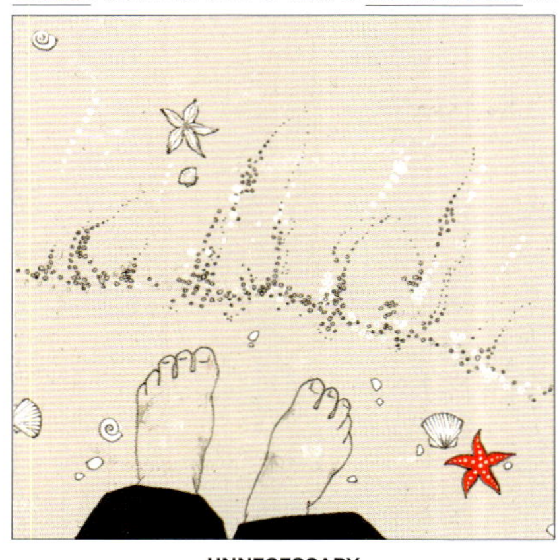

UNNECESSARY

SHOES FROM THE POINT OF VIEW OF **A BULLY** ARE

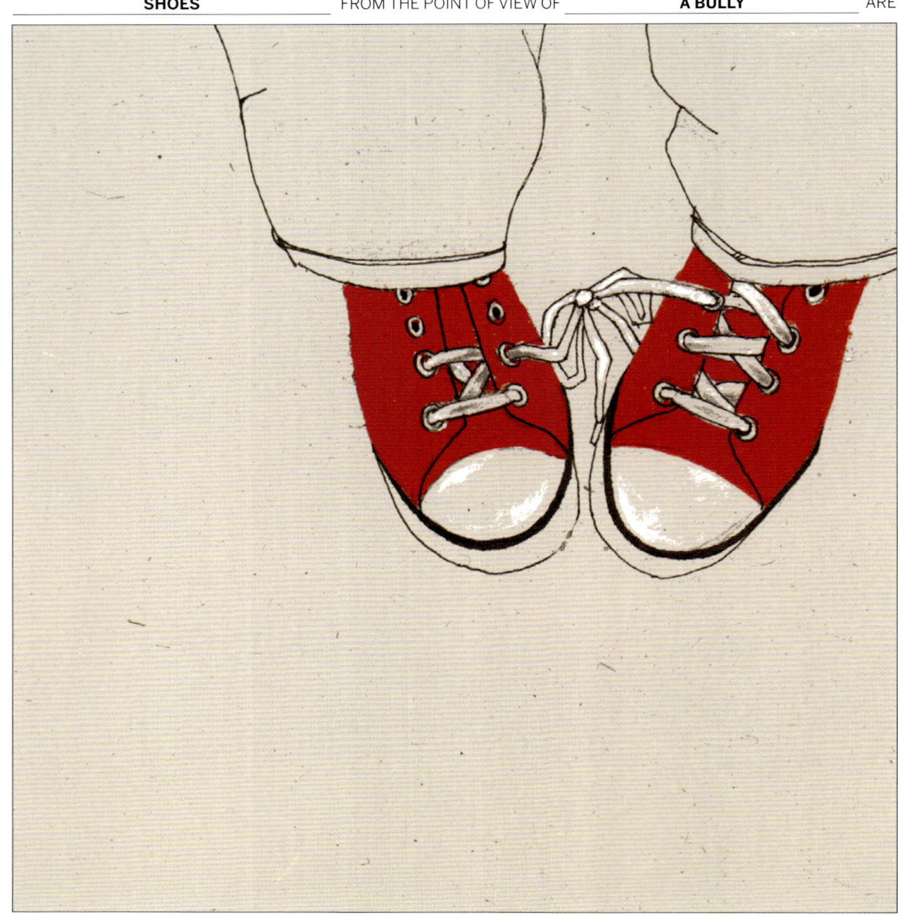

OPPORTUNITY

POINT OF VIEW SOLUTIONS:

Shoes are the subject in figures 1 through 3, whose executions rely on a highly personal drawn line, supported by minimalistic compositions and color.

Figures 4 through 6 deal with the subject of a spot, utilizing typography, literal imagery, and abstraction to execute the concepts.

A SPOT FROM THE POINT OF VIEW OF **ANYTHING ONE-OF-A-KIND** IS

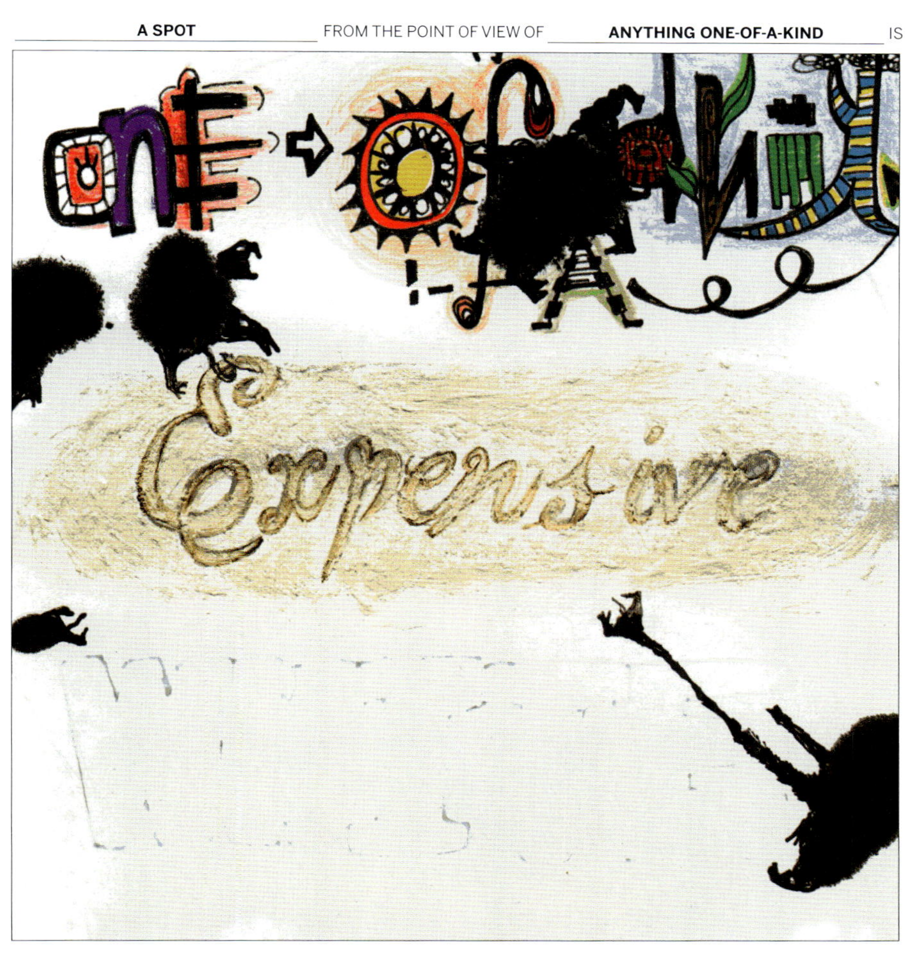

EXPENSIVE, WHITE, INEVITABLE

A SPOT FROM THE POINT OF VIEW OF **BLEACH** IS

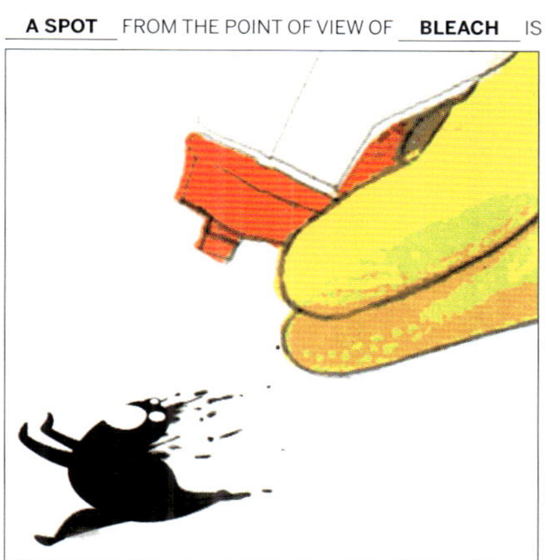

REVENGE

A SPOT FROM THE POINT OF VIEW OF **WATER** IS

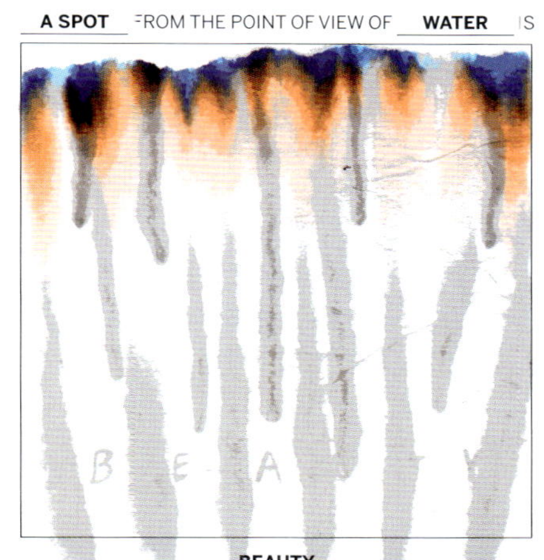

BEAUTY

1 | 3 | 4 | 5
2 | | | 6

1–3. Grace Han
4–6. Minah Kim

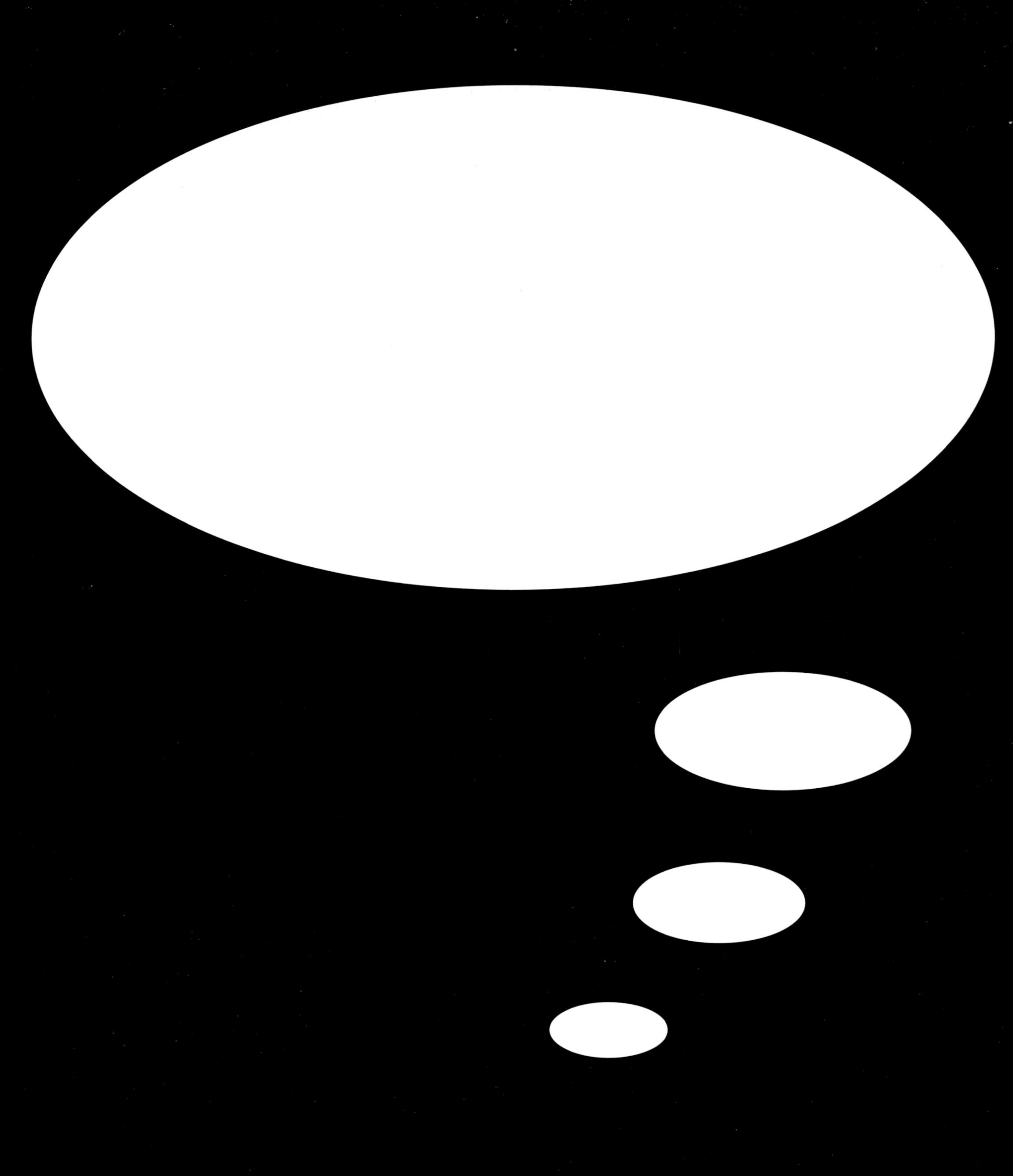

< FREEDOM FROM THE POINT OF VIEW OF A BUDDHIST MONK IS

SILENCE

A COW FROM THE POINT OF VIEW OF A COMPUTER PROGRAMMER IS

ONES AND ZEROS

A COW FROM THE POINT OF VIEW OF A GRAPHIC DESIGNER IS

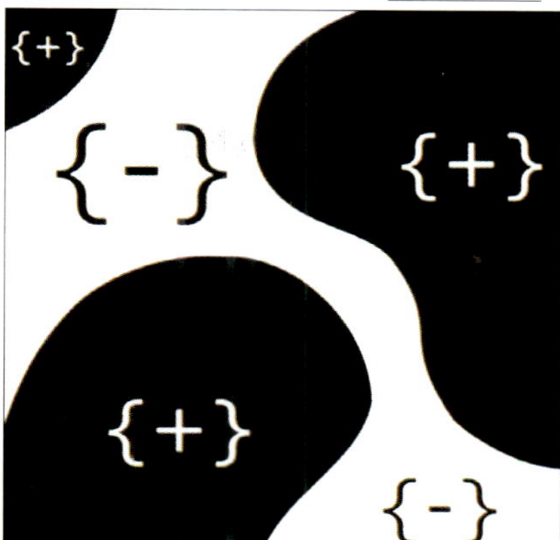

NEGATIVE AND POSITIVE RELATIONSHIPS

FOOD FROM THE POINT OF VIEW OF A LION IS

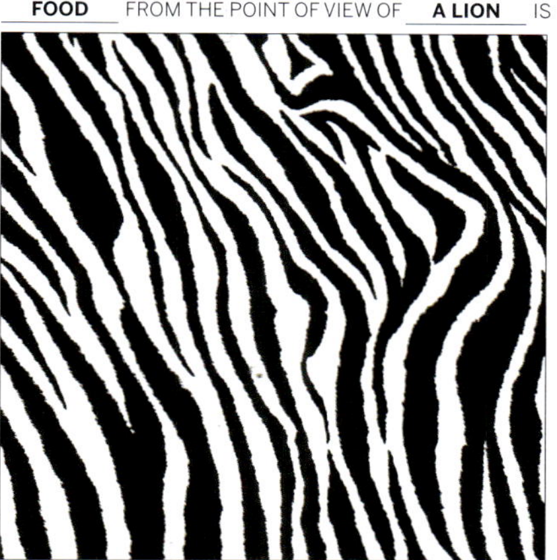

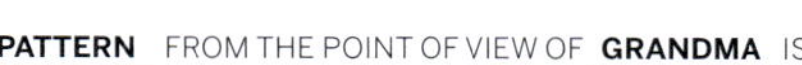

A ZEBRA

A FISH FROM THE POINT OF VIEW OF SKIN IS

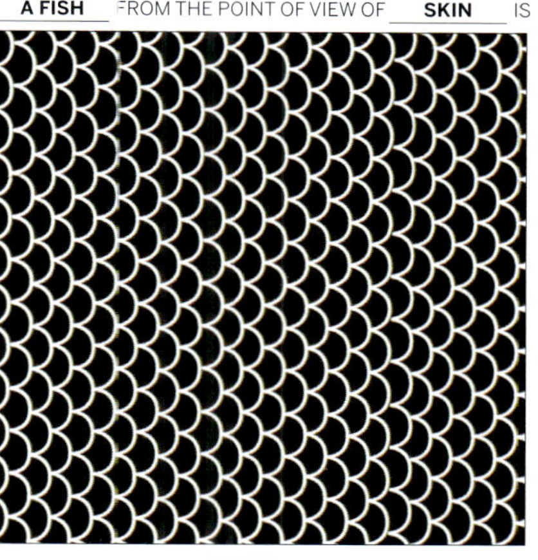

A PATTERN

PATTERN FROM THE POINT OF VIEW OF GRANDMA IS

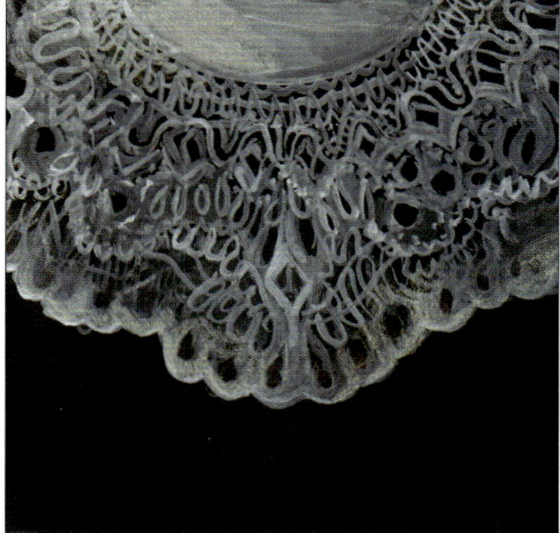

LACE

PATTERN FROM THE POINT OF VIEW OF A CELL IS

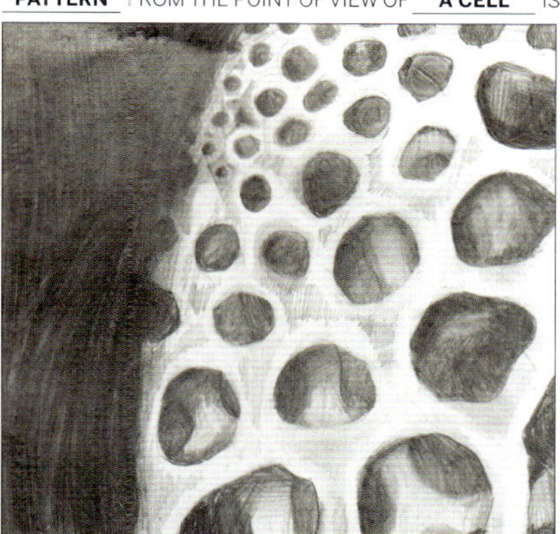

RADIOLARIA

SUNLIGHT FROM THE POINT OF VIEW OF A ROOSTER IS

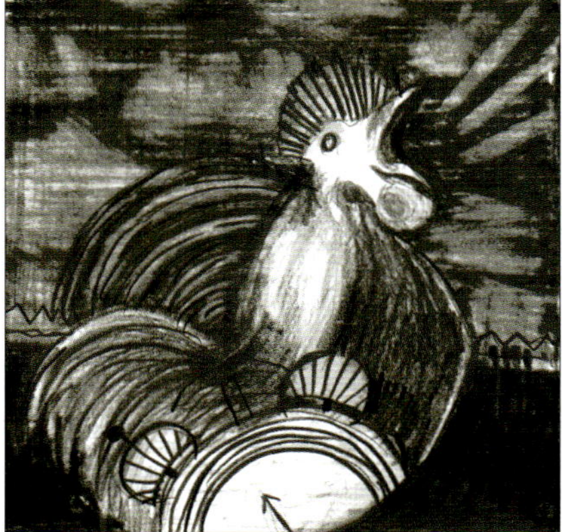

A WAKE-UP CALL

BLACK & WHITE FROM THE POINT OF VIEW OF A KID IS

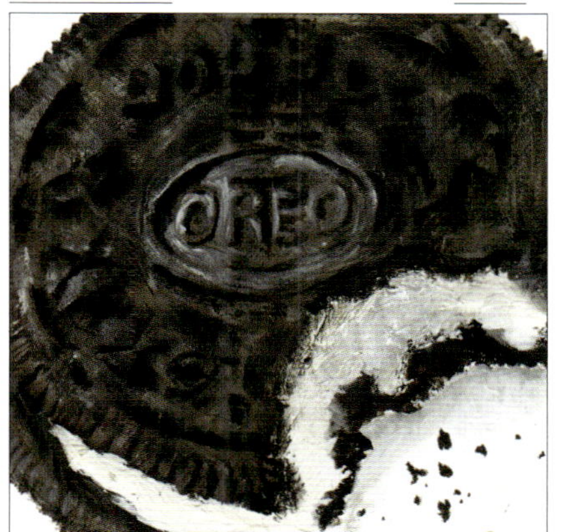

AN OREO COOKIE

POINT OF VIEW SOLUTIONS:

Figures 1 through 9 are black and white solutions.

Figure 1, whose subject is freedom, as seen from the point of view of a Buddhist monk, is a visual interpretation of the state of nothingness.

Figures 2 through 9 include the following subjects: a cow, food, a fish, pattern, sunlight, and black and white. Although the subjects vary, most of these solutions deal with patterning and textured imagery.

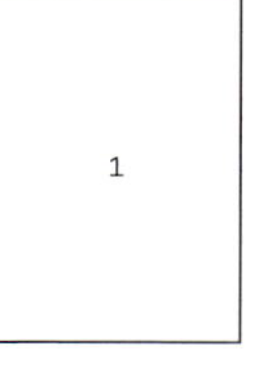

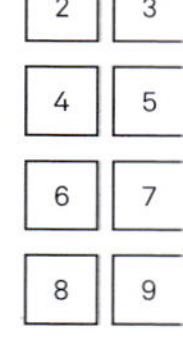

1. *Joe Coyle*
2–3. *Chris Kennedy*
4. *Artem Artemov*
5. *Hua-Chen Huang*
6–7. *Sandra Woodruff*
8. *Laurie Lipsey*
9. *Seulki Heo*

HALLOWEEN FROM THE POINT OF VIEW OF **A MUMMY** IS

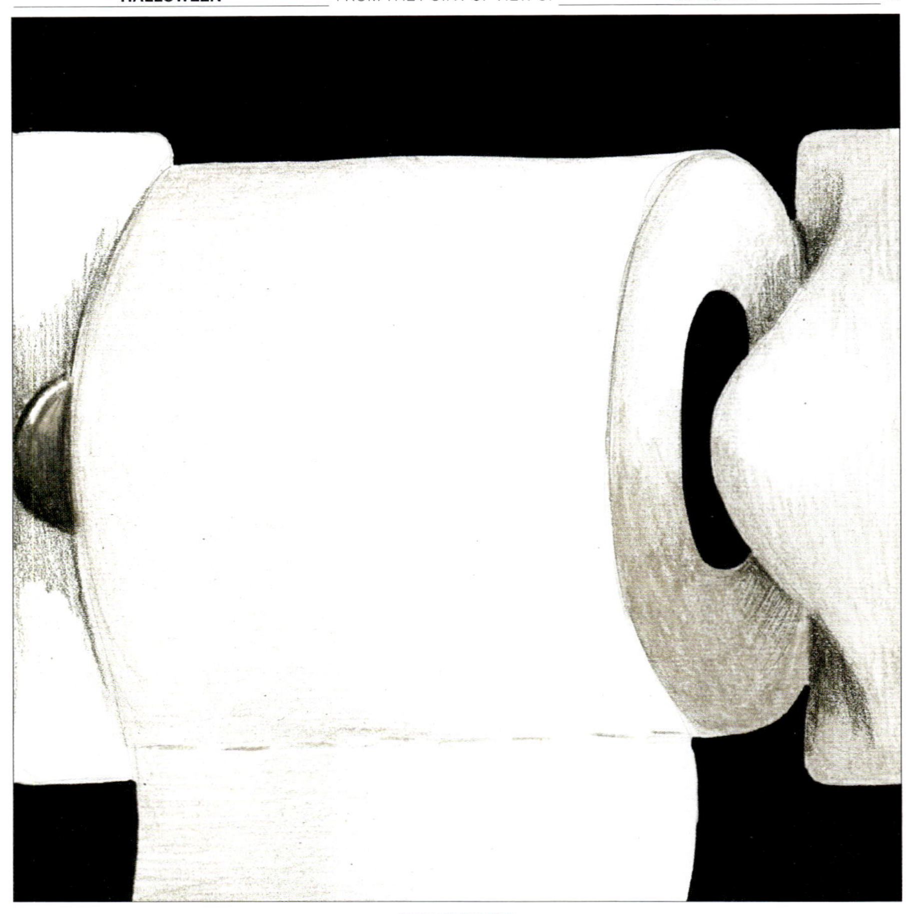

TOILET PAPER

HALLOWEEN FROM THE POINT OF VIEW OF **MONSTERS** IS

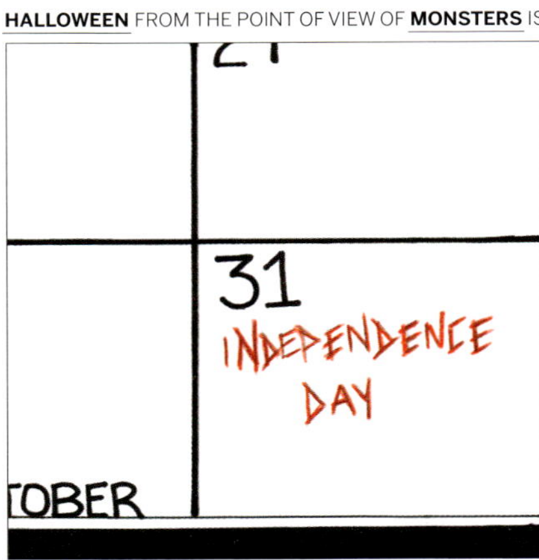

INDEPENDENCE DAY

HALLOWEEN FROM THE POINT OF VIEW OF **A WOODEN STICK** IS

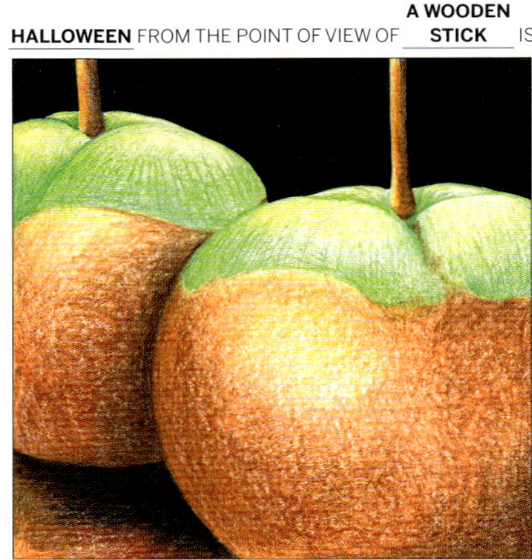

A HANDLE

SILK FROM THE POINT OF VIEW OF **A BALLERINA** IS

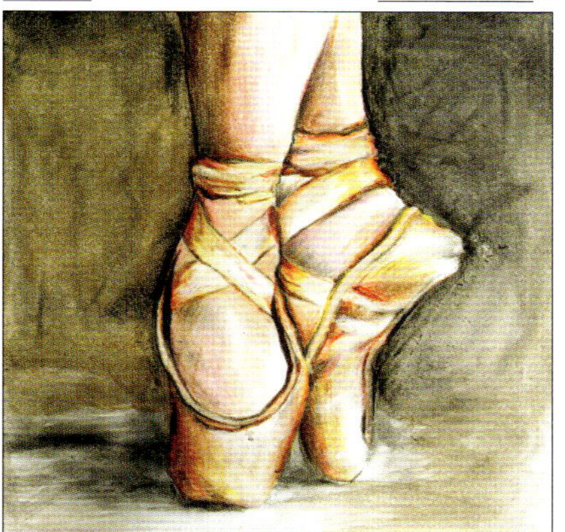

STABILITY

SILK FROM THE POINT OF VIEW OF **AN INDIAN CHILD** IS

HARD LABOR

A FOOT FROM THE POINT OF VIEW OF **AN ANT** IS

KINGDOM COME

A FOOT FROM THE POINT OF VIEW OF **A HAND** IS

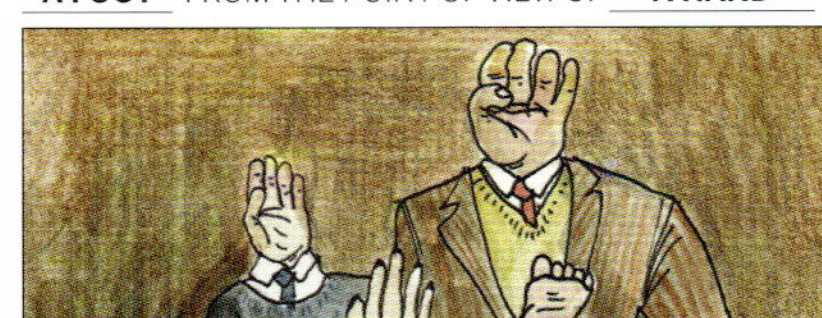

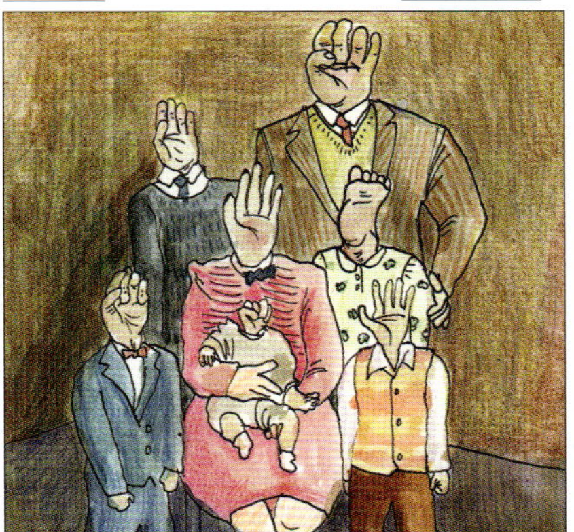

A DEFORMED SIBLING

A FOOT FROM THE POINT OF VIEW OF **DR. FRANKENSTEIN** IS

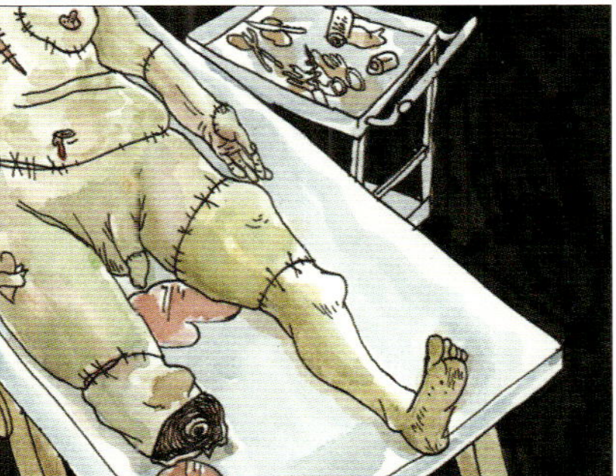

"JUST WHAT I NEED"

POINT OF VIEW SOLUTIONS:

Figures 1 through 3 depict the subject of Halloween.

Figure 2 takes artistic license by declaring October 31st as Independence Day for monsters.

Figures 4 and 5 address the subject of silk from a glamorous and tragic point of view, while figures 6 through 8 address the subject of a foot depicted through the world of the macabre.

(Figure 7 might need a closer look to discover a foot among the family of hands.)

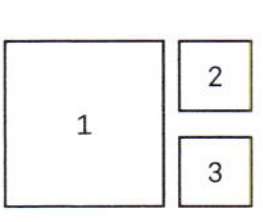

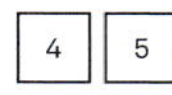

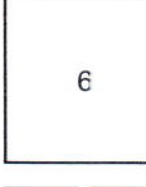

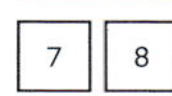

1–3. *Kimberly Yau*
4–5. *Natalie Lobel*
6–8. *Choon Teoh*

AN EYE FROM THE POINT OF VIEW OF **HELLO KITTY** IS

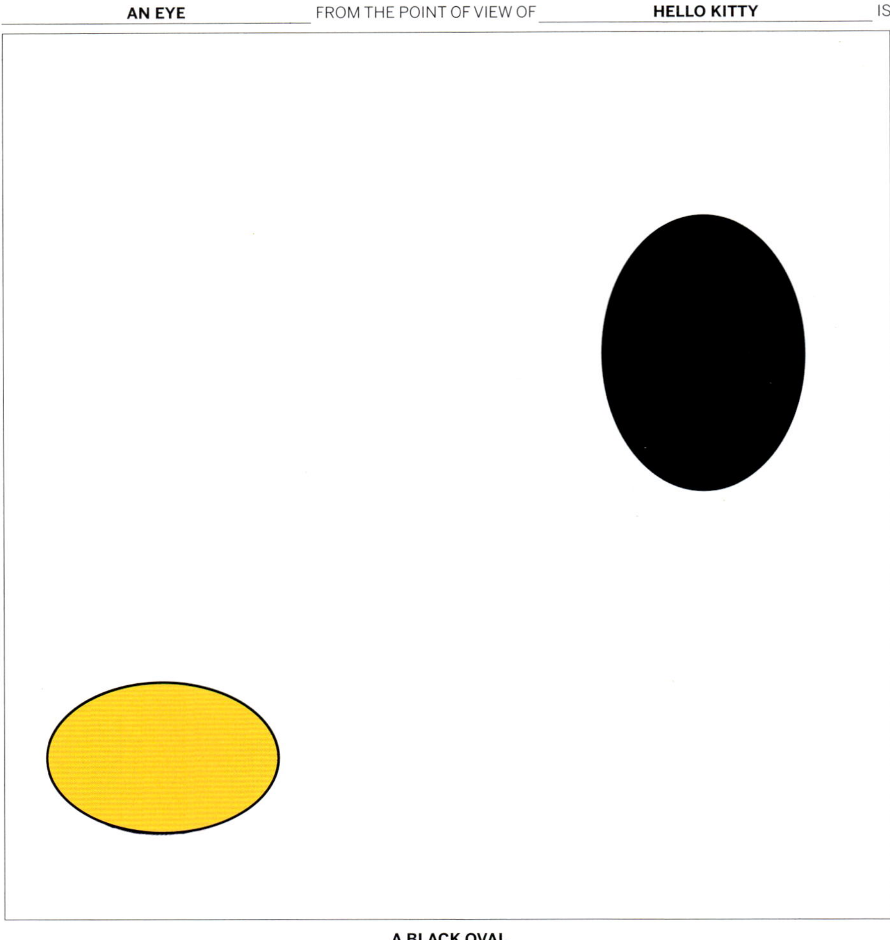

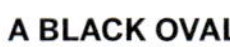

A BLACK OVAL

I LOVE NY FROM THE POINT OF VIEW OF **RICHARD WILDE** IS

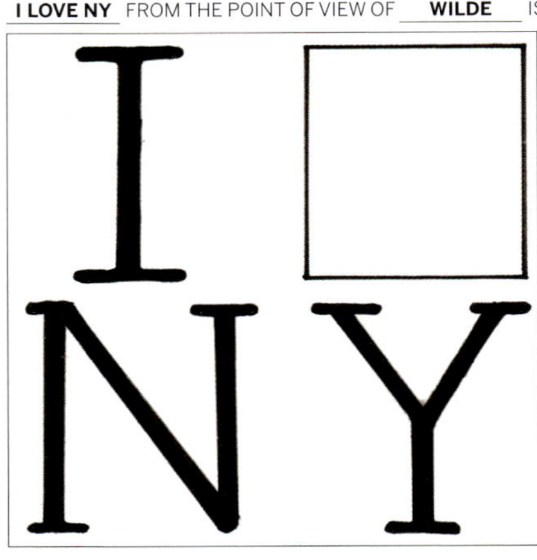

A VISUAL LITERACY ASSIGNMENT

A PEN FROM THE POINT OF VIEW OF **A BABY** IS

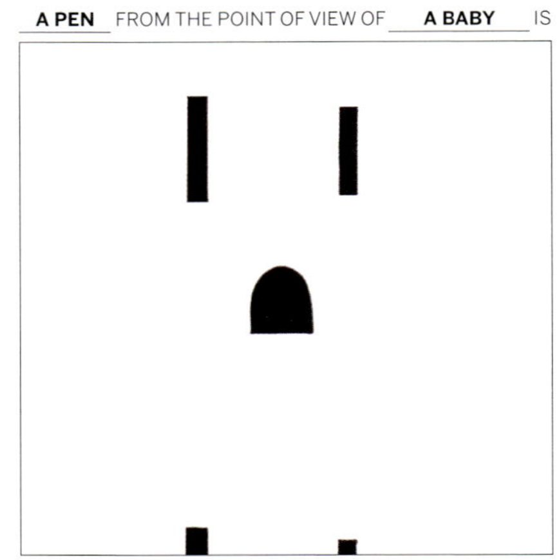

A SELF TASER

A FEMALE FROM THE POINT OF VIEW OF **A FEMINIST** IS

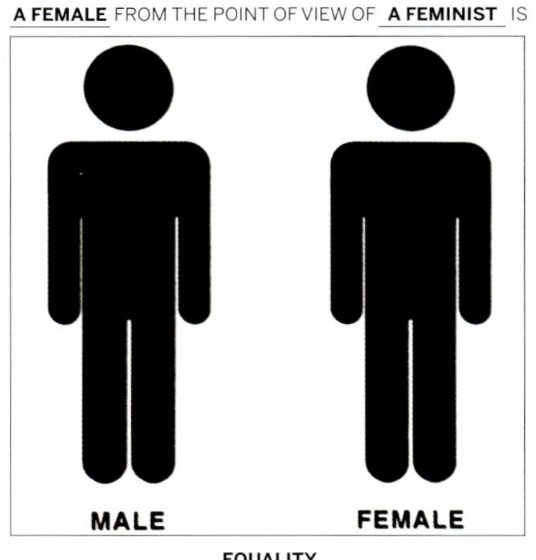

EQUALITY

A WINDOW FROM THE POINT OF VIEW OF **A PHOTO-GRAPHER** IS

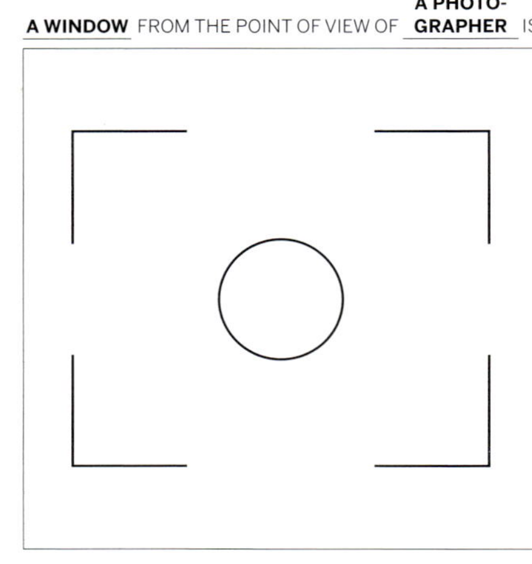

A FRAMING GRID

A WINDOW FROM THE POINT OF VIEW OF **A PRISONER** IS

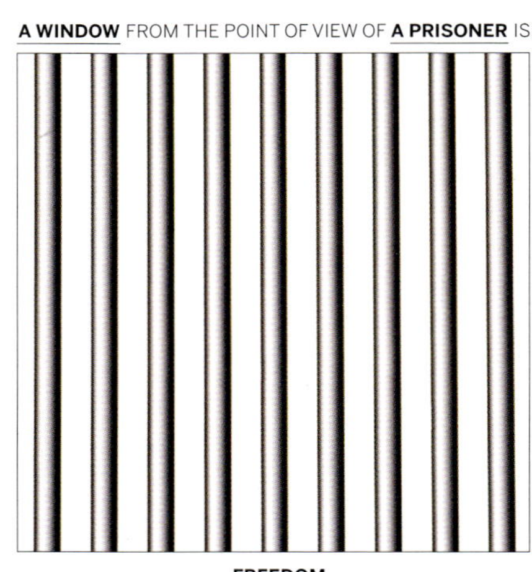

FREEDOM

POINT OF VIEW SOLUTIONS:

Figures 1 through 6 use a reductive approach to problem solving that include: an eye, I love NY, a pen, a female and a window.

Figure 2 pertains to the projects given in this book, turning the iconic "I love NY" image into an assignment where a blank space, rather than a heart, is provided for one's personal interpretation.

In contrast, figures 7 through 12 are emotionally driven spontaneously drawn images, whose subjects include an animal, hunger, a corpse, and a bear.

AN ANIMAL FROM THE POINT OF VIEW OF **A FUR COAT** IS

DEATH

AN ANIMAL FROM THE POINT OF VIEW OF **A CAR** IS

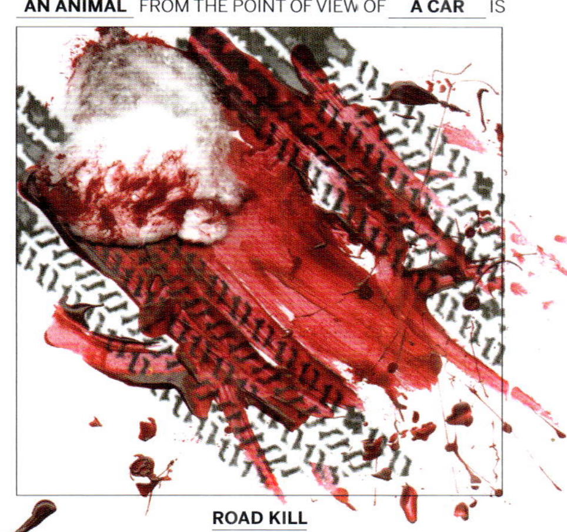

ROAD KILL

HUNGER FROM THE POINT OF VIEW OF **A VAMPIRE** IS

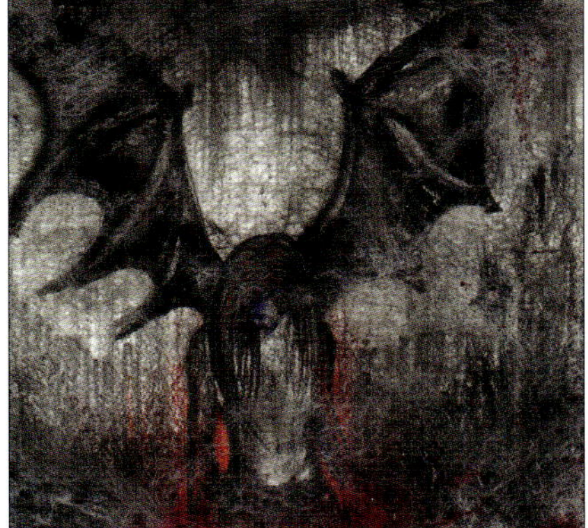

BLOOD

A CORPSE FROM THE POINT OF VIEW OF **A SERIAL KILLER** IS

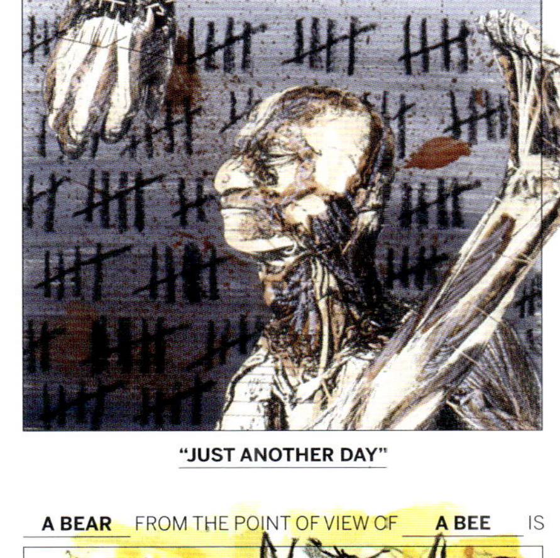

"JUST ANOTHER DAY"

A BEAR FROM THE POINT OF VIEW OF **A CAR** IS

ROAD KILL

A BEAR FROM THE POINT OF VIEW OF **A BEE** IS

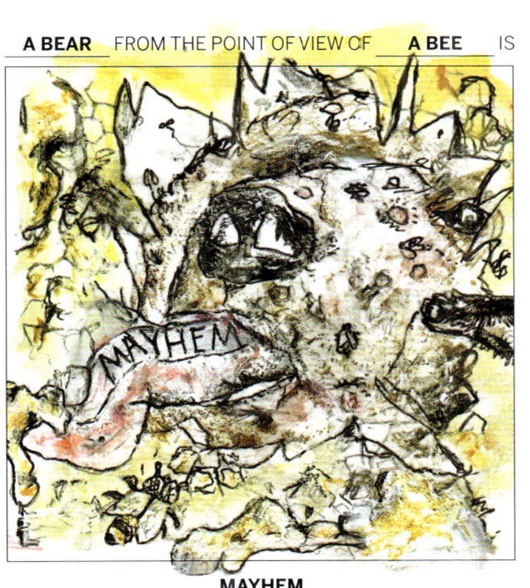

MAYHEM

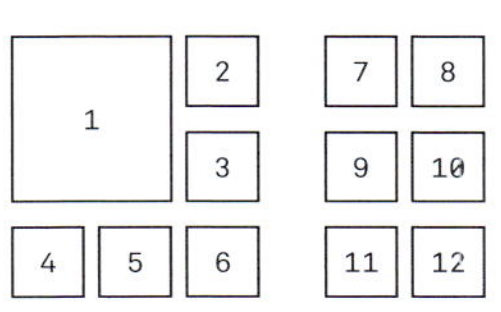

1. *Boris Rapaport*
2. *Hisa Ide*
3. *Dana Choi*
4. *Michael Scheier*

5–6. *Jason Seinkwicz*

7. *Kei Meguro*
8. *Fernando Chuqui*
9. *Eunhae Lee*
10. *Linda Kaufman*

11–12. *Kyle Fetzer*

A DOG FROM THE POINT OF VIEW OF **A FLEA** IS

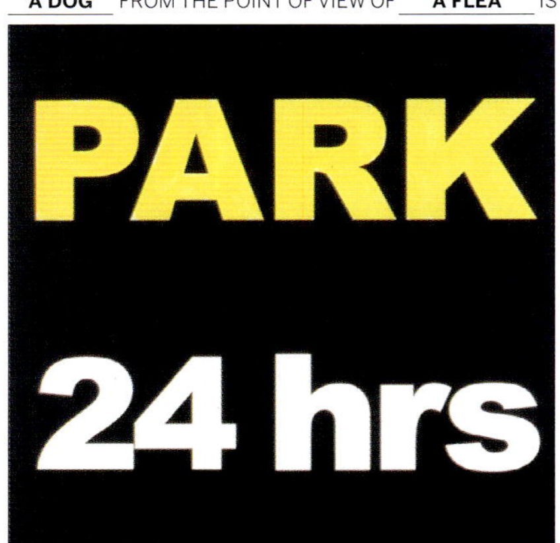

A PARKING LOT

A DOG FROM THE POINT OF VIEW OF **A FLEA** IS

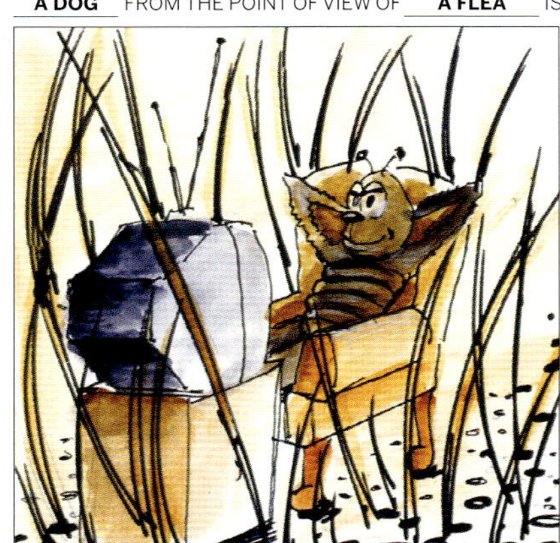

A TEMPORARY HOME

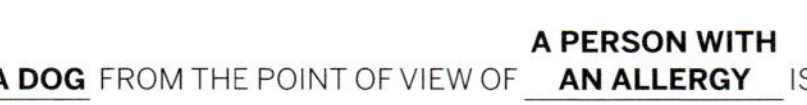

A DOG FROM THE POINT OF VIEW OF **A PERSON WITH AN ALLERGY** IS

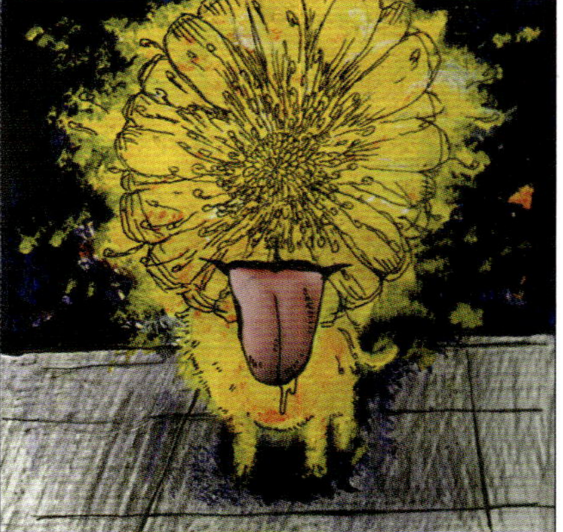

PANIC

A DOG FROM THE POINT OF VIEW OF **A BOOMERANG** IS

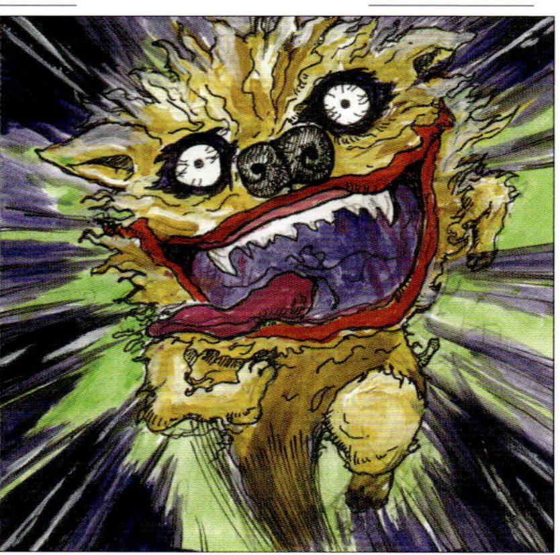

A CHASER

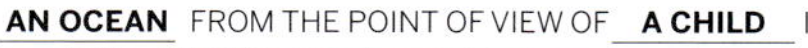

AN OCEAN FROM THE POINT OF VIEW OF **A CHILD** IS

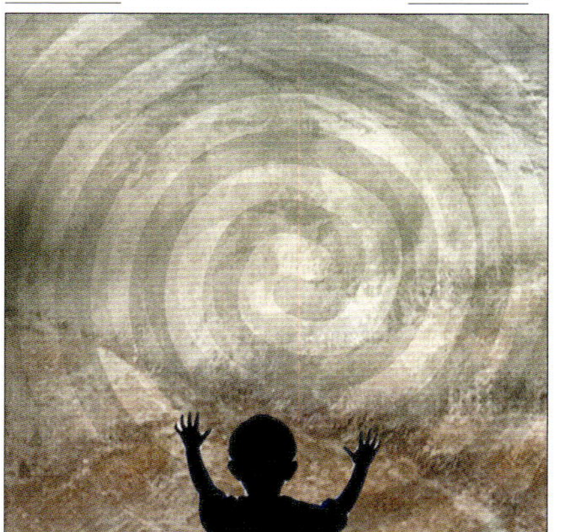

FEAR

A COSTUME FROM THE POINT OF VIEW OF **HALLOWEEN** IS

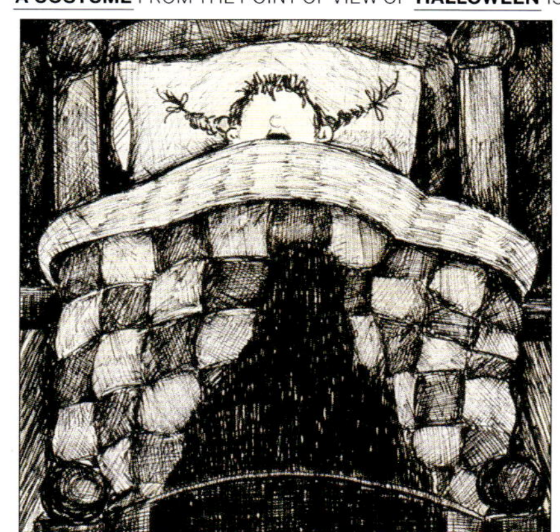

FEAR

FIRE FROM THE POINT OF VIEW OF **A FOREST** IS

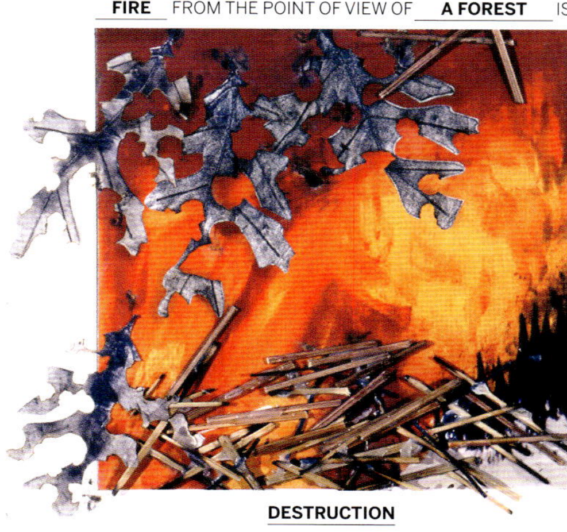

DESTRUCTION

FIRE FROM THE POINT OF VIEW OF **A CAVEMAN** IS

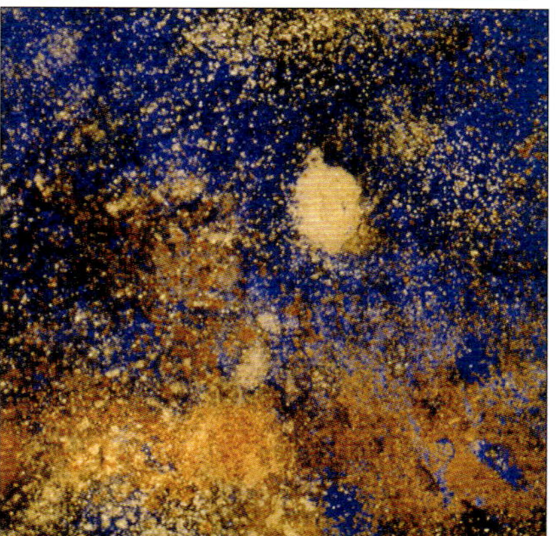

MAGIC

POINT OF VIEW SOLUTIONS:

Figures 1 through 11 deal with various subjects that include: dogs, a child, a costume, fire, fear, and a teddy bear in a scenario of executions, where humor, mystery and anxiety are dealt with.

Figures 1 and 2 are executed by two different students representing the same subject and point of view, but whose executions vary greatly.

Figure 10 depicts what is considered one of man's greatest fears, speaking in front of an audience.

A SHOE FROM THE POINT OF VIEW OF **A CHILD** IS

CONSTRICTION

FEAR FROM THE POINT OF VIEW OF **ME** IS

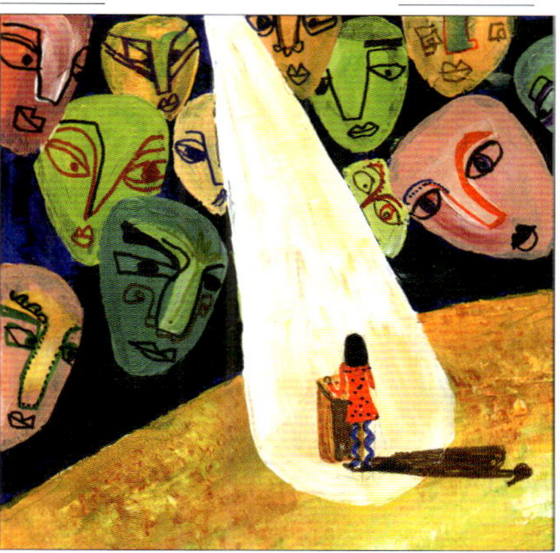

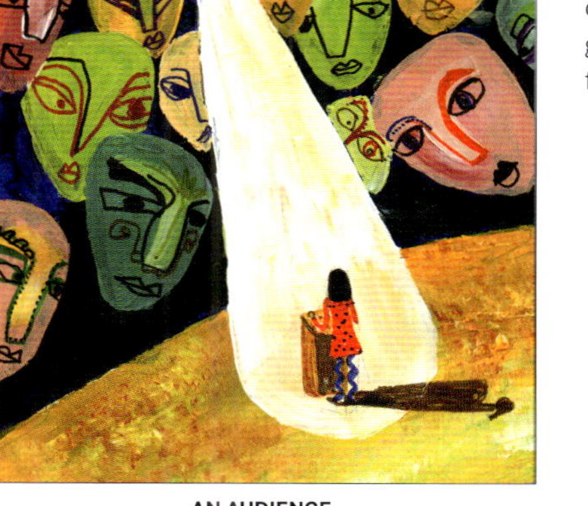

AN AUDIENCE

A TEDDY BEAR FROM THE POINT OF VIEW OF **A BACTERIOLOGIST** IS

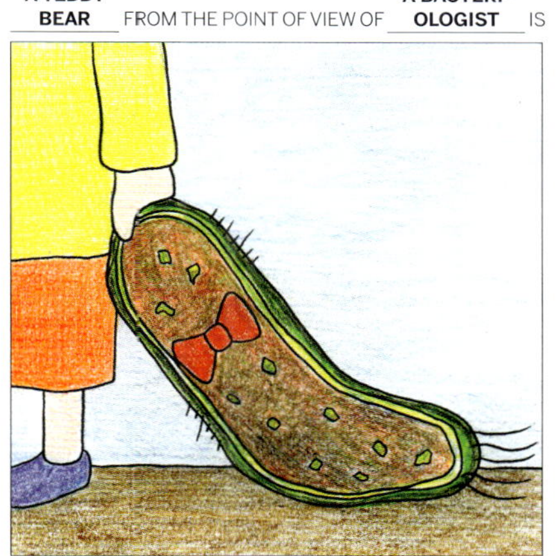

A GERM HABITAT

1. *Michael Black*
2. *Robert Freeman*
3-4. *Deukgyu Lee*
5. *Jessica Scro*
6. *Jackie Frey*
7-8. *Jessica Annunziata*
9. *Alexander Wager*
10. *Eunjung Yoo*
11. *Yerang Wi*

PEPSI FROM THE POINT OF VIEW OF **MARK ROTHKO** IS

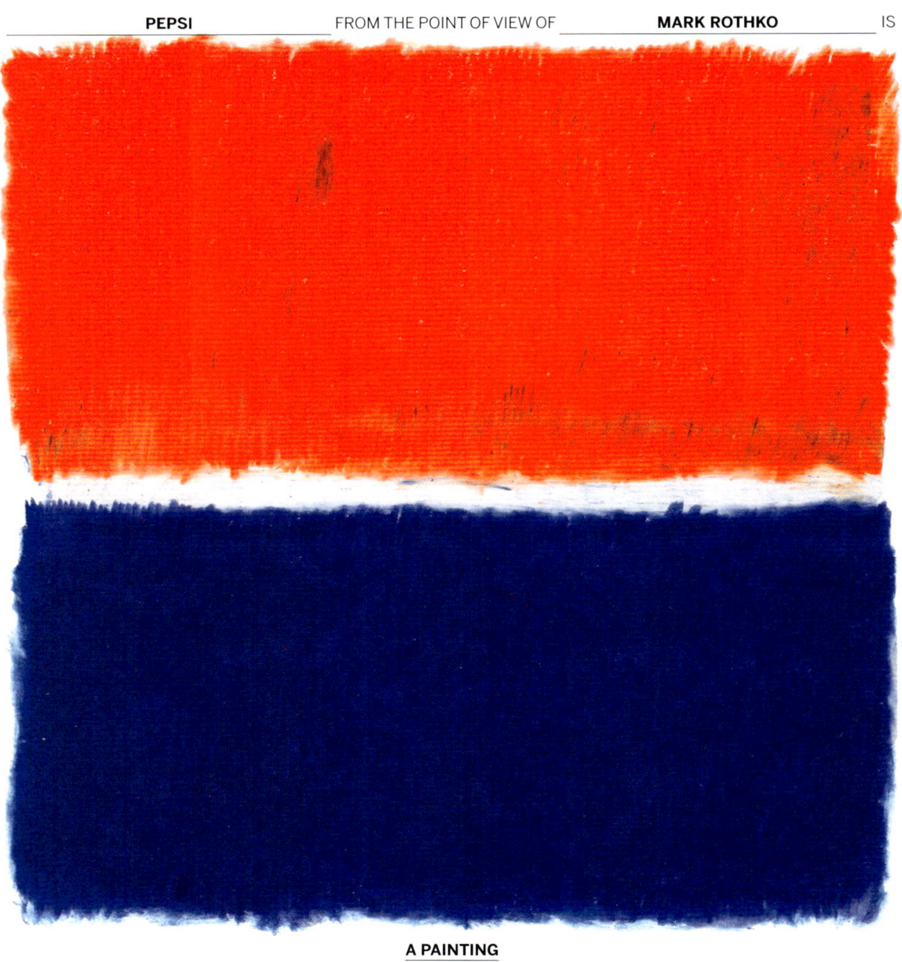

A PAINTING

DINNER FROM THE POINT OF VIEW OF **AN ANOREXIC** IS

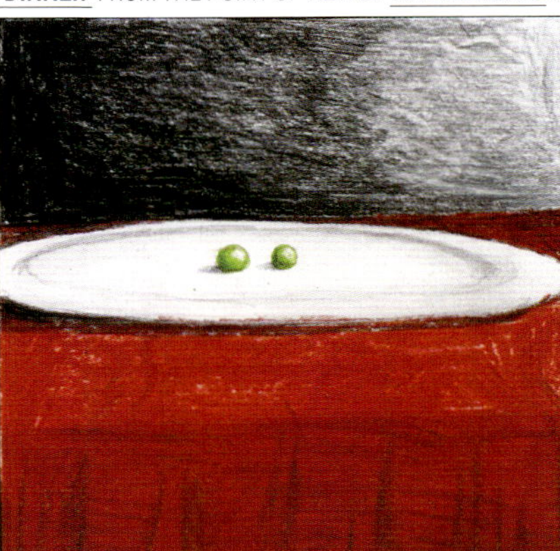

STARVATION

A PAIR OF SHOES FROM THE POINT OF VIEW OF **A COW** IS

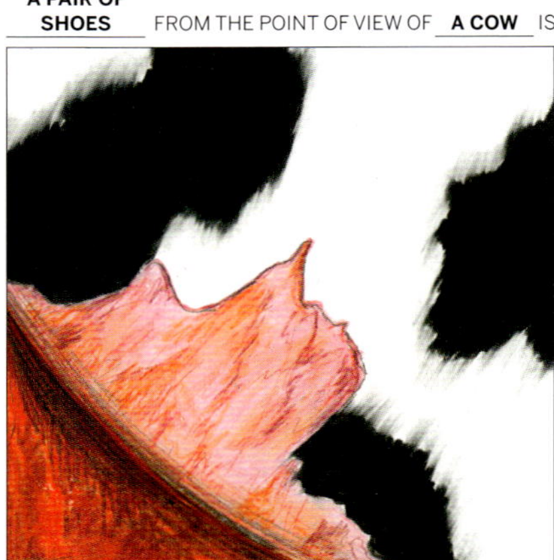

DEATH

RED FROM THE POINT OF VIEW OF **A PRINTER** IS

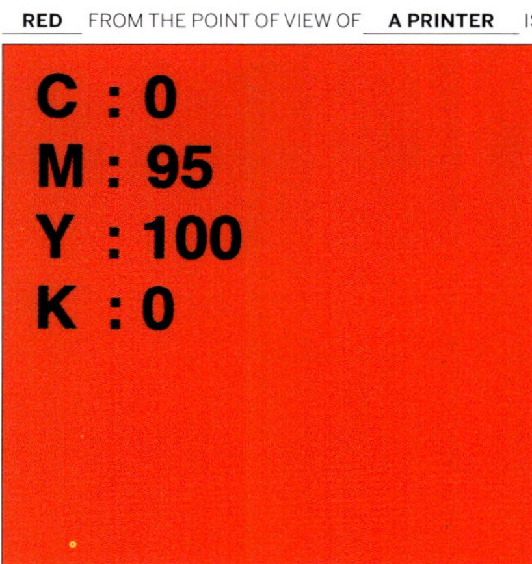

CMYK

THE SUN FROM THE POINT OF VIEW OF **ME** IS

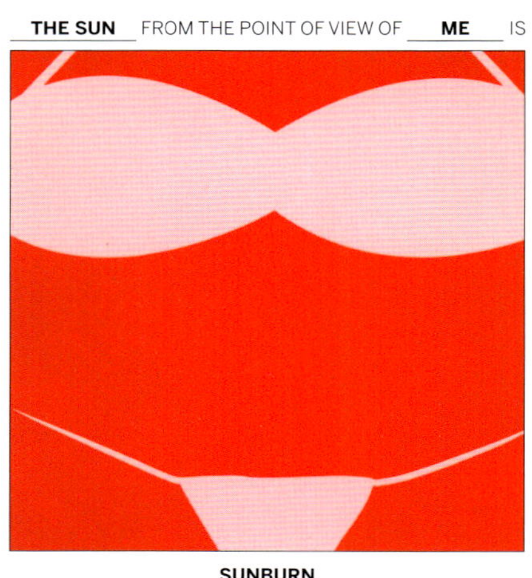

SUNBURN

TEA FROM THE POINT OF VIEW OF **JAPAN** IS

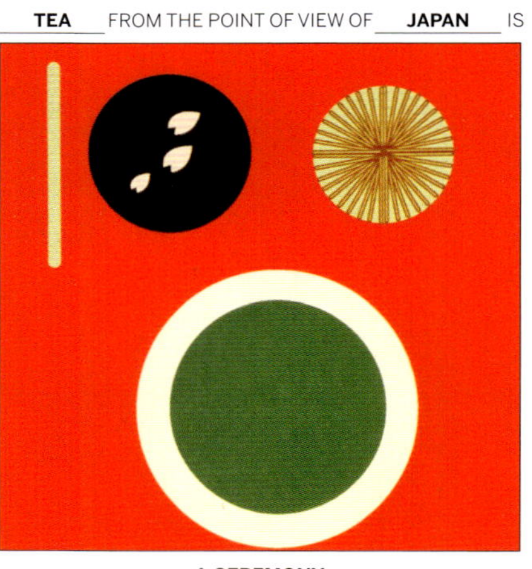

A CEREMONY

POINT OF VIEW SOLUTIONS:

Figures 1 through 6 use the color red to communicate conceptual points of view, with topics that include: a popular soft drink, dinner, shoes, the color red, the sun and tea.

Figures 7 through 12 deal with sexual connotations, ranging from the frivolous to the "practical."

SEX FROM THE POINT OF VIEW OF **MY EX-GIRLFRIEND** IS

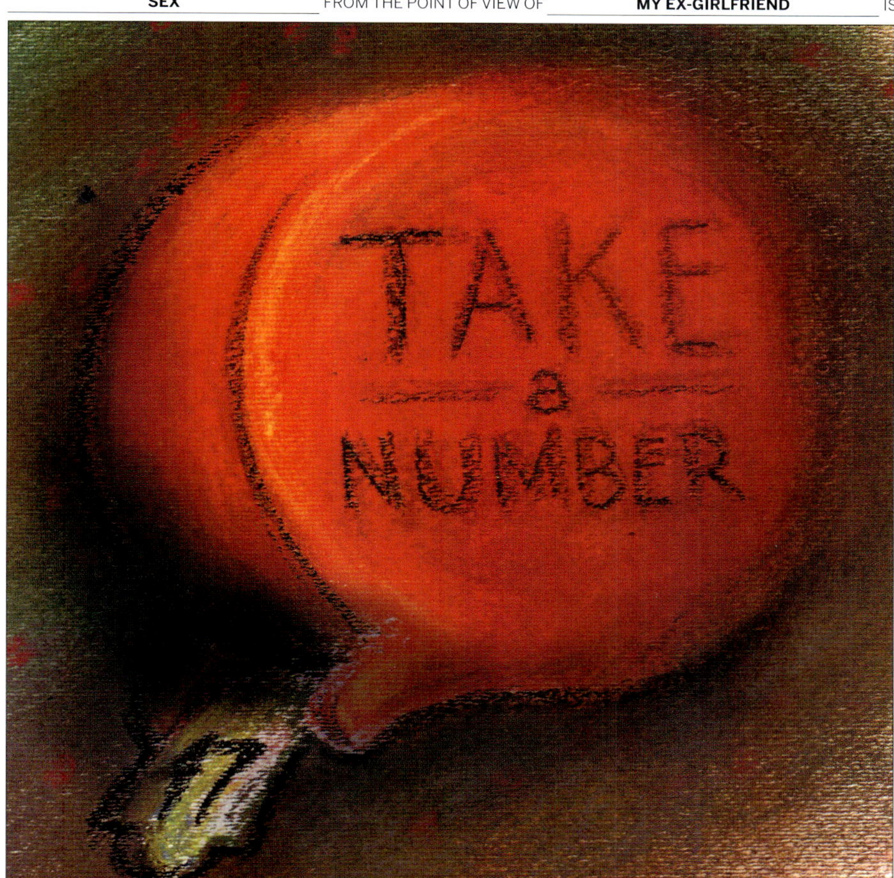

GET IN LINE

A BRA FROM THE POINT OF VIEW OF **A BOYFRIEND** IS

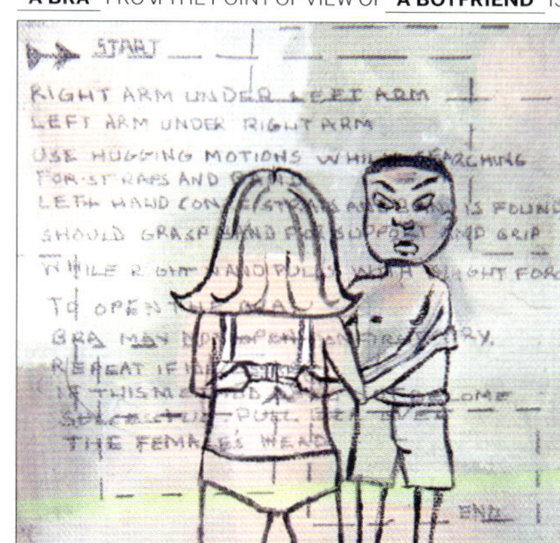

A COMPLICATED PROPOSITION

A PORN MAGAZINE FROM THE POINT OF VIEW OF **A GEEK** IS

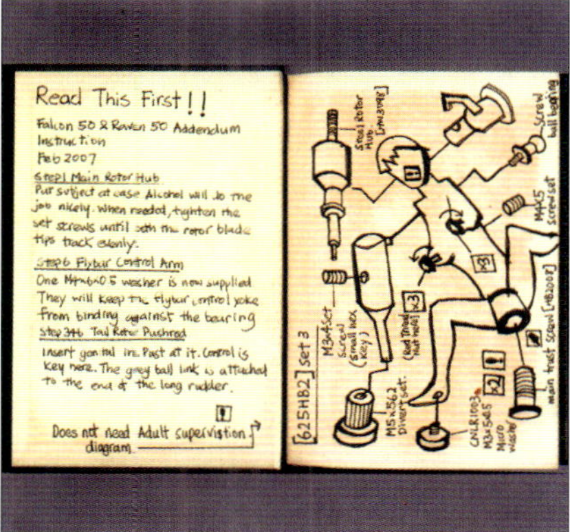

AN INSTRUCTIONAL MANUAL

A BREAST FROM THE POINT OF VIEW OF **AN ARCHITECT** IS

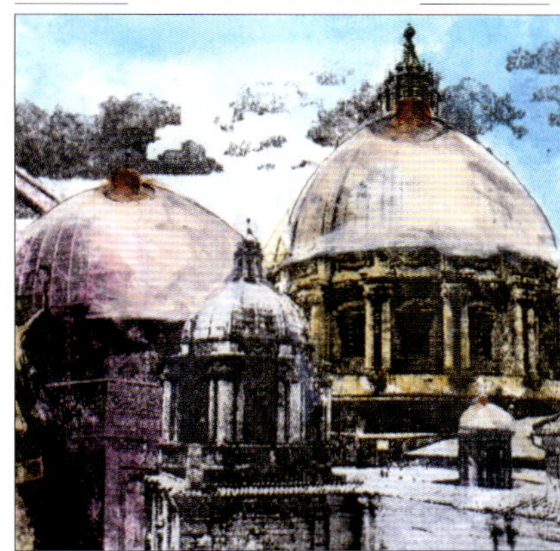

A DOME

A BREAST FROM THE POINT OF VIEW OF **AN ALPINIST** IS

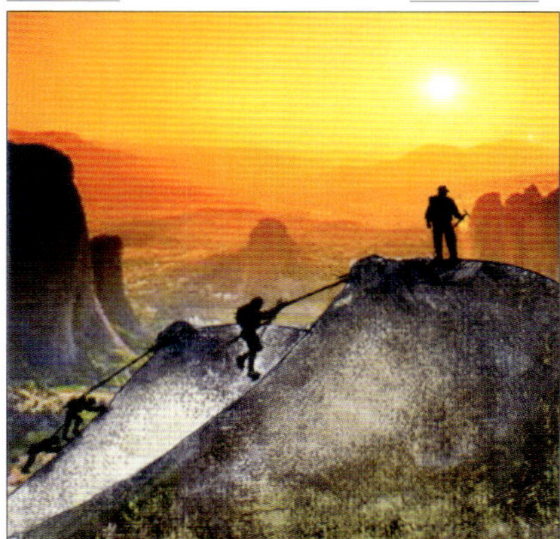

A MOUNTAIN TO CONQUER

SPERM FROM THE POINT OF VIEW OF **ANOTHER SPERM** IS

COMPETITION

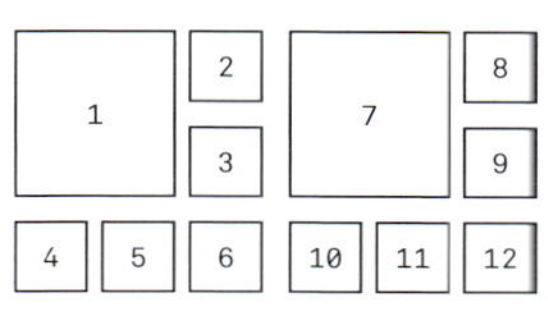

1. *Eric Ku*
2. *Deniz Yegen*
3. *John Allen*
4. *Alfred Park*
5. *Naomie Ross*
6. *Yoko Hayashi*
7. *Paul Motisi*
8. *Faith Laurel*
9. *Shing Ming Ho*

10–11. *Jinyoung Lee*

12. *Sabina Ciari*

HAIR FROM THE POINT OF VIEW OF **CHEMOTHERAPY** IS

HAIR FROM THE POINT OF VIEW OF **A TOPOGRAPHER** IS

HAIR FROM THE POINT OF VIEW OF **A PIECE OF GUM** IS

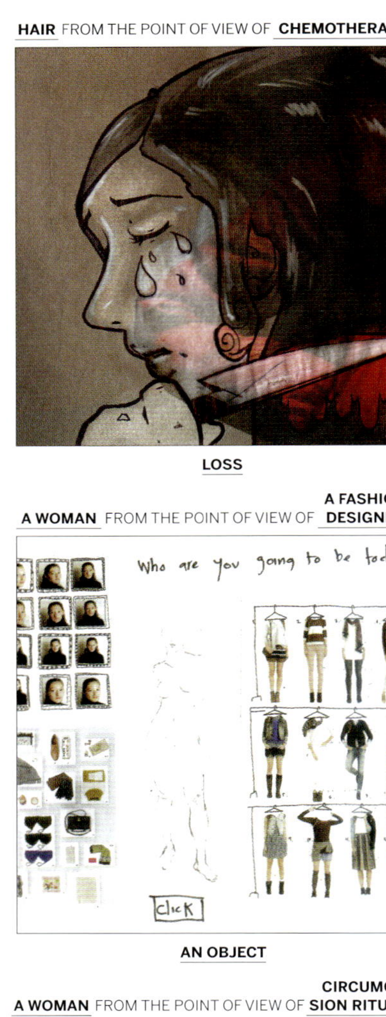

LOSS

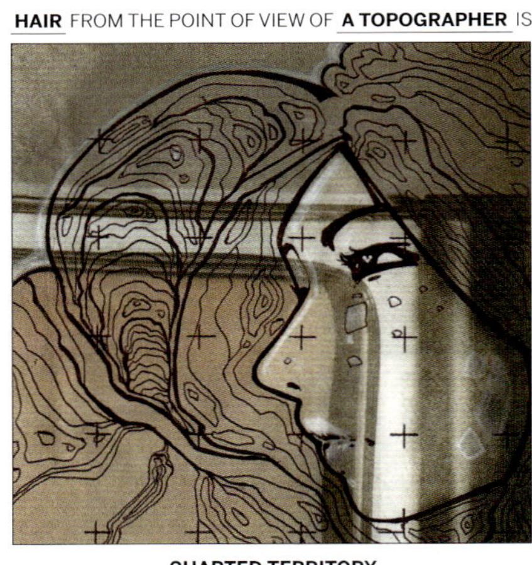
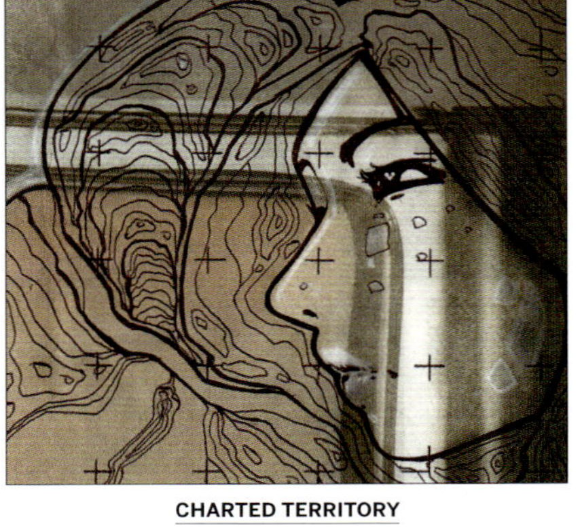

CHARTED TERRITORY

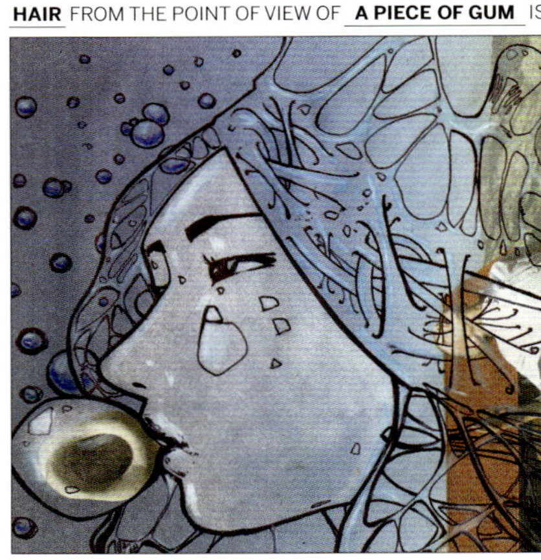

HOPELESSLY TANGLED

A WOMAN FROM THE POINT OF VIEW OF **A FASHION DESIGNER** IS

AN OBJECT

A WOMAN FROM THE POINT OF VIEW OF **CIRCUMCI-SION RITUALS** IS

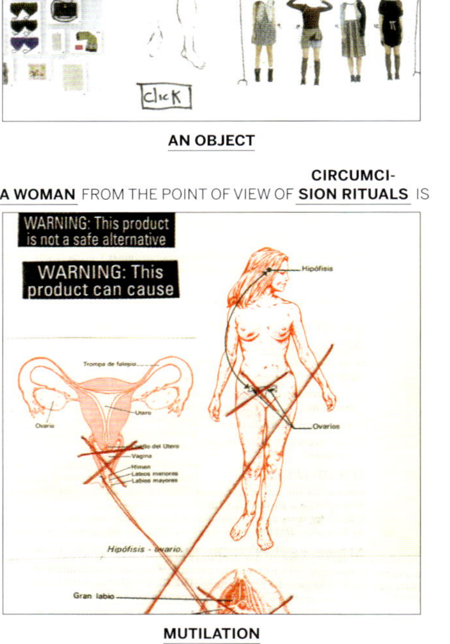

MUTILATION

A WOMAN FROM THE POINT OF VIEW OF **A GUY'S MIND** IS

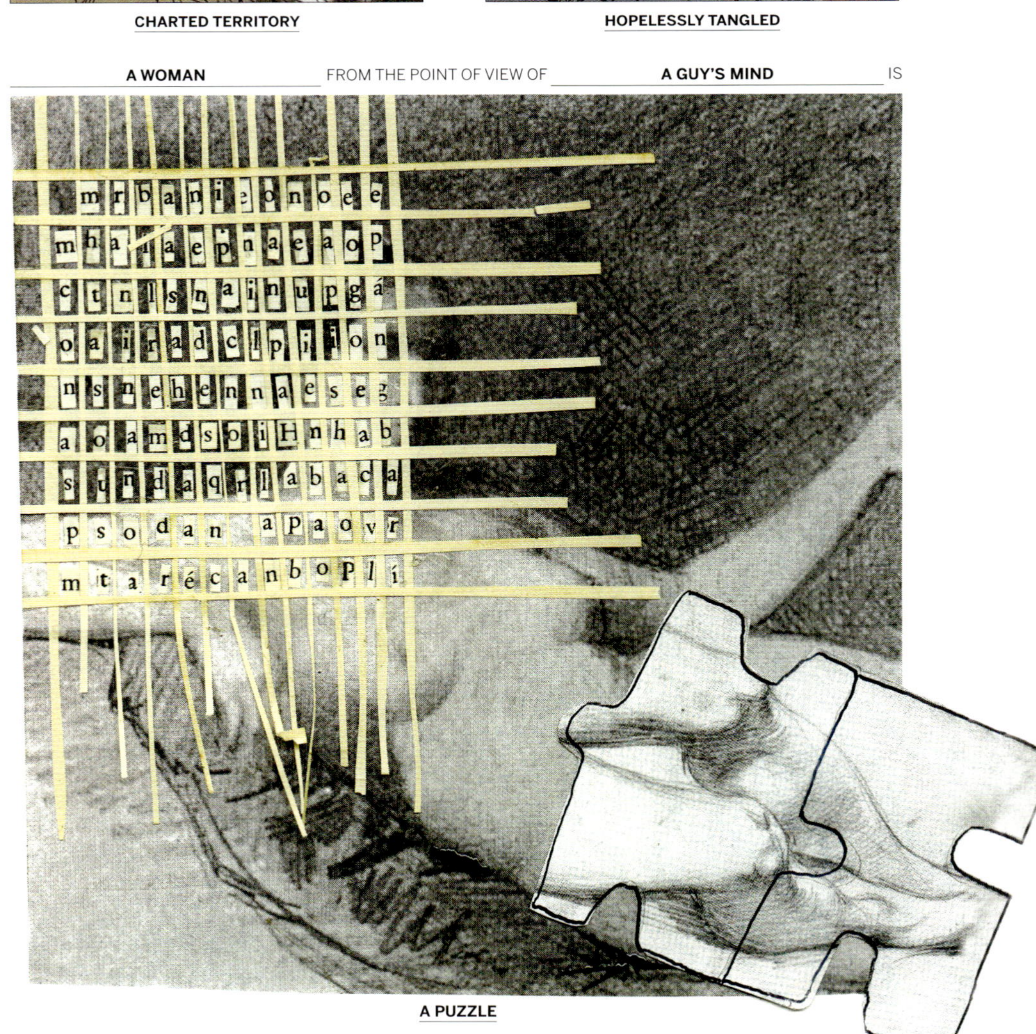

A PUZZLE

HAIR FROM THE POINT OF VIEW OF A DRAINPIPE IS

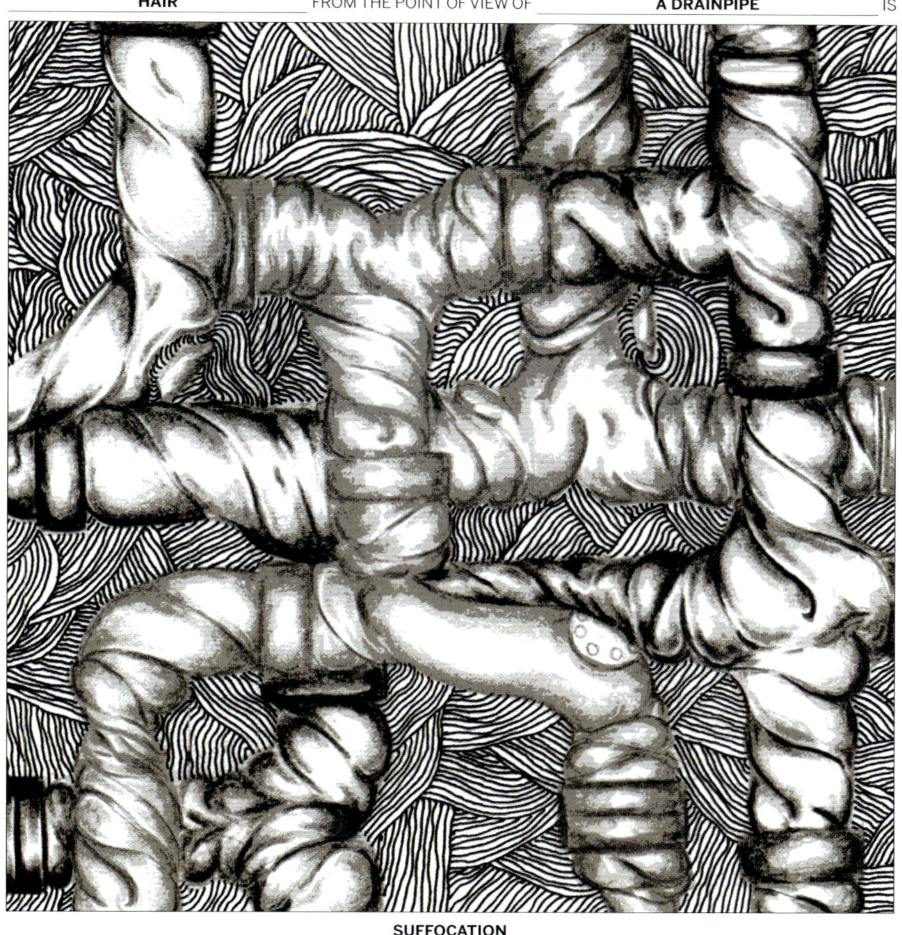

SUFFOCATION

HAIR FROM THE POINT OF VIEW OF A STYLIST IS

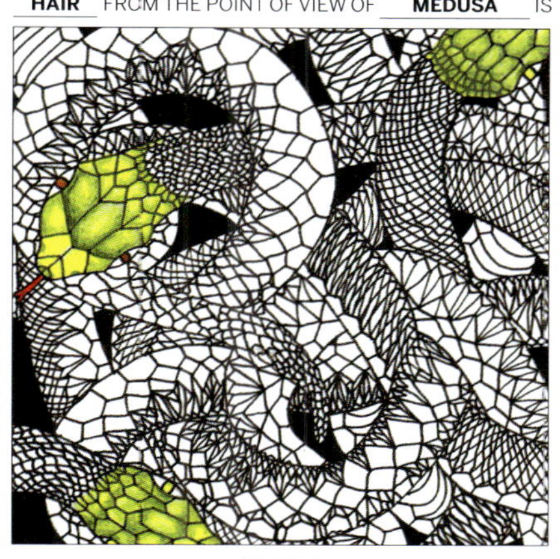

MANAGEMENT

HAIR FROM THE POINT OF VIEW OF MEDUSA IS

SNAKES

HAIR FROM THE POINT OF VIEW OF SCISSORS IS

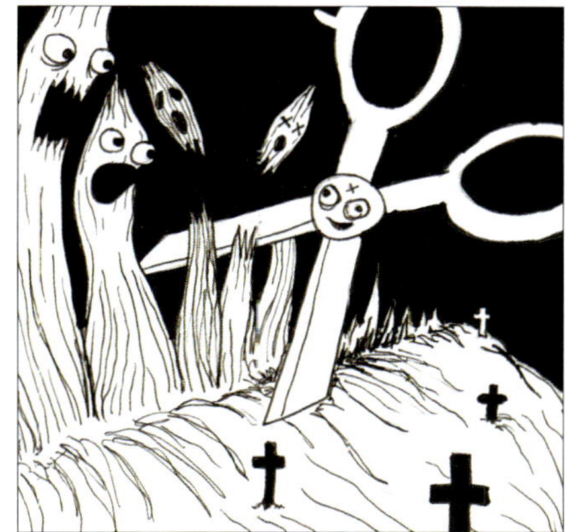

BEHEADING

HAIR FROM THE POINT OF VIEW OF A COMB IS

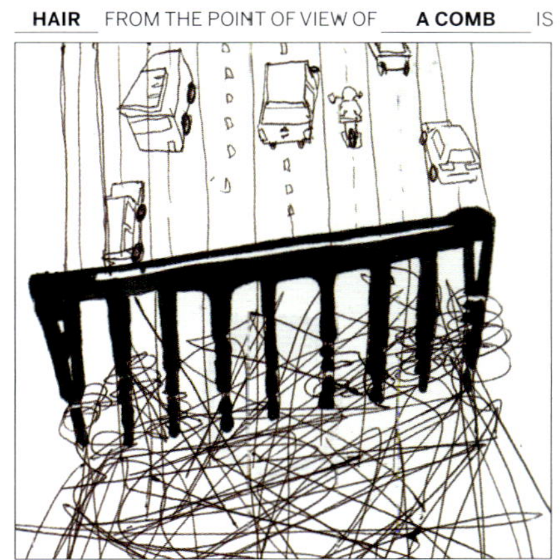

A TRAFFIC DIRECTOR

HAIR FROM THE POINT OF VIEW OF A MAGNIFIED CROSS SECTION IS

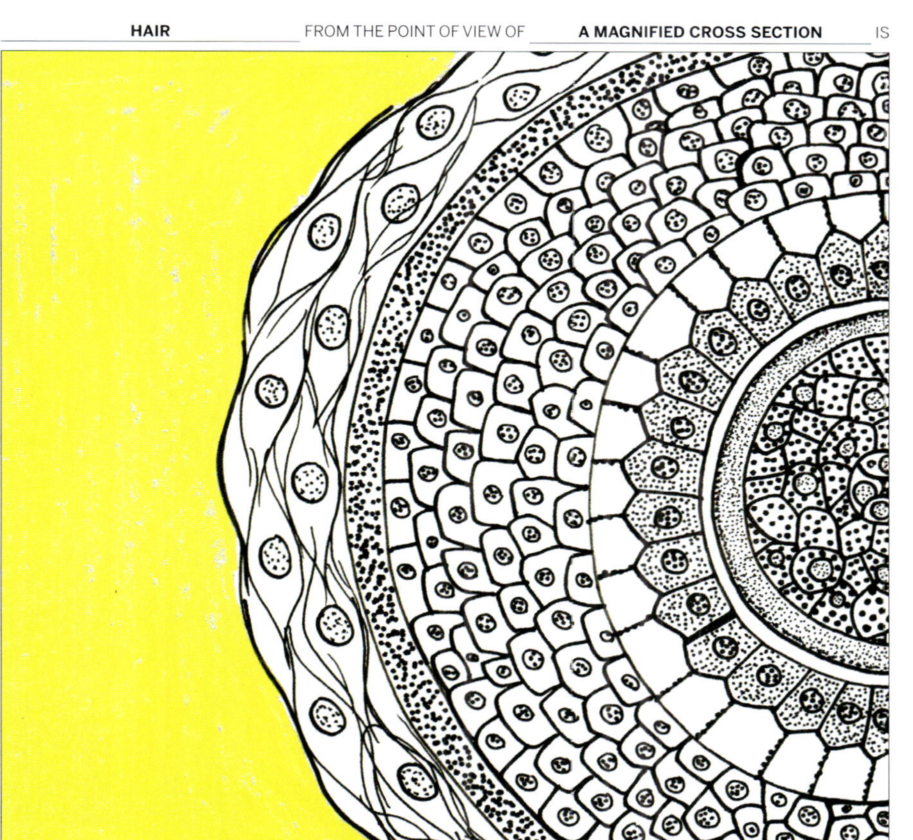

A WORLD UNTO ITSELF

POINT OF VIEW SOLUTIONS:

Figures 1 through 3 and figures 7 through 12 investigate the subject of hair.

Figure 1 deals with the loss of hair, while figure 2 deals with hair that is an imagined dimensional landscape, and figure 3 is hair that is hopelessly tangled.

Figures 4 through 6 use the subject of women to make social statements that deal with objectification, tribal mutilation, and mystery.

Figures 7 through 12 address hair from various perspectives, ranging from abstract to literal solutions.

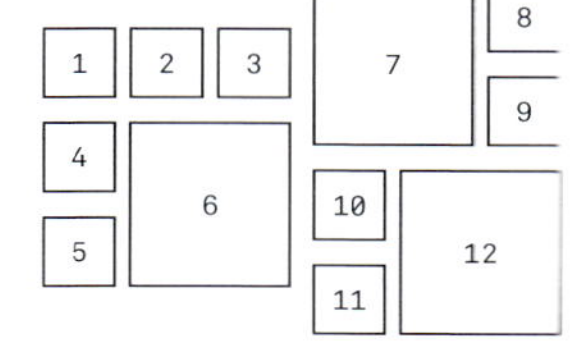

1–3. *Danjyu Ono*
4–6. *Karen Montero*
7–9. *Aerial Chen*
10. *Michael Ungano*
11. *Hyoju Hong*
12. *Aerial Chen*

THE SUN FROM THE POINT OF VIEW OF **THE UNIVERSE** IS

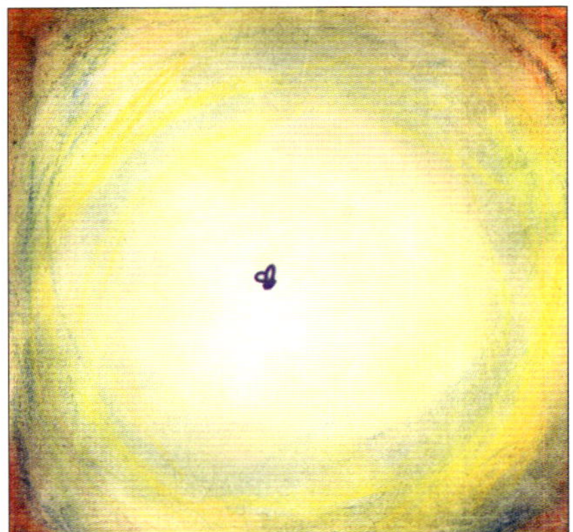

A FIREFLY

CHOCOLATE FROM THE POINT OF VIEW OF **THE BRAIN** IS

A POWER SURGE

A COCKROACH FROM THE POINT OF VIEW OF **LIGHT** IS

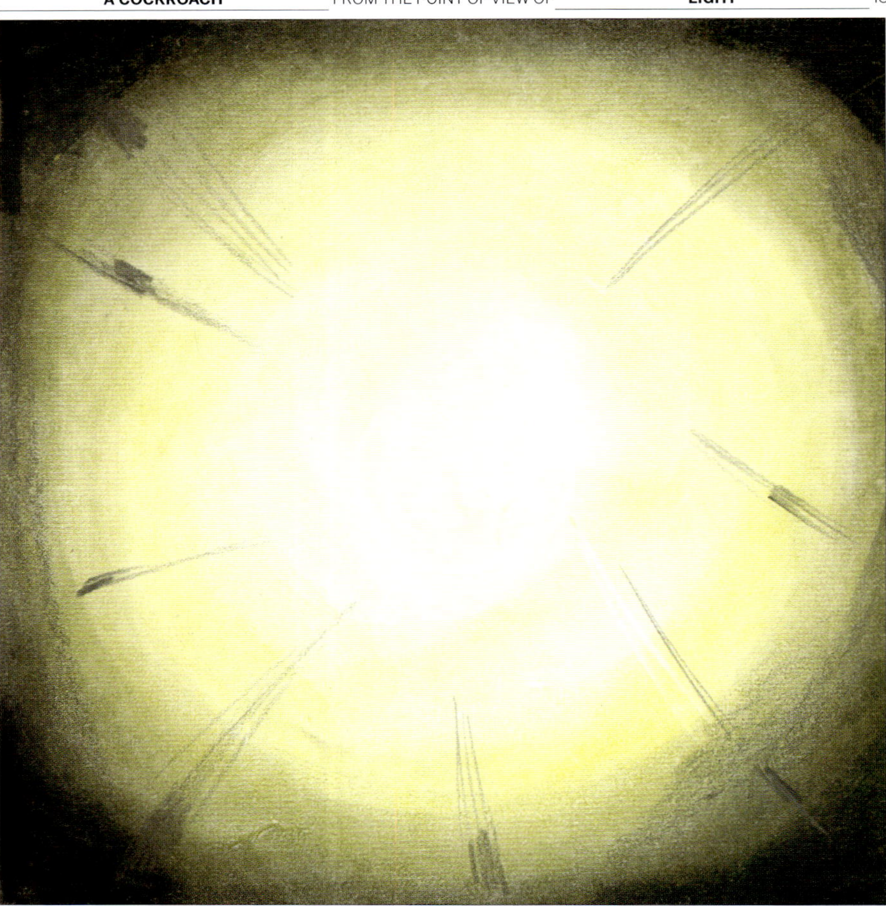

A DISAPPEARING ACT

A DOT FROM THE POINT OF VIEW OF **AN HISTOLOGIST** IS

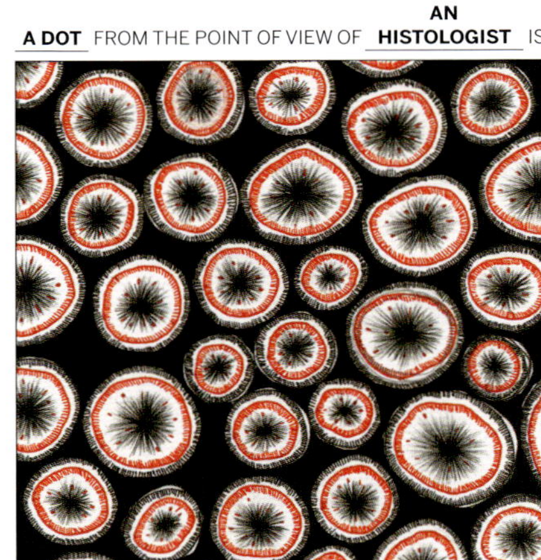

A STUDY

A DOT FROM THE POINT OF VIEW OF **A LEPIDOP-TERIST** IS

CAMOUFLAGE

A SIDEWALK FROM THE POINT OF VIEW OF **A PIGEON** IS

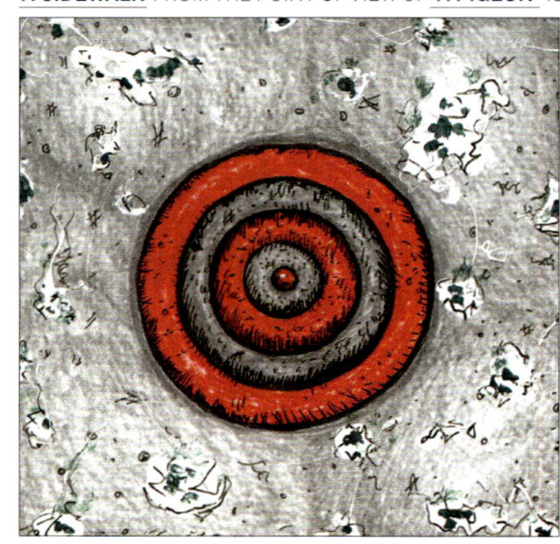

A TARGET

A DOT FROM THE POINT OF VIEW OF **A FROG** IS

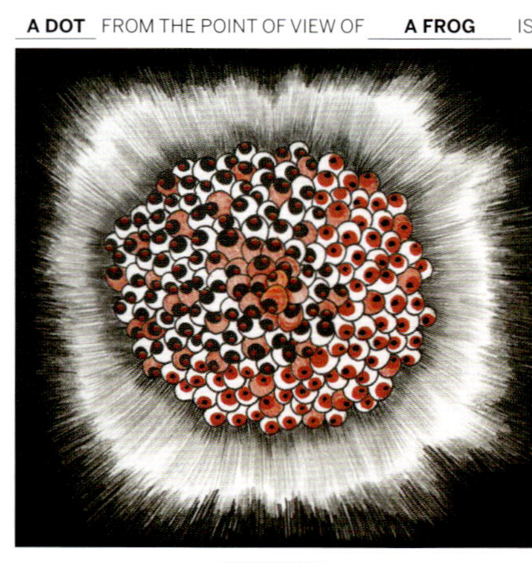

AN EMBRYO

A BALLOON FROM THE POINT OF VIEW OF A CHILD IS

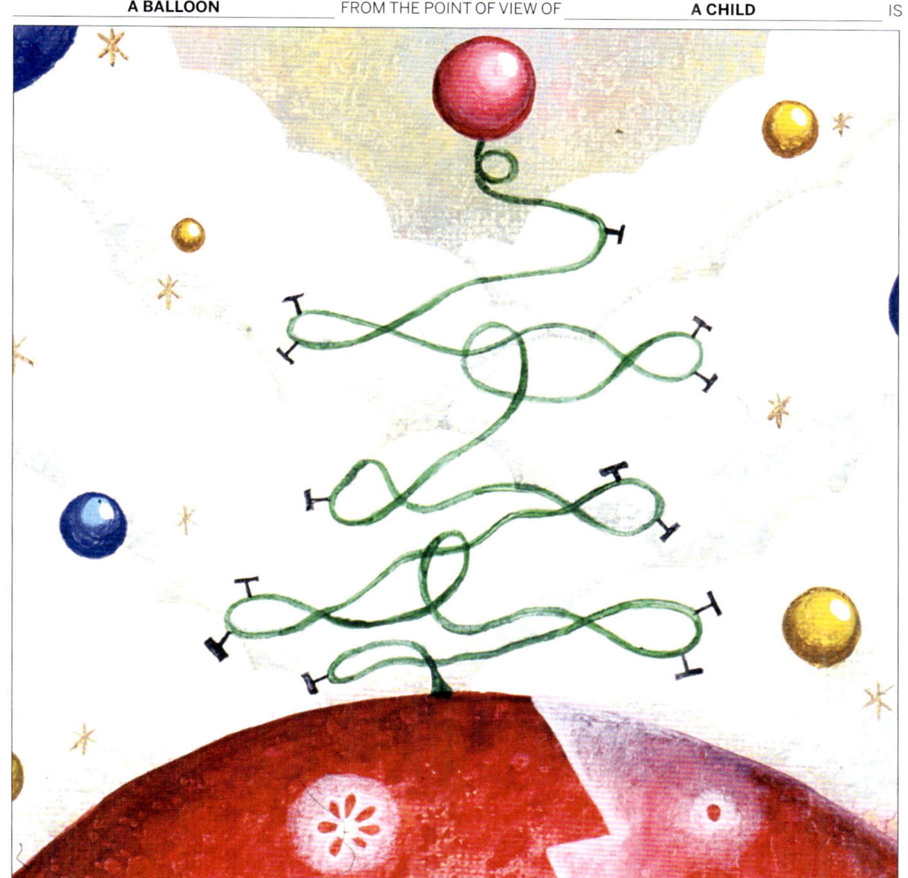

ASTONISHMENT

A RELATIVE FROM THE POINT OF VIEW OF A CHILD IS

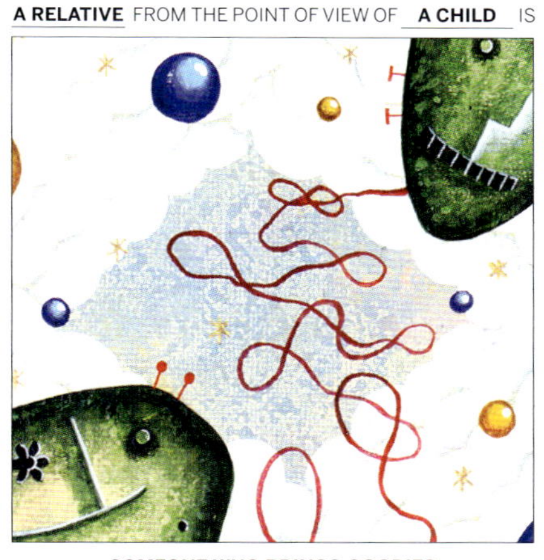

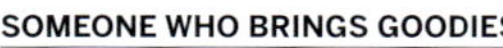

SOMEONE WHO BRINGS GOODIES

A FISH FROM THE POINT OF VIEW OF A CHILD IS

A PET

CANDY FROM THE POINT OF VIEW OF A CHILD IS

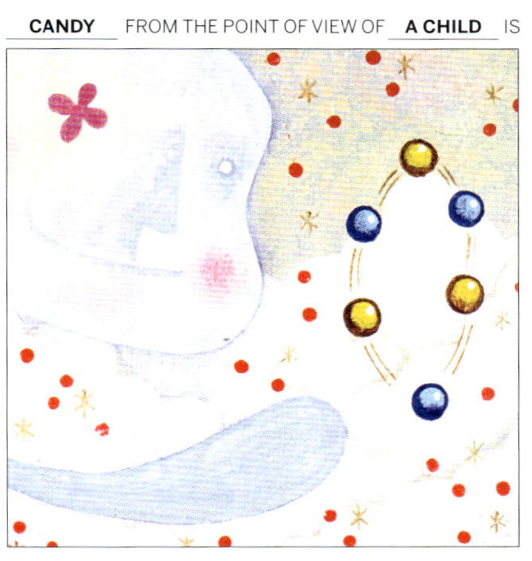

HAPPINESS

A TEDDY BEAR FROM THE POINT OF VIEW OF A CHILD IS

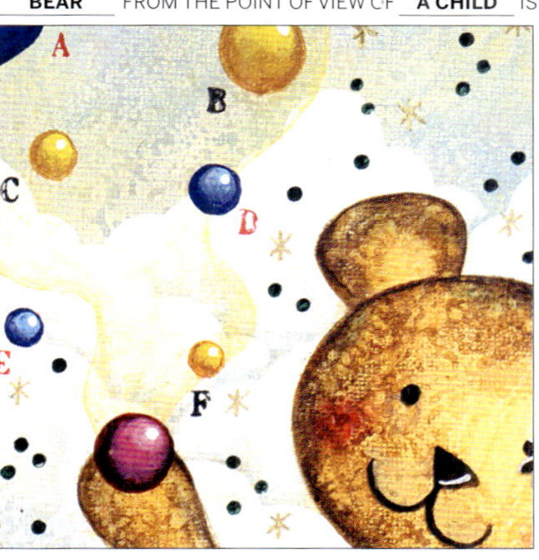

A BEST FRIEND

POINT OF VIEW SOLUTIONS:

Figures 1 through 7 concern themselves with circular imagery.

Figure 1 deals with a metaphoric approach to dramatize the concept of scale.

Figure 2 deals with the physiological effect of chocolate on one's brain.

Figure 3 addresses the effect of switching on a light to the behavior of cockroaches and figures 4 through 7 deal with circular patterns found in nature.

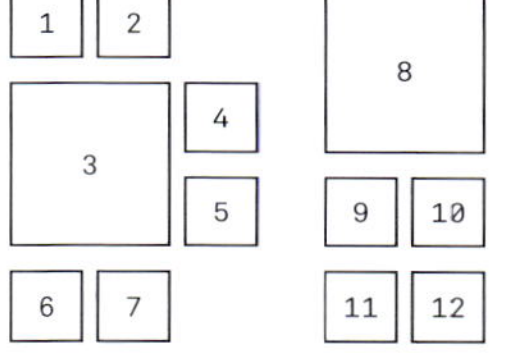

1. *Samantha Raso*
2. *Ravi Yeara*
3. *Meeseung Kim*
4–5. *Nicole Lapenta*
6. *Adam Kostman*
7. *Nicole Lapenta*
8–12. *H. Kim*

Figures 8 through 12 represent a variation on the Point of View assignment, where the initial subjects vary, but the point of view remains the same. All the solutions depict a child's vision of life.

Although the project was done in reverse, it successfully communicates a specific point of view.

A VAGINA FROM THE POINT OF VIEW OF **A FETUS** IS

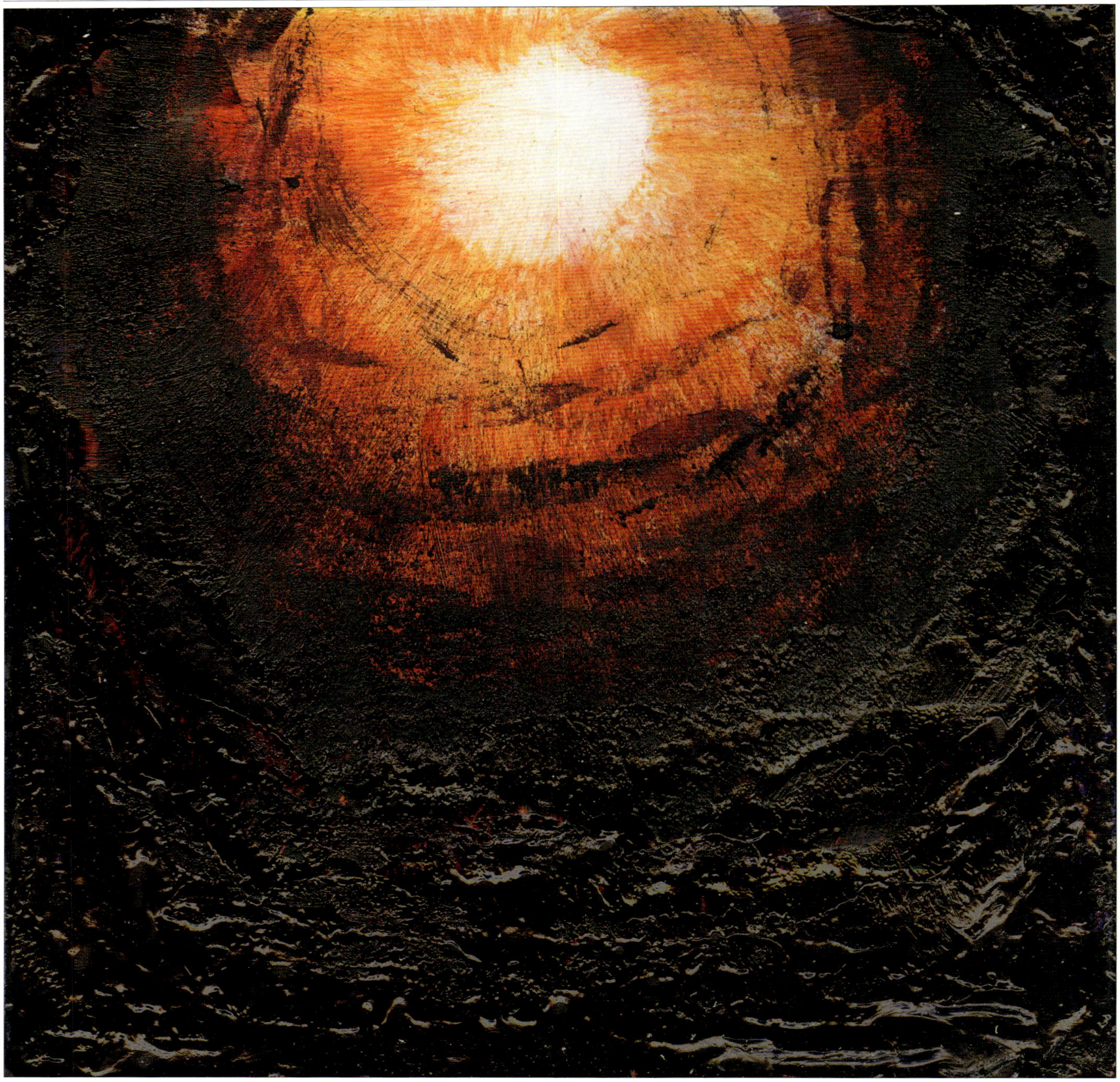

AN EXIT

POINT OF VIEW SOLUTIONS:

Figure 1 depicts an image from the inside looking out, just before the birth of a child.

Figures 2 through 4 use collage to create abstract interpretations, yet given the context of each, the narratives are evident. Solutions range from: figure 2, a sorrowful tale, to figure 3, a fly's cuisine, to figure 4, the relationship between sunlight and coffee beans. This solution could pertain to the effect of the sun on the coffee bean as well as beginning one's day with a cup of coffee at sunrise.

TRASH FROM THE POINT OF VIEW OF **A HOMELESS PERSON** IS

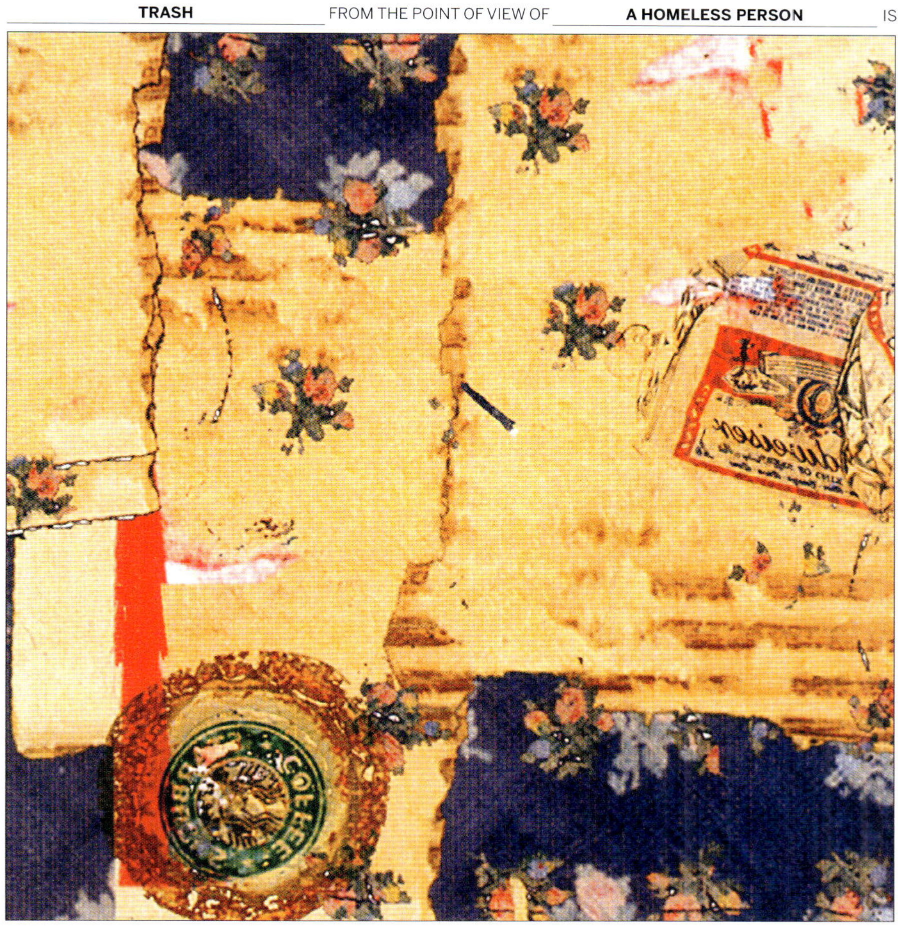

TREASURE

TRASH FROM THE POINT OF VIEW OF **A FLY** IS

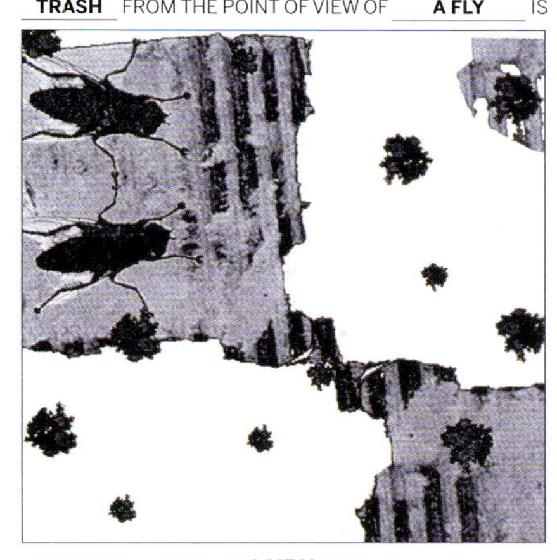

A MEAL

COFFEE FROM THE POINT OF VIEW OF **SUNRISE** IS

THE PERFECT MATE

1 | 2 | 3 | 4

1. Michael Mejia
2–3. Susan Park
4. Laura Pocier

MY PET FERRET FROM THE POINT OF VIEW OF **MY MOM** IS

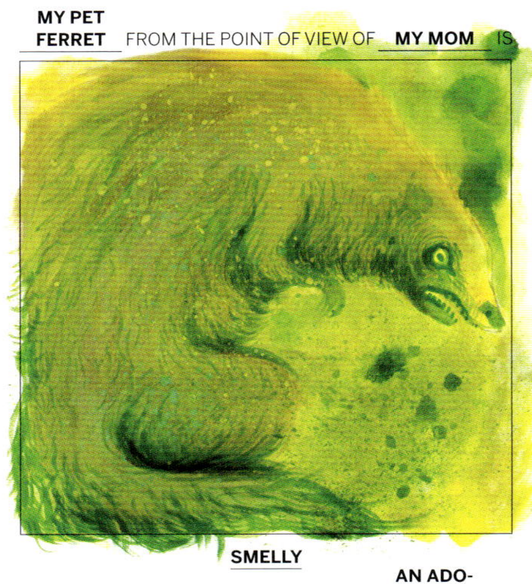

SMELLY

EVOLUTION FROM THE POINT OF VIEW OF **AN AMOEBA** IS

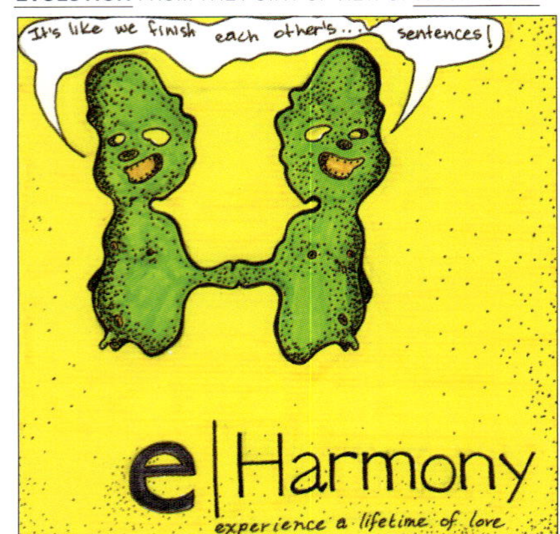

ASEXUAL REPRODUCTION

CHEESE FROM THE POINT OF VIEW OF **MILK** IS

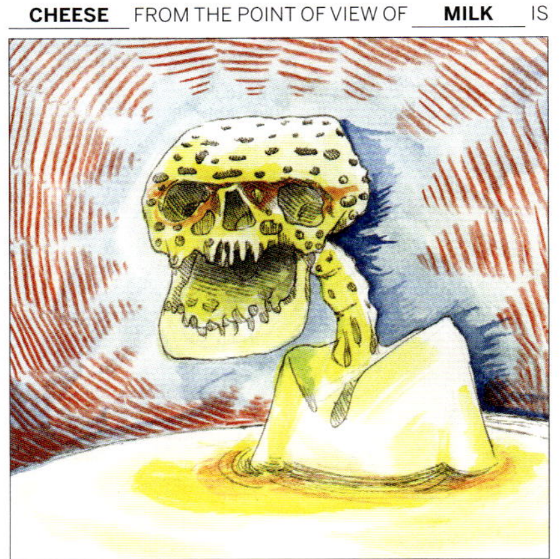

DEATH BY CURDLING

A BOTTLE FROM THE POINT OF VIEW OF **AN ADO-LESCENT'S PARTY** IS

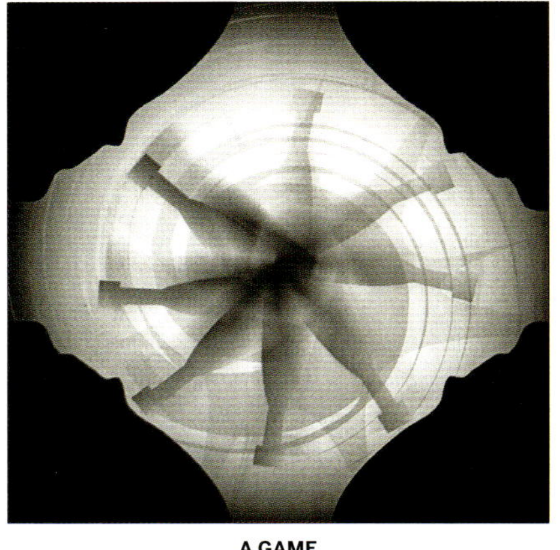

A GAME

A MIRROR FROM THE POINT OF VIEW OF **A VAMPIRE** IS

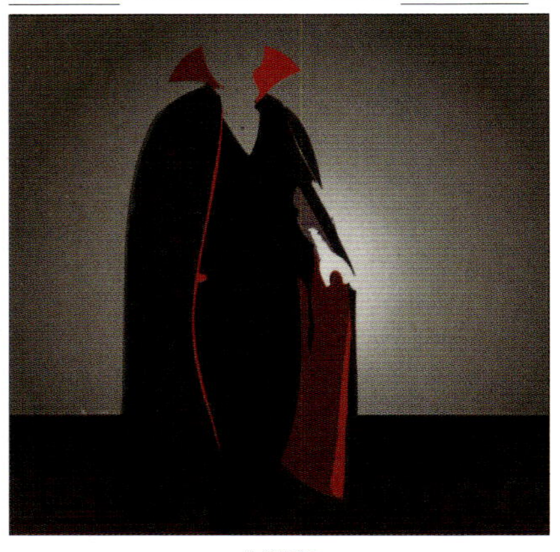

A CAPE

A SHOE FROM THE POINT OF VIEW OF **A THIRD WORLD COUNTRY** IS

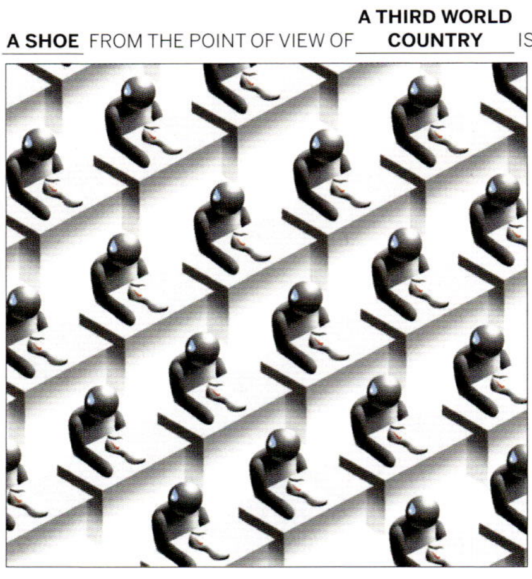

A LIVELIHOOD

PAPER FROM THE POINT OF VIEW OF **ME** IS

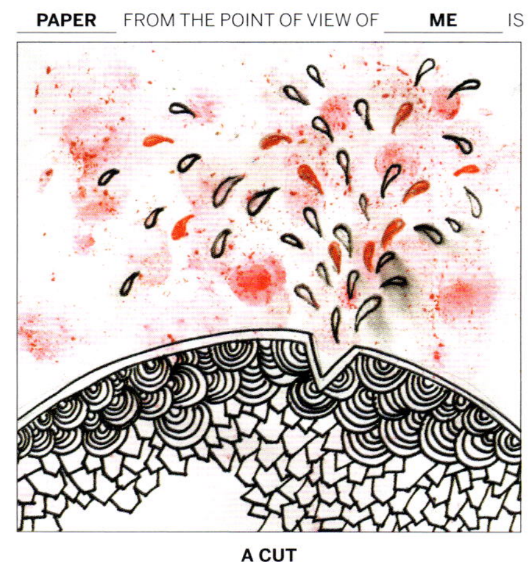

A CUT

WAR FROM THE POINT OF VIEW OF **A GENERAL** IS

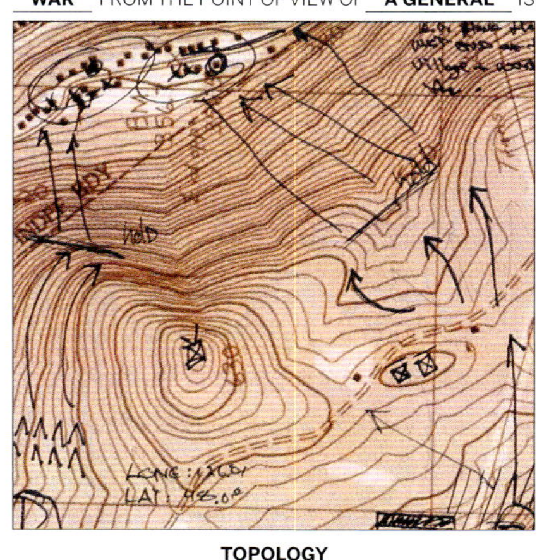

TOPOLOGY

A FRANKFURTER FROM THE POINT OF VIEW OF **A BUN** IS

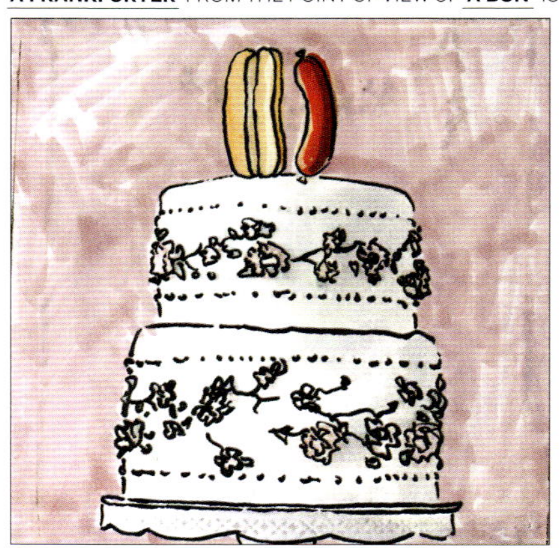

A MARRIAGE

POINT OF VIEW SOLUTIONS:

All fifteen solutions range from computer-generated imagery, as seen in figures 4 through 6, to hand-drawn executions, appearing in figures 1 through 3 and 7 through 15.

For most all solutions appearing in this project, the concept not only dictates the form, but dictates the medium as well.

GOD FROM THE POINT OF VIEW OF **A BUDDHIST** IS

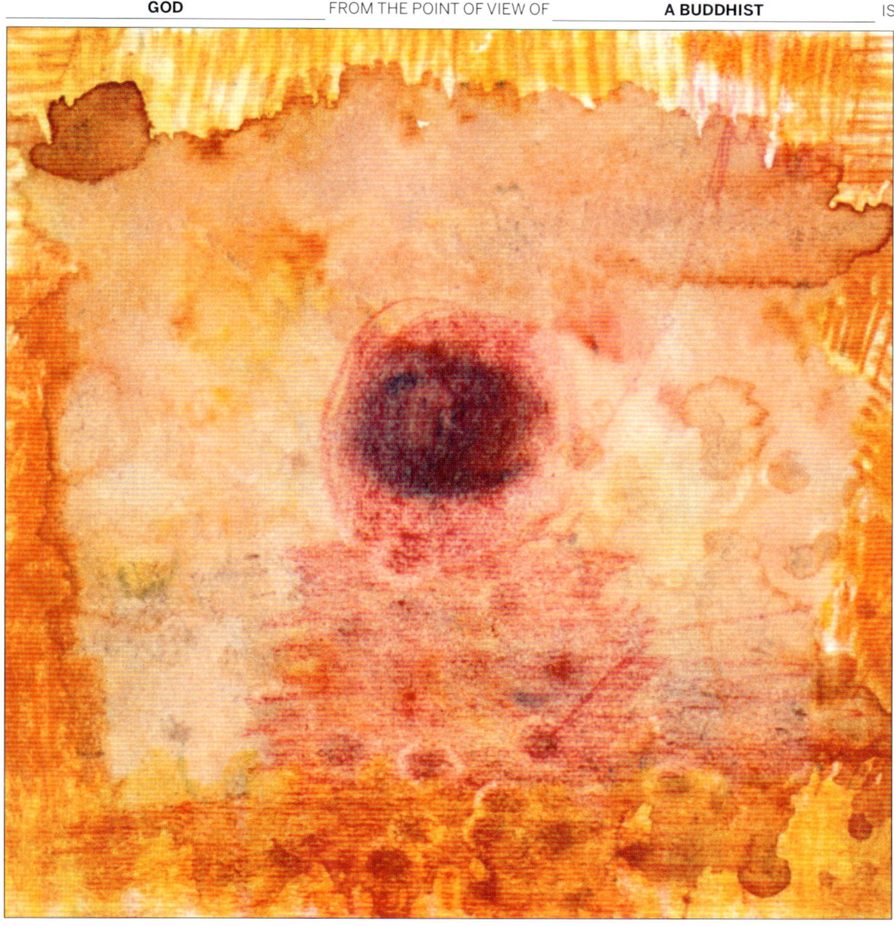

OM

THE COLOR GREEN FROM THE POINT OF VIEW OF **A CHILD** IS

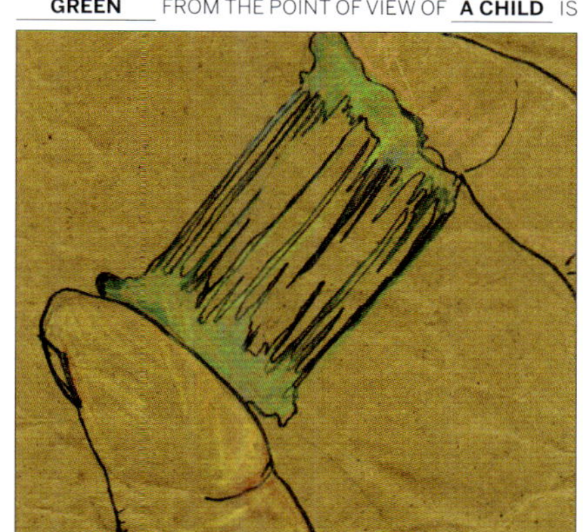
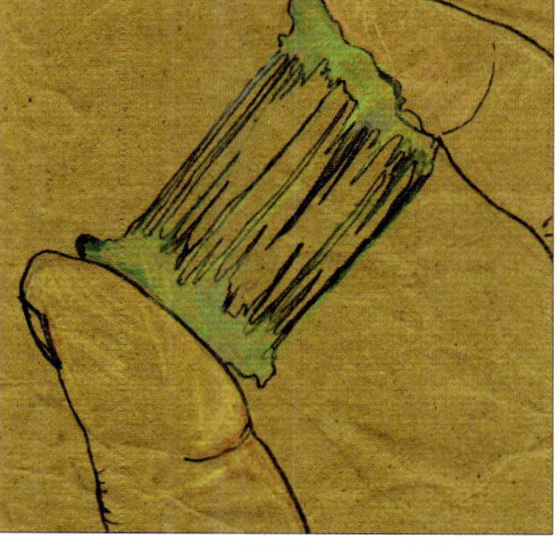
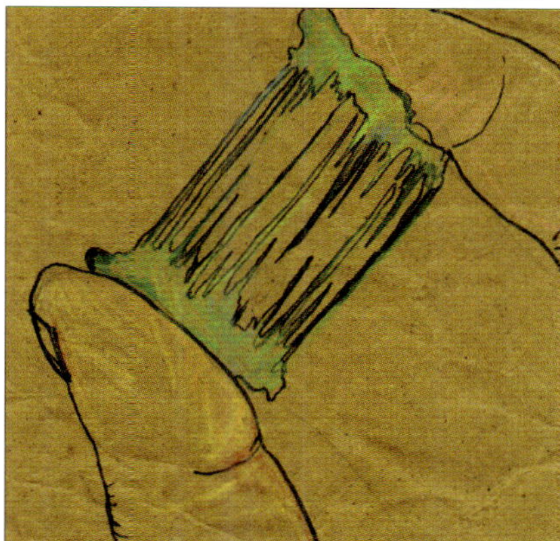

YUCKY

A DINOSAUR FROM THE POINT OF VIEW OF **A TAR PIT** IS

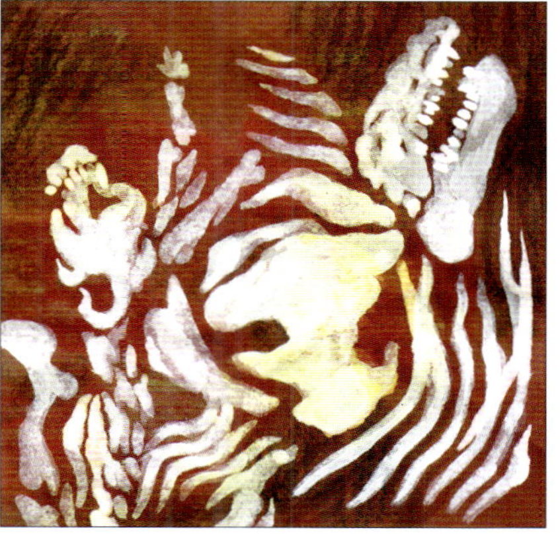

A FOSSIL

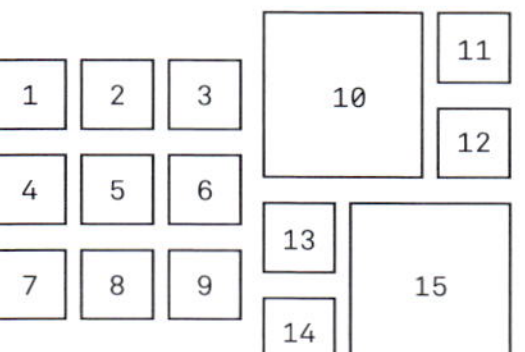

1. *Amy Churchwell*
2. *Jason Arias*
3. *Catherine Small*
4. *Sarah Nguyen*
5. *Nicholas Saint Onge*
6. *Felix Velez*
7. *Saeyoon Kim*
8. *Josh Clark*
9. *Maria Sanoja*
10. *Max Kaplun*
11. *Jeong Kong*
12. *Chris Wright*
13. *Dayeong Lee*
14. *Hyena Song*
15. *Haeree Kim*

EYE BALLS FROM THE POINT OF VIEW OF **A MONSTER** ARE

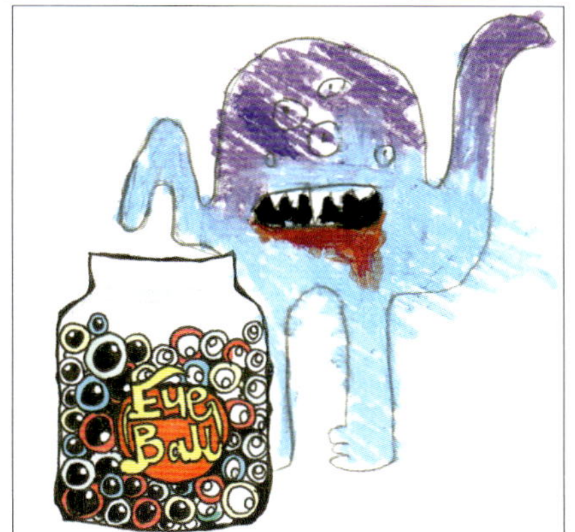

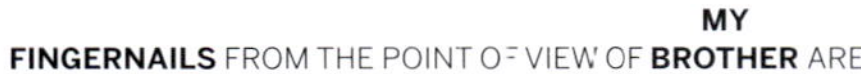

JELLY BEANS

FINGERNAILS FROM THE POINT OF VIEW OF **MY BROTHER** ARE

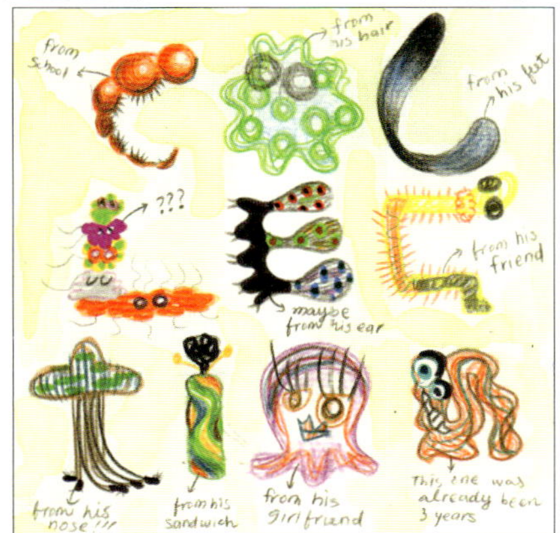

GERM COLLECTORS

HAPPINESS FROM THE POINT OF VIEW OF **ME** IS

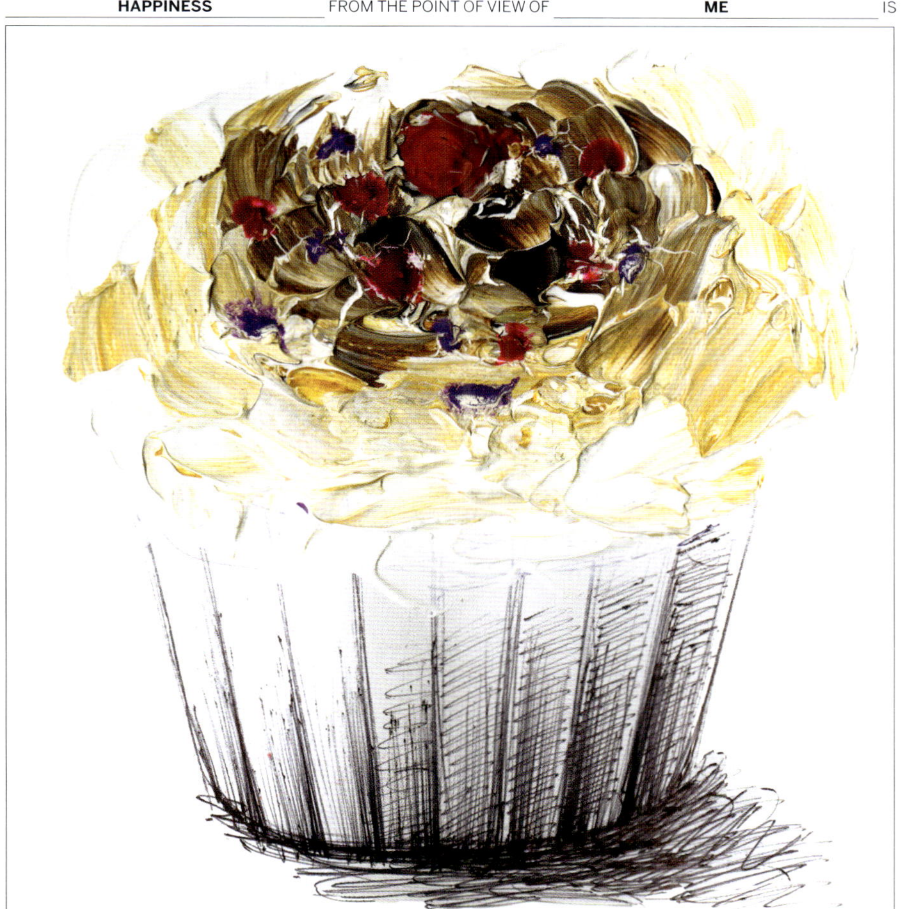

A CUPCAKE

A BOOK FROM THE POINT OF VIEW OF **A SOLITARY PERSON** IS

A FRIEND

A BOOK FROM THE POINT OF VIEW OF **PAPER** IS

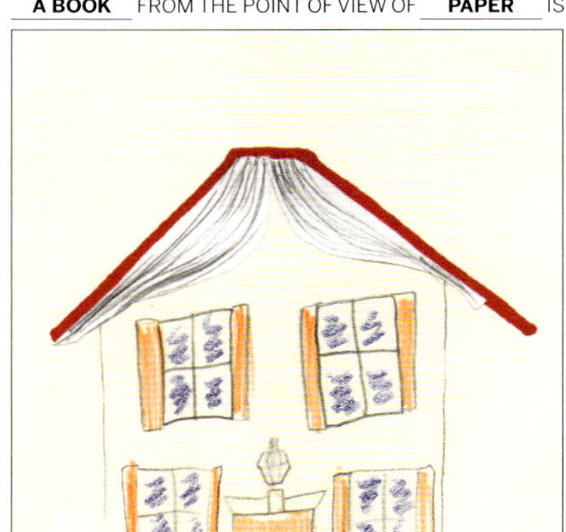

ITS HOME

A BOOK FROM THE POINT OF VIEW OF **AN AUTHOR** IS

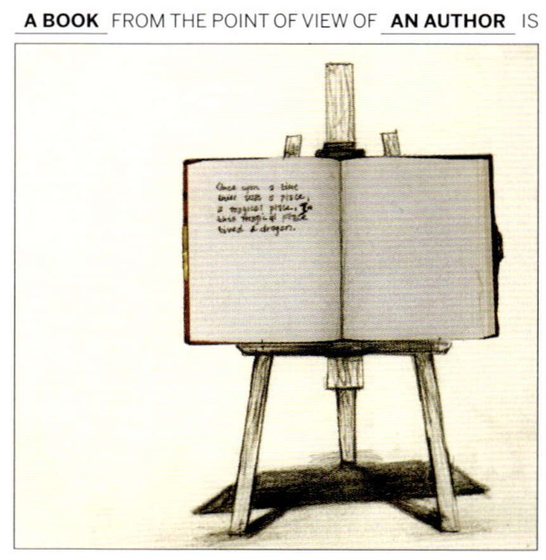

A CANVAS

LILIES FROM THE POINT OF VIEW OF **A GIRL** ARE

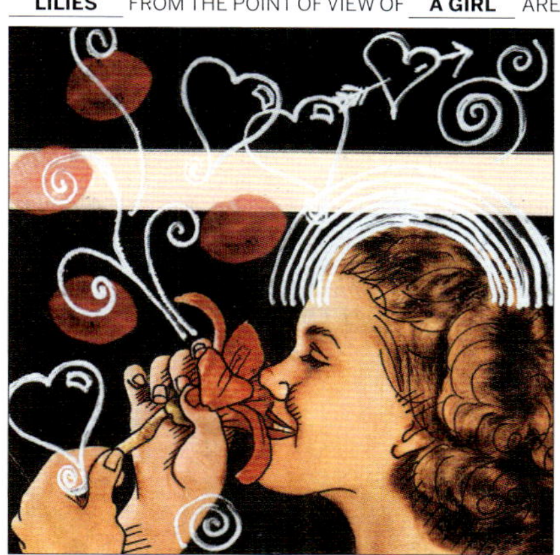

A SIGN OF LOVE

LILIES FROM THE POINT OF VIEW OF **A BOY** ARE

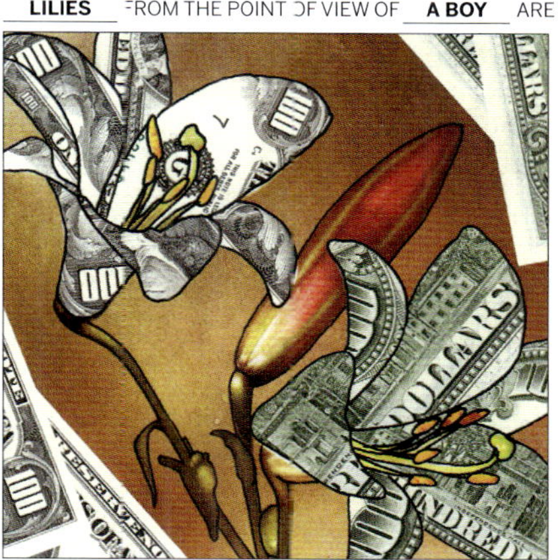

AN EXPENSIVE GIFT

AN UMBRELLA FROM THE POINT OF VIEW OF **AN ARTIST** IS

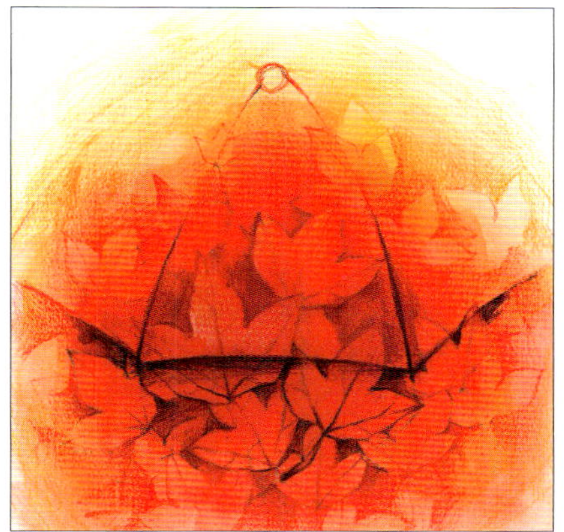

A CANVAS

AN UMBRELLA FROM THE POINT OF VIEW OF **A KID** IS

A SWORD

A NEWSPAPER FROM THE POINT OF VIEW OF **AN ENVIRONMENTALIST** IS

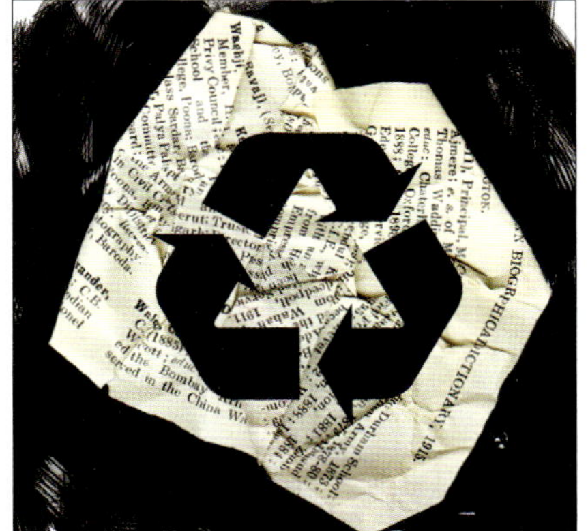

RECYCLABLE

A NEWSPAPER FROM THE POINT OF VIEW OF **ME** IS

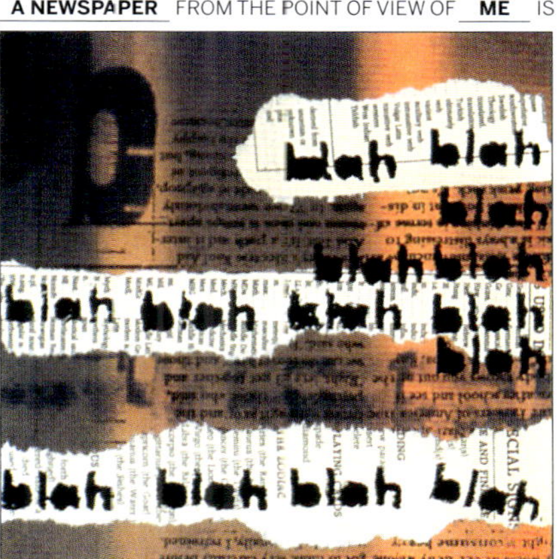

MEANINGLESS

A CHANDELIER FROM THE POINT OF VIEW OF **AN ANT** IS

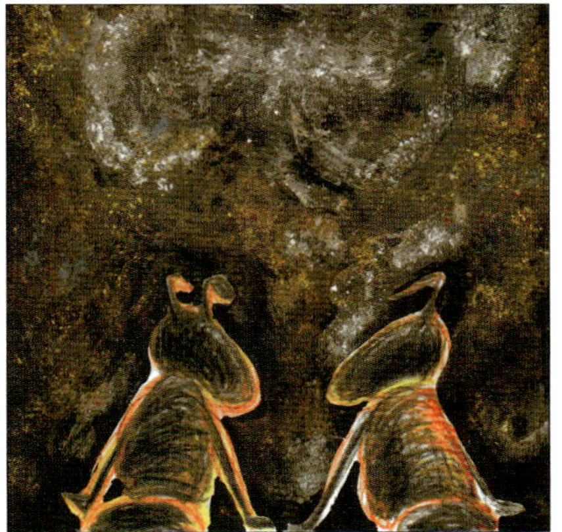

A GALAXY

A CARPET FROM THE POINT OF VIEW OF **AN ANT** IS

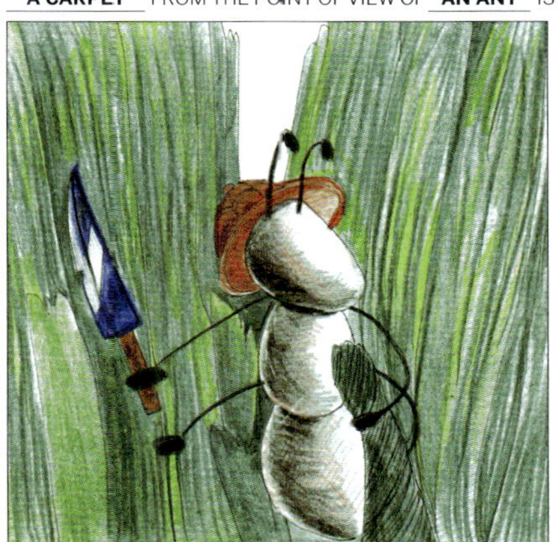

A JUNGLE

POINT OF VIEW SOLUTIONS:

Books are the subject in figures 1 through 3, which utilize sophistication, naïveté and metaphor respectively.

Figures 4 and 5 extend the collage technique with the inclusion of drawing.

Figures 4 through 11 cover the subjects of lilies, umbrellas, newspapers, and ants. Illustration and collage are the mediums used in these executions.

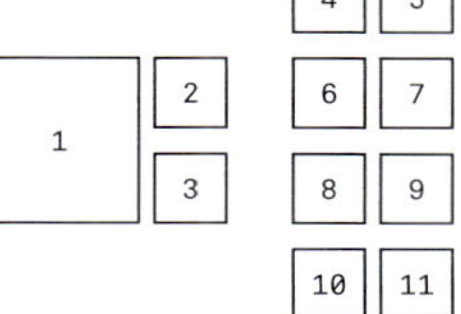

1. *Kayla Heeran Jang*
2–3. *Dylon Burns*
4–5. *Tine Wall*
6–7. *Luree Lee*
8–9. *J. Yun*
10–11. *Sinyoung Kina*

A BOOK FROM THE POINT OF VIEW OF **A CHILD** IS

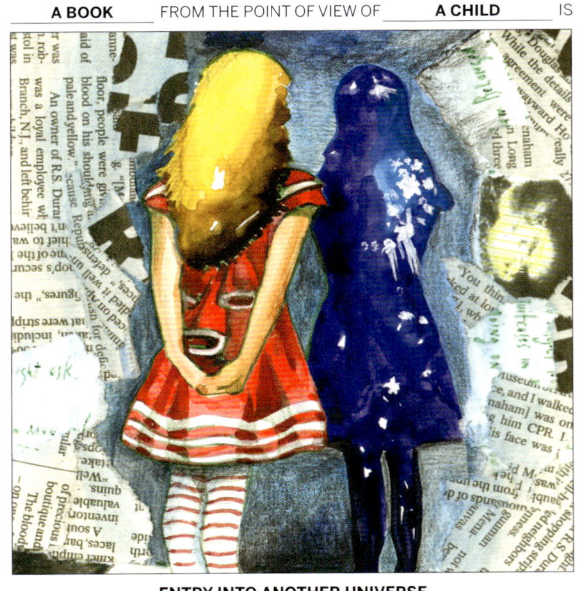

ENTRY INTO ANOTHER UNIVERSE

AN EGG FROM THE POINT OF VIEW OF **ALL THE KING'S MEN** IS

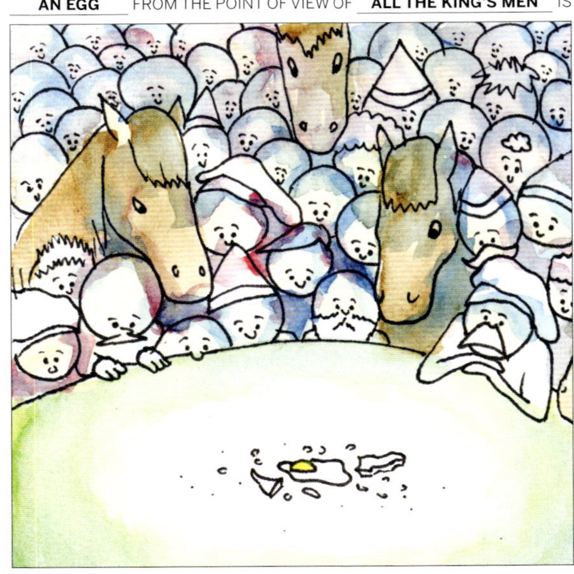

UNFIXABLE

A COW FROM THE POINT OF VIEW OF **JACK** IS

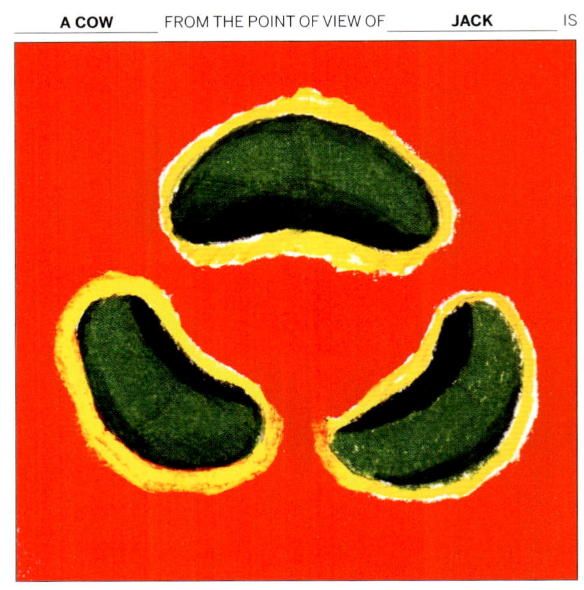

MAGIC BEANS

AN ELEPHANT FROM THE POINT OF VIEW OF **THE LITTLE PRINCE** IS

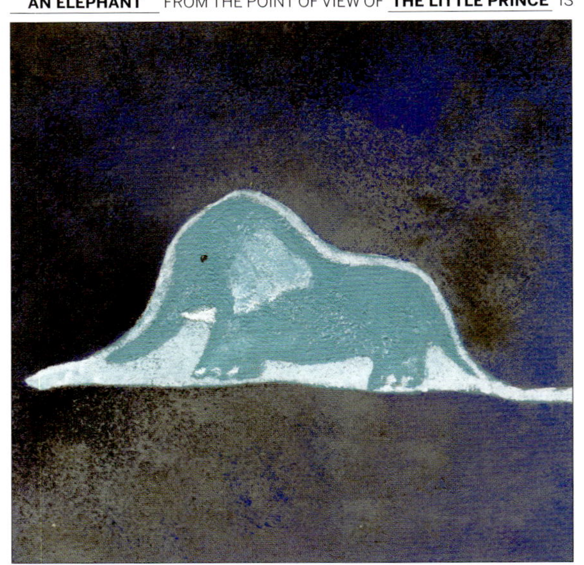

A MEAL FOR A BOA CONSTRICTOR

WATER FROM THE POINT OF VIEW OF **A WICKED WITCH** IS

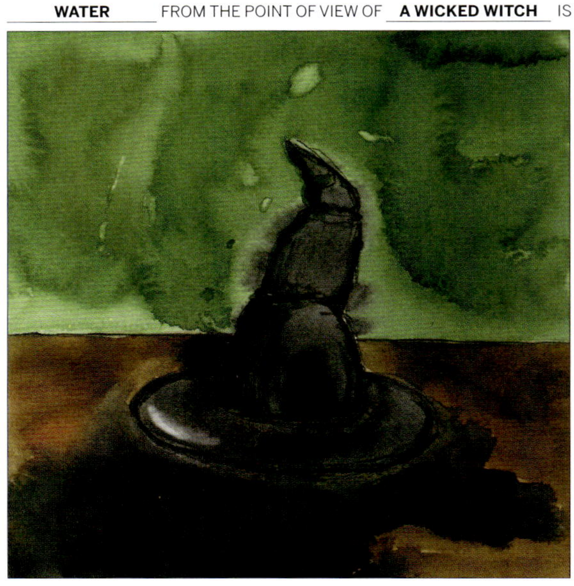

MELTING

AN APPLE FROM THE POINT OF VIEW OF **SNOW WHITE** IS

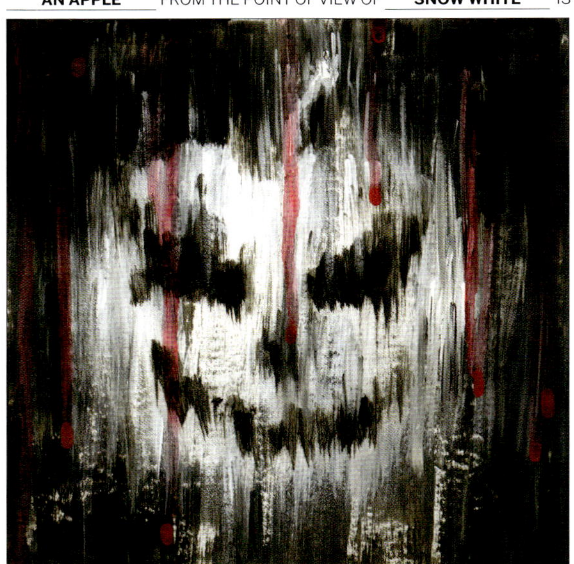

POISON

POINT OF VIEW SOLUTIONS:

The solutions in figures 1 through 6 are themes related to children, whose subjects include: books, nursery rhymes, fairy tales, and films.

Figures 7 through 12 use collage, typography, and drawing in varied ways.

Figures 10 through 12 also relate to the theme of children's imaginary worlds.

KETCHUP FROM THE POINT OF VIEW OF A KID IS

PRETEND BLOOD

KETCHUP FROM THE POINT OF VIEW OF FRENCH FRIES IS

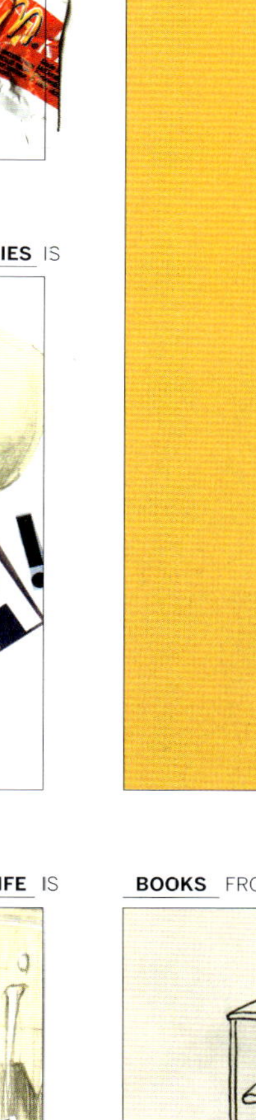

A GREAT PARTNER

A BOX FROM THE POINT OF VIEW OF A LITTLE BOY IS

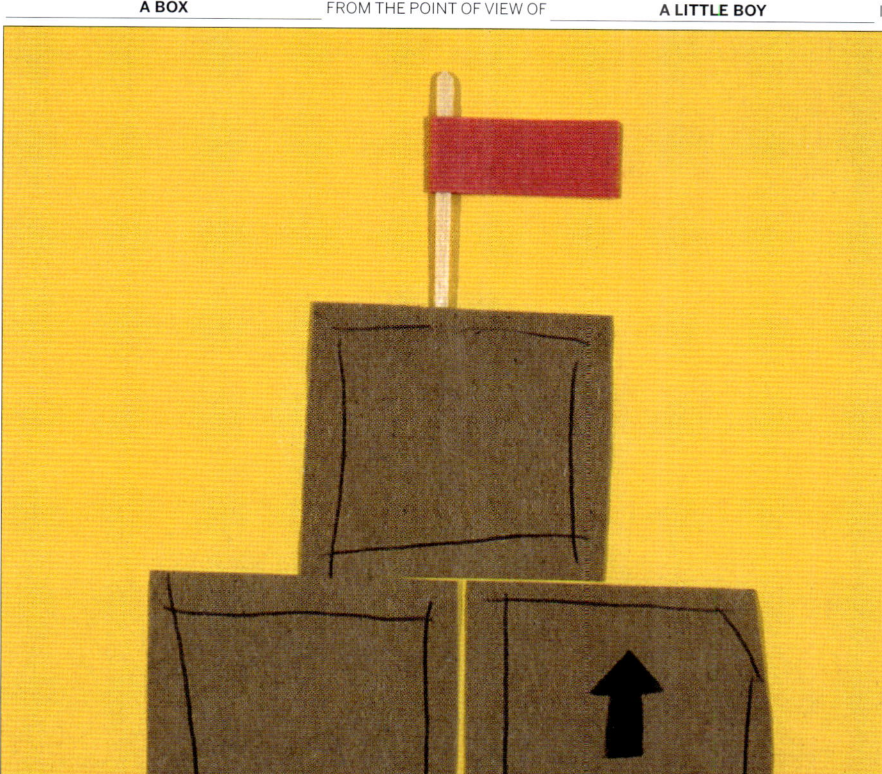

A KINGDOM

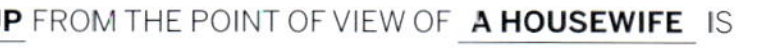

KETCHUP FROM THE POINT OF VIEW OF A HOUSEWIFE IS

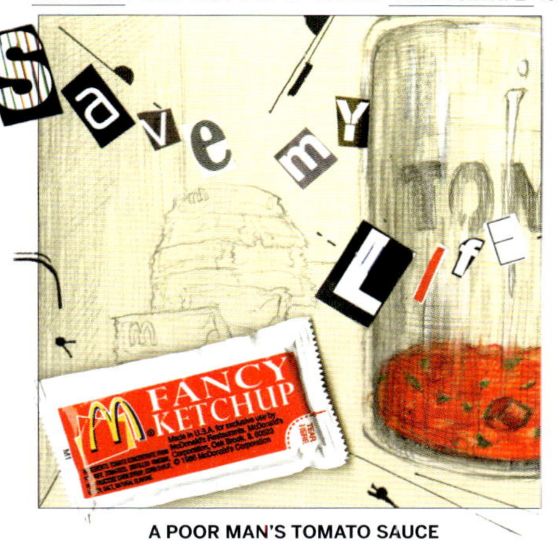

A POOR MAN'S TOMATO SAUCE

BOOKS FROM THE POINT OF VIEW OF A CHILD ARE

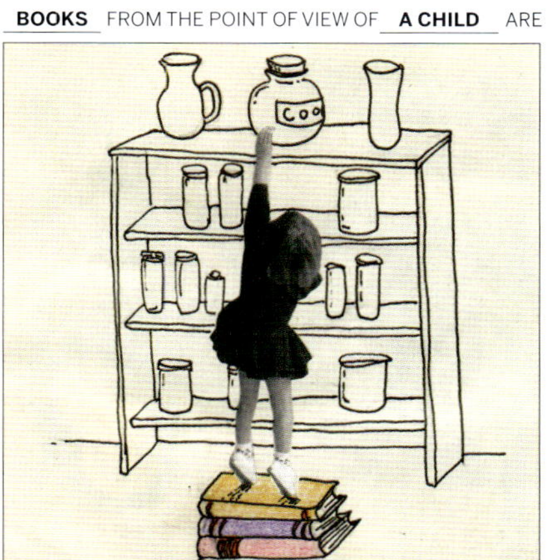

A LADDER

A NEWSPAPER FROM THE POINT OF VIEW OF A CHILD IS

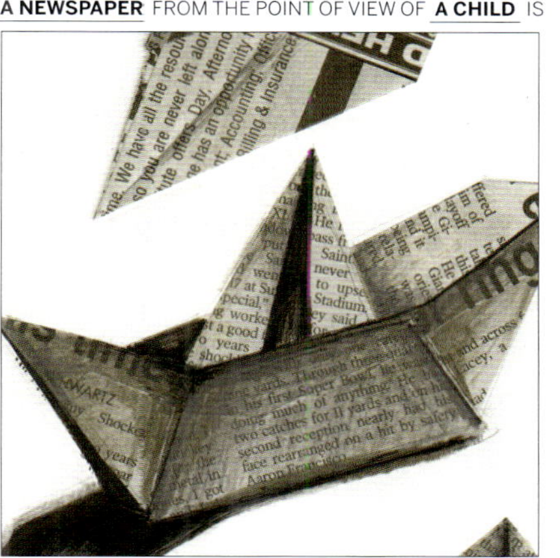

A BOAT

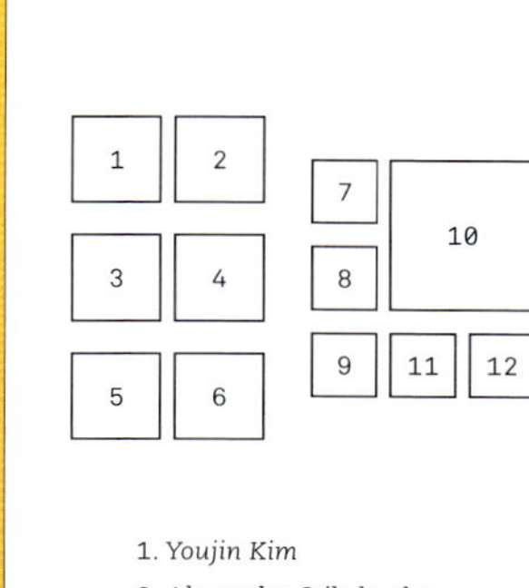

1. *Youjin Kim*
2. *Alexandra Stikeleather*
3. *Maria Jaramillo*
4. *Hyena Song*

5–6. *Vera Yorbunara*

7–9. *Kingchung Wong*

10. *Erica Demasi*
11. *Kayla Heeran Jang*
12. *Hyosun Kim*

WATER FROM THE POINT OF VIEW OF **A BAD DIVER** IS

PAIN

A CUPCAKE FROM THE POINT OF VIEW OF **A MATHEMATICIAN** IS

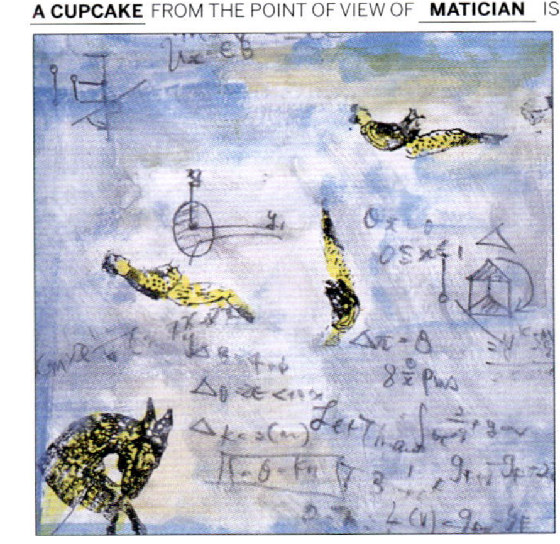

A RECIPE

A NAIL FROM THE POINT OF VIEW OF **AN AUTO** IS

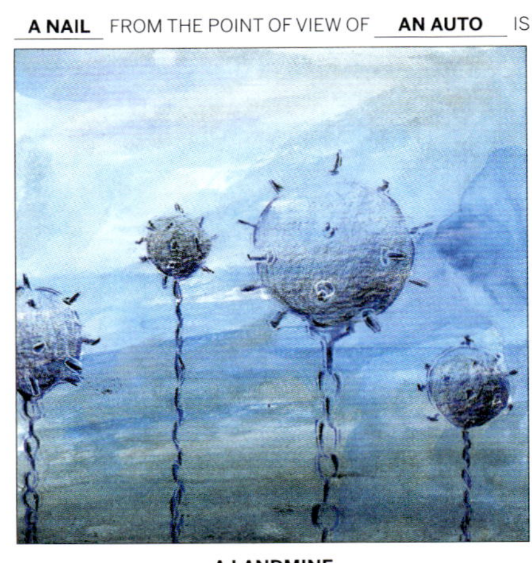

A LANDMINE

ANXIETY FROM THE POINT OF VIEW OF **AN AIRPLANE** IS

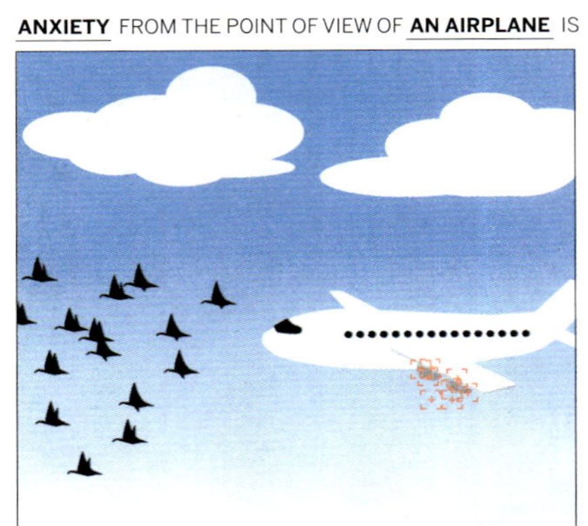

A FLOCK OF GEESE

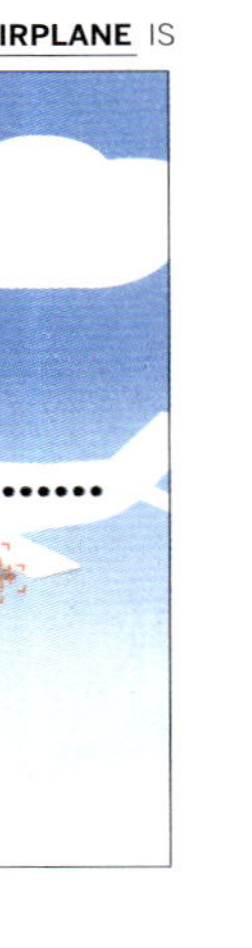

A BASS FROM THE POINT OF VIEW OF **A TERMITE** IS

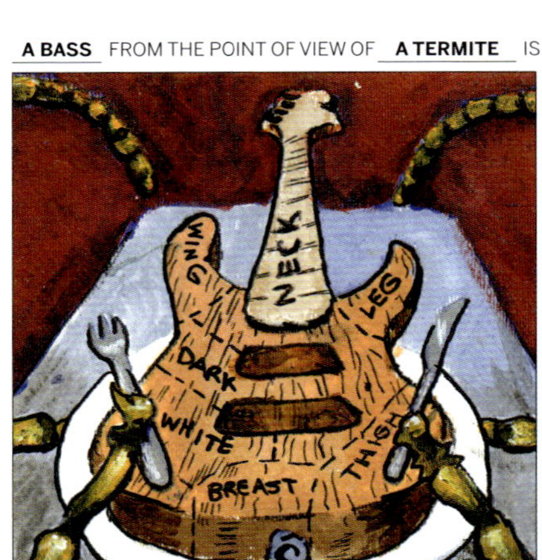

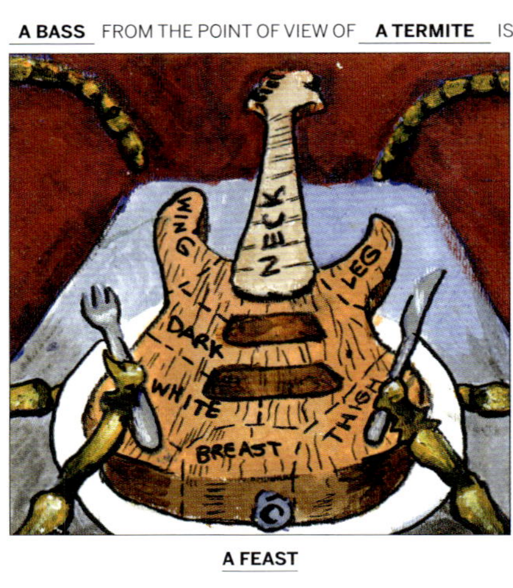

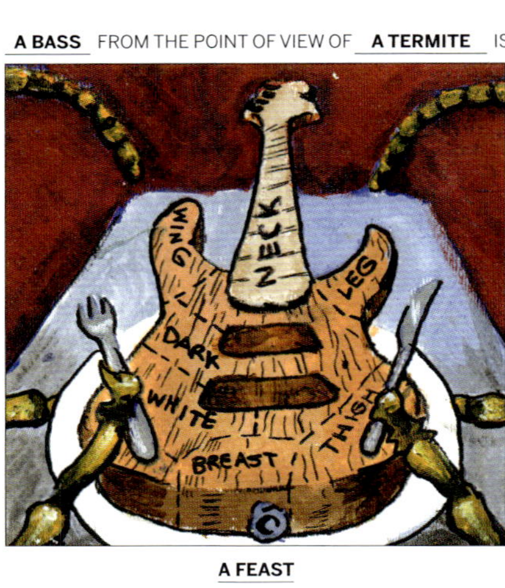

A FEAST

A DEADLINE FROM THE POINT OF VIEW OF **A DESIGNER** IS

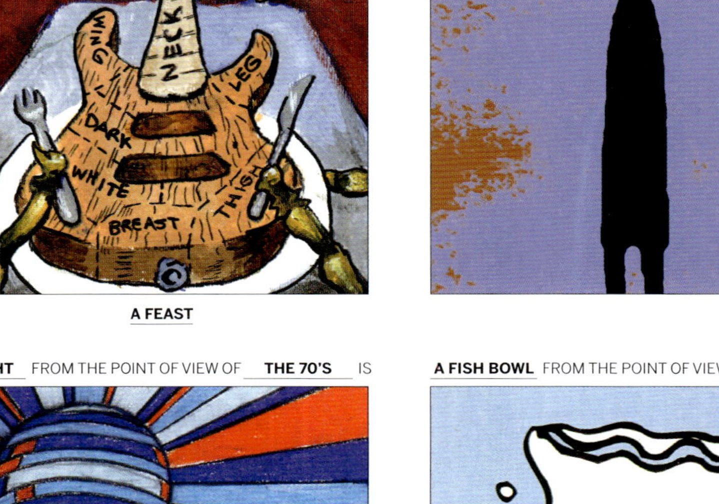

ALWAYS IN MIND

LIGHT FROM THE POINT OF VIEW OF **THE 70'S** IS

A DISCO BALL

A FISH BOWL FROM THE POINT OF VIEW OF **A FISH** IS

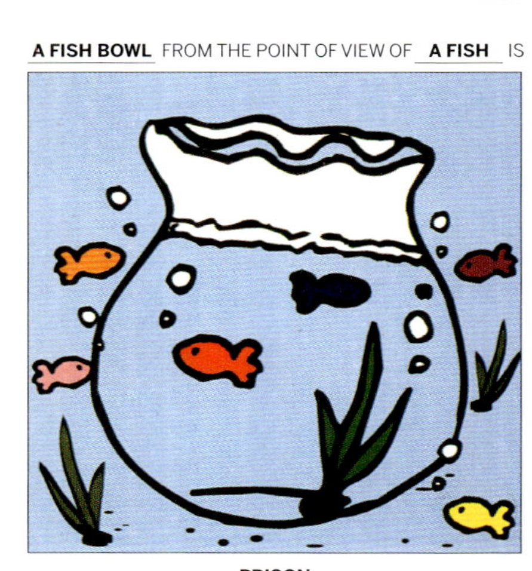

PRISON

A TOILET FROM THE POINT OF VIEW OF **A GOLDFISH** IS

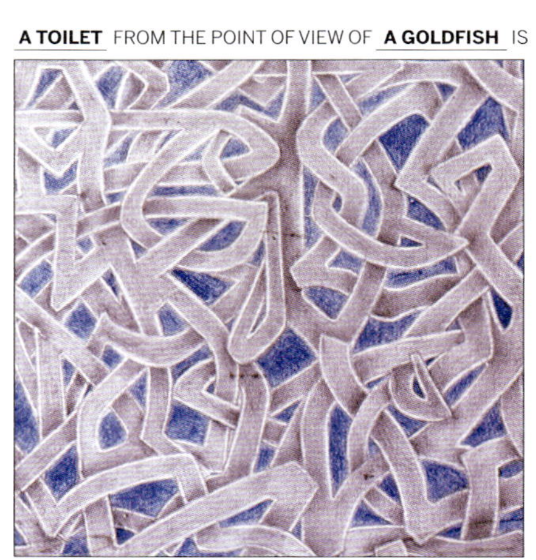

AN UNCHARTED JOURNEY

COSMETICS FROM THE POINT OF VIEW OF **A RABBIT** ARE

TORTURE

COSMETICS FROM THE POINT OF VIEW OF **A TRANS-VESTITE** ARE

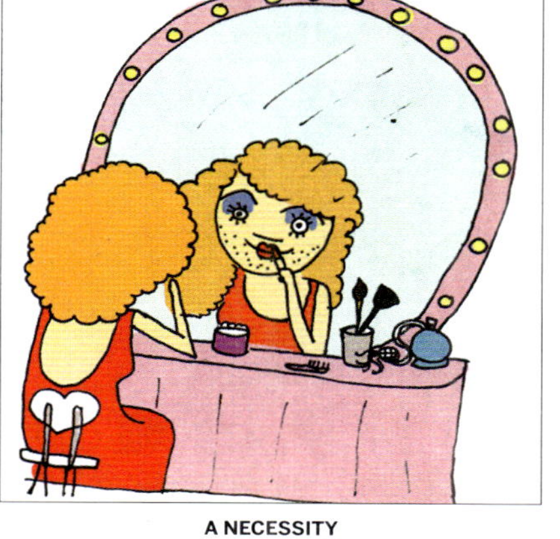

A NECESSITY

A CRITIQUE FROM THE POINT OF VIEW OF **A DEMANDING TEACHER** IS

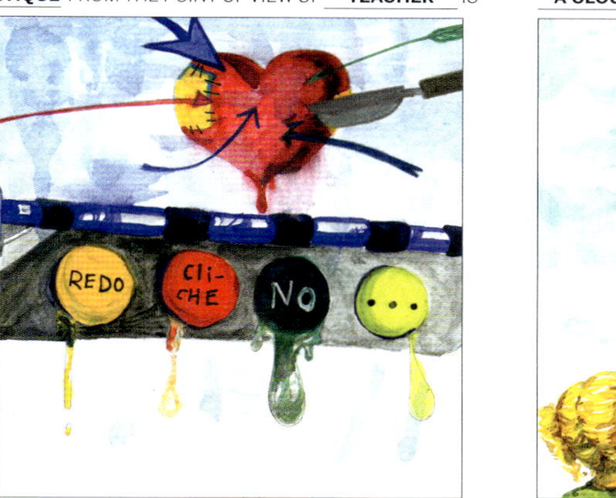

A SCARY PROPOSITION

A CLOUD FROM THE POINT OF VIEW OF **A CHILD** IS

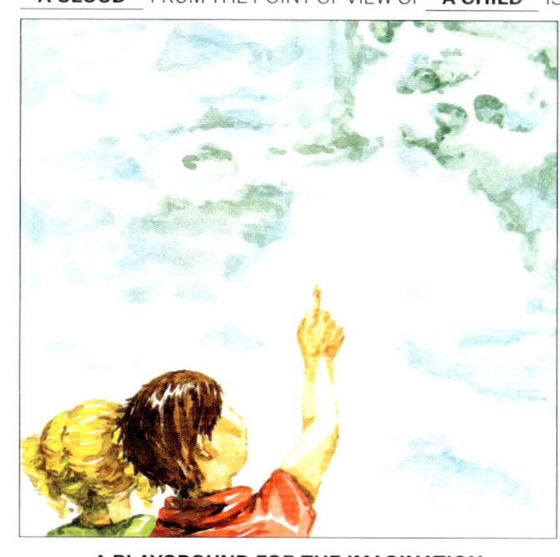

A PLAYGROUND FOR THE IMAGINATION

A SNAKE FROM THE POINT OF VIEW OF **A FASHION DESIGNER** IS

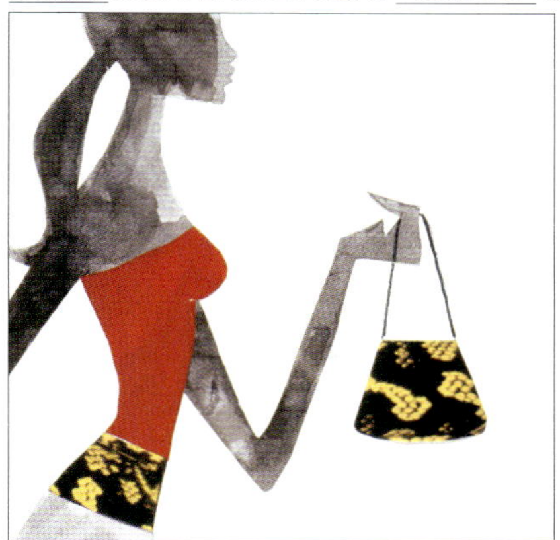

AN ACCESSORY

A DOG FROM THE POINT OF VIEW OF **AN NY RESIDENT** IS

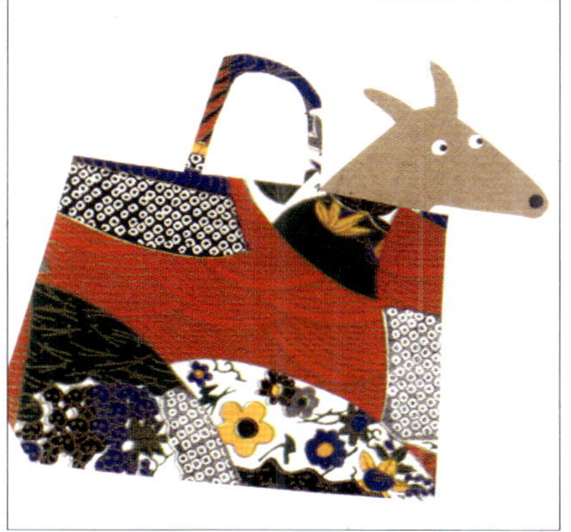

AN ACCESSORY

A FIRE HYDRANT FROM THE POINT OF VIEW OF **A DOG** IS

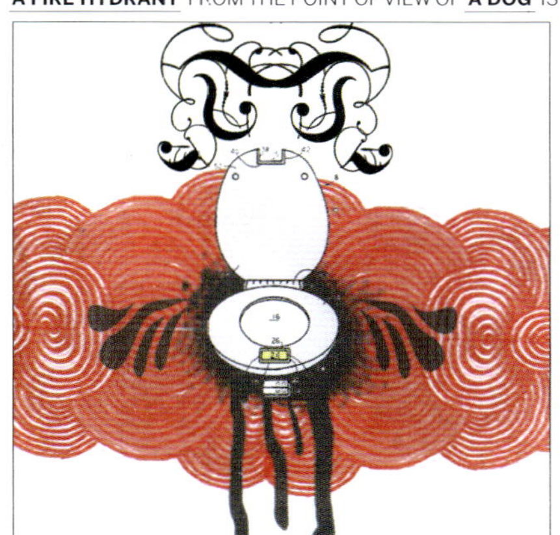

A TOILET

A DOG FROM THE POINT OF VIEW OF **AN AIRPLANE** IS

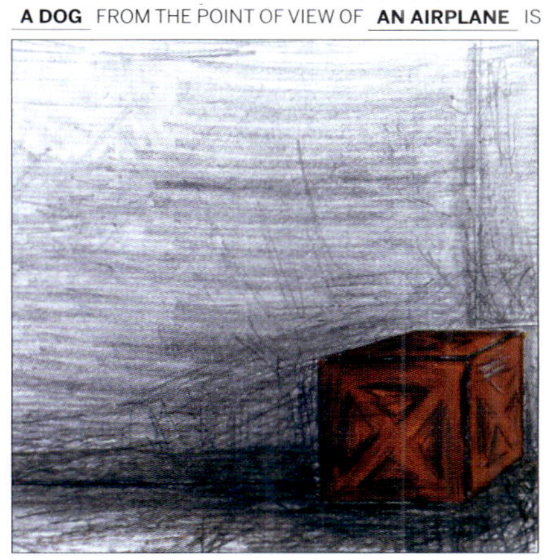

CARGO

POINT OF VIEW SOLUTIONS:

Figures 1 through 9 utilize metaphor, abstraction, and storytelling. Some themes included range from pain to imminent destruction, to time management, to imprisonment.

In figures 10 through 17, many solutions deal with social commentary.

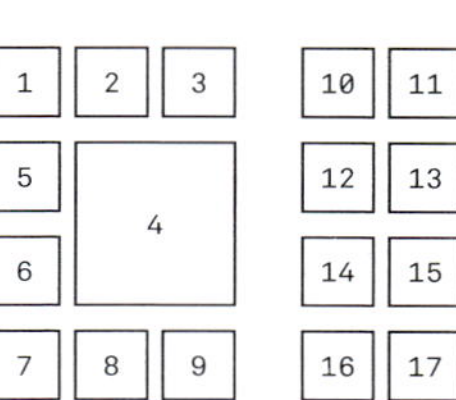

1. *Janice Frank*
2. *Fumiyo Osawa*
3. *Hoyun Son*
4. *Ren-Julius Reyes*
5. *Maria Gomez-Trujillo*
6. *Jeremy Stein*
7. *Corey Tucker*
8. *Huachen Huang*
9. *Jane Goldman*

10–11. *Erin Hookana*

12. *Elly Lee*
13. *Mee Jang*

14–15. *Rhonda Lehr*

16. *Chet Purtilar*
17. *Jane Raskin*

A RORSCHACH FROM THE POINT OF VIEW OF **AN ATHLETE** IS

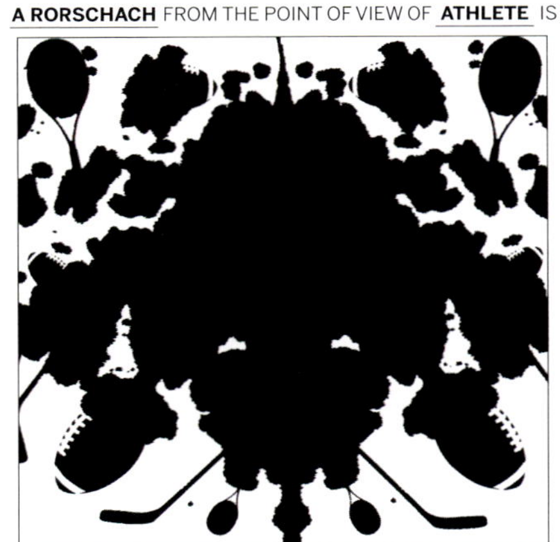

SPORTS EQUIPMENT

A RORSCHACH FROM THE POINT OF VIEW OF **A POT HEAD** IS

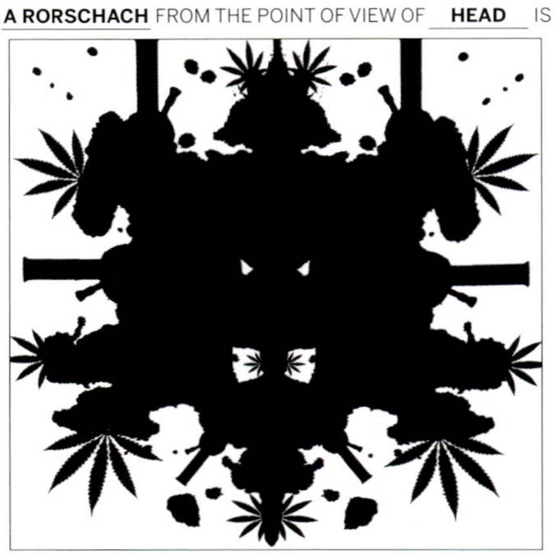

MARIJUANA

A RORSCHACH FROM THE POINT OF VIEW OF **A CAT** IS

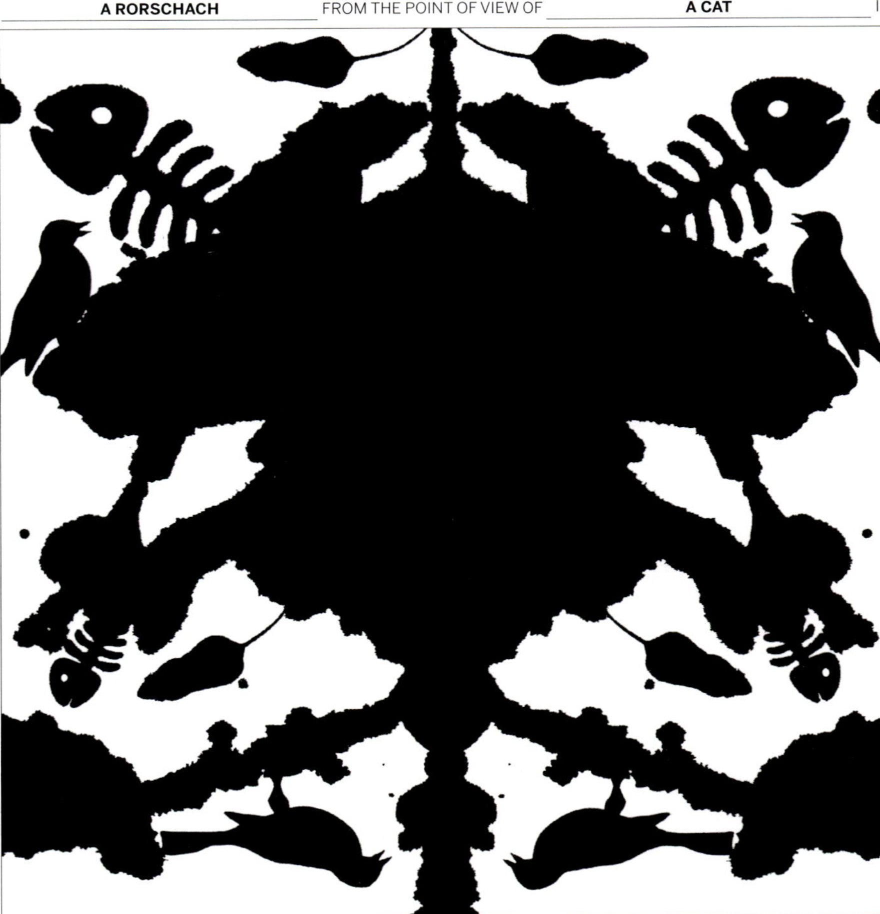

FOOD

DOODLING FROM THE POINT OF VIEW OF **AN ARTIST** IS

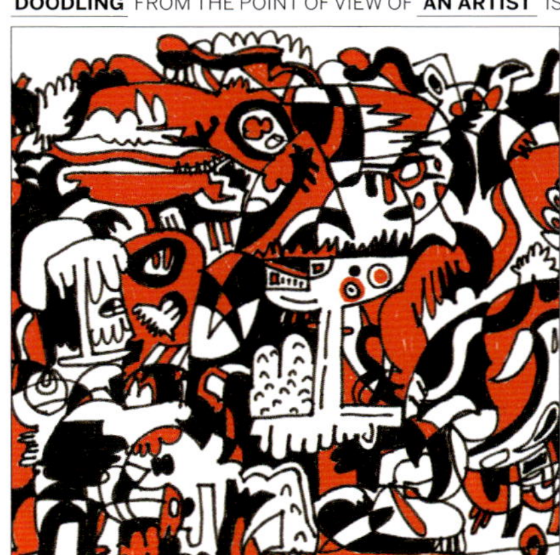

A WORK OF ART

A WOLF FROM THE POINT OF VIEW OF **THE MOON** IS

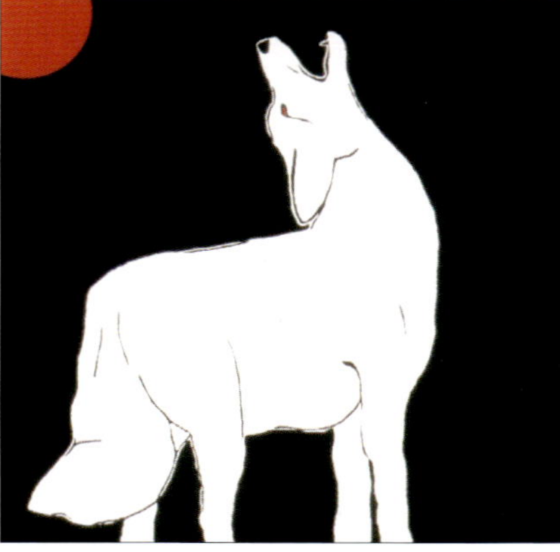

AN AUDIENCE

A CONSUMER FROM THE POINT OF VIEW OF **A RETAILER** IS

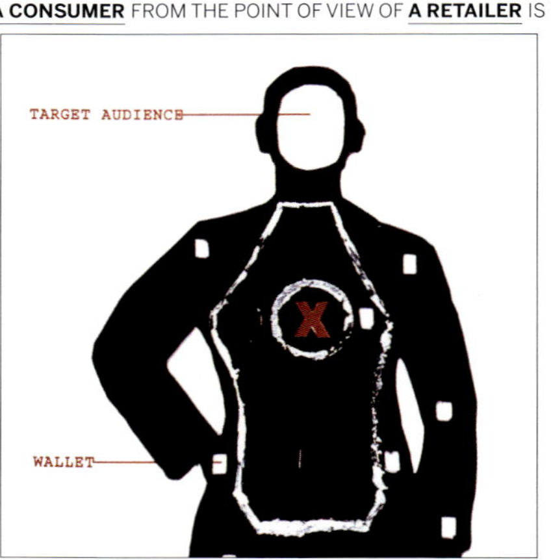

A TARGET AUDIENCE

SUNLIGHT FROM THE POINT OF VIEW OF **A MAGNIFYING GLASS** IS

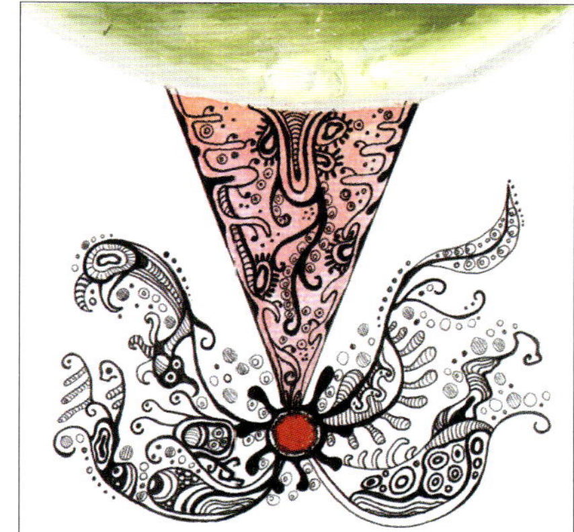

CONDENSED ENERGY

SUNLIGHT FROM THE POINT OF VIEW OF **SKIN** IS

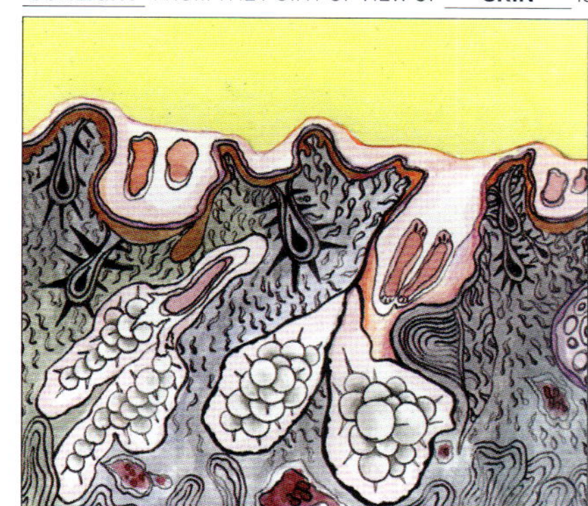

CELL DAMAGE

DOODLING FROM THE POINT OF VIEW OF **A READER** IS

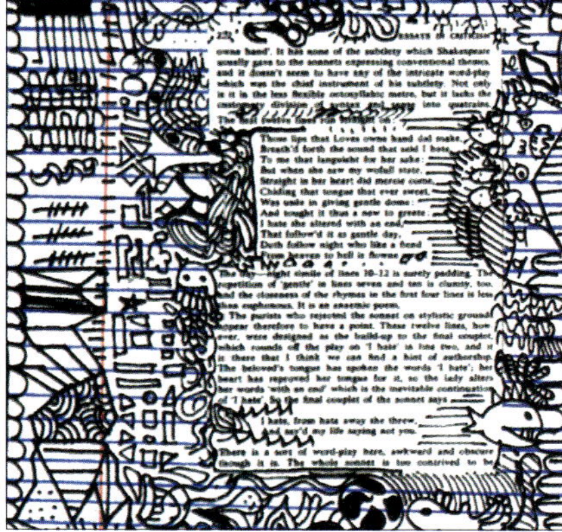

A DISTRACTION

DOODLING FROM THE POINT OF VIEW OF **A MOM** IS

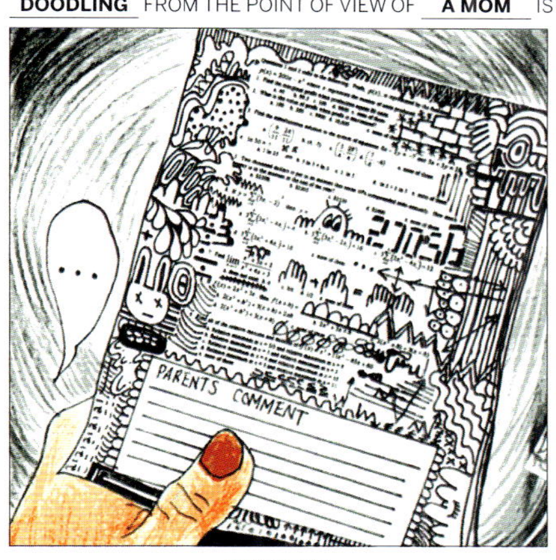

CONCERN

ME FROM THE POINT OF VIEW OF **MY MOTHER** IS

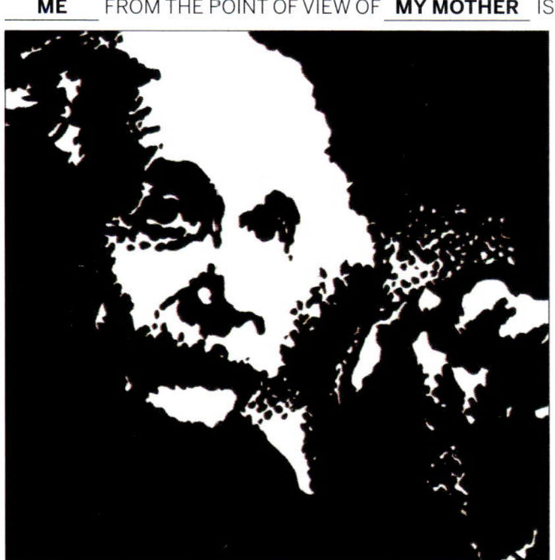

GENIUS

DUCT TAPE FROM THE POINT OF VIEW OF **A DUCK** IS

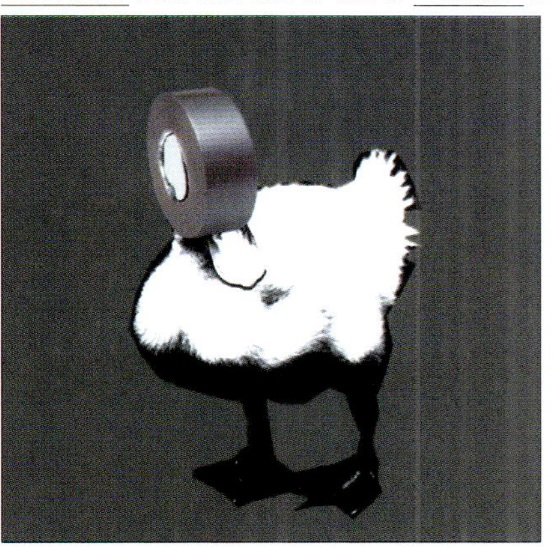

A COMMON MISUNDERSTANDING

POINT OF VIEW SOLUTIONS:

Figures 1 through 6 use a palette of black and white, and in some cases the addition of red is used to accentuate the concept.

Figures 1 through 3 use flat symmetrical shapes indicative of Rorschach inkblots used in psychological testing.

Doodling, howling, and advertising are the themes depicted in figures 4 through 6.

Figures 7 and 8 explore scientific themes through both decorative and informative interpretations.

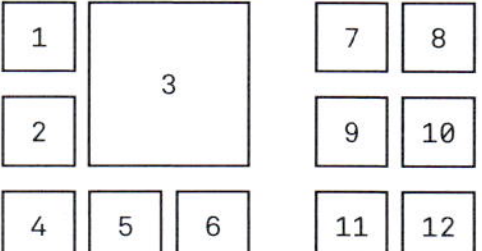

1–3. *Matthew Klein*
4. *Yujin Lee*
5. *Phillip Eggert*
6. *Jose Chicas*
7–8. *Minhee Kim*
9–10. *Yujin Lee*
11. *Jose Chicas*
12. *Jennie Lou*

In figures 9 and 10 the subject of drooling, in effect, became the directive of the execution.

Figures 11 and 12 deal with the humor of the subjects depicted.

LIGHT FROM THE POINT OF VIEW OF **A TRAIN** IS

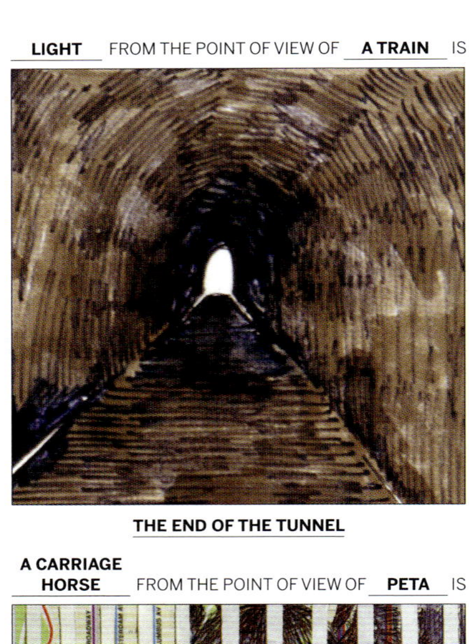

THE END OF THE TUNNEL

POLITICS FROM THE POINT OF VIEW OF **A PESSIMIST** IS

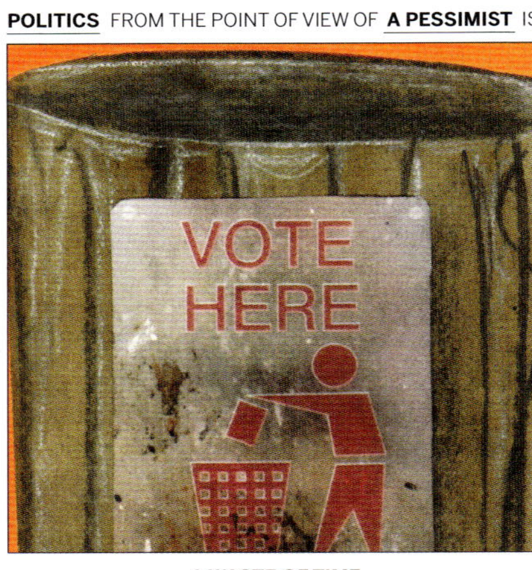

A WASTE OF TIME

A FAST FOOD CHAIN FROM THE POINT OF VIEW OF **A HIGH SCHOOL DROP OUT** IS

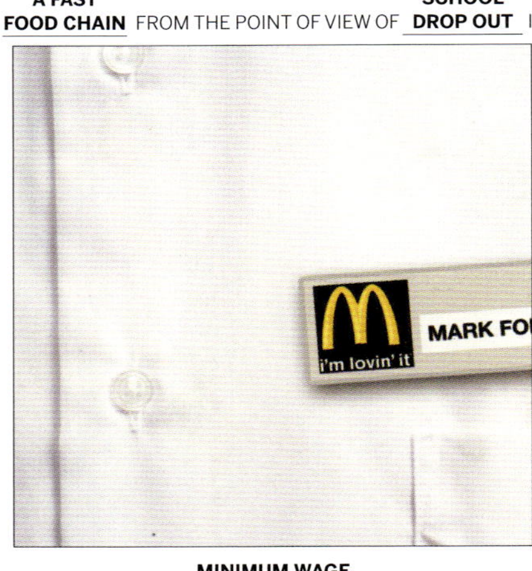

MINIMUM WAGE

A CARRIAGE HORSE FROM THE POINT OF VIEW OF **PETA** IS

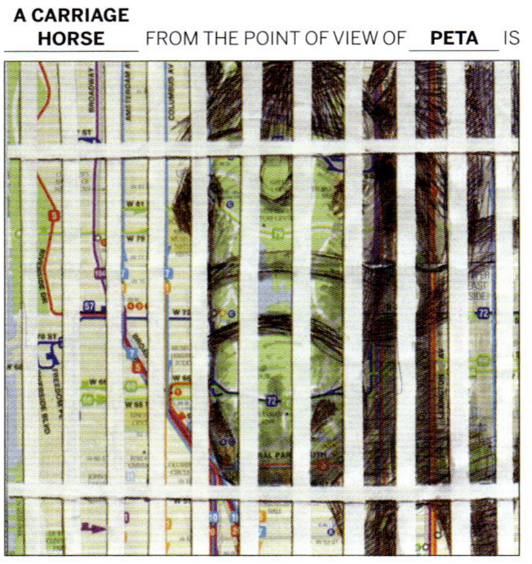

CRUELTY

THE UPPER EASTSIDE OF MANHATTAN FROM THE POINT OF VIEW OF **A COMPASS** IS

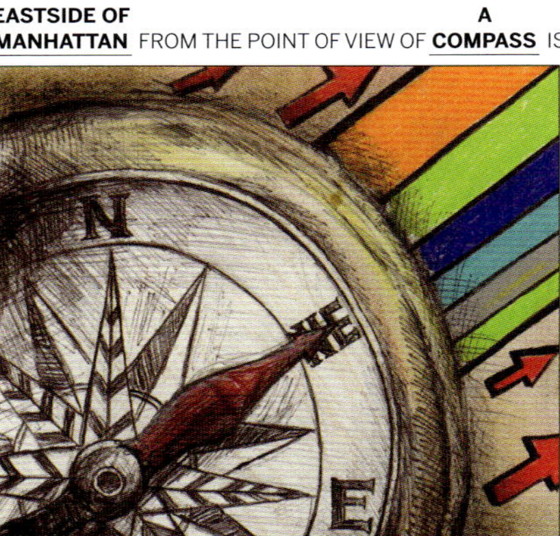

NORTHEAST

A SALSA DANCER FROM THE POINT OF VIEW OF **A FASHION DESIGNER** IS

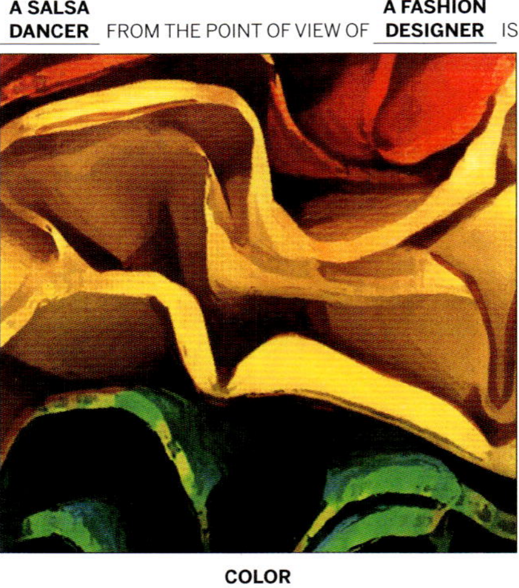

COLOR

A DANDELION FROM THE POINT OF VIEW OF **A CHILD** IS

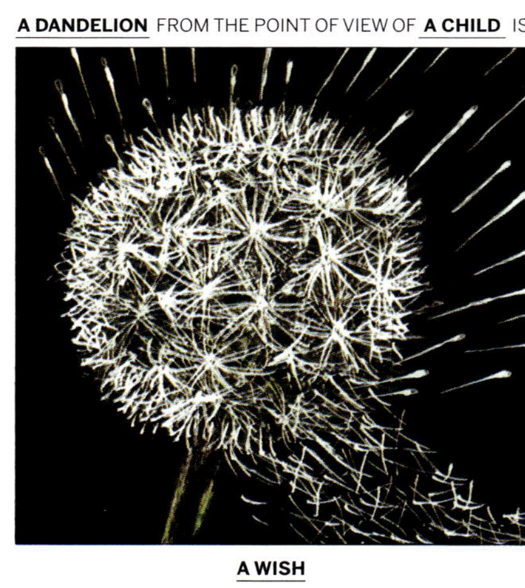

A WISH

A MICRO-ORGANISM FROM THE POINT OF VIEW OF **A SCIENTIST** IS

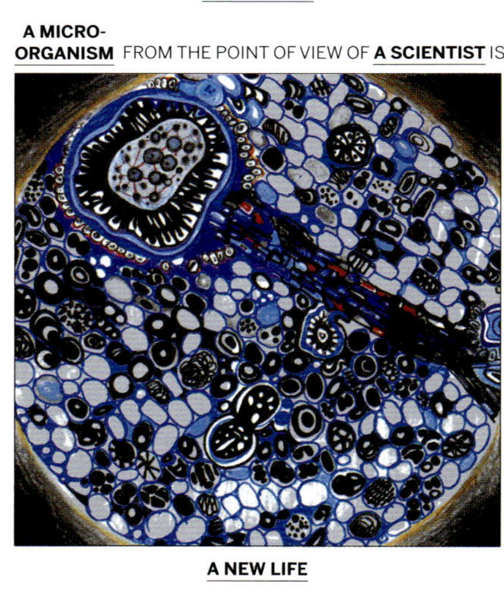

A NEW LIFE

A SUBWAY CAR FROM THE POINT OF VIEW OF **A GERMA-PHOBE** IS

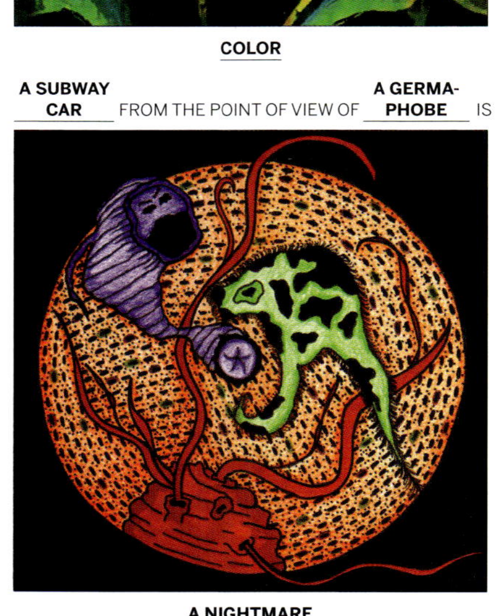

A NIGHTMARE

POINT OF VIEW SOLUTIONS:

Figures 1 through 18 deal with a variety of subjects, utilizing an array of techniques that depict social and political issues, scientific investigations, along with poetic license and humorous interpretations.

One way to measure the success of many of these solutions, as well as the rest of the solutions appearing in this chapter, is to eliminate the written explanation that appears below each solution, and see if the image by itself conveys the intended message.

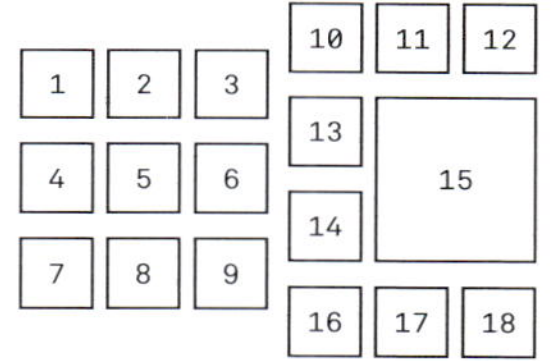

1. *Barry Seigel*
2. *Christopher Rogers*
3. *Mark Forsman*
4. *Minhee Choi*
5. *Heeseung Lee*
6. *Andreina Carrillo*
7. *Yi Chen Tsai*
8. *Minah Kim*
9. *Maria Jaramillo*
10. *Kaitlyn Komar*
11. *Alexandra Stikeleather*
12. *Charles Russo*

13–14. *Shiella Pesik*

15. *Chantal Durante*
16. *Lynne Yun*
17. *Melissa Ha*
18. *Joseph Hertz*

However, even though this is a conceptually driven assignment, certain solutions use the project as a point of departure simply to create imagery that is aesthetically pleasing and captures one's imagination, which is no less of an achievement. In this approach, the concept lies in the formal aspects of the execution.

SNOW FROM THE POINT OF VIEW OF **AN EVERGREEN** IS

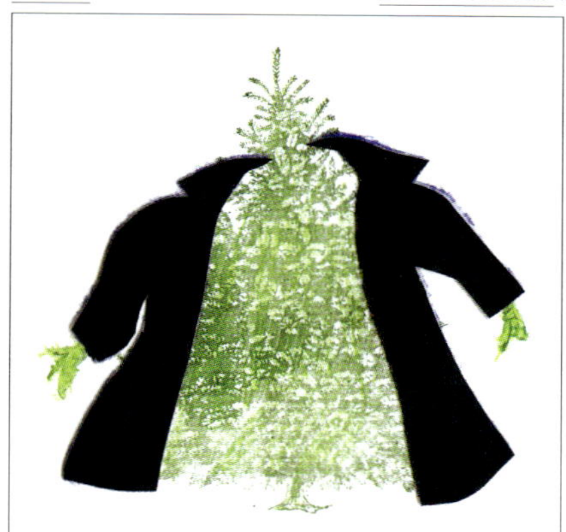

A WINTER COAT

A POWDERED DOUGHNUT FROM THE POINT OF VIEW OF **AN ANT** IS

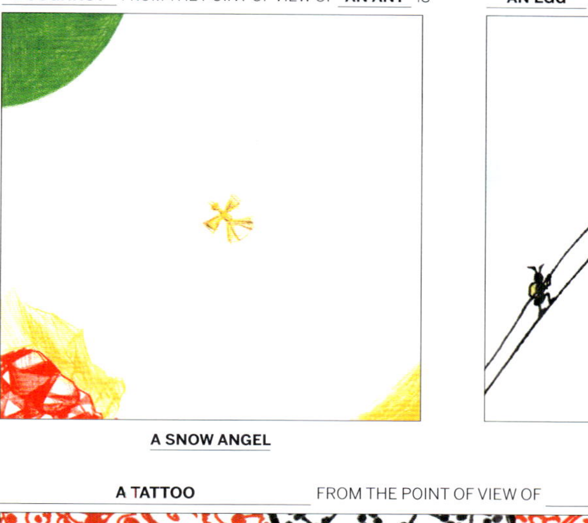

A SNOW ANGEL

AN EGG FROM THE POINT OF VIEW OF **ANTS** IS

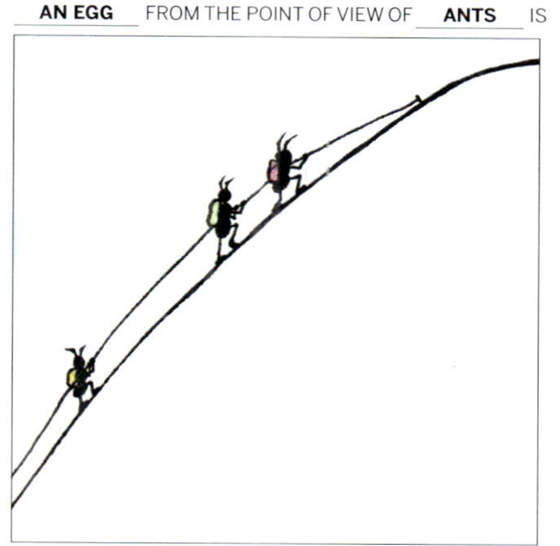

MOUNT EVEREST

A LEAF FROM THE POINT OF VIEW OF **A DESIGN STUDENT** IS

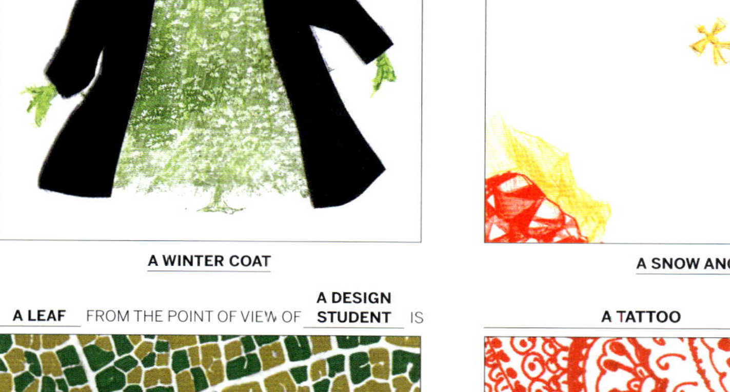

A PATTERN

A TATTOO FROM THE POINT OF VIEW OF **AN INDIAN WOMAN** IS

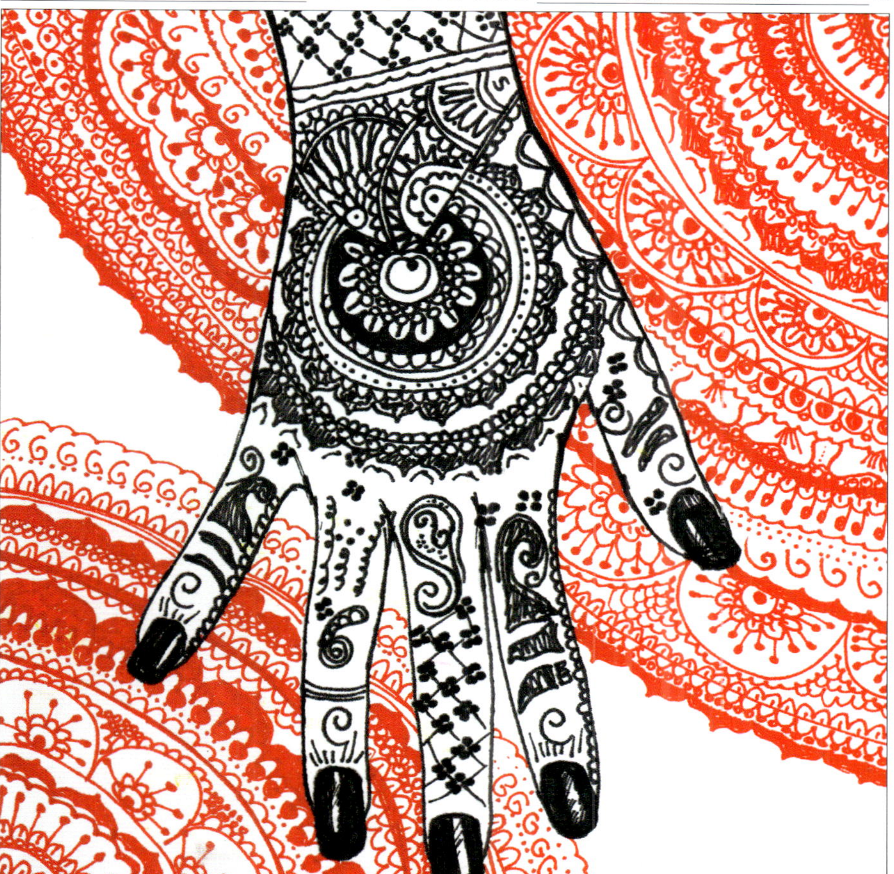

DECORATIVE

A LEAF FROM THE POINT OF VIEW OF **RAIN** IS

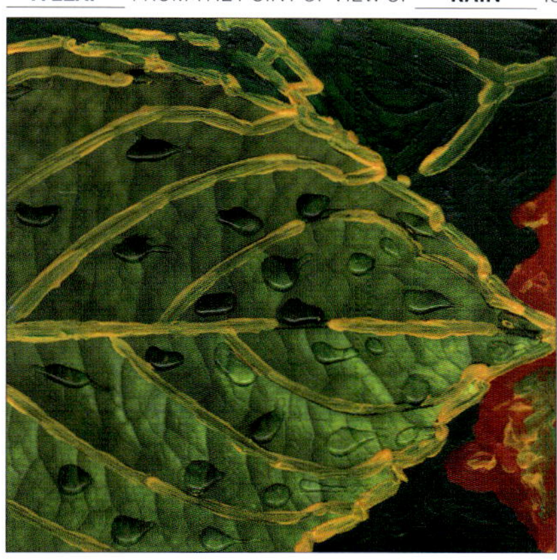

A SHOULDER TO CRY ON

A CAT FROM THE POINT OF VIEW OF **A FISH** IS

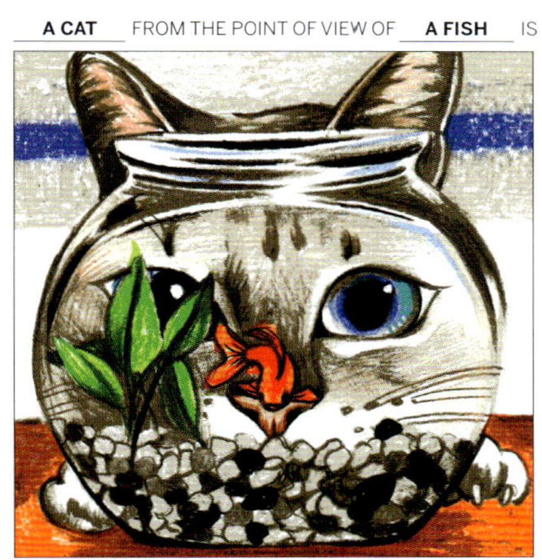

FRIGHTENING

RED OR BLACK FROM THE POINT OF VIEW OF **A BOMB DEFUSER** IS

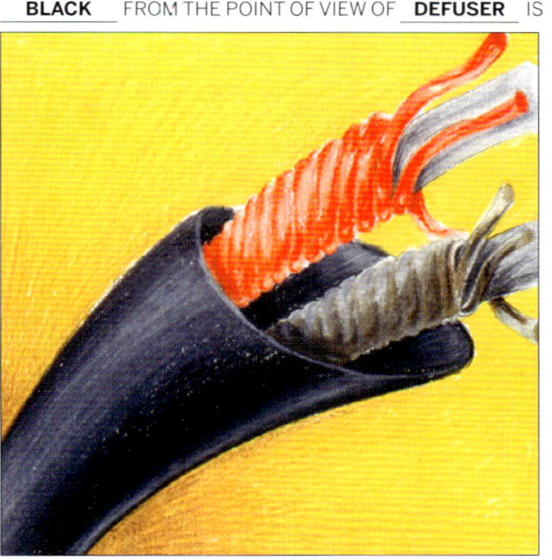

LIFE OR DEATH

WATER FROM THE POINT OF VIEW OF **FIRE** IS

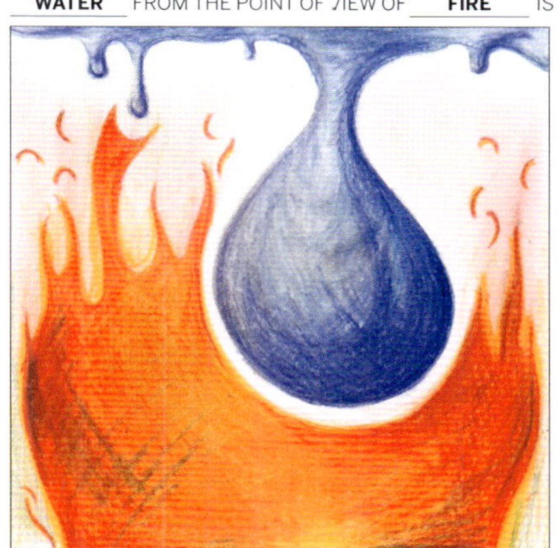

AN ADVERSARY

THE AUTHORS

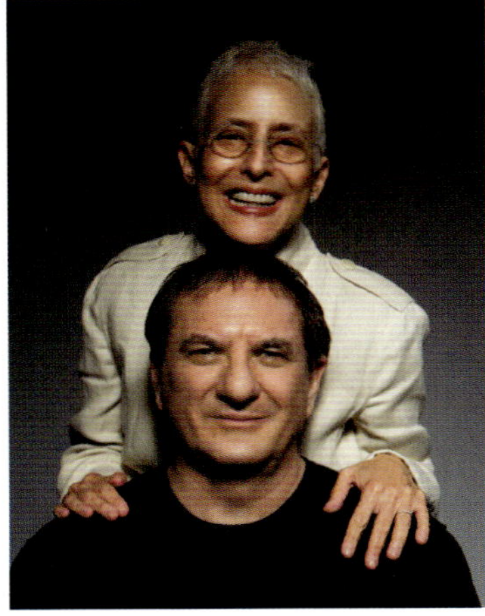

For over forty years Richard Wilde has been chair and founder of the Design department and chair of the Advertising department at the School of Visual Arts in New York City. He is a laureate of the Hall of Fame of the New York Art Directors Club and a laureate of the One Club Hall of Fame. He has authored several books including *Problems: Solutions, Visual Thinking for Graphic Communicators*, and has co-authored *Visual Literacy, a Conceptual Approach to Graphic Problem Solving* and *101 Ways to Stay Young* with Judith Wilde. Richard is the recipient of over 200 professional awards including gold medals, Art Directors Club, One Club, Andys, Clios, Society of Illustrators, and others.

Judith Wilde is an instructor at the School of Visual Arts in New York City. She is Professor Emeritus at Kingsborough Community College, City University of New York. She is a poet, author, painter, and collage artist.

Judith and Richard divide their time between New York City and the Hudson Valley. They have two children, Brandon and Trilby, and raise Koi fish, too numerous to mention by name. They work together creating experimental assignments for their design and advertising students. Richard possesses several wunderkammers, which he continually adds to. Judith is enthralled by the beauty that surrounds her daily life, which finds a way of entering her work.

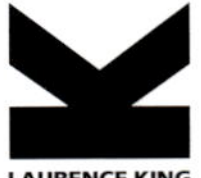

Published in 2014 by
Laurence King Publishing Ltd
361–373 City Road
London EC1V 1LR
United Kingdom
Tel: +44 20 7841 6900
Fax: +44 20 7841 6910
email: enquiries@laurenceking.com
www.laurenceking.com

A catalogue record for this book is available from the British Library

ISBN 978 1 78067 239 7

Designed by Jiwon Kim
Art directed by Judith Wilde / Richard Wilde
Printed in China

ACKNOWLEDGMENTS

Many people contributed to this book, too numerous to list, especially our students. We wish to acknowledge some without whose help this book could not have happened.

Jiwon Kim, for designing *The Process* with love, patience and fortitude, for working non-stop while maintaining design excellence. Her spirit never wavered. We are indebted to her.

Jonas Christiansen, for his critical eye, dedication to the project and his contribution to all phases of the book.

Tal Shub, for his technical and production expertise, as well as his enthusiasm, coordination and management of the project.

Yasmin Malki, for her unlimited energy, care and coordination and understanding.

Special thanks to:
Carolyn Hinkson-Jenkins and **Ingrid Li,** for their support and effort in bringing this book to fruition.

DEDICATION

To all the students who have crossed our paths on their journey of becoming artists. And to our children, Brandon and Trilby, for enriching our lives with their presence.